THE MANIA CHRONICLES

A Real-Time Account
of The Great Financial Bubble

1995-2008

by
Peter M. Kendall
and
Robert R. Prechter, Jr.

The Mania Chronicles

A Real-Time Account of The Great Financial Bubble 1995-2008

Printed in the United States of America

For information, address the publishers:
New Classics Library
Post Office Box 1618
Gainesville, Georgia 30503 USA
Phone: 800-336-1618, 770-536-0309
Fax: 770-536-2514
E-mail address for products: customerservice@elliottwave.com
E-mail address for comments: info@newclassicslibrary.com
Web site: www.elliottwave.com

New Classics Library is the book publishing division of
Elliott Wave International, Inc.

ISBN: 9780-932750-59-4
Library of Congress Catalog Number: 2004110412

THE MANIA CHRONICLES

Dedication

We are grateful to the true believers in every bubble, without whom this volume would not have been possible. It is dedicated, however, to those who will use this knowledge to make the most of future episodes.

Acknowledgments

For the past 10 years, Steve Hochberg has served as co-editor of *The Elliott Wave Financial Forecast*. Over the course of that time, Steve has applied his extensive knowledge of the Wave Principle to all of the markets covered in EWFF each month. Many of the entries that follow appeared originally in EWFF, so Steve's contribution is material to say the least. Many of the charts are his from start to finish. Steve also proofed each issue before publication; so *The Mania Chronicles* is deeply indebted to him.

Leigh Tipton, Angie Barringer, Rachel Webb and then Angela Hall handled monthly production of EWFF and *The Elliott Wave Theorist*.

The enormous task of re-assembling the entries that make up this volume was performed by Sally Webb. Sally is an indispensable, 20-year veteran of the Elliott Wave International team.

Pam Greenwood, Jane Estes, Christy O'Neal, Cari Dobbins and Angela Hall made contributions to the final layout. The jacket was designed by Clint Welsh with an assist from Eliot Bern. Thanks also to Mark Almand and Susan Walker for reviewing the final manuscript.

EWI Research Director Dave Allman reviewed every monthly issue of *The Elliott Wave Theorist* and *The Elliott Wave Financial Forecast* and offered valuable feedback from the beginning to the end of this 13-year project.

Most important, we would like to thank our families and colleagues for sharing the mania years with us. The "process," as we liked to call it, took longer and, at times, was more arduous than we earlier thought possible, but, all in all, it was an adventure we're glad we experienced.

Peter Kendall extends special thanks to Lee and Nancy Kendall for that copy of *Extraordinary Popular Delusions and The Madness of Crowds*; it came in handy.

A Note To Readers

The depth and breadth of The Great Asset Mania was so extensive that it is hard to imagine a life that was not touched by it in many ways. Since the impetus behind it was a naturally occurring wave of optimism that extended to every corner of social life, ours is a large and disparate topic with many interlocking aspects. This presents an organizational challenge. We have elected to group the mania into eight chapters. Each one proceeds chronologically from 1995 to 2008. There is abundant overlap, as many manifestations of the great mania fit into multiple categories. If you find yourself experiencing a sense of déjà vu, close your eyes and remember where you were when that particular event took place. In this way, you will remind yourself that it was not a dream. It really happened. And we all lived to tell about it.

Table of Contents

Introduction

"Given the technical situation, what might we conclude about the psychological aspects of wave V? The 1920s' bull market was a fifth wave of a third Supercycle wave, while Cycle wave V is the fifth wave of a fifth Supercycle wave. Thus, as the last hurrah, it should be characterized at its end by an almost unbelievable institutional mania for stocks and a public mania for stock index futures, stock options, and options on futures. In my opinion, the long term sentiment gauges will give off major trend sell signals two or three years before the final top, and the market will just keep on going. In order to set up the U.S. stock market to experience the greatest crash in its history, which, according to the Wave Principle, is due to follow wave V, investor mass psychology should reach manic proportions, with elements of 1929, 1968 and 1973 all operating together and, at the end, to an even greater extreme."

—Robert Prechter, *The Elliott Wave Theorist*, August 1983

Historian Jacques Barzun (*From Dawn to Decadence*) explains a shortcoming among his peers when he states that it is impossible to describe the past "as it felt when it was the present." By the time events become history, they are invariably colored by a new perspective. This is why most books on social manias look back and describe participants' behavior as a kind of temporary insanity that in retrospect appears bizarre. When each history is written, the presumed certainties and solid convictions behind each old trend are long forgotten.

Few observers have ever had the perspective to point out the extreme behavior of a social mania as it was taking place. This volume, however, stands apart. It gets around Barzun's hindsight problem because it is a real-time account of the Great Mania, written as it was happening.

Now take that idea one step further. As you can see from the quotation, *The Elliott Wave Theorist* did even better than chronicling the mania in real time. *It forecast it.*

The passage above appeared in "A Rising Tide," a report from 1983 that extended the case, made in 1982 (see the Appendix to *Elliott Wave Principle*), for a powerful bull market in stocks, just as it was emerging from the ashes of a period of caution and fear. The references there to specifically numbered Cycles and Supercycles relate to the basis for our dramatic expectations: the Wave Principle. The fundamental tenet of the Wave Principle is that collective human mood fluctuates according to an alternating 5-3 wave form at each degree of trend (see Figure 1).

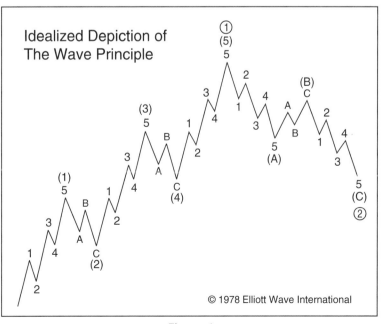

Figure 1

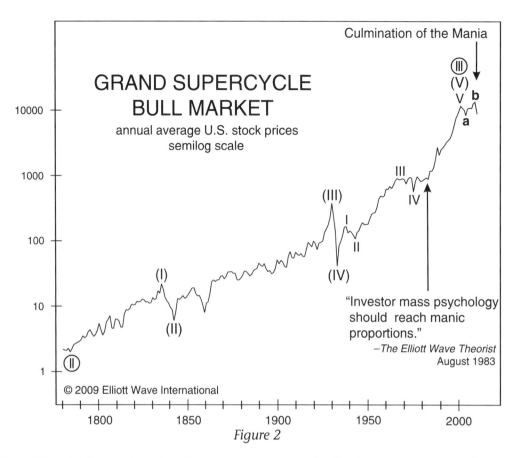

Figure 2

Waves V and (V) mentioned in the quote above are the final waves of an even larger Grand Supercycle wave that began with the formation of the United States in the late 1700s, as shown in Figure 2. The Wave Principle is not the subject of this book, but frequent references to it appear herein because our observations and forecasts flow from Ralph N. Elliott's elegant discovery. As with radio waves, we cannot see waves of social mood with the naked eye. But we certainly can see their effects, in all kinds of cultural expressions, most reliably in the Dow Jones Industrial Average. Indeed, this mania has been so powerful that financial and social trends merged into an entire cultural identity based upon stocks and investing, from the bidding frenzies for children's toys such as Beanie Babies to the bright lights of Times Square, where the NASDAQ ticker tape was installed in December 1999. The bull market ended there, but the momentum from two centuries of rising prices was so extreme that the mania kept right on going, for real estate into 2005, for stocks (at least in nominal terms) into 2007 and for commodities into 2008. These peaks occurred roughly where you see wave **b** on the chart above. For a sneak peek of the final price explosion, see the Conclusion; for a capsule summary of the Wave Principle, see Appendix A; and for a brief description of the basis for our social forecasting, see Appendix B. A review is highly recommended for non-subscribers, as our regular monthly issues assume a certain familiarity with the Wave Principle.

To understand the dynamics behind history's greatest financial bubble and its attendant social psychology, you should turn to a source that described them both *before* they happened and *as* they happened. This is the only way to be sure that the dynamics described are accurate. After all, it's easy to identify a mania after the fact, but anyone who gives you a guided tour of a mania as it unfolds knows his subject. We are unaware of any other chronicle of a mania written as it took place. The reason is not hard to fathom. When a mania is under way, the vast majority of people — from economists to academics to everyday investors — think that the conditions of the mania are perfectly justifiable if not rationally imperative. This one was no different. For every article we saw about the folly of the times, there were 1000 extolling its virtues.

In the late 1970s and early 1980s, Prechter prepared investors for a great bull market, in *Elliott Wave Principle* (1978, with A.J. Frost) and *The Elliott Wave Theorist*. As the bull market completed its long rise, I was busy writing most of the material on the mania's social expressions (thus this book) while Bob wrote *At the Crest of the Tidal Wave* (1995), preparing readers for the reversal, and *Conquer the Crash* (2002), offering a survival guide to the bear market as well as the deflationary depression that we still think lies ahead. To understand our basis for social forecasting, we highly recommend *The Wave Principle of Human Social Behavior* (1999), published at the height of the mania. As its back cover states, "Mass emotional change has a fair degree of predictability." All entries in this book are from *The Elliott Wave Theorist* and *The Elliott Wave Financial Forecast*, which illustrate that very point by having anticipated many different aspects of the greatest social mood reversal in history.

You are about to take a ringside seat at the culmination of the greatest financial spectacle of all time. Attributes of the bubble certainly appeared prior to 1995, but we begin our discussion at that time because that's when it became especially maniacal (and entertaining). Each of the following eight chapters captures a thematic aspect of the extreme ebullience that rolled through every major area of human social interaction. The mania took different forms in different institutions, individuals and social settings, but a solitary force — an uplifting sense of optimism and unity — drove every manifest action. The mania's all-encompassing aura shines in the strength and magnetism of the heroes it created, its saturation throughout the media and its geographic spread even to some of the most primitive and most fervently anti-capitalist places on the planet. During its final gasp higher, there was even a Chinese version of the tulip mania in which speculation in a certain type of tea leaf completed the passage from euphoria to desolation and loss in classic fashion. Here's The New York Times' profile from January 2009: "Over the past decade, as the nation went wild for the region's brand of tea, known as Pu'er, farmers bought minivans, manufacturers became millionaires, and Chinese citizens plowed their savings into black bricks of compacted Pu'er. But that was before the collapse of the tea market turned thousands of farmers and dealers into paupers." The bull market took a lot longer and rose much higher than we originally anticipated, but its extension had the magnificent result of expanding the exotic extremities of the mania, as well as the historical value of this book.

Keep in mind that our opinions have been utterly out of favor and still are. Conventional economists have confidently assured us that the country is locked in a self-reinforcing growth spiral, the product of enlightened credit management by the Federal Reserve (and more recently, the White House), which has created "the best of all possible worlds" for all time. As we go to press, 90% of economists still report that they are optimistic. Needless to say, our opinion is that such collective assurances are simply expressions of an elated social mood.

Toward the end of each chapter, the sensitive reader will see sure-fire signs of the major trend reversal in social mood. We can see one manifestation of it all around us today. The flood of tomes exposing the mania, published around the time the S&P was down 58% in March 2009, includes business best-sellers *A Failure of Capitalism: The Crisis of '08 and the Descent into Depression*; *House of Cards: A Tale of Hubris and Wretched Excess on Wall Street*; *The Return of Depression Economics and The Crisis of 2008*; *Meltdown*; and *The Great Depression Ahead*. We knew enough about the aftermath of manias to predict that authors would write such barrages of blame and reproach, exactly as they have. As *The Elliott Wave Financial Forecast* said in February 2000, right at the high (see Chapter 8), "The bull market's attendant accounting gimmicks will also get a lot more ink as the blinding light of the new era gives way to sober reflection and recrimination." To predict such things, one must have studied manias in advance to see that they all end in this manner. Here is Michael Pollan's take (from *The Botany of Desire*, 2002) on the literary response to the collapse of the Dutch tulip mania nearly 400 years ago:

> In the aftermath...broadsides excoriating the tulip mania became bestsellers: *The Fall of the Great Garden-Whore, the Villain-Goddess Flora; Flora's Fool's Cap, or Scenes from the Remarkable Year 1637 When One Fool Hatched Another, the Idle Rich Lost Their Wealth and the Wise Lost Their Senses; Charges Against Pagan and Turkish Tulip-Bulbs*. (Flora was the Roman goddess of flowers, who was a prostitute famous for bankrupting her lovers.)

So the more things change, the more they repeat themselves. Once you know that, you can predict all kids of social trends and events, from manias to the things people will write when they're over.

We didn't get it all right by any means. The chapters that follow offer many instances in which we were early or wrong (for a fuller discussion, see the Conclusion). One key miss, for instance, was identifying the rise off the October 2002/March 2003 lows as a second wave rather than a b-wave, which carried the Dow Jones Industrial Average to a new all-time high. But, as the second leg of the bear market — the countervailing force to the great bull market described here — takes hold, it has been common to hear that "no one saw it coming." The Queen of England, for instance, famously asked this "simple but fundamental question posed by many millions of Americans and people around the world" at the London School of Economics in November 2008. The answer is that *participants* in a mania, which means just about everybody, cannot see their folly and so cannot predict its end. But a better question is why, despite the historical literature on manias, they keep happening. We believe that the mass of investors can never gain an understanding of the dynamic involved because of the immutable nature of the human herding impulse, which is unconscious, and the resulting immutability of the Wave Principle. The Wave Principle describes the course that investors traverse as they transit from panic at a major stock market low (the very best buying opportunity) to euphoria at a stock market peak (the best time to sell) and vice versa. Somehow, the layered progression of shorter-term swings always causes investors to lose all respect for the extreme emotions that guided their decision-making at the last major reversal. The result is endless waves of social mood, from the pervasive fear such as prevailed at the lows of 1932 and 1974 to the unbridled enthusiasm of the late 1960s and late 1990s, and so on. It has been this way as far back as history is recorded.

The establishment of EWFF in 1999 increased the mania coverage available previously only in EWT, but even with a doubling in capacity, it became increasingly difficult to show the ever-more abundant evidence for a social-mood peak. To rectify that problem somewhat, this book rescues some additional mementos of the mania from the cutting room floor. So that you can tell them apart, items not originally shown in our publications are screened in gray and extended slightly beyond the margin. Together with the original selections, these "bonus features" are designed to aid the reader's understanding of the unconscious social impulses that are always at work in society and in the markets.

—Peter Kendall

CALVIN AND HOBBES ©1995 Watterson. Reprinted with permission of UNIVERSAL PRESS SYNDICATE. All rights reserved.

Chapter 1

The Classic Traits of a Once-in-13-Lifetimes Financial Bubble

This craze for shares is greater than the sum of its antecedents: This is the Tulip Bulb Mania, the South Sea Bubble and the Jazz Age rolled into one. The emphasis on hope over value becomes so overwhelming that investors rush to money-losing ventures that fly to absurd heights, then crash and burn. Some even rise again, phoenix-like, from the ash heap. With 200 years of advance at its back, the staying power of the shared financial dream is unprecedented. It lasts so long that the accompanying desire for luxury becomes the economic growth engine. The demand for SUVs, $15,000 handbags and Gulfstream airplanes is so vast that economic growth enjoys a time of extended animation. When the debt bubble finally breaks, however, all the others follow.

June 1996

A few months ago, Al Newman [editor] of Crosscurrents (Great Neck, NY) noted that while several technology stocks had matched the performance of tulip bulbs in 1634 to 1637, comparisons to the tulip mania were lacking one last lunatic high note. "What was missing was short-term action that equated to the Switser bulbs." Back then, Switser bulbs went up 2880% in a little over a month (see chart). Comparator Systems has now completed the analogy. In fact, its advance of 5600% from the low of 1/32 (about 3 cents) on May 3 to an intraday high of 1 25/32 (about $1.78) on May 7 took place even faster: in three trading days, setting all-time record volume for single-day trading in any stock ever. At this point, there is reason to believe that Switser bulbs were a better value. For one thing, a vice president of Comparator sold three million shares after the stock had risen 33% to 4 cents a share on May 3 (just before it soared).

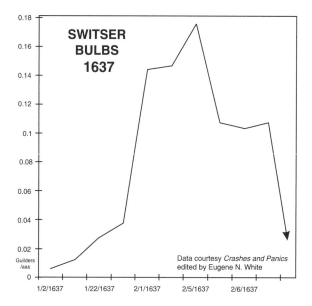

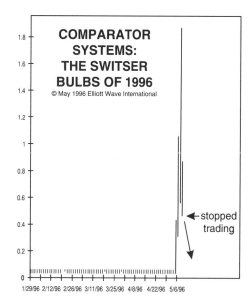

For another thing, the firm, whose market capitalization briefly surpassed $1 billion, could not even secure $2.5 million in financing. At its peak, Comparator traded at 11,866 times sales (an equivalent multiple would have Microsoft selling for $112,353 a share). Comparator is not only a late bloomer, but a fast wilter. After inquiries began, the company requested that the NASDAQ suspend trading in the stock. The SEC is investigating.

Cultural Trends

Jazz Age extravagance has broken out at nouveau riche happenings across the country as well. Charity wine auctions are sold out. What's a charity wine auction? That's where you "taste great wine and watch people really throw some money around." Such auctions raised 61% more in 1995 than 1992. "Community leaders," says one article, "are finding that an effective path to charity is through gluttony." Booming luxury sales have driven Saks Fifth Avenue to a successful public offering while retailers are scrambling to keep $5,900 Regent pens in stock and "seriously opulent" magazines like The Robb Report are flying off newsstands. "Even the icon of the 1980s, the Porsche 911, is now back in vogue." 1985 Clos Du Mesnil champagne ($300 a pop) is being rationed out in twenty-bottle consignments. A glamorous new champagne bar has opened in NYC. A subscriber says patrons of The Bubble Lounge sip flutes of vintage champagne while blowing smoke rings with a cigar. Tiffany & Co.'s profits have rocketed straight up from a loss in 1994.

Champagne Goes With Bull
The Bubble Lounge Is Manhattan's Leading Indicator

NEW YORK – Gregg Morano was already in a giddy mood before he got to the Bubble Lounge the other night.

The stock market has swooned upward, and Morano, a currency trader, called a friend to come celebrate at the chic champagne bar in Manhattan's funky TriBeCa section.

"When the markets are good, customers are in a better mood and it makes me want to come out and spend money," said Morano, 29, "When it's a bad day, I generally go home or go to a pub for a beer."

"Our sales rise and fall every day with the Dow," says Eric Macaire, a French entrepreneur who opened the Bubble Lounge in March 1996.

—*The Washington Post*, December 9, 1998

July 1996

A University of California professor has "busted the study of economics wide open" by suggesting that we are in an "idea-based" economy, which "isn't defined by scarcity and limits on growth." This opinion has been apparent in the action of this year's infamous bubble stocks, which so far have all come and gone on the basis of increasingly flimsy fundamentals. The latest, Home Link Corp., was also the first to undergo a full round trip. Home Link was up 23 times in price before regulators halted trading on June 10. When trading resumed on June 24, the stock completed a 100% retracement to $1 a share. As the media pointed out, what made "Home Link stand out from the crowd [of high flying stocks] was its complete lack of publicly available financial statements." Yet whoever purchased Home Link was simply taking the conventional wisdom to heart. Ditto Comerica, a bank, which has proposed a mutual fund composed entirely of Internet stocks.

January 1997

Cruise liners are reaching enormous new proportions. The world's largest cruise ship, the new 101,000-ton Destiny, is 50 feet taller than the Statue of Liberty, 15 feet wider than the Panama Canal and 20% larger than the Queen Elizabeth. By 1999, however, it will lose its rank as the world's biggest ocean liner. Two 130,000 ton vessels are being built by Royal Caribbean Cruise Lines.

May 1997

A mania is not simply a "big bull market." It is something else, and it not only behaves differently, but it resolves differently as well, which is why the difference is worth knowing.

Normal market behavior is the result of a chaotic feedback system, which produces a fractal movement. As long as the society involved is viable, the long term direction of the stock mar-

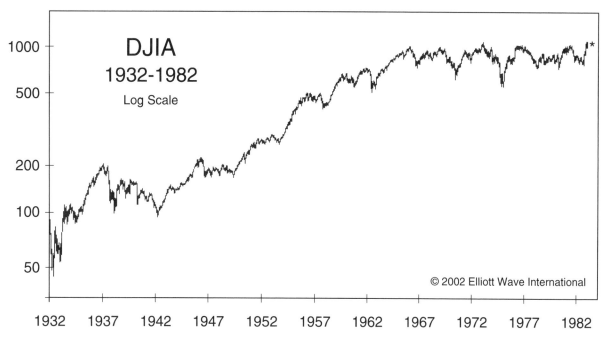

ket remains up, but it is interrupted by setbacks of various sizes. The frequency of those sizes is roughly proportional to the time between them; i.e., roughly speaking, 1% setbacks happen weekly, 15% setbacks happen annually, 50% setbacks happen twice a century, and so on. As long as the market exhibits this "breathing" phenomenon, it is healthy. Take a look at the chart of the DJIA from 1932 to 1982. Notice the irregular yet fractally patterned beat: rally is followed by correction, bull market is followed by bear market, and long rising phase is followed by long non-rising phase. The same behavior held sway from 1857 to 1921. When the market abandons this style, something else is going on.

The first aspect of a mania is that it produces a powerful, persistent rise with remarkably fewer, briefer and/or smaller setbacks. Manias are born of long term bull markets, which is to say that every mania is preceded by a long period of oft-corrected rising prices. When the time is right, the public begins to acquire the understanding that "the long term trend is *always* up" and increasingly acts as if, and ultimately presumes that, *every* degree of trend is always up.

The quotation that begins this book (see Introduction) stands as the only example in history of a mania being forecast. Most people do not even recognize manias as such when they are in them (which is why they are possible). Our purpose here is to describe the unique characteristics of a mania for the purpose of confirming that one is in force now, and more important, to display what typically follows for the purpose of forecasting what will happen afterward.

To that end are shown (on the next two pages) pictures of five market events: the Tulip Mania culminating in 1637, the South Sea Bubble of 1719-1720, the Roaring 'Twenties stock advance of 1921-1929, the Value Line index run-up in 1966-1968 and the leap in collectible coin prices in the late 1980s. The first three of these were bona fide manias. The rise in the Value Line index was not a mania, but it is the closest thing to a mania that a large number of people alive today personally experienced, which is why I show it. The rapid gain in coin prices displayed here had all the characteristics but one: It lacked broad public participation. The buying was done by brokerage firms in anticipation of public demand, which never actually materialized! The resulting picture is exactly the same, however.

The Aftermath

Webster's Dictionary defines "mania" in the individual as an "excitement of psychotic proportions manifested by mental and physical hyperactivity, disorganization of behavior, and elevation of mood." This is highly descriptive of its social manifestation as well. It is worth not-

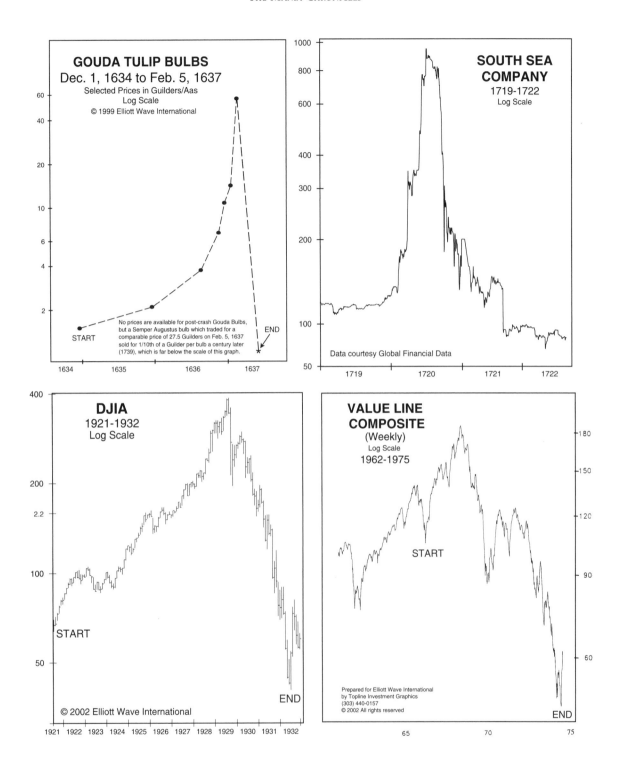

ing that the word more specifically refers to "the manic phase of manic-depressive psychosis." Is there a social parallel here, too? Apparently so, as a consistent element in these pictures brings us to this most important observation about the market's action following a mania: Regardless of extent, every mania is followed by a decline that ends below the starting point of the advance.

Considering the heights that manias reach, this is an amazing fact. Tulip bulb prices had been substantial for years and then soared in 1634-1637, reaching thousands of guilders (see top left chart).

Just one year later, city councils in Holland passed regulations allowing tulip bulb futures contracts (yes, they were a "sophisticated, modern" financial society, too) to be paid off at 3.5% of the contract price. A footnote in the book *Crashes and Panics* by Eugene N. White adds that the decline in prices was probably greater than 96.5% because many of these contracts were not fulfilled even at that price. A few decades later, a bulb could be had for 10 cents. In other words, these "investments" declined in value nearly 100%. The collapse following the South Sea Bubble (see chart, previous page) also ended below its starting point. In fact, of all the stocks listed on the London exchange at the peak, only 9% remained two years later.

Taking into account the stocks that went to zero, the average issue declined 98% in less than two years. The 1920s advance in the Dow Jones Industrial Average (see chart, previous page) began at the 64 level, while the ensuing 89% decline brought the average down to 41 in less than three years. At the top, over 800 issues routinely traded every day on the New York Stock Exchange.

Three years later, it was half that number. By 1933, many companies, municipalities and even some mutual funds had failed. The substantial public participation in the stock rise of 1966-1968 (see chart, previous page) was enough to condemn the gains to more than complete retracement as well, as the Value Line index thereafter fell 74% in six years.

Again with coin prices in the late 1980s (see chart at right), had an investor been clever enough to buy just before the explosive advance, he would currently have a loss.

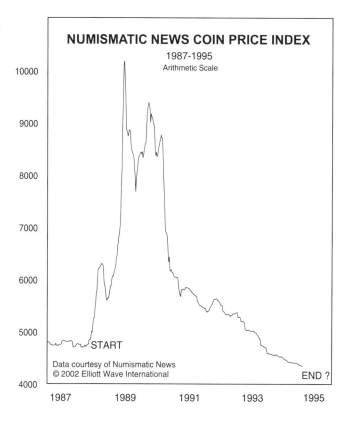

Why must a mania be more than fully retraced? The scientific explanation, I expect, has to do with the disruption of a properly functioning chaotic system. Here is a quote from "Science Watch" in The New York Times of April 15, 1997:

> Dr. Ary L. Goldberger, director of electrocardiology at Beth Israel [hospital], determined that healthy hearts exhibit *slight fractal-like irregularities — patterned variations of beating*. A heart beat that seems *abnormally smooth and free of fractal variations may actually signal an impending heart attack.* [ellipsis omitted, emphasis added]

The same thing is true of investment markets. When they become smoothly-trending and free of fractal variations, they depict an unhealthy patient and signal an impending "heart attack."

June 1997

Mania Watch

Let's examine one foreign market in depth. As noted in our May 1997 study, "Bulls, Bears and Manias," one of the things that has pushed this episode in popular delusion beyond all others is the "unprecedented depth of participation" whereby even "current bastions of Communism" are caught up in the fever. Consider these headlines about the world's most populated country: "Oblivious to Risk, Chinese Riding a Stock Market High," "Small Time Savers Make Big Time

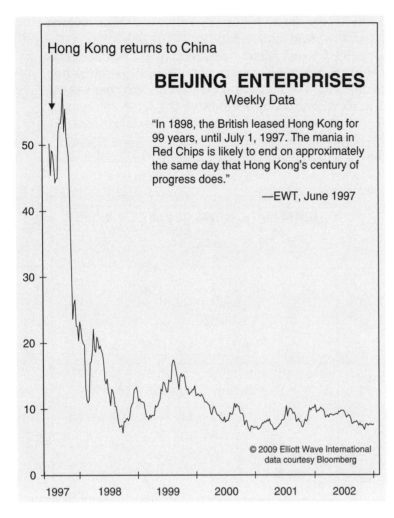

Hong Kong returns to China

BEIJING ENTERPRISES
Weekly Data

"In 1898, the British leased Hong Kong for 99 years, until July 1, 1997. The mania in Red Chips is likely to end on approximately the same day that Hong Kong's century of progress does."

—EWT, June 1997

© 2009 Elliott Wave International
data courtesy Bloomberg

Gains," "The Trading of Four Stocks Suspended After Prices Soar Much Too Quickly," and "Red-Chip Fever Hits Hong Kong Market."

Red Chips are mainland Chinese stocks that are traded on the Hong Kong exchange. As of now, names like Gitic Enterprises, Beijing Enterprises Holdings and Shanghai Industrial are not commonly known in the U.S., but the unbelievable demand for these offerings (up to 1300 times supply) and the lack of any fundamental justification for the prices being offered assures that, in time, they will be legendary. The euphoria surrounding these stocks makes the U.S. stock market seem tame. Beijing Enterprises went to the market to raise $241.6 million. Instead, it brought $31.5 billion in subscriptions.

Chinese speculators say that mathematics have been adjusted to account for the "hidden value" they see in one particular company backed by Shanghai's municipal government: "In what circumstances does one plus one equal three? When valuing Shanghai Industrial," says a Hong Kong broker. Speculators are absolutely convinced that "the government wouldn't let the market fall ahead of Hong Kong's return to China." The fuel behind the speculation is margin financing provided by Chinese banks, which "cover as much as 95% of the value of the shares to which investors subscribe." The word from the South China Morning Post is that these loans are being "channeled directly into stocks" at an increasing rate. "Lawyers, doctors and every fund manager in town are playing 'bingo,' in the words of one fund manager," says a correspondent. "People who have no idea about the trading of stocks nevertheless join the quest for shares so as not to 'miss out,'" reports a subscriber. "No one wants to be excluded."

In 1982, at the end of Cycle Wave IV, ties to China were considered stock market poison. "In 1982, [the Hong Kong] market tanked because the government sold a prime piece of land to the Bank of China at a friendship price," recollects The Asia Wall Street Journal. "Contrast that resistance to China's embrace with the present-day urge to leap into the maw of the dragon." The difference is in social psychology at a major low vs. a major high. Ironically, the buying stampede is a bet against the continuation of free markets in Hong Kong. "People don't believe China's promises to maintain Hong Kong's system after July. The inescapable conclusion is that Hong Kong companies that want to thrive after June must be prepared to jockey for political position in Beijing." Yes, the communists are coming, and this means a plunder of the island's businesses infrastructure. These stock buyers want a share of the booty, and they actually think they will get it!

Already, however, bad loans are reported to account for 20% of commercial loans in Chinese banks. Hong Kong bankers estimate that the total is probably closer to 30%. Margin debt will be the final killer when prices reverse trend. Those most plundered will ultimately be the "investors" themselves, the banks that supported them, the productivity of Hong Kong, and ultimately the

Chinese mainland and its government, as a result of the fallout. Grand Supercycle tops bring the end of multi-decade trends. As we noted in *At the Crest of the Tidal Wave*, 1896 marked a major Kondratieff cycle bottom and a major low in the Dow. In 1898, the British leased Hong Kong for 99 years, until July 1, 1997. The mania in Red Chips is likely to end on approximately the same day that Hong Kong's century of progress does.

December 1997

When the history of the 1990s is written, it will be said that until [the end of 1997] there was a lingering sense of unease with the wealth created by the great bull market. Layoffs, an uneven distribution of wealth, and retirement worries tempered the usual bull market urge to give in and go for the good life. Last February, a downtown Manhattan Lamborghini dealer summed up the hesitancy well when he told us that business was good but not "stupid good" like it was in the late 1980s. In the midst of last spring's correction, however, as cigar bars infiltrated the far reaches of Manhattan, Wall Streeters finally blew the lid off conspicuous consumption. The Wall Street Journal says they "began snapping up big ticket stuff from Park Avenue apartments to suburban mansions" to all the usual bull market trophies.

With the Dow high of August 7, the public was piling on. The list of big-ticket goods that were taking off in the late summer and early fall of 1997 ranges from fine wine (and the wine cellars to boot), $3 to $7 million second homes and picture portraits, which are hot because "newly empowered people want to underscore their status" by paying up to $250,000 to immortalize themselves on canvas. A brand new luxury magazine, Luxe, is targeted for the "corporate executive and others who market luxury brands to those wealthy enough to light cigars with $100 bills." Other newly popular symbols of wealth are alligator shoes, recording labels and, of course, fancy new homes. A subscriber notes that medium-priced homes continue to languish, while "large new homes, even if twice the price of the bargain, are selling like hotcakes. There is no fear of debt." Another reports people paying $125,000 over the asking price for a house in an affluent Massachusetts community. A California Mercedes showroom turned into a "World Wrestling Federation" match recently when it introduced its new M Class. Affluent young buyers were literally fighting over the floor models. The "M" is for "Mania," says a headline. A subscriber tells us of his yacht-broker friend who almost went out of business in 1991. He is so short of yachts today that he is offering owners big premiums to sell. The last time yachts were in such an outrageous "I-gotta-have-one-now" demand was in the late 1960s, at the top of Cycle wave III.

The fur trade is enjoying this victory. Only yesterday, it seems, Naomi Campbell and her "supermodel" friends posed nude alongside a banner that said, "I'd rather go naked than wear fur." These days, they are draping themselves with mink stoles, full-length fox and baby-blue Mongolian lamb jackets. In Harper's Bazaar, fall fur ads

---

M IS FOR MANIA
Dealers Can't Keep Mercedes' New M-Class Sport Utility Vehicle in the Showroom

At a coming-out party in Silicon Valley last month for the Mercedes M-Class 3, 2000 eager customers swarmed over the Smythe European dealership. The gridlock outside got so bad that a nearby freeway exit had to be shut down. Inside the showroom, wine guzzling customers thronged the floor models. A melee erupted later when the demonstrator models arrived. "It was like a World Wrestling Federation match," says dealership manager David Spisak. "People were screaming, 'It's mine,' 'I've got it next.'"

Mercedes dealers say a sort of madness has gripped their showrooms with the arrival of the M-Class in recent weeks, "It's been phenomenal – we're overrun with people," says Eric Hessinger, manager of Bobby Rahal Motorcar Co. in Wexford.

—*The Pittsburgh Post-Gazette*, October 11, 1997

Fashion Industry:
Fur Is Coming Out of the Closet

Perhaps it started in the spring, when model Naomi Campbell, who once posed nude for an advertisement that read "I'd rather go naked than wear fur," strolled down the Fendi runway draped in a sable-lined coat.

At Harper's Bazaar, fall fur ads for 1997 are up 87 percent from last year and are also at a 10-year high. Retailers around the country are confident that a rebound is under way.

The Seattle Fur Exchange, one of the two largest fur auction houses in North America, said mink prices at auctions this year were the highest ever.

—*The New York Times*, October 1, 1997

September 29, 1997

Fall 1997

are up 87% to a 10-year high, a figure matched by several other fashion mags. In September, the Seattle Fur Exchange experienced the most successful mink auction in its 98-year history. After hitting a low of $987 million in 1991 during the recession, fur sales climbed back to $1.25 billion last year and are expected to surpass that total easily this year. With the big autumn push, the 1987 (the last stock top, remember?) record of $1.8 billion may fall. "Like cigars, large vehicles and red meat, fur may be on the brink of returning to the fold of socially acceptable indulgences as many wealthy consumers brush off early 1990s taboos in favor of flaunting their good fortune." The costume curator at New York City's Metropolitan Museum of Art reports that "fashion is less drawn to the moral strictures that drove fur out. There is a certain cultural sense now that if it feels good, wear it." Then there is the ultimate luxury, charity. It is the hip new thing, as super-rich titans have turned their ultra-competitive streaks to handing money out rather than hauling it in. Leading the pack is Ted Turner's $1 billion in promised contributions to United Nations' humanitarian projects. George Soros followed a few days later with a $500 million gift to Russia. He dropped another $4.5 million on a group of "guerrilla philanthropists" dedicated to New York's poor. Bill Gates, the world's richest man, has also made a down payment on his promise to give all his money away before he dies with a $215 million contribution that will bring the Internet to public libraries. Meal programs, museums, university foundations and research labs are "thriving on the bull market." A new magazine, The American Benefactor, was created to court and cajole the "new wealth." As a spokesperson for the magazine says, "You get to a point where people ask how much is enough."

The point of maximum satiation, whether it is revealed by lavish gifts or indulgences, will mark the big turn. The market has become the obvious tie that binds this culture-wide celebration together. During the stock market decline of October 27, a local Lexus dealership fell almost entirely silent. On the rebound since then, business has returned, but the brief and sudden pall shows that the survival of such businesses depends heavily on new highs in the Dow. After hitting an all-time high of 48 in October, Tiffany & Co. shares are now around 38, failing to follow the November rally. Here too, Asia may be providing a peek at the future in the U.S. The Financial Times reports that a "used-to-be-rich" market now offers limousines, hydrofoils, light aircraft, and other second-hand luxury toys at "bargain" prices.

A Jungian Perspective
(by Anne Crittenden)

Carl Jung (Swiss psychotherapist, 1875-1961) believed that the psychological foundation we all share as human beings makes us susceptible to "psychic contagion" from those about us. Today, because of electronic communications and mass media, such contagion can rapidly become a full-scale epidemic. When this occurs, we are no longer responsible, sensible individuals, but a herd. This is the situation today in the stock market, particularly in the United States but virtually throughout the world. We must always be aware of the fragility of our rational capacity and must treat the unconscious with great respect and caution. If this is not done, individually, our ego can be seized and enthralled by an archetypal unconscious influence. In the grip of an archetypal idea, our ego becomes charged up by a sense of power. In Jungian terms, the ego becomes "inflated." This is bad enough in an individual, but if the collectivity identifies with an archetype, the result is mass psychic inflation, a populist mania.

Such is the situation today in the stock market, throughout much of the world. There is, alas, nothing new in the phenomenon of mass mania. Throughout history there have been many manias: political, military, religious, financial. The effect is always to over stimulate the group so that its sense of power and efficacy is abnormally revved up. Social mood becomes supercharged. The collectivity as a whole feels enlarged, energized and empowered. National self-esteem soars. It becomes extremely difficult for any individual to resist this marvelous feeling of elation and godlikeness. Jung never tired of pointing out that only a highly developed consciousness of the power of the unconscious can enable an individual to withstand the power of the psychic flood sweeping everybody along. There is nothing more isolating than maintaining one's individuality in a mass mania. When people succumb, however, they lose the capacity for independent thought and function almost solely as bearers of the prevailing psychological epidemic. Eventually, even previously responsible people can become a mindless herd governed by some collective fantasy.

May 1998

The "if-it-moves-buy-it" strategy of these new "stock market high rollers" appeared to reach a climax on April 21 and 22 when several thinly-traded NASDAQ stocks burst out of flat-line patterns and raced to gains of between 500% and 1000% (equaling the historic gain that has taken the DJIA 16 years to accomplish) in a matter of days, or in the

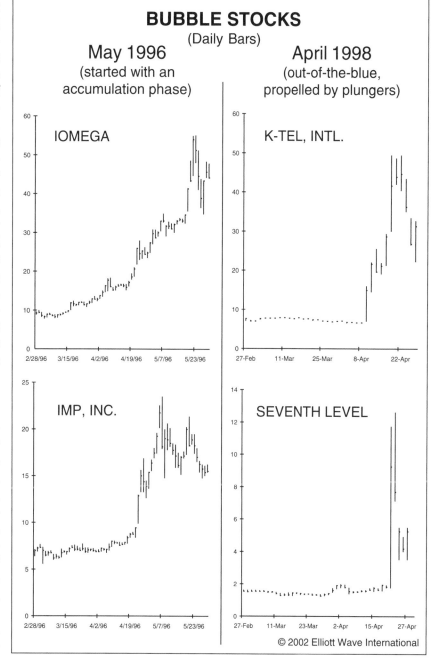

© 2002 Elliott Wave International

case of one stock, hours. When similar bull raids occurred in May 1996, *The Elliott Wave Theorist* (EWT) pointed to the sharp nature of the advances as reminiscent of the one-month run in Switser bulbs that closed out the tulip-bulb mania of 1634-1637, stating it was a sure sign of a top. It was, as the averages immediately dropped 10%, though obviously it was not the top.

The charts on the previous page show two focal points of bullish frenzy in May 1996. As you can see, the May 1996 episode was gradual by comparison, as most of the explosive rises (Comparator Systems excepted) were preceded by a slowly-rising "accumulation" phase. In contrast, the two charts on the right show stocks that in mid-April rocketed in and out of favor in a span of just six days. The message is that the recent plungers' frenzy was more intense than the last. It therefore should be doused with a correction more severe than that of July 1996. By the way, virtually all of 1996's bubble stocks now trade at a fraction of the value they attained at their May climax. Many are trading below the levels from which they began their ascent, if they are trading at all.

Even higher prices are possible in this mania. How extended is it? Well, the DJIA in the 16 years from 1982 has exceeded the previous record-setting percentage gain achieved by Japan's Nikkei index in its 15-year advance from 1974 to 1989! The Nikkei rose 1009% in that period, while the Dow has risen 1082% from 1982. This makes the U.S. stock mania the biggest in all recorded history, at least for a major market. From 1974, the same date used for the Nikkei, the Dow is up 1490%, while as of today, the Nikkei's net advance is 345.43%, one-quarter as much. Thus, from the perspective of an investor at the 1974 lows, the Dow today is four times as expensive as the Nikkei, which in my view is still overpriced.

December 1998

Nothing hones the human herding impulse in on an idea and a shared sense of optimism so intensely as the final highs in a mania. In 1720, the focus was the New World. In 1929, it was the radio. In 1968 and again in 1983, it was the computer. This time around, the Internet is the excuse for historic speculation. The difference this time, of course, is that we have had several bubbles within the bubble. We continue to believe, however, that these episodes in panic buying are totally misguided (if it were not so, Comparator and Iomega, the shooting stars of this

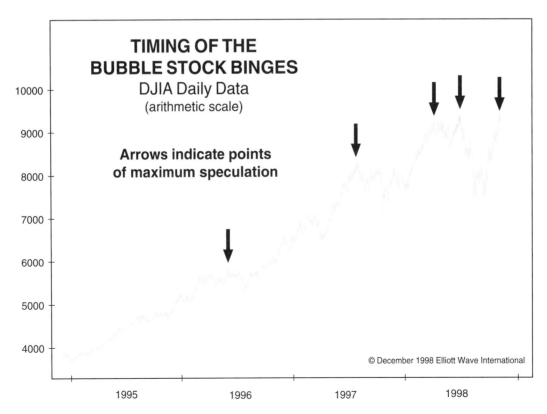

TIMING OF THE
BUBBLE STOCK BINGES
DJIA Daily Data
(arithmetic scale)

Arrows indicate points
of maximum speculation

© December 1998 Elliott Wave International

mania's first frenzy in May/June 1996, would rule the world by now) and ultimately terminal. Humankind always makes unqualified, emotional commitments to the shared vision at the wrong time.

The strength of the signal has been magnified by the number of runaway stocks, their enormous valuations and a broadening public attraction to the "risk and raw thrill" of investment, all against a weaker overall stock market. Back in April, the lightning hit a few relatively illiquid shares. Remember K-Tel? From mid-April to May 5, it went from less than $5 to almost $40 in a few days, but even at its high, the Internet retailer of Golden Oldies had a relatively modest market capitalization of $500 million. This time the valuations have hit 10 and 20 times that amount. An Internet merchant called eBay, for instance, now has a market capitalization of $8.2 billion, surpassing that of Kmart! The newly public auctioneer of collectibles is up 1036% since September 24. Another internet concept stock, theglobe.com, has been dubbed the "mania of all manias." It was offered at $9 in an IPO, opened at $90 and topped at $97, all on one day, November 13. The jump was the biggest intraday increase in the history of the IPO market, breaking the record set by Broadcast.com on July 17. Theglobe.com is now trading at about $35. A stock with the symbol AMEN went from $4 to $40 to $11 in a week.

Pinkmonkey.com, a former shell corporation that doesn't appear to have any full-time employees and on a "good day" sells $30 worth of Cliff notes over the Internet, recently rose almost 1700% from November 27 to December 2. On December 2, investors poured more than $10 million into the stock, which had a float of 370,000 shares and 14.2 million shares outstanding. It has since declined 65%.

Many more stocks than we can mention have seen eight- and ten-fold increases in a matter of days, all on 100-share lots bought by the public, based on nothing but a name and a plan, which is less equity than tulips had in 1630. This time, the errant rockets from earlier frenzies have returned for an encore. K-Tel, for instance, has had its second once-in-a-lifetime round-trip in less than a year. After returning to $5 in late October, the stock rallied all the way back to $39. It's now back at $15 and faces delisting and a rash of shareholder lawsuits.

February 1999

The great Tulip Mania of the 1630s in Holland was so remarkable that it made the history books. The popular Gouda bulb climbed to an increase of 37 times in value over the course of about two years. The popular stock Yahoo hit $455 January 11, which put its value up 100 times its offering value in 1996, a Fibonacci 2.618 times the Gouda bulb experience. What does the relatively greater speculation this time say about the historic nature of the Great Asset Mania? It says that the only alternative to this being a Grand Supercycle top is that it is of even higher degree.

Historical accounts of the Tulip Mania show that its last few weeks saw a reversal of the usual flight to quality. A dash from quality in the terminal stage of the advance reflected a "class difference" between the "nobleman, merchants, and shopkeepers...who traded in piece goods" and the rising influence of less experienced investors "trading in pound goods." In *Extraordinary Popular Delusions and The Madness of Crowds*, Charles Mackay describes this progression from the aristocrats and money changers at the outset of the mania in 1634 to "farmers, mechanics, seamen, footmen, maid-servants, even chimney sweeps and old clotheswomen" at the end, when "every one imagined that the passion for tulips would last for ever." As a result, lower quality "pound goods" (like the Switsers) replaced by-the-bulb "piece goods" prices (like Goudas) as the primary object of speculation. Switsers rose better than 25 times in value in the final month compared to a 10 times multiple gain in the Goudas. Likewise, at the end of this century's Great Asset Mania, Yahoo is lagging, up "just" 3 times from its October level compared to 6 times for the Internet Index. The quality of the late bloomers like Pinkmonkey (17 times), USA Talks (25 times), Books-A-Million (21 times) and J.B. Oxford (73 times) is so poor that Yahoo, which has a projected P/E ratio of 540, is considered a blue chip by comparison. "It sounds absurd to ask if investors would fall for a company that makes money. But that's the environment we live in

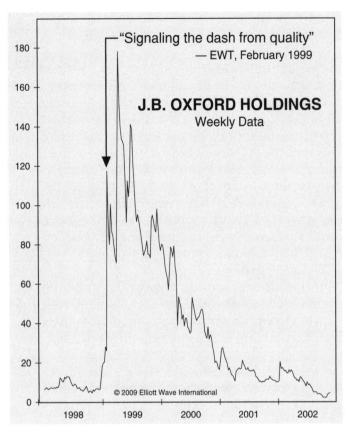

"Signaling the dash from quality"
— EWT, February 1999

J.B. OXFORD HOLDINGS
Weekly Data

© 2009 Elliott Wave International

these days," noted one analyst. E*trade, a leading on-line trading firm, is down almost 20% since January 29.

Over the same four trading days, J.B. Oxford, a brokerage that is far smaller and currently under investigation by the SEC on charges of market manipulation, jumped from $2 to $25.75. This change in leadership is signaling the same dash from quality that occurred at the end of the Tulip Bulb Mania, and for the same reason.

May 1999

In another throwback, this time to the tulip bulb mania in 1637, we are seeing more of the terminal flight from quality that EWT covered in the February issue. The latest trend appears to be successful offerings from Internet companies that not only are posting losses, but hardly have revenues.

June 1999

So what's holding up the economy? According to reliable first quarter estimates by The Jerome Levy Institute and media accounts since the end of March, the only driver left for the world economy is the American consumer's extraordinary willingness to binge on luxury goods. Back in 1988, EWT made a similar observation with regard to Japan: "Stories have been reported of rich folks sprinkling flakes of gold on their sushi in Tokyo." It turned out to be the beginning of the end for the Japanese stock bubble. Today in the U.S., newspapers are filled with stories about silver baby rattles, $10,000 teddy bears, waiting lists for $65 million Gulfstream aircraft, $15,000 handbags and the latest California rage for 10,000-to-20,000-square-foot residences that "could soon proliferate across the land." One third of Ford Motor Company's 1998 earnings came from the sale of 300,000 sport utility vehicles made in just one of its 53 plants around the world.

EWT observed in late 1997 that the luxury boom got off to a bit of a slow start as retirement worries, layoffs and worldwide disinflation "tempered the usual bull market urge to give in and go for the good life." In the second half of 1997, however, luxury spending got going in earnest. When it did, EWT noticed right away that the stock market was "the obvious tie that binds this culture-wide celebration together." At that time we added, "The point of maximum satiation, whether it is revealed by lavish gifts or indulgences, will mark the big turn." We have no reason to believe that the citizens of Japan and the U.S. are different in this regard. What better way to end more than 200 years of economic expansion than a boom made up entirely of luxuries? By definition, luxuries are not necessary, so we must be very near "maximum satiation" and thus "the big turn." One terminal sign is the sobering recognition that the "national culture of upscale spending" is itself a mania. In a U.S. News & World Report exposé of May 24, a Cornell professor calls it "luxury fever" and says many of the over-extended participants are "caught in an arms-race-like cycle in which a series of decisions, logical in themselves, add up to collective madness." If that sounds like a passage from Charles Mackay's *Extraordinary Popular Delusions and the Madness of Crowds*, it's probably because the tulip bulb mania of the 1630s had much the same effect on 17th Century consumers: "Houses and lands, horses and carriages, and luxu-

The Urge to Splurge

A booming economy is turning America into a land of big spenders.

Case study: the Ford Motor Co. in its startling new role as the purveyor of Volvos, Jaguars, and Aston-Martins. Throw in Lincolns, and Ford now offers a line of premium cars that generated 650,000 worldwide sales last year. And that's not counting the greatest moneymakers of all, the Ford Expedition and the Lincoln Navigator. With a typical array of options, these 17-foot-long, 5,000-pound behemoths carry price tags of $36,000 and $45,000, yielding luxury-style profit margins of $12,000 and $15,000, respectively. Yet Ford is selling close to 300,000 of them a year, thus turning a gross profit of roughly $3.7 billion — a third of the company's global earnings for 1998 — on the output of just one of its 53 factories around the world.

America can now lay claim to what conservative critic David Frum has aptly called "history's first mass upper class." This great burst of affluence has been a boon to sellers of jewelry and gourmet chocolate. There are waiting lists for $65 million Gulfstream aircraft and $15,000 Hermes bags. "There are more $10,000 – $50,000 watches being worn on a daily basis than ever before," says Dan Phillips, publisher of the Robb Report, a magazine dedicated to initiating the newly affluent into "the luxury lifestyle."

I'll take it. But if the country has a case of what the Cornell University economist Robert Frank calls "luxury fever," the afflicted include many Americans well outside the top quintile when it comes to either income or assets. With the economy booming and incomes finally beginning to climb for those on the middle and lower rungs of the ladder, a "national culture of upscale spending" has emerged, economist Juliet Schor writes in The Overspent American. People are running up record levels of debt, she argues, in order to acquire bigger cars, bigger TVs, and bigger houses.

To many recent home buyers, the combination of low interest rates and high incomes adds up to a "once-in-a-lifetime opportunity," as Gail Frederick, who teaches elementary-school phys ed, says.

Frederick and her husband, Jeffrey, a podiatrist, recently moved into a $500,000 custom-built home in Franklin, Mich. They would be the first to admit that they had to extend themselves financially. "We like to joke around here that the Fredericks live life in the fast lane," she says. But her husband regards the house as a pension plan. "In 30 years," he explains, "we can do a reverse mortgage or a remortgage and use it as a retirement fund for the rest of our lives." Once they decided to take the housebuilding plunge, the couple agreed that they should go all-out on such things as granite countertops, marble tile in the bathroom, a workout room, and, in short, "the full swanky," as Gail Frederick terms it. Yet their home, she hastens to point out, is far from grand compared to the one across the street. Indeed, the McMansions of the East and Midwest are dwarfed by some of those currently rising on the West Coast. Americans, says Cornell's Frank, are "trying to be as rational as they can." But they're caught in an arms race-like cycle in which a series of decisions, logical in themselves, add up to collective madness.

—U.S. News & World Report, May 24, 1999

ries of every sort, rose in value, and for some months Holland seemed the very antechamber of Plutus." In this regard, we have no reason to believe that the Americans are different from the Dutch, either.

November 1999

While this almost surely marks the end of the line for Beanies, there is a possibility that instead of concluding with the bull market, non-market speculation will press on and express itself in some even more frantic and eccentric forms. There is a precedent for a non-financial bidding frenzy after a peak of Supercycle degree in the 1838 hysteria for mulberry trees. Supercycle (I) topped in 1835, and the panic of 1837 brought a near total halt to one of the great episodes of financial speculation in U.S. history. The September issue of Horticulture reports that the burgeoning mid-1830s trade in mulberry trees continued giddily higher well into 1838. mulberry orchards sprang up in every state even though the trees were never effectively used for the intended purpose, the manufacture of silk. "In the rush to buy and plant mulberries, silk was almost forgotten; the real money was in speculating in trees." Finally, the "real problems associated with producing raw silk" became apparent. "Worse, the 'golden tree' turned out to be more delicate than its boosters knew." Sometime between late 1838 and the spring of 1839, 'the bottom dropped out of the market." During the deflationary depression of the early 1840s, "cold winters and blight killed off those few remaining trees that furious and frustrated farmers hadn't already grubbed up." "Next time," mulberry buyers must have thought afterward, "I'm going to read the prospectus."

December 1999
When the Dow Breaks...

A common assumption is that as long as the NASDAQ holds up, stocks are on safe ground. The chart shows that historically, when the NASDAQ (and its predecessor the OTC Index) pushes into record territory against a lagging Dow, the overall market is late in a long-term uptrend. Apparently, it is only after years of ascent that investors can work up the courage to jump into these relatively young names despite a weakening trend. Not shown are the Dow peaks of 1946, 1953, 1957 and 1962, which were coincident. For the duration of Cycle wave III, the OTC Index

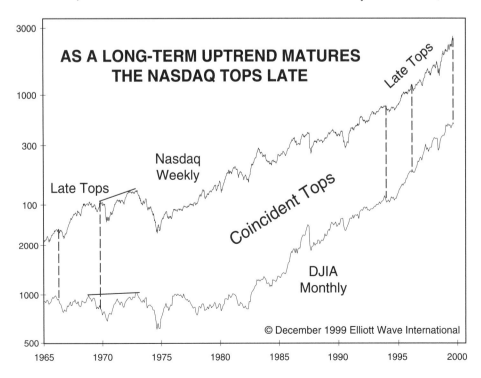

did not push to new highs beyond a major Dow peak. It did, however, peak in April 1966, three months after Cycle wave III's final high. Intrepid investors stayed with the OTC again in 1969 after the Dow double-topped in late 1968. At the January 1973 high, the two indexes peaked together, but the NASDAQ was well past its prior high while the Dow barely exceeded the high of 1968. In Cycle wave V, NASDAQ peaks were before or coincident with the Dow until 1994 when it defied the Dow by rallying seven weeks beyond the late January peak for most indices. In 1997, the NASDAQ surpassed the Dow's peak by nine weeks. In both cases, the discrepancy was resolved in a matter of days with resounding declines in all indices. A new Dow high will not change the natural hierarchy of a healthy bull market in which the big names set the pace. When the herd pursues the more speculative stocks to the virtual exclusion of the Dow, it represents a breakdown in the established order.

From a contrarian's standpoint, another good reason to keep an eye on the Dow is that the index has suddenly lost respect in the marketplace. "Ignore any forecast of the Dow or anyone whose analysis is based on the Dow," says a Forbes columnist. Fortune has created a new index it calls "the antidote to the Dow Jones Industrial Average." The Fortune e-50 index is composed entirely of Internet-related companies. The rationale behind this Dow bashing is revealed by the Washington Post business editor's response to a reader who said he had "tired of this buy-and-hold bunk." When the Dow was going down in September and early October, the editor said that he, too, thought for a moment "that the big one had arrived: that for the first time, I would have to bid farewell to the good times. But I came to my senses." His mistake, he decided, was putting too much faith in the world's most-watched index. "Sell if you must. But the swinging pendulum of the Dow should not be the dispositive factor in our decisions. If you find that you're too anxious, just take a look at what the Dow really is. It's 30 stocks of huge old-timey companies." He pointed to one recent trading day in which an earnings shortfall at IBM accounted for almost all of a 1% decline in the Dow. "How did this compare with the movement of other equity indexes? Badly. The NASDAQ composite was actually up half a percentage point. I believe we should treat the Dow like a sports score most of the time." A recent issue of American Heritage magazine has even gotten in on the trash-the-Dow sentiment with a list of complaints that have dogged the index "almost since the day it was born." The article headlined "Lies, Damned Lies, and the Dow" concludes that a single revision of the Dow had cheated the world out of untold prosperity. If IBM had not been removed in 1939, "the actual history of the stock market would have been different. For the players in the market would have reacted differently to the very different readings Charles Dow's barometer would have given them."

American Heritage is half right. The DJIA is a mass feedback loop that allows the financial community to feed off its own emotion. But as Bob Prechter explains in his chapter on "Impulsivity and Herding" in *The Wave Principle of Human Social Behavior* (HSB), this process doesn't undermine its integrity, it assures it:

> The reason is that every market is both produced by information and produces information. Each transaction, while at once an effect, becomes part of the market and, by communicating transactional data to investors, joins the chain of causes of others' behavior. This process is governed by man's unconscious social nature. Since he has such a nature, the process repeatedly generates the same forms.

As Dow Jones & Co. says, "The components may change with the times, but what the Dow represents remains constant." It is the best measure of social mood, and thus the best tool for forecasting because it comprises "huge old-timey" names like GE, Disney, Texaco and IBM. By contrast, the NASDAQ is being driven by some names that did not even exist 10 years ago. The NASDAQ is getting bigger, but the Dow is psychologically universal. The only reason the pundits of today don't like it is that another index is stronger, and, of course, only a bullish index can be valid.

January 2000
...The Cradle Will Fall

Under the heading "When the Dow Breaks," last month's *Elliott Wave Financial Forecast* (EWFF) identified the discrepancy between the languishing Dow and the ebullient NASDAQ as a classic sign of long-term vulnerability for the market. In the past when the NASDAQ rose to new highs after a floundering Dow, it has always succumbed to the Dow's lead. In 1994 and 1997, we noted that similar discrepancies "were resolved in a matter of days with resounding declines." Those drops averaged 15%, but the degree of this turn is almost certainly higher.

IS THIS THE MODEL FOR THE NASDAQ?
(updated from *Short Term Update* December 13, 1999)

NASDAQ Composite=Left Scale
Nikkei 225 (1/1/89-12/29/89)=Right Scale

Concept courtesy of Ned Davis Research, Inc.

1989 Top
NASDAQ is here?
NIKKEI 225 INDEX

Shaky Concerns Are the Talk of Chat Room

Investing chat rooms are great gauges of what is hot among today's fickle and fidgety stock traders. The chat room craze du jour is stocks of companies that are currently insolvent.

In recent weeks, investors have thronged into shares of troubled companies like Fruit of the Loom, Levitz Furniture, Loehmann's, Iridium World Communications and the Singer Company. Between January 10 and January 12, for example, Levitz furniture shares went from 5 cents to 37 cents on no news. And last Wednesday, Loehmann's stock almost tripled for no apparent reason, going from 12 cents a share to 34 cents.

Inexplicably, the chatterers seem to view these companies' depressed shares as bets worth taking. One Fruit of the Loom fan posted this message on a Yahoo board last week: "FTL's earnings were upgraded by First Call to less of a loss, this makes me believe that we have nowhere to go but up from here."

—The New York Times, January 23, 2000

Additional evidence of a very important peak is shown in the chart shown here. It places the NASDAQ 100 of 1999 over the Japanese Nikkei of 1989, revealing a remarkable similarity. Recall that the Nikkei topped on the last trading day of 1989 and subsequently fell nearly 65% over the next two years. Such analogies rarely work to perfection, but given the striking replication of a year-long trading pattern, this one bears watching.

A good example of the craziness that results in this environment is what has become of investors' benchmarks for expected returns. As "the focus of the mania narrows," "Bulls, Bears and Manias" noted, so do the benchmarks, and they become increasingly difficult to attain. In the final months of 1999, the focus was so narrow and the psychological pressure to keep up so strong that the benchmarks themselves had to be adjusted to keep pace. In November, the Dow dumped four solid, dividend-paying companies for four non-dividend paying "new era" firms, and in December, the S&P 500 added Yahoo! to its roster. Upon its addition to the S&P, Yahoo! shot up almost 150 points, and several old-line stocks tanked because money managers had to sell them to finance their purchase of the Internet search engine company. Blindly buying the index has become so central to the "management" of investment assets that fund managers throw away established companies with earnings and dividends for a five-year old firm with no dividends, virtually no intrinsic book value and a P/E of more than 600.

March 2000

Back in May, Paul Volcker said, "the fate of the world" hinges on "the stock market, whose growth is dependent on about 50 stocks, half of which have never reported earnings." Well, it is still true, but there are some new wrinkles. One big problem is that the world seems to have recognized and embraced its dependence. When the NASDAQ rallies, investors all over the globe cheer, as this headline demonstrates: "Eurostocks Strong, Enthused Over NASDAQ Rally."

An ominous development is that the stock market's leadership has changed. Even bull market champions like Microsoft, AOL and Qualcomm have deserted the cause. The NASDAQ's strength is derived from rotation among a thinning list of high-tech stocks. "The mentality is, 'Let's trim the generals and put some of that money to work among the soldiers.'" The flaw in this investment strategy was discussed at length in the December issue. Basically, it boils down to this: Investors are so bullish that they will defy their own social nature to back a leaderless army. The chart (shown on page 13) in the December EWFF shows that such transgressions generally happen only late in long-term uptrends. The resulting carnage resembles what happens in a real war when the generals abandon the fight. In January, investors got a small taste of the potential bloodbath when the NASDAQ fell more than 10% in four days. Despite this demonstration of how these discrepancies have historically been resolved, the divergence in trend between the OTC indexes and all other stocks is bigger than ever. This is a bearish sign for the overall market, including the NASDAQ.

April 2000

Ironically, as the old money reaches out for the new, the new tycoons are acting more and more like blue bloods. Silicon Valley has recently become engulfed in an air of pretense and rectitude that is so thick it's making the papers. A name change for one of the industry's trendiest annual soirées shows how mindful the newly rich have become of their treasure. The Millionaires' Dinner is now the Billionaires' Dinner. According to The Wall Street Journal, the name of the event was actually changed last year, but a year ago "many attendees insisted, the 'B' word just wasn't for them. A sense of unrealness had kept the moguls from taking it all too seriously until now. By last week, no one seemed to be bothering with such pretenses. The chatter was now full of sober discussions of the vast wealth that has been created and what to do with it." As they "come to terms" with their wealth, many are leaving the lucrative posts that are the source of their fortunes to concentrate full time on spending their money. Even though the company he founded has yet to make a profit, the founder of Red Hat Inc. has retired as a "billionaire" "at the ripe old age of 30." "He's been thinking a lot about helping others," says a Washington Post profile. "Philanthropy — he likes the ring of it. He considers it an 'interesting' way to keep occupied." "It's a huge, looming thing," says a philanthropy specialist. "I don't think most people have really grasped how consequential and transformative that money is going to be." It may be transformative and consequential

BOOMTOWN:
At the Billionaires' Dinner, Tech Stars Move to Grown-Ups' Table

MONTEREY, Calif. — Like a lot of things in the frothy Internet world, it didn't take long for an annual get-together at one of the industry's trendiest conferences to show mindboggling growth — in this case a change in its name from the Millionaires' Dinner to the Billionaires' Dinner.

When the host, New York literary agent John Brockman, added three zeros to the dinner last year, there was more than a bit of giggly discomfort among the attendees. The general agreement was that the provocative Mr. Brockman, who also runs a discussion Web site called Edge.org, was poking fun more than offering a description. The "B" word, many attendees insisted, just wasn't for them — who are really just regular people.

By last week, no one seemed to be bothering with such pretenses. And the chatter, which used to sound like gee-whiz-kids playing at business, was now full of sober discussions of financing, deals, mergers and, most tellingly, the vast wealth that has been created and what to do with it.

One of the assembled moguls, Sky Dayton, who founded the EarthLink Internet-access service (merged this year with its main rival MindSpring), zeroed in on the feeling immediately. "In a way, the whole tone of being understated was set long ago by Bill Gates and his insistence of doing things like flying coach," he said, surveying the scene. "But I think that is just about over." Now, "I think no one pretends any more that they fly coach," he laughs. "They seem less afraid to show their success."

—The Wall Street Journal, February 28, 2000

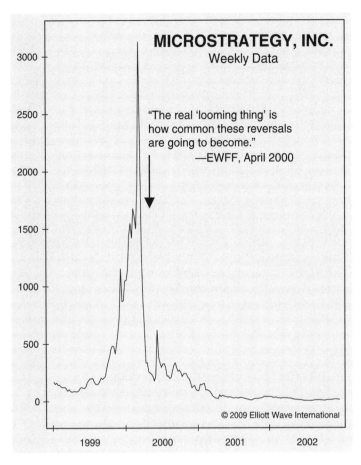

MICROSTRATEGY, INC.
Weekly Data

"The real 'looming thing' is how common these reversals are going to become."
—EWFF, April 2000

© 2009 Elliott Wave International

but not in the way the new rich believe. The problem with "coming to terms" with money is that it has a tendency to disappear soon afterwards. Luxury spending is a classic example. It always booms in the late stages of a mania, which is why *The Elliott Wave Theorist* said, "We must be very near the big turn" last June when upscale spending itself reached mania proportions. EWT has also noted that "charity is the ultimate luxury." So, philanthropy fever indicates that we are closer still. The experience of one generous Internet billionaire confirms that the Dow has indeed seen its final high. Five days after a "$100 million down payment" toward the creation of an online university that will "offer a free 'Ivy League-quality' education to anyone in the world," MicroStrategy, the Internet stock that was to fund the gift, collapsed from 226 to 72 a share. The real "huge looming thing" is how common these reversals of fortune are going to become.

May 2000

In January, we showed the NASDAQ's performance over the last year against that of the Nikkei going into its major top in 1989 (see chart page 14) and asked, "Is This the Model for the NASDAQ?" Despite its delayed start, the NASDAQ's downside is 7% ahead of the Nikkei's at the same point in 1990. The Nikkei was down 30% at its low in the first week of April 1990. After a 22% bounce through June 6, 1990, the Nikkei crashed to a decline of 50% for the year at 19,780 on October 1, which is slightly higher than where it is today. Try telling a "NASDAQ maniac" that his beloved index is higher now than it will be in 2010. The disbelief that this suggestion inspires is one good reason to suspect that the Nikkei's ten-year path may be a best-case scenario for the NASDAQ.

July 2000

The mania's continuing advance on the periphery is remarkable, because, at its core, the psychology that produced it is melting down. The charts on the next page show the historic pattern in the form of the South Sea Bubble in 1720 and Japan's Nikkei into 1989. Notice that once the ascent goes vertical and is then broken by a sharp break, every lunge back toward the peak is followed by a sharp sell-off. This creates the skyscraper form in the topping process and the ensuing panic. The more recent charts of the NASDAQ and Cisco (which is representative of scores of Internet-related issues) show that the right side of the tallest stock market skyscraper in history is very likely under construction.

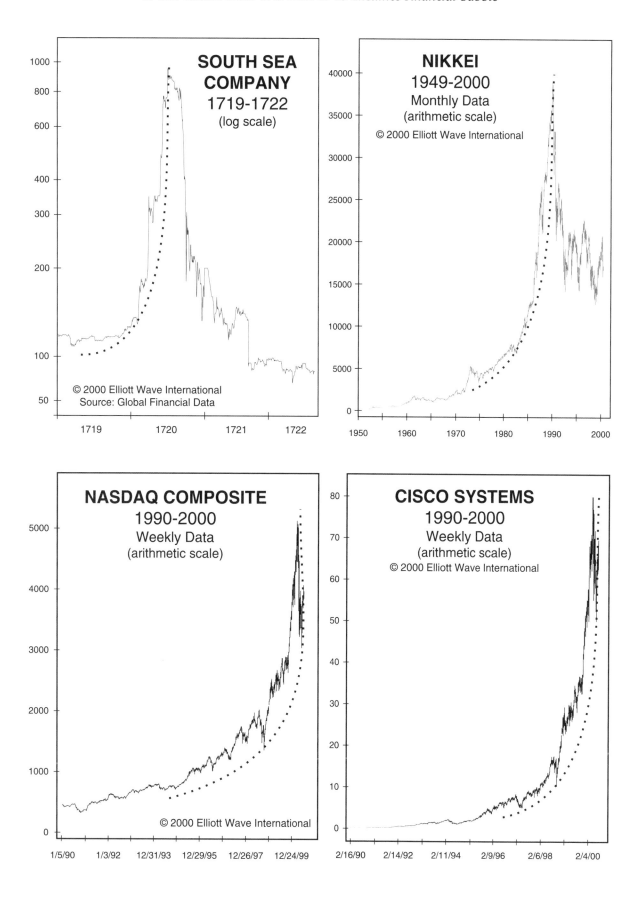

October 2000

Since January, EWFF has been tracking the NASDAQ's uncanny resemblance to the Japanese Nikkei-225 in 1989 and 1990. Now that it has fallen and bounced, it has acquired a look that is also very similar to the post-peak performance of the 1929 DJIA, the 1987 DJIA and the 1997 Hong Kong Hang Seng index (see chart). In all cases, the manic final run to all-time highs was followed by an initial leg down that led to a three-wave countertrend rebound, the classic Elliott wave signature of a correction. Look closely, and you will notice that these rebounds usually start with a big up day (sometimes on a gap) that fools the bulls into thinking that a major bottom has been recorded. The rallies last mere days, though, and then prices turn down in a crash. The NASDAQ gapped higher off its May low at 3043 and then traced out a three-wave move to the September 1 high of 4260. The decline since then has violated the trendline support that contained the entire countertrend rally. The near-term pattern may traverse this trendline in the coming days, but the clock is ticking for the start of the "cascading phase" of the pattern. Thus, prices may rally briefly, but a severe decline is likely.

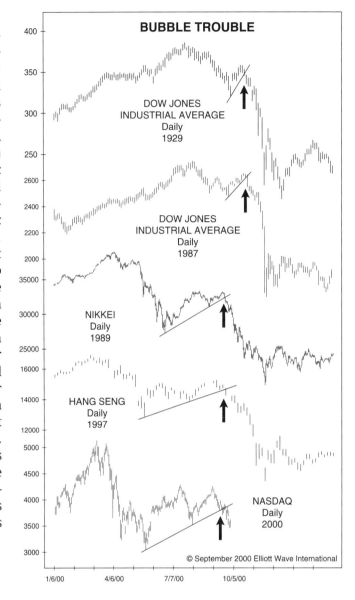

January 2001

It's Not Over Yet

> Realize that even at 50% down, the bear market will have hardly begun.
> —*At The Crest of the Tidal Wave*

The following charts display a very simple form. In fact, it is so simple, it does not show up in anyone's chart book of technical patterns. It does show up in the history books, however. In May 1997, *The Elliott Wave Theorist* dug out charts of the South Sea bubble, the Crash of 1929, the tulip bulb mania of 1637 and the coin price bubble of 1990 and presented them as the historic model for the culminating event of the Grand Supercycle bull market in stocks. The most critical conclusion of the report was, "every mania is followed by a decline that ends below the starting point of the advance." One look at the chart of the South Sea Company (upper left-hand corner) conveys the typical picture we showed.

As the charts show, some of the skyscraper patterns have already paid back most of the price for their manic booms. However, with retracements of only 50%, the NASDAQ, Cisco and many other stocks have much further to fall. Many participants continue to resist the very idea of "down," using arguments based on "fundamentals" and the future of technology. If a stock mania were a mechanical system that fed on technology breakthroughs or earnings, their hopes

THE NAMES MAY CHANGE
BUT THE PSYCHOLOGY REMAINS THE SAME

© January 2001 Elliott Wave International

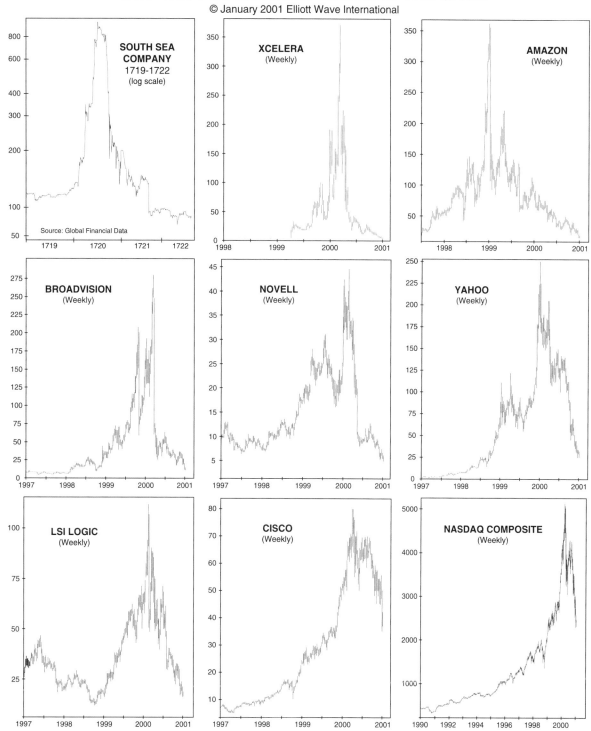

might have a basis for fulfillment. But all history reveals that the process is a psychological one, and the psychology demands a full retracement of the gains generated by the mass belief in ever-rising prices.

March 2001

Says Bob Prechter: "Tulips are a bargain compared to stocks. They have less risk and higher yield. They have much higher earnings than dot-com companies, and they last longer, too. In the past year, they outperformed the S&P by 30%."

September 2001
Infinity or Bust

How many charts of formerly high-flying stocks have we seen in recent weeks that show 80%, 90% and 98% declines? We cannot count the number. But the prospects for still more sweeping declines are confirmed by this quote from a technology fund manager whose fund has already lost 80% of its value: "I don't think $2 a share is a lot of risk. We could go down from here certainly, but over the long term, there is more potential on the upside than on the downside." The fund was started when Merrill Lynch brokers tapped clients for $1.5 billion as the NASDAQ made its peak in March 2000. During the bull market, the lack of any mathematical limit on how high a stock could go was cited as one big reason to go long and stay that way. Comments like these remind us that infinity can also actually work against bull-headed fund managers like this guy on the way down. The fund can still drop another 80%. It can then do so again and again and so on into infinity.

January 2002
It's Still Not Over Yet

Last January, *The Elliott Wave Financial Forecast* opened the year by showing nine different pictures of a mania in various stages of regress and asserted that the relentless declines that followed every major mania in history indicates that the declines of 2000 were just the beginning. With virtually every major index down for 2001 and the S&P 500 and the NASDAQ experiencing their worst two-year fall since 1973-1974, the simple, up-down form of the historic model has kept us right on track. We also reiterated this key statement from a May 1997 *Elliott Wave Theorist* study on manias: "Every mania ends below the starting point of the advance." With this full retracement yet to occur, the paramount message for 2002 is unchanged: the bear market has

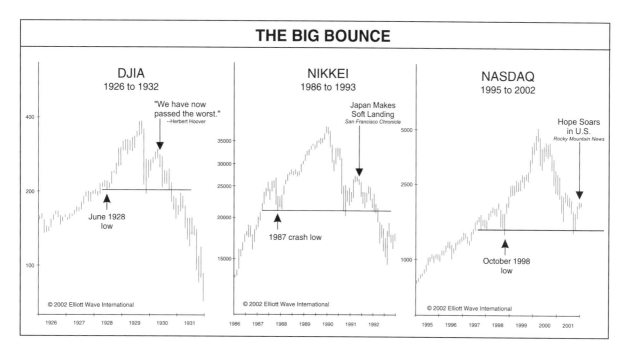

a long way to go. This is not to say, however, that it will happen all at once. While the falling phase tends to be even sharper than the advance, these charts of the Nikkei from 1986-1993 and the Dow in 1926-1932 show that it is not necessarily a straight-line affair. After an initial leg down, each experienced a three-wave bounce that covered several months and began from a level that is about even with a departure point for the preceding mania. The horizontal lines on the charts connect the start of a final thrust higher in the mania to the start of the sustained rebound. The chart on the right shows that in rising from the area of its 1998 low, the NASDAQ may have reached a similar juncture at the September 21 low. If so, the countertrend rally should continue into the first half of 2002, which would be consistent with wave patterns discussed [in this issue].

Any time stocks trade precariously near new recovery highs (as they are currently), however, it is very important to keep in mind another post-mania guideline EWT also offered in 1997: "Rallies after the top will be as brief and/or weak as the corrections have been on the way up." The last eight months have borne this out as they include two rallies of two and three months duration, or the same as the average correction from 1995-1999.

Another reason to remain alert for a possible return to free-falling stock prices is the psychology that now surrounds the rebound. The quote from Herbert Hoover (shown on the Dow chart, previous page) is a small sample of the collective sigh of relief that accompanied the Dow to a recovery high in 1930. The rally brought forward authorities of every stripe to pronounce that renewed prosperity was dead ahead, even as the U.S. was heading straight into the teeth of the Great Depression. In Japan, things were still going so well that the April 1991 issue of the San Francisco Chronicle reported, "The entire policy establishment is congratulating itself for being the first regulators in history to deflate an asset bubble without impacting severely on economic activity." The headline on the NASDAQ chart is just the barest glimpse of the positive vibrations around the year-end rally. Measured against the global economic damage and the polarizing social forces that have emerged in the second half of 2001, this sentiment is comparable to that of 1930 U.S. and 1991 Japan. Its strength is a certain sign that more unpleasant "events" are likely to revisit in 2002.

December 2002

Last Call for Extravagance

One common accessory to a mania is "luxury fever," which we covered in various issues of *The Elliott Wave Theorist* and *The Elliott Wave Financial Forecast* from June 1996 through April 2000. Luxury sales languished through the first half of the 1990s' bull market, but, in June 1996, EWT reported that luxury sales finally took off. EWT tracked the phenomenon from skyrocketing profits at Tiffany & Co. to the enormous new proportions of cruise liners and the rise in the ultimate luxury, charity. By the end of the mania, the two trends were so intertwined that EWFF used several displays of over-the-top ostentatiousness to confirm that the peak in stocks was in (see entry for April 2000).

Stock prices for most luxury goods companies peaked with the overall market in 2000, but sales of luxury goods and the extent of the stock declines to date indicate that the demand for luxury has been as slow to exit in the new bear market as it was to enter in the mid-1990s. Continued strength of the sector is signaled by Tiffany's stock, which is down a third from its August 2000 all-time high but still up more than 300% from its level in early 1996. A Bloomberg story notes that luxury brand sales are about even with their level in 2000. Another example of the sector's lingering strength is Carnival Cruise Lines. CCL stock is about where it was a year ago. On Tuesday, when one of its cruise ships returned to port with the flu bug that has besieged the industry, its stock barely budged.

A study by the Boston Consulting Group, a consumer research firm, explains the impetus behind this latent taste for high-end goods and leisure items: "People are worried about holding onto their jobs in a shifting economy and moving up the corporate ladder," says a Washington Post story about "the New Luxury." "The bottom line is that they try to get [satisfaction] in the marketplace. There are some real emotional needs being met here." In other words, people are warding off the bad feelings of the new downtrend by indulging in the opulence of the old uptrend. The urge is so strong that Porsche, BMW, Cadillac and Mercedes-Benz have introduced new entry-level luxury cars that are being snapped up, mostly by middle class buyers that are probably overextended. The splurge constitutes another form of late-stage denial that will be no more satisfying than technology stocks were in 2000.

By the end of the bear market, the cruise lines will be in drydock, Tiffany's stock will be well below its level of $6 a share at the beginning of 1996, and looking rich will be so uncool that even the wealthy few will dress down. The chart of the Value Line Composite vs. annual fur sales shows a recent downtick in the demand for luxury goods. This is surely just the beginning of a steep fall. As in 1987, when fur sales

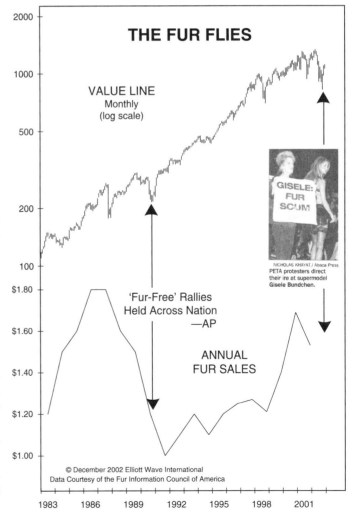

NICHOLAS KHAYAT / Abaca Press
PETA protesters direct their ire at supermodel Gisele Bundchen.

preceded the Value Line's decline by running sideways for a year, the current decline preceded the Value Line's fall. Figures for 2002 are not yet available, but the picture of a recent protest at a Victoria's Secret fashion show hints of a reversal in public sentiment. Back in 1997, one of the signals of the luxury boom cited by EWT was a change in supermodel attitudes toward fur. We noted that models went from saying, "I'd rather go naked than wear fur" in the early 1990s to draping themselves in mink, fox and Mongolian lamb. The headline describing nationwide fur protests in late 1990 (see chart) shows the broad negative sentiment toward fur (and a disinterest in other luxuries) that prevailed at the last major low. In the early 1990s, supermodel outrage against fur actually lasted well into the bull market. Supermodel Gisele's defiance of the fur protestors is yet another sign that the bottom is still to come. The final lows probably won't be in place until long after the supermodels have joined the anti-fur crowd.

July 2003

Stocks carried to one more unanticipated new high in June, but not without creating a jolt of the old euphoria that signals unequivocally that the bull market is not back as so many now claim. As *The Elliott Wave Financial Forecast* has noted many times over the course of the bear market, a second wave reconstructs the psychology that existed at the preceding peak. True to form, the speculative fires that raged at the all-time highs in early 2000 have been re-lit. The 67% percent gain in the AMEX Biotech index from March 12 through June 6 has been accompanied by daily media reports of "Another Aggressive Bull Run," a rebound in CNBC's ratings and a "daytrading comeback." "Some investors are hunting out spots in the market where you can get some big returns," says one article. In another sign of the old frenzy, Schwab and Ameritrade reported that online trading has surged over the last 6 weeks. NYSE margin debt jumped 7.7% in May to $146.38 billion. The jump was the biggest monthly percentage increase since February 2000, which was the last full month of the bull market in the NASDAQ and S&P. A June 16 Barron's cover screams "BULL RUN!" and says, "This rally is for real. Stocks are likely to be 10% higher by year end." Our wave counts in all the major averages indicate instead that it is one last whiff of the old mania.

August 2003

More All-Time Flashbacks

Like a sequel to a good movie, a wave two high doesn't always live up to the original, but sometimes it feels like the same experience. Back in March 2000, EWFF noted that leadership was falling to fundamentally weaker firms. In the final months of the mania, this progression was so pronounced that EWFF coined a phrase for it: "the flight from quality." According to Steven Desanctis of Prudential Securities, the same flight is taking place now. Desanctis reports that companies with median P/Es of 14 were up 16% in the second quarter, but companies with a median P/E of 33 gained 32% and those with no earnings were up 39%! Today's investors remain anything but conservative.

September 2003

The Smaller They Are, The Harder They Fall

Since the early 1990s, Elliott Wave International has used 8- and 12-year cycles to successfully forecast the relative performance of secondary stocks. In 1992 and 1993, EWT said that smaller stocks were likely to underperform through "1998 ± 1 year," when both cycles were due to bottom. Relative weakness persisted, as expected, into May 1999. Coming out of that low, EWT used the same cycles to predict that small stocks "should lead the market." Due to the terminating long-term pattern in the overall market, EWT remained neutral on the absolute performance of small stocks saying it was making "a forecast for relative performance." Small stocks have outperformed blue chips ever since. The strength has surprised us somewhat lately as EWFF called for the Value Line to fall relative to the S&P in April 2002. The 8-year cycle, which EWT identified as the more powerful of the two when it first introduced the cycles in the early 1990s, and the 12-year are cresting. The cycles were in a similar position as the market rolled over in 1930.

These cycles concur with the wave count calling for the broadest decline of the bear market to date. Another factor pointing to a special emphasis on the small stocks in the next leg down is investors' now fearless approach to this sector. The recent outperformance has fostered a comfort level that is totally at odds with small stocks' capacity for collapse in a drawn-out bear market. Back in the 1980s, when the bull market was young, the financial media continually warned investors about the dangers of penny stocks. These days, a low stock

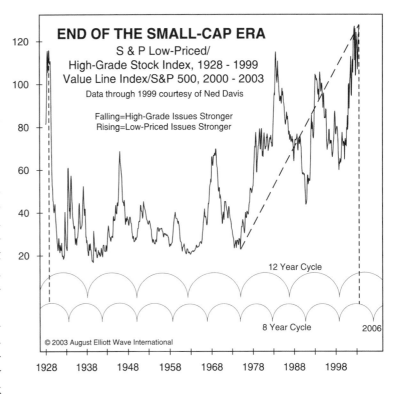

price is not a red flag, it's conclusive evidence of a bargain. One article refers to "7,000 opportunities, most for less than $1 a share," in companies that are no longer listed on major exchanges. It notes that these stocks are "an area of rising investor interest." Countless other stories sing the praises of firms because they are small. "Since small to mid-cap stocks and mutual funds have historically led the way in a new bull market," investment advisors are convinced that they "are once again the place to be." Under the headline "Small Caps Leave Others in Their Dust," one choice piece says it is the small caps that are "giving the market its juice." All this is coming over four years after the correct time to have purchased small stocks.

November 2003

A recent New York Times headline reveals that the current "flight from quality" rivals that of the all-time highs: "Bull Market 2003: The Worse the Company, the Better the Stock." Stocks with Standard & Poor's A ratings based on dividends paid and earnings reported over the last 10 years are up half as much as those rated B, which are up half again as much as stocks rated C, a category that indicates doubtful financial condition. After three years in which the bear market has undoubtedly undermined the fundamentals even more egregiously than Cycle wave V (see Chapter 1 of *Conquer the Crash* (CTC) for the story of its weakening fundamentals versus Cycle III), only the mania explains it. Its continued stranglehold on investors means those who liked stocks in March 2000 must love them now.

December 2003

From the Dow's all-time high in 2000 to its secondary peak, the most recent topping formation has covered 46 months, beyond the peak-to-peak span of 8 months for the Dow in 1929-1930, 9 months for gold in 1980 and 10 months for coins in 1989-1990. The peak of 2000 is of Grand Supercycle degree, which is higher than that of 1929. So it makes sense that the set-up for wave three down has taken longer this time. Following 200 years of rising stock prices it's only natural that the after-effect would be more protracted.

Up From The Ash Heap

One by one, the hot buttons of the old mania have been pressed, and investors have responded with the most speculative buying since 2000. In recent days, warrants or options to buy stocks that appear to be all but worthless have become some of the most active securities traded on the NASDAQ. Shares in 8x8 Inc., an Internet phone service firm, doubled in the last week of November and many of the same issues that washed out in 2000-2002 are enjoying wild rides. Theglobe.com epitomizes the driving force behind this speculation. The stock surged 600% to become the fastest rising IPO in history in 1999 then fell to a low of 1 cent in September 2001. In 2003, the stock has rebounded to as high as $2.50. On Monday, theglobe.com landed on the cover of The Wall Street Journal. Apparently, the website that was the impetus for theglobe.com's initial moonshot has been shut down, but the firm has been reborn as one of hundreds of competitors in the Internet telephone industry. Obviously, business prospects aren't what buyers of the stock are interested in. What they are buying is the memory of theglobe.com's famous IPO in 1999. Apparently, if a bubble is big enough, the notoriety created by one of its most spectacular failures is reason enough to rally a stock when that bubble returns for an encore.

January 2004

Q: Do you still see a "flight from quality"?

A: Yes, which is very specific to a mania. We are not aware of anyone else who identified this flight and, more important, its implications for the market as a whole. The public will always chase performance, but in a mania, this urge actually causes participants to give up on guessing at value and pursue the biggest risks. In 2003, the riskier the asset, the more investors wanted it. They desperately desire to "get whole" from their big losses, and they are trying to do so by shifting assets from mutual funds to hedge funds, from the NASDAQ to illiquid Bulletin Board stocks and from Treasuries to junk bonds.

A Fashion Statement for Bagholders

One of the central traits of the Great Asset Mania was a surge in the demand for luxury goods. By the middle of 1999, the demand for luxuries was so great that it actually became key to the economy's continued rise. The June 1999 issue of *The Elliott Wave Theorist* compared the fever for designer fashions, extravagant autos and other high-end goods to a similar indulgence at the end of Japan's bubble in the late 1980s and said, "What better way to end more than 200 years of economic expansion than a boom made up entirely of luxuries?" EWT traced the runaway upscaling back to the Jazz Age when "putting on the Ritz" was the attendant slang. In 1929, the sentiment and its place in the cycle were immortalized in Irving Berlin's song of the same name, which ends, "You'll declare it's simply topping/To be there, and hear them swapping smart tidbits/Putting On the Ritz." A revised version concludes, "Come with me and we'll attend the jubilee and see them spend their last two bits/Putting on the Ritz."

— *Barron's*, December 15, 2003

Figures attributing much of this year's holiday season sales increase to luxury goods and this cover from the December 15 issue of Barron's illustrate that the urge to splurge is back in full swing. The wave of luxury spending came roaring back in the fall when sales of designer goods re-ignited, the art market set several records for contemporary works, tourism turned around and New York City tax revenues bounced higher for the first time since mid-2001. "Happy days, it would seem, are here again — at least for people who can afford to spend $30 on a hamburger," said the Washington Post of a clear rebound in New York City's power lunch scene.

In some ways, the current phase is not an echo of the original article but a full-blown reprisal. Several luxury stocks continue to push to all-time highs; the Queen Mary 2, the largest passenger ship ever built, has been launched; and prices on many individual items have pressed on to outrageous new extremes. In our June 1999 write-up, for instance, we commented on $15,000 designer handbags. Guess how much Neiman Marcus wants for the one shown here? Do we hear $30,000, $50,000? Try $75,000, or five times what we called insane in 1999. For those interested in something a little less formal, Neiman is also selling "Hobo" hand bags for about $1,000. This is an appropriate name, as it foreshadows the future for many buyers of these fancy bags. Once again, the intensity of the latest luxury binge signals an approaching climax and reversal. What could be a more appropriate symbol of the boom and bust than an empty $75,000 purse?

February 2004

Question: How does a 220-year trend in stock prices change from up to down without being noticed?

Answer: Ever so slowly. The great fooler of the long-term peaking process that began in 1997 has been its longevity. The emerging Grand Supercycle bear market has thrown many of the most seasoned market observers off track by simply outlasting their skepticism. If the stock market had recovered 50% of its decline (the average of the Dow, S&P and NASDAQ's retracement) over 6 weeks instead of 68, only the perma-bulls would be bold enough to proclaim the bear market over. With its steady grind higher, however, the countertrend rally has convinced many to discount time-tested indicators even as the long-term wave count, sentiment and valuations have done everything to strengthen the bearish case. None of the news has come close to signaling a new bull market. The only question now is the date of the bear market's resumption. January 26, the day of the latest NASDAQ peak, stands a strong chance of being that date.

One defining facet of a mania is that it generates an unnatural upward thrust in prices. From the outset, some recognize the movement as unsustainable, but as it pushes higher, they give in to calls for further advance. The reversal tends to come when a large body of holdouts finally decides that the advance can, in fact, be sustained. On March 10, 2000, the day of the NASDAQ's all-time peak, this

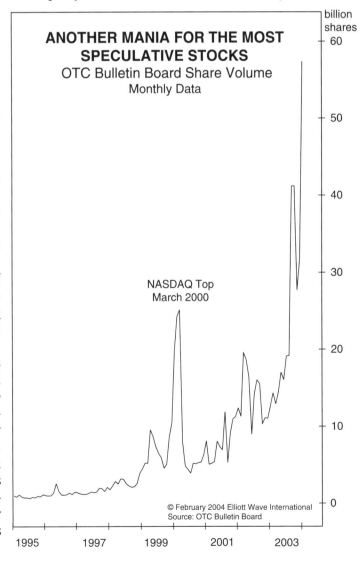

ANOTHER MANIA FOR THE MOST SPECULATIVE STOCKS
OTC Bulletin Board Share Volume
Monthly Data

NASDAQ Top
March 2000

© February 2004 Elliott Wave International
Source: OTC Bulletin Board

billion shares

principle was enshrined on the front page of The Wall Street Journal by the following headline: "Conservative Investors Finally Are Saying: Maybe Tech Isn't a Fad." In recent weeks, the same sentiment has been evident in a rush of articles about "bears" who now forecast a continuation of the rally. One story cited a host of different indicators ranging from a record high 90% of stocks above their 10-week moving averages to the lowest CBOE Volatility Index readings in almost 10 years signaling that "stocks are extremely overbought" but then added that the technicians gathering these readings had all given up on their normally reliable gauges. "All the indicators everyone has relied on for years are ineffective," said one prominent chartist. Another dismissed the significance of a 99% bullish level in a proprietary indicator saying, "I would not say that the party is over."

So many technicians' dismissive attitude toward their own tools is itself a sign that the decline will be bigger than almost anyone expects. It will have to be to produce any kind of normal bearish psychology at the low. One of the key lessons of the all-time peak is that the indicators didn't fail. By flashing longer and more brilliantly than ever, they simply broadcast the size of the reversal. The recent array of unheeded overbought readings is an extension of that display.

The amazing chart of share volume on the OTC Bulletin Board is a classic picture of the flight to risk that Elliott Wave International identified as a primary trait of the mania in 1999. Its recent reemergence as part of the mania "echo" is visible in the stunning surge of Bulletin Board volume to an all-time high of 57 billion shares in January 2004, 4.5 times the total for January 2003 and double that of the March 2000 top. By this measure, the latest episode is still classified as an echo rather than a bigger mania because the total dollar value of Bulletin Board volume last month was $7.3 billion, much lower than the dollar volume of $28.4 billion in March 2003. Of course, the 300% increase in volume means that speculators were throwing their money at much cheaper stocks, many of which were the same high flyers that fell 90% or more in the first three years of the bear market. So, in terms of the investors' willingness to pin their hopes on financial assets of deteriorating quality, the wave 2 peak ranks right up there with 2000.

May 2004

Trees don't grow to the sky, and stocks usually don't either. Normally, they go up in a measured and patterned way that roughly correlates to the value and growth prospects of the businesses they represent. What keeps them grounded is a deep-seated fear of loss, or what behavioral psychologists refer to as "myopic loss aversion." Under normal circumstances, studies show that investors weigh potential losses twice as heavily as possible gains. During a bull market, the weight of the evidence needed to overcome this fear gradually dissipates; a mania is what happens when it disappears altogether. In May 1996, when Iomega (IOM) and Comparator (IDID) were in the throes of the Great Mania's first bubble stock rally, the arrival of an absence of fear was actually documented by the following headline from The Wall Street Journal: "Risk Aversion as Behavioral Problem."

Historically, these episodes come along no more than once a generation because the painful consequence of reckless speculation, i.e., the total or nearly total evaporation of the initial investment, has always had a way of rendering permanent a participant's aversion to loss. As *The Elliott Wave Theorist* first observed in 1998, the difference this time is that soon after a group of bubble stocks breaks and returns to the dust from whence it emerged, the market has managed to recover and produce a whole new crop of bubble stocks. The collapse of bubble stocks like Iomega (96% so far) and Comparator in 1996 (99.9%) was followed by at least six more periods of frenzied, bald-faced speculation in bubble stocks. After two centuries of rising prices, including two full decades in which many participants experienced nothing but a bull market, a new condition, call it "myopic gain addiction," has engendered a Grand Supercycle sense of fearlessness. The primary symptom is a willingness to buy a stock for one simple reason — it is going up.

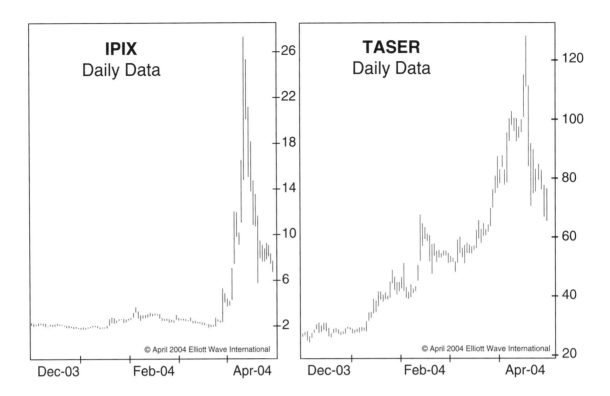

The two stocks shown here, Taser International and IPIX Corporation, are representative of the latest outbreak. Taser has gained 500% since December and 10,000% since the beginning of last year, while IPIX, formerly known as Bamboo.com, gained more than 1400% from March 19 to April 12. IPIX illustrates the progressively weaker strength of the mania effect, as its value is still a long way from its high of $462 a share on March 14, 2000. For holders of IPIX, however, the latest ride has been even more thrilling. It gained twice as much (in percentage terms), seven times as fast. Clear evidence of the old uptrend's flagging strength is suggested by the "story" behind the stock market's late windfall issues. IPIX's gain came after the firm announced that its remote video systems had been informally endorsed by a member of the U.S. House Subcommittee on Homeland Security. Instead of the new era of growth and technological advancement that underpinned the Internet boom, the concepts that now spark investors' imagination are grounded in an underlying sense of fear about the future. Taser makes stun guns that "deliver a high voltage surge of electrical pulses to the target. These electronic pulses are designed to affect the central nervous system and incapacitate an individual." Socionomics has surmised that a mania works in a similar fashion: It stimulates individuals' primitive herding instincts in a way that incapacitates the thinking part of their brains.

Back in 1998, EWFF pointed out that even when bubble-stock phases turned out to be false signals of the ultimate top, they have always tended to come right before washouts for the general market. An interesting difference this time around is that the bubble-stock fireworks followed the recent peak in the NASDAQ by two full months, which suggests once again that the last binge is grounded more in desperation than euphoria.

The resemblance to the first quarter of 2000 grows more striking. According to an article in Sunday's NY Post, "people are talking about stocks again instead of unemployment," and "day-trading ads are flooding the airwaves." And don't look now, but the ".com" moniker is making a comeback. From the second half of 2000 through 2002, the stigma of being a dotcom was so great that most companies dropped the suffix from their names. Now several companies including Salesforce.com, Shopping.com and Advertising.com have filed offerings. Headlines in Tuesday's issue of The Wall Street Journal say, "Tech IPOs Kick Into High Gear" and "Investors Ignore Scant Revenue and Big Losses." Remember how silly investors were back in 2000 when they actually bid a search engine company with a silly name up to a market valuation of almost $200 billion? YAHOO! peaked at $250 a share January 4, 2000. It's happening again as Google is about to come to market on a giant wave of expectation. Never mind that it's likely to have a market cap that is several times greater than the $2.5 billion in advertising search engine companies generate. Google, "the most anticipated initial public offering in years [has] rekindled memories of the 1990s." Rekindled memories of the decline into 2002 should not be far behind.

November 2004
The Big Boys Break Down

According to one investment web site, blue chip stocks are "inherently stable." The following charts introduce the new inherently unstable character of many stocks. The shares shown here represent kingpin issues in a broad cross-section of industries: great bull market brands like Coke and Colgate, which have been locked in to consumer psyches for more than a century; the world's largest insurance company, AIG; Fannie Mae, a linchpin to the homebuilding and financial industries and a cornerstone of the debt structure of the U.S. government. Every one of these stocks has gapped lower in recent weeks. These are the "air pockets" that EWFF labeled a "pending issue" in August. In a bull market, the "bad news" would generate little more than a minor hiccup on the way to higher levels. Since July, however, sharp price drops are being rein-

BLUE CHIPS SET THE STAGE

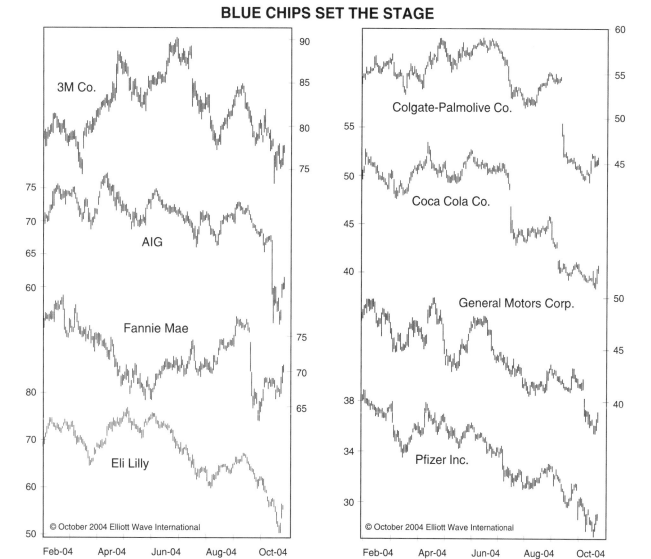

© October 2004 Elliott Wave International

31

forced by more selling. These charts expose a seeping decay, one that will surely run much deeper because it is starting in the shares that are the largest and most closely scrutinized companies on Wall Street. This kind of havoc confirms that the great bear market is back and mustering new energy. We expect the market averages to look this way soon.

The Dow Goes, and the Market Will Follow

The Dow Industrial Average is composed of the bluest of the blue chips and was once universally regarded as the single best indicator of the trend in stock prices. But a funny thing happened on the approach to the early 2000 all-time high in stock prices; the financial herd suddenly decided that the Dow was outdated. The rebellion against the Dow's status as the preeminent stock barometer took place in late 1999 as the index fell behind the performance of the rip-roaring NASDAQ. When the Dow stumbled in September of that year but the NASDAQ kept going, the business editor of the Washington Post dismissed the Dow as a bunch of "huge old-timey companies." One month before the Dow's all-time peak, the December 1999 issue of EWFF (see December 99 entry) used this widespread belief in a new stock market order to make the following forecast:

> When the herd pursues the more speculative stocks to the virtual exclusion of the Dow, it represents a breakdown in the established order and is at the very least a strike against the market's intermediate-term prospects.

In late March 2000, when the NASDAQ was one week from its all-time high, EWFF called for it to join in the Dow's decline (see Mar 2000 entry).

Well, it's happening again. This chart shows another trait that makes wave ②'s re-creation of the psychology of the all-time highs a nearly perfect facsimile. The Dow's decline from the September high carried the index to 9750 on October 25, which was not only a 30-day low but a new closing low for the year. At the same time, the NASDAQ 100 recorded a 30-day high, mimicking the early 2000 divergence, which kicked off the Great Bear Market. The decline signaled by this latest occurrence should be even more devastating because this time it marks the kick-off for wave ③, the most powerful wave in the sequence.

After languishing in the immediate aftermath of its celebrated initial public offering, Google took flight in September. Trading in shares of the popular Internet search engine closely resembles Netscape's wild ride in 1995. Netscape was the first great rocket ship of the Internet bubble. Like Google, it came out in August, then languished for a month before rising fast. Netscape gained more than 300% in less than three months. The purely

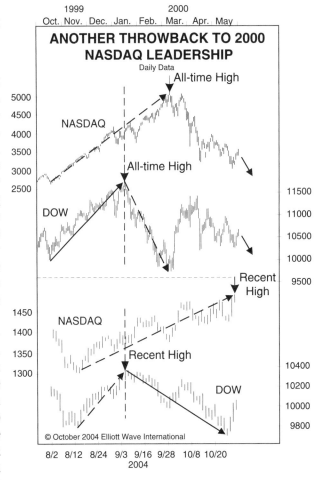

speculative nature of the rally was apparent from the start, but it became truly glaring in retrospect when Netscape went to zero, disappearing into the ether of Internet flameouts. The initial hesitation in both of these Internet stocks suggests that they will probably bracket the front and

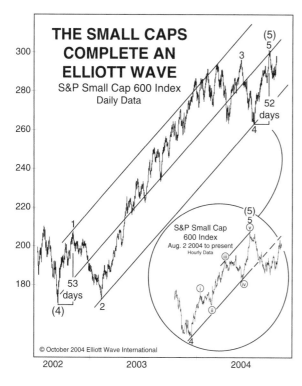

THE SMALL CAPS COMPLETE AN ELLIOTT WAVE
S&P Small Cap 600 Index
Daily Data

S&P Small Cap 600 Index
Aug. 2 2004 to present
Hourly Data

© October 2004 Elliott Wave International

back ends of the most manic phase of the great bull market. In 1995, Netscape first hesitated as investors took time to get up the nerve to give in and go with the great Internet revolution. Google initially stumbled because many investors have realized that the well of greater fools can run dry at any moment.

Small Caps: The Final High

Like junkies running low on dope, investors are crowding into smaller and smaller investment vehicles to deliver any semblance of the highs (in both senses) that they got hooked on during the bull market. The small-cap sector signals the phenomenon's persistence and utter exhaustion. In October, an all-time high for the S&P 600 Small Cap Index, the most speculative of the stocks charted by the S&P, preceded the Dow's low for the year. So, EWFF's comment about what happens when the investment community pursues "the more speculative stocks to the virtual exclusion of the Dow" is even more applicable today than it was in December 1999. It is a sure sign of a top — and not a minor one — as the divergence between the Dow and the small stocks now covers more than 4½ years. Nothing gets the old bull market juices flowing like all-time price highs. But the vast underlying weakness of the rally is evidenced by the fact that the last group to generate record highs was the one with the least liquid shares. The gaps shown in the chart on the previous page should filter down to small caps rapidly. Once they start, the price vacuums will be far more pronounced.

December 2004

The S&P 600 Small Cap index has continued to subdivide in wave 5 of (5). Wave 5 needs one more down-up move to signal the onset of a major small-cap reversal. The likelihood of a reversal is supported by a rash of small-cap fund closings, in which fund managers have shut their doors to new investors. "It's been a growing phenomenon this year," says a Morningstar analyst. Mutual funds closings were all the rage at the peak in 2000, too.

A Stratospheric Non-Confirmation

The following charts depict a re-run of Grand Supercycle delirium. As we explained in April when Taser International, a maker of stun guns, completed a five-month gain of more than 500%, these binges happen at tops when investors lose all fear and buy stocks strictly because they are going up. April's episode was an especially strong signal because, instead of reversing ahead of, or at least coincident with the larger market, TASR and a few other bubble stocks rose right through the peaks in the NASDAQ and Dow Industrials. After falling off through the summer, TASR has flared anew. In a sign of the faltering trend, however, it did not overtake its April high. However, the fervor moved on to a few other ridiculously over-valued shares that added to triple-digit gains. The relatively meager sales and earnings underpinning all of these shares illustrates once again, how stunningly detached mania-era investment is from the usual investment principles of value and growth. All it takes to score the fattest returns which the stock market has to offer is a stock symbol (preferably something that spells out some desirable attribute to traders like ABLE, PACT, TZOO, LOUD and BOOM) and a recent history of rapid price appreciation (and even the latter condition is not required).

HAVE CATCHY SYMBOL, WILL ROCKET

TASR
TASER INTERNATIONAL
Daily Data
© November 2004 Elliott Wave International

SIRI
SIRIUS SATELLITE RADIO
Daily Data
© November 2004 Elliott Wave International

ABLE
ABLE ENERGY
Daily Data
© November 2004 Elliott Wave International

BOOM
DYNAMIC MATERIALS
Daily Data
© November 2004 Elliott Wave International

PACT
PACIFICNET
Daily Data
© November 2004 Elliott Wave International

TZOO
TRAVELZOO
Daily Data
© November 2004 Elliott Wave International

LOUD
LOUDEYE TECHNOLOGY
Daily Data
© November 2004 Elliott Wave International

ROXI
ROXIO INC.
Daily Data
© November 2004 Elliott Wave International

Mar. May Jul. Sep. Nov.
2004

Mar. May Jul. Sep. Nov.
2004

As EWFF noted last month, the continued interest in more speculative shares amidst a steady deterioration for the largest and most established stocks (see November 2000 entry) is a clear sign that the overall market is on extremely shaky ground. Instead of breaking higher within the confines of a rising trend, as the bubble stocks did from 1995 to 2000, these shares have rocketed while the old leaders have stumbled badly. In the second half of November, BOOM doubled again from $8 to more than $17 while Wal-Mart, the world's largest retailer, was gapping lower in a 10% decline. Which one points the way? If BOOM was struggling and Wal-Mart were going gangbusters, it might be a tough call. But when it's the blue chips that are floundering, it's a no-brainer. History says unequivocally that it doesn't pay to bet with the cats & dogs over the blue chips.

Charity Begins at the Top
In another bearish reprisal of the great peak, some investors are so overwhelmed by their success that they are trying to decide how to give some of the profits away. According to a front page story on "The New Giving" in the latest issue of Barron's, charity is hot. The last time philanthropy was this big was back at the all-time highs in early 2000. In April 2000, EWFF alerted readers to the condition and stated that the discussions about giving back the vast wealth created by the bull market was a clear sign that much of it was about to disappear. A "philanthropy specialist" of that time called charity "a huge, looming thing." Well, it's looming large once again. Barron's cover suggests that the new non-profits might even "feed the world." We doubt it, but aggressive investors may want

to throw some money that way anyhow — this way they'll have something to fall back on when TASR, TZOO and BOOM don't work out as planned. While they're at it, they can reserve a place in the bread line.

The likelihood of a downside resolution is confirmed by the performance of the market's "generals," which, on average, continue to underperform relative to more speculative shares, the "troops." It is a war of attrition to get every bear out before the turn down, but it's been a very slow advance. The Dow Industrials have pushed back to their February high and are up 2.90% year-to-date, essentially equivalent to the yield on a 6-month U.S. Treasury Bill, which, unlike stocks, carry zero risk. The NASDAQ Composite closed today just 10 points above its January closing high. The S&P has been stronger, but it has its own problems with numerous internal divergences.

If investors had a rallying cry in 2004, it was "more risk." The movement from mutual funds to hedge funds, government bonds to high-yield offerings and into home loans that allowed consumers to plunge deeper into stocks is a manifestation of investors' urge to win back what was lost in the first phase of the bear market. These bets look like winners right now, but "yield grabs" have almost always ended badly for the grabbers, and we see no reason why history's greatest episode should be an exception. The deteriorating technical environment indicates that the markets are verging on a reversal point. Given the unprecedented disregard for prudent investment practices, when the tables turn, they should do so fast.

January 2005

One of the most compelling opportunities resides in the small cap sector. In November and December, we discussed the S&P Small Cap 600 Index, which began a fifth wave rally at the August 13 low that is near completion. The same pattern is unfolding in the Russell 2000 Index. The unmistakable five-wave form of the rise from October 2002 is a near-textbook Elliott wave. The cycles EWFF mentioned in November are shown in the chart at left. The 8-year cycle remains down and should start to bite any time. A turn lower in the 12-year cycle will add to the bearish

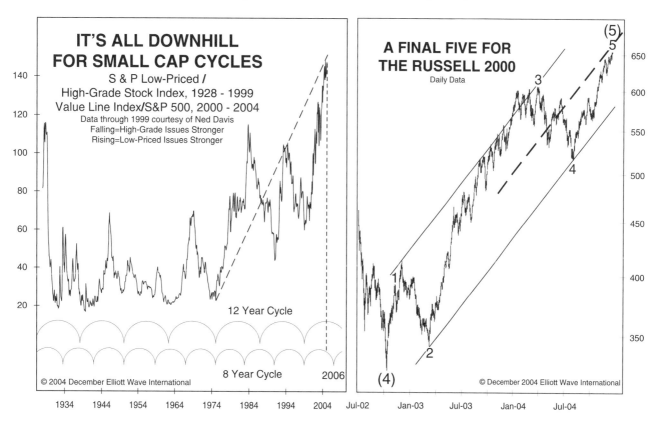

At the All-Time High 1999/2000	The Echo Effect 2004
Monetary Tightening The Federal Reserve raised the Federal Funds target rate six times from June 1999 to May 2000, from 4.75% to 6.5%, or 36.8%.	Fed tightens, again. This time raising the FF target rate five times, from 1% to 2.25%, or 125%, over six months.
Insiders Bail Out In August 2000, a wave of insider selling crested with $7.7 billion in sales, and EWFF noted, "Insiders want out. There must be a reason for it. The torrent of insider selling shows that corporate officials are not being swayed by their own earnings reports the way the public is." As usual, the insiders turned out to be right.	Insider selling hit $6 billion in November, its highest level since August 2000. One difference this time is that insiders' efforts are supported by a slowdown in earnings growth. USA Today reported on December 7, "Usually, investors react negatively to slowing earnings." But this time, "There's a curious lack of angst." Given the flight of the insiders, it is curious indeed.

cyclical picture into at least 2006. The position of these cycles and the well-defined Elliott wave pattern make this a high confidence forecast.

One big reason that the next decline appears a lock to make the history books is because the current secondary peak now forming has gradually reconstructed virtually every facet of the all-time highs. For the most part, it remains an echo of 2000, but, in recent weeks, some of the bubble era traits, like the level of insider selling and the number and speed of interest rate increases, are approaching exact clones of their counterparts in 1999 and 2000.

A Grand Supercycle Yacht Race?!

One of the saving graces for U.S. retailers this holiday season was consumers' continuing urge to gorge on luxury goods. Back in January, EWFF identified this seemingly insatiable demand for the finer things in life as one of the areas in which the bear market rally from 2002 was actually challenging the splurge of 2000. We compared it to the Jazz Age when Irving Berlin observed that many people literally spent their last two bits, "Putting on the Ritz." The picture on the following page is a monument to this sentiment and the ability of the bull market's biggest beneficiaries to literally float above the fray as the bear market intensified in 1931 and 1932. The Hussar sailing ship belonged to Marjorie Merriweather Post and financier E.F. Hutton. When it was completed in 1931, it became the biggest sailing yacht ever commissioned by a private individual, surpassing J.P. Morgan's Corsair IV (1930) by 17 feet. Both ships were surpassed

shortly thereafter by the *Savarona*, which was 408 feet long. Through the entire Supercycle bull market, from 1932 to 2000, the *Savarona* was the world's largest privately built vessel. In the wake of the Grand Supercycle peak, however, the title finally passed to the *Octopus*, billionaire Paul Allen's 414-foot yacht. The colossus, which has a basketball court, two helicopter landing pads, a music studio and its own personal submarine, was built in 2003. Observe that in both cases, the ships broke records after the market's all-time high.

The peak of the Grand Supercycle advance from the late 1700s has super-sized the same race. In the wake of the all-time highs, modern-day titans are jostling with one another to establish their place atop the social order. According to The Wall Street Journal, mega-rich software kingpin Larry Ellison increased the length of his yacht from 393 to 452 feet to beat out Allen's *Octopus*, "at least temporarily." A Saudi family is reportedly catapulting past Ellison with a 525-foot boat. The breadth of the demand is also far wider than at any time in history. "Yachts are becoming more mass-market," says The Wall Street Journal. Yacht makers are in such great demand that some are booked through 2009.

The aftermath of a great bull market is the perfect moment for "over the top" spending on yachts. While these ships record the grandeur and hope of a great bull market, they also broadcast an emerging desire for separation and detachment. Once again, a post-peak, big-boat fling appears to be satisfying this social craving, as The Wall Street Journal says it is being driven by "one important value: exclusivity. Yachts separate the seriously rich from the merely well-off." It also takes the rich from their favorite bull market pastime, mingling amongst themselves, and carries them out to sea, another symbolically potent gesture. Yachts also destroy wealth faster than just about any other asset as they are incredibly expensive to keep afloat. Given the current glut (there are now more yachts than berths world-wide), the craze for bigger and bigger boats should fade quickly, just like it did in the 1930s. The last great yacht boom was over by 1935. Due to divorce, "soak the rich" taxes and less ostentatious social conventions, even the likes of E.F. Hutton, Vincent Astor and J.P. Morgan lost their sea legs. When a bear market psychology reaches more serious extremes, these toys turn out to be great patrol boats, or in the emerging era, war ships.

The December 21 Interim Report observed that investors' rallying cry in 2004 is "more risk." This trait is epitomized by the bond market and the Phoenix-like return of Global Crossing, one of the stock mania's most famous telecom disasters. For the first time since it declared bankruptcy in January 2002, the company completed a bond sale earlier this month. In a move that Ponzi himself would have been proud of, the proceeds will be used to pay off other debt and provide cash for continuing operations, which the company says it would have run out of in just two weeks without the offering. Still, demand was so strong for the high-risk, high-yielding bonds that Global Crossing got $405 million, $55 million more than it was asking for. Back near the stock market lows in 2002, Global Crossing's famous flameout was being investigated by Congress for dishonest accounting, fraudulent swapping of assets and liabilities, and the enrichment of top executives. Employees and shareholders lost millions. Investors appear to be suffering from a condition clinicians refer to as emotional amnesia (also known as hysterical amnesia) in which psychological trauma causes memory loss. It is usually a temporary condition. As deals like Global Crossing's latest issue turn sour, the memories will come pouring back. Along with them will come another spate of scandals and the desire for corporate executives' blood.

February 2005

According to the Oxford English Dictionary, an echo is a "secondary, imitative sound produced by reflected waves as distinguished from the original sound caused by direct waves." The chart of dollar volume on the OTC Bulletin Board (next page), which is comprised of speculative shares that are not traded on any major exchange, is a graphic illustration of the difference between the imitative force of an echo and an original wave. At the height of the boom, the dollar value of total Bulletin Board shares traded peaked at $28.4 billion. In January 2004, the wave

② echo effect produced a secondary peak of $7.3 billion. Most averages went on to countertrend highs in late December, but, at $5.6 billion, a lower high in dollar volume reflects a weakening of the speculative frenzy. The total number of Bulletin Board shares traded (not shown) was also down from an all-time high of 57 billion in January 2004 to 43 billion in December 2004. At the all-time high in prices in 2000, total volume was lower at about 30 billion shares. So, by January 2004, Bulletin Board investors had to churn through almost twice as many shares to generate a fraction of the price change at the all-time peak. This past December, they were still trading like mad, but the rise was weaker still. As stocks move further from the boom, its reverberations will weaken much more dramatically.

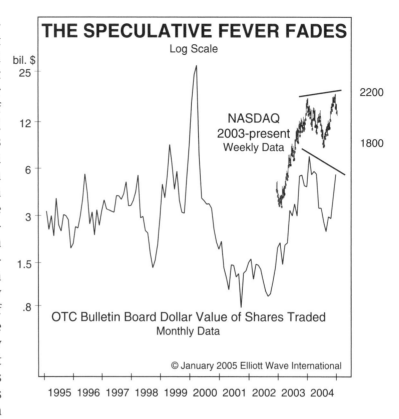

Last month, EWFF identified an investor demand for increasingly risky investments as the primary theme of 2004, but the diminishing demand for illiquid bulletin board stocks is just one sign that the start of a new era toward lower-risk investment is at hand. In the first three weeks of 2005, The Wall Street Journal reports, "Investors have turned more cautious." High yield bond funds have seen outflows, emerging market bonds have sold off and, as discussed at the start of this issue, small-cap stocks have begun to lead on the downside. Investors' new cautious streak means that the two-year bear market rally is, in fact, over. The bull market in cash should now steam higher with renewed vigor.

April 2005

In December, as speculators poured money into several high-risk shares whose primary investment virtue was a catchy stock symbol, EWFF compared the blue chips to the charts of the eight exploding unknowns and made this observation:

> History says unequivocally that it doesn't pay to bet with the cats & dogs over the blue chips.

The bubble in our composite index of eight shooting stars burst before the month was even out, a few days ahead of the NAS-

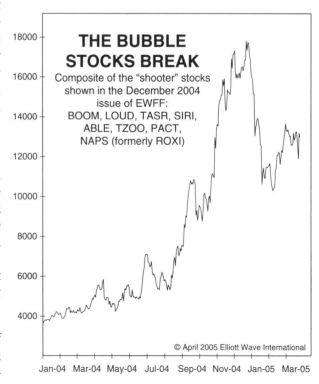

DAQ's January 3 peak. The index barely bounced into March 4-7 (a Friday and Monday), when the Dow Industrials, S&P and other major stock averages topped. But somehow, the great post-mania flight to even-riskier financial assets (rats and frogs?) pushed on for another week. On March 15, Bloomberg reported, "Money managers' optimism about stocks worldwide rose in March to the highest level in at least six years. Fund managers said emerging-market companies have the most potential to boost profits. 'People are positioned for a significant surprise in global growth,' said the chief global strategist at Merrill Lynch." The shift was so palpable that Bloomberg, which observed the positioning "for a surprise in global growth" just one day before, headlined a story about declines in global stocks, bonds and currencies this way:

Investors Flee From Risk

The turnabout fits perfectly with EWFF's January forecast for 2005: "As the market turns lower, investors will feel enormous pressure to take risk capital off the table entirely."

June 2005

The Ultimate Buy and Hold

A peak in social mood expresses itself in a multitude of extravagances, but one of the more idiosyncratic through the course of the Grand Supercycle peak is the physical consumption of gold, which *The Elliott Wave Theorist* first observed occurring in Japan in 1988. Conspicuous opulence is a classic mania trait, so when rich Japanese started to sprinkle gold flakes on their sushi, EWT said it was a sign of the top. It took another 20 months, but in December 1989 Japanese stocks reached an all-time high that remains 250% above current levels.

In the U.S., the same signal was broadcast in 1997 when the Cellar in the Sky restaurant at the top of the World Trade Center first offered a dessert featuring edible gold. Once again, it took a while for the peak to come in (30 months). Even after the peak, the outlandish staying power of the mania has continued to manifest itself in gold-laced food items. Gold's popularity as a "delicacy" continues to grow. The specialty drink at La Bete, the new nightclub in the ultra-swank Las Vegas Wynn, is a champagne cocktail sprinkled with gold flakes. Another Atlantic City casino offers Brulee, a $1000, hazelnut brownie dusted with edible gold. Searching Google for "edible gold" produces 6640 references including 1450 for "recipes" and 361 "sprays." "If you wish to impress, decorate with edible gold leaf," says one site. In London, the rich eat, drink and smear their faces with gold. "In the last four or five months there has been an upsurge in what people do with gold," says a London restaurant owner who started serving gold items in 1999. Gold facials were introduced to the British capital last September.

Traditionally, golden ages are remembered as such because furnishings, halls and other trappings end up covered in gold leaf. This time participants are so convinced of the rising trend's permanence that its affluent beneficiaries are literally gilding their own outsides and insides. Some do it because they believe the ancient Egyptians were right: eating gold is the secret to immortality. Since lean times (when you might want back the $1000 you paid for a brownie) can't possibly happen, who wouldn't want to live forever?

July 2005

Just over a year ago, the volume of shares traded on the OTC Bulletin Board, a quotation system for unlisted over-the-counter stocks, was almost three times its peak level of March 2000. At that time, EWFF identified the surge as a lesser echo of the great all-time peak. The fading strength of the bear market rebound shows up clearly in the most speculative sector of the equities market, where the dollar volume has recorded a series of three declining peaks since March 2000 (bottom line on the chart, next page). Bulletin Board share volume soared as the NASDAQ hit a new countertrend high in January 2004, but dollar volume fell to 25% of the March 2000 peak. With the higher price high of January 2005, dollar volume was down further to 18.3% of the all-time high. In May, as stock prices rose steadily, the figure barely rose to 13.2%. Investors' willingness to trade ever-more furiously was a sign that they were not giving up on the uptrend. The all-time share volume peak in 2004 displayed an amazing willingness among investors to churn through unlisted, low-priced stocks. Remember, many of these shares are the same ones that fell from the sky and got kicked off the NASDAQ exchange in the wake of 2000's great flameout. The dotted line at the top of the chart shows that share volume is sinking fast. In May, it turned down almost 50% from the peak level of January 2004. As the Bulletin Board falls silent, most of the fallen angels will disappear for good.

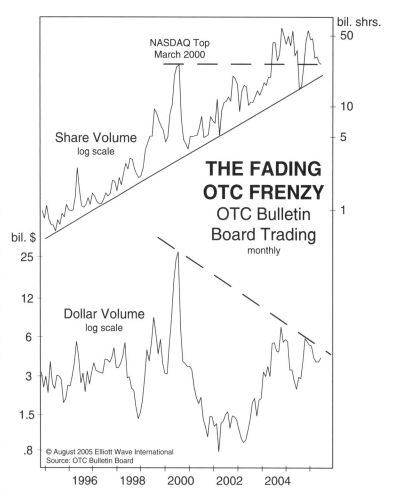

November 2005
More Evidence of a Nice Bubble

Google popped higher to more than $350 a share on solid earnings, but as EWFF noted in July, Google's rally is a far more solitary version of the upward sweep in internet stocks that took place in 1999-2000, or even 2004. Google is now pretty much alone in exploding to new heights. In a reversal from the pattern at the great Internet peak in 2000, it was a positive earnings announcement that pushed Google to its latest new high. This is a qualitative difference from the trend at the height of the mania, which moved from ever skimpier earnings, to no revenues, to "no one is to know the plan." The problem with earnings is that they remove Google from the dreamy realm of infinite potential and place the stock in a finite world where expectations apply to actual performance and disappointment will always catch up with historically unprecedented valuations.

Charity Begins at the End of a Long Rise

Within three weeks of the March 2000 NASDAQ peak, EWFF reported that charity had become "a huge, looming thing" among high-tech types. When the Valley's nouveau riche started casting about for ways to "give back," EWFF observed that "philanthropy fever" was a sure sign that the boom was at its peak. Charity is the ultimate luxury, and "luxury of every sort" has been a by-product of manias since the Tulip Bulb craze of the 1630s. One such "gift" was the proposed creation of an online university that promised a "free 'Ivy League-quality' education to anyone in the world." It was supposed to be funded by shares in Microstrategy, an Internet stock that started to collapse almost in concert with the unveiling of its endowment, which, of course, comprised shares. "The real 'huge looming thing' is how common these reversals of fortune are going to become," stated EWFF. From a (split-adjusted) high of $3330 a share in March 2000, Microstrategy fell to a low of $4.20. This is a decline of 99.9%. Along the way, it was joined by so many other 90% to 100% declines that utter collapse did, in fact, become commonplace.

Five years later, the stage is set for a whole new round of bubble-busting, as philanthropy is all the rage once again. Recent developments include the emergence of social venture philanthropy, also known as "nonprofit angel investing," women's giving circles, social events at which issues and grants are discussed and friendships solidified, and the establishment of the "First-Ever Microlending Web Site," a Palo Alto-based charity that allows visitors to "make personal loans to small businesses in developing countries." "In Silicon Valley, Doing Good Is the New Thing," says a New York Times headline. On October 12, Google, the last of the great high fliers, put what should be the finishing touch on the trend with a $265 million charitable pledge. In order to make good on a "commitment to devote a share of its lucrative public stock offering to charity and social causes," Google has targeted the problems of poverty and the environment. The focus on poverty was described as a "big, hairy, audacious goal." The long-term wave pattern says it is about to get bigger and more audacious. So does history; the only time that companies give away bucket loads of shareholder money is at the end of a social euphoria when society is about to get a whole lot poorer.

December 2005

The following clipping, which is headlined "Wall Street Goes Gaga for Google," shows how downright intolerant Wall Street is toward the old-fashioned idea of savings:

> CNBC's hyperkinetic James Cramer urged his auds last week
> to buy Google, even though it's in the stratosphere, even if
> you've only got enough cash in the bank to buy one share.

As we noted last month, the suspicious aspect of Google's furious advance is that it refuses to spread to other issues. The article, which is from the latest issue of Variety, notes that Google's gains appeared to come at the expense of the rest of the media industry. "For just about every other media company 'This is the year of panic,' says one money manager." The solitary nature of Google's blast into the heavens is a clear break from the contagion that spread so freely during the mania phase of 1999-2000. After accompanying Google into the stratosphere in late 2004, a portfolio of bubble stocks (TASR, SIRI, BOOM, PACT, TZOO, LOUD and NAPM) peaked on December 27, 2004 and is now down more than 50%. October also saw the dollar volume of trading on the OTC Bulletin Board fall again. It's now down 43% from its December 2004 high and a whopping 90% from its all-time peak in March 2000.

January 2006

In Saudi Arabia, a kingdom that bans gambling, a dot.com-style mania has broken out. "So many people crush the banks to get on board an initial public offering that the police have to be called out. Some Saudis disappear from work during trading hours, and teachers bring their laptops to class to trade stocks." The number of Saudi investors jumped from 50,000 to 2 million over the last five years. The analysis of a Saudi bank sees "no deterioration on the horizon of any of the underlying forces driving the stock market." With the most established blue chip shares continuing to falter, this blatant disregard for weakening stock market leadership actually confirms EWFF's contention that 2005 is nothing more than a supersized 1968, when an all-time high in speculative shares accompanied a smaller scale secondary peak for the Dow.

Time Magazine Covers The Top

The November issue observed a new flurry of charitable giving and concluded: "The stage is set for a whole new round of bubble-busting, as philanthropy is all the rage once again." The end of the trend, and by extension a renewed stock market downturn, is confirmed by Time magazine's "Persons of the Year," which goes to rock star Bono, and the world's richest couple, Bill and Melinda Gates, for their willingness to spread their wealth and get the rest of the world to join in. As a similar spike in early 2000 demonstrated, philanthropic fever reflects a positive social mood and is therefore a sure sign of a major stock market top.

Time's person of the year coverage is a massive double sell signal because in addition to its long history of identifying trends as they are expiring, its fawning tribute to Bono and the Gateses depicts a societal infatuation with giving that is totally out of bounds with historic precedent. In additional stories, Time reveals that the great benevolence runs deep. It tabs 2005 as "The Year of Charitainment" when "celebrity do-gooderism was in fashion." And it wasn't just the big shots: "Americans dug deep to raise billions for those who lost everything." Why? Because the end of a long bull market is the only time when people feel so confident in their future earnings that they are willing to part with more than usual amounts for charity. We have nothing against charity, it's just that when so many people are being mobilized to give by powerful social forces, society is operating under the blissed-out influence of a long advance. In December 1999, Time honored Jeff Bezos of Amazon.com as its person of the year. The choice celebrated the vast wealth gener-

ating capacity of the new information age and signaled that a major peak was at hand just as the January 2000 issue of EWFF suggested. Five years later, stocks must be at an even more bearish juncture because instead of honoring the creation of wealth, Time is recognizing the willingness to give it away. In terms of social mood, it's the perfect send-off for the next phase of the Grand Supercycle bear market.

February 2006

The small cap stocks actually continued to new highs on their own on January 25, broadcasting the same defiance that more speculative shares showed for two months into March 2000. A few days before the NASDAQ peaked in March 2000, EWFF noted that "bull market champions like Microsoft, AOL and Qualcomm" had deserted the advance and had been replaced by a thinning list of increasingly speculative shares. Today the market is in exactly the same condition. The first chart below shows just a few of the many generals that have abandoned the latest charge. Of the 30 stocks in the Dow Industrials, just four (Caterpillar, Hewlett Packard, McDonalds and Procter & Gamble) accompanied the average to its recent peak. So the same warning that EWFF sounded in March 2000 applies now.

The chart of dollar trading volume on the OTC Bulletin Board indicates a likely powerful force in the coming decline. Since

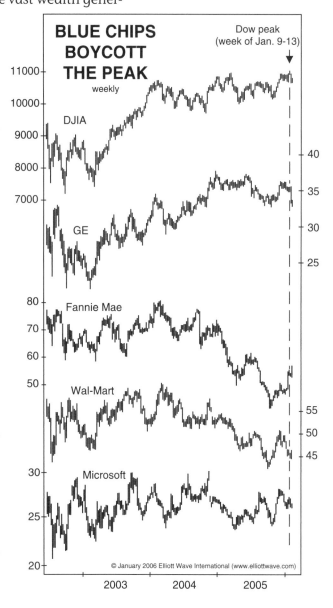

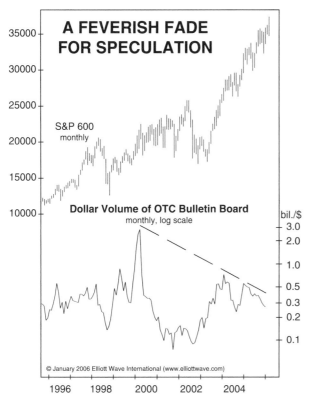

the OTC Bulletin Board is composed of stocks that are not listed on any exchange, trading in these shares represents the most speculative market action. A high level of bulletin board activity is a sign of underlying strength for the small caps indexes. Back in March 2000, dollar volume on the bulletin board surged to $26 billion, signaling that the S&P 600 Small Cap Index was on relatively firm ground. The index went on to gain another 86%. On the latest index rally however, trading on the bulletin board did not rise at all. In fact, as the indexes of listed stocks climbed to new countertrend or all-time highs through 2005, trading in the most speculative shares plunged 51% from December 2004, and down 90% from the all-time high in March 2000. This contraction is a powerful sign that investors are losing their nerve.

Last summer, when a bevy of 2004 bubble stocks failed to confirm new highs in the major averages, EWFF surmised that the pool of greater fools might be drying up. It was draining so fast that Google seemed to be the only stock generating the kind of lunatic buying that characterized the NASDAQ's all-time high.

March 2006

The Approaching Crash

The first chart below (next page) shows the Saudi Arabian stock market index for the past eight months. It shows what lies ahead for the Dow and S&P. The U.S. stock market has continued to climb almost mystically, defying sentiment extremes, momentum divergences, cycles and completed wave patterns on a short term basis. Likewise the Saudi index had been advancing relentlessly as if on a mission. Yet the SASE index just lost 28 percent of its value in 2½ weeks. This is equivalent to waking up just a dozen trading days from now to see the Dow back at its October 2002 low. Can you cite any obvious indication at the high that this market would reverse and plummet? Fundamentally, oil has been trading near all-time highs. Technically, there was no top formation, no head and shoulders pattern, no slowing of the market's ascent; in fact, the index accelerated in its final two months of rise and then further in its final few days of rise. As with the U.S. market in the late 1990s, one would have counted the waves in real time only with extreme difficulty because the corrections during the rise were exceptionally shallow. At the top all we had for certain was an extended mania, and that was enough. This year the U.S. stock market is shaping up to drop at least as fast. Generally when stocks levitate late into a market cycle, they make up for it by crashing.

Is this scenario fanciful? Take a look at the second chart. This is the Dubai Financial stock index. It has lost 53% of its value just since November. This is equivalent to waking up in mid-July to see the Dow in the 5000s. The Abu Dhabi stock index is also falling hard. No one today imagines anything like this will happen to U.S. stocks. But I am certain that it will happen when the next bear market wave kicks off. In other words, our outlook for the U.S. is happening now in other parts of the world. Pretty soon the U.S. will be in its own "now."

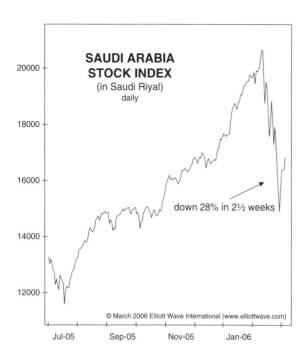

The Bond Market

Relatively low levels of bond market volatility, as reflected by Merrill Lynch's MOVE index, invariably lead to high levels of volatility. The MOVE index measures the implied volatility across the yield curve using the price of 1-month Treasury options. The index just fell to a new all-time low, eclipsing the previous low of July 1998.

The strong potential for a similar reversal is shown in the chart of the MOVE index plotted above the Confidence ratio (inverted here for clarity), which divides the yield on Moody's Corporate BAA bonds by the yield on 30-year Treasuries. When the ratio is rising, it means that investors are demanding a larger premium on lower quality debt relative to higher quality because fears of default are increasing. Notice what happened prior to the MOVE index's upward spike in 1998: the Confidence ratio was subtly rising, foreshadowing the volatility spike in both bonds and stocks.

These bearish conditions are in place as the U.S. Treasury yield curve heads into a second straight month of inversion, with the yield on 2-year Treasuries above that of 10-year Treasuries. When it first occurred briefly in late December (prior to a sustained inversion in late January), EWFF compared it to a freight train and said that holders of risky financial assets were standing on the tracks. The train claimed its first victims last week as it barreled through the distant financial outpost of Reykjavík, Iceland. Fitch Ratings downgraded Iceland's debt,

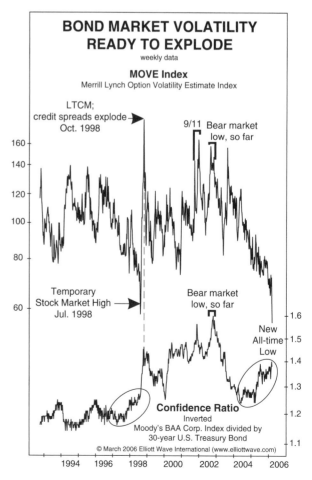

and the Icelandic króna quickly fell 9.3% against the dollar, setting off an avalanche of sell orders in emerging markets. The Brazilian real declined 3%; the South African rand more than 2%; the Indonesian rupiah and Polish zloty fell 1.5%; and the Mexican peso and Turkish lira slipped 1%. "The contagion was primarily due to traders' need to liquidate profitable positions in order to fund their Icelandic losses." This episode was only a mini-ripple, but it is a perfect illustration of the "carry trade" reversal, which the January issue of EWFF said was likely coming right behind the inversion of the yield curve. In the weeks ahead, the "end of the carry trade" will be much discussed, but it's really just another way of observing the emerging shift from a voracious mass appetite for risk to an extreme stance of risk aversion. This is the new conservatism predicted in *Conquer the Crash*. As it intensifies, liquidity will disappear, financial sector profits will be squeezed and the money supply will ultimately decline.

May 2006
All the Same Decline

Back in 2002, *Conquer the Crash* observed a correspondence in the price action between the S&P, gold, silver and the CRB and stated that the positive correlation between these often disparate markets "means that most assets lately are moving up and down more or less together, probably as liquidity expands and contracts." Subsequent issues and a May 2004 Barron's article (see next page) by Prechter and Kendall associated the liquidity bubble to a global "risk grab" and expanded the list to include junk bonds, real estate, small-cap stocks, hedge funds and emerging markets. The great liquidity wave clearly has extended until now, as April's spike high in silver and copper accompanies new recovery highs in blue-chip stock averages and a new all-time high in the more speculative small-cap sector. As we've been saying, it's all one market.

Now, however, there are very strong reasons to believe that the direction of this broad movement is shifting from up to down. In addition to the solidifying evidence of upside exhaustion in the stock market, real estate, junk bonds and several formerly surging foreign stock markets topped in 2005 and are now in decline. Granted, several of these markets are in distant corners of the financial world, such as Dubai and Iceland, but the last global "contagion" in 1998 also had obscure roots, and the straight-up to straight-down form of their reversal suggests a critical shift from risk-free abandon to trepidation among global investors. The hazard is visible in the current action on the Saudi Arabia stock exchange, which fell 28% from a late February peak, rallied 19% after a Saudi sheik announced a $2.7 billion dollar investment in Saudi stocks and then promptly fell another 31% in April. The total decline from its peak was 42% in just two months.

Where Were You When the Fire Went Out?

As the new universe of ETFs and other newfangled derivatives emerges to satisfy every speculative whim of the public, the fire that drove their creation is on the verge of a flame-out. EWFF has noted Google's relatively solitary frenzy and a general wane in investors' appetite for over-the-counter stocks as signs that the speculative heat has been cooling for months. Another potent sign of a complete dousing is now visible in a reversal of the gold/silver price ratio. *The Elliott Wave Financial Forecast* last discussed the gold/silver ratio in the September 2001 issue, forecasting a continued rise to above 63:1. On a monthly basis, the ratio topped at 80:1 in May 2003. As this chart shows, a decline from this high has traced out an impulse wave to this month's 46:1 low. As we go to press, a reversal to 50:1 is in place. This shift in relative performance is significant because, as the higher-beta metal, when silver stops outperforming gold, it signals a larger scale exhaustion of the "animal spirits" that have carried all-the-same-markets to simultaneous price highs in 2006. Conversely a strong preference for gold reflects investors' conservatism at a stock market low as well as industry's lower demand for silver in the recession that typically accompanies major stock market bottoms. The arrows under the ratio show what happens to stocks when the ratio reverses from a sharp fall as it is doing now. Major stock declines tend to

In Synch to Sink

Liquidity matters: A contrarian view on inflation prospects

BY ROBERT PRECHTER and
PETER KENDALL

PRECIOUS METALS AND COMMODITIES STARTED their climb about three years ago, yet it's only recently that investors have turned passionate about the idea that commodities are poised to enter "runaway" mode.

Hedgers, gloom-and-doomers, fund managers and now even conservative investors have embraced the idea of investing in "things."

The new believers in runaway inflation are being spurred by memories of the 1970s, which are echoed in current headlines such as "Skyrocketing Lumber Prices" and "Corn, Wheat and Soybeans Surge."

Is it déjà vu all over again? Yes, but not in the way people believe. In our view, recent market turns portend not runaway inflation, but deflation. There is an important difference between now and periods of accelerating inflation such as the 1970s and its predecessor, the 1910s.

In those periods, the trends in hard assets and financial assets went opposite ways. Precious metals — except gold, when its price was fixed — and commodities soared while stocks languished and bonds collapsed, a typical response to accelerating inflation. In the current environment, however, stocks and junk bonds have recovered right along with gold, silver and commodities.

The first two charts on the right show how tight the correlation has remained, especially over the last two years. What gives? The third chart updates one from our book *Conquer the Crash*, showing that the Commodity Research Bureau commodity index has been roughly tracking the Standard & Poor's 500 since mid-1998.

As explained in the book, "This correlation means that most assets lately are moving up and down more or less together, probably as liquidity expands and contracts."

Rising liquidity in a disinflationary environment is not only fuel for a rise in inflation-hedge investments, but also the lifeblood of the stock market, property investment and the economy. A recovering economy, in turn, supports the issuers of junk bonds and maintains investor optimism. Such a confluence of effects, as we have argued over the last several years, can occur only in a disinflationary world.

Many observers say that these classes of markets will soon decouple: Either inflation will accelerate, pushing up gold and commodities, or inflation will remain moderate, benefiting the stock market and junk bonds.

We disagree. Liquidity is everything now, and it is driving the prices of all investment classes. These markets have been going up together, and we think that when liquidity contracts, they will go down together. This outcome happens only at rare times in history when a society-wide credit expansion reaches its zenith and social psychology changes from expansive to defensive.

A change in financial market trends from up to down signals the transition — exactly the situation we face today.

There is precedent for our view. The Great Depression followed a soaring stock market and a countertrend advance in commodity prices in the 1920s, all fueled by an expansion in credit. The depression of the late 1830s and early 1840s likewise followed a liquidity spike. Even as stocks retreated from a record high in May 1835, enough liquidity remained to fuel a commodities rally into 1837. In neither period did the commodity index make a new all-time high, because the overall disinflationary environment precluded it.

The current episode gives us a strong echo of the 1830s lagged commodity rally (see final charts). The commodity-price peak in the first quarter of 1937 coincided with a march on New York City Hall, in which protestors carried signs demanding, "Bread, meat, rent, fuel! Their prices must come down!" The march devolved into a riot in which the crowd ransacked several stores.

The modern-day version of that riot is the recent rash of articles forecasting a looming storm in virtually every commodity. Headlines of the past few weeks include "China, Iraq Using Up Steel, Lumber," "Imagining a $7-a-Gallon Future" and "China Effect: Food Prices Are Rising."

And on April 20, Federal Reserve Chairman Alan Greenspan confidently announced, "Threats of deflation are no longer an issue." As veteran market-watchers know, changes in trend often occur when the majority is looking the other way. The rush into commodities by hedge funds and small investors over the past year is another sign that the supposedly approaching inflationary storm is in fact nearly over.

Back on March 17, 1837, an unexpected fall in cotton prices began a decline that soon engulfed all commodities. An overheated real-estate boom reversed, and the stock market resumed its major bear trend. Today, all of these markets are in the same position as they were just before that transition a century and a half ago. The failure of a single New York stockbroker in 1837 is said to have triggered the eventual demise of hundreds more, but the truth is that the deflationary collapse of the late 1830s and early 1840s was the ultimate resolution of a two-decade pattern of credit expansion and speculation that finally became exhausted — just the setup we have today.

All the Same Market?

▶ In a rare alignment, stocks and junk bonds have rallied with real estate, foreign currencies, gold, silver and commodities. When it ends, all these markets should turn down. Some already have reversed, indicating a possible resumption of the bear market and the onset of deflation.

Liquidity Is Everything

▶ The rough correspondence between the S&P and the CRB Commodities Index in recent years indicates that investment markets are responding primarily to liquidity flows.

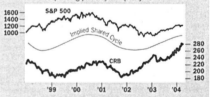

Disinflation to Deflation

▶ In the wake of the 1835 stock peak, commodity prices surged. Their reversal in 1837 signaled the start of a deflationary decline in all assets. Over the past year, the commodity rally following the peak in stocks suggests that the same outcome is due.

Source: Elliot Wave International

The resolution of all this is likely to be a credit contraction followed by a deflationary drop in most asset classes. Cash and safe cash equivalents like Treasury bonds will provide a welcome refuge from the storm. ∎

ROBERT PRECHTER is president of Elliott Wave International and PETER KENDALL is an editor at the financial-forecasting firm. You can find them at www.elliottwave.com

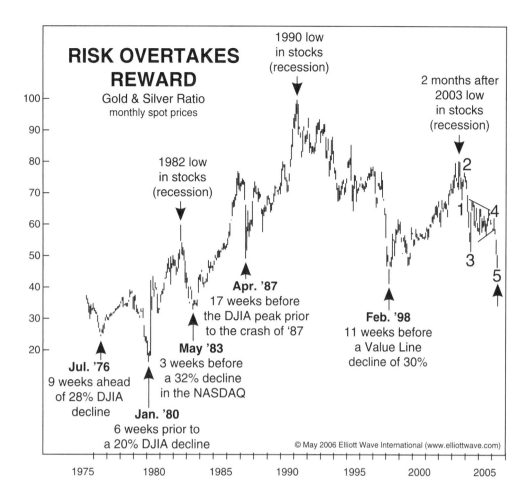

follow closely. The last shift in favor of gold in 1998 preceded a 30% decline in the Value Line Index, the LTCM meltdown and Asian currency crises. The coming financial decline should create even more turmoil because the assets involved are spread over more territory, priced higher on average and held in far weaker hands.

June 2006

The reversal from "the across-the-board rally in financial and commodity markets" to "an across-the-board decline" called for last month is now underway. It should take the form of a chain reaction in which distant and seemingly uncorrelated markets decline more or less in sync. The S&P 500 top occurred on May 5, a target date that was cited six months ago in *The Elliott Wave Theorist*. The DJIA recorded a corresponding peak on May 10 and both indexes now join the NASDAQ 100, which topped over 4 months ago, in the decline.

Liquidity and the Markets

Last month's issue anticipated the culmination of a long-standing forecast here at Elliott Wave International. It began with Chapter 21 of *Conquer the Crash* (2002) in which Bob Prechter observed a positive correlation between commodities and stocks, two historically disparate markets, and cited a "shared cycle" driven by massive liquidity flows. In a May 2004 *Barron's* article, "In Synch to Sink," Prechter and Pete Kendall showed the pattern in greater detail by stacking charts of the U.S. Dollar Index (inverted), Real Estate Investment Trusts, silver, the S&P 500, junk bonds, gold and the CRB index and said, "Liquidity is driving the prices of all investment classes. When liquidity contracts, they will go down together."

The U.S. Dollar Index (inverted) is shown in the first panel of an updated version of our stacked chart. It gets the lead spot because the reversal of our all-the-same-markets scenario began with its turn at the end of 2004. The second box in the upper right corner shows that the spread between the yield on high and low quality debt reversed to widening in March 2005. We place this graph prominently because a contraction in credit (liquidity) is the unifying force that will drive the entire multi-market reversal. The downtrend will gather much of its strength and spread into seemingly unrelated areas when investors are forced to unload even the most secure financial assets to meet margin calls and other payments due on debt.

The March 2005 issue also turned subscribers' attention to the real estate sector with another Special Study, "The Real Estate Bust Begins" (see Chapter 2). The July 2005 issue added, "There's no mistaking it now: The extreme psychology of the Grand Supercyle has taken up residence in real estate." The chart of a key housing stock index (second row, left column) shows that the statement came days before top tick in housing. Finally, our largest-ever Special Study in last month's issue of EWFF asserted that the reversal was about to reach the rest of the global financial markets. EWFF stated that the broad movement in these heterogeneous markets "is on the cusp of a turn into an across-the-board-decline."

The tout that commodities provide "diversification and inflation protection" is another indication of how perfectly positioned psychology is for our projected synchronized descent. One of the fatal misconceptions of the post-2000 drive into riskier and riskier financial assets is that they somehow offer shelter against market declines. "Diversification is gospel today because investment assets of so many kinds have gone up for so long," CTC explains, "but the future is another matter. Owning an array of investments is financial suicide during deflation." The last nine panels on the previous page show the initiation of the "kitchen sink" effect discussed in May.

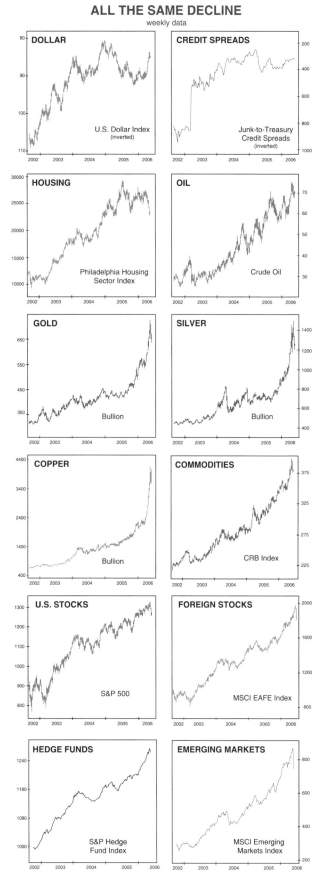

ALL THE SAME DECLINE
weekly data

Investor Psychology

One of the critical aspects of the next bear market wave that we discussed last month is the "snuffing of the speculative fires." A key indicator of this condition is the gold/silver price ratio, which tends to turn up in favor of gold ahead of stock peaks. In last month's Special Study, EWFF's long-term chart of the gold/silver ratio showed that the ratio bottoms and turns up from a steep decline anywhere from 3 to 17 weeks before stocks top. With three weeks between the recent April 19 bottom in the ratio and the May top in stocks, the relationship is right in line with precedent. As we also said last month, "The higher-beta NASDAQ's underperformance relative to the blue-chips is another signal that the market's speculative fever is breaking." Continued weakness in the NASDAQ/S&P ratio is to the point that we can now character-

ize it as downside leadership. It is clearer than ever that speculators are losing heart.

July 2006

All the Same Market

Here's the "Bottom Line" from the May issue, published on April 28:

> The across-the-board rally in financial and commodity markets is on the cusp of a turn into an across-the-board decline.

And here's the media now, catching sight of the "new mentality":

With Global Markets Jittery, Investors Decide to Rein in Risk

—The New York Times, June 12, 2006

There's "little doubt" says the Times, "that investors were dumping risk from their portfolios." It's the big new thing, and it's visible everywhere, from virtually every global stock market to a

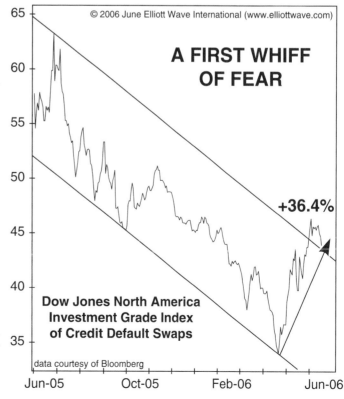

reversal in real estate to a jump in junk bond yields to a stilted performance by IPOs in the U.S., Hong Kong and Europe to a 36.4% six-week rise in the cost of insurance against bond defaults, as seen in the chart. The gold/silver ratio pushed to 58:1 last week, making significant progress toward the initial target of 62:1 that we established in May (see chart previous page). This ratio should continue its upward path until stocks bottom and a risk-timidity not seen since the Great Depression wrenches the economy into a severe contraction.

The clamor for China Bank's IPO is another indication of a terminally extreme financial optimism. Despite illegal activities by its directors and employees, which were disclosed in the China Bank prospectus, the retail allotment of the IPO was oversubscribed by a factor of 80 times! The return to financial propriety will require such excruciating pain that investors will shy away from the financial speculation store for not just years but generations.

September 2006
Losing Faith in Old Faithful

In early 2004, *The Elliott Wave Financial Forecast* argued that the speculative intensity of the Great Asset Mania was starting to dissipate. In May, as the small cap averages approached their all-time highs, EWFF took a firmer stand saying that the speculative fury that has driven investors into so many risky financial vehicles was on the "verge of a flame-out." One convincing piece of evidence was a chart of the gold/silver price ratio (see June entry), headlined "Risk Overtakes Reward." In recent days, the ratio has retraced a portion of the rise from the May low. As the stock market rolls over, the preference for the perceived safety of gold relative to higher-beta silver should quickly push the gold/silver ratio to our initial target of 62:1 and probably higher. The muted rebound in the small-caps and NASDAQ since July, two of the more speculative sectors of the market, signals that the bear market's drive toward taming investors' euphoric animal spirits is underway.

Belief in an economic "soft landing" permeates Wall Street's economic forecasts. This myth is attractive because the current mania has run so long and continually found new and generally ever riskier avenues of expression, making an actual contraction, much less a crash, seem fanciful. As far as we know, the mania's ability to continually re-invent itself is unique to history. It has been a full 10 years since Iomega and Comparator Systems captured the imagination of the investors with gains of 965% and 6233%, respectively, in the first half of 1996. It has taken a complete decade for the fever to play itself out, but the steady deterioration followed by the recent signs of decline in different speculative realms suggests that the mania is, in fact, on its last legs. As Charles Mackay said of tulips in *Extraordinary Popular Delusions and the Madness of Crowds*:

> At last, however, the more prudent began to see that this folly could not last forever. It was seen that somebody must lose fearfully in the end. As this conviction spread, prices fell, and never rose again.

Many of the most exotic, modern-day tulips will meet that same fate. But despite the unfolding contraction, this mania has persisted for so long and morphed into so many different areas that we wouldn't be surprised to see a few residual buying stampedes into increasingly obscure investment vehicles. As EWFF noted in November 1999, it happened in the wake of Supercycle wave (I) when a brief flurry of speculation in mulberry bushes followed the crash of 1837. Here's another: A record bid of $45,192 for a pay receipt signed by the original five Beatles. The wild bidding for a hand scribbled note signed by the musical heroes of the old bull market is a good example of how narrow and farcical these late blooming speculative markets are likely to be. The aftermath of this and any other post bubble geysers will offer historians a graphic illustration of what happens when investors refuse to let go of the past.

October 2006

It should come as no surprise to readers that the squeeze to "get out" started in the energy sector. Back in July, when the clamor over "peak oil" reached its fever pitch, *The Elliott Wave Theorist* took an in-depth look at the crude oil market and issued the following forecast:

> Extreme opinions, shared widely, constitute the single most reliable indicator of an impending change of direction for a market. I have never, in 35 years of watching markets, seen such a consensus about any financial trend. A setback of at least Primary degree, if not a bear market, is due now. Stay away from the long side.

Crude is down more than 21% from its July peak. The depth of belief in "peak oil" suggests a decline of much greater magnitude. Considering the number of emerging markets that are largely dependent on oil and other commodities (the CRB is also down 17%), the next domino could come in from almost any direction.

The only difference this time is the size and connectedness of the turn. The markets went up in one happy clump, and they will come down more or less in unison. But big peaks can be frustratingly diffuse, and the hair loss experienced by your editors from this one is definitely approaching Grand Supercycle dimensions. Instead of the one-fell-swoop that started the reversal in May-June, the turn is taking more of a saw tooth form in which some markets such as oil cut sharply lower while others follow more slowly and a few drift slightly higher as seeming safe havens. It is not unusual for investors to narrow their focus before they cut and run. Eventually, they always give in.

November 2006

While the S&P and NASDAQ remain beneath their March 2000 all-time highs, October took the Dow Jones Industrial Average to an all-time high above 12,000. What happened? We did not expect the Dow to buck its usual September-October swoon. Through the course of the 1974-2000 bull market, September and October were both up months only twice, 1982 and 1988. Unlike the latest case, both of the prior moves against this strong bearish seasonal tendency came after declines to relatively depressed levels.

The steadiness of the surge takes us back to 1997, when the index was in its longest-ever upward move without a 10% correction. In the midst of that experience, a classic issue of *The Elliott Wave Theorist*, "Bulls, Bears and Manias," made the following observation:

> When investment markets become smoothly-trending and free of fractal variations, they depict an unhealthy patient and signal an impending "heart attack."

This table (from Dr. John Hussman at www.Hussman Funds.com) shows the 10 longest DJIA advances without an intervening 10% correction. The third column shows the percentage declines that occurred prior to the next 10% advance. The 1997 experience actually produced the smallest percentage decline, but after a few more relatively uninterrupted bursts in the late 1990s, the big one finally arrived in the form of the 2000-2002 decline, the first leg of the bear market. At 921 trading days, the current stretch of trading days without an intervening 10% Dow decline is the fourth longest in the history of the index. Observe that these streaks do not appear to be randomly distributed

Date	Trading Days	Decline	P/E at high (S&P)	T-bond yield
9/3/1929	719	-40.00%	20.6	3.80%
3/10/1937	654	-14.90%	11.3	2.50%
5/29/1946	1020	-23.20%	16.2	2.10%
1/5/1953	617	-13.00%	9.4	2.80%
7/12/1957	960	-19.40%	13	3.70%
2/9/1966	912	-25.20%	17.6	4.60%
8/25/1987	780	-36.10%	19.7	8.90%
7/16/1990	657	-21.20%	13.6	8.60%
8/6/1997	1723	-10.60%	23.7	6.40%
11/3/2006	921		18.5	4.70%

data courtesy of Dr. John Hussman (www.HussmanFunds.com)

but instead precede some of the most important highs in market history, including the end of Supercycle wave (III) in 1929, Cycles I and III in 1937 and 1966, respectively, and the peak that preceded the stock market crash in 1987. Even the streaks in 1946, 1953 and 1957 preceded Primary and/or Intermediate-degree declines. The laws of nature have not been abandoned and the current streak should likewise lead to a major decline, similar to the preceding examples.

December 2006

The OTC Bulletin board and EWI Bubble Stock Index have been quiet. The stock market's underwhelming participation in the frenzy is another dramatic non-confirmation. Apparently it's hard to get a real party going when everyone still has a hangover.

January 2007

The chart offers a pictorial representation of the sentiment behind the freakishly even uptrend in the financial markets in recent months. The November and December EWFF issues discussed this relentless climb with respect to equities and the VIX; the MOVE index of bond volatility and the spread between the emerging market debt and U.S. Treasuries show that this same relationship applies to the debt markets. As the trend goes higher with the smoothness of a department store escalator, risk premiums collapse as fewer and fewer investors seek insurance against decline. History suggests, however, that such periods of extremely steady ascent tend to give way to bone-jarring reversals. One reason is that in such seemingly benign environments investors tend to overreach for return. This is definitely happening now. The January 2 issue of the Wall Street Journal notes that market conditions have "driven investors into riskier corners of the market." Investors' unprecedented appetite for higher yields is manifest in the frenzied issuance of new junk debt in

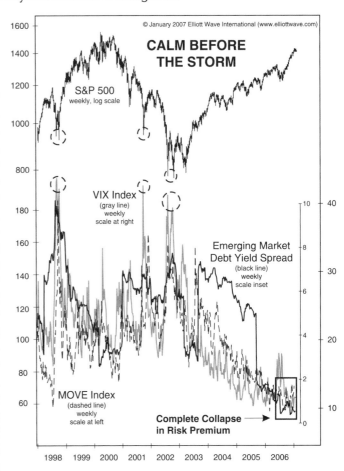

2006. According to Bloomberg, a record $163 billion of high-yield bonds came to market. The Journal notes, "junk has never been so fashionable," and adds this staggering statistic: "more than 70% of U.S. companies rated by Standard & Poor's have below-investment grade, or junk, ratings. That's a record." The love affair with lower quality credit is the perfect backdrop for a reversal from risk tolerant to risk averse.

February 2007

Chinese stock-buying frenzies are getting to be like *Rocky* movies; they keep coming and coming. Of course, there is a very important difference; they don't end happily. The original version, known as red chip fever, occurred right before Hong Kong returned to Chinese rule in 1997. At the time, the Hang Seng, Hong Kong's main stock index, was going full bore. The June 1997 issue of *The Elliott Wave Theorist* identified the spasm of buying as an extension of a worldwide rally and called for it to end around July 1, 1997, the day of the island's reunion with mainland China. The Hang Seng topped a month later and fell 46% in three months. In September 2000, when nearly half a million prospective investors "thronged" to Hong Kong banks in hopes of landing shares of a local Internet startup, Tom.com, EWFF said the potential for another break in Chinese shares was high. The Hang Seng plunged 48% over the next three years.

The last chart shows that the fever is back. And it bears a striking resemblance to exponential rockets in U.S. housing stocks in 2005 and copper in 2006. The classic, almost straight-up acceleration of this curve is the same as the one that EWFF showed on the NASDAQ and Cisco Systems in June 2000. We also showed the historic break that inevitably results, in two historic forerunners, the South Sea Co. of 1721-1722 and the Nikkei of the 1990s. "Notice that once the ascent goes vertical and is then broken by a sharp break, every lunge back toward the peak is followed by a sharp sell-off," stated EWFF at that time. The first two examples shown here compose a fascinating time-lapse version of a break down in process. If the top is not yet in for Chinese shares, it should be close. A big turn is also strongly suggested by Time magazine's "Dawn of a New Dynasty" cover story, which invokes Paul Montgomery's Magazine Cover Indicator. We love the use of the word "New," as it comes after 20 years of expansion and a 200% surge in less than 20 months. Time's "Home Sweet Home" cover in mid-2005 illustrates the deadly effectiveness of this contrarian signal.

A host of articles about an insane burst in the public demand for Chinese shares reveals the extent to which the mania for stocks is striking at the heart of the world's largest communist country. By all accounts, it is at least as feverish as that of 1997 and 2000: "Grungy-looking college students, office workers, retirees and even a pregnant woman in suede boots all jostled into the brokerage on a recent morning, eager to buy stocks and buy them now," says the New York Times. In Shanghai, one of the most popular local television programs is Stock Market Today. "Trading houses can seem like carnivals." To handle "the torrent of new clients," brokerage houses are installing computers and adding registration desks. Mutual fund business is booming. At the beauty salon, the manicurists talk about stocks, "They ask me, 'What should I invest in?" says a consultant in Shanghai. "They say they are doing research."

The frenzy's re-location from Hong Kong to the mainland stock markets of Shanghai and Shenzhen is an important leap because it shows how confidence has expanded over the past 10 years. While the Chinese economy emerged two decades ago, Chinese stock markets remained "stagnant financial backwaters, marred by scandal [and] weak oversight." As recently as a year ago, "China's markets nearly disintegrated, and one 2003 poll found that 90 percent of investors had lost money. Public confidence was so low then that half of those investors said

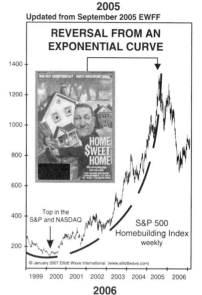

EXPONENTIAL BLOWOFF TOP OF THE YEAR AWARD
2005
Updated from September 2005 EWFF

2006

2007

they wanted to sell their holdings and abandon the market forever." But a Beijing-based investor who "lost her shirt" in the last decline says, "the market is more mature now." Even though the various officials are warning "that the market is overheating" and "there is a bubble going on," investors insist that "the government is trying to straighten things out so that the markets will become stronger" and "I don't see this as a bubble." A U.S. financial magazine seems to agree. It asks, "Are Communists The World's Best Capitalists?" It answers affirmatively with a raving endorsement of China's fearless leaders' ability "to impose controls to slow down the economy." The Times of London says Chinese "investors have dubbed the surge a 'rational bubble' and say that China's economic circumstances mean that a crash is unlikely."

Of course, at the pinnacle of an exponential rise it must be exactly so. The Chinese stock market miracle is not the work of communist planning and the credit that it fosters, but an extension of a global bull market in social mood. The false accounting and loss-generating capacities of state-owned companies are simply concealed by a haze of goodwill that every mania inspires. As the frenzy passes, these problems will make a dramatic re-entry. Chinese leaders are doing everything to "warn" investors because they remember what happened in 2000 and 1997. That's why Cheng Siwei, vice chairman of the Chinese legislature, issued a warning against "blind optimism." He added that "shares are overvalued," and suggested the government "will step up efforts to slow fund inflows." Amidst so much official concern, many argue that it can't be a bubble, but as EWFF also pointed out at the top in 2000, one of the final signs of all the great bubbles is that authorities often see them for what they are and, in trying to stem the tide, end up strapped to the mast of their sinking ship.

This is a particularly appropriate endpoint for the bull market because so many avowed capitalists have become enamored with China's ability to direct its economy. But as *The Elliott Wave Theorist* initially observed in 1997, it is really a tribute to the awesome power of the bull market. The uptrend is so strong that the market has even driven those that profess to be ideologically opposed to its existence into a frothy bid for shares. This state of unbridled acceptance will last as long as the rally does. Once it ends, the recriminations will start to fly, as they always do. The resulting turmoil will probably reshape China's political order. Then, as Elliott Wave International has previously predicted, the bottom will give rise to a globally powerful "new dynasty."

With more than a few bears retiring or otherwise expiring, the majority belief that stock prices always go up appears to be getting ever closer to unanimity. In that regard, it is interesting to note the recent passing of the world's oldest man; his last name is Mercado del Toro, which is Spanish for "Bull Market." At 115 years of age, his death probably didn't come as a surprise. But that's not true of bull markets. No matter how long they last and how slowly a peak rolls into place, people will say it came out of the blue and there was "no way" to see it coming.

Flight from Risk

Barron's Randall Forsyth probably sums up the current state of the bond market best in paraphrasing Churchill: "Never have so many paid so much for so little." The complete collapse in bond and stock market volatility has resulted in an evaporation in the yield premium demanded by junk bond speculators from a high of 10% in 2002 to a current rate of less than 3% above comparable U.S. Treasuries. Current high yield investors have no margin of safety in the case of default, which, as we showed in the March 2005 issue of EWFF, is more probable than not when it comes to junk debt. But "earnings are great, fundamentals are great, and there's an awful lot of money out in the market getting put to work right now," says a managing director of a major Boston-based mutual fund company. This assessment is true, but it is useless to investors because it says nothing about the future. Yet such statements do have forecasting value when descriptions of current conditions are being broadly extrapolated forward. This week, we heard on financial television that the economy is "perfect," "a nirvana" and "the best of the absolute best." And people see "no signs" of a reversal. The extreme extent to which this forecast is being repeated and wagered on now is a sure sign of an impending turn toward contraction and default.

This chart is the MOVE index, which measures bond market volatility and is comparable to the VIX index for stocks. Last month, we showed both indicators stacked on a chart. Here we separate out the MOVE index to highlight the extraordinary complacency that consumes the bond market. The index has not been above 72.25 since the start of 2006, by far the longest period of low volatility since Merrill Lynch started the index in 1988. There are only two periods in which the index briefly spiked below current levels. The first occurred in December 1989 (not shown), at the forefront of the S&L crisis and a significant real estate decline. The other was August 1998, when *The New York Times* reported a mysterious "decoupling of fixed income," i.e., a worldwide collapse in which investors took flight from low-grade debt. Both periods preceded major spikes in junk-to-treasury credit spreads, the latter of which is seen on the chart, and both were accompanied by an inverted yield curve, which is in place now. Another credit bomb went off in 1980, so nine years separate the credit blow-outs of 1980, 1989 and 1998; 2007 is the next year in this rhythm. The conditions are nearly ideal for a massive flight from risky bond instruments. A push above the December 2006 high of 72.25 in the MOVE index will provide a strong signal that spreads are on the rise.

All the Same Markets

One can hardly peruse a financial periodical or posting these days and not read about how "liquidity is driving up all the markets." As far as we know, we were the first firm to introduce this idea. *Conquer the Crash*, completed in March 2002, presented this illustration and accompanying commentary:

> As shown in this chart, the Commodity Research Bureau (CRB) commodity index has tracked the S&P, with a slight lag, since mid-1998. Gold and silver have also joined in the latest stock rally. As I see it, this correlation means that most assets lately

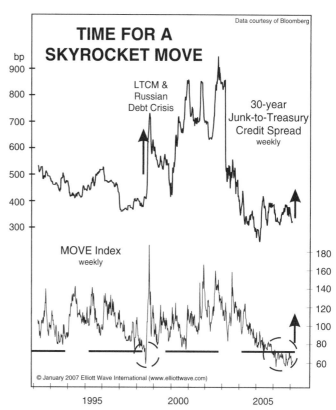

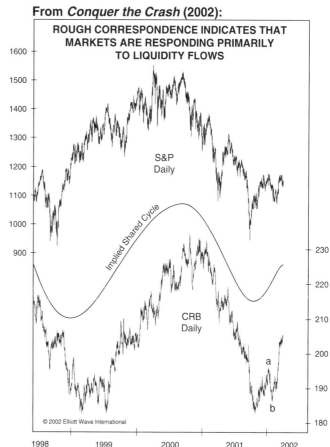

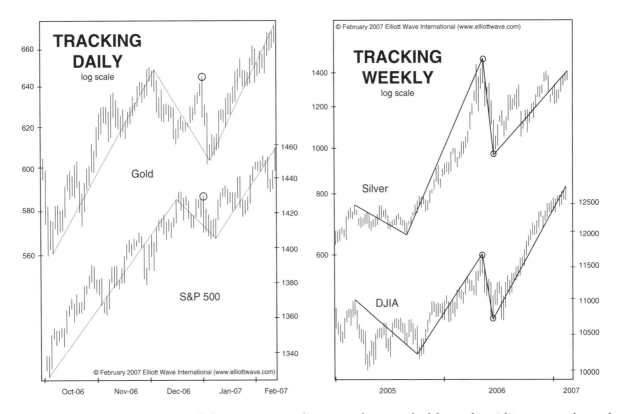

are moving up and down more or less together, probably as liquidity expands and contracts.

We began following up on this idea in *The Elliott Wave Theorist* and *The Elliott Wave Financial Forecast*, showing graphs of financial markets that were tracking each other. We published the idea in an article for Barron's in May 2004.

Our main focus has been to recognize the topping phase of this liquidity binge. We have been wrong in continually expecting the big party to end. Some parties did end when we called for a reversal. Real estate topped in July 2005, a year and a half ago. So at this point, we seem to be on the right-hand side of the topping process. Of course, the market that almost everyone cares about is the stock market, and that's the one holding up the longest. The stock market's rise since the summer has dragged some other markets such as the precious metals along with it. The charts of gold and silver over stocks show how closely these markets have tracked each other. Our overall theme, then (if not our timing), has so far proved correct. When stocks turn down, it will signal a major liquidity contraction, and all major asset classes should decline together.

March 2007

When commentators weren't faulting some mysterious computer jam for Tuesday's 500-point Dow plunge, they cited China, as this headline attests: "Stocks Tumble; Concerns About China Blamed." But readers know better. Last month, we showed the exponential rise in Chinese shares and said it was very close to where housing stocks and copper were at their peaks in July 2005 and May 2006, respectively (see February 2007 entry). EWFF also observed the euphoria surrounding Chinese stocks and stated, "This is a particularly appropriate endpoint for the bull market because so many Chinese have become enamored with China's ability to direct its own economy." Tuesday's historic 9% decline in the Shanghai Composite index is an appropriate starting point for the bear market because Chinese government regulations designed to stem the tide are being blamed for triggering the plunge. Of course, the falsity of such beliefs is also plain to readers because we talked about these measures here last month, before they even happened.

They may play an important role, however, as the flash point for the "recriminations that will start to fly" once the decline gains downside momentum.

The China Syndrome

The Chinese stock market plunge likely marks the termination of the rally that started in June 2005. In addition to bringing prices to the bowl of the exponential curve shown on the chart (see February entry), an important divergence between the Shanghai Composite and the more speculative Shenzhen Composite preceded the index's drop. Just as the NASDAQ ignored the example of the venerable Dow Industrials in early 2000, the Shenzhen sprinted ahead with a gain of 30% so far this year. The Shanghai, by contrast, is down from its January 1 intraday high. We described this classic sign of a mania in full flower and said it should mark the "pinnacle of an exponential rise." The frenzy's spread to even greener investment pastures is described in this article:

Stock Market Mania
Grips Vietnam's Middle Classes

—The Financial Times, Feb. 21 2007

Like its northern neighbor, Vietnam remains a communist country, and, with no prior stock market history, its investors are even less sophisticated than the Chinese. But the article reveals that "students, civil servants and state enterprise managers are all rushing to buy shares and dreaming of windfall profits." Bets are being made not just on Vietnam's stocks, but also on "an unregulated informal market for shares in partially-privatized state-owned companies that may or may not list on the form exchange some day." "All the chatter in Hanoi is about people investing in the market," says an economist in Vietnam's financial capital. "I don't know if anyone knows what these companies are worth, but they are buying the paper." Companies also "appear to be using surplus cash to punt on the market instead of investing in core activities. Authorities are struggling to get stock market-obsessed civil servants to focus on their day jobs." The Ho Chi Minh Stock Index is up 174% in just six months. Long-time subscribers will recognize the push into lower quality shares by less sophisticated investors. It is a phenomenon that in 1999 EWT dubbed the "flight from quality:"

> Historical accounts of the Tulip Mania show that its last few weeks saw a reversal of the usual flight to quality. A dash from quality in the terminal stage of the advance reflected a "class difference" between the "nobleman, merchants, and shopkeepers...who traded in piece goods" and the rising influence of less experienced investors "trading in pound goods." In *Extraordinary Popular Delusions and The Madness of Crowds*, Charles Mackay describes this progression from the aristocrats and money changers at the outset of the mania to "farmers, mechanics, seamen, footmen, maid-servants, even chimney sweeps and old clotheswomen" at the end, when "every one imagined that the passion for tulips would last for ever." As a result, lower quality "pound goods" (like the Switzers) replaced by-the-bulb "piece goods" prices (like Goudas) as the primary object of speculation.

So, an investment frenzy within the same Hanoi populace that was consumed by communism at the lows in the 1970s is signaling the end of the last phase in the Great Asset Mania of the 1990s and early 2000s. The urge to make profits in the stock market is so strong that Vietnamese investors are willing to bypass the relative "safety" of an exchange for "informal shares that may or may not be listed." After the Chinese market plunge, Vietnam's stock index actually rose. Despite clear and immediate contagion to other global markets, analysts ultimately dismissed the Chinese retreat as a "short-term knockback" that will likely be contained because "China is relatively isolated." But what happened to all the hubbub about an interconnected global investment world? There's certainly something to it as there's almost no such thing as an untapped investment realm (Mongolia just floated a $60 million bond offering that was 9.5 times oversubscribed). But, even in a completely free and open market, it takes time to raise a refined trading culture. As two of the world's last remaining communist countries, China and Vietnam clearly equate to the "lower quality pound goods" buyers of 1634. So, it makes perfect sense that the mania comes down to the most speculative shares in Shenzhen and Vietnam, which both managed to hit new all-time highs on Monday, the first trading day after the week-long Chinese New Year celebration. The New Year euphoria clearly played a role as 2007 is a rare

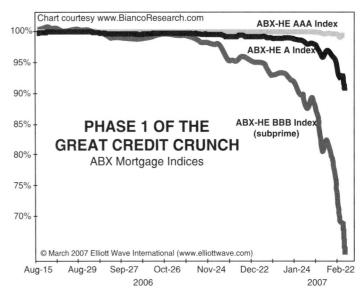

conjunction known as the year of the golden pig, which is supposed to equate to a "fat and easy life." Somehow, the celebrants haven't noticed that the last golden pig year was 1947, which was soon followed by the closure of the Chinese stock market, a communist takeover and Mao Tse-Tung's brutal 25-year reign. The unfolding decline should also produce some challenging fundamentals.

The troubles in the sub-prime loan market finally hit the front pages in early February. Since December, 27 mortgage lenders have gone "belly up" and, as columnist Caroline Baum says, "the notion that the bust part of the housing boom/bust cycle might not be quite so benign started to manifest itself elsewhere." The result is the flight from the riskiest sub-prime debt, which is shown by the lower line on the chart. The saga of the sub-prime mortgage industry is the front edge of the "massive flight from risky bond instruments" that EWFF called for here last month. Naturally, it's starting in the riskiest sectors, but it won't stop there. Eventually, even many of the currently perceived safest debt instruments will go bust.

April 2007

In last month's issue, we passed along several press accounts about the Chinese New Year and about 2007 as the year of the Golden Pig. An alert Hong Kong subscriber informs us that this is a "widely held misconception. The current year is actually the year of the Fire Pig. Volatility and uncertainty are the hallmarks of the Fire Pig." According to one website, it is a "symbol of disharmony and struggle." Sounds more accurate to us.

Luxury Boom To Swoon

The luxury boom hit some important milestones in March. These included the first $1,000 slice of pizza (at a New York City restaurant) and a $1 million laptop (from Luvaglio). At the same time, USA Today announced that luxury fever hit the masses: "Average Joes enjoy $4 cups of joe at Starbucks, guzzle bottled water, feast on Godiva chocolates, drag suitcases on wheels, sit on heated car seats and let GPS systems guide them."

But that's the old trend. To see where things are headed, look to the new leadership sector, the subprime mortgage arena. Two years ago, loan officers were flooding through a Newport Beach, Calif., Porsche dealership. These days the only mortgage industry types that come in are stopping to put their Porsches up for sale. "In the last two weeks, we've had nobody," says the Porsche dealer. Across the breadth of the markets, it took a long time for the great peak to roll in. In areas like luxury, however, where the trend is so extended and pervasive, the swing from up to down will seem to happen overnight.

May 2007

Of the three valid interpretations of the market's wave structure, the most attractive labels the rise from 2002 as wave **b**. One key reason is the undeniable bear market status of the Dow Jones Industrial Average in terms of gold, the Real Dow, which is shown at right. Notice, by contrast, the relative strength of the Real Dow versus the nominal Dow, the index in terms of dollars, from 1980 to 1982. By August 1982 when the Dow denominated in dollars bottomed, the Real Dow was rising strongly from its 1980 low, the business environment was clearing up and the first signs of a rising social mood started to appear. The nominal Dow soon played catch-up, and they both

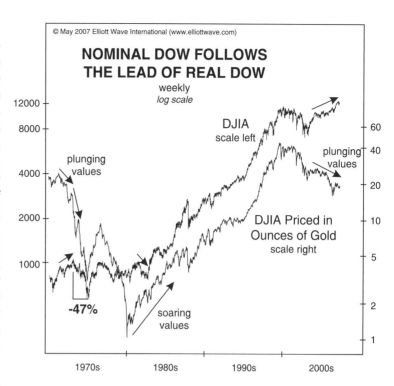

rallied more or less in sync until 1999. Now, instead of soaring, the Real Dow is crashing relative to the nominal Dow. In fact, it's barely off its low of May 2006. This dichotomy reveals the weakness that underlies the financial markets' push higher. Credit inflation is devaluing the current account in which the financial markets are denominated, the U.S. dollar, which is a large part of why nominal prices are rising. When mood turns and credit inflation reverses, the ensuing drop in the nominal value of the market should be dramatic.

Perhaps the most important dynamic of the stock market rise these days is the all-the-same-market effect, which Elliott Wave International has tracked with our stacked chart of the dollar (inverted) over the Dow Industrials, S&P, CRB, junk bonds, copper, gold and silver all rising together over the last 5 years. Over time, many financial observers have become aware of the positive correlation. "Everyone, everywhere is reinforcing one another," says noted money manager Jeremy Grantham in one widely-cited commentary. After touring the world, he says he's seen it all, and pretty much everything is in a bubble. This is probably another expression of the uh-oh effect, a moment of recognition and trepidation that tends to accompany the end of every great bubble. History reveals that these warnings are never taken seriously.

In the Lap of Luxury

[Bernard] Baruch also recognized a key similarity between 1929 New York and 1637 Amsterdam when he quoted Mackay saying, "Holland seemed the very antechamber of Plutus." The remark is a reference to the luxury binge that accompanied the runaway speculation for tulip bulbs. Back in 1999 when one writer identified a fever for luxury as a "an arms-race-like cycle" comparable to a "collective madness," EWFF examined the important supporting role that luxury plays in every mania. Of the Tulip Mania, Mackay says, "Houses and lands, horses and carriages, and luxuries of every sort, rose in value." The latest outbreak is true to form. At this point, even as the real estate depression gathers, the most expensive houses are among the few that keep rising. The

extreme luxury of the modern-day carriage is well represented by the Bugatti Veyron 16.4, the fastest, most powerful, and most expensive street-legal full production car in the world. It has a top speed of 250 miles per hour and costs $1.4 million. As for luxuries of every sort, we covered the $1000 slice of pizza last month. This month, you can get 16 steaks and 24 Donald Trump burgers for just $999. We kid you not.

Hedge funds are at the epicenter of this trend. In addition to being the prime targets for the purveyors of luxury goods, a recent Wall Street Journal article notes that they are now the driving force behind the "ultimate luxury," charity. The WSJ reveals that "big-money financiers from hedge funds and private-equity firms" are imbuing the field with many of the financial strategies that they employ in their day jobs. They are taking over non-profit boards, encouraging them "to take on more risk and debt," "demanding new recruiting goals," "pushing for bigger donations" and "orchestrating mergers of smaller chapters." In another dubious "arrival" on Wall Street, Merrill Lynch just produced a new luxury-firm stock index, The Merrill Lynch Lifestyle Index (shown at the bottom of the chart in the May 2007 entry in Chapter 5). Relative strength in the luxury sector in 2001 was a harbinger of the Great Mania's ability to morph into housing, hedge funds and a renewed stock bubble in 2002. With its latest rally to a new high, however, it confronts the top of the trend channel that contains its five-year rise. This may be the end of the line for luxury.

Investors Are Buying More with IOUs Than Money

The pyramid of debt, the extremity of optimism and the b-wave label of the advance since 2002 all portend an all-out collapse of investment prices in wave c. The decline in social mood during that wave will engender a crushing deflation in the galaxy-sized bubble of outstanding credit and ultimately a disastrous depression. Few of us will be able to side-step the effects of the depression, but we can all avoid the effects of falling financial prices and the deflation of the debt bubble by following the recommendations in *Conquer the Crash*.

When *Conquer the Crash* was published [in 2002], outstanding dollar-denominated debt was $30 trillion. Just five years later it is $43 trillion, and most of the increase has gone into housing, financial investments and buying goods from abroad. This is a meticulously constructed Biltmore House of cards, and one wonders whether it can stand the addition of a single deuce. Its size and grandeur are no argument against the ultimate outcome; they are an argument for it.

This chart depicts just one isolated aspect of the debt bubble as it relates directly to financial prices. In 1999, the public was heavily invested in mutual funds, and mutual funds had 96 percent of their clients' money invested in stocks. At the time we thought that percentage of investment was a limit. We were wrong. Today, much of the public has switched to so-called hedge funds (a misnomer). Bridgewater Associates estimates that the average hedge fund in January had 250 percent of its deposits invested. This month the WSJ reports funds with ratios as high as 13 times. How can hedge funds invest way more

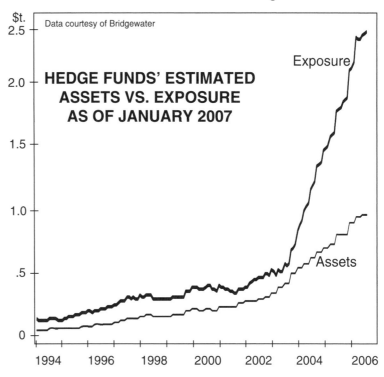

$t.

Data courtesy of Bridgewater

HEDGE FUNDS' ESTIMATED ASSETS VS. EXPOSURE AS OF JANUARY 2007

Exposure

Assets

money than they have? They borrow the rest from banks and investment firms, using their investment holdings as collateral. So they are heavily leveraged. And this is only part of the picture. Much of the money invested in hedge funds in the first place is borrowed. Some investors take out mortgages to get money to put into hedge funds. Some investment firms borrow heavily from banks and brokers to invest in hedge funds. As for lenders, the WSJ reports today, "...the nation's four largest securities firms financed $3.3 trillion of assets with $129.4 billion of shareholders' equity, a leverage ratio of 25.5 to 1."

So the financial markets today have been rising in unison because of leverage upon leverage, an inverted pyramid of IOUs, all supported by a comparatively small amount of actual cash. This swelling snowball of borrowing is how the nominal Dow has managed to get to a new high even though it is in a raging bear market in real terms: The expansion in credit inflates the dollar denominator of value, and the credit itself goes to buying more stocks, bonds and commodities. The buying raises prices, and higher prices provide more collateral for more borrowing. And all the while real stock values, as measured by gold, have quietly fallen by more than half! Seemingly it is a perpetual motion machine; but one day the trend will go into reverse, and the value of total credit will begin shrinking as dollar prices collapse.

The investment markets are only part of the debt picture. Most individuals have borrowed to buy real estate, cars and TVs. Most people don't own such possessions; they owe them. Credit card debt is at a historic high. The Atlanta Braves just announced a new program through which you can finance the purchase of season tickets. Can you imagine telling a fan in 1947 that someday people would take out loans to buy tickets to a baseball game? Instead of buying things for cash these days, many consumers elect to pay not only the total value for each item they buy but also a pile of additional money for interest. And they choose this option because they can't afford to pay cash for what they want or need. Self-indulgent and distress borrowing for consumption cannot go on indefinitely. But while it does, the "money supply"—actually the credit supply—inflates. But it is all a temporary phenomenon, because debt binges always exhaust themselves.

Virtually everyone else sees things differently. Countless bulls on stocks, gold and commodities insist that the process is simple: the Fed is inflating the "money supply" by way of its "printing press," and there is no end in sight. The Fed is indeed the underlying motor of inflation because it monetizes government debt, but the banking system, thanks to the elasticity of fiat money, manufactures by far the bulk of the credit—credit, not cash.

If you don't believe credit can implode and investment prices fall, then why did the housing market just have its biggest monthly price plunge in two decades, and why is the trend toward lower prices now the longest on record? If you don't think credit and cash are different, then why are the owners of "collateralized" mortgage "securities" beginning to panic over the realization that their "investments" are melting in the sun? Lewis Ranieri, one of the founders of the securitized mortgage market recently warned that there are now so many interests involved in each mortgage that massive cooperation among lawyers, accountants and tax authorities will be required just to make simple decisions about restructuring a loan or disposing of a house, i.e. the collateral, underlying a mortgage in default. In the old days, the local bank would suss things out and come to a quick decision. But now the structures are too complex for easy resolution, and creditors are hamstrung with structural and legal impediments to accessing their collateral. The modern structures for investment are so intricate and dispersed that a mere recession will trigger a systemic disaster. When insurance companies and pension plan administrators realize that they can't easily and cheaply access the underlying assets, what will their packaged mortgages be worth then? And what will happen to the empty houses as they try to sort things out? This type of morass relates to debt. Cash is easy; either you have it or you don't.

June 2007

By its very nature, the shift from up to down in an all-the-same-markets scenario is a big turn. EWI's forecast calls for stocks, gold, silver, junk bonds, oil, emerging stock markets, art, hedge funds, foreign companies and just about every other freely traded asset to reverse lower more or less in sync. As we noted in October, "the turn is taking more of a saw tooth form" in which some markets turn ahead of the pack. We added at the time that it "is not unusual for investors to narrow their focus before they cut and run." The housing sector topped in July 2005 (S&P Homebuilders Index). The key investment banking stocks, also known as EWI's Hedge Fund Enablers Index, peaked in January. Home prices accelerated their decline, falling substantially for the first time in the lives of many homeowners in April. The U.S. Dollar bottomed in May. The Dow Transports appear to be thrusting out of a contracting triangle in a final hurrah. The "cut and run" phase in which all indexes fall together still awaits the Dow Jones Industrial Average and other major stock indexes, which continue to push in the late stages of a 5-year rally. The year-long succession of highs accompanied by a clearly weakening economy says that when the big stock indexes do start their long-awaited decline, the weight of the world will fall with them.

The Glory of Getting Rich in China

Back in February, EWI showed an exponential rise in the Shanghai Composite Index and asserted, "If the top is not yet in for Chinese shares, it should be close." It wasn't. After a brief downturn in late February, China went back into its vertical ascent. But the higher it goes, the more certain we are of its eventual crash, as its further rise creates an even more extreme representation of a mania.

[A] key trait that accounts for the similarities between the technology bubble antics in the United States in 2000 and China today is that bubbles can cool in one area and migrate into new ones. In 1719/1720 when John Law's Mississippi Scheme petered out as the South Sea Bubble was ramping up into its most extreme phase of price acceleration. According to the book *Millionaire*, an account of John Law's role in the bubble, Mississippi Company shares peaked in late 1719 and created a run on hard assets. In 1720, authorities tried to stem the tide by banning the purchase of diamonds, pearls and rubies. "Investors turned to silver and gold, candelabras, tureens, dishes, plates, even furniture made from precious metals." When a new law prohibited the production and sale of all gold or silver artifacts with the exception of religious paraphernalia, "the price of crosses and chalices soared." A drive into gold and silver as the demand for shares declined should sound familiar. It happened here in the form of the all-the-same-market phenomenon which has sent investors scurrying into gold, silver and various other "alternative" assets. Just as share speculation leapt across the English Channel to London in 1720, the fiery core of the mania is now burning itself out on the other side of the Pacific.

July 2007

For hedge fund operators and the investment banks that enable them, the scariest moment since the 1998 fall of Long Term Capital Management hit last week when Merrill Lynch threatened to sell $800 million of mortgage securities seized from a Bear Stearns hedge fund in which Merrill held a stake. When Merrill announced that it planned to sell the securities on the open market, Bloomberg reported that the "threat is sending shudders across Wall Street." Why? "A sale would give banks, brokerages and investors the one thing they want to avoid: a real price on the bonds in the fund that could serve as a benchmark."

Later that day, Merrill decided against an open market sale. Reuters described the episode this way: "If word of the exact nature of the losses became public, it would have forced many other funds to revalue their holdings and perhaps lose money, setting off a domino effect that could rattle markets globally." Another writer called the debacle a "subprime Chernobyl" and accused banks of creating a "cone of silence" over the subprime mortgage sector. We used to think the surreal world of "structured finance" resembled the Emperor's New Clothes, but the emperor was a stark (naked) realist compared to modern-day financial engineers, who appear to believe that the debt paper they trade back and forth amongst themselves is worth what they say it is rather than what they can get for it. As with LTCM in 1998, they appear to have bailed themselves out (this time), but the effort calls to mind the following quote from a September 1998 issue of *The Elliott Wave Theorist*: "The shift in social mood is beginning to shatter the collective financial delusion."

The delusion lives on thanks to the mania's amazing ability to take asset prices higher, the construction of exotic debt instruments with ever-more-lenient terms and the occasional industry-backed bailout. But the latest episode points to a fast approaching endpoint. For one thing, at this point we are not alone any more in seeing the swamp of rotting debt for what it is. The impending credit implosion will directly lead to deflation, the central thesis of *Conquer the Crash*. As the quotes above illustrate, an expanding body of observers now recognize that the credit structure is teetering. Notes a Connecticut based broker-dealer, "Wall Street is now engineering a way to pretend that nearly worthless subprime bonds are maintaining" their original values. The whole game is highly dependent on a curtain of secrecy that is starting to be torn away by an emerging bear market mood. In May, EWFF predicted that the reversal would be marked by a "survival" mentality in which key players "turn on each other." This is starting to happen. With Merrill's threatened sale, the ranks came close to breaking. It's just a matter of time until lenders realize that it's every man for himself.

It's no coincidence that as a survival mentality emerges, the notoriously murky pricing of derivatives is becoming an issue. "The [Bear Stearns] debacle may finally provoke regulators," says one columnist. "Their focus is likely to fall on how to assign prices to complex derivatives." One supplier of price data, Markit Group, has grown to 400 employees and generated more than $100 million in revenue in just a few years. In 2007, revenues are expected to increase as much as 75%. Even the U.S. government relies on its data. The Office of the Comptroller of the Currency, a lead-ing U.S. bank regulator, checks the Markit data when assessing banks' financial health. Markit's subprime index, the bottom line on the chart, suggests that the lowest grade mortgage assets are not nearly as healthy as broker/dealer "mark to model" pricing schemes suggest. Merrill Lynch probably managed to mute the decline with its decision not to sell Bear Stearns' junk mortgages, but the subprime index's recent drop to a new low, accompanied by a sympathetic push lower by higher quality mortgages (the middle line on the chart), confirms that the trend of prices in the credit markets is now straight down.

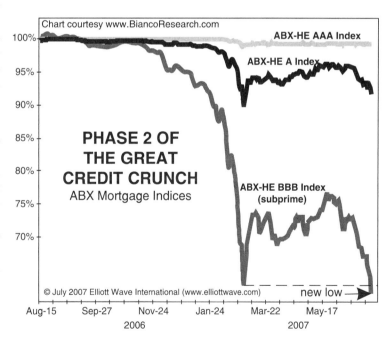

August 2007
The Credit Bubble Bursts

> When the social mood trend changes from optimism to pessimism, creditors and debtors change their primary orientation from expansion to conservation. As creditors become more conservative, they slow their lending. As debtors and potential debtors become more conservative, they borrow less or not at all. These behaviors reduce the "velocity" of money, i.e., the speed with which it circulates to make purchases, thus putting downside pressure on prices. These forces reverse the former trend.
>
> —*Conquer the Crash*

Unsettling Indications That Global Retreat From Risk Is Spreading
—New York Post, July 2, 2007

United Capital Halts Hedge Fund Withdrawals
—Bloomberg, July 3, 2007

LBO Debt Alarms

"S&P [downgrades] are going to force a lot more people
to come to Jesus," -- Institutional Risk Analytics
—Bloomberg, July 10, 2007

TIAA-CREF, Which Oversees $414 Billion, Is Boycotting Some Debt Offerings Used To Finance LBOs

Hedge Horror Lands
—New York Post, July 7, 2007

Roof Caves In
—New York Post, July 11, 2007

LBO Credit Quality Falls
—Bloomberg, July 11, 2007

Loans Pulled Over Credit
—Financial Times, July 16, 2007

—Bloomberg, July 5, 2007

Goldman, JPMorgan Stuck With Debt They Can't Sell To Investors
—Bloomberg, July 17, 2007

KKR Cancels $1.4 Billion Sale of Loans
—Bloomberg, July 16, 2007

Hedge Funds Almost Wiped Out
—MarketWatch, July 17, 2007

CDO Machine Shuts Down
—Bloomberg, July 24, 2007

Market Shock: AAA Rating May Be Junk
—New York Times, July 20, 2007

Corporations Have Trouble Borrowing

KKR's Banks Fail To Sell $10 Billion of LBO Debt
—Bloomberg, July 25, 2007

Bye Bye Borrowing
—New York Times, July 23, 2007

The issuance of high-yield corporate debt, dubbed junk bonds by Wall Street, has virtually dried up.
—USA Today, July 24, 2007

Global Corporate Bond Risk Soars
—Bloomberg, July 27, 2007

Chrysler Abandons Loan Sale
—Bloomberg, July 25, 2007

Subprime Mess Fueled By Crack Cocaine Accounting
—Bloomberg, July 25, 2007

Risk Premiums Soar as Investors Seek Safest Assets
—Bloomberg, July 27, 2007

Climate of Fear Tightens Money
—Atl. Jrnl-Cnst., August 2, 2007

Bam! Easy Credit Evaporates
—New York Times, July 27, 2007

American Home Mortgage to Close as Demand Collapses for Loans
—Bloomberg, August 2, 2007

The January issue of *The Elliott Wave Financial Forecast* started the year with a Special Section titled "2007: The Year of Financial Flameout," in which we asserted that confidence, the "psychological foundation" that supports the great asset bubble, was about to undergo the big reversal described in CTC. Through the first six months of the year, Elliott Wave International observed a succession of climactic credit events from the bludgeoning of the subprime mortgage market to a booming demand for "covenant lite" commercial loans and record narrow spreads between junk and U.S. Treasuries. EWFF identified these events as the set-up to the onset of a new conservatism that would drive the greatest credit crisis in history.

The collage of credit related headlines shows how rapidly the credit problems of late June multiplied as stocks peaked over July 13-19 and then blossomed into a full blown crisis as stocks plunged during July 23-27. The general picture, and indeed many of the specifics such as Chrysler's troubled private equity buyout, new lows for Blackstone Group's recently offered public shares, attacks on bond rating agencies and Congressional hearings on the taxation of hedge funds, are all part of the future envisioned in recent issues of EWFF and *The Elliott Wave Theorist*.

Like any great crisis, this one can now be listed as official because it continues to be officially denied. "On Wall Street, there isn't a chief executive officer who will tell you there is a crisis," says Bloomberg. "Citigroup Chief Stays Bullish on Buy-Outs," proclaims another headline. The CEO of one of Wall Street's biggest investment firms says he sees "no clear signs" of rising troubles in the debt market (see chart, next page). In various articles, the U.S. Secretary of the Treasury said the spreading aversion to risk and lower grade debt is "healthy," "global expansion is strong" and the "Rout Doesn't Threaten [the] Economy." Last month, EWFF stated, "The harder officials contest the point, the more likely it becomes."

The telling aspect of the turn is the velocity of the reversal. In May, EWFF predicted that a "vast amount of the paper [hedge funds and investment banking firms] hold and distribute will be worthless." But it was still impressive to see how fast it can happen. On July 17, Bear Stearns revealed that assets in two hedge funds were "almost worthless." As one analyst said, "the speed with which loans are going bad" is shocking. This week when two hedge funds run by Sowood Capital Management fell more than 50% and had to be sold due to "lenders demands for more

"NO CLEAR SIGNS" ?

—Wall Street CEO

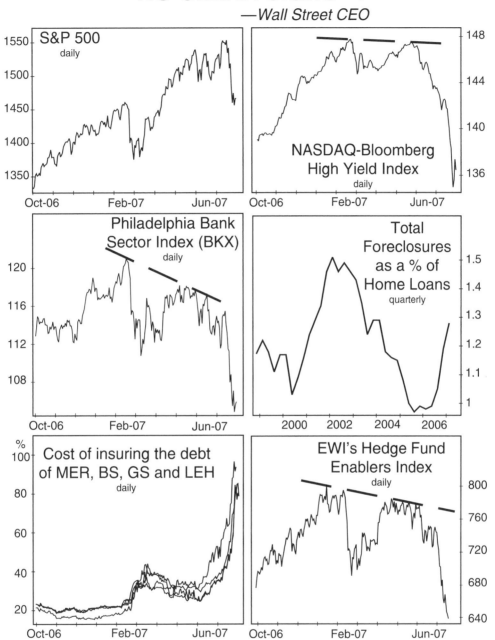

collateral," a fund manager called the rapidity of the loss "mindboggling." The chart of junk bond issuance (next page) shows the summer reversal's flick-of-a-light-switch quality.

Major magazines have a long history of signaling trend changes when they acknowledge their presence on their covers. The following cover relates to bonds in which syndicates buy up life insurance policies, securitize and sell them and collect when the insured person dies. In what "may be the most macabre scheme ever," Business Week says that investors are now flocking to these instruments. This coverage should prove fatal for "death bonds." More important, it probably signals the end of the line for the era of financial engineering. With death benefit shares on the block, what's left to engineer, odds on passing through the pearly gates? Wall Street's armies of "mathematicians, hedge fund wizards and programmers" are not even dimly aware of how dependent their schemes are on the ocean of liquidity created by the bull market. The

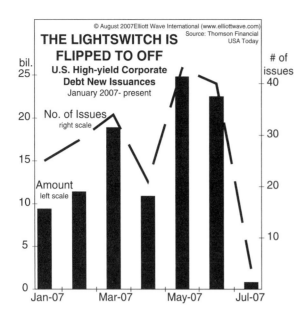

grim reaper is the perfect visage to welcome the arriving wave of liquidation; it will wreak havoc with their work. The field's dark fate is clear in one fund manager's description of what caused "forced sales" at another fund: "The models work when they look at history, but not when history is all new." What's "new" is that for the first time in the experience of many model makers, confidence is on the run. As they rob Peter to pay Paul, all assets will be impacted in negative ways that do not compute in their models.

The Bubble Loses Its Inner Engine

As EWFF mentioned in June, one of the key traits of the Great Asset Mania is its ability to cool in one market and reignite in another one. A wellspring of credit drives every bubble. The beginning of the end for the credit boom occurs upon a tightening of credit, as depicted in the collage. As the suspension of redemptions at one hedge fund after another in recent days attests, the financial markets are fast becoming a "cash only" enterprise. In coming months, this intensifying thirst for cash will dry up the well of credit that fed the global markets over the last few years. As it dries up, the seemingly endless succession of market manias will end, also.

My Boat Is Bigger than Your Plane

As the May issue of EWFF explained, a key corollary to the speculative fevers for tulip bulbs in 1637 and stocks in 1929 was a furious demand for extravagant luxuries. Here's what happened to the luxury sector as the Dow Jones Industrial Average completed its final charge to new all-time highs:

Luxury Goods Boom Goes Over the Top

NEW YORK (AP) – Forget about the $350 stilettos. Shoes with status these days come with $1,000 price tags. And $600 handbags have become so bourgeois. A-listers don't want to be seen with anything costing less than $5,000.

—Yahoo News, June 14, 2007

The boom in luxury goods is no secret. But the latest surge carries extravagance to the outer limits of human imagination. Consider, for instance, the Maltese Falcon, a sailboat that Time magazine describes as the "largest, most self-indulgent ever made" and a "vulgar ostentation." The ship is 289 feet long, 42 feet wide and 20 stories high. Then there's the first private A830 jumbo jet, which is being fitted to suit the whims of an unnamed tycoon. The plane is 239 feet long and can hold 800 passengers. "At a time when the average American is grousing about meager wage growth and feeling strapped by a 30-cent spike in the price of gas, splurging by the wealthy has risen to gaudy proportions as the super rich seek new heights in pampering, price tags and one-of-a-kind items that set them apart."

"There's this insatiable appetite for the most luxurious," said the chairman of a luxury leasing firm. There are many signs that the latest binge is a final blow-off in luxury spending. Our contention is that the final extravagant burst of luxury spending is tied most prominently to the bonuses, commissions and trading profits of financial types, and it should dissipate quickly as some of Wall Street's all-time great schemes unravel. This potential is borne out by the recent misadventures of John Devaney, founder of United Capital Markets, a hedge fund that specializes in buying and selling subprime mortgages. At the American Securitization Forum conference in late January, Devaney said, "I personally hate subprime and I'm kind of hoping the whole thing explodes." Be careful what you wish for. On July 3, Devaney suspended investors' withdrawals from his $620 million fund. On July 30, The NY Post reported that Devaney's 142-foot yacht, "Positive Carry," is up for sale, with an asking price of $23.5 million. Devaney is also trying to unload an Aspen home he bought in November for $16.25 million. He hopes to get $16.5 million for it. United Capital is just one of several hedge funds to hit the rocks. Since its early July troubles, fund problems have jumped the tracks. By the end of the month, Sowood Capital Management, which importantly "didn't own subprime loans," was gone. Its demise wiped $350 million off of Harvard's endowment and cost the Massachusetts state pension system $30 million. The chain reaction is underway.

September 2007

[People] appear to be awakening to the strangeness of one-after-the-other bubbles. The July-August credit "quake," for instance, caused one New York Times writer to ponder the "forgetfulness" of investors. "Not long ago people were slapping their foreheads, too, after the tech-stock boom busted earlier this decade. Much of the talk of new paradigms turned out not to be worth the pizza boxes that many a dot-com business plan was written on. All this raises questions: Why such short memories? Why did so many homebuyers ignore recent lessons?" The reason has more to do with social euphoria than forgetfulness. Investors are responding to the emotional conditioning of a Grand Supercycle peak. Since the beginning of Cycle wave V in 1974, it has been one long bull market in which all declines were followed by ever-higher stock prices. It includes the crash of 1987, which fed an all-consuming belief in the ultimate resiliency of the stock market. As the buy-and-hold crowd has noted ever since, the lesson of that crash is not to panic and to ride out all declines. The technology bust is not forgotten; investors remember it as another bump in the road that they managed to overcome. But this belief is actually quite dangerous because the collective experience of one bubble after another leaves investors with a heightened sense of indestructibility. As Bob Prechter explains in *The Wave Principle of Human Social Behavior*, investor expectations appear to be descriptions of present conditions "multiplied by an unconsciously calculated summation of multiple forward-weighted moving averages of the trends of those conditions." After 33 (a Fibonacci 34,-1) years, the market has positioned investors perfectly for an across-the-board financial collapse.

The Wave Principle at Work

We've been asked why we dedicate a lot of space to past entries. The reason is that the best way to get a proper perspective on a forecast is to measure it and the environment in which it was made against the present reality. We think this brings a certain amount of context to present conditions and highlights key differences between our anticipatory methods and conventional approaches. A perfect example is our case for a flight from risk, which we featured here in May 2006. This is the bottom line from that issue:

The across-the-board rally in financial and commodity markets is on the cusp of a turn into an across-the-board decline. A key element in the process is signaled by a reversal in the gold/silver ratio, which indicates that a new risk averse mentality is about to emerge among investors.

In various issues over the last 20 months, EWI continued to track the onset of a more conservative investment climate. Here's a headline that acknowledges its arrival on the street in recent weeks:

Risk Returns with a Vengeance

The August 20 story cites economists who say that fear of defaults is rising and that housing prices may decline another 5%. Unlike our own methods, which forecasted rising foreclosure rates and falling home prices ahead of their actual appearance, these observations assume a continuation of current conditions. It's a critical distinction, because this approach also extrapolates current economic conditions to conclude that the "basic economic outlook remains sound." We disagree, and a review of our original forecast for a reversal in the gold/silver ratio explains why. First, notice by the asterisks on the chart here that the forecast actually coincided with the initial upturn in the gold/silver ratio; so it is not a response to a change that was already in place. Also realize that the turn has now been in place for many months, which means risk didn't just return. It's been creeping back into the financial structure since May 2006. There was an 18-month prelude to the apparently sudden "return of risk."

Applying the Wave Principle to another market verifies the flight-from-risk forecast. The next chart is a monthly picture of the Euro/Yen. This currency

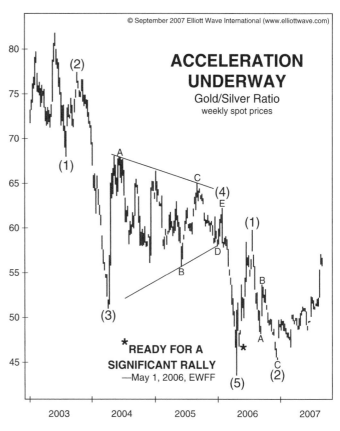

cross-rate is an excellent proxy for the yen carry trade because speculators are able to borrow yen at extremely low rates and convert them to other currencies for investment in higher-yielding assets elsewhere. Thus, an expansion of the yen carry trade necessarily results in a lower yen versus

the euro, as well as many other currencies with higher-yielding domestic financial assets. In our January 2007 Special Section titled, "2007: The Year of Financial Flameout," EWFF addressed the carry trade's role in expanding world-wide leverage and noted that the prevailing wave pattern suggests that its reversal "is close at hand." The monthly Euro/Yen chart shows a clear five-wave rise that ended in July. At minimum, the EuroYen should decline at least to the area surrounding 130, as the yen carry trade unwinds and the global markets "de-lever." In terms of Elliott, everything is coming together.

On the following page is one more chart that shows the power of these trends. As the September issue of *The Elliott Wave Theorist* points out, the Fed can lower rates all it wants, but it cannot force the issue: "When bull markets turn to bear, confidence turns to fear, and fearful people do not lend or borrow at the same rates as confident ones." The persistence of the fear that created the initial crack in the markets is evident in this dramatic chart of the spread between rates on U.S. asset-backed commercial paper and the U.S. Fed Funds rate. Despite repeated Fed statements and offers of increased lending capacity to allay credit market fears, this chart shows that the rate that issuers of asset-backed commercial obligations must pay on the open market is still way above the funds rate. It confirms a key point of our confluence of wave patterns: confidence is waning. As it continues to do so, credit will contract. In fact, the gap between overnight lending rates is already as wide as it was in October 2001, the middle of the last bear market leg. This 0-to-60 mph start signals a new trend with a great deal of horsepower. It should drive the stock and credit markets for some time to come.

October 2007

On July 9, the CEO/Chairman of Citigroup said, "When the music stops, in terms of liquidity, things will be complicated." Now wait a minute. We keep hearing that the Fed will shore up all their debts with perpetual liquidity, so how do you explain this comment? Answer: The bankers know better. Liquidity, formerly the solution, is now the problem, and the bankers know it.

The only solution that bankers, regulators, politicians and the Fed can think of is to do more of what they did to get into the problem in the first place: create more debt. They know of no other response. When the big bankers met via conference calls, "Besides hearing from senior executives from each of the big banks, the group also sought ideas from others." In other words, they are flailing for a solution to a problem that has no solution aside from taking measures to make it worse. I still think there is no better analogy to a system-wide credit binge than a person who keeps going only by gulping down amphetamines. He will collapse if he stops taking them, but if he keeps taking them he will ultimately die. Bankers always choose to ingest more speed. Their choice is to collapse now or die later. They always choose later. But they cannot avoid the inevitable result.

Speaking of the inevitable result, Bloomberg reports that a mortgage fund managed by Cheyne Capital Management Ltd. has just announced that it will fail to pay the interest immediately due on the commercial paper it issued to buy mortgages. Here's the problem: If it tried to pay the interest, it would have to sell assets to raise the money. If it were to sell assets in an illiquid market, they would fall in value, making the collateral in the fund worth less. I'll bet this company can't wait for that call from the managers of the new super fund, that is, if it owns any top-rated mortgages.

Can you see how exquisite the conundrum is for the "investors" who lent money to this firm? If they ask for their rightful interest, their principal will fall. If they don't ask for interest, they have no income. If they can't sell the assets, in truth they have no principal.

The emperor has no clothes, but so far the stock market floats

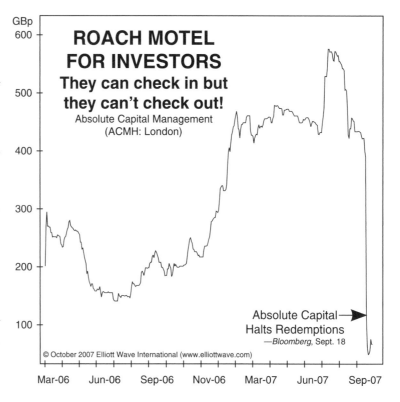

merrily unconcerned in a haze of unprecedented optimism. Someday that optimism will melt as fast as it did in the mortgage market. As the liquidity vise tightens, the great margin call of 2007 will continue to spread, and the markets for mortgages and an alphabet soup of CLO, CDO and SIV investments will constrict further. Absolute Capital Management, a manager of $2.1 billion in hedge fund assets, represents the speed and extent of the potential breaks. After the stock plunge shown on the next page, investors learned that Absolute holds about $530 billion in over-the-counter U.S. stocks "that can't be sold at the prices the firm has on its books." When clients moved to withdraw $100 million, they were told "they shouldn't expect to remove money for a year" pending a restructuring of funds. Never underestimate the power of denial at a Grand Supercycle degree peak. It is so powerful now that financiers, who got where they are today by trusting the wisdom of the market, can turn around and say to their clients with a straight face, "We'll pay you back later when the market figures out we're right."

In another burst of clarity, the Wall Street Journal reports that Alan Greenspan recently told a gathering of economists, "The human race has never found a way to confront bubbles." He then added, "The behavior in what we are observing in the last seven weeks [since mid-July] is identical in many respects to what we saw in 1998, what we saw in the stock-market crash of 1987, I suspect what we saw in the land-boom collapse of 1837 and certainly [the bank panic of] 1907." Unfortunately, Greenspan did not comment on the much larger scale of the current episode, but the reference to 1837 is somewhat surprising as most economists are generally unaware of this one. EWI long ago identified this particular deflationary implosion as the best historic model for the topping process that is now unfolding. In 1837, the real estate and commodities booms continued for two years after the peak in stocks. The recent version also experienced a secondary bubble that focused on real estate and certain commodities. Housing peaked in 2005 and now commercial real estate appears to be reversing. Here's what one Internet history says happened in 1837: "The public lost confidence in the New York banks and withdrew their deposits. Within two weeks, all of the nation's banks had suspended specie payments. This first general suspension in the nation's history started a six-year economic downturn that was the most severe of the nineteenth century." Welcome to 1837.

The End Times for Luxury

One of the gaudier by-products of a mania is the demand for luxuries, and the recent societal affinity for ostentatious displays certainly suits the high degree of the unfolding trend change. This must be the end of the greatest mania of all time because, unlike prior manias when pretentious consumers gorged themselves on their whims "no matter the price," the pretense this time is that a high price itself is what matters. "For the Love of God," a platinum cast of a human skull covered in 8,601 diamonds, probably best illustrates this principle. The $100 million sale of the piece by Damian Hirst is the highest price ever paid for the work of a living artist. It may well mark a conspicuous end to the era of conspicuous spending, and not just because it shapes a cache of diamonds into a symbol of death. The message for the art market is so resoundingly clear that Washington Post art critic Blake Gopnik points it out in a recent review:

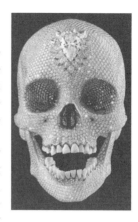

> Normally, such a record doesn't tell us much, least of all about art. But "For the Love of God" is a work of art that is all about outrageous and pointless overspending. And the best way for it to be about that is for it to insist that it is also the ultimate example of it. What could be a better time to make this piece than now? We have reached a new level of absurd consumption—in the art market, clearly, but also elsewhere. No one claims that this is even close to being a major moment in the making of art. Everyone knows it is the greatest moment in the selling of it. Price has an even more tenuous relation to worth than it has ever had.

The last few weeks have been something of "The boy is right; the emperor is naked" moment for the luxury sector as whole. A new book, *Deluxe: How Luxury Lost Its Luster*, argues that, by the standards of past luxury binges, the current bender is a cheap knock-off. The author describes a "devolution of luxury" in which brand names and high price tags themselves rather than quality are the objects of buyers' affection. "Luxury has come to mean something less than it once did," says USA Today. A New York Times article announces, "Suddenly, a Hesitation About Splurging." Thanks to subscriber Deron Kawamoto, who submitted the article and pointed out this key quote: "People just don't feel euphoric, and they don't want to be high profile any more."

This is likely the beginning of what may eventually become an outright backlash against expensive goods. In August, we noted the potential "chain reaction" decline in this sector, and the signs are starting to emerge. At that time, we also identified one hedge fund manager's forced decision to sell his yacht, "Positive Carry," as a likely trend setter. In August, he threw in his Sikorsky helicopter, asking $11 million. A sales brochure lists the reason for the sale as "changing corporate travel requirements." No doubt. After doubling in price from mid-2006 to April, trendy bag maker Coach Inc. is experiencing a fall in demand. The firm's chief executive says, "Growth in the $7 billion U.S. market for handbags may fall by as much as half next year." Given the potential for a societal rebuke of the luxury lifestyle, his forecast appears optimistic. Tastes will probably shift dramatically to more earthy fashions and lifestyles. Nobody will want a designer handbag when they've lost the money and the bling they used to haul around in it.

November 2007

They'll All Fall Down

Since 2002 when *Conquer the Crash* postulated an emerging positive correlation between stocks and commodities and illustrated "that markets are responding primarily to liquidity flows," Elliott Wave International has tracked the upward sweep of this "shared cycle." With the forecasted credit contraction very much in evidence, liquidity is clearly drying up as confidence wanes and a steady movement toward an across-the-board decline is happening, albeit slowly.

The following table presents striking confirmation to the visual evidence presented in our all-the-same-markets charts (last shown in June 2006). A +1.0 equals a perfect positive correlation, 0.0 reveals no correlation and -1.0 shows markets moving in perfect opposition to one

Correlation to the S&P 500

(1.0 = perfectly positive)

	Jan. 1980-Oct. 2002	Oct. 1997-Oct. 2002	Oct. 2002-Oct. 2007
Silver	-0.40	0.03	0.91
Gold	-0.66	-0.61	0.92
CRB	-0.53	-0.11	0.80
Copper	-0.02	0.40	0.89
Oil	0.06*	0.33	0.86
S&P Small Caps	0.93*	0.13	0.98
S&P Homebuilders	0.73**	-0.65	0.41***
U.S. Dollar	-0.56	0.11	-0.83

monthly data

* from 1983　** from 1989
*** .92 through July 2005 peak in housing index, -.76 thereafter

another. As you can see by the numbers in the first column, the S&P shows no historic tendency to move strongly in line with any of the other non-equity asset classes. But observe the strong tie that these historically independent or even opposing markets have had to stocks over the last five years. Don't forget the footnote at the bottom, as it points to a new direction for the whole lot. It relates to the S&P Homebuilding Index, which tracked stocks relatively closely from 1989 to 1997 but then ran mostly counter to them for a five-year period to the October 2002 low. At that point, the homebuilders jumped dramatically, in line with the stock market rally that started in 2002. The footnote reveals, however, that a powerful divergence emerged in July 2005 when the housing stocks peaked and headed lower against the trend for the rest of the financial world. In terms of capitalization, the S&P Homebuilding Index is a relatively small market segment, but the importance of its descent is reflected by the various other markets related to homebuilding that are now catching up to its 70% decline from the July 2005 top. First and foremost are home prices themselves, which are the most important financial asset of the most important economic entity on the planet, the American consume. Also joining in the decline are various segments of the debt markets such as asset-backed paper, high yield bonds, the rest of the real estate and a host of key sectors.

The table reveals the startling rarity of this alignment. Most observers conclude that the correspondence will end with any downturn in stocks. In an "Analysis of the Investment Potential of Precious Metals," for instance, two professors spot the shared path of gold and stocks but then conclude, "Inflation—or the lack thereof—is likely to move gold and stocks in different directions." But as the October issue of *The Elliott Wave Theorist* points out, there is only one possible explanation for the positive correlation in so many disparate markets: an all-time high in optimism fueled a credit expansion so powerful that it sent every market higher. The credit squeeze is all-important now because, as EWT explains, it shows that the great global confidence that created this phenomenon is unraveling. Everything is in place for a sweeping financial reversal in which all the correlated markets go down together. A collective tumble could happen at any time.

Transition to a Fear of Risk

The NASDAQ's relative strength versus the blue-chip stock indexes shows a surge back toward risk in this one particular area of the stock market, but there appears to be more evidence of a move away from risk in other areas, which appears consistent with the transitional phase from up to down. In fact, the fate of some of Wall Street's biggest risk takers indicates a rapid about-face from reckless abandon to abhorrence for risk. Until this summer, Merrill Lynch flourished under the leadership of now-former CEO Stanley O'Neal. O'Neal helped increase the brokerage firm's earnings to $7.7 billion, a better-than-three-fold increase in five years, by taking on "more risk" and moving the firm into "riskier" endeavors like trading for itself, private equity and lending. This headline from the October 29 issue of The New York Times announces the new mood on Wall Street: "Risk-Taker's Reign at Merrill Ends With Swift Fall." The Times calls O'Neal's departure "stunning in its speed and ferocity." The sea change toward greater conservatism is abundantly clear in the credit markets, where the big squeeze continues to unfold like

"the plot of a hundred disaster movies," according to the Financial Times. "Calamity at the end of act one leaves the submarine/aircraft/asset-backed lender in trouble. In act two—where we are today—calm ensues as the hero races to repair the damage. But time is running out...." We postulate, time has run out.

As EWFF demonstrated in the July issue, the ABX Mortgage Indexes are akin to the eerie music that starts to play right before the goriest scenes in a horror movie. When the ABX sub-prime index notched a new low on June 29, EWFF said that the move "confirms that the trend of prices in the credit markets is now straight down." The above chart shows the latest, more dramatic thrust to another new low. Again, notice the increasing downside participation of the mid- and top-grade indexes. Mounting losses and crashing share prices at Ambac Financial and MBIA, two insurers of premium-grade collateralized debt obligations also illustrate that the credit crunch is climbing the quality ladder at a rapid rate. The average stock investor is unconcerned, but an enormous breadth of apprehension among professionals is clear in stories like this one from the October 25 Financial Times:

US Companies Lose Taste for Risk

According to an FT/Treasury Strategies survey of more than 100 U.S. corporate officers, 50% became more cautious this past summer and not one took a more aggressive posture with their firm's capital. This caution is the complete opposite of the unbridled pursuit of risk that powered the across-the-board rush into global financial assets from October 2002 to October 2007.

December 2007
Last Dance for Luxury?

Last month, our table of correlations showed the extraordinary synchronization that has marked the movement of major financial sectors. Luxury is another sector that's been locked into the shared advance over the last five years. In fact, at .992 (with 1.00 representing perfect positive correlation) the Merrill Lynch Lifestyle Index of key luxury shares is the group that is

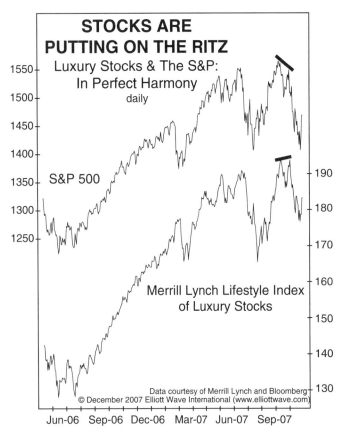

STOCKS ARE PUTTING ON THE RITZ

Luxury Stocks & The S&P:
In Perfect Harmony
daily

S&P 500

Merrill Lynch Lifestyle Index
of Luxury Stocks

Data courtesy of Merrill Lynch and Bloomberg
© December 2007 Elliott Wave International (www.elliottwave.com)

Jun-06 Sep-06 Dec-06 Mar-07 Jun-07 Sep-07

most closely aligned with the S&P 500. Even the Dow Jones Industrial Average, with a .983 correlation to the S&P, is not linked as tightly to this broad blue chip U.S. index! It is hard to imagine a closer alignment. History shows that every mania is accompanied by a fever for luxury goods. So, 1) it must be a mania, and 2) close scrutiny of this chart of the S&P 500 plotted over the Merrill Lynch Lifestyle Index reveals that it may well be over. Notice the recent divergence shown by the lines at the top of each index. While the S&P peaked on October 9, the luxury stocks managed a new high on October 31. This is similar to what happens to speculative shares at a mania peak; they tend to run higher on their own. The NASDAQ peaked later than the blue-chip DJIA in the bear market of 2000-2002. In October 2007, the NASDAQ did it again, peaking 20 days after the Dow. With the luxury stocks joining in, the Halloween peak had the distinct flavor of a final fling. When the most exuberant sectors of the market depart a deeply-entrenched tendency to follow more senior averages, the downside slope tends to be quite steep.

Even as the luxury shares bolted higher on their own, signs of the luxury-goods flame-out covered here in October continued to accumulate. After running at annual rates above 10 percent early this year, the International Council of Shopping Centers says that luxury goods' sales growth fell to 3.3% in October. Luxury brands Polo, Ralph Lauren and Coach, the largest U.S. maker of luxury leather goods, cut sales and earnings forecasts. Another big "surprise" came from Seattle-based department-store chain Nordstrom Inc., which reported a 2.4% decline in October same-store sales instead of an anticipated rise of 1.1%. "A big red flag went up with Nordstrom," said one analyst. Luxury goods makers are fighting the new trend the way that mutual fund managers are fighting the turn in stocks. The change is being called a shift to "ethical luxury," which is not about ostentation but being "ecologically conscious." "We need to replace hollow with deep," says designer Tom Ford, while the chairman of LVMH said that his trendy customers "seek discretion." These observations are all elements of a new, more bearish mindset, one that designers can try to dress up all they want. But in the end they will fail because luxury isn't about deep thoughts. It's about wearing fur and showing off, and people are just too agitated for it to succeed in a big bear market.

A New Market Index

We at Elliott Wave International invented the phrase "All the Same Market" to refer to the coordinated trends in diverse financial markets that we saw emerging in 2002. So who better to create an index that tracks it? EWT reader Joshua Hansen suggested we do it, and I thought it was a great idea.

As you can see, the ASMI contains two stock indexes, gold (i.e. real money), two commodity representatives, a real estate index, the most liquid U.S. bond, and a straight bet against the dollar in the form of the U.S. Dollar Index inverted.

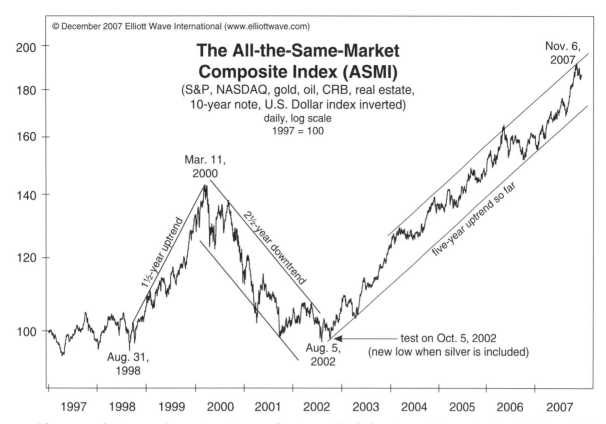

These markets are of varying sizes and prices. We did not want to make the ASMI capitalization weighted or price weighted, because the important aspect in our view is the market's psychology with respect to each component. So we counted these markets as equal partners in the index by equal-weighting them on the start date in January 1997. Then we let them range from there.

The chart shows the ASMI's 11-year history. Strikingly, this index has not meandered around but marched up and down in distinct trends. Given this noticeable order, we think our index tracks something singular and real, namely the exceedingly rare orientation of the financial marketplace in which the market treats all investments not as competing, somewhat exclusive options but rather as part of a vast array of available items on a smorgasbord where investors can graze among the offerings, blithely paying for them all with the massive amount of credit made available by the banking system.

Why is the ASMI important? To quote the former chairman of Citigroup (from last July), "When the music stops, in terms of liquidity, things will be complicated." Well, this index will tell us when the music has stopped. As long as the uptrend from 2002 remains intact, the magic levitation will continue. But when the biggest credit-fueled investment mania of all time terminates, this index will tell us so by breaking its lower trendline. At that point, it will indicate that the deflationary crash—the unwinding of the great credit bubble—is finally underway.

January 2008

2008: The Year Everything Changes

[Many say] that it was impossible to anticipate the debt crisis or the depth of its damage ahead of time. We see this assertion even in the most respectable financial services. Here's one example: "There's been a confluence of events that I don't think anybody's models captured. I don't think anybody had a model that encompassed real estate going down, and going down by the amount that it's gone down, and going down in the way that it's continuing to go down." On the contrary, real estate's collapse fits perfectly with the plunge predicted in Chapter 16 of *Conquer the Crash*, which was published before it was on anyone's radar. What's more, we used the Wave Principle to identify the perfect model, the post-stock market real estate rally of 1835-1837. As Bob Prechter and Pete Kendall pointed out in a 2004 Barron's article, the most appropriate historic parallel to what we expected was the across-the-board market and economic reversal that took full hold in March 1837 when "an overheated real estate boom reversed, and the stock market resumed its major downtrend. The deflationary collapse of the late 1830s and early 1840s was the ultimate resolution of a two-decade pattern of credit expansion and speculation that finally became exhausted—just the setup we have today."

It's taken longer than in the 1830s, but the Wave Principle explains that too; it's a Grand Supercycle top, not just a Supercycle degree turn, as was the case in the 1830s. The topping process started in late 1999 when the DJIA peaked in terms of real money (gold) and purchasing power (commodities). Observe on the following chart, the simultaneous rise in all three indexes—the Dow in terms of dollars (nominal), gold (real) and commodities (purchasing power)—from 1980 to 1999. This advance signified real gains for investors. The Dow's rise since 2002, however, occurred only in dollar terms. The Dow's new nominal high in 2006 does not represent an increase in purchasing power nor a rise in terms of real money. In fact, it is just the opposite, as the Dow denominated in each of these asset classes has been crashing. The new high in nominal terms occurred because credit inflation eroded the value in which the index is typically measured—dollars. The topping process reached the housing market in 2005 when homebuilding stocks peaked along with some commodities in May 2006. The financial flameout began when credit inflation turned to credit deflation. This process will soon devastate the nominal value of the blue chip stock indexes.

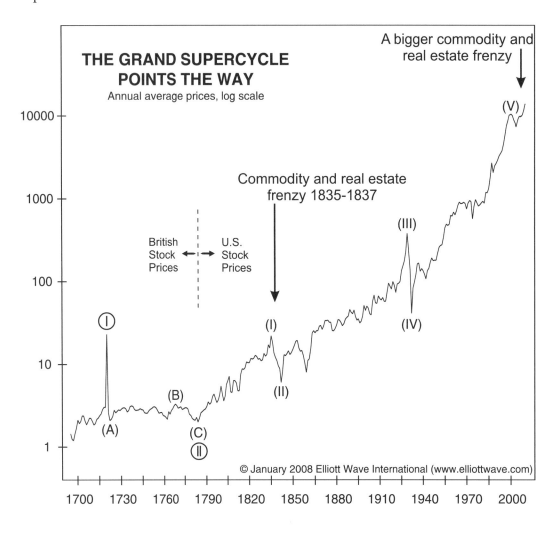

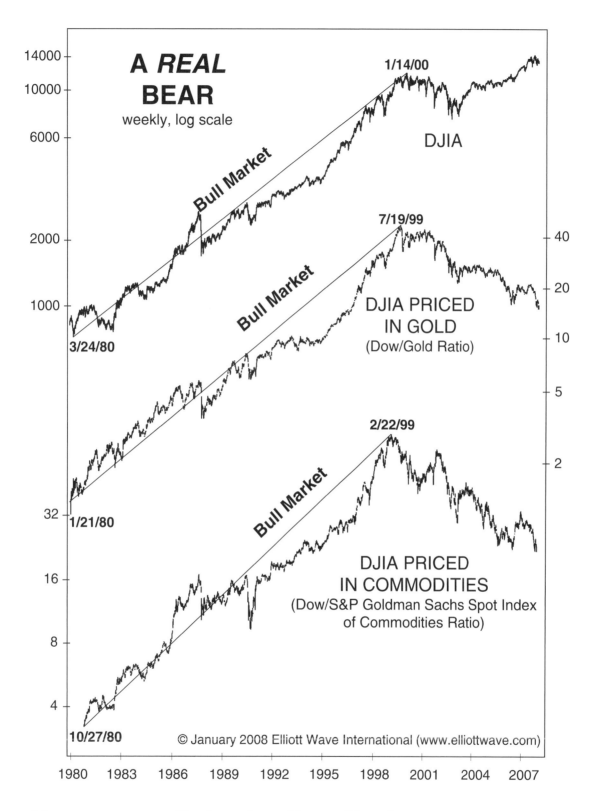

Most news accounts still refer to the problem as "the subprime crisis." In time, however, such characterization will evoke the same euphemistic quality of the housing and subprime headlines shown at the beginning of our 2007 timeline. The spread of the crisis to lenders of every stripe is clear now. The last few months of 2007 included the biggest one-month jump in auto-loan delinquencies in eight years, a $344 million quarterly loss at student loan giant Sallie Mae, a suspension of student loan securitizations and sales by The First Marblehead Corp., one of the nation's largest student loan lenders, and a 26% increase in credit card delinquencies (year-over-year in October). "It's like a game of dominoes," says the director of the Center for Consumer Financial Services at the Rochester Institute of Technology. It certainly is, and the process has reached the point of self-reinforcement. Independent Strategy, a financial consulting firm, figures that banks must shrink lending by 15-to-20 percent to return their capital ratios to pre-crisis levels. Hedge funds and brokers must curtail borrowing by $18 to $25 for every $1 lost. According to Bianco Research, newly-adopted Fannie Mae and Freddie Mac lending standards mean that "over one-third of home buyers are going to get 'crunched' by tougher standards, much bigger downpayments and interest rate 'surcharges.'"

In wave c, the second leg lower of a bear market, there's just no hiding from reality. That's where we are now. "We're at the beginning of the financial world coming to its senses after the bursting of the biggest credit bubble the world has seen, " says Washington Post columnist Steven Pearlstein, who goes on to take the words right out of *Conquer the Crash* when he describes the market for derivatives this way: "If all this sounds like a financial house of cards, that's because it is." He even concludes that the crisis may be more serious than the junk bond crisis of 1987, the S&L crisis of 1990 and the bursting of the tech bubble in 2001, but he fails to go far enough, saying this is "not the crash of 1929." CTC notes that in "the Great Depression, bonds of many companies, municipalities and foreign governments were crushed. Understand that in a crash, no one knows its depth, and almost everyone becomes afraid." Many municipalities and states are feeling the early tremors of fear. Several, including California, have already announced "fiscal emergencies." In a story that will likely become all too familiar, we learned that Springfield, Massachusetts "invested" $14 million in AAA-rated CDOs as a way of earning a higher return on their excess cash. Yesterday, The Boston Globe reported that as of now, "there are no buyers and no real market to set an actual price" for these formerly highest-rated securities, revealing Springfield's investment loss to be 100%. Last year's 2007 EWFF preview concluded by stressing the central importance of this emotional transition. "The psychological foundation of liquidity is confidence. We cannot stress this point strongly enough. When investors are optimistic, confidence remains high and liquidity expands. When this optimism goes away, the spigot will run dry." It seems that the drought here in Georgia is not the only natural phenomenon that is parching the environment beyond recognition.

Previously, EWFF spotted a rising level of caution and fear in investors' preference for gold versus silver and the spread between the yield on U.S. Treasuries and junk bonds. These indexes continue to reveal fear's expanding

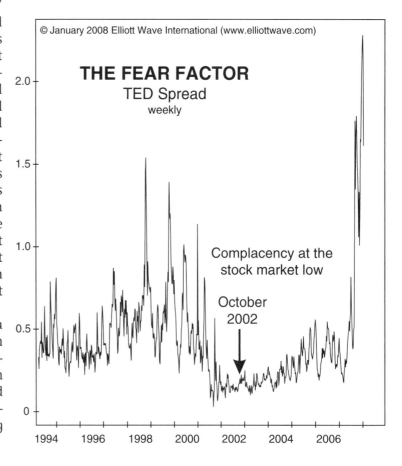

presence across the marketplace. An updated version and forecast for the gold/silver ratio is shown here. Another important measure of overall fear versus complacency is the "TED Spread," the difference between the 3-month Eurodollar yield and the 3-month U.S. T-bill yield. Eurodollars are considered more speculative investments, T-bills more conservative. As the chart shows, the spread has been surging. Incredibly, back in October 2002 when stocks were making their low, the spread was not far from the zero line. The most elemental aspect of a bear market is fear, its conspicuous absence was a clear sign that 2002 was very early in the bear market, not the final bottom. The plight of the financial sector in 2007 confirms our suspicion that wave c will produce an unrivaled abundance of fear. Stay out of its way.

Gold & Silver

Some of the most relevant information coming from the precious metals sector continues to be from the movement of the gold/silver price ratio. Its persistent rise throughout 2007 is consistent with EWFF's observations that social mood is turning toward a more cautious stance, which is the prelude to a bear market in a host of financial assets. This trend should continue in 2008.

February 2008

Breaking the Market's Animal Spirits

One of the traits that set the Great Asset Mania apart from earlier bull markets was its facility for sending stock after stock and group after group of stocks rocketing higher with reckless abandon. As far as we know, the latest rise has yet to produce any such high flyers. Google, the search engine that became a focal point for equity lust over the course of the b-wave rally, is actually down over the course of the last week. It is also down 25% from a November 7 peak. A new tentativeness is signaled by a headline that says Google is wobbling but "It Won't Fall Down ... Maybe." According to the socionomic principle of post-peak attacks against the most successful corporations, Google's slump may well turn out to be a small hint of far more intense societal pressures in the months ahead.

The dissipation of the market's animal spirits, which EWFF has shown in everything from a steady rise in the gold/silver ratio to a plunge in the dollar volume of OTC Bulletin Board stocks, continues. The latest sign of a speculative exhaustion is in the IPO market, which is now shutting down. According to Bloomberg, 24 companies froze plans for initial public offerings in January, the most in at least a decade. The private equity game is over. "Deals have dried up," says the New York Times. Merrill Lynch just decided to curtail severely its participation in the market for collateralized debt obligations, and some central bankers believe that "securitization is not coming

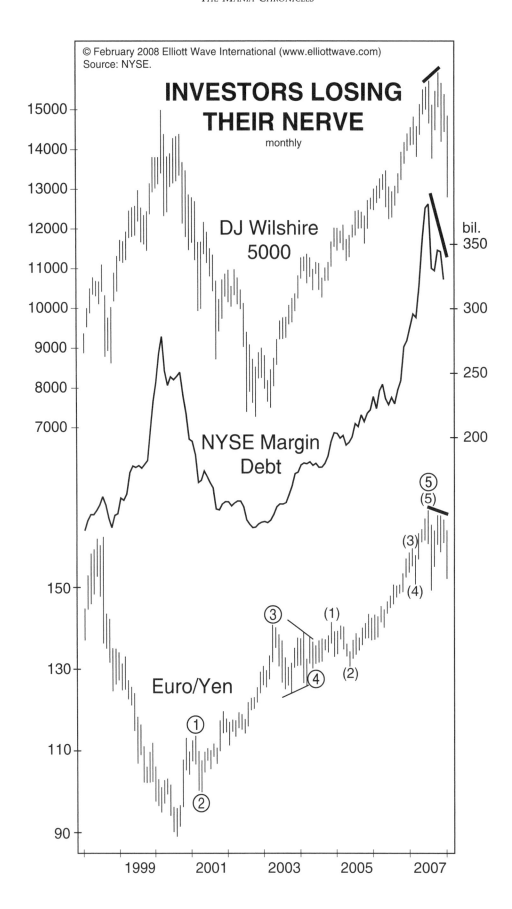

© February 2008 Elliott Wave International (www.elliottwave.com)
Source: NYSE.

INVESTORS LOSING THEIR NERVE
monthly

DJ Wilshire 5000

NYSE Margin Debt

Euro/Yen

bil.

back in any meaningful way in the foreseeable future." So the whole risk-shifting apparatus that turned the debt markets into a casino and stretched the credit bubble to extremes is suddenly endangered. Two more key measures of the marketplace's appetite for risk are represented in the chart of the DJ Wilshire 5000 over NYSE margin debt and the euro/yen cross rate. Both failed to confirm stocks' October 11 peak, topping below prior highs. As EWI has noted in the past, a failure of margin debt to expand to a new high with stocks is the "kiss of death" for a bull market. The September EWFF noted that the euro/yen is an excellent proxy for the yen carry trade, in which speculators borrow yen at low rates to buy riskier assets in distant markets. That issue showed a five-wave move from 2000, which may also be seen on this month's chart. The complete Elliott wave means that the unwinding of the yen carry trade is underway, which in turn signals that the great global yield grab of riskier assets is surely abating.

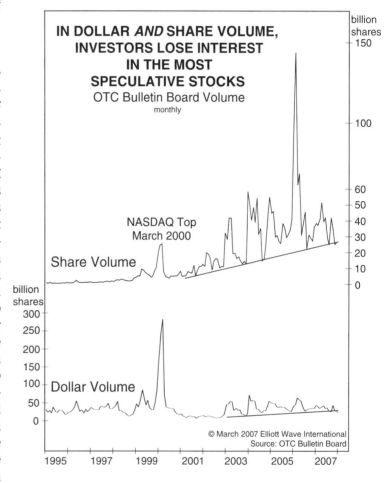

March 2008

It takes a lot of speculative horsepower to create a Supercycle-degree peak. Last month EWFF offered several signs that the internal combustion of the market is long past peak power. One measure that we mentioned is the OTC Bulletin Board volume figures. As an asset class, these shares rank as the riskiest because they are not listed on any exchange. The dollar volume shown at the bottom of the chart illustrates the much greater intensity of the 2000 bull market peak relative to the wave b rally from 2002-2003, which never carried dollar volume anywhere close to its 2000 high. The much higher share-volume totals (top line) show that through the countertrend rally, investors churned through the diciest shares even more furiously. There is evidence of further exhaustion within the rally from 2002-2003, as Bulletin Board trading volume soared to record levels in 2006 yet dollar volume failed even to surpass its rally peak of early 2004. Now, dollar and total volume are slipping through the uptrend lines created by the 2003-2007 advance.

The same trepidation that is doing so much to squelch the debt markets is seeping into the stock market. The new tone is readily apparent in the revised marketing approach of online brokerage firms. As one headline says, "Online Brokerages Stress Preserving Capital." "Active traders today aren't swinging for home runs anymore; they're happy for base hits," says the VP of active trading at Charles Schwab. The television pitch of TD Ameritrade, the same firm from which slacker/online-trading enthusiast Stuart ruled the air waves with "Let's light this candle" enthusiasm in 1999 and 2000, now focuses on "risk management" and "things to stay more disciplined."

Is the Bubble Era Over?

There are several reasons to believe that the October 11 peak in the Dow Jones Industrial Average is the end of the line for the mania days. The most compelling is that the bubble that enabled all the others—the credit bubble—is over and continues to unwind. The yield spread chart reveals the credit market's bellwether status. It shows the spread between the Moody's Corporate BAA Index and the yield on the 10-year U.S. Treasury note plotted beneath the S&P 500. The spread, inverted on the chart, started to rise back in 2005, but it really spiraled higher in July when subprime mortgage debt went into a freefall, lending standards started to tighten and the commercial paper market froze solid. The blue chip averages managed one more new high in October, but they too were sucked into the credit market vortex by October. Now the debt disruptions are coming fast. "Virtually every week we discover a new large but obscure corner of the U.S. and world financial system that, unknown to all but a few practitioners—depends on the confidence of debt buyers in order to survive," says MSN Money columnist Jon Markman. "Take, for instance, auction rate securities. These lightly regulated, trillion dollar financing programs underpin our civic infrastructure, and their possible failure seriously threatens the health of our cities, hospitals and transportation networks."

On February 21 alone, auctions of 395 out of 641 (62%) publicly offered bonds failed (i.e. there was not sufficient bidding). This total is almost 10 times the 44 failures recorded over the entire 23-year life of auction-rate bonds. The chart of auction rates shows the yield explosion that was needed to draw bidders. Real consequences of the losses are rippling into everything from the Massachusetts Turnpike, where drivers now face higher tolls, to college and hospital costs. As the debt markets unravel, regulators and credit market authorities are doing everything they

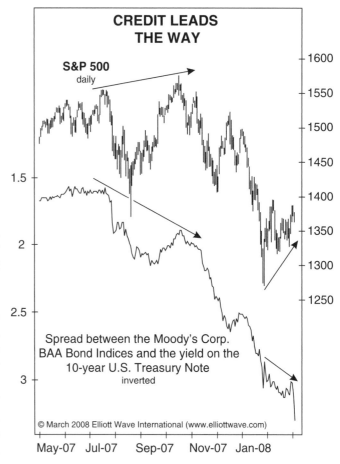

CREDIT LEADS THE WAY

S&P 500 daily

Spread between the Moody's Corp. BAA Bond Indices and the yield on the 10-year U.S. Treasury Note inverted

© March 2008 Elliott Wave International (www.elliottwave.com)

May-07 Jul-07 Sep-07 Nov-07 Jan-08

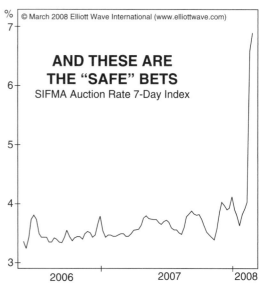

© March 2008 Elliott Wave International (www.elliottwave.com)

AND THESE ARE THE "SAFE" BETS
SIFMA Auction Rate 7-Day Index

can to curb the "slow motion asphyxiation." This week, stock indexes rallied when MBIA and Ambac averted downgrades to their respective AAA credit status by raising a few billion dollars (which was several billion less than what they said they needed only a few weeks ago). In this way, imminent disaster for a large swath of the debt market was reputedly averted. In the face of the unfolding collapse in social mood, however, no amount of shoring up or ratings agency leniency will prove adequate. MBIA and Ambac are perfect examples of the following comment from *At the Crest of the Tidal Wave*:

The next depression will cause countless bond issuers to default, even ones that today sport impeccable ratings and appear unquestionably sound. Bond ratings are doomed to announce changes far behind the market. The forces that will soon propel the U.S. into depression will devastate bond ratings.

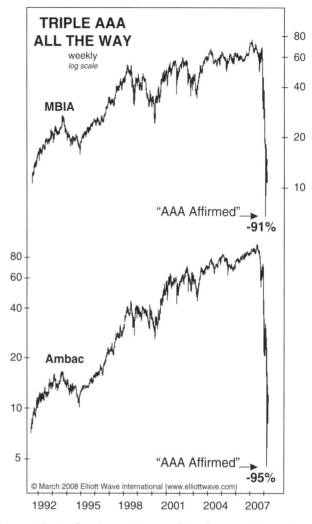

At this point, rating agencies themselves may be doomed as they are not just behind the market, but they are attempting to buck its message by endorsing the effort to shore up MBIA, Ambac and other monoline insurers. In time, the move will serve only to remind people that the market gods retain an expert sense of comic timing. The chart at right, which is updated from November, shows that MBIA and Ambac have declined over 90% from their respective peaks last year. Through the entire run up to the highs and subsequent decline, S&P and Moody's, two of the main ratings agencies, maintained a AAA rating on each company. Despite the crushing decline in the share price, ratings agencies this week "affirmed" their AAA status on both companies, maintaining the charade of financial stability. We are quite sure it will fail. For one thing, the rating agencies reveal the presence of the ultimate trend-follower, the government. A recent Wall Street Journal editorial notes, "since 1975, the Securities and Exchange Commission has limited competition in the market for credit ratings by anointing only certain firms as 'Nationally Recognized Statistical Rating Organizations.'" Over the course of the bull market, government-endorsed agency assessments of risk came to replace market-based assessments. This was not much of a problem on the way up, particularly at the end of the great bull market, because the ever-upward trajectory of prices kept even the most rickety promises afloat. But the change toward increasing pessimism means that a long-term attack on agencies and their ratings is on, and it will do for the decline what complacency did for the advance. Don't be surprised if affirmations of corporate health accompany short-term peaks and the inevitable downgrades near the bottom are erroneously seen as contributing to the carnage.

Efforts to stem the tide will be especially damaging to ratings agencies' credibility. For every hole in the unfolding default crisis that they try to plug, a slew of others are already appearing. As ratings agencies stood behind MBIA and Ambac, for instance, the leverage loan and commercial real estate mortgage markets hit the skids. "As the strength of the U.S. economy has deteriorated, it has become harder for heavily leveraged companies to meet their obligations," says Business Week. Charts of lower-tier commercial real estate mortgages show that they are priced about where the subprime securities were in the middle of last year. This item is just in: "Small and Midsize Banks Beginning To Struggle in Credit Crisis." FDIC regulators announced this week that they "are bracing for well over 100 bank failures in the next 12 to 24 months." Subprime did a great job of blazing the trail to deep writedowns and downgrades; other debt markets should implode even faster.

No Place To Go

Another sign of the end times for mania days is the conclusion of Vietnam's mania for shares, as shown in the chart. Last March, EWFF called for a peak in the Ho Chi Minh Index based on an exponential rise capped by a classic last-minute rush of small investors into the share market. This turned out to be an accurate forecast as Vietnam reversed in a matter of days and is now down by more than 40%.

At that time, EWFF added a larger point:

> An investment frenzy within the same Hanoi populace that was consumed by communism at the lows in the 1970s is signaling the end of the last phase in the Great Asset Mania of the 1990s and early 2000s.

Our reasoning was that with "students, civil servants and state enterprise managers" in one of the last bastions of communism rushing to buy shares and "dreaming of windfall profits," speculative euphoria was tapped out. Another recent confirmation is that despite Vietnam's reversal and even as the global nature of the decline becomes pronounced, "frontier markets like Vietnam" are becoming more popular. According to Investors Business Daily, "January's blood bath in the so-called BRIC (Brazil, Russia, India and China) markets has investors looking at lesser-known developing countries—the 'frontier markets'—for better returns." While BRIC equity funds experienced outflows in January, funds that focused on more remote investment outposts such as Africa and the Mideast experienced steady in-flows. Late comers may try to extend the injection of capital to even lower quality areas, but now that the ideological opposition has been conquered, the mainstream movement toward a more conservative social mood should be fiercely concentrated in the very safest financial instruments.

The Dow in Real Money Has Crashed

The Dow in Real Money chart updates our ongoing Dow/gold chart, the one that shows the trends of the stock market priced in ounces of gold, i.e. real money. The "Year 2000" edition of *At the Crest of the Tidal Wave* included a long-term bearish forecast for this chart, and unlike our outlook for the nominal Dow,

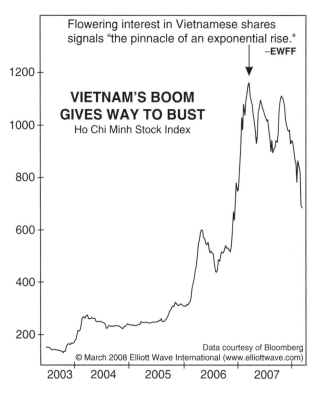

Flowering interest in Vietnamese shares signals "the pinnacle of an exponential rise."
—EWFF

VIETNAM'S BOOM GIVES WAY TO BUST
Ho Chi Minh Stock Index

Data courtesy of Bloomberg
© March 2008 Elliott Wave International (www.elliottwave.com)

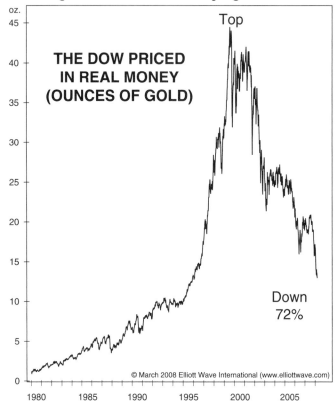

THE DOW PRICED IN REAL MONEY (OUNCES OF GOLD)

Top

Down 72%

© March 2008 Elliott Wave International (www.elliottwave.com)

this one has been on track the whole decade. As the chart shows, in recent months the real value of U.S. stock shares has plummeted for the fifth time since 1999, reaching another new low. It is now down a stunning 72 percent in fewer than nine years. Had we been smart enough to short the S&P and go long gold simultaneously to simulate a short sale in real money, we could be retired by now.

If the nominal Dow had been priced in honest money since its January 2000 top, it would be selling today at 3400. And the bears would have been properly rewarded for having the guts to go against the historically large one-way crowd that was bullish in 1999-2000. Thanks to the Federal Reserve System, however, no one who would normally be succeeding is being rewarded. Bulls think their stocks are holding up, but they are crashing in value. Short sellers should be rich by now, but they aren't, thanks to the banking system's raging credit engine, which has allowed leveraged investors to keep nominal stock prices up even as values collapse. Even people who don't care about the stock market, the poor schlubs who are simply savers, are losing purchasing power with every passing month. So dollar-credit creation from nothing robs from almost everyone. The primary winners in the U.S. fiat-money-monopoly scheme are Congress and the President, who can spend money without collecting it. That's why they created the Fed in the first place. Bankers also gain, because they have the legal privilege of draining off a percentage of the population's production every year. Ironically, even these institutions get hurt in the end.

A Portent of How Coming Price Adjustments Will Occur

According to lore, the stock market is supposed to be a "discounting" mechanism, meaning that it anticipates future events and moves ahead of them. This notion is fatally flawed. The market does move ahead of events, but the reason is that it records the changes in social mood that motivate social actions, which manifest as events.

Lately, however, markets have failed to turn quietly and slowly ahead of events, as they usually do. The sub-prime mortgage meltdown provides a case in point. *The Elliott Wave Financial Forecast* described the market's change in July 2007 from fully valuing these mortgages to considering them nearly worthless as being so swift that it was as if someone "flipped a switch." *Conquer the Crash* came out in March 2002. So five years before the "switch" was flipped, someone studying the situation could see the tremendous risk in weak debt. Moreover, the housing market topped in 2005, so two years before that change, anyone attuned to the implications of the end of a record housing bubble could have made the decision to bail out of sub-prime mortgages. But the market did not budge. Optimism remained entrenched. It was not until some lone seller offered up one of these mortgages for sale in July 2007 that the market suddenly acted as if the mortgages were toxic.

We have just had another such event. *Conquer the Crash* covered the structural weaknesses in debt and insurance companies and expressed the utter certainty that rating services would be behind the curve. So, of all things, insurance companies that insured debt, thereby jacking up the bonds' ratings, would have to be one of the most dangerous of all investments. Yet investors' optimism was so persistent and blinding that they bid up shares of the two biggest debt insurers, MBIA and AMBAC, in 2003...2004...2005...2006...and even into 2007! AMBAC peaked on May 18, just shy of two years after housing prices topped nationwide. We were stunned at the complacency. Then, in a blinding fury, these two stocks fell *93 percent* on average, in a matter of months.

When optimism toward a market continues unrestrained despite deteriorating conditions, the only possible resolution is a "light-switch" type of reversal. When bulls have committed capital to a market and borrowed more to keep investing, and when the rising prices fund even more borrowing to keep them going, there is simply no cushion when the trend reverses. There is no cash on the sidelines waiting to scoop up bargains; it has all gone into investments and the loans that back them. In addition, there is no contingent of bears waiting for an entry point, and there are no short positions to cover. So there is nothing to stem a free fall.

In the case of these two stocks—as with the sub-prime meltdown and to some degree the real estate reversal—the stock market abdicated its traditional role of turning quietly and sneakily ahead of events. The level of optimism associated with a Grand Supercycle top must be keeping investors so intoxicated with optimism that they hold onto that feeling until they simply cave in. There is precedent for this profile: The 1929 peak was a spike, and the 1720 peak was a spike.

Do not assume, though, that the stocks in this chart are "reacting" to events. The crashes in these two stocks are still way ahead of events and most people's stated opinions. If you can believe it, the two major rating services are still *confirming their AAA ratings of these two companies*. But the market has spoken: These ratings will go the way of the dinosaur, and these companies will go under. These events have yet to happen, so once again the market is ahead of events.

We had long thought that the great bear market in stocks might be swift, because over the past 300 years the bigger the investment mania, the faster has been the ensuing collapse. The peaks of 1968 and 1835 led to deep bear markets of six and seven years, respectively. The wilder Roaring 'Twenties, capping an 87-year rise, led to a deeper bear market, yet it was faster, lasting less than three years.

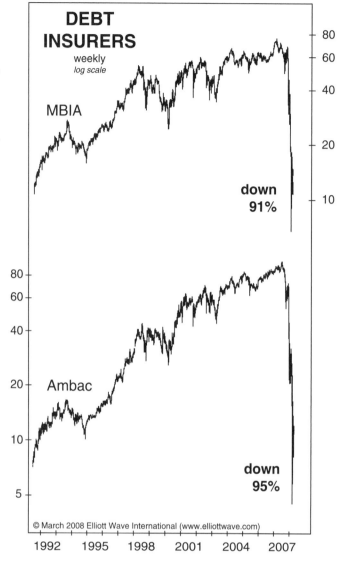

The even more dramatic South Sea Bubble, which peaked in 1720, led to a still deeper bear market, yet it was even faster, lasting only two years. So given that the past ten years of topping has produced the craziest overvaluation, the largest number of bubbles and the most persistent period of market-related optimism *ever*, by a huge margin, we are more than ever expecting a swift resolution. It would also make sense from a political perspective: The coming deflation needs to be swift enough to out-run the actions of the Fed and Congress. If it happens fast, they won't be able to act quickly enough to turn the credit deflation into a currency inflation before the former trend has run its course.

Take a good, long look at the Debt Insurers chart. This might turn out to be the profile of the stock averages when the big capitulation hits. It could happen now, or, if the averages somehow manage to reach a temporary bottom soon and scrape their way to another new high it could happen later. But with the ideal year of 2012 (±2 years) for a bottom looming near, the potential for a breathtaking plunge in stock prices—and housing and commodity prices as well—is moving from a possibility to a probability.

April 2008

History Catches Up to the Credit Bubble

Elliott Wave Principle (EWP) ends by asking, "Why does man continuously have to shelter himself from hurricanes of his own making?" It answers the question as follows:

> Apparently it is one of nature's laws that man at times will refuse to accept the rest of its laws. The Wave Principle exists partly because man refuses to learn from history, because he can always be counted upon to be led to believe that two and two can and do make five. He can be led to believe that the laws of nature do not exist, that what is to be consumed need not be first produced, that what is lent need never be paid back, that promises are equal to substance, that paper is gold, that benefits have no costs, that the fears which reason supports will evaporate if they are ignored or derided.

> Panics are sudden emotional mass realizations of reality. At these points, reason suddenly impresses itself upon the mass psyche, saying, "Things have gone too far. The current levels are not justified by reality." To the extent that reason is disregarded, then, will be the extent of the extremes of mass emotional swings and their mirror, the market. ...When the fifth wave of the fifth wave tops out, we need not ask why it has done so. Reality, again, will be forced upon us. The laws of nature will have to be patiently relearned.

The relevance of this passage is clear from the labeling of the Grand Supercycle degree chart on page 153 of the same text. In 1978 when *Elliott Wave Principle* was first published, the Grand Supercycle rise from the late 1700s was shown as one fifth wave away from completing a larger fifth of a fifth, or Supercycle wave (V) of Grand Supercycle wave ⑪. The completed Grand Supercycle is shown here. The post-peak rally to a new high is wave **b**, which re-created the euphoria of 2000 and exuded this personality trait from EWP: "If the analyst can easily say to himself, 'There is something wrong with this market,' chances are it's a B wave." As stocks advanced to all-time highs, EWT identified what was wrong with the rise: a collapse in real values. The April 2007 issue of EWFF also observed a debt structure that "is past the point of no return. Debt issuers are now in an unprecedented position of throwing horrendous loans after really bad loans to keep borrowers afloat. All it takes is for one lender to fold and the race for the exits will be on." In June, EWFF said the race was in fact "on" when Merrill Lynch put the brakes on a Wall Street effort to sweep losses in two Bear Stearns mortgage funds under the rug. The top line of the chart (next page) shows the best estimate of the damage to date, a

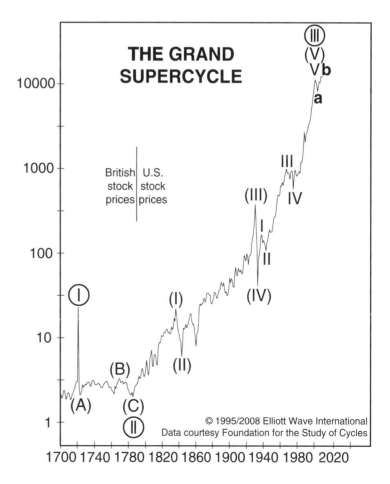

© 1995/2008 Elliott Wave International
Data courtesy Foundation for the Study of Cycles

87

55% plunge in the Hedge Fund Enablers Index. EWFF created the index last May from the shares of the eight largest investment banks based on their backing of the hedge fund industry and "fearless approach to leverage." Word of hedge fund margin calls "Even on Treasuries" and frozen or closing funds is pouring in so fast now that it is hard to keep up. At such times, it is best to let the market tell the story.

Bear Stearns' recent performance (second line on the chart) speaks volumes. The sentiment surrounding its plunge offers further insight into the depth of the delusion at a historic peak. Contrary to popular belief, it didn't happen all at once. The 98+% decline, from $172.61 to $2.84, took more than a year. Still, even sophisticated observers with ring-side seats to the debacle were caught off guard by its final two-day plunge from $57 to under $3. In the wake of the break, Bears' own economists said, "We were concerned about a run on the bank. We never imagined we would be the bank!" Other celebrated financial gurus and fund managers rushed in and were still buying the dip in Bear Stearns just days before the

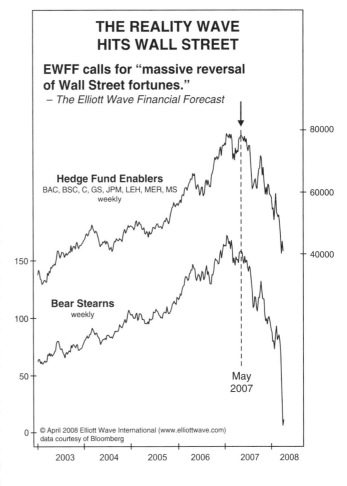

THE REALITY WAVE HITS WALL STREET

EWFF calls for "massive reversal of Wall Street fortunes."
– The Elliott Wave Financial Forecast

Hedge Fund Enablers
BAC, BSC, C, GS, JPM, LEH, MER, MS
weekly

Bear Stearns
weekly

May 2007

© April 2008 Elliott Wave International (www.elliottwave.com)
data courtesy of Bloomberg

95% two-day plunge. The damage to their portfolios illustrated "how quickly the credit crisis is transforming celebrity investors into laggards, as their traditional down-market playbooks are failing." The recent uptick to $11 a share shows that not even a 98% decline can dampen the enthusiasm of dip buyers. The current price of $11 confirms that in some circles, JP Morgan's revised buy-out price of $10 a share is considered a steal. But the effort to average down in Bear Stearns stock will backfire when Morgan's own exposure to corporate and consumer loans turns tail. Reason will not reclaim the entrenched financial kingdom in a straight-line fashion. It will do so in fits and bursts, like the lines on these charts.

The next chart shows the almost immediate descent of another stock EWFF identified as a key debt bubble barometer: Blackstone Group. Last April, when Blackstone's chairman was on the cover of Fortune as the "New King of Wall Street," EWFF declared that a proposed offering of its shares to the public meant that "the jig is very likely up" for the private equity buy-outs that depend so heavily on borrowed money. When Blackstone immediately declined from its initial offering price, the July EWFF added:

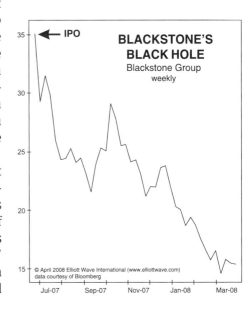

IPO

BLACKSTONE'S BLACK HOLE
Blackstone Group
weekly

© April 2008 Elliott Wave International (www.elliottwave.com)
data courtesy of Bloomberg

One week of trading does not make a trend, but the behavior of Blackstone shares is probably a good proxy for the prospects of the Private Equity/LBO craze. This telling rejection of a key element of the financial engineering craze is another sign that the great financial flameout is nigh. [It is] a glimpse of a weakening state of affairs and a turn toward a more conservative mood. Stocks may muster one more rally, but the larger liquidity bubble of the past five years appears to be drying up.

The new force of reality is recognizable in an 89% fourth quarter earnings slump at Blackstone and countless stories of a "Staggering Weight of Debt" that cripples the private equity industry. But the panic is still mostly ahead because Blackstone recently managed to raise $1.4 billion to buy bonds and loans at "fire sale" prices. Blackstone has yet to invest the money. "Our view is that things will get worse before they get better," says Blackstone's president. Even the leverage-loving kings of the great debt bubble are reticent. This is the conservatism that figured so prominently in *Conquer the Crash*'s forecast for a deflationary depression. At such times, CTC said it doesn't matter what the Fed does, lending officers will become afraid and call in loans and slow or stop their lending "no matter how good their clients' credit may be. Corporations likewise reduce borrowing for expansion and acquisition, fearing the burden more than they believe in the opportunity. Consumers adopt a defensive strategy at such times by opting to save and conserve rather than to borrow, invest and spend." The resulting economic ripple effect is clear in the chart of the year-over-year change in residential mortgage loans, commercial real estate and consumer and business loans relative to the respective changes in lending standards

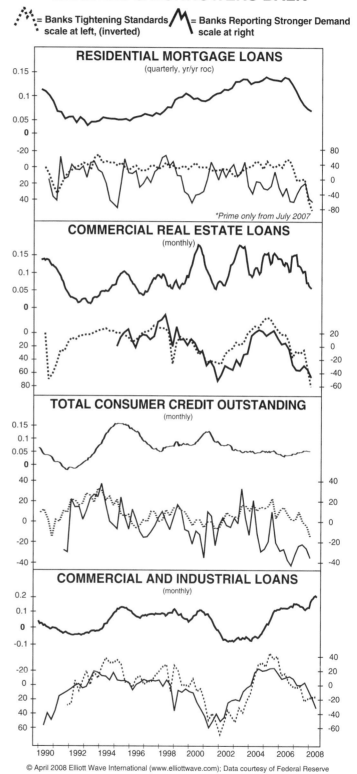

© April 2008 Elliott Wave International (www.elliottwave.com); Data courtesy of Federal Reserve

and loan demand. Mortgages lead the way with an incredible 85% of banks tightening standards and 69% reporting slackening demand; thus the sharp plunge in mortgage originations. Commercial real estate is not far behind. Consumer installment loans and business lending is still growing, but the willingness to lend and borrow in these sectors is also in well established declines. As one headline puts it, banks are "hoarding cash," and for good reason. It is only a matter of time before these rates of change cross the zero line. When that happens, the economy will tank and consumers and businesses alike will have even more reasons not to lend or borrow. Like any law of nature, there's no stopping it now.

The China Syndrome Revisited

In February 2007, EWFF pointed to an exponential rise in Chinese shares and said they appeared to be approaching a peak. Prices raced higher, but in September EWFF noted that Chinese brokerage firms were adding close to half a million new trading accounts a day and reasserted that a peak "cannot be far off." The Shanghai Composite peaked on October 16 and is down 45%. And it's not over. Even as the crashing right-hand side of the China's skyscraper pattern takes shape, sentiment continues to hold that the "downside is limited for China shares" (Asian Investor, March 26). In a classic finishing touch, some of the most exuberant expression of optimism toward China came well after its peak. The ad here appeared as a full-page, color spread in a December issue of The Wall Street Journal. Jim Rogers is an excellent student of the markets who caught a good part of the run-up in Chinese shares, but there are times when the psychology surrounding a forecast is more telling than the forecast itself. Rogers is getting such prominent placement because the world has finally caught up to his early lead and become "hog wild for China." His latest book, *A Bull in China*, came out in December and hit the Top 50 on Amazon.com's bestseller list.

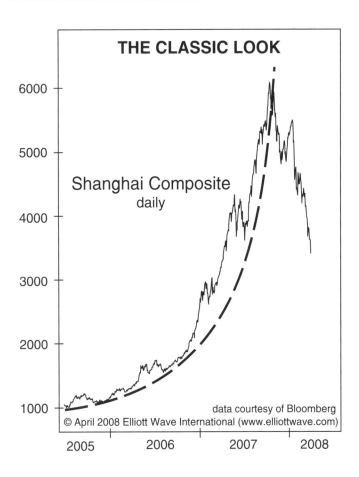

May 2008

More Signs of a Burst Bubble

The most critical expression of the mania's dissipating energy is the loud hissing sound that now emanates from the world of structured finance, where $100 billion blow-ups are becoming common. Whole classes of are disappearing. Citigroup said on April 15 that the auction-rate bond market will "cease to exist" because Wall Street firms will no longer spend their own capital to prevent auction failures. In turn, a dissolving auction-rate bond market squeezes the market for student loans, because student loans comprised more than 25% of the auction-rate market. In April alone, 46 lenders stopped offering student loans. A chain reaction in which further reductions breed faltering confidence indicating more shrinkage is in motion. There is no reversing the process now.

Financial engineering's still-booming vestiges reveal just how precarious its position is. As the credit crunch emerged in the second half of 2007, "activity in credit continued to explode." According to the Swaps and Derivative Association, the total value of outstanding credit contracts stood at $62 trillion at the end of last year, an increase of 44% from 2006 and 10 times the level of 2003. "The heady expansion—which in effect let investors protect themselves against the chance of corporate default—will delight many investment bankers," says the Financial Times. But these instruments are among the most dangerous ever devised, because they will *not* let investors protect themselves. It is a virtual certainty that the counterparties who issued trillions of dollars in insurance against default will not make good on their guarantees in a systemic rout.

A former banker, Charles R. Morris, lays out what he says could happen in *The Trillion Dollar Meltdown*, a new addition to the New York Times best sellers list. Defaults will trigger writedowns of insured portfolios, demands for collateral, and a rush to grab cash from defaulting guarantors. The credit system will suffer "an utter thrombosis" that will make the subprime crisis "look like a walk in the park." So, the credit world is most definitely coming around to *Conquer the Crash*'s forecast. But participants believe they can simply redirect their speculative energies to mine the downside the way they did the upside. This false belief is why CTC advised readers not to "get suckered into this maelstrom thinking that the bear market will be business as usual, just in the other direction. If you want to try making a killing being short in the collapse, make sure that you are not overexposed. Make sure that if the system locks up for days or weeks, you will not be in a panic yourself." Now more than ever, this advice may save your financial life.

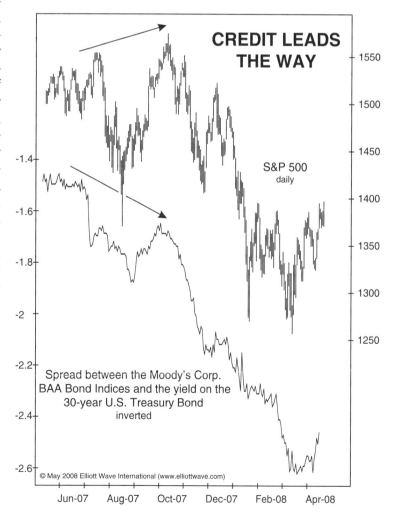

CREDIT LEADS THE WAY

S&P 500 daily

Spread between the Moody's Corp. BAA Bond Indices and the yield on the 30-year U.S. Treasury Bond inverted

© May 2008 Elliott Wave International (www.elliottwave.com)

Derivatives are as resilient as kudzu in the south, but the one thing they cannot survive is a sustained contraction in the asset values sitting at the base of the paper pyramid. This is clear from the derivative fallout that accompanied the fall in home prices. As the devastation ripples into the economy, it will expand exponentially. The front-edge of the storm is near, as stories about firms "That Should Have Failed" were it not for the incredibly easy credit standards of the mid-2000s are appearing. According to Merrill Lynch, distressed corporate bonds jumped to $206 billion worth in April from $4.4 billion in March 2007. That's a gain of nearly 4600%! As EWFF illustrated in March with a version of the "Credit Leads the Way" chart, the debt markets are leading the bear market. The meager rally in the spread between lower-quality bonds and Treasuries shows that credit quality is far from any kind of "all-clear" signal. After expanding from 145 basis points to 262 basis points, or 80% from June to March, the spread between 30-year T-Bonds and lower-grade bonds narrowed to 239 basis points with the rally in stocks. Credit is out in front of the bear market because the recent experience of debt holders connects them directly to the reality that values can disappear overnight.

June 2008

The great credit contraction, which is most immediately reflected by the waxing and waning of spreads between low-grade and high-grade debt, reliably foreshadowed the trend in equities since at least last year, when the credit meltdown preceded the October stock market peak. This is why EWFF emphasized the widening spread in our "Bottom Line" forecasts from August through December. Then we added in January that it was a sure sign that wave c was underway and would produce "an unrivaled abundance of fear." The commotion surrounding Bear Stearns' meltdown in March was just a first taste. The chart is updated from our September 2007 issue; it shows not only the ever-burgeoning fears that we forecast in January but also that credit continues to lead the way through the wave (2) peak. The low-to-high-grade credit spread has narrowed since March in conjunction with stocks' countertrend push, but it now looks ready for another round of widening. The difference this time is that stocks are in a third wave; so the rise on the chart, which looks like a complete blow-out, should carry to even greater heights.

According to the usual sources, the crisis is abating, just as it was supposed to have been back in July 2007 (see chart). Here are just a few of the headline-making declarations that recently marked its alleged passing.

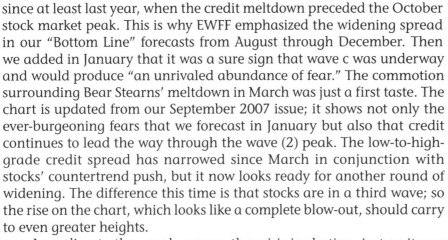

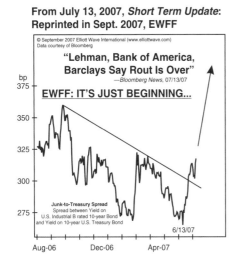

"The worst of the crisis in Wall Street is over."

—May 3, 2008, Bloomberg Television

"...the worst is over,"

—May 12, 2008, head of Treasuries trading
at New York Securities firm

"The acute phase of the credit crisis is over."

—May 20, 2008, Global hedge fund manager on Bloomberg

In a third wave decline, the eventual damage is commensurate with the depth of belief that the storm passed at the end of the preceding wave two rally. The height and breadth of official, high-level assurances has never been more pronounced; so here again, we see the outline of a coming default wave that should be truly historic.

July 2008

Throwing Good Money After Bad

A PIK toggle loan, short for "payment in kind," allows the issuer to pay interest in additional debt rather than in cash (yes, you read that correctly). Here's what EWFF had to say about this dubious bull market instrument in December 2004:

> It's probably one of the few times in history when the market has rewarded investors for taking huge risks because so many are so desperate for a big return. But historically, reaching for yield has been the death knell for investors. As the bear market in stocks reignites and the economy contracts, the junk rally of 2003-2004 will turn into a very ugly rout.

Even though the economy pressed higher, spreads between junk bonds and U.S. Treasury yields started to widen in early 2005. In March 2007, EWFF contended that the economy was running on fumes and that the PIK Toggle loan was a perfect example of the kinds of risky gambits that were extending the life of the expansion.

> With the help of the PIK Toggle, companies are issuing debt 'without the usual terms that require them to meet certain performance metrics to avoid defaulting.' In other words, dying companies can put off the inevitable by canceling payments. The PIK Toggle is a monument to what mania-era financiers have accomplished with OPM, other people's money.

PIK toggle loan originations ended with the start of credit crisis last fall, but companies are now exercising their rights to suspend cash payments on PIK bonds. The president of one of the private equity groups behind many PIK loan deals continues to insist that PIK bonds and covenant-lite loans, which were also featured here in a similar light, are "not a bull market aberration at all." In fact, he says they should be built into every leveraged buy-out because they let companies repair their balance sheets instead of defaulting, which is good for society. In the light of a reversal, however, the Financial Times now counters that PIK loans are a "sorry lesson in how banks and other creditors allowed themselves to be pressed into underpricing debt and letting underwriting standards fall." It adds that troubled companies tend to "throw good money after bad" and "will run down everything to stay in business so that, by the time there is a default, there is nothing left." The FT concludes that by suspending cash payments and loosening covenants, the private equity boom of recent years may be "storing up worse trouble for the future."

It is certainly true. In fact, this is the point we made here in our March 2007 issue. The trouble must be ready to break, because the press is catching on to the deeper meaning of PIK bonds and publishing it for all the world to see and react to. As we discussed in May, this is another example of former bull-market practices being revealed during a c-wave decline for what they truly represent. The flashes of recognition are coming fast and furious by now. Even the bastion of high-level denial, U.S. credit ratings agencies, faced the music in recent days by finally stripping the two main premium-grade bond insurers, MBIA and Ambac, of their AAA credit ratings and alerting the world that the debt of Ford, Chrysler and GM are in danger of further downgrades. In another stunning acknowledgment of the obvious, Goldman Sachs just downgraded GM to a sell after an 88% decline to a 53-year low.

The Fantasy Revealed

In November, EWFF published a chart of the crashing share price of both MBIA and Ambac and said, "the credit crunch is climbing the quality ladder at a rapid rate." In March, we updated the still-cascading prices of each company to illustrate the fulfillment of this forecast from *Conquer the Crash* (CTC):

> The next depression will cause countless bond issuers to default, even ones that today sport impeccable ratings and appear unquestionably sound.

EWFF added:

> Despite the crushing decline in the share price, ratings agencies this week "affirmed" their AAA status on both companies, maintaining the charade of financial stability. We are quite sure it will fail.

And fail it did. Last week's stripping of both MBIA and Ambac's AAA ratings by Moody's came on the heels of previous downgrades by Fitch and S&P. Ratings agencies finally confirmed the verdict that the market rendered eight months earlier via 90%+ declines in the share price of both companies. We cannot overstate the importance of this event. Ratings on much of the debt backed by these insurers must now be cut in turn, as much as $1.28 trillion worth, by some estimates. "The downgrades that we have seen so far, numerous though they have been, have yet to scratch the surface," says CreditSights.

A downgraded bond does not necessarily mean default, although, as the economy continues to contract, many bond issuers will go bankrupt. But as CTC explains, a decrease in the aggregate value of dollar-denominated debt in a credit-based economic system is deflation. With the potential loss in value of trillions of dollars worth of debt, the deflationary forces forecast in CTC continue to intensify. Says one investment analyst, "This form of systemic risk from monoline downgrades represents another negative development for credit markets." This may prove to be the understatement of the year. And it doesn't even take into account the strong potential that both of these companies themselves might declare bankruptcy. Sound far-fetched? At this point, what is far-fetched is that it could sound

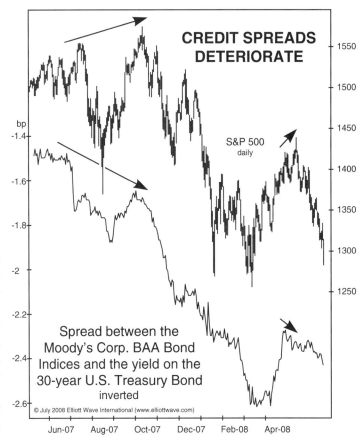

CREDIT SPREADS DETERIORATE

S&P 500 daily

Spread between the Moody's Corp. BAA Bond Indices and the yield on the 30-year U.S. Treasury Bond inverted

© July 2008 Elliott Wave International (www.elliottwave.com)

far-fetched to anyone paying attention. At below $5 a share, MBIA is now down 94% from its January 2007 high, while Ambac is under $2, down 98% from its peak of just over one year ago. The market says bankruptcy is more probable than not, and we agree with the market. Or, rather, the market finally agrees with us.

Near term, credit continues to lead the way, as EWFF noted in May. The spread between low-grade and high-grade debt started to deteriorate again on May 6, nearly two weeks prior to the wave (2) high in the DJIA and S&P. As wave (3) unfolds, spreads should remain out front, on their way toward a record widening.

August 2008

Year II of the great credit implosion continues with Merrill Lynch selling off its collateralized debt obligations for 22 cents on the dollar. But get this: analyst Jim Bianco notes that Merrill is financing 75% of the sale, so it will actually receive just 5.5 cents on the dollar, 94.5% less than par. All it would take is a five-cent decline in the CDO's price to completely wipe out any remaining value. And this is for the super-senior tranches, not the bottom tier! Such is the current state of affairs in the credit market.

More important, Wall Street recognizes the deal's much broader significance. As The Wall Street Journal notes, it "didn't just lower this price for balance-sheet purposes, it turned it into a real loss. That is tough medicine. Lots of other financial firms need a dose." Naturally, the stock market's bottom-fishers celebrated by pushing the S&P to its highest close since July 1. Some even argued that re-pricing is a good thing because it means that the "endgame for CDO risk at financial companies" is at hand. But there are times when big, growling bear market developments are exactly as bearish as they seem, and the Wave Principle says this is one such time. As we noted here last month (see July 2008 section in Chapter 8), "price discovery" on depressed debt instruments is the one thing that Wall Street fought desperately to avoid. The transaction provides a real price against which investors and accountants can now measure all other "model-based" CDO prices. Few if any models are currently pricing in 95% writedowns. Merrill's acknowledgment that "credit-crunch losses are real" immediately triggered "tougher questions about values being assigned to commercial real-estate" as well as a whole host of other debt obligations. The flood-gates between asset price deflation in the mortgage realm and the rest of the economy are now open. As the trappings of financial solvency fall away, the latest push higher in stocks should soon expire and lead to the next phase of this historic decline and unfolding economic depression.

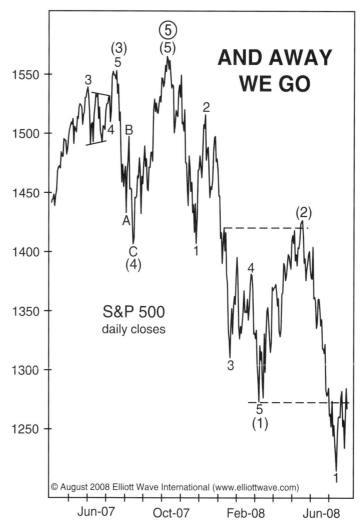

AND AWAY WE GO

S&P 500
daily closes

© August 2008 Elliott Wave International (www.elliottwave.com)

Now They Tell Them

It is sometimes said that history repeats but not in specific detail. This time around, however, the downside of the cycle is quite transparent in many of its particulars. In fact, the specifics are so close that the media is even picking up on terms EWFF previously used to forecast the now-unfolding contraction. A case in point is our June Special Section, "The Fundamental Tipping Point," in which EWFF called for an imminent break in the economy. This Wall Street Journal headline recognized the same critical economic passage a month later:

Economy Near 'Tipping Point'

This must be that break because media depictions of the economic, stock market and social environment fit the forecasts as advertised in CTC and recent issues of EWFF and EWT, in some cases to the letter. Consider this entry from a March 2007 issue of *The Elliott Wave Theorist*, which appeared under the headline "What Wave **c** Will Be Like":

> Now it's time to be prepared for wave **c**. Here is how *Elliott Wave Principle* (p.83) describes C waves: "Declining C waves are usually devastating in their destruction. They are third waves and have most of the properties of third waves. It is during these declines that there is virtually no place to hide.

Here's a picture of that reality as it greeted Cleveland residents one recent Sunday morning.

EWT added, "In C waves the news and the market are fully compatible: The trend is down, and news is bad. So we forecast a dramatic increase in the frequency and severity of bad news." The news is certainly following the script. As noted above, word of business failures and defaults has gone global, with FDIC bank seizures becoming routine. Depressionistic economic conditions "are reaching deep into the daily lives of ordinary Americans." "Can the bad news for banks get any worse?" The New York Times calls the unfolding saga "a financial crisis where the unthinkable has seemingly become routine."

A [prevailing] sentiment is the emerging disdain for "negative" forecasts among market and government authorities. Suddenly, it's not just wrong to be bearish; it is downright improper. In addition to a broadening effort to ban certain forms of short selling, there is a sense that talking

about potential declines is irresponsible. Articles in Georgia recently have reminded citizens that speaking improperly of trouble at a bank is illegal. New York banks considered suing over negative comments. "These are volatile times," says a leading Wall Street strategist. "There's a lot of moving parts here, and nobody can quite figure out how they all mesh. You're hearing a lot of catastrophic predictions." The New York Times adds, "critics of forecasting say this is a dangerous trend. The events of the last year have lent credence to the case of the heretics who say that Wall Street puts too much faith in its ability to predict the future by looking at the past." Given our study of mania parallels in recent months, we would argue that a little faith in some forms of forecasting is certainly in order. But this quote makes such studies sound like some kind of disease. What's so radical about EWFF and EWT's stance to "Get out of stocks and into cash"? Willful efforts to shut down the message of history are a sure sign that the most destructive aspects of the mania mindset are still very much in place. In 1997, *The Elliott Wave Theorist* stated that one key trait of a mania is that a knowledge of history and value comes to be seen as "an impediment to success." At this point, it is hardening into an impediment to survival itself for many.

September 2008

A slew of financial news outlets grabbed on to falling oil prices to claim a bullish case for stocks. "It's Hard to Lose Betting on Stocks as Oil Falls," said one. "Nothing bad happens if oil prices keep falling. But if oil turns up, uh-oh." Here's the same basic assessment from Market-Watch:

Cheap Crude = Bullish Mood

But there is no consistent correlation between oil and stocks. In fact, our all-the-same market scenario reveals that oil and stocks rose *together* from October 2002 to October 2007. They briefly parted ways until July of this year, but according to our forecast, they should now head lower more or less together. And don't look now, but since stocks made their wave (2) high in May, this chart shows that both oil and stocks are down, with crude falling 14.4% and stocks declining 11%. As noted, the shared decline won't necessarily happen step-for-step, as it is not unusual for a multi-market reversal to occur unevenly. When wave 3 of (3) hits its stride, however, we would not be surprised to see them tumbling jointly.

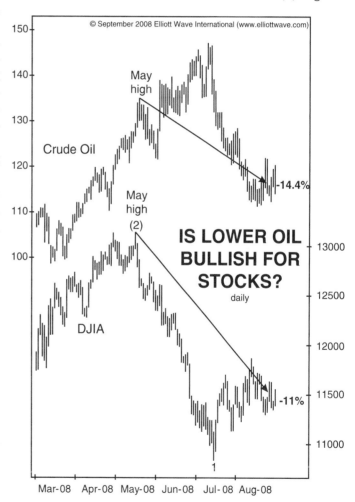

In March, we confirmed "the credit markets' bellwether status" by showing how rising spreads between U.S. Treasuries and lower grade corporate bonds have gotten out in front of declines in the S&P 500. Once again, this leadership trend spells trouble for stocks, as this chart reveals. The spread between lower-grade and higher-grade debt has already breached the July 15 low, wave 1 of (3) in stocks, and it is weakening rapidly. In other words, the fear of default is on the rise, again. This is typical C-wave psychology and it should continue, at least until Cycle wave **c** is close to completion. EWFF has hammered on this theme for months because it highlights this central tenet of *Conquer the Crash*: *get safe*. With equities on the verge of a third-of-a-third wave decline, this point takes on added urgency.

The "Impossible" Is Happening

The subtitle of *Conquer the Crash* is *How To Survive and Prosper in a **Deflationary** Depression*. Calling for deflation is still a distinctly minority opinion, which is as it should be. Meanwhile, the process that so few thought was even remotely possible is wiping out a lot of financial value. Almost every trend is down, except for the U.S. dollar. "All the Same Market" is back, this time on the downside (see charts, page 98). Smells like deflation spirit.

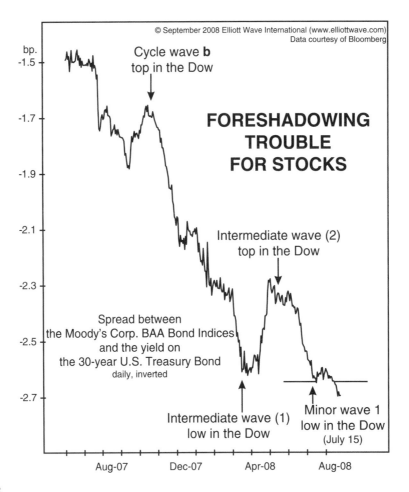

© September 2008 Elliott Wave International (www.elliottwave.com)
Data courtesy of Bloomberg

bp.

Cycle wave **b**
top in the Dow

**FORESHADOWING
TROUBLE
FOR STOCKS**

Intermediate wave (2)
top in the Dow

Spread between
the Moody's Corp. BAA Bond Indices
and the yield on
the 30-year U.S. Treasury Bond
daily, inverted

Intermediate wave (1)
low in the Dow

Minor wave 1
low in the Dow
(July 15)

October 2008

New Attitude Toward Risk Is In the Vault

In a section titled, "Where Were You When The Fire Went Out?," the May 2006 issue of *The Elliott Wave Financial Forecast* made the case that after nearly 3 years of falling, the gold/silver ratio was due for a significant rise. In November 2007, the *Short Term Update* reasserted that "the gold/silver price ratio appears set to vault higher, reflecting a continued move away from risk." After a few more sideways subdivisions, the "vault higher" started in earnest on August 11 with a series of upside gaps, as seen on this chart. A near-term pause after such a strong move is normal, which is happening now, but the boom in this ratio captures an explosion in the flight from risk. The force of the trend is obviously extreme, as all of the largest backers of risk capital have been shaken to their foundations in recent months. In March, Bear Stearns' shares fell to a fraction of their former price, and the company was forcibly absorbed by JPMorgan Chase. Last week, Merrill Lynch leaped into the arms of Bank of America and, of course, Lehman Brothers went under. This week the "survivors" rushed to convert from investment banks to commercial banks, thereby gaining access to the Fed's lending window and averting bankruptcy. As the New York Times says, it is a "new era" in which "Goldman Sachs and Morgan Stanley moved to restructure into larger, less risk-taking organizations." This necessarily implies a long period of collapsing equity prices and deflation, as the entire financial system is built upon a generation in which risk-taking became progressively more outrageous. "It is a turning point for the high-rolling culture of Wall Street," says the Times. But the chart shows otherwise. The turning point actually slipped somewhat quietly into place in May 2006, the month of our call, and the recent upside boom in the gold/silver ratio signals risk aversion's coming-out party. Wall Street is, and will be, a different place.

"ALL THE SAME MARKET" RESUMES, ON THE DOWNSIDE

daily data

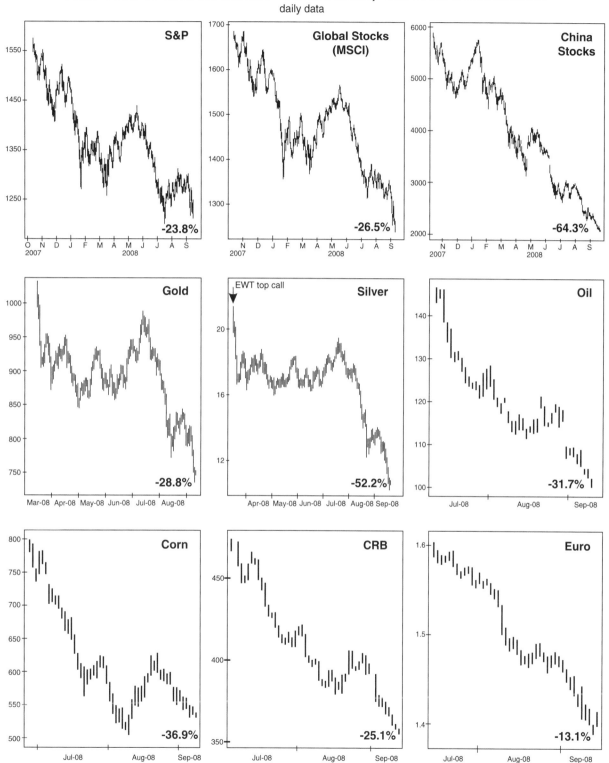

The deteriorating spread between lower- and higher-grade bonds is another key measure that keeps our subscribers on top of the flight from risk. With the help of this spread, EWFF has remained out in front of this trend since it started in March 2005. The flight from even higher grade bonds is now readily apparent in widening spreads between investment-grade corporates

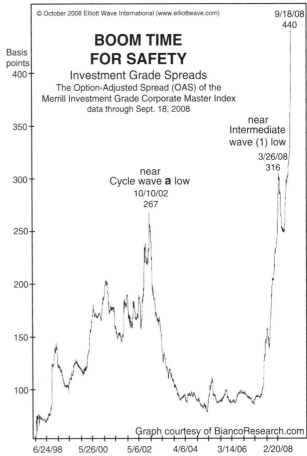

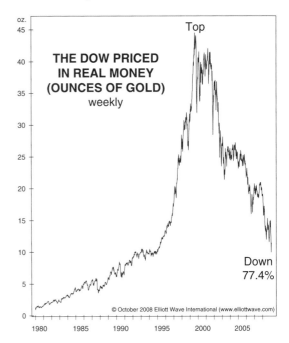

and U.S. Treasuries. The chart shows the explosion to 440 basis points on September 18, which carries the spread well past the extremes registered near the Cycle wave **a** low in stocks, as well as near the wave (1) of ① low within Cycle wave **c**. The greater severity of the unfolding Cycle wave **c** is still young, but the demand for the safest and most secure bonds, U.S. Treasuries, is already posting new records. Last week, the yield on the 3-month U.S. T-bill briefly dipped to zero percent. This shows that investors are more concerned with getting a return *of* their money than a return *on* their money, which is exactly what CTC and all of our "cash is king" advisories said would happen once the shouting started.

The chart at right shows an update of our graph of the Dow in terms of real money. As you can see, it has plunged again to a new low. In 1999, the Dow sold for 44.8 ounces of gold; last week it sold for only 9.95 ounces, a collapse of 77.4% in value. And that's with gold having fallen nearly 30 percent in its own right, which means that stocks are falling even faster. If we still had a money system, as we did before 1934, the Dow would be selling at 2650, and people would understand the true extent of the bear market. It is not likely to end until the Dow sells for less than an ounce of gold.

Have Investors Panicked and Capitulated?

Ever since mid-September, we have read that the bottom is in because investors have "panicked" and "capitulated." But market history does not support this widespread view.

A perusal of volume shows that investors have not panicked. In a market panic, the number of shares traded increases substantially on down days and bottom days. In October 1929 and in October 1987, daily volume surged to between triple and quadruple the preceding summer's average as prices plummeted. Volume recently has been quite steady, aside from two spikes. But it is important to get out the microscope and see on which days they occurred. September 19 sported all-time record volume as the market surged *upward*. September 18 had the fourth-highest volume of the summer, and September 16 had the fifth-highest, and both were up days in the market. Even though September 17 had high volume on a down day, it was a *contraction* in

volume relative to that on the adjacent up days. October 10, which is so far the low day for prices, saw the second-highest volume ever, and in some contexts would indicate an important reversal. But it happened amid hints that the G7 would meet and propose a global bank bailout, and some averages, such as the NASDAQ Composite and the two Value Line measures, closed *up* that day. Even the record and near-record volume surges of January 23 and March 20 occurred on huge up days, not down days. So most of the biggest volume days this year have been those that attracted mostly *buyers*, not sellers. This is not how volume has behaved in past panics. It is more like the way it behaves in the early stages of a bear market, when hope still reigns.

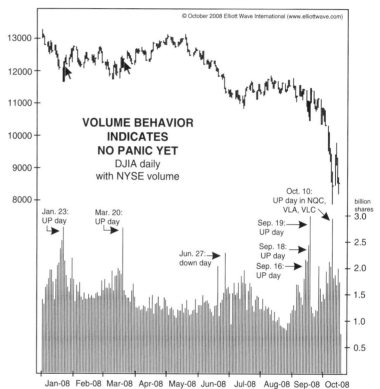

Special Report:
The Dispiriting of Speculation

Over the course of the mania years, Elliott Wave International has uncovered various indicators and averages that gauge the flow of speculative juices. Based on several key measures, *The Elliott Wave Financial Forecast* stated that the mania peaked in 2000 as the Grand Supercycle bull market in stocks ended. After the Cycle wave a decline, wave b brought a more muted strain of the mania back to life. The dissipation of upside strength is shown by the EWI Bubble Stock Index (next page), an index of eight high fliers—TASR, SIRI, ABLE, BOOM, PACT, TZOO, LOUD and ROXI—EWI created under the headline, "Have Catchy Symbol, Will Rocket" in December 2004. It turns out that December 2004 marked a price peak that was down more than 60% from the index's March 2000 high. Still, the right chart shows that the gains were pretty spectacular. The mania's slackening hold is evidenced by the subsequent steady decline in our Bubble Stock Index and a complete absence of any new boom stocks. In September, some triple-digit returns did top the leading gainers list, but all of these stocks had been decimated in prior weeks. The difference between these two groups is important. Instead of idea stocks capturing investor imaginations as they did in 2000 and 2004, the action is in fallen giants such as Fannie Mae

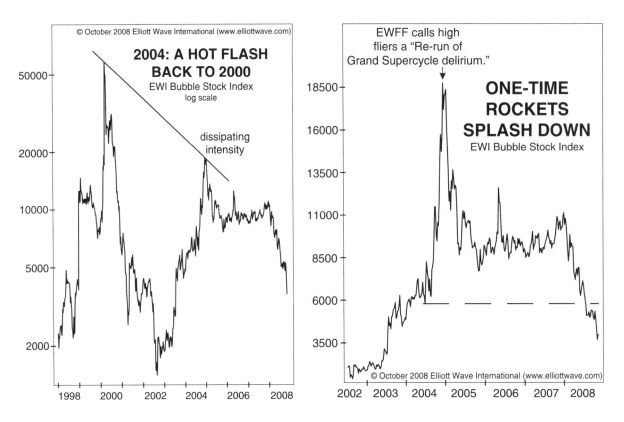

and AIG. Speculators' emphasis is on getting everything back rather than hitting it big on a great new concept. EWFF covered this bear market impulse and its tightening grip on the stock market in the Investor Psychology section of recent issues. Meanwhile, the Bubble Stock Index has broken back below the trendline on the chart showing that the most explosive part of its rise off the 2002 lows has been given back.

A Bulletin Board Message

The OTC Bulletin Board dollar and share volume shows that the dollar value of trading activity in the riskiest of financial shares, those that are not traded on any financial exchange, topped in 2000. A lower peak in dollar volume (bottom line) followed in early 2004, but share volume (top line) zoomed to an all-time high in 2006. In other words, the most aggressive plungers were churning through shares like never before as late as 2006; but the lesser *value* of those shares shows a net dissipation in speculative froth. The chart also shows that both measures are now falling in tandem. In the top line, the break of the trendline from 2001 shows that, after years of trying to scoop up over-the-counter bargains, investors are throwing in the towel.

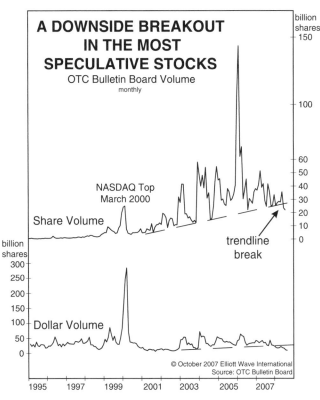

Risk Becomes a Scary Proposition

In May 2006, EWFF showed several key charts depicting a transformation from a voracious risk appetite among investors to rising risk aversion. A key to our case was the gold/silver price ratio. Under the headline "Risk Overtakes Reward," EWFF called for the gold/silver ratio to bottom and push to an initial target of 62:1 before moving higher. As it turns out, the ratio had bottomed the month before, in April 2006. The gold/silver ratio chart (on page 99) shows how its gradual rise turned into an outright explosion in August. With a recent high of almost 80:1, the ratio continues to blast skyward. The deepening aversion is now being widely observed. On October 13, the Wall Street Journal reported that investors are "abandoning anything with the tiniest hint of risk."

Another keyhole through which subscribers spied this reversal ahead of time is the yen carry trade. In early 2007, EWFF identified 2007 as the "The Year of Financial Flameout" and cited the "carry trade's role in expanding world-wide leverage," as a critical part of the forecast. In September 2007, we further noted that the euro/yen cross-rate was "an excellent proxy for the yen carry trade because speculators are able to borrow yen at extremely low rates and convert them to other currencies for investment in higher-yielding assets elsewhere." According to this measure, the global "reach for yield" held up into the middle of 2008, completing a pristine Elliott wave from 2000. This ratio is now making up for lost time. It may take out the 2000 low in short order.

Volatility Is Taking Off

Trading goes wild in a mania, but our study of history shows that the initial plunge following a mania's completion is even wilder. This is why we called for an upward spike in volatility in May: "The market should produce record-high volatility by any and all measures before wave **c** is over." At least one measure, the VIX index, is already registering an impressive spike. The Dow Jones Industrial Average finished the week of October 5-10 with an 18% decline, the worst weekly performance in its 112-year history, ending with the first one-day, 1,000-point swing in its history. On Monday, October 13 "gloom turned to euphoria" and the Dow gained 11%. This is the unprecedented volatility EWFF anticipated.

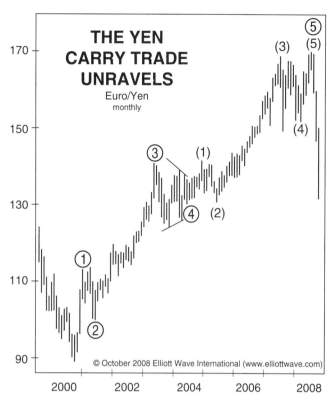

THE YEN CARRY TRADE UNRAVELS
Euro/Yen
monthly

© October 2008 Elliott Wave International (www.elliottwave.com)

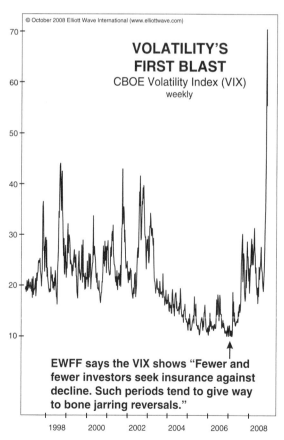

© October 2008 Elliott Wave International (www.elliottwave.com)

VOLATILITY'S FIRST BLAST
CBOE Volatility Index (VIX)
weekly

EWFF says the VIX shows "Fewer and fewer investors seek insurance against decline. Such periods tend to give way to bone jarring reversals."

Don't be fooled by the buying stampedes. They are a big bear market's method of generating a sense of relief, which invariably fuels further selling. The volatility should settle in for a long while and re-write the record books by a wide margin.

The Debt Bubble Within the Bubble

Leverage greases the gears of commerce and exchange on the way up, and its departure from the scene invariably extends and accentuates the bust. As stocks rose to their final peak in October 2007, EWFF pointed out a small but critical divergence:

> Despite the renewed enthusiasm among investors, there remain many subtle signs that the market is losing steam. There is the NYSE margin debt data. The total for August was $331 billion. This is down substantially from the new record of $381.4 billion in July.

The updated chart shows margin debt's early reversal and its continued descent. The first chart on the next page depicts a less subtle sign of a full-blown credit market rout in the expanding spread in yield between the 3-month Libor rate and the 3-month U.S. Treasury bill rate (the Ted Spread). In January when the spread was a little over 140 basis points, EWFF called the surge a new bull market in fear. It is now more than three times that high and well beyond the record high that was set during the crash of 1987. If there is a wooden stake that can be driven through the heart of the mania, it's the "credit market seizure" represented by this spike. "The money markets are completely broken," says a fixed income strategist. "There is no market anymore," says another. The Wall Street Journal adds, "The most worrying aspect of the crisis is a growing reluctance among financial institutions to offer basic loans that are the lifeblood of the economic system." Remember in the very early stages of wave **c**, credit cushioned the impact of falling stock prices. In November, *The Elliott Wave Theorist* observed, "The bear market in stocks is raging, but thanks to the system-wide credit binge, almost no one can see it." Without leverage, the financial markets and the economy will surely fall prey to the new conservatism predicted in *Conquer the Crash* and so frequently anticipated in these pages over the last several months.

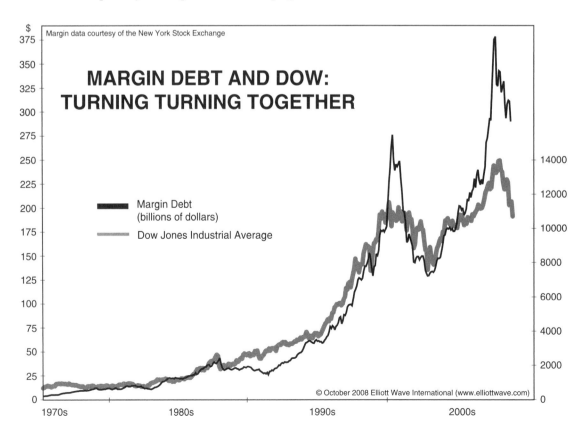

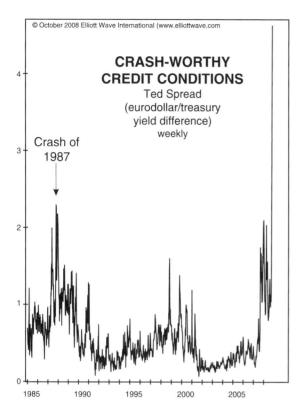

CRASH-WORTHY
CREDIT CONDITIONS
Ted Spread
(eurodollar/treasury
yield difference)
weekly

Crash of 1987

© October 2008 Elliott Wave International (www.elliottwave.com

LUXURY'S
LOST LUSTER
Merrill Lynch Lifestyle Index
weekly

Data courtesy of Bloomberg
© October 2008 Elliott Wave International (www.elliottwave.com)

How About a Luxurious Bowl of Soup?

One key mania meter, the thirst for luxuries, actually surpassed the extremes of 2000 by a long shot. Merrill Lynch's Lifestyle Index, which is an aggregation of luxury company shares, surpassed its March 2000 peak in March 2003. Its October 2007 peak of 194 marked a 115% gain from its March 2000 high. It also held up longer than the Dow, topping on October 31, 2007. But it is now falling harder than the overall market, down 52% compared with a high-to-low Dow decline of 44%. A decline back below 100 will erase all of its gains since December 2003 and put it below the level that Merrill Lynch used as its January 2000 starting point. The effects are clearly starting to be felt, as the October 9 issue of The Wall Street Journal asks: "Is Bling Over?" The article answers in the affirmative noting that luxury executives are themselves "handling the financial crisis" by "selling the yacht." "Luxury stores such as Saks suffered big sale drops" as "American shoppers went into hiding in September." On the record down day—in Dow points—of September 29, the only gainer in the S&P 500 was Campbell Soup Co. A new bare-bones mentality is clearly putting luxury on the fashion sidelines, probably for some time to come.

November 2008

Sometimes, it's not enough to know history or to know the markets; you have to know how they work together. All indicators have to be measured within the context in which they occur. With respect to sentiment readings, this means knowing that they can act differently in bull and bear phases. In early August, when the Investors Intelligence Advisors' survey showed only slightly more bulls than bears, *The Elliott Wave Financial Forecast* stated, "For all we know, these marginally positive readings may be the new 'wild optimism.'" The Dow Industrials subsequently declined 33.7%. The resulting bearish readings, such as the historically high 61% bearish reading in the American Association of Individual Investors survey, won't necessarily mark a bottom during the next leg of the bear market.

Another reason to expect greater pessimistic sentiment extremes is related to EWI's all-the-same-market theme. In September, *The Elliott Wave Theorist* illustrated this trend's powerful resumption "on the downside." The updated chart shows that the laggard commodity indexes are now catching up *fast*. There's just no way that *all* the markets that generated so much optimism last May can reverse in one fell, deflationary swoop without stretching sentiment extremes past the limits that are known to most investors. Also, the unwavering vibrancy of the buy-and-hold and buy-the-dip investment stance reveals that a bullish market psychology is intact to an extent that the survey numbers simply do not show. Consider, for instance, the tried and increasingly debilitating strategy of diversification. With the market smash extending across every investment front but cash, one might think that this concept would at least be challenged by now. But it remains a virtually uncontested truism among market advisors and their followers: "If you want to minimize your losses, hang in there and ensure that there is plenty of diversification across your entire investment portfolio." "Diversify, diversify, diversify," say recent articles in MarketWatch.com, The Reading [Pa.] Eagle, The Salinas Californian, the Southtown Star, LocalTechWire.com, istockAnalayst.com (twice) and Television Week. "Diversify," commands the nation's largest daily newspaper. "Let's be honest: The only diversification strategy that worked well in the third quarter was adding money market securities to the mix. But diversification usually works." "Usually" is a dangerous word in the investment game. It means it works until it doesn't, at which time it almost always becomes a catastrophic failure. *This is that time.* "Owning an array of investments is financial suicide during deflation," states *Conquer the Crash*.

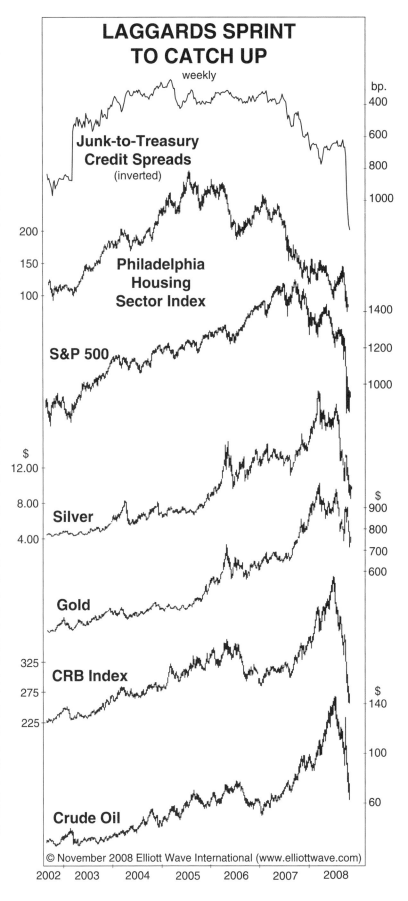

LAGGARDS SPRINT
TO CATCH UP
weekly

Junk-to-Treasury Credit Spreads (inverted)

Philadelphia Housing Sector Index

S&P 500

Silver

Gold

CRB Index

Crude Oil

© November 2008 Elliott Wave International (www.elliottwave.com)

2002 2003 2004 2005 2006 2007 2008

ASMI Confirms the Turn

In December 2007, EWT introduced the All-the-Same-Markets Index, which combines the trends of all major investment classes: stocks, real estate, precious metals, commodities, bonds and foreign currencies; that is, everything but dollar cash. Three months later, the March 14, 2008 issue noted that a "new extreme in bullish opinion is now occurring toward the investments that are most strongly considered [to be] inflation hedges—gold, silver, oil, and the inverted dollar index." We cautioned, "But this spell will break, too, and when it does *the ASMI will say so.*"

The ASMI peaked in July along with oil. The event we needed to see to confirm the end of investors' obsession with all these investments, driven by inflation (yes, including the ocean of issued bonds), was whenever "this index turns down and breaks the lower trendline of the channel that extends back to 2002." As you can see in the chart, this event has unquestionably occurred.

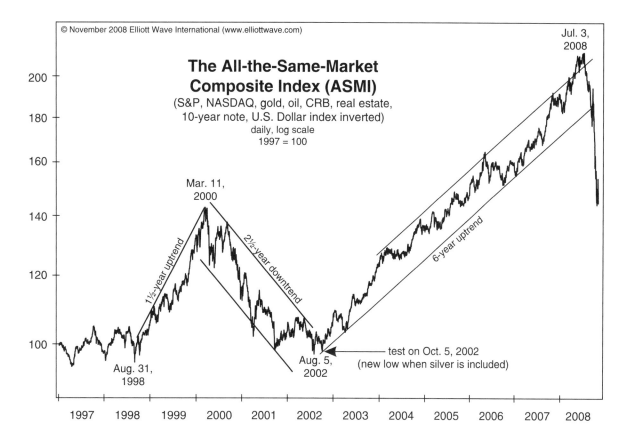

The All-the-Same-Market Composite Index (ASMI)
(S&P, NASDAQ, gold, oil, CRB, real estate, 10-year note, U.S. Dollar index inverted)
daily, log scale
1997 = 100

© November 2008 Elliott Wave International (www.elliottwave.com)

December 2008

Animal Spirits Recede Further

The October Special Report showed how many of the stocks that contributed so much to the wave **b** rally of 2002-2007 are leading the way lower. They continued to set the downside pace in November, as all of the speculative leaders such as EWI's Hedge Fund Enablers and Bubble Stock indexes beat the major averages to new lows in November.

[A] sandbagged former rocket booster is shown in this chart of Google. When Google debuted as an IPO in August 2004, EWFF called it a "speculative focal point." Like wave **b** itself, the ride lasted longer and carried higher than we expected, but the one-year decline of 67% shows that the upside of the ride is over. A suit by the U.S. Justice Department confirms that the jig is up—for all stocks. Just as the U.S. Justice Department attacked Microsoft for antitrust violations a few weeks after the NASDAQ's peak in 2000, Google must now "rein in ambitious goals for

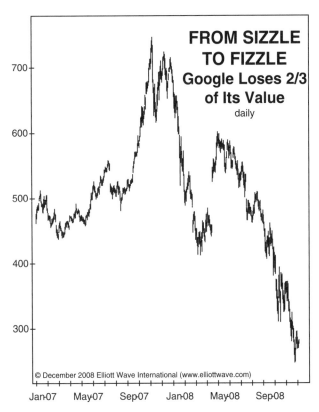

FROM SIZZLE TO FIZZLE
Google Loses 2/3 of Its Value
daily

© December 2008 Elliott Wave International (www.elliottwave.com)

expansion" thanks to the Justice Department action. The blocking of its proposed marriage with Yahoo! signals the end of the line and fits perfectly with the punitive social side effects that accompany the start of every big decline in social mood. EWT's May 2000 "Socionomic Perspective on the Microsoft Case" explained the dynamic very clearly: high degree bear market declines bring "governmental attacks against highly successful enterprises. In fact, they typically start with a major attack against the most successful enterprise of the time." Google is clearly the "most successful" major corporate beneficiary of the wave **b** rally, as it gained 770% from its August 2004 IPO to its November 2007 peak.

It will probably be the focus of further attacks, just as RCA, IBM and Microsoft were in the wake of the big peaks of 1929, 1968 and 2000, respectively. What the exact nature of this pressure will be we cannot say, but Google shares are already anticipating it. On November 5, the *Short Term Update* spotted a fourth-wave triangle in Google share prices and projected a decline from about $350 to $260 "and possibly lower." It collapsed to $247 a few days later. The potential for still lower prices is very high. In fact, GOOG should eventually fall below its initial August 2004 offering price of $85. As it does, public focus will shift from Google's benevolence and innovation during the boom to a disdain for its reputed ruthlessness and control during the bust.

Chapter 2

When All Minds Think (Dream) Alike

Technological wonder and the "demographic destiny" of baby boomers burns the message of a "New Economy" deep into the psyche of investors. Excitement based on the promise of the Internet, the "gyro power machine" and countless other technology schemes rises to a fever pitch in 2000. In the wake of the peak, the "stealth launch," in which the business of the offerer is not revealed, becomes a "standard technique" [for] "imbuing mystique." Academics take the bait, too, offering study after study arguing the merits of stock splits, emerging markets and buying and holding stocks "'til death do us part." The new intoxicant is a "heady mix of ignorance, arrogance and extrapolation." The "Great American Dream," housing, picks up where technology leaves off in 2002. Finally, in the end, high finance takes on the razzle-dazzle of the Great Mania, just in time for the final peak.

July 1995

Professors from Wright State University in Dayton, Ohio have just published a study arguing that there is no reason ever to delay stock purchases; even averaging in over time is stupid. If you get any money at all, it should go immediately into stocks no matter where you are in the cycle. "Chances of [a bear market] are pretty slim," says the Prof., and anyway, it doesn't matter; stocks always come back to new highs. A report from the University of Michigan's School of Business Administration concludes that timing the stock market is foolish because if you had bought stocks thirty years ago, you would have made lots of money. For some mysterious reason, there is no comparable report on the bond market, the Nikkei or silver. What these reports actually observe is simply that stocks have gone up for a long time. Their conclusion and advice amount to the following: "Stocks have gone up so much for so long that you should run out and buy them now." This is a siren song to ruin.

September 1995

Anecdotal evidence of a long term extreme in bullish stock market sentiment continues to pour in. On almost a daily basis, new studies assert the value of the buy-and-hold approach. Of course, none of the studies acknowledge that it is a retrospective value in one specific market, and therefore worthless. One study shows that since 1974, those who purchased stocks at a precise stock market high prior to the onset of a big decline — no matter how bad — came out on top in a few years time. So, "Even When They're Bad, They're Good," headlined a major newspaper. The article concluded that "the most important move for investors is just to get into the market — by whatever method — and stay there." Because this particular argument has only now been made, the sentence truly communicates (after the market has risen 726% in 21 years), "Get into the market now and stay there."

Fidelity's three top-selling funds all invest heavily in technology stocks, which have been the most recent focus of the overall stock mania. Indeed, ten of the top-performing equity funds with an average 65% exposure to technology issues didn't even exist last year. The August 28 cover of a major business weekly shows that the press affection for technology stocks continues as well. According to its headlines, software is "A Money Machine That's Firing On All Fronts," "Cyberspace Is The Klondike of High Tech," and "More Is More." For those readers that might miss the point, the magazine includes an editorial to stress the "value under the tech surge... Chips ain't tulips."

October 1995
Technology Manias and Their Aftermaths

How significant are high-tech manias? Technology historians refer to 1835 as the year of the "electrical euphoria." The condition was brought on by Michael Faraday's use of a horseshoe magnet, copper disc and wire to produce electricity. The public got so wrapped up in this new ability to control what the papers referred to as the "magic fluid" that all manner of eggbeaters, apple peelers and cleaning machines were invented. Many even sent the new current coursing through their bodies as a cure for ailments great and small. 1835 also saw the installation of the first air conditioner in England's House of Commons, the production of the first photograph and the invention of the reaping machine. In 1836, Samuel Morse sent his first Morse code message a distance of 50 feet. To handle the flood of new inventions, the U.S. Patent Office was opened in 1837. A host of advances like blast furnaces for the mass production of iron made the nation-wide implementation of existing technologies like railroads, power looms, indoor plumbing and telegraphy possible in the years that followed 1835. Some claimed that an electric motor would one day approach infinite velocity. How did the market respond? Its high in May 1835 marked the end of Grand Supercycle I, which was followed by an 80% drop in the averages in seven years and two back-to-back depressions. Stock prices (at least of companies that survived) did not return to 1835 levels for twenty-eight years.

From 1966 through late 1968, as the public embraced the stock market, technological wonder ran rampant. Futurists with visions of colonies on the moon, the sea floor and Mars were routinely quoted in the business press. Public fascination with such forecasts was reflected in the popularity of a prime time TV show, *The Twenty-First Century* hosted by Walter Cronkite, and a popular book, *The Year 2000*, which anticipated the conversion of sea water to drinking water and the use of artificial moons. One project that caught the imagination of reporters was "Probe," a think tank of 27 top scientists established by TRW Inc. The team used existing technologies to project moon bases by 1980, a vertical takeoff aircraft for individuals by 1977, undersea farming by 1981, and low-cost plastic injection mold housing by the mid-1980s. Of the 335 predictions TRW released to the public, not a single one came true. Six years later, the Dow was down 45% and many of the most popular technology companies among stock traders were bankrupt. In mid-1983, a lesser technology stock craze peaked. The stocks broke down six months ahead of the Dow Industrials and foreshadowed a Dow correction of 17%. Many technology stocks ultimately fell more than 70%. They did not return to a position of relative strength for ten years.

The latest run in high tech shares has been accompanied by some notions that are no less fantastic than those held in 1835 and 1968. The Internet is said to be "the most powerful force for change since the car." Medical researchers are purporting cures for aging.

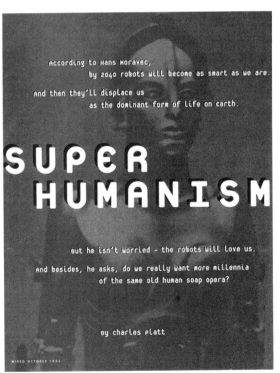

WIRED, October 1995

A company of engineers in San Diego is trying to raise $2 million to harness the torque of the spinning Earth. The prospective inventors of the "gyro-power machine" say their giant flywheel will convert the rotation of the Earth into all the power the planet needs. A Carnegie Mellon robotics professor has concluded that robots will be as smart as humans by the year 2040. He envisions a society in which machine-run corporations do all the work and generate enough wealth that people will be born into retirement. Linear and emotional thinking is what futurists use to forecast, which is why their forecasts never work out, at least not in the time frame they envision. While not always right, at least *The Elliott Wave Theorist* recognizes these events for what they are: a reflection of social mood, which in turn is a basis upon which useful forecasts can be made. This euphoric mood will lead to a stock price decline and economic depression as surely as the next depression in mood will lead to recovery and boom.

December 1995

A Newsweek cover profile makes Bill Gates sound like Thomas Edison, Henry Ford and Elvis Presley rolled into one. "It's him: the King of Comdex, if not the computer industry, if not the future itself. The richest man on the planet, and maybe the smartest: William Henry Gates III." Anchorman Tom Brokaw adds that walking through the world's most important computer trade show with Gates is "like walking through the Vatican with the pope." Gates' new book, *The Road Ahead*, is as bullish as an early Beatles song. Unfortunately, the likelihood is that it will have more significance to the road we're about to leave behind.

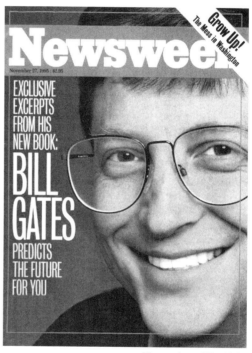

November 27, 1995

March 1996

A new study provides the "soothing news" that fund shareholders do not flee stock funds "on the first significant decline." (Of course not; they wait until the bottom.) On February 23, financial television reported yet another academic study that has retrospectively discovered positive stock market returns over every 30-year period.

May 1996

In the U.S., after six decades, landmark legislative initiatives have repealed several major laws that were enacted following the Supercycle degree low of 1932. The "freedom to farm" act was billed as the most sweeping set of farm reforms since the 1930s. With its passage, Congress will phase out subsidies paid to farmers for not farming. The bad news is that it will do so by paying them over the next seven years whether they farm or not. Nothing prevents Congress from reinstituting farm subsidies when the seven years end.

It is also reported that Congress removed a 60-year barrier to free trade in the American telecommunications markets. While it is true that they did vote to do so by a 25-to-1 margin, it is also true that the barriers had already been circumvented by technology. Before the bill was passed, long distance calls were being placed on the Internet at ridiculously low costs. Established phone companies admit that the technology to do so will only improve over time, which is why some are already pushing for re-regulation. When the law was passed, Vice President Gore cited as his goal "a computer in every home," an ambition that calls to mind the "chicken in every pot and car in every garage" motto of the Hooverites in 1928. The government's sanction of the information revolution is similar to Hoover's "New Day," which was also a glorious vision based on the economic and social potential of developing technology. As in 1929, the promise is likely to be met, but the blow to the existing business infrastructure is likely to be far more serious than is presently anticipated.

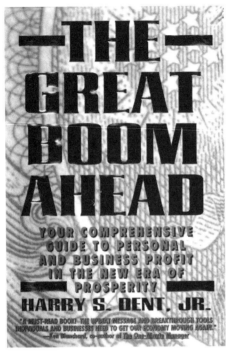

FOREIGN AFFAIRS

Shockproof: The End of the Financial Crisis
by Ethan B. Kapstein

The past year witnessed three of the most dramatic financial collapses since the Third World debt crisis of 1982. The meltdown of the Mexican peso in December 1994, the failure of the 233-year-old Barings Bank last February, and Daiwa Bank's $1 billion loss in November—apparently at the hands of a single trader—would all seem to point to a financial system that has spun out of control.

But last year the markets responded to these financial crises with little more than a "ho hum." In fact, the U.S. stock market boomed, and interest rates around the world declined.

What explains this sea change in the reaction of international markets to financial shocks? Over the past 20 years the leading economic powers have created a regulatory structure that has permitted the financial markets to continue toward globalization without the threat of systemic collapse. The elimination of financial contagion has required painstaking efforts by dedicated public servants.

January/February 1996

July 1996

It is all we can do at Elliott Wave International to remain courteous when reading from countless sources that the stock market will rise virtually uninterrupted until the year 2015 because that is when the "baby boomers" will reach retirement age. A book advancing this theory has sold tens of thousands of copies. An economics professor at Stanford calls the period until then "salad days." A finance professor has won a prize for describing the trend. A "guest scholar" at the Brookings Institution says, "The market right now is rigged for growth. For the next decade, the stock market is going to be the best game in town." Echoing these widespread sentiments, a TV anchor recently said in response to an analyst who dared speak a word of caution, "But all these boomers buying stocks! It could go on for decades!" This demographic argument has gained such widespread acceptance in recent months that hardly a magazine or newswire has failed to feature it. In response, a fund has just been created that promises to stay fully invested for the next twenty years and then sell at the top!

The argument is ludicrously weak. It is based on virtually no research. Even corner-cutting cycle analysts insist on at least two full revolutions before conjecturing on the emergence of a cycle. The "case" for a demographics-propelled market hasn't even got one full cycle to show, making it little more than an assertion. If population increases meant rising investment markets, then India and China would be rich by now. The claim is Wall Street mythology at its dumbest and most dangerous, trotted out at a time that will serve to keep potential skeptics invested. How else could you rationalize staying invested in a market yielding 2% unless you were assured that it would continue to rise for another twenty years?

Investors' belief in a long-term fundamental change in market valuation (reminiscent of 1929's permanent plateau) has grown exponentially. A brokerage firm report titled "A New Era" argues that a "paradigm shift" has taken place. The report states that new technology, legislative changes, changes in management practices and consumer lifestyles have come together to create an "obvious" environment of investment opportunity. With no historical evidence to support its contention of a great new age, the report amounts to a purely speculative list of expectations. According to the WSJ, "the explosive growth in mutual fund pension investments is transforming the economy itself."

In late May, this headline actually appeared in The Wall Street Journal: "Risk Aversion As a Behavioral Problem." The story included an economist's charge that holding any non-equity investments was "a policy for cowards." (He's so brave for saying this in 1996; we wonder where he was in 1974.) Most of the media extol the virtues of stocks. "Social Security surpluses need to be invested in stocks," demands USA Today. Foreign Affairs magazine declares the world's financial markets "Shockproof." The article, subtitled "The End of the Financial Crisis," argues that a 20-year project to construct a global regulatory structure has brought about a "sea change in the reaction of international markets to financial shocks." "Painstaking efforts by dedicated public servants" has eliminated "financial contagion," so there can never be another global financial crisis.

August 1996

'Til Death Do Us Part With Stocks

The nation's business paper says, "The last thing older people should do when the market takes a dive is panic and sell stocks pell-mell. In fact, there is every reason to be in the market for the rest of your life."

The idea that "a new generation of savers has embraced stocks" is even turning up in obscure medical journals. The June 24 issue of Medical Economics argues that the new, enlightened saver will "hold for the long term." According to "The New Upbeat Rules For Stock Investing," price/earnings ratios of 20 are no problem, low book values are unimportant, and yields are a thing of the past. "Today's buyers care more about capital gains." The old rule: "Watch out for a big crash"; the new rule: "Crash, schmash. Buy on downturns."

The average investor does not need these reminders; he knows the new rules. As stocks briefly collapsed in July, commentators noted that holders of 401(k)s, dividend reinvestment plans (DRIPs) and other "autopilot investment programs" were bullish by default. One called this condition the "psychology of staying put." Investors whose plans are in place don't have the energy to "stop buying," and "that may be the pillar that keeps this market from collapsing."

New Upbeat Rules For Stock Investing

Going by traditional measures, the bull market should be ending. But maybe traditional measures are no longer a good guide.

OLD RULE	NEW RULE
Watch out for big crash.	Crash, schmash. Buy on downturns.
When price-earnings head above 15, watch out.	Relax. With inflation low, P-E's can top 20.
A company's share price rises & falls along with the value of hard assets in the books.	Book values matter less than a company's ability to produce earnings.
When dividend yields fall below 3 percent, investors will start bailing out of the market.	Forget yield; today's buyers care more about capital gains.

Medical Economics, July 1996

Technology Manias And Their Aftermaths: Update

The November 1995 issue of *The Elliott Wave Theorist* explored the relationship between popular technology manias and stocks. We found that terminal stock rallies back through 1835 have been bound up in elaborate technological fantasies. The New York Times has even bought into the craze with a magazine piece on "How To Get to Mars (and Make Millions)." After 35 years, a "Privatized Space Program is Near." Aerospace companies are expected to scale back NASA and move quickly to make profits from satellites, space labs and even tourism. Other "space entrepreneurs" are planning to launch human DNA into space because "people will pay $45 on the hope that an alien civilization will clone them some day." The $10 million X-Prize will go to the first group to put three humans on a 100-kilometer sub-orbital flight. Space artifacts have become "a hot collectible." A new book, *The Next 500 Years*, says we will mine asteroids, colonize Mars and make love in lunar hotels. NBC has unveiled a new TV show called *Scan*. The series will focus on the way technology changes lives.

September 1996

As EWT has pointed out, the bull market tendency toward inclusionism extends even to embracing extraterrestrials. Not only science fiction, but science, too, reflects the euphoric trend of our times. Earlier this year, scientists revealed the discovery of two distant planets that raise the "likelihood that life exists elsewhere in the universe, perhaps even intelligent life." This month, scientists found "what appear to be the chemical and fossil remains of a microscopic organism that lived on Mars 3.6 billion years ago." Never mind that organic molecules found in the rock are routinely found in meteorites. The discovery fanned a deep societal need to "encounter alien life."

Less than six months ago, a Time headline wondered, "Is There Life in Outer Space?" The August 19 issue answered: "Life on Mars." Carl Sagan said the discovery will stand "as a turning point in human history, suggesting that life exists...throughout this magnificent universe." To many headline writers, it didn't matter that Sagan and others said the results still need to be verified. The President immediately called a press conference to announce a "bipartisan space summit" and report that two Martian probes would go out before the end of the year. NASA officials are talking about a manned mission to Mars. Recall that serious talk of a manned mission to the moon took place in wave ⑤ of III in the 1960s; the actual fulfillment of that vision occurred a year after the second stock market top of 1968.

November 1996

You must have seen a widely published chart called "The Spending Wave: 44-46 Year Birth Lag." It first appeared in one of the "buy-and-hold" books that now fill entire shelves in bookstores across America and has been reprinted countless times since. The chart superimposes the number of middle aged Americans produced by the Baby Boom over the bull market from 1982 and infers that the force behind the stock market is the growing sector of 44- to 46-year-olds. Since this trend runs to new highs for another dozen years, it is implied that the bull market has more than a decade left to run. Echoing other presentations, one editorial noted, "So the long-term trend of the stock market is up. We'd heard this before but had never seen it presented so persuasively." It says that this self-evident "demand component" can legitimately be expected to cause further price increases.

We have several observations. First, in order to claim the existence of a cyclic correlation, a researcher should require some evidence of it. Kondratieff enthusiasts are routinely dismissed by economists who say that "four cycles are not enough to prove anything." This chart begins in 1955

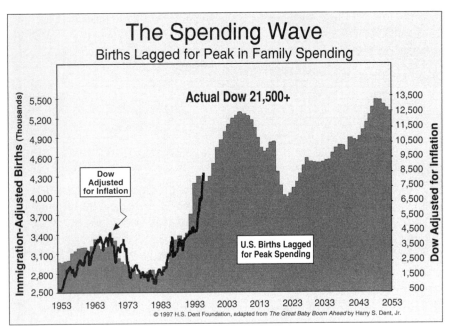

© 1997 H.S. Dent Foundation, adapted from *The Great Baby Boom Ahead* by Harry S. Dent, Jr.

and doesn't even last for one complete cycle. Second, the birth trends it depicts are also quite well correlated with concurrent inflation-adjusted stock market trends, which suggests that people simply have more babies in bull markets, when their energy and optimism wax. As usual, fundamentalists have inverted the actual causality. Finally, we suspect that the real message of this chart is not what it says, but the fact that it is everywhere. It is another aspect of the ubiquitous "new era" talk, which is a reflection of optimism.

February 1997

Whole economic frameworks are emerging to support the prospect of uninterruptible prosperity. For instance, the "new growth theory" says that knowledge, not money or history or plant is the engine of economic growth. The theory "offers a promise of 'increasing returns' as knowledge feeds on itself," or so says a front page story in the January 21 issue of The Wall Street Journal. Authorities are embracing this vision. Since November, at least 16 states, "growing tired of gathering acorns for an economic winter that many believe will never come," have or will cut unemployment insurance taxes. "Their plans," says one news report, "grow from the belief, voiced recently by President Clinton and others, that the U.S. economy has moved beyond the boom-bust cycles of the past."

The Business Cycle is Tamed, Many Say

THE WALL STREET JOURNAL, November 15, 1996

Business Cycle of Booms, Busts Tamed, Some Execs Say

THE DENVER POST
November 11, 1996

Has Boom-Bust Cycle Really Gone?

The business-cycle-is-dead school believes there has been important structural changes in the economy. For one thing, widespread use of computers makes possible a fine-tuning of stocks so that waves of inflation-inducing understocking and recession inducing overstocking are things of the past.

The Sunday Times London, December 1, 1996

ECONOMISTS EXPECT LITTLE TROUBLE IN PARADISE
BUSINESSWEEK
December 30, 1996

Can Nation's Economy Be All Boom, No Bust?
Some see no end to the country's financial expansion

The Orange County Register, November 17, 1996

U.S. Sails on Tranquil Economic Seas
Recessions No Longer Seem Inevitable as Nation, Policymakers React Quickly to Change

The U.S. economy, after more than a quarter-century of painful ups and downs, appears to have entered a new period of stability in which recessions no longer seem inevitable

The Washington Post
December 2, 1996

An Exceptionally Virtuous Circle of Expansion

FINANCIAL TIMES, November 20, 1996

The International Political Economy "After" the Business Cycle

The Journal of Social, Political and Economic Studies, Fall 1996

Is Business Cycle Tamed? Yes, Optimists Crowing — The Salt Lake Tribune, November 24, 1996

Debating A Recession-Proof Economy — The Atlanta Journal-Constitution, December 8, 1996

April 1997

"This is an important historical moment," declares a Harvard economist. (We agree, but....) "Economic growth will raise the living standards of more people in more parts of the world than at any prior time in history." This time, writers decided not even to hedge the bet, as the article itself contains few disclaimers to the "golden age thesis." While "economic thinkers" see the potential for some setbacks along the way, "The process of economic integration and elimination of controls on international capital are irreversible," says a Berkeley professor.

They are right that economic freedom "is the best thing for prosperity that you can possibly have," but when so many scholars, analysts and global visionaries agree, it is likely that they are describing the virtues of a bull market that has already happened. The seemingly endless article goes on and on, blithely painting a picture of a perfect world, quoting one professor and guru after another. "It is breadth that makes this possible third golden age so momentous," says one visionary. The article also tells the story of Intel chief Andrew Grove, who sniffed at his "new-ventures chief" for bringing him a $50 million investment idea. "Come back when you can tell me how you're going to invest $1 billion." The article closes with a word from a "skeptical" financier, who nevertheless agrees that the new boom "might last a century."

May 1997

A California finance professor offers this tip: "You have to set up a mechanistic system to stop yourself from selling."

August 1997

This past month brought the great Mars landing. When Pathfinder's first Martian image was flashed at NASA headquarters, cameras captured a room full of NASA engineers exploding with cheers and applause as the Beatles' "Twist and Shout" blared in the background. The scientists' "infectious enthusiasm" was said to have "turned all our heads upward." "Marsmania" produced more "new era in space" headlines than any extraterrestrial event since the moon landing in 1969, within months of the last social mood peak of Supercycle degree. "Space crazy" entrepreneurs are gearing up to "mine asteroids." All kinds of companies are making rockets, and investors are committing to the dream. "We're finally at a point where people are plowing their own money in." Euphoric social mood, say hello to the market.

September 1997

Have you heard of "stock-split fever?" According to the August 18 New York Times, both "ordinary" and "sophisticated" investors "believe that [stock] splits augur well for a company's future, and they quickly buy those shares on such news." We first noticed this affront to the natural order in markets last December when Microsoft gapped higher on news of a stock split. The gap came not on the announcement of the split, but on the actual split date, even though the news of it was obviously in the market. Since then, the apparent success of this strategy has created a new growth industry. "In this roaring bull market, stock splits are today's most exciting way to profit," says one of many "real-time stock split" paging services now advertising in Investor's Business Daily. Another "Stock Split Alert" has diversified into providing other "major market moving news" like "buybacks." "Beeper madness" has swept through the options crowd.

December 1997

Archetypal Symbols Involved in the Mania

(by Anne Crittenden)

The particular archetypal idea or image that enraptures people's consciousness in the stock market today is ascension or magical flight. It is not hard to see why this should be so. The market graphs have been in an overall uptrend since the Great Depression. Then, since about 1985, they have been accelerating upwards in a gravity defying way. The human mind is very susceptible to the allure of this upwardly vaulting line. We long to be able to rise up out of this world of work, suffering and death into a heavenly state of freedom, ease and bliss. The stock market is today's magic stairway by which people imagine they will ascend into a heaven where all their dreams will be fulfilled, and they and their families will live happily ever after.

While the stock market as a whole promises magical ascension, the high technology stocks embody the archetype of magical flight quite literally. Jung would have been fascinated by the magnetic appeal, to today's investors, of the high technology stocks. He always held that the presence of what he called the "cosmic element" was a sure sign of the activation of an archetype of the collective unconscious. By cosmic element he meant anything that suggested the attainment of infinity, such as extraordinary angles of flight, enormous speed, or vast extension. In today's mania, the high tech stocks obviously exhibit such "cosmic" qualities, embodying fantasies of unlimited power. The vast amount of money committed to these stocks certainly testifies to the power of this particular archetype. (A recent PBS television program interviewed a suburban lady who has put the family fortune into two technology stocks whose names she cannot quite recall. There can be little doubt that the collective unconscious is in the driver's seat there!)

In Greek myth, Daedalus, master of technology, made wings for his son Icarus. He warned Icarus that the glue would melt if he flew too high, but Icarus ignored the danger, his wings fell off, and he crashed.

March 1998

In January, a Barron's headline boldly claimed: "Demography is Destiny." We were regaled yet again with the argument that stocks will continue higher for at least another decade as 9.7 million Americans turn 45 between now and 2008. Paul Montgomery (Universal Economics) responded in a letter to the editor, noting that the $146 billion this segment is expected to bring to the market is nothing compared to the $450 billion the market took away in just one day last fall. Instead of calculating what boomers can do for the stock market, Montgomery concluded, boomers should consider "what the market can do to them." Proponents volleyed back with another Barron's feature ("Triple Play") on February 16. A long-time advocate of the demographics theory discovered another $25 trillion in inevitable stock market flows. The author's new study, "The Big Shift — Barely Begun," asserts that the stock market will triple again over the next 15 years simply by assuming that it will rise at a historical growth rate of 8% a year.

We point out that if GDP were simultaneously to maintain its comparatively meager historical growth rate of 2.5% a year, it would bring stock market valuation to 500% of GDP. The figure as of September was 125%, 50% higher than the old record set in August 1929. Are we to be concerned with such things? "With an air of satisfaction," the article notes, "The nice thing about demographics is that you're not wrong unless there's a plague." So to some, the proposed relationship of demographics to the stock market is not a theory but a law of nature: the bull market as manifest destiny.

Recent statistics show that baby boomers are not saving much, but they are saving differently. What used to go into the bank or a second home now goes right into the stock market. We think this change in behavior illustrates Montgomery's point: Investment is based on emotional, not mechanical, decision-making. We think that the demographics theory will ultimately prove to have been a rationalization of an emotional state.

April 1998

The elation over record stock prices reflects a deep emotional and even structural commitment to the bull market. The 1980-1981 issue of The Fed in Print listed only a single paper on stocks: "Inflation and Stock Values: Is Our Tax Structure the Villain?" In 1997, the Federal Reserve System was far more expansive on the subject. The Fed in Print for last year includes 28 different papers under the headings "Stock Market," "Stock Prices" and "Stocks." The titles range from "Stock Market Fundamentals" to "Rational Herd Behavior." Another 20 financial market studies can be found under "Options," "Asset-Backed Securities" and "Derivatives," which did not exist in 1980-1981. The plethora of papers reflects a broad-based academic interest in and sanction of the rise in stock prices.

Scholarly journals like the Quarterly Review of Economics and The Journal of Finance have also experienced a bull market in stock market research. In many ways, this is a good thing. At the outset of this bull market, most of the market-related revelations coming down from scholars were variations on the efficient market hypothesis. Now professors routinely explore everything from "turn of the year anomalies" in equity prices to "multi-component nonlinear prediction" systems on the S&P 500. However, many of the studies simply validate society's faith in a rising stock market. On the basis of stock price trends from 1982 to 1987, which years happen to mark the start and finish of the bull market of the 1980s, a University of Michigan study sagely concludes that the buy-and-hold approach outperforms 28 of 29 market timing strategies.

Whole groups of studies echo the stances of the brokerage, mutual fund and electronic beeper industries: circuit breakers will not effect volatility; mutual fund holders will not trigger a downward spiral in asset prices; and, contrary to pre-mania experience, one can make inordinate gains by purchasing companies that announce stock splits.

As EWT noted last September, the practice of buying stock splits has become a common and rewarding one as the mania has continued. The winter issue of The Quarterly Journal of Business and Economics documents "The Wealth and Earnings Implications of Stock Splits." The paper shows that "cumulative abnormal returns" or "CARs" are a "long-term wealth effect associated" with splits. The fallacy that underlies many of the findings is the limited time of the data. When stocks go down, they will act in ways that contradict these limited histories.

Two studies on "emerging" markets show the post-peak progression we can expect. Emerging markets have underperformed the S&P 500 since early 1995. Upon their sharp initial break in 1995 came a working paper titled, "Rethinking Emerging Markets." The paper concluded that the "investment boom [in developing countries] was not so much ill-founded as it was excessive. Now the market has had its reality check and will not behave foolishly." In the wake of 1997's mania and Asian crash, conclusions are harsher. The latest study by the Institute of Chartered Financial Analysts shows that any combination of emerging market stocks performed worse than "simply investing all your money in the U.S. market. Over the long term, the sector has therefore offered the unattractive combination of high-risk and lower returns." We will see the same conclusion with respect to split stocks after the market turns down.

J F
S D
Journal of Financial and Strategic Decisions

Volume 10, Number 2 Summer 1997

EARNINGS AND STOCK SPLITS IN THE EIGHTIES

Prior literature presents evidence on the nature of the earnings information conveyed by stock splits during 1970-1980. During 1970-1980 the information conveyed is that large pre-split earnings increases, usually viewed by the market as transitory and likely to be followed by earnings decreases, are in fact permanent. This paper presents evidence on the nature of the earnings information conveyed by splits during 1982-1989, a period of lower inflation and higher real economic growth. Results for 1982-1989 indicate that the market interprets stock splits as signals of subsequent earnings increases. Thus, the information conveyed by stock splits is time-period specific, with the market interpreting splits more optimistically during the period when economic conditions are stronger.

Eugene Pilotte
Rutgers University

May 1998

[Mutual Fund magazine] quotes two scholars from a Washington D.C. think tank offering a "mathematically-based rationale for a further explosion of equity values." According to their calculations, it would take a P/E ratio of 100 and a Dow of 35,000 to create overvaluation in today's market. "People who make bearish arguments based on history make a mistake." The quotes from these think-tank scholars are actually a restatement of their thesis presented in a March WSJ editorial, "Are Stocks Overvalued? Not a Chance," which concludes with this statement: "In the current environment, we are very comfortable in saying that pundits who claim the market is overvalued are foolish." EWT pointed out a year ago that in a mania, prudence and a knowledge of history become impediments to success. Evidently, these scholars have not allowed their brains to be a burden.

August 1998

The Wall Street Journal has just published (on 7/28 and 7/30) two stunning editorials. The first is co-authored by the director of economic studies at the Brookings Institution and the director of the Financial Institutions Center at the Wharton School, a professor of finance. Reporting the opinion of "the nation's leading academic scholars," it states, "sources of structural fragility [in the market] have been substantially, if not totally corrected, [making] a repeat of the hair-raising events of 1987 highly unlikely." I agree; the coming fall will be much worse. The structural fragility of social mood (which is what the market reflects) remains uncorrected to this day. In recent years, it has built upon its sandbar a structure that is taller than any before in history, and its foundation is fragile indeed. The second editorial, by a professor of economics at MIT, says flatly, "This expansion will run forever." At first, we thought the piece might be a parody, but it was dead serious. "The U.S. economy likely will not see a recession for years to come." Why? "We don't want one, we don't need one, and as we have the tools to keep the current expansion going, we won't have one." Our "policy team will keep it from happening.... The market won't melt down.... Just-in-time policy levers give the present expansion years of life. A recession would be an unforgivable mistake." Whew! We will simply say that this would have been a great forecast sixteen years ago, but today it is nothing but a symptom of the prevailing social dream, delivered with a frantic intensity that must be read to be believed.

December 1998

Media reports indicate that the long-term, culture-wide embrace of equity ownership was not even dented by the decline. As the bestseller status of the latest Pollyanna book, *New Rules For the New Economy*, indicates, New Era ideologies are stronger than ever. Now even the name of Kondratieff, the king of cycle theorists, is being invoked to suggest the potential for limitless growth. "Although still outside the realm of mainstream economics, a core and growing group of economists continue to see the Kondratieff framework." So says an economist in the Financial Post in Canada, adding in the very next sentence, "I believe we are in the very early stages of an upwave that will be characterized by massive investment." This kind of comment drives us up the wall. "Very early stages"? "Will be" characterized by investment? What does this person think has been going on for 24 years, reaching a record extent? This would have been a good call in 1974 or 1982, but in 1998? This is pure rationalization of the ebullience gushing forth from the emotional portion of the pre-rational brain. The Kondratieff cycle is unequivocally in its final decade, as disinflation has reigned since 1980, leaving only the deflationary years to go. The claim that it turned up in the 1970s or 1980s reveals utter unfamiliarity with its pattern.

February 1999

The cultural scene continues to be brightened by the flares of a still-rising social mood. Early 1999 will be marked by the launch of a NASA probe that will travel into deep space to retrieve "stardust" (actually a pure form of interstellar dust that is believed to be the building block of planets and human bodies).

April 1999

The Wall Street Journal, renowned for its conservative, buttoned-down look, pushed an almost unbroken history of one-column front page layouts aside to acknowledge "The first 10,000 points." The banner headline was the biggest in the 110-year history of the paper. The four-column layout of articles on the "Innovators," "Extraordinary Faith" and the "Rare [economic] Strength" that produced the achievement was also unprecedented. By comparison, the Crash of 1987, one of two other events to rate more than one column, was given just two columns. Further testimony to the giddiness of the paper's editors was the use of a color (green, of course) on the front-page of a regular section.

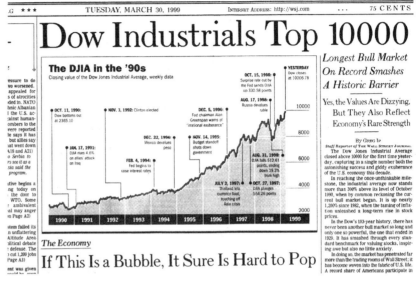

One would think the hard-nosed editors of The Wall Street Journal would be the last to succumb to euphoria. Several outlandish "new era" opinion pieces that have appeared on the paper's editorial page since a year ago show that this may, in fact, be the case. A bullish polemic, each one more self-assured than the last, has appeared after multi-month runups in prices. This chart tells the story. The most emphatic signal was fired over the last few weeks in three separate columns. Taken together, these intensifying professions of faith in the bull market comprise a long-term sell signal that discloses the extent to which the rising emotional fervor of 1999 has surpassed even that of 1929. Back then, WSJ editor William Peter Hamilton used the editorial voice of the nation's business daily to warn of an imminent break in the market before the crash. This time, the editors have invited in a pair of academicians to conclude, "Investors are bidding up the prices of stocks because stocks are a great deal." In a March 18 piece, which was headlined "Stock Prices Are Still Far Too Low," the economists used "sensible assumptions" about stocks versus bond yields to argue that "a perfectly reasonable level for the Dow would be 36,000 — tomorrow, not 10 or

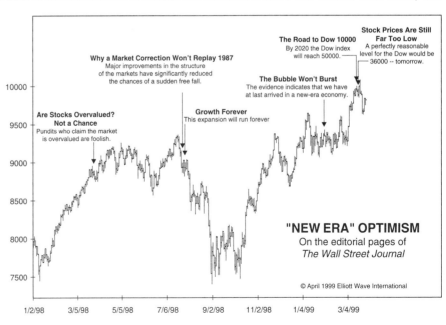

20 years from now." The authors were so sure of this number that they made it the title of their new book. The column ran in the same space where a rallying cry of 50,000 by 2020 arose a day earlier. From a sentiment perspective, these targets are dangerous because, as the euphoria over Dow 10,000 has shown, big numbers have a way of inciting the imaginations of investors.

May 1999
On-Line Opportunity at Any Price?

Two more arrows can be added to our chart showing "New Era" optimism on the editorial pages of The Wall Street Journal. The latest articles added a technological slant to the relentless drumbeat of bullish polemic described in last month's EWT. The headline over an April 6 piece asserts, "The Good Times Will Last." The article notes that the U.S. economy contracted 40% of the time from 1853 to 1953 and only 4.5% of the time since 1982. "There is ample reason to believe that the American economy will do even better in the 21st Century." We can all count on a century-long, better-than-95%-recession-free existence because "technology drives an economy forward, and the U.S. goes forward with a full inventory of inventions and innovations." Then on April 26, before readers could even get to the question of whether "conventional valuation standards apply anymore," WSJ headline writers answered with this bold assertion: "Big Profits Are In Store From The Online Revolution." The article assumes that AOL will more than double its subscriber base, increase its monthly service fees and enjoy pre-tax margins of 44% by 2004. Given the deflationary scenario described in *At The Crest of the Tidal Wave* and the Internet's role as an engine for price wars described in more recent issues of EWT, these are extremely optimistic assumptions.

It is important to note that after completing its list of rose-colored projections, the above-cited article concludes, "This brings us to about where the stock is selling today." In other words, today's stock price has discounted five years of a best-case future. How important is this observation? This chart illustrates what can happen to a technology leader after it experiences a parabolic rise like that of AOL over the past two years. As the dominant radio and then television company, RCA more than fulfilled the expectations of investors who in the 1920s saw it as the wave of the future. However, the company's prospects for over a third of a century got priced into the stock, as RCA did not return to its 1929 high for almost four decades. Even though they were absolutely right in their technological assessment, RCA investors had to endure a 13-year setback of 97%, no small correction.

As EWT has pointed out, the great Supercycle peaks of 1835, 1929 and 1968 were bound up in elaborate flights of technological fancy. In each case, investors acting

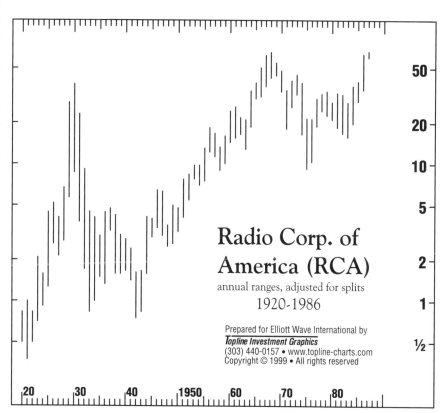

on impulsive thought born of a long bull market embraced the promise of coming advances while ignoring pitfalls that would drag down stocks a minimum of 70% in each case. Recent action surrounding initial public offerings illustrates an increasing reliance on technology fever. In the first quarter, a record-breaking total of $9.4 billion was raised in initial public offerings (data: Securities Data/Thomson Financial). Internet offerings represented nearly one-third of the total number of deals, and the percentage "is expected to rise due to a flood of first-quarter filings from companies hoping to capitalize on the online euphoria." Non-Internet firms have actually cancelled offerings, "given investors' limited interest in anything not connected to the Web."

Shown at right is a technology stock cover from the May 1999 issue of Money magazine.

September 1999

Most people who attempt to relate demographics to the stock market operate under the standard presumption that, if there is any relationship at all, demographic changes (like changes in politics, economics, cultural events, and so on) would be causal to the trends of the stock market.

This stance reflects the standard misconception of causality, i.e., the idea that social mood, and therefore the stock market, is a slave to "outside" influences. This view with respect to demographics, as with every other major social phenomenon, is precisely backward: the premise is false. We must start from the perspective on social causality. We know that social mood, as reflected by the stock market, determines the expansions and contractions in the economy. We know that extremes in social mood, as reflected by extremes the stock market, determine whether a landslide election will favor the incumbent or the challenger. We know that the direction and extent of social mood change, as reflected by the stock market, determine the extent of peace or whether there is a social mindset conducive to the outbreak of war. Is it possible to imagine that social mood also determines demographics? Most people would never pose such a question; I hope to suggest an answer.

The chart on the following page shows stock market prices plotted against birth rates from 1909 to the present. The data is shown with no lag. The first thing to notice is that there is a fairly noticeable correlation between the two sets of data.

Why would births and the stock market trend together, if they do at all? Sometimes answers can be found in subtleties. Notice that the deepest low in births this century came in 1933, the year after the deepest low in the stock market this century. Notice that the second most important low in births occurred again in 1975, one year after the second most important stock market low of this century. Why would there be a one-year lag? Well, can you think of any activity that always precedes a birth by about a year? If so, could this activity be correlated directly with people's moods and therefore the trend and level of the stock market? A rising social mood trend [correlates to], among other things, "friskiness, daring and confidence," a falling trend with "somberness, defensiveness and fear."

We now have a tenuous basis for a hypothesis regarding demographic trends. When aggregate feelings of friskiness, daring and confidence wax, people engage in more sexual activity with the aim of having children. When these feelings wane, so does the desire for generating offspring. It takes about nine months between the procreative impulse and a child's birth, which is why, at least at market bottoms, annual data on births lag annual data on the stock market by one year. The chart on the next page shows the same data, lagged by one year to reflect conceptions. The result is not the result of elaborate exercises in data fitting, as we find so often

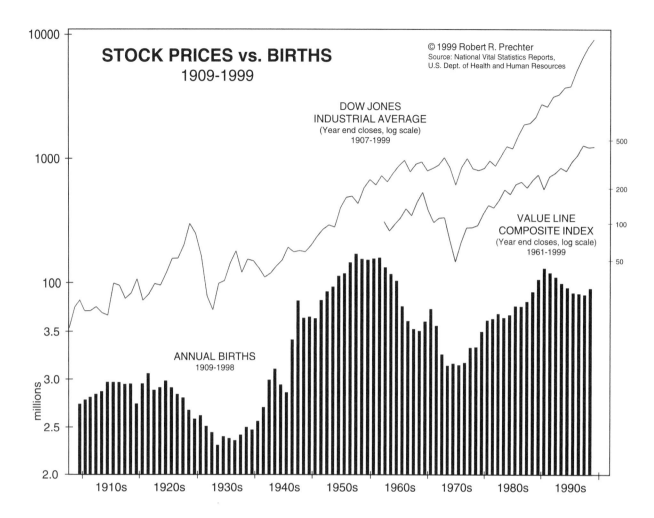

with hypotheses that demographics drive the economy. We know that a procreative decision or impulse is required nine months prior to a birth, so there is no theoretical presumption in repositioning and renaming this data. Now the two major lows line up exactly.

Let's investigate market tops. As you can see from the slash marks imposed upon the chart, the rate of procreation has declined prior to major tops in the Dow Jones Industrial Average. This is precisely the same behavior exhibited by indicators of market breath and rates of change for stock averages, which always peak and begin declining before the major blue chip averages top out.

Practical Application

As you can see from the following chart, conceptions fell persistently against rising stock market averages in 1920-1929 and again in 1956-1966, i.e., in the ten years prior to the top of waves V of (III) and III of (V) respectively, the two biggest tops of this century. After each of those periods, aggregate stock prices rapidly joined the trend of procreation on the downside. We might be tempted to suggest cavalierly that, like waning market breadth and velocity, waning procreative activity is a sentiment-based "sell signal" for the stock market because only the extremity of bullishness at an approaching major market top could make people more interested in stocks than in sex. However, it is more accurate to postulate an intimate and contemporaneous relationship between the limbic system's impulses both to procreate and to herd. Regardless of our hypothesis, the same divergence that occurred prior to previous major market tops is in evidence from 1989 to 1999, portending a reversal of like magnitude.

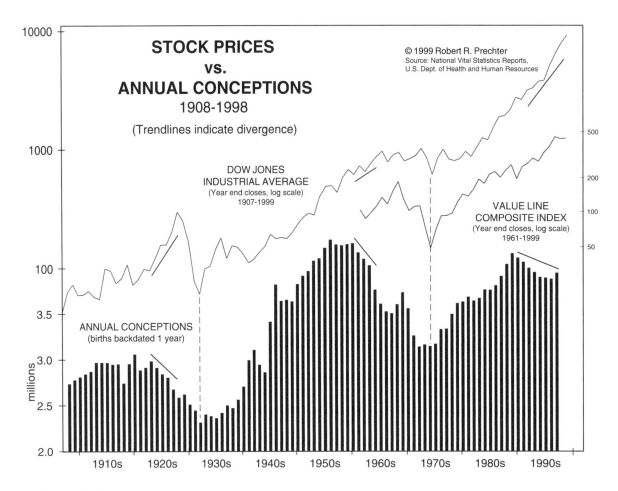

October 1999

The "new era" has been officially endorsed by the U.S. government, as the Bureau of Economic Analysis has reclassified software purchases as investments rather than spending! These are the only investments we know of that are guaranteed to fall 90% in value in three years, so why would the government do this? One answer is that the change will provide a retroactive boost to measures of economic output and thereby magically narrow the puzzling gap between the parabolic growth of stocks and the slowing growth of most economic fundamentals. Alan Greenspan even threw his weight behind the paradigm shift when he acknowledged that earnings have been understated by the move to an "idea-based" economy.

In this way, a simple accounting adjustment has rendered the prospects for future growth more brilliant than ever. "There can be little doubt that there is a new, technology-based economy roaring toward the year 2000," responded The Wall Street Journal in its latest "new-economy" opinion piece. "Compelling" academic support has also been supplied by a team of MIT researchers, who show that "stocks, in particular of technology companies," can "sensibly trade at such unprecedented multiples of earnings" because companies are "spending so heavily on 'intangible assets' such as research and development, software, marketing and computer training. Intangible assets fuel future profits just as surely as a 'tangible asset' such as a piece of equipment or a factory." That's a bold statement considering that many of the "intangibles" companies are pouring money into are Internet concepts that will compete against each other in an environment that has yet to sustain profitability.

November 1999

The ultimate concession to the "technology and information revolution reshaping of the U.S. and global economies" is due November 2, when Microsoft will be inducted into the Dow Jones Industrial Average. For most of the bull market, the world's most dominant stock was excluded from the world's premier blue-chip average. But just as RCA was added to the Dow in October 1928 (and removed in 1932), Microsoft has assumed its rightful place at the head of the pack, in time to lead the way down.

The "new era" intellectual rationale for euphoria continues to gain momentum. The authors of a 1997 magazine article on the boom ahead have reissued their thesis as a full-length book, *The Long Boom: A Vision For The Coming Age of Prosperity*. According to a New York Times review, its "quite familiar" message is, "the world stands on the edge of a global economic expansion on a scale never before experienced." This must be the back, not the front, edge of the boom because the reviewer hardly contests the point. Instead, he laments the loss of any more bad news and concludes, "Their dream looks superior."

January 2000

This item from Robert Farrell at Merrill Lynch: stocks of companies losing money rose 52% for 1999, while stocks of companies actually making money in 1999 were down 2%!

Since Internet stocks account for almost all of the gains among the money losers, it is an unavoidable fact that a psychological state, the belief in the future profitability of the Internet, has held the market up through the latest phase of the mania. This dependence on the future prosperity of an emerging technology is an interesting place for the mania to wind up because almost since its inception, *The Elliott Wave Theorist* has noted that the most important peaks of the last 200 years have been bound up in periods of intense technological advance. Specifically, we have referred to the peak of Supercycle (I) in 1835, Supercycle (III) in 1929 and Cycle III of (V) in 1966.

Even if the Internet is all that it is cracked up to be, the pattern at each of these past peaks suggests that the current prices have probably accounted for decades of future growth. After the peak of Supercycle (I), for instance, stock prices (at least of companies that survived) did not return to 1835 levels for 28 years. Compared to the innovations of that era, electricity, photography, blast furnaces for the mass production of iron and indoor plumbing, the Internet is no more than a refinement of existing technology. The great hopes of the 1920s, like commercial air flight and radio, were also fulfilled. Still, a long-term chart of RCA illustrates the tremendous human capacity for pricing 40 years of growth into one euphoric moment. We showed it in the May 1999 issue of *The Elliott Wave Theorist*. From its top in 1929, RCA declined 77%.

Of course, amidst the techno-reverie at all these peaks, there were many more wildly speculative visions that did not come to pass. In the "electrical euphoria" of 1835, the public got so wrapped up in this "magic fluid" that many sent the current coursing through their bodies, and others speculated on the eventual development of an engine that would never expire. From 1966 through late 1968, the same kind of wonderment became a popular form of entertainment. On a prime-time TV show, futurists envisioned colonies on the moon, the conversion of sea water to drinking water and the use of artificial moons. The passage into 2000 has been accompanied by a similar wave of super-bullish forecasts. The enchantment with the prospects for the human race is stamped clearly on a special multi-color Saturday January 1, 2000 issue of The Wall Street Journal. In blazing letters, the front-page headline announces: "The Amazing Future." According to a vast array of recent accounts, everything from poverty to unfulfilled sexual fantasies to common diseases will become things of the past. The basis for all this hopeful anticipation is apparent in a 200-page booklet on the potential for a "long boom" in the global economy published by the Organization for Economic Co-Operation and Development. It begins, "One of the most promising and commonly evoked vistas of the future centers on the dazzling potential of new technologies."

February 2000

> ...with growing optimism, they gave birth to a foolish idea called the 'New Economic Era.' That notion spread over the whole country. We were assured that we were in a new period where the old laws of economics no longer applied.
>
> — *The Memoirs of Herbert Hoover*

At the end of Supercycle (III) in the 1920s, the talk of a new era escalated with Hoover's election in 1928 and continued until the crash of October 1929. The following chart, depicting the number of major references to the "new economy" since 1985, illustrates this same phenomenon recurring, this time on a Grand Supercycle scale. The modern notion has been widespread for more than five full years and for the past year has been accelerating at an unprecedented rate. In 1999, the number of articles in major publications focusing on the new economy rose 2.4 times from a record in 1998. In January 2000, the annualized rate was 7 times that of 1998. As discussed below, it is no coincidence that this acceleration comes as evidence of price deflation has mounted. The February issue of EWFF showed that falling prices hit many parts of the world in 1999.

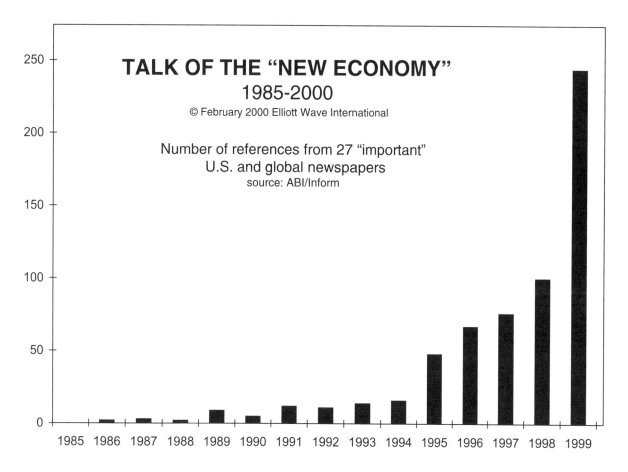

TALK OF THE "NEW ECONOMY"
1985-2000
© February 2000 Elliott Wave International

Number of references from 27 "important"
U.S. and global newspapers
source: ABI/Inform

At the Crest of the Tidal Wave first identified the connection between the gathering deflationary storm and the belief in a New Economy. "The true threat today is not inflation, but deflation," *At the Crest* said. "There is no hint of any such crisis on the horizon because economists are unanimous in their identification of slowing money supply expansion and moderated price gains as the best imaginable news for long-term economic growth." Since then, the New Economy has grown into an elaborate myth. It reflects the positive psychology of the extensive bull market in social mood, which serves as cover for the dangerous transition from inflation to deflation.

R.N. Elliott said, "It is a well known fact that prosperity and depression follow each other in cycles." It is a reality that most people admit only at market bottoms. That is why a search of 27 major newspapers finds no references to a "new economy" in 1980. As late as 1985, when the bull market entered Intermediate (3) of Primary ③, there were still no such references. Even in the middle of the 1990s, many of the references were qualified and others rightfully warned that the very idea of it was a sign of an overly enthusiastic social psychology. The dramatic quickening in the new era drumbeat recalls the drunken revelry in Troy as the Greeks' famous wooden horse was accepted inside the gates of the citadel. The more exaggerated and insistent the reports of the triumph of the New Economy and the death of the business cycle become, the more emphatically they reveal the hidden fact that the economy is back where it was in the fall of 1929, at the cusp of a great deflationary downturn.

The Miracle of Modern Productivity

A deluge of recent articles on the subject includes a lengthy Washington Post study that proclaims, "New numbers provide dramatic confirmation that the new economy not only exists but continues to thrive. The new economy is about what can be done and what can be dreamed." "Dreamed" is the key word here because it reveals the euphoric emotional tone that underlies all of these stories. Similar missives are literally daily events now. Here are two more examples from this past Monday. The one on the top is from a Business Week editorial and the one on the bottom is from the publisher of Forbes.

Business Week's faith in a productivity-induced boom borders on a religious conviction. Every week it produces "More Evidence" in the form of recent conversions. In January, it was the former chief economic advisor to the President who said, " I am rapidly becoming a New Economy convert. Productivity gains from technology have altered the economic playing field." In the January 31 "New Economy" cover story shown at right, Business Week argued that the "innovation factor" is one big reason "the New Economy bandwagon" is very likely going global.

> Is the growth in U.S. productivity accelerating? Recent figures suggest it may be, and the implications are vast: Living standards could rise faster, profits may increase further, economic growth might be higher, the budget surplus might grow bigger.
> —BusinessWeek
> February 21, 2000

> Can this benign environment last? Any history buff would say no. But the Internet offers the possibility, once slim but now becoming more probable by the day, that the good times can run a long while.
> —Forbes
> February 21, 2000

January 31, 2000

March 2000

The rhetoric that has emerged to justify the optimism is also bearish. According to this latest twist on the "new economy," the Dow is down because its "old economy" members have been left in the dust by the information age. This assertion fits perfectly with the thesis of EWFF's February 25 Special Report, "Deflation and The New Economy," which argued that the "new economy" is a cover for the transition to deflation and a Grand Supercycle turn in stock prices. The latest buzz means that the sharp upward slope in the "Talk of the 'New Economy'" chart shown in that report actually steepened even more dramatically as the Dow started down, a remarkable event.

April 2000

A page 1 Wall Street Journal story on the day of the NASDAQ all-time high confirms that the bull-market image has congealed in the heads of what had been a few remaining doubters. "Conservative Investors Finally Are Saying: Maybe Tech Isn't a Fad." "Countless bedrock American investors have undergone a transformation in recent months," says the article. "For a long time, they sneered at the new paradigm. Now these conservative investors are feeling stupid — and worse, poorer for it. They have started buying tech stocks. Others are going a step further. Conservative people, some in their 80s, are walking into their financial advisers' offices and demanding that their mutual funds or their managed portfolios begin to include a piece of the soaring new economy."

July 2000

"The mania is definitely back," says a money manager in the June 22 issue of The Wall Street Journal. Investors are "falling in love with tech again," says another article in the same issue. A USA Today article on the same date begins, "A next phase in tech is emerging — one that will be deeper, more complex and more thrilling." The Red Herring's July cover refers to it as "THE NEW AND IMPROVED ECONOMY." "It is a good thing," says the editor.

The July issue provides an in-depth portrait of a "stealth launch," used by Internet start-ups to "imbue a company with mystique." It works like this: "Some companies will selectively leak details to the press in the weeks leading up to their launch. The more brazen will hold a press conference months before their launch to announce their existence, but without saying what they do. Sometimes these succeed in whipping up a frenzy of anticipation. Other times they raise expectations to a level no company can satisfy." In *Extraordinary Popular Delusions*, Charles Mackay described a mystery offering that Mackay called "the most absurd and preposterous" of all the South Sea mania's wild promises. This time around, the media speak of multiple mystery launches as not an absurd novelty but "standard technique." Prechter and Frost forecast back in 1978 that the coming bull market would end an advance of the same degree as the one that climaxed with the South Sea Bubble. Actually, this one is crazier.

While investors are still firmly behind the Internet

Conservative Investors Finally Are Saying: *Maybe Tech Isn't A Fad*

The little light bulb came on in Charlie Wolf's brain last summer.

The 41-year-old project manager at a nuclear facility in Colorado had been meticulously building a conservative stock portfolio since the mid-1980s. Mr. Wolf felt better with solid, safe blue-chip names such as DuPont, Johnson & Johnson and Procter & Gamble. Technology highfliers seemed "outlandish." Then came his epiphany.

It dawned on him that the economy had shifted, and that companies that made diapers weren't exactly at the epicenter of the action. He was late to the party, but now he was going to dance.

Tech stocks now account for the bulk of his seven-figure portfolio. Mr. Wolf is one of countless bedrock American investors who have undergone a transformation in recent months. Now, these conservative investors are feeling stupid — and, worse, the poorer for it. They have started buying tech stocks themselves. This tectonic shift has helped push the NASDAQ Composite Index to its first close above 5000 yesterday.

In the course of a few months, many people have changed their definition of a blue-chip stock. Conservative people, some in their 80s, are walking into their financial advisers' offices and demanding that their mutual funds or their managed portfolio begin to include a piece of the soaring new economy.

—The Wall Street Journal, March 10, 2000

as an investment vehicle, a darker picture of it as a destructive technology that breeds fear and undermines the established order has begun to emerge. As one shattering headline put it, "Technology Creates Threat to Economy." In a Wall Street Journal opinion spot formerly reserved for glowing accounts of the "New Economy" and Dow 36,000, a recent column broke the news this way: "The enemy is the Internet." People "who should have known better bought into the lie that 'hits,' 'visits,' and 'clickthroughs' would magically morph into loyal customers, margins and profits." The article "reveals" a dirty little secret that *The Elliott Wave Theorist* has been quietly pointing out since 1998. In a wired world, corporations lose pricing power.

The chief executive of a financial web site traced the shift in emphasis to a very specific point in time. "After Internet stocks took a dive in March, investors changed their minds and declared they wanted profits. 'Up until April, the market was telling us to be the next ESPN. The next day the market wanted us to be a small profitable newspaper company.'" After Amazon. com declined 68%, USA Today revealed on June 23 that "investors should have seen this coming" because the online retailer has no physical storefronts. (There was no mention that the media should have seen it coming.) When the market was going up, the lack of physical storefronts is exactly what brightened Amazon.com's financial outlook and made it so appealing to investors and intoxicated reporters alike. Neither could see the change coming because the psychology that created the Amazon phenomenon is all that has changed.

December 2000
Technology: The True Story Can Now Be Told

Back in March and April, when the NASDAQ plunged, everybody said it was no big deal. *The Elliott Wave Financial Forecast* disagreed. Noting that the index's loss was the fastest decline from an all-time high by any major average in the history of the stock market, we called it "a sign that the Grand Supercycle transition is probably behind us."

It took nine months, but the bad news is now sprinting to catch up to our assessment. Startling new revelations about the scope of the meltdown have become daily events. In addition, the glorious New Era assumptions that we tried so hard to debunk as the index rose to its peak are now being picked at by a suddenly skeptical press. Media accounts now tell us that cycles matter, that Internet growth can actually slow, that nobody actually pays any attention to Internet advertising and that the public affection for bidding for stuff over the web can simply go away. Services that once toted up the number of triple-digit IPO gains now keep a running tally of the dot.com shutdowns and layoffs. By all accounts, the "death toll" is rising at an amazingly fast rate. "While industry groups have always drifted in and out of favor, it is rare to see an industry evaporate as quickly and completely as Web stocks," says one article.

This quote is devastatingly accurate, for the Web itself was never quite the industry that Web stocks were. From March 10 to November 25, the Bloomberg Internet Index of 280 stocks lost $2 trillion in market capitalization, more than twice its current value of $912 billion. To get an idea of how far down these stocks can go, re-read *At the Crest*. It's way further than anyone realizes.

The personal toll on participants is revealed in tales from the "Dot-Com's Dark Side," such as the story of the death of Aaron Bunnell, an executive with Upside.com. "According to the NYC medical examiner, this 'rising player in the on-line world' overdosed on alcohol, heroin and Valium. Still, it was not the drugs, Bunnell's father says. 'My son was a victim of the dot-com boom.'" This is another sharply accurate quote. The killer is not the decline; the killer was the boom. That is what *set people up* for devastation.

As all the high-flying IPOs come tumbling down, we read a thousand variations of Aaron Bunnell's tragic story. The 10 hottest IPOs of the last 25 years are all technology start-ups that came public within the last two years. All are down a minimum of 67% from their first-day close. The average decline is 82.7%. The top two, VA Linux and Theglobe.com, are down 97% and 99%, respectively. A year ago, PETS.COM was clearing the way for a successful launch by having its hand puppet mascot appear on NBC's broadcast of the Macy's Thanksgiving Day Parade. On the strength of this mascot, a hand puppet, PETS.COM came out at $14 a share with a market capitalization of more than $4.7 billion. Now, with PETS.COM shuttered and its stock selling for 25 cents, a 98% decline, Barron's reports that the only living vestige of the firm is an e-mail that treats recipients "to the image of a sock puppet snorting lines of cocaine through a rolled-up bill." In our opinion, this image is no match for that of the stuffy Ph.D. academics who assured us all in national newspapers that the boom would never cease. They weren't snorting cocaine but something far worse: a heady mix of ignorance, arrogance and extrapolation.

Are technology stocks near bottom? The answer is, not yet. The main reason is that the average investor is still bullish on the sector. Even though 74% of the respondents to a USA Today survey said they had lost money in the stock market this year, an incredible "85% said the NASDAQ's tumble hasn't shaken their faith in technology stocks." A lot of the experts also remain upbeat. When "the share price of a tech alpha-dog like Intel slumps 50%, history says bet the ranch," gushes the editor of Forbes. He adds that the potential for the right Internet play is "without limits." "Technology stocks will be the most dynamic growth group of 2001," says a well-known strategist. "This is a good thing," adds a banker whose technology investments just took a big chunk out of profits at the nation's third largest bank. The IPO market has slowed, but it is still pumping out the remaining dregs of the erstwhile boom. Nothing less than a complete retracement will correct the excesses of the last several years.

May 2001

The skepticism *At the Crest* calls for at the final low will look more like this: "At the bottom, despair will reign, and the trend will be projected further downward by the majority of economists. Academics will issue scholarly studies to support the bearish mindset." At this point, they are still re-stating the bullish case.

Sock Puppet Finds a New Home

The spotted mascot for now-defunct Pets.com is coming back as a spokesdog for a car-financing firm.

It wasn't his first job choice, but at least the Pets.com sock puppet hasn't joined the high-tech unemployment line.

One of the most recognizable icons of the dot-com era has a new agent and has inked a new deal for a California financing company. The black-and-white spotted dog puppet has just signed on as the mascot for 1-800-Bar None, a company that provides car financing for consumers with bad credit. The sock puppet has been out of work since online pet store Pets.com was forced to shut down for lack of funds in November 2000.

Jim Crouse, chief executive of 1-800-Bar None, said he hopes the sock puppet will send the company's message — everyone deserves a second chance — "cleverly and with a touch of humor."

—Los Angeles Times, June 24, 2002

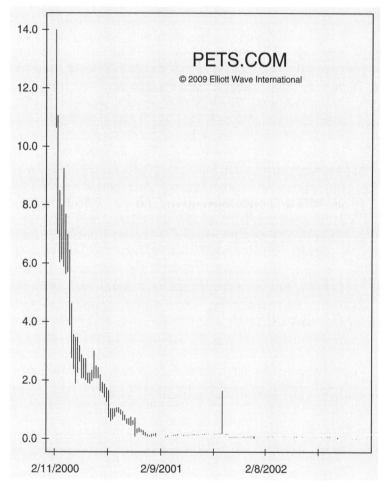

A good example is the "unreconstructed and unrepentant" bullishness of *Dow 36,000* author James Glassman. Two years ago, Glassman made it big with a Wall Street Journal editorial that argued, "A perfectly reasonable level for the Dow would be 36,000 — tomorrow, not 10 or 20 years from now." Near the March low, he reappeared on the editorial page of the Wall Street

Journal proclaiming "Dow 36,000? It's Still a Good Bet." "What I think is dangerous is for people not to be in the market," he says. This is like saying that it is dangerous for people to expect winter, even as the days get shorter and the snow starts to fly. A better title for Glassman's book might be, *The Case for an Endless Summer*. The fact that its premise continues to capture people's imagination is another sign that the toll for this bear market will eventually be higher than for any in more than 200 years.

April 2002

With golden hues and butterflies, this Newsweek cover echoes the psychology that dominated the scene right before the all-time highs. The story boldly welcomes investors back to the sector that was one of the primary killing fields through the first leg down in the bear market. Instead of pain and loss, readers get more tales of "brilliant new ideas," "schemes" and "well-thought-through deals," in other words, a revised version of the bullishness that preceded the peak in prices. In January 2000, *The Elliott Wave Financial Forecast* counted 17 similar covers and called it a "signal of the potential for a huge reversal." This story and several like it since January signal a continuation of that decline. Even the subhead of the cover, which is supposed to be something of an admonishment to former plungers, underscores that this psychology is not that far from the euphoria of old. By insisting that the crash has "saved" technology, Newsweek is reprising the "new reality" mantra that greeted the first wave of selling in April and May 2000. When

discipline, sobriety and sanity were said to be re-entering the marketplace in May 2000, EWFF identified the proclamations as a sign of the bear market's early disappointment phase. The main reason was that valuations had done virtually nothing to adjust to this new mood. Since valuations are still light years away from the emerging earthiness of these statements, we will continue to await their return to below average levels.

In February 2000, *The Elliott Wave Financial Forecast* published a special report, "Deflation and The New Economy," arguing that the "new economy" was an "elaborate myth" that reflected "the positive psychology of the extensive bull market in social mood." EWFF added that "the more exaggerated and insistent the reports of the triumph of the new economy become, the more emphatically they reveal the hidden fact that the economy is back where it was in the fall of 1929, at the cusp of a great deflationary downturn." An unprecedented acceleration in the number of "new economy" references was cited as evidence of the onset of the downturn. The updated version of that chart shows that a blow-off top in "new economy talk" came in 2000. As expected, the ebullient new-era chatter has waned with the decline in stock prices. This decline confirms that the new economy was a product of the rising social mood that has now reversed.

The new economy's latest media incarnation is further evidence. As the Newsweek cover above illustrates, the rally from September 21 has revived belief in the "magic" of high technology. "Fortified by the lessons of history," the article concludes that Silicon Valley is "gearing up to wire us more than ever. So welcome to Revenge of the Nerds, The Sequel." The most recent wave of enthusiasm for a new age strikes us as suspiciously similar to the one we observed arriving in early 2000. As we prepared our special report, Business Week kept topping itself with another editorial or cover story on the miraculous, technology-fed rise in productivity, which led EWFF to comment, "Business Week's faith in a productivity-induced boom borders on a religious conviction." Don't look now, but Business Week is back on the new economy bandwagon. Since mid-February, when a BW editorial claimed that productivity is "Galloping to the Rescue Once Again," issue after issue has dispensed proof of it. A mid-March cover story concludes, "If there is anything we have learned in recent years, it is that the U.S. economy's improved efficiency, flexibility, and quick reflexes have given it a surprising resiliency. The New Economy has shown time and again that it can deliver on its promises."

Deliver on its promises? The last time the full weight of that promise was being delivered by the media, the NASDAQ, the main measure of the new economy, fell 72%. Business Week's reaffirmation of the promise suggests that it is about to be broken once again. The rebound in the new economy is probably over.

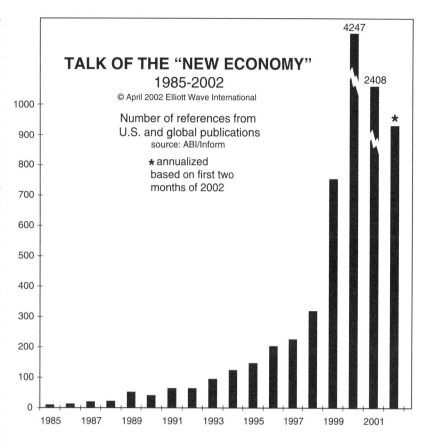

July 2002

Academic Pessimism

The search is on for a solution to the bear market. What can the president, the Fed, the SEC or anyone else do to get things back on track? The correct answer is that it does not matter what they do. The dictates of the Wave Principle are immutable. Even if it were possible for someone to think of a way out of a bear market, *The Wave Principle of Human Social Behavior* explains that it could not be instituted because the bear-market impulse of the majority always "overwhelms the power of logical entreaties from various individuals." The reason is that the social mood behind a market reversal shapes the reasoning of even the most advanced intellects just as it eventually bends the economic fundamentals. According to HSB, this happens because the neocortex, or the seat of the reason within the brain, is a "slave to the limbic system." On the way up, and in the immediate aftermath of the long advance, libraries everywhere were stuffed with scholarly treatises espousing higher and higher Dow targets and dubious bull-market schemes like the purchase of shares in companies that announce stock splits based on short-term, mania-induced price histories. "When stocks go down, they will act in ways that contradict these limited histories," *The Elliott Wave Theorist* said in April 1998. The current decline has been accompanied by a series of studies in which scholars are beginning to take back the optimistic assertions of the 1990s. With respect to stock splits, for instance, the latest study reverses the positive assessment of the last decade. After reviewing more than 10 years of history in which "various researchers view stock splits as a favorable signal," the spring issue of the Financial Management Association Journal finds "weak evidence that stock splits convey a positive signal." Other high level researchers have suddenly turned up negative correlations between stocks and the summer season, current P/Es and the ratio of consumer net worth to disposable income. Another interesting study by Hong Kong-based researchers finds that "close daily monitoring of volatile financial affairs may not be good for your mental health." The top story in the July 22 Forbes magazine focuses on an "alarming" study in the Financial Analysts Journal. Two "financial experts" have raised "the disturbing possibility" that stocks have not outperformed bonds the way researchers have been contending for the last 10 years. The story reveals that due to a "misreading of history," a purported 5% risk premium of stocks over bonds "is bunk."

Notice the timing. The studies all appeared as [the mid-2002 stock decline] got underway. This timing, in turn, supports the wave count. Apparently, if the turn is of high enough degree, the limbic system control of the group's reasoning is strong enough to acknowledge the direction of stock prices by bending the academic research itself. Also note that these revelations are still relatively mild rejoinders to the old trend. Even as it unmasks the "great stock illusion," for instance, Forbes' cover story exposing the true risk in equities offers an "alternative to abandoning equities" in REITs, timber trusts, JP Morgan and General Motors. At the time of the study at least, each had yet to taste the full wrath of the bear market. When they are sufficiently ravaged, their various weaknesses will probably be revealed in the financial literature.

The good news is that the new mood has also opened eyes to certain truths, like technical analysis. Market timing is now gaining esteem at a fast rate. Some of the sages of buy-and-hold strategies are even breaking from that camp and turning up in papers that expound the virtues of various indicators. A Financial Analysts Journal study on "Using The Yield Curve To Time the Stock Market" is an example. The discoveries come at a difficult time for many technicians. As noted above, many traditional measures and indicators are being redefined by the bear market. The FAJ's yield-curve study notes that an inverted yield curve has produced "a larger mean excess return than a stock-only, buy-and-hold strategy," but it fails to mention that the current bear market was not preceded by any such inversion. As the newly dominant social mood issues directions to the party, it switches all the signs around. This is consistent with the contrary tenets of the practice. In the wonderland of technical analysis, it makes perfect sense.

January 2003
A Year of Academic Reversal

At the start of the summer sell-off, EWFF commented on the shift from scholarly endorsements of the stock market late in the bull market to academic pessimism in the third year of the bear market. We cited a host of late-breaking studies debunking or even reversing bull market schemes like the advisability of buying stocks that are subject to splits or buybacks. We said there appeared to be some significance in the exact timing of these bear market reappraisals.

One of the greatest "findings" of the bull market was all the research concerning the "demographic" argument. You remember the claim that the large pool of maturing baby boomers would refuse to allow stocks to fall. Well, the case has been officially re-cast as a force for the bear with this headline from The New York Times:

16-Year Slump? If So, Blame It on the Boomers
—December 1, 2002

A Yale University study says demographic patterns in the U.S. call for the stock market to fall as baby boomers unload their holdings through 2018. What about all that money boomers were supposed to be socking away through 2008? The best explanation is the one offered by *The Elliott Wave Theorist* in March 1998: "We think that the demographic theory will ultimately prove to have been a rationalization of an emotional state." The latest shift proves this to be the best explanation because of the three potential theories, it is the only one that explains the popularity of both, as well as the switch from a rising implication in a bull market to a falling one in a bear. Even rigorously defined "truisms" reverse to get in line with the direction of the main trend. The great thing about socionomics is that it does not fall apart when the winds of social mood shift because it is the one social theory that explains the dynamics behind the reversal.

April 2003

A compelling sign of unfinished bear market business is clear in this chart of the relative size of the financial sector within the overall stock market. As a percentage of the S&P 500, financial issues are still near their peak level of 21% in August. The current level of 20.4% is still 4 times the level of 4.5% near the start of the last bull market. The bear market will not end until this percentage approaches or shrinks below its level at the low in 1980. Instead of pulling in their horns, financial intermediaries are intent on growing their way out of their increasing problems by expanding their use of , supplying and reaching for higher yields on riskier debt instruments and lowering credit standards. In the February issue, EWFF offered another illustration of this psychological transition: investors' jump from the mutual fund pan into the hedge fund fire. We see another example of a desperate flight to higher levels of financial risk in brokerage firms' latest "strategic plan." They intend to make up for the revenue lost to dwindling commissions by turning their trading units into profit centers.

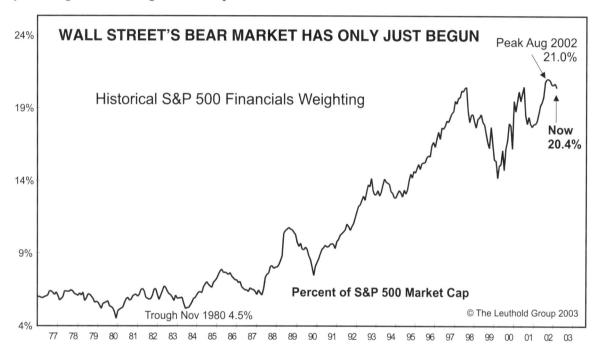

A similar article focuses on Goldman Sachs, which is "counting on trading revenue to sustain profits." By raising its exposure to market swings, the firm managed to "weather a sliding stock market." Translation: they survived last year's down market by shorting the stock they sell to clients. When the stock market vigilantes hear about this, trading department managers may be the ones being escorted out in handcuffs.

August 2003

A familiar story in July was the way that technology pushed its way to center stage. Technology's leading role in the market's May-July run was so reminiscent of March 2000 that the papers were commenting on it as the NASDAQ reached its July 14 high of 1776. "Close your eyes and it feels a little like 1999," reported the Los Angeles Times on July 13, "that giddy, amazing, lost moment when Silicon Valley was the most important place on Earth and just about everyone in it was happily adding a zero or two to his or her net worth. The stock prices of unproven Internet companies that no one has ever heard of are once again doubling in a single day. The future, once again, appears unlimited in many eyes."

On the day after the NASDAQ hit its high in mid-July, USA Today threw in a New-Era opinion piece entitled, "Economic Optimism Rises." The column is filled with one-sided infatuation with technology, which played a huge role in the mania. For any who managed to block out the memories of the premise that launched whole business magazines at the market's highs, the article highlights the following passage in big letters: "The underlying fundamentals of this economy...offer the promise not only of a strong rebound, but also a new era of economic growth and innovation." The article offers a heavy dose of the breathy, bull-market rhetoric that was omnipresent in early 2000: "Deep truths are setting the stage for a very optimistic economic future," "Wireless computing is adding a new level of convenience and ubiquity to the Internet," "The real payoff is yet to come," and "It's time for economic observers to stop whining about the losers and start celebrating." This rhetoric reflects the illusion of limitless growth based on the "intense technological advance" that EWFF identified as part and parcel of the bubble in the first quarter 2000. The rally of 2003 reveals that investors are still beholden to this fantasy. It will not survive the bear market.

Why Birth Rates Are Falling

In *The Elliott Wave Theorist*'s September 1999 take on demographic trends ("Stocks and Sex"), EWT offered the following hypothesis: In a bull market, "when aggregate feelings of friskiness, daring and confidence wax, people engage in more sexual activity with the aim of having children. When these feelings wane [a bear market], so does the desire for generating offspring." Because it takes nine months between the procreative impulse and a child's birth, EWT speculated that the trend in annual data on births should lag an important stock market turn by a year. The figures for the last three years of the bear market are in, and they clearly support EWT's socionomic conjecture. Like the stock market, the updated chart shows that conceptions

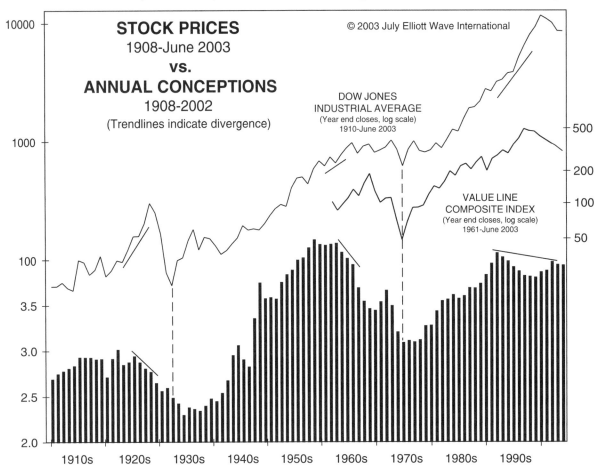

peaked in 2000 and declined in 2001 and 2002. Birth rates also confirm our forecast for a high-degree trend change in social mood, as the government reported June 25 that the per capita figure for 2002 is the lowest annual reading in the 94-year history of U.S. birth data.

Is socionomics useful in forecasting? Here's a follow-up prediction from EWT in June 2001: "If you want to have kids, hurry up. You won't feel much like it three years from now." The cover from Newsweek's June 30 issue reveals that two more years of bear market was enough to cool the interest for many couples. The headline on the story inside strikes at the heart of the matter: "Sex: We're Not in the Mood." It supports EWT's contention that, in the aggregate, procreative decisions are "more commonly impulsive/emotional than meditative/rational." This is what makes them predictable. The accuracy of EWT's analysis shows that birth rates respond to changes in social mood, as reflected by trends in stocks. In fact, a divergence against a birth rate peak in 1989 (see lines

on the chart) caused EWT to predict that the current reversal would be "of like magnitude" to sharp declines that accompanied the bear markets of the early 1930s and 1970s. The divergence has held, so the likelihood is that birth rates will fall much lower over the next several years.

October 2003

The interplay of a faltering long-term rise and an emerging bear is very much in evidence in the U.S. space program. On the one hand, NASA announced last month that the shuttle will fly again in 2004. Surveys show support for the space program is "broad but not deep." Even this moderate support is likely to wane, however. Recent headlines suggest that it may have started already, as an independent report has found that the program is "Full of Flaws," and some members of U.S. Congress are suggesting that "space flight be curtailed." This relates to one of the consequences of a bear market catalogued in *The Wave Principle of Human Social Behavior*. A falling trend quenches the desire for science and scientific exploration. Science fiction writers have already spotted the emergence of this trend in the "present depressing state of the field." "Incredibly, young people no longer find the real future exciting," said one author at the latest World Science Fiction awards. "They no longer find science admirable. They no longer instinc-

tively lust to go to space." The aftereffects of the stock market rally may get the shuttle back in orbit. But the shuttle's next run will be its shortest yet. As the bear market wears on, disdain for NASA's "risk-taking" culture and a public obsession with more earthly matters will probably ground it for a long time.

December 2003

Just as the bullish sentiment at the all-time highs concentrated squarely on technology, this mania echo has likewise focused ever more intently on dreams of the riches that await investors in high-tech stocks. Barron's November 17 cover surveyed the "tech industry's long-awaited revival," as a November 24 Newsweek cover boasted of the "Next Big Thing" alongside the happy visage of Bill Gates. USA Today also put out a technology "Bonus Section" promoting the "Next Big Thing," as well as the "future of money," "tech dreams" and "What's Emerging In Venture Capital Trends."

February 2004
The Bull Market Arrives On Mars

On January 16, USA Today reported that the "collective feeling" is that "the technology slump is history." To paraphrase EWFF's comments from six days before the Dow's all-time peak in January 2000, this is an interesting place for the mania echo to wind up. Almost since the inception of the mania, *The Elliott Wave Theorist* has noted that the most important peaks of the last 200 years have been bound up in periods of intense technological excitement. As EWT noted in 1997, it is a spectacle of anticipation that goes beyond the stock market to the far reaches of human endeavor. In 1969, it coalesced around the first moon walk, which was followed by a last lonely peak for the OTC Index and the unraveling of the Apollo space program in the ensuing bear market.

Once again, man has been "drawn to the heavens" as the small stocks have enjoyed their own lonely trip to the heavens. As three separate Martian rovers landed on the red planet, George Bush announced an "ambitious vision" calling for a space station on the moon and eventual manned flight to Mars. "We've got something positive to think about here," a tourist on pilgrimage to the Smithsonian's Air and Space Museum told USA Today. This appeal to the "American psyche" will hold up only as long as the stock market does. As EWFF observed in October, the space program's latest booster shot of optimism is a direct reflection of the mood behind the countertrend rally. The exploding U.S. government deficit shown in the chart ensures that the next giant step for man will be away rather than toward Mars. Despite the landing and Bush's initiative, polls suggest that "Mars Mania" is already dissolving. According to a CBS News/New York Times Poll released January 17, only 48% of Americans favor sending astronauts to Mars. "Up to now, Americans have been supportive of such a program. In 1999, 58% favored sending astronauts to Mars." The public opposes the building of a base on the moon, 58% do not think a permanent space station on the moon is worth the cost. As the bear market intensifies, this change in support will probably be characterized well in retrospect as a tragic loss of idealism.

Mars Mania Grips A Nation That Can't Get Enough of Spirit's Images

The hottest action hero is 4 feet tall, looks like a golf cart and stars in a feel-good Mars mania blockbuster that is gripping the nation. The arrival of NASA's spirit rover on surface of Mars Saturday night has thrown into sharp relief public and scientific fascination with this planetary neighbor.

USA Today, January 9, 2004

Plans for Space Are Realistic, Official Says

When President Bush decides on a new policy of space exploration for the nation, the goals will be realistic and achievable, the NASA administrator, Sean O'Keefe, said on Tuesday.

Mr. O'Keefe said in an interview that the interagency task force gathering options for the president in space policy was working to avoid "pie in the sky" goals that may be grandiose and exciting but impractical for financial and technical reasons.

The New York Times, December 17, 2003

Return to Moon May Be on Agenda

President Bush's aides are considering a new lunar exploration program and other unifying national goals administration officials said yesterday.

"The drumbeat is getting louder," Wendell Mendell, manager of the Office for Human Exploration Science at NASA's Johnson Space Center in Houston, said in a telephone interview. Mendell has long advocated a return to the moon.

The Washington Post, December 5, 2003

Moon Dreams

The Washington Post, Jan 11, 2004

Bush Seeks Manned Mars Trip

WASHINGTON — President Bush next week back to the moon within the next decade and then on to Mars, presidential aides said Thursday.

Chicago Tribune, January 9, 2003

April 2004

EWFF has built a case for a mounting liquidity crisis focusing on a financial sector that has become extremely dependent on derivative instruments and trading profits. By turning their trading rooms into profit centers, Wall Street firms have further stacked an inverted pyramid

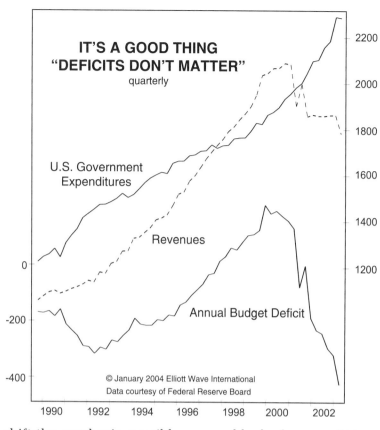

IT'S A GOOD THING "DEFICITS DON'T MATTER"
quarterly

U.S. Government Expenditures

Revenues

Annual Budget Deficit

© January 2004 Elliott Wave International
Data courtesy of Federal Reserve Board

of risky financial obligations with another layer of leveraged bets. According to Wednesday's issue of The Wall Street Journal, brokerage firms are "riding a wave of strong stock markets and low interest rates." Goldman Sachs has increased its profits to record levels, but not without tripling its risk exposure since 2000. The move to riskier financial plays is also evident in U.S. pension funds' aggressive investment in hedge funds. According to the latest study, the percentage of pension funds, endowments and foundations using "alternative investments like hedge funds and equity real estate" jumped from 12 percent in 2000 to 23 percent in 2003. As the markets fall to levels that are not even considered by Wall Street's current trading strategies, firms will be forced to reel in these bets. Falling prices will shift the emphasis, possibly very suddenly, from profit to preservation. At that point, brokers and hedge funds will do whatever it takes to stay solvent, which will only intensify the decline as it seals the fate of many firms.

As of March 5, this re-arrangement of the financial deck chairs helped lift the Philadelphia/KBW Banks Index to a new all-time peak. But the pattern of the advance suggests that the latent danger inherent in the Street's risk grab is about to become manifest. Financial stocks now account for the largest share of the S&P, more than 21%. This is the same status that the technology sector occupied at the start of the bear market. Sentiment toward high finance is also very similar to the aura that surrounded technology at the all-time highs. The similarity is captured by two headlines from The Wall Street Journal. The first is from the day of the NASDAQ's all-time high, March 10, 2000, when the Journal endorsed technology's dominant status with its infamous "Maybe Tech Isn't A Fad" headline. Four days after the S&P's latest peak, the Journal celebrated the performance of risky financial plays by showing the following headline over the image of a treasure chest that overflowed with gold coins:

Triumph of the Speculators

It's "The Death of Equities" (Business Week, 1979) in reverse.

June 2004
Financial Sector Meltdown Underway

EWFF's April call for a financial emphasis through the next leg of decline was quickly confirmed by Dow Jones & Co.'s addition of a financial stock (AIG) to the Dow Jones Industrial Average. In making the change, The Wall Street Journal's "top news editors" said that they were recognizing "the continued growth of the financial [sector]." The same accolade foreshadowed the technology sector's leadership during the first leg down in November 1999. Microsoft and Intel were added two months before the Dow's all-time peak.

In recent years, the pioneering financial efforts of traditionally cautious German investors have also been a solid contrarian signal for related markets. In September 2000, as the S&P tested its high before turning down hard, one of the developments that entered into EWFF's bearish case for stocks was that some small-cap U.S. shares were generating more trading volume in Hamburg than in the U.S. A similar signal that flashed in the wake of the all-time high was major purchases of U.S. financial interests by European banks. The October 2000 issue of EWFF had this to say about their acquisitions of U.S. brokerage firms and mutual funds:

> As we noted last month and many times in the past, foreign buying is a classic signal of the end of an uptrend. Banks are also notorious for getting caught holding the bag at the end of long-term uptrends. Now we have both together!

The Euro-fever for U.S. securities assets was also accompanied by J.P. Morgan's September 2000 purchase of Chase Manhattan. On May 6, The Wall Street Journal recorded the firing of a very similar double-barreled sell signal with a story on the "Influx of Banks From Europe." The Journal noted that the Bank of Scotland's $10.5 billion purchase of a Cleveland-based bank in May brought the total value of U.S. banks purchased by European commercial banks since 2000 to $35.9 billion, "roughly equivalent to the value of the merger between J.P. Morgan and Chase Manhattan." The Journal added that European banks used to be known as "Big Dumb Foreign Banks" in the 1980s. It added, "Nobody is cracking wise anymore," which is actually yet another sign of a peak, as such commitments always seem to make perfect sense at a top. The wise-cracking guys show up later, when the reversal is underway and a popular way of expressing the negative mood is to castigate the last man to board the old trend.

July 2004
Real Estate Broadcasts a Sell Signal

Is it a housing bubble or not? That's the question according to USA Today. A lengthy study by the Federal Reserve Bank of New York says no, but articles such as The New York Times' account of the "Ever More Graspable, and Risky, American Dream" make it clear that housing is an asset class that has slipped away from its moorings. Buyers aren't just expecting home prices to rise anymore; they are depending on it. In a typical example, the NY Times cites the holders of a mortgage that consumes more than half their monthly income. Even though they face a stiff increase in two years, the homeowners are unconcerned because they believe rising home prices will allow them to get a better loan down the road. "I'm figuring that my income will have climbed by then as well," says another expectant home owner. Mortgage brokers are "nervous, but they are pressing ahead." The sub-prime and no-down-payment categories now account for about 40% of home loans. That's up from zero at the beginning of the bull market. And the Mortgage Bankers Association reports that 30% of all new loans are now adjustable rate, up from 13.5% in January 2003, subjecting borrowers to the increased interest costs of rising rates.

Does that mean it's a bubble? No, it's not a bubble, it's the bubble, the final fireworks in the bidding frenzy that pumped everything from Pokemon cards to Picassos to ridiculous heights. The housing market is the logical sector for where the bubble should end because its positive performance during the last bear market makes it the asset class that most investors trust the most. It is also among the most illiquid markets, which means it will lock investors in during the bubble's deflation. Here's one more note that may be the sound of the final nail being pounded into real estate's coffin:

CNNfn's New Sked Axes Stox, Adds Home

Stocks are out; real estate is in. CNNfn is tweaking its programming schedule and will announce today that it will replace a stock market show with a new program devoted to real estate.

—New York Post, June 21, 2004

CNNfn is right up there with Business Week when it comes to marking the end of long-term trends. The same network created a show dedicated to the New Economy ("The N.E.W. Show") in March 2000. The "Smart Money Guide To Real Estate Investing" hit the airwaves on Monday.

September 2004

This chart shows another bank-induced gold rush that has reached its limit: real estate. As a percentage of total loans, U.S. banks' real estate lending reached 51.8 percent in May. The five-wave form of the rise, from less than 25 percent in the early 1970s, suggests that the downtick in June and July is only the beginning of a massive trend change. Chapter 16 of *Conquer the Crash* covers the precarious nature of real estate lending. It notes, "The worst thing about real estate is its lack of liquidity during a bear market." Lenders seem to have forgotten the disastrous consequences that resulted from the bear market of 1973-1974, when 75% of mortgage REITs were non-performing, not to mention the massive savings and loan crisis that accompanied a decline of just 20% in the Value Line Geometric index from 1987 to 1990.

This time, the fallout will be much greater because banks' exposure to real estate is unprecedented and the bear mar-

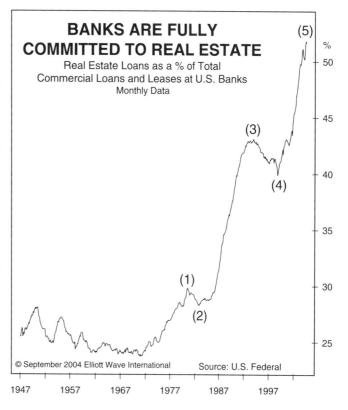

ket is of much larger degree. Also, there will be no inflation to help break the fall in prices for all that property, which will soon be repossessed by the banks out of desperation. Bankers' other big problem is that they don't have the cash-generating businesses to fall back on as they did in the past. At the stock market peak in 1973, banks had $1 of commercial loans and industrial loans outstanding for every $2.95 in real estate loans. In 2001, as the financial sector scurried to get out of the way of the bear market, the ratio reached a new all-time high of 1:3.7, and it's been crashing ever since. In June, the ratio reached a new record low of 1:5.3. The more they refrain from conventional business lending, the more furiously banks shovel funds into bricks and mortar. U.S. commercial and industrial loans are down 20 percent from their all-time peak in January 2001, while real estate loans are up 20 percent. Obviously, bankers are as convinced as the public that real estate never goes down.

January 2005

Real Estate and The Uh-Oh Effect

One of the final manifestations of the Grand Supercycle peak was a phenomenon that *The Elliott Wave Financial Forecast* dubbed the "uh-oh effect" just five market days before the NASDAQ reached its all-time high in March 2000. The uh-oh effect was drawn from the following observation from *At the Crest of the Tidal Wave*:

> There are times in history when the percentage of naive investors is so high that occasional warnings from professionals are irrelevant to net market psychology.... [It] is in fact normal behavior at the biggest tops of all.

Over the course of 2004, EWFF has charted the shift of the epicenter of the great peak to the real estate sector, so don't mistake a recent flurry of warnings about a housing bubble as a contrary sign of strength. The papers are full of references to a potential retreat in home values. Wednesday's Wall Street Journal notes, for instance, that the number of new homes on the market has swelled to a 25-year high and says the housing market "seems a bit shaky." But it adds, "A decline would be troubling. Fortunately, such a decline also is unlikely." Even those that are talking about a bubble refuse to suggest that people should sell their homes or even put off buying one. Economists at UCLA are using the word "bubble" to describe California home prices, but when it comes to forecasting the next year they see only a slight drop of about 1%. "Experts inside and outside the housing industry reject the notion that there's a housing bubble," an L.A. Times story about the study adds. "Are We Inside a Bubble Looking Out?" asks the headline in a Sarasota, Florida paper. The author of a book on bubbles concludes that the answer is yes, but says, "We are in the early to middle stages." We see the same thing occurring with respect to many stock market forecasts for the upcoming year, particularly from those who claim to be wary of the market. While some even acknowledge that the stock market is in a "secular" downtrend, they still forecast continued rising equity prices in 2005. And just to make sure that they have properly covered all the contingencies, many add the qualifier "moderately" before the word rising.

So, it's a bubble, but it's a nice bubble that home owners don't have to protect themselves against. This same complacency surrounded warnings about high stock prices in March 2000 when EWFF reported, "Even if investors have concerns as a result of hearing an occasional warning, they do not act on them." Financial bubbles by definition always pop, and one of history's great tip-offs to the fact that they are ready to do so comes when participants see the bubble for what it is and decide not to do anything about it. Real estate is there now, and that is especially relevant because the bursting of the real estate market is the last straw. Its break should mark the start of the all-out economic collapse into depression.

February 2005

Most of the largest financial stocks already appear to be anticipating the fallout that will ensue. Last March, EWFF called for a long-term reversal in the financial sector. The Philadelphia KBW Bank Index managed to make a new high on December 23 (by just over 1%), but the three largest stocks in the group, Citigroup, Bank of America and JPMorgan Chase, representing nearly 30% of the entire index, failed to join the rally. Major brokerage firms Merrill Lynch and Goldman Sachs, have also lagged. This divergence is consistent with the larger market in which key blue chip stocks stalled in anticipation of the overall market's late December peak. Back in 2003, when the largest players in the financial industry decided to make up for a slump in trading volume by beefing up their proprietary trading operations, EWFF cited it as:

> Another example of a desperate flight to higher levels of financial risk. They intend to make up for the revenue lost from dwindling commissions by turning their trading units into profit centers. We predict unequivocally that trading disasters at brokerage firms will make headlines in coming months.

This phase appears to have begun with a series of "revelations" in The Wall Street Journal about the inner workings of brokerage firms. In a series of "Open Secrets" columns, the WSJ reveals that a "stepped-up review" of Wall Street shows that "clients don't always come first." As a matter of fact, some on Wall Street "have come to believe it's their God-given right to use information about orders to make money." Brokers fill customers' orders after they do their own, use sophisticated software to anticipate and profit from customer moves and situate their proprietary trading arms within earshot of large trading floors where customer's orders are handled. When the market was going up, this was a "problematic issue." Once the losses start to roll in, it will be a source of bitterness and conflict between Wall Street and the outside world.

March 2005

The Real Estate Bust Begins

With real estate now the focus of investment clubs, a Chicago Mercantile Exchange futures instrument, full page ads in the local newspaper and best-selling books like *Building Wealth One House at a Time, The ABC of Real Estate Investing* and *The Millionaire Real Estate Agent*, it is clear that the optimism of the Grand Supercycle bull market peak attends the real estate market. As shown in the left chart below, the transference of focus from stocks to property began four days after the NASDAQ's March 10, 2000 peak, when the S&P 500 Homebuilding Index bottomed. Since then, the index has soared to more than a 700% gain, which resembles the NASDAQ's October 1998-March 2000 ascent. As with the NASDAQ in March 2000, the man on the street is now captivated by the concept of easy wealth through real estate. "Middle Class Drives Soaring Purchases of Second Homes," says a headline in Wednesday's Washington Post. The New York Times reports that "a growing number of ordinary people" are "buying and selling residences they do not intend to occupy." According to the National Association of Realtors, a stunning 25% of the 7.7 million homes sold in 2004 were purchased strictly as investments.

The potential for a serious unraveling of the housing market is confirmed by the chart on the right, which combines the stock prices of four major subprime lenders. As the most aggressive dispensers of credit to the housing industry, these firms are on the front edge of the last two remnants of the financial bubble's great surge, the debt and housing bubbles. Their bursting is signaled by the five-wave rise through January 3, followed by a similarly impulsive short-term decline, which breaks the support line of the trend channel. These clean five-wave patterns portend a fall to much lower levels. Such a retrenchment fits with the Federal Reserve's latest plans for Fannie Mae and Freddie Mac, the two government-backed engines of the U.S. housing industry. On February 17, Alan Greenspan proposed cutting back their portfolios of mortgages from $1.7 trillion to $100 or $200 billion.

Meanwhile, various other government agencies are flashing contrary signals of a nearby turn with programs designed to drive home ownership above the already historic extreme of 69% of U.S. households. The state of Arizona joined forces with CitiMortgage to create the larg-

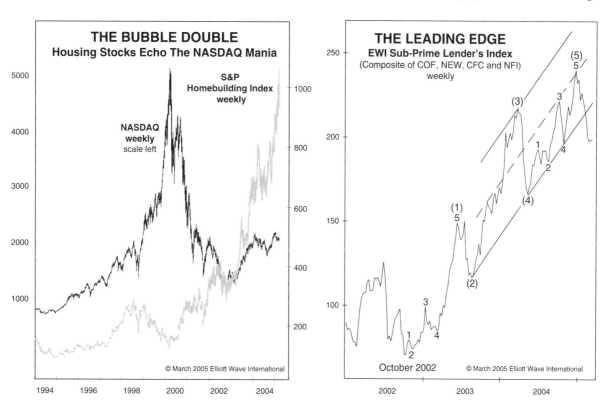

est "affordable-housing" lending program in the state's history. The aid, which is modeled after a $4.5 billion California program that was started in 2001, will allow homes to be bought for as little as $500 in paperwork costs. "We encourage all borrowers," says one lender. "We're not excluding anybody." Obviously, these lending policies are part of the reason prices have gone up so high, but the newfound zeal for universal homeownership signals that it is now time for the new environment of falling prices to overwhelm their influence. With zero equity loans, a 1% decline will put homeowners underwater. The reversal will certainly be historic as these instruments and others like them make the 1920s stock leverage look like 100% cash.

Back in the 1990s, *The Elliott Wave Theorist* designated Japan's developing deflation as the best available model for the U.S. The chart shows the plunge in commercial, residential and industrial real estate prices since the Japanese stock market peaked in 1990. Several smaller U.S. stock averages have reached new all-time highs in recent weeks. This final expression of Grand Supercycle euphoria has been sufficient enough to carry real estate to its present heights. As the next phase of the bear market digs in, the Japanese real estate experience will be replayed in the U.S. The one difference between the U.S. and Japan is that Japan had a safety net: the continued expansion of the global economy. The U.S. won't have that luxury, so the decline should happen faster.

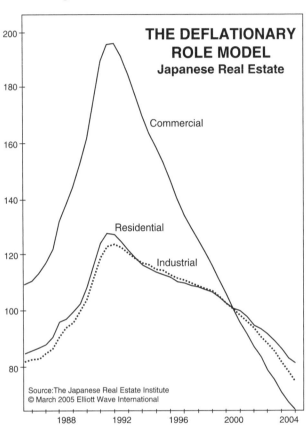

This quote from Wednesday's Washington Post demonstrates that the property euphoria is just a late-cycle extension of the Grand Supercycle peak: "I had money in the stock market, but the market always seemed to be going down, down, down. I decided to take that money out and invest it in real estate." New York Giants quarterback Kurt Warner is investing in real estate, stocks and mutual funds. "I want as little risk as possible." Asked what will become of his Super Bowl winnings, one recent champ answered, "I'm a real estate guy." From the frying pan to the fire, we say. Houses are far less liquid than stocks, and thus a more perfect final resting place for many investors' mania-era ambitions.

May 2005

Better Than Sex

Real estate's rise is now marked by the unmistakable traits of a full-blown mania. These include: day trading (some houses in Florida and California were recently bought and sold in the same day), a run of Harvard M.B.A.'s jumping into the field, and a hit show on TV, *Extreme Makeover: Home Edition*. The "buy-the-dip" philosophy even infected the sector in March, as a record one-month decline in median new home prices (9.3%) touched off a surge in new home sales. In an echo of the academic sanctions the stock market acquired in the late 1990s, a Miami realtor predicted that the boom will go on because "South Florida is working off a totally new economic model." Yes: The Fantasy Model. Back in March 2000 when "new economy" talk was omnipresent, EWFF stated that the claims were "a cover for the transition to deflation and a

Grand Supercycle" downturn. In yet another sign that sentiment for real estate is "over the top," Playboy's May Playmate of the Month says she's leaving the modeling game to go into "investment type real estate." Back in 1997 when the mania for stocks was still gathering steam, one of the key milestones covered in *The Elliott Wave Theorist* was money's replacement of sex as the primary preoccupation of many Americans. Now that the seduction is sweeping even the objects of society's sexual obsessions off their feet, a final reversal is at hand.

June 2005

The conventional wisdom about the investment buying power of millions of baby boomers is on its way out — again. The Wall Street Journal reported earlier this month:

As Boomers Retire:
Will Stock Prices Get Crushed?

The 1946-1964 baby boom = 1990-2008 investment boom equation dates to the start of the 1990s bull market extension when it was referred to us as the "Pig-in-Python theory." In 1998, as stocks were cresting, it was the subject of a second best-selling book. As EWFF noted in January 2003, The New York Times first re-cast boomers as "a force for the bear" with this headline: "16-Year Slump? If So, Blame It on the Boomers." Why now? Because we are entering a recognition phase. It is time for old bull market arguments to be refashioned into bear market arguments, as EWFF said they would be back at the all-time highs. Stock buybacks are another area of the bull market experience that is now being revised. "Beware the Buyback," reported Barrons over a story about a new study by Rockdale Research. "The most unexpected thing, but in retrospect it made total sense, was that corporations tend to buy back stocks at peaks, not troughs." EWT made the same observation in 1995 — five years before the high, not five years after — noting, "Company officers are part of the market's psychological fabric just like everyone else, and they tend to become bold when things look good, and that's usually near a top."

Another sign of the bear market is that financial bubbles are suddenly the object of widespread interest. Even the academic world is contemplating their significance. As an example, The Times of London reported on May 18 that a team of professors at the University of Southampton looked at investment patterns in the South Sea Bubble, the Japanese financial bubble and the global dot.com boom. Their research "unearthed evidence that suggests that investors can indeed go mad." "It seems that the dot.com boom-bust and the South Sea Bubble, though separated by nearly 300 years, are directly linked," say the authors. A Harvard Business Review article confirms, "Booms and busts cause economic instability." This timing is perfect. The academic world is adding fuel to the emerging bearish mindset. By contrast, EWT's special report on "Bulls, Bears and Manias," came out in 1997, giving investors plenty of time to protect themselves and a road map of what to expect. Obviously the bust part of the experience is not over as Harvard's study emphasizes that bubbles also "produced broad benefits for society." When a lasting bottom is in place, the "good side" of a financial mania will not be getting any play.

Planes, Trains and Space Cruisers

A fading veneration for science is evident in several science fiction endpoints. First recall *The Elliott Wave Theorist*'s classification of *Star Trek* as a bull market icon. Back in 1992, EWT noted that the show hit the airwaves at the end of Cycle III in 1966 and lasted through a secondary peak in 1968, which included all-time highs for the small-cap shares:

> It became popular again during the bull market of 1982 to date both in movies (along with *E.T.*) and on TV (*Star Trek, The New Generation*). The essential message of *Star Trek* is that all the creatures of the universe are a brotherhood. This ethic is a reflection of the most extremely positive social mood in a few centuries. When the bear market in stocks takes hold, *Star Trek* will go off the air and the movie sequels will cease.

In May 2005, the *Star Trek* TV and movie series flamed out. Once again, it is happening after a long peak in which the most speculative stocks are the last major market sector to make it to substantial new highs. *Star Trek*'s experience during Cycle V reflects the fact that it is also a peak of two larger degree trends. At the Cycle-degree peak of 1966-1968, *Star Trek*'s TV run covered three seasons. *Star Trek* reappeared in movie form in 1979, near the start of the bull market. *Star Trek* returned to TV a few weeks after the peak of 1987 and lasted 13 years. In 1968, fans successfully petitioned the studio to add the third season. This time, they tried to do the same thing, actually raising $3 million toward a continuation, but the trend is just too exhausted. Producers decided that the audience just isn't there. In terms of content, *Star Trek* "darkened over the decades," says a USA Today columnist. In the final version, the "universe is a hostile place filled with malevolent and treacherous aliens. Forget exploring strange new worlds. The underlying message now is survival."

The other brilliant science fiction success of the bull market, *Star Wars*, also completes its run in May 2005. As it does, it reflects the same darkening tone. By all accounts, the latest episode, *Revenge of the Sith*, is the bleakest of the six movies. From a socionomic perspective, the ingenious aspect of the most successful movie franchise in history was the decision to show the last three episodes of the sequel (Episodes IV-VI), which were the most upbeat, at the beginning of the bull market and the first three (I-III), easily the most bearish, from 1999-2005 as the Dow crashed through and then clung to the channel shown in the chart. In this way, *Star Wars* reflected the tenor of social mood and reaped the benefits of enormous popularity. Talk about timing, the original *Star Wars* debuted in July 1977, two months after the Dow Transports' Primary wave ① peak.

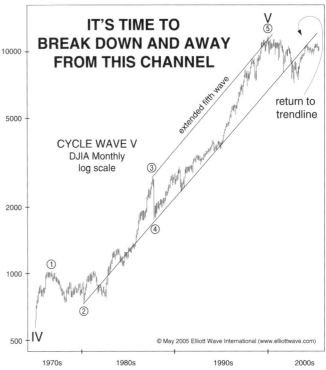

In another fascinating mood twist, Steven Spielberg, the director of *E.T.*, will bring an alien attack of Earth to theaters this summer. Back in the bull market, Spielberg said he'd never make a sci-fi film featuring hostile aliens. But he's making *War of the Worlds* now because 9/11 made him realize the relevance of H.G. Wells' "frightening vision of the future." *War of the Worlds* is considered by many sci-fi buffs to be the genre's first great work. If Spielberg's version succeeds, it may also be the last science fiction classic — for a while, anyway.

July 2005

For Real Estate, It's Time

There's no mistaking it now: The extreme psychology of the Grand Supercycle peak has taken up residence in real estate. The public demand for periodically illiquid pieces of property is an eerie facsimile of the zany excitement for stocks in 2000. It now includes a record high price of $90 million for a U.S. residential property; a TV show, *Property Ladder*, in which subjects buy houses and resell them for a quick profit; and an online trading service, Condoflip.com, where "flippers, brokers and developers come together" to trade as yet unbuilt condominiums. "Bubbles Are For Bathtubs," reads the top line on the site. While the number of stock market investment clubs has decreased 46% since its peak year of 1999, the number of real estate investment clubs is up 400% since 2002. One California club member explains proudly, "I quit my day job of 30 years. It's the wave of the future, of working smarter, not working harder." The easy-money, "I'm a wizard now" ethos of the mania is coursing through real estate as furiously as it raged through the stock market in 2000. "Get Rich Without Leaving Home," says a CNN Money headline. "If you've dreamed of investing in real estate but don't want to miss out on the kids' Little League games, [real estate] partnerships may be the answer."

The leverage upon which "the dream" is built is way beyond the record high margin levels in stocks in 2000. "I've been playing with the bank's money," says the cover girl on the May issue of Money Magazine. Forget the 30-year mortgage; 40-year home loans are now "mainstream" and 60-year, no-interest terms are offered in hot markets like San Francisco. This time there is no mistaking who the Enrons of the bust phase will be. They will be the firms now peddling adjustable-rate, no-interest/nothing-down and assorted other types of "sub-prime" mortgages. According to the ISI Group, homeowner equity was 56.3% in March, a slight uptick from the lowest level on record. A strong undercurrent of envy is another tie to the dot-com era. "Desperation is driving people," says the director of Harvard's Joint Center for Housing Studies. "People are not looking at what they are going to have to pay over the long term. They are asking what is the lowest possible payment I have to make over the next 12-months so I can get in." Says a California disc jockey, "I saw my friends and colleagues getting rich. I wanted to get rich too."

To top it off, Time magazine issued a real estate cover story in early June as the NAREIT Index was completing a five-wave rally. As EWFF explained in January and February 2000, major magazine cover stories have a "strong record of marking a trend change in the fortunes of a profiled firm, sector or market," and Time magazine's record is among the most distinguished. Back in 2000, we were referring to a slew of covers on the New Economy, Amazon, AOL and Martha Stewart that did, in fact, mark the all-time peak with glowing profiles. Here on the right shoulder of the same long-term peak, Time has done it again. It's "Home Sweet Home" cover focuses on the most ubiquitous holding in the average American's investment portfolio. Now that its editors are all on board, it is the most dangerous, too.

Some say real estate can't go down because far too many people are concerned about a real estate bubble, a worry that is now even greater than it was for stocks at the March 2000 NASDAQ peak. But as our section on "Real Estate and the Uh-Oh Effect" in January explained, it is actually another sign of a top when participants are dismissive of the warnings. The June 22 issue of Business Week asked a roster of economists if housing prices were "soaring unsustainably and due to plunge?" Not one said yes, though one did admit that the market "is caught up in the psychology of a bubble." The rest agreed that the concept of "a national housing bubble is relatively silly." The man on the street remains largely oblivious to the debate. A

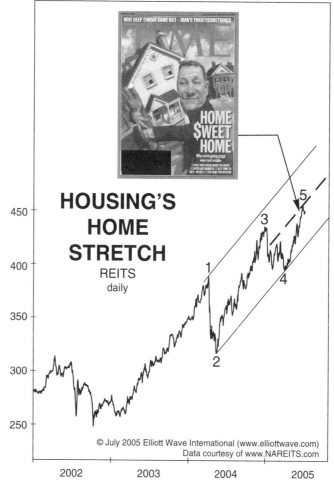

poll by the National Association of Realtors found that only 23% have heard of the potential of a housing bubble, and many didn't know what pollsters meant by "bubble." When informed, 37% said that a housing bubble is "somewhat" or "very likely." The survey may explain the uh-oh effect. Apparently, a significant percentage of the population does not know that a return to earth is implicit in a financial asset's pole-vault to record heights.

September 2005

Why The End Is Near

The July issue showed Time magazine's "Home Sweet Home" cover story over a completed five-wave advance in the NAREIT index and labeled it "Housing's Home Stretch." There are many reasons to believe that a bear market in real estate has, in fact, just begun, including the latest reading on that chart of bank mortgage holdings. At 61%, bank mortgage holdings touched a Fibonacci point of likely reversal. Another factor is the action in the EWI Sub-Prime Lenders Index, which the March issue of EWFF identified as the "front edge" of the great financial bubble. After completing five waves up at three degrees of trend in January (see chart in the March entry), the index declined in five waves, sputtered higher in a countertrend bounce and reversed in what should be a powerful decline to much lower levels. The homebuilders have also joined in with a five-wave decline of their own. The decline's break of the exponential curve formed by its near vertical rise (shown on the chart of the S&P 500 Homebuilding Index) is a powerful sign that a long, hard fall is starting.

Homebuilding company insiders apparently contributed to the fall as their sales at several key firms are running at their highest levels since 1985. Richard Bernstein of Merrill Lynch notes that the one-sided selling levels are similar to insider sales of technology stocks on the approach to their March 2000 peak. New home sales are still strong, but as the August issue of *The Elliott Wave Theorist* noted, the decline is now underway in several foreign markets and a tell-tale inventory build-up, which *Conquer the Crash* cited as the first sign of the big collapse, has started. Reports of rising inventories are surfacing from California to Massachusetts. In Sacramento, inventories rose to a 7-year high in July then shot up another 26% in August. Nationally, prices for condominiums fell for a second straight month, while the number of condos on the market rose sharply. In the once-torrid South Florida market, "the word 'correction' is being increasingly whispered" and agents report a "subtle change" in the tone of business over the last six months. More houses fail to sell and more listings expire—"something that would have been unheard of a year ago"—and asking prices are falling. "The market is turning," says a Palm Beach realtor. Houses purchased by speculators in hopes of a quick flip are "killing the market in certain areas."

Then there's the uh-oh effect, which, as our collage shows, continues to mount within the real estate sector. Noting that reversals from "the biggest tops of all" are accompanied by ignored warnings of imminent reversal, the January EWFF stated that a flurry of concern about a housing bubble is similar to concern in 2000 about high prices for NASDAQ stocks, which EWFF used

Greenspan: Housing Bubble May Burst

Bound for a crash?

Greenspan said that people were investing in houses as if they were a one-way bet, not allowing for falls. He said "history had not dealt kindly" with investors who kept ignoring risks.
—*New York Daily News*, August 28, 2005

Experts warn heavy debt threatens American economy
—207 different publications including *The Washington Post, Peoria Journal Star, Longmont Daily Times*, August 29, 2005

Eonomists Worry About Housing Bubble
—*Consumer Affairs*, August 23, 2005

Bubble Babble
It is no longer possible to pick up a paper, open a business Web site or watch a money channel without having the US housing market thrown at you.
—*The Jerusalem Post*

Michigan Likely to See Housing Prices Decline
—*WOOD-TV*, Grand Rapids, Mich., August 28, 2005

U.S. Heading For House Price Crash
Greenspan Tells Buyers
—*The Times* (of London), August 27, 2005

Bubble Talk Bursts Housing Euphoria
Market nearing peak, some experts say
—*Chicago Tribune*, August 28, 2005

Greenspan Warns Against Optimism on Homes, Stocks
—*USA Today*, August 27, 2005

WARN: Boom Can Be Fleeting
—*The Atlanta Journal-Constitution*, August 27, 2005

Debt Load Makes Americans Vulnerable
—142 different publications including *The Washington Post, Forbes, Jefferson City News Tribune*, August 28, 2005

to successfully anticipate the NASDAQ's peak in March of that year. Contrarians continue to contend that the housing boom cannot end because many pundits are worried, but the majority and its conviction are what matters. At this point, there is one key difference between concerns about the NASDAQ in 2000 and real estate worries: the effect is much stronger this time. "Talk of the current prospects for 'the bubble' has become an evening-news staple and is fueling endless cocktail party conversations and Internet blogger musings." The National Association of Realtors' web site even posted an unusual "wait-to-buy" advisory. The message was quickly removed because it was being "viewed incorrectly as a pronouncement that the bubble was popping."

December 2005
The New Economy Is Back

A big component of the hoopla at the all-time high was the celebration of the great technology wave that allegedly eliminated the down part of the business cycle. In a February 2000 special report, "Deflation and the New Economy," which came out 14 days before the NASDAQ's all-time peak, *The Elliott Wave Financial Forecast* exposed the truth about the "miracle of modern productivity." The biggest reason to suspect that the so-called New Economy was something less than the nirvana that it was being made out to be was the aura of boundless optimism that surrounded it. Expectations were universally positive, and EWFF identified this condition as a surefire sign that "in the not so distant future, we will be hearing about these less glamorous aspects of the deflationary cycle."

Within the last few weeks, the media has rediscovered the New Economy. "Let's Celebrate the Belated Arrival of the New Economy," says one headline. An editorial in a major financial newspaper reveals how closely tied the whole idea is to the movement of the Dow Industrials. Editors admit to a "loss of faith" in the new economy during the decline of 2000-2002, but now, they say, they are back on the bandwagon:

The New Economy Lives On

Traumatized ourselves by the market debacle, and then 9-11, we too started to play down the New Economy theme. But then came Thursday's report on third-quarter productivity—up a whopping 4.1%—and it all started falling back into place. The blessings that this highly productive New Economy has brought are real.
—Investors Business Daily, November 4, 2005

In another parallel to 2000, zealous technophiles are once again invoking the name of a famous cycle theorist to suggest that a whole series of innovations created during the last bull market make the economy immune to economic contraction. "Economist Joseph Schumpeter taught us years ago that gales of creative destruction generate more than usual growth, profits, and real wages. Schumpeter's gales are blowing." That they are, but as EWFF warned in 2000, they are not a one-way ticket to economic growth. This statement from the February 2000 issue of EWFF is even more relevant today:

> In time, there are several more Schumpeterisms that will be revisited. These include the "elimination of what is incapable of adaptation," the "reorganization of economic life," the "remodeling the system of value" and the "liquidation of indebtedness."

Deflation will drive all these changes, but one of the reasons that it remains largely invisible to economists and the public at large is that a 200-year Grand Supercycle bull market topping process blinds many to even its most obvious symptoms—even after the initial visions of the New Economy proved to be devastatingly false for many believers. One big misconception back in 2000, for instance, was the belief that the entry of "traditional companies" into the Internet was a positive development. EWFF noted at the time that deflationary breakdowns tend to coincide with Supercycle degree downturns. At the end of Supercycle I in 1835, for instance, innovative new technologies like the railroads and telegraph were becoming viable while Supercycle III ushered in the era of radio entertainment and air transport. At such times, Schumpeter said deflation usually begins with a broad-based "adaptation to the new things created" during the boom, producing a brutally competitive business environment. The dot-com bust of 2000-2002, in which hundreds of upstart firms vanished virtually overnight, was the first wave of the current episode.

A similar inflection point into an outright deflation may have occurred on October 30 when Microsoft's Bill Gates, the most successful innovator of the old bull market, announced, 'The next sea change is upon us." Gates told Microsoft senior managers and engineers that henceforth all of the firm's strategies would be built around Internet services. The new strategy will "impact on almost everything Microsoft does. In order to execute on this opportunity, we must act quickly and decisively." Gates is rallying the troops because the transition to a new world of cutthroat competition is happening fast. Just within the last month, Google unveiled free wi-fi services and free "enterprise class" analytics, programs that track the results of online marketing campaigns. The service used to cost $199 a month from Google and many times more than that from some vendors. "This is great information at no charge," said one competitor. Google is also initiating a free classified advertising service called Google Base. The Internet rallying cry cited by EWFF in August 2000, was "Information wants to be free." Now, we're hearing the same slogan, and it's literally true.

As king of the established order, Microsoft naturally resisted the trend as long as it could because it has enormous revenue streams tied up in the old business methods. The rising social mood was a big help because as long as the trend was up, individuals and businesses were willing and/or able to stick with the old ways. At the end of the great bull market, which stretched into 2005 in some sectors, the mood is so elevated that both the new and the old economy coexist. That's certainly true for the newspaper industry, which has tried to run on the old and the new tracks. Until very recently, revenues continued to grow even though the content of most papers is available for free on the web. In recent months, however, as the countertrend rally in stocks weakened internally, subscriptions at many papers plunged. At the San Francisco Chronicle, Atlanta Journal-Constitution and Boston Globe, subscriptions fell 16.4%, 8.73% and 8.25%, respectively, in just six months. Overall, newspaper subscriptions are down 2.6% for the half year that ended in September. In response, a slew of newspapers are putting themselves up for sale and laying off reporters; moves that will only accelerate their descent.

In any of the last 10 years, consumers could have used the web to save money and drive harder bargains in a wide variety of different areas, but they're only doing so now en masse because the bear market in social mood is assuming complete control. Almost six years after the Dow Industrials' all-time peak, consumers are eliminating extravagances like the daily paper, which they no longer read or can get on the Internet for free. There are many other signs that consumers are jumping to the deflationary track. In March, for instance, EWFF mentioned that a new community bulletin board called craigslist.org was eating into the classified revenue of California newspapers. It is now the "most popular classified advertising web site." "More People Are Selling Something Online," says a November 28 headline. On any given day, 2% of Internet users are selling online. "The Internet has evolved into a global bazaar, where people buy and trade a wide array of collectibles, knickknacks, furniture, clothes and other used items." The number of visitors to online classified sites jumped 80 percent from September 2004 to this September. This is just the set-up phase. Once the global garage sale really gets rolling, truly astounding volumes of dirt-cheap goods will be available on-line and elsewhere.

The latest projections from CNN/Money say that economists are raising forecasts and "Partying Like It's 1999 – into 2006." There is every reason to believe that the celebration will turn out to be as ill-timed now as it was at the turn of the century. Recently, the main economic driver has been the housing and home equity lending booms. In California, home sales are so essential to the economy that 2% of all adult residents hold licenses to sell residential property. Toward the end of the last major real estate boom in 1989, *The Elliott Wave Theorist* pointed out that the licensing of brokers typically reaches extremes when housing is at the end of a long rise. In fact, the top may be in. The National Association of Home Builders housing market index just suffered one of its worst monthly performances in history, tumbling 8 points to its lowest level since May 2003. Since July when EWFF declared that housing stocks were in their "home stretch," the S&P 500 Homebuilding index traced out a five-wave decline followed by a small-degree countertrend rebound. The three-wave rise probably ended November 23. Pundits aren't worried and argue that housing is simply taking a much needed breather. "The NAHB believes the market is in an 'orderly cooling process,'" states one account. Another says that investors are "so desperate for buyers that some are offering cash bonuses" but then adds, "That's a sign the Federal Reserve is succeeding in removing some 'froth' from the market."

The housing market is in the process of falling into an enormous crater, and the belief that the Fed can simply scoop away the froth while leaving the boom intact is sure sign of it. In October, home sales fell a larger-than-expected 2.7%. "It's like someone turned off the faucet," said a real estate agent. A big October uptick in the number of unsold homes is even more revealing, as it rose to its highest level since April 1986. This is the supply surge that *Conquer the Crash* placed at the front edge of housing's downward spiral:

> In the initial stages of a depression, sellers remain under an illusion about what their property is really worth. At some point, a few owners cave in and sell at much lower prices. Then others are forced to drop their prices, too.

Sellers will do anything to avoid dropping prices. They're offering prizes and having parties, whatever it takes to keep the good times rolling.

February 2006

Here's another road sign that points to a real estate plunge dead ahead:

43% of First-Time Home Buyers Put No Money Down
—USA Today, January 18, 2006

It's not the reality of easy money. *The Elliott Wave Financial Forecast* covered that ground several months ago. The significant aspect of the story is its prominence. Its appearance on the front page of USA Today shows that investors are awakening from the dream-state of ever-rising real estate prices. Another sign is this quote from an industry analyst that appeared within the article: "If a modest decline (in the housing market) turns into a rout, there's almost no bottom to that.

That's a crash scenario." We said last month that almost no one expects a dramatic decline in real estate prices, and that's still true. But suddenly there is an awareness of the potential. How long can it be from the first use of the word "crash" on the front-page of the nation's largest daily newspaper to the actual break? Our suspicion is that it will not be long. Real estate developers in Las Vegas are already scaling back their plans. "Experts now forecast that only a quarter to a half of seven dozen originally proposed [luxury towers] will ever be built," reports Time magazine.

Another key glimmer of recognition comes from Boston, where housing inventory is rising fast (up 54% from the level of January 2005). Would-be buyers indicate that they will "watch the market, hoping prices fall further." "Now, 'Buyers and sellers know the market's changed. Last year, nobody knew,'" reports the Boston Globe. This is the dawn of the new conservatism discussed in *Conquer the Crash* and recent issues. This new cautiousness is the motor of deflation.

April 2006
Whatever You Do, Don't Say D-O-W-N

February was another bad month for the housing industry, as sales of new homes plunged 10.5%, the biggest drop in nearly nine years, while prices fell and the number of homes on the market hit a record high. This has to be the real estate toboggan slide we've been expecting. In concert with the turn, the government is setting its sights on lenders. "Brokers who arrange home loans at high interest rates [are] drawing scrutiny from law enforcement authorities," and federal regulators are cracking down on the Federal Home Loan Banks in a way that threatens to shrink a subsidy long enjoyed by thousands of lenders." New rules proposed by the Federal Housing Finance Board would require the banks to retain more of their earnings as capital to build up a bigger cushion against potential losses. These news items mark a tidal shift away from the feverish "sub-prime" lending climate that EWFF profiled in the July and September issues. As Barron's notes, "Teaser rates have expired. With house prices no longer soaring, [mortgage borrowers] can't easily cash out or refi." Keep this quote from our July issue in mind: "This time there is no mistaking who the Enrons of the bust phase will be. They will be the firms now peddling adjustable-rate, no-interest/nothing-down and assorted other types of 'sub-prime' mortgages."

And still there is virtually no fear about home values. A recent national survey of homeowners by the L.A. Times shows "widespread faith in the real estate market." A question about expectations for house prices asked only about the predicted amount of future rises and did not even include a category that allowed for expressing an opinion about any decline. The worst possible scenario, that prices would "stay the same" over the next 3 years, was selected by just 5% of homeowners. That total was less than the 6% who said they expect to see a rise of "31% or more." No matter how much talk of a bubble there may be, homeowners continue to demonstrate that they have no clue about the ramifications of one. Included in the survey were respondents with adjustable-rate mortgages, a quarter of whom said they "aren't sure they'll be able to make their monthly payments if interest rates go up." Even among the financially strapped, the very concept of falling real estate prices is not a consideration. And, as the latest housing figures attest, this is in an environment in which prices actually are falling! The denial runs so deep, it's not even denial anymore. It's some kind of epic disconnect between the reality of a newly-falling housing market and an unwritten social contract that says home prices do not fall. Whatever this delusion is called, it cannot last much longer.

May 2006

There are some benefits to the ripple effect that keeps the churn of the great asset mania pushing through one asset class after another, from Beanie Babies to tech stocks and most recently through real estate. One big benefit is that, at this point, it's not hard to clearly envision where the post-peak stress fractures are going to show up. In real estate, for instance, one of the potential problem areas that EWFF cited last summer was all the new forms of "creative' financing that were springing up. When "60-year, no-interest terms" and the "sub-prime adjustable-rate, no-interest/nothing-down" loans became mainstream offerings and home buyers started "asking what is the lowest possible payment I have to make over the next 12-months so I can get in," EWFF said the top had to be close at hand. This headline from the April 20, 2006 issue of the *San Antonio Express* confirms that it is now in place:

Real Trouble In Real Estate

Local mortgage brokers have a warning for people already struggling to make their adjustable rate mortgage payments: get out of them now.

Of course, now it's too late. Rates are up and mortgage bankers are increasingly at a loss when it comes to creative refinancing solutions. The September issue showed that banks' mortgage-related assets [have risen to 61% of total assets] and said that they seemed "blind to the danger as they continue to stuff their balance sheets with mortgaged assets." Bloomberg columnist Caroline Baum reveals in a recent article that the truth can now be told—banks are in deeper than almost anyone thought. "Every time the subject of banks making risky home loans to bad credit risks—no money down, no questions asked—the usual retort is that banks sell the mortgages. They aren't at risk. That's not exactly true." Baum places the exposure at 44%, but even that understates the problem because banks still derive significant origination fees from mortgages they sell, and those fees are drying up. With the national foreclosure rate jumping 63% in the first quarter of the year (according to RealtyTrac.com), real estate, is suddenly a dicey proposition for bankers.

August 2006

In just the first half of the year, venture capitalists invested $254.9 million in blogging and online social networks. The total exceeds the investment in all of 2005, according to Dow Jones VentureOne. "The popular success of the social-networking site MySpace and video-sharing site YouTube has inspired a spate of imitators" even though MySpace and YouTube are not yet profitable. Sound familiar? The condition is a close copy of the plunge into unprofitable Internet networks like iVillage.com and theGlobe.com in 2000. In the bear market, both suffered 99% declines in their share prices. But the signal is even more bearish now because this time the mania is snaring some of the same people with the same story of limitless potential in Internet communities. There's just something about these buzzing electronic clubs that seems to magnify the siren song of a mania.

Real Estate Recognition

Here's the psychological progression that *Conquer the Crash* said to look for in real estate at the beginning of a deflationary collapse:

In the initial stages of a depression, sellers remain under an illusion about what their property is really worth. They keep a high list price on their house, reflecting what it was worth last year. This stubbornness leads to a drop in sales volume. At some point, a few owners cave in and sell at much lower prices. Then others are forced to drop their prices, too. What is the potential buyer's psychology at that point? "Well, gee, property prices have been coming down. Why should I rush? I'll wait till they come down further!" The further they come down, the more the buyer wants to wait. It's a downward spiral.

Here's a chart that shows the unprecedented inventory of the total number of new houses for sale in the United States. Already there are the headlines marking the front edge of the great cave-in:

Home Sellers Push Their Prices Down

—Boston Globe, July 17

**SUPPLY SPIKE PREDICTS
PRICE PLUNGE**
New Homes for Sale in the U.S.
monthly (thousands)

© July 2006 Elliott Wave International (www.elliottwave.com)
Data courtesy of Bloomberg

1960s   1970s   1980s   1990s   2000s

Home Prices Could Start Falling
—USA Today, July 26

Home Prices Drop
—Washington Post, July 27

This week the Boston Globe quotes a Wellesley housing economist who says that there is "no question" prices will come down, but the article notes, "Massachusetts real estate agents are increasingly discouraged by an unwillingness among clients with properties on the market to lower their listing prices." Coldwell Banker Residential Brokerage is actually holding classes in which it coaches agents in how to persuade clients to list their homes at an asking price that undercuts the competition. The article refers to the technique as "drama or energy pricing" and says that it "is a drastic measure for difficult times." But there's still no real understanding of just how difficult times will become. When a course is needed to convey the "concept" of falling prices, it is still very early in the process described in CTC. In the homebuilding sector, which should lead the upcoming economic downturn, the first signs of a downward spiral are starting to show. The Wall Street Journal reports that land-value erosion is now being recognized as a problem in an industry where book value was viewed as a "possible floor for stock prices." But the startling realization that homebuilding "companies' land might not be worth what they paid" means they face "painful write-downs," which means weaker stocks and further declines in property values.

Many of the most vulnerable property owners are those that think they just dodged a bullet by trading in ballooning payments on their old adjustable-rate mortgage plus the equity in their house, for a new adjustable-rate mortgage. According to The New York Times, $400 billion in adjustable-rate mortgages, or about 5 percent of all outstanding mortgage debt, will readjust this year for the first time. Another $1 trillion in loans will readjust next year. Home owners can put off the "day of reckoning" by refinancing with new adjustable-rate mortgages that keep monthly payments low, but by doing so they dig themselves in deeper, because payments will be even higher in the future. The headlines above mean that this "opportunity" is ending. "Everything works fine as long as there is pretty decent home price appreciation," says the director of a residential mortgage securities group. With prices beginning to fall, there's only one way out, and that's to sell, which means further price declines. Welcome to the wicked world of deflation.

Homebuilding stocks have been declining since July 2005, when Time magazine published its "Home Sweet Home" cover story about Americans going "gaga for real estate," right at top tick. A year later, the S&P Supercomposite Homebuilding index is down more than 50%, but the potential for still greater damage is evident by the fact that the chief economist for the California Association of Realtors has only recently stopped using the term "soft landing" to describe the California real estate market. "Maybe we need something new," she says. But the "illusion of what was" is obviously in place because the economist adds, "That's all I'm prepared to say. When I get a new term, I'll let you know." Based on the industry's two key measures of future business, "crash" is not too strong a word. The National Association of Home Builders Housing Market Index is down from 72 in June 2005 to 39 this month, its lowest reading since 1991. The

Traffic of Prospective Buyers Index is down from a level of 53 in the middle of 2005 to 27 now, its lowest level since March 1995.

November 2006

Wall Street Tries to Lend Its Way Out

The big top in the financial sector is visible in bank and brokerage firms' effort to horn in on the hedge fund game. On Wednesday, for instance, Bloomberg reported that Morgan Stanley made its third hedge fund purchase "in as many days." "Investment banks have increased their ownership of hedge funds to boost profits," notes the story. In an important divergence, however, the exposure is not keeping financial stocks on pace with the DJIA. Despite a rally in conjunction with the rest of the market, the AMEX Securities Broker Dealer Index's April 21 peak remains in place. Several tremors in the form of earnings shortfalls at T. Rowe Price and Legg Mason, as well as Bank of America's offering of free online trades, shook the street in October. Free stock trading "ratchets up competitive pressures," since commissions have already been slashed to the bone.

With the pool of investors stagnant, the industry's route to growth is clear—more leverage. This explains the popularity of some non-NASDAQ firms like Echo Trading and Bright Trading, which offer 20-to-1 leverage to any trader with a Series 7 brokerage license. Leverage of up to 100-to-1 is available for those that can show a "track record." In another perfect twist of timing, the SEC is planning to lower margin requirements for institutions on stocks, options and futures from 25%-50%, to just 15%! In a classic undoing of 1930s-era trading restrictions, the change will remove limits put in place over 7 decades ago to prevent "another 1929." Bob Hoye of Institutional Advisors notes that the last time a central bank lowered margin requirements was in Japan in early 1990, right after the mania for Japanese stocks. The Nikkei fell 20% in the first five months of 1990 despite a substantial rise in margin debt. By the way, the Nikkei is still down 59% from its all-time peak.

December 2006

The enormous power of the unfolding deflation is now visible in the housing sector. The median U.S. home price fell to $221,000 in October, a decline of 3.5% from a year ago, the biggest year-over-year price decline on record. It marks the third straight month that home prices have fallen compared to the same period a year ago, the longest stretch on record. The chart of homeowner vacancies shows the corresponding and totally unprecedented rise in excess housing stock. In the western U.S., whole subdivisions are already so blighted by walk-off homeowners that the president of the Federal Reserve Bank of San Francisco describes them as the "new ghost towns of the West." In Phoenix, where a year ago developers were raising prices $1,000 to $10,000 a week, the number of unsold homes has soared to 46,000. "The striking contrast tells the tale of a housing

A HISTORIC HOLLOWING OF THE HOUSING STOCK
% of U.S. Homes Unoccupied
quarterly

Source: U.S. Census Bureau
© December 2006 Elliott Wave International (www.elliottwave.com)

bonanza turned bust," says the New York Times. "It's finally catching up to me," one former homeowner told the Denver Post. "We have no place to go and no money."

Another persistent fairy tale is the belief that any decline will be confined to certain regions and sectors. Headlines like these tell a different story: "Real Estate Slump Tough on Midwest;" "Florida's Housing Hurricane;" "New Jersey Home Foreclosure Indicator Rises 44%;" "California Home Sales Plunge." The real estate collapse is clearly spreading. With prices of REIT indexes extending to new heights on November 24, the consensus is that commercial real estate will "cushion the impact of the housing slump." But it is only a matter of time before every type of property gets pulled into the deflationary spiral. REITs are not up because of real estate, they are up because of the continuing stock mania. One sign of an imminent crack is the sale of Equity Office Properties Trust in the biggest leveraged buyout in history. The firm is the largest office building owner, with 585 buildings and 108.5 million square feet of space in major U.S. cities. Some analysts criticized the firm's principal, Sam Zell, for selling too low, but it looks like a cagey exit to us. As EWFF noted in February 2000, the biggest deals tend to happen near peaks because those with the most knowledge of their industry are generally willing to surrender control only at such times. The underlying fragility of the commercial real estate market is readily apparent here in Atlanta where some of the city's signature office buildings sit virtually empty. With a vacancy rate close to 30%, landlords are offering discounts of up to 30% to new tenants. Less than 10 years ago, Atlanta was one of the leading office markets in the country. It still is, but no one wants to admit it. Now that it is leading the way down, it is labeled an aberration.

With the real estate decline so well developed and more and more evidence of an economic slowdown starting to emerge, the only possible explanation for the lack of concern is the difference between the oncoming deflationary collapse and the recessions of the past 50 years, which were all accompanied by inflation. The misdirected outlook has some very dangerous repercussions. Instead of reducing their exposure to debt, for instance, companies and individuals are increasing it. The takeover binge described above is a perfect example. Buyers are financing the deals with private equity in which 70% of the purchase price is bank debt that is held on the balance sheet of the purchased company. According to Standard & Poor's, corporations have also significantly increased their use of debt financing in acquisitions. "There has been a fundamental shift in companies' attitude towards debt as shareholders have put more pressure on them to perform," says Standard & Poor's managing director of corporate ratings. The latest deal, a reputed $100 billion buyout of Home Depot, would saddle a perfectly respectable balance sheet with $80 billion in debt. The more vulnerable the economy and markets get, the more precariously companies and individuals position themselves. In this way, the slow grind into the peak is laying the ground work for the coming decline to do immeasurable damage.

Follow Up On Financial Fallout

Last month's issue concentrated on the potential for a "big top in the financial sector"; the merger activity certainly supports this view. Finance is the leading sector with almost $500 billion in deals for 2006.

Another amazing symbol of the financial industry's ballooning size and instability is the global market for , which increased to a record $370 trillion in the first half of 2006. More threatening than the number, which is 27 times U.S. GDP, is the audacity of its financial engineers. The latest wrinkle is a Constant Proportion Debt Obligation, which uses a hefty dose of leverage to parlay the "creditworthiness" of corporate bond issuers into returns that are up to "2% better than prevailing money market rates." According to Bloomberg columnist Mark Gilbert, "The most innovative feature of a CPDO is its resemblance to a gambler at a casino, doubling up when bets go awry." If this sounds familiar, it's probably because similar "loss chasing" portfolio insurance products came out once before, right before the stock market crashed in 1987. Some blamed the instruments for the crash itself; but bigger declines in markets without portfolio insurance show that portfolio insurance didn't tank the market. Still, its appearance is vitally important because it reflects a rare level of complacency in which uncertainty itself is believed to be eliminated. At such times, the 1987 experience reveals that markets are primed for devastating hits. Hints of this potential are visible in the stocks of the biggest financial giants, as the Philadelphia/KBW Banking Index is now sputtering badly. In fact, the index's high was two months ago, on October 4. Its banishment from the last two months of rise amidst so many dazzling financial developments points to something much more serious than a brief market correction.

January 2007

2007: The Year of Financial Flameout

One of the legacies of the Cycle wave V bull market that began in December 1974 and ended in January 2000 is the conviction that speculation and financial engineering are enduring and self-sustaining engines of economic growth. Longtime subscribers know better. Way back in 1983, *The Elliott Wave Theorist* presaged the financial boom of the last two decades by observing that fifth waves are "built more on unfounded hopes than on soundly improving fundamentals such as the U.S. experienced in the 1950s and early 1960s. And since this fifth wave, wave V, is a fifth within a larger fifth, wave (V) from 1789, the phenomenon should be magnified by the time the peak is reached." Thus, the boom of the last three decades is founded on the quicksand that EWT described at its outset. The full extent of the mania for paper is captured in this chart of total financial assets held by U.S. brokerage firms and other "funding corporations" as a percentage of annual U.S. Gross Domestic Product.

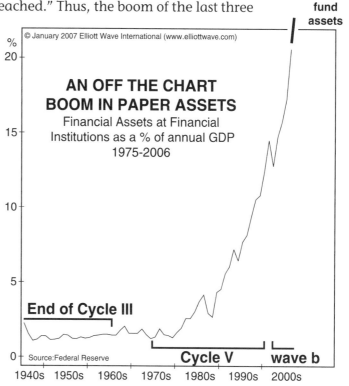

From 1974 to the third quarter of 2006, financial assets held by Wall Street firms soared from 1.3% to 20.5% of GDP. Following a rare setback in the bear market year of 2002, the ratio actually zoomed to new heights even as the major stock averages fought to get back to the highs of 2000; a feat that the NASDAQ and S&P have so far failed to accomplish. The rate of ascent is even faster than the Fed shows because their figures do not include hedge fund assets. According to HFM Week, a hedge fund newsletter, hedge fund assets hit $2 trillion in November, raising Wall Street's total assets to a mind-boggling 36.6% of GDP. We have added hedge funds assets to the total.

As EWFF has noted in the past, financial firms survived the plunge of 2000-2002 and thrived through the rebound of 2002-2006 by pushing clients, and increasingly their own capital, into riskier investments. By amplifying the leverage and rechanneling the speculative intensity of a Grand Supercycle peak from technology in 2000 to housing in 2005 and commodities in 2006, financial firms kept the fire alive. Thanks to hedge funds, leverage and financial engineering have been pushed into every available asset class. When hard assets, such as copper and silver, which were abandoned in favor of paper assets in 1980, were pulled into the fervor and pushed into exponential uptrends, the end was near. The May 11 peak in the Reuters/Jefferies CRB Index of commodities appeared to be the last bubble, but financial engineers found a new object of investor affections—themselves. Recent issues of EWFF reveal some of the myriad ways in which Wall Street became the focal point of speculation. The street's fabulous year-end bonuses are the latest example (see January 2007 entry in Chapter 6 for the emerging bear market response). Of course, the financial industry's position so close to the center of the mania can only mean one thing; it is only a matter of time before it joins tech stocks, real estate and commodities in the great turn lower.

A sure sign of a financial zenith is the recent massive media acknowledgment of the liquidity boom that underlies the Great Asset Mania. The Wall Street Journal and Newsweek opened the year with major articles extolling the virtues of a "world awash in cash." "Let The Good Times Roll," says Newsweek. "The world has been building toward this critical moment for some time. It's no accident that financial markets have flourished. Now regulators, central banks and markets around the world are poised to make moves that could turn an expansion into an explosion." Newsweek is exactly right and wrong at the same time. It is a "critical moment," but the "explosion" will come in the opposite direction than the media now project. This is clear by the evidence that it offers for a further boom. Newsweek, for instance, again cites the bullish implications of the global bidding frenzy to own financial exchanges. But as EWFF explained last month—and previously in 1999 when the major U.S. exchanges announced public offerings—a century of NYSE seat price history shows that extremes in the demand for exchanges come at major peaks.

The other incredible expanding story is the "staggering" size and volume of corporate acquisitions. Newsweek and countless other articles find the rash of "bigger and bigger" deals "Phenomenally Positive" for the stock market. Even though he "is not in the business of predicting where stock markets go," a M&A specialist says, "It really props up the market." Another article reveals that private equity firms now have enough cash to "fund the acquisition of every company on the NASDAQ and the London Stock Exchange." But as noted here last month and at the peak in 2000, one of the key signs of a peak in stocks "is the folly surrounding corporate takeovers." It can't get much crazier than this.

Back in the spring, when the papers initially discovered that the global financial markets were rising in tandem, a worrisome shudder hit the street. The Wall Street Journal and others nervously reported on possible "systemic risks." Eight months later, some of the hottest of these markets have plunged, yet the Journal now reports that nothing can stop the "river of money:"

> Even the most pessimistic economists and central bankers see little sign that the liquidity boom, and the benign financial environment that it has fostered will disappear soon. Confidence in the current environment stems from financial innovations and new financial players that have helped disperse risk more quickly and more broadly than ever before. While the argument that things are different has always been dangerous, many economists now subscribe to the brave new cycle, or a cycle in which the ups and downs have become much more muted, largely thanks to the stabilizing influence of new financial technology.

A cycle that doesn't cycle? We heard the same thing in January 2000 when belief in the New Economy grabbed hold amid assurances that the business cycle had become an anachronism. This time, "financial innovation" replaces technology as the holy grail of economic growth. Our chart shows that the influence of finance has been growing for three decades, but only now is its "magnitude and persistence" itself the reason for the boom. The psychology is so powerful, and dangerous, that many of the financial system's most fundamental weaknesses are listed as strengths: it's "easier for the less creditworthy to borrow than ever before;" "the biggest banks don't hold much debt, having sold it on to others;" securitization has distributed debts "far and wide, so no single holder has significant exposures;" insure "the holders of debt against losses." But the pervasive spread of risk doesn't mitigate it, it simply intensifies it and snares everyone.

The Journal suggests that one factor making it different this time is "How easy it is to borrow money." This certainly keeps the economy juiced, but it also explains why the trend must eventually reverse and hints at the extent of the eventual damage. Today's bullish buzz concentrates on the process by which liquidity is created, whether via the yen carry trade, Federal Reserve repos or the securitization of bizarre credit instruments. This focus completely misses the point, in our opinion. Regardless of the process, the psychological foundation of liquidity is confidence. We cannot stress this point strongly enough. When investors are optimistic, confidence remains high and liquidity expands. When this optimism goes away, the spigot will run dry, no matter what the "reasons" that people may place on it. People are bullish because they are bullish. But they celebrate the condition and come to view it as a "self-sustaining" virtue only when it is nearly over. The wave pattern discussed below suggests that point is close at hand.

February 2007

The names of two new stadiums offer another incontrovertible sign that the great financial pyramid is right where technology stocks were in the first quarter of 2000. The new New York City homes of baseball's Mets and basketball's Nets will be named Citifield and Barclays Center, respectively. Citigroup and Barclays Bank will pay $400 million for the naming rights over 20 years. The deals are reminiscent of 2000, when the stock of technology company CMGI Inc. soared to $160 a share and the company purchased the naming rights to the New England Patriots' new football stadium. Those rights were later relinquished as CMGI slipped to less than $1 a share, for a loss of 99.9% of its stock value. Enron Field is another ballpark that outlasted its original corporate namesake; the Houston Astros' stadium opened on March 30, 2000, just one week after the all-time high in the S&P.

The Real Estate Bust

In real estate as well, the forces of reversal have overwhelmed the forces of continuance. The optimism that fostered liquidity creation for property speculation has turned to caution. On Thursday, the National Association of Realtors said that in the final three months of last year, sales of existing homes fell in 40 states, and home prices dropped in 49 percent of the cities it surveyed. This is the widest price decline in the history of the survey. Crashes do not typically occur in straight lines. Even they have a structure, with periods of bounce and recovery. Each positive sign will probably be taken as the bottom. But this recent article makes it pretty clear that the environment has changed:

Toll, Centex, Lennar Join 'Moron' Speculators in Land Grab Bust

Feb. 7 (Bloomberg) — Brian Tuttle owns so much land that he paid $3.6 million to get rid of 125 acres ready for development in the middle of Florida's Palm Beach County.

"In 2005, I was a brain surgeon, and in 2006, I was a moron," said Tuttle, who walked away from his deposit on the land rather than lose even more money buying it and building homes on it. "The only good news is that I'm not alone."

The worst housing slump in 16 years made a lot of smart money vanish. D.R. Horton Inc., Pulte Homes Inc., Lennar Corp., Centex Corp. and Toll Brothers Inc., the five biggest U.S. homebuilders, said plummeting land prices cost them a combined $1.47 billion in the fourth quarter.

Builders paid more for land during the boom because home prices were rising, too. They didn't realize speculators were pumping up demand by buying houses to sell quickly. When prices reached a point where speculators quit buying, homebuilders were forced to abandon so much property they helped create a glut that drove down land prices more than 9 percent last year, according to data compiled by New York-based research firm Real Capital Analytics Inc.

Lennar of Miami, the third-biggest U.S. homebuilder by market value, incurred costs of $494 million for land write-downs and canceled options in the last three months of 2006.

Pulte, the second-biggest homebuilder, wrote down $350 million last quarter on the sliding value of land and deposits it won't exercise. The unpredictable outlook for land prices is hurting Pulte's ability to plan ahead.

"Uncertainty"

From a socionomic perspective, the most interesting sentence in the above article is, "The unpredictable outlook for land prices is hurting Pulte's ability to plan ahead." Apparently real estate prices are now "unpredictable," whereas before the peak they were "predictable." As *The Wave Principle of Human Social Behavior* (1999) postulated, terms such as uncertain and unpredictable in financial discussions are often code words for down:

> [P]eople equate uptrends with predictability and downtrends with unpredictability. The Harper's Weekly quote from 1857 includes the phrase, "never has the future seemed so incalculable as at this time." Translation: "The market has been falling for several years." The media constantly characterize market setbacks as injecting "uncertainty" into a picture of the future that presumably was previously as clear as crystal. I am not exaggerating when I say that this foible is timeless. Just this month, after a three-month decline in the Dow and a six-month decline in the Value Line index, The Wall Street Journal says, "The prevailing sentiment among investors these days appears to be confusion. And confusion is costly after so many years of predictability." Translation: "After going up for years, the market has trended down for several months." If uptrends are so predictable, then why didn't these same investors know that one had ended in April/July and another had already begun six days before the article appeared? The timeless conceit that uptrends are predictable explains why people ignore cycles in uptrends and embrace them in downtrends.

For whatever reason, most humans naturally see uptrends as normal and downtrends as abnormal. So when the trend is down, they feel lost, as if laws of the universe have been temporarily suspended. This tendency reveals one of the great values of studying Elliott waves. Trends change at all degrees; the form is a fractal. Down is just as natural as up. If you invest for an up market, why can't you invest for a down market? There should be no reason why a person cannot "plan ahead" when the trend is down just as well as when it is up.

Bizarrely, the only law of nature that seems to have been suspended for 25 years in the stock market is the regular appearance of downtrends. Except for two months in 1987 and two years in 2000-2002, the trend of stock prices has been up, and except for about two years in the early 1990s, the trend of real estate prices has been up. To most observers of the current generation, up does indeed appear normal, so you can hardly blame anyone for being "uncertain" when the trend changes. When wave c of the bear market gets going in stocks, "uncertainty" is likely to reach epic proportions.

March 2007

Many subscribers will recall our EWI Subprime Lenders Index, which *The Elliott Wave Financial Forecast* used to forecast the reversal in housing in March 2005. Here's what EWFF said at that time:

> The potential for a serious unraveling of the housing market is confirmed by [this index], which combines the stock prices of four major subprime lenders. As the most aggressive dispensers of credit to the housing industry, these firms are on the front edge of the last two remnants of the financial bubble's great surge, the debt and housing bubbles. Their bursting is signaled by the five-wave rise through January 3, followed by a similarly impulsive short-term decline. These clean five-wave patterns portend a fall to much lower levels.

The excerpt appeared right after the peak of the head and shoulders pattern in this updated chart of the index. The right shoulder finished in May 2006, and the index broke the neckline on February 9, a feat discussed at the time in the *Short Term Update*. The index was down nearly 19% in February and is off 42% from its December 2004 peak. A measured move from the neckline of the head-and-shoulders pattern targets the area surrounding the 85 level, which means

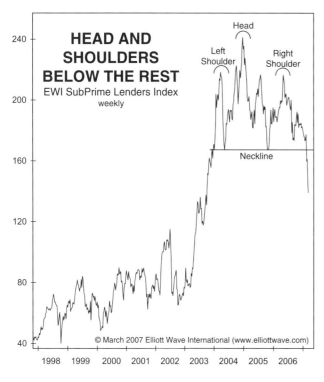

HEAD AND SHOULDERS BELOW THE REST
EWI SubPrime Lenders Index
weekly

Head
Left Shoulder
Right Shoulder
Neckline

© March 2007 Elliott Wave International (www.elliottwave.com)

there may be yet another 41% decrease in the index's value before a low is in place. One or more of these companies will probably declare bankruptcy.

Since the subprime industry's unfolding debacle is leading the decline in stocks, as well as the bursting debt bubble, there is much to learn from it. First and foremost is how important it is to ignore those who continue to suggest that the trouble is over or contained. Since late last year, when the lowest grade ABX Index started angling down and away from the 100% line, analysts have been positioning for an imminent rebound. Here's a recent Reuters offering that shows the persistence of this sentiment:

Bludgeoned Subprime Index Is Worth a Buy —Lehman

—2/26/07

Somehow the slow, relentless nature of the subprime reversal convinces many that it will stop and reverse, but its durability actually relates to the size of the implosion and its eventual extension across the depth and breadth of the credit universe. Ultimately, the economy will turn down, and AAA credits will follow the collapsing subprime line shown in the chart below. As *Conquer the Crash* noted, "When lending officers become afraid, they call in loans and slow or stop their lending no matter how good their clients' credit may be in actuality. Instead of seeing opportunity, they see only danger." As late as November, EWFF noted that this ingredient was still missing, as mortgage lenders were finding ways to work with troubled borrowers. On February 8, however, The Wall Street Journal announced, "Mortgage Refinancing Gets Tougher." Freddie Mac followed by announcing on February 27 "tougher underwriting guidelines for subprime loans." As with every credit crunch, this one begins with assurances that the new restrictions will strengthen the industry and not cause any widening credit crunch. The snowball effect is evident in the housing market, which saw a 3% year-over-year decline in prices in January and the biggest new home sales decline in 13 years. In Massachusetts, January brought a one-month record of 2203 foreclosures. And that is before the stock market peaked. In another portending mishap for the debt bubble, Metropolitan Savings Bank of Pittsburgh, a small Pennsylvania bank, collapsed this month. It's the first bank to go under in more than 30 months, closing the longest period without a failure since the FDIC was formed in 1934. According to reports, "some large depositors didn't get all their money back." Big depositors in the Metro Savings Bank of Pittsburgh will turn out to be only the first in a very long line of savers and bond holders to lose money on a sure thing. We trust you have already availed yourself of the safe banks and money market funds listed in *Conquer the Crash*.

May 2007

Not a day goes by now without some new revelation about falling [house] prices, rising inventories or the residual economic effects of a sputtering housing sector. The most important of these articles are the ones that describe a constriction in the supply of and demand for credit. Now as homeowners "Grow Wary of Tapping Lines of Credit," Congress is moving to "Toughen

Risky-Loan Standards," and lenders are put off by civic group demands for "Subprime Foreclosure Freeze," the situation will only get worse. All of these measures tighten lending. According to the Federal Reserve, the percentage of banks raising credit standards for mortgages just rose to 15%; that's the highest reading since the last real estate recession in the early 1990s. This is precisely what *Conquer the Crash* was referring to when it described "the downward spiral" in housing: "What screams 'bubble'—giant, historic bubble—in real estate today is the system-wide extension of massive amounts of credit to finance property purchases."

Notice that CTC makes no distinction between residential and any other type of real estate in this quote. The credit expansion that supported housing extends to every other sector of the real estate market, as does our forecast for the most devastating price declines of the bear market. Amazingly, even as the bear market strengthens its grip on the American housing sector, the very recent newspaper clips below show the psychology of the real estate boom blasting higher. Within the still bubbling parts of the real estate market, the collage reveals the presence of an important category of investors. Notice the foreign presence. Many will remember this principle from Japan's involvement in the last commercial real estate boom in the late 1980s. When Japanese investors purchased Rockefeller Center in 1989, many worried about their control of the U.S. real estate market. Mitsubushi, the buyer, ended up losing its entire $2 billion investment when the "Hope Diamond of world real estate" went bankrupt in 1995. EWI has long noted that foreigners are always the last to hop onboard a hot trend. Their knack for getting caught holding the bag is especially deft in real estate where the locals have the inherent advantage of proximity. Revelations about the "risk in commercial mortgages" hit the New York Times on

---

S. Korea's Overseas Real Estate Purchases Hit Record High
—Yonhap News, April 11, 2007

Alberta Real Estate: This Boom May Never Go Bust
—Globe and Mail, Canada April 28, 2007

A World Full of Real-Estate Opportunity
—Barron's, April 23, 2007

A Global Boom Converges on New York Market
Investors from Britain, Ireland, Italy, Spain, Korea, and elsewhere around the world are pouring foreign capital into the New York City residential and commercial real estate market.
—The New York Sun, April 26, 2007

Commercial Real Estate Is Still Hot in Manhattan
Retail chains expand and office tenants are paying record-breaking rates.
—Globest.com

Investors Betting on a Berlin Boom
With cheap property and a chic image, it is a European capital on the move, even if its economy isn't BERLIN —A Brit is turning a former Hitler Youth headquarters into a luxury club, Americans have bought up swaths of former communist-era apartment buildings, a German firm has transformed a red-brick prison into condos, and owners of rooftop flats have never been more coy.
—Los Angeles Times, April 29, 2007

Las Vegas Experiencing Another Big Building Boom
—International Herald Tribune, April 23, 2007

Commercial Real Estate Has Emerged as an Asset Class
the commercial-real-estate industry had emerged from the cocoon where it had slept for most of the 1990s. The situations and conditions for the sector have improved so much in recent years that institutional and high-net-worth investors, both domestic and foreign, have developed newfound trust and confidence in it as an investment.
—Investment News, April 23, 2007

May 2. As demand for space slows nationwide, ratings agencies say, "Underwriting has gotten so frothy we have to take a stand." Of course they do: social mood demands it. In recent days, the real estate debacle moved into Spain. As credit dries up, the domino topple will pick up speed and spread in all directions.

June 2007

Hints of the real estate depression are beginning to emerge. Borrowing from astrophysics, one Wall Street firm came up with a term that captures the inevitability of an intensifying crisis: "foreclosure shock cone." It refers to the number of mortgages that are 90-days delinquent, an early measure of the numbers that will ultimately go into foreclosure. The figure is up 127% from the same level in 2006. This rise is almost twice the rate of foreclosures, at all stages, which are up 60-70% from last year. This potential shock should spread fast as the triple-digit increase in delinquencies creates bankruptcies in the larger economy.

The series of charts (on the following page) depicts the chain reaction now working its way through the real estate industry. With housing affordability at historically low levels, the only thing previously driving the run to record high prices was the easy-money home loan. As the mortgage spigot closes, supply is going through the roof. This is shown by the number of homes for sale (top right) and the supply of homes unoccupied (middle left). Unoccupied housing initially created "foreclosure belts" in run-down neighborhoods, but the experience of Detroit suggests that "the pockets" will spread quickly to wealthier suburbs in all directions. As a gravestone-shaped sign on one abandoned Detroit property says, "As you are, so once were we. As we are, so shall you be." The crack in starts (middle right) and finally prices (bottom left), shows the accuracy of this statement. April's percentage drop is the biggest since 1970.

Keep in mind that many of the housing statistics are based on the official figures, which appear to be misleading due to unusually high cancellation levels. According to John Burns Real Estate Consulting, national sales figures, which are derived from the National Association of Realtors, are covering up a deep plunge in the housing sector. The firm reports, for instance, that home sales closing data show that sales are down not 9% as NAR reports, but 22% in May 2006-April 2007, compared to a year earlier.

EWI's assertion is that the housing problem will spread. The last frame (bottom right) of the S&P REIT Index captures the collapse's move into commercial real estate. The five-wave decline shown on the chart is giving way to a rebound now, but the form suggests that the bull market is over for commercial real estate as well. Prices for commercial real estate are reportedly still rising, but the financing issues that stalled housing are now evident there, too. "A more conservative view on underwriting has caused spreads to widen a bit on most loans, and lowered leverage a bit," says the head of a large real estate law practice. "In most cases, the result is a bit more equity." Bit by bit, the conservatism that *Conquer the Crash* called the true driver of the oncoming real estate depression is grabbing hold. As it shrinks the supply and demand of all credit, the economy itself will retrench in ways that many people never thought possible.

July 2007

Financial trends have a long history of creeping into the entertainment industry just in time for big tops. This tendency was amply demonstrated by the housing sector in 2005 where EWFF noted evidence of the "extreme psychology" surrounding the housing boom in *Property Ladder*, a TV show dedicated to buying houses and reselling them for a quick profit. The public's continued fascination with these shows signals the sector's vulnerability to much more dramatic losses. In fact, *Time* magazine notes that six of the top ten programs on HGTV are about real estate. In a subtle twist, however, the new offerings focus on the sell side. A rising level of desperation is evident in their names: *Secrets That Sell!*, *Designed to Sell*, *Bought & Sold*, *Get It Sold* and *Buy Me*.

One new show is clearly more consistent with the aftermath of a bubble. *12 Miles of Bad Road*, an HBO series, is described as a "real estate satire" that is "dark, dark, dark but funny." We saw

HOME IS WHERE THE HEART ACHES

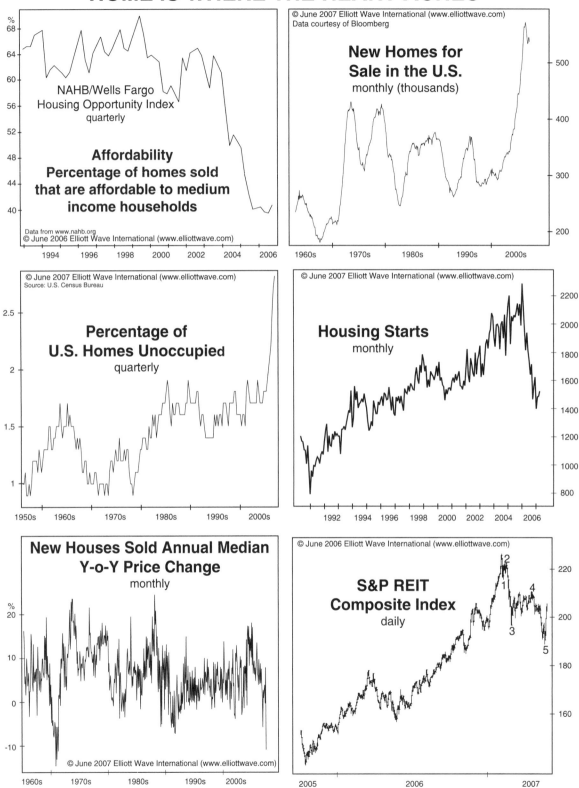

NAHB/Wells Fargo
Housing Opportunity Index
quarterly

**Affordability
Percentage of homes sold
that are affordable to medium
income households**

Data from www.nahb.org
© June 2006 Elliott Wave International (www.elliottwave.com)

© June 2007 Elliott Wave International (www.elliottwave.com)
Data courtesy of Bloomberg

**New Homes for
Sale in the U.S.**
monthly (thousands)

© June 2007 Elliott Wave International (www.elliottwave.com)
Source: U.S. Census Bureau

**Percentage of
U.S. Homes Unoccupied**
quarterly

© June 2007 Elliott Wave International (www.elliottwave.com)

Housing Starts
monthly

**New Houses Sold Annual Median
Y-o-Y Price Change**
monthly

© June 2007 Elliott Wave International (www.elliottwave.com)

© June 2006 Elliott Wave International (www.elliottwave.com)

**S&P REIT
Composite Index**
daily

something similar after the 2000 stock peak when satire became popular and society shrugged off the dot-com bubble with a TV series known as *Bull*. It lasted only a few episodes, but even that was enough to signal an exhaustion of the uptrend. This time, entertainment producers seem even more plugged in to the potential for a downturn. Viewers want to empathize with their TV stars. The transition from desperate sellers to black humor affirms their own journey. At some point, however, real estate shows will probably go off the air as they will be deemed unsuitable for family viewing.

October 2007

Financial weakness fits right in with our forecast. EWFF started the year with a Special Section, "2007: The Year of Financial Flameout," showing the importance of "An Off the Chart Boom in Paper Assets." With the sector exhibiting classic signs of a peak and the value of financial assets held by Wall Street firms soaring to 36.6% of GDP, EWFF argued that the financial sector would probably play roughly the same role in the next decline as technology played in the 2000-2002 bear market leg. It is doing all that and more as the credit crisis generated by the initial five-wave plunge in financial companies' shares is even causing many non-financial entities to slip. The clearly corrective, three-wave advance from August 16 reveals the likelihood of further damage, as shown on the "Rate Cut Fever" chart (in Chapter 6). These patterns indicate that the larger trend is down. If the DJIA and/or S&P make a new high, it will surely be unconfirmed by these three leaders, as well as the Dow Jones Transportation Average, which is also lagging. This bearish non-confirmation will signal an inevitable reversal for the stock market as a whole. This is the best-case scenario for stocks, however. If it happens, it will likely be as good as it gets for some time to come.

The Bull Market In Safe Banks

They said it would never happen again, but one of the most fundamental contributors to the financial stress envisioned in *Conquer the Crash* is in place: the bank run. The first shiver of this basest form of financial panic hit in early August when there was a brief run on deposits at Countrywide Financial's retail bank. A major cash infusion from Bank of America and a series of full page ads in which Countrywide reassured depositors that their accounts were federally insured, halted the run. In mid-September, however, the problem jumped the pond to England where "tens of thousands of frantic Northern Rock customers queued for hours to get their hands on their savings." Another massive sign of the very large degree of this reversal is evident in the year of the last major bank run at a major English financial institution—1866. Despite the assurances from the bank's Chief Executive Officer and the U.K. Chancellor of the Exchequer that Northern Rock's deposits were safe, customers panicked. "It's not that I disbelieve Northern Rock," said one of its depositors as she waited in line with her 90-year-old father outside one of its branches, "But everyone is worried and I don't want to be the last one in the queue. If everyone else does it, it becomes the right thing to do." The power of the herding instinct can overwhelm all else. The current run finally subsided when the Bank of England said it would guarantee all deposits at the bank. But the Bank of England is way too small to guarantee all British banks, so there is surely more excitement to come.

Once again, the blame fell to the U.S. subprime problem, but this time the effort to pin any and all financial flops on risky U.S. mortgages failed almost immediately. When, in the midst of the crisis, a reporter got Northern Rock to grant a $360,000 loan against an annual salary of $60,000, questions about the bank's own lending standards finally reached the surface. "Money advisers and others dealing with debt and insolvency are expressing growing concern about both the level and nature of many of the bank's loans," says a more recent account. "Indeed, some debt counsellors are surprised that it has taken this long for the problem to emerge." The long build-up and sense of complacency that still prevails around the banking industry is exactly why a series of longer and more sustained runs is very possible.

November 2007
Will Arrange Takeovers for Food

Merrill Lynch's Stan O'Neal was not alone in getting axed. The New York Post notes that "Wall Street's bloodbath has arrived in earnest with job cuts soaring nearly four-fold this year to more than 130,000." This fits with the following comment from the February issue: *"Elliott Wave Principle* characterizes C wave declines as 'devastating in their destruction,' a trait that the brokerage community should become acutely familiar with in coming years." Back in July, Merrill Lynch actually increased bonuses to new brokers "to stay in the recruiting game." With takeovers occurring at a record rate, investment bankers anticipated another record year for bonuses. That's not the case any more, as The New York Times reports that "the prospect of much smaller bonuses" looms over Wall Street and, by extension, the entire economy of New York City. The city's renaissance of recent years is suddenly under siege as budget shortfalls are appearing and cuts are being instituted. As the bear market takes full control, the dark side of old New York will emerge.

Of course, with oil pressing to new highs and commodities holding up, a peak level of enthusiasm remains for professionals in these particular areas. Tuesday's issue of the Wall Street Journal depicts the heads of Merrill Lynch, Lehman Brothers, Morgan Stanley and Goldman Sachs commodity divisions aligned in a Mount Rushmore type pose. "Commodities traders—long considered poor cousins to blueblood investment bankers—are rapidly climbing out of the trading pits and into the corner office," says the article. Another story says a shortage of commodity traders is so acute, headhunters are turning to hiring fired mortgage bond salesmen. In earlier times, bond guys epitomized risk aversion. Now bond salesmen are being recruited into the commodity trading pits? This is another sure sign that the downturn, once it comes, will last a long time.

One sure sign of housing's continued dismal outlook is how tenaciously homeowners continue to cling to their belief in home prices' ever-upward slope. In a CNBC survey, 90% of respondents said they expect the value of their homes to increase or stay the same over the next 12 months. This magazine cover story echoes the message of an imminent return to health.

Here's another headline saying that the psychology toward housing is a lot closer to the crazy optimism of the oil pits than it is to being washed out:

Foreign Buyers Grab
Depressed Real Estate
—The Wall Street Journal, October 13, 2007

As the August issue explains with respect to equities (see Chapter 7), foreigners generally jump onboard trends near their end, which in the case of real estate today means near the high.

Realize that all of these surveys and expectations of rebirth came after the median home price fell another 4% in September and existing home sales collapsed 8%—just from August! According to one source, home prices are down "nationally on a year-over-year basis for the first time since the Great Depression." Suddenly, allusions to the Great Depression are becoming more common, not because there are any strong worries of a recurrence but because it is the only real parallel to the unfolding real estate crisis. As the foreword to *Conquer the Crash* notes, the word depression is only rarely used in economic forecasts because depressions are "exceedingly rare. During the past two centuries, there have been just two periods that historians unanimously identify as depressions. …Amidst today's social psychology, merely addressing the ideas of deflation and depression is considered something akin to lunacy." We expect it will soon become downright sensible.

A series of articles about the "very high costs" of abandoning properties reveals the inner workings of the housing market "death spiral" that was first described in CTC. Walking away is "almost always a bad idea" because it damages homeowners' creditworthiness, but on the other hand foreclosure and sale for less than the mortgage amount can bring a big federal tax hit. The amount in excess of a property's fair market value is taxed as ordinary income. Either way, the vise tightens more as home prices fall.

Real estate is the trend-setter now. The story of "negative amortization" and the consequences of massive debt assumption on the basis of anticipated future price gains is one that will repeat itself throughout the economy in coming months. One other key trait that EWFF covered in September 2005 was the extent to which housing had become a "primary driver of the U.S. economy." But this role plays both ways. Skyrocketing foreclosures and new-home construction sites have devolved into "ghost towns." They are the physical manifestations of the decline in homebuilding stocks. A recent sharp fall in sales at home-dependent retailers, a drop in property taxes and a rash of foreclosure-inspired suicides are all direct evidence of a broadening effect. Within the larger economy, there is no mistaking a continued inexorable move toward outright contraction.

December 2007

According to the latest headlines, the Abu Dhabi Investment Authority rescued the stock market from its officially designated correction with a $7.5 billion capital infusion into Citigroup. As one scribe put it, "A major cash influx from Abu Dhabi made people feel better about the financial group as a whole." "Abu Dhabi has an interest in making sure the United States economy does not weaken further," explains another. But wasn't it just a year or so ago that American politicians howled against a Dubai effort to buy up a U.S. port? Now they cheer wildly as the investment arm of a Middle Eastern government files to purchase part of the largest U.S. bank. There's something wrong with this picture, and EWI's past observations about the psychology at a major top explains exactly what it is. As EWFF noted here in August and October, foreign entities, especially the investment arms of foreign governments, tend to jump on board big trends when they are over or nearly so. In this case, Abu Dhabi appears to be buying the dip in the financial services industry, just as two Bear Stearns hedge funds tried to do in the subprime mortgage industry earlier this year. It wasn't long before those funds themselves were the object of a bailout effort, which failed.

As we also noted here last month (see "High Time for a Bailout" chart in November 2007 entry, Chapter 8), many bailouts appear successful only because they tend to come at lows. The latest round appears way too close to the market's peak to be successful. It also appears to be inadequate in size. The Abu Dhabi investment won't even cover the $8-to-$11 billion write-down that Citi is expected to acknowledge in the fourth quarter. In all, Citigroup has $134.8 billion in level-three assets, which are assets that are rarely traded and therefore valued according to in-house estimates (more like guesstimates). Stocks, particularly financial stocks, bounded sharply off Monday's low, purportedly because Abu Dhabi had plugged the hole in Citi's balance sheet. But the real reason is that $7.5 billion may be just enough to help Citi conceal the full depth of its predicament a while longer. As they say, hope springs eternal, especially at the outset of a long-term bear market.

January 2008

This time last year, *The Elliott Wave Financial Forecast* began with a special section: "2007: The Year of Financial Flameout." The forecast in that section has largely come to pass. One great way to gauge the nature and full weight of the flameout is to observe the about-face in the media's coverage of the financial sector over the course of the last 12 months. A timeline and accompanying "THEN and NOW" snapshots compare the financial arena's press clippings to EWFF's commentary and forecasts. These pages bear witness to the big turn—from a full-steam-

1999

Top in Real Stock Prices
(Dow/Gold, Dow/Commodities)

2000

Top in NASDAQ

2006

The enormous power of deflation is now visible in the housing sector. [A] persistent fairy tale is the belief that any decline will be confined to certain regions and sectors.
—*The Elliott Wave Financial Forecast*, December 2006

2007

Jan.

Home Prices Seen Rising In '07
—*The Wall Street Journal*, January 11, 2007

Feb.

In the final three months of last year, home prices dropped in 49 percent of the cities it surveyed. This is the widest price decline in the history of the survey. Crashes do not typically occur in straight lines. Even they have a structure, with periods of bounce and recovery. Each positive sign will probably be taken as the bottom. But the environment has changed.
—*The Elliott Wave Theorist*, February 2007

Greenspan Says Worst of U.S. Housing Slowdown Is Over
—*Bloomberg*, February 14, 2007

Bludgeoned Subprime Index Is Worth a Buy: Lehman
—*Bloomberg*, February 26, 2007

Mar.

Fed Doesn't See Subprime Mortgages as Threat
—*Bloomberg*, March 1, 2007

Since the subprime industry's unfolding debacle is leading the decline in stocks, as well as the bursting debt bubble, there is much to learn from it. Ignore those who continue to suggest that the trouble is over or contained. Somehow the slow, relentless nature of the subprime reversal convinces many that it will stop and reverse, but its durability actually relates to the size of the implosion and its eventual extension across the depth and breadth of the credit universe.
—*EWFF*, March 2007

With Capital Plentiful, Debt Buyers Take Subprime-Type Risks
—*The Wall Street Journal*, March 27, 2008

"People ask me what kind of shock I worry about, and I say, 'If I worry about them and other people worry about them, they won't happen.—Alan Greenspan

The rising wave of anxiety over debt and default is not a "wall of worry;" it's a "wall of reality."
—*EWFF*, April 2007

Apr.

Chasing bad deals might be entirely rational, says [a Princeton economist]. "You can sell off loans very easily in the market. If others continue to go on, then you can stay on. You try to forecast when the others are getting out. You don't focus on the fundamentals. You focus on the other players."
—*The Wall Street Journal*, March 27, 2007

Good luck. All it takes is for one lender to fold, and the race for the exits will be on.
—*EWFF*, April 2007

May

THEN:

Let the Good Times Roll

The world has been building toward this critical moment for some time. It's no accident that financial markets have flourished. Now regulators, central banks and markets around the world are poised to make moves that could turn an expansion into an explosion.
—*NEWSWEEK*, January 8, 2007

NOW:

Credit Crisis Takes Heavy Toll

The credit crunch that is 2007's biggest financial story cleaved the year neatly in two. The first half of 2007 was brilliant. Then the credit crunch hit, sweeping through the New York City economy affecting everyone. More damage is expected next year. "We're definitely in one of those turning points in the economy," says [New York City's Deputy Comptroller].
—*Crain's New York Business*, December 23, 2007

THEN:

Much of that confidence in the current environment stems from financial innovations and new financial players that have helped disperse risk more quickly and more broadly than ever before. Many economists now subscribe to the brave new cycle. …Securitization takes lots of individual debt, combines it and then chops it up into small, manageable chunks that are then distributed far and wide, so no single holder has significant exposures. Derivatives, particularly in the oddly named credit default swap market which essentially insures the holders of debt against losses, also play a big role in reducing the risk from lending money. …Now, the biggest banks don't hold much debt, having sold it on to others.
—*The Wall Street Journal*, January 2, 2007

A cycle that doesn't cycle? We heard the same thing in January 2000 when belief in the New Economy grabbed hold amid assurances that the business cycle had become an anachronism. This time, "financial innovation" replaces technology as the holy grail of economic growth. The psychology is so powerful, and dangerous, that many of the financial system's most fundamental weaknesses are listed as strengths. But the pervasive spread of risk doesn't mitigate it, it simply intensifies it and snares everyone.
—*EWFF*, January 2007

NOW:

Wall Street Wizardry Amplified Credit Crisis

The use of derivatives "multiplied the risk," says the chairman of the American Securitization Forum, an industry association.
—*The Wall Street Journal*, December 27, 2007

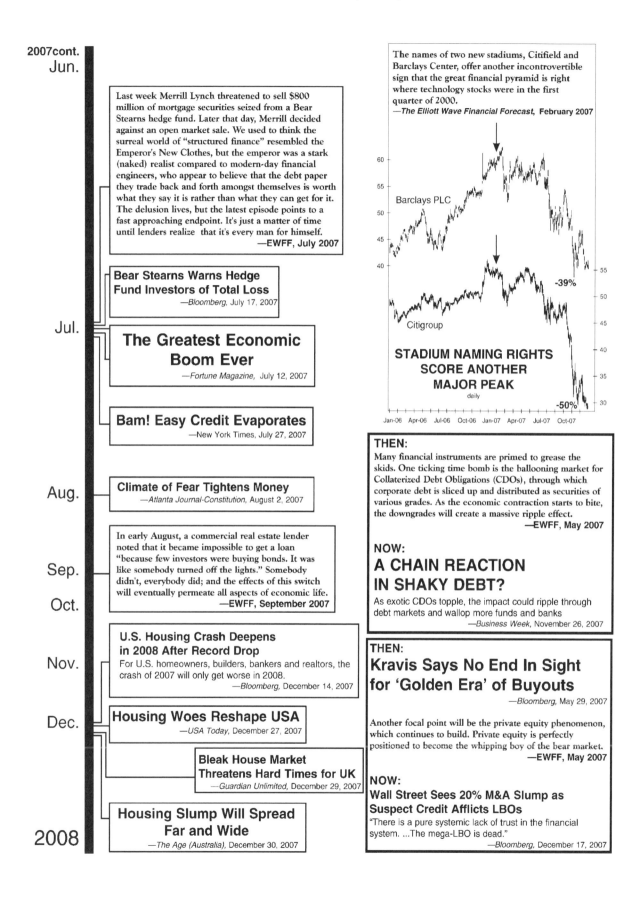

2007cont.

Jun.

Last week Merrill Lynch threatened to sell $800 million of mortgage securities seized from a Bear Stearns hedge fund. Later that day, Merrill decided against an open market sale. We used to think the surreal world of "structured finance" resembled the Emperor's New Clothes, but the emperor was a stark (naked) realist compared to modern-day financial engineers, who appear to believe that the debt paper they trade back and forth amongst themselves is worth what they say it is rather than what they can get for it. The delusion lives, but the latest episode points to a fast approaching endpoint. It's just a matter of time until lenders realize that it's every man for himself.
—**EWFF**, July 2007

Bear Stearns Warns Hedge Fund Investors of Total Loss
—*Bloomberg*, July 17, 2007

Jul.

The Greatest Economic Boom Ever
—*Fortune Magazine*, July 12, 2007

Bam! Easy Credit Evaporates
—New York Times, July 27, 2007

Aug.

Climate of Fear Tightens Money
—*Atlanta Journal-Constitution*, August 2, 2007

In early August, a commercial real estate lender noted that it became impossible to get a loan "because few investors were buying bonds. It was like somebody turned off the lights." Somebody didn't, everybody did; and the effects of this switch will eventually permeate all aspects of economic life.
—**EWFF**, September 2007

Sep.

Oct.

U.S. Housing Crash Deepens in 2008 After Record Drop
For U.S. homeowners, builders, bankers and realtors, the crash of 2007 will only get worse in 2008.
—*Bloomberg*, December 14, 2007

Nov.

Housing Woes Reshape USA
—*USA Today*, December 27, 2007

Dec.

Bleak House Market Threatens Hard Times for UK
—*Guardian Unlimited*, December 29, 2007

Housing Slump Will Spread Far and Wide
—*The Age (Australia)*, December 30, 2007

2008

The names of two new stadiums, Citifield and Barclays Center, offer another incontrovertible sign that the great financial pyramid is right where technology stocks were in the first quarter of 2000.
—***The Elliott Wave Financial Forecast***, February 2007

Barclays PLC

Citigroup

-39%

STADIUM NAMING RIGHTS SCORE ANOTHER MAJOR PEAK
daily

-50%

Jan-06 Apr-06 Jul-06 Oct-06 Jan-07 Apr-07 Jul-07 Oct-07

THEN:
Many financial instruments are primed to grease the skids. One ticking time bomb is the ballooning market for Collaterized Debt Obligations (CDOs), through which corporate debt is sliced up and distributed as securities of various grades. As the economic contraction starts to bite, the downgrades will create a massive ripple effect.
—**EWFF**, May 2007

NOW:
A CHAIN REACTION IN SHAKY DEBT?
As exotic CDOs topple, the impact could ripple through debt markets and wallop more funds and banks
—*Business Week*, November 26, 2007

THEN:
Kravis Says No End In Sight for 'Golden Era' of Buyouts
—*Bloomberg*, May 29, 2007

Another focal point will be the private equity phenomenon, which continues to build. Private equity is perfectly positioned to become the whipping boy of the bear market.
—**EWFF**, May 2007

NOW:
Wall Street Sees 20% M&A Slump as Suspect Credit Afflicts LBOs
"There is a pure systemic lack of trust in the financial system. ...The mega-LBO is dead."
—*Bloomberg*, December 17, 2007

ahead, collective embrace of risk to a new mood of "fear and risk aversion." As they say, the major trend ultimately calls the shots, and we believe that EWFF's facility for anticipating the transition testifies to the soundness of our method and ongoing outlook. But the most important elements of the forecast lie directly ahead. The great financial flameout of 2007 was a reversal toward a major financial and social downtrend, one that will change aspects of everyday life for most people.

April 2008

As far as this era's real estate collapse goes, the latest figure shows a 10% year-over-year decline in existing home sales. But a 2.9% increase in existing February sales prompted hope. "The worst is clearly behind us," said one expert in USA Today. According to the prevailing wisdom, home sellers are finally getting realistic. "They realize prices are going down." But as noted at the top of this month's EWFF, there are times of mass emotional delusion, like the present, when a pinch of reality can be a very dangerous thing for elevated prices. "This week's batch of economic reports suggest that the adjustment is finally starting to happen," says the New York Times. If the scenario sketched out in *Conquer the Crash* is right, "the adjustment" is likely to be far more jarring than almost anyone expects. Remember that CTC anticipated the bout of "stubbornness" as well as the upward blip in sales, saying: "At some point, a few owners cave in and sell at much lower prices." This is not the end of the spiral, but the beginning, as CTC adds, "Then others are forced to drop their prices, too." Buyers are quickly learning to play an exploding supply of sellers against each other and, more ominously, to wait for lower prices. Lower prices breed the desire to wait for lower prices.

May 2008

Meltdowns in the housing and the financial sector are not aberrations but the wave of the future, one that is closer than ever to hitting the broadest possible range of markets.

July 2008

The latest housing how-to book, *Foreclosure Investing for Dummies*, captures the breadth of the belief that a decimated asset is a buying opportunity. Its appearance surely means that the housing debacle is hardly closer to ending than it was in January 2007 when EWFF cited its predecessor, *Flipping Houses for Dummies*, as a sure sign that the downturn in housing was about to get nasty. (See January 2007 entry in Chapter 6.) Another illustration of the incredible depth of this belief is in the financial sector, where many companies continue to raise capital by selling shares. Despite the start of the biggest credit crisis since the Great Depression, North American banks raised $158 billion in capital since the third quarter of 2007. The total almost matches the $175 billion in losses they reported during the same period! Washington Mutual offers a case study in how these early-bird investments are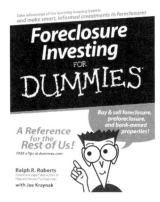
panning out. After falling from a 2006 high of $47 a share to $13 in late 2007, investors agreed to pump in $7 billion. The enticement was a 33% discount from the market price at the time. Shares now stand 41% below the $8.75 "deal" that new investors got for their piece of WaMu. The stock was recently quoted at $5.13. "Investors who jumped in early are down materially," says the The Wall Street Journal. "The smart money isn't looking so smart."

The headlines over that Journal article suggests that the next, far more serious, phase is arriving: "Investors Hide as Banks Come Knocking." According to the Journal, the "window for capital raising is closing" and investors "are tired of trying to catch a falling knife." As of today, the nominal Dow, denominated in U.S. dollars, is below its high of 8 years ago in January 2000 while the nominal S&P 500 and NASDAQ are down 17.5% and 53%, respectively, from their 2000 peaks, and the "real" Dow, as measured in terms of its gold value, is off by over 70%. In a bear market, some will slowly catch on to how much safer (and much more fun) it is to just stand on the sidelines and watch the knife catching than it is to take part. The sooner that they recognize the advantages of this approach, the more capital they will conserve and the smarter they will look at the bottom when the genius of getting out and staying out is finally recognized.

October 2008

Every major U.S. investment bank is now gone. In a span of seven months, five firms between 70-165 years old were forced out of the investment banking business, or went bankrupt. The Grand Supercycle implications of this bear market are starting to appear.

Financial Leadership

Most people forget, but back in January 2007 when *The Elliott Wave Financial Forecast* called for a "Financial Flameout," enthusiasm toward the financial sector was as positive as it had ever been. In fact, the crescendo of positive vibrations was so resounding that EWFF spent the better part of a Special Section just describing it. We even included a chart showing how financial assets had risen to a record high of 20.5% of annual GDP. After adding $2 trillion in hedge fund assets to the total, EWFF further showed how Wall Street's size in relation to the economy was literally off the chart at 36.6%. Calling the situation a "financial zenith," EWFF concluded:

> Today's bullish buzz concentrates on the process by which liquidity is created, whether via the yen carry trade, Federal Reserve repos or the securitization of bizarre credit instruments. This focus completely misses the point, in our opinion. Regardless of the process, the psychological foundation of liquidity is confidence. We cannot stress this point strongly enough. When investors are optimistic, confidence remains high and liquidity expands. When this optimism goes away, the spigot will run dry, no matter what the "reasons" that people may place on it. People are bullish because they are bullish. But they celebrate the condition and come to view it as a "self-sustaining" virtue only when it is nearly over. The wave pattern suggests that point is close at hand.

In October and November 2007, EWFF revisited the now-reeling sector and added, "Declines in the financial services should set the tone." The first eight charts in the nine-stock panel on the following page show the decimation that has followed. The net rise shown since 2006 in the ninth stock, Wal-Mart, is representative of the rest of the economy, which is still afloat. We are convinced as ever, however, that the financial stocks have simply "set the tone" for a decline that will be just as hard on the rest of the market. Look for the bricks and mortar of the economy to feel the force of this move at any moment.

Special Report:
Anticipating the End of a Relentless Mania
Technology and Real Estate Tell the Story

History shows us that a mania invariably ends when everyone becomes convinced that it will last forever. One unique aspect of the Great Asset Mania is that it continually fell away only to rise again, so that by the end, many were convinced that it would always emerge somewhere else. We have seen this belief expressed as recently as September 20 in the Times (of London):

And the Next Bubble Is
... Exotic Investments

Knowledge of this trait of mania peaks may never be of use to many investors, as few are likely to live long enough to see it repeated. It may be useful to know, however, that while the shifting focal point of the mania—technology in 2000, real estate in 2005, finance in 2007 and commodities

"Declines in the financial services should set the tone."

—EWFF, November 2007

(all percentages from peaks)

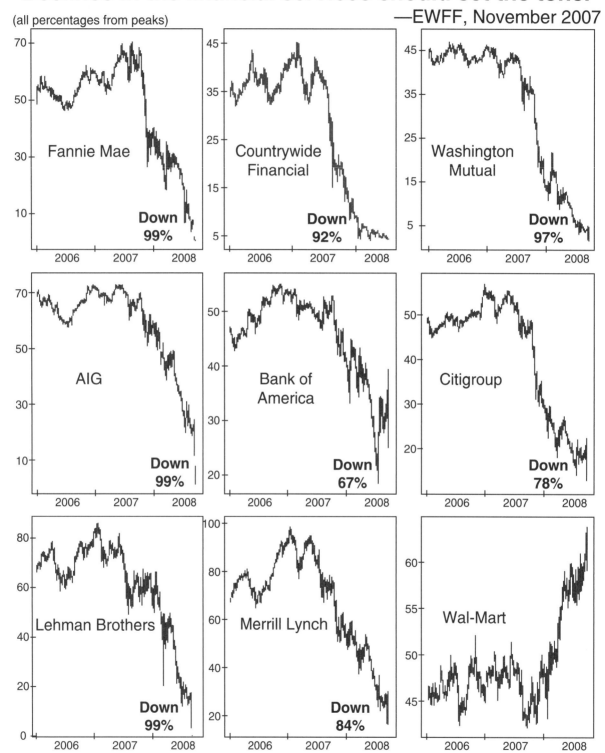

in 2008—never regained the favor and speculative intensity they generated at their respective peaks, they continued to trade in a fashion that offered important clues to the larger trend. With respect to technology, for instance, The charts shown here and the following page show how the precise form of the NASDAQ helped EWFF and *The Short Term Update* stay on top of the big reversal in the overall market. The first chart identified the NASDAQ's top just days before it took place on October 31, 2007. It was followed by this comment from the November 9 issue of STU: "The NASDAQ rushes higher on its own late in long-term uptrends. This observation helped us call the tech bust in 2000. The NASDAQ's dominance has the same meaning now." In March, EWFF offered the "Model Bear Market" chart showing a perfect Fibonacci retracement on log scale and called for a wave (2) countertrend rally that "could take weeks." When the Dow Industrials stopped rising and the NASDAQ continued higher in May, the STU returned to the same observation that confirmed the peaks of March 2000 and October 2007: "There's something awfully familiar about the NASDAQ's willingness to charge to new highs. It was this very trait that helped us confirm the importance of the highs for STU subscribers back in early November."

From the October 24, 2007 STU:

As shown in April 2008 EWFF

173

Trend Reversed!
(NSDQ 100 Index, Weekly Bar)

October 2007 top

67 weeks

64 weeks

66 weeks

67 weeks

October 2002 bottom

Copyright, October 2008
Elliott Wave International
www.elliottwave.com

Source: CQG, Inc. © 2008 All rights reserved worldwide. www.cqg.com   Tue Oct 14 2008 16:47:13

The chart at left updates the formation that initially alerted subscribers to the decline. The NASDAQ's decline hit 45% on Friday, but it should fall much farther.

The UnReal Estate Sale

Housing gave us another big picture window into the future. Just days before the S&P Supercomposite Homebuilding Index reached its July 22, 2005 peak, EWFF published the forecast shown on the chart and stated: "There's no mistaking it now: The extreme psychology of the Grand Supercycle peak has taken up residence in real estate." The decline now stands at 85%. It's come a long way, but substantial downside potential remains. As the quote from "Bulls, Bears and Manias" (see Conclusion) points out, manias are always completely retraced. At minimum, this index should fall through the March 2000 low of 127, another 50%. So, the critically important message behind this forecast is that the decline in the market as a whole and in other parts of the real estate industry is still young. Vornado Realty, for instance, which EWFF slated for collapse near its February 2007 peak, shows the ample downside potential on the commercial side. It was somewhat frustrating waiting for the final top to come in, but the size of the mania has its advantages on the way down. It spreads out the opportunities.

NO SHELTER
FROM THIS STORM
S&P Supercomposite
Homebuilding Index
weekly

← EWFF:
"It's Time"

-85%

Data courtesy of Bloomberg
© October 2008 Elliott Wave International (www.elliottwave.com)

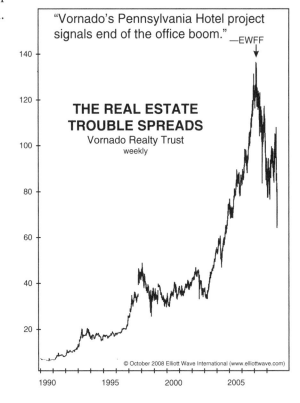

"Vornado's Pennsylvania Hotel project signals end of the office boom." —EWFF

THE REAL ESTATE
TROUBLE SPREADS
Vornado Realty Trust
weekly

© October 2008 Elliott Wave International (www.elliottwave.com)

174

Chapter 3

Equity Culture:
The Sweep Higher Reshapes the Social Order

For fashion designers, sports teams, pro wrestlers and rock 'n' rollers, the market is transformed into a way of life. As equities and capitalism triumph, bull market TV shows, "money camps" for kids, and bidding frenzies for everything from JFK's golf clubs to Mars rocks make the scene. At the all-time high, stocks become the brightest light on Broadway, and everybody wants to be a millionaire. An index of culture stocks reflects the rebound to a lower peak in 2004 and a renewed washout in 2008.

June 1995

An article in Smart Money says, "Get invested right now." "Stocks Are A Good Bet For the Long Term," says the Wall Street Journal headline. "Market seers find no disasters in Wall Street's tea leaves," says The New York Times. The London Financial Times reports in an article called "The Cult of the Equity Persists" that 76% of U.K. pension fund assets are in equities. German investors have "a new-found enthusiasm for equities," says the paper, as IPOs rise and "An Equity Culture Starts To Take Hold."

April 1996

Centuries-old religious doctrine is being reinterpreted to cast stock holdings in a favorable light. Until recently, Islamic law disapproved of equities. But "more and more scholars have looked deep into the matter and now accept equity investment." A British investment bank says it plans to tap this new source of demand with a fund for Islamic investors.

Edward R. Dewey was a pioneer in observing cyclic phenomena. One indication of economic peaks he noted was the "skyscraper indicator," which is that tall buildings are built at the end of economic booms. The largest free-standing tower in America is expected to open in Las Vegas in April. The Stratosphere Corp. is funding the construction of the Stratosphere Tower with (of course) a series of public stock and bond offerings. It will surpass the height of the Sears Tower, which was built in 1972 on the approach of the stock market top of January 1973. That building surpassed the height of World Trade Center I, which was built through the market top of 1966. That building in turn surpassed the Empire State Building, which was built through the market top of 1929. The world's tallest building is now under construction in Kuala Lumpur. China is planning to surpass it in 1997 with the Chongqing Tower in Sichuan.

June 1996

At The Crest of the Tidal Wave reviewed EWT's prediction of the early 1990s slump in art and collectibles prices and noted that "increasingly questionable quality was instrumental in concluding that the top was at hand. The situation was analogous to some 'B' waves in the stock market, when high flying 'cats and dogs' are a classic sign of heavy public involvement, and by definition, an approaching peak." *At the Crest* predicted that the decline would be followed by

$772,500 Golf Club Par for Jackie Auction

JACKIE MANIA

Auction more than a sale, it's 'a happening'

People are paying "100 times the value for objects that are amazingly mediocre."

—USA Today
April 25, 1996

Kennedy's cachet sizzles in offering

NEW YORK — Not to be outdone by a sizzling market for initial public stock offerings, the Kennedy children are putting the wraps on their own blockbuster deal. At last count, stuff worth about $5 million was selling at auction for 10 times that much, or $50 million.

That's a markup worthy of any IPO. If the Kennedys were a company, its initial price would be a healthy 10 times book value.

At 10 times book value, the Kennedy IPO isn't up to standards set by Planet Hollywood, whose star-studded IPO last week went at 51 times book. But 10 times is still a hefty value.

To some, owning a piece of the Kennedys may be worth 200 times intrinsic value or 870 times original cost, just as owning a piece of Planet Hollywood entrepreneurs Sylvester Stallone and Arnold Schwarzenegger may be worth a premium. But the Kennedy auction and other IPOs point up one thing for sure: It's a great time to be selling assets. All the better if they have novelty value.

—USA Today, April 26, 1996

another "B" wave rally. The Jackie Kennedy auction has probably just marked the end of that "B" wave. During what some called a "four-day mania," a new cat-and-dog standard was established when actor Arnold Schwarzenegger bought a set of golf clubs for $772,500, 96,463% above Sotheby's pre-auction estimate of $800. Other sales included (with original expectations in parentheses) photos of portraits: $68,500 ($88), another set of golf clubs: $387,500 ($800), a necklace: $101,500 ($250), fake jewel necklace: $48,875 ($125), fake jewelry: $112,500 ($300), a fake pearl necklace: $211,500 ($600), a "stroke counter" for golf: $28,750 ($75), a candy dish: $29,900 ($175) and three silk cushions: $25,300 ($75). A desk upon which President Kennedy signed a nuclear test-ban treaty went for $1,432,500.

Newsweek attributed prices to the excitement of the moment, noting that almost everything sold at the auction probably dropped by "half or more" immediately afterward. Our forecast is for a 99% drop on average, within ten years.

August 1996
Cultural Forces At a Grand Supercycle Peak

Business is celebrated in bull markets. Remember Calvin Coolidge's "the business of America is business" in the bull market of the 1920s? The biggest heroes of this bull market have been Bill Gates and the information revolution. The culmination of the pro-business attitude has been symbolized by the 1996 Olympic committee's goal, which is "the total privatization" of the Games. The movement from a non-business orientation to a business orientation is clear in contrasting today's attitude with those of the first modern games, which were established in 1896 at a depression low in the DJIA. The focus then was to honor the amateur athletes of the world. Today, fourth place participants receive cash payments ($7,500), advertising is everywhere, and the 1996 games opened by honoring a parade of millionaire athletes.

Mirroring the stock market, this pro-business trend appears to be reaching a culmination at the same time that counter forces are setting in. The Olympic games have endured conflict on the business front. Street vendors, unable to unload their overpriced wares, have marched on City Hall, and the games' original sponsors, who paid $40 million for exclusive selling rights, are fuming over last-minute deals that allowed "sub-category" sponsors in for a fraction of the cost. These are only early signs. By the time it is over, the bear market in stocks will usher in an anti-business attitude like the one that existed in the late 1960s and early 1970s, when conglomerate IT&T was considered by countless people to be the country's single greatest threat.

September 1996
Cultural Trends

On August 4, The New York Times ran a long article contemplating the "symbolic power" of skyscrapers. Efforts to build the world's tallest building "are assertions of power," the article asserted. "Striving for great height is a sign of an arriviste culture." In April, EWT reviewed the "skyscraper indicator," which observes that record high buildings arrive on the scene at the end of big bull markets. They are often occupied after the bear market has begun. The Times maintained that the mantle of tallest had passed to Asia where the Shanghai Financial Center is now scheduled for completion in 2001. A week later, however, Donald Trump announced his plan "to build to record heights." Could there be a more fitting monument to the bull market than Trump's planned 1,792 feet (1/3 mile) high New York Stock Exchange Tower? The building, which would be 200 feet higher than the Shanghai structure, is expected to get "extraordinarily strong backing from the state and city."

Of all the cultural relationships we consider here, the link between stock prices and the tallest buildings is one of the most fascinating because it is literally etched in stone. It's so obvious that even the media will make the connection, albeit a few years after it might help an investor. As precedent, we find that The New Republic hit upon the social significance of the Chrysler Building and Empire State Building in July 1931: "The material embodiment of the late bull market remains in our metropolitan structures of towering heights. They soar boldly above a surrounding mesa of roofs, very much as the spire-like graph of 1929 equity prices. The same causes explain both pinnacles." That was two years after the fact. In contrast, *The Elliott Wave Theorist* is relating the significance of the widespread skyscraper-building impulse now, in time to benefit from the knowledge.

The NYSE Tower was announced even as the value of another towering architectural monument to the bull market was crashing. In April, EWT noted that Las Vegas' Stratosphere, the highest free-standing tower in North America, was about to open for business. It had a market value of $1 billion. Since then, grand opening "euphoria" has given way to an "astonishingly fast" decline. Stratosphere shares are off 87%. The Stratosphere's fall to virtual bankruptcy took less than six months; all it took was a Minor degree correction in social mood.

Coffee Talk

On a trip to New York, after just a few years away, we were amazed at the number of coffee shops in Manhattan. They're everywhere. There are two here in Gainesville, Georgia, pop. 20,000. "Today's coffee shops market themselves as hip gathering places for the whole community," says one publication. The coffee break "is becoming the coffee escape, with employees dashing out to their favorite java huts once or twice a day." TV's popular show *Friends* takes place mostly in a coffee house. Does EWT need to ruminate about the possible significance of the popularity of social gathering places for the ingestion of stimulants? Hardly. There is ample historical precedent in fifth waves of Cycle degree and higher. Readers of R.N. Elliott's biography in *R.N. Elliott's Masterworks* recall that the "tea room" was so ubiquitous in the 1920s that Elliott himself wrote an accounting column for a magazine devoted to that one industry. Little, Brown & Co., a major house, published his book on the subject in 1926. Can we go back further? You bet. In the book, *The South Sea Bubble*, John Carswell reveals that in the years leading up to the great speculative washout of 1720, "There was a new sociability, whose symptom was the coffee-house."

Folks, if you could go back to Roman times at social mood peaks, you would see the same thing. That is, if you had your eyes open. At a recent gathering of market professionals who honored R.N. Elliott for his pioneering technical work, George Schade gave a presentation on Elliott's life. The mention of his accounting advisories on tea room management elicited chuckles from the crowd, as the term "tea room" sounds so quaint. Undoubtedly, the next day, the same people gathered at Starbucks to discuss whether they should stay in markets or buy a franchise. At the next Supercycle peak, people will be rolling their eyes at the quaint phrase, "coffee house," while they slurp the beverage of the day in tea boutiques or java joints. Our goal in studying social history is to identify the parallels that are just different enough in their particulars that people can't see how obviously social behavior repeats at similar junctures in the social mood. Strictly from the evidence of today's coffee house popularity, we can write the following formula: 17-teens » 1920s » 1990s. Hmm. That's the same formula indicated by the wave pattern in the stock market!

November 1996

No longer bound by measures of overvaluation or over-optimism, investors can and are putting their faith in stocks' ability to solve their long term financial problems. According to the latest Business Week, hundreds of people are quitting their jobs and taking courses on day-trading. An agriculture magazine urges farmers to supplement their income by speculating in stocks. "The quick, easy way to profit from adding value to raw farm products is to buy stock," says a September Progressive Farmer editorial. Increasingly, the local paper is filled with queries and comments that show the market has tapped into a totally new and ignorant class of investors. The general interest Q&A section now gets stock market questions. A phone-query section begins, "A funny thing about the stock market..." A 13-year-old reader asks the Kid's Page, "Why do they call the stock market a bear or bull market?" A query about the importance of earnings gets this response: "Stock prices are determined largely by earnings expectations." History clearly shows this is false. It's hard to say which are more troubling, the questions or the answers.

Another sign of renewed optimism is the rebirth in real estate of Donald Trump, the real estate hero of the 1980s. His ability to resurrect his name with bankers, gossip columnists, tenants and the public is an echo of the psychology of the last advance. As we noted in September, Trump plans to construct the world's tallest building, with the New York Stock Exchange as his anchor tenant. Trump has unveiled similar plans before. He presented blueprints for the world's tallest building in Chicago in 1989, which presaged the collapse in real estate and his own bankruptcy. This time, his dream tower, which wave patterns suggest will not go past the blueprint stage, foreshadows a major fall in stocks as well as another slide in real estate prices. By the way, we just heard today that London is now planning Europe's tallest building.

December 1996

Art and Collectibles

In mid-1990, *The Elliott Wave Theorist* forecast the end of the mania for art and collectibles. Since then, everything from coins to paintings to baseball cards have collapsed in price. At the time, we also bemusedly noted the sky-high prices for meteorites. While data is scarce, this bull market still appears to have some life to it. A recent New York auction of three meteorites from Mars drew a record bid of $1.1 million. However, in an amazing show of bullish sentiment, the sellers refused to accept the money. They held out for at least $1.5 million. Because of that demand, no sale took place. Equally interesting is the fact that the number of reporters covering the event was several times the number of bidders. This double victory for hype over substance is one more sign that the widely hoped-for resumption of the bull market in collectibles is being supported by little more than out-of-this-world expectations by the owners of rocks from Mars.

Mars Rocks for Sale at Astronomical Price

Auction Block: Since scientists saw signs of life in a chunk of the Red Planet, every millionaire on Earth seems to want a piece.

When three small Martian meteorites go on the auction block Nov. 20, the man greasing the skids boasts they'll sell for $1.5 million, $2 million, maybe more.

"These will probably go down in history as the three most precious pieces of stone that were sold by man," the mysterious figure who owns them told The Associated Press in a phone call.

—The Atlanta Journal-Constitution
November 11, 1996

January 1997

The global bond market had a very interesting 1996. There were several issues of 100-year corporate bonds and several companies made plans to issue long term zero-coupon bonds early in 1997. We saw debt sold by many formerly communist countries, most for the first time ever, at surprisingly small spreads to U.S. Treasuries (like 100-year Chinese bonds in April at 9.13%). By the end of the year, this trend reached all corners of the earth, as demonstrated by the tiny Argentinian province of Tierra del Fuego (population 90,000) arranging to issue $160 million in bonds backed by oil and gas royalties. A neighboring province did so at just 4% above U.S. T-bills. The asset-backed bond market has reached an even zanier state, with the issuance of various bonds representing bets on such things as royalties from taxicab medallions, Italian cemetery revenues, future record sales by 1970s pop icon David Bowie, moneygrams from Mexican workers in the U.S. to relatives back home, and future payments for nose jobs, hair transplants and breast enlargements. This is insanity on a historic scale, but it seems normal to the participants while it's happening.

More Evidence of a Grand Supercycle Peak

The search for genes that affect mood and personality took an important step forward last month "with the first identification of a genetic mutation that makes people more susceptible to anxiety and depression." The research is expected to shorten the time it takes for anti-depressants to take effect. Banning depression is one thing; inducing energy is another. Caffeine, "the safe stimulant, is all the rage in the beverage industry." New drinks include caffeine-spiked orange juice, water and sports drinks like Krank2O and Zapped. Coca-Cola has introduced Surge, a new high-caffeine citrus soda, and Pepsi is test-marketing Pepsi-Kona, a blend of Pepsi and coffee.

April 1997

A record high 43% of American households are in the market. Most of the newcomers have been mentally overwhelmed by a bull market propaganda machine that is still gaining momentum. In 1996, $1.8 billion was spent on financial ads, making them the fastest growing share of the advertising market. Mutual funds led the way with an all-out advertising assault. Ad budgets expanded 80% in one year. The big new thing is television, as financial salesmen bought a record $140 million in TV time last year. New investors don't get their information from Buffett or Biggs; they get it from sources like the National Association of Investment Clubs, which says with all seriousness in its February magazine, "History shows quite consistently that it is more dangerous to be out of the market than in it."

People have taken these messages to heart. A recent Frontline documentary, "Beating the Market," asked one couple why they put their life savings into two volatile technology stocks. "Because we're working way too hard and not furthering ourselves. It's too slow. We have to do something aggressive." What stock did they buy? Says the wife, "To tell you the truth, I don't even know the name of it. I know the call letters are AMLN. It's supposed to double by August." In this way, the couple hopes to "pay off credit cards, set up retirement and college for the children." On the day of the March high, the top of the front page of the Wall Street Journal directed these words to bosses everywhere: "EMPLOYEES NEED EDUCATION." What type of education? "Employers should help workers learn that in a downturn, 'the worst thing to do is sell out.'"

In a tangible sign of the connection between this bull market and the mass urge to recreate, which probably rivals that of ancient Rome, Formula One plans a $4 billion stock offering. In this country, motor sports are also big stock market news, as 65% of Winston Cup races are held on tracks owned by publicly held racing companies. At a March "motor sports investment conference," the head of NASCAR, the U.S. stock car race sanctioning body, said a "new Winston Cup date" has "roughly the value — in Wall Street terms — of a drug that instantly cures baldness."

More Evidence of a Grand Supercycle Peak

When Tickle Me Elmo bidding took prices to ridiculous extremes, we guessed that the only possible explanation "was that the act of buying, or more precisely, of pushing up prices, is turning people on." The frenzy has reached the literati, as competitive bidding for the memoir of a 100-year old Kansas laundry lady just pushed its price to more than $1 million. Everyone involved admits that it would have received no consideration if a story about the woman had not appeared on the front page of The Wall Street Journal. Said one Simon & Schuster executive who read the book, "It was so boring it was unbelievable." But the bidding was exciting, wasn't it?

May 1997

The depth of investors' affection for stocks is displayed by a series of love poems to the Dow that were published in Slate, Bill Gates' electronic magazine, on April 15. Here is a selection:

> In harmony with the Dow, the skies are clear and clean,
> In harmony with the Dow, memory serves no purpose;
> At one with the day's momentum, forgetting all history.
> '87 is but a pale shadow, '73 a warm breeze.
> The Dow is all-loving. That is why everyone loves it.

Today's investment mania is far broader than past manias, at least as far as I can discern from a cursory reading of history. It is certainly not limited to stocks. In the past decade, almost anything that can pass for an asset has been fair game for a bidding war: real estate, coins, art, baseball cards, President Kennedy's golf clubs, Cabbage Patch Kids, Tickle-Me-Elmo and Beanie Babies.

The hysteria to own Beanie Babies has brought the frenzy to speculate to its lowest common denominator. Kids everywhere are using their allowance money to buy the $5 items in hopes of landing a rare version like Peanut the elephant, whose "investment" price has soared as high as $1,500. "I've been through a lot of things, Transformers, Cabbage Patch Kids. There's never been anything like this," said the owner of a Virginia toy store. We can vouch for the intensity of the Beanie Baby craze. Bob's daughter was about to purchase one in a small Florida town when the store manager snatched it out of her hands and said that the owner had just called, demanding two of each for her personal collection. Upon emerging from the store with several others, she was met with shrieks from women on the street, who shouted, "They've got Beanie Babies in there!" While the Beanie Baby buying panic is the most widespread yet, it is also the one in which buyers have the least chance of selling at a profit. The toy maker continues to re-supply stores and McDonald's is selling 100 million smaller but authentic versions in its "Happy Meals." The illusion of scarcity and insatiable demand have been mastered.

June 1997

The social embrace of the stock mania is reflected by the rise of the celebrity shareholder. A Wall Street Journal feature of late May covered the stock picking abilities of Capitol Hill politicians. "I picked them through the gut," (surely a tried and true method) says Sen. Alan Simpson of his stocks. Another feature noted that "a galaxy of superstars [is] demanding and getting stock or options as compensation for their services." Michael Jordan, Cal Ripkin Jr., Greg Norman and "even 'Tuff' Hedeman, one of best rodeo bull riders, [have] joined the equity rush." The cast of *Seinfeld* held out for $1 million per episode per star but then settled for as little as half that amount when General Electric stock was thrown in. "NBC had little choice but to bow to the stars' wishes," noted the Journal.

In 1989, the year the Nikkei topped out, EWT reported that in Tokyo, some prosperous Japanese were sprinkling gold flakes on their cereal. Today in the U.S., in the equivalent 15th year of a stock mania, the Cellar in the Sky restaurant at the top of the World Trade Center has begun offering a dessert featuring edible gold.

SEINFELD
The economics of a TV supershow

It is the first TV series to command more than $1 million a minute for advertising — a mark previously attained only by the Super Bowl. Its growing strength has helped a smart network dominate prime time — and news, mornings, and late nights, too. It has shattered the ceiling of what a network will pay to keep a show and even its supporting actors.

As the "Hallelujah Chorus" from Handel's Messiah resounded through an auditorium filled with advertisers, the network presented its new fall schedule. NBC Entertainment President Warren Littlefield did little to downplay the importance of the show to the network. "Praise the Lord!" Littlefield shouted. "Seinfeld's back."

The return of the show was anything but assured, since the three supporting-cast members had demanded a combined $66 million for their services. But after the concerted efforts of the NBC brass, featuring the offering of GE stock options and appearance by GE Chairman John F. Welch, a deal was struck.

—Business Week
June 2, 1997

To keep the euphoria going, the world's movers and shakers are flying high on stimulants. Do you know how to make a mania cocktail? Mix caffeine and Prozac.

September 1997

Some commentators have noted renewed vigor in the market for paintings and real estate and concluded that it is an early warning of an inflationary episode. Don't bet on it. *At the Crest* anticipated "wave two" rallies in many markets that would "culminate with the upward force of the tidal wave." *The Elliott Wave Theorist* has continued to maintain that these rebounds are a bear market rally. The chart of Blue Chip paintings below illustrates the "wave two" nature of the rebound. While volume (the number of lots sold) is up to new highs, prices are nowhere near those of 1989. This is the same pattern exhibited by the stock market during its famous B-wave rally into 1930. *Elliott Wave Principle* notes that another characteristic of B waves is that they are "sucker plays, orgies of odd-lotter mentality." Nothing reflects a sucker play better than the overall market for collectibles. Latecomers have utterly ignored historically legitimate collectibles such as coins and baseball cards, which have barely bounced from their lows, to speculate in celebrity bric-a-brac ($1,500 for a Grateful Dead "medicine bag," for instance) and potential but unlikely collectibles like $4 bean bags that are mass-produced in China. We are certain that the Beanie Baby market is turning down because on rural routes in Georgia, we see hand-lettered signs advertising their availability. It was along these same roads that the baseball card shacks appeared as the bottom dropped out of the card market in 1992.

October 1997

EWT has long argued that social mood underlies both the stock market's trends and those of popular culture. At this point, the bull market has penetrated so deeply into the social fabric that investors have actually come to embrace enterprises that are strictly devoted to trends in popular culture. These pure plays in pop culture include: stocks in restaurants like Planet Hollywood; sports teams

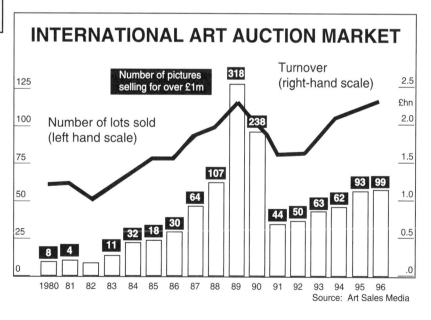

like the Florida Panthers, Miami's National Hockey League franchise; and fashion issues like Gucci. Historically, restaurant, sports or fashion businesses have been too mercurial for public ownership, but today, even transient public fascinations are deemed worthy to come to market. Yet

Planet Hollywood Reels As 'Eatertainment' Fades

Planet Hollywood, the fast-growing Orlando-based chain of celebrity-themed restaurants, this week announced that it will post a big unexpected loss for the fourth quarter and slash expansion plans.

Coming only days after another theme restaurant company, Rainforest Cafe, announced disappointing results, Planet Hollywood International's pullback raises questions about the viability of the "eatertainment" business.

Entertainment lets operators charge more for ordinary food in exchange for an offbeat environment.

The announcement sent Planet Hollywood shares tumbling to a record low on Thursday. On Friday, it slipped another 12.5 cents to close at $7. That's down from the 52-week-high of $27.25 on July 25.

—The Wall Street Journal
September 6, 1997

GREEN BAY PACKERS, INC.

COMMON STOCK

OFFERING DOCUMENT

COMMON STOCK DOES NOT CONSTITUTE AN INVESTMENT IN "STOCK" IN THE COMMON SENSE OF THE TERM. PURCHASERS SHOULD NOT PURCHASE COMMON STOCK WITH THE PURPOSE OF MAKING A PROFIT.

Football Stocks

There is a spring in the step of English football. Manchester United saw off Juventus last week and there are high hopes England will do the same to Italy tonight. Alas, the good news has not seeped through to football stocks. Yesterday Nottingham Forest closed its first day trading 13 per cent below the issue price, a continuation of the pattern whereby 11 of the 14 stocks listed over the past 18 months are trading below their issue price. The market, meanwhile, has risen 30 per cent over the same period.

—Financial Times
September 6, 1997

Ice Hockey Fans May Make a Fast Puck

When Tommy Soderstrom and his Djurgarden team mates take to the ice later this month, they hope to emerge from the clash with arch rivals AIK not only as leaders of the Swedish league but as Europe's first quoted ice hockey team.

Directors of the Stockholm club say victory in the derby game, marking the start of the ice hockey season, could be vital in wooing a new breed of fan — stock market investors attracted by the idea of making a fast puck.

A winning streak would be the ideal fillip for Djurgarden, 14 times champion of Sweden's elite hockey league, as it prepares to raise $27 million through a share offering. If fully taken up, the offering would enable the club to fund rising salary demands from its players and help stem the exodus of stars to North American teams. The need to match the pay cheques offered by the likes of the Toronto Maple Leafs or Florida Panthers was underlined this summer when Djurgarden's long-haired star, Espen "Shampoo" Knutsen, announced his departure for the Anaheim Mighty Ducks of the US.

—Financial Times
September 6, 1997

a survey of those mentioned above and others like Nike, the sportswear firm; Jenny Craig, a chain of weight-loss clinics; and Manchester United, an English soccer team, shows the emergence of a clear pattern. These "pop culture" stocks are well off the pace of the overall market. Most are actually in clear downtrends. This underperformance is fascinating because it hints that the mood behind the buying will prove as transient as the fads it temporarily supports.

Golf shares, now a legitimate stock market sector with no less than 29 issues, illustrate this divergence from the overall market trend. To understand it fully, let us provide some brief history on golf's pedigree as one of the great bull market games. The first major American golf tournament was played in 1895, eight months before the initiation of the Dow Jones Industrial Average and 10 months before a low that still stands. In each successive wave of rising stock prices, golf's popularity has surged. In the 1920s, country clubs sprang up across the nation. The Depression, "of course, put a pinch on the country-club lifestyle. But by the late 1950s [during wave III], the concept was ready for a comeback."

March 10, 1998

In the 1980s, Japan's booming mood coincided with an outrageous golf craze (noted by EWT in February 1989), and since 1989, the number of golf communities in the U.S. has more than doubled. The game's popularity is so clearly in lock-step with the stock market that Barron's noted in a golf section earlier this year, "We can now report that there appears to be a definite connection between golf and stocks." The very fact that Barron's has supplemented its financial coverage with a golf issue is itself further evidence. Business Week and The Wall Street Journal have also added golf advertising sections, just as The Magazine of Wall Street mixed golf ads with its stock market coverage in 1929. Golf heroes are also a feature of bull markets. On the pro tour, Tiger Woods has established himself as the sport's dominant player, just as Jack Nicklaus did the mid-1960s and Bobby Jones in the late 1920s. "Tigermania" has coincided with an unprecedented middle-class enthusiasm for the game.

Despite golf's soaring popularity and its 100 years of dependence upon a positive social mood, only two of the 29 golf stocks accompanied the Dow to its all-time high in August. All others topped out months or even years ago. As a group, the golf stocks, which trade under ticker symbols like PAR, GOLF, EDGE and TEE, have demonstrated an amazingly consistent pattern. Like the other "pop culture" stocks discussed above, they go public, enjoy a brief moment of price appreciation, and then go into a swoon. Some have come to rest at pennies a share and now seem to await the extinction that is sure to come with an actual downturn in social mood.

November 1997

Pop culture and the stock market were unofficially wed on October 27 as stock market reporter Maria Bartiromo appeared as a guest on "Late Night With David Letterman." Stock market jokes have become regular fare in the nightly comedy monologue of Letterman and Jay Leno. Cracks Letterman, "Daylight savings ended this weekend. And we're all supposed to turn our clocks back...to 1929." Ba-Da-Boom.

January 1998

The Shanghai stock exchange has just moved into a "vast blue-glass and chrome monument to the market economy." Stock market dignitaries from around China sent bronze, crystal and mahogany bulls as tokens of goodwill to celebrate the opening of the building, which draws its architectural inspiration from the Arc de Triomphe.

More Evidence of a Grand Supercycle Peak

In another sign that the rising social mood is having its last laugh, *Seinfeld*, the #1 show on television, will end its run with the current season. Jerry Seinfeld turned down a $5-million per episode offer to stay on. Why? He says he "wants to go out on top. It's time."

NOW YOU CAN OWN A PIECE OF YOUR FAVORITE $TAR!

National Examiner
March 10, 1998

According to an NBC/Wall Street Journal survey, stockholders now outnumber non-stockholders, as 51% of adults say they own shares directly or through mutual funds. Equities account for 43% of household financial assets and 28% of all household assets, passing the all-time highs of 39% and 26% in 1968. As it uncovered these figures showing higher public participation in the stock market than at any point in the history of the republic, The New York Times proclaimed "the democratization of capitalism."

A sizable share of the economy's growth can now be traced directly to the rise in stock prices. A catch-all category labeled "other services" by statisticians who tally up the GDP has topped $1 trillion for the first time. The category was "driven by a 30% increase in inflation-adjusted spending on brokerage and investment counseling fees." In other words, the 2.5% annual growth in GDP that is so dramatically lagging the 8% rate of gain in stock prices is itself being sustained partly by spending on investment services, which is hardly production in the classic sense. What a house of cards investors have built!

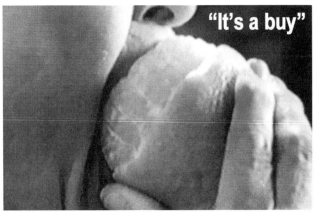

Commercial for Minute Maid Orange Juice
Spring 1998

The investment craze has infiltrated the culture. According to Competitrack, a firm that measures ad spending, mutual funds increased their record high ad budgets of 1996 by 68% in 1997. Look elsewhere and you see reminders of the enthusiasm for financial assets in less obvious places. The fluorescent greeting in the window of our ATM machine says, "we can help with your long-term financial plan." The entry for 59 Across on The New York Times crossword puzzle is clue: "put," answer: "stockoption." A prime-time ad for Minute Maid hooks customers by subjecting its product to the scrutiny of an investment club. "It's a buy," concludes a shrewd Beardstown Lady lookalike. A billboard in our neighborhood lures the eye with the phrase "High Yield Bonds" in bold letters, a pun on family togetherness from a non-profit group. A full-page ad for a desk calendar engages potential buyers with this line: "Invest Now While Stocks Last." There are Rock 'n' Roll bonds. There is *Buffettology*, an unauthorized take on Warren Buffett's investment technique by his ex-daughter-in-law, and one of ten investment books on Business Week's best sellers list.

Financial products aim at every conceivable social group, including women, blacks, children, the elderly, gays ("They Have Cash," a New York Times headline explains), animal rights activists and Hispanics. A car introduced at Comdex allows drivers to get real-time stock quotes by just saying the name of a company. Fine art pays tribute to "The Big Board." Wall Street Creations is a catalogue devoted entirely to assorted financial memorabilia and bric-a-brac. The Daughters of Charity, an order of nuns, has shut

September 30, 1997   January 7, 1998

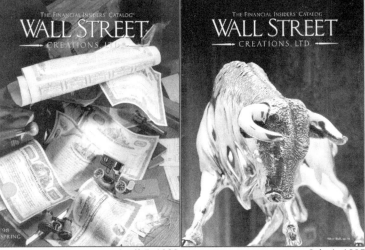

April 7, 1998   July 1, 1997

down a fifth of its hospitals as it increased its investment portfolio to $2 billion. We have a National Week of Investment (April 20-24). Better Homes and Gardens has created a new investment magazine called Family Money.

The U.S. is not alone. The Financial Times reports an "Equity Culture Growing Fast" throughout Europe. Euro-fever has even swept up risk-averse Germans who "can't seem to get enough [financial information] anymore." In the last year, "it's become fashionable to be a shareholder." Europe's traditional laggards, the Mediterranean nations, Italy, Spain and Portugal, now "epitomize" the opportunities of intentional investing, says the Christian Science Monitor. The idea of ownership in publicly held firms is universally appealing.

The golden era in the U.S. extends beyond the economic to the philosophical. A Financial Times columnist refers to "America the Triumphant. Europe in the 19th Century had two dreams: socialism and America. The first illusion has collapsed. The second has bloomed and become universal." Greed is good again, asserts John Stossel in an ABC television special. Greed works because "the end result is both parties profit." In China, the Communist Party School "recently reported that Karl Marx's doomsday assessment of capitalism was in error."

Spring 1998

April 1998

When people feel good, they like to get out, be seen, eat well and drink socially. This makes restaurants a focal point for the expression of a bull market mood. In our town, chain restaurants now seem to spring up a row at a time, which led us to dig up the following highlights in the history of the restaurant industry. Data show that the urge to eat out has been synonymous with the urge to buy stock for the duration of the Grand Supercycle bull market. The first true restaurant was the Grande Taverne de Londres, which was established in Paris around 1782, approximately the year that we believe Supercycle (I) began. Delmonico's, the first American restaurant, was established during the final leg of Supercycle (I). Between its establishment and the stock top of 1835, the Delmonico brothers and two other proprietors became the first to "operate multiple restaurants which functioned as a complex organism — the use of the same name, almost duplicate menus, and similar genetic consistencies to create clones," according to the book, *From Boarding House to Bistro*.

Through the middle of the 19th Century, restaurants became more common, but the choppy stock market conditions were reflected in a high failure rate. Of the 497 different addresses in New York City from 1850 to 1860 only 11, or 2%, were open under the same proprietor in both years. True chains appeared after the Civil War, as Supercycle (III) began its steady advance. In 1875, in the middle of wave (III), the Harvey House restaurants, which ultimately grew to a highly standardized family of 50 restaurants, revolutionized the industry. "Like the Delmonicos, Fred Harvey was at the right spot at the right time," records *America Eats Out*, a history of the restaurant business. "[His] effect was immediate, populist, and spread through the entire country, [setting] the course of culinary history."

In the bull market of the 1920s, cafeterias, speakeasies and White Castle hamburger joints spread rapidly across the country. Howard Johnson, Marriott Corp. and countless other "white box" hamburger stands tapped into the mass appeal that White Castle had uncovered.

The next "revolution" was called "fast food," which *From Boarding House to Bistro* dates to 1949, the exact year of the start of Supercycle wave (V) in inflation-adjusted stock prices, when the McDonald brothers established a walk-up hamburger stand. In many ways, "McDonald's story was a re-enactment of the [White Castle system] in the 1920s." In 1954, as the "third of the third wave" entered its acceleration phase, Ray Kroc bought the franchise rights, capturing the S&P restaurant index because it remains one of just four well-established restaurant-chain stocks. Appropriately, however, in this final leg of the advance, the public has assumed much of the risk that is inherent in catering literally to tastes. In the current bull market, the number of restaurant stock offerings has mushroomed into the hundreds, financing an unprecedented boom in restaurant industry growth. Almost 45% of the money spent on food now is spent in restaurants. In some multi-purpose establishments, dining has been upgraded to a full-sensory experience known as "eatertainment." At the Rainforest Café, patrons are treated to an "environmentally conscious 'family adventure' featuring live tropical birds, simulated nature sounds, waterfalls, aromatic scents and a gift shop retail area." Planet Hollywood packages its fare around the aura of celebrities from movies, sports and music. Both are publicly traded.

The stock market is an advance-warning device, so it is of interest that the stocks of these two companies have fallen substantially. In fact, it's hard to find a restaurant stock that is still participating in the bull market. Even McDonald's is struggling to regain "its golden touch." Over the last two years, McDonald's shares have been flat versus a 70% gain in the S&P. Suddenly, "the company that once seemed a half-step ahead of pop culture" cannot even "construct an appealing new lunch sandwich." Our view is that McDonald's and the restaurant business are powerful reflections of a positive social mood. The quantity, diversity and increasing complexity of restaurants reflect the same aspects of the bull market. The inability of their stock prices to match the bull market hints of a coming retrenchment in the industry. That, in turn, portends an end to the economic uptrend that has supported their success.

May 1998

Stocks make up 43% of all households' financial assets (including bonds, money funds, bank deposits, etc.). There is more money in stocks than in homes for the first time since the top of the low-priced stock craze in 1968 (which was probably the only other time in U.S. history that it happened). Just before the 1987 crash, U.S. households had 13% of their assets in stocks, less than half of today's percentage.

June 1998

In a closely related phenomenon, the Beanie Baby delirium has moved on to an even higher plane. Last year, when the craze started, we called the speculation in stuffed toy animals "a classic sign of heavy public involvement, and by definition, an approaching peak." Knowledgeable collectors have tried to quell the hysteria by explaining that value in the field is created by a fondness for a product and a scarcity that develops over time. A common toy that is in demand as an investment instantaneously has zero "long-term collectibility," according to a columnist for Antiques & Collecting magazine. The columnist noted that the Beanie Baby phenomenon is the result of "an artificial demand" created by a toy company's manipulation of "the gold rush mentality" that permeates society. "When future historians write the history of collecting in the 1990s," he says, "some may name the decade after a new species of collector that developed during this time: collector ignoramus."

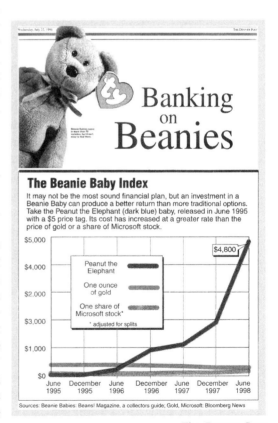

The Denver Post
July 22, 1998

Beanie Baby speculators are confusing their own intense faith in the moneymaking potential of cute beanbags with scarcity. *The Beanie Baby Handbook*, which projects how many thousands of dollars various Beanies will be worth in 2008, had sales of 1 million in 1997 and 1.1 million so far in 1998. The durability of the Beanie frenzy is unprecedented, but it doesn't change the transitory nature of the beast. Seasoned collectors have watched in amazement as naïve "investors" have made this same mistake time after time in the 1990s. First, it was baseball card sets, then the "Death of Superman" comic book, the Elvis stamp, Mighty Morphin Power Ranger toys and Tickle Me Elmo dolls. All these experiences ultimately offered the same simple lesson: Anything everybody wants is not worth having. Thus it is that Antiques & Collecting can say with total assurance that "individuals who pay more than $5 for a Beanie Baby will discover the correct words to describe their purchases are 'stupid,' 'idiotic' and 'foolish.'"

A year ago, McDonald's disappointed collectors by giving away just 100 million Beanie Babies. This time around, the company is determined "to meet expectations." It has raised the total for its four-week giveaway to 240 million, or just about one for every man, woman and child in America. On May 23, a local McDonald's was shut down by the fire marshal when 600 collectors crammed into the restaurant for Beanie Baby Mania. In retrospect, we may decide to call the 1990s the "beanie brain decade."

July 1998
Real Estate

A developer has plans to bring the title of "world's tallest building" back to Chicago with a 2000-foot-high rocket-ship-shaped office tower. Two years ago, when Malaysia was building the world's tallest building and China planned to top it, *The Elliott Wave Theorist* observed that "record-high buildings arrive on the scene at the end of big bull markets." In 1997, Malaysia's Petronas Towers did, in fact, become the world's tallest, and the Malaysian economy did, in fact, fall under the weight of the country's towering hopes. In 1996, EWT characterized the world's tallest structures as monuments to peaking social mood. Shanghai's 94-story tower has been postponed, which shows how weak its long-term trend has turned. The very idea of making a tall building, rather than its actual construction, may have been enough to signal a reversal there.

Collectibles

In collectibles auctions, we see signs of both wild topping behavior and exhaustion, some of which are downright freakish. Consider the $29,900 slice of cake. From the wedding of the Duke and Duchess of Windsor, the cake was purchased inside a box, which could not be opened without destroying the cake. When asked why he would pay almost $30,000 for something he couldn't even see, the winning bidder told CNBC, "I acquired this piece in the spirit of Dada surrealism." How about this for tempting fate? On June 16, Sotheby's auctioned off a series of tulip bulb artifacts commemorating the Tulip Bulb Mania of 1637. The first-ever auction of tulip bulb art actually went for 50% above high estimates.

May art auctions managed to hit the auctioneer's targets, but most of the sales took place at the low end of the expected range. The PR spin was on how fast the items sold. "There were exceptions to the ennui," notes a Wall Street Journal review. Apparently, a "completely new" crowd of "nouveau collectors" displayed a fondness for accessible works such as Andy Warhol's silkscreen of Marilyn Monroe. The orange Marilyn sold for about $17.3 million, which was more than four times the amount that a red Marilyn brought

'Orange Marilyn': $17.3m

Andy Warhol's "Orange Marilyn," a silkscreen portrait of Marilyn Monroe, has been sold in New York for $17.3m — more than four times the previous highest price paid for a Warhol.

FINANCIAL TIMES
May 17, 1998

in 1989, when its sale announced the end of the 1980s art splurge. Finally, in the heading-for-the-exits department, there was the sale of Christie's itself. Unloading the biggest piece was Joseph Lewis, described by The New York Times as one of the world's foremost currency traders. The buyer was a Frenchman, who became the first foreigner to own the auction house in its (Fibonacci) 232-year history.

More Signs of a Grand Supercycle Peak

One of the "big books" getting a resoundingly positive reception in the first half of 1998 is *The Commanding Heights*, by Daniel Yergin and Joseph Stanislaw. *Heights*, according to a review in the Economist, tells the "fascinating tale" of the free market. "Almost everywhere," even the liberals "are much like traditional moderate conservative parties.... In this new consensus, markets have the upper hand."

The Romance of the Marketplace

Not so long ago, there was a real war between the state and the market. A new book explains why the conflict seems settled.

The Commanding Heights, by Daniel Yergin and Joseph Stanislaw, is a big book. The book reveals the temper of our times. From India to Israel, from Mexico to Moscow, it has become a truism that economic activities should be dominated by market forces.

Around the world, nominally left-of-center governments advance what used to be thought right-wing economic policies. The intellectual climate of the era has been transformed.

—Newsweek, May 4, 1998

The Age of Friedman

America's most influential living economist since World War II was once isolated and ignored.

IT IS ONLY IN THE PAST 10 OR 15 years that Milton Friedman has been seen for what he is: the most influential living economist since World War II. For decades, Friedman–now 85 and long retired from the University of Chicago–was regarded as a brilliant outcast. He extolled "freedom," praised "free markets" and attacked big government. He was a cheerful dissenter in an era when government seemed the solution to most social problems. Confident of his views, Friedman would debate almost anyone, anywhere, but he was widely dismissed as a throwback.

Not anymore. Friedman's impact has been so huge that he's approaching John Maynard Keynes (1883-1946) as the century's most significant economist.

—Newsweek, June 15, 1998

REVERSAL:

Once upon a time, Keynes was king and Friedman was ridiculed; now, his free-market theories rule the roost.

—BusinessWeek, July 13, 1998

Marxist Comes To Market

Building private-sector wealth is a new concern for prime minister

Question: You had a reputation as an Albanian-style Marxist. Now you have embarked on market-driven reform. Is your heart really in it?

Answer: I have never believed in sharing poverty but I have always felt wealth should be shared as equitably as possible. What I've come to realise is that private-sector driven economies are the only viable sources of creating wealth, and unless you create wealth you cannot share it. The program we are currently undertaking is the only realistic option.

—Financial Times
May 4, 1998

188

On May 4, the day of the DJIA high to date, Newsweek took note: "From India to Israel, from Mexico to Moscow, it has become a truism that economic activities should be dominated by market forces." For now, it says, the debate between Adam Smith and government interventionists is over. In the middle of its review, Newsweek showed a picture of Thatcher and Reagan dancing merrily and stated that they "led the triumph." In another article, it adds that Milton Friedman, the economist who dared to extol free markets and was widely dismissed as a throwback until the 1980s, has approached "John Maynard Keynes as the century's most significant economist." Economists, in general, have become the superstars of academia. A bidding war broke out April 7, when Columbia offered $300,000 a year for the services of a prominent Harvard economist. "The market for top economists is starting to look like those for movie stars, basketball players and bond traders. It carries all the trappings, too — complex negotiations, signing bonuses and highly organized raids." A record total of 40% of the University of Chicago MBAs are taking positions in the financial services industry.

We applaud the triumph of the idea (but not the grudging and inadequate implementation) of capitalism and laissez-faire. However, as social scientists, we know what the implications of the celebration are: that trend is ending. History shows that government intervention tends to wane in bull markets and grow in bear markets, so this trend and that of the stock market are likely on parallel paths.

Speaking of which, on May 14, The Wall Street Journal surveyed the scene and pronounced in a front-page headline: "Capitalism Is Giddy With Triumph," but then went on to ask, "Is It Possible to Overdo It?" "The march to the market confronts America with a question that hasn't provoked serious debate in generations: Is the market penetrating too deeply into American life?" This is The Wall Street Journal talking now. It concludes that the "early stirrings of a backlash against the market are in sight." Indeed they are, as the U.S. Justice (sic) Dept. is suing Microsoft and Intel for their success, just as it sued IBM in 1969, within months of the great Cycle wave III top in the Value Line index.

January 1999

The front page of The Wall Street Journal reported on America's "Culture of Optimism" on December 22. Here, under the banner "Joy To the World," the WSJ records that the S&P and NASDAQ attained all-time highs despite political chaos, dropping bombs and fraying economic fundamentals because of "the ebullient national personality of the U.S., an immeasurable quirk that without question adds to the gross domestic product and to social harmony." America, the "most optimistic nation on earth," has an irrepressible natural resource, or "good feelings premium," which it places on the economy, political figures who project optimism and Internet stocks.

From our perspective, it is an amazing article because it accurately identifies the driving force behind the bull market. The economy is a reflection of "a generic, almost metabolic, human optimism," says the author of Optimism: The Biology of Hope. The dean of one of the nation's top business schools adds, "When I'm optimistic, I'm more likely to make commitments of capital, to spend and to take risks.'" As The Elliott Wave Theorist has always stressed, this positive group emotion is in fact the root of all bull markets. What the article does not say, however, is that there is a natural countervailing pessimism (also known as a bear market) that enters the picture from time to time.

In that light, we note that the article characterizes Americans with the same unwaveringly positive traits that Japanese writers attributed to their country's people in 1989. In November 1989, a month before the Nikkei's peak, for instance, the author of The Japan That Can Say No appeared in Time suggesting that Japan's bull market was a racial trait. Japan's leadership in technology would help it "build a new world history." At Japan's great peak, countless other articles and books on both sides of the Pacific extolled the virtues of Japanese management techniques and declared its business habits and educational system far superior to its slothful

American counterparts. Now that the S&P is at an all-time high and the Nikkei is down more than 65%, the situation is reversed. We believe the outcome here will be the same as it was there.

March 1999

The "world's most prestigious" exchange made several moves to accommodate the public's seemingly unquenchable thirst for equities. With the help of nearly $1 billion in city and state funding, the Big Board will expand its trading floor into a nearby building. It is the NYSE's first major expansion since 1987, when plans for the New Blue Room were put in motion. Construction of the original Blue Room began near the peak of 1968. These two previous expansions were initiated at the zeniths of the last two great speculative binges and opened for business in the far more subdued trading environments of 1988 and 1969. In an unparalled action, the NYSE also announced a tripling in the length of its trading day. "The growth of global investing will not allow markets to be competitive if they constrain themselves to a time clock," explained the chairman. The NYSE will open for business in European shares at 5 a.m. and add evening hours through midnight "to embrace a consumer group that traditionally has been shut out." The NYSE is also making plans to begin trading popular shares on the NASDAQ.

Equity Culture Revisited

On March 9, the NYSE will present one more symbol of the stock market's complete integration into every corner of American life. Barbie will celebrate her 40th birthday by ringing the bell to start trading. Wall Street will be renamed Barbie Street for the day and traders will sport pink vests. Read this item from the real-life fashion world: "When models, photographers, hair and make-up artists and Sports Illustrated editorial staffers were on location in the British Virgin Islands to shoot the 1999 swimsuit issue, it seems most of them had at least one thing in common. CNBC says everyone gathered around the TV each day so they could watch satellite feeds of *Power Lunch* and *Market Watch*." It has now been one full year since EWT observed that "the investment craze has infiltrated the culture" of the U.S. and Europe. Like an immense wall of white noise, this flood of financial images and information has grown stronger even though the global and broader U.S. markets have been declining for much of this time. The stock market's ascendant pop status was captured nicely in this report from New York magazine:

> The triumph of stock-market culture is visible everywhere you look in the city. A decade ago, Times Square was an archaic neon jumble of small business peddling sex and novelties. Walking through Times Square now feels like stepping inside a spreadsheet: The famous news zipper at 1 Times Square is sponsored by Dow Jones. NASDAQ will soon have its own mammoth stock-quote screen directly across the street, rising three stories high on the face of the Condé Nast building; there will also be a gallery, a lá the *Today Show*, that's part TV backdrop and part tourist attraction, featuring live traders. Five blocks north, on Morgan Stanley's headquarters, huge glowing orange stock fractions and corporate symbols move so fast they're unreadable. The unavoidable New York conversation has been about the stock market, exposing just how obsessed and market-savvy this city has become.

But it is not just a New York thing. In many circles, the stock market has replaced the weather as the No. 1 topic of conversation. It hardly even makes our ears ring anymore when the local weatherman says, "Temperatures are going up as fast as some of those Internet stocks." A Melbourne McDonald's has installed a stock ticker. In Germany, where a short time ago individual investors were considered too cautious for equity investment of any kind, the Neuer Markt, one of four new European stock markets for start up firms, is red hot even though the blue chips have been flat since last March. "Anything that's listed there these days seems to go really crazy. No one pays attention to any fundamentals. They just get carried away."

A major breakfast cereal has sponsored a contest in which the winner gets to invest $5000 in "stocks/mutual funds." "A bull market in old tunes is slowly emerging" as a wave of rockers ranging from Crosby, Stills & Nash to Michael Jackson line up to sell rock-and-roll investments secured by royalties from their hit songs.

April 1999

Dining establishments had record revenues of $337 billion in 1998, and the nationwide boom is looking so strong that the Department of Commerce has designated 1999 the year of the restaurant. At $10 million, Restaurant Daniel in New York is believed to be the most expensive new restaurant in the history of the city. New eateries are opening so fast that critics say they cannot keep up, and still, reservations at many of the hottest establishments must be made months in advance. Despite the boom, however, the equity valuations for many of the late 1990s' most celebrated restaurant industry IPOs have been almost totally extinguished. Boston Chicken's decline leads the way, down 98.3%. The list of disasters over the last few months includes Koo Koo Roo (down 95%), New York Bagel Enterprises (down 95%), Planet Hollywood (down 96%), Rainforest Café (down 81.3%), Lone Star Steakhouse (down 85%) and Jerry's Famous Deli (down 94%). Read those percentages again and note that they reflect *At the Crest's* outlook for the market as a whole in the coming bear market.

In January 1997, EWT linked the mania for stocks to the runaway bids for objects like Tickle Me Elmo and Jackie O trinkets by observing, "that the act of buying, or more precisely, of pushing up prices, is turning people on." A recent article on Internet auctions revealed that these "passions" continue to run as strong as ever. As one self-professed auction junkie put it, "Buying is an actual high for us." In its more formalized outlets, however, the popular celebration

A Thriller On Wall Street

Michael Jackson periodically pops into public view, his emergence often stage-managed in minute detail, including the well-placed tabloid leak.

The King of Pop is turning up in a new venue – Wall Street. He is hoping to pull off a high-finance coup to the tune of $100 million or more. How? Float Jackson bonds.

The financial move would be slick but simple. Selling the bonds would allow Jackson to, in effect, borrow against future royalties from golden oldies, including early Beatles hits, that he owns. The eccentric performer began to consider the strategy last year, several music-industry executives say. Former EMI Capitol Music boss Charles Koppleman, backed by Prudential, now has the inside track to underwrite Jackson bonds. In an interview, Koppleman was mum on Jackson, but said he is poised to announce $250 million worth of music-royalty deals.

On Wall Street, a bull market in old tunes may be slowly emerging.

—*Newsweek*, November 23, 1998

of rising prices is subsiding. Since April, the Absolute Beanie Index is down 26.4%. Another bull market standard, the Barbie doll, is also in a free fall. "Barbie investment has crashed in the last year," reports Gannett News Service.

June 1999

Art patrons are throwing money at that market with an abandon not seen since the Japanese exited the scene in 1990. What are they buying? "If there is an artistic movement that could be called 'sunlight breaking through green trees,' it would be the dominant one now," noted a WSJ art critic. "Collectors are paying hefty amounts for such sun-dappled landscapes, often regardless of who painted them (as long as the name is famous), the degree of skill shown or the painting style. Good Camille Pissarros of a rainy day are selling for less than bad Alfred Sisleys of a sunny one." The almost giddy content of popular art is another unhappy signal for the market. As EWT noted in its Pop Culture report of 1985, "light, bright, positive mood" works of art are "found in extremes at market tops."

August 1999

The "striking thing about the stock market speculation of 1929 was the way it became central to the culture," wrote John Kenneth Galbraith in *The Great Crash*. "It follows that to be out of touch with the market, ever so briefly, was a nerve-wracking experience. Happily, this was not often necessary. Ticker service was now nationwide." Today, people watch financial TV, carry electronic quote machines with them and follow every tick over the Internet.

Investors know that the market won't go down, but they also know it may occasionally "correct." If it does, they know what to do: "Delay all sales until the market recovers." This message, reiterated yet again in the July 13 Wall Street Journal "Getting Going" column headlined, "Why You're Never Too Old for Stocks," was taken to heart by investors long ago. In a period of market volatility last year, 97% of Fidelity clients said they were in the market for the long term, meaning 10 years or more. All but 6% said they had no plans to take any money out of the market in the event of further declines. We think that this resolve will dissolve some time in the next few years as the biggest bear market since 1720 takes hold.

Since many people apparently plan to hold until the day they die, why are they so interested in the minute-to-minute gyrations of the stock market? The answer, as this cartoon suggests, is that people just like to bask in the positive aura of a rising market. This day-at-the-beach attitude is borne out by the books vacationers will be taking with them to the shore. In addition to *Dow 36,000, Dow 40,000* and *Dow 100,000*, publishers have or will put out no less than 30 different books on day trading. This mass fixation is an odd combination of dangerous and laughable.

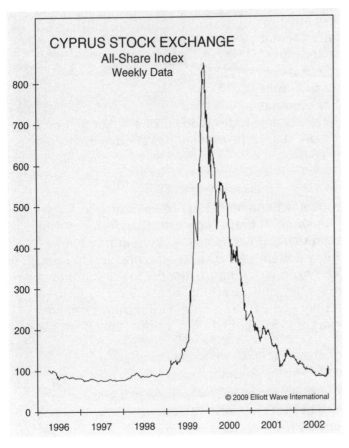

September 1999

In two other signs that bullish sentiment hit all-time highs with the Dow, the price of a seat on the New York Stock Exchange reached a new record of $2.65 million, and speculative fever has jolted "the once sleepy Cyprus market" where "not many even knew the island had a market" until recently. Now, state television broadcasts prices live during the 90 minutes of daily trading, and "islanders joke that even a poor village shepherd would sell his goats to buy shares." The story says, "thousands of Cypriots" are "throwing caution to the wind" and abandoning the safety of deposit accounts that have traditionally been the dominant investment choice. The newspaper seems to recognize the dangerous naïveté of these islanders.

In the U.S., however, where investors responded to the decline of July-August with a "we've seen it all before" attitude, the media is totally supportive of the speculative impulse. "The biggest thing is, don't panic," said a 45-year-old retiree with a sizable share of her portfolio in Internet stocks. The same woman used to hyperventilate from nervousness when she first started buying stocks, but now she is "eager to buy more Net stocks." In a society obsessed with "Bold Bets," it is presumed to be a sophisticated reaction.

In an important article from August 1, The Wall Street Journal explains "How Life On The Edge Became Mainstream In Today's America." It tells the story of Barbara Harkness, a child of the 1930s Depression who "went from thinking banks were the best place for my money to the worst place" over the course of the last ten years. "From cautious saver to citizen speculator in just a decade — that's quite a trek across the spectrum of financial risk. But if it's extreme, Ms. Harkness's journey points to something indicative of American behavior in the 1990s, in investments, careers and social life: a growing appetite for risk." The paper cited "barometers of cockiness" ranging from a 150% four-year increase in the percentage of Harvard Business grads joining high-tech or venture capital outfits to the "extraordinary interest in 'hard adventure' travel,'" to the historically high 75% stock allotment in the average individuals' investment portfolio.

As we said here last month, the striking thing about the stock market today is how "central to the culture" it has become. The cultural environment was similar in 1929, the only difference being the greater degree currently, which is why many of the manifestations of today's peaking mood would make a 1929 stock market speculator blush. In downtown Chicago, for example, local artists have populated the sidewalks and squares with a herd of 300 life-size fiberglass bulls. On network television, the surprise hit of the summer is *Who Wants to Be a Millionaire?*, a game show in which ordinary contestants get a chance to walk away with a million dollars. The show got the highest ratings of any summer series. Money camps for kids have surged in popularity. The "high point" for some happy campers was "the futures-trading course." Due to the enthusiastic response of attendees, the Future Investors Club of America hopes to go national and extend its camps into the school year. "When 8-year-olds in our community are giving presentations on financial markets, the sky's the limit," said the group's president. Actually, unless rhesus monkeys can be enticed into the investment arena, financial presentations by 8-year-olds will probably mark the Grand Supercycle limit in the demand for and belief in market information and analysis.

The pull of stock market culture is so strong that it is roping in economists. "Economists Give More Weight to Effect Of the Stock Market in Their Forecasts" says an August 15 headline, the reason being that it has "become more important." Is it actually more important, or has the force of the crowd made its lure irresistible? One economist admits that despite disbelieving the idea that stocks are driving the economy, she is "sticking her toe into the world of looking at stock market values because I'm getting so many questions."

November 1999

Back in 1997, when Tickle Me Elmo became the object of an intense holiday bidding frenzy, *The Elliott Wave Theorist* noted that one of the more direct social manifestations of the mania for financial assets was the way in which the thrill of "pushing up" prices was spilling over into society at large. Since then the creation of price bubbles has become a popular form of public recreation. EWT has observed its movement through everything from Mars rocks to $5 bean-bags. The latest craze is Pokemon, cartoon monster cards that have turned playgrounds everywhere into trading floors. "What distinguishes Pokemon from other toy crazes is its intensity," notes a recent story. "Young devotees spend countless hours arranging card trades — on-line bidding is popular — with the most prized cards fetching far more than the average allowance." It is a "rehearsal for life," says the chief of child psychiatry at Massachusetts General Hospital.

These extra-market bubbles have become so big that they now spill back into the financial realm. The Pokemon sector was one of the few groups to keep rising through the September decline in stock prices. "Grand Toys International, maker of Pokemon balls and school supplies, saw its stock rise 50 percent [in one day]. Pokemon is a cultural phenomenon."

As we noted last spring, bidding passions are planted so deep in the psyche of the public that even Internet companies have managed to make money mining them. Of course, that will get a whole lot harder as the phenomenon fades with the market and the number of new Internet auctions sites continues to mushroom. Now Microsoft plans to enter the business that already includes hundreds of firms making markets in just about everything. Even trivia has joined "The Web Auction Craze" with InfoRocket.com, a firm that hopes to make big money brokering facts and advice. "There's a constant auction going on out there" for employees, college tuitions or even stock market opinions. The fascination with the auction process runs so deep that TV shows draw viewers by dramatizing appraisals. On *Treasures* and *The Antiques Road Show*, a parade of hopeful owners wait with expectant faces as the value of their goods is estimated. In another popular Treasures segment, viewers tell about "a collectible that changed your life."

There is some evidence of a slackening in this trend. In late July, right after the S&P 500 peak, a baseball autographed by the pope failed to sell. Organizers of the auction "expected a bidding war of biblical proportions" but "got a lot of curious onlookers and not much else. Only two out of several hundred in attendance placed bids on a Pope John Paul II-signed baseball. Both bids came woefully short of the $50,000 asking price." Since then, offerings have tested the limits of human imagination, as Ty Cobb's dentures, Babe Ruth's underwear and a human kidney have been auctioned off. Bidding for the kidney topped $5.7 million before executives at eBay yanked the illegal posting. On Wednesday, we saw the purchase of a photograph for $837,400, the most ever paid for a photo. The total was ten times the expected amount, but it was the subject of the photo that strikes a portentous chord here. The object of bidders' enthusiasm was a 1955 shot of the Mediterranean coast called Grande Vague, or Big Wave. (A Big Wave is exactly what is poised at its peak culturally.)

The most important sign of a possible termination for auction fever came August 31 when Ty Inc. suddenly announced, "All Beanies will be retired" at the end of the year. Any question of the subconscious herding impulses behind the Beanie Baby craze was removed when collectors reacted angrily to the news. "As word spread that the maker of Beanie Babies would 'retire' all of the pint-size stuffed animals by the end of the year, many consumers were outraged, [saying] they were furious at being manipulated by the maker of Beanies." Beanie Baby buyers' limbic systems must be in control, because the reasoning parts of their brains would tell them that in limiting supply, the company is making its first legitimate effort at creating value. To celebrate the first light of sanity's return, we decided to help mark the top. We purchased the last Beanie Baby, a black bear named "The End." It is pictured here.

December 1999

The longer-term fools-for-stock psychology has now dwarfed that at the highs of 1968 and 1929 by a margin that is hard to comprehend. Stock market capitalization as a percentage of GDP is now 144% vs. 81.4% in 1929. A more qualitative comparison is the 1990s parallel to the Ladies Home Journal "Everyone Ought To Be Rich" article of 1929. The current mania matched the audacity of the Ladies Home Journal when Reader's Digest printed, "You Can Make A Million [in the stock market]" back in July 1996. Since then, millionaire-hood has become the common goal of the nation. It advanced from a new notion to a popular form of veneration in late 1996 when "You Can Make a Million" became a book, *The Millionaire Next Door*, a best seller in 1997. Then came a rush of stories about "secret millionaires" who got in early, lived frugally and died with millions squirreled away in stocks. At the end of 1997, newspapers discovered that the "millionaire population is growing 20 times faster the general population," and a wave of stories celebrating this fact followed. "Millionaires: Just a Dime a Dozen" was a headline in the L.A. Times. As many stocks reached their all-time high in July of the next year, aspirations seemed to escalate by a factor of 1000. The New York Post headline of July 8, 1998 was "High-tech Billionaires: They're a Dime a Dozen."

A Millionaire Moment

The publishing industry, eyeing dollar signs, is pumping out feel-good tomes on building a stash

HERE'S A GET-RICH-QUICK TIP: If you want to become a millionaire, perhaps you should consider writing a book about millionaires. After all, millionaire mania has become the "Harry Potter" of personal-finance publishing. The just-released *The Millionaire Mind*, by Thomas J. Stanley, is lodged in the number-four slot on The New York Times best-seller list. It's the sequel to his *The Millionaire Next Door*, which has been on best-seller lists for more than three years. Publishers are finding any excuse to put "millionaire" in titles these days. Amazon.com lists dozens of such books, including *The 401(k) Millionaire*, *365 Ways to Become a Millionaire (Without Being Born One)* and, of course, *Who Wants to Be a Millionaire*.

More than four out of every 100 households has a net worth of a million bucks or more, and many more are well on their way. While greed got a bad rap in the '80s, in this incarnation it's good, clean family fun, even a game show. Publishers say that makes for a promising, and growing, category of books.

Tip number 32 from *365 Ways to Become a Millionaire* advises: "Trust is the foundation of all good relationships."

"These books are really modern religious manuals. They tell us how to be virtuous," says Paul Schervish, a sociology professor at Boston College.

—Newsweek, March 13, 2000

Expanding Club
Millionaire households have quadrupled over the past four decades

HOUSEHOLDS WITH NET WORTH OF $1 MILLION OR MORE (IN 1995 DOLLARS)

4 million
3
2
1

1962   83   92   99*

*ESTIMATE. SOURCE: EDWARD N. WOLFF, NEW YORK UNIVERSITY

WILL WORK FOR MILLIONS

WE SUSPECTED IT for some time, but now we have proof: Today's college students are spoiled, and proud of it. Just view the latest informal Web poll of 2,000 undergraduates at recruitment site jobtrak.com: 25% of the respondents said they expected to be millionaires by 30. An additional 27% said their millions will come by the wrinkly age of 40.

—BusinessWeek
April 24, 2000

Newest 'Millionaire' Ratings Bliss for Fox

The entire landscape of network television was changed by the success of ABC's game show *Who Wants to Be a Millionaire*, and Fox's show this week proved that variations on that theme can reach similar ratings heights.

Fox's two-hour special featured a parade of would-be brides competing to be chosen by a multimillionaire, and it culminated in an on-the-air wedding presided over by a Nevada judge. Drawing stunning ratings, it attracted more young viewers–especially female viewers–than even ABC's *Millionaire*.

—USA Today, November 17, 1999

HOOKED on 'MILLIONAIRE'

The party should have been just another university faculty get-together, the kind where people consume wine and cheese, gossip about their rivals and argue the fine points of King Lear or Greek history. But when a group of Syracuse professors gathered recently, all they could talk about was *Who Wants to Be a Millionaire*.

Yes, it's true: Even ivory-tower denizens watch television, including TV game shows such as *Millionaire*, the ABC phenomenon now sweeping the ratings, the country and otherwise rational people off their feet.

"It's almost impossible to quit watching, it's so compelling," says Robert Thompson, director of Syracuse's Center for the Study of Popular Television, who attended the party. "It's the programming equivalent of crack cocaine."

And apparently, much of the USA is addicted to the high-tech, multiple-choice quiz show, hosted by Regis Philbin.

—The Denver Post
February 17, 2000

The game-show smash, *Who Wants to Be a Millionaire*, may be the culmination of this whole process. "It's almost impossible to quit watching. It's the programming equivalent of crack cocaine," said the director of the Center for the Study of Television. During one key ratings week, the show accounted for half the viewership of the Top 10 shows. Another prime-time example of the mania's rising entertainment value is this exchange on the December 1 episode of the TV show *Law & Order*:

> Officer (about a cabbie): "A guy's bleedin' to death in his back seat, he's makin' day trades."
> Partner: "Gotta run with the bull."

Food Fights and The Seattle Mob

As in 1906 and 1968, much of Coca-Cola's turmoil is rooted in emotional fears about food. The campaign against genetically engineered "Frankenfoods," which people have been consuming for years with no evidence of harmful side effects, started in Europe and spread to the U.S. in recent weeks. As in 1908 and 1969, government hearings have been called to discuss the health risk in food. "The second of three FDA hearings on the safety and regulation of biotech foods is expected to be as contentious as the first meeting [on] November 18." "Growing resistance to new technology" has prompted the public forums. At the World Trade Organization conference in Seattle, protestors attacked a McDonalds, smashing its windows and unfurling a banner protesting the genetic engineering of food. Nobody seems to know what triggered the wave of irrational fears but many are taking action. "Once Quick Converts, Farmers Begin To Lose Faith In Biotech Crops." Even when the "customer is wrong, the customer is right," says a farmer who has decided not to plant genetically modified seed next year.

In the middle of the unexpectedly explosive world trade summit, Ralph Nader himself resurfaced and grabbed more public notice than at any time since the Nader's Raiders days. In countless other ways, the events of Seattle over the last few days have provided clear signs of a reversal in the long-term trend in social mood. What was supposed to be an inclusionistic tour de force, the biggest free-trade meeting in history, has been all but shut down by a well-organized amalgam of eco-terrorists, union agitators, food phobes, students and protectionists. With tear gas hovering over crowded streets, a call out of the National Guard, law-and-order types decrying the "mob tactics" of their adversaries, and the sudden labor unrest, a whole host of long-dormant, cultural manifestations of a bear market have emerged.

The National Association of Manufacturers tried to head off the demonstrators by calling an army of Fortune 500 CEOs to the front. Before the WTO meetings even started, however, it was obvious that the world's corporate heroes would be powerless against the protestors. "We're never going to compete with thousands of Naderites rappelling and chanting," said a NAM spokesman. This is what happens in a bear market; the emotional forces of the crowd simply overwhelm the established order.

NASDAQ ⊕ AMEX

Press Release

The Nasdaq-Amex Market Group, an NASD Company
1735 K Street, NW
Washington, DC 20006-1500

December 28, 1999

New Nasdaq MarketSite Tower to Light Up Times Square Largest Video Screen in the World Mayor Giuliani and NASD CEO Zarb to Light at 5 p.m. Today

New York, NY—The Nasdaq Stock Market® will formally open its new Nasdaq MarketSite Tower—the largest video screen in the world—in the heart of New York's Times Square this afternoon at five o'clock.

New York City's Mayor Rudolph W. Giuliani and NASD Chairman and Chief Executive Officer Frank G. Zarb together will throw the switch to light-up the Nasdaq MarketSite Tower.

Mayor Giuliani commented, "I can think of no better place for the new Nasdaq MarketSite Tower than right here in Times Square—The Crossroads of the World. This is a great addition to the New Times Square, and will no doubt become one of its greatest attractions. The MarketSite Tower serves as a symbol of New York City's leadership in finance, and is another example of what makes New York City *The Capital of the World.*"

The Nasdaq MarketSite Tower: A prominent feature of the new MarketSite will be its large video screen, referred to as the "Tower." The Tower will be the largest video screen in the world, specifically:

- 8 stories tall
- 90 feet by 120 feet (10,736 sf, or ¼ acre)
- state-of-the-art, light emitting diode ("LED") technology
- number of LEDs: 18,677,760
- life-like, clear, high-resolution presentation
- display real-time, full-motion video, multiple video replay, text, and special effects with animated high-intensity graphics.

A Dow Stock Case Study: Coca-Cola

In 1993's *For God, Country and Coca-Cola*, Mark Pendergrast dates the start of Coca-Cola's "golden age" to 1923. With a push into global markets and a new age of mass media, Coke soared to heights of wealth generation previously unimagined for a maker of a 5-cent item. The real "secret," of course, was the company's primitive but powerful understanding of its underlying attractiveness. Ad man Archie Lee, "one of the first to realize that a product's image was more important than the product itself," came up with the "Pause that Refreshes" campaign in 1929. It is to that moment in time that anthropologist Clifford Geertz dates Coca-Cola's crossover from a soda fountain and syrup making company to "a system of symbols which acts to establish powerful, pervasive and long-lasting moods." The company "promotes a particular, satisfying, all-inclusive world view espousing perennial values such as love, peace and universal brotherhood. As a sacred symbol, Coca-Cola induces varying 'worshipful' moods, ranging from exaltation to pensive solitude, from near-orgasmic togetherness to playful games of chase."

The corporate history behind Coke's long rise shows that the company's old jingle is actually pretty accurate. Things really do go better with Coke. Unless, of course, the thing is a bear market. At such times, things don't go so well, not even for Coke. The firm's history is a living illustration of this passage from page 168: "Trends based upon subjective mental imagery undergo violent reversals when the imagery dissolves." Like the Dow Jones Industrial Average, Coca-Cola took off in the mid-1890s when its founders realized that there was more future in the beverage as refreshment than medicine. "We found we were advertising to the few when we ought to advertise to the masses," said one of the firm's original leaders. By the turn of the century, the company was burrowing deep into the public psyche as it "pioneered celebrity endorsements" to become "not simply a soft drink, but a phenomenon." The first big setback for Coke was the passage of the Pure Food and Drugs Act. Its date of passage was June 1906, five months after a Dow high that would not be materially exceeded until the 1920s. At the outset, Coca-Cola loyalists referred to proponents of the "pure food movement" as "cranks" and "misguided fanatics," but they had far more clout and staying power than expected. Their leader was Harvey Wiley, a man Pendergrast calls the Ralph Nader of the early 1900s. In 1907, Wiley took aim at Coca-Cola with the formation of a new "Poison Squad." Coke's annual report of 1907 reflected a coincident downturn in the company's prospects. As the bear market dragged on, Coca-Cola was beset by woes. In 1908, the U.S. government filed suit over its labeling and employment practices.

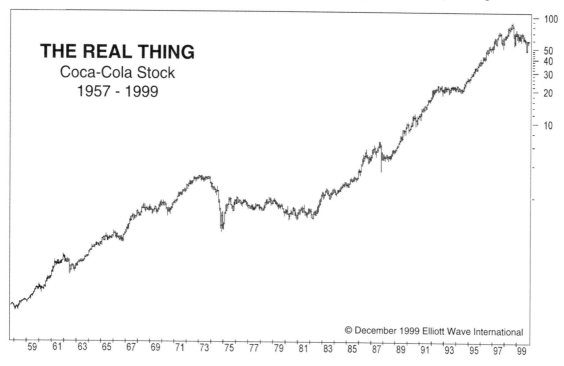

THE REAL THING
Coca-Cola Stock
1957 - 1999

© December 1999 Elliott Wave International

By 1949, the end of the bear market in inflation-adjusted terms, Coke was experiencing the same anti-Coca-Cola sentiment that had pulled it down in the 1910s. In Paris, mobs overturned Coke trucks, and "the level of hysteria reached such a pitch" that the wife of Coca-Cola's French president worried that her house might be bombed. "Coca-Cola faced similar threats and rumors at mid-century around the world." In Japan, the drink was said to sterilize women.

In the 1950s, the drink got back on track with the bull market. "Consumer behavior was often irrational, based on subconscious psychological motives," Pendergrast writes. "For the first time, the company attempted to plumb the depths of the subconscious mind." Coca-Cola was soon riding high again. In 1966, the end of Cycle wave III in the Dow and a long advance for Coke, the company "suddenly became a hot political topic" and nearly lost the Jewish market by refusing to grant an Israeli bottling franchise. The crisis was forestalled until late 1968 when the Dow topped and the resulting Arab boycott went into effect. In 1969, Ralph Nader surfaced with attacks in a hearing before the Select Committee on Nutrition and Human Needs. Shortly thereafter, "the Food and Drug Administration sounded another theme of the approaching seventies by revealing alarming results of tests on cyclamates." Coke's "perfect harmony" ad campaign of the early 1970s helped carry it to a final high with the Dow in 1973, but after that, it was all downhill as the company lost its long battle with the FTC, internal morale fell to an all-time low and "cozy relationships with dictators blew up one after the other." "No one would have guessed that a hopeful new era was about to commence."

By 1995, Coca-Cola would be the world's best known brand, with nearly half of the world-wide soft drink market. The perfection with which the "peace and harmony" of its commercials reflected the public mindset is captured in the stock's price climb from 1982 to 1998. Since its peak in July 1998, however, things have changed in ways reminiscent of past stock market tops. Coke has been shaken by a continuous stream of mysterious corporate crises that range from mold scares to the French government's rejection of its bid to buy Orangina to an assortment of unfavorable court rulings. In one case, the Belgian government successfully forced Coke to stop selling its beverages at a discount.

The true nature of Coke's problems is revealed by another recent snafu, an outbreak in which several Belgian school students reported feeling bad after buying Coca-Cola from a vending machine. Some were hospitalized, but no medical problems were ever diagnosed. Even though the company analysis showed "consumers were generally limited to subjective symptoms," massive recalls followed in Belgium and then France. "The pattern of this epidemic is consistent with a clinical entity which has been described as 'mass sociogenic illness.'" In socionomic terminology, this translates to "We're in a bear market."

January 2000

Look what Forbes has in giant type on its cover: "Everyone Ought to Be Rich." The title is repeated from the August 1929 issue of the Ladies Home Journal in which John Raskob argued that it is impossible not to get rich buying stocks. Forbes' December 27 issue argues that Raskob was absolutely right! "Yes, the market could collapse to 5500 two years from now (and would still be at the high end of historical multiples of earnings, dividends and book value). If you are young and thrifty, you would be benefited, not hurt, by such a collapse." The article insists that anyone can dollar-cost average his way to millions. It's not about smarts; it's about guts.

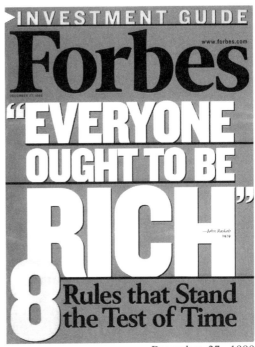

December 27, 1999

This mentality has created a carnival atmosphere that is evident in the promotions and gimmicks used to draw the public deeper into stocks. On-line retailers now put a portion of the money customers spend on toys, compact discs and other items in designated mutual funds. In December, a brokerage firm placed online trading PCs on the slopes at Vail. A spokesman for the firm explained, "More and more people are self-directed in their investing. Part of their responsibility is to be in touch with the markets."

As never before, celebrities are used to amplify the magnetic attraction of the market. Bigger and bigger names are lending their auras to the opening ceremonies at the NYSE. From mid-December through the first week of January, a group of top-tier celebrities including Hank Aaron, Rev. Desmond Tutu and Muhammad Ali have sounded the opening bell. According to Business Week, the NYSE "bell-ringing ritual on TV is now the single-most widely viewed daily event." A host of other music, movie and fashion stars have started to take stock in exchange for associating their images with companies. The practice has become so common the William Morris Agency has set up an entire division to match stars with firms. Cindy Crawford has a deal with eStyle. "Everyone wants to be involved in the web," she says. Ice-T, William Shatner and Jason Alexander "hold Internet paper, too." A most egregious example of the linear extrapolation of this trend is from Newsweek's user's guide to the 21st Century, which predicts, "The stock market will take over just about every aspect of society" (as if that is not precisely the current state of affairs).

February 2000

In another bull-market breakthrough, CNBC attracted more viewers than general news leader CNN in the fourth quarter. The first-ever daytime ratings victory for the financial network probably represents the completion of what Fortune described recently as "the great cultural transformation of our lifetime." There is a higher "level of awareness — and a level of sophistication — about the market that is simply unprecedented. It has become part of the popular culture." The term "sophistication" is inaccurate, as investors are not so much educated in markets as they are entertained and hypnotized by them. As we explained in last month's EWFF, the market has become a form of popular amusement.

Cultural Trends

The February 7 Newsweek cover story asks why professional wrestling is "No. 1 in Cable, Videos, Toys & Books." *The Elliott Wave Theorist* answered this question fifteen years ago, back in 1985, explaining that pro wrestling, "with its well-defined representatives of good and evil," is popular in bull markets. Definitive morals and heroes accompany a bull market; blurred morals and mixed heroes accompany a bear market. Indeed, the history of the World Wrestling Federation, as described by Newsweek, parallels that of the bull market. The modern era began in 1982 (the year of the low in inflation-adjusted stock prices), when Vince McMahon took control of the company and started its expansion. "In the mid-1980s, it grew more popular than ever. For a 1987 show at the Pontiac Silverdome, the company sold 93,000 tickets. Then trouble struck." It lasted a little past the stock market's correction in 1990. Since 1996, "wrestle mania" and stock mania have actually become indistinguishable in some ways as "wrestle mania" has exploded to become the dominant

February 2, 2000

199

form of cable television entertainment and a publicly traded stock with a market capitalization of $1 billion. On February 5, WWF president McMahon appeared on CNBC and announcing a new plan to expand into professional football said, "I don't think we can fail." "Performers can make $5 million, plus stock options," Newsweek reported. In one insightful, behind-the-scenes note, Newsweek quoted a veteran wrestler boasting about his investment performance. Another wrestler, who plays the lovable Mankind and the redneck psychopath Cactus Jack, said "When a new guy comes in, I try to give him financial tips." He has also written a book, which is No. 3 on The New York Times nonfiction list. His nemesis, the Rock, has a book, too, and it hit No. 1 on January 30. As Paul Montgomery (Universal Economics, Legg Mason Wood Walker, Newport News, VA) has noted, the standing of these books indicates "that public interest in pro wrestling could not get any greater than it is right now." That sentiment precisely reflects the stock market's level of popularity as well.

March 2000

Further reflecting the depth of this vision, a major network has decided to make the mass belief in the birth of a new era the basis for a new television show. *The Hollywood Reporter* announces that a news show "dedicated to 'the new economy'" will go on the air in March. It will be called *The N.E.W. (New Economy Watch) Show*.

The story's Hollywood dateline is also significant, as it shows that the financial bubble is now fully established in the entertainment capital of the world. In December, EWFF noted "the mania's rising entertainment value," and the rapid progress of its show-biz career has been duly recorded in every issue since then. This month, the market became a prime-time staple, as "Hollywood succumbed to the allure of Wall Street," reports USA Today. "Given our current infatuation with the stock market and Internet trading, the merger of dot-com and sitcom is marketing perfection."

Unlike *The N.E.W. Show*, a number of the programs currently being added to the TV schedule are fictional dramas, including *Bull*, an hour-long series about investment bankers and brokers. Another breakthrough for financial television is contained in a New York Times piece headlined, "The Money Culture Is Now Everybody's Business." According to this story, "Humor coexisting with finance might once have seemed a reach. [But] *Squawk Box* [which opens CNBC's day-long market coverage] changed the way business news was reported: not as dry, arcane number-crunching — though that, too — but as entertainment. That it is one of the funniest shows on television is hard to explain to anyone who hasn't seen it."

May 2000
Show Me a Sign

Speaking of surreal, did you see the glazed looks on the faces of New Yorkers as they gathered outside NASDAQ's MarketSite in Times Square April 14? One NASDAQ commentator said that he didn't have to look at the tape. He could tell when the market hit an air-pocket by the level of shock staring back at him from the street. As the market tanked, the media zoomed in on those faces to articulate what its army of financial commentators were suddenly at a loss for words to express. A picture in Time magazine called it "Ground Zero" and said, "Even live from NASDAQ's own TV studio, it was hard to describe the action." Newsweek's April 24 weekly recap opened with this headline quoting a woman "as she watched the NASDAQ signboard in Times Square:"

Oh my God, oh my God, oh my God! Agghhhhh!

If only someone had shown them a sign. Actually, all they had to do was take a few steps back and look up. A whole host of long-term sell signals would have literally flashed before their eyes. The biggest and most radiant is the new NASDAQ billboard they were standing under. It is on

the left in this picture of Times Square. The $37 million stock market beacon was turned on within days of the January peak in the Dow (see press release, December 99 entry). It is now the largest, most technologically advanced and most expensive display in Times Square. The sign beams NASDAQ prices out on Broadway in more than 16.7 million distinct colors to elicit "wonder and amazement, from tourists and denizens alike."

As we showed in last month's Cultural Trends section, this stretch of Broadway historically has been tuned to the stock market to a surprising extent. This history dates all the way back to the turn of the century, when a bull market raged and the area emerged as New York City's theater district. It became known as the Great White Way because of the brilliant white sign lights that appeared at that time. In the bull market of the 1920s, the same streets exploded in color as neon signs were popularized. The finishing touch was a giant Warner Brothers sign that was "reputed to be the largest electrical advertisement in the world." The sign was going up as the market was crashing in 1929.

The latest, all-time greatest Times Square sign is of even greater weight as a signal of a peak stock market experience because this time, it is actually firing out market information. "Its purpose is a garish display, adding to the bright lights and scrolling news zippers blanketing Broadway and grabbing the attention of tourists likely to walk away with a NASDAQ key chain or coffee mug." With this display, the stock market is beyond popular. It's the 8th wonder of the world.

The NASDAQ board is just one piece of a wide panorama. As the picture shows, it is located directly across from the Dow Jones zipper, which is right above Pokemon's tribute to price bubbles as a popular form of public recreation (see bottom right of the picture). The Dow zipper went up last year, replacing the original, which was first erected in 1928, one year before the crash. On the jumbo TV screen shown above the zipper, CNBC appears through most of the market day. As Business Week said recently, these days, "CNBC is more than popular — it has become a cultural phenomenon."

In Times Square, you can watch commuters coming up out of the subway look up and lock onto the network's giant talking heads. Also visible from the spot where this picture was taken are the new Reuters financial tower, a blinking Bloomberg sign and a new "Disneyesque" visitor's center that is being added to the NASDAQ site. Turning north, Morgan Stanley Dean Witter's rapid-fire streamer flickers out stock prices at the far end of the square.

Another unmistakable sign of how the financial markets have subsumed the world's most famous entertainment district is the fact that many big brokerage firms have abandoned downtown Manhattan and even Wall Street itself for this part of town.

In 1983, *The Elliott Wave Theorist* identified the drive "to clean up 42nd Street" as a sign that the bull market was in its early stages. From pickpockets and porn in 1980 to a financial phantasmagoria in 2000 may not necessarily constitute a cleansing, but, by capturing the dazzling glow of Broadway, Times Square's financial makeover certainly exceeds the ebullience achieved during any prior stock market advance. When the surviving brokers have shuffled back to Wall Street, the NASDAQ's sign has gone dark and the underworld has reclaimed Times Square, that will be a lasting bottom and truly a great time to buy the pullback. How many will be positioned to do it? We hope that you, as a reader of EWFF, will be among them.

A Socionomic Perspective on the Microsoft Case

In 1890, a year after a new all-time peak in stock prices that would last a full decade, Congress passed the Sherman Act, which in vague language outlawed "trusts," which in fact means companies that service a large market without significant competition. Take a look at the comments above the graph of stock prices below. Observe that the government's antitrust suits against U.S. corporations, particularly the landmark suits that make the history books, consistently come near stock market peaks, usually slightly afterward. Often the correlation is so close as to be within weeks of a major top that leads to declines in the averages of 50% or more.

Railroads were arguably the most successful U.S. industry in the late 19th century. On the run-up to the stock market peak of June 1901, the stock of Great Northern Pacific railroad, which later became part of Northern Securities Co., increased more than ten fold in less than a month. Shortly thereafter, the government sued Northern Securities Co. in the first major application of the Sherman Act. In 1906, the year of a peak that was not exceeded for ten years, President Theodore Roosevelt filed his famous suit against one of the country's largest company, Standard Oil. During the Panic of 1907, the President offered no objection to a merger involving U.S. Steel when asked to do so and explicitly directed his attorney general not to bring an antitrust action against International Harvester. In 1911 and 1912, after stock prices had recovered, President Taft's antitrust division filed suit against both companies.

A month after the all-time high of 1929 and before the crash, the U.S. attorney general announced that the Justice Department would deal "vigorously with every violation of the antitrust law." In 1930, the Justice Department filed suit against one of the biggest success stories of the 1920s bull market, RCA. In 1937, the year of a major top in stock prices, the government sued aluminum maker Alcoa.

The antitrust movement saw little action throughout the nearly two-decade long bull market of 1949-1966/68 until the very end, when the stock market reached a top of the same Elliott wave degree as that of 1937. In 1967, the government ordered Proctor & Gamble to divest itself of Clorox, and in January 1969, a single month after the most speculative bull market peak since 1929, the Justice Department sued the country's most successful company, IBM.

From 1982, antitrust activity again virtually disappeared during nearly two decades of bull market. On May 18, 1998, just one month after the final high in the advance-decline line, which had risen for 24 years, the Justice Department sued the world's most successful company,

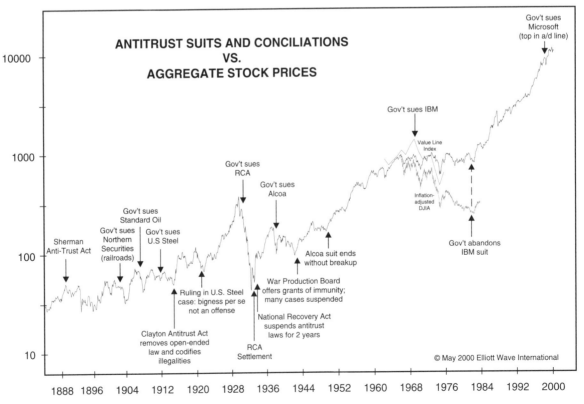

Microsoft. On April 3, 2000, a single week after the closing high in the NASDAQ 100 index, the court sided with the U.S. Justice Department in ruling that Microsoft had unlawfully violated the Sherman Act. Like his predecessors at prior historic turns, U.S. District Court Judge Thomas Penfield Jackson, representing "the people," has pursued and denigrated Microsoft with a fervor that borders on the evangelical. His desire to break up the most successful company of all time as measured by percentage gain in value per year by a major corporation is a passion born of the passing of a social mood peak of even higher degree than that of 1929. As you can see from this century-long history, major antitrust suits coincide remarkably consistently with the passing of major stock market tops.

The social mood shift that occurs at the transition from bull market to bear includes a change in general attitudes toward the financial success of others. Society moves from a feeling of support toward one of resentment. During a bull market, the social mood is directed toward rewarding achievement; during a bear market, it is directed toward punishing it. The bear market mood begins to creep into collective thinking late in a bull market. Democratic governments are instruments of egalitarianism. At some point, their representatives cannot stand watching some companies succeed wildly more than most others. When the bull market reaches exhaustion, the old supportive mood begins to crumble, and the new punitive mood bursts forth. One result of this metamorphosis in social character is governmental attacks against highly successful enterprises. In fact, they typically start with a major attack against the most successful enterprise of the time.

This socionomic perspective is quite comfortable with the fact that Microsoft tripled after the suit was announced. The environment of stock market tops is one of rampant speculation fueled by a manic psychology. Reason and outside event causality are no part of this landscape. Bullish fever among speculators and righteous anger among egalitarians can coexist for brief periods as major social mood tops are being formed, thus producing the anomaly of a soaring stock price for a company that is being attacked in court by its own government.

June 2000

The Equity Culture Expands

The routine use of stock market terms and images as a marketing gimmick shows how deeply the equity culture has permeated mainstream thought. In recent weeks, stock market optimism has produced some of the most flagrant manifestations of the equity culture to date. On May 3, the Taco Bell chihuahua rang the bell to open trading on the New York Stock Exchange. The appearance was part of a "promotional stunt" for a new menu item, a chip Taco Bell calls its "initial public offering." ABC has constructed its entire fall television schedule around four weeknight episodes of *Who Wants to Be a Millionaire*. StockGift.com, a new electronic registry, signs up brides and recent graduates to receive stock as gifts. The really revealing thing is not the service itself but the faithful endorsement of it by the media. The Wall Street Journal, Fortune, Money and Forbes have all spread the word. Even the Chronicle of Higher Education quoted StockGift's founder, who says, "It's a passive way to ask for what you really want."

Be Careful What You Ask For

If you know where to look, you will find that countless seemingly disconnected fashion and social trends reflect the same underlying impulse. That was certainly true throughout the mania. In recent months, one of the most powerful

HOLD THE BLENDERS!
We'll take Microsoft

The designer cheese grater was the last straw. Georgetown University MBA student Gino Heilizer, 31, was adding the gizmo to the wedding gift registry for him and his fiancee, Christina, 29, a photo editor, when he realized it was "ludicrous," he says, for a couple awash in kitchenware but short of cash to sign up for future dust magnets. "I thought, 'Why not register for something we really need?'"

Emily Post might not applaud his solution, but Warren Buffett probably would: Heilizer started StockGift.com, where those planning a birthday, wedding day or graduation day can put shares of companies such as Microsoft or Disney on their wish lists – to be bought with the click of a button.

— People, July 3, 2000

changes in psychology has been a turn away from the image of prosperity. This impulse is showing up in many places. As Bob notes in *Prechter's Perspective*, 1967-1970 marked years in which bell bottom jeans, long unkempt hair, sloppy shirts and boots became the style for baby boomers, and the VW became the car of fashionable choice.

> The wearers insisted they merely wanted to be comfortable, not fashionable. Not co-incidentally, that dramatic shift from the neat look took place as the stock market was making its final run into 1968. That was late in the topping process for Cycle III. The fashions of 1967-70 preceded the first recession in a decade. The mood behind fashion is father to the outcome. In 1969, people wanted desperately not to look prosperous, and lo and behold, a few years later, they weren't. Fashion signaled a mood change, which had tangible results.

Here at roughly the same juncture in Cycle V, the very same people are "dressing down," as companies have gone casual to "mirror and match clients." "This uniquely '90s phenomenon [has] penetrated most corners of corporate America." The final holdouts, "white-shoe" Wall Street firms, gave in to pressure in April and May as junior staffers threatened to quit if they were not granted the right to come to work in casual attire. This change is socionomically of at least Supercycle importance, and it portends a long setback in social mood.

In a similar leading-edge fashion note, the House of Dior has come out with a spring-summer haute couture collection described as "homeless chic" by The New York Times. "Dior models who starve themselves posed as the starving. They came down the runway raggedy and baggy, some swathed in newspapers, with torn linings and inside-out labels, accessorized with empty litter green J&B whiskey bottles, tin cups dangling from the derriere." The designer's inspirations were the "hobos" he sees as he jogs along the Seine, the mentally ill and "the Rag Balls of the 1930s, when French socialites wore tattered duds." A more intense replay of the 1930s, financially speaking at least, lies dead ahead.

Reflecting exactly the same socio-psychological trend, tastes in autos are also ratcheting down. "With Today's Cars, It's Hip To Be Small," says USA Today. The reversal actually started in May 1998, one month after the peak in the advance/decline line, with the advent of the new VW Beetle, an updated version of the same car that *Prechter's Perspective* identified as the turning point for car fashion in 1968. Now, Chrysler's "PT Cruiser is causing a mania that easily rivals what the New Beetle stirred up two years ago." This "mania" is actually a crashing reversal of the old mania. Meanwhile, discounting has become rampant in the market for super-sized "sport utility vehicles," and a rising chorus of protest against SUVs is gathering steam. The chairman of Ford, William Clay Ford, even joined the ranks by bashing his own company's line of super-sized autos at the firm's recent shareholders meeting. The performance "baffled shareholders, stunned Wall Street, angered dealers and left observers wondering if the latest Mr. Ford is not a proud tycoon like those who preceded him."

This summer, A-list movie stars Nicholas Cage, Kevin Spacey, Bruce Willis and Chris Rock will undergo a role reversal that also seems to pluck long-dormant chords in the recesses of the collective mind. All four $20 million-per-movie players will be transformed in movies "extolling the virtues of poverty." The theme in each of their latest films: "Money not only can't buy happiness, it impedes it. 'Having it all,' in other words, only proves you don't. ...Money is depicted as a sinister, toxic force." Or how about *Who Wants to Be A Millionaire*'s June ratings loss to *Survivor*, a "gladiatorial concept" show in which 16 people scramble for food and shelter. What's the attraction? "It's the Machiavellian twist" on the concept of becoming a millionaire overnight. Over the course of weeks, contestants vote one another off the island until there is a single million-dollar winner and 15 rejects. "It's the suffering, the mean-spiritedness, the humiliation. ...Despite *Survivor*'s gross-outs, its dark premise and its wall-to-wall cheesiness, viewers have embraced the desert-island soap with fascination and bemused contempt."

Here's another headline that also hints at a 180-degree turn:

Give Me a Break!

*With the economy booming, more Americans are demanding
the ultimate perk: a long breather from work.*

The article quotes one burned-out, high-tech executive explaining, "I had gone over the top." The founder of iVillage said she could not care less about the nosedive her company had taken in recent weeks. "Everyone talks about the bubble bursting. I say, 'Who cares, when am I going to get some sleep?'" These managers should be careful. The last time people threw the culture into reverse with fashion and lifestyle statements as evocative as these; they got a much longer winter's nap than they bargained for. Workers, to be sure, are on the verge of more free (literally) time than they ever imagined possible.

July 2000

New Assault On U.S. Corporations Confirms Microsoft Sell Signal
In May, *The Elliott Wave Theorist* analyzed more than a century of U.S. antitrust activity and found the government's case against Microsoft to be socionomic confirmation of a significant stock market peak. The chart (see May 2000 entry) shows the succession of antitrust "breakthroughs" at the start of major bear markets since 1889. Our "Socionomic Perspective On The Microsoft Case" explained that a market top of Cycle degree typically starts with a "major attack against the most successful enterprise of the time." Within days, Judge Thomas Penfield Jackson brought "the harshest penalty possible" against Microsoft, the dominant firm in the fastest growing segment of the U.S. economy. By ordering a break-up of the software power, the conservative Reagan appointee "rubber-stamped" every aspect of the U.S. Justice Department's proposed penalty and issued one of history's most definitive long-term stock market sell signals.

August 2000

Last month, *The Elliott Wave Financial Forecast* identified a host of cultural shifts like the movement to casual fashions and smaller cars as possible trend change signals. We said they were throwbacks to 1969 when "people wanted desperately not to look prosperous, and lo and behold, a few years later they weren't." Since then, we have noticed the emergence of several more social images that hint at a regression to even more distant bear markets. The following headline marks a retreat from a bull-market social norm that dates back at least a century:

Get Dirty, America: Experts Warn of Danger of Cleanliness

After five years of "compulsive health consciousness," concern about the "problem of excessive cleanliness" has suddenly become "a craze," according to a geneticist who has earned minor celebrity status for theorizing that scrubbing and sponging may actually be weakening our immune systems. "The public is just gobbling it up," he added. "There was a bandwagon, and it got bigger and bigger and bigger." Here is another item from an even more distant bear market: "Good news for gladiator fans: after 1,500 years, you can now get the same center-stage view of the imposing Colosseum the celebrated fighters had moments before they met a bloody death." For the first time since the start of the Dark Ages, live performances are taking place in the "home of howling Roman mobs." The first production will be Oedipus Rex, a classic in the annals of human self destruction.

What's going on? Our best guess is contained in the "Theories and Observations Relating to Impulsivity and Herding" chapter of *Human Social Behavior*. Page 168 discusses the possibility that a reversal in social mood can find initial expression as "shared fantasy images [that] are an intermediate step between mood change and resulting action." This was labeled "social visioning:"

Since mood is expressed immediately in countless ways other than buying or selling stock, expressions of the prevailing mood probably do include public visual images. These images would reflect mood quite immediately, before the public could mobilize itself enough to act in the economic or political arenas.

As noted last month, one of the most visible images of a mood shift was the change at the top of the TV ratings. *Who Wants to be a Millionaire*, the former No. 1, held out the promise of prosperity through knowledge. In the new most-watched show, *Survivor*, the objective is the same, $1 million, but getting it is a matter of physical endurance in which participants eat rats and ultimately kick each other out of the "tribe."

What holds the group together (and the attention of the audience) is the shared sense of deprivation. The same basic theme is prominent in two other new shows in which people voluntarily surrender basic human rights and conveniences for the camera. In *Big Brother*, 10 strangers are forced to take full-time occupancy of a single residence for 89 days while *1900 House* forces a modern family to withstand the rigors of a turn-of-the-century, Victorian lifestyle. They call these shows "reality" TV, which recalls this description of "social visioning" from HSB: "[People's] minds adapt to the group's changes in attitude as if reality itself had changed (and as a result, it usually does.)"

The Equity Culture Lives

For now, most people's reality is still firmly grounded in the bull market in social mood. That is why CNBC had a higher daily audience than CNN for the first time in the second quarter. "New Nielsen data showed that CNBC had become the highest-

MASS OPIATE?

Wall Street's Ubiquity on TV May Be Sending Sell Signal

Popular culture is rife with references to Wall Street, and there may be no greater evidence of its having found its way into the great mind of the masses than this fall's offering of two television dramas on the subject. The question is, does this indicate a market top, a la *Dallas* and *Dynasty*, which appeared at the top of the oil market?

The hourlong shows, *Bull*, which premiered in August on Turner Network Television, and *The $treet*, which the Fox Network will air in November, both focus on the high-powered world of traders and investment bankers.

"It goes to something we call the equity culture," says Peter Kendall, co-editor of *The Elliott Wave Financial Forecast*. "We do think it's a long-term bearish development," Kendall says of the Street showing up on the tube. He notes that *The N.E.W.*, a show on the new economy, aired shortly before the Nasdaq's 36% plunge off its March high. Kendall wrote last December of "the mania's rising entertainment value." Indeed, Michael Chernuchin, creator of *Bull*, was recently quoted in USA Today as saying, "Wall Street is no longer a mystery. Even cabdrivers are reading Barron's."

Be that as it may, Bob Prechter, president of financial forecasting firm Elliott Wave International, points to the old story about the shoeshine boy and the elevator operator looking for stock tips before the Crash of '29. The similarity to the current zeitgeist doesn't necessarily inspire confidence. Kendall cites a commercial for *The $treet* in which an exotic dancer is asked what she wants in return for her services. Her reply? Equity.

But what of timing? Kendall says Chernuchin has been pitching the idea for *Bull* since 1990. "He couldn't do it at the bottom; here it is the top and now they're ready for it." The shows will probably have their run "in what we think is the beginning of a bear market," Kendall says.

—Barron's, September 4, 2000

TONIGHT!
THE STOCK MARKET CRASHES AND A DESPERATE GAMBLE TO SAVE THE FIRM COULD MEAN LOSING EVERYTHING.

BULL

TONIGHT 10 PM ET/PT

TNT

TNTBULL.COM
AMERICA ONLINE KEYWORD: BULL

rated news and information network on cable television, cementing its reputation as a leading media organization of the new economy." *Bull*, an hour-long fiction series on TNT, is another indication of the public's undisturbed faith in the bull market. This is the series EWFF mentioned a few days before the NASDAQ's all-time high. It is all about the new economy and the people making big profits in it. At least, that is what the ads promoting its August premiere now say. The very idea of the show coincided with a 35% decline in the main New Economy index. Its actual broadcast may not be much kinder. When a bottom is really at hand, the fictional traders on *Bull* will be scornfully recalled as the only ones who ever made any money on the New Economy.

January 2001
Be Really *Careful What You Ask For*

Back in July and August, this section applied socionomic theory to the changing cultural scene. We identified a number of shared social visions that appeared to reflect the new bear market mood "quite immediately" and speculated that these images might be suggesting the direction of economic and political events before the public was able to mobilize itself in the direction of the new trend. Many of those signals are now taking on a more concrete form. One that appeared to be flashing a big hint of a 180-degree turn came from workers, particularly high-tech workers, who were "demanding" the ultimate perk, "a long breather from work." "Be careful," EWFF warned, "the last time people threw the culture into reverse with fashion and lifestyle statements as evocative these, they got a much longer winter's nap than they bargained for. Workers, to be sure, are on the verge of more free (literally) time than they ever imagined possible." The layoffs, particularly within the Internet economy, have now begun.

Here's another emerging vision from the "chic, palm-lined streets of the Riviera:"

'Death to Money'

– Declaration by EU Protestors, 12/7/00

Note the date. It was within hours of Alan Greenspan's tilt toward lower interest rates. The market was up 300 points, so Greenspan carried the day. With headlines and rallying cries like this one, however, the collective mind continues to issue signals that suggest it will win the war against manipulation. As Jim Grant says, "Money is of the mind." When the collective mind wants to make it disappear, there is nothing Alan Greenspan or anybody else can do about it.

February 2001

One of the most direct cultural manifestations of the mania for financial assets was the appearance of price bubbles in speculation for children's play things. It started right before Christmas in 1996 with Tickle Me Elmo. As expected, Tickle Me Elmo quickly fell by the wayside, but the speculative horde did not disperse. It found a new outlet in Beanie Babies, which were embraced with an even more passionate frenzy. Particularly around the holidays, the creation of price bubbles for certain toys became a popular form of public recreation. The following chart shows the progression from Elmo to Beanie Babies to Furby and finally to Pokemon in 1999. As EWFF noted in November 1999, Pokemon was the ultimate extra-market bidding frenzy because it turned playgrounds everywhere into trading floors that the media said were a "rehearsal for life." The following article illustrates, however, that, in the end, the life-long lesson of this episode will be the exact opposite of what the child psychologists had in mind when they touted Pokemon back in 1999:

Pokemon's Market Crash Holds Lesson For Young Traders

Back in 1999, when the Pokemon fad was the talk of every playground, Mike's collection of cards was worth hundreds of dollars. But like investors in dot-com flameouts and other once-highflying technology stocks who thought the NASDAQ could rise forever, Mike sat on his assets and watched them dwindle away. "I should have sold," Mike said. A year ago, Pokemon cards were the most popular plaything on the planet. Now the card market has virtually collapsed and Pokemon "thousandaires" have watched their net worth be wiped out.

Here is what we find significant: This past Christmas, no new trading fad emerged to take its place. The distinguishing trait of the 2000 holiday season was its lack of a "must-have toy" and its attendant speculation. Retailers were so thrown by the absence of a new craze that many reported their final sales figures in Pokemon-adjusted terms, i.e. "excluding Pokemon comparisons, same-store sales were down 2.3%." Retailers expect "sales comparisons to be adversely affected by [last year's] Pokemon sales through the second quarter." The absence of a new toy-buying bubble has greater meaning than anyone knows. It is a critical non-confirmation of the buying panics that have re-visited the NASDAQ and junk bond markets in recent weeks. It shows that in the deepest recesses of the public mind, the mania has lost its grip.

March 2001
As Advertised: The End of an Era

The content of many current ads is another tip-off to a big reversal. Instead of informing potential customers about the benefits of the product, many modern-day ads are designed simply to entertain. By the end of this year's Super Bowl, the ratings showed that more people were watching the commercials intently than the game. Advertisers call this approach the soft-sell. After an 80-year bull market, the pitch has softened to such an extent that it is sometimes difficult to tell what is being sold. According to the book *Advertising in America: The First 200 Years*, a softer style was also popular at the end of the bull market in 1929. But the depression brought a swift change in tone as "advertising went for the hard sell." Instead of spacious life style ads, companies packed their ads with content that explained the benefits of their products and tried to entice buyers with contests, prizes and promotions. For the first time since the beginning of the century, skepticism about the efficacy of advertising and its effects on consumers became rampant. Government agencies were called in to supervise and control the practice.

As the bear market unfolds, advertising will experience a similar shift. Look for the advertisers to go back to the basics with pitches that get in your face and tell you exactly why you need their products. The government watchdogs will also be back on the scene in short order. Companies will slash their budgets and seek cheaper, no-frills approaches to get their name in front of the public. Eventually, for the first time since the turn of the century, the very idea of advertising will be under assault.

A number of ads seem to reflect this future in extremely graphic ways. The following article is about a commercial in which a heart-attack victim's life flashes before his eyes. It's from the February 2 N.Y. Times:

Advertisers Make Use of Death and Dying

Toshiba's spot, called "Flatline," represents a new trend in marketing. Like many other recent pitches seeking attention, it eschews prurient themes, instead embracing subjects that are even more shocking and taboo — death and dying. And while others who have ventured to this final advertising frontier leaven their references to death with heavy doses of humor or satire, the Toshiba campaign, which began last week, offers little of that. It is so realistic, in fact, that while the heart attack victim's open eye at the commercial's end is meant to show that he survived, viewers may not be so sure.

Examples of the lighter approach to mortality abound. There is the FedEx commercial in which "The Crocodile Hunter" keels over dead from a snake bite. And there's the Discover credit card commercial, widely seen on television lately, in which the nurses and doctors in an emergency room at the fictional St. Sophie's Hospital wait to attend a patient until his credit is approved.

Or how about the Nike ad where the Texas Chainsaw Massacre man chases after a female runner? Then there's a whole spate of ads that "pit Man against Bear in Faulknerian struggle for supremacy." "Bears are everywhere," says an ad critic. "It's a really weird phenomenon." But to us it makes perfect sense. According to the theory of social visioning, which EWFF has presented in the Cultural Trends sections of the July, August and January issues, it may be normal for a

AD TRENDS

Experts Agree: It's a Bear Market

SEX SELLS, BUT SO, APPARENTLY, DO HAIRY BACKS AND GRUBBY PAWS. A SPATE OF ADS pit Man against Bear in a Faulknerian struggle for supremacy—and the beer-guzzling SUV drivers triumph every time. "Bears *are* everywhere, it's a really weird phenomenon," says Peter Beckman, founder of adcritic.com. And with spring on the way, the National Park Service hopes campers don't get overconfident. "We're worried about the cartoonish aspect of these ads," said Scott Gediman, a park ranger in Yosemite, where inappropriately stored food is a surefire bear magnet. "They need to know that if a person gets into a fight with a bear, the bear is going to win."

▲ **Bear Meets 'Matrix'**
Southpaw tries to protect his catch from sneaky John West Salmon employee.

▼ **Bears Eating Salad?**
Yup. While 'tough' men drive Toyota Tacomas. Don't try this one at home.

▲ **The New Face of Wendy's**
What about the redhead? She didn't share her nuggets.

◄ **Cruising for A Boozing**
Ursine muncher and rugged outdoorsmen battle over Smirnoff Ice. In the end, one human is sacrificed so the other can drink in peace (with two hot women).

▲ **Wish You Were Here**
Da, da, da—with fangs. VW reps confirm yet another bear sighting.

multi-year cultural shift to be foreshadowed by images that get out in front of the public with immediate expressions of the new mood. Ad makers are in the business of pushing emotional buttons, so it stands to reason that they would be among those foreshadowing the future, especially their own future, in starkly accurate terms. Of course, until very recently, these visions have always been presented with a humor that recalls the light-hearted highs of the late bull market. We can only echo the dead-serious Yosemite park ranger who responded, "We're worried about the cartoonish aspect of these ads. They need to know that if a person gets into a fight with a bear, the bear is going to win." Amen, brother!

April 2001

The Bear Takes Cultural Form

Over the course of the last eight months, as the stock market continued to make new lows, *The Elliott Wave Financial Forecast* cited a litany of emerging cultural images that offered subtle evidence of a change in mood. In recent weeks, however, many social spheres have dispensed with the subtleties. The public is now exhibiting the unadulterated effects of a bear market in social mood. For example, the fear over the spread of hoof and mouth and mad cow diseases is anything but subtle. As herds in Europe were rounded up for slaughter and new scares swept the world, a Cambridge professor received an advance of more than $300,000 for a book titled, *Our Final Century*. The author speculates that improving technology will render humans obsolete as lethal "engineered" viruses and atomic experiments go awry. The book places the odds that humans will survive the century at 50/50.

In another clear sign of a darkened public mood, Monday night's Academy Awards show earned its lowest rating in history. At the spring fashion shows in Paris, the offerings were "almost entirely black." The mood was so bleak, in fact, that a NY Times review warned, "Black Mood in Paris: Watch Out for Bad Times."

These fashions are the results of the downturn in social mood, not a harbinger. But don't expect the dark fashions, disease scares and total disinterest in traditional Hollywood starlets to be as fleeting as the bearish cultural manifestations of the early 1990s. Whatever form the bear market ultimately takes is likely to shape the social scene for years to come.

A Baseball Forecast

In 1985, *The Elliott Wave Theorist*'s original study on "Pop Culture and the Stock Market" asserted, "Trends in sports reflect the prevailing mood." The emergence of a bull market produces an escalating energy level that is physically embodied in the organization of athletic competitions. As the rise in social mood progresses, people share the optimism of the time by heading out to the ball park in larger numbers and constructing elaborate events. The leagues and their champions become increasingly sophisticated and revered. Eventually, massive stadiums are constructed to house the widespread public obsession with sports. EWT theorized that a reversal by a dominant bull market sport like baseball could be "an advance indicator of important fundamental events." In late 1992, EWT put this theory to the test by publishing the following forecast for baseball:

A Top In Baseball?

Signs of a turn are there. If you're an investor, take profits on baseball. If you're a player, sign a long-term contract. If you're an owner, sell your club.

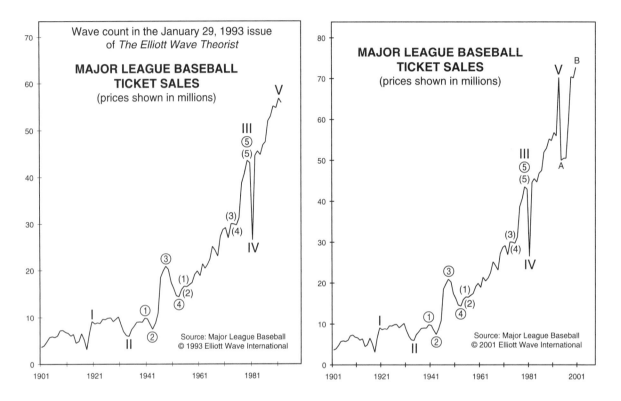

In early 1993, we counted a five-wave rise in total baseball ticket sales since 1901 and concluded, "At minimum, baseball faces its largest percentage drop in attendance since it became the national sport." The wave count from 1993 is displayed in the chart with an updated version showing that total ticket sales collapsed in 1994 then rebounded to a b-wave high. At 73.4 million, the 2000 total is slightly higher than the total for 1993, but it is labeled a bear market rally for several reasons. The key factor is that the implied attendance growth is illusory. First, observe the lack of a new high in the per-team ticket sales below. The number of tickets sold in the average major league city peaked in 1993, the season following EWT's forecast. Further, the sales totals shown in these charts represent tickets sold, not actual attendance. Brokers report that demand for seats has plunged. In fact, so many season tickets are not being used that scalpers sell some of the best seats in the house at "60% to 80% below face value."

Another clue to the major change in the primary trend in baseball's fortunes is the plunge in television ratings for the All-Star game and World Series. The total number of fans tuning in to baseball's two most important annual events actually topped the year before baseball's 1993 attendance peak, the same year as EWT's forecast. After successfully foreshadowing baseball's initial decline in ticket sales, TV ratings have continued to contradict a slight new high in total sales with a decline to their lowest level in history. This is a bearish non-confirmation of the new high in total ticket sales. The five-wave pattern of this decade-long trend announces the onset of a major bear market.

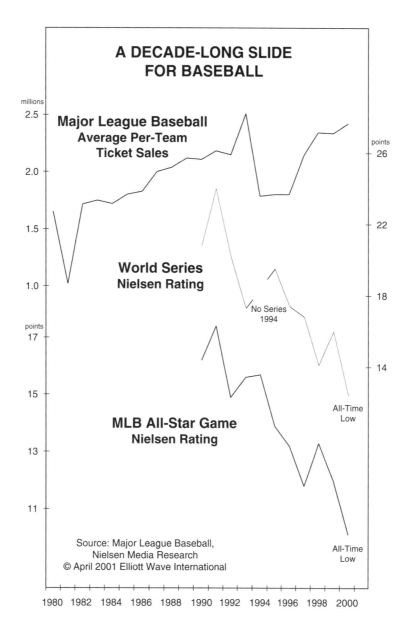

A DECADE-LONG SLIDE FOR BASEBALL

Major League Baseball Average Per-Team Ticket Sales

World Series Nielsen Rating

No Series 1994

MLB All-Star Game Nielsen Rating

All-Time Low

All-Time Low

Source: Major League Baseball, Nielsen Media Research
© April 2001 Elliott Wave International

May 2001

Cultural Trends

Here is an interesting forecast from the April 17 issue of The Wall Street Journal:

Theme Parks Predict Summer of Thrills, Few Chills

Industry experts are forecasting "mostly sunny skies" saying amusement parks do well no matter what happens to the economy. Is it a coincidence that investors are now saying the same thing about stocks? We do not think so. A little socionomic detective work explains why. First, you have to look at the current state of the industry. The big news is that there is no big news in the amusement park business this year. For the first time since at least the middle of the 1990s, no park has unveiled a momentous ride that will break all the records. "Roller coasters debuting at many parks in 2001 herald a departure from the emphasis on height, speed and distance records prevalent the past few years," reports Amusement Business magazine. Where else but in the past two decades in the stock market is it news when records aren't set? Another coincidence? History says no way.

The deeper you dig, the more you discover that the amusement industry is a finely tuned instrument in the orchestra of the century-long bull market in social mood. Some of the highlights include the development of the nation's first major park on Coney Island in 1897 (the Dow bottomed in 1896) and an explosion in the number and sophistication of roller coasters during the bull market of the 1920s. By all accounts, the Golden Age of roller coasters ended with the crash of 1929. Like the Dow, the amusement park industry did not recover from this near vertical plunge until the 1950s, i.e., after the end of the bear market in inflation-adjusted terms that occurred in 1949. A decline in the number new of roller coasters ended in 1980, at the end of the stealth bear market of the 1970s. In the second half of the 1990s, growth accelerated to a full-fledged boom in which billions of dollars were spent on attractions of ever-more-thrilling dimension.

The downturn in social mood has started with the amusements themselves, but it will soon filter into the financial performance of the parks. Contrary to the opinion of amusement industry experts, roller coasters are not on an ever-upward path. The business should experience a deep depression in the first half of the 2000s. If you own an amusement park or amusement park shares, sell this year.

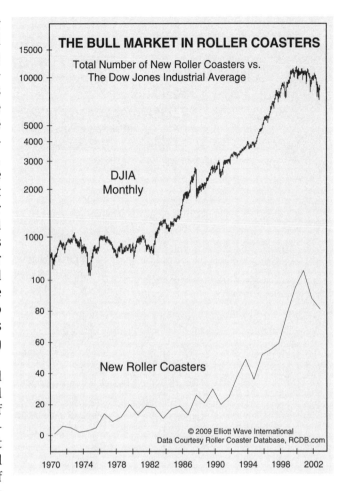

July 2001

Apparently, General Electric has let chairman Jack Welch's subscriptions to *The Elliott Wave Theorist* and *The Elliott Wave Financial Forecast* lapse. If Welch was subscribing, he undoubtedly would have retired with his status as one of the untarnished heroes of the bull market firmly intact. Instead of packing it in at GE's mandatory retirement age, however, Welch stayed one more year to complete the world's biggest merger between GE and Honeywell. The result is a year of aggravation that culminated with this headline on June 15:

Welch Underestimated Antitrust Issue

In May 2000, *The Elliott Wave Theorist* analyzed more than a century of U.S. antitrust activity and showed that major bear markets in social mood over the last 110 years have been confirmed by an immediate escalation in antitrust activity. With a quick glance at the chart (see May 2000 entry), Welch would not have underestimated the European Union's effort to block GE's proposed merger. The chart starts with the Sherman Antitrust Act of 1890, which preceded a bull market peak that was not exceeded until 1899, and ends with the start of the U.S. Justice Department's case against Microsoft, which occurred a month after the NYSE advance-decline line peaked in April 1998.

Over the last 100 years, no corporation has enjoyed the sustained success of General Electric. Another quick study that could have sent Welch riding off into the sunset was the series of charts that appeared in a July 2000 Special Update (see entry in Chapter 5). The charts show that since the beginning of the last century, merger activity has always receded with major downturns in stock prices. A then current "outbreak of anti-merger fever" indicated that it was "open season" on merger proposals. In rejecting GE's deal for Honeywell, The Wall Street Journal said that the EU was "relying on antitrust theories that were discarded in the U.S. 30 years ago." That sounds about right, as 30 years ago, the U.S. was in the middle of its last Cycle-degree bear market (which is where the NASDAQ is right now).

In recent weeks, many more signs of rising antipathy toward corporate success have emerged. Some, like price controls on California utility rates and "Eat The Rich!" signs at the latest free trade conference, are not the least bit subtle. Others, like a ban on handkerchiefs, gas masks and anything that could "interfere with effective gassing" outside free trade conferences, divulge an escalating level of hostility.

According to Reason magazine, opposition to the "expansion of 'corporate power'" is becoming increasingly sophisticated. The effort to block the free trade movement, for instance, reportedly took a big step toward legitimacy on February 24 when a newly formed neo-Luddite group staged an elaborate "teach-in" hosted by a "veritable Who's Who of anti-technology and anti-free market activists from around the globe." The group espouses the regulation of all new technologies based on criteria like whether the technologies are "needed" or "too socially disruptive." This is the face of the "new punitive mood." The disjointed band of protestors that marched on Seattle on the approach to the early 2000 highs (see December 1999 entry) is turning into organized entities that will eventually help accomplish their goal of eating the rich. By the end of the bear market, the few remaining rich will be sitting ducks on the menu.

August 2001

Remember this headline from the May issue?

Theme Parks Predict Summer of Thrills, Few Chills

EWFF responded with an immediate sell signal saying, "The bear market in social mood will soon filter into the financial performance of the parks." Industry experts were not swayed. As the amusement park season entered full swing in June, they were still insisting that the roller coaster business was on an ever-upward path. In late June, an analyst with a major Wall Street firm called the industry "nearly recession proof." The following headline appeared a few days later:

Theme Park Attendance Slip Blamed on Economy

Within the cultural realm, the transition to a bear market is picking up speed. In recent weeks, subscribers have passed along lots of clips that testify to an accelerating downside rate of social change. There are many more than we have room to mention. Here's another recent example that speaks for itself:

Dracula to get theme park
Developers hope terror theme park will boost Romania's Tourism Industry

September 11, 2001
Elliott Waves and Social Reality

As terrible as today's tragedy is, we must pause to point out another tragedy, which is that so few understand why it happened, what will happen next and what they can do about it. Sometimes it takes an appalling drama to stir people from lethargy and make them pay attention to matters of grave importance. Comfort and safety come from understanding. If you can see the big picture clearly, both past and future, you will be able to make fruitful decisions calmly.

Forecasting Styles of Social Events

Social mood repeatedly traces out five waves up followed by three waves down. The negative themes in "wave four" within the "fives waves up" presage those that will dominate, more dramatically and on a much bigger scale, in the ensuing "three waves down."

This is true of the styles of cultural trends. For example, Psycho came out in 1962, at the end of a fourth wave correction of Primary degree. In the larger bear market of 1966-1982, slasher films (the Halloween and Friday the 13th series) were a dominant theme.

It is also true of the character of social events. In an earlier fourth wave from 1916 to 1921, collectivists took over Russia. In the larger fourth wave that followed, from 1929 to 1949, collectivists took over nearly half of the earth's population, in Germany, Italy, Eastern Europe and China.

In the current case, the most recent fourth wave of Cycle degree or higher took place from 1966 to 1982, roughly, "the '70s." Aside from a slew of terrorist incidents in the 1910s,[1] a decade dominated by a long bear market in stocks, the idea of "terrorism" as a social force began with the 1966-1982 bear market. A 10-volume chronology of American social history over the last 100 years (American Decades) lists no acts of terrorism in the 1920s, 1930s, 1940s, 1950s or the 1960s. In early 1970, when the Dow was in year four and the Value Line Composite in year two of a Cycle-degree bear market, the age of terrorism began. An Arab terrorist strike killed one person and injured 23 in Munich. On February 21, 1970, another group of suspected Arabian terrorists hijacked a Swissair flight and crashed it. The worst of it ended approximately when the bear market did, as Iran finally released U.S. hostages in January 1981. In those first terrorist acts committed against the United States, we caught a glimpse of the style of conflicts that we would have to endure when the bear market of next bigger size arrived, which it certainly has.

Neither is this point made only in retrospect. Page 435 of *At the Crest* lists 43 speculations as to specific social actions that will take place during Grand Supercycle wave ⅳ. Several of them have already come to pass. One of them reads:

"Foreigners will commit terrorist acts on U.S. soil."

Here is a summary of today's event, which truly is "more dramatic and on much bigger scale" than those that occurred during the previous fourth wave of the 1970s:

> New York, Sept. 11 (Bloomberg) — The attacks on the World Trade Center and Pentagon today are the worst acts of terrorism ever on U.S. soil and change the scope of foreign policy, experts say. Never before has a large-scale terrorist attack on the U.S. been coordinated successfully in more than one U.S. city.
>
> "It's just an attack of extraordinarily sophisticated planning," said Michael R. Fischbach, a professor of history specializing in the Middle East. "The world that we know has now changed."
>
> "Americans' whole attitude about daily life, about foreign policy will be forever changed," Fischbach said.

"The world that we know has changed" is a correct statement, but it did not change "now." It changed between January 14 and March 24, 2000, a two-month period during which the three major U.S. stock indexes signaled the end of a Grand Supercycle uptrend that had been in force for 216 years. We are only now beginning to feel the lagging results of that change. We are at the beginning of a long period of social unrest, and while it will wax and wane with the waves, overall it will intensify. The best time to prepare was two years ago, but it is not too late to do so now.

---

[1] The first act of terrorism listed in *American Decades* is the explosion of the Los Angeles Times Building in October 1910, which was linked to organized labor. The last one of note was a bomb that rocked Wall Street on September 16, 1920. The scars of that blast can still be seen in the façade of 23 Wall Street, then as now the offices of J.P. Morgan Inc. The financial attack centered on Wall Street became physically manifest. Almost the same thing has happened today.

A Side Point

During the 1990s, we studied the history of skyscraper construction and issued several reports on the correlation between the erection of tall buildings and the late stages of positive long-term social mood trends. As EWT stated in April 1996, "Of all the cultural relationships we consider here, the link between stock prices and the tallest buildings is one of the most fascinating because it is literally etched in stone." We concluded that skyscrapers are "monuments to peaking social mood." Some people take such studies as frivolous. They are not. Now that we are in a negative social mood trend of greater magnitude than any since the construction of the first skyscrapers in the 1890s, we should hardly be shocked that the forces expressing the emerging downtrend in mood have aimed their sights at these towering structures, symbols of the productive optimism of Grand Supercycle wave ⓘⓘⓘ.

October 2001

The Public Hangs In

The papers continually compliment the public on their amazing resolve. In recent weeks, they have also taken to castigating the "Wall Street Big Wigs" for not acting the same way. On September 19, for instance, the New York Post ran the following headline: "Fast-Buck Wall St. Bigs Foil Patriotic Buyers." As we noted last month, historically disinterested investors are "being lured in as never before," and the effort to combat the impact of terrorism by channeling the public into stocks is just an extension of that effort. We know of no precedent, but the peddling of stocks as a call to arms certainly strikes us as a late-cycle phenomenon. Its blatantly emotional tone signals that, beneath the surface, the suddenly grim public determination to own stocks is breaking down. A less subtle indication is the steady movement out of equity mutual funds, which have been leaking cash since July. Another crack appeared Monday, September 17, when "shaken 401(k) participants fled stock funds in unusually high numbers." According to Hewitt Associates, large 401(k) plans recorded nine times the normal activity on September 17. The current wave pattern and the market's extreme oversold condition indicate that the dam should hold for now, but it is getting closer to giving way. When it does, probably during wave ③ in the NASDAQ and S&P, the line on the chart (showing the public commitment to the stock market, Chapter 4, October 2001 entry) will crash harder than in any of the prior downtrends.

December 2001

Psychology and The Coffee Break

The popularity of coffee houses like Starbucks offers a case study in how one branch of the service sector, the local coffee shop, is likely to fare as deflation starts to bite. The line at the top of the chart shows Starbucks' stock price since its inception in 1992. It is no coincidence that Starbucks, the biggest benefactor of the 1990s' coffee-house craze, caught fire in 1996. As the mania took flight, coffee bars were springing up everywhere. EWT identified the phenomenon as another expression of the surging bull market in social mood (see entry from September 1996). We illustrated a direct parallel to two prior fifth waves of Cycle degree: the tea rooms of the 1920s and the coffee houses that actually hosted much of the stock trading during the South Sea Bubble in 1720. The top of the chart shows how Starbucks rode the sentiment to a 500% gain from early 1996 through late 2000, the last year of the mania. Notice, also, that coffee itself was falling out of bed. Even as coffee prices suffered the biggest bear market in the history of the commodity, coffee houses were enjoying a huge bull market. This is because people do not go to Starbucks just to get coffee. They go for the convenience, ambience and social interaction. In other words, it's not the beverage, it's the psychology. A reversal of that psychology is now reflected by Starbucks' completed five-wave rally and its break of an uptrend line that has been in force since its inception in 1992. As the bear market and deflation gain steam, demand for the Starbucks experience will wane a lot more. Our advice: Sell Starbucks. When the downturn finally hits bottom, the $4 cup of coffee and probably Starbucks itself will be long gone.

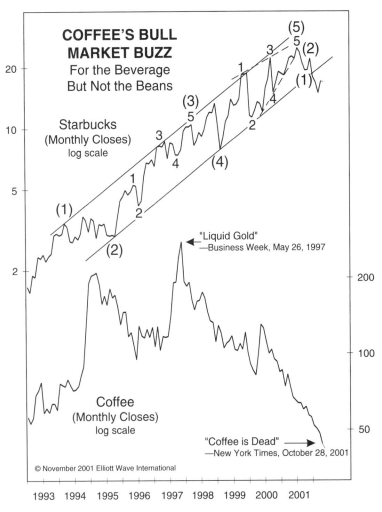

COFFEE'S BULL MARKET BUZZ
For the Beverage But Not the Beans

Starbucks (Monthly Closes) log scale

"Liquid Gold" —Business Week, May 26, 1997

Coffee (Monthly Closes) log scale

"Coffee is Dead" —New York Times, October 28, 2001

© November 2001 Elliott Wave International

Psychology surrounding the commodity appears to be approaching [a negative] extreme. Prices are so low that the Association of Coffee Producing Countries, the group that controls 70 percent of world supply, has decided to shut down in January. "The announcement ends eight years of coordinated, international attempts to maintain prices." As one trader said recently, "Coffee is dead." So as the coffee house craze crashes and coffee growers throw in the towel, coffee is likely to muster its first big rally since the highs of May 1997. That's collective human psychology at work. You gotta love it.

January 2002
Real Estate

Look at these news clips. The July-to-December progression marks two important transitions. For the real estate market, it is a giant sell signal. Donald Trump put forward a blueprint for another "world's tallest" for the same city in 1989, right before the real estate decline of the early 1990s and his own bankruptcy. In late 1996, he proposed the New York Stock Exchange Tower, which was also slated to become the world's tallest. Within 10 months, commercial real estate put in a top that still stands. As EWFF noted in October, the REIT indexes have rallied, but for several reasons cited in recent issues, we are convinced it is a bear market rally that will soon expire if it hasn't already. Trump's scuttled plan confirms that real estate is in big trouble.

Chicago Sun Times
MIDWEST'S BEST-READ NEWSPAPER

WEDNESDAY, JULY 18, 2001

WORLD'S TALLEST BUILDING
THAT'S WHAT TRUMP, SUN-TIMES WANT TO BUILD AT RIVERSIDE SITE

Wednesday, December 12, 2001

Trump Downsizes Plans For Skyscraper

In the aftermath of the terrorist attacks of Sept.11, New York developer Donald Trump has scuttled plans to build the world's tallest building in Chicago. Instead of a 1,500-foot-tall structure, Trump will announce plans today for a 78-story skyscraper that rises 1,073 feet. The building won't rank among the 20 tallest in the world.

Even more important is where this proposal places the "skyscraper indicator," which is Edward R. Dewey's observation that the tallest buildings are built at the end of economic booms. *The Elliott Wave Theorist* has noted that it is not the towers themselves, but the decision and will to reach for record heights that mark the big peaks. Most of the world's tallest buildings like the Empire State in 1929 and World Trade Center I in 1966 were conceived and begun at the highs and occupied later when bear markets were underway. The underlying weakness of the fundamentals through the latest bull market is represented by its inability to actually see constructed any of the "world's tallest" edifices that it inspired. This confirms this comment from EWT in 1998: "The very idea of making a tall building, rather than its actual construction, may have been enough to signal a reversal."

Together Trump's abandoned plans make an interesting triumvirate. They came right before, during and right after the last great run of a 200-year bull market. In the aftermath of the World Trade Center's destruction, the middle proposal, which was to be a 1/3-of-a-mile high monument to the stock market, is particularly inconceivable. It cannot be built because a New York Stock Exchange Tower would be too big of a target. Trump is not building grass huts yet, but his revised tower will only be the fourth largest building in Chicago, which is a giant step away from the statement of "symbolic power" that he was trying to achieve just five months ago. As *The Elliott Wave Theorist* pointed out on September 11, the quick and seemingly permanent swing away from extremely tall buildings is also a powerful symbol, one that shows we are in "a negative social mood trend." This retrenchment may not inspire the same awe, but it should command more respect.

March 2002

In December 1999, protestors rattled the World Trade Organization by staging a series of raucous demonstrations on the streets of Seattle. At the latest World Economic Forum in New York, people voiced the same "chaotic multitude of complaints." But the streets were quiet by comparison because the "dissent against corporate America has moved indoors." The "undercurrent of resentment to the U.S. corporate establishment" is so entrenched that The Wall Street Journal now places it within an "aura of social change." This is the backlash against business institutions and icons that *The Elliott Wave Theorist* anticipated in 1998. Over the course of the topping process, EWT and EWFF have chronicled its tightening grip.

The next, more-personal phase of this process will focus on the individuals that benefited the most from the rising mood. The transition is foreshadowed by the plummeting popularity of *Who Wants to Be a Millionaire*. The TV game show that dominated prime time at the highs is down to its last weekly slot. The New York Times notes that interest in the attainment of instantaneous wealth has been replaced by a "Nervous Hunger for Torture Shows and Gross Out Stunts." A minute ago, everyone wanted to be a millionaire. In another, everyone will want to beat one. As shown by this note from Investment News, a weekly newspaper for financial advisors, the injuries will be even worse than the insults: with $3 trillion in losses from June 2000 through June 2001, wealthy investors are absorbing the bulk of the damage from falling stock prices. Say hello to the sadistic side of social mood.

April 2002

As the negative social psychology of the bear market grabs hold, one of the key social forecasts featured in *At the Crest of the Tidal Wave* was a call for a global trade war:

> Political manifestations will include protectionism in trade matters. Tariffs will become popular, regardless of the fact that virtually everyone knows they are dangerous and wrong, because they are a consequence of an increasingly negative psychology involving fear, envy and a misguided attempt at self defense.

On March 5, George Bush "set the wheels in motion for a global trade war" by imposing stiff tariffs on imported steel. The move "triggered retaliation the world over."

The new tariff is another direct parallel to the "recovery" of 1930 when the Smoot-Hawley trade tariff bill worked its way through Congress against a backdrop of recovering stock prices. Bush "contradicted his own free trade advocacy" for the same reason Hoover signed Smoot-Hawley into law in June 1930. Not doing so would have been political suicide. Obviously, George Bush knows these tariffs are dangerous and wrong. Just six weeks before he imposed them, he was attacking protectionists for holding out a "false comfort." Like September 11, it is a harbinger of the global tension, exclusionism and xenophobia that will mark the real "new era." It is also another great reminder of how fast reason can fly out the window, when the emotional reality of a bear market slaps the unprepared across the face.

May 2002

The article inside Smart Money's April effort advocates a "three pronged approach: large stocks, small stocks and foreign stocks." Even though they never abandoned stocks in the first place, many of these publications are brimming with advice on how to charge back in. The cover of Bloomberg Personal Finance insists investors are returning by filling its cover with these letters: "I'M BUYING AGAIN." The data, however, confirms what EWFF has been saying all along. Most investors stayed with stocks. According to the Sindlinger & Co.'s poll of U.S. households in equities (see chart in Chapter 4, October 2001 entry), the percentage of U.S. households in the market is 57.3%, or about where it has been since the fall of 2000, and only 0.5% from the all-time high of November 2000.

Cultural Trends

When monitoring the direction of social mood through the prism of cultural trends, it is important to keep in mind that the trends themselves are results of social mood. This means that many cultural manifestations will lag the social mood itself. It has been more than seven months since the stock market advance began. Is this enough time for cultural shoots of a new positive trend to show? Appearing less than six months after the low of August 1982, the social commentary in *The Elliott Wave Theorist* of February 7, 1983 resoundingly answers yes. Back then, the cultural trends were so bullish that EWT issued its inaugural cultural trends section. It was titled "social phenomenon" and cited the emergence of "Roaring '20s parties," "conservative values" and "a move to clean up 42nd Street" in concluding that the social scene was in line with EWT's forecast for a great bull market. "All are part of the typical social background in the early stages of a long bull market," EWT stated. At this point, no such evidence is emerging. In fact, almost all of the social forces that EWFF has tracked over the course of the last 25 months have been impervious to the countertrend rally.

In many areas, bear market psychology is picking up speed. A typical example are the harbingers of exclusionism and xenophobia discussed last month. On April 13, we got word of a wave of anti-Semitic attacks in Europe. According to a new study, 2001 and 2002 "stand in contrast to a steady decline in anti-Semitic activity that continued from 1995 to 1999." On April 23, Jean-Marie Le Pen shocked the world by taking second place in France's preliminary presidential vote. "Le Pen is a symptom of a wider political malaise: fear of globalization, gloomy declinism, ugly xenophobia," reports the Washington Post. The Post added, "When it comes to France, this resentment is most loudly expressed as hatred of America." Along with Latin American condemnation of the U.S. over a failed Venezuelan coup, the spread of anti-U.S. sentiment can be seen fanning out across the globe. Obviously, it is gaining a foothold in contingents that are thought to be far less radical than those that attacked the World Trade Center on September 11. This is the opposite of the global embrace that the U.S. and its democratic, free-market ideals enjoyed during the bull market.

Here's another recent news flash that fits right in with our studies calling for a sharp reduction in the demand for the bull market game of baseball (see April 2001 entry): "Baseball's April Attendance Picture Filled With Empty Seats." Bloomberg reported May 1 that Major League Baseball's rush to embrace new ballparks with spacious concourses, sushi bars and playgrounds has suddenly stopped packing in the fans. "As the ballpark honeymoon effect wears off, many seats are going unfilled." Attendance for 20 of MLB's 30 clubs fell from April 2001. "Everything's contributing to the general malaise," said a sports marketing expert. In Denver, Baltimore and Cleveland where "large crowds once flocked to new parks for baseball-as-social event, plenty of good seats are available." In Cleveland, where the Indians sold out a record 455 straight games from 1997 through 2000, April attendance was off 22 percent. "We rode the wave for as long as we could ride it," said the Indians general manager. He added, "It's not as if our attendance is falling off a cliff now. This is more like a market correction." Where have we heard that before?

Baseball Sliding Toward Oblivion

Since the day we called for a boycott of every major league stadium, the movement to unite fans has exploded. The Internet is your entry point to a world of anger: www.baseball fans unite.com, www.wethe fans.com, www.mlbfan strike.com. All three Web sites advocate a multi-tier strategy against Bud Selig and Donald Fehr, which is to stay away from the ballparks.

—The Record
July 10, 2002

Staying Away in Droves
Depressed Attendance

When attendance across the majors was down slightly early in the season, baseball officials had plenty of excuses – poor weather, a slumping economy, lack of marquee matchups. Nothing to worry about, they said. It's too early to jump to conclusions.

It's time to worry. The weather has turned warm and most traditional rivals have played at least two series, but through Sunday attendance had dropped 6% compared with last year's. Worse, 20 of the 30 teams were behind last year's pace. The Orioles, averaging 32,161, were on track to pull fewer than three million fans for the first time since Camden Yards opened in 1992. The Indians, among baseball's top-drawing clubs since '94, are down 22% at the gate. The Reds, despite a surprising run atop the NL Central, have seen a 12% drop. Hardest hit have been commissioner Bud Selig's own Brewers, who drew an average of 23,401 to their first 29 home dates — a 30% decline just one year after Miller Park opened.

The extent to which fans are staying away is troubling: Does anyone think the prospect of a work stoppage will have them flocking to the parks?

—Sports Illustrated, June 10, 2000

June 2002

Culture Stocks Set the Bear Market Pace

A recent issue of the Financial Times says, "The equity culture is alive and well in the United States." It is certainly true. But as the message of this cartoon suggests, the equity culture lacks the vitality that characterized its appearance in the second half of the 1990s. This divergence reveals two important facts: 1) The bear market is not over; 2) It is well on its way toward the completion of one of its primary missions, the extinction of the equity culture that flourished in the second half of the 1990s.

In the late 1990s, bull market cultural trends lifted sports teams, fashion houses, restaurants and even fads like Pokemon so high that they became freely traded stocks. This accomplishment was in and of itself one of the ultimate signals that the great bull market was in its final days. Investors were so sure of the bull market's permanence that they purchased shares in inherently volatile diversions, or even outright fads, with no record of the underlying's success as publicly-traded enterprises. One of the biggest hints to their ultimate fate was how poorly they performed once they hit the market. In October 1997, *The Elliott Wave Theorist*

recognized this chronic under-performance and used it to predict that "the mood behind the buying will prove as transient as the fads it temporarily supports."

An analysis of one representative group covered in 1997 reveals that the bearish message behind this phenomenon persists. Back in 1997, EWT noted that shares in golf-related companies had become "a legitimate stock market sector with no less than 29 issues" and said that it offered an excellent illustration of the culture stocks' divergence from the overall market trend. "Like the other 'pop culture' stocks, they go public, enjoy a brief moment of price appreciation, and then go into a swoon." EWT concluded that the golf shares "await the extinction that is sure to come with an actual downturn in social mood." Running down the same list today, we find that ten have gone bankrupt, four have been acquired and three generate "no available price information." One went private and converted to a dot.com. Of the eleven that still trade, all are down at least 50%. The biggest decline is 99%, and the average drop is 78%. Here's the

important point, however: Golf stocks are still kicking. From late 2001 through April, the surviving golf shares staged a rally. Compared to the decline from its 1997 peak it may not look like much, but the September-to-May bounce in Callaway Golf was a 75% gain (see chart). Notice, however, that the pattern into that high was clearly corrective. Callaway now appears to have resumed its impulsive decline that should eventually take it below its initial price of $2.12 in 1992.

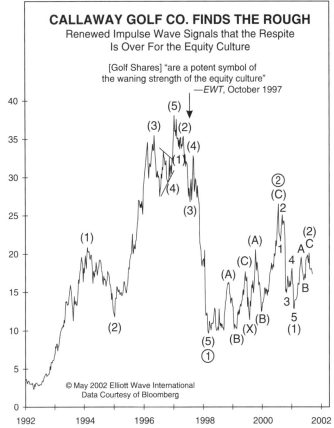

This is similar to the action in a host of other equity culture stocks. Fashion, restaurant, sports and other entertainment issues have recovered from the lows of September, but they appear poised for renewed downtrends. As the volatility of these businesses collides with the purging of the public's appetite for risk and speculation, these shares and the equity culture that they represent will join long-gone golf issues like PARR, GOLF and PUTT in oblivion.

September 2002

The Equity Culture Crumbles

The move through the head-and-shoulders neckline in late 1985 brought the first sprouts of the equity culture that went on to rule the world by the end of Cycle wave V. In the summer of 1986, *The Elliott Wave Theorist* reported that the bull market was working "its magic on general thinking patterns:"

> Newspaper clippings from June, July and August told the story. 'Money,' said a media expert in the WSJ, 'is becoming the new sex,' a source of 'endless fascination.' 'A new crop of celebrities will be picked from business,' said another. Even the new board games reflected the focus on finance. 'Last year it was murder; this year it's money,' said a New York merchandise buyer in the 8/28 WSJ. New game titles this summer included 'Condo-moneyum,' 'Go For It,' 'Your Money' and 'The Bottom Line.' Even the media joined in, like catfish in a feeding frenzy. 'Television is suddenly bullish on business news,' said a 7/30 article entitled 'Lineup of TV Business Shows Expands.' 'Local Stations are Giving

ANOTHER LONG-TERM NECKLINE GIVING WAY IN THE CONSTANT DOLLAR DOW
Updated from *The Elliott Wave Theorist*, August and December 1985

© September 2002 Elliott Wave International

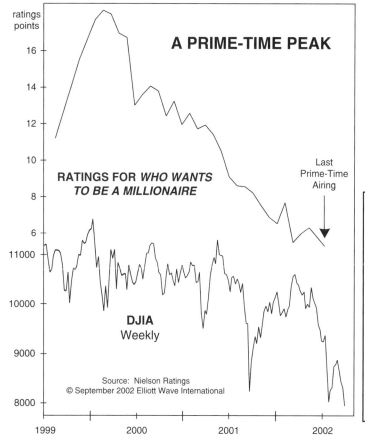

A PRIME-TIME PEAK

RATINGS FOR *WHO WANTS TO BE A MILLIONAIRE*

Last Prime-Time Airing

DJIA
Weekly

Source: Nielson Ratings
© September 2002 Elliott Wave International

Business the News…And the Viewers Like It,' read another headline. After decades of near total ignorance of business, television flooded the market with business and market news this year. Why? Because Cycle wave V of Supercycle (V) is in force.
—EWT, October 1986

The public thirst for all things financial grew so strong that by the end of V of (V) in the first quarter 2000, *Who Wants To Be a Millionaire* was a prime time smash, and several stock market dramas were in production. In December 1999, millionaire-hood became "the common goal of the nation," and EWFF said that its unprecedented popularity "may be the culmination of this whole process." The chart at right shows that this assessment turned out to accurate, as the shows ratings peaked with the Dow a month later.

The equity culture didn't end with the bull market, however. The entry from the August 2000 issue (see *The Equity Culture Lives*) records its continued dominance for several months.

When the next leg down started in early September 2000, the equity culture finally rolled over. *Bull* [an hour-long fictional TV series about traders in the "New Economy"] didn't make it to the end of 2000. After the rally from the September 21, 2001 lows a year later, the equity culture predictably enjoyed a brief moment

---

'Who Wants To Be A Millionaire' closes out prime-time ABC run

In early 2000, "Millionaire" held the top three spots in the Nielsen ratings. By fall 2001, "Millionaire" was down to two nights a week and earlier this year, it was cut to one. Finally, last month, ABC pulled the plug in prime time. Even the show's executive producer, Michael Davies, had decided the show's time was up and asked ABC to end its run.
—Seattle Times, June 27, 2002

of rebirth, but its extinction has clearly begun. As the S&P approached its neckline in late June, *Who Wants To Be a Millionaire* left prime time. The final episode aired June 24, two weeks before the S&P's broke its H&S neckline at 952.

The exhibits below offer more evidence of veneration for stocks being displaced by disgust.

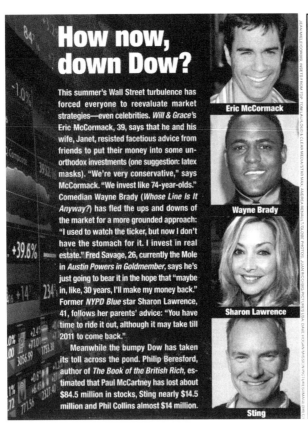

How now, down Dow?

This summer's Wall Street turbulence has forced everyone to reevaluate market strategies—even celebrities. *Will & Grace's* Eric McCormack, 39, says that he and his wife, Janet, resisted facetious advice from friends to put their money into some unorthodox investments (one suggestion: latex masks). "We're very conservative," says McCormack. "We invest like 74-year-olds." Comedian Wayne Brady (*Whose Line Is It Anyway?*) has fled the ups and downs of the market for a more grounded approach: "I used to watch the ticker, but now I don't have the stomach for it. I invest in real estate." Fred Savage, 26, currently the Mole in *Austin Powers in Goldmember,* says he's just going to bear it in the hope that "maybe in, like, 30 years, I'll make my money back." Former *NYPD Blue* star Sharon Lawrence, 41, follows her parents' advice: "You have time to ride it out, although it may take till 2011 to come back."

Meanwhile the bumpy Dow has taken its toll across the pond. Philip Beresford, author of *The Book of the British Rich,* estimated that Paul McCartney has lost about $84.5 million in stocks, Sting nearly $14.5 million and Phil Collins almost $14 million.

Eric McCormack

Wayne Brady

Sharon Lawrence

Sting

Me Incorporated: I Quit!

In the 1990s, the responsibilities of a personal CFO became even heavier as firms dismantled professionally managed defined-benefit pensions. We employees had to take on the management of our 401(k) portfolios. By 1998, $1.5 trillion resided in those accounts, every penny of which, we were repeatedly reminded, escaped evaporation only because of its owner's unwavering oversight. We should renounce this 24-7 baby-sitting job.

When Charles Schwab runs that commercial with Jackie Collins reading a romantic passage in which the heroine, on a balcony, pushes her lover away, explaining, "If you don't understand portfolio allocation, Nick, you don't understand me," we should stand shoulder to shoulder with Nick. And resist the hortatory message in another Schwab spot, in which a rock jam session comes to a halt when the anonymous lead guitarist can't come up with a lyric that rhymes with "ela–tion." Sitting behind his drum set, Ringo Starr offers a solution: "Dividend reinvestment participa–tion." An instru- mental version of "Money" fills the soundtrack, and Ringo continues: "Market capitaliza–tion. European market fluctua–tion. Industry globaliza–tion. Asset alloca–tion." I can hear the whirring sound of John Lennon spinning.

Flaunt fluency in finance-ese? On Wall Street, Bartleby the Scrivener provides the best all-purpose response: "I would prefer not to."

—U.S. News & World Report, August 5, 2002

After the break of its neckline in November 1985, the stock market went on to unprecedented levels of popularity. By the end of the bull market, the market's star power was so strong that A-list celebrities basked in its warm glow. Remember when the gossip columns swirled with rumors about Barbra Streisand's stock picks? "Honest, the media now vies for the inside scoop on Babs' 'stock picking prowess,'" EWFF reported in September 1999. One hot scoop revealed that Streisand "was so eager to snap up shares of TheStreet.com, a hot Internet IPO, that she called up the company's CEO offering tickets to her concert in Las Vegas." With the break back through a long term neckline, words like "down," "sell" and "real estate" have entered the vernacular of the celebrity. The People magazine article reports that Paul McCartney, Sting and Phil Collins have lost millions. Still, the concept of "loss" is long way from acceptance in the public mind. The "Scoop" section of the magazine reveals, for instance, that half the celebrities interviewed are banking on a market rebound. Another clue is the big smiles on the faces of these celebrity shareholders. They are the remnants of the grin-and-bear-it stage EWFF predicted as the bull market was drawing to a close in December 1999. At that time, EWFF noted that the immediate aftermath of the bull market would probably be accompanied by an effort to laugh off the initial drop. "The desire for comic relief will expand rapidly in the weeks ahead," EWFF said. We even added that it might lead to the "start of a whole new genre of social satire." This forecast has proven accurate, as every wave of selling has been met by a rush of cartoons depicting the absurdity of the mania and its resulting washout.

The Blondie comic depicts the effect, but it also shows that the equity culture has yet to expire. When cartoonists first discovered the stock market in the heat of the mania, EWFF main-

tained that investors would be a lot less inclined to laugh off their losses at the end of the bear market. One of the reasons is that capitulation carries a level of contempt and anger that is just not funny. When the selling is over and the public's investment have collapsed to worthlessness, no one will be laughing about the stock market.

The New Fashion in Stock Indexes

Another sign that the extraordinary bullish sentiment of the mania years is about to be pulled out by its roots is that stocks dedicated to bull market cultural trends are leading the way down, once again, as EWFF has anticipated in recent months. On May 31, EWFF called for "fashion, restaurant, sports and other entertainment issues" to set the bear market pace as "the S&P detaches from the right shoulder of the head- and-shoulders topping pattern." The indexes of restaurant, fashion and entertainment stocks all display relative weakness versus the Dow. From the lows of July 24, all experienced weaker bounces and returned to new lows. Bloomberg's golf index (not shown) also reached a new, all-time closing low September 19. This downside leadership confirms that the public trading in many culture stocks will not survive the decline.

The social scene is littered with additional signs of the polarizing, dissonant, ugly and destructive themes of a bear market in social mood. The results range from an emerging interest in unions and a return of labor strife to escalating levels of shopping and road rage and a sudden lurch forward for separatist campaigns

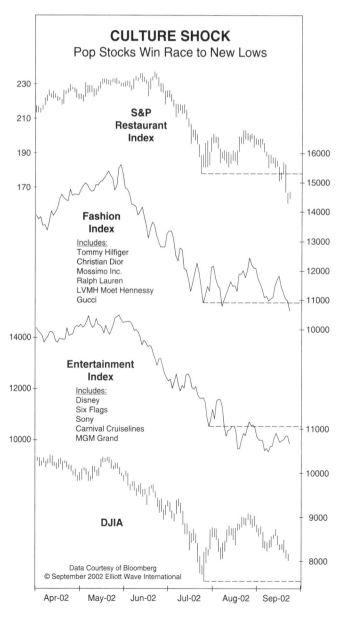

CULTURE SHOCK
Pop Stocks Win Race to New Lows

S&P Restaurant Index

Fashion Index
Includes:
Tommy Hilfiger
Christian Dior
Mossimo Inc.
Ralph Lauren
LVMH Moet Hennessy
Gucci

Entertainment Index
Includes:
Disney
Six Flags
Sony
Carnival Cruiselines
MGM Grand

DJIA

Data Courtesy of Bloomberg
© September 2002 Elliott Wave International

Apr-02   May-02   Jun-02   Jul-02   Aug-02   Sep-02

from Kashmir to the San Fernando Valley. In addition to its own falling stock prices and the omnipresence of long skirts in the latest catalogues, the fashion industry offers a number of confirming indicators. These include an end to casual dress codes and a "shocking blood-spattered dress" and "death hoods" at a recent fashion show. The burqa-look was part of a show in Spain where models sported "nooses, execution-style hoods and body covering bandages." Bear market momentum must still be building, because instead of embracing the gloomy style, the audience broke up the show with boos and whistles. Still, the impulse behind it is clearly bearish, as the basic instinct of fashion in a declining phase is to cover up. The urge to veil the face and head — a part of the human anatomy that has been on display for centuries — and the angry response to it probably speaks to the high degree of the trend change. So, don't count the "hooded look" out.

At the outset of the long topping process, *At the Crest of the Tidal Wave* said the downturn would lead to the creation of a whole new bear market social order. These cultural seedlings will eventually become the "dramatic upheaval" called for in the final chapter of *At the Crest*. So far, the effects have only impacted a small percentage of the population. Eventually, the forces will reshape the lives of just about everyone. When all is lost and these things can only get worse, the bottom will be in place. The first signs of the clearing skies won't be perceptible until the market is rising again in a third wave.

March 2003
Calling the Whole Thing Off

A February 20 Financial Times article says that in Europe, disillusioned followers are deserting the "Cult of the Equity." Two years ago, Schwab spent millions setting up a European operation to get a piece of what was expected to be a burgeoning demand for financial products. Now, Schwab's "plans have turned to dust. Schwab's sorry experience reflects the shattering of the dream that Europe was about to be transformed into a US-style, share-owning democracy." The article notes that Germany's Neuer Markt closed after its market capitalization collapsed from $233 billion to $20 billion in a little more than two years. The conversion of risk-averse German investors to traders of speculative shares was one of the high-water marks of the equity culture. Back in September 2000, when the NYSE was at its all-time high, one of the factors cited in EWFF's bearish case for stocks was that some U.S. shares were starting to generate more trading volume in Hamburg than in the U.S. EWFF claimed that it was a sure sign that the mania had run its course. After the next wave of selling, volume should dry up even further. At that point, the equity culture will go into a deep slumber that should last for years to come.

August 2003
Sexual Ambiguity Hits Prime Time

Alternate sexual lifestyles is another bear market theme that has advanced to the forefront of popular culture in recent weeks. This connection was first suggested by the 1985 Special Report, "Popular Culture and the Stock Market," EWT's initial study on the relationship between mood and its manifestations. One of the relationships EWT noticed right off the bat was that in bull markets, gender idols are sexually distinct and stereotypical (John Wayne and Marilyn Monroe in the 1950s; Arnold Schwarzenegger and Madonna in the 1980s), while their bear-market counterparts are mixed and blurred. Remember the "caring male" of the 1970s? He's back. A USA Today article cites a "growing trend by men to move into professions long dominated by women. More men are finding careers as librarians, secretaries, nannies, preschool teachers, nurses, paralegals, typists, dressmakers — even lactation consultants or midwives." "The Days of Sex Stereotyping are Quickly Crumbling," a headline reports. The gender-bending even extends to the "macho sport" of professional soccer where David Beckham, the world's most popular player, conducts himself with a "stylish androgyny" that has pushed the sport past "lines of sports and sexuality that are rarely crossed by elite athletes."

A new, unrivaled popularity for gay themes was signaled by an early June USA Today headline that declared, "It's 'In' To Be 'Out' These Days." "Mainstream entertainment has fallen head over heels for gays and lesbians." The buzz actually rose to the level of mild frenzy this week when a cable TV show, *Queer Eye for the Straight Guy* was such a hit that NBC re-ran a shortened version in prime time. *Queer Eye* is a show in which five gay men apply their well-developed fashion sense to the make-over of a straight man. The next step is a TV reality show called *Boy Meets Boy*, which debuts Tuesday. The matchmaking format calls for a gay star to choose a partner from a group of contestants. The twist is that he doesn't know it but some of the candidates are heterosexuals. The idea "to test the boundaries between gay and straight" is a classic example of the blurring of sexual identities that EWT anticipated with its initial observations in 1985.

The acceptance of open homosexuality appears to be a bear market trait. The initial spark for gay rights came in June 1969, seven months after the speculative peak of Cycle wave III, when gays locked arms against a police raid of the Stonewall Inn in Greenwich Village, New York. According to *The Readers Companion To American History*, "Almost overnight, a massive grassroots gay liberation movement was born." By the time stocks bottomed in 1974, anti-gay statutes were being rescinded, the first gay politician had taken office and "the lesbian and gay world was no longer an underground subculture but a well-organized community." New York's Gay Pride Parade was started in 1970 to commemorate the Stonewall Rebellion. In late June, The New York Times reports that this year's version, "now known as New York City's Lesbian, Gay, Bisexual, Transgender Pride March," went off with a heightened sense of progress. "Crowds cheered louder, political groups marched in greater numbers and parade goers seemed more party-prone." The revelers celebrated two significant "advances in gay rights, the U.S. Supreme Court's ruling to strike down laws against sodomy and the decision in Canada to allow same-sex marriage." Newsweek's July 7 cover shows that it is rapidly becoming a mainstream topic in the U.S. as well. The "celebratory" nature of this year's parade and the rising cachet of gay-themed entertainment illustrate an inclusionistic sentiment within society that reflects the still-dominant bull-market psychology. But a bear market also brings polarization so we can expect that a conflict with opposing forces lies ahead.

November 2003

Cultural Trends

When baseball attendance and playoff TV ratings experienced a late-season spike, it was cited internally as a result of the rally in stock prices. This observation was challenged as an example of two-armed socionomics. If the result is positive, an in-house skeptic charged, it's a consequence of a recent rise in stock prices; when it's negative, it's the effects of a longer-term decline. Are we having it both ways? Not at all. To understand why, you have to step back and look more broadly at the prevailing trends. Scan the headlines and one glaring aspect stands out: the current social scene is riven with cross currents. On the one hand George Bush has raised more money than any other politician in history and is considered a shoo-in for re-election. On the other, his approval rating slipped below 50% for the first time in September and he is generating a level of anger and "hatred" that makes Clinton's opponents seem tame by comparison. Publishers have discovered that readers "can't get enough of ideologues"— on the left and right. The two sides trade punches by selling books with titles focusing on *Liberal Treachery* and *Lies and the Lying Liars Who Tell Them*. A Virginia minister says the "most powerful voices now speak from the far right and left" and adds that the effect extends to a "shrinkage of the moderate religious middle." The Anglican church may split in two. On the same day that Iran agreed to allow its nuclear facilities to be inspected by the U.N., a secret agreement calling for Pakistan to supply nuclear arms to Saudi Arabia was reported.

Entertainment reflects the same dichotomy. The best selling movie of the year was the Disney cartoon *Finding Nemo*. But the box office surprise of the summer was "consumers' thirst for gore." The new trend was announced by *Freddy vs. Jason*, which had the biggest opening ever for a horror movie. October brought the successful debut of *Kill Bill Vol. 1* and a remake of *The Texas Chainsaw Massacre*, which came out in the bear market year of 1974 and spawned a whole new genre known as the slasher film. *Kill Bill*, "the most violent movie ever made by a major studio" got a four-star rating in the local paper. On the contemporary music scene, the battle between saccharine-soaked balladeers and edgier hip hop and hard rock artists continues to play out (see Chapter 6, February 2002 entry). This week the more traditional and syrupy side moved back into the top spot, as Clay Aiken of *American Idol* fame hit No. 1, but edgier rap artists have become increasingly dominant on the pop charts. Right behind Aiken are rappers Ludacris, Hard Edge and OutKast.

This is exactly right for the current point in the downtrend as the year-long bounce combined with the aftereffects of a 200-year bull market are battling the emerging influence of a long-term bear market. The effect is very similar to the raucous interplay of social forces that were said to create a "world upside down" in 1969. The world of sports illustrates how deep the symmetry runs. In 1969, the New York Jets "shocked the world" by becoming the first team from the upstart American Football League to beat a team from the more established National Football League in the Super Bowl. This year, the Tampa Bay Buccaneers were the underdog winners of the Super Bowl. After years of frustration, the Bucs became the first team that was not a member of the original NFL or AFL to win a Super Bowl. In golf, for the first time since 1969, all four major Professional Golfers Association tournaments were won by golfers who had never won a major before.

In baseball, 1969 was the year of the Miracle Mets. After a decade of futility, the Mets overcame the powerful Baltimore Orioles to win their first World Series. This year, the Chicago Cubs and Boston Red Sox, two clubs that have not won titles since early last century, made their strongest bids in more than a decade. For the first time in years, TV ratings and the emotional involvement of fans shot higher as both teams came within a game of winning the pennant. According to the oddsmakers, however, there was an even more unlikely candidate, the Florida Marlins. With the help of a dropped fly ball in a game six divisional playoff and the interference of a fan in game six against the Cubs, the Marlins beat the Yankees in six games to win the Series. As the deciding game six played out, Yankee fans (as well as the Yankees' starting pitcher) were convinced that the psychological pressure of Yankee stadium would get to the Marlins. "But the ghosts didn't show." A team with a payroll that was one-third the size of the Yankees' became the first team to win a Series in Yankee Stadium since the bear market year of 1981.

Like 1969, 2003 was a year in which baseball rebounded from two straight down years (in attendance). To generate excitement, baseball had to overthrow its own order. Ratings show that fans were more interested in the lovable losers than the Yankees, a team that dominated through the course of the mania as well as the last century of rising stock prices. Sustaining a dynasty in a bear market is much more difficult because unstable social forces make it almost impossible to maintain a winning balance. As the Series played out, a new item was added to baseball's burgeoning list of troubles. Several of the game's biggest stars have been called to testify in a "designer steroid" case that will tarnish the image of several major sports. The list of witnesses includes Barry Bonds, who smashed the single season home run record with 73 home runs two years ago. The steroids were not discernible by testing until recently, so just as financial performance has been called into question by slack accounting standards, the home run record has been tainted. With the market near new highs, the story's been stuck on page 3.

Look for it to rise toward the front page as the downtrend intensifies. The precise findings of the investigation matter little. Once the bear market resumes, baseball will be tried and convicted in the court of public opinion.

More Similarities and a Big Difference
Here's another flash that goes straight back the vibrant pop scene of 1969:

Pretty in pink
..and yellow, orange, green and other colors of the rainbow

The fashionistas in the audience might be garbed in their perennial black, but designers are in a more upbeat mood, sending out a bouquet of garden-fresh colors for next spring. The fashion industry seems to be saying that if women would just wear a pink suit or a floral party dress, the world would be a happier place. In show after show being staged during New York's Fashion Week, vibrant color was a hallmark. Zac Posen avoided doing any clothes in black, preferring beachy shell pinks and seafoam green. "Designers are looking at spring as a time of revitalization and optimism," says the director a color-matching service. For those who still didn't get it, "Let the Sun Shine In" — lyrics from the Broadway classic "Hair" — on the soundtrack hammered home the point.

—The Denver Post, September 21, 2003

One of EWI's original observations on manifestations of a peak psychology was that "bright colors are associated with market tops and dull, dark colors with bottoms." By the way, "Aquarius/ Let the Sun Shine In" was a No. 1 hit in 1969. In two additional throwbacks to the late 1960s, Simon and Garfunkel are on tour and The Beatles, who had their biggest selling album in 1969, are expected to make a commercial comeback in the fall. Tuesday's issue of USA Today says:

Beatlemania Returns

This is not the first Beatlemania replay since the start of the bull market in 1982. But the re-release of *Let It Be* (without the orchestral arrangements) will take fans back to a very important point in time, 1970 and the Beatles' last act as a combined entity. Don't be surprised if it is their final encore for a long while.

In countless other ways — from the acceptance of openly homosexual lifestyles (see August entry) to the escalating military entanglement in Iraq, the rising sense of outrage against corporate America, labor unrest and an increasing willingness to take social demands to the street — the parallel to 1969 is palpable. In some cases, the details are slightly different. In 1969, for instance, the corporate targets were ITT and IBM. Now they are Wal-Mart and Microsoft. So far, the anti-war demonstrations have been peaceful, but violence has flared on the California picket lines, celebratory riots following football upsets and Montreal, where youths rioted when informed that a concert by a punk rock band was cancelled. As one participant explained, "'Someone yelled, 'Riot!' and everyone jumped in. People were just full of rage. There is obviously something else inside of them. It can't be just because of a show."

The exact details are less important than the direction, which should be toward confrontation, mayhem and destruction of the old order. As writer Geoffrey Colvin has noted of the late 1960s, "The Old Culture and the New Culture were at war in the larger society. And the New Culture won." Of course, there are some key differences between 1969 and 2003. In October 1969, for instance, the Concorde took off and flew at supersonic speed for the first time. A Fibonacci 34 years later, the Concorde has had its last flight. Forbes magazine called the grounding, "Another giant step backward for aviation." In 1969, it was the U.S. that was making great strides in space with the first moon landing. This time around, the forward momentum is all China's as it launched a man into space on October 15. After a decade in which the U.S. was the lone superpower, China's successful space shot symbolizes the return to a bi-polar geopolitical order. As the world adjusts to the strength of a second pole, the potential for social disruption is far more extreme than it was in 1969. This undoubtedly reflects the higher degree of the current trend change. At Grand Supercycle degree, this change is two magnitudes higher. Ultimately, it should make the cultural revolution of the 1960s look like a minor happening.

February 2004

Real estate billionaire Donald Trump has turned up as the focal point of a TV show called *The Apprentice*, which features 16 contestants vying for a position in Trump's firm. *The Apprentice* is a manifestation of the mixed social forces that took over as the countertrend rally from October 2002 played itself out. One article headlined "Survivor Meets Millionaire" described the program as a cross between *Who Wants to be Millionaire* and *Survivor*, which replaced *Millionaire* to become the No. 1 show in the first few months of the bear market. At that time, *The Elliott Wave Financial Forecast* identified the change at the top of the TV listings as "one of the most visible images of a mood shift." The prize is the same, $1 million, but the emerging influence of the bear market is evident in *Survivor*'s format and setting. Set in desolate jungles and deserts, *Survivor* is about physical endurance and the elimination of opponents. *Who Wants to be a Millionaire*, on the other hand, was an appeal to the public's fascination with instant wealth. While *The Apprentice* celebrates the idea of money and the glamour that it buys, the basic idea is closer to *Survivor*. Most episodes highlight bickering contestants and lame appeals to Trump's vanity. Each show ends with Trump firing a contestant. In Trump's words, the essence of the show is "brutal and real," which makes it more reflective of the mood behind a bear market.

The training of the spotlight on Trump is perfect for the final high of the long-term topping process. Trump, one of the great heroes of Primary ⑤, is a master at climbing into the limelight near important market peaks. Three other books, *Trump: The Art of the Deal* (1987), *Trump: Surviving At the Top* (1990) and *The America We Deserve* (2000), all appeared within a few months of peaks at all-time Dow highs. Today Trump announced his latest book: *How To Get Rich: Lessons from 'The Apprentice' and Other Big Deals*. It's a how-to-book, Trump explained, "I think that's what people are looking for." For Trump, the title will probably turn out to be as ironic as *Surviving At the Top*, which was soon followed by his own near bankruptcy.

In another cultural flashback to a peak experience, ABC has decided to bring *Who Wants to Be a Millionaire* out of retirement for brief reprise in late February. From 1999 to 2002, *Millionaire*'s ratings tracked the contours of the stock market with uncanny precision (see chart in Sept 2002 entry). If *Millionaire*'s brief rebirth stamps the end of wave ② as successfully as we think it will, it may go down as one of most highly refined cultural symbols of the great peak.

No Gain, Lots of Pain

Back in the 1980s, one of the very first cultural trends *The Elliott Wave Theorist* identified as a by-product of the bull market was the move toward physical fitness: "There was a new energy building in the early 1980s, and humans had to express it by running, lifting and jumping up and down." In the late 1990s, the corresponding forecast was for more sedentary lifestyles to grab hold. The dynamics behind the transformation are described in *The Wave Principle of Human Social Behavior* (1999). Ample evidence of its arrival is captured in the chart of the premier fitness stock, Bally Total Fitness, which fell almost 90% to a low of $4.36 in March 2003. Since then, it has rebounded somewhat, but as with Trump's TV show, the rally in fitness has been accompanied by all kinds of evidence of a falling rather than a rising underlying trend. Instead of a grassroots jogging or aerobics craze, for instance, the hot new thing in exercise has been toward regimens with bearish overtones such as kick boxing and military style workouts. According to a recent issue of the Wall Street Journal roughly 700 gyms now offer boot-camps:

'Drop, You Maggot, and Give Me Twenty'

Gyms Push Extreme Workouts To Counter Exercise Ennui

Sounds like a good reason not to exercise: Getting up before dawn and crawling around on your belly in Central Park, while getting hollered at by an ex-Navy Seal. It turns out that a growing number of people are willing to pay good money for workouts like that. In the latest response to the health-club industry's perpetual dilemma of how to keep workout-averse patrons working out gyms and personal trainers are pushing an array of aggressive fitness plans based on everything from U.S. military boot camps to Soviet-style weightlifting regimens.

In an alternative bear-market survival technique, fitness clubs have embraced the racy sexual mores of the bear market making striptease workouts the new thing. Strip Workouts for Every Woman is a strong seller on Amazon.com. In another effort to literally broaden their appeal, Bally's has started to highlight "full bodied fashion models" in its ads. "Americans are gaining weight, and health clubs don't want to be left out." Many fitness clubs have also added cooking classes to their offerings. In other words, the meager, one-year uptick has more to do with self-indulgence, self-defense and punishment, than self-improvement. The genuine article, a fresh grass-roots passion for getting fit, will come again, but not for years and not until people swear off finance as the best road to self-improvement.

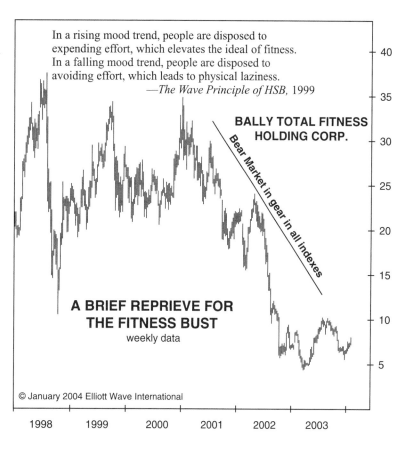

In a rising mood trend, people are disposed to expending effort, which elevates the ideal of fitness. In a falling mood trend, people are disposed to avoiding effort, which leads to physical laziness.
—*The Wave Principle of HSB*, 1999

BALLY TOTAL FITNESS HOLDING CORP.

Bear Market in gear in all indexes

A BRIEF REPRIEVE FOR THE FITNESS BUST
weekly data

© January 2004 Elliott Wave International

1998   1999   2000   2001   2002   2003

March 2004

A clear winner of the cultural tug-of-war covered in the last four issues of *The Elliott Wave Financial Forecast* appears to be emerging. One big sign of the victory for the bear market trend was this week's "blockbuster" opening by *The Passion of the Christ*. *The Wave Principle of Human Social Behavior* observed that religious conviction escalates in a bear market. On this score, the controversy and strong emotions that swirled around *The Passion* before it was even released signaled the downtrend's strengthening grip. Another bear market connection is that in spite of its religious theme, the movie is one of the most violent ever made, which is right in line with this prediction from the October issue of *The Elliott Wave Theorist*: "Films will break new ground in horror, probably with themes that include torture." *The Passion*, says one reviewer, "is graphic beyond belief, and unrelenting. Basically, the entire second half of the film is spent watching Jesus endure physical torture never before seen in a movie." Many other write-ups referred to the treatment of Jesus as torture.

April 2004
The Waning of 'Millionaire' Magnetism

Another Supercycle-degree indicator that served us well back at the all-time highs was the social cachet of the word "millionaire." In December 1999, one month before the all-time peak in the Dow, EWFF detailed myriad ways in which "millionaire-hood has become the common goal of the nation." By that point in time, book sellers, newspaper editors and even TV show producers discovered that the word had an almost magical ability to stir the public's financial fantasies. It started back in 1997, when newspapers found out that the "millionaire population is growing 20 times faster than the general population." With the following entry, EWFF noted that the phenomenon had gone way beyond The Ladies Home Journal's article of 1929, "Everybody Ought To Be Rich:"

> The game-show smash, *Who Wants to Be a Millionaire*, may be the culmination of this whole process. 'It's almost impossible to quit watching. It's the programming equivalent of crack cocaine,' said the director of the Center for the Study of Television. During one key ratings week, the show accounted for half the viewership of the Top 10 shows.

This obsession has clearly returned, as USA Today's top selling business book is *The Automatic Millionaire*; advertisers are pitching a get-rich quick scheme by asking "Does the idea of becoming a Weekend Millionaire intrigue you?"; and, as we covered in the February issue, Regis Philbin has returned to prime time with a new version of *Millionaire* called *Super Millionaire*, which appeared three days after the Dow's February peak. Over its five-day run, it had an average Nielsen rating of just under 10, about where it was in mid-2001 when the Dow was last in the same area, near 10,700. *Super Millionaire*'s lesser popularity confirms that the rally is a countertrend move that cannot recapture the fullness of the old peak. An important recent divergence in the trend is shown by this bar chart of "millionaire" references in five major newspapers. Notice the explosive increase as the market peaked in 2000. After falling with the market in 2001 and 2002, the number of prominent "millionaire" mentions

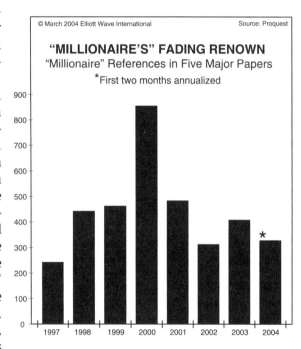

rallied in 2003 but fell as stocks peaked in early 2004. This happened even as *Super Millionaire* debuted in February. The chart depicts an important waning in the social fascination with millionaires, which is in perfect socionomic concert with the bear market.

The fall-off is significant because it shows that the public is losing its connection to a term "millionaire" that dates back to 1720 and John Law's creation of modern finance near the last Grand Supercycle peak. According to the book *Millionaire*, it was first used to describe the wealthy beneficiaries of the Mississippi Company: "Law sparked the world's first major stock-market boom, in which so many made such vast fortunes that the word 'millionaire' was coined to describe them. The term 'millionaire' exerted a seductive appeal. The idea that money could be made from speculation rather than drudgery was printed indelibly on the popular consciousness." The counterbalancing principle, that money could go up in smoke even faster, was made just as indelible by the subsequent bursting of Law's bubble. But the public is unable to keep both ideas in mind at the same time. So, it vacillates between the two, and every 300 years or so it repeats the transition in a fashion that is so uniform and grand that, for those few observers that are able to watch it happen in real time, it is a wonder to behold.

May 2004
Springtime for Ursa

One of the great things about the Wave Principle is its tremendous scope. Users can take the stock market count and, by examining changes in the culture through similar wave positions in the past, do quite well at forecasting the social future. Readers certainly seem to appreciate this value. It can work the other way, too. There are times when broad changes in the social realm can be used to confirm the wave count. This appears to be one of those moments. There is no mistaking the footprints of a big bear market in the changing social landscape. One of the most prominent changes is the shift away from the permissiveness and feelings of alignment with others to a sudden public fetish for restriction and control. Here's how *The Wave Principle of Human Social Behavior* described some of the key traits that create this reactive, bear market craving for regulation and revenge: "A waxing negative social mood appears to correlate with a collective increase in discord, exclusion, unhappiness, anger, opposition, depression, destructiveness and a desire for power over others."

Bear markets are necessary because they correct the excesses of the preceding rise. At big turns, like the one that began in 2000, they bring a wave of reality that breaks down many of the illusions of the bull market years. By the end of the current bear market, baseball will be back on a level playing field, third graders who can't read won't be advanced to the fourth and the airwaves will be safe for the ears of children. But the sobering process is never smooth because virtually every restriction or call for retribution creates a response by an adversary in the same negative mental state. After Israel assassinated Hamas leader, Sheik Ahmed Yassin, a Hamas official responded, "Words cannot describe the emotion of anger and hate inside our hearts." When Yassin's successor was also assassinated on April 18, the headline said, "Hamas Vows 'Volcano of Revenge.'" The more progress the U.S. forces make in Iraq, the more non-aligned parties join the fight and the more terrorists it creates. Another problem is overzealous implementation: The FCC's new rulings caused radio stations to pull songs like Lou Reed's Walk on the Wild Side, which has aired for years without complaint. In this way, even wise and well-conceived bear market reforms and dictates tend to have unintended negative consequences.

Social Visioning: Take Two

In its chapter on "Theories and Observations" on impulsivity and herding, *The Wave Principle of Human Social Behavior* discusses the idea of social visioning, which is the supposition that an emerging trend can find initial expression as "shared fantasy images [that] are an intermediate step between mood change and resulting action." The emergence of *Survivor* and "reality TV" is one of several examples that EWFF cited right before a decline labeled Intermediate wave (3) in 2000. Based upon that big market drop, the principle of social visioning has so far been upheld.

Our August 2000 piece titled "Be Careful What You Ask For" put forward a rising incidence of management-level sabbaticals as evidence of a socially envisioned downtrend. Bloomberg reported on March 29 that a similar phenomenon is sweeping through the ranks of money managers. In "Hey, Where's the Boss Gone? Off on a Sabbatical," one manager said, "I seek a break. It may be six months. It may be forever." In 2000, the trend focused on high-tech executives. Its shift to money managers may be another indicator of the next bear phase's special stress on the financial sector.

Another social vision that seems to be pointing squarely at the potential for a burgeoning employment problem is the way the phrase, "You're Fired," has caught on. Since Donald Trump started using it as the climactic line in his reality TV show, *The Apprentice*, it has been affixed to hot-selling t-shirts and become a common punch line for cultural discourse like this cartoon. Since changes in social mood cause changes in the economy, the phrase, "You're Fired," may become even more common though undoubtedly much less popular.

MUTTS

by Jan Eliot

June 2004

Picasso's $104 Million Sell Signal

Add paintings to the list of "things" that have again become the object of investors' affections. The art market just had its biggest month since May 1990. In addition to the all-time record price for a painting, $104.2 million for Picasso's "Boy With a Pipe," new records were set for works by a host of contemporary artists such as Jackson Pollack and 13 others. The obsession with paintings and other collectibles is an extension of the panic for stuff. It is a twin to the high of May 1990,

which was also accompanied by a spike in commodity prices and a brief burst in consumer prices. As disinflation re-asserted itself, however, a debacle referred to in art circles as the "nightmare of 1991" ensued. This time, the problem is not disinflation but outright deflation, so the coming downward pressure and collapse in art prices should be far deeper than in the early 1990s.

The art market's rise in the wake of the 1987 stock market crash showed that art prices are not strictly commodities. Their price is also influenced by social mood as reflected by stock prices and regulated by the Wave Principle. Art prices appear to save their boldest moves for the aftermath of big advances, as well-heeled investors can afford to bid up "quality" works of art. The first great blow-out bid for a work of art, for instance, came right after the end of Primary ③ in 1987. On November 11, 1987, Australian entrepreneur Alan Bond made his famous, and eventually ill-fated, purchase of Vincent Van Gogh's "Irises." In November 1989, just one month after a record high in the Value Line Arithmetic Index, two more big-ticket paintings were sold. In May 1990, when the Dow Jones Composite, NASDAQ and Value Line had all recorded important peaks that would soon be confirmed by the Dow Industrials, the art market reached its great peak with the highest sales volume in history and a record price of $82.5 million for Van Gogh's "Portrait of Dr. Gachet." Here's what *The Elliott Wave Theorist* said about the explosion as it was taking place:

> What we are witnessing is one mania, an investment mania, with various outlets, art being one of them. What might surprise people is how closely the timing of their impulses and corrections is related. When the stock market finally tops out, art prices won't be far behind.

The forecast was quickly followed by a washout for stocks (particularly in the Value Line and Dow Transport averages) that was even harder on buyers of art. Once again, the art market has carried to new heights in the wake of a Primary degree peak. A comparison to the peak of 1990 reveals many internal signals that the rally is on much weaker footing than its 1990 predecessor. For one thing, even though Picasso's "Boy" finally broke the record set by Van Gogh's "Dr. Gachet," Artprice.com's paintings index shows that the overall market for paintings is still below its level in 1990.

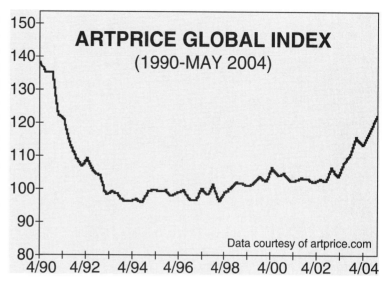

This inability of the art market to substantially surpass the old peak, despite ten years of bull market and a world awash in financial liquidity, suggests an extremely unstable uptrend. The death knell may have been a May 10 Barron's article headlined, "Young Buyers are Plunging Into the Market." It reveals that impressionists and old masters are being ignored for contemporary works that are "far more likely to double or triple in value in a short period." This narrowing focus on objects of lesser quality is a dead ringer for the latter stages of the mania, when investors ignored stocks with long histories and established earnings records to flood into penny stocks with small floats and thus potential for a quick profit. Like investors who gave up on the Dow to ram the NASDAQ higher in February and March 2000, the new "collectors" have "little or no interest in works by what they call 'dead artists.'" Descriptions of the atmosphere surrounding the "crazily hot" art scene are almost indistinguishable from those of the day-trading arena in 1999. "It's about adrenaline," says an art advisor. "It's a fast-paced world, it's exciting, it's new. In a funny kind of way, collecting is the new cocaine."

The focus of the rise is another important socionomic clue to the impending downswing. In May, abstract expressionism, the influential American art movement of the 1950s and 1960s bull market, topped the bill at the most prestigious contemporary art auctions. According to the Artlex Art Dictionary, the whole point of that era's abstract expressionism was to "show feelings and emotions. It was generally believed that the spontaneity of the artists' approach to their work would draw from and release the creativity of their unconscious minds." The upward thrust of Cycle wave III, one of the most bullish periods of the entire Grand Supercycle advance, was so powerful that artists completely dispensed with any semblance of geometric form. Painting left the realm of the tangibly real and focused purely, and some experts say impeccably, on emotion. It makes perfect socionomic sense that, at the last stop for the euphoria of the Grand Supercycle peak, investors would reconnect with the emotion of Cycle III by bidding up the works that embody the energy and excitement of that quintessential bull market time.

It makes no financial sense, however, because the prevailing emotions, and thus tastes, are about to swing dramatically away from those that reigned through that time, so these high prices will not be maintained. The striking aspect of the Picasso that sold for $104 million is that it is so realistic. It is from 1905, two years before Picasso helped pave the way for abstract expressionism by founding the cubist movement. Ironically, in bringing such an extravagant price for a more traditional work, the market has managed to foreshadow, once again, the more prudent and conservative mood that is slowly working its way to the fore.

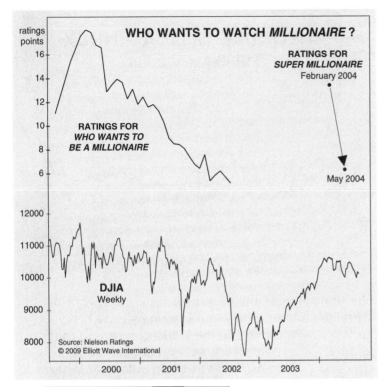

WHO WANTS TO WATCH *MILLIONAIRE* ?

RATINGS FOR
SUPER MILLIONAIRE
February 2004

RATINGS FOR
*WHO WANTS TO
BE A MILLIONAIRE*

May 2004

DJIA
Weekly

Source: Nielson Ratings
© 2009 Elliott Wave International

July 2004

The public fascination with money and finance is falling away as ratings for *Super Millionaire*, ABC's hyped-up version of the mania-era smash *Who Wants to Be a Millionaire*, crashed from an average rating of 13.5 in February to 6.1 in May. Lethargy and disinterest are dangerous traits for stock holders, as they are totally at odds with the energy and intense financial focus that carried stocks to the heights they still occupy.

September 2004

Much of Las Vegas's late-cycle real estate strength is due to its status as the nation's gambling capital. As this recent Time cover says, Las Vegas is "hotter than ever." Gambling has certainly gained unprecedented stature. The number of states with lotteries has risen to a record total of 41; poker is so "hot" that its become a cable TV staple; and California Gov. Arnold Schwarzenegger is attempting to stave off financial ruin by building a casino near San Francisco that will be larger than any in Las Vegas.

In 1992, *The Elliott Wave Theorist* explained that gambling is a bear market manifestation of "the urge that in a bull market results in investment and speculation." The gambling binge is a bear market expression of the speculative fire that burned through the first quarter of 2004. The main function of a bear market is the destruction of capital, and few "investment" venues are quicker and more thorough at this than gaming tables, lotteries and slot machines. In 1996, EWT predicted that gambling would persist through the start of the bear market, but, as the bear market progressed, it added that the industry will "probably get seedier" and fall on hard times like everything else. So, Time's cover is probably performing its usual function and indicating that Las Vegas' best days are now behind it. The transition from a glamorous getaway to a seamy resort where former investors come for one last roll of the dice may already have started.

October 2004

Donald Trump also has another book out. Back in February, when he announced his last book, *How To Get Rich*, *The Elliott Wave Financial Forecast* said it was "perfect for the final high." The Dow peaked less than three weeks later. His latest book, *Think Like A Billionaire*, came not eight days after the recent peak in the small-cap stocks. The chart shown here shows the timing of past Trump tomes. As EWFF noted in January, Trump simply has a knack for training the spotlight on himself at the end of long uptrends. Pride comes before the fall, and nobody expresses the virtue of the unbounded ego better than The Donald. This is clearly the most pronounced signal yet. In addition to being the only double sell signal in one year, *Think Like a Billionaire* is Trump's cheesiest and most self-serving book to date. It consists of page after page of glossy color photos featuring Trump, his supermodel fiancée and fellow celebrities.

Trump's public image is way too straightforward to survive the bear market. Back in 1988, when the stock market was traversing a fourth wave correction, *The Elliott Wave Theorist* explained that declining waves are periods in which "more complex role models and antiheroes emerge." This budding affinity for underdogs and antiheroes is apparent on many levels of society, but one where it is now being systematically mined is the comic book market. DC Comics is currently running a series called "Identity Crisis," in which Batman, Superman, the Flash, Wonder Woman, Green Arrow and other classic characters are "put through an emotional hell. The story line has electrified comic readers by immersing the Man of Steel, the Caped Crusader and their fellow good guys in pain, guilt, anger, fear and realistic violence and consequences."

"These days, people no longer seem to want 'gentle and old-fashioned' superheroes," one comic book columnist explains. "They want their heroes meaner and more complex, with good and evil sketched in various shades of gray rather than in the previously comforting black and white. Comic heroes often share many similarities with their arch villains. As these characters become more knotted and multidimensional, the good and bad impulses that drive the story forward play more and more in the psyche of the protagonist." Similarly the good and bad impulses of the market are beginning to play more and more on the psyches of investors.

December 2004
Skin Is On the Way Out

Back in September 2002 when stocks were approaching a low and long skirts temporarily reestablished themselves in many women's wardrobe, the burqa made a brief appearance as a suggested fashion accessory. *The Elliott Wave Financial Forecast* offered the following analysis:

> Bear market momentum must still be building because instead of embracing the gloomy style, the audience broke up the show with boos and whistles. Still, the impulse behind it is clearly bearish, as the basic instinct of fashion in a declining phase is to cover up.

One of the clearest cultural signs of the bear market's reemergence over the course of the last eight months is a avant-garde shift away from the bare styles that pushed exposure of the female form to its natural limits in 2003 and early 2004. The trend was first spotted by USA Today in the aftermath of peaks for the major averages. In April, the paper used the very words EWFF used in 2002 to describe the new direction within certain avant-garde fashion circles:

It's the Great Hollywood Cover-Up!

Celebrities are toning it down (though not totally)

Since then, a steady stream of fashion observers have said: "Goodbye to bare sexiness;" "People have overdosed on bare bellies;" and "Slutwear is so last year." In September, the Wall Street Journal and USA Weekend both dubbed the trend "The Big Cover-Up." The November issue of In Style notes that hemlines, the quintessential coincident cultural indicator, are falling again.

The "though not totally" comment in the subhead above is an important caveat, however. It reveals an oncoming trend, not an established one. When we mentioned it as the look of the future at the Atlantic City Money Show in August, a veteran retailer insisted that more modest fashions wouldn't sell. Fashion conscious teens "won't wear it." Establishment retailers probably said the same thing about maxi-lengths skirts in 1968. But their expectations are the reason that these styles are inevitable. Just as investor bullishness has reached its upper limit, the skimpy fashions have progressed so far that even really large farm women are wearing them. To retain the element of surprise and reflect the bear market, fashion has to turn. At the bottom, the average retailer will eschew a projected rise to knee-length skirts as too risky.

Player/Fan Tension? Right On Cue

As EWFF explained in July when the Detroit Pistons defeated the Los Angeles Lakers to earn the National Basketball Association title, the Pistons' tradition of winning in bear markets and their bruising style of play fit perfectly with the transition to a renewed bear market trend. Their fans also stepped boldly into the new mood when they got into a "player-fan brawl that shocked the nation" on November 19. The violent outburst was endlessly replayed on most major TV stations. The April 2001 issue of *The Elliott Wave Theorist* anticipated this behavior:

> On and off the field, the games should be characterized by an increasingly rough tone. Player-on-player, fan-on-player, and fan-on-fan violence should continue a rise that has already begun.

The forecast was based on observations from EWT's 1996 special report, "Basketball and the Bull Market," which noted that in the early part of the century, the character and rules of basketball were "more bearish." EWT quoted one basketball pioneer saying its was common "in highly industrialized cities" for fans to "flip stove bolts at out-of-towners." Our report also noted that the game was originally played in wire enclosures known as cages. In the wake of the Detroit brawl, several commentators noted that basketball may want to bring back the cage. So far, the NBA has no such plan, but it is working up a "fan conduct code that could even regulate what hecklers can yell at the court." This is right in line with another change covered in the May issue: bear markets bring a shift "from permissiveness to a sudden public fetish for restriction and control."

January 2005
A Scandal Waiting To Happen

A November Interim Report from *The Elliott Wave Theorist* compared George Bush's re-election to that of Richard Nixon's in 1972 and said that Bush "will probably experience something very like Nixon's second term but worse: a bigger slide in the stock market, a drop to lower levels of popularity and ultimately ousting by some method." Nixon was Time's Man of the Year (with Henry Kissinger) in 1972, and in a continuation of the parallel between the two men's fortunes, the latest Time cover shows that Bush has just received the same distinction for 2004. As with Nixon, Bush's re-election has been accompanied by a stock market rally. The Nixon-era bounce

ended in January 1973 and led to the most dramatic stock market decline since the Depression.

In an interesting divergence, however, Nixon's peak approval rating occurred with the peak in stocks in January 1973, while Bush's current approval rating is down to 49% from a January 2004 high of 60%. The greater strength of the next leg in the Grand Supercycle bear market already appears to be tugging on the popularity of the President. If Bush's star continues to follow the Nixon path, 2005 should mark the beginning of an epic political decline for the president.

Squeezing the Juice Out of the Long Ball

What's the difference between the steroids' controversy in baseball and the accounting crisis at Fannie Mae? From a socionomics perspective, there is none. The slackening of accounting rules that allowed corporations to pump up their financial statements and the use of performance-enhancing substances by professional baseball players are just separate mediums through which the peak mood of the 1990s and early 2000s "juiced up" the social environment to reflect the end of a 200-year bull market. One key attribute of a fifth wave is that it lacks the underlying strength of the preceding third wave. But what fifth waves fail to produce in substance they make up for in an abundant optimism. Apparently, when it is a fifth wave of Supercycle degree, the positive outlook is so rigorously imposed on society that long-established social institutions such as professional baseball or industries such as the mortgage field stretch conventional standards to allow the achievement of record-high results, or at least the impression of them. As *The Elliott Wave Theorist* explained with regard to the financial fundamentals in September 1998, one key attribute of the last leg of the great bull market was its ability to get novice, as well as professional observers, to explain away, ignore and deny a long list of financial measures that were clearly weakening in the bull market's waning days (see Chapter 1 of *Conquer the Crash*).

A bear market is the path through which historical standards and values are re-established. The first phase of this movement focused on Enron, and the front edge of the next wave is being signaled by a series of events that Bloomberg magazine is calling "Fannie Mae's Fall From Grace." Back in 2001, when Fannie Mae was still just below its all-time high, Money magazine tabbed Fannie CEO Franklin Raines "the most confident CEO in America." *Conquer the Crash* responded, "His stockholders, clients and mortgage-package investors had better share the feeling, because confidence is the only thing holding up this giant house of cards." With the Dow Industrials still above 10,000, confidence remains historically high. However, regulators showed that it is clearly teetering when on December 22, they managed to remove Raines from the chairmanship of Fannie Mae.

It is no coincidence that the steroids scandal in baseball also rose to the fore in December. Like many of Fannie Mae's accounting tricks, widespread steroid use by major league players has been an "open secret" for some time. It is generally thought to date back to the front-end of the bubble era. Observers say they first noticed a suspicious bulge in homers and player physiques in 1995, the year the first bubble stocks appeared and the most manic phase of the long bull market began. In 1998, when the left shoulder of the great peak was formed by a preliminary high for most of the major averages, the Chicago Cubs Sammy Sosa and St. Louis Cardinals Mark McGwire both surpassed Roger Maris' single-season home run record in an epic bid for that season's home run crown. McGwire won with 70. In 2000, Major League Baseball set the all-time record for total home runs with 5,693, which marked an incredible 71% increase from 1990. In

2001, Barry Bonds broke McGwire's single-season record with 73 homers. In 2004, he crossed the 700 mark for his career and moved within striking distance of the most venerated record in sports, Hank Aaron's all-time home run record of 755. But his accomplishments, as well as the integrity of the game, were called into question earlier this month when it was revealed that Bonds had admitted to using steroids ("unknowingly"), during the 2002 season. The admission was a "scales falling from the eyes" moment for the game. Suddenly, the media had to face the fact that Major League Baseball looked the other way as Bonds and a host of other bulked-up stars effectively neutered the game's cherished record book. "Baseball's numbers are sacred. So now, if you can't believe the numbers, what's left to believe in?" asks one scribe.

In the same vein as stock "bears" who nevertheless call for a continued market rise in 2005 and those recognizing real estate as a bubble yet call for real estate to remain buoyant, many sports columnists are incensed by the steroid revelations, but say there will be little or no effect on the game in 2005. They continue to track a high level of indifference on the part of fans. At this year's winter meetings, player salaries again notched higher, and teams report no discernible effect on season ticket sales. "Fans Don't Care About Steroids," says one headline. What these writers do not understand is that the overriding force behind baseball's popularity was the long bull market, and the current indifference is the result of a countertrend rally. As its influence fades and the bear market returns, the baseball crowds will thin out and the disgust will come pouring out. The effects of a deepening negative social mood will undoubtedly extend onto the field since most players took steroids for the same reasons investors bought stocks: to make money, to mimic one another and, as author Carl Elliott explains, to avoid "the risk of being left behind." "This may be less about the desire to succeed than the desire to avoid shame and humiliation," says Elliott. The fear of shame and humiliation is a powerful motivator. But it totally re-orients itself in a bear market. As steroids and other performance-enhancing drugs themselves become a source of shame, not to mention severe punishment, their use will wane. This will probably reduce the size of the players (as forecast in the April 2001 issue of EWT) and home run counts, but it will get the game more in line with its roots, which is what bear markets are all about.

May 2005

> San Francisco in the middle sixties was a very special time and place to be a part of. There was a fantastic universal sense of inevitable victory over the forces of Old and Evil. We had all the momentum; we were riding the crest of a high and beautiful wave. So now, less than five years later, you can go up on a steep hill in Las Vegas and look West, and with the right kind of eyes you can almost see the high-water mark — that place where the wave finally broke and rolled back.
>
> —*Fear and Loathing in Las Vegas* (1971)

Hunter S. Thompson probably didn't know it but he was reflecting on a third wave of Cycle degree, which topped exactly where he remembered it, in the mid-1960s. In fact, with the help of the Dow Jones Industrial Average he could have put a date on it, February 9, 1966, when the average hit an intraday high of 1001.10. But by facing the west for the place where the wave finally stopped and rolled back, Thompson looked the wrong way. To the east, he would have seen the last vestiges of the bull market peak in the burgeoning skyline of Las Vegas. The city's ascent started in 1967, a year after the completion of Cycle III. That was the year Howard Hughes bought his first casino (the New Frontier) and laws were changed to allow publicly traded companies to own casinos. Within three years Hughes amassed a "casino empire" and multi-story resorts were rising above the strip. In 1969, the Landmark, a 31-story tower, and the 1500-room International (now the Las Vegas Hilton) opened. At the time, the International was the largest hotel in the world.

As EWFF explained in September, gambling fever blossoms in a bull market when the societal urge to give in and go for broke is strongest. It continues to gain stature in the early phases of a bear market, thus providing the great Vegas explosion of the 1990s, and its continuation to this day. On April 25, Steve Wynn opened the "world's most expensive casino." The 2,700 room hotel features a $130 million man-made mountain, rising as high as seven stories, with pine trees and other landscaping that includes 100-foot high waterfalls, dancing fountains and other special effects. With its lavish accommodations, the Wynn marries the mania-era craving for luxury with the thrill of the high-stakes gaming tables. As home to the last of the big spenders and the last of the big risk takers, the Wynn will stand as a monument to the greatest wealth peak and subsequent destruction in history. Once again, Las Vegas marks the spot where a great wave rolled back.

The Tone of the Culture Is Changing

Can you feel it? The change in cultural expression that we predicted is coming to pass. Horror movies are pouring out of the studios. "Film noir" has turned ultra-violent. The latest *Star Wars* film is rated PG-13. Exclusionism is rising in the form of anti-Semitism and anti-immigration protests in Europe. Free trade coalitions are fraying as "the costs of trade have become more important to many voters than the benefits" (Washington Post, May 13). Volunteers patrol the border in Texas and California. The Chinese are in a fit of rage over actions taken by the Japanese government over half a century ago. The U.S. has been mired in war for three years. A new wave of anti-U.S. sentiment is

MS-13 gang branches out across U.S.

The rapid spread of vicious street gangs such as MS-13 is causing alarm in cities and suburbs nationwide, inspiring a comprehensive anti-gang bill in Congress.

Branches of the Mara Salvatrucha (MS-13) gang, 2004

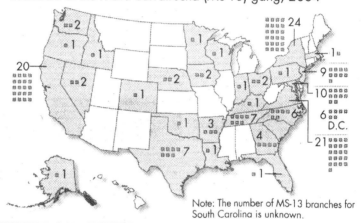

Note: The number of MS-13 branches for South Carolina is unknown.

SOURCE: Fairfax County, Virginia Police Department   AP

spreading. On May 27, Islamic groups will observe the first "international anti-U.S protest day." Riot police are battling anti-U.S. mobs in South Korea. Mexico's president is denouncing U.S. immigration laws. The popularity of religion is soaring. Clinical depression is on the rise. The electorate is polarizing into "red" and "blue" states. Pornography spam is turning to themes of brutality. In entertainment reviews, praise is yielding to criticism. Automobile styles are changing from angularity to the squat, rounded lines of the 1930s. Vicious street gangs are proliferating throughout America, just as in the 1930s. They are financed by severe market imbalances due to prohibition, just as in the 1930s. We anticipated these trends—some very specifically—back in the 1990s when the bull market was raging and no one else could see around the corner. This is the power of socionomic understanding. You can bet that many more, and more extreme, expressions of negative social mood are on the way.

Meanwhile, the downtrend in mood is affecting the economy. Delta is nearing bankruptcy. Ford and GM's debt has been downgraded to junk. Real wages in the U.S. are falling at their fastest rate in 14 years. The price of lumber, which bounced after the write-up in the October EWT, is again falling fast, foretelling of a decline in construction.

Yet the dream-state continues. The administration is pursuing a "guns and butter" policy, just as Johnson did at the major mood peak of the 1960s. Investors are buying junk bonds in record relative quantities. Housing prices are sky-high, and builders are giving us the tallest condo in the world (in Miami) and the most expensive resort in the world (in Las Vegas), at which only the toniest brands have stores. Spam headlines touting stocks outnumber those touting Viagra. And the Dow is still above 10,000.

July 2005

The public's interest in the stock market is waning. One sure sign of the market's approaching estrangement from everyday life is the Chicago Sun-Times' decision to eliminate stock tables from its pages. Since stocks peaked in 2000, several papers have cut back on stock coverage, but the Sun-Times is the first major paper to eliminate the listings altogether. "Expect more papers to join the fray," says an Editor & Publisher columnist. Back at the all-time highs, advertisers loved to place their appeals inside the stock tables because it allowed them to associate their message with the euphoria that surrounded stock prices. Now, as circulation and ad revenues hit the skids, quotes are the first thing to go because instead of a warm, fuzzy feeling, the stock tables are a source of agitation.

Cultural Trends

Can you feel it now? In May, *The Elliott Wave Theorist* observed that the change to a decline [in social mood] is expressing itself across the cultural realm. June brought a wide array of cultural changes that shine an even brighter light on the path of social mood. A natural consequence of the bear market is a reversal in the public consensus from "for" to "against" the war in Iraq. A similar reversal to greater than 50% against occurred with the Vietnam war in 1968, when new all-time highs in many of the small-cap averages accompanied the Dow's test of its Cycle wave III peak. The same variety of small-caps were among the only stocks to carry to new all-time highs in 2005.

Back in November 2003, EWFF fully discussed parallels to a similar cultural transition in 1968/1969. One trend in the fall of 2003 that EWFF traced "straight back to the vibrant pop scene of 1969" was a fashion preference for bright colors. That trend is now giving way. According to the latest headlines, the transition is to darker tones. "In fashion for the coming fall, black is back," says a June 2 Wall Street Journal column headlined, "Going Over to the Dark Side." In an effort to "boost sales," U.S. retailers are pushing "more shirts and jackets in dark tones including black and burgundy after bright color fashions lost some appeal last year." This Saks catalogue cover expresses the extent to which darker, bear market styles are taking over. It is completely filled with hollow-eyed, disinterested models striking somber poses in dark pant suits and skirts, which have fallen below the knee. In a December entry titled "Skin is On the Way Out," EWFF stated that a cover up is an "inevitable" consequence of the bear market.

In a related shift, the "macho man is an endangered species." This fits perfectly with EWT's 1985 treatise "Pop Culture and the Stock Market," which noted that the "falling transition" phase of a bear market is characterized by "feminine caring men." "Today's male is more likely to opt for a pink flowered shirt and swingers' clubs than the traditional role as family super-hero." "All the traditional male values of authority, infallibility, virility and strength are being completely overturned," says a consultant to the French fashion industry. On June 19, The New York Times notes the move to pastel shirts and other "Queer Eye for the Straight Guy" looks and says, "You can't rely on gaydar anymore." "Many men have migrated to a middle ground where the cues to pigeonhole sexual orientation are more and more ambiguous. The poles are melting fast."

The movie box office offers some even more compelling evidence of a bear market acceleration. According to *The Wave Principle of Human Social Behavior*, two dominant bear market movie themes are anti-heroes and horror. Among the few successful offerings are *Batman Begins* and George Romero's *Land of the Dead*. The lineage of both films fits right in with the start of a major bear phase. Batman goes back to 1939 when the comic book version of "The Dark Knight" first appeared as an antidote to the classic bull market hero of Supercycle I, Superman. A campy TV version emerged at the end of Cycle III in 1966, but *Batman Begins* "positions its hero at the dark end of the street. It's a film noir Batman, a brooding, disturbing piece of work." In a nod to more down-to-earth bear market sensibilities, the latest Batman's lack of "super powers" is part of the marketing appeal. *Land of the Dead* is Romero's "long-awaited return to the horror genre he invented, beginning with the seminal *Night of the Living Dead*" in October 1968, shortly before an all-time peak in the Value Line index that stayed in place for 15 years. Back in 1999, EWFF cited the box office success of a single scary movie, *The Blair Witch Project*, as "the strongest evidence that a sudden social mood trend change" was in the cards. Now the same signal is flashing, only many times stronger, as horror has become Hollywood's one reliable money-maker. "The genre's raging success has led to some almost frightening developments of late," says The New York Times. "Horror is now very much filmdom's stylish inner track." "You'd be shocked at who's calling and wants to be in these movies," says a producer.

It's somewhat incongruous to see the horror movies rise to the level of full-fledged industry while many bull market institutions and icons press on to new highs. The bull market sports of baseball and basketball, for instance, are holding up relatively well. Basketball enjoyed a slight uptick in regular season attendance this year, to a new record high, while 2004 brought out a record number of baseball fans, also by a slight margin. But the bear market dike appears ready to burst. League-wide scoring droughts, failures by teams that dominated through the course of the old bull market and player/fan altercations have marred both sports. For basketball, the potential for a stunning reversal is evident in 2005 apparel sales. After rising 30% in each of the last three years, NBA licensed jerseys, T-shirts and jackets fell by a third so far this year, according to SportScan. TV ratings for the NBA finals were down as much as 35% from 2004 levels. "Someone has abducted the fans who used to watch the NBA finals," reports The New York Times. In baseball, the steroids controversy finally moved to page 1 with the March peak in the major averages. As it has, the game's greatest player, Barry Bonds, has gone to the bench, his assault on the all-time home run record sidetracked by injury and steroid allegations.

Given their troubles, it's amazing that baseball and basketball still have fans. But there's a simple socionomics explanation: the Value Line Arithmetic index hit a new all-time high June 17, just as it did in May 1968. This lift in the small-cap stocks was strong enough to produce an uptick in the fortunes of these games, which historically have been extremely sensitive to a rise in social mood. As the bear market descends, a relentless series of unfortunate events will befall baseball, basketball and the whole bull market sports establishment.

Speaking of bull market heroes, did you catch Michael Jackson flashing the victory sign as he walked out of court a free man earlier this month? The bear has already turned Jackson into a shell of his bull market self. "He will never be able to get by as any more than a vastly talented eccentric," writes Daily News columnist Stanley Crouch. "He has now joined the ranks of the great freaks of our age and has no one to blame other than himself and his own willingness to play with the carnivorous forces that created his illusion." As the musical hero of a large-degree fifth wave, Jackson's public image is extremely susceptible to the negative force of the bear market. It actually started slipping back in 1991 when he was considered "a national treasure" and Sony signed him to a $1 billion contract. At the time, *The Elliott Wave Theorist* said the contract marked the "peak in his valuation." As Jackson is effectively bankrupt, it was a pretty good call.

August 2005

After establishing a parallel between the number and sophistication of roller coasters through the bull and bear markets of the 20th Century and pointing out their "ever-more-thrilling dimension" through the bull market of the 1980s and 1990s, the May 2001 issue of *The Elliott Wave Financial Forecast* issued the following recommendation:

If you own an amusement park or amusement park shares, sell this year.

Jackson Released on Bail After Arrest on Molestation Charges

Michael Jackson, the international pop sensation whose career has been eclipsed by his increasingly erratic behavior, surrendered to authorities Thursday and was booked on multiple counts of child molestation.

After being booked and surrendering his passport, he posted $3 million bail and was released, flashing a "V" sign before being driven away in a black SUV under police escort. *Los Angeles Times*, November 21, 2003

Never-Never Land

What Mr. Jackson has tried to sell the public is the waif-like innocence of his Peter Pan-persona. What he has succeeded in doing is to mask clumsily the highly stylized, thoroughly uninteresting decadence of a middle-aged potentate who possesses the tastes of an uneducated, indulged teenager. He strikes the public as both a monstrous deformity and a misguided wretch. It comes as no surprise that he should be accused of being a child molester. He seems in his public statements and behavior to have almost been courting such charges. That the man who wishes to be a sexless child himself, like Peter Pan, whirling in the air as an untouchable sex object to Wendy, Tiger Lily and Tinkerbell, should be accused of taking advantage of children, must seem to every thinking person, not the ultimate irony, but the ultimate decadence. THE WALL STREET JOURNAL
December 2, 2003

The cover photo of Michael's piercing, glassy-eyed stare and ultra-unnatural chiseled face was just plain spooky. This is not the Michael I knew and loved when I was a teenager. Some people ask, "Where's Waldo?" I ask, "Where's Michael?" **People** MailBag
December 29, 2003

How 'thriller' lost its thrill
Newsweek
December 1, 2003

Michael Jackson Charged
JET
January 12, 2004

The Cuffed One

On Wednesday, Santa Barbara County district attorney Thomas Sneddon Jr. announced with unsuppressed glee that he had issued a warrant for Jackson's arrest, apostrophizing, "Get over here and get checked in." The next day Jackson flew in from Las Vegas on his private jet and was put in manacles. The Gloved One had become the Cuffed One.

TIME, December 1, 2003

Farther and Farther Off the Wall

IT'S A SHAME THIS page doesn't bestow a Newsmaker of the Year award, because Michael Jackson deserves some kind of recognition for keeping our staff fully employed. In the last week alone, Jackson generated stories on claims that the Santa Barbara police abused him, concerns that the Nation of Islam has taken over his life, allegations that CBS paid him $1 million for a "60 Minutes" interview and counterclaims (complete with videotape evidence) that he exaggerated the abuse charges. Newsweek
January 12, 2004

Michael Jackson pleads not guilty to child molestation charges
ALL THINGS CONSIDERED, January 16, 2004

Michael Jackson Indicted
Pop Star's Attorneys Say He Will Plead Not Guilty
abc NEWS, April 22, 2004

Thanks to the Roller Coaster Database (rcdb.com), we now have a chart of coaster growth back through 1901 when the bull market of the 1900s was beginning and the first roller coaster went flying into action on Coney Island. The chart confirms the socionomic premise that EWFF presented in 2001. While the number of new coasters led the market on the way down in the late 1920s and lagged coming off the lows in the 1940s and early 1950s, roller coaster booms and busts over more than 100 years conform nicely to the ups and downs of stock prices. As the chart shows, EWFF's forecast for a peak in construction with the all-time high in stocks proved accurate.

As EWFF also anticipated in 2001, the business is now anything but amusing to owners. Since we issued our warning on amusement park shares, the stock of Six Flags, Inc., the purest roller coaster play, is down 77%, from $23.73 to $5.25. The bear market rally in the blue-chip

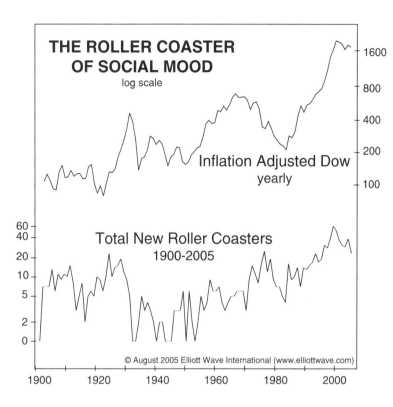

THE ROLLER COASTER OF SOCIAL MOOD
log scale

Inflation Adjusted Dow
yearly

Total New Roller Coasters
1900-2005

© August 2005 Elliott Wave International (www.elliottwave.com)

stock indexes has barely registered in the price of Six Flags shares and the total number of new coasters, but there is a massive evidence of it elsewhere. Measuring 45 stories, Kingda Ka, the world's tallest and fastest coaster, opened at Six Flags Great Adventure in Jackson, New Jersey earlier this year. Riders go from 0 to 128 miles per hour in 3.5 seconds then take a 90-degree turn and soar 45 stories straight up followed by a 41-story nose-dive. What better way to get the adrenaline rush of a bull market? Right now, we can think of one group that would offer an alternative, but in a few weeks as the Value Line index locks into its straight-down phase, small cap investors will wish they had stuck to the amusement parks.

September 2005

The July issue cited a rise in the "feminine, caring" male role models and noted that the drift toward less stereotypically masculine fashions and lifestyles is a classic response to a bear market in social mood. When *The Elliott Wave Theorist* first identified this correlation in 1985, it also noted that a rise in "masculine," "liberated" women is the flip side of this bear market trend. So far, it's been a relatively quiet assault, but, in many areas, women have already moved beyond the in-roads created with the help of the women's lib movement back in the 1970s. A highwater mark for female athletes during the last bear market, for instance, was Billie Jean King's exhibition tennis victory over Bobby Riggs. In 1973, as the biggest bear market since the Great Depression was getting underway, King defeated Riggs in the famous "Battle of the Sexes." Women are challenging men on their own turf, once again. But this time it's not an exhibition. "Female athletes—from golf's Michelle Wie and Annika Sorenstam and auto racing's Danica Patrick to bowling's Liz Johnson and minor-league hockey's Angela Ruggiero—are taking on the men

and receiving their greatest receptions." With a fourth-place finish in the Indy 500 and a subsequent spot on Sports Illustrated's cover, Danica Patrick replaced Janet Guthrie, the first female Indy car driver (also during the last Cycle-degree bear market of the 1970s), as the most accomplished female car racer in history. A USA Today headline reveals that 15-year old golfer Michelle Wie is "No Sideshow But A Real Threat to Gender Line."

It's not just the playing fields, as Bob notes in *Prechter's Perspective*, but "In every field, women gain dominance

243

in bear market periods." The extension to the highest levels of society is evident in a full color picture of Hillary Clinton in a recent issue of USA Today. She's standing confidently in front of two GIs in a pose that all but declares the former first lady fit for the role of commander in chief. As "the first female presidential frontrunner in history" she's already the most accomplished female candidate for the presidency in history. Clinton's ability to secure the 2008 Democratic nomination remains an open question, but with "tough talk on defense" and an array of "pro-military" stances, Clinton has solidified her prospects.

November 2005

As the November 2004 EWFF explained, Donald Trump thrives right at peaks in mood, which explains the higher ratings for his version of *The Apprentice*, which first appeared on the left side of the countertrend rally's peaking

With troops: Sen. Hillary Rodham Clinton visits U.S. forces at Bagram Air Base in Afghanistan in 2003

Can Hillary be elected commander in chief? Tuesday, July 19, 2005

Pro-military views inspire guessing about 2008 run <u>Cover story</u>

process in January 2004. But now Trump is sinking. Trump's audience is down to 9 million, a 50% drop from its peak in 2004. In recent days, he became the target of a mini-media firestorm when he blamed Martha Stewart for his show's decline saying, "I never thought it was a good idea." One critic called him a "hypocrite" and "a pretentious, self-absorbed narcissist with an acute inability to admit mistakes." The New York Times reflects a souring public mood with a recent story about Trump's negative net worth back in the early 1990s. The story contends that Trump took out a loan from his father's estate to stay solvent. Trump called the story "a pile of crap." Maybe so, but Trump and other luminaries of the old bull market should take it as their cue to beat a fast retreat. Society is moving on to the phase of the cycle when its members derive pleasure from the misfortunes of once-exalted stars. It's going to be a tough crowd.

January 2006

When the trend in social mood changes from up to down, society is impelled to turn on the most abundant beneficiaries of the old positive social mood. The May 2000 issue of *The Elliott Wave Theorist* titled, "A Socionomic Perspective on the Microsoft Case," first fully described this aspect of a bear market. In a section on "The Timing of Attacks on Successful Corporations," EWT observed that when social mood shifts from a bull to bear market, "general attitudes toward the financial success of others" shifts, too.

> During a major topping and declining mood trend, all kinds of sociological forces work against corporations that are visibly successful. For example, in the bear market environment of the early 1970s, countless people were apoplectic over an irrational fear that ITT (the International Telephone and Telegraph company), which had begun a program of taking over smaller companies, would "take over the world." It was considered an immense threat. College students fretted over it, and talk show hosts discussed it continually.

ITT's "mistake" was being a conglomerate in 1968. At that time, conglomerates were a focal point of a big rally in stock prices and thus the ensuing bear market. Microsoft was in a similar position in 2000 when technology was at the center of the bull market's final phase. As EWT pointed out in 2000, the new punitive mood tends to "objectify" itself by striking at the "most successful enterprises." Microsoft was found guilty of anti-trust violations and became a very prominent target through the early stages of wave **a** down. Patterns point strongly toward [a similar focus on] the consumer in the next phase of the bear market; thus the commencement of hostilities toward the world's most successful retailer, Wal-Mart. "There is a drumbeat every day that's building," says a political operative. "The question of whether Wal-Mart is good for America is being pushed to the forefront of a national debate." At right is the headline and graphic from a recent USA Today article.

Growing opposition frowns on Wal-Mart
World's No. 1 retailer fights to keep smiley face on image

The story points to a critical parallel: "Wal-Mart is facing the most formidable opposition to a retailer since the 1930s, when a campaign was waged against Great Atlantic & Pacific Tea (better known as A&P), which subsequently lost its domination of the retail market." This is important because it reveals the truth about Wal-Mart, which is that it is no more of a threat than a good grocery store. The source of its emerging opposition is the mood behind a bear market of at least Supercycle degree. A&P suffered the same fate in the 1930s because it was the most successful developer of the new, more efficient supermarkets. Now Wal-Mart represents another giant step forward in efficiency and economies of scale, but it is under fire for offering low wages, discriminating against women, hiring illegal aliens and hurting communities, small businesses and the environment. Subscribers know the real reason: a negative social psychology that is grabbing hold. It must be a powerful one, because the animosity extends well beyond Wal-Mart to business in general. According to a recent New York Times story, "Americans do not trust business or the people who run it." Polls clearly show that animosity toward business and executives "as a class seems to be rising to a new level." Don't look now, but "politicians are picking up on the antibusiness scent." The "rampant distrust" speaks to the breadth of the oncoming decline. In one way or another, it should impact just about everyone.

February 2006

Another strong sign of a reversal in Google shares and the market as a whole is a sudden series of attacks on Google's good name. Until recently, Google was known for its "don't be evil" motto and the efficiency of its Internet search engine. But now a flood of stories inform us that it is colluding with communist oppressors in China and being sued by the U.S. Department of Justice. Google's "Once Brotherly Image" has turned "Big Brotherly," says a recent USA Today headline. "Google's Reputation at Stake in Fight With Government," says another from January 22. The transformation is a classic illustration of Elliott Wave International's observation of the "attacks on the most successful corporations" that come with major downturns in social mood. The emergence of a new strain was covered in last month's Cultural Trends section (which was an update to the May 2000 EWT, "A Socionomic Perspective on the Microsoft Case.") It is now attaching itself to Google because when the mood shifts from a bull to a bear, society at large besieges the most prosperous corporate beneficiary of the uptrend. The same thing happened to RCA in 1929, IBM in 1968 and Microsoft in 2000. By the way, you can tell that the current market peak is occurring within an existing bear market because, after settling with the government in the depths of the initial leg of the bear trend, Microsoft is attracting its wrath once again. On Tuesday, the Justice Department announced that "Microsoft is failing to move quickly enough to comply with its antitrust settlement with the government." The announcement was called the "strongest show of impatience" since Microsoft and the U.S. government reached an anti-trust settlement in September 2001. So, the fire still burns and Google's experience shows that it is starting to spread fast.

April 2006

The following article from Good Morning America reflects the fact that establishment advisors are all for the involvement of the little guy.

Expert: Get in the Red-Hot Stock Market

March 20, 2006— It's not only time to jump into the red-hot stock market, it's time to stay, says a chief economist [with a major brokerage firm]. We've got the strongest overall profit performance in 30 years, and these are real profits, not the fake ones we saw in the late 1990s.

With the morning news shows recommending stocks, the equity culture is definitely alive and kicking.

Planet Earth's Big Stress Test

The January issue of EWFF pointed to one of the last mania outlets for the Grand Supercycle-degree peak, Saudi Arabia, and said:

> With the more established blue chip shares continuing to falter, this blatant disregard for weakening stock market leadership actually confirms EWFF's contention that 2005 is nothing more than a supersized 1968, when an all-time high in speculative shares accompanied a smaller scale secondary peak for the Dow.

The chart showing a 28% decline from a late February peak (shown in March 2006 entry in Chapter 1) from *The Elliott Wave Theorist* confirms this assessment. A closely related hyperbolic rise and an even steeper 53% plunge occurred in the Dubai Index. As EWT asserted, these rumblings are not likely to remain distant for long. The depth of the link to 1968 is underscored by a Fidelity Investment advertisement for its International Discovery Fund, which displays the fund's latest performance numbers against a psychedelic, flower-power cartoon background a la Peter Max. The ad features Iron Butterfly's 1968 hit, "In-A-Gadda-Da-Vida," a song that accompanied the stock market top in 1968. *The Elliott Wave Theorist* explained the importance of this and other heavy metal progenitors way back in 1985:

> Then in the fall of 1968, as the secondary stock bull market was preparing to enter its top, 'heavy metal' music entered the scene, as hits by Iron Butterfly, Deep Purple and Steppenwolf all entered the charts concurrently. The sudden popularity of this new style foreshadowed the stock market top in December 1968.

Fidelity isn't one of the world's largest mutual fund families for nothing. It knows how to harvest the fruits of a peak social mood. In this case, the parallel to 1968 comes with an ironic twist. Fidelity is using the counter-culture ethos of that era to promote the establishment practice of buying stocks. As EWFF has said many times before, average investors buy foreign shares only at the end of a long rise. The ad is a massive sell signal because it shows how totally established the once-risky practice of investing in international stocks is.

While the set-up has much in common with 1968, other factors suggest that the extent and speed of the upcoming decline will be more like that of 1929-1932. One literally massive piece of evidence is the construction of the world's tallest building in Dubai (for more on this see below). Another screaming parallel is the response to the initial plunge in Dubai and other once-remote financial outposts. The chief investment strategist for a major Wall Street firm termed the Dubai's 53% collapse "an adjustment phase" and told a Dubai daily newspaper, "We believe that Dubai is the Shanghai and Hong Kong of the Middle East." He'd better hope not. The Shanghai Stock Index remains down 42% from its bull market peak nearly five years ago, while Hong Kong's Hang Seng index is still down 13% from a peak in March 2000. Tuesday's Wall Street Journal reports, "Analysts say the selloff in the Gulf shows few signs of spilling over broadly." It's a global "What, me worry?" in a mad world.

Cultural Trends

The longer the countertrend rise in social mood continues, the more closely it comes to resemble the chaotic clash of bull and bear market forces in the late 1960s. More than two years ago EWFF stated that growing "labor unrest and an increasing willingness to take social demands to the street" was making the parallel "palpable." Just this week, Delta pilots in the U.S. engaged in a "practice strike" at the same time that a huge pension strike of 1.5 million government workers spread across Britain. At least a million protesters poured onto the streets of France on Tuesday, "in a mass effort to pressure the embattled Prime Minister to withdraw a new jobs contract for younger workers." Some contrary-minded observers doubt that it can be a top because the social scene is too tumultuous. But it's important to remember that this is not the end of the bull market but an important secondary peak for the major averages coupled with a new all-time high for more speculative shares. The best prior example is what happened after the end of Cycle wave III in 1966. So it is perfectly appropriate that, as many stories have noted, "France is being rocked by one of the biggest social upheavals since the student rebellion and workers' general strike of 1968." The year 1968 marked a major secondary peak in the U.S. blue-chip stock indexes and the start of a bear market decline that was led by the more speculative Value Line Composite Geometric Average, which fell 75%. So, vive les Francais. There is a good chance that their passion for social protest boils over at a very precise and important moment in the course of social mood.

A Bull Market Goodbye From Dubai

How big is this peak? The next chart captures the remarkable heights that human ambition is scaling at the greatest top of all time. The closest precedent is what happened in the late 1920s. Here's a description from a review of the book, *Higher: A Historic Race to the Sky* by Neal Bascomb:

> At the tail end of the 1920s, the Jazz Age was in full swing, and Americans experienced an unprecedented level of prosperity with no apparent end in sight. Though the Great Depression would soon wipe out many of those gains, three landmark buildings on the New York City skyline—the Chrysler Building, the Empire State Building, and the Manhattan Company Building [40 Wall Street]—remain as tangible reminders of the enormous ambition and exuberance that characterized the era.

All three buildings were conceived in the bull market and built through the peak, only to open for business amidst the worst market for office space for decades on either side. That great race to be the world's tallest is the building frenzy Edward R. Dewey used to identify the Skyscraper Indicator back in the 1940s. The latest "race to the sky" also features three contenders, in Malaysia, Taiwan and Dubai. But this time, the first two skyscrapers actually held the title of world's tallest for only a few years, eventually exceeded by an even taller monument to another regions' euphoric surge in social mood. Dewey originally observed that the "world's tallest" sell signal for stocks is given when a tower is conceived because construction takes a while to complete. A new world's tallest building is invariably occupied only in the aftermath of the bull market that gave rise to its creation. All three of the new ones fit this profile, as the Malaysian market doubled-topped in 1994 and 1997, before the completion of the Petronas Towers; Taiwan peaked in 2000 ahead of the 2004 completion of the Taipei 101 building. As our discussion of the Arab stock markets over the last three months indicates, everything points to a similar fate in Dubai, where the Burj Dubai is now being built through the wreckage of a crashing Dubai Stock Index. As with the contestants for the world's tallest

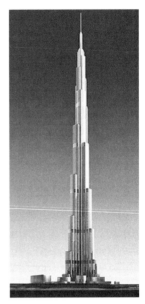

building in the 1920s, "The Burj Dubai's height is a closely guarded secret." The latest projection is 800 meters, which would be a 77% increase from this era's first record breaker, the Petronas Towers. Billed as "the world's greatest vertical mega-project," the Burj Dubai is designed to "beat all records and on a scale that will be a dramatic testament to Dubai's faith in the future." The same kind of rhetoric surrounded the move toward the heavens in 1929.

The latest sell signal rates as even more potent than that of 1929 for several reasons. A major one is the sheer audacity of the last and most dramatic tower. At 800 meters, the Burj will be close to half a mile high, more than doubling the Empire State Building's 381-meter height. Also, in addition to the incredible repitition of the signal, there is its geographic spread and distance from the hub of the mania, New York City. In 1929, the projects were all within a couple miles of the New York Stock Exchange. Dubai is 6,420 miles away. And it is a city of less than 1.5 million people that was virtually nonexistent just 50 years ago. It's also situated in the midst of an unstable region. The Burj Dubai is just one of a wide range of wildly exotic projects now being constructed in Dubai. Others include: the first luxury underwater hotel; "a man-made archipelago of private, residential islands (yes, the biggest development of its kind) that will resemble a map of the world when seen from above"; a set of man-made resort islands shaped to look like a palm tree when seen from above; the first commercial spacecraft flight center; Dubailand, a sprawling tourist attraction that is geared to be a combination between Disney World and Las Vegas; and Eco-Tourism World, which will present "natural" environments and biosphere structures to create a "place that celebrates the natural beauty of our planet."

But, the bear market is wasting no time throwing a monkey wrench into the works over in Dubai. Here's the latest news from the Burj Dubai building site:

> Asian workers angered by low salaries and mistreatment smashed cars and offices in a riot that interrupted construction Wednesday on the site of a building meant to be the world's tallest. The violence, which caused an estimated $1 million damage, illustrated the growing unrest among foreign workers who are the linchpin of Dubai's breathtaking building boom.
> —Associated Press, March 23, 2006

Thanks to extremely low labor costs, the developers will undoubtedly work through this dust up. But the depth of the excess in this once forsaken desert town suggests that the Burj Dubai may not make it to its rumored height of 160 stories. It was a small riot, but it will probably go down as the first important sign that something turned rotten in Shangri La.

A big difference between this peak and those of the last century is that no new heights are being scaled in the United States. Since 1996, a handful of plans to construct the world's tallest building in the United States have been announced only to be derailed for one reason or another. It takes a high level of social cooperation to pull off a tallest building because they are less efficient than smaller structures (and, as it turns out, excellent terrorist targets in bear markets). In a divergence from the dramatic harmony at the end of Supercycle wave (III) in 1929, developers just cannot pull the pieces together the way they did in the heart of the Grand Supercycle bull market. Through the peak of Supercycle (V) in 2000, the aspirations are just as grand as they were in Supercycle (III), but at this point antagonism between developers, lenders, governments and other parties is making it hard to even replace the towers of the World Trade Center that were destroyed on September 11, 2001. Originally, the Freedom Tower, which is being built on the site of the World Trade Center, was supposed to win the

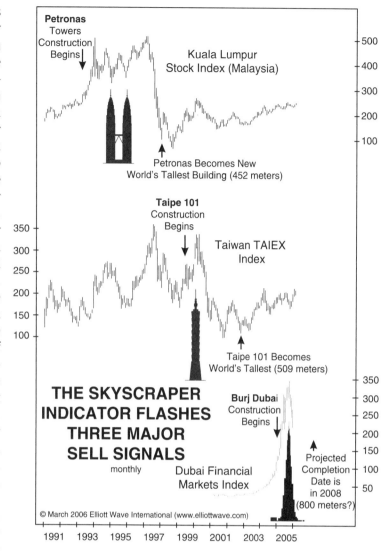

crown of world's tallest building at 540 meters, but the project has been continually delayed. A NY Post columnist describes the effort to date as a failure that is "Homeric in scale. The paralysis can only be explained by a heart that was never really in the job, or gross incompetence—or both." As a Daily Show "news" commentator dryly noted, Bin Laden may have brought down the Towers but he did nothing to destroy the bureaucracy that will keep a new tower from ever being rebuilt. All of this is evidence that on a Grand Supercycle scale, the U.S. has begun to lose its world dominance.

May 2006

Since late 2003, EWFF said prevailing cultural trends were "very similar to the raucous interplay of social forces" that persisted in the late 1960s. Beside the prominent similarity in the averages (a new all-time high in the Value Line Index accompanied by a secondary peak in the Dow Jones Industrial Average), "a war has gone awry," the streets are filling with social protests and the president's popularity is plummeting. Notice the uncanny resemblance in the trend of presidential approval ratings between the front edge of a 16-year bear market in 1966-1968 and 2000-2006. Except for a spike to above 90% in the wake of the September 11, 2001 bombing of the World Trade Center towers, presidential popularity has traversed the same straight-down course that it took as the Dow stayed aloft and more speculative stocks soared in the late 1960s. In both cases, it started at just above 60% and fell into the mid-30% range.

THE PRESIDENTIAL DIVERGENCE: 1968 AND 2006

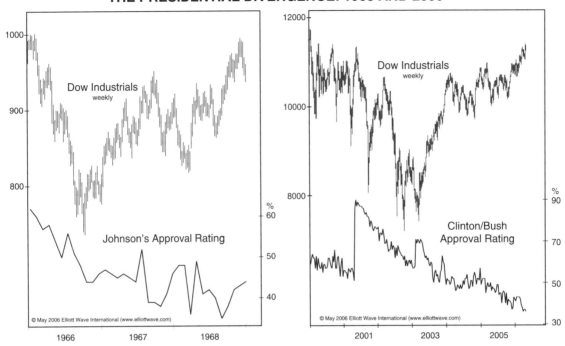

The big difference between Bush's readings vs. the stock market and those of Johnson is that this time the discrepancy has been building for roughly twice as long. A longer social divergence equates to a bigger turn. As EWFF said in November 2003, "the potential for social disruption is far more extreme than it was in 1969. This undoubtedly reflects the higher degree of the current trend change." As we have noted here before, there are many more cultural transformations than we have room to cover, but one critical change that signals the depth of the change is in religion. A New York Times article, "Rebel With A Cross," describes a burgeoning "counterculture" that calls to mind a similar experience in the late 1960s. In fact, with their "extreme Christian clothing," their own music and "alternative churches," The Times says the new followers are "the heirs in spirit of the 60s' Jesus people." "The 'Jesus freak' was certainly the most curious social phenomena of the late 1960s and early 1970s," says a "History of the Jesus Movement." The article dates its inception to 1967, one year after the start of the bear market, and says it "effectively ended by the mid-1970s," along with the bear market.

As we noted in back in March 2004 when the blockbuster movie, *The Passion of the Christ*, came out, "religious conviction escalates in a bear market," and the strong emotions that swirled around *The Passion* were an early indication of a strengthening in bear market psychology. May brings *The Da Vinci Code*, a movie based on the best selling book that is described as a combination conspiracy theory/religious thriller. (Conspiracies are another emerging passion that appeals to what *The Wave Principle of Social Behavior* refers to as the "magical thinking" of a bear market.) The non-fiction work on which *The Da Vinci Code* is based came out at the end of the last bear market in 1982. Suddenly, after years of neglect, this controversial challenge to the core belief of Christians is all the rage. But it has also generated a wave of "interest in the early history of Christianity." The papers are filled with a steady stream of religious themes. A week ago, every newspaper in the country covered the drive to revise Judas Iscariat's "most despised place in history." This week the Time cover story focuses on "The Ways of Opus Dei, [a] powerful ultraconservative Roman Catholic faction." Clearly, the public is "getting religion," and the media is reflecting that bear market impulse.

July 2006

A Picture of Peak Social Mood

The art market has done it again, producing a new all-time high price for a single painting in the aftermath of an important stock market peak. At $135 million, Gustav Klimt's "Adele Bloch-Bauer" becomes the highest price ever paid for a painting. Bidding for the six most expensive paintings on record all took place in the wake of stock peaks. Our graph shows the progression. *The Elliott Wave Theorist* of May 1990 first made the key point: "When the stock market finally tops out, art prices won't be far behind."

The Mei Moses Art Index traces the value of major artwork back through the beginning of the last century. Over that span, art prices have tracked stock prices almost precisely except for two key periods: the 1920s, when stocks rose and artworks declined, and the 1990s, when stocks also soared to new heights unaccompanied by art prices. This time around, the art index managed to join the Value Line Arithmetic Index at new all-time highs, probably because of the higher level and greater breadth of speculation at the end of Supercycle V. As happened in the 1920s, however, the relative underperformance of art prices through the bull market probably foreshadows a coming deflationary era. Art is extremely illiquid in periods of decline, so art prices should suffer greatly in the years ahead.

Another sign of an approaching trend change in art and art prices is the "flight from quality" that *The Elliott Wave Financial Forecast* discussed in June 2004. Notice the difference between the stature of the artist at the beginning of the art boom in 1987 when Van Gogh's work was the object of the bidding frenzy and this year's recipient, Gustav Klimt. Compared to the other artists shown on our chart, Klimt is relatively unknown. According to *The Wave Principle of Human Social Behavior*, tastes in art progress from traditional in a healthy bull market and colorful and "alive" at a peak to "anarchic – anything goes" in a bear and deliberately ugly at a bottom. The frenzy for "Adele Bloch-Bauer" is a subtle sign of the move away from traditional tastes. A not-so-subtle sign of bear market tastes is "Exhibit 1201" at London's Royal Academy of Arts. It is the work of an artist who entered a sculpture into a field of 9,000 applicants for exhibition in the Royal Academy. His sculpture was rejected, but the stand he had put it on won entry to the Royal Academy. In the judgment of The Wall Street Journal, the actual sculpture of a laughing face, "One Day Closer to Paradise," lost because of its "emotional content." The "laughing head is not only fatally well rendered but exudes a sense of joy and hilarity, and the overtly evocative is déclassé. How much more sophisticated a stoic square of slate [is]." In a bear market, tastes crash from the "alive" phase of the peak to an emphasis on death at the bottom. The judges' preference for the inexpressive over "joy and hilarity" indicates that the re-ordering of the art world is underway along with the re-ordering of financial values.

August 2006

I Get A Kick from Ultra Jolt

Back in 2001, *The Elliott Wave Financial Forecast* offered a two-pronged forecast for coffee prices, saying that the price of coffee beans was heading higher, while the biggest chain of retail java shops, Starbucks, was headed much lower. We were right about coffee, which more than tripled, but very wrong about Starbucks. Still, the historic link between the popularity of coffee houses and big bull markets (discussed in December 2001 entry) remains in place, as Starbucks accompanied the Value Line Arithmetic index and several global indexes to substantial new all-time highs. It has also turned down from a May 5 peak in a form that is consistent with a long term peak.

As EWT noted with respect to Microsoft near its all-time high in late 1999, major peaks are followed by societal attacks against the most successful corporate beneficiaries of a bull market in social mood. So it is now with the world's biggest coffee chain. Starbucks is "in the sights of the so-called 'food police.' The Center for Science in the Public Interest plans to take action against the popular coffee chain" for the high-fat products it sells. Energy drinks are another bull market beverage that is suddenly under fire. "Energy Drinks Are Fueling Concern," says the June 19 issue of The New York Times. Energy drinks complemented the bull market peak perfectly. They first hit the market at the 1987 high, when Jolt Cola

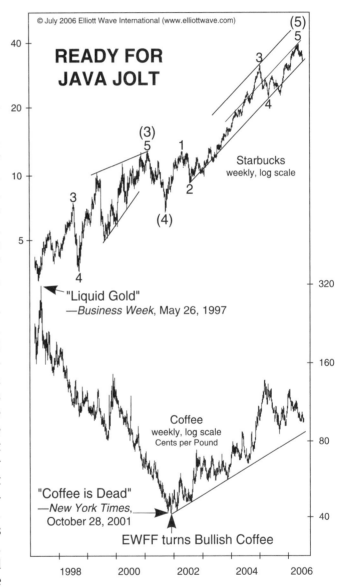

and Red Bull were introduced. At the end of the greatest top-building process in stock market history, drinks with even more bullish sounding names— such as Extreme Energy Shot, EndoRush and Ultra-Jolt—and four times the caffeine of a traditional bull market beverage, Coca-Cola (see December 1999 entry), comprise the fastest growing segment of the beverage industry.

Now, check out the latest twist, which literally cans the cross-currents of an expiring bull and a revitalized bear:

252

Energy Drinks Add Another Kick–Alcohol

—The Atlanta Journal-Constitution,
June 11, 2006

It picks you up and slows you down at the same time, the perfect cocktail for celebrating the all-time peak in the Value Line and the initiation of a third wave decline in the S&P. In a collective toast to the greatest top of all time, people everywhere are knocking back Tilt, Sparks and Liquid Charge. How long can it be before we hear: "Bartender, give me an energy drink, but hold the energy?" Not long, we bet.

September 2006

Here's another index that reflects the dissipating excitement for equities. EWI's Culture Stock Index includes four stocks: Bally Total Fitness (BFT), Callaway Golf (ELY), World Wrestling Entertainment (WWE) and Martha Stewart Living Omnimedia (MSO). All four stocks are pure plays in bull market social phenomena and thus are representative of one of the most ebullient aspects of the bull market, the public's belief that it can profit by investing in its own whimsical tastes in pop culture. The Culture Stock Index peaked in early 2005, shortly after the Dow Jones Industrials' cumulative advance/decline ratio topped in December 2004, and then failed to exceed that level later in the year. A second upside effort exhausted itself at still lower levels in March, well ahead of the Dow, S&P and small cap peaks. The culture stocks actually fell through most of the summer-long countertrend rally and are down 22% from their April high, violating a long uptrend support line.

Another measure of a late-cycle, go-for-broke mentality that has dominated the bear market's countertrend rally is the gambling boom. For this trend, Las Vegas is probably the most reliable gauge. In May 2005, EWFF observed that in the wake of Cycle wave III in 1966, a Las Vegas boom marked the final transition to a much more serious bear market and suggested that Vegas appears to peak when "the societal urge to give in and go for broke is strongest. Thus the great Vegas explosion of the 1990s, and its continuation to this day." But now Vegas appears to be coming off its highs. Signs of slack are apparent in Las Vegas real estate, car sales and gaming revenues. "Everything is changing," but no one appears to believe that the growth could actually stop. It should not be long before they are proven wrong. Contrary to popular belief, there is no such thing as a "soft" bust.

Cultural Trends

In some ways, it's not hard to spot the onset of a big bull or bear market. When the last bull market was a few years old, for instance, *The Elliott Wave Theorist* pointed to the jogging fad, which had turned into a full-blown craze for physical self-improvement, the blockbusting popularity of the movie *Rocky* and success-oriented self-help regimens as cultural evidence of the new mood. The following quote is from the *The Elliott Wave Theorist* in August 1985:

253

The first big victory for the positive mood forces in general was the public adoption of 'bootstrap' psychology. It was as if people had tired of the negative and were determined to pull themselves, each as an individual, out of that mood.

As *The Elliott Wave Theorist* explained at the time, people simply said, "I'm sick of hearing the negative!" Conversely, one of the first big victories for the negative mood forces is a spate of books that openly attack basic bull market traits such as speed, materialism and happiness for its own sake. These volumes include *Doing Nothing, In Praise of Slowness* and *Out of Control: Finding Peace for the Physically Exhausted and Spiritually Strung Out.* "The pendulum has now swung the other way," says the author of Slowness. "Speed is doing more harm than good." USA Today reveals that employees' emotional health, "a topic that once seemed incongruous with the survival-of-the-fittest corporate arena," is "no longer taboo." The list of "mood disorders" that employers are advised to "watch for" is strikingly similar to the components of bear market mood listed on pages 228-229 of *The Wave Principle of Human Social Behavior.* It includes, "persistent sadness," "loss of interest in or pleasure from activities," "decreased energy," "feelings of hopelessness or pessimism," "feelings of guilt," "thoughts of death," "irritability," "excessive crying" and "difficulty concentrating, remembering or making decisions."

It's the opposite of 1985; people are hungry for the negative. On Monday, The New York Times announced the latest downer title: Pessimism*: Philosophy, Ethic, Spirit* saying "these are ideal times" for its release. The book aims to "rescue pessimism from the philosophical sidelines, where it has been shunted by optimists of all ideologies." The NY Times reviewer describes the book as "seductive, because pessimists are generally more engaging and entertaining than optimists." The mindset will fit perfectly with a shrinking money supply and a retrenching demand for housing and luxury goods. It's no accident. Social mood always accommodates society with a disposition that conforms to its direction.

The Flagging Fixation on Millionaires

Back in April 2004, EWFF observed that one of the anecdotal signs of the uptrend's waning strength was the fading "social cachet of the millionaires." EWFF noted a return to a societal obsession with the term but found it muted by comparison. As this headline from the August 15 USA Today attests, the collective preoccupation, which first appeared in France to describe the boom-time beneficiaries of John Law's Mississippi Scheme in 1719-1720, is in place at the current highs:

$1 Million

What's the Infatuation With That Number?

But here again, the "infatuation" is losing its grip on the public. The key parallel to the highs of early 2000 and early 2004 is the emergence of another prime time TV show in which contestants vie for a $1 million prize. In 2000 and 2004 it was *Who Wants to be a Millionaire*. Now USA Today notes that *Deal or No Deal* is the vehicle through which Americans observe their "obsession with bagging the magic $1 million." But the obsession is obviously a lot less riveting now, as *Deal's* typical rating of 9.8 is only about half that of *Who Wants to be a Millionaire* at its peak in late 1999 and early 2000. In fact, *Millionaire* was so popular that NBC had it on most weekday nights. *Deal* is on just once a week. Another subtle sign of more powerful bearish forces is that no one has come close to winning a million on *Deal or No Deal*. Finally, there is the fact that *Deal* is pretty much a straight gamble whereas *Millionaire* offered the promise of prosperity through knowledge. This is a concise expression of the view of wealth causality in a bull market vs. bear.

USA Today has done its part to puncture the allure of "millionaire mania" by pointing out that a million dollars just isn't what it used to be. As a matter of fact, it's "almost pocket change for some Wall Street bankers. In pricey markets, it will barely get you a two bedroom house." "Nor does $1 million guarantee long-term happiness beyond the initial euphoria," says the author of *Money and the Meaning of Life* in the vein of the downer-theme titles listed above. The author adds that having $1 million is a "cheap symbol of success," one that fails to feed "one's inner life, moral value and spirituality." Here too, social mood is self-sustaining. It provides all kinds of routes to wealth destruction, which thereby tends to rouse a former millionaire's inner life.

The emergence of a bearish twist on the concept of becoming an instant millionaire is another important connection to the summer of 2000, when the first leg of the bear market was in the same wave position as the current decline is now. The July 2000, EWFF stated that one key pop culture clue

that "hints at a 180-degree turn" was *Who Wants to Be A Millionaire*'s June 2000 ratings loss to an emerging new show called *Survivor*, a "reality" program that offered $1 million to the lone survivor of a grueling jungle contest. The socionomic implications of the latest *Survivor* series are even more starkly bearish. In the current edition of the show, contestants for the $1 million prize will be divided into four teams — blacks, Asians, Latinos and whites. The racial format has "enraged" many who say it promotes divisiveness. As we said in March, the "coming trend of negative social psychology will be characterized by polarization between and among various racial" groups. Protestors want the show banned, an impulse that also betrays the shift of the trend from up to down. As EWFF said in July 2000, "one of the most visible images of a mood shift" is being broadcast on network TV. So be sure and stay tuned.

October 2006

> *To achieve harmony in bad taste is the height of elegance.* — Jean Genet

Stocks are up, and hemlines are rising with them as they generally do, but Bergdorf Goodman's fall fashion catalogue is anything but bullish. Yes, some short skirts are back, but there's nothing alluring about the cold, almost comatose look of the models In July 2005, EWFF argued, "Bear market styles are taking over." The fall season marks another step in fashion's inexorable movement toward truly bearish styles. No matter how much leg they may show, a September 19 fashion article from the Washington Post observes that the fall lines are not about "sex appeal:"

Clothes Reflect Dark Times

This fall, fashion takes a journey to the dark side. One industry watcher calls the new look "reflective chic." It looks as if Jessica Simpson and Lindsay Lohan soon won't have much to wear. The fall season's runways were a sea of monochromatic, often monastic gray and black dresses, tops and jackets. There were some cheeky platform shoes in the mix, but on the whole, the shows made ritzy, revealing starlet style seem about as fashion-forward as parachute pants.

Designers have been churning out darker themes for some time. Of course, the public has yet to embrace them, but the stark contrast to, and steady movement away from, the colorful and revealing styles of 2000 when the NASDAQ and S&P reached their all-time highs is a powerful sign that the bear market is laying the groundwork for broad public acceptance of mostly longer skirts, darker colors and various body coverings of the last few years.

The one whimsical item mentioned in the Post article, platform shoes, fits right in with the stock market transition from a bear market rally to a renewed downtrend. Back in May 2001 when Japan was enjoying a major platform shoe revival, we showed a pair of our own vintage 1973 platforms and said:

> The bear market is still in mid-trend [in Japan]. One cultural clue is the emergence of 'super-platform' shoes. Last year, platform soles of up to nine inches became popular among "girl fashion gangs" and women who want to emulate the gangs' look. A similar excess for men hit the U.S. footwear market in 1973 when the bear market in inflation-adjusted terms was only about half over. For the Japanese market, then, this appears to be cultural confirmation that the bear market has a ways to go. The message for people who remember 1970s relics, don't buy stocks on the Nikkei too soon.

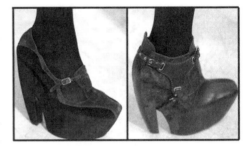

The Nikkei promptly fell another 40% by October 2002. An Internet "History of the Platform Shoe" records that other than the last bear market of the 1970s, the only "in" phase for platform shoes was the 1930s. So, the style coincides with the two most bearish decades of the last century.

According to one couture writer, platform shoes are "dangerous to say nothing of gaudy," which is why they've always been a fashion faux pas in uptrends. But they go great with downtrends because, as EWFF noted in September 2002, "Poor taste is a hallmark of a bear market." At the end of a rally phase of a bear market, the fashionable literally lift themselves back toward former heights with several inches of corked footwear. Another possible aspect of social mood is touched on in this observation from the New York Daily News: "Platforms uncover women's inner fierceness. Can't the world use a little of that right now?" Of course it can, because as EWI's cultural studies attest: "Women gain dominance in a bear market." What better way to express this than platform shoes? If history is any guide, soles will rise as the Dow falls.

November 2006

In another parallel to the March 2000 peak when HBO unveiled *Bull*, a TV series about "people making big money," two new television shows focus on hedge funds, their proprietors and all the money that they are rolling in. One is a documentary series, *Wall Street Warriors*, which appears on cable network INHD, and the other is an as-yet-untitled drama that will tell the story of a forty-something hedge fund trader. Like *Bull*, money is the real star of the show. Or as the show's creator puts it, "New money, the kind you don't inherit—puts you on a different stratosphere, and that's what I think will be interesting in this show. What happens when you've made all this money? What kind of stress does it put on your relationships." He also says it will be based on "real events in the hedge fund world." If that's true, the stress produced by falling from the stratosphere should make for fascinating story lines as the financial markets accelerate lower in unison.

December 2006
The New Era of Wealth Destruction

Back in November 1999 when Bill Gates' net worth equaled 1% of U.S. GDP, pundits latched on to a growing gap between the rich and poor. *The Elliott Wave Financial Forecast* said not to worry, these situations invariably take care of themselves:

> In the 1930s, the wealth distribution problem was "solved" by a falling market and tax rates of better than 90% for the wealthiest Americans. In the second half of 1999, the same social forces can be seen stirring, as the "growing gulf between the haves and the have-nots" has suddenly become an issue. The seeds of a new social movement were visible in a rash of headlines like this one: "Income Inequalities Reach 'Grotesque' Gap, U.N. Says." A bear market is nature's way of redistributing wealth, but apparently, at a trend change as big as this one, people just cannot wait to get in there and lend a hand.

The timing of the last wealth disparity alarm makes a more important point. They tend to arrive at big peaks. The first order of business for the new Democratic-led Congress is raising the minimum wage. The consensus surrounding the first increase since 1997 shows that politicians are "beginning to address the growing wealth disparity." A raise is the one item on the Democratic agenda that President Bush says he can accommodate. At this approaching peak, even the rich are starting to resent the rich. Over the course of the last two weeks, The New York Times has run a series of stories on how the "Very Rich Are Leaving the Merely Rich Behind." "The moment has arrived for a battle" between the rich and the superrich, says another Times article. The "divide has emerged" due to "windfalls tied largely to expanding financial markets" and a newfound belief that "making money out of money" is a crass way to make a living. This headline points to the driving sentiment behind the collective angst over wealth: "Rich Now Envy the Superrich." As *The Elliott Wave Theorist* pointed out in 1997, envy plays a big role in the very biggest peaks. In 1999, *The Elliott Wave Theorist* reproduced a Newsweek cover that identified the "Whine of '99" as "Everyone's Getting RICH But Me!" At the follow-up top now forming, the cry is a less comprehensive, "Some people are getting even richer than me!" But it's the same basic emotion, one that will guide the proceedings as the social mood turns down. In the words of Emmanual Kant, envy "aims, at least in terms of one's wishes, at destroying others' good fortune."

The global scope of the issue is evident in a stream of reports from around the world. "Economic Gaps Grow in Mexico," says a recent headline in the Austin American-Statesman. While 47% of Mexicans live on less than $4 a day, "Mexico's wealthiest residents inhabit a parallel universe of fortified mansions, posh shopping malls and separate movie theaters. They live in surreal mini-cities of gleaming, geometric towers. And most are breathing a big sigh of relief that next week conservative Felipe Calderon will be sworn in as president instead of Andres Manuel Lopez Obrador, who vowed to end the privileges of Mexico's elite." Obrador lost and continues to contest a close election, but radical populists have taken control in Bolivia, Venezuela and Ecuador. In Nicaragua, Daniel Ortega, the socialist leader who battled the United States from 1979 to 1990, just won re-election. Recent headlines extol the dangers of expanding "wealth gaps" in Asia, Africa, Afghanistan and the Mideast. According to a recent World Bank report, China's poor "grew poorer at a time when the country was growing substantially wealthier." This is nothing new, as the article points out that the gap has been growing since 1980. What's new is the recognition and growing desire to "do something" about it. In the Persian Gulf, where the condition is almost as old as the world's reliance on fossil fuels, the ruling elites are addressing the issue head on. Here's the latest from the Arab News agency:

Fair Distribution of Wealth Assured

JEDDAH, 15 November 2006 — Crown Prince Sultan, deputy premier and minister of defense and aviation, yesterday emphasized the government's plan to ensure fair distribution of wealth by establishing new development projects all over the Kingdom.

Ironically, one of the biggest projects is the encouragement of stock ownership and the establishment of exchanges throughout the Mideast. Like the Dubai Financial Market, these markets are all getting hammered. So far this year, Saudi Arabia's main index is down 60% while Qatar is down 44% and Jordan is off 36%. Government efforts to spread wealth are always counterproductive. The harder it tries, the more it ruins. Locking the less wealthy into stocks in a bear market will be the last nail in their coffin.

One More Wacky Time for Bidders

Apparently, when it comes to toy crazes, the great mania wants to leave off right where it started. For the first time since Christmas 1999, there's a bona-fide bidding frenzy surrounding a must-have toy—Elmo TMX, or Tickle Me Extreme. The toy is actually the 10th anniversary edition of Tickle Me Elmo, which sparked the first holiday bidding frenzy in 1996.

So far, Elmo TMX is not generating the price appreciation of the original. The range on eBay appears to be $50 to $140. Still for an item that is probably overpriced at $40 retail and likely to fall fast after Christmas, it bears the unmistakably daffy thumbprint of the great mania.

Other tried and true manifestations of the craziness have appeared in the usual places. After some relatively tame seasons, contracts for baseball and soccer players are skyrocketing again. Manchester United's Wayne Rooney just signed a £100 million, six-year deal that will make him the highest-paid player in British football history. A 14-ounce bottle of Scotch whisky from the 1850s just sold for $28,700 at auction in London, beating the top presale estimate by almost 50%. The fall art sales broke all the records. More than $1.3 billion in works of art were sold in two weeks. The all-time record performance exhibited "broad strength throughout the market." "Experienced dealers were astonished by some of the prices paid," reports the Financial Times. "The worldwide boom shows no sign of slowing, with hedge fund managers providing a fresh pool of buyers." As EWFF has previously noted, art price spikes marked stock peaks in 1990 and 2000.

January 2007
The Peak Etches Out a New Skyline

No matter how wobbly, the stock averages indicate that the direction of social mood is up. This trend is evident in the further spread of the skyscraper boom that was covered here in April. We followed with a December 22 SocioTimes.com post, but even this recent update is out of date. According to a CNN article, over the next 10 years, 434 new buildings of more than 50 stories are expected to be built around the world. That compares to the construction of 630 buildings of similarly lofty proportions during the past 100 years. In a 160-story representation of the peak in the U.S. housing and equity markets, the Chicago Spire is set to surpass the Sears Tower as the tallest building in North America. It will be 300 feet higher than the Sears Tower and consist entirely of condominiums. In Manhattan, the financial peak anticipated in this month's Special Section is signaled by Vornado Realty's latest bid to entice financial tenants with five floors (100,000 square feet) of trading space in its latest project. The height of the building is still being worked out, but the firm plans to replace the Hotel Pennsylvania across from Penn Station with an office building that is roughly the size of the Empire State Building.

In England, a rapid succession of new projects are leading a "renaissance in British high-rise architecture." London, Birmingham, Manchester, Liverpool, Leeds, Brighton and Edinburgh are "vying for the buildings with the best superlatives." By 2010, London's skyline will be dominated by the London Bridge Tower, a 310 meter (1,017 feet) building that will surpass the 235-meter Canary Wharf to become the tallest building in Europe. Work is also planned on five other London skyscrapers. Similar building panics are in progress in China, India, Russia and, of course,

Dubai, where several towers including the world's tallest tower are now under construction (see chart in April issue). The unprecedented global burst into the skies marks a dramatic transition from 2002, when EWFF noted that the very concept of skyscrapers was under siege. In the heart of a bear market, extremely tall buildings no longer made economic sense. "After terrorists crashed two commercial jets into the Twin Towers in New York City we read many stories about how the age of skyscrapers had ended," says one account of the new boom. With the latest peak in social mood, this thinking is being turned on its head: "Building vertically instead of horizontally makes sense because a building that takes up the space of one city block can house an entire community." In bull and bear markets, reason slides with the trend. The lightning fast transition from the "end of the skyscraper" to the tallest construction binge on record only hints at the depth of the next downswing.

February 2007

One of the most ominous trends that EWFF covered in each of the last two issues is a rising global wealth discrepancy between rich and poor and, more important, the public's emerging impatience with the divide. In a January 22 cover story, however, Barron's describes the trend as a long term reality that presents "exploitable investment opportunities." It offers a basket of luxury stocks that includes Coach (COH), Sotheby's (BID); Polo Ralph Lauren (RL), Tiffany (TIF); Four Seasons Hotels (FS); Bulgari (BUL.Italy); and LBMH (MC.France). Stocks "of this ilk already have outpaced the broad market over recent years." The key phrase in this forecast is "already have." In the "era of wealth destruction" that EWFF described in December and January, luxury stocks will set the pace. But it won't be in the direction that these investment strategists expect. The effort to cash in on the wealth gap is a late-stage phenomenon. The same stocks will fall faster than the markets when the bear trend resumes.

March 2007
Broadcasting A Sell Signal

In another reflection of the blazing optimism represented by the arrows on the Stock Market Orgasmatron chart (in Chapter 4's entry for March 2007), the total number of financial television networks is about to double to two. News Corp. announced the launch of a new cable financial network: FOX Business Channel. In announcing the decision to challenge CNBC, Rupert Murdoch said, "We have long considered the business television market to be underserved." Ironically, the decision finally to commit confirms that some riveting financial drama is about to take place. If FOX gets on the air soon it will be able to report some of the most dramatic footage in stock market history. In another unmistakable indication of an oncoming train wreck for stocks, CNBC's lead news anchor Maria Bartiromo filed to trademark her "Money Honey" nickname with the U.S. patent office. Bartiromo intends to use the moniker as a brand on mouse pads, jigsaw puzzles, dolls, backpacks, school supplies and other items. Just think how great a Money Honey pen and pencil set will look next to our collection of Beanie Babies.

May 2007

The Dow and S&P are floating higher with amazing persistence. A big reason for the persistence is that there appear to be no earnest sellers left. Even long-time bears are throwing in the towel. This week a colleague of ours received a request from one of the shows on CNBC begging him to appear as a bear because bearish analysts are so scarce they can't find any. A day later,

Bob Prechter got a similar request. They probably found about a third of the remaining bears right there.

In the social realm, the difference in trends [between the 2000 peak in the Real Dow—Dow Industrials divided by gold—and the 2007 peak in the nominal Dow] is evident in the sagging popularity of the U.S. president. From August 1980 to August 1982, the approval ratings for the president increased from 32% to 42% even though nominal stock prices went lower. Since the peak in 2000, presidential approval has gone the other way, falling from 59% to 35% even as the nominal Dow has risen. These popularity trends followed the Real Dow. The roster of bear market consequences also includes an increasingly unpopular war, a cultural fascination with horror movies and the erection of walls in Tijuana, Baghdad and Gaza. When the bull market was in mid-form, the walls were coming down. After the fall of the Berlin Wall in 1989 EWT explained, "When times are bad, intolerance for differences grows, and people build walls and fences to shut out those perceived to be different." As the rally in the nominal Dow exhausts itself, the fences are going up. As we know from the early 1980s, a powerful trend can get ahead of itself in various ways, but prices always catch up.

It's Root, Root, Root For the Stock Market

At the really big tops, distinct elements of a bull market have a tendency to connect with each other. A good example is Martha Stewart's equitization, as Martha Stewart Omnimedia two months before the January 2000 peak. In a sign that the developing high is a twin to that

peak, the premier issue of a new Conde Nast investment magazine, Portfolio, reports that the first public stock market that trades in professional athletes is being constructed by a well-financed company in Silicon Valley. According to the plan, athletes will eventually "be able to sell 20% of all future on-field or on-court earnings to a trust, which would, in turn, sell securities to the public." The author notes that fans already have tremendous "emotional" and "speculative" ties to athletes, as they are objects of fervent observation and wagering. The ability literally to invest in sports figures marks a coalescing of positive mood forces, as EWI previously identified baseball and basketball as bull market sports in 1985 and 1996, respectively. As Portfolio says, "The analogy with the stock market holds." A big top is the perfect moment for sports stars to be re-packaged as investments because it is the point of maximum distance from an understanding of how painful it can be to lose everything, not to mention the risk of adding insult to injury when the asset you once had no more than a rooting interest in turns out to be a bum.

Call us crazy, but we believe that the conversion of fans into investors is very likely an extreme in the equity culture that cannot long endure. As EWFF has illustrated in the form of a weak rebound in our chart of key culture stocks Martha Stewart Omnimedia, World Wrestling Entertainment and Callaway Golf (see preceding entry for September 2006), the culture-wide incursion into the stock market has actually been tiring for some time. Further evidence appeared recently in Russia, where President Vladimir Putin attempted to fuel enthusiasm for equities by using televised speeches and press conferences to tout shares of state-controlled companies OAO Rosneft, Russia's second-biggest oil company, and OAO Sberbank, its largest bank. Another news item that suggests frustration rather than the cultural adulation that characterized the equity culture in 2000 is the story of the Iowa machine shop worker who sent threatening letters and pipe bombs to investment firms, "in an effort to drive up stock prices." The man threatened to harm executives and their families unless shares of Navarre Corp. and 3Com, both of which were down substantially from earlier peaks, did not rise. He was caught without incident last week.

Here's one more mixed signal from the equity culture: The woman accused of running a prostitution ring serving Washington's elite turns out to be "something of a stock picker." Deborah Jeane Palfrey asked a federal judge on Monday for permission to sell almost 5,000 shares of Dolby Laboratories that were in an account frozen by the government. "I believe it's reached its peak," she told the judge. The stocks quickly dropped almost 20% in less than a week before recently rebounding. Her liquidity problem is clearly unique, but Washington's madam is at the forefront of the future. The fear of being locked in to a falling stock is one that will be widespread in the next major phase of the bear market.

June 2007

The legacy of 1719/1720 is borne out by the latest flare-up in the veneration of millionaires. Recall that EWFF has tracked the phenomenon back through the Mississippi scheme itself. In fact, the word "millionaire" was first used there to describe the nouveau riche that the bubble created. The fascination with the term regained its grip over the public imagination in 1929 and 2000. In September, EWFF noted a return to a societal interest in "millionaire-ness" but found the obsession muted by comparison to the *Who Wants To Be A Millionaire* frenzy of 2000. This may not be the case in Asia where a million goes a lot further. The latest lifestyle magazine, MillionaireAsia, was launched with a lavish May 13 bash. "MillionaireAsia is dedicated to the celebration of the Millionaire lifestyle where money is no object," says the magazine. It's truly amazing how thoroughly the tapestry of the Great Asset Mania weaves the threads of past bubbles into its framework. There is, of course, one missing piece, which is the most important element of all. This was also covered in the EWT's Special Report of May 1997: "Every mania is followed by a decline that ends below the starting point of the advance." The advance is exciting, but the decline should be even more compelling human drama. While the bubble markets flare in succession, the move below the starting point should culminate in unison.

July 2007

This is the 40th anniversary of the Summer of Love, which came a year after the end of Cycle wave III. To the extent that it can replicate the good feelings of 1967, the summer of 2007 may try to deliver the same type of optimism. But any flower child of the 1960s can tell you, "everything changed" after that. With social mood so tightly wound and a turn of much higher degree at hand, the coming change should be much more dramatic.

Gordon Gekko Rides Again

Here's another parallel to the last big peak from the March 2000 issue of *The Elliott Wave Financial Forecast*:

> Like the peak of 1987, which was soon followed by the movie *Wall Street* and Gordon Gekko's "greed is good" credo, the current stock-market peak now has a cynical, feature-length motion picture to encapsulate its excesses. In a story "to match the giddy heights of the Dow," *Boiler Room* is a "gritty" drama that explores "the shady side of Wall Street."

Boiler Room included scenes from *Wall Street* and came out in February 2000, when the Dow Jones Industrial Average was a month past its high. Now the word is that Gordon Gekko himself is returning to the silver screen signaling an even more important top than that of 2000. A sequel to *Wall Street*, to be called *Money Never Sleeps*, is in the works. It's still a ways off, but the original *Wall Street* (there are several movies with similar names) also went into production before the top and didn't actually appear until December 1987, four months after the Dow's August 1987 peak and as the dust from the crash was still in the air. A previous *Wall Street* came out right after the crash in 1929. Another movie drama, *Wall Street Tragedy*, appeared in 1916, just as the Dow was completing a multi-year counter-trend rally. All three Wall Street movies explore similar themes of greed, ruthless capitalism and ruination.

Every mania has elements of greed and envy, but it is only near the end of the advance that the public becomes aware of them. Where the rising mood conceals these darker emotions, the

decline draws them out. As anger grows, they become a common preoccupation. Thus occurs the epic "fall from grace" for many high flyers. Those that leverage the rising mood with debt or unethical investment practices are the most vulnerable when the trend changes. In addition to *Money Never Sleeps*, CNBC's latest primetime effort, *American Greed*, signals a reviving fascination with the sordid side of high finance. The series, subtitled "Scams, Scoundrels and Scandals," "examines the dark side of the American Dream." When stocks top and the mood turns darker, series like this one hold the potential to be a smashing success.

One of the more prominent signs of a rising bull market is "the public adoption of 'bootstrap' psychology." Back in 1985, *The Elliott Wave Theorist* first recognized its influence at the start of Cycle V: "It was as if people had tired of the negative and were determined to pull themselves, each as an individual, out of that mood." A classic example of this impulse is the success of self-help books, which is a bull market genre if ever there were one. It was pretty much born with *How to Win Friends and Influence People* and *Think and Grow Rich* at the end of Cycle I in 1936 and 1937, respectively. In the 1950s a slew of titles including the all-time biggest, *The Power of Positive Thinking*, coincided with a series of third-wave rallies. It gave voice to the century's most powerful blast of positive mood.

The latest self-help smash is *The Secret*, a book and 90-minute DVD that's been raking in the sales since right before the Dow Jones Industrial Average moved to a new all-time high. Like *Think and Grow Rich* at the end of Cycle I, *The Secret* is a smash hit that is capping a five-year rise in social mood. There are, however, some important differences. For one thing, *The Secret* is no secret. It is a rehash of past self-help advice. Another distinction is the approach that it advocates. Unlike *Think and Grow Rich*, in which readers had to think and plan to attain their dreams, *The Secret* espouses a "law of attraction," which says you can have whatever you want if you will only imagine yourself having it. "The explicit claim," observes columnist Jerry Adler, is that you "can manipulate objective physical reality—the numbers in a lottery drawing, the actions of other people who may not even know you exist—through your thoughts

and feelings." At the end of the long rise, the idea of "pulling yourself up by the bootstraps" has given way to a world in which gaining material possessions is possible through three mental steps: "Ask, believe, receive." "If you keep saying it the way you want it to be, the universe will line up and give you exactly what you've said you wanted." The approach is a perfect set-up for complete failure in a bear market.

October 2007

The dramatic departure from the strictly positive course of the late 1990s and 2000s has been the multi-month key reversal in cultural trends. We tabbed this the "social divergence" and in May noted that it is largely a reflection of the bear market behavior in the DJIA priced in terms of real money, which is gold. These two charts explain why we like to call this ratio the Real Dow. History shows that the Real Dow has a way of sifting out the underlying trend in social mood. The top chart (next page) shows a positive divergence from 1980 to 1982 when the Real Dow held up against a fall in the nominal Dow. The arrows illustrate various key manifestations of the positive mood that was unfolding according to the Real Dow. One of the most important was the election of an optimist, Ronald Reagan, to the office of President. Reagan would go on

to become one of the most revered U.S. presidents (according to a 2006 CBS News account, the most admired since 1945). Other developments reflecting an emerging optimistic time in the face of a net decline in the nominal Dow were the initiation of space shuttle flights, sales of the first personal computer by IBM and a breakthrough moment for Michael Jackson, who would go on to become the musical hero of the 1980s bull market. Another clear expression of developing optimism was the blockbuster debut of *E.T. The Extra-Terrestrial* in June 1982, two months before the final low in the nominal Dow. *E.T.* was the biggest box office hit in history. The movie about a boy who bonds with a creature from outer space expresses an inclusionistic view of the universe, which is a bull market trait. As *The Wave Principle of Human Social Behavior* explains, "A rising mood leads to feelings of social brotherhood and acceptance among races, as well as toward animals, plants and proposed aliens."

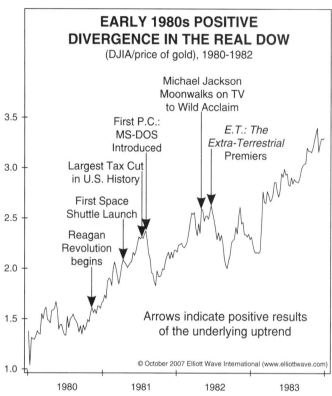

The chart chronicles the effects of the huge decline in the Real Dow the last seven years. There are many more negative mood developments than we have arrows—everything from the emergence of no-holds-barred Ultimate Fighting as the sport of the future to rising tension over immigration. The chart shows some of the most important bearish manifestations. Like World War II and the first Persian Gulf War, the war in Iraq actually started right after a major low and was initially popular in the United States. But it has grown steadily less so ever since. The trend toward unpopularity follows the Real Dow instead of the nominal Dow. According to various headlines, the "surge" failed by June, and public approval of George Bush's handling of the war in Iraq reached an all-time low of 22% in July.

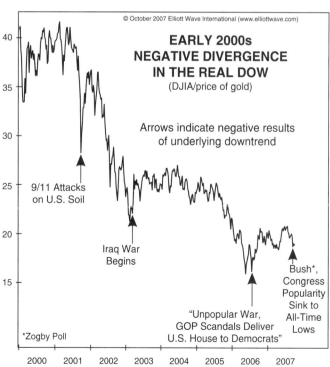

Here is another revealing set of statistics: From an initial bottom in April 1980 to the low of August 1982, the Gallup Poll approval rating for the U.S. president actually rose, from 39% to 42%. From the peak in 2000 to the peak in July, presidential approval plunged from 63% to 29%. According to the Zogby poll, Bush just slipped to a new low (also 29%). "The public mood is not just dark. What's darker than dark?" says pollster John Zogby. "The mood is getting ugly."

The Real Dow and its foreign counterparts forecast political unrest around the world. This is exactly what we do see, as most major democracies are undergoing leadership changes or have done so within the last 18 months. Decidedly bearish political pressures are driving many of the changes. In Japan, for instance, "nationalistic ideas" were "heretical in postwar Japan but have gathered public support in recent years." Among other things, USA Today says that Japanese nationalists want to "rewrite history, erasing bits about sneak attacks and massacres." The "main political ambition" of the new prime minister, Yasuo Fukuda, is to "restore Japan's national pride which it lost with the military defeat of 1945."

After 11 years in office, conservative Australian PM John Howard is expected to fall to a Labor Party challenger before the year is out. The country's newly formed Protectionist Party hopes to institute tariff barriers against cheap foreign imports and implement a zero-net immigration policy. In Switzerland, the Swiss People's Party hopes to introduce a penal code that will allow judges to deport foreigners who commit serious crimes. For offenders under 18, it wants to kick their families out, too. "It will be the first such law in Europe since the Nazi practice of Sippenhaft—kin liability," reports the Independent. These are still fringe parties, but they show a clear splintering effect that HSB identifies as a bear market political trait. These are just the political expressions. In sports, fashion and most other social fields, the bear market is asserting itself in ways that will provide lots of fodder for the future study of bear markets.

January 2008

Considering the significance of the big turn, it figures that it is finding some exquisite ways to express itself on the big screen. As one critic noted, movies "were awash in dark themes and violence" in 2007. Among the most acclaimed is *Sweeney Todd: The Demon Barber of Fleet Street*. The musical starring Johnny Depp just premiered to glowing reviews, but its bear market pedigree actually dates back to 1846, when the U.S. was still dealing with the social manifestations of Supercycle wave (II) and British stock prices were locked in a long bear market. Sweeney Todd was the key character in *The String of Pearls*, a melodrama based on a Victorian pulp horror book. Bear markets demand their anti-heroes, and *Sweeney Todd* represents something of a bear-market breakthrough. According to playwright Montagu Slater, Todd was "unique among bad guy protagonists because he showed no remorse for his evil deeds and his motivation was entirely selfish." In the original stage adaptation, dramatist George Dibdin Pitt "made the great discovery that there was no need to whitewash the criminal; on the contrary, he was better blackwashed. The important thing is to make him a supreme criminal, a demon." In 1979, when the Dow Jones Industrials were near the end of a Cycle degree decline (in inflation-adjusted terms), Stephen Sondheim scored a huge hit by bringing *Sweeney Todd* to Broadway. The play won eight Tony awards and ran through the March 1980 stock market low. This time the bear market is two degrees larger, so the film will not mark a low. Much more violent fare will accompany the bottom.

Nevertheless, there could hardly be a more appropriate moment for the film version. N.Y. Times' critic A.O. Scott reveals that its creators, Sondheim and goth film director Tim Burton, have "systematically subverted" two of the most optimistic genres of popular art: movies and musicals. On the one hand, *The Demon Barber* appeals to the lingering influences of the long bull market by wringing "some grim, boisterous comedy out of both the impulse for vengeance and the bustling spirit of commerce." But with a "subtext of anxiety and alienation," the NY Times review says, "Sweeney is as much a horror film as a musical. It is cruel in its effects and radical in its misanthropy, expressing a breathtakingly, rigorously pessimistic view of human nature."

Another aspect of *Sweeney Todd*'s bear market appeal is its attack on industry and "obtaining and keeping profits." A second release in which the bear market appears to be foreshadowing an approaching antagonism toward business and markets, as well as picking up where the last Cycle degree bear market left off, is *The Mist*. The movie is adapted from a Stephen King short story that first appeared in 1980. Unlike some of the "tearjerker" King stories, like *Stand By Me* (1986), *The Shawshank Redemption* (1994) and *The Green Mile* (1999) that made it to the big screen in the bull market of the 1980s and 1990s, this is a classic horror story. The film is set in an idyllic Maine coastal town that becomes enveloped in a giant mist. As it sets in, the protagonist and his son find themselves among horrified shoppers at the local market. As the world outside the storefront disappears in the fog, co-star Laurie Holden says "the monsters inside of the store turn out to be more frightening than the creatures outside." Sounds like the current-day derivatives markets.

Take Me Out to The Ballgame (So I Can Boo)

Here's the case *The Elliott Wave Financial Forecast* made in 2005 for a link between the game of baseball and the mortgage giant Fannie Mae:

> What's the difference between the steroids controversy in baseball and the accounting crisis at Fannie Mae? From a socionomics perspective, there is none. The slackening of accounting rules that allowed corporations to pump up their financial statements and the use of performance-enhancing substances by professional baseball players are just separate mediums through which the peak mood of the 1990s and early 2000s "juiced up" the social environment to reflect the end of a 200-year bull market.

After levitating in the face of one accounting scandal after another, Fannie Mae shares cratered last month. This month, it's baseball's turn. After years of simmering in the background as baseball continued to make marginal new highs in attendance, the steroid scandal hit page 1 in mid-December on just about every newspaper. Even though the Mitchell Report was composed mostly of previously reported stories and allegations about the use of "performance-enhancing drugs," the charges resonated like never before." "This has not been an isolated prob-

lem," said former senator George Mitchell. "Everyone involved in baseball over the past two decades—commissioners, club officials, the players association and players—share to some extent the responsibility for the steroids era." As USA Today's front-page of December 14 emphasizes, it was a "collective" experience that took place in a "culture that allowed it." Why? Because early bull market standards erode and cheating proliferates in the final stage of a long bull market. It's almost as if people have to break the rules to keep pace with their enthusiasm.

Another factor is that society becomes so permissive that otherwise law-abiding and conservative participants bend the rules to keep pace with their neighbors and colleagues. Punitive and reactionary bear market forces re-establish the old order, usually with jarring force. The clamor surrounding the Mitchell Report suggests that the collective experience is changing fast. As many commentators noted, steroids in baseball is old news. Baseball's years-long resiliency caused one columnist to estimate that the scandal will be "vanishing from the public's mind within weeks, maybe days. In fact, by spring training, most folks will be discussing balls and strikes more than syringes and HGH." On the contrary, stumbling stock prices and the sudden momentum behind the steroids scandal suggest strongly that the public, which is entering a new trend toward negative social mood, is now ready to deal with the rumors in a tangible way. As long as the Dow was rising, baseball fans were willing to "look the other way." No one stepped in to stop Barry Bonds from breaking the all-time home run record. On November 15, Bonds was indicted for lying under oath to a grand jury four years ago. Some argue that baseball and federal authorities are finally putting the pressure on Bonds to "protect America's pastime from the harm it deserves." A USA Today/Gallup Poll says that 60% of fans think that baseball should "punish" drug users. As the Dow falls hard, attendance will fall sharply and the complacency of recent years will stand in stark contrast to the anger of many former fans. Baseball will probably survive, but as social mood finally bottoms out, the jeers will so overwhelm the cheers in many ballparks that many will warn of its demise.

June 2008

Back in 1996, when the Great Asset Mania was starting skyward, *The Elliott Wave Theorist* looked around at a proliferation of coffee shops and back to a similar trend at two very important historical counterpoints. During the South Sea Bubble of 1720, Charles Mackay's *Extraordinary Popular Delusions and The Madness of Crowds* records that brokers operated out of coffee houses, and the career of our own R.N. Elliott took a turn toward the tea room rage of the 1920s. EWT detected the following pattern in the demand for stimulating drinks:

> Strictly from the evidence of today's coffee house popularity, we can write the following formula: 17-teens ≈ 1920s ≈ 1990s. Hm. That's the same formula indicated by the wave pattern in the stock market!

The blue chip exploiter of this bull market's coffee binge is, of course, Starbucks. Like the bull market that it represents, Starbucks is a coffee business of gargantuan proportions with more than 15,000 stores in 44 countries. Its expansion started in 1987, when Starbucks opened its first stores outside of Seattle, as the middle wave of the great bull market was peaking. When it went public in 1992, it had just 165 outlets. Through the 1990s and the first half of the 2000s, Starbucks' stock exploded. It was coming off an all-time high in May 2006 when EWFF spotted the completion of a

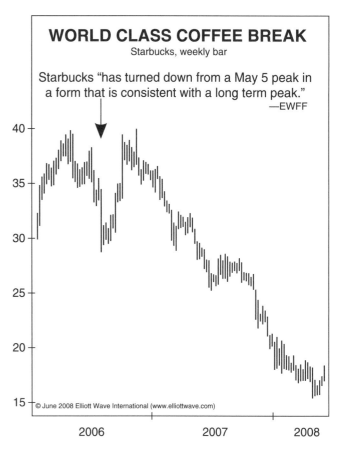

WORLD CLASS COFFEE BREAK
Starbucks, weekly bar

Starbucks "has turned down from a May 5 peak in a form that is consistent with a long term peak."
—EWFF

© June 2008 Elliott Wave International (www.elliottwave.com)

five-wave rise followed by an initial impulse wave down and called a top. Starbucks staged one more rally to a new intraday high, but it failed to exceed the May 2006 peak on a closing basis. Since that November intraday high, Starbucks is down 55%. As usual, the market is out in front of the fundamentals, as sales of Starbucks' "premium coffee experience" are now beginning to fall off; profits plunged 28% in the first quarter. Starbucks "blames its recent disappointing performance on a new unwillingness among coffee drinkers in California and South Florida to pay top dollar for stimulants." Socionomically this translates to: It's time to wake up and not smell the coffee. It's a bear market.

We further theorize that there is a similar bull market affinity for restaurants in general. Here's the reasoning that EWT offered in 1998:

> People feel good, they like to get out, be seen, eat well and drink socially. This makes restaurants a focal point for the expression of a bull market mood.

Here too, EWT has traced the connection back hundreds of years. One key parallel is to the first true American restaurant, Delmonico's, which began operations at the end of Supercycle wave I in 1835. At the end of a Grand Supercycle uptrend, the urge to dine socially and the urge to invest in stocks was so broad and powerful that the two manifestations of a rising mood merged into one phenomenon: the restaurant stock. In recent months, most restaurant stocks have suddenly fallen on hard times. Stocks of companies such as Brinker International (Chili's, Macaroni Grill) and Darden Restaurants (Longhorn Steakhouse, Red Lobster) are down 30% and 40%, respectively, as "people are treating themselves less often." The industry reports that the number of diners is down and orders are smaller. According to the National Restaurant Association's Performance Index, which tracks the health and outlook for the entire U.S. restaurant industry, the slowdown began last year. As the chart shows, the industry crossed into contraction early this year and is now below the lowest rate established in late 2002. So here again, a contraction is already below its level at the end of the last recession. This quick weakness confirms that the budding contraction is no recession but something much larger. By the time it is over, many of the restaurants that line the malls and highways of the country will be long gone.

The restaurant chart is interesting because it reflects the course of many bull market cultural icons and activities over the last few years. Most rebounded from depressed levels in 2001-2002 but then failed to move back to the heights achieved in 2000. After trailing off in 2004-2007, many have fallen off dramatically in recent weeks. These range from playing golf (according to the New York Times "More Americans Are Giving Up Golf") to watching Oprah, whose feel-good talk has dominated day-time TV since the bull market of the 1980s hit its stride. This week it emerged that average audiences for the The Oprah Winfrey Show fell nearly 7% in 2008 from a peak in 2004. Oprah's approach and message are the same, but suddenly, she can't seem to do anything right. *Oprah's Big Give*, a prime-time philanthropy show, was launched with huge fanfare before Christmas, then lost a third of its audience during an eight-week run. Circulation at her magazine, O, is down 10% over three years. "The universal adulation that turned Oprah into the most popular TV host in history is

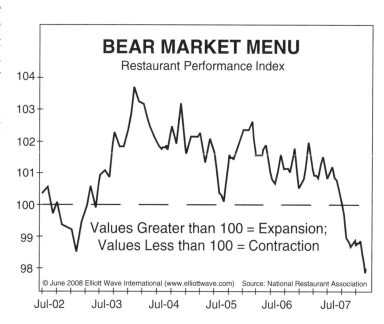

no more," says one review. "Her longstanding Midas touch is vanishing fast." But what's really vanishing fast is the positive social mood that supported both stock prices and Oprah. Upbeat public symbols and personalities just don't play well in a beaten-down social environment.

July 2008

In January, EWFF identified 2008 as the "year everything changes." Recognition of the reversal's stunning depth is finally starting to appear in the cultural realm as well. In "Everything Seemingly Is Spinning Out of Control," the Associated Press connects a "dour powerlessness" to an "onslaught of dispiriting things" such as global warming, floods, food scares and a television writers strike and says that it is "chipping away at the country's sturdy conviction that destiny can be commanded by sheer courage and perseverance." Of course, this comes as no surprise to the average consumer. According to most sentiment surveys, their level of confidence is already back to where it was in the early 1980s, when the Dow was 10,000 points lower. At this point, an ABC News-Washington Post survey finds that just 14% of respondents believe the country is moving in the right direction. That's the lowest total in the 30+ year history of the survey.

The AP article asks "There's always sports, right?" Our answer is that, on paper at least, sports still reflect a long bull market in social mood. The bull market game of basketball just completed a successful season, with a championship series between the Boston Celtics and L.A. Lakers, a rivalry that also capped the bull markets of the 1960s and 1980s. The Celtics won the series. *The Elliott Wave Theorist* described the Celtics as the consummate bull market team in a 1996 report, "Basketball and The Bull Market." Major League Baseball says it is headed for a fifth consecutive attendance record. In a "sky's the limit" sign for the sport, its blue chip franchise, the New York Yankees, just raised its ticket prices for the best seat in the house to $1000 a game. Next year, when a brand new Yankee Stadium opens, the top ticket will rise again, to $2,500. The chart shows the exponential curve of New York Yankees' top ticket prices. As we showed with respect to similar upward arcs in tech and housing stocks, a massive decline cannot be far off. So far, no amount of bad publicity seems to dent the popularity of these games. What they cannot survive, however, is a full-scale bear market. As the major indexes plunge, the stars of the playing fields and courts, and the prices they can command, will crash en masse with them.

Much of the ground work for a reversal has been put in place over the course of the social mood peak. The AP notes, "The moorings seem to be coming loose" in sports, too. "Baseball stars Barry Bonds and Roger Clemens stand accused of enhancing their heroics with drugs. Basketball referees are suspected of cheating. Stay tuned for less than pristine tales from the drug-addled Tour De France and who knows what from the summer Olympics." We couldn't have said it better ourselves. The media senses it because a reversal of monumental proportions is grabbing hold.

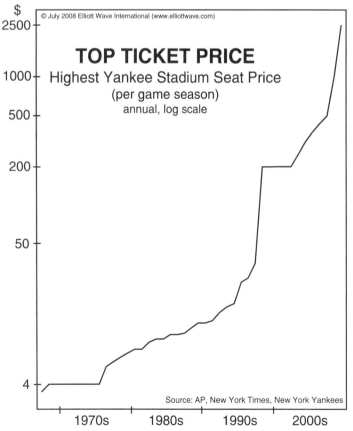

© July 2008 Elliott Wave International (www.elliottwave.com)

TOP TICKET PRICE
Highest Yankee Stadium Seat Price
(per game season)
annual, log scale

Source: AP, New York Times, New York Yankees

August 2008

Wall Street may be covering its eyes and berating the bears, but fashion is mining the styles of the 1930s and pushing them into the mainstream.

> The duds say it all—and it's depressing. Taking a cue from the grim economy, this fall's fashions at Banana Republic, Gap and H&M are featuring a distinctly Depression-era trend of cloche hats, pencil skirts, conductor caps and baggy, vintage-style dresses. One of the most popular styles appears to hark back to the impish, newsboy getup of the 1930s: baggy trousers, caps, pinstriped vests, oxford lace-up shoes and utilitarian handbags.
>
> —The New York Post, July 28, 2008

"The loose pants are like the dropped hemlines of the late '30s, and there's no bling," notes one observer of the newsboy look for women. Another says he "hates the look—it covers far too much for his taste. He also predicts it won't last." Of course, it won't. It's still too frivolous. Fashion will go darker and reveal even less as social mood continues lower.

That's for the ladies. For the men, it's suddenly a "sea of sequins, silk and all things pink as Paris designers increasingly blurred gender boundaries." The gender bending fits perfectly with the *The Elliott Wave Theorist*'s original 1985 assertion of a pop culture preference for "masculine" women's and "feminine" men's fashions in some corners of a bear market. But even here there is too much frivolity. Men's fashions should get darker and more conservative, too.

Speaking of dark, has the word ever been used more exhaustively than it has in connection with *The Dark Knight*, the new Batman movie? It fits, of course. With his lack of super powers, vigilante approach to crime fighting and bear market origins (1939), Batman is the right superhero for these times. The "darkest superhero film yet" is smashing box office records. Several bearish aspects of the film helped it score with critics and movie-goers alike. Not only does the villain, the Joker, steal the show with lines like, "When the chips are down, these civilized people, they'll eat each other," but the actor who portrayed him, Heath Ledger, died of a drug overdose in the aftermath of its production. Unlike the decidedly campy television version at the end of the last Cycle degree bull market in 1966, this version is true to Batman's bear market roots. A N.Y. Times reviewer predicts, however, that *Dark Knight's* success will "represent a peak" for the "superhero genre as it currently exists." He is surely right. Big budgets, moral rectitude and superhuman feats are bull market fare. Besides, all that action would get in the way of more complex plot lines, morally ambiguous characters and nihilistic messages, coming soon to theaters near you.

October 2008

As we eye the social scene, one set of observations that is conspicuously absent is anything that resembles the equity culture that occupied so much of this publication in the late 1990s and early 2000s. When we last spotted its fraying manifestations in May 2007 ("It's Root, Root, Root For the Stock Market"), athletes were trying to turn their "20% of all future on-field or on-court earnings" into stocks. EWFF said, "Call us crazy, but we believe that the conversion of fans into investors is very likely an extreme in the equity culture that cannot long endure." We also cited Vladimir Putin's effort to pump up certain stocks in speeches and television appearances and a shop worker's effort to do the same by sending pipe bombs to investment bankers, as finishing touches on the equity culture.

We ended that issue by stating, "The fear of being locked into a falling stock is one that will be widespread in the next major phase of the bear market." The flip side of the equity culture is now very much in evidence. People are bummed out, and they link their anxiety directly to what's happening on Wall Street. "Anxiety was palpable in the financial community all day Monday," said CNNMoney on September 21. Even before the latest series of market-shaking events, various mental health agencies were reporting months of increases in calls from "those seeking help for stress from financial pressures." In July, "money worries" were behind a 75%, 11-month increase in calls to the Hopeline network for people with depression or suicidal thoughts and a 21% year-over-year increase in calls to ComPsych, the world's largest provider of employee assistance programs. The American Psychological Association finds that three out of four Americans are suffering from financial stress. "A tidal wave of anxiety is washing over America," concludes Bloomberg. The dream is "shattering," most dramatically for those that bought most fully into the equity culture and reached aggressively for big paydays by day trading in 1999 or flipping houses in 2005.

As in the mania days, the stock ticker is a national compulsion. But the happy feeling that accompanied the obsession in 1999 is now driven by a mix of trepidation and anger. People are caught between a fear that the market will tank before Congress can iron out the details of the latest and biggest bailout plan and a swelling anger over the administration's effort to rush the fat-cat bailout through Congress. According to the The New York Times, a tidal wave of one-sidedly negative e-mails and phone calls is besieging Capitol Hill. Some are finding creative ways to vent their frustrations. Sarah's Smash Shack is a San Diego shop where customers pay to smash tableware like dinner plates, wine glasses, intricately lined sashimi plates, brightly colored vases and goblets. Since the shop opened a few days after the Dow peaked in October, business has been "steadily increasing." The bull market in "rage channeling" is on.

"Knock it off, fellas...you're scaring me!"

The Culture Turns on Equities

As the last leg of Supercycle wave (V) was coming to an end, the January 2000 issue of *The Elliott Wave Financial Forecast* noted that one clear sign of an unprecedented social infatuation with the stock market was the celebration at the start and finish of every trading session on the New York Stock Exchange:

> As never before, celebrities are used to amplify the magnetic attraction of the market. Bigger and bigger names are lending their auras to the opening ceremonies at the NYSE. From mid-December through the first week of January, a group of top-tier celebrities including Hank Aaron, Rev. Desmond Tutu and Muhammad Ali have sounded the opening bell.

The just-published October issue of EWFF offers a first glimpse of the equity culture's "flip side." To those observations we can now add what happened on September 29, the day the Dow suffered its single biggest point drop in history: The opening bell failed to sound. At the close, actress Missie Pyle, "who appeared as the buxom Laliari in the cult hit *Galaxy Quest*" (talk about a step down from 2000), was supposed to ring the bell, but failed to do so saying she "decided to let the day be about the market and not about having a celebrity ring the bell." These days ringing in or out the trading day "can be a little bit like being asked to blow the foghorn on the Titanic," says a corporate communications advisor.

An index that shows the excitement for equities literally breaking down is our Culture Stock Index, which originally consisted of four stocks: Bally Total Fitness (BFT), Callaway Golf (ELY), World Wrestling Entertainment (WWE) and Martha Stewart Living Omnimedia (MSO). It is down to three now, as Bally Total Fitness went under last year. We combined these four because they "are pure plays in bull market social phenomena and thus are representative of one of the most ebullient aspects of the bull market, the public's belief that it can profit by investing in its own whimsical tastes in pop culture." The index peaked in early 2005 and it's been tapering off ever since. The break of its bear market low in 2002 is another definitive sign that the mania's breaking point is past.

© October 2008 Elliott Wave International (www.elliottwave.com)

POP GOES THE CULTURE STOCKS
EWI's Culture Stock Index
weekly

The Art World Holds Out

One of the purest cultural encapsulations of the social frenzy for price appreciation is what happened in the art market. As art prices accompanied stocks and virtually every other financial instrument higher, art buyers went wild for increasingly recent works. We thought the bidding reached an endpoint in 2004 when the buying focused on abstract and pop art pieces from the 1950s and 1960s. The trend was very much in line with the larger financial flight to risk, because younger pieces have less time to establish their masterpiece status and are therefore susceptible to changes in taste, which invariably follow in the wake of a large-degree bear market. But the stock market plowed higher, and as it did the art market moved on to an even riskier proposition, works by living artists. A few days before the Dow Jones Industrial Average reached its all-time high in October 2007, EWFF identified a possible sign of the top in a parallel high water mark for the art market: a diamond-encrusted skull.

> The $100 million sale of the piece by Damian Hirst is the highest price ever paid for the work of a living artist. It may well mark a conspicuous end to the era of conspicuous spending, and not just because it shapes a cache of diamonds into a symbol of death.

As previously noted, art tends to hold up for a while in the wake of a major peak. This is probably because extremely wealthy art patrons recognize the unfolding storm and acquire iconic images as a hedge against decline. Invariably, however, the downtrend catches the art crowd, and the industry's post-peak record ends up being top dollar. In September 2008, a block sale of Hirst's

271

works likely marked the conclusion of the bull market in art. "Against the surreal backdrop of a severe financial market collapse, 'Beautiful Inside My Head Forever' was a conclusive success. The groundbreaking sale collected a grand total just shy of 200 million dollars, beating the previous record for the auction of a collection by a single artist formerly held by Picasso by roughly ten times." One dealer called the sale a "magnificent triumph. At a time when other markets are reeling, the people with the free cash and the will have ignored the storm warnings and the voyage goes on." But we think that the sale of one item, Hirst's "Golden Calf," a bull calf with 18-carat gold horns and hooves preserved in formaldehyde, captures the art market's prospects quite elegantly. It went for more than $18 million even though Hirst's signature 1991 piece, a shark-in-formaldehyde, had to be replaced because it was "disintegrating." Metaphorically, the bull market is in the same state. Sotheby's artists may be doing well, but Sotheby's itself is not. The chart of Sotheby's crashing stock price (below) is a peek into the art market's future.

Knowing When To Fold 'Em

Another revealing collapse is that of casino titan MGM Mirage. The urge to risk it all helped lift MGM to an all-time high of more than $100 on October 10, 2007, one day ahead of the peak in the Dow Industrials. MGM's rapid descent fits with our forecast for a bear market in Las Vegas and gambling in general. "Once believed recession-proof, casinos are proving to be highly vulnerable to the economic downturn." The society-wide conservatism called for in *Conquer the Crash* explains the reversal. Remember the poker boom? According to the latest reports, it's long gone, too. "An overall disinterest in the game" has sparked a decline in tournament sponsors and "steep declines in popularity." The U.S. government is now pulling out the stops to free up spending and revive chance-taking. The effort will not succeed because, at a very deep level, rolling the dice just doesn't charge people up the way it did during the late-boom and early-bust phases.

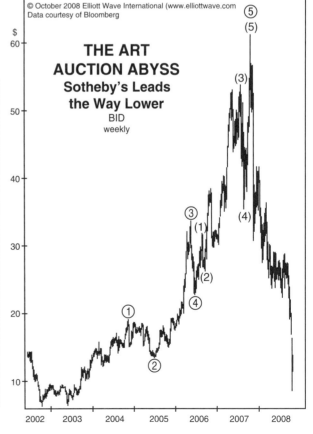

November 2008

Just Don't Take Me Out of The Stock Market

As the October issue explained, the society-wide, investment cocktail party that we call the equity culture is coming to an end. But it doesn't just turn on a dime. It is initially transformed from an outlet for social euphoria to a wellspring of collective angst. You've seen the recent photographs in the daily papers of bewildered traders covering their faces, rubbing their eyes or praying, which is evidence of the metamorphosis. A series of 12 different grimacing traders on the Style page of the Washington Post shows the depth of the stock market drama. "The hapless broker may or may not stand for the whole of America—and you and me and the future, too," says the story. We know that the equity culture still lives on, because the story appears not in the financial page but in the Post's "Style" section. Toward the end of the bear market, only hard-core financial types will be reading about stocks, and the stories certainly won't be in the Style section.

Another Style section article actually describes the start of society's break with equities with a story saying that many are literally turning away from the stock market. "There is a new way to tell people apart: there are those who can bear to look and those who avert their gaze; those who follow the nose-diving value of their investments and those who want to close their eyes and hum until the noise stops." The story quotes a visitor to Times Square who says her husband is the first type but he did not want to come into the city because "he thought there would be people jumping out of windows." Instead he stayed home to "look for bargains. He's on the computer trading." Obviously, the outright death of the equity culture is a ways off. History teaches that it will not survive the bear market.

After pyramiding people's hopes up to such a high pinnacle, however, equities cannot go out of style without commanding center stage. According to an AP-Yahoo News poll of 2000 respondents, "financial worries have permeated all corners of society." Another story says, "Across the country, authorities are becoming concerned that the nation's financial woes could turn increasingly violent, and they are urging people to get help." This concern is probably misplaced, because violence tends to come later in a bear market, but falling out of love with equities is now so pronounced that Hollywood is "rushing to tap America's fixation with the financial crisis and anger at the Wall Street executives blamed for it." Here's a quote from the March 2000 issue of EWFF showing what happened at the peak in March 2000:

> This month, the market became a prime-time staple, as "Hollywood succumbed to the allure of Wall Street," reports USA Today.

Stocks didn't make it in the entertainment industry in 2000, and something tells us *Confessions of a Wall Street Shoeshine Boy*, a Time Warner offering slated for 2009, and other movies about the stock market's dark side, won't catch on either. By the time they come out, the detachment from equities will be further along so that people simply will not care.

In many areas, the market's downside is actually revealing the full depth of the connection between the financial and social realm. Sports and markets is another intersection point that EWI has long monitored. In mid-2007, when future athletic achievements were literally being "equitized," most people probably didn't even notice, but EWFF said it was surely a sign of "a big top." Now that social mood is in retreat, Sports Illustrated reads a little bit like a financial sheet. Recent stories cover the financial turmoil's creation of "storm clouds" over the winter Olympics in Sochi, Russia, "economic woes" for NASCAR and a shifting "focus to soccer's growing problems." "Almost every [college] athletic department in the nation must deal with the fallout from the recent economic plunge," says another SI story. Here's another headline that marks a big bear market starting point:

Yankee Stadium Memorabilia Not Selling Well

EWFF identified a New York Yankee high water mark in July, when top tickets at Yankee stadium were raised to $2,500 a game. Here's what EWFF had to say about it:

> So far, no amount of bad publicity seems to dent the popularity of these games. What they cannot survive, however, is a full-scale bear market. As the major indexes plunge, the stars of the playing fields and courts, and the prices they can command will crash en masse.

Evidence of a huge reversal arrived on October 18, when the last home run ball from a game at Yankee Stadium failed to sell at auction. The ball, one of several Yankee "artifacts" that went unsold, was expected to fetch up to $400,000. The ball's failure to even get the $100,000 opening bid is another air pocket, like those that appeared in the prices of financial stocks. The damaged, intertwined fate of stocks and baseball was apparent in the World Series locker rooms, where players were reputedly as interested in stocks as they were in the World Series game they were about play. "Millionaire baseball players trying to win the World Series are talking about the stock market's plunge in between discussions about hitting breaking balls or stealing bases," reports Bloomberg. Philadelphia Phillies relief pitcher Brad Lidge told the news service that he's checked in with his financial adviser throughout the Major League Baseball playoffs. "We are paying more attention now than we ever have. We are all aware that maybe we should be moving stuff into real estate right now. You take a hit but you have to ride the storm because eventually it's going to bounce back. If you take it out, you won't be there for the gains, only for the losses." Even as it slips away, the grip of the equity culture gets tighter than ever.

December 2008

The market for art was one bidding venue that EWFF listed as a holdout in October. But here's the latest headline from the November auctions: "Bottom Falls Out of the Art Market." "Experts now fear the bubble may finally have burst after museum quality paintings failed to sell." Total sales were well below Sotheby's and Christie's lowest estimated prices. So art prices have clearly entered the "disintegration" phase foreshadowed by Sotheby's stock price (see chart in the October entry above).

The great skyscraper race, which EWFF last discussed in July, leaves behind several architectural monuments to the size and suddenness of the reversal. The Trump Tower, the second

tallest building in the U.S., and the Burj Dubai, the world's tallest building under construction in Dubai, extend to their full heights now; so they will likely be completed. But construction on the Chicago Spire, a proposed 150-story condominium that was slated to become the tallest building in the United States, and the Russia Tower, a 1,970-foot building that was supposed to be the tallest in Europe, came to a halt in recent weeks. The Mile High Tower, a proposed "superscraper" in Jeddah, Saudi Arabia, illustrates the full magnitude of the peak. The tower was initially projected to more than double the 2,684-foot height of the Burj Dubai. In May, it was scaled back by 1,500-feet because of soil conditions. In October, however, the unveiling of the final plan failed to happen. The reason is that the bull market is over, and every big bull market ends when the world's tallest structures are conceived and initiated but not yet complete. In the current case, economic ambition is so monumental and out of whack with the capabilities and burdens of economic participants that the Mile High Tower will not make it past the blueprint stage. The extreme height that the tower plans soared to even as the "light switch" change was flipping its way through the financial system represents the gargantuan delusion seen at the final highs. It took a full year to move from the banks and capital markets to the brick and mortar of the economy, but social mood has been pointed straight down, and everything must follow.

Yo Ho Ho and a Bottle of Downers

The contracting economy may be the most visible result of the change in social mood, but many totally unprecedented changes that Elliott Wave International predicted over the course of the last few years are moving into place. As far as we know, for instance, *The Elliott Wave Theorist* is the only forecasting service to say—in 2003—that pirates would be a pop-culture hit. When pirate images and movies started to spring up in 2005, Sociotimes.com, our web catalogue of developing bear market trends from 2004-2007, made the following assessment:

> Of course, an interest in pirate books and movies is not the same thing as outright piracy. Still, it makes sense that a higher level of social acceptance would precede a rising incidence of the real thing. If it is, the uptick in software and intellectual property piracy over the last few years should be the start of a bull market for plunder.

Pirates are, in fact, back on the high seas. Bands operating off the coast of Somalia now hold hostage a Saudi supertanker with $100 million in oil as well as at least 12 other ships, and they "are becoming more brazen." Earlier this week, they went after a U.S. cruise liner with 1,000 vacationing passengers on board. After a recent meeting in Cairo, diplomats "expressed anxiety toward the growth of the phenomenon of piracy." The "phenomenon of piracy," who'd a thunk it? Due to the Grand Supercycle-degree of the turn and the history of the pirate game, we did.

Here's another wacky forecast from the August 2006 issue of *The Elliott Wave Financial Forecast*:

> How long can it be before we hear: "Bartender, give me an energy drink, but hold the energy?" Not long, we bet.

Last week brought a seemingly random news item; one that fits perfectly with our forecast:

Anti-Energy Drink Fuels Concerns

First came Red Bull and Monster Energy, giving a high-octane boost to late-night parties and study sessions.

Now the anti-energy drinks have arrived, carbonated beverages that promise to help you "slow your roll" or "lean with it."

Even in these small yet striking examples, you can see the power that comes from understanding socionomic causality. Once again, the transition took a little longer than we thought. But given the violence of the decline, it was kind of nice to have a little extra time to prepare. Being ready is the best antidote to the depressionary funk that rides in on a bear market.

Chapter 4

The Little Guy Trades His Way to the Top

Day trading takes off as "buy the dip" becomes the rallying cry. Rather than sell, an auto mechanic at the "All Transmissions Shop" contemplates a Coney Island honeymoon. Stocks are the new sex, and margin is the aphrodisiac. When stocks start down, the love affair gets even more intense. An unnatural, unrelenting optimism precedes the final turn.

June 1995

After the bear market of 1929-1932, the federal government passed a law making it illegal to borrow more than 50% of the value of collateral stock to finance stock speculation. The Washington Post reports that Wall Street investment firms and banks are beseeching Congress, the Fed, the Treasury and the SEC to have those restrictions removed. They are making so much money in the bull market that they do not want it to end. The more the public can buy on credit, the higher it could go, they conclude. True, but the faster it will unravel when it falls.

July 1995

I had thought it impossible for anyone to say anything more bullish than the oft-repeated "it's the best of all possible worlds for stocks and the economy," but someone did, on June 20, telling Reuters, "It's a perfect world." At Dow 790, it was a scary world. If a scary world is a buying opportunity, what is a perfect world? Know this: A scary world is perfect for stocks and a perfect world is scary for stocks.

October 1995

Polls reveal that a whopping 95% of mutual fund investors proudly state that they are "in for the long haul," while over 3/4 claim that they will not sell stocks if they plunge. In the first eight months of 1995, moreover, 70% of mutual fund inflows went into retirement accounts. Taking these statistics at face value, analysts and money managers tell reporters that the public is "a stabilizing force," providing "an ideal situation for fund managers." They conclude from the public's conviction that investors will continue to buy stocks no matter what, and thus keep the market from falling. The only problem with this assessment is that people have minds, which they are inclined to change from time to time when dealing with investments.

Do you remember 1980, when the public finally became convinced to own gold, silver, and mining stocks? Investors then vowed never to sell. They knew that the dollar was doomed and only hard money could save them over the long run. Did they keep their word? No. Like that lady on *Saturday Night Live*, they later said, "Oh.... Never mind!", and sold out at far lower prices. Today we are witnessing precisely the same phenomenon. Its focus is simply over pieces of paper called stocks and bonds instead of pieces of metal.

O.K., the bulls might say, so it is possible that investors could change their minds and sell their now-beloved stock market mutual funds. But is it likely? Yes, and the reason is provided in a wonderful little booklet called *One-Way Pockets*, published in 1916, which described the progression of the typical investor's temporal outlook on the market through a market cycle. The author, a broker, found that his clients were skittish and near-term oriented in the first two-thirds of a bull market and confident and long-term oriented from near the top to halfway down in the next bear market. Human nature hasn't changed. The same thing happened in the gold market from the early 1970s to the early 1980s, and it is happening again in the stock market. Throughout most of the 1980s, the public was afraid of the stock market as a long term investment, but since 1991, it has fallen in love with the idea.

The public's shift in attitude, rather than being a "stabilizing force," is in truth a devastatingly bearish indicator of where the market is in its cycle. It was the public's fear and disinterest that guaranteed a continuation of the bull market back in 1979, 1982, 1984, 1988, and most of the years on either side. On the other hand, widespread public enthusiasm for an investment (particularly after it has risen over 500% in thirteen years, as this one has) is a classic sign of a top. Yet money managers have called today's investor "far more market-savvy than believed" for suddenly committing to the long haul.

When the tide turns, these investors will do just what their fathers did when the great 1969-1974 bear market began. Some will panic and sell their funds, if they can get past the busy signals. Some will stand frozen like a deer caught in headlights. Others will squeeze cash out of their credit cards and buy more stock, following the advice of their bullish heroes. But ultimately, they will sell out at much lower prices. When the next era of widespread bearish public conviction arrives, they will be a part of it, regardless of (indeed, because of) what they believe today. Then they will wish they had never invested in a mutual fund at all. They will wish that someone had explained that investing is not saving, and that investment success, as in any paying endeavor, demands knowledge and experience. Yet all will not be for naught. As a result of their financial adventure, some of today's youngest participants will learn enough to become invested before the next 500% rise, not after. Then when today's market environment recurs, they will take their profits and keep them.

January 1996

Corrections have been met with more optimism than concern. During the three-day NASDAQ slide of 6.4% in early October, and despite deep drops in technology stocks, fund managers pounced on the decline as an opportunity to buy. "Valuations were quite reasonable before this started, and now they are compelling," said one buyer.

March 1996

A Long Island artist knows the litany: "If the market fell sharply, I'd gather together every penny I could get my hands on and put it in the stock market. History shows that, over the long term, prices will recover."

April 1996

One casualty of the entrenched bullish conviction is the presumed value of historical precedent. A rising chorus of observers now say that today's investment psychology is not bearish as is classically assumed. "I'm not saying it's different this time," the Boston Globe quotes one market psychologist as saying in an outright lie, "but I think the psychology of investing has changed. You can't in this day and age use past statistical data to figure out what is going to happen in this market." Two other psychologists turned market analysts agree: this is not a mania. There is no consensus desire involved, they imply, just facts and reason. After all, stocks must rise because "boomers are well aware there is no place else to put their money if they hope to retire." So in the new psychology, fear propels stock prices up, not down. Call us old fashioned, but we conclude that the fact that hope, greed and fear are all allied on the side of buy-till-you-die bullish conviction reflects an emotional extreme confirming that we are in the vicinity of the greatest stock market top in nearly three centuries.

May 1996

On-line access has opened up a whole new world of trading through cheap commissions. For just pennies a share, Internet investors can now compete with experienced traders due to the extremely low transaction costs.

July 1996

One subscriber notes that a single day's trading on the NYSE and NASDAQ exchanges now surpasses the volume for all of 1929, yet the population of the U.S. has only doubled since then. This data suggests a far greater level of public participation today than in 1929.

August 1996

The correction of 1996 has come, and everyone is resting easy. Large speculators haven't budged; their stock futures holdings remain at "major top" levels. Both professionals and the public, it seems, were emotionally prepared. "Forget about selling...instead, think about what you can do to ensure you stick with your stocks," says one commentator. "Make no mistake: This is the healthiest thing that could happen," says a chief investment officer. "A classic bull market correction... a walk in the park," says a mutual fund manager. The nation's largest general interest daily editorialized that brief routs are "a common occurrence" and should not be feared. Why? Because "the market is to today's savers what bank savings accounts were to their parents and grandparents. The nearly $140 billion in mutual fund inflows through the first six months of this year matched the nation's net savings rate." This is a terribly bearish fact reflecting historic stock market optimism, yet people are assuming it is bullish.

When the "long awaited" 10% correction occurred, it held at 10% for only a half hour (1:00 to 1:30 on July 16). The violent upside reversal that day illustrated and bolstered investors' now unshakable faith in their new savings vehicle. In a series of man-on-the-street interviews, USA Today quizzed nine people on what they did when there was "havoc" in the stock market. Every one let his stock investments ride. "A paper loss," said one. "I'm going to close my eyes and just leave it in," said another. Several intend to seize the opportunity. "Now might be a good time to buy," said a lawyer from New Jersey. A pilot from Indianapolis is "eyeing investments abroad, China in particular." A Tampa sportscaster wishes that "it would go down even more." (Don't worry; it will. Just be patient.) Outright gratitude in the face of such a broad-based decline is a sign that the bull has set his hook deeply. When he hands the rod to the bear, the fish will have no chance. We will know that the process of contraction has run its course when price declines strike fear into the hearts of average investors and the "old rules" apply once more.

HOW TO MAKE A MILLION PAGE 25 · July 1996 · $2.25 · **Reader's Digest** · *World's most widely read magazine · Over 27 million copies in 19 languages bought monthly*

You Can Make A Million

"I'M LIVING PROOF that anybody can become rich," says Arnaud Loustalot. With $4 million in stocks, Loustalot and his wife, Mildred, live in a Falls Church, Va., retirement community on $200,000 a year earned from their portfolio, not including his pension and their Social Security benefits.

Each day family members put their pocket change on a table, and Loustalot's mother took all the dimes to put away in savings. From her example, he developed the habit of saving 10% of his salary and investing in stocks, then reinvesting the dividends and holding on to his shares through high and low price cycles.

Today almost five million households have a net worth exceeding $1 million. That's nearly twice the number of millionaires in 1989, and the numbers are increasing 15 percent a year. Most of these people still live in middle-class neighborhoods, and 80 percent are first-generation rich.

Instead of buying a $1 lottery ticket every day, invest it in a stock fund. "The risk of loss is almost total playing the lottery," says investment manager Joel Whittenberg. "But the payoff from investing is a near certainty."

Cautions Jonathan Clements, financial columnist for The Wall Street Journal, "If you sincerely want to be rich, focus on socking away [in stocks] as much as you can."

Striking it rich in America is within anyone's grasp
BY RANDY FITZGERALD

—July 1996

Commentary on the "Motley Fool" web site on the Internet is rife with 1) desperate hand-wringing about why Iomega (which wags around here call IOU Mega) is falling in the face of good earnings and 2) novice rumination about why it has to soar soon and make its dedicated owners rich.

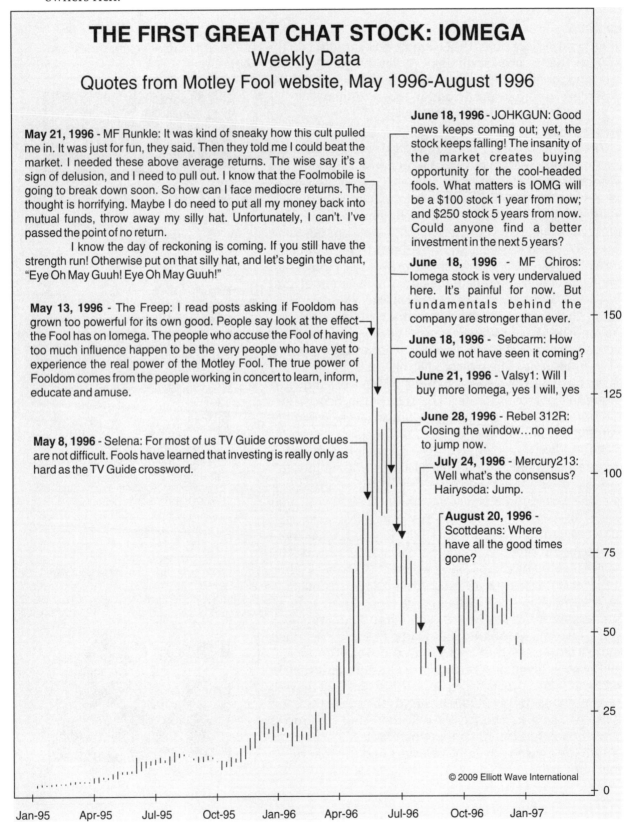

THE FIRST GREAT CHAT STOCK: IOMEGA
Weekly Data
Quotes from Motley Fool website, May 1996-August 1996

June 18, 1996 - JOHKGUN: Good news keeps coming out; yet, the stock keeps falling! The insanity of the market creates buying opportunity for the cool-headed fools. What matters is IOMG will be a $100 stock 1 year from now; and $250 stock 5 years from now. Could anyone find a better investment in the next 5 years?

May 21, 1996 - MF Runkle: It was kind of sneaky how this cult pulled me in. It was just for fun, they said. Then they told me I could beat the market. I needed these above average returns. The wise say it's a sign of delusion, and I need to pull out. I know that the Foolmobile is going to break down soon. So how can I face mediocre returns. The thought is horrifying. Maybe I do need to put all my money back into mutual funds, throw away my silly hat. Unfortunately, I can't. I've passed the point of no return.
    I know the day of reckoning is coming. If you still have the strength run! Otherwise put on that silly hat, and let's begin the chant, "Eye Oh May Guuh! Eye Oh May Guuh!"

June 18, 1996 - MF Chiros: Iomega stock is very undervalued here. It's painful for now. But fundamentals behind the company are stronger than ever.

May 13, 1996 - The Freep: I read posts asking if Fooldom has grown too powerful for its own good. People say look at the effect the Fool has on Iomega. The people who accuse the Fool of having too much influence happen to be the very people who have yet to experience the real power of the Motley Fool. The true power of Fooldom comes from the people working in concert to learn, inform, educate and amuse.

June 18, 1996 - Sebcarm: How could we not have seen it coming?

June 21, 1996 - Valsy1: Will I buy more Iomega, yes I will, yes

June 28, 1996 - Rebel 312R: Closing the window…no need to jump now.

May 8, 1996 - Selena: For most of us TV Guide crossword clues are not difficult. Fools have learned that investing is really only as hard as the TV Guide crossword.

July 24, 1996 - Mercury213: Well what's the consensus? Hairysoda: Jump.

August 20, 1996 - Scottdeans: Where have all the good times gone?

© 2009 Elliott Wave International

November 1996

As the November rally advanced, a front page article in USA Today noted, "so good is the environment for stocks that some are likening it to nirvana. And there is talk that the stock market entered a new age where century-old measures of value are no longer relevant." [Emphasis added.] A front page article in the November 15 Wall Street Journal also makes the case for what in 1929 was called "a permanently high plateau": "From boardrooms to living rooms and from government offices to trading floors, a new consensus is emerging: The big, bad business cycle has been tamed." In an interview with David Brinkley, President Clinton agreed. One analyst has been quoted calling for Dow 750,000 by 2096 because "in the final analysis, the market, despite fluctuations along the way, goes only in one direction — up!" We agree about one thing: this kind of talk may prove to be the final analysis that many investors ever care to hear.

January 1997

In a throwback to the bucket shops of the 1920s, small trading houses are springing up across the country by offering the guy on the street the "opportunity to operate like institutional money managers." "Clients dart in and out of the stock market, accumulating profits on a rise of as little as 1/8 of a point. The clients, or traders, are mostly young men, many just out of college, who are ambitious and not averse to taking risks..." The effort to skim profits from market moves was made possible by NASDAQ's Small Order Execution System. The system was instituted after the 1987 crash because many small investors were unable to get out of the market that day. A trader who made $6250 in one day (less $3000 in commissions) by buying long in the morning and selling short in the afternoon said, "They call us day traders, but we're more like minute traders. It takes all the long term risk out."

Another actually welcomed the idea of a crash: "Market Crash 'Would Benefit US Economy.'" The story quoted a study by a UCLA professor saying, "A decent collapse in the stock market would be nice right now." In a 14-page USA Today "Guide to Investments," an expert analyst said (using a phrase typically applied to the Bible and not inaccurately addressing the bull market as a religion), "Look, we're in the midst of the greatest story ever told. Corrections dampen exuberance and are healthy, particularly when the background music is very, very favorable as it is now."

> # BAD BOYS of Capitalism
>
> Block Trading's office on the third floor of a Houston shopping mall exudes the dimly lit quiet of a pool hall, suggesting an activity that is as purposeful as it is questionable. Twenty-eight customers sit staring at the dance and flicker of numbers across computer screens. Stephanie Clark is one of them.
>
> Thin, blond, and getting richer by the minute, Clark only 18 months ago was a 28-year-old secretary at Oppenheimer & Co. in Houston, where she grew tired of watching men make money while she answered the phones. Now, thanks to the alternative created by Block Trading cofounders Chris Block and Jeff Burke, she's a "SOES bandit" – SOES (pronounced sews) standing for the Small-Order Execution System, which gives individual investors both direct access to stock prices and near-instantaneous executions on NASDAQ. "Bandit" is the epithet conferred by the established market makers who create and support markets in stocks, and who want to keep the individual traders out – off their turf and away from their profits.
>
> But it's too late for that. For Clark and the other bandits, this has become their day job. On a good day a SOES trader might make a grand or two. On a bad day he or she will give it back. The only sure thing is this: no matter how much their enemies huff and puff, the bandits are here to stay.
>
> —Inc., January 1997

July 1997

The best illustration of this market's ability to tolerate unprecedented bullish sentiment is the countless versions of the phrase, "the best of all possible worlds." Analysts have been using it to describe the financial picture for four years now. Naturally, it has thus become embedded in the lexicon. The lead story in the Financial Times of June 14 offered a typical example: "It is the best of all worlds for the financial markets." A June report on the U.S. economy has this title: "The Best of All Possible Economies." A brokerage firm report proclaims, "Paradise Found." To emphasize its stance further, the cover includes a full-color portrait of a lush tropical setting. In normal times, the market would punish this graphic display of enthusiasm. But as noted in May these are not normal times, and the market has allowed such talk for nearly half a decade. This affront to the paradox of market sentiment is an irony in itself because "the best of all possible worlds" comes from Voltaire's 1759 book, *Candide*. It was first uttered by Candide's mentor, Professor Pangloss, from whose name a word for reckless optimism is derived, to describe conditions right before Candide is beset by earthquakes, floods, starvation, flogging, and assorted other disasters. But now even Barron's, which has put a skeptical slant on the bull market for as long as we have, is wondering, "Could it be that Dr. Pangloss has finally got it right?"

Does this mean that the value of sentiment as an indicator is lost? No. True, caution due to the optimistic extreme has contributed to our inaccurate anticipation of a top. But even in this context, its extent speaks to the degree of the approaching trend change. At turns of Primary and Cycle degree, extremes in sentiment can be posted up to three months ahead of the actual turn, as the "magazine cover" interpreters have long observed. This time, the extremes have been in place for years. This persistence is a measure of the degree of the top and the size of the bear market to come.

Will sentiment change immediately after the top? This clip illustrates how the slightest provocation will trigger a return to the "best of all possible" belief long after the Grand Supercycle bear has begun. It's about a recent technology conference that started out in a morose mood because of a 35% decline in the sector from May 1996 to May 1997. Despite losses of more than 1/3, bulls "dared to hope" that the 1997 conference could turn out to be a bottom rather than a top. Untethered optimism leads inevitably to a psychology in which all outcomes, even losses, are causes for celebration. Pangloss was the first to point this out when he noted that "in the best of all possible worlds, even private misfortunes make the public good, so that the more private misfortunes there are, the more everything is well."

> ## Tech Investors Turn Upbeat at Conference
>
> Many of those attending said they grew steadily more optimistic, as a number of the 260 presenting companies offered credible evidence that their business backlogs were strong and that they were staying on top of the lightning-fast technological changes in such areas as networking and multimedia.

October 1997

Leverage in the Modern Financial World

According to the weekly poll by economist Al Sindlinger, new investors have been jumping into the U.S. stock market at a rate of 300,000 a week for the last 16 weeks. This brings the stock market's penetration of U.S. households to 45%, twice the highest estimates for 1929 and easily the highest total ever.

The evidence of unprecedented public interest now runs the gamut from the proliferation of arcade-type brokerage offices in which novice traders "try their hand at winning and losing fortunes, in a matter of minutes," to cheddar cheese options, now available on the Chicago Merc. Other evidence of over-trading includes fantasy stock market contests in newspapers across the country, college courses in which students manage real funds, securities that allow investors to bet against catastrophic events like hurricanes and earthquakes, and death futures, by which speculators try to profit by purchasing the life insurance proceeds from the terminally ill.

Small investors are behind the explosion in on-line trading and the popularity of new software that helps the novice trade "like a professional without being one." A New York Times editor has filed with the SEC to start a mutual fund as, "In today's world, you don't have to have any experience to manage a mutual fund." A former police lieutenant has traded in his holster "and hung out a shingle as a financial adviser," according to a front page WSJ article on how "Retirees, Lawyers, Even Cops" have spurned their brokers and now "Dish Out Investing Tips." At the nation's financial daily, front-page features on the roping in of new participants and the average investor's do-it-yourself resolve have become weekly features.

One such article is headlined, "Market's Ride Has Everybody Buzzing." It begins by noting that investing has replaced sex as the lunch-time preoccupation at the "epicenter of world finance."

AMERICA'S CONSUMING LOVE AFFAIR WITH STOCKS
A study by Montgomery Asset Management in San Francisco shows that Americans expect a 34 percent annual return on stock funds for the next 10 years.

—The Christian Science Monitor, October 17, 1997

Actually, the sentiment is universal. A recent survey showed 47% of all Americans think more about money than sex. (Could this be within the same 45% of households that are invested?) A pair of long-running commercials for a discount brokerage firm appeals to potential customers by implying that trading is better than sex. CNBC's New York Stock Exchange correspondent is being compared to Sophia Loren. In the many articles chronicling her newfound stardom, Maria Bartiromo never fails to mention that there is a "sexy element" to the markets. "Thus does Bartiromo radiate gusto and glamour even as she defines her primary mission in these crisp business-like terms: 'I try to give my viewers, particularly the small investor, an advantage. That's the point.'" That's also the trap, the same seduction of the little guy Adam Smith warned of in 1776. But dusty admonitions are no match for Bartiromo's big brown eyes fluttering at viewers from the floor of the stock exchange. After all, while she handles the finance part well, sex still counts for something.

September-October is witnessing the launch of a "mini" Standard & Poor's 500 contract, which is 1/10 the size of the standard contract, as well as futures and options contracts based on the Dow Jones Industrial Average. These debuts mark the point at which the little guy meets leverage, entwining the two great aspects of a mania. This merger, after 101 years of Dow Jones trading, may be remembered as the day the nickel slots came to the Great Asset Mania. The exchanges' bullish bias (a necessity in attracting the public) is reflected in their daily price limits, which go into effect on declines but not on corresponding advances.

Leverage availability is seeping into the market through a host of avenues. In the last year, bankers say mutual fund managers have doubled their reliance on bank credit to maintain low-cash positions. The state of New Jersey has finalized plans to borrow $2.8 billion at an interest rate of 7.6% so that it can invest the proceeds in the stock market. MasterCard International has documented the public's use of credit card debt to supplement stock and mutual fund purchases. Total outlays are not known, but CNBC reported recently that studies show cardholders are augmenting their holdings of financial assets with more charges. "It may sound daring, but it's not uncommon," said a reporter.

Another popular route for leverage is the home equity loan, which can now be extended beyond the value of the home by 25 percent. But not to worry: "You are effectively paying 7.8% on the money you borrow, but if your return is 22%, you can see how you will come out way ahead," blithely notes a financial columnist. Or how about this "opportunity to make a small fortune," as identified in the August 17 Miami Herald? "You borrow $100,000 at an after-tax cost of 5%. You reinvest the money at an after-tax return that exceeds 8%. Each year — and this works best if you plan to participate for the long haul — you reap a compound return on money that's not even yours." The article goes on to extrapolate the return to "roughly $300,000 over 30 years." Such a deal! No one asks why some fool would lend the money at 5% if 8% is a sure thing. "The caveat, of course, is that this loan must be secured by your house, so if you fail to pay, you lose your home." In another miracle of modern finance, First Security Capital gets people leveraged by lending up to 90% of the value of their stocks. It does so by hedging the transaction with an array of financial derivatives and plowing the cost of the hedge back into the interest rate on the loan.

Remember how some cheesy property-investment gurus used the "miracle of leverage" to bind small investors to real estate's collapse in the 1980s? The very same pitch is being used today in infomercials that help viewers "Discover Exchange Traded Options." In excited tones normally reserved for Vegematics, Ginzu knives and Ab-rollers, leverage is touted as "an alternative to enhance stocks and mutual funds." (Come to think of it, maybe they are the same people.) These headlines from a recent newspaper show how financial advisors are rolling (in both senses) people ill-served by the last mania into this one:

Couple's Real Estate Investment Not Paying Off

Planner: Sell Houses, Focus on Funds

— USA Today, August 4, 1997

The public is ripe for this message. As one of our subscribers reports, "None of my friends and colleagues are worried. The naivest of the naive have of late plunged into S&P futures, IPOs and naked option speculations. Many are saying, 'If this keeps up, I can take early retirement.'"

November 1997

On Tuesday of this week, a local financial planner was on TV saying that she told all her clients to buy because "you are supposed to buy when blood is running in the streets, and that certainly happened yesterday!" Yet what the formulator of that maxim meant was blood actually running in the streets. Then, it is truly hard to buy. But these days, fantasy rules all, and a 7% down day near an all-time high is "blood in the streets." On October 28, phone banks at brokerage houses and mutual funds were "overwhelmed" when people jammed the lines to buy. Prior to the fall, polls indicated that up to 84% would buy on a 1,000-point drop in the Dow and as few as 2% would sell. The volume on October 28 suggests that they did just what they said they would.

The headlines and news clips shown from before and after the October 27 slide, are, in our opinion, a call to the cliff. Notice the progression from "it can't happen" or "if it does, it's meaningless" before October 27 (top left hand corner) to "don't be frightened" (top right) to

"bargains, bargains, bargains" on October 28 and 29 in the bottom half. What's missing here? The panic. Nobody said, "Run for your life!" Wall Street unleashed an immediate ad blitz "geared to soothe jittery investors." Instead of precautionary "stand asides," journalists eased readers' pain by telling them what to think ("Don't Panic") or predicting the storm's passing ("Market May Stay Bullish, But Ride Will Be Bumpier"). Journalists will be on the opposite side when the bear market passes its halfway point. In contrast to these headlines, our recommendation to bulls is: Panic early and avoid the rush.

December 1997

Remember that chic pale stare that characterized the majority of fashion ads through most of the 1990s? According to an October New York Times article, it has gone the way of grunge. "Sullen got old. The attitude now is fabulous." "Happiness is back in a big way." "Happy" has replaced "Obsession," "Poison" and "Opium" as the new perfume. According to its creator, the new fruity floral fragrance represents a "breaking through the doldrums." "A brighter, sunnier and, yes, happier attitude seems to be emerging."

Even perpetually oppressed American laborers have experienced a break to the upside as "most of America's 32 million blue collar workers" have "halted their long forced retreat in pay and jobs." This story is headlined, "Rising Tide Finally Floats Workers." "Call it the bleaching of America's blue collar." To celebrate, a recent WSJ story says many are dipping into their 401(k) nest eggs to live better. "It Isn't Always a Terrible Idea." "In fact, one-third of all workers with 401(k)s currently have loans outstanding." In the long run, the backsliding and underlying edginess of the 1990s will prevail, but not before a period of triumph for old-school indulgence.

Last year, when a major financial columnist suggested that people should buy stocks and hold them until the day they died, we figured expectations had hit the ceiling. We were wrong. Apparently, in a mania of this magnitude, even the bounds of mortality can be surpassed. The Luxembourg-based Prometh Societé is offering "reincarnation accounts" to people who are not willing to let death stand in the way of their financial planning (minimum account size is $30,000). When the claimant returns in the next life and provides a few key facts, he can claim the account, which will presumably have grown to quite a size at the generally expected 30% per annum compounded.

This degree of faith in the long haul, despite a spreading global financial crisis, shows a total detachment from the tremendous potential for falling prices.

March 1998

Investors' confidence in picking their own stocks, which abounded in 1987, is back. Investors' interest in direct ownership is reflected in NYSE seat prices, which reached a new all-time record of $1.8 million in February. "More investors want access to the market," explains a money manager.

Cultural Trends

The "new optimism" has rekindled "a passion for pink." "Think Pink," says Seventeen. "In With Pink," shouts Vogue. "Pink is the perfect color for the late 1990s, a time when people are shifting gears from the misery years." Pink was the "color of the Roman Empire," says the author of new book called *Pink*. "It is the gay color. It is the color of power, and it is also the color of pigs."

May 1998

According to a Gallup poll, "two-thirds of Americans think stock prices will rise in the next six months." But read the papers closely, and you will see that many investors have narrowed their time horizons for expecting higher prices to something like the next 10 days. A spate of stories on the wonders of speculation have redirected the spotlight from patient long-term investors to newly aggressive market players like Rich Ferguson, a Utah-based mortgage loan officer with 50 to 100 call options in his portfolio. In a story about the rising popularity of options ("Betting on the Bull"), Ferguson said, "Absolutely, this market is going higher. I don't think I can go wrong with calls." Says the article, "It's clear that America's abiding faith in the stock market — key doctrine 'be in to win' — has opened up a new world of options trading, once considered too risky for most individuals."

June 1998

Do not miss the May 22 USA Today article, "Lawyers Heed Market's Siren Song." It describes the "new breed" of traders, everyday people who are quitting their day jobs for the leisurely life of stock trading.

> ## A New Breed of Traders
> ### *Pizza guys to lawyers heed market's siren song*
>
> For most at-home traders, a big draw is the work style it affords, allowing them to work in bathrobes, with their feet on their desks, with no boss save Mr. Market.
>
> Humera Aliuddin, of Lincolnwood, Ill., recently quit a job at First Chicago bank after six months. "I wanted to stay home and trade," says the recent graduate of Loyola University in Chicago. It's doubtful that any bank would let her work at home with two TVs on, one for CNBC, the other for soap operas, especially Days of Our Lives. She doesn't want to miss a thing. On her PC, she monitors the market with TradeStation software, and is frequently on the phone with her J.B Oxford broker and her cousin, who works for a brokerage. She controls a personal portfolio of about $150,000 and trades private accounts for two friends. And "I'm teaching my mom to trade," she says.
>
> —USA Today, May 22, 1998

September 1998

In the six years after the top of Cycle wave III in 1966, financial institutions, thinking they had found "bargains," nearly doubled their stock holdings, only to get killed by the biggest bear market in 40 years.

The past month is a microcosm of that psychology. In place of the fear that marked the 10% corrections of 1994, 1996 and 1997, there is a celebration of the wisdom, nerve and wealth of the little guy. One day off the high, this headline appeared: "Some Investors Enjoy a Market Decline Despite the (Temporary) Financial Hit." "Most folks get upset when the stock market dives. I like it, and I am not alone," says the WSJ's resident bull, referring to people like himself who are "loaded to the gills with stocks." On August 4, a 300-point down day with 541 new lows and 21 new highs, he added, "It is foolish to sell stocks just because prices are lower." Another article confirms, "stock pickers are breathing a sigh of relief over the sharp decline in stock prices, recalling the old mantra that smart investors love a down market." In the past two weeks, as the Dow has fluctuated dramatically, there has been no wavering in the public determination not to panic. "I was actually hoping it would go down some more, so I could buy more stocks," says a guy from Muskegon who has "seen the markets go down before and then come back."

The incredible expanding confidence shows up in the premiums on puts versus calls. On August 4, the day of the (then) third biggest point decline in Wall Street history that capped a 7-day decline of 850 points, the ratio fell to 0.29%, a low for the last five years! As investors keep telling us, they are invested for the long (keel) haul!

> ## *How to Double Your Money Every Month with Stock Split Strategies!*
>
> Spend an exhilarating evening with stock market expert and entrepreneur Lea Lerman and learn about stock splits – a proven method for making big money in the stock market! Stock splits occur daily in all kinds of companies. Lea will show you how to get information on stock split announcements the second they occur. This tried and true method has a 95% success rate – if you know what you're doing! This invaluable seminar will cover the ins and outs of stock splits.
>
> You'll also become an expert on covered-call writing and options on stock-split companies. This class is for beginners as well as experienced investors!
>
> —NYC Learning Annex Catalog, Summer 1998

October 1998

The author of the book, *What Works on Wall Street*, classified the decline in August as "the buying opportunity of a generation." One investment mantra of September 1998 is, "They are only paper losses until you sell." Like domesticated animals released into the wild, today's investors, who have been pampered in the sheltering arms of a 24-year bull market, have no respect for the speed at which a bear market can ravage one's savings.

February 1999

Carpenters, hair stylists and personal injury attorneys have abandoned careers to strike it rich as day-traders in the market. The number of on-line investors rose 34% in the fourth quarter alone and now stands at 5 million. Like the Dutch who believed "the passion for tulips would last forever," many of these new players (23% by one survey) really do believe Internet stocks cannot go down. "You gotta have faith," says a 49-year old retired cop. "My goal is a 1000% return by 2000," says a former waiter. One chat room includes a forum for traders with day jobs: "Working all day, but trading behind the boss's back."

Investors are so sure of the Internet's long-term prospects that Amazon.com, which has no credit or profit history, has floated a debt security that is viewed as a nearly risk-free way to play an Internet stock. Amazon.com sold $1.25 billion in convertible bonds at 4.75%, just 10 basis points above 10-year Treasury bonds! If you have access to the web, check out techstocks.com, the "world's largest financial discussion site." It is a living display of the exotic forms of bullishness that could only blossom in the heat of a Grand Supercycle top. If you're not on-line, catch one of the many accounts featuring the exploits of day traders. Forbes, Newsweek, The New York Times and The Washington Post have just featured illuminating articles on the Internet gold rush. These stories reveal beyond all doubt that trading has now advanced to the level of a common addiction. The accounts also confirm that the leverage in the market is far higher than the margin figures show, as countless "financial guerrillas" have raised their grubstakes with credit cards and second mortgages, which is another throw-back to 1637 when "people of all grades converted their property to cash and invested it."

This tidbit from The Washington Post hints at the size of this iceberg: "In January, Massachusetts filed suit against a day-trading firm that allegedly used $32,000 in cash to generate $99 million in debt-financed transactions." An enlightening glimpse of the intense pain to come was the story about "web traffic jams" the week of the DJIA high. Even as the market was rising, "online investing became a nightmare for the cybersavvy," as heavy trading volume overwhelmed brokerage firms. By January 15, just about "every major Internet trading house" had "experienced Website slowdowns or downright outages." This glitch will surely be magnified many times on the way down.

March 1999

One key measure of psychology, the price of stock exchange memberships, is surging. A seat on the American Exchange sold for $660,000 on February 16, a 15% increase from the record high of January 6. On February 11, the price for a Chicago Stock Exchange seat eclipsed a record that had stood since 1929. The New York Stock Exchange also surpassed its record with a $2.6 million sale on March 1. The sale, which does not include options trading rights, was a 23% increase from the record for a full membership, set in March 1998. "It's a resounding vote of confidence in the future of the New York Stock Exchange," said an economist. As the chart here

NYSE SEAT PRICES
Yearly Bars
(log scale)

Data courtesy David Toth, NYSE

shows, however, such resounding votes have proven excellent sentiment signals at all the great speculative climaxes of this century. Peak prices for NYSE seats signaled the turns of 1906, 1929, 1968 and 1987.

May 1999

To gauge long-term public sentiment, all you need to do is get out in public. What about the guy who fixes your car? If he is like the auto mechanics at the All Transmissions shop in the blue collar New York City suburb of Nanuet, you are paying him $40 an hour to split his attention between your valve job and his stock portfolio. "Each morning, even before getting their hands dirty underneath any chassis, the All Transmissions team logs on and starts looking for ideas on what stock to play." Two guys repair as the third "tracks stock prices while dealing with customers." When stock prices are moving rapidly, "they banter virtually nonstop about the market, often with their customers."

One of the three blew much of the savings he set aside to pay for his May 15 wedding. He had $25,000, but in a week, he lost $12,000, leaving $13,000, or exactly what he owes in expenses for the wedding. He could get out now and be out from under his debt. Judging from the article, however, this thought does not appear to have occurred to him. Having to ask his fiancee "how she'd feel about a honeymoon in Coney Island rather than Hawaii" clearly has. If he could, he indicates that he would dig in deeper: "Right now we're so strung up with our other investments we can't do much."

> ### SHIFTING GEARS:
> #### *Auto Mechanics Lose Big*
>
> NANUET, NY – On Monday, the three auto mechanics at All Transmissions shop in this blue-collar New York City suburb had a busy day: They rebuilt transmissions on a BMW M6, Volvo 240, Ford Explorer, Dodge Intrepid and Ford pickup.
>
> And on a Compaq laptop computer they keep at the counter to trade their stock portfolios and monitor the Internet chat rooms, they watched in dismay as the value of their stock holdings plummeted.
>
> How and why three auto mechanics working in a shop behind a strip-shopping mall became so enamored with the stock market says a lot about America's love affair with the stock market in the late 1990s. For many people, it has become an enthralling preoccupation that they indulge in while working at their real – often more mundane – occupations.
>
> Each morning, even before getting their hands dirty underneath any chassis, the All Transmissions team logs on and starts looking for ideas on what stock to play.
>
> —The Wall Street Journal
> April 21, 1999

The "newest Internet craze [is] called 'Minute Trading.'" "Minute Trading (for you Neanderthals who buy stocks and hold them for more than 24 hours) is buying a stock, holding it for only a matter of minutes, and selling for a quick profit," reports Bloomberg.

June 1999

The latest figures show that April witnessed the largest one-month percentage jump in margin debt in history. The increase to $181.94 billion was from a record high in March. In normal times, particularly given the background of slowing upside momentum, these figures would constitute an unequivocal "sell signal." Only the words, "It's a mania," keep one from 100% confidence that the market will do the normal thing and turn into a bear. Though it is too early to say, perhaps our next observation will be, "It was a mania."

Corporations are discovering that much of the American work force has been diverted from production, as "millions of wage earners, managers and entrepreneurs [are] obsessing about Wall Street." The New York Times reveals that the orgy of intra-day trading, which "far eclipses the speculative 1920s," has become a big personnel problem at many companies. Charles Schwab's website now averages 33 million visits a day, a 37.5% increase from the fourth quarter of 1998. Its busiest hours are right after the open and right before the close. A dentist tracks stocks between patients, sometimes even between X-rays and fillings. A freight-company manager logs on to a financial web site for four to six hours of his workday. A designer gets so absorbed in the market that his billable hours fall by 25%. This is evidence of a collective investment sophistication that is plummeting, not rising.

Instead of warning people of the danger thus implied, brokerage firms and other financial industry interest groups are fanning the flames with promotions. Have you seen the commercial in which the truck driver turns out to be a world-class trader who is so wealthy that he owns his own island? Earlier this month, it beat out over 300 entries in a contest sanctioned by the Financial Communications Society. The award honors "the best creative solutions to marketing and advertising challenges in financial services."

July 1999

The word "trader" is bandied about these days as if it meant something other than "buyer." A buyer is not a trader. Stocks such as America Online and UBid that move down 29% or 82% should be "darlings of day traders." Those are huge moves; their direction is irrelevant. An actual trader could make money from them. But a buyer cannot. "A former can't-lose day trader" in this context means a former couldn't-lose bull. The very idea that the novice legion buying internet or any other stocks are traders is ludicrous. They are bullish maniacs, caught up in the mania. The proof is that a measly 6% pullback in the Dow can ruin them.

We know this type of people because we found ourselves surrounded by them at the Las Vegas Money Show a few days after this article appeared. If we could put a name on this year's conference, it would be "Invasion of the Day Buyers." In place of the mutual fund companies that used to dominate the Bally's convention center floor, on-line brokerage firms, software trading companies and data providers hawked

Net Stocks' Fall Injures Day Traders

TYSON'S CORNER, Va. – A former can't-lose day trader, who bought lots of stock "on margin" — meaning with borrowed money — just got hit with a "maintenance call." Her account at the All-Tech Investment branch office here has dwindled so low that she must put up more cash or sell her five remaining stocks — at steep losses. Well, she doesn't have any more cash, so she sits in front of her trading station trying to sell out of OneMain.com. She would be happy to get $20 a share now for her 2000 shares, though she bought it months ago at $42. At the All-Tech office here, some customers seemingly vanished. As the Internet stocks plunge like pricked helium balloons, many of the day traders who gorged on such stocks are in near-shock. Many are facing large portfolio losses. Many of those who buy on margin are being hit with margin calls. Now, the Internet winners are rare.

—USA Today, June 1, 1999

fast and easy access to the market. Workshops were titled "Double the Dow," "40% Annual Gain From Value-based Momentum Stocks," and "How to Become a Millionaire in Short-Term Trading." A Vegas casino was the perfect setting. As we studied the electrified air created by the crowd of 10,000, we could not help but think of the way the June 1 USA Today story had closed, with the featured trader "determined to start over. She is selling her town home and plans to devote much of the proceeds to day trading. 'It's addictive,' she says. 'I am convinced I can come back.'" When the market sinks relentlessly one of these days, the people we observed will surely suffer from the same conviction.

Based on the most consistently available measure, the number of people in the market is now nearly twice as great as it was at the last all-time high in 1987. This is based on Sindlinger Inc.'s (Wallingford, PA) survey of stock ownership by American households. We consider this to be the most definitive measure of the number of U.S. investors because Al Sindlinger has been compiling the figures on a regular basis since 1957. The chart shows the weekly percentage back through 1974. In

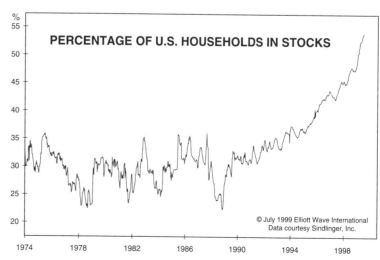

PERCENTAGE OF U.S. HOUSEHOLDS IN STOCKS

© July 1999 Elliott Wave International
Data courtesy Sindlinger, Inc.

January, the total crossed 50% for the first time ever, and it has continued to rise to an all-time high of 54% as of June 24. The total reflects 104.7 million people, an increase of more than 14 million since the stock market's momentum peak in April 1998. Prior to the 1990s, the highest figure ever recorded by Sindlinger was 36%, or 53.4 million, which came two weeks after the August 1987 stock market peak. The swelling of the ranks of buyers after the high is classic crowd behavior, and it's happening now.

The historical significance of Sindlinger's survey is enhanced by similar polls done on an intermittent basis beginning in 1939. Of particular interest is the first survey, a series of more than 500 in-depth personal interviews conducted by Sindlinger in various cities. Based on these interviews, Sindlinger determined that approximately 21% of American households were in the market in 1929. Since it was derived 10 years after the fact, the figure lacks some reliability. The current peak is 54%.

August 1999

The ultimate evidence of the ticker tape's magnetism is the on-line investing boom. Day trading is nothing more than a bullish reaction to the "excitement and challenge" of rising prices. That was EWFF's assertion last month, and it was confirmed by a series of July 18 New York Times interviews with day traders across the country. Prices are down, so the day traders' accounts are, too. Since the Internet stocks peaked in April, selectivity, caution and even nervousness have crept into "this preternaturally optimistic community." "In the old days, it was free money," said one "trader." None seemed ready to pack it in, however. "This has been a big reality check, but people forget. Once some frenzy starts, people will go back to the old style."

Internet stock trading is not the only outlet for stock market gamblers. The Chicago Board Options Exchange reports that individuals have driven the average daily volume of options to a record high. Discount broker Charles Schwab had an 80% increase in its options business in the second quarter. "Investors are swarming to seminars [that cost up to $4000] to learn the tricks of options trade."

If the histories are right, and participants in the mania will recover their senses "one by one," we should not expect to see any windfall of recognition at the peak. This comic strip seems about right. It suggests that a few vaguely recognize the risk and absurdity that underlie the whole affair. Today's late afternoon All-Tech tragedy, in which a day-trader "concerned about financial losses" took 12 lives in Atlanta, occurred just a week and a half later. The rate of movement from the funny papers to the front page suggests the repercussions after a year of falling prices will be far more severe.

According to a California man, to trade options these days, "You have to be able to take $10,000 in your fist, stand at the edge of a cliff and throw it off." The "edge of a cliff" describes the sentiment of a surprising number of investors now. As the market heads down, look for this image to assert itself more strongly. Regardless of the risk they subliminally feel, many investors continue to play because they are being impelled by their impulse to herd with the crowd.

FOXTROT   By Bill Amend

290

September 1999

Mild consumer confidence is not dangerous to the stock market, but an extreme confidence has been stock market poison. The Consumer Sentiment Index shows a progression from tentative expressions of confidence in the 1950s to the current period, in which consumers have displayed extreme confidence for almost two and a half years. Prior to today, the longest period of high confidence lasted a year and occurred at the end of Cycle wave III. The current phase is the first to sustain readings above 100 since the 1966 peak, and it has held there for a longer time and reached a higher level despite a lesser rate of economic growth. Another measure, the Consumer Confidence Index, offers further historical context. The all-time high for the CCI, which dates back to the mid-1960s, was registered in October 1968, two months before the Dow reached a peak that was not materially surpassed for 14 years. The next highest reading was registered on June 30, 1999.

October 1999

Investors have a stronger commitment to this market than their stated levels of bullishness. The Commitment vs. Belief indicator measures investors' actual investment against their bullish expectations by subtracting the percentage of bulls in the American Association of Individual Investors sentiment survey from AAII member equity allocations. Basically, it shows how willing individuals are today to ignore their own negative sentiments toward the market and stick to the buy-and-hold-no-matter-what philosophy they have so long espoused. The chart shows that over the last 12 years, investors have gradually succumbed to the idea of staying in the market against their own unfavorable judgments about direction. In a way, 1999 has marked a supreme accomplishment, as the spread stretched to 40%. The peak reading came in February, when

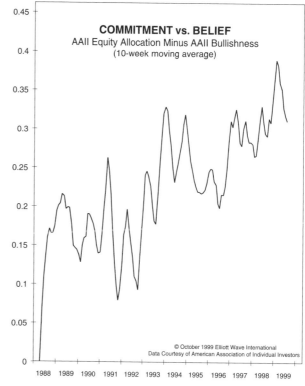

72% of AAII member assets were allocated to stocks or stock funds and only 31% were bullish. At the beginning of Primary wave 5 in late 1987, individuals were actually more bullish than they were invested. In a bull market, people learn to ignore their misgivings about the market as conflicts between high levels of stock ownership and lower levels of bullishness have continually been resolved positively by the market, at least until the final high.

November 1999

Last month, EWFF showed a headline (see Chapter 5) marking the stock market's elevation to the level of national pastime. This status has been confirmed by TV coverage of the World Series, which featured as many advertisements for trading services as innings. According to the October 28 New York Times, "On-line investment firms, many of which did not exist two years ago, have collectively bought more World Series ad time than any other industry, displacing even GM, the marketing monolith of sports. During nearly every inning break and throughout the pregame shows, Fidelity is pitching its offerings against E*Trade or Merrill Lynch, with Datek and Ameritrade also vying for a slice of baseball fans' household income." "Baseball is very American and apple pie," said an executive of a firm that entices would-be traders with, "Be your own sugar daddy." "People are taking control of investing themselves, and that's very American, too." One ad for Datek Services showed a modern-day investment mob crashing through the doors and windows of the New York Stock Exchange as an announcer proclaims, "the tools of serious trading" are "now available to everyone." Most of these ads are humorous, which suits the stock market's new role as the ultimate plaything.

Further evidence comes from Playboy's new growth strategy, which will be "heavily skewed to money, sports and sex, a place where surfers can check out their stock portfolio, their favorite sports team or super-model Naomi Campbell." The firm plans to take its on-line business public early next year. These pop culture enticements and offerings are significant because they are generating a whole new wave of enthusiastic and totally unsophisticated investors. Joe Granville called this class of investors the "bagholders" because it always appears at or after a market peak with an aggressive attitude that demands, "Gimme that bag!"

FORTUNE
OCTOBER 11, 1999

The Hunt For The Youth Pill • Inside the New China • The Hottest Chip Stock

Trader Nation

At work, at home, all day, all night: Everybody wants a piece of this stock market. It's more than a bull gone mad. It's a new set of rules. They can break you or make you _rich ..._

A Nation of Traders

What we have here is nothing short of a revolution. Power that for generations lay with a few thousand white males on a small island in New York City is now being seized by Everyman and Everywoman. Our new national fixation with investing can't be written off as simply a sign of a market top (you know, where the rubes all rush into the market).

—Fortune, October 11, 1999

January 2000

Sentiment can be summed up in two words: "party on."

December's Consumer Confidence reading of 141.4 is the highest since October 1968, two months before the start of a 6-year collapse of 74% in the Value Line index. The Gallup Organization also recorded a dramatic escalation in the public's short- and long-term expectations in December. On a long-term basis, investors' anticipated annual return from stocks over the next 10 years hit 19%! This expectation was up from 16.2% in November, which was already the highest figure recorded by Gallup. Short-term optimism soared even more dramatically based on the Gallup Index of Investor Optimism. The latest reading of 167 is the highest since the poll began in October 1996. 72% said this is a good time to be buying stocks.

February 2000

In mid-January, Gallup measured an astounding total of 82% bulls on the stock market. That record figure came upon a leap from 71% in December. Gallup's Index of Investor Optimism also hit a record at 181, a 14-point pop from December's all-time high. The monthly Index had a baseline of 100 when it was created in October 1996.

A more established measure, the Consumer Confidence Index, confirms the long-term significance of these new marks with a record high of its own. The figure of 144.7 in January surpasses the previous high of 142.3 in October 1968, little more than one month before the Dow hit a peak that was not be materially exceeded for 14 years and the Value Line registered a top that was not exceeded for 15 years. Consumers' assessments of their present conditions and job prospects also hit their highest levels ever.

With the race for the U.S. Presidency officially underway, the pundits are out in force to get the pulse of America. Many have commented on the "staggering" optimism that now prevails. Several have even pointed out that the "feel-good mindset" is the antithesis of the atmosphere in 1980 when Ronald Reagan asked voters, "Are you better off today than you were eight years ago?" Voters' resounding "no" got Reagan elected. It also provided an ideal example of the kind of sentiment that precedes major stock market advances.

Gallup has no comparable figures for the two periods, but it notes in a release that the "ebullient mood at the beginning of 2000" is the reverse of 1980, which is exactly the message of the Elliott Wave Principle. A Gallup comparison between today and the start of the upwave from 1992 quantifies a similar contrast: "Today, the mood is strongly upbeat with 83% of Americans satisfied with the state of the economy, 71% rating the economy excellent or good, 69% saying economic conditions are getting better. ...In 1992, 25% of Americans were satisfied with the state of the economy, just 18% rated the economy as excellent or good and only 29% felt the economic condition were getting better."

These two charts present more graphic illustrations of the spiraling commitment to the bull market. The first shows the hours that the average manufacturing employee must work to buy a share of the S&P 500. The parabolic rise since the mid-1990s means that it will take a decline of about two-thirds to bring the measure back to where it was at its peaks in 1966 and 1987. The other shows the record high in margin debt against the long rise in stock prices. Notice that the recent blast to $228 billion in December represents an increase of 62%, or about three times the Dow's growth over the same span. In the last nine months, moreover, a 32% increase in margin has been accompanied by no net gain in the Dow. Even a slowdown in the rise in margin debt should lead to falling stock prices.

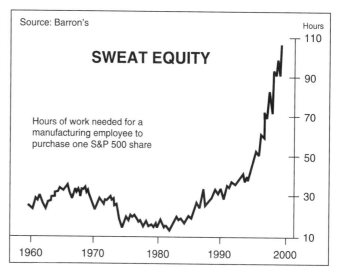

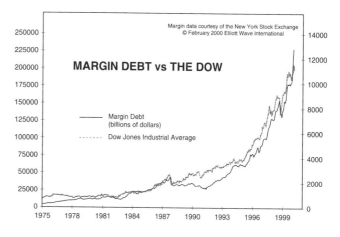

March 2000

Gallup's Index of Investor Optimism has climbed to another record high of 184 in February, its highest level ever. 73% of those surveyed say it is a good time to invest in stocks, a 10% increase from January. Gallup's latest stock-market poll also uncovered the addition of some interesting new converts to the buy-the-dip club, as its index of female investors' sentiment jumped 50 points to a record high of 179 despite the Dow's fall since mid-January. Sentiment measures show that the dip-buyers have moved beyond fearless and actually become excited by falling prices. In the week of February 25, the Dow's 16.3% decline from its all-time high produced an average put/call ratio of .42, which is lower than the five-day ratio at the January 14 peak! Declines of just 10% in October 1997 and August 1998 produced put/call ratios that were almost twice as high, at .79 and .86 respectively.

The Uh-Oh Effect

The record surge in margin debt has led more than a few to speculate that Wall Street may be on a "Drunken Borrowing Binge." Then there are the discouraging words of the nation's premier credit rating agency. Standard & Poor's made an even more negative assessment when it put the U.S. on a ratings watch list that includes Cyprus, Panama and Egypt. The S&P is worried that equity prices could be overstated. "A sharp correction in the stock market could lead to a hard landing for the economy and, thus, banks."

We do not view this sentiment as a contrary indicator, however, because even if investors have concerns as a result of hearing an occasional warning, they do not act on them. According to the American Association of Individual Investors' most recent survey of equity allocation, the average investor is 77% in stocks, the highest equity exposure ever. "Let's be real. Lots of people are feeling skittish these days," says a Wall Street Journal article on investment strategy. But acting on such an opinion might mean missing something on the upside. "'The average person must ride it out,' says [a] Nobel Prize winner. A 'very bearish' investor who normally has an 80% stake in stocks might trim that to 70%." Quotes such as these will deserve preservation in bronze when the bear market is mature.

As *At the Crest of the Tidal Wave* said, "There are times in history when the percentage of naive investors is so high that occasional warnings from professionals are irrelevant to net market psychology.... [It] is in fact normal behavior at the biggest tops of all." For some perspective on how big this peak might be, consider Alan Greenspan's ongoing battle with lawmakers, reporters and the public over his concerns about "irrational exuberance." The Fed sounded similar alarms about the sustainability of stock prices at the peaks of Supercycle (III) in 1929 and Cycle III in 1966. In those cases, the warnings from key Federal Reserve figures preceded the peak by a few months. This time, Greenspan's skeptical observations actually began more than three years ago. So, even when it comes to the duration of the uh-oh effect and the accompanying annoyance over its expression, we appear to be facing something larger than the Supercycle degree peak of 1929.

Dollar Trading Volume of Equities

The great thing about this chart of Dollar Trading Volume as a % of GDP is that it actually quantifies the sentiment at the unfolding Grand Supercycle-degree turn against that of 1929. *The Wave Principle of Human Social Behavior* noted that by comparing the total value of shares

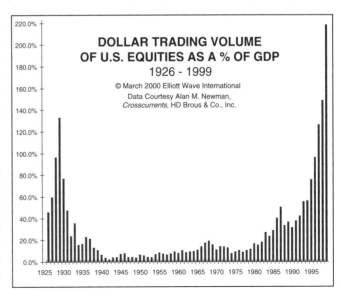

traded to the value of goods produced, this ratio measures the national involvement in the stock market. "The higher the degree of the wave that is ending, the more extreme will be the value of trading activity relative to the value of production." So far, the volume/GDP ratio has surpassed the high of 1929 by about 65%. The final figure will almost certainly be closer to 100%, however, as the reversal should be accompanied by a tremendous surge in volume. On the biggest day of the 1929 crash, for instance, volume was four times the average daily level for the prior two months.

April 2000

In another interesting manifestation of the mania, a Gallup poll of 1003 people found that a Fibonacci 61% of Americans had some form of investment in the market. The survey was initiated the day of the NASDAQ peak, March 10. The same figure was recorded by Gallup in their poll of January 10, four days before the Dow's all-time high. Chapter 12 of *Human Social Behavior* displays several studies and experiments linking 61.8%, the Fibonacci ratio or phi, to the stock market. A built-in sampling error and an answer of "no response" by 2% of those polled is enough to speculate that the percentage of investors has reached a perfect Fibonacci level of participation as a result of the greatest stock buying mania of all time.

A second example of the "Fibonacci tendency in decision-making" turned up in the answer to another question from the same poll. 62% of respondents said the recent volatility in the market is "the normal type of fluctuation to be expected and not a sign of a long-term change in the direction of the market." This entry from HSB offers an intriguing possible explanation for the high level of affirmative answers:

> Opinion is predisposed to a 62/38 inclination. With respect to each individual decision, the availability of pertinent data, the influence of prior experiences and/or learned biases can modify that ratio in any given instance. However, phi is what the mind starts with. It defaults to phi whenever parameters are unclear or information insufficient for an utterly objective assessment.

May 2000

Though the NASDAQ experienced one of the most dramatic reversals in U.S. stock-market history, the bullish resolve of investors was hardly dented. Within days of the culminating 10% decline of April 14, the American Association of Individual Investors' level of bullishness was 63.7%, which was 27% higher than it was on March 15! Investors Intelligence's measure of bullish advisory sentiment was 50.5%, just 3.5 percentage points lower than it was a month earlier. On April 14, 54.9% of advisors were bullish, which was higher than its level at the January peak in the Dow.

Until the final moments of the NASDAQ decline, several major mutual fund companies reported no net redemptions. In fact, tracking services reported that money was actually pouring in as late as April 11, when "stock funds focused on aggressive growth stocks — mainly technology companies — took in $6.7 billion in the five days." After the April 14 rout, Fidelity Funds told the Boston Globe that its customers were turning "their money over to its stock fund managers at rates unheard of just a few years ago. ...Mutual fund companies, under strict orders from clients, are shoveling money into the stock market even as the market lurches. Once a trickle, mutual fund investments have grown into a flood of money."

The Scudder Kemper funds plans to lure investors with a $4 million ad campaign focusing on its superbullish lead fund manager. Bill Froehlich is a big believer in "boomernomics" and the author of a book called *The Three Bears are Dead!* Business Week says the reason Scudder is "branding itself by featuring Froehlich is that he's an unabashed bull. ...His visage is even etched upon an aromatherapy candle in the shape of Mt. Rushmore. 'The candle's scent is meant to calm investors who are agitated by the market volatility.'" As the bear market drags on, similar "stay-in-the-market-no-matter-what" products and services will undoubtedly become very

Did the markets really "lose" trillions in the recent slide? No, not really. The losses were almost certainly temporary, like losing your glasses.
The Objective American, April 1, 2000

Buyers Out There, Everything's on Sale
USA Today, April 18, 2000

RETURNING TO EARTH ISN'T SO BAD, PROMISING INVESTMENTS ABOUND
BusinessWeek, June 26, 2000

A Day of Margin Calls and Bargain Hunting

Mark Lyan, owner of Chef Wang, a Chinese restaurant in Dallas, keeps a computer above the cash register in his restaurant so he can trade during the day. But despite losing $100,000 on paper in the past few days, he figures he hasn't lost money until he sells.

"We're having an incredibly rational resolution of a major market imbalance, which the market has a really good track record of doing," says Ed Kerschner, chief investment strategist at PaineWebber, who thinks the overall market is reasonably valued but the "new new" tech stocks aren't. "You have to kill this 'new metrics' mania."
THE WALL STREET JOURNAL, April 5, 2000

Market Rout Ushers In Opportunity
THE WALL STREET JOURNAL, April 17, 2000

When asked to assess the mood of their companies in light of Nasdaq's meltdown, CEO after CEO explained why so steep a decline in their stock was actually a good thing.
Newsweek, May 15, 2000

"Stocks haven't suddenly become tulip bulbs"
THE WALL STREET JOURNAL, April 17, 2000

Equities are finally looking more reasonable and profits are still going strong
BusinessWeek, June 26, 2000

popular, but they have yet to take off. Demand is still running much higher for "opinions" that validate investors' decision to buy the decline.

That's the genius of Kemper's new marketing strategy. The firm doesn't have to pay a penny to get its bull-market "cheerleader" in front of the public. One market day after the NASDAQ April 14 retreat, Froehlich was making the "Case for Tech Stocks" on the cover of The Wall Street Journal's investment section. "He's more convinced than ever he's right," reported the Journal. "The NASDAQ slide, he scoffs, is 'the bear's brief day in the sun.' In a month, he predicts, investors will kick themselves for not snapping up their favorite stocks at a 20% to 50% discount. Says Mr. Froehlich: 'This is the greatest opportunity for individual investors in a long time.'" The comments appeared next to a chart showing a 51.2% decline in Yahoo!

After Iomega and the first tier of bubble stocks cracked in July 1996, the dip-buying public said the same thing, and they were right. They were right again in the Octobers of 1997, 1998 and 1999. And, yes, it could happen again, but there is reason to suspect that this continual affront to the natural order in markets has finally spent itself. For one thing, at this bottom, fear had been replaced by an overwhelming belief that the decline was the "best thing that could happen." It was "a little dose of reality" or a "good and healthy thing." A Business Week cover called it "healthy flight." It shows investors are "sane," according to a Wall Street Journal opinion piece; "the remaining bullish sentiment is more mature and tested." In Silicon Valley, the loss of countless billions was greeted with a "We-Needed-That Sigh." The chief scientist for an Internet software company explained, "It's like a forest fire. A clearing out is very, very healthy." That is, unless it consumes the whole forest.

The gradual spread of major peaks, from the advance/decline line in April 1998 to virtually every other sector of the global equity market, suggests that this fire has, in fact, encircled the forest. Still, the exhortations to diversify into as many different equity instruments as possible are pouring in. The chairman of one of the big online-trading firms even put out a memo reminding customers, "Don't forget to diversify." So, even as the strategy breaks down, its magnetism as a panacea for losses grows stronger. This trap was covered in the last chapter of *At the Crest of the Tidal Wave*: "Diversity is not going to save people this time. Diversified portfolios will be guaranteed losers." *At the Crest* has a paragraph in "How to Handle the Coming Environment," a great explanation for why people fail to take defensive action (or, in this case, continue to take offensive action) against the slow sweep of changes that are in violent opposition to their expectations. The passage concludes with this observation from stock market historian John Brooks about the 1929-1933 experiences:

> It came with a kind of surrealistic slowness...so gradually that, on the one hand, it was possible to live through a good part of it without realizing that it was happening, and, on the other hand, it was possible to believe one had experienced and survived it when in fact it had no more than just begun.

June 2000

The main trends in consumer confidence have always been tuned to stock prices. The first major peak above 100 ended in early 1966, right after the peak of Cycle wave III in February 1966. In the bear market that followed, consumer sentiment continued to track stock prices, hitting bottom a few weeks after the two lowest points in the sixteen-year decline. Together, these points (shown by the line on the bottom of the chart) produced a divergence that may explain what is happening now. As you can see, a higher Dow low in March 1980 (vs. December 1974) accompanied a lower low in the sentiment of consumers. Just as pessimism overshot on the downside then, optimism has slipped its moorings at the all-time peak. Since the Dow topped in January, consumer sentiment has been running at its highest level in the 50-year history of the survey. "The current optimism is like a virus that is spreading and has no treatment," states The Washington Post.

After interviewing 3000 investors between April 21 and May 12, pollster Dick Morris concluded, "There is a tremendous resiliency. It's an in-depth, long-term confidence." 62% said that if the market

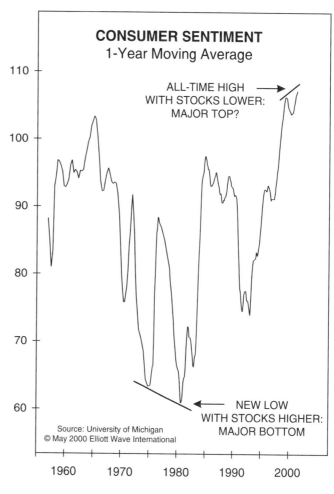

fell another 20% they would see it as opportunity to buy stocks at reduced values. "Everybody knows that we need lots of rain to make things grow," says a Motley Fool lesson called "The Logic of Hoping for a Bear Market."

Wall Street professionals have also been feasting on plunging stocks. In an April 28 survey of Wall Street strategists, Richard Bernstein of Merrill Lynch recorded an average equity allotment of 60.6%, a total that has only been materially exceeded once before in the 15-year history of the review. Bernstein said that the remarkable thing about the survey was that it was the first time "analysts got more bullish in response" to falling prices. The one higher reading came in early 1994, before a year-long retrenchment in stock prices.

Lack of fear is also readily apparent in the S&P Commitment of Traders data for Large Speculators (the trend followers). Large Specs have bought nearly the entire decline from the

March 24 peak. They now hold their largest net long position since the January 1992 high, a peak in prices that led to a nearly year-long correction. The occasional plunge is part of the fun now. After the April 14 decline, The Wall Street Journal reported that Internet enthusiasts were literally raising their arms up "like a kid on the Space Mountain ride at Disneyland" to demonstrate their approach to the stock market. Another article notes that Internet fund shareholders can "stomach the thrills and spills" of relatively risky Internet funds. "It's exciting," said one Internet stock fund holder. "It's like estrogen for women." "Such thinking has helped the mania for such funds to continue unabated and, it appears, unsated." This is classic psychology for the lower peak of the rally after the top.

August 2000

Investors still love stocks. According to the American Association of Individual Investors, 66.6% of its members were bullish in the week ended July 20. This reading is the next-to-highest reading in the 13-year history of the AAII survey, second only to the outrageous record high of 75% eight days before the January peak in the Dow Industrials. The third-highest total of 66% was recorded at the peak in August 1987. The public [is] bullish, which is not bullish for the market.

September 2000

In bear markets, "wave two" rebounds can induce a bullish psychology that equals or exceeds what existed at the high. One sure sign of a second wave peak is the appearance of new sentiment extremes after a choppy, corrective-type move. This is the case now. The latest S&P 500 Commitment of Traders report (www.bullishreview.com) shows that Small Traders, who are usually wrong at significant turns, had all-time record net-long positions in August. Meanwhile, the smart-money Commercials, who are usually right, hold near record net-short positions. This combination of positions reveals the most bearish technical situation (by this measure) ever, which fits the Elliott wave case that a Grand Supercycle degree wave is topping.

The Margin Monster Waits

Here's an important fact. According to Bloomberg, margin debt as a percentage of total stock market capitalization (NYSE, NAS-DAQ & AMEX) has barely budged from its high of 1.59%. Here's another. The high came not with the

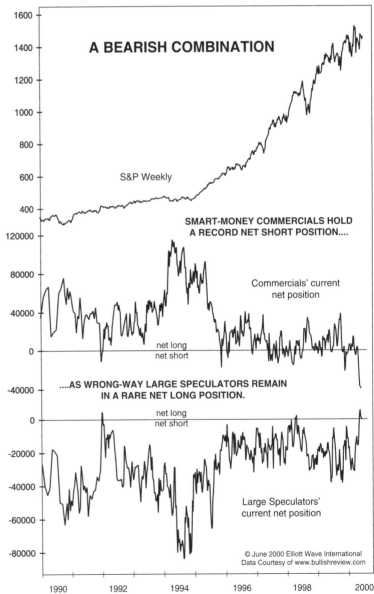

A BEARISH COMBINATION

S&P Weekly

SMART-MONEY COMMERCIALS HOLD A RECORD NET SHORT POSITION....

Commercials' current net position

net long
net short

....AS WRONG-WAY LARGE SPECULATORS REMAIN IN A RARE NET LONG POSITION.

net long
net short

Large Speculators' current net position

© June 2000 Elliott Wave International
Data Courtesy of www.bullishreview.com

NASDAQ's peak in March, but on its low in May. Clearly, the stock market's staunchest supporters have not lost faith. The WSJ story of a podiatrist/trader who now depends on his trading income to pay the bills bears this out. When the NASDAQ plunged on April 14, the doctor's account was down $1 million, 80% of his heavily margined portfolio. "Just three months after margin debt fueled his portfolio's collapse, [he] is once again borrowing heavily to boost his returns."

In a similar story, a 36-year-old, stay-at-home mom in San Antonio also got rocked hard by margin calls. She wishes she "could go back to 1999…and never day-trade and never get myself into this mess." She cannot quit because she says she is addicted to trading. Obviously, however, the addiction is not to trading, because falling prices would not put a true trader in de-tox; she would be short. What these people are hooked on is hope. Margin debt's persistence near its peak suggests that investors have been anxiously holding out for another big upleg. The result is an undercurrent of nervous tension that makes the sideways action of recent months far more dangerous than most observers realize. The longer it goes on, the more strung out these hopium addicts become.

This weight on the market is even heavier than the margin figures show. As *The Elliott Wave Theorist* has noted, the bull market has leveraged its ascent with a unique array of financial devices. In the past, EWT has pointed to the derivatives industry, which has created untallied trillions of dollars of exposure to market risk. The near-meltdown of August 1998 shows the instability that can result. In various ways, mortgages have also become a vast source of hidden margin. Consider Wall Street's latest mechanism for doubling down on the American Dream, a mortgage that allows borrowers to use stocks as collateral to buy a house. Says The Wall Street Journal, "Imagine: You pay nothing down on your house while the money you would have spent rides up and down with the latest dot-com or your favorite blue chip." One financial planner says it is "betting the farm — literally," but others say "the products are actually quite useful."

November 2000

For probably the first time since 1987, the weeks leading up to October did not include a major story drawing parallels to the crashes of 1929 and 1987 and reminding everyone that October can be a frightful month for stocks. On October 18, the Dow was down 10% for the month, and murmurs of concern finally crept into the media. Yet even as the Dow plunged into the 9600s for the first time in 18 months, advisors magically turned a bearish month into a bullish one, arguing that Octobers provide opportunities to buy. (Any one who bought during October 1973 might wish to argue that point.) "We are very near the end of an ugly period that began last April," said one investment strategist. "Within the next week to 10 days we will make a bottom."

One day later, the media spin centered on the whipsaw reversal from "Panic Selling To Bargain Hunting." Newspapers wondered, "Is Bottom Here?" and "Has Dow Finally Hit Bottom?" A wire service asked, "October Spooks Investors; Is Rebound Next?" After one more day of rising prices, another paper had a definitive answer: "History Predicts Markets Will Rally." Even though it seems anomalous, the bear market has strengthened the buy-the-dip mentality. Like teenagers who have been through the haunted house one too many times, investors just aren't frightened by "boo!" anymore.

> ### Market Turbulence Does Little to Curb Investors' Optimism
>
> The get-rich-quick hysteria of recent years may be gone, and in the last six weeks stocks have looked fragile amid fears that economic growth is slowing and corporate profits will fall short of expectations.
>
> But a raft of evidence, both anecdotal and statistical, suggests that exactly six months after the technology-heavy NASDAQ composite index suffered its worst week ever, Americans remain optimistic that stocks are the best place for their money.
>
> The confidence is striking.
>
> Investors remember that big drops in 1998, after the Asian financial crisis, and 1987 proved to be little more than great buying opportunities, said Charles Geisst, finance professor at Manhattan College and author of "Wall Street: A History."
>
> "Everybody, including myself, views this as a short-term blip," Mr. Geisst said.
>
> —The New York Times, October 15, 2000

December 2000

Another extenuating factor for this leg of the bear market is the margin problem covered in prior issues. In relation to the size of the market, margin debt is still almost as high as it has ever been. As of October, margin debt as a percentage of total market capitalization was still slightly higher than its level of 1.58% at the NASDAQ's March high. This means that investors have used every last drop of credit to buy the "pullback."

January 2001

The bottom fishers are certainly out in force. The following headline is from a financial column that recommended purchase of five of the worst-performing stocks of 2000 "in the belief that what goes down almost invariably goes up — and goes up big:"

Down 78% — We Call That Stock a Buy

Even though they have been burned the worst over the last nine months, high-risk investors are the most bullish. According to one survey, 66% of aggressive investors think the NASDAQ will be higher in a year and 70% think the Dow will be up. Meanwhile, calls for "choosing widely diversified stock funds," "good defensive stockpicking" systems and a "return to value" are more prominent than ever as soothing the nerves of the "buy and hold" crowd has become a page-one priority.

Since the unfolding contraction must also destroy the equity culture that emerged in the 1990s, the desire to pick up bargains extends beyond the stock market. Any asset that is well off its high is considered a potential buy. Despite its worst year since at least 1987, for instance, junk bonds are drawing all kinds of interest. "Junk Bonds Are So Cheap, They Look Good," says one of several bullish headlines. In fact, "the wish" of many is that "things will get just a little bit worse," according to The Wall Street Journal. "A lot of Americans see an upside to the economic downturn: a chance to finally swoop in on some relative deals."

At this point, the prime targets are "homes, luxury cars, high-end electronics and vacations — the very things that often suffer first in a slump." In an appropriate epithet, the Journal tabbed this phenomenon the "vulture culture." This "culture" embodies the post-peak psychology described in *At the Crest*. It is the reason readers were admonished, "Be prepared to resist the relentless drumbeat of hopeful opinion." The drums are pounding it out today at deafening volume.

February 2001

Another measure that hints at the extent of the next downturn is consumer expectations. In December, Consumer Sentiment plunged below 100, and in January, that decline extended to 93.6. The plunge is significant because it marks the first time the index has been below 100 for two months in a row since 1996; it also confirms the end of history's second sustained rise above 100. The only other era of comparable good feelings ended with Cycle wave III in 1966. At four years and eight months, the most re-

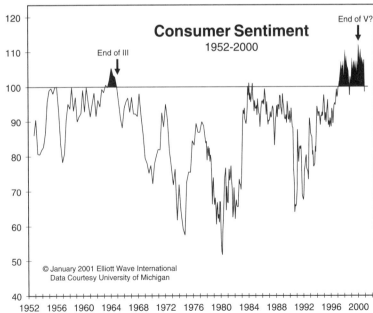

cent phase was a Fibonacci 2.6 times the length of the other persistent consumer euphoria in 1964-1966, which was followed by a succession of lower highs and lower lows that lasted for 13 years. The record-long persistence of optimism beyond the peak in stocks despite the weakening fundamentals of Cycle V (see Chapter 1 of *Conquer the Crash*) suggests once again that the coming contraction will be more serious than the one that followed Cycle III in 1966. This type of decline is something even the most pessimistic consumers are totally unprepared for; the University of Michigan's latest monthly poll also found that among those Americans expecting recession, 74% believe it will be mild.

Volume Revs Higher

In March 2000, EWFF showed the chart of dollar trading volume of U.S. equities as a % of GDP on and noted that the ratio had surpassed the high of 1929 by 65%. We added that the "final figure will almost certainly be closer to 100%, as the reversal should be accompanied by a tremendous surge in volume." In 2000, dollar trading volume exceeded the high of 1929 by more than 150%.

With wave ③ down in the Dow still ahead, we expect this ratio to rise still further. In already pushing so far beyond

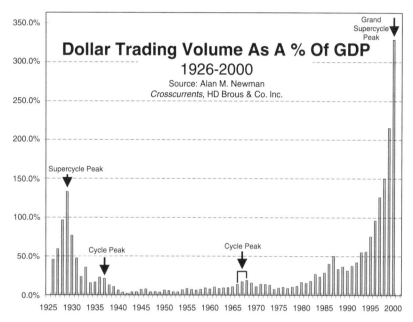

the record high of 1929, however, the volume figures for 2000 accentuate the whole point we made about this chart in *The Wave Principle of Human Social Behavior*. The latest figure is clearly commensurate with a volume peak of at least one higher degree than the Supercycle peak of 1929. It also argues strongly that a price peak is in place, because 2000's unprecedented volume surge was accompanied by a down year for the Dow, NASDAQ and S&P indexes.

April 2001

Despite the uptick in near-term bearishness, a wellspring of hope continues to gush through Wall Street. Nothing exemplifies this fact better than the reaction to the 100-point decline of March 22. With a late rally, the Dow closed at 9389.84 or a net decline of 19.9% from its all-time high. Even though the Dow was down 100 points and declining NYSE stocks outnumbered gainers by more than 3 to 1, a big cheer went up on the floor of the exchange because the late surge had pulled the Industrials "Out of the Bear's Jaws." As the Wall Street Journal reported the next day, the "bounce kept the average barely out of its first bear market in more than 10 years, by the commonly accepted definition of a 20% drop from a closing high (only a close in bear-market territory counts; intraday visits to bear country don't)." Never mind that the NASDAQ was down more than 60%, the S&P 25% and the Dow Transports 30% at the time. Or that 20% is an arbitrary level that has only been "commonly accepted" in recent years (in the old days a bear market began when people started losing money). Or the fact that a quantitative definition for a bear market is ridiculous, implying that 19.99% is not a bear market but 20% is. What we watch is psychology. The very real sense of relief that accompanied the move back across 9389 is an important long-term indicator because it shows that the belief in the transitory nature of losses is alive and well.

The "new era" is over, but the delusions that created it are not. Confirmation of this observation still arrives from all kinds of extra-market sources. The Weekend newspaper magazine and TV Guide both featured "soothing financial advice" from TV anchormen. A call-in query to local consumer advocates offered further proof. The frightened stock holder wanted to know if it is a good idea to meet a margin call with credit card debt.

May 2001

The Uh-Oh Effect Revisited

Another reason to expect this bear market to blow through many negative developments is that an undercurrent of skepticism has actually accompanied the decline from its very inception. Even as the March peak for the S&P and NASDAQ approached, EWFF observed "more than a few" concerns about overly high margin levels and Standard & Poor's placement of the U.S. equity markets on its ratings watch list. We added, however, "We do not view this sentiment as a contrary indicator." Instead, we said it was another reason to expect a large-degree bear market. We dubbed this phenomenon the Uh-Oh Effect. Well, as often happens, you read tomorrow's headlines in EWFF. This Fortune magazine cover uses our expression to describe an "alarming" crash in consumer confidence. Can bearish magazine covers stave off depression? No, but just as episodes of extreme bullishness marked short-term peaks in the Dow on the way up, outbursts of pessimism will appear at short-term lows. The long-term trend will weave its way around signals of this type.

Another big clue to the dimension of the downturn is the enormous punishment investors willingly absorb. How far do stocks have to fall before they will take flight? The experience of the Pro-Fund Ultra OTC fund suggests that it may never happen. In a recent column, Floyd Norris reports that a decline of 95% failed to shake the faith of UltraFund buyers. "The lower the fund goes, the more money is invested in it. About twice as many shares are outstanding now as there were when the fund was at its peak last year." In March, the NASDAQ was down 68%, and many issues had declines of 90% or more.

Small investors are clinging to the buy-and-hold tenet of the bull market. "Despite one of the worst bear markets in history, few investors have sold stocks over the last six months and fewer still plan to do so in the next six months," says an Investor's Business Daily poll published April 18. "If anything they plan to buy more, believing market conditions will improve even if the economy doesn't. All in all, the poll paints a picture of an investing public that buy and hold, come what may."

Even though this stance has already cost many fully-invested pensioners years of retirement, it is universally applauded by professionals as the right thing to do. "It's encouraging to see that investors are seeing these funds as long-term holdings," says the spokesman for a mutual fund tracking company. Unfortunately, this is another confirmation of a much bigger decline ahead.

October 2001

The case for the eventual resumption of a waterfall decline is made by a quick study of one chart, the percentage of U.S. households in stocks. It shows that the public faith in stocks is still virtually unshaken. According to the weekly poll of Sindlinger & Co., the severe damage to every major stock market in the world over a period of more than four years has done virtually nothing to drive a solid majority of Americans from the market. Even after the September 11 attack on the World Trade Center, 57% of U.S. households were in the market, a total that was higher than at any point in the first quarter of 2000 when the Dow and NASDAQ made their all-time peaks! The total was down only slightly from the all-time high of 57.8% in November 2000. No matter how many of the fundamental assumptions and icons of the bull market get kicked out from under them, Americans cling to the promise that stocks always go up in the long run.

The very bearish significance of this stance is evident in its extreme contrast to the trepidation and mistrust that was the consensus among U.S. households through the first 13 years of the bull market. In 1975, after the first six months of a bull market that had 25 years to go, the percentage of households in stocks peaked at 35% (first dashed line on chart). The rally continued on for another year and a half. In late 1982, when the next major leg kicked off, the public was not much braver. As the

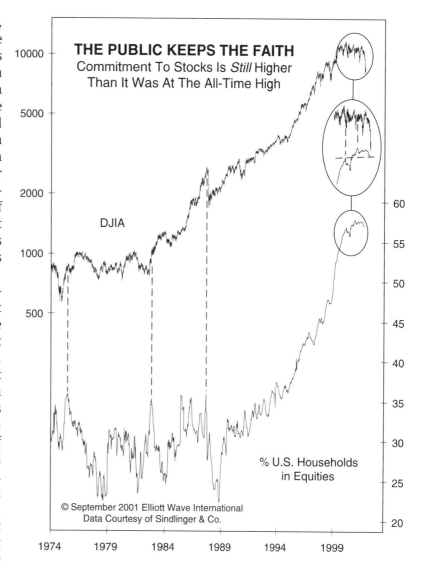

Dow broke through 1000 in November 1982, involvement peaked again at about 35%. This time, the average household missed another full year of rising prices.

The public did not hold stocks beyond an important Dow peak until September 1987 when it did so for one week. After the Dow's August 1987 peak, the percentage of households in the market edged to a slight new high of 36%. Notice that it took all of the upward thrust from 1984 to 1987 to produce a very tentative new high in the percentage of households holding stock (see the third dashed line). Also notice that that ever-so-slight overstay of the investor in 1987 was followed by a prompt market decline of 40%. The inset shows the recent experience. In addition to establishing a record that was 60% higher than that of 1987, involvement rose for 11 months after the Dow's peak, and it is still higher than it was at the Dow's January 2000 peak!

March 2002

A Flying Leap for Stocks

Several recent features on individual investors' abiding devotion to the stock market confirm that a tenacious "Belief in Stocks" is alive and well.

Individual Investors Remain Loyal

—USA Today, February 22, 2002

Small investors are "down, but not out" of the market, says The Wall Street Journal. "In the long run, where else are you going to go?" says a retired sociology professor. The graphic is representative of Money magazine's current "Leap of Faith" on stocks.

Source: Money Magazine

"Buying any stock takes faith," says Money. "But sometimes an extra-large helping of hope is required." In a phrase coined years ago by Bob Prechter about gold and as EWFF explained in January, every bear market descends a "slope of hope." The perilous quality of the current slope is signaled by the graphic and Money's qualifying statements, which encourage investors to abandon all reason and go with their hearts "because of the complexity of a company's operations and the opacity of its financial statements." "The answers to key questions surrounding" stocks like General Electric "are to some extent, unknowable. If you have faith in GE, this is a good time to buy." We will stick with objectivity, the Wave Principle and the short position it put us in near GE's all-time high in late 2000.

Damn the Torpedoes!

Further proof that reason has virtually nothing to do with most investors' approach to the stock market is a nationwide telephone survey of investors with a median income of $100,000. The poll found that even though the percentage of people who say that the S&P 500 will rise this year has declined from 62% to 49% from a year ago, "most people are not taking any steps to lessen risk. Only one in four has ever sold a mutual fund because of poor performance."

The emotion behind the market's long rise is still so overwhelming that many investors do not seem to realize that they did not profit by it. An analysis of Federal Reserve data by Professor Edward Wolff, a New York University economist, reveals that two-thirds of American households have failed to increase their retirement wealth "at all since 1983." According to the study, which includes neither the boom of 1999 nor the bust of 2000-2001, the retirement wealth of the median household actually fell 13 percent despite the fact that stocks were in a bull market over the entire 15-year span! The reason is that the median household has continually bought the highs and been shaken out at the lows. Performance has been dismal, "questions about earnings and accounting" are pervasive and fears that even the safest stocks "could soon blow up, or even disappear" are mounting. "And yet," The Wall Street Journal notes, "many not only are soldiering on, but they are putting even more money into stocks." Investors still have their "resolve," and they are going to use it no matter what.

April 2002

Another match with the post-peak environment is the emergence of the dip buyers. This index from Professor Robert Shiller of Yale University offers objective confirmation that they are out in force. On the rally from September 21, Shiller's Buy-On-Dips Confidence Index shows that the percentage of investors who share this reflex expanded to a height that is well beyond its level in the midst of the mania. Almost 80% of investors now say they expect the market to rebound one day after a decline of 3%. The trajectory of Shiller's data is fascinating because it verifies a phenomenon that *The Elliott Wave Theorist* and EWFF have documented anecdotally since the brief 10% decline of July 1996. The chart shows that during the mania, prompt stock market rebounds implanted an instantaneous buying response in many individual investors. As EWT noted in January, the stance is one for which the financial press praises the public as "sophisticated." The more stock prices fall, the more logical it is to buy stocks because stocks are falling. This is the ingenious investment plan that guides the average investor. The following chart shows that he's sticking to it.

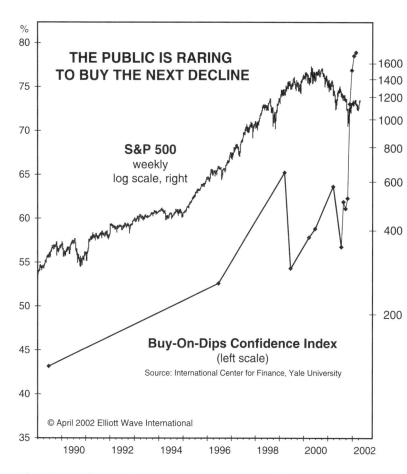

THE PUBLIC IS RARING
TO BUY THE NEXT DECLINE

S&P 500
weekly
log scale, right

Buy-On-Dips Confidence Index
(left scale)
Source: International Center for Finance, Yale University

© April 2002 Elliott Wave International

May 2002

The Problem With Staying Put

Liquidity doesn't light the fire under a bull market, but it can certainly provide fuel. The chart on the next page shows that it did just that during the mania of the 1990s. Liquidity, as defined by the Federal Reserve and compiled by Ed Hyman at ISI Group (New York City), pushed steadily higher from February 1993 through January 3, 2000, which was just 11 days before the all-time peak in the Dow. Since the all-time highs, however, ISI's measure of liquidity has fallen dramatically. In fact, on April 8, the measure went negative with a reading of -1.4%.

The crossing of this threshold brings to the fore the liquidity issues EWFF first broached in March 2000. This observation from the February 2002 issue of *The Elliott Wave Theorist* explains why we continue to view liquidity problems as a huge threat: "For prices of assets to fall, it takes only one seller and one buyer who agree that the former value of an asset was too high. All that everyone else need do is nothing." As indicated above, this is a great portrait of the current mindset. An April 28 Associated Press article describes investors in this very way: "Doing nothing is the strategy many investors are using." The measures of optimism are as high as they were at the all-time peaks, but instead of the utter confidence that they displayed at the highs, many "uneasy bulls" are literally afraid to look. The AP reveals that some do not even open their financial statements any more. This is classic denial, another aspect of the current debacle that is perfectly consistent with the mania history books.

We are beginning to see what Charles Mackay meant and why it was such a problem when he said in 1852 that men go "mad in herds" then recover their senses "one by one." By clinging to the sidelines, investors feed the illiquidity.

The toll is starting to become visible across the financial spectrum. In the market for private companies, for instance, Inc. magazine has observed the telltale sign, that "deer in the headlights" look. "Would-be sellers are paralyzed. Since they aren't willing to lower their expectations, they've taken their companies off the market and hope for better days." The market for derivatives is in similar straits. According to reports, "dwindling implied volatility" has left Goldman Sachs, Morgan Stanley and other brokerage firms sitting on "substantial unrealized losses in their equity derivatives books." According to traders, the trouble is due to "reduced volume, customer flow drying up since Enron's collapse and hedge funds sitting on the sidelines." As sellers give in and accept lower prices, values are hitting air pockets that astound participants. A recent one-month plunge of 40% in CBOE seat prices is a prime example. After hovering around $350,000 a seat for a full year, prices suddenly fell to $250,000 on March 25. A few days later, seat holders were getting just $200,000. Seat prices are among the first victims of the emerging liquidity crisis because they are extremely sensitive to the shrinking volume and volatility on the exchange. It hints that, in the months ahead, SLS (Sudden Loss Syndrome) will become a common sensation in many more areas.

The recent performance of NYSE margin debt is another indication of how quickly the speculative juices are evaporating. From the peak of March 2000 through September 2001, this huge source of financial leverage fell 48%. The clear five-wave decline to $144.6 billion in September 2001 has been followed by a measly rebound of 3.2% through March. As *The Elliott Wave Theorist* noted way back in 1980, a failure of margin debt to expand in an advancing market is the "kiss of death" to a bull trend. In fact, back in February 2000, just a slowdown to a 32% rise over nine months led EWFF to comment that falling stock prices would soon follow. A month later, the S&P and NASDAQ started declines of 39% and 72%, respectively. Keep in mind that liquidity

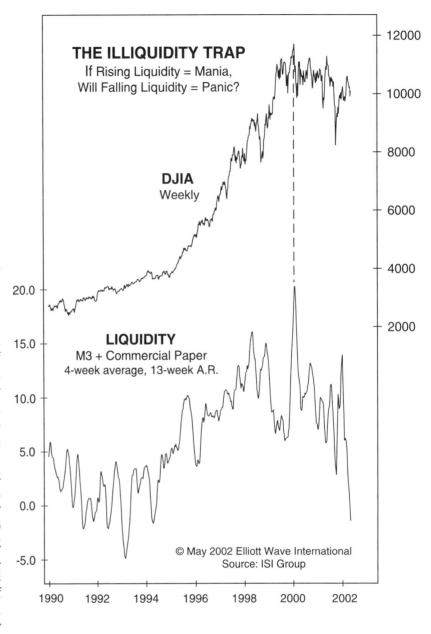

growth was only slowing until March. Now that it is actually drying up, it will inhibit the financial system in ways that few can currently even imagine.

June 2002

The Liquidity Vise Tightens

May brought the lowest non-holiday NYSE volume since the grinding declines of August and early September. This is just one more sign of the looming liquidity problem discussed in last month's issue. Overall volume is still running at relatively high levels, and it will probably spike to an all-time high in the next wave of selling, but, before the bear market is over, an extreme intolerance for risk will choke off investors' still-robust craving for speculation. Charles Biderman keeps a running tab of liquidity in his publication Liquidity Trim Tabs (www.trimtabs.com). By subtracting takeovers and buy backs from new offerings and insider sales, Biderman finds that the total trading float of shares has been building at a bearish rate of more than $3 billion a week since February. And that's still on the supply side.

Going forward, the bigger liquidity issue will come from demand. Last month, we noted, for instance, that disruptions in the demand for transactions were starting to appear economy-wide. This has been confirmed by the latest income tax flows. Trim Tabs says this indicator reveals a "sharp unexpected across-the-board decline in incomes that is currently unappreciated by the great mass of financial professionals." The precarious financial straits that this puts many American consumers in is hinted at by another recent study from the Consumer Federation of America. The CFA found that a quarter of U.S. households are "wealth-poor," which means they have net assets of less than $10,000. This group of mostly younger, well-educated households has higher incomes and more assets, but their debts are even larger. The study says paying those debts leaves many "liquidity constrained."

For many, the only way out is to unload assets acquired over the course of the bull market. Many corporations are in the same boat. Six months ago, Dynegy was maneuvering to buy Enron Corp. at what was believed to be a sale price. While Enron went on to become the biggest corporate collapse in history, Dynegy dodged a bullet and its focus shifted to selling off whatever assets it can to "bolster its liquidity."

The more these economic agents look to sell, the harder that it gets for them to make any money on whatever it is that they are trying to unload. The self-reinforcing nature of this cycle illustrates why it is not possible to get air back into a financial bubble. As participants awaken to the threat and take action to put themselves on firmer ground, they make things that much shakier.

September 2002

Almost everyone who held stocks at the all-time high holds them now. Sindlinger & Co.'s latest survey of U.S. households with equity holdings fell to 56%, or just below the level of 56.3% at the March 2000 high for the S&P and NASDAQ.

November 2002
The Best of All Possible Bear Markets

The farther the market falls, the more convinced investors are that a big new bull market is underway. The extent of the decline is one of the big reasons that many are betting on a rebound. "Losses This Big Suggest Gains Will Follow," reports a Bloomberg article. To sum up the prevailing view, forget about the wave pattern, forget about valuations that are still scraping against the outer limits of their historical boundaries and forget about the stock market's rigid adherence to bubble retracement patterns that have historically swallowed every bit of the preceding advance. Equities will come back, not in spite of the damage to date but because of it. To understand the sentiment behind this stance, we have to go back to 1997, when the mania was blooming and analysts everywhere adopted the mantra, "It's the best of all possible worlds" to describe the prospects for the economy and financial markets. At that time, *The Elliott Wave Theorist* noted (see July 1997 entry) that the phrase comes from Voltaire's 1759 book, *Candide*. It was first uttered by Candide's mentor, Professor Pangloss, from whose name the word for reckless optimism is derived. Voltaire put the words in Pangloss's mouth to describe the environment that prevailed right before Candide is beset by assorted calamities. EWT explained: "Untethered optimism leads inevitably to a psychology in which all outcomes, even losses, are causes for celebration. Pangloss was the first to point this out when he noted that 'in the best of all possible worlds, even private misfortunes make the public good, so that the more private misfortunes there are, the more everything is well.'" EWT used Voltaire's insight to conclude that bullish sentiment was unlikely to change after the all-time highs were in place because "the slightest provocation will trigger a return to the 'best of all possible worlds' belief long after the Grand Supercycle bear has begun." That insight has proved eerily accurate right through today.

December 2002
Another Visit From Prof. Pangloss

Last month, we covered investors' strange willingness not only to absorb punishing declines, but to embrace them as "causes for celebration." Here's another entry that affirms the masochism of modern-day investors:

Increasing Your Index for Pain

"Hurts So Good"? John Mellencamp's classic rock ditty comes as close as anything to explaining what's driving investors in today's topsy-turvy markets.

Watch what they do, not what they say.

Even as investors claim now is not a good time to invest in the markets, they poured $85 billion into a select group of index funds – not including Vanguard's index fund, which is the world's biggest – in just five days last week. Considering that the major stock indices have plummeted this year, it seems there are lots of people who enjoy pain.

Clearly, Americans are saying one thing – "we are hurting" – while doing a completely different thing. They're buying stocks, funds, houses, autos and other stuff like there's no tomorrow.

—New York Post, November 10, 2002

January 2003

The chart of the percentage of U.S. households in stocks shows that almost no one has gotten out of equities. At 56.7%, Sindlinger & Co.'s weekly survey is exactly where it was at the Dow's all-time peak on January 14, 2000. USA Today notes that investors pulled just $19.9 billion from stock funds in 2002. The total is less than 1% of fund assets at the start of 2002. This is one of the truly remarkable feats of the bear market. Despite three years and a brutal 75% decline in the NASDAQ index that was the focal point of the public's affection for stocks, virtually everyone that was in the market at the all-time high remains in the market now.

March 2003

Another indication of a flagging demand for equities is the decline in New York Stock

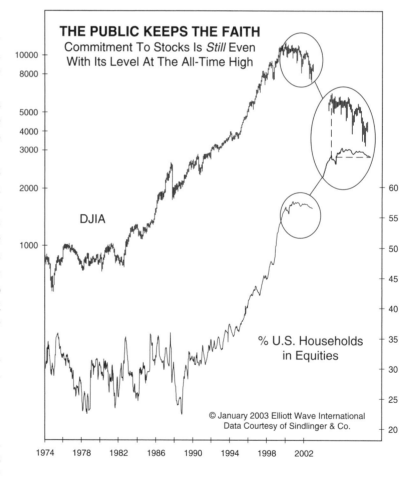

THE PUBLIC KEEPS THE FAITH
Commitment To Stocks Is *Still* Even
With Its Level At The All-Time High

DJIA

% U.S. Households
in Equities

© January 2003 Elliott Wave International
Data Courtesy of Sindlinger & Co.

Exchange seat prices, which have fallen 23% from October to early February. The drop is undoubtedly related to the unfolding liquidity crisis covered in recent issues as well as the shrinking volume on all the major exchanges. "Trading stocks was a popular activity at the height of the bull market," notes a financial columnist. "At the peak in 2000, customers of discount broker

Charles Schwab made an average of 349,000 stock trades per day. In January 2003, daily trading volume fell to 126,000. In the first 10 days of February, it dropped to 103,000." The columnist rightly concludes, "America's love affair with equities is seriously on the rocks."

Back in September 2000, when the NYSE was at its all-time high, one of the factors cited in EWFF's bearish case for stocks was that some U.S. shares were starting to generate more trading volume in Hamburg than in the U.S. EWFF claimed that it was a sure sign that the mania had run its course. After the next wave of selling, volume should dry up even further.

August 2003

A final, familiar nail from the old bull market's coffin is the public's rediscovery of leverage. Back in March 2000, EWFF noted that a surge in the use of NYSE margin had been accompanied by numerous signs that Wall Street was on a "Drunken Borrowing Binge." In a replica of that progression, EWFF noted last month that NYSE margin debt in May had its biggest one-month jump since February 2000. This month, a re-emerging willingness to literally bet the ranch is apparent in articles like this one:

Borrowed Funds, Buffed Returns

Is it time to leverage your house on long-term profits? In late 1999, day traders and novice investors alike mortgaged their homes for money to put into a soaring stock market. The folly of that strategy, in hindsight, is painfully obvious.

Yet with near 45-year-low mortgage rates, a new capital gains tax cut and a recovering market, borrowing against a home to add to stock investment could now be a prudent course – if investors stay committed for the long-term, some financial planners say.

— CBS MarketWatch.com, July 11, 2003

A financial advisor says the strategy is "really a smart move" because it "holds limited long-term risks compared to 1999. We're seeing a lot of people starting to do this lately." Betting the house on the stock market is almost always as stupid as it sounds. But when investment professionals are endorsing it as a sound course of action and "a lot of people" are doing it even though many just got burned by similar schemes, it stands virtually no chance of success.

September 2003

Here's a good example of a recent headline that is really a notch more extreme than the day-trading psychology at the all-time peak: "Out of Work? Become an Investor." At least back then, day traders who quit their jobs to trade had a reasonable expectation of finding another job when it didn't work out. Now they don't, but the advice is to lay one's life savings on the same line that proved so disastrous in 2000, 2001 and 2002. Another amazing thing about the current psychology is that it still reaches way beyond the stock market's usual circle of involvement. The cover of this month's Reader's Digest is a good example. It plugs the story inside on how to "Catch the Next Boom." The answer is the "Invest Now" story shown here.

October 2003

Over the last three months, EWFF has discussed countless other areas in which the countertrend rally from October has managed to regenerate the level of expectation and commitment that ruled the stock market at the all-time peak. Many of these manifestations, like on-line trading activity, stratospheric valuations and casual conversation about the stock market, have continued to rise through the recent September 19 high. The latest surge in the use of margin has also generated a sell signal. On September 15, the NASD's

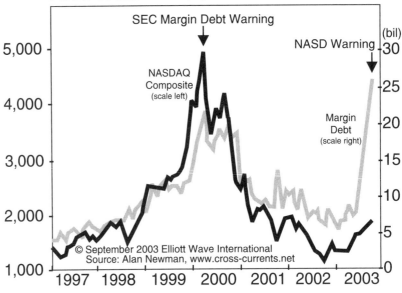

ANOTHER MAJOR MARGIN CALL

president of regulatory policy and oversight officially warned investors of the "consequences that can result" from the purchase of stocks on margin. "The NASD's big concern is that many small investors don't understand the full implications of margin calls." The chart shows that the rush to buy stock with borrowed money has been even more rapid and impulsive than it was at the end of the bull market. In 1999/2000, it took about a year for margin debt at NASDAQ firms to go from under $10 billion to more than $20 billion. This time, it sprang from the same level to an all-time high of more than $25 billion in just two months, without a setback. As a percentage of the NASDAQ market capitalization, the figure is about three times its level in March 2000.

The NYSE's dismissal of Dick Grasso, its former president, is instructive because it speaks to the size and strength of the downswing. Several news outlets have noted that Grasso's fate is similar to what happened to the exchange's leader in the wake of the last Supercycle peak in 1929. Richard Whitney was nabbed for embezzling stock exchange funds as president from 1930-1935 and jailed in 1938. In an apparent reflection of this turn's larger, Grand Supercycle degree, Grasso's departure happened much faster and did not involve any crime. In fact, Grasso's only "sin" was being awarded the amount of money the NYSE board decided to pay him for doing such a good job. When the figure was released, the public outcry was so great the board had no choice but to force Grasso out even after he gave a big piece of it back. Of Grasso's departure, The New York Times said, "It will by no means put an end to investor scrutiny of the big board." By Tuesday of this week, a spirit of "revolution" at the NYSE had advanced to the market-making mechanism itself. USA Today reports that critics are now "taking aim" at NYSE specialists. The NYSE board is also being wiped clean. This is what happens to former bull market icons in large degree bear markets, and it is predictable.

November 2003
Pouring Sludge Into the Market Machine

The most recent price of a New York Stock Exchange seat fell by a third from a high of $2 million in September. The September sale had pushed seat prices to within reach of the all-time record of $2.65 million in 1999. The reversal is another similarity to 1969 when the speculative overshoot from a long bull market took NYSE seat prices to a peak of $515,000. Once the post-peak party gave way, however, Wall Street suffered one of its greatest liquidity crises in history, and seat prices fell by 87% to $35,000 over the next eight years. The framework for a similar drop is clearly in place as the Money & Investing section of The Wall Street Journal is stuffed with stories about court cases against Wall Street research and investment bankers, mutual fund trading practices and "Tense Times" for the Big Board and its specialist system.

December 2003

The persistence of the bullish consensus for stocks has now surpassed any prior period in history. Last month, EWFF reported that the percentage of bullish respondents to the American Association of Individual Investors' weekly survey had surpassed 50% for 11 straight weeks to tie the record set through the Dow Industrials' all-time high. With six more 50%+ readings through the first week of December, the new record is now more than twice as long as the old one. The Investors Intelligence weekly survey shows that a majority of investment advisors have now been bullish for 31 straight weeks, which is also an all-time record. The Investors Intelligence survey goes back to 1963.

The stability of bullish opinion reminds us of 1997, when stock market corrections became virtually nonexistent and *The Elliott Wave Theorist* noted that a properly functioning chaotic system requires periodic disruption. In a special report, "Bulls, Bears and Manias," EWT compared the market's straight-ahead rhythm to a dangerously regular heart beat and cited research showing that a heart beat that is "abnormally smooth and free of fractal variation" may actually signal an impending heart attack. The observation proved accurate, as a financial heart attack hit in 2000-2002. The emergence of bullish expectations that are now even more "abnormally smooth" than those of the all-time peak is a sure sign that another, bigger onslaught lies directly ahead. Back in the salad days of the mania, the weakness was signaled by relentlessly rising prices; this time it is the expectation of rising prices that is relentless. Prices themselves are well below their level of 2000 and have risen only about 5% since the AAII statistics went over 50% in August. Despite the weakness in real gains, investors have felt better about the prospects for stocks longer than they did at any time during the course of the mania. This is a critical difference.

January 2004

Of course, the mania environment has made one thing quite clear: sentiment extremes don't always trigger an immediate move in the opposite direction of the consensus expectation. In lingering, however, an extreme psychology is a comment on the scope of the next trend change. The longer the extreme persists, the bigger the reversal is likely to be. Back in 1994 and early 1995, for instance, the implication of 44 straight weeks in which Investors Intelligence registered more bearish advisors than bullish ones (shown at by the circle at the bottom left of the chart, next page) was borne out by the stock market's ensuing advance. The youthfulness of the current major bear trend is signaled by the fact that bears have briefly outnumbered the bulls just three times since stocks peaked in 2000; at the lows of September 2001, July 2002 and October 2002. Another compellingly bearish fact is that 40 years of Investors Intelligence surveys have never produced a bullish extreme like the current one. Bullish advisors have outnumbered bears by more than 30% for 35 straight weeks.

February 2004

The steady hum of hopeful optimism continued through January. The American Association of Individual Investors' bullish percentage hit 69.5% as the Dow approached its January 26 high. The old record of eight straight weeks of better than 50% bullishness was also set as the Dow reached its all-time peak. That record has now been shattered by 25 straight weeks of more than 50% bulls. According to the Yale School of Management's measure of one-year confidence, 95% of individuals and 91.74% of institutions believe that the market will rise over the next year. The figures are both the highest in 15 years of polling.

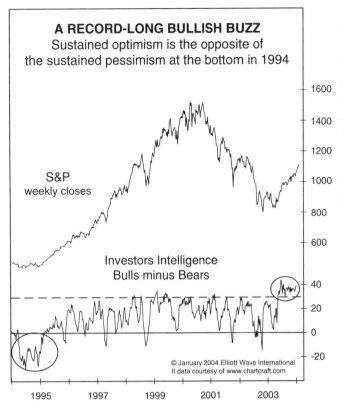

A RECORD-LONG BULLISH BUZZ
Sustained optimism is the opposite of
the sustained pessimism at the bottom in 1994

S&P
weekly closes

Investors Intelligence
Bulls minus Bears

© January 2004 Elliott Wave International
II data courtesy of www.chartcraft.com

**CONSUMER CONFIDENCE
IS BACK TO PEAK READINGS**
DJIA Monthly Data
log scale
1952-present

III

IV

Consumer Sentiment
1952-2003

End of III

End of V

Wave ②

1990

© January 2004 Elliott Wave International
Data Courtesy University of Michigan
Updated from the September 1999 issue of *The Elliott Wave Financial Forecast*

A good example of a warning signal that flashed early and more insistently as the all-time peak approached is shown by the updated chart of the University of Michigan's Consumer Sentiment Index. In September 1999, *The Elliott Wave Financial Forecast* noted that a rise through 100 signaled the end of Cycle III and speculated that the second sustained move through that level was likely to accompany the end of Cycle V. It stayed in high territory for a while, but the high of 112 was reached in January 2000, the month of the Dow's all-time high.

As EWFF noted in June 2000, the most telling aspect of extremes in the Consumer Sentiment figure is how consumers respond to the reversals. The long-term trend is generally ready to change course only after consumers overreact and sentiment goes to a new extreme unaccompanied by stocks. In 1980, for instance, Consumer Sentiment sank to a substantial new low as stock prices held above the low of 1974 (see lines on chart). This divergence was an early tip-off to the bull market of the 1980s. This time, the divergence points down for stocks as Consumer Sentiment failed to approach its October 1990 low despite a bigger percentage decline in stocks. Last month, Consumer Sentiment roared back above 100 with a 10-point jump. This bounce through the fateful 100 line is another sign that a "knock-out punch" is still ahead for consumers and investors alike.

March 2004

One of the truly amazing facets of the bear market rally is how efficiently it has manufactured enthusiasm for stocks. In just 15 months, the rise from October 2002 produced some exquisite sentiment measures like the latest bulls-minus-bears reading from Investors Intelligence, which favors the bulls by a whopping spread of 42.5% (www. chartcraft. com). "Since we consider 'normal' to be a 10% difference," Investors Intelligence says with understatement, "the current readings show excessive optimism." Some measures have now pushed way beyond the extremes created by the decades-long rise in stock prices that ended in the first quarter of 2000. Investors Intelligence's bullish percentage stayed above 50% for 27 weeks in late 1999 and early 2000. This time it has been above the 50% level for a record 43 straight weeks.

The once-cautious members of the American Association of Individual Investors have also been locked into an unusual affection for equities. To understand the freakishness of this spell, we have to go back to January 2000 when *The Elliott Wave Financial Forecast* noted that a majority bullish opinion within the cautious ranks of AAII was an extremely rare event.

Based on five straight readings of better than 50% bulls, EWFF called for a significant market decline, noting that a surrender on the part of these "normally conservative investors" was an "extraordinary" signal of an imminent downturn. The Dow peaked seven days later, and the AAII survey went on to register a record 11 straight 50%+ readings before investors realized that a bear market was indeed underway. In 2003-2004, that record has been obliterated by 29 straight readings (2.618 times as many!) of more than 50% bulls. As the chart reveals, the 26-week moving average rose to a record high of 59% in the first week of February. The first-ever crossing of the 50% level occurred on March 31, 2000 (shown as the vertical dashed line on the chart), one week after the start of the bear market in the S&P. Eight 26-week readings of better than 50% accompanied the start of the first leg down.

July 2004

Despite the sell-off and a relatively shallow bounce from the May low, the brokerage community seems convinced that happy days are here again. Profits at the biggest investment firms hit record levels in the first quarter and several articles have noted recently that the party is definitely back in full swing on Wall Street. With Street bonuses pouring in once again, several articles have noted recently that all of Manhattan is back on its feet. Rolls Royce Phantoms, which go for $325,000, are flying out of the showroom doors, and a $1,000 frittata has appeared on a restaurant menu. As EWFF noted right after the last major peak (May 2000), Wall Street always saves its biggest celebrations for the biggest peaks. A hint of the heightened risk to the financial sector is suggested by mounting pressure on specialists, who must serve as the buyers of last resort if bids suddenly disappear. "The bright spot," according to the chief executive of one of five NYSE market makers, "is that the equity markets will come back and volume and volatility will come back." Well, we do agree with the second half of that statement.

It should not come as a surprise that the financials may have tipped the scales. EWFF noted in April that, at 21%, the financial sector had replaced technology as the largest share of the S&P. In terms of profitability, Bianco Research (www.BiancoResearch.com) reports that the financial sector is even more critical, accounting for a huge 40% of all domestic corporate profits! The total does not even include the finance arms of major industrial companies such as General Motors and Ford. A breakdown of car company bottom lines makes the depth of the economy's dependence on the now-stumbling financial sector glaringly apparent. Last year GM got 87.5% of its profits from GMAC, while Ford would have had a loss of more than $1 billion without the $1.8 billion in profit from its credit extension operations. As the credit bubble deflates, financial stocks will mimic the performance of technology stocks from the mania's 2000 peak. In other words, the slope of the sector's decline will resemble the NASDAQ from March 2000 to September 2001.

August 2004
The Storm After the Calm

With the Dow Jones Industrial Average trading at 9966, or within 4 points of its average weekly level since January 1999, USA Today welcomed readers to the "age of 'dead money.'" It went on to cite advisors who declared that stocks are in a "no-where market" that was likely to last 6 months to 6 years. The graphic shown here is from The Wall Street Journal's second-quarter mutual fund report. It shows that underneath investors' calm exterior, anxiety levels are rising. Mutual funds' "meager returns" in the second quarter are way below expectations. One recent survey showed that 58% of investors still anticipate returns of 10.4% per year. The gap between what investors are counting on and reality will push many to the breaking point.

The Wall Street Journal
July 6, 2004

The problem for the bulls is that the stock market is currently constructed for speed and constant action. Like a well-oiled machine or athlete, it will break down without the activity it was designed for. In many ways, the situation is the opposite of the early 1980s when the mechanisms of the bull market appeared. In a August 1983 Special Report on the start of the "Superbull Market," *The Elliott Wave Theorist* observed the building blocks "falling into place" this way:

> In 1978, an Elliott analyst had no way of knowing just what the mechanisms for a wild speculation would be. Well, to be honest, we didn't know. But now look! The entire structure is being built as if it were planned. Options on hundreds of stocks (and now stock indexes). Futures contracts on stock indexes, which promise to deliver nothing, have been created for the most part as speculative vehicles with huge leverage. The financial arena is becoming the place to be. And, as if by magic, the media are geometrically increasing coverage of financial news. New financial newsletters and magazines are being created every few months. Financial News Network is now broadcasting 12 hours a day, bringing up-to-the-minute quotations on stocks and commodities via satellite and cable into millions of homes.

A Hurricane of Paper Draws Near

The term "air pocket" originated in the early days of aeronautics and was adopted by the financial world in the middle of the 1929 crash. It was perfect for describing the vacuums that sucked prices lower as bidders failed to appear in one stock after another. *Conquer the Crash* covered the re-emerging potential for "air pockets" and other trading breakdowns with this comment:

> Today's system — much improved to be sure — is nevertheless a recipe for an even bigger mess during the panic. The investors will be so nervous that they will screw up their orders. Huge volume will clog website's servers, disrupting orders entered on-line. Orders may go in, but confirmations may not come out. Quote systems will falter at just the wrong time.

The other pending issue is how complex the "speculative vehicles with huge leverage" mentioned above have grown over the course of the bull market. This chart of settlement failures was brought to our attention by analyst Thomas Peterson at Bulls Eye Research (www. bullseyeresearch. com). It shows the total number of failed bank settlements in the markets for U.S. Treasuries, agency debt and mortgage-backed debt. A settlement failure occurs when securities are not delivered on the date agreed at the time of a sale. Notice the clear uptrend in the number of settlement failures and an increasing tendency toward upward spikes since the start of the bear market in the first quarter of 2000. The first explosion came right after September 11, 2001. The last two were triggered by bearish reversals in bond

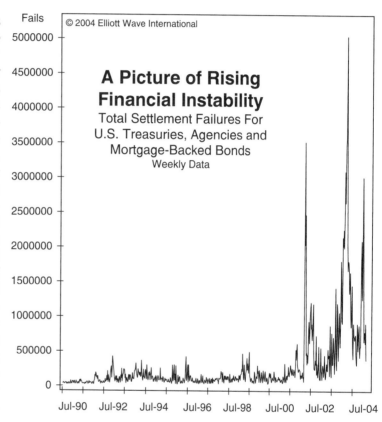

prices into August 2003 and May 2004. Peterson correctly notes that these settlements "eventually did get completed," but the events of September 2001, August 2003 and May 2003 are nothing compared to the chaos of a full fledged financial panic. With the complexity and incidence of failure already on the rise, it is easy to see how the mayhem predicted in *Conquer the Crash* will overwhelm the financial infrastructure.

October 2004

The Party Crowd Is Keeping Its Day Job

A semblance of the old mania's lunatic fringe has re-surfaced. On October 19, The Wall Street Journal revealed a trendy burst of late-night trading in the DAX, Germany's blue chip index. The article explains that the DAX is the latest "hot spot" for day traders because it has everything they need: quick swings, low account minimums and "best of all, hours that let day traders trade at night." Since this is just an echo of the mania, traders are hedging their bets — they're keeping their day jobs. The article ends with a quote from an electrical engineer/trader who has "lost faith" in corporations, mutual funds and NYSE stocks, but still hopes to hit it big in trading the DAX overnight. "I'd like to quit my full-time job and move into this," he says. The dream, faded though it may be, lives on.

Investor Psychology

With four additional weeks of net positive readings in the Investors Intelligence poll of investment advisors (www.chartcraft.com), the bullish consensus among newsletter writers has extended past the two-year point! Even as the Dow closed at a low for the year on October 25, the percentage of bullish advisors outnumbered the bears by more than two to one (56.4% to 25.5%). The chart shown here shows how investors actually became more bullish as the decline extended into October. The last net negative reading came on October 11, 2002, the same week as the low in most of the major averages. Advisors have been bullish ever since. This immediate and relentless bullish bias toward stocks refutes the spate of stories that celebrated October 10, 2004 as the second anniversary of a new bull market. In the media, it's taken for granted that it's a bull market, a classic second wave assumption.

In the 1980s and early 1990s, when major averages' best days were still

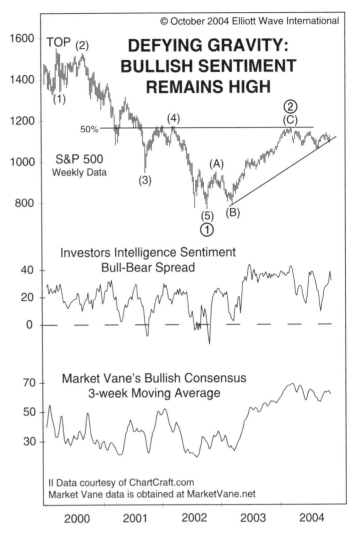

ahead, Investors Intelligence data often reached net bearish levels. The longest hiatus was a one-year stretch that ended right before the stock market crash in October 1987. We keep saying it, but the significance of the optimism keeps expanding: the longer the bullish buzz lasts, the harsher the bust is likely to be. It's been 502 weeks since the last extended period of net-bearishness ended, in February 1995. Over that span, bears outnumbered bulls just 5% of the time (26 weeks), despite the worst bear market since 1929-1932. This is a chilling indictment of the market's supposed bullish prospects.

December 2004

The lines at the bottom of this chart of the S&P capture two outstanding aspects of investors' current hopes for the stock market. One 17-year-old measure, the 10-day Daily Sentiment Index (MBH Commodity Advisors, trade-futures.net), has never been higher, reaching 89.3% bulls on November 17. Even the euphoria at the all-time highs in 2000 failed to get traders as excited about stocks as they are right now. The second line averages a whole year of American Association of Individual Investors surveys to show the extremity of long-term optimism over the course of 2004. Back in January 2000, when the AAII poll experienced its first series of sustained readings above 50%, EWFF cited the break from a long history of "steadfast caution" as a sign of an imminent downturn for stocks. The signal was well-timed, as the Dow registered its all-time peak a week later. Notice the acceleration of the downtrend as the 52-week average broke back below 50% in the later part of 2000. Now notice the much higher and more sustained bullishness

316

of 2004. Despite a recent uptick in bullishness, the 52-week AAII figure has fallen back below 50%. The last time that happened, the Dow, S&P and NASDAQ followed with declines of 30%, 38% and 58%, respectively. A similar break soon is a high probability.

On November 15, The Wall Street Journal captured the sentiment with the headline, "Optimism Reigns." Overseas, the bullishness is even stronger, as this headline from an Australian daily testifies:

Raging Bulls Set To Go on Stampede

Unless this is one of the rare instances of an accurate headline forecast, the rush will surely be out of and not into the stock market.

January 2005

By at least one measure, the bullish sentiment surpassed the level generated at the all-time highs. The chart at the bottom of this page shows the latest three-week average of the percentage of bullish advisors (as compiled by Investors Intelligence.com), and its rise to a new 17-year high in late December. Even in the bull market's most manic days, advisors were never as united in pushing investors into stocks as they have been over the last month.

February 2005

Margin Debt is Outpacing the Dow Again

One of the signals that helped *The Elliott Wave Financial Forecast* decide that the Dow Industrials' all-time peak was in place back in January 2000 was a discrepancy between an explosion in NYSE margin debt and a slowing rise in the Dow. The same phenomenon is in place now as the Dow gained just 3.1% in 2004 while margin debt jumped 17.3%. At $203.8 million, NYSE margin has now retraced a Fibonacci 50% of its decline through September 2002. Margin debt's only other trip above $200 million started in November 1999, within weeks of the Dow's all-time high. It remained above $200 million for one year. Given the heightened exposure to riskier assets, the higher levels of leverage through alternate

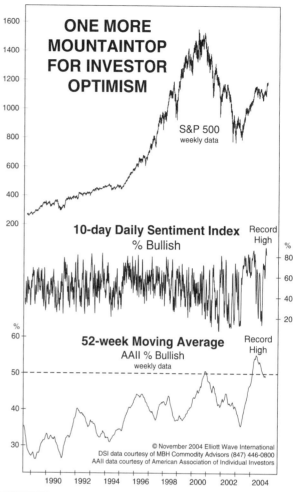

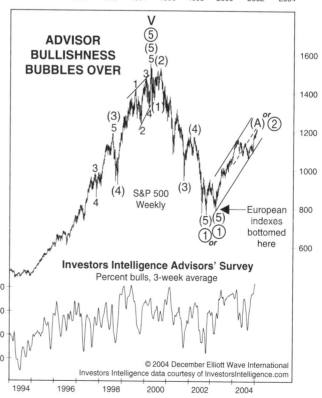

instruments like second mortgages and hedge funds and the potential for a sudden, street-wide aversion to risk, margin calls will surely rain down on the market at an unprecedented rate once the S&P breaks its 2002 low. Margin debt is just the tip of a pyramid that extends way beyond the markets. Its contraction will help burst the economy-wide debt bubble.

May 2005

Sentiment figures are off from the bullish extremes registered in 2004 and early 2005, but, as we note in the momentum section, it will take more than a few weeks to work off years of excess optimism. Selling is the sincerest form of bearishness and there is little evidence yet of a lessening in the public's commitment to the stock market. According to AAII's allocation survey, 67% of the individual investors' portfolios remain invested in stocks. The figure is 24 percentage points higher than it was at the October 2002 low and 4 points higher than the average over the last five years. Sindlinger's poll of U.S. households shows that Mr. and Mrs. John Q. Public remain locked into equities, with a near record 57.4% of households continuing to hold shares.

An Uh-Oh Update

If you were with us back in March 2000, you know something that's already been lost to history: The bear market did not sneak up on everybody as so many commentators contend. In fact, a few days before the NASDAQ's peak, Standard & Poor's, the world's "foremost provider of independent credit ratings" was among those voicing concerns about the potential for a "sharp correction." Given the Fed's exhortations on "irrational exuberance" three years earlier, EWFF noted that the caution was an outsized parallel to 1929 and, therefore, another hint of an even larger bear market. One week before the NASDAQ's all-time peak, EWFF labeled this the "uh-oh effect" and cited the following passage from *At the Crest of the Tidal Wave*:

> There are times in history when the percentage of naive investors is so high that occasional warnings from professionals are irrelevant to net market psychology.... [It] is in fact normal behavior at the biggest tops of all.

Now the caution lights are flashing more persistently than in March 2000. On March 13, for instance, when many averages were still just a few days off their countertrend rally peaks, the Financial Times ran this headline:

Growing Fears Credit Boom May Implode

The article quotes the president of Citicorp, the world's largest financial firm, saying: "The possibility of a liquidity bubble around the world concerns me. A very cautionary thing is that it feels like the world is changing and traditional indices may not give a complete picture." On April 6, the International Monetary Fund, which is famous for putting a bullish face on even the direst financial calamities, issued a warning "on investments and the global economy. The IMF stated that the huge and growing market for credit derivatives and other complex securities could suffer a serious and 'disorderly' decline if conditions turned negative." The notice was widely reported in the press. In a separate report, the World Bank "warned that the global economic recovery has peaked." A diehard bull through the course of the bull market now offers "Seven Reasons Why the Bears Might Be Right." "What Comes after a Bubble is Seldom Pretty," said one of many headlines about a possible real estate debacle. Another bubble story hints at potential trouble for "the totality of our economic and financial world:" "Hot Financial Markets Giving Rise to Talk of Collapsible Mega-Bubble."

Talk of a bubble is so prevalent that more experienced investors say they are reassured; it can't be a bubble if so many people are worried about one. "People are on bubble-watch," says an analyst. But the all-time highs confirmed EWFF's assertion that worry is not an antidote to financial crisis. In third waves, news and fears develop concurrently with the trend, and that's what's starting now.

Screaming Sell Signals from Wall Street

A historically reliable sign of concern is selling by corporate insiders. EWFF's observations about spikes in insider buying in June 1998 and April 2000 preceded big declines. Insider sales data effectively quantifies the uh-oh effect. This chart shows Thomson Financial's insider sales-to-buys ratio back through March 1996. For most of the last decade, the figure has been running at high levels. Historically, Thomson Financial reports that a 20:1 level at any time is considered bearish; the average since 1996 — nine years ago — is 23.6:1. The arrow on the chart shows EWFF's bearish take on insider activity back in August 2000, at the start of an S&P decline that ultimately cut the index's value in half. The ratio reached a high of about 30:1 right before the start of a third wave of Intermediate degree. The doubling of the ratio to 60:1 in March supports our forecast, which now calls for a third wave of one higher degree. As EWFF noted last May, there tends to

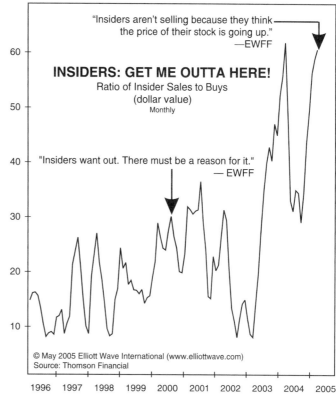

be a one-year lag between a high level of insider sales and a significant stock market decline. The ratio experienced an initial spike to 60:1 in March 2004; so the stock decline that started in March 2005 is consistent with the one-year lag observation. The return to 60:1 in March shows that top corporate managers see something nasty on the horizon. As we've said before, there may be many reasons why insiders sell their shares, but one of them is not because they think the price of their company's stock is going to go up. Unlike the larger body of investors, they're not waiting to take defensive action.

The exchanges are now racing against the strengthening power of the bear market. Here, too, the story goes back to the other side of the all-time peak. Back in the summer of 1999, the New York Stock Exchange and NASDAQ announced plans to become publicly traded companies. The New York Times was particularly smitten with the NASDAQ's potential offering, calling it one of the "most intriguing investment opportunities of the next decade." The cited reason was the "magic" of the market. With the NYSE, after 207 years of tight control by insiders, the public was going to own the exchange mechanism itself. *The Elliott Wave Financial Forecast* identified this supposed big break for the little guy as one of the ultimate signs that the mania's "terminal phase" was at hand. Within five months, the Dow reached its all-time high and the exchanges scrapped their IPO plans. Thanks to the lingering strength of the old bull market, however, the NASDAQ managed to slip into the public domain through private placements in 2000 and 2001. In December, a month before the NASDAQ's countertrend high, the insiders who purchased the OTC exchange's private placement filed to sell $100 million worth of shares. On April 20, the New York Stock Exchange revealed that it had also found a back door to public ownership. If it can complete its purchase of Archipelago, the NYSE will finally become a publicly traded firm. After two centuries of rising stock prices, the public gets to own the NYSE. These deals are even more bearish than the exchanges' efforts to go public in 1999. For one thing, the exchanges are far more desperate than they were back at the highs. At this point, it's not about the "magic" anymore; it's about survival. With NASDAQ and the NYSE essentially offering duplicate services, "a long and brutal battle for dominance in stock trading" is underway. Throw in the deadly listlessness

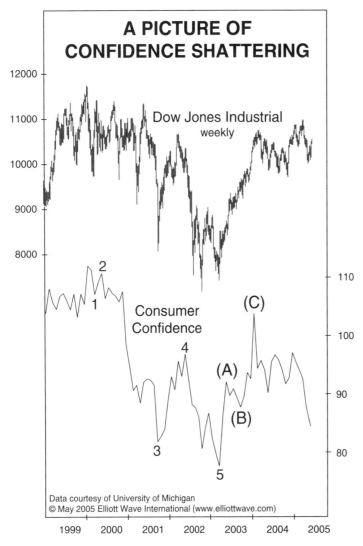

A PICTURE OF CONFIDENCE SHATTERING

12000

11000

Dow Jones Industrial
weekly

10000

9000

8000

2

1

Consumer
Confidence

(C)

110

4

(A)

100

90

(B)

3

80

5

Data courtesy of University of Michigan
© May 2005 Elliott Wave International (www.elliottwave.com)

1999   2000   2001   2002   2003   2004   2005

that will follow in the dog days of the bear market, and the writing is on the wall. We predict that at least one of these two entities will not survive the decline intact.

June 2005

In finance, desperation and hope are an explosive combination. Violent disappointment is the usual result, and the following chart of consumer sentiment is a picture of the fuse being lit on one of the world's largest bombs. EWFF has tracked the consumer's arc through the nether reaches of extreme optimism since shortly before the Dow's all-time high in 2000. In January 2004, when sentiment popped back above the "fateful 100 line," EWFF identified the burst as a sure sign that a "knock-out punch is still ahead." The key to that forecast was the 5-3 form of the action since the all-time highs. As it turns out, sentiment's three-wave rally was complete at that time. The chart at right also reveals a close tie between consumers' vitality and stock prices. Both the Dow and consumer confidence peaked in January 2000 and bottomed in March 2003, along with the European stocks and many U.S. averages adjusted for dollar weakness. The March peak for stocks has been accompanied by a decline of almost 10% in the confidence index. Since this is a third-wave decline for consumer confidence, a downside explosion that alters the face of the U.S. economy should occur over the next few months.

August 2005

The mid-July peak in stock prices generated an upward spike in bullish sentiment. Expectations among traders at Lowrisk.com popped from 28% bullish to 52% bulls. The one-week jump was the biggest since December 1999, right before the all-time high in the Dow. The American Association of Individual Investors survey also leapt to 57.9% bulls, its highest level since January. Since the start of the bear market, AAII readings of better than 50% are more common, but, as EWFF noted a few days before the Dow's all-time peak, AAII "is a notoriously cautious group that rarely displays a bullish majority." Apparently mom and pop investors are as ready as ever for a continued stock market rally in coming weeks.

But it's an edgy bullishness. The manic nature of the optimism is well expressed by the guru of the day, "CNBC's loudmouth stock swami," Jim Cramer. To his credit, unlike the patron saints of investing back at the all-time highs, Cramer buys and sells. He's also an entertainer, beginning every episode of "Mad Money" in a straitjacket, then ranting his way through hundreds of investment decisions. But Cramer clearly has a talent for catching the turns in the market with popular investment appeals. His *Handbook of Internet Stocks* came out at the end of 1999, as the Internet boom was ending. *You Got Screwed, Why Wall Street Tanked* and *How You Can Prosper* appeared in November 2002, one month after the bear market low in the Dow. His latest book of investment tips, *Jim Cramer's Real Money*, is designed to help "investors on the wrong side of Wall Street's recent shakeups find the courage to get back in the game."

Whatever You Do, DON'T PANIC!

In the wake of the London subway bombing. The FTSE, an index of 100 of the most highly capitalized companies on the London Stock Exchange, experienced a one-day sell-off that was quickly retraced. "Investors Have Learned Not To Panic," proclaimed a USA Today headline. "If historical trends are any guide," on the day of the blast Bloomberg reported, "The impact on the U.S. stock market may not last long." "I thought, hmmm, time to buy," said Fox News' top anchorman. No matter how bad the news gets, or even because it's so bad, investors have become conditioned to see the sunny-side of the stock market.

EWFF has shown how the neocortexes of high-level researchers continually find ways to intellectualize the sentiment of mania-era investors. A new study of brain-damaged investors in the journal, Psychological Sciences, proposes that individuals with an impaired ability to experience emotion are better at making financial decisions. It's great to see this type of research. The focus on emotion is a clear advance toward the core issues of finance and socionomics.

But there's a more immediate message in the media's coverage of the study. According to the headlines, "Investing and Emotion Are a Bad Mix" and "A Brain Damaged Investor Is a Smart Investor." The New York Post somehow interpreted the findings to mean, "more risks translate into more rewards." Buried deep in just one story is the revelation that the damaged participants only outperformed in a simple coin-tossing experiment. In more complex settings, they did not fair so well; in fact, "three of four experienced personal bankruptcy." Real world experience exposes the flaw in the media's interpretation. The best way to combat emotional barriers to smart investing is not emotional castration but an understanding of the emotional framework that guides markets. Based on this approach, the importance of the study is not what it says, but the press' infatuation with it. While buying into an atmosphere of fear is generally advisable, the Wave Principle explains that there is a point, in the middle of a bear market impulse wave, when this is a bad idea. In third wave declines, fear can be a useful thing. At least, it is to those that listen to it and sell. These studies are further testimony to the ingenuity of social mood. With Primary wave ③ pending, papers ranging from The Wall Street Journal to MaineToday and The Hindu, India's national newspaper, are focused on bolstering the conviction of investors. Many will conquer their fear and be locked in for the duration of the bear market. When the headlines finally say, "Go ahead and panic," a bottom will be at hand.

October 2005

Like a camel stores up water, the stock market sometimes stockpiles extreme emotions in preparation for long hauls to much higher or lower levels. This is what happened in 1994 and early 1995 when the Investors Intelligence advisor's survey showed that the percentage of bears outnumbered bulls for 45 straight weeks, right through the start of a historic bull market that took the Dow Industrials from under 4000 to 11,000 in five years. Today the bear market's tank is clearly filled to the brim for a long trip to much lower levels as advisors are in their 154th straight week of net bullishness, the longest sustained consensus in the 42-year history of the survey. The potential for a trip to Dow 7000 and far below is highlighted by the fact that the latest streak is only part of an even longer stretch in which the number of bulls has exceeded the number of bears for 353 of the last 361 weeks, a period of almost seven full years dating back to October 1998!

The tip-off to a long-term rally in 1995 came when investment advisors stayed bearish despite a subtle uptick in the averages. Last time, it was an 11-month rise of 300 Dow points. This time optimism persists despite a decline of 500 points in 7 months.

Peak Seat Prices and Another Backoffice Logjam

As the chart illustrates, New York Stock Exchange seat prices are back to an all-time high, just as they were in the peak years of 1906, 1929, 1968, 1987 and 1999. The latest peak of $3 million is most reminiscent of 1968 because that was also a point at which smaller and more speculative shares soared to substantial new highs but the Dow Industrials only managed to approach its 1966 peak of 1000, where Cycle wave III ended.

In another striking parallel to the late 1960s, the latest new high in seat prices is also accompanied by one of the biggest trading backlogs in history. In the aftermath of Cycle III, the Value Line Geometric Average rose to a substantial new high in May 1968, OTC stocks peaked in September 1969 and share trading on the NYSE churned so furiously that Wall Street suffered a "record-keeping crisis." The backoffices of

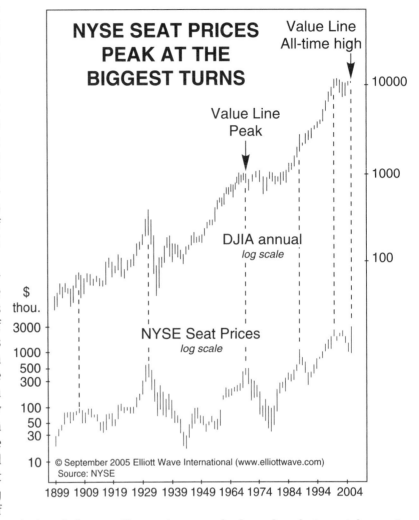

investment firms were so overwhelmed that staff members worked weekends to catch up. In recent months, derivatives transactions have strained Wall Street's ability to process the trading. According to the latest reports, for instance, it will take *eight months* to clear a backlog of unconfirmed trades in the credit derivatives market. The head of the New York Federal Reserve says the problem "poses risks not only to the financial institutions which use [derivatives] but to the financial system as a whole." It is no coincidence that the booming market for the credit derivatives market is a big culprit. Credit derivatives allow participants to shift the risk of default on debt from primary lenders to third party "insurers." After exploding more than eightfold in the three years that ended last December, the International Swaps and Association reports that credit derivatives grew another 50% to $12.43 *trillion* in just the first half of 2005. For perspective, the entire annual Gross Domestic Product of the United States is $11 trillion. A general rule of thumb is that the farther a loan gets from the originating lender, the more complex the counterparty claims become and the higher the risk of default. With the weight of deflation and widespread default bearing down on the economy, those risks are rising fast. The explosion in credit derivatives is an effort to "manage" the escalating risk. It cannot end happily, however, because no one now trading credit derivatives (except possibly some of the traditional lenders that are selling susceptible credits into the market) envisions the unprecedented default rates to come. When they can't even figure out who *owns* what, figuring out who owes what will be nearly impossible. As the economy heads south, the great derivatives fiasco and the implications discussed in *Conquer the Crash* will be close behind.

November 2005

The Market Itself Is on Offer

Back in 1999, when the NASDAQ and NYSE started making noise about going public, the NY Times reported, "On its face, it's hard to imagine a less appealing investment." Still, the Times concluded that the deal "could become one of the most intriguing investment opportunities of the next decade." The reason cited was the "magic" of the market. *The Elliott Wave Financial Forecast* identified the exchanges' IPO plans and the media's belief in them as a clear-cut sell signal for stocks. Last month's century-long chart of NYSE seat prices illustrated very clearly that the main trading mechanism of the market is always most prized at important peaks. When the speculative fires are burning so hot that the exchanges themselves are being bought and sold, a truly enormous peak is at hand. The top formed in the major averages a few months later is still very much in place.

But with the small-stock averages working their way to new all-time highs in early August and many stocks rallying to countertrend bear market peaks at the same time, the enthusiasm for markets, by some measures, has actually exceeded the level of 1999. All the major financial exchanges have gone public. The NASDAQ went public through the back door in 2002 with a private placement that was later converted to public shares. The New York Stock Exchange will do likewise with its pending acquisition of Archipelago, an electronic trading platform that is already public. The Chicago Mercantile Exchange went public in a December 2002 IPO and has soared more than 1000%. The CBOT is the last to make it. It did so through a successful offering on October 18. The still ascendant appeal of financial paper and its exchange is evident in the CBOT's aftermarket performance. The stock rose sharply from an initial price of $54 to $134. The bear market of 2000-2002 followed just the idea of a publicly-traded stock exchange; a complete equitization of the major exchanges constitutes a much more powerful sell signal.

The discrepancy between the exchanges' unprecedented valuations and the rising vulnerability of their business speaks to the severity of the next decline. Since 1999 when the NY Times characterized the NASDAQ as fundamentally unpromising, the viability of traditional exchanges has deteriorated. For one thing, their monopoly right to trade certain shares and instruments is eroding. As trading becomes entirely electronic, the threat of obsolescence and competition among themselves and others is also rising. Another risk is the rising wave of financial reprisal, which is focusing ever more sharply on traders and financial instruments like derivatives. In the next phase of decline, as government sinks its hooks into this free-wheeling business, exchanges will experience a big increase in costs and a loss of efficiencies due to new regulation and oversight. Then there's the biggest challenge of all, a deep retrenchment in financial activity that still lies ahead. During the last Supercycle decline, the slackening demand for equities outlasted the bear market by a full decade. Speculators' slow response to that decline was evident in the course of NYSE seat prices, which fell 70% between 1929 (from an all-time high of $625,000) to 1932 when stocks bottomed, and then another 80% before bottoming in 1942 (at $30,000).

More Evidence of a Nice Bubble

Another subtle precursor to an even bigger bust is the enormous number of bubble references now being bandied about in polite society. An Atlanta Journal-Constitution writer notes, "The biggest bubble of all is the 'bubble' bubble—the use of the word, mostly by the media, as a metaphor for any activity driven by irrational exuberance. We've seen an SUV bubble and a bubble in reality TV programming. A Google search on the word 'bubble' brings up 35.1 million hits of every kind: stock market bubble, housing bubble, oil price bubble and hurricane bubble." This appears to be a variation of the uh-oh effect, which EWFF observed at the all-time highs and in recent months. The uh-oh effect is a brief point of recognition at the very end of a long rise when some participants glimpse the enormous potential for a devastating reversal. Bubble references appear to be an extension of this vague sense of peril to the social realm except that, after so many years of frenzied price advances, users have lost respect for the meaning of the word bubble; "a speculative scheme that comes to nothing." This lack of appreciation is very apparent in real estate, which *Conquer the Crash* identified as the last bastion of the Great Asset Mania. Bubble talk in this market is off the charts, but it is now fashionable to reply that real estate is a "balloon not a bubble." The difference? According to the Rocky Mountain News, "Bubbles inevitably burst. Balloons slowly let air out." According to the outgoing Federal Reserve Board chairman there's "no national bubble in home prices, but rather 'froth' in some local markets." With years of central bank leadership under his belt, Alan Greenspan knows how to hedge his bet by acknowledging a measure of ebullience. The headline in today's Washington Post credits Ben Bernanke, the incoming Fed chairman, with a categorical denial:

There's No Housing Bubble to Go Bust

The article is probably the first hint of what is likely to become an extremely strained relationship between the Fed and the public. After Manhattan real estate prices collapsed 12% in the third quarter, the NY Post asked: "Could it be the bursting of the real estate bubble? Not exactly. There are no indicators that this is the beginning of a crash. Think of the current kinder, gentler bubble, not a catastrophic burst, but a reality check, a skimming of the froth, a round of requisite price corrections that is seen as a welcome necessity." This is the last great myth of every financial euphoria; that the excess can be slowly "unwound." It is exactly what was said about technology stocks in May and June of 2000. Here's how the July 2000 issue of EWFF recorded the phenomenon:

> There is a common theme in the press now. Writers are calling the stock market setback a "new reality," or "rational exuberance" or "the culling of the weak." "It's a good thing," says the editor of The Red Herring. "It is a sure sign that the increasingly delusional psychology that created the mania has stopped waxing and begun to wane."

At the time the NASDAQ in fact had begun a wipe-out of 78%. Another definition for bubble is that it is simply an "illusion." Once it is replaced by an accurate reflection of the world, it cannot be skimmed back or undergo a slow fade; it ceases to exist.

December 2005
Another Month, Another Exchange IPO

This month, the Intercontinental Exchange (ICE), a market in commodity futures, came out with another initial public offering. After quickly trading up to a high of more than $44, ICE fell to $32. These shares should fall hard with stocks as a whole.

January 2006

Without a single week of more bears than bulls in the Investors Intelligence (II) sentiment survey, 2005 marks the third straight year of a bullish plurality, the longest streak in the survey's 40-year history. Not even the salad days of the Great Mania, 1995 through early 2000, elicited as many consecutive weeks of net advisor optimism as the current one. Stocks were continually making new all-time highs from 1995 to 2000, but the latest and longest streak takes place with all three major stock indexes, the Dow, S&P and NASDAQ, still beneath their 2000 all-time highs. This week's 60.4% bulls is especially noteworthy because it is occurring with the Dow and S&P essentially flat for the month of December. Investor optimism is increasing as the market is stalling, a classic sign of a reversing trend.

February 2006
Bullish on Volatility

Last Friday's 213-point drop in the Dow Jones Industrial Average is the first daily move of 2% or more in almost three years. The sell-off is a shot across the bow for traders who expect last year's record, tight trading range to persist through 2006. The lack of volatility is the rea-

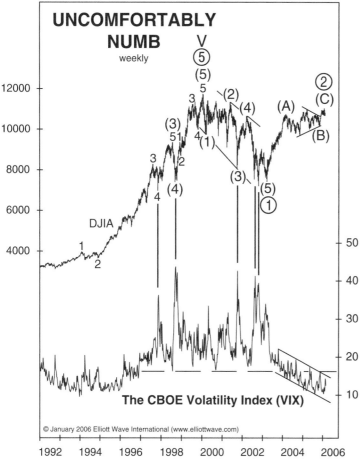

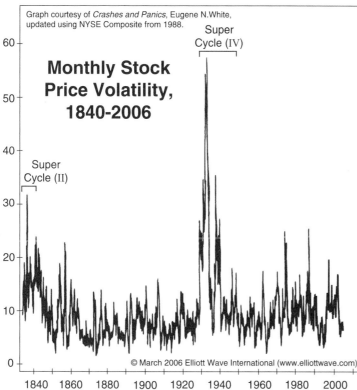

son that the CBOE Volatility Index (VIX) is locked in a downtrend that has drawn the index to its lowest level since December 1993. When volatility evaporates, the premium on at-the-money options shrinks because most investors linearly extrapolate the current trend, believing that volatility will stay low for the foreseeable future. Ironically, these are the exact conditions which lay the groundwork for a return of volatility. This year should mark a change toward a sharply rising VIX. The only time that a rise in the VIX has failed to trigger a substantial stock market decline was in late 1995-early 1996 when a doubling from about 10 to 20 accompanied a stock rally. The anomaly is not likely to repeat because investor optimism remains lopsidedly bullish, a very bearish sign for stocks. The record streak of bullish plurality in the Investors Intelligence Survey of Advisors is now at 171 weeks, whereas leading up to the 1995-1996 period, bears outnumbered bulls for 46 straight weeks, providing a springboard for the market's advance. In other words, this indicator is three times as bearish as it was bullish at the end of 1994.

March 2006

The Coming Volatility Boom

Last month we looked at a 12-year low in the CBOE Volatility Index and adopted a strong bullish stance on volatility. This month's chart adds another 150 years of data to our case. It's from the book, *Crashes and Panics* (edited by Eugene N. White, 1988); we've updated it here using monthly figures for the New York Stock Exchange Composite. There are several pertinent aspects. First and foremost, the largest upward spikes occurred in the mid-1830s and the 1930s, in line with what Elliotticians label as

Supercycle wave (II) in 1835-1842 and Supercycle wave (IV) in 1929-1949 (in inflation-adjusted terms). Of course, the bear market that began in the first quarter of 2000 is not just a Supercycle degree bear market; it will be even bigger: a Grand Supercycle decline. Therefore it is a near certainty that at some point volatility will be even more extreme than it was in the 1930s when 24 of the 25 most volatile months in U.S. stock market history occurred.

While Supercycle (IV) offers the best clue to the extent of coming volatility, Supercycle (II) is turning out to be a better key to the *stages* of the reversal process. *The Elliott Wave Financial Forecast* first discussed the similarities between Supercycle (II) and the current bear market back in April 2004, noting, "The Panic of 1837 is a perfect model for the decline in wave ③." Like the bear market that began in 1835, and unlike that of 1929-1933, the initial decline from the all-time high of 2000 failed to douse the speculative fever of the old bull market. After stocks' initial retreat in 1835, investors plowed into riskier speculative vehicles such as commodities and real estate, just as they have since 2002. Also similar to the mid-1830s, the reflationary phase of the advance focused around a property mania. In yet another apparent parallel between the two periods, a wave of popular unrest related to high prices for fuel and other commodities accompanied the peak in real estate speculation in 1837. A wave of fear in which mobs took to the streets to demand lower prices actually preceded the deflationary depression that resulted from Supercycle (II). As EWFF noted in April 2004, "The protestors got their wish, and suffered for it." A similar event occurred in conjunction with this era's real estate reversal when in late August and early September fears of runaway prices touched off panic buying at gas lines, fist fights and "No More Oil" headlines in supermarket tabloids. It has taken three times as long now as it did in the aftermath of Supercycle (I), (66 months versus 22 months in 1835-1837), but, once again, prices appear to be accommodating the crowd. Oil peaked with the gas line fisticuffs in late August of last year and many other commodities seem to have peaked as well. The volatility data show that the Panic of 1837 hit stock prices in earnest in July of that year, three months after the commodity price protest. Once the wild ride lower begins, don't look for any let-up. July 1837 is the only month outside of the 1930s to crack the top 25 most volatile. But the five remaining months of 1837 are all among the 52 most volatile in the 172-year history of the data. One online history of the episode explains, "The wild speculation ended, and a panic concerning the stability of the financial markets, the banks, and even in the government, spread across the nation." If the correspondence to 1835-1837 holds and it takes three times as long now for the selling to move from Main Street to Wall Street, we should see the same mayhem by summer.

Investor Psychology

The all-time peak in 2000 was unprecedented in terms of extreme stock market psychology. The final upward twists of the current countertrend advance may not be generating an exact replica of that period, but it's pretty darn close. One common facet of both peaks is a gusher of money from individual investors. On February 23, The Wall Street Journal reported that small investors "are moving into the stock market at a stronger clip than has been seen in years." According to the Investment Company Institute, equity mutual funds received $31.8 billion of net inflows in January, the sixth largest monthly total in history. The only bigger months were the first four of 2000 and January 2004, when the bear market rally was a few days from a peak. The surge represents a major capitulation to the uptrend. Trading in individual accounts at several key firms also jumped 30% to 40% from December to January. Discount brokerage firms are seeing "record levels of activity." At Fidelity Investments, net flows into stock funds surged $5.6 billion versus just $400 million in January 2005.

April 2006

As the great risk aversion spreads, declines in one country will feed the rate of descent in others. In one more vestige of the peaks of 1929 and 2000, even those who glimpse the big break ahead for what it is are unconcerned. This is the uh-oh effect, the phenomenon by which observers see but do not heed the substantial evidence of a collapse that is at hand. "The emerging markets look like they're getting close to the scalding point," writes a Bloomberg columnist. "You can tell by the bubbles – the torrid price action in single country mutual funds from India to Brazil, the hot money going into almost any stock fund with 'international' in its name. Is this column predicting an imminent disaster? It most certainly is not." Almost no one does, until it's too late. Eventually, the selling will sweep in from the periphery of the financial world to the global financial capitals in stunning fashion. (See Saudi Arabia/Dubai March 2006 entry in Chapter 1.)

May 2006

As the following collage illustrates, investors are anything but wary. Back at the all-time high, a 75% reading in sentiment surveys was about as hot as optimism toward stocks got. At this point, however, silver sentiment, the red hot speculative tip of the latest surge, hit a peak reading of 98% bulls on April 19, a level that analyst Paul Montgomery aptly described as "cartoonish." On a 10-day basis, Market Vane's Bullish Consensus peaked with 95% of investors convinced of further highs in silver. This white metal is definitely the focal point of the frenzy as even long-time gold bugs are expressing a preference for it: "Silver will not be just twice as

profitable as gold in the next few years, but many times more profitable—maybe ten times more profitable," said one famous gold bug. (See gold/silver ratio analysis May 2006 entry in Chapter 1.) Just as the pension funds were rewriting their by-laws to get more fully invested in stocks in the late 1990s, funds and university endowments are making a big push into commodities. A plethora of new exchange-traded commodity funds are also coming on line to satiate current demand. Much of the bullish sentiment in silver focuses on a new Barclays silver ETF that was approved yesterday and starts trading today. "I don't think I could have dreamed up anything more potentially bullish than the Barclays ETF," said one silver analyst. The word on the street is that billions of dollars in new silver interest cannot "flow smoothly into the silver market. It's like trying to stuff ten pounds of ice cream into a one-pound container. This is the reason why I was sure the regulators would reject the silver ETF. By the time this silver story plays out, the $50 Hunt Brothers episode will merely be a footnote in silver history." But the craze about the silver ETF's arrival suggests strongly that any positive effect on prices is completely played out in the rumor of the offering, and the actual appearance of the fund will be accompanied by nothing but selling. Rather than observing the unfortunate result of similar pension fund commitments to the stock market in the late 1990s, the fund movement into commodities is almost universally viewed as proof positive that commodities will continue still higher. "The main buyers are new investors like pension funds starting from scratch in commodities, and for them the actual price level is not relevant. Nothing can stop it," said one hedge fund manager. The first sentence is true; the second one isn't.

The whole theory of "peak oil," which blossomed around crude oil's third wave high in August, is now being exported to the metals markets. "Investors should take a clue from the boom in oil prices and a theory called Peak Oil," says one financial writer. "'Peak Metal' argues that the boom in the prices of metals and metal stocks is a long, long way from over. Factors could produce even sharper and more sustained price increases for Peak Metal than for Peak Oil." The September issue showed a panoply of "peak oil" books, noted that fears about shortages are typical of commodity tops and said that oil would soon fall. Oil dipped 14% immediately, but it has since surpassed its high by 7%. The depth of belief in "peak oil" suggests, however, that a much larger and more sustained decline is in the offing. With supply worries expanding to all kinds of metals, the psychology of last September is spreading out, which means that the retreat that it portends is likely broadening as well. Another critical element of the sentiment picture covered in September was a simmering public rage over high gas prices. The fury is even stronger now. The President just halted additions to the strategic oil reserve and launched an investigation "To Quell Anger Over Gas Prices." Fears about runaway commodity prices now match the riotous levels in the spring of 1837, after which an across-the-board deflation took hold in the United States (see March 2006 entry earlier in this chapter and April 2005 entry in Chapter 5). Then as now, it is the perfect segue to a deflationary era.

Return of The Margin Monster

In February 2000, *The Elliott Wave Financial Forecast* showed a chart of New York Stock Exchange margin debt having risen to $228 billion in December 1999 and said:

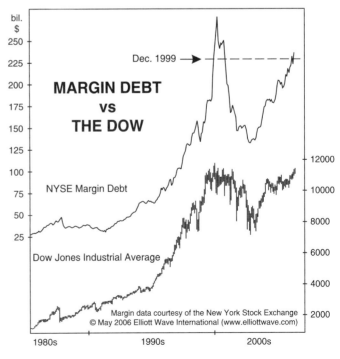

In the last nine months, a 32% increase in margin has been accompanied by no net gain in the Dow. Even a slowdown in the rise in margin debt should lead to falling stock prices.

The reversal in stocks was already underway. The revised chart here shows that margin debt hit $237 billion in March, taking it past the $228 billion level that EWFF was remarking on in February 2000. At this point, the willingness to leverage bets on stocks must be even more bearish than it was in the euphoria of the Dow's January 2000 peak because the level of NYSE margin just charged through the same late 1999 level accompanied by no net gain in the Dow Jones Industrial Average for six whole years! Another type of margin, loans to individual investors backed by their stock portfolios, is also back. "Such borrowings, also known as margin loans, were used extensively in the dot-com era by investors seeking to bulk up their portfolios. They fell from favor after the market crash. Now, margin loans are gaining renewed popularity. But brokerage firms say investors are increasingly using securities-based loans as a quicker and cheaper way to pay for a variety of purchases, not just stocks and bonds." This time, wealth managers say investors are using stocks to finance real estate, cars, artwork and boats. One client borrowed money against his investment portfolio to buy a jet. This is another example of how the bullish psychology of wave ② is fanning out into riskier and riskier areas. It also shows why the next decline will be felt far more broadly than wave ①. Such behavior implies a tremendous wave of bankruptcies in the offing.

Margin is also playing a big role in many foreign stock markets. This is confirmed by Vietnam's ministry of finance, which recently expressed "alarm at the volume of bank lending being used to finance the purchase of shares in the country's tiny, overheated stock market." The Vietnam Stock Exchange is up more than 100% so far this year. "You've got a lot of people who think it is not possible to lose money, find it easy to borrow to buy shares and don't understand the risks," says a manager of Vietnamese stocks. In India, where the Sensex Index has also doubled over the last 12 months, the use of margin is expanding fast. In fact, it's happening so fast and controls are so slack that banks may already be beyond their allowed 40% exposure to capital markets. "The lure of quick bucks is pushing many enterprising people to avail of credit to pump into the booming stock markets," says the Times of India. "It's made easier by banks that are ever willing to dole out loans at reasonable interest rates (19-21%) to people—especially those with salary accounts and a clean credit card history." The connection of the word "reasonable" to rates of 19-21% suggests a level of financial naiveté that probably even surpasses the gullibility at the height of the dot.com mania. The mountain of margin debt is going to lead to a valley of insolvency.

June 2006

Investors Bank on Stocks, Again

There's something about the final phase of a big stock market rise that makes some investors want to have their cake and eat it, too. This quote from the November 24, 1999 issue of The Wall Street Journal is a great illustration of the urge that seems to overwhelm them and their bankers:

> Everything old is new again — or that is the way it often seems on Wall Street if you just wait long enough. Take one of today's hot products, the market-indexed certificate of deposit. This hybrid CD, which promises to protect an investor's principal while offering the potential to share in further gains in stock prices, actually had its debut in the months before the 1987 stock-market crash. While today's products are somewhat different from those of a decade ago, the concept is the same.

A sudden demand for these products preceded the crash of 1987 and the initial leg of a great bear market in 2000. Guess what? Stock-linked bank accounts are back. The New York Stock Exchange reports "an increase in the sale of market-indexed CDs and is concerned that some customers don't understand the difference between these hybrid products and traditional CDs." We are not surprised. In this day and age, many economists don't understand the difference, either. That's why they continue to argue for a change in the traditional definition that would consider gains in stock portfolios as savings. This mentality is a result of the long bull market in social mood. Near the end of such periods, thoughts of loss are banished from the realm of the possible. A related capitulation to the social mood is an FDIC decision to raise to $250,000 the ceiling on the insured level of some bank accounts. If government regulators believe that the risk of loss is so remote that it's safe to increase the maximum coverage, then it must be time for a bank-shaking bear market.

Fuses Get Short at the Stock Exchange

The New York Post reports, "In the days leading up to the New York Stock Exchange's landmark bid for Euronext, the Chairman of the Big Board lashed out at a vocal shareholder who had publicly questioned the wisdom of a big merger deal. 'You are a f***ing idiot.'" The statement was made to a man whose fund owns 3% of the total NYSE shares. This is all anyone needs to know about the intensifying pressure for profits that is starting to exert itself on the trading community. Back in March when the Big Board was about to go public, EWFF identified its IPO as one of the areas "where the hues of the latest stock market euphoria were even more vivid" than they were at the top in 2000. We added that the NYSE's offering "is one of the most bearish imaginable signals." The stock (NYX) is already down 38.7% from a March 16 post-offering peak price of $90.35 a share. The NASDAQ's stock (NDAQ) is down even more, 41%, since a January 30 high price of $46.75. The stock of the Chicago Mercantile Exchange (CME) may be the most attractive to short sellers. It's down just 13% since an April 24 high, and sells now for $439 a share. Time will tell who the *@#!! idiots are.

July 2006

Today, even the slightest hint of negativity is regarded as a sign that the market is ready to resume its climb. After just one week of equality between the number of II bulls and bears (35.6% bulls to 35.6% bears), many analysts used the figure to make the case for a sustained rally. Here is one of several articles that cited the supposedly bullish implications of the flat reading:

Ready Set Soar? As Bears Growl, Some See a Rally
—NY Post, June 25, 2006

Instead of any hair-raising sense of fear, the leg down triggered a wave of what Bob Prechter calls "aggressive complacency." "NASDAQ's Slide Signals Opportunities for Investors," says a typical piece in the Wall Street Journal. Here's the WSJ's corresponding headline from the bottom of the first plunge down in April 2000: "Market Rout Ushers In Opportunity." The NASDAQ subsequently lost 65% of its entire value. "A Slowdown Investors Should Cheer, Not Fear," chirps Business Week. "Commodity Selloff a Panacea," relates The Globe and Mail. Even in places like India where the damage to stocks was more severe (down 30% from May 11 to June 14), the "drop in risk appetite has a silver lining." In a series of profiles from an Internet cafe in Mumbai, a June 21 WSJ story captures the uncanny resemblance to U.S. day traders in wake of the NASDAQ's initial plunge in April 2000. "Piggybacking on the stock market's historic run higher is no longer the no-brainer it has been. 'I was stupid. I should have sold,'" says a former real estate broker. What she and fellow traders "haven't lost is the bug." A former salesman insists that he "makes more money buying on dips than in his old day jobs." Another article from the Dubai exchange displays the universal, post-bubble urge to win it all back. It says that a group of female traders "from across the globe have united. They speak only one language: money. And the recouping of their life savings."

In Saudi Arabia, where declines in the stock exchange index exceeded 50%, there's anger, indignation and finger-pointing. Many small investors sport bumper stickers that rail against

"Big Thieves." "Ordinary folks like me lost, and what fault is it of ours?" asks a Saudi Arabian investor. "The market regulator is to blame." In "a move aimed at pumping liquidity" into the market, Saudi regulators lowered "trading commissions by 20 percent, allowed further discounts" and legalized share buybacks. More dramatic measures such as the outright reimbursement for losses and a suspension of taxes on gains are also rumored to be under consideration. The more governments do to stem the tide, the longer and deeper the consequences are likely to be.

August 2006

In our discussion of "aggressive complacency" last month, we observed that the decline can generate enthusiasm for shares even as stocks fall. Barron's "Time To Buy" cover may turn out to be a good example. "After two months of downward pressure applied by turmoil in the Mideast, pumped-up energy prices and worries about U.S. interest rates, there are bargains to be had," says the article.

In March 2000, EWFF observed an "uh-oh" effect in conjunction with the all-time peak in the NASDAQ and noted that it is normal for many observers to recognize the reversal of manias. The [August 2006 entry in Chapter 5] covers its appearance again in a society-wide awakening to the popping of the debt and real estate bubbles. Here's another strain that is directly parallel to the March 2000 highs:

Internet Bubble May Burst—Again

The amount of money being invested in startups reminds some of the situation before the dot-com bust.

October 2006
More Credit on the Way

If the sentiment figures show that bulls are numerous and committed, how could the market go any higher? Well, the same type of credit expansion that fueled the final rush in the property mania might do the same for stocks. As happened in real estate, it would become available only because prices are rising in the first place. In case you haven't heard, the SEC is expected to re-write margin requirements that were established in reaction to the 1929 crash. Back then margins were as low as 10 percent. Leverage contributed to the run-up, and its unwinding contributed to the ensuing collapse. Since then—for over 70 years—margin requirement has been at 50 percent. Now the New York Stock Exchange has asked the SEC to let the Federal Reserve lower it back to 15 percent for institutional investors. When investors buy stock on credit, they put up stock as collateral. You can see what a house of cards this borrowing scheme can create. Of course, investors have already found ways around the margin requirement, by borrowing from home equity, on credit cards, etc., and institutions borrow money from banks. But now they won't even have to go through those machinations, or, worse yet, they can borrow money in the first place, then give it to a broker and leverage it again. You don't need more bulls to fuel more rally in this circumstance; you need only provide the already bullish majority with more credit.

December 2006

The Dow's advance into the short-term peak of November 22 induced one of the more brazenly optimistic trading environments we can remember. After the unprecedented run of 90% readings in the Daily Sentiment Index, the DSI began another run on November 14. The march through the November 22 high was accompanied by eight straight 90% readings among S&P

and/or NASDAQ traders. So readings of 90% bulls occurred in 27 out of 43 trading days through November 23. Persistent bullishness is expressed on a longer term basis by the Investors Intelligence survey of investment advisors where the bears have not exceeded the bulls for more than 4 years. At 58% on November 21, the percentage of bullish advisors hit its highest level since December of last year. Once the main stock indexes turn definitively lower, the weight of these extremes will keep stocks tumbling for a long time to come.

Another classic sign of a top is the unprecedented craze for financial exchanges themselves. In addition to a NASDAQ bid for the London Stock Exchange and a tripling in the price of seats on Brazil's Sao Paulo Stock Exchange over the last four months, the NYMEX, the world's largest energy market, became the top performing IPO of 2006 with a 125% rise from its initial price on November 17. According to one report, the offering gave the NYMEX a market cap that was about 175% that of the Chicago Board of Trade even though the CBOT trading volume is five times that of the NYMEX. More confounding is a $435 million offering by the Dubai Financial Market, Dubai's stock exchange. Even though the Dubai Financial Market Index is down 65% for the year, the IPO is 300 times oversubscribed! Back in March, when the NYSE went public, EWFF called it "one of the most bearish imaginable signals." NYSE shares' ability to accompany the Dow to a new high certainly surprised us. But the latest runup in exchange prices magnifies the strength of this signal several times over.

January 2007

At various times, wave **b** has pushed psychology to the outer limits of the bullish range, but here's a sentiment measure showing that traders entered an out-of-this-world phase of optimism over the course of the last several weeks. The line at the bottom of the chart at right is a long-term 60-day average of the percentage of bears from the Daily Sentiment Index (courtesy of MBH Commodity Advisors, futures-trade.net), inverted and plotted on log scale. Toward the left side, the horizontal line shows the optimistic extremes reached throughout wave V (the true bull market) and to the right, the extremes reached during Cycle wave **b**. Need we say more? Virtually no one is bearish stocks now, which must be a trend extreme.

Ringing In A Bear Market

Likewise, Wall Street strategists are all in. "Even Skeptical Money Managers Fall In With Stock-Market Bulls," says a recent Wall Street Journal headline. According to a Bloomberg survey, it's unanimous: 12 out of 12 strategists

at the largest Wall Street firms agree that the market will rise in 2007. Several converts to the bullish view were "among the most bearish analysts" on the street. A larger Russell Investment Group survey of 87 money managers found that 80% are bullish on U.S. stocks. "The bulls are running," says Russell's chief strategist. One headline captures the sentiment this way:

Wall Street 'Belongs to the Bulls' In 2007

Here's another from the January 1 issue of the New York Post:

'07 BULL RUN
THE TIME OF NO FEAR

"There are no major stumbling blocks ahead for the stock market," says a market strategist. "There is too much cash waiting to be put to work to allow a sharp drop." USA Today opens the new year with a massive spread offering "10 REASONS WHY THE S&P 500 COULD HIT A RECORD HIGH IN 2007." A day later, it followed with "UP, UP, UP" in which "10 out of 10 market gurus interviewed by USA Today say stocks will post gains." Some of the coverage was tempered with mild concerns, but the only salient one was the observation, "There wasn't a single bear. No real pessimists. No one calling for a loss." Here's another headline that places the fearlessness on the same plane as that of January 2000:

'Irrational Exuberance' May Now Be More Rational

February 2007

Sentiment appears to be building in a kind of symphonic crescendo in which one class of investors soars to impossible heights, such as the traders' run of 90%+ days mentioned here in December (DSI), followed by others who fully hitch their lot to the bandwagon of optimism. According to the UBS Investor Sentiment Index, for instance, investor optimism popped 13 points to 103 in January, the measure's first reading over 100 since 2004 and only the fifth reading above 100 since 2000. The Conference Board's Consumer Confidence index just pushed to 110.3, its highest reading in five years. Another survey of top executives produced a five-year high in confidence over global business conditions. According to The Economist Intelligence Unit, nine out of ten top executives rate prospects good or very good over the next three years. Keep in mind that the dwindling percentage of bears in the NASDAQ Daily Sentiment Index shown in the chart is a 60-day average. Notice how much more extreme the paucity of bears is now versus levels at the January 2005, August 2005 and April 2006 highs.

The final clash of the symbols may be a quick spike in the AAII poll. We were starting to wonder if small investors would join in the party this time around, and the American Association of Individual Investors jumped to 57.5% in the middle of January. That's the highest reading since the end of 2005, which was quickly followed by a NASDAQ high in January 2006.

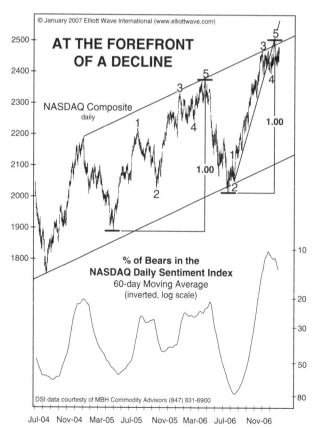

Don't Worry, There's Too Much To Worry About

Last month's Special Section made the case for the downside in the long boom in finance in general saying, "It is only a matter of time before it joins tech stocks, real estate and commodities in the turn lower." This month, a host of admonitions hit the street about an unsustainable liquidity bubble and surging demand for derivatives and junk debt. After noting that derivatives' use was growing at the fastest pace in eight years, an economic minister from India made the sage observation that "people don't have much experience" with these instruments in declining markets. The founder of a buyout firm notes that the spread between high-yield bonds and Treasuries is as narrow as it's ever been and says, "Investors are simply not being paid for the risks they're taking." He goes so far as to add, "We're able to borrow at unusually low spreads. I'm not sure I'd want to be the buyer of that high-yield paper."

From a contrary perspective, it's a little eerie how many of the warnings emanate from the most exposed quarters. China, which is experiencing the classic mania depicted in the February 2007 entry in Chapter 1, elicits the most pronounced outbreak of candor. Zhu Min, the executive vice president of the Bank of China frankly admits that "much of the money is flowing to Asia where people have no idea what risks they are taking." At the annual economic forum in Davos, Switzerland, U.S. and European regulators "expressed concern" that investment banks are allowing hedge funds to increase "borrowing capacity using collateral that could lose its value rapidly in a financial crisis." Suddenly it's all too apparent that Wall Street firms allow hedge funds to use illiquid credit default swaps and other derivatives to reduce margin requirements. "Is this inherently dangerous? Yes it is," says a consultant. A governing member of the European Central Bank warned that financial markets need "to move back to more adequate risk pricing and maybe forgo a deal even if it looks tempting. There's a danger of a 'rush to the exit' if investors wait too long." The problem with this plea is that it is absolutely too late to apply a remedy.

Once a mania has detached values from their earthly moorings, there is no comfortable way to re-attach them. These warnings are another prime example of the "uh-oh" effect, a phenomenon that *The Elliott Wave Financial Forecast* first identified at the peak in the NASDAQ in March 2000, as "normal behavior at the biggest tops of all." As we noted in March 2000 and at the peak in the housing bubble in 2005 (see collage in the September 2005 entry in Chapter 2), one critical aspect to forming a top is that no matter what the weight of the authority or how well reasoned the argument, these warnings are not heeded. This is clearly the case now as the outcry about the "scary risk of something systemic happening" is being quickly dismissed. One hotbed of concern was the World Economic Forum in Davos, Switzerland. Here's how Bloomberg characterized the overriding sentiment at this year's event:

Davos Elite Brushes Off Policy Makers' Warnings of End to Boom

Bankers, investors, and executives last week arrived at the Swiss resort of Davos giddy about record profits and bonuses. After five days of hectoring by policy makers that they are too complacent, they left just as happy.

"The mood has been totally upbeat," the chairman of India's largest mobile-phone operator said. "I've never seen a mood like this."

Warnings by central bankers were batted away by dealmakers like Michael Klein of Citigroup, and David Rubenstein at the Carlyle Group Inc. buyout firm. They were confident in their ability to cope with the inevitable slowdown.

—Bloomberg, January 27, 2007

Another columnist described the concern as "warmed over prudence" and added "the most striking thing about the growing derivatives markets is the stability that has come with them."

An added concurrence with 2000 is a return to the glorious, easy-money life of day-trading. Although "day trading activity doesn't resemble the frenzy of the late 1990s, it is heating up again," says the January 16 Los Angeles Times. "Rising stock prices and new highs in major stock indexes have tickled investor interest." In a fitting echo of 2000, a January 26 CNBC article confirms the finding with a story hailing "The Return of the Day Trader." The head of an online-trading firm insists, however, that the revival is not being driven by speculative money because all the fast money is "tied up in the condo market in Miami." There's certainly some truth to this, but the difference is probably just another example of the comparative weakness of a B-wave peak.

March 2007

Any one of these sentiment signals in conjunction with a 61.8% retracement in the S&P 100 would probably be worth heeding. All of them in succession (most of which are shown on the chart) over the course of two months suggests a peak of no ordinary magnitude.

- The 10-day S&P DSI (courtesy of MBH Commodity Advisors) hit an all-time extreme of 91.1% bulls on December 15, 2006. The 60-day DSI has been above 85% since November 22, 2006 (over 3 months!), by far the longest and most extreme optimistic stance since the start of the data series on April 2, 1987. 30-day DSI has likewise held near or above 85% since October 18, 2006, a record optimism.

- December cash-to-asset levels at U.S. mutual funds hit 3.9%, below the low of 4% at the March 2000 peak and slightly above the all-time record low of 3.8% in September 2005.

- From September 26 to January 16, the percentage of bulls in DSI's daily survey was over 90% in the NASDAQ and/or the S&P on 42 out of 75 days.

- On January 18, 2007, the American Association of Individual Investors poll hit 57.5% bulls, a historically high level for this traditionally cautious group.

- In January, NYSE margin debt exceeded $285.5 billion, surpassing the old record of $278.5 billion, which coincided with the all-time high in the NASDAQ and S&P in March 2000.

- The CBOE Volatility Index (VIX) closed the week of February 12, 2007 at 10.02, its third lowest close in history. The first and second lowest closes came December 1993 and January 1994, right before a sharp 11% market decline.

- On February 23, the Large Speculators' (hedge funds) futures position hit a record net long 21,708 contracts in the DJIA and the smart-money commercial

hedgers took a correspondingly bearish record net short position of 39,834 contracts.

- The percentage of Investors Intelligence bulls has been equal to or greater than the percentage of bears for a record 228 straight weeks. The streak of bullish weeks is now 50% longer than the second longest streak, which took place through the all-time highs in 2000 and was followed by a devastating decline to the lows of 2002/2003.

- Market Vane's Bullish Consensus scored the second highest 10-day average on record, 72.3%, with data going back to October 1988. The record 10-day average is 78.1% on June 20, 1997, which preceded a 16% decline by about a month.

- Consumer Confidence just hit 112.50, its highest reading since August 2001.

Add the fact that these extremes were registered as the S&P was completing its longest streak without at least a 2% correction in more than 50 years, and the psychological set-up is clearly ripe for a resumption of the bear market of Grand Supercycle degree. The latest action confirms this assessment. The December issue of EWFF stated, "High volatility tends to follow low volatility." On Tuesday's decline, the VIX spiked a whopping 64%, closing at 18.30. This is probably the start of the "high volatility" era. Near the end of wave **c**, the VIX should reach levels that investors cannot currently fathom.

Three Cheers for Market Volatility

What's striking about Tuesday's big sell off is how ready investors were to exploit it. "Yea! Stocks are on sale," one analyst said on a local TV news show. Turns out that many supposedly avowed bears were just looking for a decline to buy and, for some, the dip into Tuesday's low sufficed. Virtually no one thinks that the market has returned to the bear trend, one that will be a long and protracted decline. We heard various explanations for the trading glitch that erased more than 200 points from the Dow Jones Industrial Average at 2:59 on Tuesday—a surge caused by a Dow Jones switch to a back-up computer system, a big options trade gone awry or concentrated ETF selling—but none strikes us as very reliable. What was unmistakable, however, was how completely unfazed investors were by the plunge. Once the dust settled, traders didn't hesitate to jump right in. "There was a glitch on the NYSE," said a CNBC message board respondent. "But this is just a hiccup. I'm standing pat." To a CNN survey that asked, "What do you think about the stock market slide?," 71% said it was "Just one of those things." "U.S. Stock Volatility Welcomed by Traders," says a Bloomberg headline. The rout "creates a great opportunity. We can sift through the wreckage and see what we have." To repeat: There are few serious bears. There are bulls and bulls looking for a correction to buy.

April 2007

Last month, margin debt finally surpassed its March 2000 high (see following chart). Record margin buying while the Dow is only marginally higher than it was seven years ago and the S&P and NASDAQ are actually down from 2000 is classic B-wave behavior. It fits perfectly with the following description from *Elliott Wave Principle*: "B waves are phonies. They are sucker plays, bull traps, speculators' paradise, and orgies of odd-lotter mentality."

The February peak did little to stem the feeding frenzy for buyouts of financial exchanges. The Chicago Board of Trade is the focus of a bidding war between the Chicago Mercantile Exchange and the Intercontinental Exchange. As it stands, the ICE is outbidding the Merc, but the Merc refuses to increase its offer, saying ICE's deal is "significantly inferior" as its shares represent a "weaker currency." The NASDAQ, NYSE, CME, ICE and NYMEX all peaked between November and February. The CBOT appears to have topped this month. Post-issuance action in NYMEX stock, which went public last November, is revealing. After it doubled its market capitalization with a November 17 stock offering, NYMEX "has been dead money for anyone who wasn't part of the IPO." Since November, the cost to rent NYMEX trading rights has plunged from $20,000 to around $8,000 "as electronic markets made inroads." This is exactly what EWFF has been saying is so fishy about the public's sudden access to exchange shares after 200 years of member-only

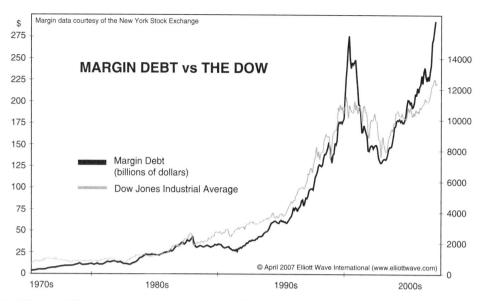

ownership. The public never gets an even break. Considering Blackstone Group's recently announced IPO, anyone involved in the frothy realm of private equity buy-outs should keep this aphorism in mind. When the firm that is famous for taking companies private goes public, the jig is very likely up for that whole game, too.

May 2007

Credit derivatives doubled in size over the past year for the third straight year. The International Swaps and Derivatives Association reports that the global market for credit grew to over $34.5 trillion in 2006. The overall derivative market is now reputed to be $370 trillion, or 10x the total financial assets of the United States. This is a mind-boggling figure that will unwind when investor optimism, as measured by the stock averages, turns toward pessimism. It will contribute mightily to the coming deflation. In the meantime, investors' motto is "party on, dude." But the party has already gone on too long, and dawn appears to be creeping over the backyard hedge.

While stocks retain the potential to roll still higher here, our view is that turning bullish is not an appropriate course. Doing so would align one with the most lop-sided, extreme, across-the-board optimism in the history of the financial markets. The shared affection for stocks and gold, for instance, is shown by their almost simultaneous 90% bullish readings

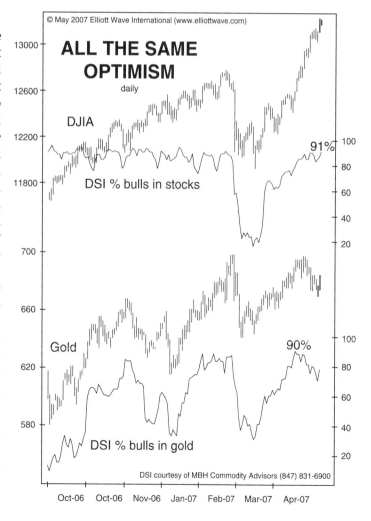

(Daily Sentiment Index, MBH Commodity Advisors). Since in the past these two markets commonly moved in opposite directions, this is an extremely rare confluence of optimism. The same lofty expectations are present in other markets, too. Over a two-week period in April, readings of at least 90% bulls—a rare level in any market—were also registered in the Canadian dollar, British pound, copper, German DAX, Dow Jones EuroStoxx 50, the euro and platinum! Nearly everything is rising, and, even more importantly virtually everyone is bullish, in fact very bullish, which means that by now they've all acted on their impulse to buy. A bear market is the process through which investors re-commit to the sell side. With so many so fully committed to the long side, it cannot be far off.

Extreme Optimism in the Face of Looming Disaster

We just returned from a speaking engagement at a financial conference. The conference began years ago as a hard-money-oriented group, and the theme was usually bearish. What a difference today! According to several attendees and one of the conference organizers, there were no super bears on the stock market until we showed up. They had difficulty finding speakers who would volunteer for the bear side in a panel debate, but they finally found three. So while investors have bought into the idea of perpetual liquidity, so have most of the experts. The record readings reported in *The Elliott Wave Financial Forecast* of "90 percent" bulls among traders and the unprecedented duration of net bullishness among advisors are not just numbers; they reflect exactly how lopsided market opinion is these days.

June 2007

Bullish commentators point to slack mutual fund sales as a sign of the little guy's disinterest. But he's not disinterested; he's already fully invested in mutual funds and hedge funds. The American Association of Individual Investors asset allocation survey shows that individuals allowed their portfolios to dip below 50% equities only briefly in late 2002 and early 2003. Over the last three years, the share of portfolios in stock has hovered just below 70%. In April, bullishness increased just 1% to about 40%, but the AAII allocation survey says that investment in stock mutual funds jumped more than 8 percentage points, bringing the total stock market allocation to 68.53%. This is not as high as the 77% allocation in early 2000, but it is a historically high level.

Another area where investors are expressing a wild-eyed optimism rivaling that of 2000 is

in their use of leverage. The chart shows that April brought another surge in the use of NYSE margin (shown as a percentage of market capitalization). A similar push accompanied the S&P 500's big top in 2000. The six-month rate of change at the bottom of the chart depicts a rare 4% surge in the use of margin. Again, the figure is not as high as it was in 2000, but it is high.

Considering the debt that is being used to fund buyouts and some of the more exotic derivatives plays, margin is probably higher than at any time in history. We may never know the full extent of the leverage, but we'll know the resulting margin call when we see it. It should be vicious.

In Chinese, Uh-Oh Means Uh-Oh

One of the biggest reasons cited for the continuation of the uptrend is the belief that way too many people are worried about what will happen if things go wrong. Recent weeks have brought a loud chorus of warnings about derivatives, debt and high share prices. China is probably the biggest worry. Today's issue of the Shanghai Daily says, "Chinese financial authorities in the past month took a string of measures to cool the high-flying stock market." The central bank raised interest rates while Chinese securities regulators issued public warnings against investment risks. Chinese bank regulators also launched a "campaign to prevent people or companies from channeling bank loans illegally into the equity markets." A stamp duty on stock gains was raised from 0.1% to 0.3%. That's not much, but Chinese authorities pushed through a similar increase, to 0.5% from 0.3% in 1997, right before a big smash. Here again, we see an unmistakable parallel to the Mississippi Scheme crack-down in 1720. Not to mention the U.S., where worries of overheating accompanied a similar effort to slam on the brakes with interest rate increases in 1929 and 2000.

In fact, the architect of the U.S. government's effort to stem the tide in 2000, Alan Greenspan, is among the latest financial heavyweight to weigh in against Chinese shares. The Chinese market ignored Greenspan's warning, just as the Dow did back in January 2000. Here's what February 2000 issue of EWFF said about the market's response: "In finally succeeding to tune out the sincere concerns of Alan Greenspan, the foremost financial hero of the bull market, the public has signaled that its potential to experience tragedy is now fully formed." The Dow completed its last burst shortly thereafter. In China today, the response, is much the same. The more authorities worry, the more convinced investors become that the market won't crash. "The increase in stamp duty and the crack down on irregularities 'can trip a short-term correction,' but it won't suddenly turn bearish," said an analyst at the nation's top broker." "Wen Jiabao [the prime minister] won't let it drop. He's afraid of that," says a Chinese investor. "Look at the benefits—stamp-duty revenues, more money for the government from IPOs, plus the hot stock market is creating jobs." Here too, China's mania is exhibiting a highly developed version of the "uh-oh effect" that typically appears in the final phase of a bubble. With China's history of reliance on social engineering, the effort to stem the tide may be more pronounced than in other countries. Any such action will magnify the effect of the eventual decline.

August 2007

In a bullish report titled "Five Reasons Not to Panic," a chief market strategist says, "Earnings growth is poised to rebound" and "The economy has managed a 'soft landing.'" Even the bears are unable to wrap their arms around the full depth of the situation. One famously "dour perma-bear" who says the world is in the midst of a "global bubble" and "has never been so bearish," is "still bullish on emerging market stocks." Under the headline "Time to Sell?" one columnist extols the "genius" behind a recent sell signal, but adds, "As for me, I'm not selling anything." After a generation of mostly rising stock prices, being bearish is one thing, but selling is quite another.

If anything, the initial round of debt liquidation contributed to an aura of long-term optimism. One story claimed, "The biggest losses in equity and credit markets in five years are making U.S. stock bulls more bullish." On Monday July 30, two separate Bloomberg articles stated that investors were diving in. "Stock Bulls Grow More Bullish" read one headline, while the other declared, "Bulls Load Up on Stocks." "The world's largest investors say last week offers them even more opportunities to profit." Brief upticks on July 30 and 31 added to the dip-buyers' delight. "Stock Strategists View Sell-Off as Bargain Sale," said a typical headline.

From our perspective, one of the more interesting bullish arguments is that the reversal is happening way too fast to be for real. "You don't tend to go to new highs and then immediately start a bear market," said the chief investment strategist at Charles Schwab. "Markets don't tend to turn on a dime." Of course they do. How else could they turn? But we also observe that the turn in the long term trend has been a slow process. The big top described in *Conquer the Crash* started back in 2000 with the NASDAQ's peak and has advanced through the housing market in 2005, the commodity markets in 2006 and finally to the Dow Industrials and global stock markets last month. It's the most diffuse and dangerous top in history, but it took so long and extends so broadly across the breadth of the financial markets that many on Wall Street still can't even see it.

Another finishing element is a sudden intellectual fondness for bubbles. In recent months, various articles and the book *Pop! Why Bubbles are Great for the Economy* appeared, describing the positive attributes of financial manias. It's true, bubbles aren't all bad. As Elliott Wave International pointed out years ago in our exposition on the technological and investment manias, all the great bull markets involve bursts of innovation, and the biggest always feature a public euphoria for technology and its future benefits. But as EWT explained in 1999, the problem with manias is that they tend to price in decades of future progress. Hurricanes have positive attributes, too. In the summer they provide much needed moisture to parched southern states. But try telling that to a former resident of New Orleans' Ninth Ward. Bubbles always end up with a bad name because their aftermath ruins so many people.

The only time that bubbles get good press is at a peak and the very early stages of a bust. We noticed a series of similar reviews in mid-2000 when stocks were off their highs and it became hard to argue that the rise of the late 1990s was normal and sustainable. At that time, *Famous First Bubbles*, a dissertation on the fundamental basis behind the Tulip Bulb, South Sea and Mississippi manias, was released to positive reviews. The book contends that it was not madness but a zealous regard for fundamental value that drove these manias. This probably happens because, at such moments, focusing on the bright side of a bubble assuages the embarrassment caused by holding stock in the likes of Pets.com and DrKoop.com. The positive PR of recent weeks comes at roughly the same juncture; it probably won't turn out to be any solace either.

October 2007

Optimism in the Stock Market

The latest reading from Investors Intelligence shows 62 percent bulls among newsletter advisors, the second-highest reading over the past 21 years, a period that includes the tops of 1987 and 2000. And this is not the most extreme figure relating to investor sentiment. The duration of net optimism is the longest ever by many measures.

October 19 is the anniversary of the biggest down day in the 1987 crash, so let's compare some of the technical readings at the 1987 pre-crash high with today's. The table shows five different measures (the first two lines express the same thing) of optimism. Low valuation of dividend payouts indicate optimism, because when investors don't care about receiving dividends, it

	Aug. 1987	Oct. 2007
DJIA Annual Dividend Yield	2.6%	**2.0%**
Price of $1 dividend	$39	**$50**
Duration Div. < 1929	3 months	**13 years**
Price/book value	1.73	**4.04**
Advisors net bullish (>97%)	156 weeks	**468 weeks**
Daily readings > 90% bulls	3	**51**

means they are counting on capital gains to get rich. By all these measures, the persistence of optimism going into October 2007 dwarfs that of August 1987.

The chart shows how the greatest tops of the 20th century compare in terms of the duration of optimism. The X axis records the length of time that bulls consistently outnumbered bears by a ratio of at least 50/52 in Investors Intelligence's weekly readings. (We estimate that at the tops in 1929 and 1937, bulls had outnumbered bears continuously for about 2-2.5 years.) The Y axis records the length of time that the dividend yield from the Dow was less than it was at the 1968 top, the peak with the highest dividend payout among these five tops. As you can see, the other major tops cluster around an area of 2-3 years for a lopsided bullish consensus and 7-11 months for extremely low dividend payout.

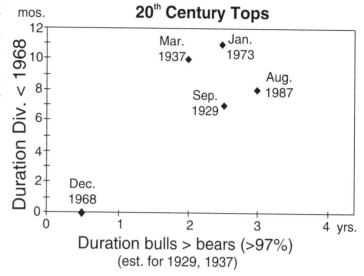

Now look at the left chart below. This is the same graph but with two added data points representing the top of January 2000 and now. Compared to past market tops, the current juncture is nothing less than grotesque. We hope you can see some reasons why we have expected a major top at each interim peak.

The figure on the right is even more striking. It uses the greatest top in U.S. history (in 1929) as a value benchmark. At the 1987 high, just before the crash, bulls had reigned for 3 years. Then, just three months after the annual dividend yield from the DJIA fell below that of 1929, the market crashed. At the 2000 high, dividends had been below the 1929 level for a full six years, but the duration for a preponderance of bulls was only 1.25 years. That was enough for the S&P to fall in half and the NASDAQ to collapse 78 percent.

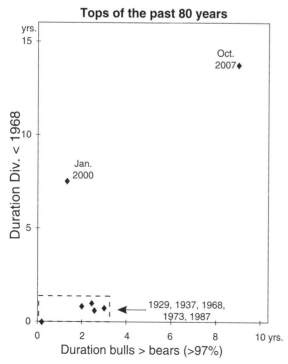

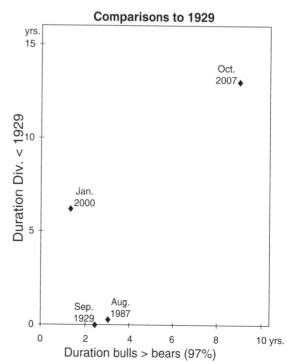

But the situation in October 2007 dwarfs all these experiences. Advisory bulls have consistently outnumbered bears for 9 years, by an incredible 51/52 ratio, and the dividend yield has been below that of 1929 for 13 years. Thus, optimism is not only historically extreme in terms of extent but also—by a huge amount—in duration.

And remember, this graph uses the peak reading of 1929, the greatest top of the 19th and 20th centuries, as a benchmark. Forget comparing today's values and psychology to past bottoms.

November 2007

The stretch in which the weekly percentage of bullish advisors surveyed by Investors Intelligence exceeds the percentage of bearish ones extended to a fifth full year this month. This is by far the longest period of uninterrupted bullish plurality on record. For the week of October 16, the bullish advisor reading of 62% relative to 19.6% for the bears means there was a rare ratio just as the DJIA reached its October top: three bulls for every bear. In fact, other than a single more extreme reading in June 2003, the last time that the survey generated a stronger surge of optimism was in August 1987, as the stock market topped prior to the October 1987 crash. Again, it is worth keeping in mind that the 1987 peak was accompanied by a bullish plurality for just 10 months, so the current persistence of optimism dwarfs that of August 1987.

The celebration surrounding the twentieth anniversary of Black Monday is a testament to the remarkable depth of complacency concerning a big bear market. The bottom line of various reminiscences is that "the market always bounces back." "Passivity was the best course," explained one advocate of "blissful ignorance." Funny, as we recall at the time, there was not a whole lot of blissfulness and few commentators advocating any such course. A generation later, the hold-for-the-long-term lesson is so thoroughly established that investors are perfectly tenderized for a bear-market roasting.

January 2008

No matter how riled the debt markets become or how close the economy gets to an outright contraction, the belief in rising stock prices stays rigidly in place. According to Investors Intelligence, the percentage of bullish advisors was greater than 50% for every week in December, even though the market was down for the month. "Despite widespread worry, the subprime mortgage crisis and resulting problems in the credit markets," Wall Street analysts say that there will be no recession in 2008. "Instead, most strategists expect slower-than-normal growth in the first half of 2008, followed by a pickup in the second half." In a Newsday sample of strategists for eight major Wall Street securities firms, the average forecast is for an 11.8% rise in 2008. "Even the most bearish strategist in the group recommends that investors keep a majority of their assets, 60%, in equities." "Be Ready To Buy on the Word 'Recession,'" says a Wall Street Journal headline. "The biggest money managers are closing their eyes and buying," says Bloomberg. The article quotes a Dallas-based fund manager who tripled his holdings of Bear Stearns and is hanging on to interests in Merrill Lynch, JP Morgan Chase & Co. and Citigroup. "This is close enough to the bottom," he says. "You may suffer for a while if you buy now, but then within a year, these stocks will outperform the market." And if you stick your finger in a light socket and leave it there, it probably won't hurt forever. After a while, we suspect you just go numb, which is what we see as the next stage for investors. When we really are close to the bottom, we will recognize it by the selling sensation that finally sweeps through the ranks of Wall Street's "strategists."

The Uh-Oh Effect

The most important headlines in the timeline shown at the beginning of this issue (see Chapter 2) are the most recent ones. They illustrate that a new level of realization is sweeping into the marketplace. Here's how Christopher Thornberg, a founding partner with Beacon Economics, described the phenomenon in the December 28 issue of the Los Angeles Times:

Realty Reality: Housing Prices Headed Way Down

There are 'experts' out there who once preached that there was no bubble; they now preach that all real estate is local and that prices in your neighborhood won't be affected by foreclosures and price declines elsewhere."

The cold, hard truth is that foreclosures are serving only to hasten the painful process of shifting housing prices back to a level the market can sustain. Prices must and will fall. Everywhere. When making important financial decisions today, be realistic and factor those declines in.

As *Conquer the Crash* explains, such recognition is a critical psychological component in the establishment of a downward spiral. It is an all-important inflection point in which buyers experience a shift in incentive. According to CTC, they say, "Well, gee, property prices have been coming down. Why should I rush? I'll wait till they come down further." The media alarm is clearly intensifying. The question now is whether housing's troubles are leaking into the overall economy. Another month of data does nothing to alter our view that the economy is on the cusp of a contraction. In fact, the latest Institute of Supply Management factory index says that manufacturing in December shrank for the first time since April 2003. The ISM index fell 3.1 percentage points to 47.7. A reading of 50 marks the line between growth and contraction.

February 2008

With house prices falling and a recession brewing, it should come as no surprise that investors are getting a little skittish. The American Association of Individual Investors survey registered just 19.63% bulls on January 10. That's the fourth lowest weekly total over the last 15 years. On the other hand, the allocation part of the same survey shows that the average AAII member has 64% of his investments in stocks. So they may be bearish, but AAII members are a long way from being scared off, which is what we will finally see near an important bottom.

The party must be over because the five-year stock rally left behind lots of conviction that the bull market will never end. The clippings shown here depict a mad rush to add to positions or at least "hang in there" at the recent low. Like the Texan in The Dallas Morning News article, investors stepped in and "bought stocks all day." The great "bargain hunt" depicted here is an ideal response to the first stop in a long trip to much lower stock prices. An English subscriber reports that the Gartmore funds, managers of the only bear funds available in England, announced their closure at the end of January. When asked why the funds were closing, a Gartmore representative said it was not poor performance "but the nearly total lack of interest in them from investors." At the end of the bear market, bear funds will be all the rage.

Bargain hunt amid the turmoil
—*Toronto Star*, January 22, 2008

Dallas Business Leaders Snatch Up Stock Bargains

"I'm a big buyer. I've bought stocks every day of last week, and I bought all day today," said Harold Simmons, Dallas' richest man.
—*The Dallas Morning News*, January 23, 2008

Market Drop, Fed Cut, Create Opportunities For Cherry Pickers
—*The Wall Street Journal*, January 23, 2008

Five Good Reasons Stocks Are Attractive Despite Downdraft
—*The Wall Street Journal*, January 23, 2008

Best move may be to just hang in there.
—*USA Today*, January 24, 2008

Investors swoop in to buy bargains
—*USA Today*, January 24, 2008

Bargain-Hunting Investors Are Just Getting Started
—*The Washington Post*, January 27, 2008

Bargains await long-term investors who can shake off their seasickness. Ten tempting stocks at rock-bottom prices.
—*Barron's* Cover story, January 28, 2008

March 2008

As EWFF explained in May 2000 when the initial wave of accounting scandals hit, a first order of business for the bear market is to snap people out of the dream state that persisted through the last upward thrusts of the Grand Supercycle bull. The bars on the chart show that the number of financial bubble articles boomed as the bear market began in 2000. When the mania re-ignited, the bubble talk receded briefly, only to re-emerge last year as the housing crash started to bite and the credit market imploded. The secondary bubble of 2003-2007 should be over, because bubble references are once again rising fast. Projecting forward January's total, the number of 2008 articles should spring higher and challenge the peak year of 2002. In the years ahead, the spiking interest will probably become a whole new field of bubblenomics.

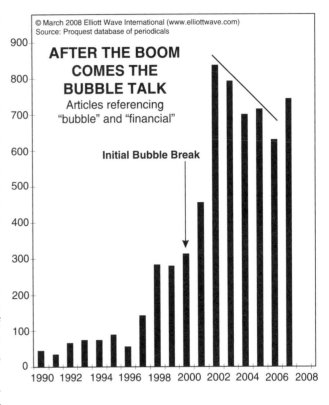

© March 2008 Elliott Wave International (www.elliottwave.com)
Source: Proquest database of periodicals

AFTER THE BOOM COMES THE BUBBLE TALK
Articles referencing "bubble" and "financial"

Initial Bubble Break

April 2008

The record string of bullish plurality in the Investors Intelligence advisory surveys finally ended on March 11 when 33% of advisors were bullish and 43% bearish. If a countertrend rally is, in fact, underway, this reading may provide a short-term tailwind. But five and a half years of net positive readings (shown on the chart, next page) strongly imply an opposite reaction that should ultimately hold bullish advisors below bearish ones for weeks or months on end. As the downtrend intensifies, the consensus will be pinned to the floor, just as it was pinned to the ceiling from 2002 to 2008.

The Word on the Street Is Bearish

One of the strange things that happens at the end of a mania is that many people actually seem to clue in to the fact that there may be costs associated with a lunatic era of price appreciation. This is a phenomenon that EWFF identified as the "uh-oh effect" in March 2000 when the NASDAQ was just seven days from completing the great technology boom. Here's a more recent manifestation:

Think Bubble Trouble Is Over?
Keep an Eye on Commodities

The commodity bubble could be the next to burst. Oil prices had one of their sharpest falls ever last week, and other markets seem to be teetering. Bulls argue that demand from rapidly developing countries like China and India justifies the high prices. But in reality, commodities have become the last refuge for speculators as other bubbles have popped.

—The Wall Street Journal,
March 25, 2008

The Journal even correctly notes that the commodity markets are the last in a long line of bubbles. This is important, because a bubble in any corner of the financial markets has helped cushion declines across the board. The bursting of the last bubble means that the complete retracement of manic upward movements can now commence across the breadth of the financial markets.

As the opening passage from *Elliott Wave Principle* in the Chapter 1 entry for April 2008 explains, when the fifth of the fifth wave is over, reality will assert itself. The Journal's use of the word *bubble* is another hint that a bear market experience is underway. As our chart in last month's issue, "After the Boom Comes the Bubble Talk" shows, bubbles always get far more publicity after they are over. According to the Proquest database of newspapers and journals, 214 articles used the word "bubble" and "financial" over the last three months. That projects out to an annual total of 856, which will surpass the high in the last post-bubble, bear-market year of 2002. "Bubbles are a topic of great importance," says a recent issue of the The Review of Financial Studies. The article "sets out a taxonomy of approaches used to explain the nature of bubbles." Every day brings more insight. Here's Wednesday's item from the WSJ, "Wanted: A New Policy For Bubbles." The article says, "Here's one area that needs closer attention: managing bubbles." Let the bubbleology boom begin.

In March 2000, EWFF also observed that while there was a noticeable surge in warnings about overstated equity prices, even the most skittish investors were not acting on them. One reason is that even as the media take note of obvious imbalances or bearish parallels, it also dismisses the danger. This "not to worry" aspect is very clear in number of recent articles that compare the current scene to the Great Depression. Here's one example from the March 20 Los Angeles Times that expresses the sentiment with the most famous last words ever spoken on Wall Street:

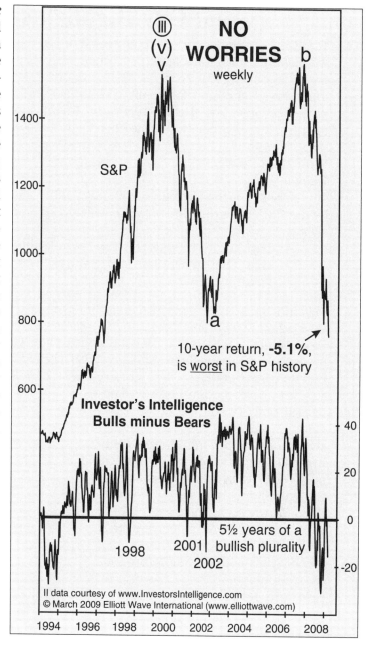

A New Great Depression?
It's Different This Time

"The global boom is ongoing, unemployment is low and the government has new tools to address the downturn," concludes the article. But a USA Today/Gallup poll reveals that the "uh-oh" effect has reached the man on the street. Half of respondents fear that "the downturn could become a depression." But a major NY Times piece responds, "The odds of a full-blown depression are almost nonexistent." The article concludes, "We are unlikely to see the bread lines, shantytowns and dust bowl of the Great Depression." The BBC finds, however, that one of these depression era icons is already back:

Tent City Highlights U.S. Home Crisis

Tent City, which lies about 40 miles east of Los Angeles in Ontario, California, is still relatively small with just 300 people. But it fits perfectly with EWI's portrayal of the oncoming depression, and it is growing fast, from less than two dozen last summer. As more people lose their homes and run out of money for hotels, a volunteer says, "more former homeowners could end up in place like Tent City." He is surely right. Foreclosure "ghost towns" are springing up across the country; their former occupants have to go somewhere.

May 2008

Volatility

Here's how the December 2006 EWFF characterized historically low volatility as measured by the CBOE Volatility Index (VIX), which uses premiums on options to measure expected price swings:

> High volatility tends to follow low volatility, and volatility is always greater on the downside. The "impending 'heart attack'" should generate some of the most pronounced volatility in history.

The anticipated rise has occurred, as shown on the chart. Some claim that the heightened volatility is a sign of a bottom: "Volatility Means Stocks Are Near A Low" (Barron's, March 31). But the Wave Principle tells us that the roller coaster ride will get a lot wilder as stocks fall further. By one measure, the number of trading days with a price range of 1% or more (52% of the sessions in the first quarter of 2008), the U.S. stock market is as volatile as it's been in 70 years. According to the VIX, however, volatility is still well below the highs of 2001 and 2002. Data from Jim Stack at InvesTech Research shows that average intraday volatility in the Dow Industrials passed the level of the 1987 crash, but it is still shy of the volatility generated by the 2000 downturn in stocks and the 1929-1932 bear market. Since the current bear market is of larger degree than that of 1929-32, the market should produce record-high volatility by any and all measures before wave **c** is over.

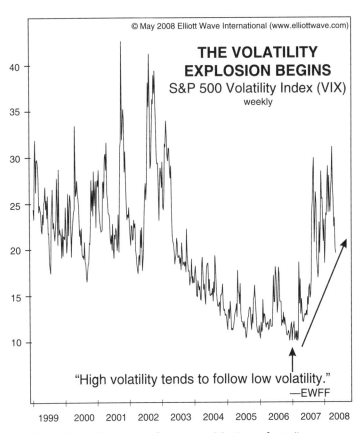

© May 2008 Elliott Wave International (www.elliottwave.com)

THE VOLATILITY EXPLOSION BEGINS
S&P 500 Volatility Index (VIX)
weekly

"High volatility tends to follow low volatility."
—EWFF

Seasonality

Bear markets can bring a whole new trading tone, and the uptick in volatility is not the only sign that things are different now. This is what EWT was banking on in December when it made the following observation about "Backwards Seasonals": "It has been fascinating recently to watch the stock market turn in the opposite way from normal seasonal patterns." EWT listed a series of instances in which the market moved in the opposite direction of seasonal norms. Noting that "everyone knows" that the market is always up in years ending in 8 and election years, EWT called for a

2008 decline. So far, so good, as the main stock indexes are down from approximately 4% to 10%. EWT's observation about a reversal in the seasonals is certainly holding true according to Mark Hulbert. He reports that one seasonality-based timing system, which gets in and out of stocks according to the calendar, lost 15.5% in the first quarter of 2007, the third worst performance of 186 monitored strategies.

There's still plenty of time to position against seasonal optimism. The NY Post notes, "It's a well-reported fact that the stock market historically does well in the last seven months of a presidential election year like this one, up 13 of the last 14 times." Of course, a bearish decline into the election would be consistent with the historic pattern of May-November stock relative weakness, but the following headline from the Financial Post suggests that investors are anxious to bet against this bearish pattern:

Don't Sell in May and Don't Go Away
Those who sit in cash this summer likely to miss out

As EWT said in December, it's about time for the majority to get fooled on seasonals. So far, it's happening. Given the seasonals' freakishly long hot streak, it may keep happening for some time to come.

Investor Psychology

In a bear market, the purpose of upward corrections is to alleviate extreme negative sentiment, and that is exactly what the rally from March is doing. The percentage of bulls in the Investors Intelligence survey of advisory sentiment returned to a positive plurality on April 18 (39.1% bulls to 35.6% bears). The most recent American Association of Individual Investors survey recorded 46.7% bulls to 27.5% bears. This is not an overwhelming bullish consensus, but as the bear market progresses even moderate pluralities should lead to extended declines.

Returning to the bullish camp requires "shrugging off" treacherous economic conditions. Many investors are having no trouble doing just that. A Money magazine article notes that "the economy is in trouble," "banks and other financial companies are posting huge losses," the Fed engineered "a rescue of Bear Stearns," and "home prices are sinking." Still, it offers "A Strong Case for Market Optimism." After laying off more than 24,000 employees and writing down $54.2 billion in assets, the heads of Goldman Sachs, Citigroup, Lehman Brothers and Morgan Stanley say that "the credit-market contraction is winding down." "The worst is behind us," says Lehman CEO Richard Fuld. "Signs of fading headline risk abound," says USA Today. "The last time an opportunity of this nature existed to buy bank stocks this cheap was in 1990," says a bank analyst. "The next time will be in 20 years. This is a once-in-a-generation opportunity." Actually, the willingness to pounce on the March lows says that this is a bad time to buy stocks. With so many "worst since the Great Depression" economic mishaps at hand, it's a really bad time. The "worst-is-over" bullish sentiment that restores the bullish resolve of a long rise is the most dangerous kind of bullishness there is. It's a perfect example of wave two optimism that comes right before the bottom drops out. For some it will be the last pleasant thing that happened before a rout sets in that will be remembered for generations to come.

July 2008

Watching financial TV, where the stock market recovery begins every hour on the hour, it is not hard to find economists, analysts and fund managers who are eagerly snatching up perceived bargains. The proof is in the percentage of cash in mutual funds, which is still below 4%. Many of the buyers are value investors like Bill Miller of Legg Mason and Kirk Kerkorian, both of whom built careers on buying low and selling high. Kerkorian's big target is Ford Motor Company. At just over $5 a share, the conventional wisdom is that the struggling auto maker can hardly go lower. But we've seen this shared "belief in rock bottom" before. In fact, it was only a few weeks ago that everyone was up in arms over JP Morgan's $2 a share offer for Bear Stearns. The supposed low-ball offer so incensed the Street that the offer was quintupled to $10. "Well, it now appears possible that Morgan may have grossly underestimated how terrible the Bear bond portfolio may be." Sam Zell, another legendary investment vulture, finds himself in a similar trap thanks to his early 2008 purchase of the Tribune Co. With ad sales plunging faster than any point in the last 37 years, S&P now says the company may be in default on billions of dollars worth of debt by the end of the year. Bank and brokerage stocks reputedly find their bottom—on a daily basis. As wave **c** intensifies and carries assets from low to unimaginably low levels, many will rue the "instincts" that served so many value buyers well through the bull market.

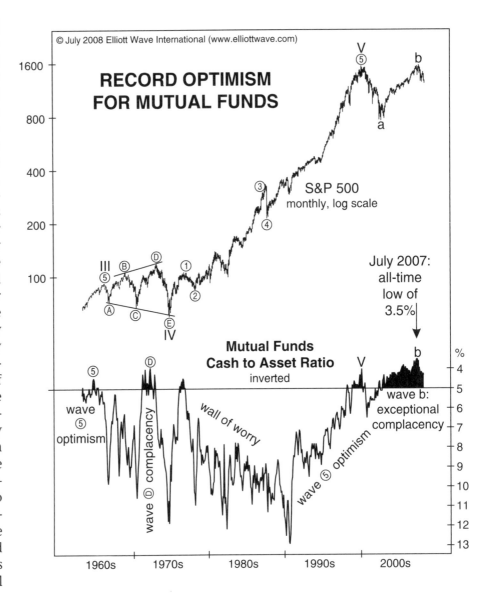

In April, EWFF noted that "bubbles are generally only spotted and discussed openly when they are ending." Since this is also the end of a long succession of bubbles, EWFF added, "Let the boom in bubbleology begin." This is certainly happening because The Wall Street Journal used that very word, "Bubbleology," in a page one story stating, "The study of financial bubbles is hot." Here's another headline that captures both this rare moment of clarity and the insanity at the end of a rise:

Don't Fear the Bubble
—Business Week, June 11, 2008

"Heap praise" on market bubbles, says the story. This is a prime example of the "nice bubble" phenomenon that EWFF first identified with respect to housing in January 2005, when several articles classified the run up in housing prices as the "early to middle stages" of a bubble. But in truth, there is no such thing as a nice bubble because bubbles eventually take down everyone involved. The size and volume of the bubble talk confirms that the Great Mania itself is approaching its final moments.

August 2008

Bullish stock market investors may be bruised and battered, but there is no evidence that they are throwing in the towel. This headline from MarketWatch.com captures the prevailing mood:

Investors Hanging in There

Under the same headline, a CNN.com story says, "Investors aren't happy with the current bear market, but they are not panicking; they are sticking with their investment strategies." A financial planner says, "It's very strange; people really haven't been all that concerned." "Focus on the horizon, not the waves," says another. Thankfully, R.N. Elliott did not take this advice.

One of the most important nuances added in EWP to Elliott's discoveries is the revelation that C waves are times in the middle of a major stock market move when the news should be taken at face value. As the July issue of *The Elliot Wave Theorist* observes, this is consistent with the current scene, as the fundamentals are starting to fall apart.

Ironically, many investors choose such moments to take a contrary stance. This quote from the CNN.com article offers a classic illustration: "The market has really held up fairly well with the news, the confluence of different things and the degree of it. I really think that more of the bad is behind us than in front of us." No matter how bad things get, investors have been unshaken in their belief that they are about to get better. "Most of the downside U.S. growth risk has been discounted," says a global strategist. Four months ago, a financial weekly answered the question, "Have the Bank Stocks Finally Hit Bottom?" with a largely positive review. On July 21, the KBW Bank Index was down by *another third* when the publication issued another "Buy Banks" cover story. The article concludes, "However bad the conditions for financials may be, they strike us as unlikely to get worse." Every rally feeds the shared belief that "the worst is over," confirming this critical long-term point from the July Theorist: not only is the decline not over, but it's still only just beginning.

Breaking Down The Bubble

One glaring sign that a big bear market is still just starting is the boom in bubble references, which we discussed in the March, April and July issues. As noted earlier, bubble talk blossoms in that moment of clarity that comes at the end of every manic rise, when people recognize the irrational enthusiasm for higher and higher prices and openly talk about it. The updated bar chart shows the volume of articles referencing "bubble" and "financial" and the current year's projected break of the record references set in 2002, the last year of the wave **a** downtrend. The July *Theorist* notes that C waves are what happens when "people can no longer fool themselves that it's an old bull market or that the market is going to go back to new highs." They also no longer believe that the previous rise to fundamentally irrational levels was anything other than a classic bubble; thus the recent spate of stories offering "bubble lessons." One article, "Inexperience May Feed Bubbles," discusses a new academic study that shows inexperienced managers do, in fact, contribute disproportionately to manias and suffer the biggest losses when they end. So, at least at some level, the swing back to an appreciation for knowledge of history and value is starting.

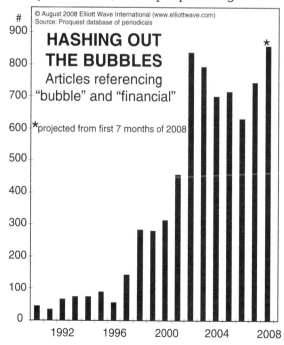

© August 2008 Elliott Wave International (www.elliottwave.com)
Source: Proquest database of periodicals

HASHING OUT THE BUBBLES
Articles referencing "bubble" and "financial"

*projected from first 7 months of 2008

October 2008

According to an MSMoney survey, 74% of respondents said they plan to "do nothing" in response to the news of the current financial turmoil, and a Fibonacci 62% said they will continue contributing to retirement accounts. This is true even though 44% said they expect their personal finances to be worse off a year from now. The survey's respondents are generally following the advice of "experts" who almost to a person say selling now is the worst possible move even as they "caution that this crisis is more serious than earlier drops."

The "Slope of Hope" is the expression that Bob Prechter coined several years ago to describe the sentiment that investors cling to as stocks move through a bear market. An AP story recently noted that the current financial atmosphere is "one of uncertainty, not despair. People haven't given up hope that opportunities to make money are still out there, somewhere." And as far as we can tell, the succession of bailout attempts is not needed to grease the market's skid, but the government's moves appear to be doing just that. USA Today reports that "investors rushed giddily back into stocks," as the latest government "rescue plan is being credited with transforming the mood on Wall Street from fear to hope." A brokerage firm "Strategy Report" offers the usual invest-for-the-long-term response to turmoil saying, "Market declines are a normal part of the investing process." (Our point exactly. But how does that translate to "hold your stocks"?) It continues, "Veteran investors who have been through tumult before know that their first knee-jerk reaction to sell everything is not correct." The prevailing attitude is that the market is down so far that it has to go up. From our perspective, the market always heads in the opposite direction of where it "has" to go.

Even as they note that the financial events of recent days are completely without precedent, the media assures readers that this is just another one of those financial tumbles that happen all the time. "Wall Street's Old Hands Not Rattled by Financial Crisis," says an Associated Press headline. "Naked Shorting Rule Means Time To Buy Stocks," says another headline. An "ace" fund manager, who normally lets his funds' quarterly filing "do the talking about what he's buying," revealed that he's loading up on financial stocks. On one particular day, stocks rallied "in response to an array of government actions," according to media accounts. The rally petered out, however, and the market ended up lower still. Don't tell anyone, but the knee-jerk bailout buying has been going on for more than a year now. We are starting to wonder if anyone will ever notice that it has yet to pay off.

A seller of bull statuettes at 40 Wall Street says he is "confident things would turn around soon enough. When the market is down two days out of three, people aren't out spending. They're paranoid. But they'll be back. Wall Street is all about optimism." Apparently, that's true no matter how bad the financial contraction. But history conclusively shows that pessimism plays a role, too. In time, it will appear and even grow to an extreme. Until that extreme is reached, share prices will keep falling.

Have Investors Panicked and Capitulated?

The dominance of hope over fear indicates that investors have not capitulated. Capitulation is in evidence when investors finally abandon their hopes based on presumably bullish external factors. During September and October to date, investors have expressed immense faith in purportedly bullish news events. The chart on the previous page displays market actions to confirm this point. From September 1 through today, no fewer than half of the trading days found investors so excited about buying stocks that they drove closing or overnight futures premiums to record or near-record levels and/or concentrated their buying so intensely as to create large opening upside gaps in the futures market. You need not take my word regarding investors' temporarily euphoric reaction to each news event; just flip through the news reports. This morning (October 21, 2008) AP reports, "Wall Street surged on a burst of optimism Monday, [on] comments from Federal Reserve Chairman Ben Bernanke." The Washington Post agrees: "The stock market soared in response to Bernanke's remarks...." Socionomic theory accommodates brief market reactions to emotional stimuli, but we also know that otherwise the market's trends are entirely in the grip

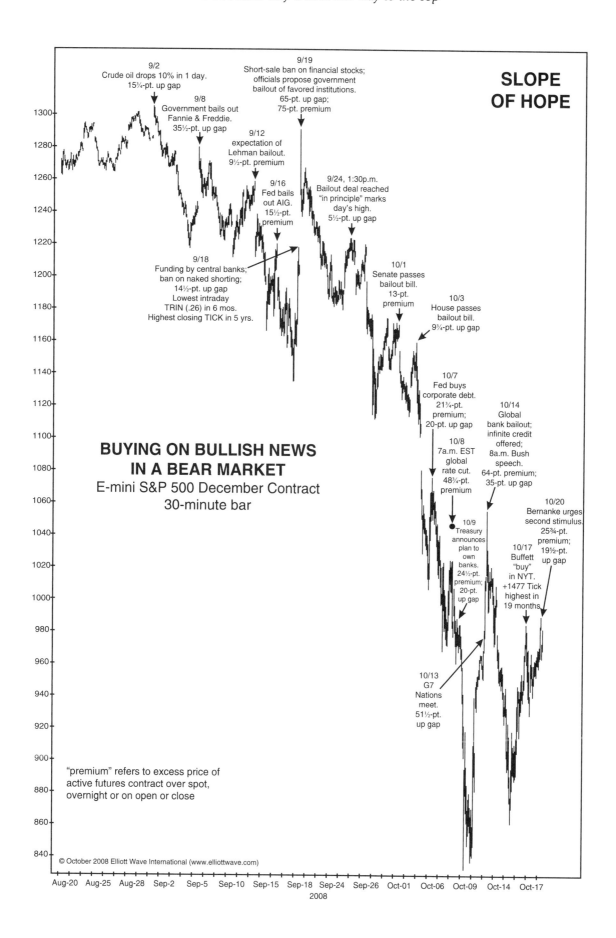

SLOPE OF HOPE

9/2
Crude oil drops 10% in 1 day.
15¾-pt. up gap

9/8
Government bails out
Fannie & Freddie.
35½-pt. up gap

9/12
expectation of
Lehman bailout.
9½-pt. premium

9/19
Short-sale ban on financial stocks;
officials propose government
bailout of favored institutions.
65-pt. up gap;
75-pt. premium

9/16
Fed bails
out AIG.
15½-pt.
premium

9/24, 1:30p.m.
Bailout deal reached
"in principle" marks
day's high.
5½-pt. up gap

9/18
Funding by central banks;
ban on naked shorting;
14½-pt. up gap
Lowest intraday
TRIN (.26) in 6 mos.
Highest closing TICK in 5 yrs.

10/1
Senate passes
bailout bill.
13-pt.
premium

10/3
House passes
bailout bill.
9¾-pt. up gap

10/7
Fed buys
corporate debt.
21¾-pt.
premium;
20-pt. up gap

10/8
7a.m. EST
global
rate cut.
48¾-pt.
premium

10/14
Global
bank bailout;
infinite credit
offered;
8a.m. Bush
speech.
64-pt. premium;
35-pt. up gap

10/9
Treasury
announces
plan to
own
banks.
24½-pt.
premium;
20-pt.
up gap

10/20
Bernanke urges
second stimulus.
25¾-pt.
premium;
19½-pt.
up gap

10/17
Buffett
"buy"
in NYT.
+1477 Tick
highest in
19 months

**BUYING ON BULLISH NEWS
IN A BEAR MARKET**
E-mini S&P 500 December Contract
30-minute bar

10/13
G7
Nations
meet.
51½-pt.
up gap

"premium" refers to excess price of
active futures contract over spot,
overnight or on open or close

© October 2008 Elliott Wave International (www.elliottwave.com)

351

of social mood, which cares naught for news. That is why we analyze waves of social mood, not news, except as it gives us hints about market psychology. Since every one of these days of excited rally had an excuse for buying based on news, it is clear that investors have yet to abandon their bullish bias or to give up hope that external factors will revive the bull market.

The main reasons that market observers are giving to support the case for a bottom are that momentum indicators are oversold and short term sentiment measures show that most traders are bearish. We know about these readings and show them on *The Short Term Update*. These indicators are tried and true, to be sure, but one must interpret them in context. Recall how often these same indicators registered an overbought condition or traders' optimism from 1995 to 2007. If we are correct that Elliott waves identify that period as the end of the largest-degree advance in nearly 300 years, setting up the largest-degree bear market since the 1700s, then current short term sentiment and momentum readings do not count for much. While they could support a near-term rally, the bear market is likely to bulldoze right over them eventually.

More Support for the Case that the Bear Market Is of Very Large Degree

A week ago, governments from around the world met and promised banks infinite liquidity. Sounds like a plan! So the market had its biggest two-day rally of the entire bear market to date. We decided to investigate the import of large daily moves in the market.

The following two charts mark most of the points over the past century at which the Dow had its 18 biggest up days and 18 biggest down days. Such days do not occur at specific times in market trends so reliably that one can use them to identify a near-term wave count or a turning point. But these charts are informative nevertheless, because they show that by far the largest up and down days occurred during a four-year period encompassing the Supercycle-degree decline from September 1929 to July 1932 and its immediate aftermath. In other words, as might be expected, bear markets of that degree tend to usher in more volatility than bear markets of lesser degree.

The market's penchant for such days seems to have resumed again. One such day occurred on September 17, 2001, in wave **a**, and here in 2008, there have been three such days in the past three weeks. So the probability is great that (1) our long term Elliott wave interpretation that a bear market of very large degree is in force is correct, and (2) there will be many more volatile days ahead. It is of some interest also that the period from June 1931 to June 1932, as the market fell relentlessly, contains fully half of all the past hundred years' record *up* days and only one of its record down days.

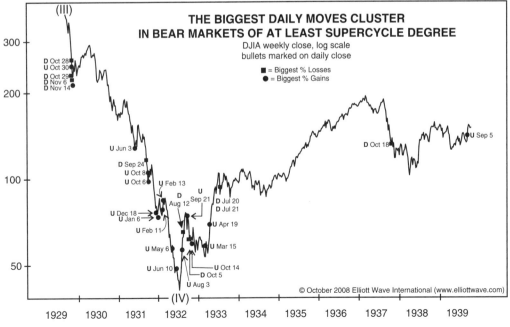

352

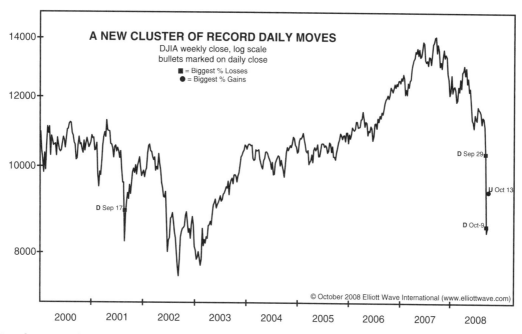

For the record, 1917 sported one dramatic day in the middle of a panic, and the 1987 crash had a stunning four such days at its end, including the biggest down day ever, on October 19 that year. These events show that big daily movements can occur occasionally within corrections of degree as low as Primary. The 1987 example is perhaps one of the reasons why people think that recent volatility indicates panic and that the bear market is over. There are no quantitative absolutes to rely upon in market analysis, but clearly such extreme daily volatility at Primary degree is the exception, not the rule, so it would not be prudent to place recent action in the same category as the 1987 crash, on the basis of either volume or volatility.

The chart at right shows a study we found at ChartOfTheDay.com. It plots the percentage losses over the first twelve months of 15 bear markets. Observe the confluence of the three biggest opening declines and the time-honored Elliott wave interpretations of those bear markets and their respective degrees. 1937 kicked off a bear market of Primary degree; 1929 kicked off a bear market of Supercycle degree; and 2007 (if we are correct) has kicked off wave **c** of (a) of a bear market of Grand Supercycle degree. The increasingly large initial declines of these bear markets are right in line with our Elliott wave labels and lend more support to our case that a bear market of Grand Supercycle degree is underway.

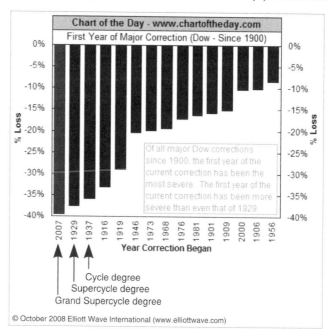

The Public Gets Locked In

Many cite low levels of bullishness and investors' nervousness as reasons that the market should rally. According to the American Association of Individual Investors, more than 55% of investors were bearish on October 2, a historically high number. Over the next seven sessions, the Dow fell another 27% to new lows. How can the market be going down as "Investors' Fear Rages Higher?" A reversal from a mania explains it. Just as the market moved higher in the face of

353

unprecedented levels of bullishness, the market now drops despite a "menagerie" of negative investor emotions including "anxiety," "despair" and "despondency."

Keep in mind, however, that one of the reasons a contrary approach works is that buying at the point of maximum pessimism usually means investors are out of stock to sell. This time, despite all their fears, most investors have yet to sell their first share. An army of media pundits and advisors continually instructs them to hold, or better yet buy, because stocks must be near a low. On October 8, a fifth straight day of falling prices, the tag lines on CNBC alternated between "Is the bottom in?" "Stocks Plunge to 5-year lows" and "Is this a buying opportunity?"

The more anxious and unsure investors get, the more vociferously advisors warn them against retreating to the sidelines. Even the most dire news about the credit squeeze, the latest economic conniption or a new muni-bond default is invariably followed by admonitions not to sell. The effort to keep the public on board is illustrated by this article from the Atlanta Journal-Constitution:

Sell? No. Buy? Maybe. Nervous? Yes

Q: Is this a good time to buy?

A: "Don't react—act. There's a fire sale on right now," says a senior partner [in an investment firm].

Q: Is it OK to be nervous?

A: "Screw up your courage," said a long time advisor. "My emotional side of my brain told me it was very fearful. My logical side of my brain told me it was a good time to invest."

According to the Washington Post, a whole new "niche industry of psychologists and behavioral economists" instructs advisors on handling their clients' emotions." Investors are "fluctuating between fearful, freaked, impulsive, obsessive-compulsive, outraged, disgusted, despondent, contemptuous, and sometimes all of the above," but there are ways to alleviate stress. The techniques offered by professionals in the Post article reveal that the whole idea is to keep investors from doing the one thing that really will alleviate their stress, not to mention save their bacon — sell stocks. Here's what they advise:

- Listen empathetically, to understand the clients' irrational behavior and build a bridge to wise action.

- When a client calls and says, "I want out," reply, "You've lost 10 percent since you started investing. You feel like now is the time to fold." Show an understanding of the issue by repeating it back. Then fire up the empathy. "We didn't expect this to happen, but it's happening. It's really hard to have your dreams look further."

- Put the market drop in perspective, maybe mentioning that it is starting to feel like the bottom.

- Show a chart on how stocks did in the 10 years after a collapse [when bull markets were in force].

- Make the client see the opportunities that emerge at the bottom of markets and to not miss them.

- Move from the primitive survival mode to the adult, rational-thinking mode [in which selling stocks is always stupid].

- Relaxation and visualization techniques can be helpful. Sit back and visualize lifestyle or retirement goals: the house in the leafy suburbs, the boat, the private schools.

- Say, 'Let's sell a little bit of one position and let's put it somewhere else.' That's an opportunity."

The essential buy and hold credo of the mania surely lives because the Post ends with the following tip: "Get them to think about the purpose of saving money, for their dreams and their vision of the future. You don't achieve that dream by selling out at the bottom." The columnist then reveals the vast depth of belief that lingers by stating, "If all else fails, we can at least keep dreaming." So there's still no recognition that the dream and the shared passion for it might be the problem or that clinging tighter ensures that a very real nightmare will get more intense.

November 2008

In March 2007, *The Elliott Wave Theorist* described the "personality" of wave **c** by noting that it should be a "devastating" decline of high degree. It offered the following quote from *Elliott Wave Principle*: "It is during these declines that there is virtually no place to hide except cash." This must be a C wave of high degree, as EWP's description is now echoing up and down Wall Street.

Textbook Wave C

"There really is no place to hide in these markets."
—*Reuters*, October 5

"There's been no place to hide.""There's nowhere to hide."
—*Bloomberg*, October 8   —*Motley Fool*, October 9

"There has been almost nowhere to hide in recent weeks."
—*The Wall Street Journal*, October 12

"Once that bubble popped there was nowhere to hide."
—*MarketWatch*, October 21

"Fund managers found there was no place to hide."
—*The Wall Street Journal*, October 24

Chapter 5

Herding Euphoria: Instruments of the Uptrend

IPOs, the media, mutual funds, pensions, government and other agencies create "an almost supernatural aura of prestige and power." The public goes to the front "of the line with the institutions" and gets trapped as soon as it is let in the door. Hedge funds up the ante after the 2000 peak.

February 1995

Stock market mutual funds lost an average of 1.7% in 1994 (dividends included), yet the public poured $124 billion into them, nearly matching 1993's record of $130b. So on a long-term basis, the public remains historically optimistic on the direction of share prices.

April 1995

Some subscribers have asked whether "contrarian" stock market mutual funds will be profitable in a bear market. The answer is no. The only thing most contrarians are contrary about is what stocks to own, not whether to own them at all. On the other hand, funds that are short should do well.

May 1995

Consumer Reports magazine generally rates products such as cars, sunscreen lotion and microwave ovens. The May issue rates mutual funds.

The number of mutual funds of all types (stock, bond, money market; open and closed) has been soaring, and has now climbed all the way to 8135, well more than twice the 3420 individual stocks traded on the New York and American stock exchanges combined. Because assets of stock funds have risen 60 times, those in finance have figured out that forming a mutual fund means instant wealth. This trend is reminiscent of the mad rush to own a real estate license in the mid-1980s, and will end the same way.

Corporate pension funds now have 57% of their assets in the stock market. Presuming they hold some pittance in cash or real estate, their stock percentage is up to double the bond percentage. So corporate pension funds have swallowed hook, line and sinker the idea that stocks are like some sort of long-term savings account with high interest.

July 1995

A Democratic and a Republican senator have jointly introduced a bill to allow Social Security to put 25% of its "trust fund" into the stock market. The goal is to "save Social Security." Government is the embodiment of the crowd. If Congress allows the move, the Social Security program will die faster than otherwise.

The dollars in stock mutual funds reached $1 trillion in May, doubling since February 1993! (To put that amount in perspective, the total value of mutual funds at the top of the public stock mania of 1968 was $50 billion, one-twentieth as much.)

August 1995

Newspapers, which are generally content to report other people's opinions on the market, have lately taken to forecasting. The Wall Street Journal sported this headline on July 21: "Rocky Stock Market Should Smooth Out In the Longer Term; The Gains Won't Be as Big, Neither Will Declines." The first sentence of the article is "Relax." USA Today on July 17 offered this advice: "The stock market is high now, so what should investors do? It certainly isn't time to dump everything. If you're investing for a long-term goal, hang on and enjoy the ride." Novice investors, as noted above, claim to have their feet dug in. "Poll: Market Investors In For Long Haul," says one headline. "Little Guys Hang Tough," says another.

The Wall Street Journal, July 1995

September 1995

The general public is displaying an insatiable appetite for information about mutual funds. Several million people now subscribe to a new breed of monthly financial magazines that continually recycle cover stories and ratings on the hottest funds. For those that cannot wait a full month, the WSJ will soon join the fray with a weekly mutual fund tabloid. Charles Biderman of Mutual Fund Trim Tabs noted that the first half of the 1990s has witnessed the biggest media push into the financial realm since Business Week and Fortune were launched in late 1929 and early 1930.

October 1995

Reflections of the extent of the equity mania are available on the business bookshelf of your local bookstore. Each month brings new books on buying stocks. The latest are *The Hometown Investor*, *The On-Line Investor*, and one book just for Fidelity Fund investors. There's even *The Complete Idiot's Guide To Making Money on Wall Street*, a timely book, to be sure.

December 1995

USA Today's Daniel Kadlec mentioned that on the same day he received one copy of *At the Crest of the Tidal Wave*, he got his fifth review copy of *The Warren Buffett Way*. We would add that *At the Crest* is the only bearish book in print, while *Buffett* is one of about thirty bullish books to have hit the shelves recently, another telling ratio.

Grant's Interest Rate Observer reports that New York State in July 1994 adopted a new "prudent investor" doctrine by a vote of 202 to 1 (a good reflection of the bulls-to-bears ratio among the public). The new law pertains to trustees of other people's assets. Gone is the standard in force for 165 years that stressed safety. The new, modern standard emphasizes the desirability of total return, which translated means that anything goes — IPOs, futures, options, foreign stocks, anything — as long as you are trying to make a profit. The implication of the new rules is that those trustees who simply want to *preserve* capital *are no longer considered prudent*.

February 1996
Parallel With the Peak Social Mood of 1968

Mutual funds are now a cultural phenomenon. These days, it's not just financial magazines that are splashing fund rankings all over their covers to jack up newsstand sales. General interest magazines do it, too. The January 29 cover of U.S. News features the "Best Mutual Funds." The last time funds attained the status of a cultural mania was 1968. In that peak year, the inflation-adjusted (to 1995 dollars) average investment in stocks was $45, 1/22nd of the value of the average portfolio, worth $1000. In 1995, the average investment was $447, 1/9th of the value of the average portfolio, worth $4,074. "It looks like this mania is a lot bigger," notes The New York Times.

March 1996

At the Crest cited the proposed plan for the government to invest Social Security "contributions" in the stock market as a sign that optimism had captured all quarters. The Advisory Council on Social Security has split into three separate groups on the question of how to restructure the Social Security System, but all three camps "have one common feature: they recommend equity investment to improve returns," in fact, as high as 40% of assets. "Such discussions would have been unthinkable just a few years ago," notes The New York Times. Instead of pondering the effect of a possible stock market decline on the Social Security trust fund, headlines speculated only on the bullish implications, on how many billions Social Security "Could Shower on Mutual Funds."

It is not as if mutual funds need the money. The public threw a record $29 billion at stock mutual funds in January, more than twice the money that went in during all of 1990. February's inflows are running just shy of that rate.

A national non-financial columnist on February 15 promises, unequivocally, the moon: "People are asking, 'Is it too late now to get rich in the stock market?' Answer: Never. If you're in the market, stay. If you're not, get in now." A public television commentator adds that long-term bears should be "sued for consumer fraud." TV anchor on February 28: "These liquidity flows could go on forever, or at least as long as baby boomers are saving for their retirement." Guest: "Obviously that's true, but you also have to ask, where else can you put your money? There is no other place."

CNN advises viewers with $20,000 to leverage their stock investments by going long S&P futures contracts in perpetuity. CNBC runs a program on February 9 entitled, "Will the Stock Market Go Up Forever?" Well, snorts a columnist, stocks will go down occasionally, but "it's a prospect regarded more as a petty nuisance than a cause for alarm." In his own good time, the clever bear, who has overstayed his hibernation to lull his amassing quarry into complacency and sloth, will spring forth and reveal this utter hubris for what it is.

April 1996

At the federal level, when the Social Security advisory council went before Congress, the plan was met "without criticism from any member of Congress or any of the experts on pension policy." Pension & Investments magazine says that pension "plan sponsors have learned that cash is bad. There is a growing pressure to remain fully invested." The states of Indiana and South Carolina are trying to amend their constitutions to end 100-year-old bans on buying equities. Several cities such as Milwaukee have passed laws raising the percentage of funds available to equity investment.

Even lay financial writers are on the bandwagon. When the market fell sharply on March 8, columnists leaped to advise their readers. "A full blown market crash would be mighty rewarding," noted one business daily. Another called the 3% decline the crash he had been waiting for and instructed readers to "buy or hold, but do not sell" because "the stock market always comes back." "The greater risk" said another, "is not being caught in a falling market, but being out of stocks when the market starts to soar."

Here's a cultural trend: Readers of Playboy magazine can now say, "I don't subscribe for the pictures, I get it for the mutual fund coverage." The funny thing is, a lot of them would probably be telling the truth.

May 1996

Forbes magazine has invited subscribers to enroll in the Forbes Stock Market Course. The offer notes: "It's easy to make money in the stock market!"

Themed mutual funds are back as well. According to one industry expert, themed funds come to market when "attention (shifts) away from fundamentals to dreams of the future." The highly specialized funds are targeting small market segments like landfill stocks or heart transplant stocks. American Diversity Growth Trust will invest in firms owned or controlled by African Americans. The fund will attempt to overcome African Americans' traditional disinterest in stocks and bonds. It will be distributed through churches and other social organizations.

Among the most compelling and dangerous means by which investors are joining in at the top is an IPO fever that will rank among the greatest, if not the greatest, of all time. In addition to

April 1996

$3 billion raised by Lucent Technologies in the biggest initial public offering ever, the new issues boom includes Planet Hollywood, a leading purveyor of "eatertainment," a fashion designer, Donna Karan International, and Embassy Acquisition, a firm that admits in its prospectus that it has no definite plans for the $8.28 million it raised from the public. Despite this admission and the fact that insiders paid 6 cents for stock that cost the public $6, shares in Embassy rose in the aftermarket.

One financial writer says that "Trendy, gimmicky offerings are ubiquitous among current IPOs." While lame "idea stocks" have had their runs in the past, never before have investors paid so much for so little. The public owns just 18% of Planet Hollywood, compared to an 18.5% stake that went to movie stars for occasionally appearing at its 30 restaurants. The public's stake in Yahoo!, a "pioneer Internet directory service," is about 10%. If Yahoo!'s $1 billion market capitalization, total lack of profitability, and exclamation point aren't scary enough, consider this quote from the IPO Maven (New York City): "I had 80-year-olds calling me up and saying, "I want to buy Yahoo!!" The market has been plumbing the depths of unsophistication to find new investors. Has it finally attracted yahoos?

Forbes, January 1996

The red carpet continues to be rolled out to new investors in other ways as well. Spring Street Brewery, a micro-brewery that failed in bids to go public with investment through barroom solicitations and sports page advertising, has succeeded by offering a market in its shares over the Internet. Since Spring Street raised $1.6 million, 500 firms contacted its president for guidance on setting up on-line trading floors in their own shares.

June 1996

In recent weeks, more indications of manic behavior among institutions have appeared. The Supplemental Benefits Program of Alaska (the state opted out of the Social Security system in the 1970s) will raise the equity exposure of some participants to 90%. In Canada, a team of high-profile advisors has recommended that the Canada Pension Plan (their Social Security), which currently invests only in government bonds, should be allowed to "play the market to get a better return."

Boeing's Employee Retirement Plan has decided it no longer wants to give its pension holders the option of variable payouts based on the performance of the stock market. The stated reason is to standardize administration, but one pensioner says the real reason is that Boeing now wants to keep excess stock market returns for itself. The company is apparently so convinced of endless market profits that it has announced it will pay a 35% bonus on all accrued benefits in return for fixing the plan's payout! As an EWT reader, our inside source says he's more than happy that the company has paid him 35% for the privilege of guaranteeing his benefits through the coming bear market.

NESDAY, JULY 3, 1996   ARTERLY   MUTUAL FUNDS   THE WALL STREET JOURNAL   R   REVIEW

© 1996 Dow Jones & Company, Inc. All Rights Reserved.

MUTUAL-FUND STAMPEDE

August 1996

Virtually no one sees the downside potential of any current financial arrangement. As another example, because investors' stock holdings are tied up in IRAs and 401(k)s, the headlines say that "Stock Gyrations Won't Damage Economy," but that is precisely a recipe for economic contraction. When stock prices fall, IRAs will fall in value, people will feel less wealthy, and they will spend less money.

October 1996

For those "investors who would rather watch the Golf Channel," but who nevertheless must do the prudent thing and invest in stocks, the mutual fund industry has started to push funds of funds. So far this year, 11 new funds of funds have been introduced, a 23% increase in the total. Think about this: The rationale for creating these additional funds is that there are too many funds. "Investors don't have time to pick from the more than 7000 funds now available." Why the sudden increase? Regulatory restrictions put in place after abuses in the 1920s and 1970s are being eased. One must always examine the quality of a mania as well as its quantity to determine if an extreme has been reached. If we can speculate that a fund of funds of funds is an unlikely coming product, then we may conclude that the very idea of funds of funds logically signals an extremity in sentiment.

January 1997

As our Popular Culture Special Report of 1985 pointed out, one of the classic signs of a bull market top is that fears rampant at the preceding corresponding low are overcome. It is significant, then, that circuit breakers that were put in place right after the 1987 crash by the Chicago Mercantile Exchange and the New York Stock Exchange have suddenly been eased.

On the Supercycle scale comes a revision of rules that for decades has kept banks out of the securities, insurance and real estate businesses. The Treasury Department's issuance of new banking guidelines reverses restrictions that were put in place after the crash of 1929. Treasury Secretary Robert Rubin says the repeal of the Depression-era laws will reduce risk and make banks stronger...which are the same reasons given 62 years ago for enacting the laws.

March 1997

If we added a hundred pages to this publication, we still would not be able to express adequately the perilous extreme that sentiment achieved on the Dow's rise past 7000 in mid-February. The editors of the Post were so enthralled with the market's effect on the portfolios of bull market heroes Bill Gates, Warren Buffett and Nike CEO Phil Knight that they pushed word of Michael Jackson's baby to page 3.

May 1997

In late February-early March, the depth of commitment to stocks was recorded in a nationwide survey of 750 mutual fund investors. The survey showed that fund owners are counting on a 16.7% return in 1997 and an average 22.2% per year over the next 10 years, which means that they expect the market to continue accelerating its rate of gain, which has averaged 15.2% annually for the last five years and 11.2% for the last 60 years, about half the current expectation.

February 14, 1996

There has been a flood of cartoons featuring Wall Street themes in recent months. "Doonesbury," "Dilbert," "Frank and Earnest," "Thatch" and numerous editorial page cartoonists have been observing nuances and ironies of the investment world. Even those little wax paper comics that come with Bazooka bubble gum featured a stock market joke. On the surface, it might not be immediately clear that the market's arrival in the comics is a bearish development because many of these portraits focus on losses. But a survey of several cartoonists has led us to conclude that when the market makes it to the funny papers, the message is bearish regardless of the cartoonists' theme. Cartoonists say they never mentioned the stock market much before because not enough people would get the joke. Successful cartoonists make their living crystallizing the everyday experiences of life. The repeated use of in-

FRANK AND ERNEST By Bob Thaves

March 1997

April 1997

October 1997

THE NEW YORKER
March 31, 1997

vestment themes shows how deeply the market has reached into the mainstream of American life. As for the loss-oriented nature of many cartoons, Tom Toles of the Buffalo News suggests that cartoonists are contrarian by nature. Profits aren't funny, but losses are. It is worth noting that whatever their natures, all four of the cartoonists surveyed said they were in the market.

The U.S. Investment Mania

This mania has something very rare: official sanction. Two of the greatest manias of recorded history, the South Sea Bubble in England and the Mississippi Scheme in France, both of 1720, were initiated by government action. From an Elliott Wave standpoint, the current mania is ending a two-century advance, the same "Grand Supercycle" degree rise that ended with the South Sea Bubble, which is why I forecasted a mania in the first place. Perhaps manias require official sanction to create excesses of this degree. While it did not initiate today's mania, there is no question that government has supported it. Indeed, the start of the runaway phase of the current mania emerged after the market's digestion of the rumor that the Fed had intervened in the stock market on October 20, 1987 to stop the panic. No U.S. agency had ever done that before. It put stock investing in a new light. The mighty Fed had exhibited a vested interest in stopping declines, a fact that was not lost on the psyche of investors.

In the same spirit, Congress and the Securities and Exchange Commission have repealed or relaxed numerous laws and rules governing investment that had been in place since the 1930s (in response to the aftermath of the last mania). In recent months, the Social Security Administration has expressed interest in buying stocks to keep the government's retirement guarantee system from going bankrupt. National officials and agencies have thus placed their stamp of approval on the advance.

Numerous subscribers have asked about the idea that the Federal Reserve bank will prevent a crash or bear market by buying S&P futures, which it apparently did on October 20, 1987, at the bottom of that crash. Strategic Investment newsletter reports that on January 14, Alan Greenspan, speaking in Belgium, said, "We have the responsibility to prevent major financial market disruptions through the development and enforcement of prudent regulatory standards and, if necessary in rare circumstances, through direction intervention in market events." On February 23, The Washington Post reported that a "Working Group" consisting of "high level officials of federal agencies and Alan Greenspan" has "a confidential plan" to prevent a crisis. I have four points to make with respect to this claim.

1. Remember that the Fed did not prevent the 1987 crash. It happened. Many claim that the Fed averted further collapse, but in our opinion, it acted on the day the market was due to bottom anyway, the evidence being that *The Elliott Wave Theorist* said in print four days earlier that the 2-week cycle was due to bottom on October 20.

2. Given all the other parallels to 1929, it is interesting that we appear to be on track for a replay of what happened then, when a consortium of bankers amassed a pool of money to halt the October decline. On the strength of that buying and the resulting euphoria, stocks soared...for one day. Then they fell even harder, utterly ignoring a second attempt at "organized support" on the 28th. So history knows of a failed attempt to stop a market collapse.

3. The Fed's apparent success in 1987 will make it confident that it can stop the next crash, but this time, it won't work (more than briefly, anyway) because the wave of selling will be much bigger. When the Fed itself, then the professionals and soon afterward the public realize that the Fed's attempt is failing, the overall panic will increase, at minimum negating any bullish effects of the action.

4. While it is true that the Fed has an unlimited power to create fiat credit, it cannot create liquidity, as the debt already outstanding can fall in value faster than the Fed creates new credit, effecting deflation regardless of the Fed's desires. So as we see it, there are only two possibilities: The Fed will act on the bottom day of the coming collapse and appear to have been effective (watch our dates for such action), or it will try to stem the tide early and fail. Either way, the market's ultimate destiny will be unaffected. Only people's thinking will be affected (adversely), so that hope-filled bulls will hold on for the slaughter and irresolute bears will give up their positions. In other words, the main effect of this soothing news will be to produce a psychological deterrent to proper investment action.

June 1997

For the first time since 1969 (the year after the historic peak in the Value Line index), the federal budget is scheduled to be balanced in 2002. The famous "budget deal" of May 1997 was called a "golden moment for America" by the chairman of the House budget committee.

It was made possible not by hard-nosed spending cuts but by "last minute estimates" from the Congressional Budget Office. According to the CBO, better than expected tax revenue is being generated by unexpected strength in the economy and the stock market. Now that the windfall is a "permanent trend," "political enemies are working together" and everything from a capital gains tax cut to 80% of the administration's proposed spending initiatives is feasible.

July 1997

Realizing that experts have been too conservative and the public correctly fearless, financial reporters and even editorial page writers have taken it upon themselves to cajole every last investment dollar into the market, for good. Many have dispensed with the formality of professional attribution. "There's no reason to think stock prices can't go up indefinitely," noted one Wall Street columnist. "Even if they drop back, they can be expected to rebound and rise still more. Those who wait until the bear market comes and goes are losers, in this view." A gain of 1000 points in two months was the proof of what happens when investors hesitate. "Don't wait. Don't try to 'time' the market," said another. "Buy stocks and stock funds and hold onto them through thick and thin."

Another writer noted that since 95% of mutual funds have underperformed the S&P 500 so far this year, investors can do quite well just by taking free advice available in brochures and web sites. "Cookie-cutter approaches to investing" are "money in the bank." A USA Today editorial assured its readers that the Dow's dramatic rise was fundamentally sound because of the expanding global economy.

December 1997

(by Anne Crittenden)

The investment scene as a whole is so archetypally excited at present that deep emotions that we would normally consider religious now flow into, and add great power to, financial longings. Wall Street itself has become a place of numinous power, a "World Center" where people worship the gods who decide human fate. It is as much a sacred precinct as were the great temple-complexes of ancient Mesopotamia, with their ziggurats climbing into the heavens. For the first time since the Great Crash of 1929, Wall Street once again radiates what anthropologists call "mana" — an almost supernatural aura of prestige and power. The irrationality of this situation is evident to a detached observer. However, the collective consciousness is so dominated by unconscious projections that people will not accept that there is anything irrational about their rapturous faith in the financial markets. They justify themselves by pointing to past performance — about which they know virtually nothing beyond a few slogans provided by Wall Street. They believe they are acting rationally, but reason is in fact just the dazzled dupe of the whole mana-messiah-ascensional flight archetypal complex that holds the populace transfixed.

At the end of the current stock market mania, Wall Street's current aura of mana will be replaced by loathsomeness. It will be regarded as a World Center of everything evil and corrupt.

February 1998

Everything you need to know about long-term stock market sentiment is available in living color on the country's premier financial TV station, CNBC. Advertisements play to the average investor's "passion" for the market. One vendor peddles loans of up to $150,000 for "hot stocks." Others push products and services like stock options, commodity futures, "guaranteed" trading systems and up-to-the-minute market information paging services. In one brief station identification video, a bull charging down Wall Street is mounted by a character who rides off into the horizon.

Some commentators have mastered the art of heightening the urgency of their information. While holding the phone to his chest, one says, "Looks like I'm going to get some interesting information on the banking industry." Then after a commercial break in which a woman appears to be making love to her on-line trading device, the commentator returns to say, "the banking industry may have as much as 50% upside." Why? "I haven't gotten all the reasons. At this point, they're simply saying the fear (in the industry) isn't justified."

March 1998

Advertisers are introducing messages that are consistent with the golden era theme. According to The New York Times, the "new" motto, which in fact is recycled from 1988 when a song of that title was a #1 hit, is "Don't Worry, Be Happy." The hip new thing among fashion advertisers is "bright-eyed, optimistic campaigns." Even Calvin Klein, who until recently was renowned for his sullen and salacious ad imagery, says, "People don't want that now. Everything is prettier, healthier, cleaner, attractive." A youth-marketing consultant calls the attitude "sunny-side-up, a focus on a positive, upbeat outlook."

Life insurers report that people are examining their personal mortality tables and now "worry more about outliving their savings than about dying prematurely. This has led to sluggish sales of conventional cash-value life insurance and soaring popularity of mutual funds." To combat the absence of growth in its industry, Prudential Insurance, the nation's biggest life mutual, has no choice but to go public. An offering will give its agents something to sell: Prudential stock. "In dangling the prospect of a share distribution to customers, Prudential is giving its demoralized agents a powerful marketing tool." Other big mutuals that combine for hundreds of years of rock-solid financial performance have no choice but to follow Prudential into the stock market.

April 1998

The Depression-era restrictions on banks have already been effectively circumvented by banks' purchases of brokerage firms, but the banks' return to the securities markets is about to become sanctioned by law. Barriers to bank involvement in stocks and bonds were erected after the crash of 1929, a few years after the disaster they were designed to prevent. At that time, research undoubtedly showed there was no other way to safeguard savings. Today, bank deposits are an anachronism, and the House Republican Conference has concluded that the new Financial Services Act "will tear down outdated laws that separate banking and other financial activities." We expect that this change will be no less historically ill-timed than the imposition of the laws in the first place.

May 1998

On the surge past 9000, another classic signal flashed in the form of a Newsweek cover story, "Married to the Market."

June 1998

In recent months, several separate classes of savvy professionals have been beating a hasty retreat from the stock market. Last month, we showed Commitment of Traders charts revealing that commercials, or smart-money traders, have been persistent short sellers for the first time in at least 12 years, reaching an extreme in April. Bob Gabele of CDA/Investnet has been tracking insider transactions since 1983. Last year established a new one-month record for insider sales of stock at $3 billion; this year, sales are averaging $3 billion per month. Gabele says that he has never seen a

April 27, 1998

sustained selling pattern like the current one. Lesser waves of selling have always preceded important declines. The mutual fund field is littered with fund managers who are bailing out or handing their ownership interests off to the public in a rash of mutual fund IPOs. More than 100 have sold part or all of their firms in the past two years and the rate is accelerating. The sellers are often nowhere near retirement age. Notably, they are asking for most of their payments in cash rather than stock. When Michael Price, 47, sold Mutual Shares to Franklin Resources, he took less than 10% of his total selling price in Franklin stock.

The incredible spike in corporate mergers is another example of this trend, as each one represents a management team's decision to sell out. Historian Robert Sobel has pointed out this is the 20th century's fourth "merger mania." The first concluded in 1904, two years before the end of the bull market that kicked off the century. The second began in 1922 and ended with the crash of 1929. Sobel dates the beginning of the third wave to 1949, or the start of Cycle wave III, and says it lasted one year past the highs of 1968. The current binge began in, you guessed it, the "early 1980s." As we mentioned last month, the cash-financed portion of these deals has fallen to 13.4%, the lowest total in at least 10 years. This "seems to suggest," notes The Wall Street Journal, "that corporate America has a lower opinion of the value of stocks than individuals these days, although that doesn't necessarily foretell an imminent fall in the market." True, "highly probable" does not mean "necessary."

Speaking of crafty market veterans, we notice that one of the entities selling out is Norman Fosback's Institute for Econometric Research. The key asset in the deal is Mutual Funds Magazine, which was launched in 1994 and now has a subscription base of 750,000. The June issue included "Superbulls: 'You Ain't Seen Nuthin' Yet.'" The article quotes two scholars from a Washington D.C. think tank offering a "mathematically-based rationale for a further explosion of equity values." According to their calculations, it would take a P/E ratio of 100 and a Dow of 35,000 to create overvaluation in today's market. "People who make bearish arguments based on history make a mistake." The quotes from these think-tank scholars are actually a restatement of their thesis presented in a March WSJ editorial, "Are Stocks Overvalued? Not a Chance," which concludes with this statement: "In the current environment, we are very comfortable both in holding stocks and in saying that pundits who claim the market is overvalued are foolish." EWT pointed out a year ago that in a mania, prudence and a knowledge of history become impediments to success. Evidently, these scholars have not allowed their brains to be a burden.

Everybody knows what it means when Time or Newsweek has a bull on the cover. How bearish is the signal when both do, as happened in late April? We think it is even more bearish that the buyer of Mutual Funds Magazine is Time Inc. When Time *buys a bull market magazine*, it must be a sell signal, and a rare one! The popularity of bullish market media was corroborated by CNBC's highest ratings month ever in April (up 80% from year ago levels). We also note the appearance of more books about the coming boom. Publishers have discovered that nothing excites the popular imagination like a big stock market number, and their authors now outbid each other with bullish projections. Harry Dent's latest effort, *The Roaring 2000s*, predicts the "greatest boom in history" and a Dow of 35,000 by 2008. According to *Dow 40,000* (published by Mass Market Paperbacks), Dent is too bearish by 5,000 points. *Prosperity* says he has underestimated the duration of the boom by a good ten years. All these books re-hash the new-era talk of technology, education, free trade and demographic destiny, which today is accepted wisdom. Actually, their market forecasts reflect a mass delusion born of a Grand Supercycle degree top in social mood.

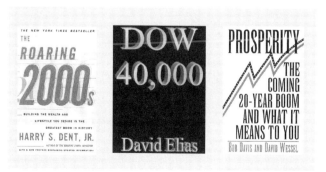

Government is always the last sector of society to catch on to a trend. Usually it embraces a trend after it is over. Perhaps the State of West Virginia will prove to be an exception, but its Consolidated Public Retirement Board is sending out warning letters to people who do not plunge their retirement savings into the stock market.

In a letter to one of our subscribers, who had chosen the safety of a money market account for his retirement funds, the board asserts, "This type of investment is usually not appropriate for the long-term investment of retirement funds." To add further emphasis, it skips to a new line and switches to all caps and an underline: "YOU NEED TO MAKE WISE INVESTMENT CHOICES NOW." Finally, it compares the cash account's return of 5.48% to a Fidelity growth fund that was up "over 40.76%" in the same year. Obviously people who won't buy stocks must not be good with numbers, so it adds that 40.76% is "more than seven times greater than the return" in the money market.

July 1998

A 40-page junk mailer on why "The Doomsayers on Wall Street are Dead Wrong" keeps reappearing in our mailbox. "Minor Market corrections? Of course. Big Bad Bear Market? No Way!" exclaims the mailer on "Undiscovered stocks [that] will make you rich!" CNBC's ratings for the key 25- to 54-year old group passed CNN's for the first time.

In late 1997, stock holdings of insurance companies and pension funds passed bond holdings for the first time ever. We say ever because while no figures exist, the great size of the bond market in the 1800s and first half of the 1900s, along with the paucity of stock shares, suggests that bonds were the dominant financial asset before 1952. The chart from Bianco Research (Barrington, Ill.) reflects an unprecedented institutional embracing of the stock market.

Current figures actually under-represent bullish conviction because many people have given up on life insurance and started "pouring money into investment-like mutual

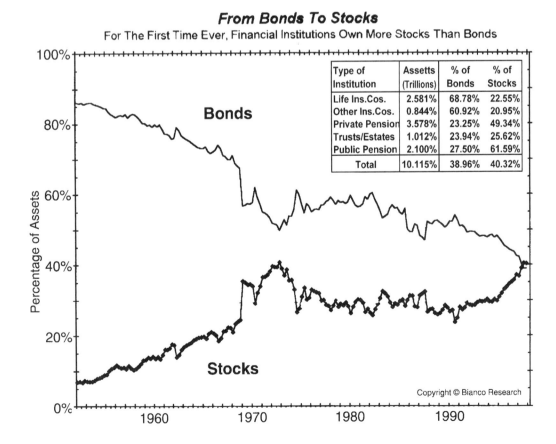

From Bonds To Stocks
For The First Time Ever, Financial Institutions Own More Stocks Than Bonds

Type of Institution	Assetts (Trillions)	% of Bonds	% of Stocks
Life Ins.Cos.	2.581%	68.78%	22.55%
Other Ins.Cos.	0.844%	60.92%	20.95%
Private Pension	3.578%	23.25%	49.34%
Trusts/Estates	1.012%	23.94%	25.62%
Public Pension	2.100%	27.50%	61.59%
Total	10.115%	38.96%	40.32%

Copyright © Bianco Research

funds and variable annuities. The shift in attitude, which has been building gradually for years, has now reached critical mass, sending life insurance into something of a free fall" just in time for the peak in the market. To remain relevant, life insurance companies have dropped the word "insurance" from their name and started hawking investment advice.

A subscriber who consults with pension fund advisors says many retirees are being far more aggressive than the 40%/39% split shown in the following "bonds to stocks" chart. A typical example is one of his clients with a niche helping blue-collar employees handle their 401(k) rollovers. The average recommended mix during retirement is 66% stocks and 33% bonds. "I was able to get the local community hospital out of the market early this year," our subscriber says. "They lasted two months. They panicked back into stocks in April. The reason was that our advisors insisted that we had a potential liability by taking a position that no one else was taking. Basically, you can get sued for thinking these days."

Another subscriber sits on the board of a low-income day-care center with a $150,000 endowment. For the last two years, he has been trying to keep the rich matrons who run the foundation from plunging the foundation into the market. "They have won," he said. Half of the money has been moved to stocks and stock mutual funds. "This is an endowment fund that is supposed to be invested prudently!" Well, some say that being in the stock market has become a fiduciary responsibility. "Bulls say they have debunked an investment superstition, fueling their view that stocks are on their way to more levels once thought impossible," a recent WSJ says, referring to the notion that stocks are riskier than bonds. The article carries this headline:

Classic Rule of 'Risk Premium' For Stocks Comes Under Attack
— The Wall Street Journal, May 26, 1998

Every top has its magical words and formulas that keep people intensely bullish. According to our man in the pension business, retirement planners across the country are "pitching the Harry Dent rationale for loading up on stock mutual funds." Research scholars, quoted extensively, contend that the gains in the market are due to a mass realization that stocks are no more volatile than bonds over the long term.

February 1999
Remember back in late July when The Wall Street Journal editorial page embraced the new era economy with a pair of glowing editorials, including "Growth Forever"? At the time, we called the editorials a reflection of the "prevailing social dream" and suggested that their "frantic intensity" was another sign of euphoric sentiment. That was within days of the July high. On January 12, four days after the latest Dow high, The Wall Street Journal opinion editors may have done it again with "Overvalued? Stocks' Price is Finally Right." Markets in all of recorded history, it says, have been wrong about P/E and price-to-dividend ratios, which now, for the first time ever, are finally correctly valued. On February 3, an article by a former Fed governor suggests that we are, in fact, "living in a new-era economy." According to this view, technology is too fast and the Federal Reserve too smart to allow the economic problems overtaking the rest of the planet to cross the border into the U.S. The piece was headlined "The Bubble Won't Burst," which managed to instantaneously expose the false dichotomy of this New York Times editorial of the same day: "Is That A Bubble, or Is the Outlook Fabulous?" The answer to both, says the WSJ writer, is yes.

March 1999
A subscriber and investment planner from Australia tells us he was "audited" by that country's Investment and Securities Commission because too many of his clients were following his instructions and withdrawing cash. "As a result of the audit, I was advised to refrain from such advice. If our clients are still in this position in 12 months, it will be suggested that I be counseled."

The chart shown here from Alan Abelson's Barron's column expresses everything there is to know about government and markets. The effort to save Social Security from default by putting the national nest egg in the stock market is another excellent example of what happens when extreme optimism meets fundamental shortcomings in a fifth wave. That is when the weakest hands with the most to lose climb on board rickety enterprises. In this case, pensioners may actually get pushed on board by the U.S. government. The drive to get Social Security in the market is one of the few current political initiatives said to have a chance of making it through Congress because some form of stock market investment is the only thing Democrats, Republicans and the White House agree upon.

In Capitol Hill hearings, Richard Anderson Jr. became the youngest person ever to testify before Congress. "If you want to retire, you must save and invest," he said. When, after three generations of rising stock prices, a 6-year-old boy is brought in to do the bidding of politicians, what is really being testified to is the termination of the advance.

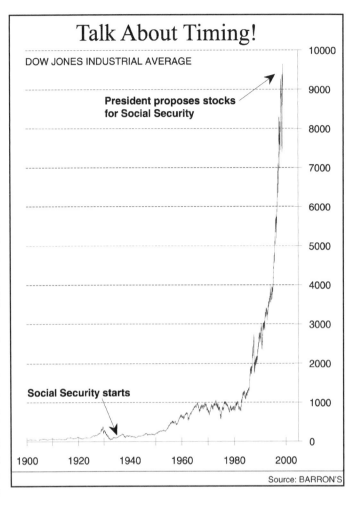

Advisors' incredible and expanding comfort level with the stock market was illustrated by a personal finance reporter who grew concerned when she found out her mother had 100% of her assets in stocks. She was "aiming for retirement in seven years." "Mom, I can't believe this," said the reporter. On her mom's behalf, the reporter called in the experts who said, "I would want 100% in stocks. Today, you have to protect your buying power at (retirement) age." A second opinion also produced "no shrieks of concern." "So, Mom, it looks like you could be in the clear," concluded the reporter.

May 1999

At least 17 of the 52 Internet deals waiting to go public have either no revenues or sales of less than $1 million. iChargeit Inc. is an Internet concept company with $30,000 in revenues, a float of 200,000 shares and no financial statements. Its only real corporate asset is an Internet stock picker turned "investor relations specialist." The stock has increased more than 700% since February.

Additional evidence of a last grab for shares is apparent in Internet IPO asking prices. "Investor enthusiasm for Internet-related IPOs has emboldened Internet startups to go for more money. Even the most obscure Internet firms are finding they can sharply increase the amount of money they raise." iVillage nearly doubled its offering price, which gave the Internet publisher $87.6 million instead of $51.1 million. Meanwhile, however, 1999 issues have been quietly running "out of gas," as people who buy these offerings find that Net issues are now posting aftermarket returns of only 29% compared to 157% last year.

One offering making its way toward a $50 million capital infusion is the health information web site of C. Everett Koop. Dr. Koop intends to use the money for brand promotion, content development, working capital and strategic alliances. In other words, the former U.S. Surgeon General will figure out what to do with the money once he has it. Much of the capital being raised is not earmarked for any specific purpose. After Amazon.com raised more than a billion dollars in equity and debt, the big secret was what the firm was going to do with all the cash. The flood of money to the Internet is reminiscent of the South Sea Bubble offering that Charles Mackay in his *Extraordinary Popular Delusions* identified as "the most absurd and preposterous of all, and, which shewed more completely than any other, the utter madness of the people." The offering was entitled, "A company for carrying on an undertaking of great advantage, but nobody to know what it is." To that state we have returned. As one pundit said on CNBC this week, "The stock market is a national casino." Indeed it is, as investors shun speculation for gambling. There is no work or knowledge behind their buys; they're just a roll of the dice, a spin of the wheel.

June 1999

The public is not going it alone; the financial press is its faithful sidekick. Several years ago, we noticed that many journalists had stopped pretending to be unbiased observers of the financial scene and become strident bull market boosters and forecasters to boot. A recent example, from a Wall Street Journal column, challenges the advice of mutual fund titan Jack Bogle. Of Bogle's caution against foreign stocks, the columnist says, "I believe that not only is his argument wrong, but also his timing couldn't be worse. Foreign stocks will come roaring back." If there is any analysis behind this assertion, we are not apprised of it.

Finance had made some journalists far more famous than financiers; now it is making them far more wealthy. "Stop the Presses! Some Reporters are Getting Rich," shouts a recent issue of Newsweek. "Journalism is suddenly emerging as a rather unlikely rocket to riches." Among the newly wealthy scribes is a "former rank-and-file Wall Street Journal reporter" who saw his net worth scream past $9 million when the financial Internet site that employs him went public. Then there is the "self-taught Wunderkind of Wall Street," a 23-year-old "journalist/financial commentator" who admits that he got started as an investor because "the notion of being able to make money without actually doing much of anything jazzed me to no end." His advice, which involves diversification, the miracle of compound interest and buying and holding stocks, is straight off the Barnes & Noble bookshelf. Nevertheless, The New York Times says that Jonathan Hoenig "has burst onto the scene" with a radio show that "sells young people on investing" with a mix of "common sense," "fraternity-style wit," irreverence and sex. His new book, *Greed Is Good*, resurrects the sentiment that helped Michael Douglas win the best actor Oscar as ruthless financier Gordon Gekko in the movie *Wall Street* (which came out in the rather interesting year of 1987).

Instead of improving or getting "wiser," the coverage gets cruder as its volume increases. The following "scoop" from a sports page on May 14 affords an example:

> INGLEWOOD, Calif. — A CNN camera crew waits patiently to speak to Chris Antley. But the jockey who won the Kentucky Derby earlier this month aboard Charismatic isn't ready. He wants to dispense investment advice first.
>
> "Hang on a sec," he says to a member of the crew. "I'll be right with you." Then comes the hot stock tip: "Here's my Triple Crown," Antley says. "AOL, Yahoo, CMGI. Buy now."
>
> Antley, in high demand for both his riding abilities on the race track and his investment advice on the Internet, hopes to win the Preakness aboard Charismatic on Saturday. A vic-

tory there would put him within one of achieving something only a handful of jockeys have ever done — win horse racing's Triple Crown. Yet, he's a guy who takes his investment advice as seriously as any ride he might get at the track. Perhaps it foreshadows something momentous; his stock market tips were winners earlier this week.

As our book says about market analysis, when "anyone can do it," the trend is over. If there actually is more upside to go in this stock mania, maybe reporters will next be asking the horse for advice.

August 1999

For millions of people, turning bearish and selling is literally not an option, as they have built their careers around rights to company stock options that do not vest until 2001 or later. "Bound by these silver handcuffs, many workers are sticking with jobs they may not want or putting off life plans in hopes of striking it rich." Others cannot bear the thought of a decline because their retirement is riding on a rising market.

One investment consultant argues that the "current stock market does not fit the definition of a classic speculative bubble" because too many investors need the money. "They are buying not because it is discretionary investing but rather because it is compulsory investment for the 401(k) retirement plans." This is rationalization to the max. A column on how hard it will be to break the "habit" of confidence begins by wondering if "Wall Street and Main Street" have "combined forces to build a perpetual moneymaking machine for the USA" and concludes that even "a crash" in stock prices will not "effect the mentality of baby boomers" who "will push the stock market to pay for retirement lifestyles as lush as today's." If greed and/or purported need were the key to perpetually rising prices, then they would have begun upon the dawn of civilization. We'll stick with the Wave Principle, which says that all it takes to topple confidence is the completion of a fifth wave.

IPOs: The Happy Daze

Traditionally, offerings start to dry up ahead of a downturn in the Dow. With all the other classic divergences registered by the Transports, Russell 2000, mutual fund flows, etc., it was a little surprising to see the IPO market hold up right through the Dow's [August] high. However, there are reasons to believe that we could see a coincident or even a later peak this time around. For one thing, offerings tend to top out closer to more important peaks. The one previous time that offerings held up to within a month of an important Dow peak was July 1987, ahead of the August 1987 high in the Dow. No definitive record of IPO performance in 1968 is available, but based on the aftermarket records that are available, it is the only IPO market that is even remotely comparable to this one. The record shows that it topped out very near the December 1968 high. In fact, several of the famous "shooter" stocks of 1968 actually peaked out well after the Dow.

On top of this, there is the flight from quality, which EWT identified in February as one of the distinguishing characteristics of the final thrust of a mania. Basically, at this late juncture, investors prefer not to be constrained by old-fashioned concepts like fundamentals or past market performance, and nothing is more unseasoned or fundamentally unbound than an Internet IPO with a business plan. Oops, too late; the latest concept according to the WSJ is to "do the deal and worry about the business plan later."

Even in June, when the IPO aftermarket was down from its April high, investors were screaming to get a piece of an IPO. We witnessed it firsthand at the Las Vegas Money Show when a young man barked into his cell phone, "Get me some shares of the offering. It's hot, and it's going to fly on the open. Just do it!" Later, while seated at the back of a workshop, we heard the head of a start-up Internet provider woo a room full of potential investors with this pitch: "Our goal is not so much to achieve profitability as to position ourselves to go public." Did you hear about the head of an IPO offering company who got a call from Henry Winkler? That's right;

he's the guy who played Fonzie on *Happy Days*. The Fonz said, "Aaaay!, can you put me down for a few shares?" The president of the company said, "Sure, why not?"

Another sign of the mania's terminal phase is the successful conclusion of a three-year campaign to get the public into IPOs. The little guy is suddenly being cut in on the action. The once-exclusive domain of institutional and wealthy investors has been pried open by a combination of technology and unrelenting popular demand. In the newly democratized IPO market, an electronic system sells each issue at market prices on a first-come, first-serve basis, or, for those times when the crowd is just too overwhelming, there are new lotto-type offerings in which lucky customers win the right to shares. An Internet investment bank that calls itself an "IPO pipeline for the masses" has taken out a two-full-page ad in The Wall Street Journal. "We're letting the public in." The public could not be happier. "It's such a great feeling because IPOs had always been this bastion for the big, fat-cat investors," said an excited investor. Another said that by providing access to IPOs, on-line brokerages were essentially "giving away free

Since the beginning of IPOs, they've been a private club that the average investor wasn't invited to join. Oh, you got in eventually. But not until a lot of money had passed hands.

It's always seemed wrong to us. And as one of the leading underwriters in the country, we're in a position to do something about it. Simply put, we're letting the public in. Right at the outset. Up to 50% of our allocation in which we're the lead or co-lead will be set aside for you. You'll be right there first in line with the institutions.

Join us. It's going to be an exciting ride.

—The Wall Street Journal
full page ad, July 22, 1999

money." "Smaller investors think they have finally crashed the party," says an article. Tell us, do you think the Wall Street fat cats, after 25 years of rising prices, are really giving the public a deal? As Joe Granville used to say, the public is screaming, "Gimme that bag!" and the sellers are politely accommodating them.

Desperation may be driving some events. After its stock fell 50%, CMGI, an Internet venture capital firm that depends heavily on the IPO market, announced that it will "reward small investors" by setting aside 5% to 10% of every IPO it brings to market for its shareholders. CMGI stock temporarily retraced half of its prior price loss on the news. Then there is the crush of companies that have rushed to public sale even though the aftermarket has been losing momentum for two months. UPS, the 92-year-old delivery company that has insisted "for decades" that it performed best without having to deal with "nettlesome Wall Street analysts" decided July 21 to offer itself to the public. In exchange for proceeds of at least $3 billion, one of the highest totals ever, subscribers will get 10% of the firm. By striking "while the coals are still hot," firms are all but conceding that they will take whatever aftermarket support they can get.

In the same spirit, the stock market itself is going public. The New York Stock Exchange announced within days of the July high that it will abandon its 207-year-old seat membership system and go public by November. The move came days after a consortium of brokerage firms decided effectively to establish its own electronic exchange and weeks after the NASDAQ revealed its own IPO plan. Of the NASDAQ plan, the New York Times had this to say: "On its face, it's hard to imagine a less appealing investment: a cyclical, capital-intensive business, rapidly losing market share to newer, more nimble competitors not subject to its strict federal regulation." A NASDAQ official even cited the "mood of urgency" to bring the deal forward. Still, the Times concluded, "It could become one of the most intriguing investment opportunities of the next decade." The reason is the "magic" of the market itself: "The idea of a NASDAQ IPO has generated excitement, much of which can be traced to the financial reward that attaches itself to those three magic letters." Would a newspaper have written such a thing at the bottoms in 1974 or 1982?

September 1999

IPOs: Cleared for Re-Entry?

The corrective potential in this market is far greater than its participants realize. In dollar terms, 1999 is running slightly behind the record year of 1996, but due to the declining quality of IPOs and the anemic strength of the overall market, this sector is far more vulnerable than it has ever been. When the value of stock offerings is measured against the public's financial reserves, the all-time high of 1996 pales by comparison. In fact, as Ned Davis Research shows in the accompanying illustration of offerings as a percentage of personal savings, the extreme readings of 1999 are literally off the chart. The line stops at the end of 1998 when offerings were about 750% of savings because the ratio actually went to infinity. Personal savings levels hit zero in the first quarter of 1999 and have since been running at negative levels, which cannot be captured on this long-term chart. Whatever the figure, it probably hit another all-time high in May as IPOs expanded while the personal savings rate fell to a record low of minus 1.2%.

"Americans have let their savings rate fall into negative territory because the stock market is at record highs," the Associated Press notes. As the chart shows, the draining of bank accounts right before final highs is a time-honored tradition. Dramatic peaks in consumers' willingness to bet on the future instead of conserve for it have been forerunners to almost every important stock market high since 1970. We have no doubt that the ratio will re-enter the more normal realm of this chart and thereby create a colossal version of the more earthbound peaks of 1972, 1976, 1983, 1987 and 1990. The low on the chart offers some perspective on how risk-averse and frugal Americans can become. A few weeks before the Dow bottomed in December 1974, offerings were just 2.024% of total savings, infinitely less than today.

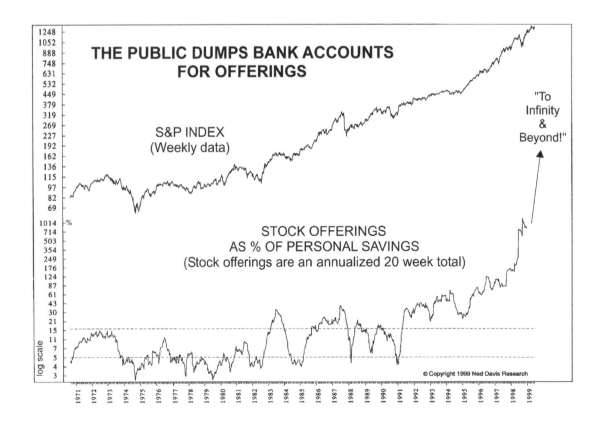

374

October 1999

Wildly bullish expressions of the long-term high in sentiment, such as plans by the NYSE, Martha Stewart and World Wrestling Federation to go public have not been affected by the market's persistent erosion. Ever-more-ambitious designs, like a proposed offering from the New York Yankees, continue to emerge. That deal would be one of the biggest IPOs ever. So, this headline from the Associated Press is true literally as well as figuratively:

Stock Market Becomes The National Pastime

Indeed, watching financial television these days, it is hard to tell if it covers the stock market or a sporting event. With its endless stream of statistical analysis, the "Halftime Report" and action shots from the floor of the NYSE, the only thing missing is the instant replay. CNBC anchor Sue Herera reports that her performance draws the adulation of a superstar athlete. She is "so besieged that she registers at hotels under her maiden name and asks her husband to pick up Chinese take-out. 'I'm trying to get out of there with my food, and the cook's asking, 'What's with Intel?'" The coverage reflects the audience, which now comprises fans rather than investors. The belief in an endless season of rising stock prices remains unshaken.

November 1999

"The ultimate bag-holder," *The Elliott Wave Theorist* has noted, is government, because it "is the last sector of society to catch on to a trend. Usually it embraces a trend after it is over." The U.S. government may have just provided one of its greatest-ever demonstrations of this principle. On October 21, the Glass-Steagall Act, which purportedly protected the financial infrastructure by separating the bank, insurance and brokerage industries, was effectively repealed. The Financial Services Act of 1999 "follows several failed efforts to do away with the Glass-Steagall Act over more than two decades." The bill basically reopens the door to the securities business for banks and insurance firms. Glass-Steagall shut the door in 1933, the year after the bear-market bottom. So, after totally missing the bear market it was supposed to prevent and protecting banks and insurance companies from six decades of rising prices, the U.S. government will free banks and insurers to take part in a financial consolidation that promises to be one of the biggest in history.

A REQUIEM FOR GLASS-STEAGALL
—BusinessWeek, November 15, 1999

Playful Postmortem Ices Cake At Glass-Steagall Repeal Party

The reaction on Capitol Hill to passage of the financial reform bill last week ranged from revelry to morbid humor.

To mark the historic occasion, House Banking Committee Chairman Jim Leach played host to a group of his closest collaborators on the bill, including Federal Reserve Board Chairman Alan Greenspan, Treasury Secretary Lawrence H. Summers, Comptroller of the Currency John D. Hawke Jr., Treasury Under Secretary Gary Gensler and Rep. John J. LaFalce, D-N.Y. They joined staff members, lobbyists and reporters in drinking champagne and devouring a large cake, which bore an epitaph for the Depression-era separation of commercial and investment banking that the bill undoes. It read: "Glass-Steagall, R.I.P., 1933-1999."

—American Banker, November 8, 1999

In our opinion, this is once again perfect timing, one year after the top in most stocks and mutual funds. This long-term signal of the most entrenched, government-backed market consensus in at least 65 years was seconded by an Associated Press story that revealed that political candidates have become "more bullish about investing campaign contributions in stocks. 'Little lights have gone off in various campaign treasurers' heads as they watched the stock market go up, up, up.'" These lights are a long-term sell signal if ever there was one.

December 1999

At this point, the mania is downright funny. The following take-off is excerpted from the Onion, an Internet lampoon:

Species of Algae Announces IPO

LAKE ERIE—Seeking to capitalize on the recent IPO rage on Wall Street, Lake Erie-based blue-green algae Anabaena announced Tuesday that it will go public next week with its first-ever stock offering.

Anabaena, a photosynthesizing, nitrogen-fixing algae with 1999 revenues estimated at $0 billion, will offer 200 million shares on the NASDAQ exchange next Wednesday under the stock symbol ALG. The shares are expected to open in the $47-$49 range.

"For every company that has a successful IPO, there are 10 others that flop," said Brian Baum, head of online consulting for Ernst & Young. "But blue-green algae has a history of steady nitrogen production, as well as a very strong relationship with fungi, an environmental power player with whom it produces many common lichens. And with the number of living organisms on the planet rising every day, the demand for Anabaena's many products and by-products should only grow."

Some of the real deals we have seen are almost as laughable. The desire for comic relief will expand rapidly in the weeks ahead, so this piece probably marks the start of a whole new genre of social satire.

February 2000

With the break into record territory, some of the most brazen bets yet on the bull market have been assumed in an almost subliminal manner. The absence of the words "could" or "might" from this recent Reuters article explains what we mean:

Legal Changes to Boost Value of Nobel Prizes

The story is about the Nobel Prize committee's decision to raise its equity holdings from an already high level of 70%. The reasoning is simple, says the director of the organization that grants awards to the world's great thinkers: "More equities means more money to laureates." The depth of this belief in the permanence of rising stock prices is clear from the Reuters report, which passes along the upside bias of the Nobel prize committee as plain fact. The story begins by stating, "Sweden's prestigious prizes are set to increase in value" just as soon as the legal maneuvers are out of the way.

Popular cartoons like Doonesbury have been covering the mania on an almost daily basis. On one level, the cartoons work because a mania is pretty funny. The cartoon is one small example, there are many more than we have room to show here.

Doonesbury
BY GARRY TRUDEAU

We must add that as a reflection of a dangerously extended extreme in social mood, the flood of cartoons is also perilous because it is yet another feedback loop that magnifies the effects of the mania. One of the striking traits of this mania, which EWFF also pointed out last month,

October 1999
October 1999

is how it has taught investors to ignore the experts. The *Doonesbury* cartoon shown here is a great illustration of this phenomenon. As comics have crossed over into market commentary, we have seen countless others poke fun at the performance and integrity of investment profession-als. A few weeks ago, *Barron's* ran a story in which the illustrator of Dilbert was the one giving the advice: "Dogbert's creator is skeptical of actively managed funds. Index funds, he argues, are the way to go."

The Merger of the Century?

There are many reasons to suspect that the union of AOL and Time Warner will mark the end of the mergers and acquisition boom. The primary one is this chart of the number of an-nounced deals. It updates an earlier version that called for the completion of a fifth wave in *At the Crest of the Tidal Wave*. While the total number of deals has been falling for more than a year and a half, the value of mergers as a percent-age of GDP has continued to climb rapidly,

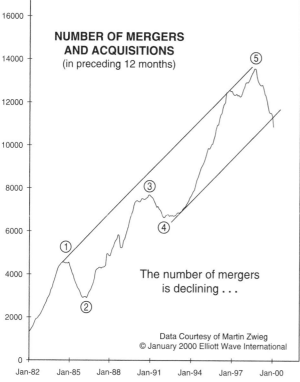

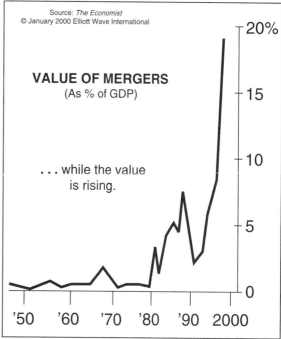

as the next chart shows. So, just like the overall stock market, merger activity has been divided into the broader market, which has been falling since the middle of 1998, and the total value of acquisitions, which has continued to accelerate on the strength of a few blockbuster deals. The decline through the lower trend channel on the number of deals, however, indicates that a bear market at all levels of the M&A business is near.

The euphoria surrounding AOL's purchase of Time Warner may mark the top. As The Wall Street Journal put it, "The deal was heavy with superlatives and symbolism. It would be the biggest merger in history — yahoo!" Even though it has a book value of just $3 billion, AOL's inflated stock price allowed it to bid $156 billion for Time Warner. The price represented a record 70% premium over Time Warner's pre-announcement market value. Business Week posted a picture of AOL's leaders on its cover and declared them "Men of the Century." The colossal expectation built into the merger is represented by the fact that the century was less than three weeks old at the time. As we noted last month and many times in the past, Business Week cover stories attesting to the strength of the long-term trend have a history of marking important peaks. Time magazine's record is even more distinguished, so its corporate parent's willingness to surrender control to an Internet upstart is indeed probably the "crowning" achievement of the new economy, as so many media outlets have asserted. Another signal of an imminent reversal in the bull market for mergers is the establishment of a new daily newspaper that will chronicle the M&A business "the same way Variety does for show business."

More important, there is a broader message in this reversal. As *At the Crest* noted, one of the main ways "companies express optimism is by taking over other companies. ...Such activity is indicative not of minor bull market tops, but of ones that precede prolonged and devastating bear markets." As the chart shows, lower peaks in value as a percent of GDP anticipated downturns for stocks and the economy in the 1970s and the early 1990s.

March 2000

The December issue of EWFF predicted the emergence of "a whole new genre of social satire," which is appearing now in different forms. Business Week's latest bull-market book list includes *How to Get Filthy, Stinking Rich and Still Have Time for Great Sex*. Another humorous takeoff, *The Trillionaire Next Door: The Greedy Investor's Guide to Day Trading*, is classified as a "funny little book savaging the nation's obsession with making easy money in the market." Like the peak of 1987, which was soon followed by the movie *Wall Street* and Gordon Gekko's "greed is good" credo, the current stock-market peak now has a cynical, feature-length motion picture to encapsulate its excesses. In a story "to match the giddy heights of the Dow," *Boiler Room* is a "gritty" drama that explores "the shady side of Wall Street." Its best moment, according to one review, is when its huckster brokers watch "Michael Douglas and Charlie Sheen in Wall Street on a giant TV and mouth their words from memory."

July 2000

One way legal historians have quantified progress and regress in the U.S. antitrust movement is the amount of merger activity. As antitrust activity rises, many have documented an inverse relationship, in which mergers "disappear." In our research for the May issue, we found the data on mergers for the first three of the charts in a book on federal antitrust policy. The data for the most recent bull market is updated from February issue of *The Elliott Wave Financial Forecast*. If you put each of these charts up against EWT's May chart of antitrust suits and conciliations (see Chapter 3), you will see how beautifully they fill in the blank spots, i.e. the major bull markets. In light of this century-long correlation between the number of mergers and rising stock prices, another major confirmation of a reversal in social mood is a recent outbreak of anti-merger fever.

Within the last few weeks, the U.S. authorities have blocked WorldCom's purchase of Sprint, H.J. Heinz's purchase of BeechNut Nutrition and the $6 billion combination of the Burlington

NUMBER OF U.S. CORPORATE MERGERS AGAINST THE DOW

© July 2000 Elliott Wave International

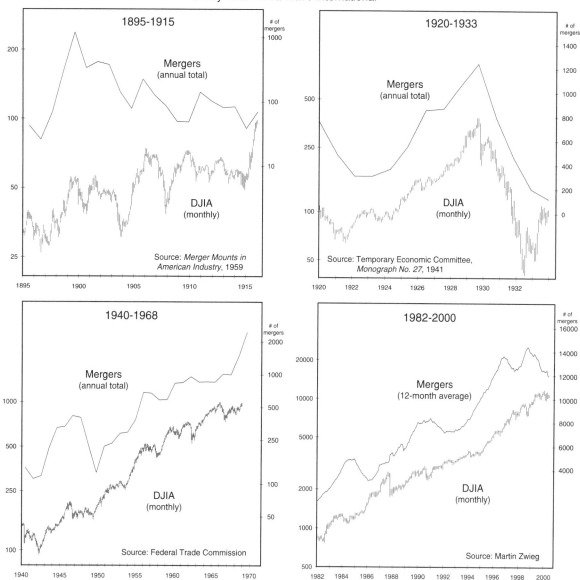

Northern Santa Fe and the Canadian National Railway, which would have been the biggest railroad combination in history. Several other deals that would have met with no resistance in the late 1980s and 1990s, including United Airlines' buyout of US Air, AOL's merger with Time Warner and Bell Atlantic's bid for GTE, are now being challenged by various federal agencies. The SEC and Federal Accounting Standards Board have undermined the potential for any more record breaking deals with an attack on the "pooling of interest" accounting method that has allowed countless firms to make acquisitions with their inflated stock rather than cash or debt. During the topping and declining mood trend, support, cooperation and synthesis give way to divisiveness and resentment. In the last two months, the speed and scope of this social change has clearly accelerated. Once the judge threw the book at Microsoft, it was as if he had declared "open season" on mergers and cooperative business relationships. This massive social change in attitude is consistent with the transition to a bear market in stocks.

The still unbroken promise of the NASDAQ is represented by a 500-page business technology magazine called the Red Herring.

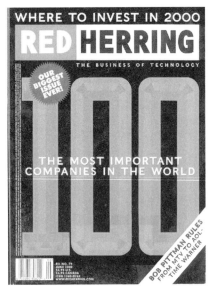

June 2000

"The market's been so volatile lately ... by the time I hit the ground I might be a millionaire again!"

June 2000

Another sign of a major mood change is the "gallows humor that prevails" around Wall Street and Silicon Valley. Last December, *The Elliott Wave Financial Forecast* predicted that a "desire for comic relief" would lead to a "whole new genre of social satire." The cartoon shown here is one small example. Cartoonists are cracking up readers with similar pieces at such a steady rate that the editor of a digest of cartoons at cagle.com has established a Wall Street section to which he posts five or six additions each day.

A former TV writer has just published *The Trillionaire Next Door*, a twisted look at day trading, and established a new web site called www.sexytrillionaire.com. Newsweek says, "He has developed a weird new niche: satirizing the financial pages." Modern Humorist, a producer of web-based parodies, has put out several wicked takes on the financial world, such as "The Fortune 5" issue of "Misfortune" magazine. "Depression, defeatism, despair... 'Bring It On!'"

In more ways than one, truth is turning out to be stranger than sarcasm as the firm, which has no revenue, has attracted a cult following and $1 million in venture capital. After Esquire printed an April Fools Day prank about a bogus concept company that planned to give away cars plastered with ads, it was flooded with calls for the new advertising vehicles. One company called to say the author had ripped him off. FreeCars.com really does plan to give away cars as ads. In June, the firm's founder was raising money in anticipation of "a July launch date." Meanwhile, Free-Wheelz.com, Esquire's mock company, is also on-line, and the author of the story says he is accepting offers for the rights to it. "If somebody could get it to work, I'm a willing partner." Reality may be on its way back, but it still has a long way to go before it is re-established.

October 2000

Another statistic that has reached a new high is the number of United States households owning mutual funds. The total "climbed 4.5 percent, to a record 50.6 million this year, as the popular investment continued to attract new money. 'In spite of the chaotic markets of the last 12 months, the reach of mutual funds continues to expand,' said [the] president of a fund research firm. 'If the first eight months of this year hasn't discouraged people, nothing will.'"

In an important divergence, however, the flow of funds into equity mutual funds has not returned to the record high of February when investors ignored the January peak in the Dow and flooded their fund accounts with more than $40 billion in net contributions (see dotted line on the bottom chart). The same thing happened from April to September 1987, leading to the crash. A more precise analogy is to the Cycle-degree peak of February 1966 and its more speculative twin of December 1968. In both cases, net mutual fund inflows topped one month after the all-time Dow peak (see dotted lines in the top chart). The key to this parallel is the steadfast dedication that greeted those respective highs. Inspired by eighteen years of rising prices, mutual

Cartoonists Satirize Stock-Market Foibles
Who Knew Nasdaq Was so Funny?

Good news for the president, for Bill Gates, for John Rocker and the rest of the famous or flawed people who usually dominate editorial cartoons: The nation's cartoonists are in love with the foibles of the stock market.

In fact, not since the stock-market crash of 1987 have there been so many editorial cartoons in mainstream newspapers, trying to generate yucks at Wall Street's expense. And what is noteworthy is that the witty doodles have shown — as have small investors themselves — a marked sophistication about the workings of the markets.

"Until recently the market wasn't a mainstream topic for cartoons. It seemed kind of specialized and there weren't that many people in the market," says Mike Luckovich, editorial cartoonist for the Atlanta Constitution. Now, he says, the market has become as familiar to Americans as "Who Wants to Be a Millionaire" on TV.

Cartoonists like the unpredictable nature of Wall Street, which gives them plenty to parody.

THE WALL STREET JOURNAL, April 20, 2000

USA TODAY
June 9, 2000

The Times, April 13, 2000

Getting Down to Funny Business

Former TV comedy writer Andy Borowitz has developed a weird new niche: satirizing the financial pages

Disney/ABC to air 'Millionaire' eight days a week: In an effort to maximize profits for its "Who Wants to Be a Millionaire" franchise, Disney/ABC will air the series eight days a week, sources close to the network say. The extra "Millionaire" broadcast will be scheduled by creating a new day, tentatively called Fruesday.

Newsweek, June 26, 2000

Backers See Value in Wicked Parodies

Get this: A couple of Ivy League wisenheimers put up a Web site on a lark, the site causes a sensation and the duo become budding new media moguls with no revenue but venture capital to burn.

It's the kind of dot-com folk tale that Modern Humorist's Web site would mercilessly spoof, except that it is, in fact, the brief history of Modern Humorist itself. Specializing in wickedly funny parodies, Modern Humorist is the brainchild of two Harvard graduates, Michael Colton and John Aboud, and, without revenue, has attracted a cult following and $1 million in venture capital.

"We figure the end of the economy is here if idiots like us can get money," says Mr. Aboud, the 27-year-old co-president of Modern Humorist Inc.

THE WALL STREET JOURNAL, May 25, 2000

By Nick Anderson, The (Louisville) Courier-Journal, The Washington Post Writers Group   USA Today, March 10, 2000

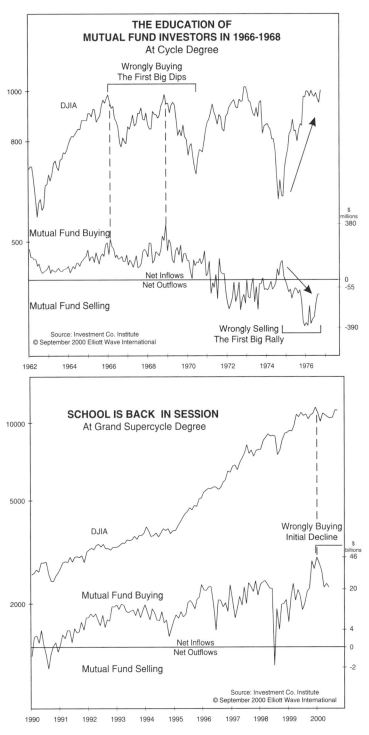

fund contributors were buyers in every month of the 1960s. The bottom chart shows that, with the exception of two brief outflows, mutual fund holders did the same thing during the long-term uptrend in the 1990s. Mutual fund investors are now as psychologically impervious to falling prices as they were at the end of Cycle wave III in the late 1960s.

At the lows in April 1994, October 1997, September and October 1999, mutual funds had robust inflows of more than $10 billion. February's all-time record was actually established during the worst month of the year for the Dow. The NASDAQ's March plunge dented the net inflow, but wave (2) has clearly done its job. This August quote from a fund consultant illustrates how firmly investors are held within the grasp of wave two psychology: "Every dip in the NASDAQ has proved in hindsight to be a buying opportunity. Until you really see a significant negative event, I don't think you'll see this voracious appetite for stock funds diminish." Clearly, investors have the fortitude to ignore even the most significant negative events, which means they are primed for the same bear-market disappointment that took place in 1966-1975.

The bracket across the top of the Dow shows the initial phase of this very painful process. Even though there was no net progress in the Dow, mutual fund holders piled in through the declines of 1966, 1969 and 1970. Net outflows did not appear until May 1971, five years and three months after the

Dow's initial failure at 1000. Another way to look at the present condition is this: If record flows of money into mutual funds could not get the averages to new highs, what will it take? And how long will it be until these investors run out of money?

The bear market's eventual re-education of mutual fund contributors can be seen by their response to the start of Cycle wave V, when a generation-long bull market commenced. The arrows show that when the market finally turned up for good in 1975, investors sold, eventually in record amounts. As then, there will be no sustained advance after this top until the public has completely lost confidence in the long-term prospects of their mutual fund holdings. A subtle but vital distinction between these two periods is shown by the value of the net flows on the right hand axis of these two charts. Fund flows have jumped from the millions in the 1960s and 1970s to the billions today. At the high in February, inflows were nearly 100 times those at the peak in January 1969. This difference reflects the difference between Cycle degree and Grand Supercycle degree peaks.

December 2000

One simple measure of investor psychology may be found in the latest issue of Business Week. First, there is the sheer weight of it, a 30% increase in heft from a comparable issue at the beginning of the year. Remember, that's when Business Week's ebullient tone and rationalization for the New Economy contributed to our forecast for an imminent peak for stocks. While Business Week's editorial content suggests some re-thinking of the New Economy, its advertising betrays an even heavier reliance on technology. At this point, technology supplies the dominant share of the magazine's ad revenue by a whopping margin. In fact, our pie charts show that technology advertising is almost ten times what it was at the beginning of the bull market in 1974 (and that's using a 1974-era definition of high tech to include calculators, plastics and "two-way radio-telephones").

BUSINESS WEEK AD CONTENT

© December 2000 Elliott Wave International

% of Ad Pie By Sector

	2000		1974
Technology	65%		6.8%
Brokers, Mutual Funds, and Other Investment Services	11%		1.1%
Manufacturing	0%		27.8%
Hard Liquor	0%		5.7%
Other Includes:			
Auto	3.9%		5.7%
Non-Profit/ Philanthsopic	2.6%		0.76%
Consumer Credit	1.9%		0.0%
Insurance	1.3%		6.8%
Bank	0.7%		9%
Energy	0.4%		6.8%

November 20, 2000 — Technology, Equity Services, Other

December 7, 1974 — Technology, Manufacturing, Other, Liquor

Another interesting difference between the current issue and that of December 1974 is in the ads for brokerage firms, mutual funds or other stock market services. In 1974, they were almost nonexistent. Recent issues, by contrast, are still imbued with all the optimism of the equity culture.

Merrill Lynch's "Be Bullish" advertisement from November 22 illustrates the almost imperative nature of this societal focus.

In the December 1974 issue, the only real stock market mention is a negative reference in an ad for cheap cologne. "There's nothing like a bearish market to make men look for solid value," says the ad. The pitch sounds a lot like the current headlines about how much "Value Investing Suddenly Makes Sense" (WSJ, November 27). We expect Business Week's advertising to head back toward its mix in 1974, when manufacturing accounted for 27.8% of its total. The current issue includes zero manufacturing ads, which is another sign

Be wired.

Be bullish.

Merrill Lynch Advertisement
October 1999

383

of the vast potential for decline; unfortunately, the U.S. virtually abandoned manufacturing in favor of "services," so we might have to rebuild the economy first! Another sector to watch is the hard liquor group. At the bottom in 1974, it was actually the sixth largest advertising segment, with 5.7% of the pie. Today, there are no liquor ads. Look for the bear market to put the booze back in Business Week.

March 2001

As Advertised: The End of an Era

Back in December, EWFF noted that Business Week had actually increased 30% from its size at the time of the bull market's peak in early 2000. Further analysis of BW's ad content prompted us to call the November 20 issue "another sign of the vast potential for decline." That potential is now being realized, as the number of ad pages in the February 19 issue of Business Week has plunged more than 50%, just since the end of 2000. Economists, after finally admitting the economy is in decline, say that it will be bouncing back by the middle of the year.

This chart of real per-capita advertising expenditures suggests, however, that advertising's decline (and that of the economy which it usually leads) has only just begun. It shows a clear five-wave rise that began with the first "golden age of advertising" in the 1920s. Not yet recorded on the chart are expenditures for 2000. In addition to Business Week's boom through the first year of the bear market, everything from record high ad rates to the encyclopedia-sized issues of previously non-existent magazines suggests that 2000 will show on the chart as a blow-off top.

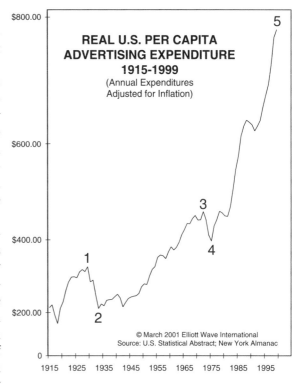

Another clue to advertising's suddenly perilous future is the pivotal role it came to play in the virtual economy. In the dream that was the New Economy, the promise of future ad revenue justified countless web vendors' lack of profitability. In the fourth quarter of 1999, $1 billion in actual cash was spent on advertising. The venture capitalists got so excited that they raised billions more and spent much of it on conventional ads that would build Internet "brand presence" and generate traffic. Once the top was in, studies came out showing that Internet advertising did not even work. Three days after the NASDAQ's March 10 peak, for instance, Internet Week reported, "The notion that web users would be steered to e-commerce sites" was "a fairy tale."

April 2001

Eventually, hostility and retribution always replace the shared rapture of a bubble. With the dissipation of a mania, objects of the public's former affections become engulfed in this negative emotional backlash. On Monday, for instance, The New York Times put out a piece on the "slings and arrows of the market's slide" that are now being aimed at CNBC, "once the pounding heartbeat of the economic expansion." CNBC stands "accused of covering the fall so heavily that it is adding to an inordinate sense of doom." In a recent issue of the New Yorker, an economist charged that CNBC "distorts the way the market works and helps turn what should be a diverse, independent-thinking crowd of investors into a herd acting upon a single collective thought (in this case, SELL!)." CNBC is not controlling the market. The market is controlling CNBC's image.

May 2001

Some contrary-minded subscribers are wondering how the market can go down as far as it is due to go when they are already seeing negative Wall Street images in the comic section of their daily newspaper. Subscriber Michael M. notes that the funny pages now carry continual references to fallen stock values and the ineptitude of bullish investment advisors. He writes:

> In the February 2000 EWFF, there was a lengthy article about cartoons and the market with numerous bull market examples. The MSN home page has cagle.com with page after page of gloomy toons (many NASDAQ related). Is this bullish? Second, the article from EWFF quotes an earlier one from the May 1997 EWT that "the message is bearish regardless of the cartoonists' theme," i.e. however despondent the prevailing mood of market-related cartoons, it's to be interpreted bearishly. Does that really hold true?

The Atlanta Journal-Constitution
January 3, 2001

Toronto Globe and Mail
January 1, 2001

The exceptional thing about these cartoons is not what they say but that they exist at all. They reflect an intense public interest in the equity markets. In a bear market, it is commonly held that the public goes from greed at the top to fear at the bottom. In a larger degree turn, however, there is another important stage that investors must reach before a major advance can begin: total disinterest. At the bottom, the average person will go back to being oblivious of the market. Cartoonists won't attack the stock market because it will lack relevance to every day life. Bearish cartoon images show that the public is anything but ambivalent about stocks.

June 2001

The chart at right shows the shift in psychology in representative headlines through the NASDAQ's slide and the Dow's recent rise. [It] shows that even at the April and October 2000 lows, the media never relinquished its bullish bias. Page-one stories on the decline were relatively rare until March 13, when the NASDAQ's "Historic Dive" finally filled the whole top half of USA Today's front page. By then, the NASDAQ was down 62%. On April 4, when the Dow had already begun its advance and the NASDAQ was on its low, the same paper offered a story on the market's "dismal" prospects, finally adding a bearish forecast to its headline for the first time, at precisely the wrong time.

The following chart shows the doubts that dominated the headlines through the rally. It also shows how erroneous assumptions such as the importance of earnings in market forecasting will cost many investors buckets of money over the next few years. As the fundamentals worsened following the market's low, the formerly intrepid financial press was filled with "alarms," warnings of trouble ahead and forecasts of "more tough times." Even at the end of a clearly impulsive,

385

five-wave rally to within a few points of the all-time Dow high, caution has reigned, indicating substantial potential for higher highs in coming months.

With respect to the long-term trend, however, there is another subtle but critical difference between these two sets of headlines. During the decline, reporters continually asserted their buy-and-hold beliefs as facts; in fact, we can think of two major articles in which reporters interviewed reporters on the topic. On the rally, in contrast, journalists were careful to attribute bearish sentiments to analysts, stock pickers and other experts. The following quote from *The Wave Principle of Human Social Behavior* addresses this phenomenon:

> When trends reach extremes, reporters no longer require the services of financial professionals to express an opinion; the continuation of the trend is so obvious to them that they become convinced that anyone can do it, and they take on the forecasting themselves.

We saw this outcome in spades throughout the major top dating from 1998 and have yet to see it on the downside. This is a socionomic hint that the long-term bear market in most issues has much further to go.

Unfortunately for many journalists, the now-broken promise of the NASDAQ is a story they cannot report. They've been laid off. Layoffs among technology and business magazines have snowballed in recent weeks. The Red Herring let go 56 employees in May and has now reduced its staff by one-third. The page count on the June

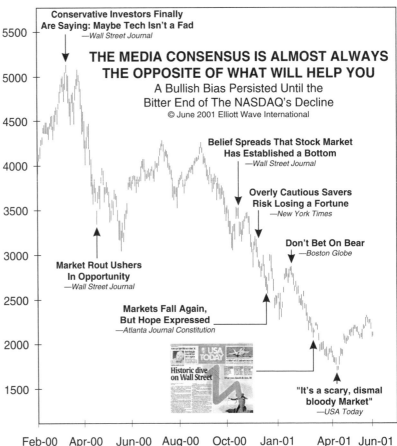

2001 issue is down more than 85% from the previous June's. "The extent of the industry correction was literally inconceivable in the valley," says the magazine's editor. "None of us thought it would be this bad." His use of the word "correction" is evidence that the long-term decline is not over. Another is the fact that the Red Herring is still in business. However, the cutbacks and the cracks in the rampant optimism that flowed from the June 2000 issue are consistent with a temporary reprieve.

Media capitulation to the old downtrend is also apparent in a 25% reduction in the financial coverage offered by the Seattle Post Intelligencer, CNBC's decision to delay the construction of a new headquarters/stock market tourist attraction and Merrill Lynch's decision to cancel its "Be Bullish" ad series. A sample ad from the $150 million campaign was shown in the November EWFF as an illustration of the "almost imperative nature of the societal focus" on the bull market. So here again, the media are finally reflecting a shift from euphoria to apprehension. Together, these reversals form a composite picture of a market that has reversed its trend, at least for now. Keep in mind the context of these observations. Longer-term sentiment is still too optimistic, reflecting the Grand Supercycle top in progress.

August 2001

An interesting aspect of a bear market in social mood is that it is not just the direction of the trend change that causes trouble. The speed of change is itself a problem, particularly for slow moving, consensus-driven entities like governments. A prototypical example of the miscalculations that can result from being behind the curve of a bear market is the California energy crisis. As EWFF mentioned last month, California's effort to control utility rates is a classic response to a downtrend in social mood. By July 12, the "new punitive mood" (for a complete description see the May 2000 entry in Chapter 3) had clearly come to a full boil in California as its legislature was working on a bill that "would make it a felony for natural gas or electric power producers to curtail production or to sell energy 'at prices above marginal cost.'"

By this time, however, the downturn in the economy actually had solved the energy crisis. Or it would have, if California hadn't tried to "control" utility rates by buying up power. These efforts created a "new problem, [a] sudden surplus of energy." In its frantic effort to rein-in rates, California had lined up contracts to buy power as far out as 2011 at 8 to 16 times the going rate! So, this ill-conceived effort to "stabilize things" should help destabilize the state for years to come. This is called making the worst of a bad situation; in a bear market, it is a very popular sport. In fact, by the time this one is over, measures designed to counter the bear's effects may do as much damage as the bear market itself.

October 2001

No matter how many measures and milestones return to the 1930s, economists refuse even to acknowledge the possibility [of a depression]. "Forecasters now predict a short, mild recession, with things beginning to turn around by next spring," said the September 18 Washington Post. "Although the word 'recession' has recently taken on an ominous tone, it's not the kind of prolonged, deep economic decline that people associate with the Great Depression, or even what Japan has been going through for the past decade." If anything, it is worse. This reality is clear from another headline that appeared in the September 3 issue of Advertising Age:

Ad Fall May Be Worst Since Depression

Ad Age said advertising expenditures are expected to fall 4.2% in 2001, which would be the biggest decline since 1938. This fall should come as no surprise to EWFF readers. We have been focused on advertising as an important reflection of "the vast potential for decline" since the December issue. In March, when economists were still saying the economy would be on the mend by summer, we asserted that the performance and content of the advertising industry argued otherwise.

The big tip-off was a clear five-wave advance in real U.S. per capita advertising expenditures over the last 80 years. Go back and check out the chart [in the March entry]; it speaks volumes. It says in unequivocal Elliott wave terms that the downturn to date is just the beginning of a severe bear market for the advertising industry. Of all the throwbacks to the 1930s, the biggest ad loss since 1938 is the most important, because in addition to showing where the economy is, advertising signals where it is headed, which is into a deeper decline. At a minimum, the decline should equal the 33% retracement that announced the Great Depression.

June 2002

The chart of the last great merger of the bull market and merger and acquisition totals since the high, depict what happens when caution pushes liquidity and the leverage that feeds it out of the financial system. *The Elliott Wave Financial Forecast* identified the pricking of the bubble with this comment in February 2000: "Euphoria surrounding AOL's purchase of Time Warner may mark the top." AOL is now down more than 80% from its late 1999 high while the total number of mergers has fallen about 65%. The merger total will fall further as this "broader message" covered in *At the Crest of the Tidal Wave* continues to play out: blow-off peaks in merger activity are indicative "not of minor bull market tops, but of ones that precede prolonged and devastating bear markets." The size and relentlessness of these declines confirm that this bear market is a colossus that is still revealing its full stature.

Cultural Trends

As we have noted many times, government is an institutionally rigid social organism that is driven by consensus. It is always among the last to conform to changes in the direction of social mood because it takes time for power to change hands, laws to be enacted and rescinded and bureaucracies to give way. Government is so rigid that it can respond to even decades-long trends of Supercycle degree after they are over. The Glass-Steagall Act is a classic example. The law erecting a wall between commercial and investment banking was a response to the downtrend in social mood that started in 1929. It did not go into effect until 1933, the year after the Supercycle degree low of 1932.

After 60 years of advance in Supercycle (V), it came to be virtually unanimously believed that Glass-Steagall was an anachronism. In the late 1980s and early 1990s, Congress chipped away at the division, but an outright repeal did not gain steam until the late 1990s. As the measure worked its way toward law in 1998, *The Elliott Wave Theorist* stated, "We expect that this change will be no less historically ill-timed than the imposition of the laws in the first place." The Financial Modernization Act of 1999 recognized seven decades of rising stock prices by repealing many aspects of Glass-Steagall in November 1999, when the bull was 99.998% complete. Now that the fires of the next bear market have jumped to all sectors of the financial landscape, the firewalls are once again under construction. More than two years after the start of the bear market, the attorney general of New York has forced Merrill Lynch to pay a $100 million fine for issuing bullish research reports in stocks their analysts secretly did not like. The "settlement" will settle nothing as commentators on all sides of the political spectrum have belittled it as a slap on the wrist. The universal belief is that more needs to be done to protect investors from the avarice of investment bankers. Once a bottom of some importance is at hand, Congress will undoubtedly do it.

On a daily basis, we see additional evidence that government, driven by the increasingly hostile public attitude toward Wall Street, markets and corporations, is falling in line with the bear market program called for in past issues. One example, which also parallels the experience of 1930s, is the re-establishment of farm subsidies by the Bush administration. On May 14, President Bush signed into law a bill that will provide $190 billion in subsidies to U.S. farmers and "officially closed the book on the nation's experiment with free market policies." This is what *The Elliott Wave Theorist* figured on when the depression-era subsidies were "swept away" in 1996. The May 1996 EWT cited it as evidence of a peaking social mood and noted, "Nothing prevents Congress from reinstituting farm subsidies when the seven years end." As it turns out, Congress is a year ahead of schedule.

The suddenly ballooning federal budget deficit is another reversal that EWFF alerted readers to in July 1999. At the time, the government projected an "elimination of all federal debts by 2015." Given its size and the speed of its growth (by one of the government's own estimates, it is already over $500 billion in debt), Bush was reportedly and rightfully "sheepish" as he signed the bill into law. As we said with regard to Bush's protectionist makeover in April, it's now time for logic to lose a lot of battles to the bitter sensibilities of a bear market.

At the state level, where budgets must actually balance, taxes are rising. This report from a May issue of the Wall Street Journal illuminates one more piece of our long-term forecast that is slipping into place. "Faced with deteriorating budgets that show few signs of recovery, states are expected to raise taxes and fees a combined $2.4 billion beginning July 1, reversing an eight-year run of cuts. And that's just the tip of the iceberg." In many states, such as Missouri, "gloomy forecasts turned out to be not gloomy enough." To make up its extreme cash shortage, Missouri has told 415,500 taxpayers that their refund checks are "on indefinite hold." Alabama has also put off returning overpaid taxes to corporate taxpayers "until the economy rebounds." If a private financial institution froze people's money in this way, someone would go to jail. As unbelievable as this theft seems, however, it is a predictable consequence of the reversal. Back in 1998, when the front edge of the topping process was nibbling away at the fringes of the financial world, *The Elliott Wave Theorist* issued this warning about "Politicians' Attack on the Money World:"

> Beware the approach of financial fascism. Russia has decided that in order to satisfy the IMF, it will impose price controls on goods and currency controls on citizens. Likewise, Brazil's plan to entice an international bailout package involves raising taxes. Government screws up, and the citizens pay. Even the U.S. will not be immune to such impulses when financial pressures increase.

The pressure is rising like never before, and that means that Missouri's appropriation of $167 million in taxpayer rebates is just the start of a new era, one that will probably bring new meaning to terms like subsidy, fiscal irresponsibility and government boondoggle. As a long essay in the May 24 issue of Grant's Interest Rate Observer reveals, "In the world in which we live, the politicians are gaining on the capitalists." The abuse is likely to be so blatant that many will blame the government for the bear market. But government doesn't cause changes in social mood. It's just so slow and stupid in its response that it appears culpable. Of course, it can aggravate a bear market's effects. This time, it appears to be gearing up to compound them in historic ways.

October 2002

Pension Fund School Is In Session

Investors' biggest problem is that they cannot accept losses. This is the first thing most traders must learn to do. In fact, a common event in the careers of many great traders is a big early mistake that wipes them out. *Market Wizards*, Jack Schwager's book of interviews with top traders, shows that big, early failure is a rite of passage in the career of many successful traders. In just about every interview, champion traders tell about the catastrophes that helped launch them on their way. Schwager reports that one "remarkably successful professional" lost money for a decade before he hit his stride. In many cases, these lessons are preceded by quick gains that turn out to be a setup for the initial loss. Most pension fund investors are still working on that first trade. They went long on stocks a decade or more ago and then just kept adding to that initial position. As the boom intensified, and even now as it turns to bust, pension funds have upped the ante with riskier and riskier moves into junk bonds, foreign stocks and real estate. This reckless pyramiding of pension fund assets is one of the big ingredients in *At the Crest of the Tidal Wave*'s case for a Grand Supercycle-degree peak. In addition to the lack of experience, *At the Crest* argues that the potential for disaster is signaled by the urgency behind the trade:

ASSAULT ON RETIREMENT PLANS

Pension Fund Alert: Beware of the Bear
—Atlanta Journal-Constitution, September 15, 2002

Pension Funds: The Next Crisis?
—Dallas Morning News, September 23, 2002

Pension Funds Not Immune to Bear Market
—The Los Angeles Times, September 22, 2002

RETIREMENT AT RISK
—The American Prospect, September 23, 2002

> Today's pitifully uninformed investor, who insists he cannot abide anything less than a double-digit return on his investments, has proclaimed, "Give me yield...and give me death!" For the promise of a high yield, either by coupons or by capital gain, he has bought stocks, which will fall 90%, he has bought municipal and junk bonds, whose issuers will default, and he has bought second and third world stocks and bonds, the perceived value of which hardly in fact exists. To some degree, these are acts of desperation over declining CD yields, weak household finances and fear of future costs of college and retirement. Acts of desperation by the unknowledgeable usually result in far greater catastrophes than they thought they were facing before they acted.

Another theme that Schwager's subjects continually return to is that trades motivated by anxiety or need are almost always doomed from the start. As super trader Paul Tudor Jones says, the most important thing for the average trader to focus on is protecting what they have rather than making money. Obviously, this is even more important when it comes to retirement assets. But the one-way rise of the 1990s has robbed many pension fund holders of any selling instincts. This is why the response to an average hit of 50% in so many pension fund portfolios has been so extremely passive.

These media accounts represent the sharp snap of the pension fund trap springing shut. Suddenly, those who have held on for so long are realizing that they can no longer afford to retire. Every day brings another story about a huge reversal of retirement fortunes. Since the end of 2000, Delta Air Lines' pension fund has swung from a surplus of $1.14 billion to a deficit of $2.36 billion. Since 1999, General Motors' fund has gone from a $7 billion surplus to a $9 billion deficit. The growing list extends to municipalities and states, which are already reaching into taxpayers' pockets to fund spiraling shortfalls. Some stories reveal that the losses will weigh on profits just as they drove them higher in the bull market. This flip-flop to an "enormous weight on growth" is exactly what EWFF said to expect when the surpluses were pumping up profits in October 1999. The September 20 issue of The Economist says, "Governments are not the only ones feeling the strain over the rising cost of pensions. Falling stock markets are increasing the pressure on companies' pension schemes. Only a rebound in equity markets or an increase in the retirement age are likely to bring relief."

The implausibility of relief is signaled by a shift in pension fund management that is supposed to be the "good news" for many corporations. Over the course of the last 20 years, companies have established 401(k) plans that place the money management responsibilities in the hands of retirees. In passing these duties on to their employees, many companies have continually counseled the importance of staying in the market for the long haul. Most pensioners have followed this advice. This comment from a production manager for Business Week magazine reveals the impotence pensioners feel in the face of falling prices: "I know things could change, but if they keep going this way, we'll be eating cat food in our golden years." As the media onslaught intensifies, some will finally abandon the buy-and-hold ideology. But since they have no idea how to cut their losses efficiently, they will take their cues from one another and thus contribute mightily to the nightmare that they so dearly wish to avoid.

December 2002

Bull Market Machinery Breaks Down

Two months ago, EWFF said the pension fund trap was "springing shut." Since then, Merrill Lynch has warned that 98 percent of the 346 companies in the S&P 500 that offer defined-benefit pension plans will find their plans underfunded by the end of this year, pension funds have become the "hot-button" accounting issue that will be a drag on earnings for years (just as the EWFF suggested in November 1999), and the state of New Jersey is suing four public companies for more than $150 million in state pension system losses. The suit will take the finger pointing EWFF has been chronicling since the outset of the bear market to a whole new level, but we can also see that the wave of recrimination still has a way to go. No one has yet noticed that the amount New Jersey is suing for is just a small fraction of the $20 billion New Jersey taxpayers have lost over the past three years. In the third quarter alone, the state lost $6 billion. By the end of the decline, the pension funds themselves will be under the gun for being in stocks in the first place, not to mention staying exposed to them as the market spiraled relentlessly lower.

The long-term repercussions of the bear market's devastating impact on pensions are finally starting to register among pensioners. A front-page USA Today article says, "Un-retirement is under way, with many seniors putting together resumes for the first time in decades and heading back to work." When counselors at a senior citizens' expo set up a job placement booth, they were amazed at the crush of retirees that lined up for advice. Most are heading back because they got "blind sided" by the stock market declines.

In a related miscalculation, annuities with investment guarantees based on the performance of the stock market are turning out to be far less than the industry "saviors" they were claimed to be. "Given what we now see the market can do," an actuary says, insurers who earlier were inexplicably blinded to 300 years of stock market history, are eliminating the product from their sales mix. CIGNA Corp. will take a loss of $720 million stemming from "its failure to take into account a steep stock market decline." "CIGNA guaranteed benefits while expecting the stock market to continue to rise." The error behind these expectations is apparent across the breadth of the insurance industry. This is an important counterpoint to the spring of 1998 when Prudential Investments, the nation's biggest mutual life insurer, said it had no choice but to go public. The March 1998 issue of *The Elliott Wave Financial Forecast* reported, "An offering will give its agents something to sell: Prudential stock. 'In dangling the prospect of a share distribution to customers, Prudential is giving its demoralized agents a powerful marketing tool.' Other big mutuals that combine for hundreds of years of rock-solid financial performance have no choice but to follow Prudential into the stock market." Prudential's offering spanned the breadth of the topping process. It was finally completed in December of last year, just weeks before the rally ended in the S&P. In recent months, Prudential tried to sell its brokerage unit. After failing to find a buyer, it has initiated layoffs. So far, 5% of the firm's staff has been let go. Brokers say the cuts are just a sign of what's to come.

The decline in stock-based annuities, pension fund stock market allocations and insurance company involvement in the stock market all show that long-term structural support is being torn away from the stock market. History shows that there is lots of room for further reductions. In 1950, the end of the last Supercycle-degree bear market in inflation-adjusted terms, notes Bob Djurdjevic of Annex Research (http://www.djurdjevic.com/index.htm), state and federal pension funds were not even allowed to play the stock market. Private pension funds accounted for only $1.1 billion, or 1% of the total value of U.S. equities. In the third quarter of 2001, pension funds accounted for $2.7 trillion, or 20% of U.S. equities (12% private, 8% government). When the bear market is over, pension fund involvement in the stock market will be closer to the levels of 1950 than 2001.

Another bearish sign is that fund managers are still convinced that the decline to date is the opportunity of a lifetime. The director of Canada's public pension fund says, for instance, that stocks "now present one of the best buy-in opportunities in a century. A falling stock market is a boon to a cash-rich and patient investor" (an extinct species). "In the face of this downturn," says an article, Calpers, the giant California state pension fund, "has barely blinked. The fund recently asserted it would stick with its heavy reliance on stocks — about 58 percent of its portfolio." Ted Benna, the originator of the 401(k) retirement plan, says it is "absolutely wrong" for a person with a 20% loss to sell. "They should be jumping into the market and buying." These confident pronouncements by the scorched stewards of "conservative" investment accounts confirm our bearish wave count. When their guidance proves devastating to many pensioners, these directors will feel the full wrath of a bear market backlash.

February 2003

One of our contentions regarding the rally from the October low was that many investors were making the classic mistake of trying to win back losses with increasingly precarious bets on an imminent rebound. This sentiment became more evident than ever in stories about the rising popularity of hedge funds.

Hedge Funds For the Masses

As Scrutiny Grows, New Breed of Fund Lowers Ante for Individuals
—The Wall Street Journal, January 23, 2003

The Wall Street Journal reports that Citigroup's private banking division is now increasing exposure to hedge funds. "Hedge funds are a good potential diversifier and return enhancer," says the chief investment executive at the bank. Twelve securities firms and mutual fund companies have "put a public patina on the loosely regulated world of hedge funds" by registering new hedge funds with the SEC. "We're moving mainstream," says one fund manager. But even as the interest in hedge funds takes off, performance is so bad that many are shutting down "or being forced to do so." Just one day after it reported the mass discovery of hedge funds, the Journal followed with this story about one of the industry's star performers in 2002:

In 7 Days, A Hedge Fund Lost All Value
—The Wall Street Journal, January 24, 2003

The Eifuku Master Fund "took huge bets with borrowed money on a limited number of trades that went wrong." After recording a gain of 76% in 2002, the $300 million hedge fund lost everything in seven trading days. It's collapse snared "one of the savviest hedge-fund managers" today, George Soros, who reportedly had about $180 million dollars invested with the fund. Most of the bets were leverage plays on Japanese stocks. The Journal noted that the collapse of Eifuku, (Japanese for "good fortune" or "prosperity") "underscores just how thinly traded even the largest shares in the Tokyo stock market can be, making large, leveraged bets particularly treacherous." Maybe, but we prefer to think that the English enunciation of the fund's name stood as an unheeded warning.

> # Wall Street Avoiding Risk, Hah! –Firms Are Making Bigger Bets
> *Securities firms that traditionally have shied away from heavy bets have begun to give traders more money to invest.*
>
> —The Wall Street Journal, March 12, 2003

As the public finally loses faith in mutual funds, it is pushing on to these riskier vehicles. Hedge funds now embody the urge to win it all back with a roll of the dice.

April 2003

It is important to realize that even as the volume of financial news shrinks, it is still dominated by enthusiasm for stocks. Some typical headlines from recent days include: "Wall Street Investors Respond To War With Optimism," "War Brings Back Wall Street Bulls" and "Experts: War Rally Will Be Tough To Derail." These headlines attest to the power of the old bull market. No matter how bad the consequences of the bear market become, the media still can envision a return to the days when stocks only went up. Fortune's latest cover boldly asserts, "AFTER WE WIN" and presents, "The Case For Optimism." CNBC's hottest new show illustrates how the bear market has tempered but not broken the bull market spirit. Kudlow & Cramer is hosted by two tarnished but re-claimed heroes of the old advance. While they point an accusing finger at analysts, company executives and Wall Street research, their central focus never wavers from a conviction that a new bull market is underway.

June 2003

Government Pensions Locking In Losses

On the subject of government and stock market trends, *At the Crest of the Tidal Wave* had this to say:

> The false belief that government can affect trends, i.e., change a bear market to a bull market, often causes people to stay invested in a bear market. However, government does not act; it only reacts, and it is always the last institution to react, because it is the ultimate crowd.

Public pension funds now offer a superb illustration of this principle. Since the start of the bear market, they have actually outperformed their private counterparts, but only because they didn't get as fully invested in stocks by the end of the bull market. Instead of heeding the message of this relative strength, however, the following headline reveals that government-run pension funds have decided to chase the old trend:

Public Pension Funds Will Put More Money Into Stocks

The weight of this bearish signal is magnified by the motivation behind it and the leverage that pension funds intend to use to enact it. The reason that funds are increasing their exposure to stocks is that 79 percent of U.S. public pension funds are underfunded. To bail themselves out, governments plan to issue bonds and buy stocks with the proceeds. A Bloomberg columnist calls the pressure on states and localities "irresistible. When bankers and politicians decide that selling bonds is the thing to do, woe to the critic who gets in the way. He gets steamrolled. The even funnier thing about pension-obligation bonds and those who advocate them is their sense of certainty. Sell the bonds now and you can resolve your pension liabilities."

At the all-time highs, investors couldn't afford not to be in stocks. At the current wave two Dow high, government is feeling the same pressure. Bloomberg's columnist wrongly assumes that the effort will "certainly" benefit the stock market. Pension-obligation bonds reek of a last-gasp bid to save the old stock bubble by marrying it to the debt bubble, which is itself receding. When the ultimate crowd goes into hock to buy stock and bail itself out of a tight financial spot, it can only lead to one thing — the ultimate margin call. Eventually, the effort will surely backfire on the people who buy these bonds, the government entities that issue them and the purchasers of the shares.

August 2003

The IPO market also has the same character as its year-2000 predecessor:

Activity Wave Signals Bull's Return
— Financial Times, July 8, 2003

IPO Market: Hope is In the Air
— The Wall Street Journal, July 1, 2003

The chart of quarterly IPOs reveals that activity is nowhere near the levels of 1999-2000. June took the level of IPO issuance to over $1 billion for the first time this year and the first 15 days of July has put the month on track for the highest total since the middle of last year, when the S&P produced a $7 billion month. July's surge is reminiscent of April 2000, when the monthly record of $14.8 billion followed all-time peaks in the major averages. On a quarterly basis, the chart shows that IPO activity peaked in late 1999, consistent with EWFF's September 1999 forecast for a sharp fall.

At that time, one of the big tip-offs to an imminent termination of the IPO craze was a big push to open the IPO market to the public. In August 1999, EWFF reported, "The once-exclusive domain of institutional and wealthy investors has been pried open by a combination of technology and unrelenting popular demand" and argued that the "successful conclusion of a three-year campaign to get the public into IPOs" was a sure sign

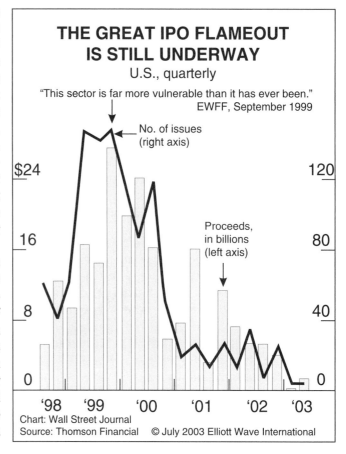

THE GREAT IPO FLAMEOUT IS STILL UNDERWAY

U.S., quarterly

"This sector is far more vulnerable than it has ever been." EWFF, September 1999

No. of issues (right axis)

Proceeds, in billions (left axis)

Chart: Wall Street Journal
Source: Thomson Financial   © July 2003 Elliott Wave International

that the market was ready for a sharp drop. In an analogous development, the latest bear market rally has been capped by a $1 billion settlement that will compensate IPO investors for some of the losses they suffered in the IPO washout of 2000-2002. In exchange for a tiny fraction of the money they lost in the last IPO crash, individuals dropped scores of class-action lawsuits. A few days later, a company called Yell, which had to withdraw the same offer a year ago due to a tepid response, raised $2 billion in its first public offering. This success by the British telephone directory was hailed "as a sign the IPO market is about to make a comeback." Before the bear market ends, the IPO industry should fall into an extended slumber that takes the quarterly totals to near zero for several periods.

A second July surge in the "activity wave" reappeared in "corporate executives' urge to merge." For two days in early July, the M&A business actually regained the glory of its all-time peak as a flurry of big takeover offers were announced: EMC's $1.2 billion bid for Legato Systems; ArvinMeritor's $2.2 billion overture for Dana Corp.; and Yellow Corp.'s $966 million proposal for its larger rival, Roadway.

September 2003

The financial press is using the imperative tense again, i.e., "GET BACK IN" almost as freely as it did in January 2000. Considering the market decline and resulting layoffs that have since transpired at Smart Money, the "STOCKS ARE BACK!" cover is strong evidence that, adjusted for the damage that has been delivered by the bear market to date, investors are actually even more bullish than they were at the all-time highs.

September 2003

December 2003

As the boom-time reverberations clanged still louder in November, the media jumped back on board the old bull with both feet. USA Today expanded its Money Section "coverage of technology, investment and senior management" and even scandal monger Matt Drudge joined in with a series of positive market headlines. Word of the S&P's slight new high on December 1 was accompanied by the most upbeat grouping of Drudge headlines in memory. From the top of his web site, they screamed, "Stocks Jump; S&P 500 Hits 18-Month High, Factories Hum, Construction Booms, Manufacturers Hit 20-year Record Pace."

EWFF has been commenting on the schism between the rising tide of financial scandal and investors' willingness to buy and hold stocks for several months, but the latest wave of mutual fund investigations has raised the dissonance to epic levels. According to one survey, 84% of investors refuse to sell, or plan to buy more, even though 67% of the same group doesn't trust corporate management, 65% doesn't trust auditors and 79% questions the reliability of corporate financial statements. In an article headlined, "Rich See More Risk Everywhere, But Stocks Offer Some Solace," The Wall Street Journal reported that "a real dynamic tension" exists between investors' position in the market and their rising concern about financial security. A story on a similar survey was headlined, "Wealthy Investors Losing Faith in Wall Street." But respondents said that they still "believe there will be positive returns." By strategists' conservative estimates that means a "normal" up year of "10 to 12 percent gains." The survey was called a "powerful wake-up call for Wall Street." Any further advance will only heighten the tension, which means that the real wake-up call will be the torrential stock market decline that comes when investors finally move to align their portfolios with their increasingly "negative attitudes" toward the financial world.

Leaving The Little Guy Out In The Cold

The SEC's cleanup of mutual funds could shortchange small investors

Business Week, December 22, 2003

The Feeling Is Not Mutual

The current mutual fund scandal involves billions of manipulated dollars many that went into the pockets of someone and left the individual investor the poorer. Just when we thought we'd seen the worst, put the bubble behind us, the market had some nasty new surprises.

Once again, the game proves to be rigged. We should be angry. But perhaps we have moved on to the more seemly response: chargrin at our innocence. We are properly embarrassed at our willingness to be seduced by a world we didn't fully understand.

New York Times Magazine
December 7, 2003

The mutual-fund scandal: Guide to what happened

If you own mutual funds, there's a very good chance you've been robbed.

That's right, robbed.

Nobody knows exactly how much was taken. But robbery is, in essence, what the widening mutual-fund scandal amounts to.

Seattle Times
November 23, 2003

The Mutual Fund Scandal: Unfair Fight

Mutual funds were supposed to be the smart, safe choice for small investors. But the latest scandal shows how Wall Street big shots make profits, while the little guys take a beating.

Newsweek, December 8, 2003

March 2004

One More Big Finish For Mutual Funds

Another important area in which the excess of 2000 has been matched or exceeded is mutual fund in-flows. In January, $60 billion gushed into stock and balanced funds, $4 billion more than the previous record month of February 2000, the month between the peak in the Dow (January) and the S&P and NASDAQ (March). The total amount of money residing in stock and bond mutual funds hit $8 trillion, also a record. Mutual funds were the primary vehicle through which the public entered equities in the 1990s and thus are the ultimate symbol of the old bull market. The simple fact that January's demand surpassed the record set one month after the Dow's all-time peak is extremely bearish. What's even more bearish is the complacency that surrounds the surge. After noting that money is now flooding into mutual funds at a "stunning pace not seen since the frothy period of early 2000," one news outlet nevertheless opined, "Investor buying is different this time." The director of a research firm that tracks mutual fund flows insists, "This isn't hot money. Money is going to many places, not to narrow sectors." We would say: many risky places. It is necessary yet always amazing how people are impelled to rationalize manic behavior.

As EWFF has also noted in recent issues, investors' willingness to overlook the scandals that continue to swirl around the fund industry hints at a vast pit of psychological denial. The drumbeat sounds right through to today, as Eliot Spitzer announced another suit against FleetBoston Financial on Tuesday. The firm's managers have been targeted for violations of "the trust that mutual fund investors placed in them." CBS MarketWatch noted that investors were "shrugging off" the "murky business practices at many [fund] companies."

The chart of mutual fund cash levels is an updated version of the one EWFF showed on March 3, 2000, 7 days before the NASDAQ's all-time peak. Our headline read, "Cash is Dead...

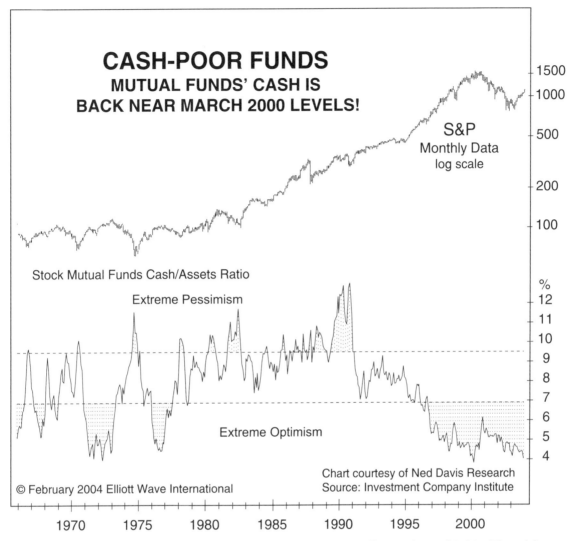

CASH-POOR FUNDS
MUTUAL FUNDS' CASH IS
BACK NEAR MARCH 2000 LEVELS!

S&P
Monthly Data
log scale

1500
1000
500
200
100

Stock Mutual Funds Cash/Assets Ratio

Extreme Pessimism

%
12
11
10
9
8
7
6
5
4

Extreme Optimism

Chart courtesy of Ned Davis Research
Source: Investment Company Institute

© February 2004 Elliott Wave International

1970   1975   1980   1985   1990   1995   2000

Long Live Cash." It was in that month that the ratio hit its all-time low of 3.8%. The old record came in 1972, right before the bear market of 1973-1974. The total lack of any readings above the shaded "extreme optimism" zone on the chart shows that, on a historic basis, mutual fund managers have experienced nothing of the fear that stamps a true long-term low. The latest reading of 4% (as of December 31) is slightly above the all-time low. This predicament combined with the public's indifference to shady fund practices suggests that the latest, near-record-low cash readings will mark the height of mutual-fund lunacy.

How Quickly They Forget

Another direct parallel to the all-time highs is the skyrocketing volume of mergers and acquisitions over the last two months. Since the beginning of the year, deals totaling $370 billion, more than in all of 1999, have been proposed worldwide. Among the bids are Cingular's $41 billion purchase of AT&T Wireless and Comcast's hostile $54 billion play for The Walt Disney Company. Comcast's pursuit of media giant Disney is reminiscent of another big media deal in the month of the all-time high, AOL's purchase of Time Warner. The February 2000 issue used that deal and other signs of excess in the M&A field to call for a downturn in mergers as well as the market as a whole:

A front page headline in Wednesday's New York Times proclaiming "The Day of the Big Deal Is Back" is indicative of a prolonged bear market that is about to make an explosive reappearance. The article from yesterday's Times goes on to say, "With memories fading of the disastrous deals during the last stock market boom, big-time Wall Street deal making is back." Memory loss is the No.1 contributor to stock market loss. That's why we write this stuff down and compare what's happening to what was going on at past market tops.

April 2004

Just as the last breath of air pop's a balloon, the charts below show that financial bubbles of Supercycle degree remain intact until one last inflation. The peak in Supercycle (I) was followed by a great reflation that pushed commodity prices to a multi-year high after stock prices reversed. Likewise, Supercycle (V) has been followed by the biggest surge in commodity prices since the great peak of December 1980. In both cases, commodities rallied to below previous inflationary highs. The chart shows that the basic progression – from two decades of disinflation and mostly rising stock prices in stage ①, to reflation and a scramble into "alternate" investments in stage ②, to an across-the-board deflation in stage ③ – has been developing exactly as it did back in the first half of the 1800s. The best evidence of a turn to the deflationary phase is the fear of permanently high prices that is now swirling through the commodity pits. Within the last few days, the papers have been filled with clamor about "the looming storm" in virtually every commodity: "Get Used to Paying A Lot at the Pump" (Barron's, March 15), "China, Iraq Using Up Steel, Lumber" (Arizona Daily Star, March 15), "Soaring Global Demand for Oil Strains Production Capacity" (The Wall Street Journal, March 22). The potential for a reversal is highlighted by the fact that the man who wrote *Dow 36,000* three months before the Dow's all-time peak and a whole chapter against investing in commodities in October 2002, now says commodities are a solid hedge against uncertainty. In Sunday's issue of The Washington Post, the former poster-boy for Dow 36,000 says, "It's not unreasonable to make at least a small bet on things."

THREE STAGES OF A SUPERCYCLE TREND CHANGE

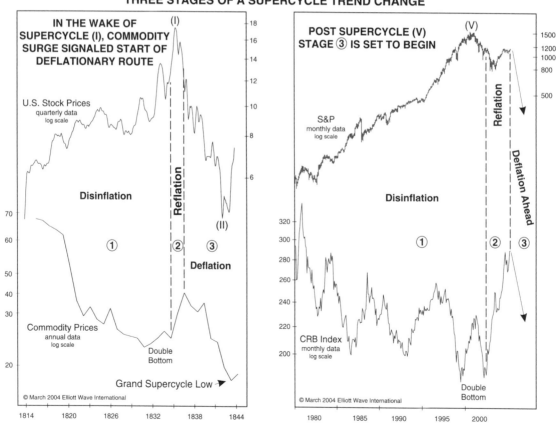

Today's mania for "things" is the modern-day equivalent of the wild commodity spike that came two years after the 1835 peak of Supercycle (I). We have only annual data, so the chart doesn't show its full height, but the history books make it clear that the peak in the 1830s came in February or March 1837. According to *Gotham, A History of New York City*, the reversal was preceded by a march on New York City Hall in which protestors carried signs demanding, "BREAD, MEAT, RENT, FUEL! THEIR PRICES MUST COME DOWN!" The fear of rising prices was so overwhelming that the demonstration devolved into a "flour riot" in which the crowd ransacked several stores. On March 17, 1837, an unexpected fall in cotton prices triggered a broader decline that soon engulfed all commodities, as well as an "overheated real estate boom" and the stock market. So the protestors got their wish, and suffered for it. The Panic of 1837 is a perfect model for the decline that EWFF and *The Elliott Wave Theorist* have been anticipating in wave ③. The failure of a single New York stockbroker in 1837 is said to have triggered the eventual destruction of hundreds more, but the truth is that the deflationary depression of the late 1830s and early 1940s was a patterned response to the two decades of speculation that preceded it, just as it is today.

So far, commodities are the one holdout in Elliott Wave International's call for a "rare alignment" of falling markets. In 2000, the CRB peaked on October 12, a full month after the peak of wave (2). They should be similarly close behind wave ②, also. Several economically sensitive commodities appear to be finishing advances. Crude oil managed to violate the upper limit of the bearish count shown in January, but its pattern continues to reflect a topping process. Base metals, such as zinc and nickel, have topped. Most other commodities should join in. Once they turn, there will be no place left to hide. That loud thumping noise will be the sound of falling brokers and hedge funds that sought refuge from the storm in these highly speculative markets.

The Bull Market in Satire

Back in December 1999, one of the subtle hints of a peak was a sudden uptick in the number of stock market send-ups. The cited example was a spoof of the IPO market from one of the first Internet parody web sites. After recounting the mock public offering by a species of blue-green algae, EWFF said, "The desire for comic relief will expand rapidly in the weeks ahead, so this piece probably marks the start of a whole new genre of social satire." EWFF tracked the first wave of the new bull market in parody with follow-ups in the March and July 2000, March 2001 and October 2002 issues. The start of an even larger wave of social satire is probably signaled by this headline from March 9:

'70s Spoofs 'Wacky Packages' Are Back

'Wacky Packages,' the hot 1970s fad parodying popular household products." "Poking fun at things, making parody, is a long accepted form of entertainment," said a VP of new products at Topps, "one we think transcends generations," just like bear markets. In fact, Wacky Packages have flashed in and out of existence with bear markets for almost 40 years. They seem to express, in a light-hearted way, the public's increasing animosity toward corporations, which EWFF has been tracking since 2000 (see Chapter 3, May 2000 entry). When the tide turns, Jell-O becomes "Jail-O, Sing Sing's favorite dessert," Gravy Train is "Grave Train" and Minute Rice is transformed into "Minute Lice." The product was added to Topps' bull market line of baseball cards in 1967, the year after Cycle wave III topped out. Popularity was limited, as the market rallied in a speculative blowoff through 1968, but when Wacky Packages were brought back in 1973 they enjoyed "booming popularity." After the market bottomed in 1974, demand fizzled and the product was cancelled at the crest of wave ① in 1976. It made brief comebacks in the early 1980s and 1990s, both near stock market lows.

A good illustration of this irreverent impulse is Monty Python's decision to re-release *The Life of Brian*, a take-off on the story of Christ. The movie, which originally appeared in the bear market year of 1979, is being put out "to counter the success of *The Passion of the Christ*." In a darker twist on this emerging cultural tendency to counter itself with lampoons and take-offs, the movie that just replaced *Passion* at the top of the box-office charts is *Dawn of the Dead*, a remake of another bear-market classic from 1979. The movie guide describes the original *Dawn* as a "satiric, metaphorically rich" zombie movie. The original *Dawn of the Dead* was itself a sequel to *Night of the Living Dead*, a horror classic that came out in 1968. EWFF has established in recent issues that the current peak is very analogous to 1968. One movie historian describes the series as a "very powerful image of middle-class America eating itself," which is a pretty good description of what happens in the wake of a mania for stocks.

A USA Today story headlined "Nostalgic Frights are Comforting" says a slew of similar fare is on its way to theaters. As we have noted since the genre first re-appeared in 1999, horror will get a lot scarier and more original before the bear market ends. By the same token, satires are likely to get more irreverent and insightful. In fact, the experience in the wake of the South Sea Bubble indicates that some of the greatest satirical works in history will be turned out in the years to come. The Literary Encyclopedia (litencyc.com) notes that "capital satires" became a popular literary form in the late 1720s. These works included *The Dunciad* by Alexander Pope, *The Beggars Opera* by John Gay and *Gulliver's Travels* by Jonathan Swift. According to the encyclopedia, *Gulliver's Travels*, which is widely considered the high point in literary farce, is "a political satire in which Gulliver's expanding and shrinking dimensions constitute a metaphor for rising and falling markets." Swift, Gay and Pope were all investors in the South Sea Company. One benefit of the great boom and its unwinding is that it will undoubtedly inspire similar great works of amused disgust.

June 2004
John Q. Public Gets a Fair Shake

In July of last year, *The Elliott Wave Financial Forecast* identified the secondary topping process as an echo of the all-time peak. Since then, EWFF has identified no less than 25 characteristics of the latest peak that are direct parallels to the psychology that ruled at the all-time high. According to *Elliott Wave Principle* (p. 77), the calling card of a second-wave peak is a rally that convinces investors that the bull market is back to stay. One crystal-clear similarity is the continuing flood of money into IPOs of dubious worth. Many have no profits, and some aren't even expecting to have a product to sell for another two years. "While the excitement may be reminiscent of the dot-com era," writes a still-credulous reporter, "there are significant differences." The only difference we can see is the stage of the signaled decline. This wave is likely to put a more permanent dent in people's willingness to believe in a free lunch.

Another reverberation from late summer of 2000 is a sudden flood of "opportunities" contending that the playing field has finally been leveled on Wall Street. The September 2000 issue of EWFF recorded that, at the start of (3) of ① down, the little guys were finally given a crack at hedge funds, venture capital and other "forbidden fruits" of the investment world. Now once again, formerly inaccessible "deal making" opportunities are being made available to the public. The doors to the "once-exclusive" world of corporate buyout funds, for instance, have suddenly opened wide. According to The New York Times, Kohlberg Kravis Roberts and more than a dozen other titans of the leveraged buyout industry are "tripping over one another in a race to sell funds to the public." Morningstar, a privately held mutual fund research firm that has been unprofitable for four of the last five years, is preparing a public offering. "It looks like some of the company's biggest investors are looking to cash out," says an industry consultant. Something similar happened in 2000. That's when the October issue of EWFF observed a flood of mutual fund sell-offs with "no end in sight."

Google's IPO is being hailed as a similar opportunity by which small investors will finally get access to the "near-exclusive domain of institutional investors and wealthy individuals. Individual investors with as little as $2000 in assets now have a chance." According to an editorial in the nation's largest selling newspaper, the offering will show "Wall Street a Better Way of Selling Stock." "We're in a different world now," a securities law professor told the Washington Post. Google's employment of a "Dutch auction" style initial public offering is totally appropriate. Some have wrongly stated that it brings the financial markets back to the original financial mania because it is the way the Dutch traded tulip bulbs in the early 1600s. But a Dutch auction actually precludes a mania because buyers don't bid prices up; sellers lower offers until they find a buyer. The skyscraper-shaped trading pattern for tulip bulbs in 1637 is evidence that a Dutch auction was definitely not in use. In fact, the Dutch auction, which is how the Dutch sell cut tulips now, was probably employed as an antidote to buying frenzies.

July 2004

Why is the government clamping down on its own mortgage operations when housing is the only remaining engine of economic growth? The answer is found in this quote from *Conquer the Crash*: "The psychological aspect of deflation cannot be overstated." As EWFF pointed out in November 2002 when the crackdown on Fannie and Freddie was starting to mount, the government is doing exactly what it did at the end of Supercycle (I) in 1835 when it "turned off the spigot" by eliminating the first national bank and tightening credit to effectively end another easy-money era for real estate. This is also a Grand Supercycle peak, so it has taken longer, but the backlash against the mortgage giants is building in the form of Congressional, Federal Reserve and Bush administration demands for greater financial disclosure and constraints on Fannie, Freddie and their counterparties. In the latest issue of Business Week, the governor of the St. Louis Fed admits that Freddie Mac and Fannie Mae "expose the economy to systemic risk" and that "the problem is going to be greater going forward." The European Central Bank has already eliminated its holdings of bonds issued by Fannie and Freddie and urged other European banks to do the same. Reform efforts "lost steam" last fall as the countertrend rally approached its 2004 peak, but as the market reverses, the nation's mortgage books will be pried open, and the conservatism cited above will finally derail the home-loan gravy train.

According to the stock market, Fannie Mae's been a bad investment since December 2000 when it peaked at $89.38 a share. Despite the 45-year low in interest rates and the biggest mortgage explosion in history, Fannie Mae's stock price has already declined by more than 20%. It may survive the bear market, but probably not without a complete round trip to $1 a share, which is where it was at the beginning of the bull market.

August 2004

One sign that the next phase of the reverse process of demolition is underway is the fall in viewership at CNBC. "In recent months," The Salt Lake City Tribune reports, "ratings have deteriorated so relentlessly that CNBC, which was the top-rated news-information network in the daytime hours just four years ago," is reaching outside the stock market for its programming. The network that capitalized on the increasingly insatiable appetite for financial information in 1983 and had ingrained itself in the culture at large by 2000 is trying to lure viewers with talk shows featuring a comedian and a former tennis player. In a fitting acknowledgement to what's ahead for Wall Street, both shows are bombs. The network's plummeting fortunes are attributed to "lost interest in the stock market." Ironically, CNBC's ratings could spike one last time as the next wave of selling reaches fever pitch. With investors' underlying apprehensions confirmed, however, CNBC will probably be de-listed from millions of living-room channel changers. Many will go to their graves with nary a glance back at the station's once-ubiquitous ticker.

October 2004

The Pension Wind Reverses

Remember back in the bull market when pension funds were considered to be overfunded and corporations were using the surplus stock gains to pump up their earnings? And whatever happened to the rising wall of baby boomer retirements that was supposed to drive stock prices higher until at least 2008? In late August, Alan Greenspan blew the whistle on the pension "miracle." According to one account, the "most famous economist in the country put out a red flag" and declared that "increasingly stark choices" must be made to avoid a boomer-induced meltdown. "We must recalibrate our public programs." The President and Treasury Secretary parroted Greenspan with compatible public statements.

The following clips show that Greenspan's comments were just the leading edge of a wave of agitation over "pension woes" and revelations about the Pension Benefit Guaranty Corp.'s wobbly finances. With the government's pension insurance fund already running a deficit of $9.7 billion and the airline industry on the verge of raising its obligations by another $31 billion, the threat of "one or more generations retiring in poverty" looms. On September 14, the agency's former economist called the fund "the ultimate Ponzi scheme" in The New York Times. His projections show that the Pension Guaranty Corp. will go under even if the airlines don't. This inevitability is explored in Chapter 11 of *Conquer the Crash*, which includes this excerpt:

> In Argentina in recent weeks, the government suspended state pension payments to 1.4 million retired state employees. It had no money to pay because times got tough, and it had never saved when times were good. The same thing could happen to many governments around the world, whether national, state or local, which pay billions of dollars annually in pensions. All of them are dependent either upon wealth transfer or upon managed funds that may or may not be properly invested.

March 2002

> Then there is the problem of major corporations' unfunded pension plan liabilities. Companies have promised billions of dollars in fixed-income pensions, but their plan assets will fall so much in value that they will have to fund those pensions from their operating budgets. How much of those liabilities will turn into debt is unknown, but the risk is large and real.
>
> **— CONQUER THE CRASH**

September 2004

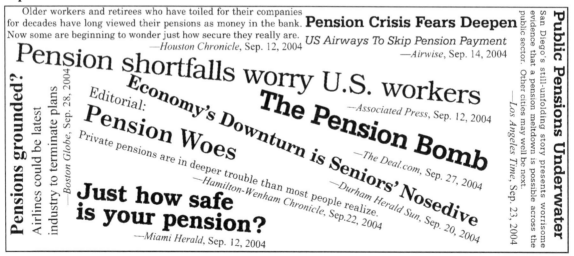

The potential for exponential growth in pension turmoil is clear from the travails of the City of San Diego, where a $1 billion pension fund shortfall is finally being addressed. For 16 months, a whistle blower's effort to expose the "ticking time bomb" was ignored. "When people finally started listening, San Diego became engulfed in a scandal that now threatens to push the country's seventh-largest city into bankruptcy." The latest reports reveal that San Diego is "far from unique." In fact, it is widely considered to be a "model of fiscal probity." As more cities which have strayed into exotic and illiquid venture capital and real estate partnerships measure their obligations against their investments, the damages will rise rapidly. Long-time readers should be safely protected already, but you may want to use the emerging crisis as a reminder to review retirement accounts as discussed in Chapter 13 of *Conquer the Crash*. Know everything there is to know about their structure, sponsors and penalties for liquidation. As the depression develops, be prepared to forego any tax advantages for the safety of a rock-solid annuity, government bills or bank account.

Third waves are "recognition" waves in which investors grasp the implications of the dominant trend. Pension-dependent seniors are prime candidates to lead the charge out of stocks because they have more immediate needs and at least some experience with the ferocity of a bear market. The potential for several more years of bear market is no stretch to older investors because they experienced a bear market that lasted from 1966 to 1982. 81% of pension funds are already underfunded, so retirees will probably opt to beat the boomers to the punch and bail out. In an article headlined, "Older Investors Jittery as U.S. Markets Disappoint," The New York Times reports that many "who thought that 2004 would repeat last year's 26 percent rise in the S&P are beginning to face the fact that their expectations will not be met." For the first time in years, there are reports that "some investors may finally be dumping the shares they have held so patiently." In a rare moment of lucidity, a 70-year old Florida retiree confessed to selling a stock: "I just held on too long. I had Lucent when it was up to $62 a share. I sold it at $3." Self-preservation is a powerful, non-rational instinct. The wave count depicts a market that is tightly wound. As a few more investors "face the fact that their expectations will not be met," a chain reaction of limbic-inspired selling should ensue.

November 2004

In a late-breaking sign that the bubble is slipping it's hold, CNNfn, which was launched in December 1995 when "business news was hot," announced yesterday that it is going off the air. At this point the wild speculation is so concentrated that it really is more of a nostalgia wave for the bubble. This impulse was captured in Tuesday's issue of USA Today: "For anyone that misses the late '90s, there's an easy way to get a flashback fix. Check out Google stock."

December 2004

A Note on Hedge Funds

One common misconception in the marketplace today is that markets are awash in liquidity. What they are is rife with hedge fund operators who are not shy about leveraging the dwindling liquidity that still exists to drive markets from normal overbought or oversold levels to historically unheard of overbought or oversold levels. *Conquer the Crash* notes "Hedge funds are only as good as their managers. Some fund managers use huge leverage and can blow up, losing everything on a bad bet." One effect of the countertrend rally has been to populate the world with an overabundance of dangerously inexperienced managers.

February 2005

Another sign of investors' cooling temperament toward risk is apparent in this headline from Monday's Wall Street Journal:

The Wild West of Hedge Funds Becomes Tamer

The great hedge fund boom of 2003-2004 was driven by investors' burning desire for higher returns. Throughout much of 2003 and all of 2004, investors were climbing all over each other to get on board these risky funds, even though in many cases they had very little knowledge of what hedge funds do with their money. In just four years, hedge-fund assets have expanded from $400 billion to $1 trillion. As pension plans, charities, insurance companies and small investors have gotten in, the total number of funds has reached 8000, roughly equaling the total number of mutual funds. According to The Wall Street Journal, it is not unusual for a hedge fund to borrow $4 for every $1 it holds. In recent months, the leverage has been expanded because investors themselves have been borrowing to boost the size of their investments. Eton Park, a start-up fund, epitomizes the craze. The fund, which had a minimum investment of $5 million, raised what appears to be a record total of $3 billion without divulging any details about its trading strategy. Investors must stay invested in the fund for as long as 4½ years or face substantial penalties. With lower reporting standards and regulatory monitoring, hedge funds have been big drivers behind the advances in the commodity, small-cap stock, junk bond, real estate and mortgage markets over the last two years. A study by Greenwich Associates shows just how dominant hedge funds have become in "less liquid markets." According to the study, hedge funds control a third of the junk bond market and credit derivatives and 82% of the distressed debt markets. Many specialize in stocks, but they have moved "into exotic pockets looking for a chance to earn outsized returns." During wave ③ of the bear market, the leverage and liquidity constraints will put intense pressure on these markets. As hedge funds and their investors look elsewhere for cash, all the popular financial markets will be exposed to jarring declines.

April 2005

In other signs of a waning patience with stocks, PBS cancelled Wall Street Week, the original stock market TV show, and the effort to move U.S. Social Security funds into the stock market ran into a "brick wall." According to one account, the wall emerged with a striking suddenness: "The speed with which Bush's Social Security plan was declared 'in danger' and then 'mortally wounded' is surprising. Indeed, the more Bush pushes his plan for private Social Security accounts, the less the public seems to like it." This headline from the front page of the March 23 USA Today explains what's behind the sudden change of heart:

Most Americans No Good at Investing

*When it comes to managing money, studies show that
most Americans don't know what they are doing.*

This represents a departure from the mania-era confidence investors exhibited just a few weeks ago as they poured into the bubble stocks shown by the composite chart (see April 2005 entry in Chapter 1). Back in 1997, *The Elliott Wave Theorist* observed that a big part of what sent stocks soaring in the first place was the public sense of stock market mastery. "Indeed, the professional with a knowledge of history and value is eventually judged as an impediment to success," said EWT. Ironically, the attainment of a proper respect for value and history will cost the public dearly and probably drive them from the market for the rest of their lives.

June 2005
Hedge Fund Hysteria

As the bear market resumes, hedge funds are rapidly assuming the same kind of notoriety that pools and investment syndicates acquired in the wake of 1929. Scary headlines, such as "Markets Shaken By Hedge Fund Rumors," "Hedge Fund Blowout Threatens World Markets" and "Hedge Fund Woes Downplayed," fill the financial pages above accounts that seem to raise more questions than they answer. One story on "Why You'll Feel Hedge Fund Pain" boils it down to this: "In the space of a few hours, an unknown amount of highly leveraged hedge fund money that probably totaled in the billions of dollars went poof!"

Here's a headline that touches on the key point: "Hedge Funds Rush To Sell Assets." The article notes that the movement of prices in "unusual ways caused liquidity in some corners of the financial markets to evaporate." As clients demand their money back, managers must sell even more than the returned amount because most hedge fund assets are leveraged investments. When they can't sell collateralized debt obligations, they have to sell something else, thus the domino effect. As illiquidity spreads, the margin calls rise and selling begets more selling. Thus the stage is set for a classic decline.

Bear Market Revisionism

Here's what *Conquer the Crash* said about captive corporate retirement plans back in 2002:

> If you have money in an employee retirement plan, investigate the rules that pertain to cashing out and decide your next course of action.

In many areas, wave ③ is picking up right where Primary ① left off. With respect to pension funds, for instance, Jane Bryant Quinn reports:

Fresh Worries on Pensions

—Newsweek, May 23, 2005

After United Airlines "dumped its plan" in the largest pension default ever, "a collective shiver went down the backs of 36 million working stiffs," writes Quinn. A similar rush of pension fund anxiety hit in late 2002 when the first leg of the bear market was in force and the media suddenly realized that most firms' pension funds, as well as the Pension Benefit Guaranty Corp., the federal government's pension insurance fund, were underfunded. According to news accounts at the time, many retirees suddenly faced the realization that they were being "unretired." The countertrend rally may have helped re-retire a few, but the March-April drop in stocks has quickly triggered deeper worries about a "pension fund implosion." The Kansas City Star now reports, that the government's pension insurance plan is "going broke" and will need a savings and loan type bailout. Of course, it grossly underestimates the scope of the problem, saying, "The agency will run out of money in 2021." The reality is that the PBGC cannot meet obligations to its current pensioners, let alone those of workers from the newly bankrupt firms that are now falling into its paper-thin safety net. As the economy contracts, PBGC will be quickly overwhelmed.

Government: Enforcing the New Mood

Right after bull markets of at least Supercycle degree, when it is time for rampant speculation and credit growth to stop, history illustrates that government is very good at slamming on the brakes. The South Sea Co. is a good example. Four days after the South Sea Co. peaked at just over 1000 pounds per share on July 8, 1720, *Extraordinary Popular Delusions and the Madness of Crowds* tells us that England's Lord Justices dissolved "all the bubble companies."

In 1836, a year after the completion of Supercycle (I), an epic era of speculation closed with the shuttering of the Second Bank of the United States, which had helped finance the preceding boom. A host of other lending practices that financed the boom were also banned. According to Fred Foldvary, a professor at the John F. Kennedy School of Management, "On May 29, 1837, the Illinois banks suspended specie payments, backed by a special act of the legislature. It became impossible to borrow money on real estate or to renew existing loans." The panic of 1837 followed. Then in August 1929, a few weeks before the peak of Supercycle III, the Federal Reserve raised the discount rate to 6%, nearly doubling its level from 20 months earlier.

This time, government is attacking the bubble with a variety of different measures. In addition to a dramatic tightening of short-term interest rates (the Fed Funds target rate is up 200% in less than a year), the U.S. government is pursuing deep cuts in public housing. According to The New York Times, the changes could result in "one of the biggest cuts since Washington began subsidizing housing." A sweeping new bankruptcy law that will "make life harder for debtors" takes effect in October. The change is the first revision of the bankruptcy code since more lenient standards were enacted in 1978, near the beginning of the bull market. In response, major credit card companies just doubled the minimum monthly payment from 2% to 4%.

In another clampdown on two of the government's most powerful bull market financiers, the White House now backs limits that "could substantially reduce the size of Fannie Mae and Freddie Mac." The measures are "part of an accelerating push to shrink the size and influence of the mortgage companies." According to one independent assessment, the latest U.S. Treasury proposal will turn Fannie and Freddie into "shadows of their former selves." Another key source of leverage that is suddenly being targeted by authorities is the sub-prime lending industry, which enjoyed a five-fold volume increase from 2000 to 2004. New York attorney general Eliot Spitzer announced in late April that sub-prime lenders are the object of his latest investigation. The Federal Reserve is also instituting new disclosure rules for issuers. The changes are designed to "Flush Out Discriminatory Rates," but our bet is that they will mark a complete flush of the "sub-prime" home loan industry. When "it's time," the herd changes course, and government is more a part of the herd than any individual.

August 2005
Hedge Fund Considerations

> In 1927-1929, banks formed affiliates for the purpose of exploiting intensively the diverse opportunities for profit associated with successful stock operations. The additional gains which accrued from guiding the price upward dulled the bankers' realization of the danger in such tactics. Though the operation was obscured by the complexity of the process, the bank was actually engaged in stock rigging. It was easier to advance further sums to assure the success of the venture, than to write off an initial loss. Before the bank officials realized the situation, they were so heavily committed that retreat was impossible.

This quote is from the chapter on "Pool Operations" in *Ten Years on Wall Street*, which came out in 1932, three years after a Supercycle degree peak capped a 75-year stock market advance. Five years after a Grand Supercycle peak, which completes a rise of more than 200 years, similar coteries of big money, brains and Wall Street experience are at work in the marketplace. In a fascinating reflection of the higher degree of this peak, however, the size, complexity and range of hedge fund investments is much broader and more complex than those of the pools and syndicates in 1929. Another key difference is that hedge funds didn't peak with the major averages in 2000; they have continued to expand through the first rebound in the bear market.

Due to hedge funds' secrecy about their operations, the exact extent of their "affiliation" with the banking industry is unknown, but it is almost surely commensurate to that of pools in 1929. According to The Banker, a banking industry journal, banks have increased their exposure to hedge funds through prime brokerage services, which includes credit in the form of direct loans and stock, sales and trading on behalf of hedge funds and myriad forms of "proprietary trading" in which they trade directly with hedge funds. Many have also become entwined through direct investment or money management relationships. According to a recent Wall Street Journal exposé on Goldman Sachs and its burgeoning hedge fund/trading business, the firm "got more than a third of its stock revenue last year from doing business with hedge funds." Proprietary trading, which is sometimes used as a code word for banks' internal hedge fund operations, now accounts for two and three times the total generated by investment banking. After an extensive study through the early part of 2005, Charles Prescott, managing director of Fitch Ratings, concludes that problems at hedge funds "could lead to the development of systemic risk."

Monday's Wall Street Journal reveals that there are now no less than 8000 hedge funds in existence. "It's impossible to find a name that isn't taken," says the operator of an as-yet unnamed start-up fund. In 1929, *Ten Years on Wall Street* notes that in "the later stages of the bull market" one of the last things to happen was that pools "lost their gains." One actually "closed its book by distributing stock to its members." In the first half of 2005, the hedge fund game appears to have reached the same juncture. The S&P Hedge Fund Index gained just 0.13% in the first half of the year, and three funds "liquidated" in June: Baily Coates, Aman Capital and Marin Capital Partners. Due to a shortfall in trading revenues, Goldman Sachs' quarterly profits fell for the first time in three years.

Some regulators see hedge funds "as beneficial, because they assist market liquidity and can dampen volatility." In fact, this was Alan Greenspan's position as late as May when the Financial

Times reported that he "extols the hedge funds' ability to make markets more efficient." In June, however, Greenspan suddenly changed his tune. In an address to the International Monetary Conference in Beijing, he stated, "Most of the low-hanging fruit of readily available profits has already been picked by the managers of the massive influx of hedge fund capital." "To hear from Mr. Greenspan, hedge funds are headed for a fall," reported the June 10 issue of The Washington Post. The market was unfazed by these remarks, as the Dow rallied a couple hundred points over the next week. In mid-July, Greenspan offered an even more pointed assessment: "Risk takers have been encouraged by a perceived increase in economic stability. History cautions that the long periods of relative stability often engender unrealistic expectations of its permanence and, at times, may lead to financial excess and economic stress." Again, the market rallied.

During the crash of 1929, the editor of The New York Times noted that the "surrender of the professional pools, though they believed their positions to be impregnable," contributed greatly to the "successive convulsions" of the crash. He added that it was, however, "only proportional to the duration and extravagance of the period of illusion." By this metric, the ensuing fall should outdo even that of 1929.

Ever-More-Exotic Tools of the Trade

As EWFF noted in May, a derivatives fiasco is likely to play a big role in the next phase of decline. In July, the New York Mercantile Exchange announced a new financial instrument that is so purely speculative that it may well mark the highwater mark for derivative "innovation." The NYMEX now offers "same-day options" in natural gas and crude oil. Each morning's option buyers can bet on what they expect the near-month settlement price to be at the end of the trading day. As Howard Simons at Bianco Research puts it, "The person who convinced the CFTC of the commercial need behind such an option is very underpaid." Oil equities, shares of stock that trade based on the price of oil, opened on the London Exchange yesterday. The NYMEX and Philadelphia Stock Exchange are also developing similar "securities" that will trade based on the value of other commodities. Even commodities are equities now!

September 2005
Hedge Fund Considerations

Suddenly, all the growth in the hedge fund industry is concentrated in one of two camps of investors. One camp is "growing impatient" with slight returns and "starting to demand that managers take on a little more risk to boost returns." A story headlined "Make My Investment Riskier, Please" describes this group as "investors who think that under all circumstances, higher risk equals higher return." The other camp is even more antsy — it wants its money back. After $400 million turned up missing at a Connecticut-based hedge fund, the August 29 issue of The Wall Street Journal labeled the situation, "Hedge Fund Havoc." "What we're now seeing is an increase in what could be called hedge fund fraud," says a lawyer in the New York Times version of the same story.

The discovery of illicit activities in the hedge fund industry marks its advance to the same breaking point that hit the accounting and Internet industries in mid-2000. At that time, EWFF cited the emergence of the first wave of market scandals as confirmation that the bear market was underway. As we explained at the time, scandals break in the wake of a mania as participants snap out of their compliant trances, look critically at their holdings for the first time and begin channeling the negative emotions of a falling social mood toward the entities in which they were formerly so enthralled. After the collapse of the Internet stocks, everyone wondered how "people who should have known better bought into the lie." The same wonder is being expressed today as big money investors with exclusive access to hedge funds (at least until very recently) bought into even bigger lies. Well-organized pockets of investment capital, like the investment syndicates of 1929 and the hedge funds of the late 1990s and 2000s, appear to be able to facilitate the formation of multiple extremes at the end of bull markets of Supercycle degree and higher.

Some of the reasons noted so far are the extraordinary leverage employed, targeting of specific issues and sectors, and hedge fund managers' extraordinary inclination to herd.

Another factor is their ability, due to an almost complete lack of oversight within the industry, to flat-out lie. According to the suicide note of a principal in the latest hedge fund blow-up, his firm's fraud dates back to 1998, when the long-term topping process started. The managers of the fund probably didn't expect to lose money. But once they did, they took full advantage of lax regulations and stayed in business by simply claiming a profit and paying those who wanted out with the money they got from those who wanted in. Thanks to the Grand Supercycle peak and its aftermath, money continued to flood in. Wisps of the old fervor were revived, but an overall waning effect is visible in a dramatically reduced speculative frenzy. Here's another headline from a July 30 Washington Post story that suggests a turn from bull to bear:

Fraud Invades Booming Housing Market

The scandals in both areas should go much deeper than anyone now imagines.

October 2005
Hurricane Force Complacency

Ironically, as one of history's greatest financial storms continues to build, investors are ditching CNBC for the Weather Channel. The following headline records the investing public's obsession with Mother Nature:

Stock Trackers Become Master Storm Trackers

According to the September 20 article, "Investors are becoming more cognizant of the impact of the weather" and have an "intense demand for weather related insights." But from August 26 when the National Weather Service first warned that Katrina was a "potentially catastrophic and life-threatening" storm and a possible "direct strike" on New Orleans through September 12 when the full extent of Katrina's impact was known, the Dow Industrials rallied almost 300 points. When all was said and done, Katrina and Rita accompanied a decline in oil prices and a rise in the Dow Jones Property and Casualty Insurance index. Home Depot, reputedly one of the primary beneficiaries of hurricane rebuilding efforts, fell more than 5%. So, as past issues of *The Elliott Wave Theorist* have noted, the divinely-favored investor with perfect foreknowledge of these events would have been foiled once again by a market that refuses to heed the laws of external cause and effect.

Another irony is that much of the financial news coverage focused on buying the pockets of perceived opportunity created by the storms. In a healthy bull market, the looming potential for massive loss probably would have shaken out weak hands with at least a quick washout. The effort to capitalize immediately on the supposed bright side of the catastrophe reflects a historic fearlessness that is anything but healthy for stock prices.

Self Esteem Heads for New Lows

Editorial page cartoonists, along with a small handful of astute stock market technicians, are probably the only commentators to offer anything close to an accurate depiction of the folly that has ruled the financial world over the last 10 years. Way back in 1997, *The Elliott Wave Theorist* noted that they were the only social observers blurting out the emperor-has-no-clothes nature of the rally in stock prices. In February 2000 when the major U.S. averages were within a month of their all-time peaks, so many cartoons focused on the bubble that EWFF added, "At this point, the message is extremely bearish, as popular cartoons like Doonesbury have been covering the mania on an almost daily basis." The sketch shown here from Bruce Beattie of the Daytona Beach News Journal shows that a few cartoonists continue to capture important

aspects of the experience that are lost on almost everyone. Like several other cartoons,
it makes the connection between the bubble
in real estate and the ongoing mania for
stocks. Another shows a fat woman, labeled
"real estate," admiring her reflection in a
mirror marked stock bubble and proclaiming, "Better." Cartoonists are the only social
visionaries to connect the dots because their
job is to capture the essence of a situation,
and there is no way to do that without coming to the simple conclusion that the big bust
is still to come.

By Bruce Beattie, News-Journal, Daytona Beach, Fla., Copley News Service

As EWFF noted near the all-time high
in 2000, the bear market is really just a reality wave that will destroy the illusions of the mania
phase. The decline in 2000-2002 started at the top of the corporate ladder and brought many CEOs
down from stratospheric levels of personal power and prestige. One former CEO/ex-con who now
lectures business school students on ethics describes the herding pressure of the "New Era" as a
world of "relative morality" in which "'Everyone does it' became the mantra. His advice to future
business leaders: Don't let success inflate your ego." The contracting force of the next bear phase
is penetrating more deeply. A story from an early 2005 issue of USA Today, "Yep, Life'll Burst That
Self-Esteem Bubble," shows that it has already infiltrated the U.S. educational system. The article
says the tide has turned against easy A's and "phony praise." Now "overpraised" kids are being
"stunned by criticism." "In college and the workplace, observers are watching them crumble at
the first blush of criticism." Obviously, the root cause of the breakdowns is the bull market, as
the "feel-good movement" started more than 20 years ago when "raising self esteem became a
national concern." Educators can actually pinpoint the beginning of the feel-good generation,

as those "born in 1982 and later," the same
year the Dow Jones Industrials soared past
1000 for the first time. A neuropsychologist
likens some students "to tiny bubbles—on the
surface they seem secure and happy, yet with
the least adversity they burst." Don't worry
about the kids, a bear market is the very best
antidote to an "inflated sense of self."

Listen closely and you can almost hear
the hot air of the bull market hissing away
across the breadth of society. In the boardroom, schools and the profession of baseball,
where steroids and other performance-
enhancing substances pumped up the game,
a face-the-music mindset is grabbing hold.
"Reality Can't Be Altered Or Ignored," says

a headline from the political front. One of the best examples of the unfolding reality and its
potential is expressed by changing perceptions of the federal government. With the situation in
Iraq spiraling out of control and an ineffective hurricane relief effort in the wake of Katrina, the
cracks in one of the biggest Grand Supercycle degree icons are already starting to show. All it took
was one quick spike in the level of catastrophic losses to push people's belief in the government's
ability to bail out victims to the breaking point. In the next phase of decline, the crises will come
so fast and furious that the social safety net established at the end of the last Supercycle degree
bear market will be in shreds so fast that emergency relief will not be possible.

November 2005

Refco's collapse is the prototype for the new order on Wall Street. It certainly shows how fast the fallout from bear market psychology can change things. In just one business week, from October 10 to October 14, Refco, a world leader in the market for derivatives, went from a "$4 billion stock market darling to carcass." Within another week it became apparent that Refco's bankruptcy meant that, sadly, investors in some funds, such as Rogers International Raw Materials Fund, "won't be able to get their money out anytime soon." This is why *Conquer the Crash* continually urged readers to "arrange your finances and your life in order to survive the depression." Cash and only the most secure cash equivalents are the priority now because, in the whirlwind of a deflationary collapse, seemingly reliable financial entities with no connection to a given financial firestorm will get burned just the same in the blink of an eye.

But even as the flight of Refco clients evokes a memory of depression-era bank runs, and as a federal investigation expands rapidly to "auditors, underwriters, lawyers" and other Refco officials, "vultures are picking over Refco the way hyenas gnaw on the remains of wildebeest." The hearty appetite for financial roadkill is yet another sign of a peak. In 1998, when Long Term Capital Management collapsed, there were no suitors waiting to buy up its remains. At the September 1998 low, the Federal Reserve was forced to "engineer a rescue" "because it was concerned about possible dire consequences for world financial markets if it allowed the hedge fund to fail." Now there is no such concern, meaning that the market is not at a bottom. Mr. Cramer sums up the prevailing sentiment in Business Week: "Refco was a false blowup. This is not Long Term Capital." He's absolutely right, LTCM's implosion marked a bottom, while Refco simply sets the tone.

February 2006

Hedge Fund Considerations

The Japanese stock market's temporary shutdown at the end of a 6% two-day decline last week calls to mind the following admonition from *Conquer the Crash*:

> Trading systems tend to break down when volume surges and the system's operators become emotional. Do you think the experience will be "smoother" because modern computers are involved. I don't. In fact, today's system is a recipe for an even bigger mess during a panic.

Hedge funds stand to be a main ingredient in the panic. Many didn't even blink when the Japanese exchange shut down with 20-minutes of trading still to go on January 17. Apparently they just see it as a buying opportunity. "Because hedge funds have been big players in Japan, one might expect the trouble in Tokyo would have them yelping in pain. Instead, it has got them drooling like Ivan Pavlov himself was ringing the bell."

A few weeks ago Centrix Capital started limiting customer withdrawals "to keep institutional investors from fleeing." Centrix packages sub-prime auto loans for which there is no liquid market. "The sudden rush for the doors is a result of two of our larger investors needing to raise cash at once, for their own reasons." One of the options being discussed is to pay investors back "in kind" with the loans in its portfolio. This is going to be a sight: "Sorry, Mr. Fund Investor; we don't have your money, but here are some I.O.U.s on used Cavaliers and Focuses in Arkansas. Maybe you can collect. Good luck!" Welcome to the new investment world where bad paper, systemic breakdown and "I'll pay you next Tuesday" will be common themes.

In Germany, Deutsche Bank took "the unprecedented step of freezing one of its so-called open-ended" real estate funds. The $7.2 billion fund was "frozen" on December 16 "to prevent a run." It was the first such move in the 40-year history of property funds in Germany. The closure sparked anger and the threat of lawsuits. This is only the beginning. In addition to the reversal in assets, the wide range in the estimates of the average hedge fund's performance in 2005 hints at another potential problem. The aggregate figure ranges from 2.3% to 9.4% depending on whom you ask and whether defunct funds (which accounted for 6% of the industry in 2005 alone) are included in the tabulation. Business Week says the annual return is only a guess because "some ne'er do well funds might overstate results." With so little oversight and so much pressure building, the predicament of even the most upstanding hedge fund manager calls to mind the Lehigh University sophomore who played second cello in the university orchestra and worked in the chaplain's office. Due to his addiction to poker, he ended up robbing a bank. When panic sets in, history shows that the urge to lie, cheat, cook the books and do whatever it takes to stay afloat seduces many. The first leg of the bear market attests to the scandal-generating capacity of this Grand Supercycle bear market. Temptation will get the best of many overwhelmed hedge fund managers. With more than $1 trillion in assets to manipulate, it should be no small affair. Move over Enron, Tyco and Martha Stewart; the really big scandals are ready to start popping.

Investor Psychology

On January 11, the financial media mill produced a bouquet of bullish pronouncements and conversions. One bullish "Supermarket" op-ed piece in the January 12 edition of The Wall Street Journal marks a re-blooming of a classic theme from the end of the old bull market. The Wall Street Journal hit the same bullish note at several key highs in 1998-2000. Said EWT in 1999, "These intensifying professions of faith in the bull market comprise a long-term sell signal that discloses the extent to which the rising emotional fervor of 1999 has surpassed even that of 1929." In 1929, the WSJ used technical methods to warn of an imminent decline in an editorial titled, "A Turn in the Tide." But the case for still higher stock prices in the current WSJ guest editorial is entirely fundamental. The writer maintains that high profits indicate that the market is "more undervalued than at any time in modern history," echoing an editorial that the paper published in 1999 calling for Dow 36,000. The contrast to William Peter Hamilton's 1929 editorial should go down as one of history's great advertisements for technical analysis.

On the same day, USA Today's editorial page offered the same opinion: "Stock Market Still Is Best Bet You Can Find." A day earlier, the Christian Science Monitor reported, "The stock market is now reflecting an optimism not seen in years," and offered the following assessment from a market strategist: "The stock market hasn't looked this good in a long time." On January 12, one analyst "went from being among the most bearish equity strategists on Wall Street to one of the most bullish," citing economic strength, productivity gains, moderate inflation and demand for machinery from China, all of which have been in place for a decade. So what changed? Nothing, except the analyst's psychological need to give in and get with the bullish crowd. The burst of optimism in January represents a widespread capitulation to the uptrend, which is typical at the start of a long move in the opposite direction.

Pension Fund Follow-Up

An October 2004 EWFF analysis of the pension fund field concluded, "The potential for exponential growth in pension turmoil is clear." A year later, Time magazine and the New York Times concurred that the "day of reckoning" was, in fact, at hand for broken U.S. pensions. The magazines noted that even healthy U.S. corporations were starting to "freeze" defined benefit pension plans. In January, pension fund permafrost set in as IBM, Verizon Communications, Hewlett-Packard and Sears announced the end of traditional pre-set pension benefits.

"Remember that stock I was going to retire on at 55? Well, my retirement age is now 350!"

Unhealthy companies are abandoning pensions altogether, "leaving millions of Americans at risk of an impoverished retirement." Actually, this quote from a Michigan auto worker makes it clear that it is much closer to a reality than a risk: "For guys who can't quite retire yet, all they think about is, 'Boy, give me a chance to get out of here.'" The statement smacks of the desperation and hope that serve as a powerful tonic in the early stages of a bear market. This cartoon is from an early 1970s edition of Changing Times magazine, in the previous era of runaway pension-fund fear. When thoughts of early retirement on the beach give way to fears of having to work in a burger joint for the rest of one's life, stocks can fall further and for a longer time than people now imagine possible.

A transition of pension funds from bull market booster to bear market drag is just what EWFF forecast in 1999. The changeover is all but complete. The New York Times already places the underfunding at a "staggering" $450 billion, and that's with some stocks still rising. To compensate for slowing returns, pensions have recently pushed aggressively into commodities, foreign stocks, hedge funds, low-priced shares, real estate, venture capital and junk bonds, all of the most liquidity-dependent sectors of the financial world. These rash moves will make retirement a nightmare or an impossibility for many people.

March 2006

In a perfect world, everyone would have his own hedge fund, and the stock market would drift higher forever. In the imperfect estimation of this newsletter, however, there are limits to how many hedge funds and how much higher and longer the Dow Jones Industrial Average can rise.

Two more features of the 2000 all-time highs—IPOs and corporate buyouts—are hotter than at any time since. According to Thompson Financial, 2005 was the strongest year for global mergers and acquisition activity since 2000, with $2.7 trillion in deals globally, $1.13 trillion in the United States alone. Business Week says the "buzz" is back in the IPO market; "Hungry investors are making 2006 the busiest year for new issues since the tech crash." The focal points of the latest boom, restaurants, retail and energy stocks, signal the inevitable calamity; they are bull market businesses that are in line for a serious thumping as the next phase of the decline kicks in.

Another parallel to the all-time peak is the appearance of a major financial satire, *Dave Barry's Money Secrets*. This financial advice parody is currently among the best selling business titles. A major financial peak occurs when the delusionary antics of a large-degree fifth wave collide with the reality of a new bear market. It seems to follow that in the shift from up to down,

some of the more absurd bull market ideas about risk and financial management are finally exposed as false dogmas through the less-threatening instrument of humor. We first alerted subscribers to this transitional phenomenon back in December 1999, when EWFF cited a rise in stock market send-ups and stated, "The desire for comic relief will expand rapidly in the weeks ahead." Two months later, EWFF noted the presence of *How to Get Filthy, Stinking Rich and Still Have Time for Great Sex* and *The Trillionaire Next Door: The Greedy Investor's Guide to Day Trading* on Business Week's business book list; we called them signs of a peak. It turned out to be more than a trivial aside, as the NASDAQ started a 78% decline a few days later. Now comes the biggest financial farce yet, a tome in which "Barry lances many preconceptions about finances." Barry's publicity tour offers confirmation that the trance-like, magnetism of the bull market advisor is holding fast. During radio appearances, he says many listeners call to "ask him serious financial questions." A turn must be near because, at this point, investors are so credulous "that even completely idiotic advice sounds reasonable."

Sadly the best advice comes from the one guy who admits he doesn't know what he's talking about: "You still have time to salvage your retirement!" says Dave Barry. "All you need to do is develop some fiscal discipline, develop a realistic budget, avoid frivolous spending, pay off your debts and start putting away a meaningful amount of money each month for the future. Don't be discouraged, you really can do it, if you put your mind to it and use your magic time-travel ring." Yes, the part about the "magic travel ring" is a joke, but isn't it amazing how well the rest of this social satire would have served the average person over the last six years and how they have utterly ignored it?

In some areas, the hues of the latest stock market euphoria are even more vivid now. One peak experience that has carried to historically unprecedented levels is the breadth of commitment to the New York Stock Exchange. After 213 years as a partnership of members, the NYSE will become a publicly traded entity under the ticker NYX on March 7. More than a century of seat-price records tell the story; exchange ownership is valued most highly at major tops. Subscribers were apprised of the link in 1999 when the exchange made its first move toward a public offering, just prior to the bear market swoon in the blue-chips. The success of the latest effort to get the exchange into the hands of the public undoubtedly heralds an even more dramatic reversal. The upcoming volatility explosion will make stock trading go out of style for a long, long time. The survival of the exchange itself will likely be threatened. In a nutshell, the public offering is one of the most bearish imaginable signals.

June 2006

A final corroboration [of a decline] will come with a concerted turn lower in the hedge fund index (see "All the Same Decline" chart in June 2006 entry in Chapter 1). In June 2005, EWFF identified hedge funds as a "key player in the reflation levitation." They are super-organized investment groups with access to vast amounts of leverage. By piling into many of the same markets at the same time, they jam some of them higher. But the following article from May 13 shows that chaos is poised to wrest power from the hedge funds:

Banks Face Vast Losses in Copper Mayhem

The spike in copper prices over recent weeks has left a group of banks and operators on the London Metal Exchange nursing vast losses, raising concerns about the stability of the commodities market.

—The Telegraph, May 13, 2006

David Threlkeld, a copper trader who helped blow the whistle on the Sumitomo copper scandal in 1996, says that hedge fund speculation has driven copper prices way beyond fundamental value. Near last week's peak, things were so out of whack that there was a whopping $5097 per tonne discrepancy between the near-term 3 month futures price ($8875 a tonne) and the April 2011 long-term futures price ($3778 a tonne). "The LME has been seduced by hedge funds, [which have] pushed prices to levels unsupported by fundamentals," Threlkeld said. "The crash could set off a chain of margin calls running through the whole commodities sector. We've got a crisis on our hands, and it is a lot bigger than copper." As we noted last week, at the end of every bubble, the marketplace always seems briefly to glimpse its fate. After the peak of the Great Stock Mania in 2000, other even riskier realms were available to investors. This time, all markets but cash should be locked in decline.

Investor Psychology

Another telltale throwback to the rarefied investment euphoria of 2000 is the commitment of new money to stock mutual funds (see chart next page). The public almost always makes its biggest move into stock funds at tops and subsequently liquidates their positions at bottoms.

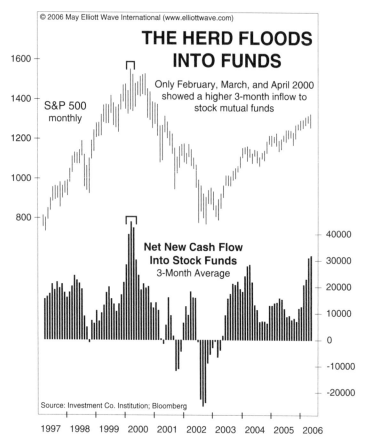

THE HERD FLOODS INTO FUNDS

© 2006 May Elliott Wave International (www.elliottwave.com)

S&P 500 monthly

Only February, March, and April 2000 showed a higher 3-month inflow to stock mutual funds

Net New Cash Flow Into Stock Funds
3-Month Average

Source: Investment Co. Institution; Bloomberg

This is how the herd operates. The chart shows this dynamic in action. The three-month average net flow into stock funds hit $31.8 billion in March, a figure that is higher than every three-month period with the exception of February, March and April 2000, the top of the Great Bull Market. Once again, the public is grabbing the "bag" just in time to hold it through the bulk of the decline.

July 2006
Hedge Fund Considerations

Conquer the Crash provides a great description of banks' "shockingly large exposure to leveraged derivatives" such as futures, options and now "collateralized debt obligations (CDOs)," through which investors lend money to a managed pool of assets, about which they have no knowledge. From 2004 to 2005, CDO issuance increased 60% to $251 billion. "Many banks use derivatives to hedge against investment exposure, but that strategy works only if the speculator on the other side of the trade can pay off if he's wrong," CTC warns. Once the credit bubble stops expanding, CTC contends, deflation will puncture the bubble that supports this complex universe of financial instruments. In the case of CDOs, for instance, the value of collateral will drop precipitously, and holders will find themselves with a shared interest in broken-down factories, pools of defaulted mortgages and/or other "synthetic" CDOs, which will not be worth the proverbial paper they are written on.

There are many signs that the era of financial engineering is approaching its endpoint. The mania-era mindset behind a celebration of speculative abandon is visible in "Hedge Fund Toddlers," a Business Week story about kids "right out of college" giving hedge fund management a try. "Opening a hedge fund is easy: It's just paperwork," says a 30-year old managing partner. The statement reminds us of June 2000, when investment experience was also being shunted aside. We stated then that many investors were "absurdly overmatched" and, borrowing from humorist Dave Barry, faced getting wiped out by forces they did "not even dimly comprehend." With mania-era financial wizardry at the helm of many hedge funds, a bout of wealth destruction seems once again assured, except that now it can happen even faster and to more people at once.

Another screeching alarm is the fact that the public is being drawn into the derivatives game. The June 21 issue of The Wall Street Journal reports that Wall Street is pushing

Complex 'Structured Products,' Long Aimed at Institutions, to Individuals

The article says that individual investors are snapping them up. Well, they snapped up the New York Stock Exchange IPO in March, and the shares have already collapsed more than 40% from their post-offering high. This decline is undoubtedly closely related to the NYSE's drive to do everything in its power "to move further into the lucrative derivatives market." Over more than 25-years of "financial innovation," the separation between issuers, who are intimately familiar with default possibilities, and holders has gotten wider and wider. The passing off of "structured products" to the public shows that they are now completely divorced. A quote from the June 16 issue of The American Banker explains the danger: "By cutting [a derivative] up in so many ways or complicating it by so many levels, do you still have clarity...on the nature of the underlying risk? It's not clear that we haven't gone, in some ways, too far." This comment is from the "dean of derivatives," Louis Ranieri. Ranieri got the ball rolling with the securitization of mortgages at the beginning of the bull market in 1980.

The hedge funds are driving a quick reversal from explosion to implosion in the derivatives industry. Back in September, EWFF observed that hedge funds were in danger due to fund managers' unprecedented use of leverage and the "extraordinary inclination to herd." This predicament made its news debut in a June 22 article in The Wall Street Journal, "Hedge Funds Hit Rough Weather But Stay the Course," which cited the credit and herding issues. The article told the story of two hedge funds, both of which have lost 80% of their assets due to "heavy borrowing" and "so called crowded trades." Apparently, stock markets like that of India, "which were easy to trade when the direction was up, lurched lower in jerks and tumbles in recent weeks as everyone sought to exit." It turns out that "risk models" underestimated "how hard it is to get out when the exits are stuffed with folks trying to do the same thing." According to the Journal, the problem would have been more widespread but "many hedge funds have made it tougher for investors to withdraw money," and Wall Street brokers are not cutting credit lines the way that they did to Long-Term Capital Management in 1998. One of the losing funds borrowed up to six times its available cash in an effort to trade its way out of its predicament.

Banks are hesitant to pull the liquidity plug completely on hedge funds because they are up to their eyeballs in leveraged bets themselves. Michael Hintze, the manager of CQS, a London-based hedge fund, says that banks are "many times more leveraged than we are." Ironically, Stephanie Pomboy of MacroMavens.com notes that bank stocks actually outperformed the market until very recently, largely because of a belief that they had "offloaded all their risks in the great securitization of the last few years." But since the beginning of the year, banks have been gobbling up mortgage-backed securities at a 48% annual rate. And as EWFF pointed out last September, banks are already hugely committed to real estate (43% of assets as of March). In other words, their stocks are a horrible investment right now. Those that may escape the coming derivatives debacle still face a deadly exposure to real estate. Now get this: According to recent reports, the government is disbanding many FDIC bank closure teams due to a lack of bank failures! Socionomically, it can only mean one thing: boom time for bank failures is fast approaching.

M&A Fever and Buy-Backs are Back

Despite the May-June stock slide, companies are busily swallowing each other up. "Merger Monday" is the term that came to be associated with big announcements that would flood the wires every Monday "back in the go-go days of mergers in the late 1990s." This past Monday fits right in with the go-go days as $110 billion in worldwide deals produced the requisite opening pop in the stock market. Tuesday's Wall Street Journal announces,

Blizzard of Deals Heralds New Era of Megamergers

After noting various similarities to the merger frenzies of the late 1980s and 1990s, it concludes, "This is fairly early in the wave." The article adds, "Things are different this time," and the "current boom appears more sustainable than its two predecessors."

Worldwide mergers and acquisitions are on pace to break the record set in 2000 and would do so if the market could hold up all year. Today, "buyers including hedge funds, corporations and private-equity firms all compete to buy businesses rather than build them." In a related phenomenon, corporate buybacks are also running at record levels ($367 billion for the year ended March 31). Like the urge to merge, buy-backs allow corporate officers to express their boundless optimism toward the future even as they reveal that the prospects for their own bottom-line business growth aren't what they used to be. If they were, they would plow capital back into their businesses rather than buy competitors' or their own shares. James Grant recently referred to the last few years as an "Age of Suppressed Deflation." Mergers and buyouts are instruments of that suppression. This fact was duly noted here in our special report on the coming deflation in February 2000: "Much of the early contraction was concealed in the form of corporate restructurings, buy-backs and mergers that pumped up stock prices at the expense of revenues and companies' prospects for long-term growth." In and of themselves, buy-outs and mergers serve no real purpose other than to raise the level of the inverted debt pyramid. Once again, the near panic to "do deals" signals a massive reversal for mergers, buy-outs and the market itself.

August 2006
Hedge Fund Considerations
Everything anyone needs to know about the end of the era of financial engineering is contained in the "lifetime achievement" award that was presented by an alternative investment newsletter to John Meriwether, who founded Long-Term Capital Management and was at the helm when LTCM blew up in September 1998. We didn't mention it last month because we thought it had to be a tongue in cheek honor. Turns out the newsletter was completely serious in recognizing Meriwether for devoting "his life to pushing the envelope of investment strategies."

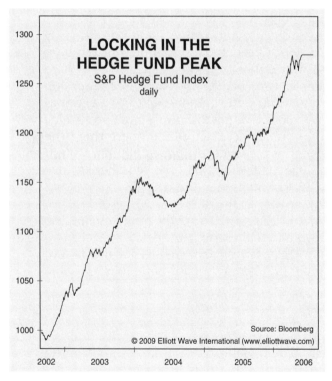

Another illustration of how perfectly positioned the hedge fund industry is for a shocking turn for the worse is what happened to the four-year-old S&P Hedge Fund Index, which we showed in June (Chapter 1, "All the Same Decline"). Standard & Poor's halted publication of its index on June 30 "due to the collapse of the fund that provided data for it." Apparently, establishing prices in the baffling world of hedge funds is so complex (quotes were already delayed by a few days because it took that long to gather "prices") that S&P doesn't even know how to track the sector. In June, EWFF stated that a "final corroboration" of a reversal in the all-the-same market scenario will come "with a concerted turn lower in the hedge fund index." Obviously, now we won't "officially" know when we get that turn. But each day our Bloomberg terminal continues to post the hedge fund price as the 1279.14 all-time high that the index achieved on June 30. It sits there like a monument to the second great craze, the first being so-called "day trading" in 1999.

The move toward increasing hedge fund regulation is evident in the credit markets, where the latest feat of financial engineering is a prolonging of the easy money phase of the credit cycle. Last month, EWFF explained that the reversal to a widening spread between the highest quality U.S. Treasuries and low-grade corporate bonds would probably be happening faster if it weren't for credit-default swaps, which are now widely used as insurance against default in lieu of selling the distressed bonds outright. The July 14 issue of James Grant's Interest Rate Observer

(Grantspub.com) finds more evidence that "a super-accommodative lending environment" has "borrowed time for innumerable bankrupts of the future." According to Grant, many bankruptcies were averted in the first half of the year due to extreme leniency on the part of creditors and hedge funds' "willingness to refinance almost anything." One source discussed a technique that industry insiders call the "loan-to-own strategy." According to this approach, creditors are actually hoping for a default that will transform their debt into equity. "Loan-to-own practitioners assume their new equity will be worth significantly more than the pre-bankruptcy debt," says Grant. Yet equities, particularly riskier ones, are still below their 2006 peaks and spreads continue to widen from the low on May 15 (see July 2006 entry, Chapter 1, top chart). Creditors' assumption about the value of equity despite these ominous signs reveals the boundless optimism that supports the great debt pyramid. Our forecast for the deflating of that optimism that inevitably occurs in a third wave remains intact.

October 2006

In mid-September, the first of what should be many major hedge fund disasters hit when Amaranth Advisors lost $6 billion in bets on natural gas prices. Even more telling than the size of the loss, which was 50% larger than that of Long-Term Capital Management in 1998, is the marketplace's complacent response. A spokesman for the London-based Alternative Investment Management Association calls Amaranth "very much a one-off where the strategy has gone wrong for one individual trader rather than any kind of systemic problem." As fellow newsletter writer Ian McAvity is fond of saying, "When complacency reigns, we all get wet."

Our opinion is closer to that of the FBI, which just identified hedge funds as "an emerging threat." Amaranth's trouble provides a window of what's to come. For one thing, there is the stunning speed of its reversal. In the same week that its meltdown started, the fund's chief operating officer was reporting a net gain of 25% for 2006. Two weeks later, investors "focused on getting what's left of their money out of the troubled hedge fund as soon as possible. But current redemption rules for the fund basically stipulate that it's now up to the firm to decide when to return their money." Amaranth's founder says they can't have it.

Then there's the contagion effect. Reports from the trading floor indicate that once Amaranth realized its predicament, its "traders began dumping large stakes in convertible bonds and high-yield corporate debt, securities that could be sold without disrupting the market." A few old hands now attest to the potential for disaster. Steve Cohen, a "trailblazing star of the hedge fund boom" admitted to the Wall Street Journal, "a rush to the exits could spell trouble. There will be a real decline that may devastate hedge funds that have crowded into the same stocks. Hedge funds are bigger than they used to be. Their positions are bigger. I worry that if everyone were to sell, could we get out?"

November 2006

"Out of the Blue" Hedge Fund Fury

Like "day trading," a phenomenon of the late 1990s, hedge funds are a key instrument of the uptrend that is perfectly positioned for an epic swing from adoration to abhorrence. As EWFF discussed in last month's issue, hedge funds are at the center of the reversal in the all-the-same markets scenario. The emerging tempest in this sector is now verified by the tone of editorial page attacks in newspapers across the country, which warn: "If something isn't done, investors who have nothing to do with funds could pay a hefty price" (USA Today, October 3). The N.Y. Times' version, "Closing in on Hedge Funds," reveals that hedge funds now account for "roughly half of all trading on the New York and London exchanges" and says, "Over the past several years, largely unregulated hedge funds have become a towering presence. It is time for Congress and federal regulators to come up with enforceable rules and laws to ensure the overall soundness of the financial system." A stream of articles reveals the emerging intensity of the media's new passion:

ECB Turns Up the Heat on Hedge Funds
—Reuters Italia, Oct 26, 2006

Investors Dissatisfied with Hedge Funds
—VNUNet.com, UK, Oct 25, 2006

Hedge Funds Can't Escape the Regulatory Spotlight
—Reuters Italia, Oct 19, 2006

The last story begins: "Almost out of the blue, hedge funds are facing a chorus from policymakers for greater regulation. In the space of only a few days, hedge funds have faced calls from those alarmed at potential systemic risks to global markets." The unfolding inquisition is already shaping up as a replay of the scandals that rocked Wall Street after the 1987 crash. As in the late 1980s, insider information is a key element; newspapers and the Securities Exchange Commission are zeroing in on trading irregularities that suggest hedge fund returns may be "juiced by insider trading." Hedge funds offer an added twist but the unfolding scandal cycle will also feature the same leveraged buy-outs (now known as private equity deals), junk bonds and real estate that made Gordon Gekko, Drexel Burnham Lambert and the savings and loan industry famous during the 1987—1990 time period. Of course, this decline is three degrees larger, so the financial disruption should be much, much greater.

As they did with the warnings about NASDAQ stocks in March 2000 and real estate in late 2005/early 2006, investors are happily complying with the advice to ignore all alarms. "Stop worrying about hedge funds," says a financial columnist. "There are so many of them in so many different areas, no single one is likely to rock the boat." The stock market's continued rise in the wake of Amaranth's September blow-up is put forth as the ultimate proof that hedge funds are a self-correcting phenomenon. "The financial market continued to operate seamlessly, without a hint of any sort of systemic risk," says a newspaper commentary that equates hedge fund reforms to "Regulatory McCarthyism," concluding:

> Precisely because of enormous diversity, the investment strategies of hedge funds cannot pose systemic risk. The economy has a fully diversified portfolio of hedge funds. When some do well, others are bound to do poorly because their investment strategies are in no way correlated.

But if the industry is perfectly counterbalanced, how did it balloon to assets of $1.2 trillion in so short a time? This myth ignores the fact that the miraculous growth coincided perfectly with the liquidity bubble of the last five years and the one-way (up) markets of the same period. Then there is the timing of Amaranth's implosion, which was one of several quiet hedge fund shutterings over the last four months. All are direct consequences of the initial downturn in the all-the-same-markets scenario EWFF has been tracking (see Chapter 1). Liquidity is the hedge fund industry's oxygen supply. As the overall contraction continues, hedge funds will do the same. Only then will we see whether the "enormous diversity" poses "systemic risk."

Investors' undeterred hopes for their hedge fund investments signals hedge funds' pivotal role in the current psychological environment. In fact, they are as robust as the extreme expectation that enveloped the stock market at the March 2000 peak. A recent poll of 600 advisors by Morningstar Inc. reveals that 65% expect more than double-digit growth in alternative investments, "every year for the next five years!" This aggressive assumption equals that of mutual fund investors at the S&P's all-time peak and calls to mind this quote from *At the Crest of the Tidal Wave*: "Today's pitifully uninformed investor, who insists he cannot abide anything less than a double-digit return on his investments, has proclaimed, 'Give me yield...and give me death!'" The lack of double-digit hedge fund returns since 2003 signals the potential for even greater damage than the NASDAQ experienced from March 2000 to October 2002. Still, hedge funds attracted a record of $44.5 billion in the third quarter, a total that is eerily close to the record monthly total of $44.4 billion in mutual fund inflows by stock funds in March 2000 (since surpassed).

Financial Chill Spells Economic Winter

It's not yet extensive, but the collateral damage from Amaranth is instructive. According to the N.Y. Times Deal Book, the failure is reverberating in the Greenwich, Connecticut cab trade. "Amaranth's collapse may not have roiled world markets, but it is taking its toll closer to home. For some local taxi drivers, the fund's size and location made it a prime source of fat fares. Now those fares are drying up. The cab drivers' plight is just one small example of how Connecticut's huge hedge-fund industry can affect its larger economy. It may also illustrate why Connecticut's governor has shown such a keen interest in keeping Amaranth's soon-to-be-former workers in the state."

According to recent accounts, the average Wall Street job now pays $289,664 and creates two additional jobs in New York City and one in the suburbs. Panics in 1837, 1873, 1907 and 1929 produced quick turnabouts from economic prosperity to economic crisis. With the U.S. industrial base depleted and even service industry jobs moving off-shore, the fallout from a financial sector implosion will hit faster and strike deeper than in any prior crisis. In a foretaste of the work that's generated by a financial upheaval, Central Taxi's dispatcher says the firm still snags an occasional fare to the offices of Amaranth: "Now I think we're bringing lawyers." Once the lawyers are through, there's never much left.

December 2006

After a summer lull, IPO volume and prices rose furiously in September and October. November is on track to be the biggest month since 1999, the final year of wave V, when stocks peaked in real terms. Bloomberg's index of aftermarket performance for IPOs came within 1% of its all-time high of March 10, 2000. By 1990s standards, however, the participation within the stock market is muted.

Takeovers Pinpoint The Weak Links

Another revealing scene is the folly surrounding corporate takeovers. The current environment is reminiscent of February 2000. When the belief in the bright future of technology so overwhelmed the investment world that Internet up-start AOL purchased Time Warner, the world's largest media company, *The Elliott Wave Financial Forecast* declared, "There are many reasons to suspect that the union will mark the end of the mergers and acquisition boom" as well as the peak of the stock market's overall advance. The dynamic behind the forecast was captured in a series of charts showing a century-long correlation between the number of mergers and each of the big bull markets of the 1900s (see July 2000 entry in this chapter). The chart at right shows the influence of the current rise. Just as AOL's deal focused on the most prized, and vulnerable market sector, the November 20 deals for U.S. Trust, Phelps Dodge and Equity Office Properties focus on

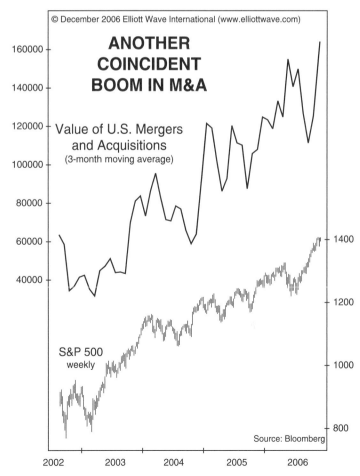

© December 2006 Elliott Wave International (www.elliottwave.com)

ANOTHER COINCIDENT BOOM IN M&A

Value of U.S. Mergers and Acquisitions
(3-month moving average)

S&P 500
weekly

Source: Bloomberg

three centerpieces of the rally over the last four years: finance, commodities and commercial real estate. The purchases push the value of total U.S. mergers to $3.46 trillion, several billion more than 2000's record total. "Unlike the stock driven, tech-merger boom of the 1990s, this one is wide-ranging," says The Wall Street Journal. This difference probably foreshadows the wider breadth of the next decline. Levels of IPO and M&A activity are manifestations of investor optimism and pessimism, similar to the various sentiment measures we regularly discuss. Record deal-making reflects an extreme in optimism, which is a precursor to a record reversal.

Another indicator of the advance's approaching exhaustion is hedge fund managers' response to flat returns: assume more risk. To compensate for their sagging performance, fund managers (says Bloomberg) are moving into "emerging markets once considered exotic," such as the apparently no-longer-exotic country of Mongolia. "Rapid economic growth, driven by copper and gold mining, is attracting investors willing to tolerate corruption and unpredictable regulation." Another article records a "growing interest in 'frontier markets'—so called because it is not even clear that they deserve to be called emerging. Hedge funds have taken to scouring through sub-Saharan Africa." Hedge fund managers' willingness to dig their clients in deeper is truly a wonder to behold.

March 2007

Thomson Financial reports that January leveraged buyouts totaled over $189 billion, the highest January total since the 2000 peak. One money manager calls it "insanity," and the inmates are indeed running the debt asylum now. They will probably try to continue to stretch the boundaries of credit creation to unrivaled extremes even as it collapses in on itself. The use of credit-default swaps is an attempt to avert defaults, which The Elliott Wave Financial Forecast covered in August, is a good example of the "creativity" that debt engineers are using to push the boundaries of the debt bubble further past those of 1720 and 1929. A similar "innovation" in the LBO area is the "payment-in-kind toggle note," which allows the issuing firm to defer payment on a bond until it matures, when it must pay in full at a higher rate. With the help of the PIK Toggle, companies are issuing debt "without the usual terms that require them to meet certain performance metrics to avoid defaulting." In other words, dying companies can put off the inevitable by canceling payments. The PIK Toggle is a monument to what mania-era financiers have accomplished with OPM, other people's money.

As long as confidence remained robust and investors are convinced that the underlying economy is growing at a strong enough rate to bail them out, the debt bubble could expand ever larger. But there are now definite signs that such convictions are waning. Suddenly, the credit default markets in the U.S. and Europe are contracting, and prices for the assets are crashing. "We're seeing a repricing of risky assets," says a European bond manager. Fears of "further contagion" are spreading fast. Right before the latest financial tumult hit on February 27, the same firm that lit the fuse on the last LBO washout, Kohlberg Kravis Roberts, announced a "record" transaction, a $45 billion offer for Dallas power producer TXU Corp. The deal is being done with just $8 billion in actual equity (as if a billion was something to sneeze at). A similar KKR deal for R.J. Reynolds Tobacco Co. was the ill-fated lodestar of the original LBO craze in 1989.

May 2007
At the Pinnacle of the Great Pyramid

We know from the "pool operations" of the late 1920s that it is possible, near the end of the very largest bull markets, for bank-backed affiliates to create large pools of capital and employ very complex financial instruments and schemes that spin outsized investment returns as they seem to guide the markets higher. As The Elliott Wave Financial Forecast noted in August 2005, the only difference this time is that "the size, complexity and range of hedge fund investments is much broader and more complex than those of the pools and syndicates in 1929." But even the miracle of modern debt financing will encounter limits.

One limit is now apparent in the housing market. Last summer when the industry's bust was still under the radar, many claimed that the situation was not serious because the industry's high levels of securitization, i.e. the ability to package loans and sell them, meant that the risks were widely spread and thus less dangerous. But our contention was that the "innovation" was more likely to broaden the impact of decline, not contain it. In July of last year, when the public was being drawn into the market for these complex structured debt products, EWFF noted that the "separation between issuers, who are intimately familiar with default possibilities, and holders has gotten wider and wider. The passing off of structured products to the public shows that they are now completely divorced." We also offered the following quote from the "dean of derivatives," Louis Ranieri: "By cutting [a derivative] up in so many ways or complicating it by so many levels, do you still have clarity…on the nature of the underlying risk? It's not clear that we haven't gone, in some ways, too far."

Nine months later Ranieri answered his own question when he told the audience at the Milken Institute Global Conference that, for the first time in history, the median home price in the United States is likely to decline in 2007. He added that rather than mitigate the fall, securitization will likely compound losses because there will be greater difficulty in working out defaults. He said that the vast majority of problem loans are securitized, as opposed to individual portfolios in past credit crises. Instead of a single lender, there are now many, many interests in most mortgages. This means that more parties must comply with the terms of each default. The May issue of EWT notes that as the decline gathers steam, this will slow down decision making enough to turn even a mild recession into "systemic disaster." In this way, the financial engineering that pushed debt levels, valuations and investor optimism through the roof on the way up reverses and will foster an atmosphere of rising caution, falling prices and ill will.

Derivatives' transitioning role from intensifying the effects of the rise in house prices to multiplying the pain of the descent is now being recognized because the downturn is well developed. Yesterday's Wall Street Journal fleshes out critical differences between the way many structured products traded on the way up and the way they may or may not trade on the way down. When prices fall hard, liquidity disappears and even the people that make the right directional bet lose out. In the first quarter of 2006, for instance, many hedge funds that positioned for the rising cost of protection against mortgage defaults "underestimated the sticky nature of these that can trade infrequently due to the complexities in valuing them." Says a fund manager, "It looks like a great trade but it isn't a profit if you can't get out. Investors had a naïve belief in liquidity thinking just because you buy it, you can sell it. The person who thought this was like trading equity futures is extremely angry."

Many other financial instruments are primed to grease the skids. One ticking time bomb is the ballooning market for Collaterized Debt Obligations (CDOs), through which corporate debt is sliced up and distributed as securities of various grades, from triple-A through double-B-minus and unrated junk. As James Grant notes in his latest dissection of the debt debacle (Grantspub. com), the trouble with these tranches is that banks must allocate substantially more capital for lower grade CDOs. Whereas triple-A paper requires a capital allocation of .6%, a Double-B-minus requires a 52% allocation. So, as the economic contraction starts to bite, the downgrades that inevitably follow will create a massive ripple effect as banks are forced to raise capital. "To us," says Grant, "this sounds like a setup for the mother of all margin calls." Considering the size of the developing economic contraction and the exploding popularity of CDOs, this strikes us as an understatement.

Another focal point will be the private equity phenomenon, which continues to build. Private equity is perfectly positioned to become the whipping boy of the next bear market. For one thing, private equity deals rely on tightly knit syndicates that have a long history of catching the eye of the Justice Department in bear markets. After the last Supercycle decline, in fact, figurative lynch mobs pursued investment banks for similar practices until well past the end of the Great Depression. Bankers didn't slip out of the noose until stocks entered the middle of the Cycle wave III rally in the 1950s. In 1955, when the bull market was in a third of third wave up, Federal Judge Harold Medina dismissed Justice Department charges for collusive practices against seventeen leading investment banks. But as the final peak of this Supercycle top approaches, the next assault on investment bankers is brewing. Josh Lerner, a professor of investment banking at Harvard, says "Modern-day trustbusters have again launched an investigation into collusion in financial services, this time focusing on private-equity firms." The behavior in the Justice Department's "crosshairs" is deal sharing, the process by which firms syndicate offerings. Sounding a lot like last summer's mortgage securitization exponents, Lerner says "deal sharing benefits us all" because it "helps investors make better investment decisions" and "helps limit risk." A falling market will completely discredit both arguments. The public enemy status of private equity and the hedge funds that drive it will be compounded by the results of these deals. The deals that get done will saddle companies with horrendous debt loads at the worst possible time. The ones that are not complete when the market turns lower will feed the stock market decline as they come undone and trap arbitrageurs in highly leveraged long positions.

In a recent e-mail, an industry insider revealed that his careful study of syndicate activities in 1929 confirms that the parallel is solidly in place: "As for the late 1928-1929 'pool operation' analogue, I have never seen or read about such financial sector combinations as exist today. Official Washington and the gullible public can only marvel at their 'sophistication' as stock, and still many property prices, especially commercial and high-end residential, continue to go up. In the latest quarter, it became abundantly clear to me that eight core poolers (Citigroup, Bank of America, JP Morgan, Goldman Sachs, Lehman, Merrill Lynch, Bear Stearns and Morgan Stanley) literally will go to any extreme to expand their balance sheets. If they can just keep adding and 'carrying' more securities, often financed by very short term borrowings and rap-

idly unhedgeable basis risk, they can skip over any business cycle trough." When the trough turns out to be a way station on the way to depression, vast amounts of the paper these firms hold and distribute will be worthless.

Hedge funds are not shy about leveraging the markets' ascent. Their fearless approach has helped large investment banks, shown as the Hedge Fund Enablers Index on the chart (middle line), boost their return over the course of the 2002-2007 rally. While the pattern of the rise is essentially the same as the S&P 500 (top line on the chart), the index is up more than twice as much. So as EWFF has noted, it's all the same market. But thanks to all that leverage, it's been more than twice as good to investment bankers and even better to providers of luxuries for clients, owners and employees of investment banks. Notice, however, the banking group's subtle inability to surpass its February peak. This is a critical divergence that should eventually be followed by a massive reversal of Wall Street fortunes.

MAKING THE MOST OF THE SAME MARKET RALLY
weekly

S&P 500 105%

Hedge Fund Enablers Index 211%

Merrill Lynch Lifestyle Index of luxury stocks 230%

Data courtesy of Bloomberg
© May 2007 Elliott Wave International (www.elliottwave.com)

July 2007

Last Friday's Blackstone Group IPO shows further dissipation of the market's "animal spirits." It was met with immediate selling pressure, driving the initial $38 share price of the new issue down 23% to below its $31 initial public offering price. One week of trading does not make a trend, but the behavior of Blackstone shares is probably a good proxy for the prospects of the Private Equity/LBO craze. This telling rejection of a key element of the financial engineering craze covered here in May and is yet another sign that the great financial flameout is nigh.

Recent actions by ratings agencies offer another sure sign that reality is gaining fast on Wall Street. Ratings agencies were slow to act at first, refusing to lower their respective ratings on subprime offerings even as many subprime issuers closed down and delinquency and foreclosure rates climbed to their highest levels in years. Now, however, they are beginning to "bow to the inevitable and revise their opinions." The Economist adds:

> In the first of what is expected to be a wave of downgrades, Moody's has cut the rating of 131 subprime bonds because of higher-than-expected defaults. It is reviewing hundreds more. Meanwhile, as more loans turn bad, it is dawning on the banks, hedge funds, insurers and pension funds that hold 'senior' portions of CDOs that their investments may not be as bullet-proof as they thought.

As an aside, a story that is whispered but not talked about is that Moody's and other ratings agencies derive a good portion of their revenue from the very companies that they are rating. The obvious conflict of interest in this cozy arrangement facilitated the very excesses that a ratings agency was supposed to rein in. What irony that the reversing trend now dictates that they should step up their vigilance and thereby contribute to the coming rash of downgrades.

We said in May that subprime problems would spread, and the harder officials contest the point, the more likely it becomes. The latest to refute it were the CEO of Merrill Lynch, treasurer of Freddie Mac and the CFO of Lehman Brothers, all of whom said at a London conference on Wednesday that they are "seeing little risk of wider fallout." But strong whiffs of an inevitable and deadly spread to junk bonds, commercial loans and private equity are clearly in the air. The July Economist echoes earlier comments in EWFF when it notes an uncanny resemblance between leveraged loans to companies and the high loan-to-value ratios in subprime and 'covenant-lite' commercial loans and interest-only/negative-amortization mortgages. The very latest headlines from the private equity sector mark the beginning of the end for private equity: 'Dark Side to Leverage' Slows Buyouts" (USAToday, June 28, 2007), "Market's Jitters Stir Some Fears For Buyout Boom" (WSJ, June 28, 2007) and "Private Equity Faces Investor Revolt" (Financial Times, June 27, 2007). Says an industry analyst, subprime might well be "a dress rehearsal for something bigger and scarier." This is happening while the Dow Industrials are less than 2% from their June 1 high. So these are still just the trailers. The full-length, credit implosion spectacular starts when the bear market in stocks resumes.

Government Gets On Board

Down through the years, EWT and EWFF have demonstrated government's knack for committing to long-term trends when they are finally ending. Here's how *The Elliott Wave Theorist* initially made the observation in 1991:

> *The Last Believers*
>
> When government gets into the act of speculation, the top is usually way past having occurred. Government is the ultimate crowd; every decision being made by committee. It is always acting on the last trend, the one that is already over. (For example, the Federal government passed securities laws to prevent the 1929-1932 crash...in 1934.)

The Glass-Steagall Act was passed right after that Supercycle degree low. After 60 years of advance in Supercycle wave (V), Glass-Steagall came to be universally regarded as an anachronism and was finally repealed in the form of the Financial Services Act of 1999. It was on the basis of this legislation that the November 1999 issue of EWFF made the following forecast:

So, after totally missing the bear market it was supposed to prevent and protecting banks and insurance companies from six decades of rising prices, the U.S. government will free banks and insurers to take part in a financial consolidation that promises to be one of the biggest in history.

The new freedoms were enacted just in time for the 2000-2002 decline when the major stock indexes lost 38%-78% of their value. Near the lows in 2002, government hinted at the upturn by establishing a range of new investor "protections" in the form of Sarbanes-Oxley and new fire-wall restrictions on brokerage firm research operations. Last month, the following headline from The Washington Post signaled a trend reversal:

SEC Votes To Soften Scope of Audit Law
Board to Revise Reporting Rule in Sarbanes-Oxley

The SEC voted 5-0 to allow companies to review only their most critical financial policies for possible fraud and abuse. The removal of some restrictions is just one of a rash of government-sponsored endorsements of the long rise in stock prices. The SEC also increased the amount of money securities firms can invest in riskier assets and voted unanimously to revoke the uptick rule that prohibited short sales on a downtick after a decline in prices. The rule was instituted in 1938, during the second economic contraction of the Great Depression.

The establishment of "sovereign wealth funds" is another sign that a downturn is falling into place and that governments are doing everything in their power to make the worst of it. These funds, which dozens of countries have established in recent weeks, invest a country's reserves and natural-resource earnings in global financial assets that are much riskier than the extra-safe bonds that governments have traditionally owned. Based on current rates of formation, projections show these investment pools rocketing from current levels of $1.5 trillion to $20 trillion over the next 20 years. On the basis of these forecasts, many Wall Street analysts now envision a "multi-trillion dollar industry" that will "transform the shape of the world economy, and provide a massive boost for share prices in coming decades." Says one e-mailer to these offices, "Think of the vast sums of money that could flow into the U.S. stock market." But as we said last month with respect to one of the initial sovereign wealth fund investments—China's investment in Blackstone—these kinds of investments are not bullish; they are a "classic precondition to a reversal." They express how utterly conventional the drive into riskier financial instruments has become. With governments making the move, complacency toward risk has surely attained an extreme.

Speaking of China, a June 28 Bloomberg article offers the following redundancy: "China at 45 Times Earnings Buoyed by 'Herd Mentality,' Trust in Government." It ends with a quote from a factory-worker-turned-investor known as "Big Account." He says, "There's no way the government would let the stock market crash." How quickly they forget Japan's herculean post-1990 effort to prop up its stock market, which fell anyway by 80%. Here's another headline that offers an additional twist in our discussion here last month about government efforts to cool China's red hot stock market :

Chinese Officials Gambling Public Funds On Stocks

It is forbidden for public funds to be invested in stocks, but the Shanghai High People's Court revealed this week that Chinese officials have found crafty ways to divert government money to bet on the markets.

From 2003 through 2006, the Shanghai court handled 105 such cases involving over $820 million. "It was the first time Chinese authorities have admitted that money embezzled from the Shanghai pension fund was funneled into stocks." Until now, there's been "no effective mechanism to supervise the operation and management of public funds," but, just as scrutiny of hedge funds is now appearing, China is "coming to grips" with the graft that did so much to drive prices higher. This is how the ultimate crowd operates. When the time is right, it awakens to the seamy side of the mania that it helped create; just in time to help pull it down. It's what happens when the trend changes.

August 2007
Stocks Import Record Buying, Big Top

Last month EWFF discussed governments' knack for committing to a trend when it is finally ending. A front page article in the July 24 issue of The Wall Street Journal titled, "Governments Get Bolder in Buying Equity Stakes," confirms the strength of this very dependable sell signal.

September 2007
Good to the Last Bubble

The cartoon quality of modern finance reached such extremes in recent weeks that it produced a deluge of cartoon takes on the financial implosion; a few even offered accurate insights into the inner workings of a mania. The flurry takes us back to a similar series that appeared in February 2000 when the Dow Jones Industrial Average was a month into a bear market and the NASDAQ was a month from its all-time high. At that time, EWFF surmised that the extreme manifestations of the mania were penetrating so deeply into ordinary society that its nuances were finding their way into general interest editorials and comics. When Doonesbury creator Garry Trudeau offered a series of frames that discussed the underperformance of actively managed portfolios over the prior decade, EWFF said, "At this point, the message is extremely bearish, as popular cartoons like Doonesbury have been covering the mania on an almost daily basis."

The **"Lawrence Welk Economy"** image shown here recognizes another peculiar element that appears most relevant at Grand Supercycle degree peaks: their capacity for sliding the extraordinary behavior of a mania from one market to another. As we noted here in June, this trait is somewhat rare, probably because burned investors are generally twice shy about reexperiencing the loss and humiliation that comes with a bust. They tend to learn from their own experience or by witnessing it in others. But there are times when one mania seems to breed another, most notably at the last Grand Supercycle degree peak in 1720 when the South Sea Bubble expanded in London as the Mississippi scheme unraveled in Paris. Political cartoonist John Trever illustrates the Great Asset Mania's enduring capacity for capturing new investment populations and markets even after a succession of widely observed pops. His "Turn Off The Bubble Machine!" plea reveals the presence of a rising popular distaste for speculation. It also foreshadows the bullseye that the Fed will have on its back as the bear market progresses.

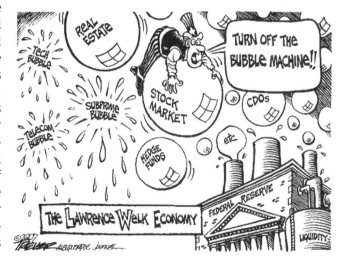

The only bubble that continues to expand is that in the Chinese stock market. The following statistic suggests strongly, however, that its peak cannot be far off: In the week of August 13-17, Chinese investors set up new trading accounts at a rate of 450,000 per day. Meanwhile, China's central bank raised interest rates again, and it is doing everything in its power to stop the frenzy. The U.S. Fed did the same at the peaks in 2000 and 1929. Government efforts to cool stock prices amidst an unprecedented flood of public involvement tend to occur near the peaks of manias. Chinese stocks may skirt higher in the short run, but wave **c** is a global affair that the Chinese will not miss out on. As the last and, in some ways, the most manic of the bubble-era advances, it should be among the most spectacular busts.

November 2007

The following page one revelation from the October 12 issue of The Wall Street Journal perhaps captures the most striking measure of the unbridled fearlessness that traders managed to attain over the course of the bull market: "Way less than half of all securities trade on exchanges with readily available price information." In the future, when a full-bodied backlash against the forces of the financial mania is in place, the investigations will probably represent this single statistic as evidence of monumental collusion. Up until now, the sufficiency of mark-to-model accounting attested to the level of trust that prevails at the end of a Grand Supercycle bull market. But as more markets top out, the revelations of fraud should spike as drowning traders flail to stay above water.

The corollary to trust in a bull market is mistrust in a bear, and we see the beginnings of this wariness in the debt market reports concerning the volume of off-the-books assets as well as questions about "what those damn things are worth" (Ben Bernanke, October 14). It seems that every day brings more signs of constriction. Alan Greenspan is reportedly "moderating his enthusiasm for derivatives." A proposed change of law in Congress will grant the Federal Energy Regulatory Commission authority over the commodities market—that's in addition to the CFTC's current authority. The commission will be empowered to levy fines for "allegedly manipulating prices." In other words, just the perception of manipulation will be enough for a fine, regardless of whether an inquiry actually finds any. As the decline spreads to all markets and picks up steam, the political response will be swift and devastating.

February 2008

As EWFF has noted several times over the last few months, government involvement in markets is a great signal at tops because it takes a very strong consensus opinion to cause a lumbering bureaucracy to take action. In recent months, the edicts and initiatives of various government entities places them squarely on board the bullish bandwagon. A new Department of Labor directive offers a perfect example, as it will force 401(k) plan sponsors to push riskier stock and bond investments on participants who fail to choose a default investment option. Here is an excerpt:

> It is the view of the Department that investments made on behalf of defaulted participants ought to and often will be long-term investments and that investment of defaulted participants' contributions and earnings in money market and stable value funds will not over the long-term produce rates of return as favorable as those generated by products, portfolios and services included as qualified default investment alternatives, thereby decreasing the likelihood that participants invested in capital preservation products will have adequate retirement savings.

In other words, according to the U.S. Department of Labor, investors need to be invested in stocks and various corporate bonds for the long haul; truly safe assets such as U.S. Treasuries are a bad investment! In another recent sign that this peak is fully endorsed by the government, lawmakers are pressuring universities to spend some of their "soaring" endowments to help defray tuition increases. "Full Coffers Could Help Ease Costs," says a USA Today headline. The story lists double digit returns at five major universities—through June 30, 2007. Since then, however, many of the riskier alternative assets that juiced endowment returns over the last decade started to sour in what we suspect is the beginning of a huge bear market. Congress' effort to "go after" college nest eggs will probably mark the beginning of a massive shrinkage in the asset values of these endowments.

March 2008

The "little guy," who did so much to create the years-long market froth, is suddenly preoccupied with rising house payments and diminishing job prospects. His predicament is evident by what he's doing to another cornerstone of the great bull market, the 401(k). According to several large retirement plan sponsors, more and more workers are "dipping into 401(k) accounts." Despite the fact that hardship withdrawals are taxed as income and subject to a 10% penalty for workers under 59½, "the nation's largest retirement plan administrators, such as Great-West Retirement Services and Fidelity Investments, are seeing double-digit spikes in hardship withdrawals and increases in loan requests, a sharp departure from levels that traditionally varied little." In addition to the psychological shift away from markets, the exodus from 401(k)s marks a very real dissipation of resources that will grow profound as the bear market deepens.

Switching Off Financial Television

Meanwhile, interest in ticker tape TV appears to be waning. Recall that it was this time last year that Fox announced its new business news station. Under the headline "Broadcasting a Sell Signal" EWFF argued that the new channel reflected a "blazing optimism" and was a sure-fire sign that "some riveting financial drama is about to take place. If Fox gets on the air soon it will be able to report some of the most dramatic footage in stock market history." As it turns out, Fox Business News nailed the peak, debuting October 15, two trading days after the Dow's October 11 high.

On the approach to the peak, Fox appeared to have a sure-fire hit on its hands. "A host of changes have made business and financial news—traditionally one of the least sexy fields of journalism—into a hottie," said USA Today. As EWFF observed in November 1999, this is what happens at big peaks, big media go after a "whole new wave of enthusiastic and totally unsophisticated investors." We now know that at a peak of exceptionally high degree, the come-on can be downright lurid. Back in 1999, the Dow was a few weeks from its January 2000 peak when Playboy announced a "new growth strategy" that would be "heavily skewed to money." One of Fox's initial business shows is a post-closing-bell offering called *Happy Hour*, in which women wearing low-cut dresses sit around a bar and gab about the markets. The station is drawing dismal ratings. According to the initial Nielson numbers released at the beginning of the year, the Fox Business News is bringing in just 6,300 viewers. As one pundit noted, the station's "anemic ratings are in danger of being surpassed by large city public access channels."

Government Goes For Broke

Speaking of desperate, yet another government-sponsored confirmation of the peak in financial assets is visible in a U.S. Pension Benefit Guaranty Corp. decision to step up investment in riskier assets such as equities to plug a $14 billion deficit. "The move, quietly announced on the President's Day public holiday, will mean the PBGC will double its equity allocation to 45% of total assets." This is a long-term sell signal if ever there was one. To those in need, stocks are no kinder than the roulette wheel. With the government itself doubling its holdings, stocks are positioned for a decline of huge proportions.

Investors Can See Clearly Now

If the current decline is a c wave that will retrace a long-running mania, it should be accompanied by flashes of recognition. This is certainly happening, as the financial press now offers glimpses of the dire straits investors and consumers are headed toward. According to the latest stories, consumers are fraught with anxieties; many Americans feel "a vague but persistent dissatisfaction;" hedge funds "are products of a bull market" that will necessarily tank as the markets collapse; and "America's Economy Risks the Mother of All Meltdowns." The majority of economists are still keeping the boom-time faith, but the mythology of economic supremacy and financial engineering, which was so integral to the boom, is now the object of skepticism and worry about the potential for systemic failure. Wages failed to keep pace with consumer demand, and the debt-fueled growth of recent years leaves the economy far more vulnerable than at any time in decades. In other words, the case for a "demonstrably weaker" economic expansion as described in Chapter 1 of *Conquer the Crash* is on the table.

May 2008

IPOs are being cancelled at a record rate as "concerns about a recession sapped demand for new shares." The waning speculative interest of investors, which EWFF showed in the form of anemic demand for OTC Bulletin Board shares in the March issue (Chapter 1) and a decline in NYSE margin debt in February (Chapter 1), clearly extends to initial public offerings, as 83 companies pulled IPOs and 24 delayed share sales in the first quarter.

Enthusiasm for company buy-back plans is another component of a healthy mania, as the public always screams its approval of such efforts in the heat of the frenzy. Once they end, however, the cheers invariably turn to jeers because a peak means that companies paid top dollar for shares that are losing value, proving that corporate managers are subject to the same herding mentality as all other investors. When the bear market in the S&P still had another 40% to fall, EWFF identified the beginning of the last buy-out, flame-out phase: "Buy backs are being recognized as a bad idea," said the July 2001 EWFF. We went on to cite the following headline evidence: "Share buybacks Hit a Wall of Fear." This downturn's version of the same disenchantment appears in an April issue of the Wall Street Journal: "Buyback Boom to Buyer's Remorse." The subhead adds, "Share Repurchases Weren't Such a Good Investment." Buy backs sour at the end of most booms, but the size of the latest swing signals the potential for a really big bust. Last year, companies in the S&P 500 repurchased a record $589 billion of their own shares, up 36% from 2006 and more than quadruple the level of 2003, according to S&P. "It's a dramatic turnabout," says the Journal. "Investors years from now may look back with awe on a period when companies went on a spending spree unmatched in corporate history." In many cases, they even borrowed money to buy the shares that are now falling in value.

July 2008

The approach of another scales-from-the-eyes moment is clear in this headline:

Hedge Funds Gird for Withdrawals
As Redemption Requests Roll In

According to the June 12 Wall Street Journal story, hedge funds are "bracing for a wave of withdrawals" on June 30. "The redemption trend could have ripple effects in the markets in coming weeks as managers raise cash by selling investments common to many portfolios." Count on it. As the thirst for cash becomes all-consuming, the bath water, the baby, the tub, the bathroom and the whole house will be made available for sale; that is, if the house is worth anything. This is why it is important to resist the too-early urge to snap up assets with even the most impeccable credentials.

Here's another big story that suggests energy trading has reached an important mania era endpoint—the point of parody. First, recall that a similar bout of silliness broke out as stocks topped in 2000. As the Dow was about to peak in January of that year, EWFF recorded the same "prices are so high it's funny" effect with respect to IPOs. In March 2000, as the NASDAQ and S&P were peaking, EWFF noted that spoofs on day trading and otherwise getting "filthy rich" in stocks were popular. Here's the latest satiric financial take from Bloomberg's David Pauly.

Dazzling Dandelions Foment
New Commodities Craze

Pauly's mania send-up of alternate energy schemes is among the best ever offered, as he displays a deft touch with some of the nuances of a bubble. He says, for instance, that the dandelion craze may look like a bubble, but "people who should know the market say it isn't so." This is, in fact, what happens when a bubble is ready to burst. People can see it so clearly that they produce humorous odes, books and TV shows that reflect some of the fundamental absurdity, (later, as the selling intensifies, the efforts tend to get more literary and scathing) and still participants do almost nothing to extricate themselves (that comes when much or most of the price damage is done).

August 2008

The hedge fund world is another bull market wonderland that is suddenly in perfect stride with the bearish future laid out for it in *Conquer the Crash*. July was the "worst month in at least five years" for hedge fund performance. With CTC's warning in mind, last September EWFF posted this headline: "Roach Motel For Investors, They Can Check In But They Can't Check Out!" over a decimated hedge fund stock (shown in Chapter 1) and said it "represents the speed and extent" of the hedge fund liquidity problem. Investors are belatedly discovering this little hitch in hedge fund ownership, as the WSJ just reported on hedge fund's "'roach motel' nature, where once investors get in, they can't get out." Check-out time has come and gone. The only reason that many hedge fund investors don't realize it is that they have not yet had the opportunity to check out. When many are finally able to liquidate their positions, actual roaches may be all that's left.

Recession-Plagued Nation Demands New Bubble To Invest In

WASHINGTON—A panel of top business leaders testified before Congress about the worsening recession Monday, demanding the government provide Americans with a new irresponsible and largely illusory economic bubble in which to invest.

"What America needs right now is not more talk and long-term strategy, but a concrete way to create more imaginary wealth in the very immediate future," said Thomas Jenkins, CFO of the Boston-area Jenkins Financial Group, a bubble-based investment firm. "We are in a crisis, and that crisis demands an unviable short-term solution."

The current economic woes, brought on by the collapse of the so-called "housing bubble," are considered the worst to hit investors since the equally untenable dot-com bubble burst in 2001. According to investment experts, now that the option of making millions of dollars in a short time with imaginary profits from bad real-estate deals has disappeared, the need for another spontaneous make-believe source of wealth has never been more urgent.

"Perhaps the new bubble could have something to do with watching movies on cell phones," said investment banker Greg Carlisle of the New York firm Carlisle, Shaloe & Graves. "Or, say, medicine, or shipping. Or clouds. The manner of bubble isn't important—just as long as it creates a hugely overvalued market based on nothing more than whimsical fantasy and saddled with the potential for a long-term accrual of debts that will never be paid back, thereby unleashing a ripple effect that will take nearly a decade to correct."

"Every American family deserves a false sense of security," said Chris Reppto, a risk analyst for Citigroup in New York. "Once we have a bubble to provide a fragile foundation, we can begin building pyramid scheme on top of pyramid scheme, and before we know it, the financial situation will return to normal."

The calls for a new bubble are only going to get louder.

"America needs another bubble," said Chicago investor Bob Taiken. "At this point, bubbles are the only thing keeping us afloat."

—The Onion
July 14, 2008

The Next Big Bubble?

These are the economic bubbles Americans would like to foolishly invest in to take their minds off the current fiscal crisis most.

- Carbides
- Some sort of fund
- Debt refinancing
- Postmodernism
- [No preference]
- Atmospherics
- Illegal immigration futures
- Freight—yeah, that sounds about right. "Freight"

Source: University of Chicago

It will probably take years to complete, but to give you an idea of just how far mania scholarship has to go, the most informative bubble exposé that we've seen is a wicked spoof from the satirical website, The Onion. The article's headline is, "Recession-Plagued Nation Demands New Bubble to Invest In." For one thing, its publication constitutes a double sell signal. As we explained with last month's dandelion mania parody, lampoons typically come at the end of the rise when satirists appear to exploit their considerable comic potential. "Once we have a bubble to provide a fragile foundation, we can begin building a pyramid scheme on top of a pyramid scheme," says The Onion. This is a great description of the financial structure now in place. And it is certainly true that the only possible way out now is another financial bubble. With the last holdouts—commodity markets—finally toppling, however, there is no "spontaneous make-believe source of wealth" to fall back on.

September 2008

The entrenched belief is that a deeper decline simply begets better deals. Why else would banks and brokerages be the leading promoters of financially related exchange-traded funds? Financial ETFs raised $8.67 billion in the first seven months of 2008 even though the shares they buy have posted "their biggest declines in almost five decades." In a similar vein, the NY Post reveals that "the value of bank-owned foreclosed homes has dropped so low that the smart money—including a sovereign wealth fund—expects to pocket a whopping 45% profit on its investment." Notice the mention of a "sovereign wealth fund," a state-run investment fund that manages the excess cash of some foreign Treasury. In July 2007, EWFF called the establishment of these entities "another sign that a downturn is falling into place and that governments are doing everything in their power to make the worst of it." As Bob Prechter said in 1991, "government is the ultimate crowd," and there is little doubt that one of the great examples of this principle is the Pension Benefit Guaranty Corp., the U.S. government guarantor of corporate pension plans. In order to "fix" a $14 billion deficit, the PBGC will shift money from safe bonds to stocks, real estate and hedge funds. In a NY Times story, some questioned the PBGC's contention that the move would reduce risk, but even the critics said all three asset classes would provide excess returns over the long haul. According to our assessment, the PBGC's very willingness to take the plunge in the wake of substantial losses in all three categories is in and of itself a sure sign that stocks, real estate and hedge funds are in long-term declines.

And it's not just the PBGC. "Public pension funds in the U.S. are increasing bets on high-risk hedge funds and real estate in an attempt to fill deficits in retirement plans and make up for their worst performance in six years." Now that the "yield grab" strategy of the mid-2000s is coming up short, public pension funds are upping the ante with a classic "double down" strategy. Ask any trader/gambler: It never works.

October 2008
Credit Default Swamps

To get an idea of just how much bigger the problem is than any possible solution the federal government can come up with, let's look back at a financial instrument that we first introduced to EWFF readers in May 2005, the credit default swap (CDS). When EWFF first discussed these instruments in connection with the economy's unavoidable advance toward the purge phase of the interest rate cycle ("Interest Rate Spikes Create Crisis" in the September 2008 entry in Chapter 8), we also noted the appearance of "some whole new risk exposures such as credit default swaps, which by some estimates now total more than $8 trillion, or 2/3 of GDP." At that point, the CDS boom had only just begun. The bar chart shows the exponential growth that has since taken place. At $62 trillion, credit default swaps' value hit 4.3 times annual U.S. GDP at its peak last December.

The extraordinary part that these instruments played at the very end of the Great Asset Mania's peaking pro-

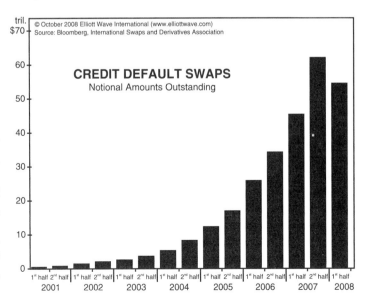

cess revolves around credit's pivotal role in the boom-bust cycle. Every boom runs higher when the willingness to lend disconnects from the value of the underlying collateral. Borrowed money ratchets up demand, pushing up prices and increasing the supply of credit. The bust comes when optimism finally wanes and the cycle reverses. Tighter credit reduces demand, driving down prices and the attendant collateral values. But the CDS introduced an intermediate step by allegedly allowing bond holders to insure against default, which they did in droves. We say *allegedly* because, as *Conquer the Crash* points out, default itself will nullify many insurance and derivatives contracts, even those that were supposed to pay off in the event of non-payment. In the summer of 2006, EWFF noted that CDSs were being "widely used as insurance against default in lieu of selling distressed bonds outright." In other words, the CDSs delayed the selling that otherwise would have come naturally, a fitting component of the **b**-wave rally. The CDS market was obviously becoming a casino unto itself because total issuance eventually grew to be six times the total value of U.S. corporate debt. Its size and wild swings in value caused EWFF to issue several warnings:

> Sudden prices swings of 30% and 80% in credit default swaps signal the potential for a violent reversal. The volatility was due to changes in corporate structure. The damage done by an economic contraction will undoubtedly be catastrophic.
>
> —EWFF, September 2006

> The use of credit-default swaps in an attempt to avert defaults is a good example of the "creativity" that debt engineers are using to push the boundaries of the debt bubble further past those of 1720 and 1929.
>
> —EWFF, February 2007

> The numbers suggest that the subprime problem could be small by comparison.
>
> —EWFF, February 2008

> The sky is the limit for this mushroom cloud.
>
> —EWFF, September 2008

And here are the press clippings that introduced John and Jane Q. Public to these exotic instruments after the U.S. government was forced to take over AIG in an overnight transaction:

Credit Default Swaps At Meltdown's Heart

> The Federal Reserve bailed out AIG because top officials were unwilling to risk the collapse of a web of interconnected derivative contracts, known as credit default swaps, the scope of which is vast, but unknown, experts said.
>
> —Investor's Business Daily, September 17, 2008

> Most people have never heard of these , and even fewer understand them, but they are at the core of the financial crisis roiling the global economy.
>
> —Houston Chronicle, September 20, 2008

All it took was one major credit event to bring down the CDS house. The failure of Fannie and Freddie tipped the first domino, AIG. In the chain reaction that followed, Wall Street firms used the instruments to drive each other out of business or into drastically different financial entities. According to Bloomberg, "The swaps became a one way bet on the demise of the financial institutions as traders hedged the risk that their partners might implode." The SEC now promises to "crack down" on the unregulated CDS market, but any such move should prove superfluous, as credit default swaps will go away just as portfolio insurance disappeared after the 1987 crash. The first tick down after seven straight years of growth has already occurred. CDS's will, however, be long remembered as a monument to the level of complacency at a Grand Supercycle-degree peak.

Wall Street Grins and Bears It

Playwright Samuel Beckett said, "Nothing is funnier than unhappiness." Seldom do more people have this condition thrust upon them as violently as they do when a financial bubble breaks. Thus the hilarity boom at the end of a mania. EWFF first observed this phenomenon in 2000. Here's what we said about a stream of stock market cartoons that suddenly appeared in February 2000.

> Popular cartoons like Doonesbury have been covering the mania on an almost daily basis. On one level, the cartoons work because a mania is pretty funny. There are many more than we have room to show.

The boom in comic relief is even larger now. In fact, there are so many market-toons flooding the news and the Internet that Daryl Cagle's index of professional cartoons now lists them in separate categories, "Wall Street Stress," "Wall Street Collapse," "Bailout Passed" and "Bailout Bust." For a look at just a sampling go to http://www.elliottwave.com/wave/cartoons. On the way up, money and markets are inherently unfunny. Getting rich is serious business. But once the curtain gets pulled away and the backlash against the money world begins, nothing is better at skewering the financial world than the pen of the satirist.

The magnitude of the current decline is broadcast by a much deeper interest on the part of the entertainment industry. Wall Street send-ups are now a regular feature on *Saturday Night Live*, for instance. The first picture at right is of a sketch in which a broker offers soothing investment advice as he jumps out of a window and falls toward the pavement. It's actually from the first leg of the bear market in March 2001,

Saturday Night Live—Financial Parodies

"It's a great time to invest."
Originally appeared in March 2001;
now popular on the web.

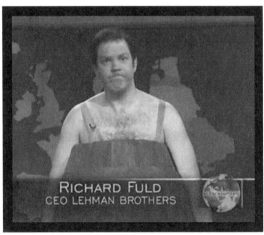

**"Lehman Brothers Richard Fuld
on Weekend Update...in a barrel."**
—September 27, 2008

but it is enjoying new popularity on the web. The second is from a recent episode. Riskcenter. com's offers a long list of Wall Street jokes "to keep us all entertained during these trying times," including: "What's the difference between a credit default swap and a Beanie Baby? You can still sell a Beanie Baby." When the bear market was just getting started in July 2000, EWFF cited Andy Borowitz's *The Trillionaire Next Door*, as a evidence of the "gallows humor that prevails" on Wall Street. The same guy is at it again. Writing in The New Yorker, Borowitz now lampoons the bailout measures by requesting "a bailout from the Federal Reserve. Like many of our nation's financial institutions, I am simply too big to fail." As the irony deepens with the bear market, the comedy and satire should develop further. The last Grand Supercycle bear market gave us *Gullliver's Travels* (1726) and *Candide* (1756).

Special Report:
Refashioning Bull Market Tools
The Door Slams Shut on the Hedge Fund Game

It is truly amazing what can be accomplished in an atmosphere of unbridled belief. The mania fostered the creation of—and then electrified—all kinds of instruments that did its bullish bidding. One of the most important was the hedge fund. Month after month, EWFF and *The Elliott Wave Theorist* discussed the leading role of these woefully misnamed financial pools. It was frequently argued that they could survive a down market because of their investment flexibility. But Bloomberg lists 20 different Hedge Fund Research indexes, and virtually every one looks the same as the composite shown here below at left. So far, the index is down 20.5% from a July 2007 high. The EWI Hedge Fund Enablers Index, which EWI compiled to measure the aggregate value of the main lenders to hedge funds, signals a much more dramatic decline. Per the chart below at right, the Enablers are down more than 75% and just took out their 2002 low. The trend in the number of its members is also instructive. With Bear Stearns wiped out, Merrill Lynch acquired and Lehman shares slated for extinction, the number of hedge-fund enabling banks is down by

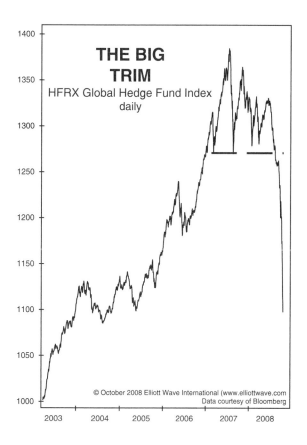

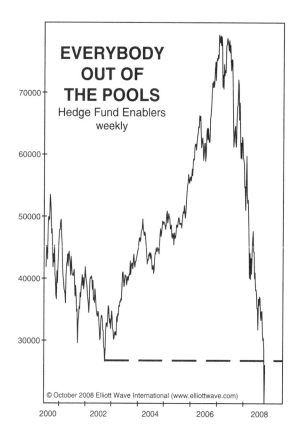

more than 37%. Bank of America, Citigroup, Goldman Sachs, J.P. Morgan and Morgan Stanley survive. Hedge funds are doing everything in their power to lock in investors. Some are even offering to reduce their fees "if investors agree to stay put." But it won't work. As the bear market presses lower, the hedge fund ranks will be decimated even more dramatically than the banks.

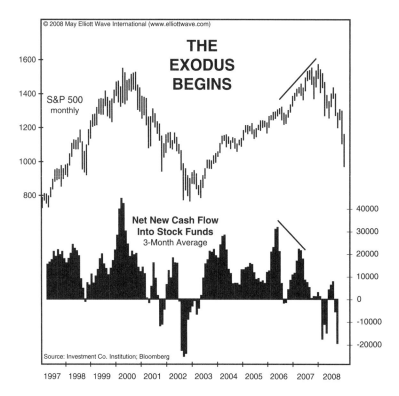

The Mutual Fund Slide

Before hedge funds captured the public's fancy, mutual funds were the bullish investors' ticket to wealth. The chart of net new cash into stock funds shows a critical tapering in the manic frenzy to own equity funds. As the S&P 500 marched to a new high in October 2007, flows did not come close to the high of early 2006, which in turn was well below the peak of 2000. At the rally high in May, flows barely managed a positive reading on a three-month basis. In the bear market of the 1970s, equity fund flows went negative for the better part of a decade. So, fund flows will probably be mostly underwater for some time to come.

Buybacks, Mergers and Pensions

Buybacks, pensions and corporate mergers are three more key financial instruments that are being reshaped by the bear market. So far this year, 3,007 merger deals worth $790 billion are in the works. At this time last year, Wall Street was on its way to a record year with 3,945 transactions valued at $1.33 trillion. Once the clean-up takeovers such as Bank of America's acquisition of Merrill Lynch are out of the way, merger volumes will crash toward zero. U.S. pensions are already down by $2 trillion, says the top of the front page of USA Today on October 8. It also reports on how foolish 25% of over 45-year-olds are for stopping their 401(k) contributions. "Workers who ditch their stock funds and move their money to low-risk investments are making a mistake." We think they are the smart ones, at least until the nation's No.1 daily hoists stories about the virtue of T-bills to the top of the front page.

With respect to buybacks, here's what EWFF said in May, "Buybacks sour at the end of most booms, but the size of the latest swing signals the potential for a really big bust." And here's the headline that marking a full reversal in attitudes toward firms that invested in their own shares:

Share Buybacks Look Foolish in Retrospect
—BloggingStocks, October 6, 2008

The Wall Street Journal points out that General Electric bought back $29 billion dollars of its own stock at an average price of $36 a share. It's now trading at about $20 a share. Lehman is now becoming infamous for investing $4 billion in its own stock a few months before it went under. As we noted in May, buybacks are always jeered after the boom, but this time the bitter buyback pill will go down even harder because the scale of buying was so much greater and many firms financed their efforts with borrowed money. In every way possible, this is no ordinary bust.

Going Public Is Going Away

Another once-sizzling, now-fizzling expression of the reversal is the market for initial public offerings. According to Deallogic, the third quarter total of 119 IPOs was the lowest number since it began tracking in 1995. The Bloomberg IPO Index, which monitors the aftermarket performance of 59 offerings, is down more than 50% from its October 11, 2007 peak. If the speculative fever is broken, the very concept of public ownership should be under review. Recent events on Wall Street itself —the failure of Lehman and Bear Stearns—show that this process is clearly underway. "Going public was a deal with the devil," says one retrospective. "It meant exposing themselves to what was, in effect, a minute-by-minute referendum, in the form of the stock price. This was fine as long as things were going well—the higher the

stock price, the richer everyone got—but, once things started to go bad, that market referendum started to look like a vote of no confidence. And that made the problems the companies were facing much, much worse."

One particular group of offerings—the stock exchange deal—captures the Grand Supercycle degree of the peak (see charts, next page). After decades, or, in the case of the New York Stock Exchange, centuries, member-owned exchanges became freely traded in the 2000s. When the New York Stock Exchange went public in March 2006, EWFF stated, "In a nutshell, the public offering is one of the most bearish imaginable signals." Previously, EWFF cited two key fundamental problems with the exchange business: competition and rapidly evolving trading technologies. Another problem is that the volatility boom will eventually give way to deadly dull trading sessions. Surviving as for-profit entities will be a challenge. The dramatic declines to date—80% in the NYSE, 55% in the NASDAQ, 68% in the Intercontinental Exchange Inc. and 60% in the Chicago Merc—show that these shares sense the peril.

December 2008

The hedge fund field shows what a minefield the bear market is for former bull market heros. Already, it is strewn with casualties. According to the Hedge Fund Implode-O-Meter (hf-impolode. com), 96 funds have closed since the middle of 2007. The NY Post reports that "industry stars are falling back to earth" amid the "worst ever" returns, "fleeing" investors and a mounting inquisition from regulators and Congress. (The Italian government is talking about an outright abolition.) Fortress Group, a publicly traded hedge fund that EWFF identified as a symbol of "hedge funds' critical role in the unfolding drama" when it came public and traded up to $35 a share last year, is down 96% from its high, to $1.87 per share.

THE MARKET IN STOCK MARKETS IS CRASHING

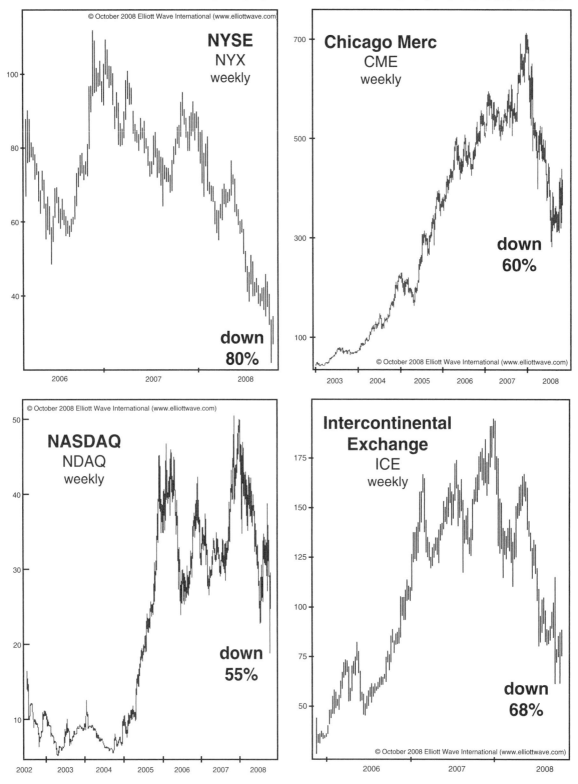

© October 2008 Elliott Wave International (www.elliottwave.com)

NYSE
NYX
weekly

down 80%

Chicago Merc
CME
weekly

down 60%

NASDAQ
NDAQ
weekly

down 55%

Intercontinental Exchange
ICE
weekly

down 68%

A Cartoon-Quality Turn

As EWFF noted in October, cartoonists of all stripes now comment on the stock market's bursting star, in some cases to a "T." EWFF first observed the stock market's appearance in the comic pages in 1997, noting that some cartoonists do a better job of identifying the operative psychology than most financial analysts. In the strip below, *Cathy* captures the average investor's effort to cope with the prevailing anger and fear as well as the irrepressible urge to "jump back in."

The bear market is obviously breaking new ground, as a negative cartoon portrayal of the investment world is breaking out to a new venue, the London stage. *Alex*, a play about a "bullish financier" who started as a comic-strip character, skewers the financial realm. The play focuses on Alex's desperate bid "to keep his job, marriage and Maserati." In other words, it's an irreverent but basically accurate portrayal of real life. Socionomically, it is perfectly appropriate that Alex takes on human form and graduates to the theater now. The cartoon first appeared in 1987, as the market was setting up for that year's crash.

Chapter 6

Plumbers, Sheiks and Fools:
New Market Wizards and Their Heroes

From Alan Greenspan to the Beardstown Ladies, the bull market creates a whole galaxy of new financial stars. The movement is toward less and less sophisticated idols. Kids are schooled in stocks, and everyday people embrace an ever-more benevolent money world. The broker-age industry declares, "Retail is king." When Wall Street meets Easy Street, however, the bear market gets rolling and the toppling of bullish icons begins. Faith in the Fed falls hard as the big break of 2008 ensues.

July 1995

Today there are a record 30,000 investment clubs in the U.S. Every single week, there are 100 new investment clubs formed, double the rate of the 1980s. The latest hot invest-ment book is one penned by 16 honest-to-goodness little old ladies subtitled, "How We Beat the Stock Market — and How You Can, Too." Their investment club made money by buy-ing stocks in companies that sell products they like. They like chocolate, so bought Hershey's. They like kitchen bowls, so bought Rubbermaid, etc. The most-owned stock among invest-ment clubs (by a full 30% above the #2 stock) is McDonald's because everyone eats there. "Buying stocks of companies you know" has been touted as a good investment approach for the typical investor. Any "method" works in a bull mar-ket. It takes a bear market, though, to teach you why such approaches are bogus.

The number of brokerage offices has doubled in four years, from 29,000 to 58,000.

August 1995

Who said this to The Wall Street Journal?: "The market grows over the long term, and I'm in there for 20 or 30 years." A portfolio manager? A stock picker? An analyst? No, a col-lege employee in her twenties. Is there a soul left who has not swallowed, digested and incorporated this line of thinking into his reasoning for buying stock that is historically overvalued? The extent of this belief is such that a Gallup poll found 92% of re-spondents describe themselves as "long term investors aiming for a comfortable retirement." 90% have no plans to cash in on stock gains, and over 3/4 would not sell stocks if they plunged.

While in truth this poll is a devastatingly bearish technical indicator, all assessments pub-lished in newspapers are the opposite: "Market experts were surprised by findings showing investors are far more market-savvy than believed."..."This is a very positive poll." Today, to be "market savvy" means to be clueless about market fluctuations, valuation and history, and to buy and hold stocks without a second thought. The truly savvy people took such action in 1974, 1979 and 1982 (when *The Elliott Wave Theorist* said to "buy and hold" for the long term), not 1995.

September 1995

For several years, *The Elliott Wave Theorist* has characterized the veneration of heroes as a hallmark of a bull market, and their tearing down as the hallmark of a bear. The modern trend toward the tearing down of heroes began with the bear market in the late 1960s, accelerated with the hounding of Richard Nixon from office in 1974, the year of the low, and continued weakly in the late 1980s with a spate of tell-all books. The trend has subsided recently, as Primary wave ⑤ in stocks rekindles the respect for heroes that was so much stronger during the third wave. For instance, Mickey Mantle and Jerry Garcia, who died recently, were characterized as near-deities, though their self-indulgent lifestyles were not censored.

The stock market, however, provides today's biggest heroes. The fame of billionaires Warren Buffett, John Templeton, Bill Gates, Peter Lynch and George Soros has risen to heights normally reserved for a select group of movie stars and athletes. Incredibly, each of these five people currently has two to four books by or about him currently in print (when has that ever happened?), some of which have made a financial or overall bestseller list. "In the past, there were astronauts pioneering outer space and capturing the collective imagination," says The Wall Street Journal. "Today, Bill Gates, the genius behind Microsoft Corp., is the hero." In lending his presence and fame to the heavily hyped introduction of Windows 95, Gates has achieved a "ubiquitousness rivaled by few chief executives." In June, he was on the cover of a major news weekly alongside the headline, "Master of the Universe." Soros was on the cover of the [international editions of the same magazine] in July as "The Billionaire Who Would Save the World." The magazine cover indicator has yet to flash a sell signal on Buffett's fame, but he has been called a "human investing machine," "a cult," and "an affront to the efficient market theory" in major financial publications.

By the bottom of the bear market, the public regard for these men will have changed (whether or not the men themselves have changed), and their fortunes and images will have shrunk considerably.

Today, a growing number of kids are learning the lesson at summer camp that "you're never too young to invest in the stock market." USA Today listed six camps where "kids can cash in" on programs that teach them about investing. At one Florida school, "savvy campers" take a limousine to class where they get advice like this: "Invest early and often in solid, reliable stock funds." Have people ever before, in any other investment mania, gone as far as to indoctrinate their children to join in?

December 1995

There are twelve full pages of personal finance ads in the November 20 issue of Time magazine, indicating that the laws of market psychology have been stretched to their limit. Among them is an ad that is about as close to an advertisement for a bear market as you will ever see. It urges investors to consider automatic dollar cost averaging, debit programs in which mutual funds electronically debit your bank account and other investment and re-investment plans that require no effort on the part of the investor. The caption contends that "auto-pilot plans" are "an easy, guaranteed way to build your savings," yet another example of the irresponsible claim that savings and stock ownership are one and the same thing. Notice that the man in the picture is facing backwards. He's looking back at what the stock market has done.

Time Magazine, November 20, 1995

More Evidence of a Major Peak in Social Mood

The Elliott Wave Theorist has long regarded the wave V bull market that began in 1982 to be a nostalgia wave, a fifth wave that would attempt to re-create the glory years of wave III from 1949 to 1966. It has already followed this description in politics, which went from conservative to middle-of-the-road to liberal in both periods: Eisenhower (two terms) to JFK to LBJ in the first period and Reagan (two terms) to Bush to Clinton in the second. The nostalgic aspect is revealed in the harking back to earlier times, Reagan to the stable '50s in the middle of wave III and Clinton to the glory days of the Great Society at the top of wave III. It is similarly appropriate that the popular musical stars of the 1960s topping process in social mood, The Beatles, should now appear for a gentle rekindling of Beatlemania. In November 1995, they are once again the top-selling act in the music business by a huge margin. Thus, they have made it to the top, at the top, again. While ABC's three-part television anthology was well received, it was still a far cry from live performances drowned out by screaming teenage girls and/or watched by the biggest television audience in history, which was the scene in 1964-1965. The difference fits our long-standing description of this fifth wave as a "hollow echo of the third." The power of the social goodwill at the peak of Cycle wave III in February 1966 is well reflected by these comments, from the show's director: "There will never be a band as big as the Beatles. It happens very seldom in history that everything comes together... It was a good vibe."

In 1989, EWT chronicled the progression of popular singers during the advancing waves of Cycle Wave III: Frank Sinatra in Primary wave ①, Elvis Presley in Primary wave ③, and the Beatles in Primary wave ⑤. Michael Jackson was the pop music craze of Cycle wave V. All four are again very much on the scene. Sinatra has a TV special, a Life magazine cover and a new 40-CD set, the biggest package of music by one artist ever assembled. Warner Brothers has a new picture book on Elvis, "A glorious tribute to The King," while the box set of his 1970s material completes a multi-CD volume spanning his musical career. Finally, Michael Jackson airs his only U.S. concert of 1995 on December 10 on HBO. That is a *lot* of nostalgic pop musical activity for a single four-week period, and reflects a culminating wave V.

April 1996

The full embrace of equities by the insurance industry is illustrated by three recent events: (1) Primerica Financial Services has altered its commission structure so that agents earn less from the sale of a policy that does not include the sale of mutual fund products; (2) John Hancock (see ad next page) now markets its services beneath this headline: "In 1929, George Myers was ruined because he had his money on Wall Street. 67 years later, the same could happen to his granddaughter if she doesn't"; (3) Gerald Tsai, chief executive of Delta Life, has "seized a central theme for today's markets" with the sale of annuities backed by a big mutual fund family. Tsai first made a name for himself in the mutual fund mania of the late 1960s. When his Manhattan Fund crashed, his name became synonymous with the mutual fund flame-out of 1969-1970.

1929, George Myers was ruined because he had his money on Wall Street. 67 years later, the same could happen to his granddaughter if she doesn't.

When the crash came, it was as though life had fallen into a monetary abyss. A dark and joyless place where the fruits of a lifetime were swept away virtually overnight.

How ironic, then, that the very thing that once contributed to the downfall of an economy now stands as our best and brightest hope for financial independence.

There are those who would suggest that choosing not to invest your money isn't just risky – it is the height of folly. A perspective which anyone who understands the financial realities of our time can appreciate.

Yet, how is one to balance the need to invest one's assets with the no less important need to protect them?

Might it surprise you to learn that the answer may well lie with an insurance company? At John Hancock we believe that while exceptional returns are desirable, exceptional risks are not. Choice and flexibility, yes. Excessive volatility and reckless speculation, no. To that end, John Hancock offers a wide range of investment and insurance opportunities. The disciplined approach offered by our family of mutual funds. Or, if tax-deferred savings for retirement or protecting your family is your goal, our variable and fixed annuities and variable life insurance.

To learn more, see your John Hancock representative or your personal financial advisor.

INSURANCE FOR THE UNEXPECTED.
INVESTMENTS FOR THE OPPORTUNITIES."

John Hancock
WORLDWIDE SPONSOR

May 1996

In the mid-1970s when the bull market began, investment clubs were shutting down. In 1975 and 1976, 2000 of them gave up on the common goal of wealth through stock ownership. According to the National Association of Investors Corporation, investment clubs didn't start forming as fast as they dissolved in 1975-1976 until 1987, when 987 clubs were formed. The annual total did not surpass 1000 until 1992. In 1995, investor interest in pooling resources and stock-picking skills went parabolic, as 5,298 clubs were started (see chart). Now NAIC officials say new clubs are being formed at an incredible rate of fifty a day, the fastest pace ever. As of March 31, the total stood at 21,172, 50% higher than the old record set in October 1970.

Warren Buffett's Berkshire Hathaway is [a] hot [stock] issue, even though Buffett himself has washed his hands of responsibility by strongly implying that he would not buy it himself at current prices. The only reason Buffett has agreed to sell the class B shares at about $1100 each (regular shares are $33,500) is that if he does not satisfy demand among small investors, someone else will. He intends to "fully satisfy" that demand. To do so, Berkshire has already increased the size of the May offering from 100,000 to 250,000 shares. He may raise it further. Wherever this offering crests, it is sure to leave a fascinating high-water mark for this bull market by showing to what extent the public will pay homage to the world's richest man by violating the very philosophy that he used to generate his wealth.

June 1996

The public's expectations are being bid up rapidly by hard sell artists. Just six months ago, a teenage boy hit the business best sellers list by extending the promise of a 34% annual return on the cover of his book. *Wall Street Money Machine* (see next page) targets the same 34% return, but, says its ex-cab driver author, a year is way too long. He says you can "consistently" acquire that return monthly.

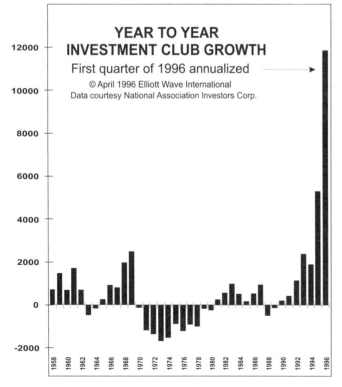

YEAR TO YEAR INVESTMENT CLUB GROWTH

First quarter of 1996 annualized

© April 1996 Elliott Wave International
Data courtesy National Association Investors Corp.

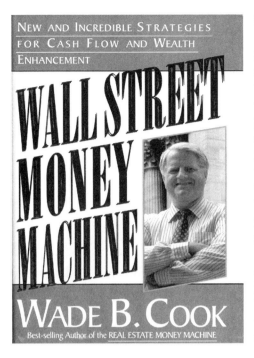

October 1996

A September 13 Newsweek article, reflected summer sentiment by declaring that "the Federal Reserve Board has come close to perfection." The Fed's icon status has been a clear reflection of the Grand Supercycle peak mood. Retaining that status will not be possible in the bear market. Once the money supply passes zero inflation, the Fed will not be able to stop the trend, as all it really does is follow the rates set by the market. The most damaging charges of mismanagement will come later, when the Fed is blamed for the ruination of the economy due to what many will call an overly restrictive monetary policy. With assets of $451 billion and 25,000 employees, the Fed will make a big potential target for a populace angered by a bear market and politicians eager for someone else to blame.

The NASD now has 527,000 registered stock brokers. That's a 80% increase from 1987. The number of Certified Financial Planners has tripled in ten years to 31,572 at the end of 1995. The number of Certified Financial Analysts has also tripled over the same time. A record number of 24,800 candidates took the CFA exam in 1996, a 27% increase over 1995 and a number greater than the total number of analysts currently holding the CFA designation.

This is more than just interesting news. Back in 1989, EWT chronicled the fact that in Connecticut, the real estate boom was so pervasive that more people were applying for brokerage licenses than there were licensed brokers in the entire state, an exact reflection of today's situation with respect to CFAs. That event marked top tick in the property boom in the Northeast, which thereafter fell into near-depression. Nationwide, the number of dues-paying members of the National Association of Realtors peaked with the real estate market at 829,000 that same year.

November 1996

Most of the time, a thorough knowledge of a subject pays off. In the realm of mass market psychology, there are times when those least knowledgeable appear as geniuses and roll in ledger-entry money. Today, I almost wish we had been among those people, but when the tide turns, their stress and disappointment will be worse than what we are going through now, if you can imagine that. Here on the left side of the top, knowing that we will avoid their fate seems a negligible comfort. On the right side of the turn, we will feel very different, I can assure you.

To keep up with the manic hype in this B wave, this once staid industry has even found a new and even more flamboyant financial hero. Ethan Pennar, a 35-year-old mortgage banker, has "emerged as one of the most powerful men on Wall Street." Pennar has become the "Michael Milken of the 1990s" after failing as a bond trader in the 1980s and getting bounced from his last firm "following a controversial loan." His three-year rise is attributed to a penchant for "snap decisions," "funky loans" and big risks. Pennar creates huge mortgage pools out of a relatively narrow mix of commercial property loans. Like all financial heroes, he has achieved the big bucks through innovation. His big breakthrough? Getting rating agencies to grade mortgage-backed securities with a dangerous concentration of real estate risk. How'd he do it? Simple, he just packs so many loans into a deal that rating agencies figure it's too big to go bad all at once. We'll revisit this attitude in a year or two.

Major companies (the same ones that adopted the disastrous "portfolio insurance" in 1987, perhaps) are betting that the stock market can be handled risk-free. Life insurers are aggressively marketing programs that guarantee "stock market exposure with downside protections." Aetna's "variable annuity account" promises at least to return an investor's money when the annuity comes due. Jackson National Life provides an equity-linked deferred annuity that helps investors to "stop losing sleep." This competition for the no-risk dollar requires products that promise a free lunch (only in the long run, of course).

January 1997

Alan Greenspan's early December warning about "irrational exuberance" triggered some crash talk in mid-December. The gloom dissipated rapidly on the ensuing rally.

> **ALL HAIL GREENSPAN!**
> —BusinessWeek, February 5, 1996

The underlying theme of a 32-page personal finance supplement to The Wall Street Journal, "A Parent's Guide to Money," is that mothers and fathers need to get their kids into the market, for two reasons: 1) to make money for their future and 2) to learn about the importance of buying and holding. Why are these observations important? So, you can see the setup for an arrogant complacency lasting months into the next bear market.

As of September 30, the number of employees on Wall Street set a new record of 262,460, beating out the previous high of 262,000, which was registered just before the crash of 1987. One more telling throwback to 1987: index funds first burst on the scene that year, and in 1996, they ruled. "This year, index funds have outperformed almost every other mutual fund group," noted one article. Another notes that the index funds left "active money managers in the dust" over the past two years. In response, Intel Corp. fired all 11 of its active managers and turned its $1.2 billion pension fund portfolio over to an in-house index fund. Two observations: First, index funds outperformed because blue chips outperformed the broad list of stocks. Second, indexing requires being fully invested, and those investors comfortably indexed will soon find themselves indexed to a bear market.

Recent articles show that once again, the market question has shifted to matters of relative rather than absolute performance. One subscriber calls the current rumination on managers' chances of beating the indexes in 1997 the Lake Wobegon Effect, because all stocks, like the children in Garrison Keillor's fictional Minnesota town, are now above average. For most people, this orientation holds only in a bull market. Customers of funds that lose only 19% in the next 20% decline will not be thrilled.

Cultural Trends

According to an annual survey by an executive search firm, 97% of U.S. companies planned to hold a holiday office party this past December. That is an immense change from just 16% in 1990, at the end of a stock market and social mood correction. At up to $400 cost per person, Wall Street Christmas parties are rivaling those of the late 1980s. Wall Street veterans have noted that the size of the shrimp at the holiday party is a pretty good indicator of the Street's fortunes in the coming year: the smaller the shrimp, the better the market's prospects. This year the shrimp were as big as shrimp get. Of course, many revelers probably didn't even notice because they never got past the lobster, caviar, Davidoff cigars and free flowing $190-a-bottle Cristal champagne. A 27-year-old Wall Street broker insists, however, "No one wants to seem ostentatious. We watched the crash and burn in the '80s. We don't want that. This time we want to be sophisticated. So it will last forever."

February 1997

For the recently formed Zoar Economically Able Ladies (ZEAL) investment club, the stock market is a religious experience. "It was weird," said one club member. "I wasn't really looking for anything to do. I had heard of the [Beardstown Ladies] before, but when I saw them on TV, it was just something I had to do. It was just something I had to do." Another said she was "led by God to join." Members have resolved not to "panic when the market takes a nose dive, but will allow themselves to get excited if the index soars."

March 1997

The Street's embrace of the public's supposed savvy was certified by the merger of Morgan Stanley and Dean Witter. Says one article, "Dean Witter, the brokerage firm that once sold stocks among the socks in Sears

CLASS MEETS MASS ON WALL STREET

Morgan Dean Witter could change the balance of power
—BusinessWeek, February 17, 1997

stores, said it will merge with Morgan Stanley, the white-shoe descendant of J.P. Morgan's banking empire. On Wall Street, retail is king."

Late-coming novice investors are now termed "increasingly shrewd households." According to a survey of retail investors, the number of U.S. citizens in the stock market has doubled to 43% since 1990. Merrill Lynch is trying to lure them with a new "Emerging Investor" account for those with no more than a few hundred dollars. In March, it will open a mutual fund "supermarket" that will let investors choose from more than 1000 different funds. A wave of institutional money managers like PIMCO, insurance companies like Transamerica and banks like Brown Bros. Harriman are heading down Main Street with a whole new series of aggressive mutual funds, which they will pile on top of the more than 8000 funds already available.

"Wall Street Values Its 'Uninformed' Investors,'" said one headline. Sometimes it's hard to tell who is more uninformed, the offerers or the offerees. The bull with bicycle grips for horns shown here is from a two-page, full-color ad campaign by a large life insurance company. Its new stock market annuity promises a 45% return over the next seven years plus half the upside above 7% a year. "You get the ride without the risk," the ad says. The Annu-A-Dex is "no wild, new idea" according to the ad. We're not sure we agree with that assessment, but we do recall that in 1987, a product similarly guaranteeing safety was sold to institutions under the name of "portfolio insurance." It didn't work out.

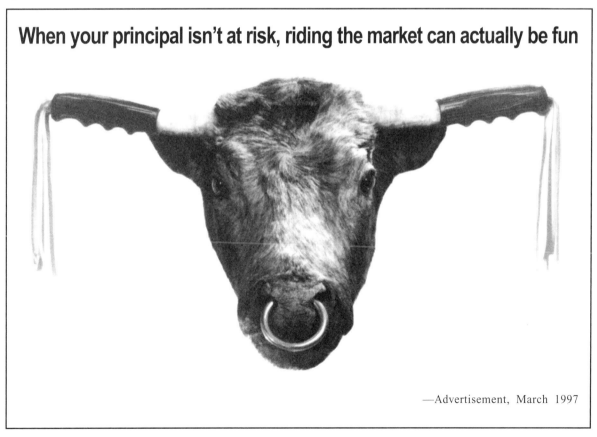

When your principal isn't at risk, riding the market can actually be fun

—Advertisement, March 1997

Another classic sign of over-extension is the free flow of money at Wall Street firms. In the last year, mutual fund portfolio managers have seen their average compensation rise 55%, to $370,800. 24 years ago, a similar adjustment took place near the January 1973 high, as brokerage firms bid up the salaries of the "Nifty Fifty" corporate fundamental analysts just in time for a decade of decline and underperformance by those stocks. Compensation for senior stock analysts (who are underperforming the market) is up 16% from 1995. Year-end bonuses totalled a record $8 billion. London traders are being tempted with advertised salaries of up to $1.6 million for a global head of quantitative research, "management experience not necessary." Another quantitative trading position promised "unlimited" pay. In 1994, Andrew Fisher, a Salomon Bros. trader, created a "firestorm" within the firm when he made $30 million trading mortgage-backed bonds. In 1996, he made another $25 million and nobody said a word. "The bull market came along, and pay wasn't an issue any more." At age 39, Fisher has decided to retire. His decision to play golf and drive his Ferraris "shocked" colleagues.

April 1997

As we said last September, Alan Greenspan has a very specific role to play in this unfolding drama. The Fed is an icon of the peak mood. A new book, *Back From the Brink* is billed as "the enthralling story of how the nation's economy was pushed to the precipice but rescued from disaster [after the crash of 1987] by the world's most important central bank and the impressive man at its helm." The depth of faith in the Federal Reserve Board Chairman is almost unfathomable.

Small Investors' Advice to Greenspan: Butt Out
—The Wall Street Journal, March 7, 1997

But a funny thing happened in February when Greenspan reiterated his famous warning of "irrational exuberance." The hero worship was replaced by "widespread hostility." It started a few days after the S&P's February 19 all-time high. A host of economists contradicted Greenspan's view. The criticism snowballed into "with all due respect, would Alan Greenspan please shut up" on March 4. On March 5, Greenspan, feeling the pressure, said something that the media could construe as bullish. He was immediately forgiven, and his status among editorial writers returned to superhuman: "He has clout mere mortals don't." A careful read, however, shows that Greenspan's view that the market is overpriced has probably not changed. Despite lip service that if earnings estimates prove correct, then stock prices are "not unreasonable," his main comment was, "We don't view monetary policy as a tool to...prick a stock market bubble," which is apparently still his view of things.

His temperance, however, was enough to let most bullish dreamers slip back into REM. Other true believers were not comforted. Wayne Angell, the Fed's onetime resident hawk on inflation, said on March 7 that if it hadn't been for this kind of overzealous monetary policy, the 1920s would still be going on. Like so many others, Angell has seen the light of a "new era brought on by a favorable economic environment." He begged Alan Greenspan to "please, please, stop worrying about the stock market." USA Today's front page later wondered, "What Did Greenspan Do To Upset So Many People?" He flicked a single drop of reality in their faces, that's what. And they hated it. Their dream was disturbed, and it took all their willpower to conjure it back.

Some insist that the Fed should feed the dream with intravenous sleeping pills. An economics professor writing in the March 23 New York Times suggests that every time the S&P falls 12% from a record high, the Federal Reserve should "buy stock index call options and futures" in order to "both send a signal of confidence and help stabilize prices" to "prevent excessive pessimism."

Meanwhile, in the real world, some other astute members of the financial community have started to sweat the decline and are catching flak for it. Barton Biggs stated that Microsoft was vulnerable. In response, a big technology fund manager cut back on trading with Biggs' firm.

Warren Buffett said "virtually all stocks" were overpriced. "Market Timing Isn't How Buffett Got Rich," responded one steamed columnist; "Legendary investor. Second richest man in America. He must know where the stock market is going. Wrong!" As Greenspan said, "No one can jawbone the stock market; anyone who thinks they can has just not looked at the evidence." *The Elliott Wave Theorist* has argued this point several times in the past, and it is true. If the market falls, his and others' warnings will not have been causal, just well-timed. However, most people cannot stand taking responsibility for their losses. As we noted in September, the Fed will make a big target for an angry populace when the tide turns.

May 1997

Bullish sentiment continues to topple stock market milestones. In the first week of April, Banker's Trust purchased a Baltimore brokerage firm "in the most visible sign yet of the breakdown of the Depression-era law that separates commercial and investment banking." The NASD has unveiled The Wall, a 55-by-11 foot wall of video images and market information designed to give the exchange a physical presence. Merrill Lynch, the nation's largest brokerage firm, reported its highest quarterly earnings ever.

Merger Talk Expands On Wall Street

Deal for Oppenheimer Could Hit $500 Million

—The Wall Street Journal
May 8, 1997

SBC Set to buy Dillion Read

US BANK BOUGHT FOR $300 MILLION AFTER COLLAPSE OF DISCUSSIONS WITH ING

Swiss Bank Corporation is to pay $600 million to buy Dillion Read, the Wall Street investment bank, as part of its attempt to become one of the world's leading investment banks.

—Financial Times, May 16, 1997

Bankers Trust in $1.6bn deal

Commercial and investment banks in record link-up

—Financial Times, December 9, 1998

The Insidiousness of a Mania

Historians characterize manias as a kind of madness that takes hold of a population. The widely shared illusion of endless huge profits that propels a mania also produces another kind of madness: anger. Though the media report new highs in the averages with a giddy demeanor, it is a clown mask that hides a miserable soul.

A very human aspect of manias is that no prudent professional is perceived to add value to a client's investment experience. Indeed, the professional with a knowledge of history and value is eventually judged an impediment to success. The reason is that the investments that are the focus of the mania are widely accepted as the benchmark of normalcy. Therefore, only a professional who "beats" that benchmark is considered successful. As the focus of the mania narrows, that task becomes impossible. This is yet another difference between a normal bull market and a mania. In a bull market, professionals can add value relative to the benchmark, which is usually conservative (the short term lending rate, for instance). In a mania, no one can add value. That is the situation today.

Let's review five types of professionals who have an approach that, in competent hands, "works" in most market environments and see how they are faring today.

　　1.　*Market timers*: Look back at the DJIA from 1932 to 1982 (see Chapter 1). For half a century, the stock market ebbed and flowed in such a way as to make good market timing a significant added value. Today, with the trend having gone one way for an entire decade, there has been nothing to time: nothing significant in the way of waves, cycles, or bear markets.

2. *Value buyers*: From 1932 to 1983, stocks that appeared undervalued by the market when priced against dividends, book value and earnings typically returned to greater valuation, providing an advantage to the investor who purchased issues meeting those criteria. The demoralizing story of this bull market for such investors is how substantially such stocks have been lagging the averages and indeed falling in recent months while the S&P soars.

3. *Quants and "diversifiers"*: Diversification into several asset classes, regardless of the weightings, has guaranteed significant underperformance relative to the S&P.

4. *Money managers*: Managers of money market funds, bond funds and mixed funds have obviously underperformed the S&P. Even 100%-stock fund managers cannot keep pace. In the past year, 80% of stock mutual funds failed to outperform the S&P. So far in 1997, the figure is 96%.

5. *Stock brokers*: Competent brokers have had a role to play in assisting investors, but in the current environment, nothing formerly prudent works. In the past year, brokerage firm research departments have repeatedly recommend $20 stocks that go to 6. Trading customers mostly sell short, trying to catch a pullback that is "long overdue," then join the advances too late out of desperation, losing in both directions. The firms' managed funds have gone up, but they lag the S&P.

In all these cases, the client becomes livid. "How can my market timer not see that stocks always go up?! How can this stodgy value buyer sit year after year in stocks that are stuck in the mud?! Why does my advisor have my account 40% in bonds and 10% in bills when obviously the action is in the stock market?! What's wrong with my broker? Almost everything he picks goes down! How come my fund is lagging the S&P by so much? What am I paying those guys for?! Everybody's getting rich but me!"

The result is that every professional who knows bull and bear markets but not manias, and every client thereof, is to some degree stressed and unhappy. In recent conversations, brokers have told me, "These are the worst months of my life." "My clients are getting killed." A money manager confesses, "I am chronically depressed." Market timers have few subscribers left and wonder if continuing is worth the effort and anxiety. This situation is totally different from that of a healthy bull market, where good money managers, timers, brokers and their customers are happy. In a mania, those who spent a professional lifetime studying the typical ways of the market are fools, and their utterly unknowledgeable novice clients tell them so, month after month.

Because a mania is so psychologically powerful, the clients have become dictators to the professionals, at least to the vast majority who have succumbed. The choice is not how to play the game (as it is in a bull market), but whether to play it. Money managers who refuse to accept the market's ultimatum to become heavily invested in mania stocks lose most of their customers. The only players who feel like (and are) winners are index fund managers who can spell the 500 names in the S&P index, the "momentum" buyers who chase whatever stocks are racing upward, and the investors who plunge into the vortex. These people are positively euphoric, and for good reason. Month after month, indeed year after year since 1992 when the fund craze took hold, they have reaped what looks like free money, and all of it can be attributed to their guts and acumen.

Ultimately, however, a mania and its aftermath have everyone for lunch: first the bears and contrarians, then the prudent professionals relying on long term studies, and finally the plungers who fancy themselves clever investors and pour most of their funds into the market in its final run. Even among prudent professionals who remain in business, the aftermath is no kinder than was the mania itself. A competent money manager's greatest claim on the way down will be that he is losing a lesser percentage of his clients' money than the averages, which is something the clients will not want to hear. Suddenly the "benchmark" that seemed so sensible on the way up is no longer acceptable. "The averages don't matter! Stop losing my money!" Market timers cannot provide much value on the way down, either. Post-mania declines are typically as persistent as the mania was on the way up. There are no significant advances, no "getting even," no way to take advantage except to sell.

June 1997

In Omaha, 7500 investors "flocked" to see the king of investors, Warren Buffett. The three-day festival surrounding Berkshire Hathaway's annual meeting was dubbed "Buffettmania," by Newsweek. The sage himself called the event "the Woodstock of Capitalism." Even though Buffett reiterated that there is no value left in the market, there were no visible signs of distress among attendees. The wave of positive emotion and its ultimate effect were summed up by a Buffett shareholder, who in reference to the infamous Jonestown incident said proudly, "We're like a cult. Warren just hasn't told us to take the poison yet."

July 1997

The media's best guess as to where the Dow is headed is derived from actuarial assumptions rather than market history. As a monitor of money management performance, Roger Ibbotson has measured managers against the market for two decades. Until recently, his name rated little more than a footnote in the fine print of managers' financial reports. These days, however, the bull market has pushed the standard so high that even the guy who sets the bar is a hero. Ibbotson's image has been boosted by a willingness to extrapolate the market's performance over the course of Supercycle (V) well into the next century. "What sets Ibbotson apart is the passion with which he preaches the equities gospel," notes a recent profile. "His view: you ain't seen nothing yet. By 2015 it will clear 34,000. In 2020, look for the average to hit 53,000."

August 1997

In keeping with the historic literature on manias, bearish analysts contesting the "obvious" logic of the rise must be shown to be dunces. In his *Short History of Financial Euphoria*, John Galbraith noted, "It is said that [the bears] are unable, because of defective imagination or other mental inadequacy, to grasp the new and rewarding circumstances that sustain and secure the increase in value." In keeping with this tradition, The Wall Street Journal ran a front-page article on July 17 that playfully taunted the bears as the objects of "intellectual sport." Another article on the public's bullish resolve concludes by quoting a man who actually wants a 20% decline

Advertisement
August 1997

because it's an "opportunity. If you don't see it that way, you are a fool." After market sage Ray DeVoe mentioned on CNBC that median valuation levels project a Dow decline of 35%, every guest that followed questioned his mental health or wondered if he was "living on another planet." "Every critic of the magical stock market must be demeaned, insulted or vilified," says DeVoe. The pressure has obviously gotten to a few former bears. The August 13 economic forecast of one well-known holdout presented a complete reversal of opinion. "Recession Forecast is Rescinded," it says.

Then there's Wade B. Cook's latest book, *Bear Market Baloney*. Cook, a former taxi cab driver and real estate guru, is the author of the best seller, *Wall Street Money Machine*. He also offers an investment seminar in which he promises to "double his [sic] money in 2½ to 4 months." (Relish the precise "2½.") As it happens, he is also the world's foremost advocate of buying on the announcement of stock splits. After bashing the bears, he offers up a host of highly sophisticated investment tips. Some, such as "avoid negativism," are psychological pleas to embrace the mania.

January 1998

Market functionaries usually know better than to tamper with the free flow of prices. Playing to the collective dream is an urge that not even the most tradition-bound, market-centered institution can resist. Just before the highs of October, the chairman of the New York Stock Exchange described a scenario in which the market would rise to 10,000, fall slowly back to 8,000 and then begin another long rally. "The adjustment would eventually lead to another bull market that could see the Dow reach 18,000," reported one of several editors and publishers to hear the chairman's address. He went on to insist that he "doesn't make forecasts." The NYSE had a long-standing tradition of not taking a position on the direction of the market. In the 1960s and early 1970s, the general rule according to a former NYSE economist was that the exchange "religiously and judiciously said nothing." This time-honored policy was established in the 1950s after the NYSE *cautioned* small investors about the possibility of a correction and regretted doing so.

In the fall of 1997, however, the NYSE chairman came not to warn the little guy, but to encourage him. At a national convention for investment clubs, the chairman appeared on a panel that included one of the Beardstown ladies. Under a headline documenting the exchange's unofficial stance ("Bullish on the Stock Market"), he guessed that the "extraordinary opportunities" of the last 15 years have another 15 years to go. Upside bias on the part of a Big Board spokesman is not entirely unprecedented.

In 1928, then-NYSE president E.H. Simmons said, "I cannot help but raise a dissenting voice to the statement that we are simply living in a fool's paradise and that prosperity in this country must necessarily diminish and recede in the future." Today's chairman admonishes dissenters with a strangely similar but even more strident rebuke: "This is a time, some say, of unparalleled risk if you're in equities. I would say there's great risk in being out of them." The Wave Principle provides a way to identify parallel times in history, and 1928/1997 is one of them.

March 1998

As noted in last May's "Bulls, Bears and Manias" special report, one of the perverse effects of a mania is that "no prudent professional is perceived to add value." The public, with its heightened sense of financial confidence, is even beginning to eschew its beloved mutual fund managers. "More investors, looking for better returns than even mutual funds can provide, are building their own portfolios with individual stocks. It's easier and cheaper than ever." An "exploding number" of do-it-yourself buyers are using on-line accounts, no-load stocks and 401(k) brokerage plans that permit the purchase of individual stocks to build their own portfolios. "This is a wonderful and empowering trend," says an expert.

April 1998

Even as the finishing touches are applied to the great monuments of this bull market, the mythology that created one of its icons has been stripped away. The Beardstown Ladies, we are now reading everywhere, did not generate the 24.3% annual return they claimed on the cover of their first book. In fact, this idolized 1990s' investment club actually earned only a 9.1% return against an S&P average of 15%. The "Beard-

---

Beardstown Ladies Overdressed Their Success

Beardstown, Ill. The Beardstown Ladies, those homespun, grandmotherly investors whose supposed success created a mini-industry, are being called frauds. Their total returns were nowhere near as robust as claimed.

—The Atlanta Journal-Constitution
February 28, 1998

---

stown Boo Boo" was attributed to a computer entry.

The far more fascinating aspect of this "revelation" from our point of view is that it isn't one. The inclusion of club dues in the Ladies' "return" was reported in a few places at the outset. We knew it shortly after the book came out. At least one columnist reports having published the fact three years ago. The major media have simply ignored the fact! A regional president with the National Association of Investment Clubs now tells us she had concerns in 1995, "but decided not to speak out." Apparently, she didn't want to contradict the Financial Times, which crowned the ladies the "Golden Girls of Illinois" and wrote, "Warren Buffett? Forget him. George Soros? He's history. The real investment gurus are 16 elderly ladies..." And so it went until now. The years it took to disseminate the truth illustrate how cherished is the mania-friendly idea that ordinary people can be stock market savants.

May 1998

Concurrently, the great merger of Citicorp and Travelers, in addition to being the biggest ever, has effectively demolished the Depression-era laws that separated the insurance, banking and brokerage industries. The principle at work here is simple: bear markets break things apart and bull markets bring them together. On April 15, regulators quintupled the size of a one-day DJIA decline that they will allow. It now takes a 20% decline after 2 p.m. or a 30% decline earlier than that to close the market for a full day. Before, it took a 550-point (currently 6%) drop to close the market. The triggers for one- and two-hour trading halts were also increased, to declines of 10% and 20%. It is interesting that the limits were so dramatically expanded at this point in the wave structure.

Forget the Beardstown Ladies; the new man, er, boy, on the block is Aaron Siegel, a "teenage day-trader" who turned "A Faux $10,000 into $212,109." His big winner was Foodarama, a thinly traded NASDAQ stock. His stroke of genius was pouring his "entire mock portfolio" into the stock after Foodarama reported dramatically higher earnings. Droves of grown men and women aren't just day trading on paper. A local business newspaper calls them "entrepreneurs" and says their number is "growing throughout the country." In our area, we have two of these trading shops, and a third is coming to town because Atlanta has all the ingredients for speculation: plenty of participants, money and, most important, "youth." The word is that it also helps to "be adept at video games."

June 1998

Let the Children Play...the Stock Market

On late-night network TV, half-hour-long infomercials patiently spell out the basics of futures trading in "Dick and Jane" cadences, stressing its normalcy and prudence. Because of the time of night, we presume that these are aimed at novice adults, not kids. Still, their tone assures us that making money is child's play. Perhaps that is why millions of kids are being lured into the market with comic books, board games, cartoons and TV stock-picking contests. April was National Savings Month. To celebrate, Merrill Lynch issued a full-color comic called "Savin' Dave and the Compounders." A companion piece called "Kid's Guide To Savings" asks, "How Does

To Boy, 5, Investing is Elementary

CNBC's financial news has turned kid into market guru

NEW YORK - When the chairman of the New York Stock Exchange wanted a stock tip, he turned to a young but savvy market observer who can rattle off names from the Dow 30 and describe the best investment vehicles.

The New York Sock Exchange's chairman, Richard Grasso, said that upon meeting Keith Anderson, Jr. in early April, he pinned his chairman's identification badge on young Anderson and transferred his title to him.

So what did young Anderson do as chairman for the day?

"I opened it up," he said.

Excuse me?

Grasso said "9:30, open it up," and with that, Richard, at age 5, became the youngest individual to ring the opening bell of the New York Stock Exchange.

Grasso spent the morning with Richard – a fourth generation entrepreneur in the making with his own business card – spreading the gospel of stocks and bonds to students, television reporters and floor traders who surrounded him and delighted in his jokes.

Asked for tips, the young owner of mutual funds (but no stocks and bonds) offered up AT&T, Merck, Caterpillar, Coca-Cola and McDonalds – all components of the Dow Jones Industrials.

Richard began his financial education at age 2 when, as punishment, his father would tell him he couldn't watch his cartoons and instead had to watch CNBC, the financial news and talk show network.

—The Detroit News, May 18, 2998

Forget Boomers–
Real Action Is With the Kindergarten Crowd
—Barron's, April 6, 1998

Your Money Grow?" and answers with a big chart showing the doubling of Barnes & Noble stock from January 1997 to February 1998. A flat line reveals the comparable yield from a piggy bank. In other words, "savings" has become a code word for "buy and hold stocks."

As far as we can tell, targeting kids with stock market propaganda is an unprecedented event that supports our conclusion that we may be witnessing the biggest mania of all time. In all the histories of financial manias, we cannot find another case in which children were drawn into the euphoria. Even in 1720 and 1929, there is no record of juveniles as active participants. The only possible parallel we could find was to 1213. According to Charles Mackay's *Extraordinary Popular Delusions and The Madness of Crowds*, it was in the spring of that year that as many as 30,000 kids got swept up in the Crusades and "undertook the journey to Palestine." Children may have participated in other bull-market delusions, but, until now, the most pronounced episodes tended to come at social-mood bottoms rather than peaks. The best example occurred in Germany at the bottom of Supercycle (IV) in 1932. According to The German Youth Movement, "Hitler's assumption of power signified in a very real sense the victory of youth," which had terrorized the country with chaos and violence in the months before Hitler's election. As part of the institutionalization of the angry social mood of 1932, Hitler Youth became a powerful part of German life until the end of World War II.

Today's stock market youth are the antithesis of the Hitler Youth. Their prominence represents a faith in the benevolence of social mood and an utter lack of respect for its potential savagery. Since we are in uncharted mania territory, there is no way to know how deeply this phenomenon can penetrate, but kindergarten must be pretty close to the bottom. This headline is from May 3: "To Boy, 5, Investing Is Elementary." According to the Detroit News, "watching CNBC" has turned 5-year-old Richard Anderson "into a market guru." Anderson, who became the youngest person to open the NYSE in April, "began his financial education at age 2 when, as punishment, his father would tell him he couldn't watch cartoons and instead had to watch CNBC." One day soon, we opine, this will be considered cruel and unusual punishment.

July 1998

Another messenger pushing all the right buttons is Abby Cohen, who made the cover of Business Week. Business Week calls Cohen "The Prophet of Wall Street" and "America's favorite bull." She is also a beloved, tenacious and courageous "spiritual leader" who, the article implies, will always be there to prop up the market because she "cannot envision doing a 180-degree turn." It tells the story of a day back in 1996 when "it was as if the world were falling, and Abby came in and lifted [the market] up again." The article ends by suggesting that she will do the same "any day now" if the market needs lifting. Take it from someone who has been through the guru mill, this beatific image is not a realistic picture. In the person of Abby Cohen, the public sees its own sagacity. The unprecedented height of her star (has a market forecaster ever before been on the cover of Business Week?), which has been propelled by a one-way forecast for stock prices after years of rise had already occurred, suggests that the warts in this reflection will soon show. For Cohen's sake, we hope that she is prepared for the inevitable backlash.

June 1, 1998

Goldman Sachs has decided to go public in the largest IPO ever. In late 1997, stock holdings of insurance companies and pension funds passed bond holdings for the first time ever. We say ever because while no figures exist, the great size of the bond market in the 1800s and first half of the 1900s, along with the paucity of stock shares, suggests that bonds were the dominant financial asset before 1952. The chart on the next page from Bianco Research (Barrington, Ill.) reflects an unprecedented institutional embracing of the stock market.

Current figures actually under-represent bullish conviction because many people have given up on life insurance and started "pouring money into investment-like mutual funds and variable annuities. The shift in attitude, which has been building gradually for years, has now reached critical mass, sending life insurance into something of a free fall" just in time for the peak in the market. To remain relevant, life insurance companies have dropped the word "insurance" from their name and started hawking investment advice.

From Bonds To Stocks
For The First Time Ever, Financial Institutions Own More Stocks Than Bonds

Type Of Institution	Assets (Trillions)	% Of Bonds	% Of Stocks
Life Ins. Cos.	2.581	68.78%	22.55%
Other Ins. Cos.	0.844	60.92%	20.95%
Private Pension	3.578	23.25%	49.34%
Trusts/Estates	1.012	23.94%	25.62%
Public Pension	2.100	27.50%	61.69%
Total	**10.115**	**38.96%**	**40.32%**

October 1998

The second biggest star in Cycle wave V's galaxy of financial lights is Bill Gates. Until the latter stages of the bull market, Gates enjoyed fawning coverage. In 1996, Newsweek referred to him as the "richest and maybe the smartest man in the world." Gates recent press is anything but favorable: "Did Bill Gates Lie?", "U.S. Accuses Gates," and "Microsoft Tactic: Like A Visit by Don Corleone." In opening its anti-trust case against Microsoft, the U.S. Justice Department set out to "paint a portrait of a sinister Gates." The suit has parallels to the department's attacks on Standard Oil in 1906, the year of a long-term peak in stock prices, and on IBM in 1968, again at a market top. The turn against Gates is not restricted to the government. At an October 15 computer conference, the "beloved geek who built a computer empire" was "under fire." Gates drew hisses from his own customers. At the next big computer show, where Gates usually reigns supreme, he was a glaring no-show.

January 1999

As EWT noted in 1997, one of the "very human aspects of a mania is that no prudent professional is perceived to add value." This condition has become increasingly acute as the Internet "Has Bred a Culture That Values High-Speed Speculation," the market advance has gotten thinner and mutual fund performance has fallen further behind the S&P 500. According to a story headlined "Many Unhappy Investors Think They Can Do Better Buying Shares Themselves," over the past five years, 273 of 294 actively managed funds have lagged behind the S&P 500.

Another full-page WSJ essay declares victory for the little guy, saying that the idea of the average investor always buying heavily at market peaks is "a myth." "There's just one problem with these comments about investor incompetence: They aren't true." At this point, this comment appears accurate, as the average investor has been right since 1992, when the mutual fund craze took hold. For the little guy, this is undoubtedly a record for his longest period without being dead wrong on the market. What counts, however, is the degree of the reversal that the market is approaching. By the time the coming Grand Supercycle bear market ends, public investors will not only be losers but the biggest losers in over two centuries. The environment of speculation during this decade has simply set them up for this inevitability.

March 1999

The "world's most prestigious" exchange made several other moves to accommodate the public's seemingly unquenchable thirst for equities. With the help of nearly $1 billion in city and state funding, the Big Board will expand its trading floor into a nearby building. It is the NYSE's first major expansion since 1987, when plans for the New Blue Room were put in motion. Construction of the original Blue Room began near the peak of 1968. These two previous expansions were initiated at the zeniths of the last two great speculative binges and opened for business in the far more subdued trading environments of 1988 and 1969. In an unparalleled action, the NYSE also announced a tripling in the length of its trading day. "The growth of global investing will not allow markets to be competitive if they constrain themselves to a time clock," explained the chairman. The NYSE will open for business in European shares at 5 a.m. and add evening hours through midnight "to embrace a consumer group that traditionally has been shut out." The NYSE is also making plans to begin trading popular shares on the NASDAQ.

What Investors Know Can Hurt Them

One of the biggest hazards of the mania is that it has instilled in investors what James Grant calls "a sense of mastery... They believe that, in partnership with Alan Greenspan, they control events." A housewares merchant says, "being involved in the stock market has absolutely changed the way I think. It's given me a feeling of control over my life." The day-trading explosion epitomizes the danger. "Watch Out!" says a Forbes teaser, "Five million ordinary investors are empowered with new trading tools." Watch out is right. The central component of these bull-market belief systems is apparent in a recent CNNfn Internet survey of 9000 investors. When asked "If a familiar stock dips, do you buy it?" more than 80 percent answered "Yes."

The February issue of Ticker, a new magazine for individual investors, expresses how far the discipline of investing has strayed. The article is about a psychologist who invested his life savings in a stock based on a dream. "I was in Palm Springs and someone told me, 'Don't worry, ICOS is going to $36.'" The stock hit $24.50, and the psychologist has since "programmed his mind" to dream about stocks by meditating before bed, praying for guidance and asking his "dream mind" to send images that express a particular stock's potential. In a bear market, the average investor's mind will be filled with nightmares, all courtesy not of REM sleep but of reality.

The Bullish Imperative

At this point, everything rides on the continuation of America's collective dream state. As one observer put it, "There is really no alternative to keeping the American bubble bubbling along for at least 12 months. It's a matter of good international policy. The reality is there's no other growth locomotive in the world." The Time magazine cover shown here expresses the consensus view that Greenspan & Co. are up to the task.

The article includes a centerfold in which "The Three Marketeers," Greenspan and U.S. Treasury officials Robert Rubin and Lawrence Summers, are portrayed as "economist heroes" who have, in fact, prevented a global slide. A similar article in USA Today is even more fawning. It says that Greenspan is "extremely smart," "extremely fair," "a great patriot," a "human computer" and "extremely devoted to his mother."

February 16, 1999

In neither article is it mentioned that none of the countries that have purportedly been saved with $180 billion in bailout funding have actually turned their economies around. In Brazil, where the latest line in the sand was drawn, the word is that the economy has tumbled into recession "Amid Few Indications of Any Turnaround Soon." While the "committee to save the world" is still "putting its faith in the markets," the rest of the world "from Brazilia to Beijing to Tokyo" is talking "about how to get out of the globally integrated economy. Indonesian rickshaw drivers and Chinese steel makers are demanding that their governments take care of them. Suddenly, the market forces that were seen as the path to national salvation have become the enemy of national sovereignty." The difference between the new international tone and the American resolve to stick by the market is simply the difference between the end of a bull market and a developing bear. As Paul Montgomery (Universal Economics), has shown, the cover of Time is in and of itself a reliable sign that the last line of defense has or will shortly succumb to the forces of reversal.

May 1999

Go to a nearby college campus and check out the kids with the fancy laptop computers. "Students and professors say student day-traders are evident all over campus. Students can be spotted monitoring their accounts on public terminals in graduate school hallways, discussing their investments with other student traders over lunch, and even purchasing stocks from their laptops during classes."

Where do college students get the money? Not "from savings or a rich uncle — but from the federal government's student loan program." A Virginia Commonwealth business student paid his $1600 tuition with his $7700 student loan and deposited the balance in his brokerage account. This semester, he has more than quadrupled his money and expects to pay the government back the day he graduates: "The financial aid office should be overjoyed," he says. A voice of caution says, "Anyone who takes the chance of losing their loan money is stupid," this from the author of a weekly column for student investors. On the collegiate investment scene, however, such admonishments constitute "conservative advice" which "grad students at Columbia and elsewhere ignore." Instead, "they look to the Internet for tips. BuckInvestors.com, for instance, is intended just for students. Others act on tips from friends. Some go much higher. 'I pray. I believe God will steer me in the right direction,'" says a taxpayer-backed student/trader.

Some of the most conspicuous cashing in has come from the brokerage sector, which has a long history of reaching for the brass ring near peaks. Goldman Sachs has increased its IPO to as much as $50 a share. By selling off just 14.5% of the firm, Goldman's top three executives will increase their net worth by $700 million. The last time the 130-year-old partnership was this close to selling itself to the public was last July, and the market had its biggest correction since 1990, derailing the offering.

The U.S. stock exchanges themselves, "which have operated as not-for-profit membership organizations for two centuries," are also considering converting their seats into shares "that could be traded publicly."

Charles Schwab has published what could be "the most conspicuous help-wanted ad ever run by a brokerage firm." The full-page ad solicits 1000 workers who will "demystify" the stock market and make it "every man's market."

June 1999

Brains or a Bull Market

Is the bull market getting "smarter?" A recent Business Week cover story answers affirmatively. In and of itself, a major magazine's front-page endorsement of "the wiser bull" is evidence of the opposite.

As EWT has observed two years ago, "a very human aspect of manias is that no prudent professional is perceived to add value to a client's investment experience." We also stated, "A

mania plays the genius for a fool and the fool for a genius, and then slays the fool for believing it."
Yes, that was two years ago, and there's been no slaying yet, but the foolishness has gotten much
more ingenious. The latest and greatest sign of the public's faith in its own acumen is people's
new willingness to abandon their beloved mutual funds to pick stocks. Many publications have
noted a nine-month decline in net new purchases of stock mutual funds and a corresponding
increase in direct stock purchases. An article headlined, "Investors Take A Direct Approach," says,
"a significant psychological shift" means "many investors now view mutual funds as passe."

The case of a suburban New Jersey housekeeper reveals the powerful human herding instinct
behind the breakthrough. She started to pay attention to stocks when she noticed her employers "frequently vacationing in Europe and buying huge homes just minutes from her house. To
pick up some pointers, she began tuning in to business-TV channels in the houses she cleaned,
ratcheting up the volume so she could hear over the noise of the vacuum cleaner. She once would
have been a prime candidate for mutual funds. Instead, she is a stock jockey. Holding stocks
directly 'gets me nervous, but it also gets my adrenaline going,'" she says. "Funds are seen as
fuddy duddy," says a mutual fund consultant in another article. "People want to own the stocks
that that guy at the cocktail party owns."

September 1999

Money camps for kids have surged
in popularity. The "high point" for some
happy campers was "the futures-trading
course." Due to the enthusiastic response
of attendees, the Future Investors Club of
America hopes to go national and extend
its camps into the school year. "When
8-year-olds in our community are giving
presentations on financial markets, the
sky's the limit," said the group's president.
Actually, unless rhesus monkeys can be enticed into the investment arena, financial

> ## More Youngsters Put Stock in Investing
> ### *Savvy kids take advantage of easy access to markets*
> Megan Tooley reads the newspaper every morning because she wants
> to know how her stocks are doing.
>
> Tooley's interest in Wall Street isn't unusual, given America's love
> affair with stocks. What is unusual is her age — 12. She buys shares of
> Nike and Delia's Clothing Corp. using money earned from pet-sitting
> and teaching karate to neighborhood friends.
>
> A recent Merrill Lynch poll showed 11% of youths ages 12 to 17
> own stocks, and a slightly higher percentage own mutual funds. A year
> earlier, 7% owned stocks and 9% had mutual funds.
> —USA Today, August 16, 1999

presentations by 8-year-olds will probably mark the Grand Supercycle limit in the demand for
and belief in market information and analysis.

The New Bull Market Heroes

Remember back in the early days of this mania when investors had value-minded billionaires like Warren Buffett to admire? As the bull market has gotten thinner and thinner, so have
the quality of its legends. The front page of the August 19 New York Daily News offered a good
example. It featured "WHEELER DEALER" Carlos Rubino, a 42-year-old New York cabbie who "is
cashing in on the Wall Street boom between the ticks of his fare box." "Safety first," says Rubino
in a Newsweek quote. "I stop the cab at the side of the road if I have to make a trade." "Wall
Street brokers are usually impressed with his knowledge," reports The Wall Street Journal, "but
the feeling generally isn't mutual." Even though the only evidence of success was the high-tech
equipment in his cab, the Daily News declared the immigrant from Brazil "a walking, talking,
driving American success story" based on his prediction that he will be "a millionaire within
five years." This is after Mark Barton introduced the world to the desperate underside of day
trading.

Remember when The Wall Street Journal used to swirl with rumors about what George Soros
or Warren Buffett were buying? Well, now the rumors are on the gossip page, and the financial
wizard they are trying to pin down is Barbra Streisand. Honest, the media now vies for the inside
scoop on Babs' "stock picking prowess." After the New York Post printed brokers' estimates of a
decline in the performance of stocks picked by Streisand in the June issue of Fortune, USA Today

reported that Streisand told CNBC that the Post story was based on a static account. "Streisand has bought and sold since she gave the interview," explained USA Today. In another hot scoop, it was revealed that Barbra "was so eager to snap up shares of TheStreet.com, a hot Internet IPO, that she called up the company's CEO offering tickets to her concert in Las Vegas." The CEO got Streisand to up the offer to "a private dinner," but "Streisand hasn't lived up to her end of the deal..." If actors can be investment geniuses, we surmise that Soros will soon debut in a musical on a Broadway. Why not?

October 1999

The public's market savvy is now established and broadly advertised as fact. "The explosion of financial information is creating smarter investors," says the AP without attribution or qualification. On-line brokerage firms are continually reinforcing the notion with television spots that celebrate the little guy's wisdom in ditching their brokers to go it alone. One calls its services, "The smart tool for smart investors." Another is building "a world of smarter investors." Do not look now, but the message is going to get several times louder. In response to a slowdown in on-line growth, brokers will pour $1 billion into additional advertising over the next year. That should be just enough to set the stage for everything investors know about the market to turn out to be absolutely wrong.

November 1999

In another interesting post-peak twist, the few bear market analysts that actually survived the recent highs are not getting much credit for catching the turn. As a matter of fact, New York Post columnist John Crudele reports that several have been shown the door or muzzled. "The more dangerous the stock market seems to get, the less Wall Street wants anyone being frank with clients," says Crudele. This comment from an unnamed Wall Street strategist is as good a sign as any that, in at least one dangerous respect, the grip of the mania is as tight as ever: "It's suicide to be rational in an irrational environment."

January 2000

Until very recently, the near-term enthusiasm of seasoned investors has been more restrained. The chart of bullishness among members of the American Association of Individual Investors depicts a relatively steadfast caution on the part of more experienced investors. Despite the acceleration in stock prices since 1996, the AAII has seldom recorded a bullish majority among its membership. The

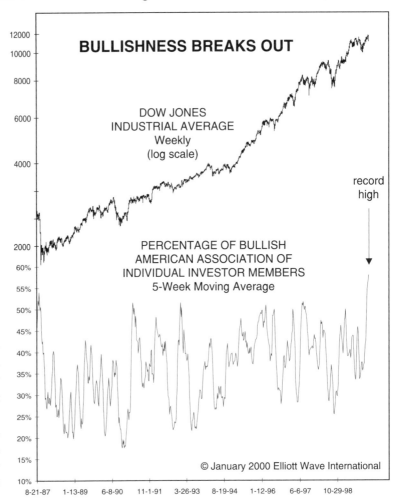

BULLISHNESS BREAKS OUT

DOW JONES
INDUSTRIAL AVERAGE
Weekly
(log scale)

record high

PERCENTAGE OF BULLISH
AMERICAN ASSOCIATION OF
INDIVIDUAL INVESTOR MEMBERS
5-Week Moving Average

© January 2000 Elliott Wave International

8-21-87 1-13-89 6-8-90 11-1-91 3-26-93 8-19-94 1-12-96 6-6-97 10-29-98

1990s did not see a sustained move above 50% until 1997, when an eight-week stretch that ended in the middle of August was followed by an immediate Dow decline of 16% and the onset of the Asian contagion. In December 1999, it happened again, as the AAII had five straight readings in which a majority of this historically cautious group was bullish. By the end of the month, AAII bullishness had reached a record high of 58%. The old record of 54% was reached in the middle of the only other sustained breach of 50%, which lasted six weeks and ended on October 9, 1987, at the start of the 1987 crash.

This latest surrender on the part of normally conservative investors brings the last four years of extraordinary stock market sentiment to a fascinating juncture. As *The Elliott Wave Theorist* pointed out several years ago, one of the perverse aspects of manic financial episodes is that prudent money management gradually comes to be seen as an obstacle. As EWT said in its May 1997 report, "Bulls, Bears and Manias," "A knowledge of history and value is eventually judged an impediment to success." The AAII data show that in the run to 11,500, reason was simply no match for bullish psychology.

February 2000

Because it believes the public's "refusal to panic has steadied the market in rocky times," the media heralds this development as another giant stride forward. The truth, however, is the opposite. The potential for a rapid and chaotic descent has been enhanced by the loss of strong hands to orchestrate an orderly liquidation of asset prices.

The market's response to Fed Chairman Alan Greenspan's latest warning about the stock market signals a complete loss of respect for financial authority. "This could be one of the euphoric speculative bubbles that have dotted human history," he said January 13. Days later, The Wall Street Journal noted, "Stocks have historically taken a hit after Mr. Greenspan said something skeptical about the market. But more and more it sometimes lasts no more than a few hours. In this case, there was no hit at all." In finally succeeding to tune out the sincere concerns of Alan Greenspan, the foremost financial hero of the bull market, the public has signaled that its potential to experience tragedy is now fully formed. When the bear market starts, we will see how sophisticated the little guy has become.

March 2000

People have lost respect for market authorities. As we said again last month, "The striking trait of this mania is how it has taught investors to ignore the experts." A front page article in the February 25 issue of The Wall Street Journal reflects the public's ambivalence toward warnings of any kind. "Signs of a Market Top Come and Go: The Bull Market Just Pushes On." The presence of a professional wrestler in the guru-of-the-day seat on "Squawk Box" probably marks a new record high in the public disdain for market experience.

April 2000

It's not just Main Street. Hard-core Wall-Street types are bowing to the mania, too. According to a story headlined, "Hedge Funds Shift Strategy to Equity Bets," many well-known funds that are considered to be the most sophisticated players around have "ditched their complicated investment strategies in favor of plain-vanilla equity bets, in many cases becoming pure stock funds." Even the Rockefellers have decided to cash in. The Wall Street Journal reports, "For the first time, the Rockefeller family is eager to exploit" its name. Rockefeller & Co., the money-management firm that serves the 178-member Rockefeller clan, has a new logo, website and marketing plan to capitalize on the "most powerful brand name for wealth in U.S. history." "We're trying to move toward a brand-name image," says Rockefeller & Co.'s chief executive officer. "The family is even considering attaching its name to its own mutual fund product."

May 2000

The chart of Wall Street employment shows the increasing numbers that have been lured by the bright light of the market. As that light flickers and then fades, this line will turn down fast. (Yes, we can see a clear five up, but lacking data from before 1960 we will refrain from placing a wave count on it.)

A recent rebellion by "oppressed" junior level analysts indicates that sentiment within the industry is also extremely ripe for a downturn at any moment. Executives at several firms recently capitulated to demands for more meal money, better laptop computers, casual dress codes and access to the company gym on weekends. "It wasn't that long ago that to become an analyst was to trade your life for a career path." Wall Street only rarely intersects with Easy Street. The problem with careers that begin near these intersections is that they tend to stop suddenly. The chart shows what happened in 1968 and 1987. This time, the damage will be far greater, and it will probably be reflected on the streets of the world's financial capital in record time.

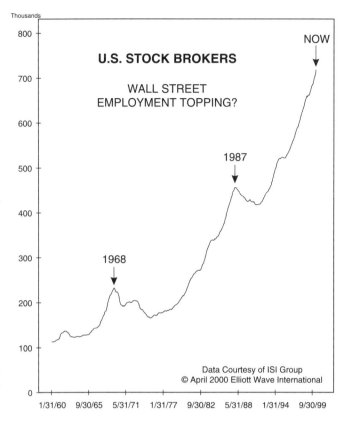

U.S. STOCK BROKERS

WALL STREET EMPLOYMENT TOPPING?

Data Courtesy of ISI Group
© April 2000 Elliott Wave International

The Casual, Coddling, Brand-Corporate Culture of Wall Street

Merrill Lynch & Co. canceled the free lunches it traditionally had doled out to its deskbound traders and salesmen. Then Lehman Brothers followed suit.

It was the fall of 1994, and though the mealtime savings were small, the symbolism was not. Wall Street, it seemed, had finally gotten religion. A new era of bottom-line, shareholder-focused discipline had dawned.

Click on the year 2000. In December, Merrill Lynch will cut the ribbon at a new state-of-the-art fitness center on the ground floor of its World Financial Center headquarters. Lehman Brothers is flying its junior bankers business class on coast-to-coast trips and offering more money for meals with colleagues. Meanwhile, J.P. Morgan offers stressed-out employees three free sessions of psychological counseling (by either phone or office visit), provides massages at its gym and is trying out a fancy concierge service that will arrange to pick up the dry cleaning, plan parties and even wait for the cable guy. So much for discipline in high finance.

—Institutional Investor, August 2000

June 2000

The New Market Wizards

"A very human aspect of manias is that no prudent professional is perceived to add value. Indeed, the professional with a knowledge of history and value is eventually judged as an impediment to success." This statement, first published in "Bulls, Bears and Manias," bears repeating as it has never been truer than it is now. The brightest lights of the investment kingdom, Warren Buffett, George Soros, Stanley Druckenmiller and Julian Robertson, have all been humbled in recent weeks. Time magazine calls it the "Fall of the Mighty."

When Robertson frankly admitted he was shutting down his fund because he could not find any value and did not understand the market, the media shot back with personal attacks. "Robertson didn't invest competently." "He's a sad shadow of the Robertson of the 1980s." "The Buck Stops With Julian Robertson, Not the Market." When Druckenmiller left the business two weeks later, the media said it was because of bad bets on technology. Buffett, on the other hand, had a bad year because he refused to make "even small bets" on technology. Buffett is in too deep to walk away, but he admitted that he is now focused on unloading his exposure to the stock market. Ultimately, he hopes to reduce his equity holding to just 10% of his portfolio. Soros has admitted that he "may not understand" the market any more and initiated a new lower risk investing style. "Maybe the music has stopped, but people are still dancing," he says.

As these distinguished investors bow out, the stature of those left to bask in the financial limelight says volumes about the current stock market juncture. EWT speculated that the last players to fall would be the "plungers who fancy themselves clever investors and pour most of their funds into the market in its final run." These days, the positive front-page profiles have fallen to the Motley Fools, whose whole philosophy calls for investors to "ignore the experts in pin-stripe suits" and a Saudi prince who calls himself the "Buffett of Arabia." "When Panic Hits Wall Street, the Prince Buys — A Lot." Unlike the secretive Buffett, however, the Prince puts out releases that announce his purchases. On April 6, he bought $1 billion in stock. On May 15, he dumped another $1 billion into a list of broken down Internet stocks. Both investments preceded market declines to new lows. His latest buys "illustrate the royal verdict that in today's break-all-the-rules stock market, so called 'value' investing is no longer limited to stocks bearing drowsy price-to-earnings ratios."

Another profile trumpets the investment sagacity of professional baseball player Jose Canseco, who has 90% of his portfolio in technology stocks and a forecast of NASDAQ 5000 in eight months. Then there's the story of Barton Biggs' plumber. The Morgan Stanley Dean Witter strategist got in trouble with the media for representing a real life plumber as an apocryphal symbol of the average investor's faith in the stock market. A Bloomberg article on the flap reveals, however, that the real problem is that Biggs has been wrong for a long time and his plumber has been right. It adds that the plumber is now "considering an offer to write a column for Bloomberg News."

These profiles in stock market courage fit perfectly with our expectations for the immediate aftermath of the mania. As we said in May 1997, "These people are positively euphoric, they have reaped what looks like free money, and all of it can be attributed to their guts and acumen." The bear market's mission is to reveal the ignorance and naivete that are the true source of their profits. Think of how delighted Papa Grizzly must be to awake and see what's on the menu: plumbers, sheiks and Fools! Most investors are so absurdly overmatched that even humorist Dave Barry picked up on it in his column last Sunday:

> If you own stocks, you have the excitement of knowing at any moment you could be wiped out by economic forces you do not even dimly comprehend. This is called "owning a piece of the pie," and it is the dream that has millions of hard-working Americans investing everything in the stock market. You should get in on this immediately. It's easy!

In another propaganda breakthrough for the bull market, a bill in Congress will allow the Secretary of Education to fund "financial literacy programs." The need was established by a test

that reputedly showed high school seniors "do not know the ins and outs of finance." According to the Associated Press, when they were asked "the best place to park money," less than a quarter "correctly answered 'stocks.'" This is an outrageous statement that refers to nothing but the recent past. This extreme optimism against lower highs in the stock market is the flip side of the deep worry among consumers in 1980, at which time consumers undoubtedly would have agreed to a man that stocks were the worst place to park your money. It will be ever thus.

September 2000

The small investor is suddenly catching all kinds of breaks. The SEC just passed "fair disclosure rules" that promise to put "Small Investors In The Info Loop." The law will "crack down on companies that share important information with a select handful of stocks analysts or large shareholders before giving it to the stock market youth." Here's a headline that shows just how low Wall Street's pursuit of the little guy can go:

Money-Savvy Youth Capture Finance Industry's Eye

Market camp teaches bear necessities
Wall Street 101 tutors teens in basics of finances
—USA Today, August 8, 2000

More Teens Making Trades – on the Stock Market
Investing: More youths are buying and selling shares

In some schools, students spend their lunch hours at computers checking stock prices. Some high schools now offer courses and clubs devoted to the market.

Thus far, schools say that investing with real money or play money is far more popular with boys than girls. Just as fast-paced computer games have a huge audience among young males, the competitive thrills of online stock -picking have become a hot draw.

—The Los Angeles Times, October 3, 2000

Readin', Writin', and Stockpickin'
Kids are trading biotech shares, not baseball cards
—Business Week, September 25, 2000

Kids never too young to learn investing

Forget lemonade stands and piggy banks. We're talking the stock market for kids in Wow the Dow. The mantra: It's never too early to teach kids money-management fundamentals.

—USA Today
October 23, 2000

In High School, Hallways Buzz With Stock Tips

"The jocks, the cheerleaders, the druggies – they all want to talk about the market." "They're giving them access to a very powerful – and socially acceptable – avenue to addiction."

—The New York Times
January 14, 2001

According to the August 11 article, "A rising tide of mutual fund companies, financial planners and other investment organizations are starting to tailor their products and services squarely for youth. At no other time have America's kids been more interested in money." Prior to the 1990s, stock ownership among sub-20-year-olds "was essentially zero." Now, 35% of 8th through 12th graders own stocks or bonds and 20% own mutual funds. The figures confirm *The Elliott Wave Theorist*'s contention from 1998 that "targeting kids with stock market propaganda is an unprecedented event" that constituted compelling evidence that we were "witnessing the biggest mania of all time." We added that there was "no way to know how deeply this phenomenon" would penetrate, but now with 200 Merrill Lynch financial consultants combing the schools with stock-market comic books, it seems likely that the last of the late-cycle investors are being mined.

Cultural Trends

Jocks know stocks? Money Magazine's September cover story, **"All-Star Investors,"** insists that it's true.

The article begins with the following observation: "Discipline. Intense preparation. Experience. Mental Toughness. All the things that you need to make it as an athlete also come in handy as an investor." Even though the discipline, preparation and experience needed for success in these two fields have almost nothing in common, and there is no documented case of a famous athlete ever sustaining above average returns outside of the mania phase of a bull market, no justification for this claim is offered. The magazine simply follows with this statement: "Lately, some of the biggest names in big-money sports have become obsessed with the stock market."

Undoubtedly, but is it therefore self-evident that "many superstars are knowledgeable investors"? Why else would designated hitter and "rabid tech investor" Jose Canseco accept 107,000 shares of BarPoint.com (an Internet stock that is down 90% since March) as a down payment for his $3.5 million home? And race-car driver Dale Earnhardt certainly wouldn't spend $2 million for a seat on the NYSE if he was not an "authority" on "a range of investments." Then there is NBA MVP Shaquille O'Neal. He likes tech stocks, so he definitely knows what he is talking about. Detroit Red Wing's star Sergei Fedorov "loves Nokia." He has three of their phones "and I use them every day. It's a no-brainer." Indeed.

Obviously, these sports guys are the ultimate trend followers, not investment Einsteins. This truth is revealed at the end of the story, when another hockey star, Luc Robitaille of the Los Angeles Kings, explains his methodology. He buys on "tips from friends and teammates." Money notes that the Kings' roster is "filled with stock junkies." "Nobody used to talk about stocks 10 years ago. Now that's all they talk about."

The glossy images of Anna Kournikova and Michael Jordan are on the cover of the issue also, but "not even the savviest sports stars manage all their own finances." These "top athletes leave the real work of wealth management to a pro." So why put them on the cover? Because they are superstars that reflect the brilliant light of the great bull market. As *The Elliott Wave Theorist* has continually pointed out, the popularity of sport and the fame that it brings its greatest stars are results of the same impulsive advance in social mood that produces a bull market in stocks. After a 200-year rise and an unprecedented mania, it makes sense that superstar athletes would be written up as market wizards. Remember, the "heroes of each major social psychological wave exit the scene when the wave is over" (EWT, May 1993). What better way to kick the pedestals out from under bull market heroes than to thrust "big money" stars into an arena where they cannot possibly succeed?

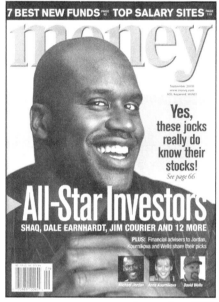

September 2000

October 2000

Wall Street's Urge to Merge

In April 1998, EWT called the merger of Citicorp and Travelers a bearish development:

> The great merger of Citicorp and Travelers, in addition to being the biggest ever, has effectively demolished the Depression-era laws that separated the insurance, banking and brokerage industries. The principle at work here is simple: bear markets break things apart and bull markets bring them together.

That comment came within days of the peak in the advance-decline line. Now, we see J.P. Morgan selling out to Chase Manhattan. Morgan is actually the commercial banking unit of the original bank, which was severed from its investment banking division by the government at the bottom in the 1930s. So, here again, we have a potent symbol of the bull market redoing at the top what was undone at the bottom.

January 2001

By some important measures, optimism is still rising. According to the "Sell Side" Consensus Indicator of Richard Bernstein (Merrill Lynch), brokerage industry strategists are now allocating a record 64.8% of their clients' assets to the stock market. As the chart shows, the total is easily the highest in the history of the indicator. In year-end survey after survey, Wall Street analysts talked up the prospects for stocks. One Wall Street Journal outlook had 11 out of 11 "top-name analysts" calling for the bull market to come back to life in 2001.

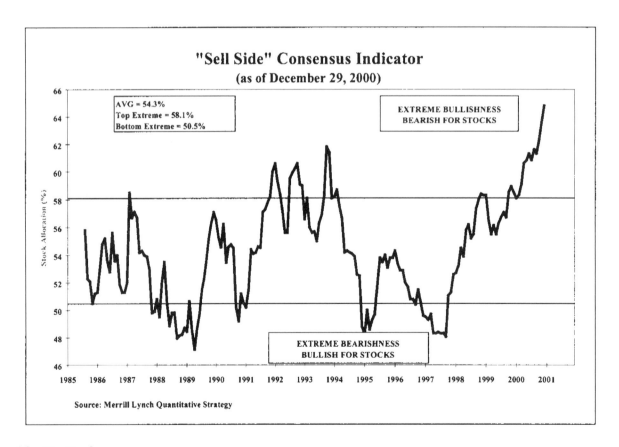

"Sell Side" Consensus Indicator
(as of December 29, 2000)

AVG = 54.3%
Top Extreme = 58.1%
Bottom Extreme = 50.5%

EXTREME BULLISHNESS
BEARISH FOR STOCKS

EXTREME BEARISHNESS
BULLISH FOR STOCKS

Source: Merrill Lynch Quantitative Strategy

The Big Hook

A year ago, EWFF published a chart of the Japanese Nikkei 225-stock index and asked, "Is this the model for the NASDAQ?" Apparently so, as the NASDAQ's decline has been closely aligned with the Nikkei's decline from its 1989 peak. So far, the resemblance even extends to

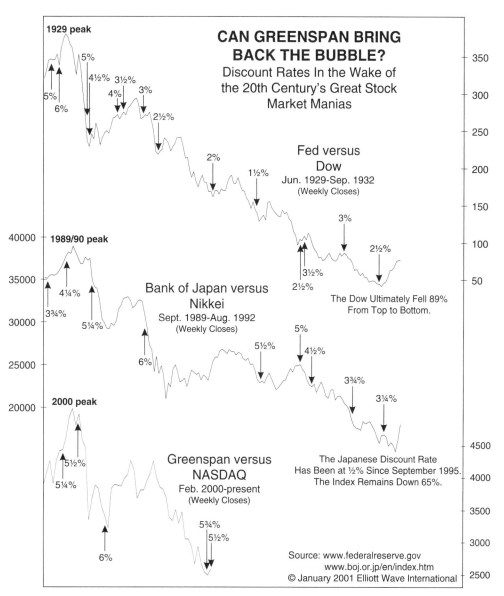

CAN GREENSPAN BRING BACK THE BUBBLE?
Discount Rates In the Wake of the 20th Century's Great Stock Market Manias

1929 peak

5%
6%
5%
4½% 3½%
4%
3%
2½%
2%
1½%

Fed versus Dow
Jun. 1929-Sep. 1932
(Weekly Closes)

3%
3½%
2½%
2½%

The Dow Ultimately Fell 89%
From Top to Bottom.

1989/90 peak

3¾%
4¼%
5¼%
6%

Bank of Japan versus Nikkei
Sept. 1989-Aug. 1992
(Weekly Closes)

5½%
5%
4½%
3¾%
3¼%

2000 peak

5½%
5¼%
6%

Greenspan versus NASDAQ
Feb. 2000-present
(Weekly Closes)

5¾%
5½%

The Japanese Discount Rate Has Been at ½% Since September 1995. The Index Remains Down 65%.

Source: www.federalreserve.gov
www.boj.or.jp/en/index.htm
© January 2001 Elliott Wave International

central bank policies. Take a look at the chart above. The Fed raised rates in the wake of the NASDAQ's initial decline, just as the Bank of Japan tightened during the first leg down in the Nikkei. It wasn't until the Nikkei was down nearly 45% that the BOJ dropped its discount rate. The NASDAQ was off 55% when the Fed finally cut rates on January 3, so the Fed is even further behind the curve than the BOJ was in 1990.

The chart shows that no amount of easing stemmed the post-bubble selling tide in Japan, where the discount rate hit 0.5% in September 1995. It has been there ever since, yet the Japanese economy is mired in a slump and the Nikkei is off 65% from its all-time high. What will they do next, pay people to borrow? In 1929, the Federal Reserve's response to the crash was almost immediate. Four straight rate cuts appeared to pay off for a few months, but in April 1930, the stock market rebound ended. Steady cuts from 6% in October 1929 to 1½% in May 1931 did not stop the Dow from falling almost 90% through the middle of 1932.

Despite the historical evidence, the belief in the Fed's ability to pump air back in the bubble is stronger than ever. Consider what happened December 5 when Alan Greenspan announced a new policy "tilt" toward lower rates (even though he perceives the current danger as "no way comparable" to that of October 1998). As this front-page banner from the next day illustrates, everybody knew what the action meant:

Economic Euphoria

—Rocky Mountain News, 12/6/00

In the wake of the big news, however, a funny thing happened. The market went down. As a matter of fact, despite every indication of an actual easing at the next Fed meeting, the NAS-DAQ fell another 20%. The "emergency" rate cut of January 3, took the Dow up 300 points, as investment bankers everywhere broke into high fives, analysts were quoted saying "Hallelujah!" and investors concluded in a matter of minutes that "a new bull market" was underway. We'll see. A section on "hooks" in *At the Crest of the Tidal Wave* anticipated the unyielding faith in the Fed's ability to bring back the bubble. "Hooks are conditions at important turning points that command investors' focus and force them to conclude that a reversal is impossible." *At the Crest* also noted that when the market is after a really big fish like the one it has been reeling in since the a-d line peak in April 1998, it uses a really big hook.

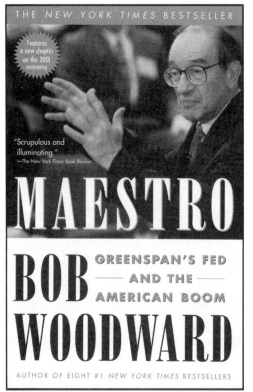

As Paul Montgomery (Universal Economics), points out in his January 1 letter, the near universal esteem toward the Fed is the opposite of the populist ire the Fed faced in the wake of the 1980 bottom for stocks. Montgomery dates the low in antipathy toward the Fed as December 7, 1981 when a distraught man entered the confines of the central bank with a sawed-off shotgun. According to one account, the assault finally convinced Paul Volcker that a full-time bodyguard was a good idea. "Clearly, the Fed chairman has transmuted from a hated devil to be taken at gunpoint to the Giver of all Good Gifts," notes Montgomery, as today, the "depth and pervasiveness of Greenspan worship is unprecedented."

Maestro: Greenspan's Fed and the American Boom is a current bestseller now being marketed as the story of "the real president of the United States." According to Montgomery's bestseller indicator, the book is at a major sell signal; its idolatrous tone marks a positive extreme for the Fed, the boom it symbolizes and its mythological power over the market. The divide between the Fed chairman's popularity and central banks' historic post-mania impotence is a recipe for grand disappointment. Look for his image to fall hard. The first hints of trouble should show as soon as the Fed-induced buying frenzy of January 3 subsides and the bear goes back to work.

February 2001

On December 5, the Federal Reserve adopted an easing bias toward short-term interest rates, and the Dow surged toward 11,000. Last month, as *The Elliott Wave Financial Forecast* went to press, the Dow had reached 11,000 again on a half-point rate cut. EWFF identified the push past 11,000 as a bear market rally that would end "within days, if it has not done so already." The market had, in fact, already reversed. After a sell-off through mid-month, it has now headed back towards 11,000 to celebrate another rate cut. Will the third time be the charm? 11,000 may be exceeded, but for all the reasons cited in last month's section on "central banks' historic post-mania impotence," we think there is virtually no chance that Greenspan can re-ignite the boom.

March 2001

As the bear market in the NASDAQ completes its first full year, many sentiment measures that have helped keep *The Elliott Wave Financial Forecast* on the right side of the entire decline are still at or near historic extremes of optimism. According to the "Sell Side" Consensus Indicator of Richard Bernstein, brokerage firm strategists actually upped their recommended stock market allocation to another record of 66.4% in February! (For the full history see the long-term chart in the January 2001 entry.) This is normal behavior at the onset of a bear market, yet it's weird to watch.

What's Wrong With Alan Greenspan

In January as investors were breaking out the party hats to celebrate Greenspan's surprise rate cut, we speculated, "The divide between the Fed's chairman's popularity and the central bank's historic post-mania impotence is a recipe for grand disappointment." We added that the first hints of trouble would show as soon the "bear goes back to work." The bear did, and the forecasted response from the media was immediate. Suddenly, we learned that Greenspan was too tight last year. He was too loose in 1998/1999. He used to be against tax cuts, and now he's for them. "The Fed has lost control." As we said in January, the time has come for Greenspan's image to take it on the chin.

The more important point is why it is due now. The answer is that for the first time in his tenure as Federal Reserve Board chairman, stocks are in a Cycle degree bear market. As any practicing socionomist can tell you (there are at least three of us), this is an extremely painful position to be in. On February 28, for instance, the market tanked when Greenspan failed to deliver an "unexpected" interest rate cut. Investors want another surprise party, and they want it now! For the Fed chairman's image, there is no way out.

April 2001

Articulate rationalizations of limbic-system responses would drive us crazy if there wasn't so much money to be made in mining them. Bob's book, *The Wave Principle of Human Social Behavior*, explains, "A conventional analyst asks, 'What will the Fed's actions do for, or to, the stock and bond markets? The socionomist asks, 'What will stock and bond market action do for (or to) the reputation of the Fed?'" Back in January, with knowledge of the historical pattern of recrimination, we suggested that Alan Greenspan was about to become a punching bag for disgruntled investors. The pounding started almost immediately.

As the decline accelerated last month, we added, "For the Fed chairman, there is no way out." This month as the March 20 rate cut approached, word spread that the third cut is the magic one that produces the big upward jolt in stock prices. This time, there was a moderate rally as the announcement neared. When investors got the "expected" 0.5% cut rather than the "hoped for" 0.75% rate cut, the market went into a three-day 900-point swoon and critics were lining up to take shots at Greenspan. This headline is from the Houston Chronicle on March 21:

Greenspan Gets Blame For Slump

"Greenspan's legacy is suddenly at stake," says Business Week's latest issue. "Nobody knows what the heck Greenspan is doing," adds talk show host Bill O'Reilly. "There is a growing concern that this stunning decline was man-made." O'Reilly's diatribe is significant because he has become the hottest name in the news business by giving voice to the public's welling anger. "Alan Greenspan is out of control," he rages.

Only one public commentator gave the proper perspective. In a revealing piece in March 22 issue of The Wall Street Journal headlined "So You Thought the Fed Set Interest Rates," Arthur Laffer illustrated that Greenspan was never in control to begin with, never has been, and never will be. To illustrate, he showed the following chart. The Fed's discount rate cuts follow the trend in short-term Treasuries, and, as Laffer lucidly explains, it cannot do anything else. The market,

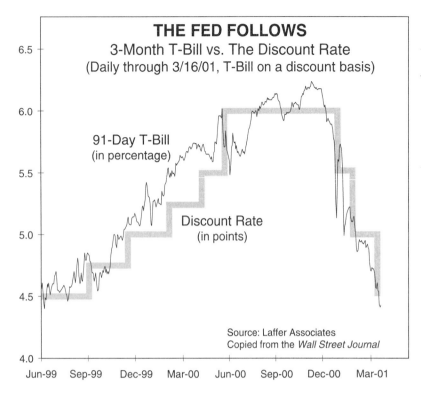

THE FED FOLLOWS
3-Month T-Bill vs. The Discount Rate
(Daily through 3/16/01, T-Bill on a discount basis)

91-Day T-Bill
(in percentage)

Discount Rate
(in points)

Source: Laffer Associates
Copied from the *Wall Street Journal*

not Greenspan, is in control. *The Elliott Wave Theorist* has been saying the same thing. In April 1997, for instance, after four months of rising market rates, the Fed raised the discount rate and EWT noted, "The Fed has always followed rates set by the free market. We watch the market, which leads the Fed."

If you would like another illustration proving the point, just look back at the chart of the irrelevance of central bank machinations in the aftermath of past stock manias (see January 2001 entry). Laffer's article will either serve to de-mystify the Fed, or people will ignore it and blame the Fed anyway. Either way, the exalted image of the all-knowing, all-powerful Fed is disintegrating. A final note: If the market does rally for months from strength in the 3.3-year cycle, Greenspan and the Fed will get a reprieve. However, it will be moderate and short-lived.

Another great example of the recrimination phenomenon is evident in all the grief that is now being heaped on Wall Street earnings analysts. The backlash has been building since the middle of last year, but media criticism for overly optimistic "market cheerleaders" escalated to the level of outright disdain in recent weeks. The Wall Street Journal, The New York Times and The Washington Post have all done major stories decrying the performance of the same analysts they showered with uncritical acclaim on the way up. Here again, there is absolutely no news in any of these stories. Brokerage house analysts have been trend-following shills for their corporate finance departments since the beginning of time. The difference is post-bubble psychology that has turned reporters against the money world they so recently venerated.

July 2001
The Witch Hunt Takes Flight

It is no coincidence that as the backlash gathers steam, analysts and other economic thinkers are a special point of focus. In 1999, economists —scratch that; we mean bullish economists — emerged as the new "superstars of academia." Now a Newsweek column calls economics "the illusion of knowledge" and reveals, "Economists are clueless." In June, Congressional hearings were conducted to dissect the inaccurate opinions of securities analysts. A team of professors from four major California universities produced a paper showing that the stocks analysts liked the most fell 31% in 2000, while their least favorable recommendations rose 49%! The detailed analysis calls into question the "usefulness of analysts' stock recommendations."

As we said months ago, this is not news. Has there has ever been a time when average Wall Street analysis has been useful as anything more than a contrary indicator? The news is how much of the academic and media firepower that supported Wall Street notions is now directed against Wall Street. This defrocking appears to be an inevitable response to the reversal of a mania. As HSB points out, people tend to "live in the limbic system, particularly with respect to fields such as investing where so few are knowledgeable and the tendency toward dependence is pervasive." This was at least doubly true in the mania, as even the most highly developed neocortex was at a loss for prior experience to draw upon. The failed images of the previously bullish social mood now induce jilted investors to destroy the advisors upon whom they have grown so dependent. It is fascinating to see how much sense the neocortexes of the attackers can make as this irrational, limbic-based process plays itself out.

Studying The Money Honey

CNBC financial correspondent Maria Bartiromo's recent appearance on The O'Reilly Factor illustrates that this unmasking process still has a long way to go. As EWFF has pointed out several times in the past, the public's affinity for the financial channel's "money honey" is a reflection of the long uptrend in stock prices. The fact that she was warmly received on a general interest news show by the usually acerbic O'Reilly is evidence that the affinity for equities is still deeply rooted in the culture. O'Reilly even cited a study by two Emory University finance professors and said, "If Miss Bartiromo favorably mentions a stock on CNBC and you buy it within 15 seconds, you'll make money." Bartiromo explained the study's findings this way: "I think what I have carved out for myself is being able to separate what is valuable and what is good analysis versus what is noise."

Bartiromo is a diligent journalist, we don't doubt that. She may even have a better than average nose for financial news. But we would offer an alternate possibility. One of the keys to our explanation is the timing of the Emory study. It was conducted from June through October of last year when the public was still operating under the illusion that the stock mania was intact. Our theory is that the positive returns are due to a bullish bandwagon effect around Bartiromo's presentation of the news rather than the news itself. Over the course of the study, all Bartiromo had to do to unleash the speculative juices was open her mouth. The study appears to support our case. To make money, it says purchases had to be virtually instantaneous. To earn $300 on a $77,000 trade, a buy order had to be in place within five seconds. Executing orders within fifteen seconds produced a gain of $123 on the same size trade. "Beyond fifteen seconds, average returns are no longer statistically significant, and beyond twenty-five seconds, average returns are negative."

Bartiromo espouses the virtue of good analysis, but the study really attests to the opposite. Anyone who took as little as 25 seconds to analyze the stock lost money.

August 2001
Wall Street Rolls Over

The chart on the next page presents a time-lapse picture of Wall Street accelerating into a turn of Grand Supercycle degree. The bear market's role is to bring down the wall of confidence represented by headline Nos. 1 through 9 on the rising side of the NASDAQ chart. In 1996, the first full year of the mania, Wall Street finally brought back everyone that was fired in the wake of the 1987 crash and began an unprecedented push for the business of small investors. By September 2000, when the first leg of the NASDAQ's bear market was half over, the bidding for the public's stock-buying business was still climbing.

In addition to a litany of Wall Street excesses, the story under headline No. 9 mentioned a flurry of merger activity in which banks paid premium prices for Wall Street firms: "Chase Manhattan Corp. announced it was buying J.P. Morgan & Co. for a steep $34.3 billion. Two Swiss banks, Credit Suisse and UBS AG, are paying some of the highest prices Wall Street has seen to acquire two of Wall Street's remaining independent firms: DLJ and PaineWebber Group Inc." This activity constituted a long-term sell signal on a host of different levels as the October 2000 EWFF demonstrated by saying, "Foreign buying is a classic signal of the end of an uptrend. Banks are also notorious for getting caught holding the bag at the end of long-term uptrends. Now we have both together!"

In purchasing J.P. Morgan, Chase was acquiring the assets of an institution that had been hacked into pieces by the government at the bottom in the 1930s. As EWFF further noted, "So,

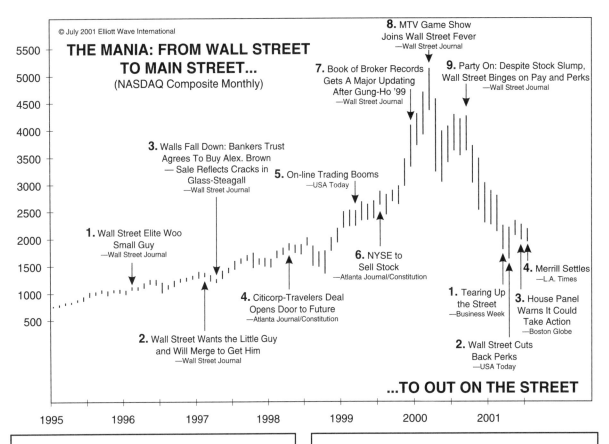

© July 2001 Elliott Wave International

THE MANIA: FROM WALL STREET TO MAIN STREET...
(NASDAQ Composite Monthly)

8. MTV Game Show Joins Wall Street Fever
—Wall Street Journal

7. Book of Broker Records Gets A Major Updating After Gung-Ho '99
—Wall Street Journal

9. Party On: Despite Stock Slump, Wall Street Binges on Pay and Perks
—Wall Street Journal

3. Walls Fall Down: Bankers Trust Agrees To Buy Alex. Brown — Sale Reflects Cracks in Glass-Steagall
—Wall Street Journal

5. On-line Trading Booms
—USA Today

1. Wall Street Elite Woo Small Guy
—Wall Street Journal

6. NYSE to Sell Stock
—Atlanta Journal/Constitution

1. Tearing Up the Street
—Business Week

4. Merrill Settles
—L.A. Times

4. Citicorp-Travelers Deal Opens Door to Future
—Atlanta Journal/Constitution

3. House Panel Warns It Could Take Action
—Boston Globe

2. Wall Street Wants the Little Guy and Will Merge to Get Him
—Wall Street Journal

2. Wall Street Cuts Back Perks
—USA Today

...TO OUT ON THE STREET

1995 1996 1997 1998 1999 2000 2001

BULL MARKET ACTIONS

1. "Blue chip Wall Street firms that have long shunned small investors are now seeking them."

2. "Yesterday's merger announcement by investment banking blue blood Morgan Stanley and brokerage behemoth Dean Witter represents the final ascendence of a key player on the American financial landscape: the individual investor."

3. The biggest merger ever between a bank and a brokerage is the "most visible sign yet of the breakdown of the Depression-era law that separates commercial and investment banking."

4. "The great merger of Citicorp and Travelers, in addition to being the biggest ever, has effectively demolished the Depression-era laws that separated the insurance, banking and brokerage industries."*

5. The boom is marked by an all-out ad blitz that inundates the public with images of easy money. The mentality of a typical online brokerage pitch is summed up this way: "Open an account with us, and you'll get rich."

6. The New York Stock Exchange announces that it will abandon its 207-year-old seat membership system and go public by November. The move comes on the heels of a similar announcement by the NASDAQ. Says the NY Times, "It could become one of the most intriguing investment opportunities of the next decade."

7. "If there is a record on Wall Street that hasn't been broken this year, it would take a detective to find it." Wall Street's unprecedented stature within the culture is symbolized by its move uptown to Times Square, which now houses many of the Street's most prominent firms and, as of late December, a new NASDAQ billboard and media center. The $37 million sign is the largest, most technologically advanced and expensive display in the history of Times Square.

8. "Thanks to a prolonged bull market that has penetrated the psyche of even young America, Wall Street is almost as hot as the Backstreet Boys. The youth-obsessed MTV channel is now doling out credits, instead of cash, for online stock-trading through E*Trade Group, as prizes on one of its most-popular game shows."

9. "Financial firms are getting into bidding wars over high-priced talent, launching megamergers, expanding into fancy new buildings and hiring Hollywood stars to entertain them and their clients. The level of expenditures these days is striking, even by Wall Street's gold-plated standards. Almost every major mutual-fund group is expanding or building new facilities. Vanguard Group has announced a $500 million construction plan. Pennsylvania's governor says it is the state's biggest job-creation project in 25 years."

BEAR MARKET REACTIONS

1. "The bear's toll on investment banks and brokerages is devastating."

2. "Wall Street investment bankers are being warned to cut spending on trophies and other time honored perks used to celebrate the closing of big deals. Lucite trophies that mark big deals generally cost about $50 apiece."

3. "The poor investor is a very unprotected investor. It is not good enough to simply say, 'Buyer beware,'" says a New York Democrat. "The cards are stacked against him."

4. "Settlement with client who alleged tainted Net-stock advice opens door for more legal challenges on Wall St."

*Quotes correspond to sources listed on the chart except for #4, which is from the NY Times.

470

here again, we have a potent symbol of the bull market redoing at the top what was undone at the bottom."

The seeds of the next dismantling can be seen in the bottom right hand corner of this chart. As the bear market progresses, succeeding lows will produce a toll that is far more extensive than the items shown, but the basic transition from binge to purge has occurred. Recent Congressional hearings, the NYSE postponement of its stock offering and Merrill's record settlement with a disgruntled customer only hint at the changes to come.

Remember back in 1997 when the blue-bloods at Morgan Stanley fell prey to the blue-collar crowd at Dean Witter (see second headline on chart)? On April 2, Morgan Stanley dropped the Dean Witter name. According to an executive with the branding firm that advised Morgan Stanley, the name Dean Witter, "the brokerage firm that once sold stocks among the socks in Sears stores," was dropped partly "to appeal to an increasingly important base: institutional investor clients." In other words, the retail customer was king, but the institutional investor has reclaimed the throne.

An interesting parallel to the current juncture is shown by the chart of Wall Street employment. The beginnings of the wave 2 and 4 declines in Wall Street employment also lagged important stock peaks. In fact, wave 2 started at a temporary market low in September 1969 and wave 4 started in February 1988 when the Dow had also resumed an uptrend. Apparently, when stock prices stop going up after a long rise, Wall Street's initial response is to keep the pedal to the metal. After the initial bout of selling, in its typical trend-following fashion, the Street slams on the brakes. The result is the start of a wreck that eventually leaves behind a twisted heap of lost jobs, scandals, lawsuits, investigations and, ultimately, if the turn is of large enough degree, reforms designed to protect investors from a bear market that has already run its course.

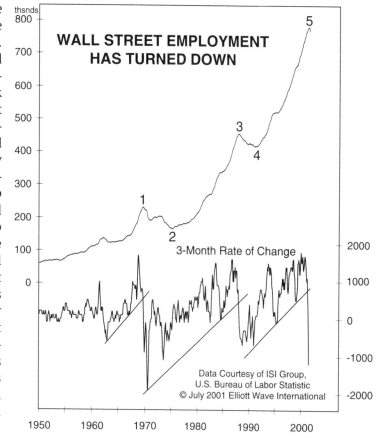

At the bottom of the chart, notice how the three-month rate of change has broken the trend-line that underpinned the hiring rate of the 1990s. Similar breaks occurred in 1969 and 1988, at the start of the two biggest contractions of the last half-century. The loss of more than 1000 jobs since the Dow bottomed in March 2001 is the steepest quarterly decline since 1969, the aftermath of the last speculative blow-off of Cycle degree. The chart shows that when employment reverses to the extent that it has over the last three months, the decline has further to go. *The brokerage industry should now experience the largest contraction in its history.*

471

September 2001
Stock Clubs Show Long-term Trend Change

The chart of the Dow over investment club totals since 1958 depicts an excellent indicator of the true long-term trend in stocks. As the chart shows, a rising number of investment clubs has rarely failed to follow the stock market to new highs. The only missteps were a couple of two-year stretches beginning in 1963 and 1988.

The current downturn has been deeper and longer than either of those episodes. In fact, in just the first half of 2001, more investment clubs disbanded than in any year in history. The 10% annualized decline was also deeper than the highest rate-of-decline in 1963 or 1988. The accelerating rate of investment club breakups is also a departure from 1963 and 1988. It indicates that a long-term decline like that which began in 1969 is taking place. The decline through 1980 reduced the total number of clubs by 75%. This time, the carnage among investment clubs should be even more severe.

Investment clubs' unique sensitivity to the main trend of stocks probably relates to the role of consensus thinking in their formation and operation. Investment clubs are social units that actively organize around a shared objective of getting rich, picking stocks by way of a collective decision-making process.

The depth of the herding instinct at work is revealed by a chapter on investment clubs in Jesse Jackson's guide to personal finance, *It's About the Money!* "One of the best ways to learn about investing is through joining an investment club," says the book. "This is an especially good technique for those who enjoy the do-it-yourself approach." Jackson's profile of a typical club illustrates their tendency toward consensus in the extreme. While its bylaws allow for the purchase of any investment based on a simple majority vote, the club "usually gets 100% support on all stock purchases." In another glimpse into the bull market essence of the investment club experience, the book adds, "The emphasis is on making the meetings exciting and keeping the level of interest high."

Jesse Jackson's book on *How to Achieve Your Financial Dreams* and the collage of recent investment club articles illustrate that historically "disenfranchised" investors are being lured in as never before.

We have noted numerous times in the past that one of the last things to happen at the end of a mania is that the least-experienced investors are drawn into the fray. This time it's happening after the party has all but ended. In the foreword to his book, Jackson calls on African-Americans to accept "investing and building equity" as the final movement in a "Freedom Symphony" that

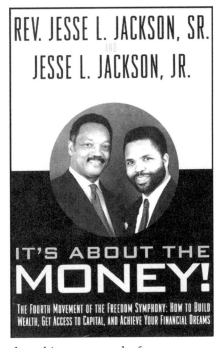

INVESTMENT CLUB BREAK UPS SIGNAL BREAKDOWN FOR STOCKS
© August 2001 Elliott Wave International
Data Courtesy of National Association Investors Corp.

DJIA Monthly

Total Number of Investment Clubs

Year to Year Investment Club Growth

First 6 months of 2001 →

Blacks Joining Clubs To Practice Financial Basics

S. Florida Churches Inspire Members To Invest

Last year, when Cynthia Todd of Miami started "Ureap," (U retire early and prosper), an investment club for African-Americans, she practically had to beat applicants off with a stick.

South Florida Sun Sentinel—Aug 5, 2001

Women find clubs good investment

Chicago Sun Times—Jul 22, 2001

Ministry members learn how to invest

Seattle Times—Aug 6, 2001

Blacks look to invest

"Invest for Success" workshops [are] being held across the country by the National Urban League, Coalition of Black Investors and Investment Company Institute. The Expectation Investment Club is made up of 21 African-American men who have pooled their money in stocks.

Chicago Sun Times—Jul 15, 2001

will deliver them from slavery. He adds that the market is a great thing because it does not know the race or gender of its participants. True, but the market does have its biases, and one of the most pronounced is to move against group expectation.

In normal times, the inherent risk to a vulnerable people prevents promotion of the stock market as a "way out." In a mania, or possibly even in the aftermath of one, politicians, reporters and club enthusiasts are somehow blinded to the enormous risk. The late focus on stocks as the final step in a centuries-long march toward the liberation of an entire race is another signal that the peak is of very high degree.

November 2001

The rally from September 21 has pushed several sentiment measures back to levels that are nearly equal to and in some cases greater than those recorded near the May 22 high. The American Association of Individual Investors survey hit a high level of 61% bulls. Back in January 2000, EWFF noted that AAII investors have historically been a notoriously cautious group. Until December 1999, for instance, the percentage of bulls had surpassed 60% just three times. Since then, however, the 60% level has been exceeded 12 separate times. The latest episode is unlikely to work out much better than the other 11, which were followed by heavy selling. The following release from the Gallup Organization captures the resurgent enthusiasm of investors:

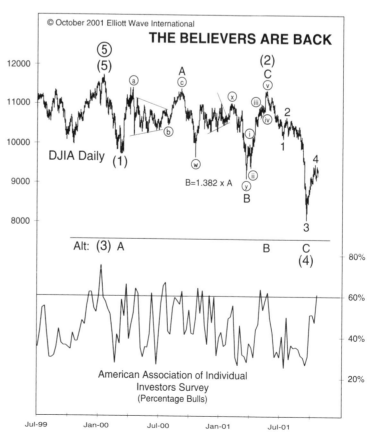

473

Investor Optimism Surges in October

According to the October UBS PaineWebber/Gallup Index of Investor Optimism, U.S. investors appear optimistic. In October, the Index surged 67 points and now stands at 130. Seven out of ten investors think that the stock market will be 'much higher' or 'somewhat higher' a year from now. Three out of four investors think that now is a good time to invest in the financial markets — the highest percentage of investors holding this view since September 2000.

Yes, investors are still bullish, but it is a different kind of bullish. Instead of the outright euphoria that prevailed at the highs, there is an edgy sense of desperation to the public's stock market obsession. This Dilbert cartoon illustrates some of what we mean. It is one of several in a series among a whole host of comedy routines, web sites and other non-financial forums that routinely poke fun at investment advisors and the process of investing. While investors are still willing to grin and bear their losses, beneath the surface, this cartoon reveals a seething anger. Anger is what happens when people bottle up their emotions. People undoubtedly feel like selling, but they have not acted on this emotion because they know holding stocks is the right thing to do.

The best example of this is the determined buying of the patriotic investors we talked about last month. On October 17, the major indexes recovered everything that was lost in the wake of September 11, but the red-white-and-blue rationale for buying stock is still gaining steam. A new non-profit group calling itself "Invest in US" was formed to "do something to bolster our country's morale in this dark time." The group of "individuals from all walks of life" including "many communications professionals — writers, illustrators, filmmakers" is running ads in major daily papers urging people to "Bring back the Bull." A poster series includes the slogans "Don't Keep the Dow at Half Mast" and "We are the soldiers. And our investments are our weapons." Today's issue of USA Today carries the analogy further: "On Wall Street, the generals may have fled, but the soldiers are holding their ground." The battlefield imagery accurately conveys the danger represented by this extreme state of denial.

February 2002

Cultural Trends

A favorite quote of ours is Plato's cautionary note about changes in musical styles from Book IV of *The Republic*. Here's another interesting translation we've come across recently: "The methods of music cannot be stirred up without great upheavals of social custom and law." Two more versions on page 255 of *The Wave Principle of Human Social Behavior* offer that when the modes of music change "the laws of the state change with them" and "the walls of the city shake." Reading deeper into Plato's account of a connection between music and social change, we find that, like most modern-day commentators, it inaccurately assumes a causal link.

> [A new] form of play makes itself at home little by little, and gently overflows upon manners and practice; from these now stronger grown, it passes to men's business agreements; and from business it moves upon laws and constitutions in a wanton flood, until at last all public and private life is overwhelmed.

Of course, Plato had an excuse. He did not have the stock market, which *The Elliott Wave Theorist* has identified as the most precise recording of social mood and thus the most important tool of socionomic research. In 360 B.C., translator H.D. Rouse notes in his preface, there weren't even books or newspapers. But there was music. In fact, in Plato's time, music was probably the most precise recording of social mood. Rouse notes, for instance, that it literally subsumed the marketplace, which was Athens' "central fount" of social interaction. This would explain the reversal in the perceived direction of cause and effect. In the quote above, notice that instead of ascribing social changes to shifts in business or politics as many erroneous observers do today, Plato's dialogue assigned the root cause to the music itself. This is another honest mistake as music can be an incredibly accurate barometer of social change. If we didn't have the advance-decline line and other major indicators to chart the course of the topping process, we'd probably be listening to the music a lot more intently ourselves.

Looking back across the long stock market topping process, the same "little by little" change Plato witnessed in ancient times can be seen overflowing "upon the manners and practices" of the music industry. The transition has been going since at least 1998, when the New Music Express, a well-established music industry trade publication, produced an eight-page report saying that the business appeared to be "in the early throes of a depression which could be terminal." A London Times music writer inadvertently identified the approaching "meltdown" as a bear market when he said it resembled its status in "the pre-punk 1970s," the disco bust of the early 1980s and "the early 1990s when sales were static and everything from computer games to comedians were being touted as 'the new rock 'n roll.'" All three periods featured coincident declines in stock prices. The music industry steadied itself through 2000, but 2001 brought unmistakable evidence of decline. The most obvious is a sales decline that left the record industry with its "worst performance in at least a decade."

Another sign is a sudden loss of interest in musical acts that had been cash cows during the bull market. The latest crater came on January 24, when Mariah Carey's $100 million contract was terminated. Carey was dumped when her latest album sold 501,000 copies. Glitter was "the first bomb in a dazzling career" that began in 1991, the start of the last leg of the bull market. As this clip reveals, there are many more victims from much deeper in the bull market:

Record Labels Are Shedding Big Names

Star singers and musicians are increasingly being dumped from their record labels. Rod Stewart, David Bowie, Tori Amos, Sinead O'Connor and Anita Baker are among established artists who have found that they do not sell enough records to justify the overhead.

—Financial Times, December 24, 2001

Late in the year, musical icons Mick Jagger and Paul McCartney put out albums that have already disappeared from the charts. The two biggest sellers of Cycle V, Garth Brooks and Michael Jackson, also put forward albums that fell almost immediately from the Top 10. Back in 1989, EWT identified Jackson as the pop music idol of Cycle V. He earned the title on the strength of a string of mega hits in the 1980s. But like many wave V cultural manifestations and music in general, Jackson has been losing momentum for years. In fact, he peaked with *Thriller*, which came out a few months after the start of the bull market in 1982 and went on to sell 52 million copies, the most in history. On November 13, in the middle of what may well be the Dow's last failed bid for its final highs, Jackson experienced his own last hurrah with a 30th Anniversary show. The TV special was the highest rated network concert in six years. (The show that Jackson could not beat out was *The Beatles Anthology* featuring the Cycle III musical heroes). At the same time, Jackson's "comeback" album *Invincible* opened at the top of the Billboard 200. But then it slid to No. 3, right behind a greatest hits album from Pink Floyd, a bear-market band EWT has previously identified as "the strongest-selling group in 'downer theme' history." Another sign of the emerging downturn was the reception that the album received in the media. Critics savaged the release as "Bizarre," "Invincibly Awful" and "Downright Creepy."

A shorter-term signal is being given by the suddenly failing fortunes of teen pop sensations like 'N Sync, Britney Spears, the Backstreet Boys and Christina Aguilera. All are off the fast pace of recent years. In November, for instance, Britney's new album opened at No. 1 on the charts with sales of 746,000, far short of her last album's opening tally of 1.3 million in May 2000 and 'N Sync's July total of 1.8 million. As one headline notes, "Teen Pop's On the Way Out." Like the Beatles in 1965-1969, Spears is now engaging in a desperate bid to turn with the tide. Her version of the Beatles' persona-shifting Lonely Hearts Club band in 1967 will take full form in her first movie, which comes out later this month. The film features sex, rape, underage drinking and teen pregnancy. "It's a far cry from the Miss Priss image Spears has tried to cultivate," says the NY Post. "The flick features the sultry songbird dancing in her underwear, getting drunk and losing her virginity to an ex-con."

Meanwhile, the bulleted albums on the Billboard 200 reveal an emerging demand for darker fare. Among surprises in recent months is *The Great Depression, The Sickness* and *Iowa* by a band called Slipknot that has "risen out of obscurity" with the help of a "dark grinding sound" and "grotesque masks." This progression from bubble gum at the highs to grinding guitars and dark lyrics is a replay of the transition from 1965-1969 as described in EWT's 1985 report, "Popular Culture and the Stock Market." During that peak, the old uptrend, characterized by "studio manufactured 'Bubble Gum' hits, a sickly-sweet extreme in trend," competed with the emerging bear market, which supported "bands whose accent was on the negative, [with a] noisy, foreboding sound." As the second major leg of Cycle wave IV got rolling in 1969, bubble gum made a quick exit. This era's lingering teen sensations should now do the same. Spears' slackening sales and makeover suggest that that is exactly what is happening. Time magazine reports that a "rap-metal fusion" album by Linkin Park "shocked the record industry by selling 4.8 million copies of its debut album to eclipse 'N Sync and Britney Spears as the top selling act of 2001." The band's themes of "alienation, frustration and loneliness" seem made to order for a post-bubble and a post-bubble gum world. A lot of the band's lyrics could be titled Ode to the NASDAQ: "I tried so hard and got so far/but in the end it doesn't even matter/I had to fall and lose it all."

Or, how about this one for a drastic shift in musical style? After 66 weeks on the charts, a collection of blues and folk songs from the 1930s rose to No. 10 on in the latest Top 200. "In an era of teen pop and rap/rock, only a complete nut job could have predicted the genre-hopping, cash-register-ringing success of *O Brother [Where Art Thou?]*," says a recent article. OK, we're nut jobs. Back in 1989, in a discussion about what to look for on the other side of the tidal wave, *The Elliott Wave Theorist* said, "Styles from the 1930s and 1940s will become adopted in or influence music." Call us crazy, but we suspect the ancient Greek philosophers would take more than just a passing interest in the meaning of *O Brother*'s popularity.

March 2002
School's Out For Investors

The plummeting IQ of the average investor is another interesting characteristic of this decline. There appears to be an exact inverse relationship between how befuddled investors are today on the way down and how smart they were on the way up. As the market roared through the second half of the 1990s, EWT and EWFF chronicled the "empowering" effect of runaway stock prices in an endless litany of anecdotes about nonprofessionals' newfound financial acumen. It started with the Beardstown ladies. In 1997, the investment matrons rose to the level of market folk heroes on the strength of their *Common Sense Investment Guide*. By the middle of 1998, even the public's beloved mutual fund managers were getting the cold shoulder as investors abandoned mutual funds to pick stocks on their own.

In 1999, day trading was the rage. Prime-time commercials filled the airwaves with vignettes about the "little guys' wisdom in ditching their brokers to go it alone." Remember "Let's light this candle!," or the one about the truck driver who had his own island? Three months before the all-time high in the Dow, on-line brokers decided to spend $1 billion on advertising and

EWFF concluded that it was probably "enough to set the stage for everything investors know about the market to turn out to be absolutely wrong." As the market fell, investors were, in fact, struck dumb.

And the rally from September 21 has done nothing to revive investors' once robust investment faculties or even return formerly beloved advisors to good standing. Yesterday, a "Big Goof" in which the Beardstown ladies misstated their financial returns resulted in a class-action settlement by which $16 million in *Common Sense Investment Guides* will be returned to the publisher. Investors have gone from believing that no one can add value at the peak to no one can be trusted. Signs of this classic "everybody's a bad guy" bear market sentiment (see negative mood traits in the chart on page 232 of *Human Social Behavior*) are everywhere. A CNBC special series titled "Who Can You Trust?" and this recent Business Week headline illustrate:

Can You Trust ANYBODY Anymore?

The cover story says, "Many feel misled by Wall Street, corporations and accountants. Everything hinges on winning back their confidence." The harder Wall Street tries to retrieve it, the more it seems to spiral out of control. "Investors lobbied for companies to 'tell all.'" Now, they're worried that the "new openness will further erode confidence." "Trust no one," concludes another page 1 story on Enron.

Suddenly, everything hinges on "confidence," "faith," and "trust," in other words, the illusive raw material of a bull market. Investors cannot get it back, because the only way to bring back a bull market is for the public to stop believing in it. This is the investment secret that the average investor can never know.

April 2002
For Bull Market Types: A Vicious Cycle

The reigning monarch of the dip-buying crowd is the Saudi Prince that EWFF profiled back in May 2000. On April 6, 2000, when the bear market in the S&P was less than a month old, the "nephew of King Fahd" jumped in with a highly publicized purchase of stocks valued at $1 billion. A month later, right before another short-term peak, the prince took another $1 billion swing at catching the lows. According to press reports, the prince continued buying right through the highs of September 2000 when the market turned down decisively. On March 11, 2002, the billionaire prince completed the acquisition of another billion in stock that has the potential to be as ill timed as his first billion.

The role of bullish pride over reason in these buying campaigns is evident from media accounts like this recent Wall Street Journal item about the prince's infatuation with Priceline. com: "Two years ago, the prince invested $50 million in Priceline.com, when the shares were trading in the $40 to $50 range. Now, the company's shares are at about $5. The prince said he had not gone forward with a complex plan to purchase $50 million in Priceline shares — at $25 a share." The prince's latest purchases included another $100 million in Priceline.com shares. Somebody needs to slip the prince a subscription to EWFF. It probably won't keep him from buying, but maybe it will give an understanding of the manner in which a declining mood trashes the reputations of bull market luminaries.

The prince's backfiring effort to publicize his stock-picking prowess and the Wall Street Journal's coverage of his Priceline debacle shows how the expectations that lift bulls to prominence in a bull market become ammunition for their destruction in a bear market. This is a big part of the process we were referring to last month when we talked about the rising backlash against bull market icons, "The next, more personal phase of this process will focus on individuals that benefited the most from the rising mood." Another taste of this bear market force was evident in Louis Rukeyser's tumble from his perch as the host of *Wall Street Week*. Rukeyser was fired after he refused to accept a devaluation to the level of a senior correspondent. One way or another, bear markets mess the hair of "venerable bulls," not to mention lighten their wallets. Just ask another part-time bull market TV commentator, Jack Welch. The former chairman of General Electric, who signed recently to serve as an occasional guest host on CNBC, is being sued for divorce and half his $1 billion fortune after a fling with the editor of the Harvard Business Review.

The bear market's encroachment on bull market terrain also includes a number of new books and memoirs that deliver "dazzling body blows" to once-revered icons. *Dot.con*, a scathing history of the Internet bubble, accords "lots of real estate to the biggest boosters of the bubble stocks, the ever-perky faces of CNBC. " Another coming tell-all will sully the names of some of its top talents. "Legendary hedge fund operator and CNBC commentator" Jim Cramer is the target of a scathing, behind-the-scenes expose. "Jim would do the opposite of what he was saying on television," says the author, a former employee of Cramer's hedge fund company.

Trading With the Enemy also takes swipes at anchor Maria Bartiromo and analyst David Faber, contending that Cramer used them to talk up stocks that the hedge fund had purchased. "No sooner would Maria be thanking us for the help than we'd be getting a payback — a quick hit thanks to our friends at CNBC." CNBC defended its team with this comment: "Any insinuations [that] our reporters' journalistic practices have been anything less than completely ethical are outrageous." The tone of the response, along with Rukeyser's outburst at his former employer in his last *Wall Street Week* appearance, are clear signs that a bear market is very much in force. It makes perfect sense that, at the end of the transition from a virtuous bull to a vicious bear, fits of indignation are a common stopping point.

May 2002

Another bear market trend that is getting hard to keep up with is the unraveling of bull market icons discussed last month. Stories about former paragons of the rising trend being laid low flood in. Two days ago it was former world-beater Bernie Ebbers getting the boot from Worldcom. Yesterday it was Hershey's Foods' CEO, who has become a "bitter issue" in a candy strike that is the first acrimony between union and management in 22 years, or near the end of the last bear market. Today, the cracking of bull market pedestals is so loud that the backlash itself made the front page of USA Today. The article is actually about the fact that "examples of corporate misdeeds bombard investors nearly every day." It notes, for instance, that Congress will be "flaying oil executives on charges of keeping gasoline prices artificially high by manipulating supply."

The anger is so intense that major articles have appeared in recent weeks exploring mass public attacks on accountants, doctors, priests and, most importantly of all, chief executive officers. This week's Business Week cover story says, "The Crisis in Corporate Governance." "Evidence is mounting that the golden age of CEOs is over," says another USA Today piece. George W. Bush, the nation's top chief executive, is the primary target of *Stupid White Men*, a new book by anti-free market activist Michael Moore. In recent weeks, the book, which publishers refused to print during the rally last November, hit the top of the New York Times bestsellers list. It signals the start of a swoon that should make the earlier George Bush's 1991-1992 fall from power look like a picnic.

Three months ago, we covered the music scene and noted that another icon of the old bull was failing to measure up to his own bull market standards. At the time, Michael Jackson's *Invincible* was languishing on the charts. Since then, it has slipped into oblivion and Jackson's personal fortune has followed. According to reports, he had to pawn a $2 million watch to meet payroll. It was exactly eight months after the bottom in 1982 that Jackson's *Thriller* hit the top of the charts with its first No. 1 hit, "Billie Jean." *Thriller* went on to become the best-selling album of all time. As we noted in February, Jackson was the pop music idol of Cycle V; his accelerating tumble is a powerful sign that main trend has turned down.

Another is that while *Invincible* disappeared, *O Brother [Where Art Thou?]*, the collection of Depression-era blues and folk songs that was also covered in February, went on to clean up at the Grammys and claim the No.1 spot after 70 weeks on the chart. The album is holding steady in the Top 10.

March 2003

Last month, EWFF theorized that one of the big reasons that a bear market does so much damage to so many people is that it dulls their decision-making ability and causes them to compound the effects of, and their exposure to, the natural consequences of a falling social mood. We cited a "big surge of fuzzy thinking" that has produced an outbreak of witch hunts, Elvis encounters and widespread media accounts of a totally unsubstantiated human cloning claims by a religious sect that says it has been visited by beings from outer space. In February, additional evidence surfaced in everything from anti-war activists' plan to serve as human shields in Iraq to Michael Jackson's decision to let a filmmaker follow him around with a camera for eight months.

May 2003

Michael Jordan has played his last game and been "fired" from his position as an executive with the Washington Wizards. At the all-time peak in the stock market, when Michael Jordan became a part owner and president of basketball operations with the Washington Wizards, EWFF noted, "[Jordan's] career has kept an uncanny rhythm with the bull market." His first two breaks from the game, an early retirement in November 1993 and his final appearance with the Chicago Bulls in June 1998, occurred right before big drops in stock prices. He reached an agreement to become part owner and an executive in charge with the Wizards on January 14, 2000, the day the Dow hit its all-time high of 11,750. For Jordan and the Dow, it's been downhill since. Both regained some of their old form in the fall of 2001 when stocks reached a temporary bottom and Jordan announced that he was coming out of retirement, but EWFF said right off the bat that both efforts would fall short of the old bull market standards. In a November 2001 piece titled "Say It Ain't So, Michael," EWFF said, "[Jordan] may be back, but without the Bulls or the bulls, he will not climb as high." Jordan's two-year comeback was an apt metaphor for stocks. He displayed flashes of his old brilliance but never regained the form that produced six championships during the 1990s. Of his retirement, Jordan said, "It's time, I feel it." In 1996, when *The Elliott Wave Theorist* predicted that Jordan would go out with the bull market, we stated that when the bull market ended, he would "retire or become less effective." In another exquisite reflection of the trend in stock prices, he has done both, retiring at the front end of stocks' 5-year topping process, returning in time to play less effectively as the first countertrend bounce unfolded and then retiring again as stocks' last effort to reach the old highs failed. If the alignment holds, the last act of the drama took place on May 7 when the Wizards "abruptly dumped basketball's most popular figure." "Imagine that, an NBA team showing Michael Jordan the door. Even he was shocked," reported the Associated Press.

Jordan should go to the bench happily. He is not the only bull market hero to fall on hard times, and his aren't so bad. Fellow icons are falling as never before. In March 2002, EWFF said that

Jordan 'shocked' by firing

An angry Michael Jordan drives from meeting after Washington Wizards severed relations

USA Today, May 8, 2003

the bear market backlash against bull market idols would intensify as wave ③ took the market lower: "The next, more personal phase of this process will focus on the individuals that benefited the most from the rising mood." An ill wind kicked up immediately and proceeded to tarnish corporate heroes that ranged from Jack Welch to Martha Stewart. Monday night, the intensification of this trend was aired in the form of a made-for-TV movie, *Martha Inc.*, which took the battering of Martha Stewart's public image to a new level. Actress Cybill Shepherd remade the "doyenne of stylish living, the first self-made, female, stock-market billionaire" into an angry and ruthless seeker of wealth and status. Shepherd's one-sided portrayal calls to mind this forecast from *The Elliott Wave Theorist* in December 1997: "The investment heroes who are now adulated as saviors will be reviled as traitors. In retrospect, their present charisma will seem demonic." Said Shepherd of the transition: "I know what it is like to be that famous. I know the feeling of the power, and I know what it's like to have it suddenly turn on you." When it turns on a whole phalanx of bullish role models, it confirms the full force of the bear market.

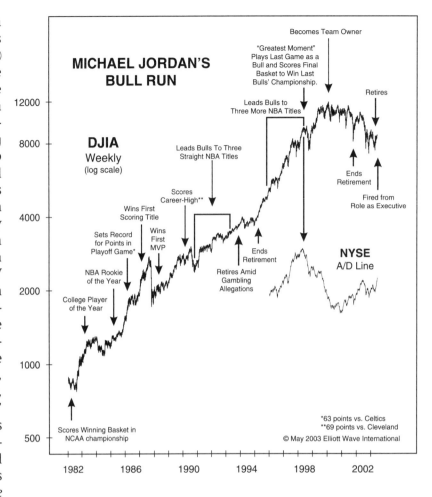

The following column from the May 9 issue of the Financial Times shows that the attack has progressed to a gale force level which is bearing down even more intently on financial targets:

Wall Street: A Rudderless Ship

Here is a small, but revealing anecdote about how far the mighty have fallen. Kathryn Harrigan, the Henry R. Kravis professor of business leadership at Columbia Business School, recently asked her incoming MBA class to list the people they most admired and disliked in their industries. Twenty years ago names such as Rockefeller, Rohatyn or Volcker would have appeared in the "most admired" column. This time, however, every one of the candidates from the financial services industry listed only villains. "They don't have any leaders the admire anymore," she says.

It seems that Wall Street has run out of heroes.

Even Richard Grasso, the chairman of the New York Stock Exchange, has been knocked off his perch. A probe is under way into possible malpractice by specialists on the trading floor. Grasso's reported $10m-plus pay in 2002 has also raised eyebrows when executive pay is under a fierce spotlight.

Bull market analysts Jack Grubman and Henry Blodget have been attacked by Congress and barred from the industry. Frank Quattrone, the investment banking "star" of the Internet era, has been indicted by the attorney general of New York. Chief executives are being forced out in record numbers. Bill Bennett, who rose to prominence as a member of the Reagan and Bush cabinets, gained fame as the best selling author of the *Book of Virtues*. Magazines reported earlier this month that Bennett lost $8 million over the past decade to Las Vegas slot machines and video poker. Even though Bennett's gambling exploits have been in the news since at least 1996, he is now being attacked as a hypocrite for "accepting $50,000 fees for lectures on morality."

The reason behind the attacks is the one that Michael Jordan identified in his decision to retire: "It's time." The "toppling" dynamic is so strong that a cartoonist addressed the trend with this recent effort. This quickening is further evidence that the bear market is about to make a dramatic reappearance. The continued popularity of two key icons, Alan Greenspan and President Bush, confirms this cultural sell signal. President Bush's approval rating is still 70%, and Alan Greenspan remains so popular

Atlanta Journal-Constitution, May 11, 2003

that Bush has said he will renominate him to his post as chairman of the Federal Reserve.

As EWFF noted in March, the U.S. presidency is a lightning rod for a bear market in social mood. Big bear markets eventually always strike at the popularity of the president. On the decline from December 2, George Bush's approval rating fell to 57% in February, but the rally from March 12 has brought it back to 70%. Greenspan's image has also bounced with the market. In February, the pundits were calling for his head. In recent days, Business Week reported, "Three-fourths of those polled who have an opinion about the monetary maestro think Bush was correct to choose him for a fifth term." The bear market won't be over until the warm and fuzzy feelings for Bush and Greenspan are transformed into focal points of popular contempt and blame. The cracks exposed by the brief winter decline should re-emerge and lead to the first signs of outright crumbling for both the market and the images of these leaders in the weeks ahead.

June 2003

A subscriber wants to know how Michael Jordan's abrupt exit from the professional basketball arena could be considered an early sign of a renewed downtrend. How can the fate of one person signal a change in a collective phenomenon? To be impelled by Elliott waves, a system need only be complex and living. It is our belief, developed over years of observing the standing of cultural figures who demonstrate a heightened relationship to the trend in social mood, that a lone individual is sufficiently complex to reflect Elliott waves. When the trend changes, we have shown that "stars" in totally distinct cultural galaxies are transformed or doused and ones that are uniquely suited to the new mood arise. At the current turn, Michael Jordan may not be changing, but the social structure that created his basketball legend certainly is. Many examples of individuals who "personified" the bull market in mood have been covered in recent issues. Jordan gets special treatment because his star rested most precisely on the rising tide of social mood.

July 2003
A Smarter Public?

A recent story in The New York Times notes, "Three years of stock market torment seem not to have shaken the long-held view that stocks are best for the long haul." The story goes on to state that one of the rationales for a new uptrend is that individual investors "learned a great deal since the stock bubble burst." A Boston lawyer says, "The public is a lot wiser about what the investment banks were up to in the '90s. The public is more Internet savvy than they were a few years ago." Back in mid-2000, several renowned investors stepped aside and a host of less established plumbers, sheiks and Internet gurus were lauded as the market's new wizards. At the time, EWFF said, "The stature of those left to bask in the financial limelight says volumes about the current stock market juncture. The bear market's mission is to reveal the ignorance and naivete that are the true source of their profits." Obviously this mission is not yet accomplished. The reputed uptick in the average investor's I.Q. simply indicates that school has been out of session.

September 2003
The Kids Are Back On Wall Street

Another classic and, as far as we know, unprecedented indication of the mania's hold on the public was the emergence of a stock market youth movement. In 1998, *The Elliott Wave Theorist* cited the growing belief in the stock market wizardry of younger and younger gurus as a sure and unhealthy sign of a bullish psychology that was pushing the mass financial delusion to new heights. Its persistence is signaled by the fact that many of the programs — like state-sponsored, stock-based college "savings," summer money camps, stock-gifting services and investment websites for kids (see teenanalyst.com for a typical example) — are in full swing. As EWT said in 1998, these instruments betray a complete "faith in the benevolence of social mood and an utter lack of respect for its potential savagery." The bear market will not be over until these aberrations have been abolished and someone instead has written a book about the harm that involvement in the stock market does to the development of a child's psyche. Instead, recent weeks have brought another push to get kids in stocks. The only difference between the current crop of investment protégés is that they are slightly older and a lot less precocious than the babes that appeared when stocks were still in a bull market. *Teenage Investor* is the latest offering. It's by another 13-year old "whiz kid" who explains "what stocks and bonds are, where to find them, how to buy them." When the author of *Teenage Investor* appeared on CNBC, his responses were so trite that the interviewer appeared ready for a long nap.

Then there's the story about the 20-year-old Los Angeles youth who is determined to become the youngest money manager in history. He appears to be trying to accomplish this feat through the media. Believe it or not, he is close to succeeding. After several guest spots on investment talk shows, including *Wall Street Week*, the boy wrote the LA Times expressing disappointment "that my own newspaper has yet to acknowledge my presence in the financial world." The paper did exactly what was appropriate for the tail end of a financial bubble. It wrote him up in a slightly skeptical way that will nonetheless advance his effort to become the manager of a fund that has $50,000 in investment assets and is the "worst performing mutual fund in the country." One of the big reasons he is likely to get the job is that he is willing to invest all of his own money and his parents' $50,000 retirement account in the fund. "Is that wise?" asked the columnist. "'No, it's stupid," came the answer. So why do it? Because throwing good money after bad is what the limbic system demands at the front-end of a bear market.

December 2003

Roy Disney, the former chairman of Disney's feature animation division, issued a blistering challenge to Eisner's leadership for the first time since Eisner took over near the start of the bull market in 1984. The fight pits the founding family of one of the great companies of Supercycle (V) against one of the great CEO heroes of Cycle V. The battle reminds us of that scene from *Blazing Saddles* when the good guy gets chased into the movie lot. This is the entertainment industry's big problem; in bear markets, the negative social forces that it depicts rarely fail to ravage the mediums in which they are rendered and many of the messengers that portray them. Just ask Michael Jackson.

February 2004
A Bell-Ringing Bank Merger

In the late 1990s another extremely accurate indicator of the approaching bear market was the banking industry's remarriage to the securities industry. Back in November 1999, two months from the Dow's peak, Congress officially repealed the Glass-Steagall Act, a Depression Era law that split the banks and brokers.

On January 14, 2004, Morgan-Chase announced another mega-merger with its purchase of Bank One Corp. Considering bankers' knack for committing fully to a trend once it is over, the deal makes perfect sense. Its bearish overtones were revealed by analysis of the merger in The Wall Street Journal, which distinguished the deal as a victory for the "once shunned" strategy of building banks around consumers. The merger sets up a "battle of financial titans for the little guy" with Citicorp, the world's largest financial institution. The "now hot" strategy of "catering to the small fry" is the equivalent of brokerage firms' merger binge in the late 1990s, which was built around retail investors. Now that the banking industry has aligned itself along the same lines, look for consumers to face the music of deflation. As they pay down debt and act in ways that should make a conservative banker proud, they will lay waste to bankers' grand plans.

March 2005

The full page ad shown here is a sure sign of the markets resonating appeal. One important nuance of sentiment at the all-time high was the rejection of more experienced market voices for novices and man-on-the-street opinions. The NASDAQ is down 60% over the last five years, but this ad illustrates that the bear market's mission is far from complete. The ad reveals that the belief in easy money is alive and well. Even a 12-year-old soccer player, says the ad, can make 355% in six months. Another recent article offers investment advice from "once-fleeced" NFL players.

More Storm Clouds Over the Corner Office

Don't be fooled by reports of besieged corporate leaders; it is only a preview of coming attractions. The latest executive compensation surveys reveal that, by at least one key measure, the infatuation with corporate leadership reached record levels in 2004. According to Mercer Human Resource Consulting, the average CEO bonus rose to a new high of $1.14 million. The bonuses represent a 46% increase from 2003. Based on CEO compensation, the bear market has yet to begin.

April 2005

The deepening severity of the next phase of decline is evident in the bear's latest targets, two of the bull market's loftiest icons, Alan Greenspan and Warren Buffett. As one Washington observer notes, "The knives are out for Alan Greenspan." The Federal Reserve Board chairman is being blamed for failing to pop the stock market bubble, helping create "America's budget mess" and "confusing the markets." The U.S. Senate Minority leader called Greenspan "one of the biggest political hacks in Washington." Meanwhile, Warren Buffett is suddenly gravitating toward an insurance scandal that EWFF described this way in November: The investigation "marks the re-emergence of a new cycle of antitrust attacks and, thus, a renewed downtrend. It is likely to spread rapidly." On Monday, it produced the ousting of Hank Greenberg, "the insurance industry's most powerful figure for decades." The Securities and Exchange Commission, the Justice Department, New York attorney general Eliot Spitzer and regulators in Ireland, Britain and Australia are now looking at Berkshire Hathaway, Buffett's firm.

Says a front-page headline in The Wall Street Journal:

Buffett Is Called In For Questioning

In an apparent confirmation of EWFF's thesis that there is no difference between the scandals surrounding bull market accounting practices and the baseball steroids controversy (see Chapter 3), one columnist offered the following advice: "Here's a tip from Mark McGwire, Oracle. Don't begin by saying you're not there to talk about the past. And don't rant and rave to the cameras outside like Barry Bonds that you're tired and you may never return." The net for trapping bull market heroes of all types is clearly widening.

May 2005

Screaming Sell Signals from Wall Street

The fight for control of Morgan Stanley offers more proof that a bear market that is equal-but-opposite the upward force of the mania is on the loose. First recall what the pundits said in 1997 when Morgan Stanley hooked up with Dean Witter, a firm that once sold stock at Sears stores. With Philip Purcell, Dean Witter's leader, assuming control over the combined operation, the union was hailed as a great victory for retail investing. One observer noted, "On Wall Street, retail is king." In January of this year, however, as the NASDAQ reached its countertrend rally peak, the same blue-blooded "descendants of J.P. Morgan's former banking empire" that in 1997 surrendered to the rising power of smaller investors, revolted against Purcell and the Dean Witter side of the business. The uprising is symptomatic of a fading promise of riches for the average investor. Eventually, the public will flee and the managers on the institutional side will win all the turf battles. It should ultimately prove a pyrrhic victory.

November 2005

As the market heads lower, sentiment won't stay at the extreme net bullish levels of the last three years, but near the outset of downside surges there should be a moderate level of optimism and a re-supply of newly committed bulls who see the setback as a correction and therefore a buying opportunity. As this story shows, this is certainly evident today:

Super-Bulls Set Sights on Dow 40,000

—MSN Money, October 12, 2005

"A growing group of forecasters see a monster-sized rally just ahead," says the article. "If you have any cash, invest it right now," writes a newsletter publisher. "The next few weeks will be phenomenal." A cadre of analysts says the market is on "the verge of a historic breakout."

484

This is true, but the big breakout should be down, not up. The edgy, manic quality of the current optimism telegraphs the inevitability of such a move. This aspect is best represented by CNBC's *Mad Money* stock jockey, Jim Cramer, who sometimes entertains a live studio audience with his barrage of stock picks. In recent weeks, Cramer has emerged as a "stock star." One reviewer says his approach represents the future of financial television: "*Mad Money* is a departure from CNBC's typical business programming and may represent a new strategic direction for the network." Within days of the recent peak in the S&P and NASDAQ, EWFF asserted that his popularity signaled a peak. This opinion is now reinforced by the latest cover of Business Week, which well captures Cramer's in-your-face style. As Paul Montgomery originally pointed out in the 1970s, Business Week covers have an uncanny knack for focusing on market moves, trends and personalities at the peak of their popularity.

Cramer is described as an "obsessive stock lunatic;" the perfect persona for selling a jittery and desperate public on the last gasps of a multi-year peak in stock prices. "This is what the bottom looks like!" he hollers on a recent episode. "You need to start buying 'cause stocks are going to rise!" Cramer sums up the whole purpose of *Mad Money* this way: "I want to keep you in the game — keep you from getting discouraged." "Our job is to seduce," says the show's producer. They do it by interspersing an array of "cartoonish sound effects," animal noises and "a hideous clip of a screaming man flying out of a glass building" with rapid-fire stock picks. And it's actually working. Thanks to *Mad Money*, CNBC's after-market ratings are up from oblivion. But we think its success is a function of a last-fling affection for stocks. It will quickly fade, after the next free-fall in stock prices.

Investor Psychology

In another Wall Street reprisal, The New York Post reports that the "Fat Cat is Back." In May 2000 when the first phase of the bear market was about where its resumption is now, *The Elliott Wave Financial Forecast* stated that stocks were "extremely ripe for a downturn " because even junior level analysts were demanding and getting lavish perks. Said EWFF at the time:

> Wall Street only rarely intersects with Easy Street. The problem with careers that begin near these intersections is that they tend to stop suddenly.

Wall Street is once again veering down the Easy Street off-ramp. Annual bonuses are expected to approach record levels, and New York City real estate agents and Ferrari dealers are being inundated with calls from expectant owners. The president of Gotham Dream Cars reports that bankers and traders are lining up to drive the yet-to-arrive 2006 Ferrari F430, which will sell for $250,000: "I have certainly been getting a fair share of Wall Streeters—mostly in their 30s but some in their mid-20s—looking at buying in anticipation of bonus time." Here too, the likelihood of a more serious crack-up is high because, this time, the brokerage community is spending its windfall bonus before 2005 is even complete. A change in the market's fortunes will cause many to rue or cancel their Ferrari orders.

December 2005

As EWFF noted last month, the only time Wall Street ever intersects with Easy Street is near major peaks. Another sign of such a crossing is a "hiring surge" that has brokerage firm staffing "back to levels not seen since before the 2000 recession." MBA enrollments, which suffered in 2001 and 2002 "because the bubble was a very MBA-intensive phenomena," is also rising again. The Dean of Dartmouth's Tuck School of Business says salaries for graduates are "back to bubble-level." "I was surprised at how fast it happened." The "New Tycoons" cover is from Penn State's alumni magazine. It takes us back to 1999, when college kids all over the country were financing their day-trading habits with student loans. The quick campus revival of get-rich-on-Wall-Street ambitions demonstrates that the market is still a long way from its ultimate lows. As *The Elliott Wave Theorist* commented in the late 1990s, a youthful enthusiasm for finance is what happens at the end and not the beginning of a bull market. As the bear market matures, colleges will go back to churning out social workers (and socialists).

March 2006

This image of Warren Buffett is another sell-signal not to be dismissed. It is the lead element in *The Secret Millionaire's Club*, a DVD cartoon series featuring the words, voice and likeness of Buffett, one of Cycle wave V's most revered heroes. His animated likeness will be used to dispense financial advice to children as young as five. "We could not have asked for a more inspirational partner," says the company making the videos. It's not a satire, but it will probably seem like a spoof in retrospect. In the depths of the bear market, stocks will become instruments of evil and the use of Buffett's folksy demeanor to peddle financial advice on defenseless children will be viewed as a perversity. The shepherding of the pennies of school children into the market through a cartoon of Warren Buffet attests to a deep societal need to keep the herd locked in through the final phase of the top. Columnist David Carr has noticed the same thing about CNBC's show *Mad Money*. He says the anchor presents a "funhouse mix of fear, anxiety, bravado and certainty. There is abundant, throbbing need in the presentation, while the bonhomie of the calls affirms a we're-all-in-this-togetherness." To us, it's more like, "We're all locked up together in a carnival house of horrors."

April 2006

The consensus among investors is that the stock market will continue to rise because earnings are solid, the U.S. economy is expanding, and the Fed is likely to soon stop raising the Fed Funds rate. Does the end of a series of rising rates provide a tailwind for equities, as so many people claim? Back in July 2004 EWFF published a chart showing that the Fed raises rates only after short-term market rates and the stock market start to rise. In other words, the actions of the Federal Reserve lag freely-traded markets. The opposite holds true, too. The Fed stops raising rates after the market is finished going up. The relationship is shown beautifully in this chart from Ned Davis Research (www.ndr.com), except that we have added the labeling for a classic impulse pattern. The graph portrays the average DJIA price action in the months after the completion of the 16 previous Fed rate-tightening cycles since 1920. The average mean return 6 months later is -4.9%, while the average mean return 12 months later is -3.87%, contradicting the current bullish consensus. Also of interest is the average date of the Dow's top relative to the Fed's final rate hike; it occurs about two months prior to the end of the Fed tightening cycle, corroborating our

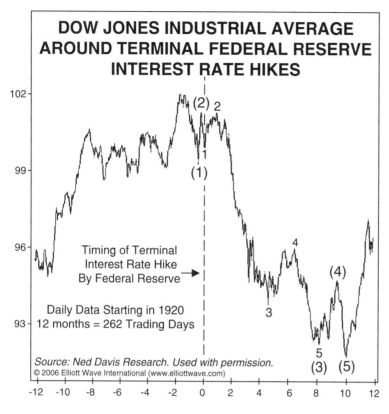

DOW JONES INDUSTRIAL AVERAGE AROUND TERMINAL FEDERAL RESERVE INTEREST RATE HIKES

Timing of Terminal Interest Rate Hike By Federal Reserve →

Daily Data Starting in 1920
12 months = 262 Trading Days

Source: Ned Davis Research. Used with permission.
© 2006 Elliott Wave International (www.elliottwave.com)

thesis that the market leads and the Fed follows. This timing makes sense because the Fed raises rates when it is confident about the economy. As EWP explains, "wave 2" psychology is the final point of optimism in the wave structure. Some project the end of the rate tightening cycle to be in May or June. Regardless, the correct timing sequence is that a stock market top of some consequence is due prior to the Fed's last rate hike, which means anytime now.

In an effort to prop their markets up, powerful interests appear to be borrowing their talking points from 1929. On October 29, 1929, as the first wave of selling was crushing stock prices, John D. Rockefeller issued the following statement: "Believing that fundamental conditions of the country are sound and that there is nothing in the business situation to warrant the destruction of values that has taken place on the exchanges, my son and I have for some days been purchasing sound common stocks." On March 15, 2006, Prince Alwaleed bin Talal issued a statement that implies even higher authorities are on the side of rising Saudi stock prices in 2006: "His Highness said that the Saudi economy is strong and fruitful and is backed by the Custodian of the Two Holy Mosques who supports the small investor. Buy and participate in companies that are respectable."

Like Rockefeller in 1929, Alwaleed bin Talal said he is getting in with a $2.7 billion investment in the Saudi market. Should investors take this as a bullish sign? In April and May 2000, after the initial fall in dot-com stocks, the same prince made the same bold $2 billion play – on Internet stocks! "When Panic Hits Wall Street, the Prince Buys A Lot," proclaimed a USA Today headline at that time. EWFF said the move and other brazenly public efforts to step into the fray were more evidence of a major peak: "These profiles in stock market courage fit perfectly with our expectations for the immediate aftermath of the mania. The bear market's mission is to reveal the ignorance and naïveté that are the true source of [less experienced investors'] profits. Think of how delighted Papa Grizzly must be to awake and see what's on the menu." Of course, the NASDAQ had already begun its record-breaking collapse of 78%. Now papa must be even more excited; a whole world of fat and happy investors to feast upon.

A quick outbreak of palpitations is already giving many investors heartache. A Saudi newspaper headline, "Hospitals on Bull Run as Markets Go Down," hints at the hidden vulnerability behind many investors' confident exteriors. "A horde of Saudi investors have ended up in hospitals with high blood pressure and acute stress after being unable to digest their losses," says the dispatch. An e-mail from a Pakistani subscriber describes the same phenomenon there. After a haircut of just 10% through March 8 in the Karachi 100 Index, he wrote, "My friend has just called me from the stock exchange where he tells me grown men have been reduced to tears. There are no buyers in the major blue chips." The tender trading psyches of Pakistani investors have been assuaged by a market rebound, but it should be temporary. We expect to see more of these kinds of psychological breakdowns. Last month we called for a domino effect that would resemble those of 1997 and 1998. Those episodes started with currency disruptions in emerging markets like Thailand and Russia, respectively. The same thing is happening this time. The Icelandic krona, Australian and New Zealand dollars, Turkish lira, Polish zloty and other currencies, mostly of emerging countries, are getting hit. This is the wave of financial conservatism called for in *Conquer the Crash*. The Financial Times notes, "These are all signals that investors are taking risk off the table."

May 2006

Another big sign of a U-turn for all the financial markets is that after more than four years of rise, a few key observers are suddenly recognizing our long-argued theme. In April, the Federal Reserve held a two-day conference in Atlanta and offered a starkly accurate assessment of the danger. "Systemic Risk Has Grown In U.S.," reports a Reuters story on the conference. "There is a dark side connected to financial integration," stated a director of the Bank of England. "If shocks are large enough, the financial system becomes a risk-transmitter rather than a risk-disburser." Back in March 2000, as the S&P and NASDAQ were putting in their all-time highs, high-level foreboding was also afoot. EWFF explained that this is one time in history when the concern should be taken at face value: "We do not view this sentiment as a contrary indicator, however, because people have lost respect for market authorities." When Alan Greenspan stated, "This could be one of the euphoric speculative bubbles that have dotted human history," one day before the Dow Jones Industrial Average's January 14, 2000 peak, here's what the February 2000 issue of EWFF had to say about it:

> The market's response to Fed Chairman Alan Greenspan's latest warning about the stock market signals a complete loss of respect for financial authority. Days later The Wall Street Journal noted, "Stocks have historically taken a hit after Mr. Greenspan said something skeptical about the market. But more and more it sometimes lasts no more than a few hours. In this case, there was no hit at all." In finally succeeding to tune out the sincere concerns of Alan Greenspan, the public has signaled that its potential to experience tragedy is now fully formed.

Once again investors are dismissing the Cassandras. "Many believe these correlated markets are a sign of a brewing systemic risk," argues one analyst. "We believe it is the opposite." Now consider the latest headline: "Asset Prices Will Fall, Greenspan Says." According to the article, Greenspan made his assessment of a likely fall in "uncharacteristically blunt terms." In a pointed reference to our all-the-same-markets scenario, Greenspan even stated, "I don't know when the liquidity is going to decline, but I am reasonably certain that what we're looking at is an abnormal situation." Once again, the financial tragedy can commence because the markets completely tuned out Greenspan's April 12 warning and staged an across-the board rally in stocks and commodities.

Investor Psychology

Unanticipated rallies like that of April can be frustrating, but, sometimes, when things go against you for the right reason, it can be somewhat reassuring. In April, for instance, the stock market's strength was attributed to "Investors' Rate Euphoria." As the Dow approached its April 21 high, USA Today reported, "A new kind of 'one-and-done' rally is alive on Wall Street," whereby the market's advance is based on the view that the Federal Reserve is at the end of its cycle of interest rate hikes. But as the chart from last month's issue illustrates (see April 2006 entry), the Dow's average performance in the wake of 16 prior tightening cycles since 1920 shows that stocks, on average, do not rise after the Fed finishes raising rates; they almost always fall. Investors' eagerness to swallow the interest rate bait is a good sign, in our estimation. It confirms that the hook, line and sinker are being set very deeply.

Interest Rate Signal

Peter Eliades (P.O. Box 751060, Petaluma, California 94975) reports on a study by Ned Davis (600 Bird Bay Drive West, Venice Florida 34285) showing that interest rate hikes to 6 percent or above have occurred very near major tops in the stock market. Until today, there had been only seven such instances in history. In every case except 1929, the hike took place after the high in the Dow. This is logical from our point of view because the chronology of events shows that the Fed does not create interest-rate, stock-market or economic trends; it follows them. Today's hike is the eighth instance since Congress authorized the Fed in 1913. If our May 4-11 time for a closing high in the Dow is correct, this hike will coincide with the peak in the stock market more closely than ever. Given the public's obsession with Fed-watching and the belief that Fed meetings are akin to miracles, we should not be surprised to see essentially coincident events as investors have loaded up on stocks prior to the announcement.

June 2006

An Era of Reckoning for the Fed

Last month, we stated that the market was going against us "for the right reason." The reason was all the hype and excitement surrounding the potential end of the Fed's rate-raising cycle. But as we showed in our rate hike chart (shown with April 2006 entry) and in this chart of rate hikes to 6% or higher, historically when the Fed raises the discount rate to 6%, which happened on May 10, or finishes a series of short-term rate hikes, which may have happened on May 10, the DJIA almost always goes way down. The Dow's decline started on the same day the Fed did exactly what investors were so hopefully anticipating. The history captured in those charts says the market should continue to fall. As it does, watch how investors forget that the last rate hike is exactly what they were cheering for at the top. Instead, they will pile blame on Ben Bernanke's doorstep. Given the degree of the peak, it will surely rise to monumental levels.

An Inside Look at the Great Reversal from India

Earlier this month, revelations about the use of margin debt in India caused EWFF to suggest that the "level of financial naïveté probably even surpasses the gullibility at the height of the dot.com mania." On May 19, we got the following update from an astute subscriber in India:

I have been following your socionomic messages for a while and have some observations from India: The Bombay index is hitting all time highs now. Compared to Indian real estate gains in last five years, US real estate appreciation is a pittance. The young generation is spending heavily (India is usually a saver's society) and feeling very good about the future. The skirt lengths are the shortest ever. If you follow Bollywood movies the skin shown is very generous even though India historically has been a very conservative society. India's top private bank is announcing [India's] tallest residential tower:

65-Floor Fantasy Tower Will Rise

MUMBAI—A four-acre plot is being readied to become the site of India's tallest residential building of 65 stories.

—DNA News, April 25, 2006

India is on a high. Wonder what will follow? —Srinivasa Allapathi

Readers who caught our April update of the skyscraper indicator (Chapter 3) know that the question is rhetorical. The market wasted no time confirming what's to follow; here's what came off the newswire two days after we received Srinivasa's socionomically enhanced perspective:

Indian Stocks Plunge, Trade Halted

India's main stock exchanges halted trading for an hour on Monday after the market fell more than 10 percent as brokers dumped stocks to cover margin requirements.

—Reuters, May 22, 2006

Another article says that police are patrolling the lakes and canals "For Suicidal Brokers." "Gold has turned into brass. We are finished," said one broker who lost millions of rupees in two hours of trading. "I don't know how I will I repay my loans," said a small investor. But the worry over suicides is misplaced. Abject hopelessness comes later, when stocks are closer to a bottom. Apparently, the suicide watch lasted just one day as the next story from India had money pouring back into shares. "Share Slide Offers Chance to Buy—Fund Managers," said the headline.

July 2006

The Pros Are Staying In and Piling In

In the U.S., another echo of the post-peak atmosphere of 2000 is the belief that buying the first big decline is the professional thing to do. "With the markets gyrating and investors fretting," Barron's says, a panel of "cool, calm investment pros" indicates that there is "really good news: lots of stocks look cheap." Last month, we echoed *Conquer the Crash*'s admonition about the gospel of diversification: it is suicidal in the unfolding financial environment. But after four years in which the biggest investment bang was in emerging markets, small stocks and commodities, experienced hands

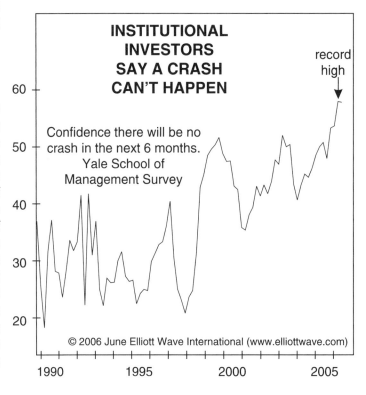

are almost ordering investors to stick to their guns: the bigger the dip, the bigger the opportunity. "Don't Dump Small Caps in Haste, Analysts Say," says one typical headline. Yes, "all sorts of leveraged strategies have cratered in the past month" says one columnist, but a rally may be underway already. "Since hedge funds do things so much faster than most investors of yore, it follows that the decline could run its course very soon." Hedge fund managers "need less time to recover from the shock of a sudden market drop." And our favorite, a quote for all time: "[It is] quite plausible that the whole process of deflating a speculative bubble might have been completed in scarcely more than a month."

Based on valuations and expectations for stock returns over the coming year, institutional investors are as bullish as they've been in the 17-year history of a Yale School of Management survey. Their confidence that there will be no stock market crash over the next six months is also higher than at any time on record. Comparisons to the conditions preceding the 1987 crash "are probably wide of the mark," says a brokerage firm strategist. Markets are consummate con artists: they always get their marks brimming with confidence right before they go in for the sting.

October 2006

The Jocks Are Back!

Over the years, EWI has shown how the fame of various bull market personalities seems to conjoin itself to an advance in social mood. On the court, basketball star Shaquille O'Neal is a good example. The 340-pound, 7-foot-1 perennial all-star has won all four of his NBA championship rings over the course of the long-term peaking process, including one in 2000 and another this June. From an investment standpoint, an even more precise coincident measure of an extremity in a bull market may be his status as an "expert investor." Back in September 2000, when the stock market was rolling over in the first big downleg of the bear market, O'Neal was on the cover of Money magazine next to the headline "Yes, These Jocks Really Know Their Stocks." As the chart shows, O'Neal is, once again, making a mark in the investment world. The guiding hand of the financial mania is apparent by the fact that his investment interests have evolved from technology stocks in September 2000 to commercial real estate in this September 19 Bloomberg article:

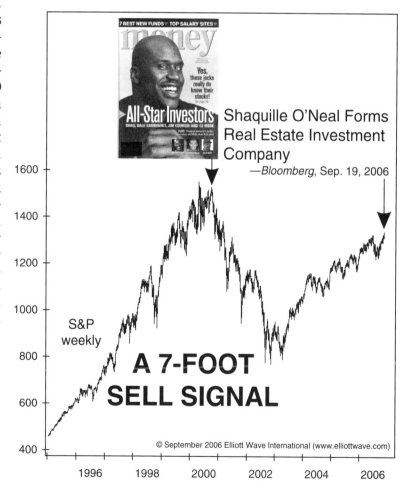

Shaquille O'Neal Forms Real Estate Investment Company
—*Bloomberg*, Sep. 19, 2006

S&P weekly

A 7-FOOT SELL SIGNAL

© September 2006 Elliott Wave International (www.elliottwave.com)

Shaquille O'Neal Forms Real Estate Company

Basketball star Shaquille O'Neal started a real estate company to invest in projects in New Jersey, South Florida, Louisiana and Los Angeles, including a residential, hotel and retail complex in Miami, where he plays for the Heat.

Back in 2000, O'Neal was quoted as one of several "All-Star Investors," athletes who were similarly praised for their stock market savvy as well as their athletic prowess. O'Neal's best move was sticking with the basketball thing. The S&P declined 50% from the 2000 peak, and it's still down from the day of Shaq's Money cover story. A definitive sell signal for commercial real estate is evident by the fact that he is not alone in this venture. O'Neal "is joined by fellow athletes such as tennis stars Andre Agassi and his wife Steffi Graf." Agassi Graf Development is partnering with former AOL Time Warner Chairman Steve Case to develop "luxury resort communities." Case was on the cover of Time on January 24, 2000, 10 days after the Dow's all-time peak. Like we said, really big tops are magnets for "peak" performers. Another celebrity basking in the glow of the current peak is Howie Mandel. We covered the Grand Supercycle significance of his hit TV show, *Deal or No Deal*, in last month's issue (see Chapter 3). In a USA Today interview, Mandel offered up the central misconception of the investment infatuation with real estate:

Q: How do you invest?

A: I'm risk averse. I'm not in stocks or even mutual funds. I'm into real estate and mortgages.

This quote captures one of the latest and greatest miscalculations of the current peak. After getting a bitter but non-fatal taste of the bear in 2000-2002, many believe they have dodged the downside by stashing their investment assets in "safe" real estate. Amazingly, these statements are being made even as the papers start to acknowledge the real estate reversal: "Home Prices Likely to Fall More" (USA Today September 26). Some say home prices may go down, but commercial real estate is safe. *Conquer the Crash*'s forecast for declines of 90% or more includes no such distinction. Many thought they were scurrying to higher ground but by flooding into assets that are likely to be far less liquid than stocks, they've probably already sealed their bearish fate.

Forbes 400: Every One's a Billionaire

By the way, we spoke too soon last month when we said *Deal Or No Deal*, the wealth fantasy game show of the current rally, was failing to live up to the peak level appearance rate of *Who Wants to Be A Millionaire* in 2000, which was on every night of the week in prime time at the stock market's top. For the week of September 18-22, five separate editions of *Deal or No Deal* hit the airwaves. On the other hand, with an average Nielsen rating of 8.74, it's pulling in just half the audience that *Millionaire* did at the 2000 high. In another shortfall from the peak experience of 2000, the show has yet to produce a millionaire.

There is one measure by which the social obsession with wealth accumulation has broken to a new high: For the first time since it was started at the onset of the Great Bull Market in 1982, Forbes' list of the 400 richest Americans contains all billionaires. "It is the age of the billionaire," says one joyful account. It may be instructive to realize that more than a third of those who made it on the 2000 list have fallen off the Forbes 400 pace. Among those no longer included is none other than Steve Case and a host of his fellow dot-com tycoons. Their replacements include a number of real estate and hedge fund operators. The latter group's wealth may be even more vast, but its experience also promises to be even more tumultuous than that of the class of 2000.

November 2006

The latest real-world hedge fund scheme has investors contributing $470,000 for the right to buy a piece of the next potential soccer star. Hero Investments and Sports Asset Capital plan to buy stakes in player contracts and profit from the transfer fees that clubs pay to obtain players.

So far, they have raised almost $300 million. Last month, we covered all the star athletes who are making a big splash in real estate funds; this month, funds are reaching into the pockets of star athletes for even more dubious long-shots. This is one of the more devious aspects of the market rally and its focus on "alternate" investments. One of the things that keeps the process going is the expectation that surrounds the lure of the next pocket. But investment stunts like Hero Investments demonstrate that the uptrend is running out of pockets to pick.

January 2007

> "Corporate America, beware. Sooner or later, shareholders and clients are going to rise up and reject you for so obscenely rewarding people who already have so much with even more."

This quote is from a letter about the "obscene" $53.4 million bonus that went to Goldman Sachs CEO Lloyd Blankfein. It's from the operator of a Leavenworth, Kansas soup kitchen. Last month's EWFF covered the outbreak of alarm over a growing wealth disparity, and Goldman's year-end bonus pool of $16.5 billion, or $623,418 per employee, proved to be a lightning rod for the emerging public anger. After top traders received as much as $100 million, ABC News responded to the "bonus bonanza" with a list of all the things $100 million could buy including the feeding of 800,000 children for a year ($60 million). In London, the cleaners of Goldman's offices threatened to strike, claiming they were being squeezed by staff cutbacks. As noted here last month, the conflict is another sign of a peak, and its focus on the financial sector confirms the vulnerability discussed at the top of this letter (see January 2007 entry in Chapter 2).

The chart shows how CEO cash pay has increased to more than 100 times the average worker over the last 36 years. When benefits and stock options are added, CEO pay is closer to 500 times that of the average worker. Even though these ratios have been climbing almost every year for this entire span, the issue is now being described as "unfair, unjustifiable and harmful." Why? Because the focus of social psychology is shifting from the harmony of the bull market years to a bear market focus on conflict. The alarm registered in a recent Bloomberg/Los Angeles Times poll in which Americans "overwhelmingly" said that the growing gap between rich and poor "has become a serious national concern." Even though poll respondents expressed optimism about the economy and little concern about a housing-market collapse (just 15% said they expect home values in their neighborhoods to fall), almost three-quarters of respondents called income inequality a major issue. So, the shift is not due to an outward change in economic conditions but a spontaneous shift toward "alarm." The article says the anxiety crosses income and political divisions. The rich-poor divide now "unites Americans." The latest outburst over a $210 million severance package for Home Depot CEO Robert Nardelli "may be the catalyst for legislation that tries to rein in executive pay." Congress and the SEC are zeroing in on the issue. As EWFF has shown in various ways, nothing expresses the anger of a bear market like an assault on those who are on top at a top.

Recall that in December 1996 Alan Greenspan's initial observation about irrational excitement on the part of investors produced a sharp market decline. It wasn't until January 2000 that a similar warning fell on deaf ears. When the Dow rallied to a January 14, 2000 high, the February 2000 EWFF observed the nonchalance and stated that the public's willingness "to completely ignore the sincere concerns of Alan Greenspan signaled that "its potential to experience tragedy is now fully formed." In early December 2006, stocks rallied straight through the 10th anniversary observance of Alan Greenspan's original remarks. A belief in a "more rational" irrational exuberance parallels 2000's lack of concern. The same complacency opens the door to a similar market response.

Out Go The Insiders/In With the Public

Corporate insiders are anything but complacent. While Wall Street loves stocks, the chart shows that those closest to corporate prospects are selling their own shares more furiously than at any point in the last decade. According to various services, insider sell/buy ratios are at their highest level since 1987, right before a stock market crash. Lower levels of insider selling helped EWFF identify selling opportunities in July 1998, April 2000 and July 2002. Sales by Bill Gates of Microsoft, Eric Schmidt of Google and others are characterized as "asset diversifications." This may be so. But one thing we do know is that they are not selling their shares in such volume because they think the price of their stock is going up.

In another critically important "coincidence," a host of previously privileged market perches are suddenly being opened to the public. In addition to their newfound capacity for owning financial exchanges, a whole world of complex financial instruments is suddenly allowing "small

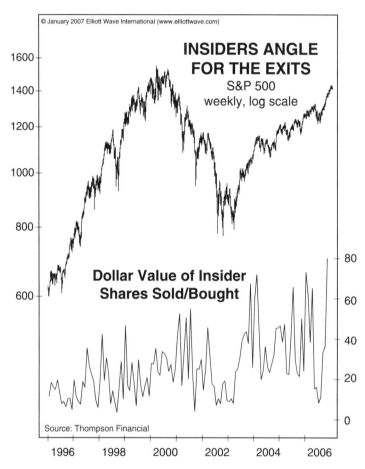

investors to invest like bigwigs." Thanks to an array of new instruments, exchange mergers and rule changes, small investors can get easy access to foreign shares, private equity and the exploding universe of derivatives. Just one example is "a weighted index of energy futures contracts designed to attract small investors" from the New York Mercantile Exchange, the world's largest energy market. The same thing happened with respect to IPOs in 1999.

Now it's the hedge funds that "have gone retail. Copycat mutual funds that mimic the 'alternate' investment strategies" of hedge funds are being "rolled out to attract the 401(k) crowd." For just $500, the little guy can "cover corners of the market that had been considered esoteric and risky in the past." "Hedge funds are on the public radar," the NY Times observes. "They even have their very own 'Dummies' book." This "democratization" of the riskiest assets stamps the trend as a mania. It is the part of the sequence that *The Elliott Wave Theorist* dubbed the "insidiousness of a mania" back in 1997. In a mania, knowledge of history and value are "judged an impediment to success," and the advantage falls to the "utterly unknowledgeable novice." Thus we see *Hedge Funds for Dummies*, which came out in October. The final weeks of 2006 brought several additional titles that imply a much broader turn. Apparently, commodities, exchange-traded funds and "flipping" real estate (published a year too late) are also "for

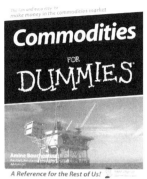 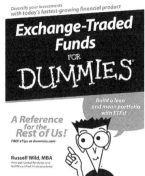 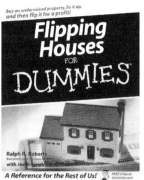 

Dummies" now. All three themes represent critical components of the liquidity driven, all-the-same-market forecast that has been slowly falling into place over the course of 2006. A quadruple whammy of "Dummies" books fits right in with the across-the-board, all-the-same-decline that EWFF has been tracking. Ironically, the financial sophistication that many are working hard to acquire will undoubtedly do more harm than good in the coming environment. Getting in cash and staying there just isn't that complicated. But we'll know that the market is near a low when "Cash for Dummies" comes out.

February 2007

This chart of Wall Street employment offers another example of the current peak's failure to recapture the full resonance of 2000. After noting that similar speculative explosions in 1968 and 1987 produced the only corrections on the chart, the May 2000 issue of *The Elliott Wave Financial Forecast* stated, "This time the damage will be far greater." So far, this is not the case, but the clear five-wave form of Wall Street job growth remains intact. After peaking in early 2001 and declining into 2003, Wall Street jobs retraced about 55% of the preceding decline. Employment tends to lag the market, so it will probably push a bit higher. We wouldn't be surprised by a reversal near the Fibonacci 61.8% retracement. *Elliott Wave Principle* characterizes C wave declines as "devastating in their destruction," a trait that the brokerage community should become acutely familiar with in coming years.

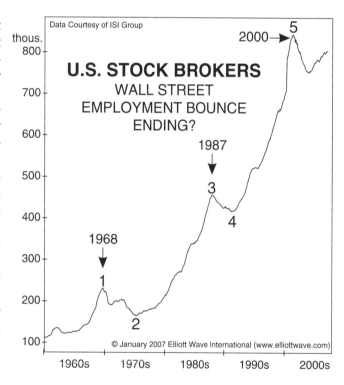

April 2007

Former Fed chairman Alan Greenspan, one of the premier magnets of bull market veneration, appears to have a role to play. One key feature in EWFF's bearish forecast back in January 2001 was the prominence of Greenspan's public image. At that time, *Maestro: Greenspan's Fed and the American Boom* was a best seller and was called the story of "the real president of the United States." In February, Greenspan was feted as the "2007 American Hero." But after the market fell

495

and he offered negative assessments on the economy and the potential spread of the subprime lending debacle, Greenspan caught flak. "Who Thinks Greenspan Should Pipe Down?" says one representative headline. A March 1 USA Today editorial ran his picture under one of Mayberry deputy Barney Fife. On Capital Hill, where the usual post-bubble blame game is revving up, Greenspan is a favorite target. Senators and congressmen charge Greenspan with a "pattern of neglect" that fostered the unfolding crisis. Instead of riding off into the sunset, Greenspan stayed to bask in the glory of the final highs. It will undoubtedly prove costly to his legacy. The rising chorus of angry politicians is nothing compared with what's to come.

The Financial Party Goes On

Everything continues to point to 2007 being "the year of financial flameout" that *The Elliott Wave Financial Forecast* called for in the January issue. The illustration below of bobble-headed investment firm leaders pumping their fists, clapping and snifting their brandies captures an aura of exaltation that is almost indistinguishable from the same condition that gripped Wall Street in 2000. Back in May 2000, EWFF asserted that a top was at hand when brokerage firm executives "capitulated to demands for more meal money, better laptop computers, casual dress codes and access to the company gym on weekends." The current "war for talent" shows up in average MBA starting salaries. According to the Graduate Management Admission Council, the average salary and signing bonus hit a record high of almost $110,000 last year. Starting salaries for MBA graduates from the most prestigious universities will exceed $150,000 this year. "I see demand just going through the roof," said one dean. In an effort to snare between 300 and 400 MBA students, Citigroup will bring as many as 70 professionals to each university event. Of course, this has always been the way on Wall Street. Careers that begin when the balloons and confetti are flying usually don't last very long.

June 2007

One key characteristic is something EWT dubbed "The Insidiousness of a Mania" back in 1997. This refers to investors' maddening facility for separating price from any principle of valuation. At such times, EWT said, "a knowledge of history and value is eventually judged an impediment to success," and market wizardry is ascribed to investors of lower and lower levels of sophistication.

In this respect, everything pales in comparison to what's taking place in China. China will likely be remembered as the place where the Great Asset Mania breathed its last gasp because it is the place where the most naïve investors have become convinced of their financial genius. It has certainly produced the largest mass of unseasoned investors on record. Investment accounts are now being opened at a rate of more than 300,000 a day. Since the beginning of 2007, the total number of accounts has jumped to more than 100 million, a 33% increase. About 10 percent of Shanghai maids resigned in recent weeks "because they make more money trading shares." China's latest hero investor is Shi Changxing, a 50-year-old monk who made headlines by simply opening an account to trade stocks. We're pretty sure that praying over a stock trade is not the path to riches or enlightenment. The accounts are owned almost exclusively by individuals. "Unlike in the west, where big institutions are the main market movers, the supercharged growth in China is being fuelled by individual investors. People are buying stocks to boost their retirement funds, students are speculating to pay for their education and housewives are borrowing from banks to expand their families' share portfolios." Debt, once again, is a major factor.

Among the preferred stock picking strategies are ticker codes containing a double eight. "Numerology is a basic trading strategy in China," reports the *Wall Street Journal*. Trading tips include wearing red cloths because they "are representative of a hot market, eating beef to sustain the 'bull' run and avoiding references to 'dad' since the word in Chinese is a homonym for 'drop.'" "We often choose stocks very blindly" admits a Shanghai investor. To an unprecedented degree, the Chinese bubble is fueled by "get-rich-quick stories and accounts of the extremes to which investors are willing to go to finance trading." "I only need to pay 9,000 yuan interest for the loan I got, but I think I can make at least 70,000 yuan a year by investing that money in stocks," says one office worker. "So why not? I see almost no risk." Can there be a better way to celebrate the final vestiges of a Grand Supercycle peak than to let loose a mania on a society that is less than a generation removed from peasantry? Add in huge amounts of leverage (no one is quite sure how much because technically it's illegal to buy stocks with bank loans) and notions of a virtuous cycle of re-investment created by China's recent commitment to the Blackstone Group's hedge fund IPO, and classic preconditions to a reversal appear to be in place.

July 2007

One subtle way to track the more advanced stages of a mania is to monitor the level of sophistication of the most celebrated investment "authorities." The less they know about markets, the later in the game it tends to be. In June 2000, for instance, as the bear market was just settling in, *The Elliott Wave Financial Forecast* noted that the more distinguished gurus were falling away and that "the stature of those left to bask in the financial limelight says volumes about the current stock market juncture." Included in the group was "a Saudi prince who calls himself the 'Buffett of Arabia.'" With a splash of publicity, the prince dove in, buying up scads of tech stocks at what turned out to be a brief respite on the way to a disastrous decline. As one headline put it, "When Panic Hits Wall Street, the Prince Buys a Lot." To be fair, some of the Prince's investments have been winners, but in recent days he is making another big media push. This time the coverage constitutes an even stronger sell signal because it is connected to a public offering. The prince's Kingdom Holding Co. is selling $840 million worth of its own shares to the public. As EWFF has continually demonstrated, when the public gets in on the action, the end of the line is generally at hand.

A related hallmark of an expiring mania is its tendency to elevate younger and younger investors to the ranks of the investment elite. *The Elliott Wave Theorist* initially uncovered this phenomenon and its Grand Supercycle implications in June 1998 when the market was a month away from the first major setback in the long-term topping process. As EWT asserted at the time, the prominence of young investors betrays a misplaced "faith in the benevolence of social mood and an utter lack of respect for its potential savagery." In a rekindling of this spirit, The Wall Street Journal offered up "Tales of a Ninth-Grade Fund Manager" on June 23. In a nod to the all-important role of fund management in the final phase of the mania, the story focuses on a 14-year-old fund manager who has "taken on many of the conventions of a professional investment." As the Journal notes, the boy manager's "story suggests that some child investors are now hitting a new level of sophistication, and sometimes obsession." He's 14 years old and he's been investing since November. How sophisticated can he be? But at the end of a manic rise, the demand for new blood is strong. In fact, it is so overpowering that children who aren't even allowed to play on their own street are allowed to play on Broad and Wall.

September 2007

The Unwonderful Wizardry of the Fed

Citing "increased downside risks," the Federal Reserve reduced the discount rate half a point on August 17. The market celebrated this seemingly bullish event with a quick 300-point burst that was followed by another 500 points over the next 6 trading days. According to various media accounts, the "sigh of relief" rally "fixed the damage" and returned "stability and calm" to the markets.

With respect to the timing of the Federal Reserve Board rate cuts, we need to reiterate one key point: The market, not the Fed, sets rates. This chart of the Federal Funds rate (dashed line) and the 3-month U.S. Treasury Bill yield shows how obediently the Fed's mandated rate follows the lead of the freely-traded T-bill market. This relative timing is consistent with our discussion in the June issue of government's role as the ultimate trend follower (see Chapter 5). The Fed's latest effort to stem the retreating financial tide came after T-bill rates had fallen and after the Dow Industrials completed a 10.7% decline. In other words, it was a response to a market decline that was already in place.

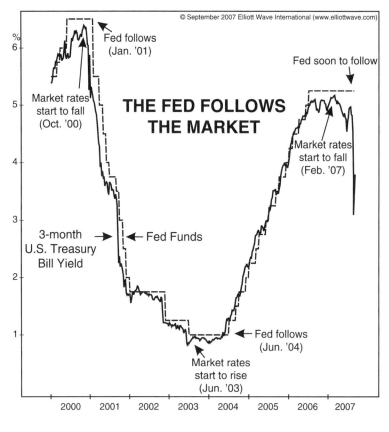

Within the longer-term scheme, the Fed's recent actions return it and its faithful followers to the position they were in on January 3, 2001. While the worst of the bear market was still ahead at that time, the Fed attempted to "intervene" with a "surprise" rate cut designed to snap stocks out of their nascent tailspin. Although a big rally followed, the January 5, 2001 issue of *The*

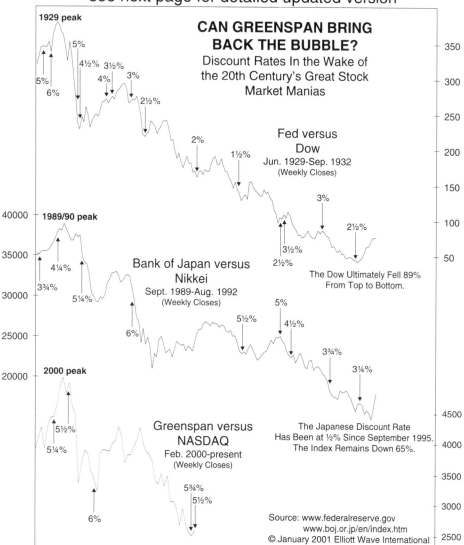

As published in January 2001 EWFF
—see next page for detailed updated version

CAN GREENSPAN BRING BACK THE BUBBLE?
Discount Rates In the Wake of the 20th Century's Great Stock Market Manias

Fed versus Dow
Jun. 1929-Sep. 1932
(Weekly Closes)

The Dow Ultimately Fell 89% From Top to Bottom.

Bank of Japan versus Nikkei
Sept. 1989-Aug. 1992
(Weekly Closes)

The Japanese Discount Rate Has Been at ½% Since September 1995. The Index Remains Down 65%.

Greenspan versus NASDAQ
Feb. 2000-present
(Weekly Closes)

Source: www.federalreserve.gov
www.boj.or.jp/en/index.htm
© January 2001 Elliott Wave International

Elliott Wave Financial Forecast pointed out that the Fed and the Bank of Japan did the same thing following the peaks of 1929 and 1990, respectively, and stated, "No amount of easing stemmed the post-bubble selling tide. The crash in the NASDAQ is not over." After rallying through the end of that month, the NASDAQ subsequently declined another 54% as the Fed tried to pump life back into the market with a succession of rate cuts. *The Elliott Wave Financial Forecast* has pointed out in myriad ways that the global advance that ended in mid-July featured the traits of a mania. In some ways, it was more extreme than that of 2000, so history says quite plainly that any near-term positive response to a Federal Reserve rate cut will be short-lived.

The initial burst of enthusiasm for the August 17 rate cut confirms this view. It persists despite the clear historical precedent that our charts show. The central bank actions you see span several generations, yet the results are the same. In the wake of a great mania, no amount of central bank easing can change social mood once it turns from extreme optimism toward pessimism.

Even though history indicates otherwise, investors jumped in or at least held on because, as various gurus maintained, "the Fed won't let" the markets, economy or any major financial institution fail. This blind faith in the Fed's power to hold up the economy and stocks epitomizes

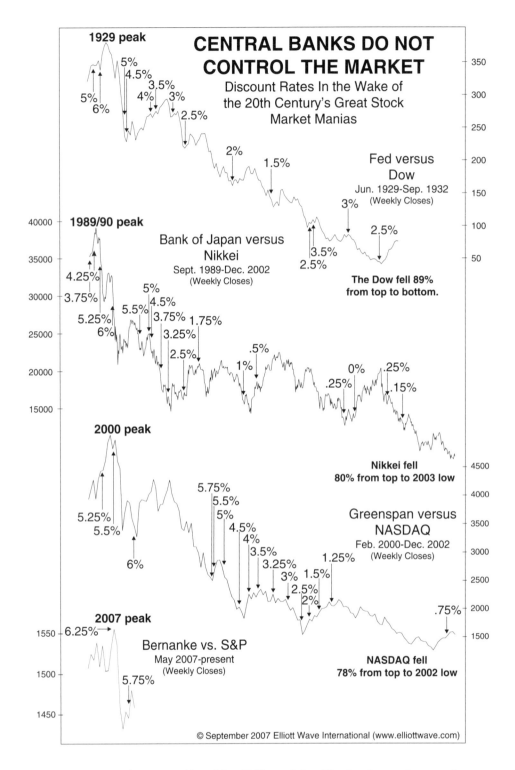

the following definition of magic offered by Teller of the illusionist and comedy team of Penn and Teller: a "theatrical linking of a cause with an effect that has no basis in physical reality, but that — in our hearts — ought to be." In the wake of another manic peak, economists' and the public's belief in the Fed's magical ability to rescue loans and stock prices is as strong as ever. In fact, it is so extreme and so deeply rooted in the public's collective psyche that we strongly suspect one of the roles of the bear market will be to sever this psychological attachment. By the end of the bear market, the public's faith in the Fed will be so shaken that its survival will probably be an open question.

Can't Buy Enough...of That Junky Stuff, or, Why the Fed Will Not Stop Deflation

We hear it every day: "What about the Fed?" The vast majority of investors and commentators seems confident that the Fed's machinations make a stock market collapse impossible. Every hour or so one can read or hear another comment along these lines: "the Fed will provide liquidity," "the Fed is injecting money into the system," "the Fed will be forced to bail out homeowners, homebuilders, mortgage companies and banks," "the Fed has no choice but to inflate," "the government cannot allow deflation," "the Fed will print money to stave off deflation" and any number of like statements. None of them is true. The Fed is not forced to do anything; the Fed has not been injecting money; the Fed does have choices; the government does not control deflationary forces; and the Fed will not print money unless and until it changes its long-standing policies and decides to destroy itself.

A perfect example of one of these fallacies recently exposed is the widespread report in August that the Fed had "injected" billions of dollars worth of "money" into the "system" by "buying" "sub-prime mortgages." In fact, all it did was offer to stave off the immediate illegality of many banks' operations by lending money against the collateral of guaranteed mortgages but only temporarily under contracts that oblige the banks to buy them back within 1 to 30 days. The typical duration is 3 days. Observe three important things:

1. The Fed did not give out money; it offered a temporary, collateralized loan.

2. The Fed did not inject liquidity; it offered it.

3. The Fed did not lend against worthless sub-prime mortgages; it lent against valuable mortgages issued by Fannie Mae (the Federal National Mortgage Association), Ginnie Mae (the Government National Mortgage Association) and Freddie Mac (the Federal Home Loan Mortgage Corporation). The New York Fed is also accepting "investment quality" commercial paper, which means highly liquid, valuable IOUs, not junk.

As a result:

1. The Fed took almost no risk in the transactions.

2. The net liquidity it provided—after the repo agreements close—is zero.

3. The financial system is still choking on bad loans.

4. Banks and other lending institutions must sell other assets to raise cash to buy back their mortgages from the Fed.

These points are crucial to a proper understanding of the situation. The Fed is doing nothing akin to what most of the media claims; like McDonald's, it is selling not so much sustenance as time, in this case time for banks to divest themselves of some assets. But in the Fed's case, that's all it's selling; you don't get any food in the bargain.

As we have said before, the Federal Reserve may be large and complex, but it is a bank. It has private owners: member banks, whose shareholders can be anyone. (For an excellent primer, see http://www.libertyunbound.com/archive/2004_10/woolsey-fed.html.) The Fed's stockholders exploit the banking system through access to easy loans and the Fed's 6%-guaranteed stock dividends. Member banks do not want to see their nurturing enterprise destroyed. Although Bernanke probably received distress calls from mortgage lenders, he probably also got calls from prospering member banks saying, "Don't you dare buy any of that crap and put it in the long-term portfolio."

In the early 1930s, as markets fell and the economy collapsed, the Fed offered loans only on the most pristine debt. Its standards have fallen a bit, but not by much. Today it will still lend only on highly reliable IOUs, not junk. And it doesn't even want to own most of those; it takes them on only temporarily as part of a short-term repurchase agreement.

The Fed's power derives from the value of its holdings, which are primarily Treasury bonds, which provide backing for the value of the Fed's notes. What would a Federal Reserve Note be worth if it were backed by sub-prime mortgages? The real value of U.S. Treasury debt is precarious enough as it is, but at least it has the taxing power of the government behind it. But if the Fed bought up the entire supply of sub-prime mortgages, its notes would lose value accordingly. So will the Fed bail out mortgage companies, as the optimists seem to think? No, it won't. Those who think the Fed will buy up junk with cash delivered by helicopter are dreaming.

Ironically, of course, the Federal Reserve System and the federal government—both directly and via creations such as privileged mortgage companies and the FDIC—have fostered all the lending and the junk debt that resulted. But these entities want only to benefit from the process, not suffer from it. As we will see throughout the bear market and into the depression, the Fed is self-interested and will not brook losses in its portfolio. Those who own the bad loans, and perhaps some foolish government entities that try to "save" them, will take losses, but the Fed won't.

Does the Fed have secret tools to stave off deflation? Yes, to the same extent that Hitler, hiding in a bunker in 1945, had secret weapons to stave off the Allies. The Fed has only one tool: to offer credit, and its arsenal is depleted because it will offer credit only on terms good to itself. And borrowers will borrow only if they think they can pay back the debt after selling assets. You can bet that the Fed is lending only to banks that it believes have the necessary assets to survive its loans' repayment provisions. If not, well, it will be the FDIC's problem. The Fed is not engineering a system-wide bailout; it is just re-arranging deck chairs.

Interest rates are higher than they were in 2002. Many people say that the Fed therefore has lots of room to bring rates down and keep the economy inflated. Do lower interest rates cause recovery? No, they simply reflect a crashing market for credit. The market makes interest rates rise and fall, and the Fed's rates typically just follow suit. Sometimes central banks force the issue, as when the Fed in the final months of 2002 lowered its discount rate to 0.75 percent, staying a bit ahead of the decline in T-bill yields. But its systematic rate drops didn't stop the S&P from losing half its value in 31 months. When the Japanese central bank lowered rates virtually to zero in the 1990s, doing so likewise did not prevent Japanese real estate prices from imploding and the Nikkei from proceeding through its biggest bear market ever by a huge margin. Rates near zero, then, did not constitute a magic potion. Zero was simply the price of loans at the time; nobody wanted them. So the "room" the Fed presumably has may or may not matter. If the market decides to take rates to zero or below, the Fed will simply follow and then have no power.

The Fed does not "inject" liquidity; it only offers it. If nobody wants it, the inflation game is over. The determinant of that matter is the market. When bull markets turn to bear, confidence turns to fear, and fearful people do not lend or borrow at the same rates as confident ones. The ultimate drivers of inflation and deflation are human mental states that the Fed cannot manipulate. The pattern of the stock market's waves determines the ebb and flow of these mental states, and now that a bear market has begun, nothing will stop the trend toward falling confidence and thus falling asset prices, credit deflation and economic depression.

The truth is that the Fed's supposed tools of adding liquidity, such as the limit suspension just granted to the big New York banks, are formulas for total disaster. The terrible secret is that every one of the Fed's tools is nothing but a mechanism to make matters worse. Just because it has taken 74 years to get to the point at which this fact is once again about to become obvious does not mean that it wasn't true all along. The Fed is short-sighted, and its schemes to foster liquidity for short-term crises have served, and are continuing to serve, to insure the ultimate collapse of most of the nation's banking system. The storm clouds are getting dark, so that time may have arrived.

The market is certainly poised for a panic. Confidence has held sway for 2½ decades, during which time investors have become utterly unconcerned with risk. They hold a number of misconceptions that foster such complacency. The day the Fed lowers one of its rates or engineers a major temporary loan and the stock market goes down anyway is the day that investors will become utterly uncertain of what they believe about market causality, and panic will have no bridle. Sadly, Ben Bernanke will be blamed for the debacle, when all he will have been guilty of is serving an immoral monopoly, bad timing and failing to understand the forces at work. The third item pertains to almost everyone.

The Fed Is Not Smart Enough To Stop Deflation, Even If It Could

The dab of grease on the gears in the form of the recent discount-rate cut did not come as part of the Fed's normal policy. According to a Bloomberg article of August 17, the surprise discount rate cut was "an extraordinary policy shift." In other words, the Fed did not know what the hell was going on. It was caught off guard and had to react. In fact, right through July the Fed's spokespeople were all saying that the number one threat to the economy was inflation! Like virtually all futurists, the Fed's economists extrapolate trends to derive forecasts. They never look at underlying indications of coming trend change. That's fine; it helps those of us who at least try to do so. But the idea that the Fed comprises a group of masterminds who "get it" at some deep level and can thereby control things is miles off the mark. For more on this theme, see the "Potent Directors Fallacy" discussion in *The Wave Principle of Human Social Behavior.*

October 2007

The Federal Reserve's seemingly aggressive half-point Federal Funds rate cut to 4.75% on September 18 was unexpected to many. But with the yield on 3-month U.S. Treasury bills already trading under 4.00%, viewers of last month's "Fed Follows the Market" chart should not have been caught off guard. In getting closer to the T-bill rate, the Fed simply chased the market the way it always does, confirming the ever-present "Fed soon to follow" arrow we placed at the top right hand corner of the chart. T-bills point to more doses of "shock therapy" in coming months because at 3.69%, they are still more than a

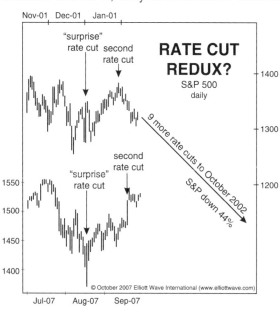

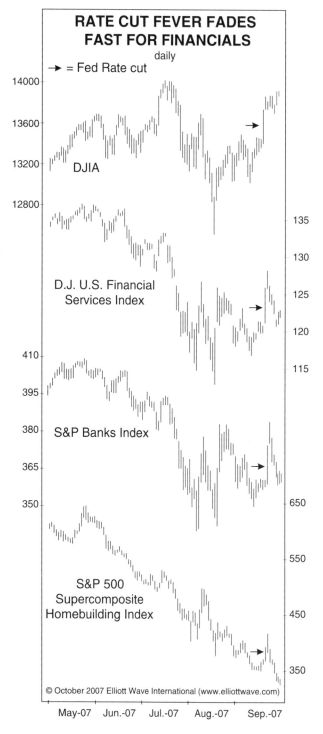

full percentage point lower than the Fed Funds rate. The market sets the rate; Alan Greenspan actually let this secret slip in the midst of a September media blitz. When asked by CNBC if he kept "interest rates too low for too long" in 2002-2003, Greenspan replied, "The market did."

While rate moves are almost always foreordained by the market, investors' responses to them are not. The prevailing psychology in the wake of a rate change can provide critical clues to the underlying sentiment of investors. As we noted here last month, the universal glee over the initiation of the latest rate cut is a dead ringer for what happened on January 3, 2001 when a quick surge higher in the major stock indexes accompanied a similar "surprise" Fed rate cut. The advance continued through January 31 of that year, when another rate cut convinced investors that "the Fed will do whatever it takes to reignite growth." The second cut however, turned out to be the set-up for a decline in which the S&P lost 44% despite 9 more rate cuts. Just like last time, a "surprise" rate cut, in this case a Discount Rate reduction on August 17, led to a one month rally and a follow-up rate cut in which the Fed is said to be making it clear that it "is willing to take extraordinary measures to boost confidence and to restore liquidity."

The performance of the sectors that are the object of the Fed's supposed rescue attempt verifies the frailty of the latest rise. The Fed's bigger-than-expected rate cut was presumed to help the financial services and the bank sectors the most, but as the taller chart shows, they are going the wrong way just as they did well ahead of the overall market's July peak. In fact, they have given back nearly the entire rally from September 18, the day that the Fed acted and the DJIA surged 336 points. Housing stocks, which have been pointing the way even lower for even longer (down more than 69% over the last two years), also shrugged off the Fed's efforts to stave off further deterioration and have fallen to a new low.

October 2007
Greenspanning the Great Peaks

Another reason to suspect that the latest Fed move is a replay of what happened in 2001 is that, like the January 2001 experience, the current episode is accompanied by a huge wave of idolatry for the Fed itself. As financial TV made the rate cut announcement and stocks started to scamper higher, commentators raved that the move was "the perfect solution for stocks" and "great news for the economy and consumer. God bless the greatest central bank on earth."

The most sustained applause didn't go to the current chairman, but to the former one, Alan Greenspan, who managed again to steal the limelight from his successor Ben Bernanke by releasing his biography, *The Age of Turbulence*, between the first and the second rate reductions. The praise that sustains the latest Greenspan media blitz is not as universally positive as it was in 2001. At that time, EWFF cited an unprecedented depth of Greenspan worship noting that *Maestro*, Bob Woodward's bestseller about the Greenspan Fed, was being marketed as the story of "the real president of the United States." EWFF called for Greenspan's image to "fall hard." He definitely took some heat near the lows in 2002. But he is clearly back on top along with the stock averages. On his latest junket, Greenspan still drew "a few detrac-

tors and hecklers," but judging from a "throng of 500 people" who turned up "to get a gander" at the great man as he signed books at a Manhattan Barnes & Noble, his rock-star status is intact.

In one more sign that the peak in finance is the focal point of the unfolding debacle, an AP reporter noted that the crowd was "full of financial services employees." One crowd member said that he needed to follow the Fed "in order to converse with his wealthy clients." Another said, "Everything that Alan Greenspan says is followed by everyone." Ironically, in the book, Greenspan admits much of his official testimony should have been ignored. In a CBS *60 Minutes* interview, he stated that he invented "fedspeak," a dense language of "purposeful obfuscation," to get around saying "no

comment" and "I can't answer that," thus the famous tendency for his words to be cited as both bullish and bearish. In a downtrend, people will probably object to being misled, but, for now, there is no denying the height of Greenspan's public standing. The Newsweek cover story reflects that status, and, as financially-related covers in general interest magazines usually do, it signals a likely reversal. As we said here last month, the decline will probably transform nearly universal Fed worship into demonization. As the head potentate of the great bull market, Greenspan's role will probably morph into the work of a great satan.

In Between the Fedspeak

As Greenspan's "the market made me do it" comment on CNBC shows, he is capable of surprising candor at times. On more than one occasion, for instance, he has said things such as "values reflect waves of optimism and pessimism" (Fed symposium, Jackson Hole, Wyoming, August 1999). Of course, he carefully chooses his spots to come clean. One came recently, in an appearance on Comedy Central (irony knows no bounds). He was asked about the recent financial turmoil and here is his reply:

> I'm looking at what's going on in the last few weeks. If I could figure out a way to determine whether or not people are more fearful or changing to more euphoric, and have a third way of figuring out which of the two things are working, I don't need any big mathematical models of forecasting the economy. I could forecast the economy better than any way I know. Forecasting 50 years ago was as good or as bad as it is today. And the reason is that human nature hasn't changed.

Of course, it hasn't. Its permanence is what makes the Wave Principle so exciting. It unlocks what R.N. Elliott called "a phenomenon that has always functioned in every human activity."

January 2008
The Whip Comes Down on Wall Street

Since EWFF's "financial flameout" call last January, the S&P 500 Financials Index is down about 26%, but this is still just the downpayment on this sector's full decline, which will last at least the next few years. The seeds for a serious fall were actually planted back at the lows of 2003 when the largest players in the financial industry decided to make up for a slump in trading volume by beefing up their proprietary trading operations. At that time, EWFF was absolutely clear on what we thought of the industry's bid to trade its way to higher heights of prosperity. Here's what we said:

> [It's] another example of a desperate flight to higher levels of financial risk. They intend to make up for the revenue lost from dwindling commissions by turning their trading units into profit centers. We predict unequivocally that trading disasters at brokerage firms will make headlines in coming months.

Naturally, these disasters waited for the next market top to pass before making their appearance. Here's the latest:

Wall Street Retreats After Black Box Blow Up

NEW YORK—Some U.S. investment banks are losing their appetite for betting their own money on trades as Merrill Lynch & Co Inc and Morgan Stanley reel from massive losses on mortgages. Morgan Stanley became exhibit No. 1 on Wednesday for proprietary trading gone wrong. So wrong the investment bank reported a $3.6 billion loss from continuing operations in its fiscal fourth quarter.

—Reuters, December 20, 2007

But this is just the tip of a very large iceberg. While the mammoth losses at Merrill Lynch and Citigroup cost their respective CEOs and many employees their jobs, Goldman Sachs continues to post profits, with a modest gain in the fourth quarter. But the exception proves the rule, as Goldman's success points to the eventual appearance of a much larger public relations problem in the future. According to The New York Times, losses in the firm's core business were "offset by the firm's bearish bet on the mortgage sector." In other words, Goldman's positive fourth quarter came at the expense of its own customers, who are now suffering mightily. In the negative-mood times that accompany bear markets, conflict of interest charges will come pouring out. We already see signs that the populist anti-Wall Street sentiment is starting to flare. Here's a small sample that appeared in our local paper's "vent" section.

F2/ Sunday, Dec. 16, 2007

SundayVent

I strongly believe that there is one employment sector in which massive layoffs, in fact, total layoffs, might be a boon to the economy and the stock market: Wall Street analysts.

Last we heard, colleges were still turning out record numbers of aspiring investment bankers. In the new economy, social work and plumbing will surpass financial pursuits in popularity.

February 2008
The Fall of the "Potent Directors"

The U.S. president and Congress revealed that they will do whatever they can think of to hold things up by rushing forward a $150 billion stimulus plan. The Fed chipped in to this "stimulus" by springing a "surprise" rate cut on the market on January 22. The rally that followed did not catch readers of the Short Term Update off guard. A week before the Fed's cut, STU stated that "recent market action makes a 'surprise' rate cute highly probably before [the Fed's] next meeting. If so, expect a large rally with the announcement." There were two reasons for our forecast. First, T-bill yields were significantly lower than the Fed Funds rate, and as EWFF and EWT have repeatedly demonstrated, the Fed follows the market. So they needed to play catch up. Second, the market had been falling precipitously, closing lower six out of seven consecutive days, and was nearing a short-term low. As expected, the final downward thrust over the last two days of the decline panicked the Fed, causing it to act. On January 22, the biggest inter-meeting cut since the 1980s coincided with the onset of a 7.5% rally over the course of the next four trading sessions. Here's the headline that appeared right before a follow-up, 50-basis point rate cut on January 30: "Buyers Bet Big on a Fed Cut." Sure enough, the announcement pushed the counter-trend rally to a new recovery high by adding a quick 150 intraday points to the Dow. However, before the trading day had ended, the market retraced the entire intraday push and ended the day lower. The Fed-inspired bursts point out the completely emotional nature of the response. After six straight rate reductions, the Dow closed that day at 12,442, below the low that it rallied from when the whole process started with a discount rate cut on August 16.

As shown in the charts in EWFF's September Special Section, "The Unwonderful Wizardry of the Fed," the reversal from a mania may coincide with some temporary upward responses to rate cuts, but "no amount of central bank easing can change social mood once it turns from extreme optimism toward pessimism." To see the ultimate impotence of the Fed, we need to go back only one month. In December, the Fed set up its Term Auction Facility, a series of four $30 billion auctions in which central banks essentially gave banks free passes to make money through arbitrage in the LIBOR market and elsewhere. One paper called it "the biggest coordinated show of international financial force since Sept. 11, 2001." If the bear market is on, however, *The Elliott Wave Theorist* insisted the scheme will fail:

> The outcome is predicated on psychology. If wave **c** of the bear market has begun, nothing the Fed does will engender confidence. On the contrary, everything it does will be interpreted, in the trend toward negative social mood, as something bad. The Fed's failures will not create fear; fear will create the Fed's failures.

Wave **c** must, in fact, be underway because the introduction of the auction plan was quickly followed by a Dow plunge from 13,700 to 12,650, today's close. The large degree of the decline is confirmed by a flood of Fed criticism. Consider some of the Fed's latest reviews: "Fed Move Reflects Alarm," "Stock Market Tumbles as the Fed Fumbles" and, from the January 25, 2008 Wall Street Journal, "Criticism of Rate Cut Mounts." One pundit says, "Bernanke is making a 'terrible, terrible, terrible mistake' by cutting rates," and another pushes the opposite view: "cut interest rates more and faster." The Fed has taken the United States "into a terrible crisis," says presidential candidate Ron Paul, one of whose campaign promises is to get rid of the central bank altogether. As the offering at left from hedge-fund manager Bill Fleckenstein illustrates, whole books are now railing against the Fed and its "powers."

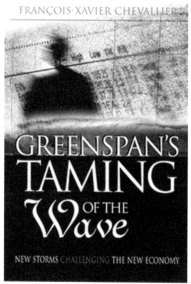

The contrast to the last major peak in 2000 is startling. Two weeks after the Dow's January 2000 top, the U.S. Senate Banking Committee chairman, Phil Gramm, helped renominate Fed Chairman Alan Greenspan to a fourth term by stating, "If you were forced to try to narrow down the credit for the golden age that we find ourselves living in...I think your name would have to be at the top of the list." Later that year, *Greenspan's Taming of the Wave*, by Francois–Xaiver Chevallier, hit bookstores. We're quite sure the author was not referring to the taming of the Elliott Wave, because there is a section in the book that says "1973 to 1997 qualifies as the down wave of the latest cycle." Thanks to the afterglow of the great peak, Greenspan didn't really face any dissension until 2002, when stocks were bottoming. But the rally from that low easily repaired the damage to his image. As the Dow approached its final high in October 2007, EWFF observed Greenspan's near canonization in a Newsweek cover story and a series of fawning interviews. We added that the celebration "signals a likely reversal. As the head potentate of the great bull market, Greenspan's role will probably morph into the work of a great satan." Fleckenstein's book and this Bloomberg article reveal that the vilification we forecast is underway:

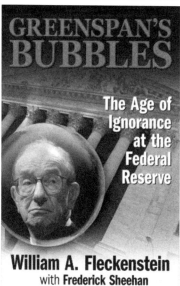

Greenspan's 'Superstar' Status At Risk

Hailed as perhaps the greatest central banker who ever lived when he left the Federal Reserve in 2006, Greenspan is under attack from critics ranging from the New York Times to economists at the American Enterprise Institute.

Greenspan missed his chance to ride off into the sunset. The harder he tries to defend his legacy, the more damaged it will become. And the more the Fed tries to reverse the market and the economy's slide, the more damage will occur and the larger the scorn and derision will become. Eventually, rate cuts will fail to generate any enthusiasm at all. When the public finally pays no attention to the "man behind the curtain," the downtrend's "point of recognition" will be at hand.

July 2008
When Bad Things Happen To Super Successful People

One of the most important (and predictable) side effects of a burst bubble is society's attack on former icons and instruments of the expired bull market. As the fallout surrounding firms like Enron, WorldCom and Tyco demonstrated in wave **a** down, such scandals are the primary means by which participants in the prior uptrend vent their newfound negativity and shriveled hopes. Even though we forecast the latest episode in conjunction with wave **c** and observed its onset with entries like "The Devil Wears Pinstripes" here last month (Chapter 8), it still amazes us to see the power of the shift from reverence and veneration to antagonism and persecution.

In November, EWFF stated, "revelations of fraud should spike," and sure enough, the financial authorities are moving in for the big financial bust right on cue: "In a program dubbed 'Operation Malicious Mortgage,' the government has brought 144 [Fibonacci] mortgage fraud cases in which 406 defendants have been charged with crimes." This month, the biggest case to date hit when two former Bear Stearns executives, Ralph Cioffi and Matthew Tannin, were "nabbed." They were taken off in handcuffs to a Brooklyn courthouse and charged with nine counts of securities, mail and wire fraud. The funny thing is that the reputed crime took place well over a year ago, and as one columnist said, "What Cioffi and Tannin allegedly did is pretty much standard operating procedure on Wall Street." In fact, the transgression for which they are now charged, driving two subprime funds into the ground, happened in full view of the world this time last year. Subscribers may remember the event, as we covered it in our July 2007 issue (Chapter 1). Recall that the pair successfully tabled an $800 million takeover and subsequent sale of the funds' bonds by Merrill Lynch, one of its investors. As EWFF noted at the time, a sale of the bonds was the last thing Bear Stearns and the rest of Wall Street wanted because, at that point, any form of price discovery "would give banks, brokerages and investors the one thing they want to avoid: a real price on the bonds in the fund that could serve as a benchmark." Within a matter of days, the credit crisis was on and the fund lost its entire value. Still, for a full year after the event, the managers faced no reprisal. The reason is that the stock market and the social mood that drives it stayed mostly positive.

At the time, one writer referred to the debacle as a "subprime Chernobyl," but EWFF explained that the "delusion lives on thanks to the mania's amazing ability to take asset prices higher." Today, the mania must be over, because the guys that managed to keep a "'cone of silence' over the subprime sector" are under arrest. Their indictment and potential vigorous prosecution is a sure sign that the new negative mood is digging in for a long-term stay. It comes as the headlines whirl with a quickening succession of stories about Congressional efforts to investigate and/ or ban commodity speculation, a startling 40% jump in stock frauds and profit rigging on the London financial markets, the sacking of top executives at Lehman Brothers and AIG and, "in a broad condemnation of its business practices," a major lawsuit against the nation's largest mortgage company brought by the states of Illinois and California. By now the post-peak pattern is so familiar, today's Wall Street Journal says, "Whenever the investing public suffers staggering losses on Wall Street, we can expect to see someone hauled off in handcuffs. The real question is not why it happened, but where it will end." We beg to differ. "Why did it happen?" is *the* most interesting question, one that socionomics answers, allowing us to be a full year ahead of the news. Believe it or not, the latest headline arrests are still just the preliminary "perp walks" in what promises to be a long, nasty stroll down the seamy side of Wall Street.

September 2008

Don't Get Even, Get Out

Isn't it fascinating how the market is backing sophisticated investors into the same corner? In a recent report to shareholders, Bill Miller, a top mutual fund manager, kidded that he and fellow value investors "needed a 12-step program to cure us of our addiction to beaten-up stocks trading at large discounts." He then reiterated the core belief that guides a generation of successful Graham & Dodd advocates: "Lower prices today mean higher future rates of return." Miller says Warren Buffett encouraged the group by saying, "We should be happy if stock prices declined a lot more, so we could buy even better bargains."

But there is big problem with this approach. In a depression, many broken-down stocks go to zero. Major bear markets have a nasty tendency to drag on for years, as our "Long-Term Strategy Must Account For The Moves in *Both* Directions" chart (see March 2008 entry in Chapter 8) illustrates. This is surely one of those times, as the public faith in Buffett and the urge to buy beaten-down values is as strong as ever. "Regardless of what's happening with earnings, the cash is still rolling in and prices are down," says a New Jersey money manager. "It's Buffett time." Another magazine cover addresses "Why BUFFETT is BUYING" and says he plans to "boost flagging growth." No one seems to notice that shares of Buffett's Berkshire Hathaway are down 25%. Or that fellow bottom feeders, Kirk Kerkorian, Sam Zell and T. Boone Pickens, are in similar positions (see June and July issues). We can certainly relate. On the way up, it was the other way around as the manic rise swept through one seeming historic selling opportunity after another. But every action breeds an equal and opposite reaction. *The Elliott Wave Theorist*'s May 1997 "Bulls, Bears and Manias" report explains it this way: "Ultimately, a mania and its aftermath have everyone for lunch," even "the prudent professionals relying on their long-term studies." There comes a time when "there are no significant advances, no 'getting even,' no way to take advantage except to sell." A lifetime of bull market experience tells these old guns that it's always darkest before the dawn. On rare occasions, however, it is darkest right before the storm hits; this appears to be one such time.

October 2008

A Fat Cat a Day

The cartoon announces the dawn of a new era for the "Wizards of Wall Street." Cagle's cartoon website now has a whole section dedicated to "Wall Street CEOs." Seems like little more than a week ago that the men now being dragged in to testify on Capitol Hill were the kings of finance. Every day brings the grilling of a former captain of industry. On October 6, it was the ex-CEO of Lehman Brothers. Not so long ago, he was ranked best CEO in America by Institutional Investor, but now he is being lampooned

THE WIZARDS OF WALL STREET

on *Saturday Night Live.* To add injury to insult, he got punched in the face in Lehman's gym after it was announced that Lehman was bankrupt. On October 7, Rep. Henry Waxman tanned the hide of former AIG executives for "wining and dining at one of the most exclusive resorts in the nation after taxpayers rescued" the firm. This trend has been building for some time, but railing against former financial wizards is fast becoming a new national pastime. The street-level explosion in outrage is captured by the call-in section of The Atlanta Journal-Constitution.

THE VENT [emails and calls to editor]

"**I have a feeling** that those of us who pay our mortgages and bills each month are going to get screwed in this bailout."

"**How many fat-cat executives** are going to walk away with their golden parachutes totally intact after running not only their companies, but the economy into failure?"

"**Americans have been** robbing Peter to pay Paul for so long…he's all petered out."

"**Let me get this** straight. $700 billion (that's with a B) is too much but $850 billion is OK. Throw all the bums out!"

"**Proposed new title for** highly-paid execs of companies failing due to mortgage debacle: Thief Executive Officer."

"**I suggest we vote** against ALL incumbents."

"**I better not see** any of these 'Financial CEOs' getting year-end bonuses for their work."

"**Someone asked** – 'Is there any such thing as LEGAL gang members' – YES, take your pick, Wall St. Bankers or Congress."

—*Atlanta Journal-Constitution*, September 2008

This is the backlash that follows every mania. It's hard to measure its exact size, but based on the storm now hitting the Capitol and the "financial crisis" takeover of the political stage—in the final weeks of a presidential election no less—we can say that it is much bigger than the retributive social force that held sway in 2001-2002. In every measure, including this one, the bust will eventually match the upside force of the boom. Over time, the outrage should coalesce into powerful social forces that change Washington and the capital markets in fundamental ways.

November 2008
The Stock Market Endgame

Back in 1998, *The Elliott Wave Theorist* called the aggressive "targeting of kids with stock market propaganda" a surefire sign that the current mania was the "biggest of all time." In another sign of the mania's end, the predicted reversal of fortune for stock market youth is now appearing. About 700,000 4th through 12th graders are still playing the "Stock Market Game," but, The Wall Street Journal reports, "Kids Are Losing a Lot of Play Money." As the bear market rolled in, we knew that kids' migration back to cartoons, baseball and dolls would happen, but it is surprising to see how the process transpires. At this point, the kids are actually gaining some valuable bear market lessons. A 17-year-old high schooler says that "in the real world" he will stay in cash rather than invest in stocks. An economics teacher is dovetailing October stock losses with lessons about the Great Depression. Funds managed by a team of students at the University of Virginia are frozen, much like those of many hedge fund investors. The big winners are on the short side. The Stock Market Game's leaders in Pennsylvania went from $100,000 to $220,000 in a few weeks by shorting Wachovia Corp., ironically a national sponsor of the country-wide contest. "They're short selling," says the game's organizer. "I don't like it." When the bear market finally arrives to round out the investment lesson, it is the grown-ups who lose heart. How long before these investment games ban short selling, just as it was in markets around the world? In the end, participation will eventually crash, and these investment games will be discontinued for lack of interest, just like the real world. Except in the real world, the game never ends.

December 2008

As *Conquer the Crash* so boldly counseled, prosperity entails managing one's finances and livelihood so as to be in tune with a 1930s' style deflationary depression. But conventional wisdom disagrees. "There's no comparison" to the Great Depression, says the world's leading financial authority, U.S. Federal Reserve Chairman Ben Bernanke: "I've written books about the Depression. We didn't have the social safety net that we have today. So let's put that out of our minds."

He cites as evidence a 25% unemployment rate, a one-third decline in U.S. GDP and a 90% decline in stock prices, all of which occurred during the 1930s' depression. Unfortunately, what Bernanke's managed to do is put one important word out of his mind—*yet*. Like the rest of the "this is no depression" camp, he fails to note that his cited figures are the extreme readings of that era. Bernanke also ignores the critical fact that today's bear market is actually ahead of where the stock market was at the same point during the 1929-1932 decline and that the economy is lurching lower in a manner suggesting strongly that it will have little trouble keeping pace with the economic contraction of the 1930s.

The Sound of Pedestals Cracking

As *The Wave Principle of Human Social Behavior* explains, "Public heroes are of their times, and their images become vulnerable when the wind changes." The flagging public image of many financial legends reflects a still burgeoning bearish trend. One of the most elevated of all the bull market stars was Alan Greenspan. Back in 2007, as the Dow approached its all-time high and Greenspan released his memoirs to widespread acclaim and a fawning Newsweek cover story, here's what the October 2007 issue of EWFF—issued days before the all-time high in the Dow— said about a Greenspan world tour:

> In a downtrend, people will probably object to being misled, but, for now, there is no denying the height of Greenspan's public standing. This Newsweek cover story [The World According to Greenspan] reflects that status, and, as financially-related covers in general interest magazines usually do, it signals a likely reversal. As the head potentate of the great bull market, Greenspan's role will probably morph into the work of a great satan.

It's now open season on his legacy. "Liar, Liar" says the headline over one NY Post profile. According to a flood of other re-appraisals of his tenure as Fed chairman, Greenspan is a "dunderhead" who "built the bomb that blew us up." The descent of Greenspan's image still has a long way to go, as he is only now being joined by other key members of the pantheon of bullish heroes. Robert Rubin, the former U.S. Treasury secretary, who "has been surprisingly bullet proof until now," is suddenly "engulfed" in scandal for his role in the near-collapse of Citigroup. Disgruntled shareholders charge that Rubin and other top Citi executives operated "a quasi-Ponzi scheme" that kept Citi stock afloat while insiders bailed out. Lawrence Summers, the third member of the triumvirate that Newsweek described in 1999 as the "committee to save the world" (March 1999 entry in this chapter), is making a comeback after getting sacked as the president of Harvard in 2006. Summers has decided to return to the scene in the role of top White House economic advisor. Obviously, years of bull market conditioning have gone to his head. If he understood the intractable nature of the unfolding economic crisis, he wouldn't take the job. Then again, with unemployment skyrocketing, he may need it.

Jim Cramer, the most prominent investment guru of the b-wave rally from 2002, was "pilloried" for issuing a relatively mild sell signal on October 6 (he said to take out "whatever money you may need for the next five years"). "Cramer Should be Suspended," said one writer. "Financial advisors across the nation have been trying to clean up the mess that Jim Cramer made." This New York Times headlines captures the basic dynamic behind the denunciation:

Jim Cramer Retreats With the Dow

**NON SEQUITUR
BY WILEY**

The seriousness of the decline is apparent by chinks in the armor of another more entrenched bullish idol, Warren Buffett. Until very recently, the world's richest man was clearly in the ascent. With the release of three new Buffett books, including a No.1 New York Times bestseller, Buffet now has 47 books with his name in the title, more than any living person aside from major political figures and the Dalai Lama. Authors say they are being "pressured by publishers" to get his name or photo onto their book jackets. But EWFF alerted subscribers to a new vulnerability in recent months, and there are now hints that even the irrepressible Mr. Buffett is sinking. One misstep appears to be his October "I'm buying" op-ed piece in the New York Times, which, if our analysis of the market's wave structure is correct, will probably go down as a bad macro bet. His rock star status, his effort to get the bullish word out and an initial five-wave decline in Berkshire Hathaway stock, all suggest much further declines for Buffett and the stock market as a whole. A Wall Street Journal article confirms that a Buffett retrenchment may be underway, as it says that Buffett "failed to see how bad the market was going to get," booked losses on derivatives exposures in 2008 and used options to make bad directional bets on equities. The damage to the other "old pros," such as T. Boone Pickens and Kirk Kerkorian, is more severe. "Market upheaval is throwing the prominent graybeards for a loop, a sign the playbooks of even top investors needs a thorough updating," says the Wall Street Journal. This "riches to rags" reversal is exactly what we were referring to in September when we said that years of bull market experience would hurt "these old guns." They've been around a long time, but not long enough to experience a bear market of Grand Supercycle degree.

This comic strip perfectly captures the move away from a consensus belief in the old bull market wizardry. In some ways, public disillusionment is a good thing, as it should energize the attack on bogus elements of modern financial theory, such as the Efficient Market Hypothesis and the importance of earnings and analysts' estimates for ascertaining the direction of stock prices. A recent Business Week article actually offers a critical, though disputed, appraisal of "buy and hold."

Of course, a bear market produces its own impediments to sound analysis. One difficulty is that a falling trend produces what *The Wave Principle of Human Social Behavior* calls "magical thinking." This is already evident in the market for financial guidance. "Psychics and people who channel spirits" say "business is thriving as clients turn to them for financial advice." According to the NY Times, lawyers, doctors, chief executives and other people with day jobs that require rational thought processes are now turning to swamis of all sorts and asking, "What is your accuracy rate?" So here again, psychology is at the helm and moving the crowd further out on a financial limb. After it snaps, more viable financial theories, possibly even socionomics, will take root.

Chapter 7

The Glo-bull Village:
Inclusionism Conquers the World

The long rise brings peace, atonement for centuries-old transgressions, a worldwide passion for American ideals, and advancing stock markets to most areas of the planet. When the bubble breaks, globalization turns out to be a source of conflict. Tension mounts among trading partners, historical rivals, faiths and political groups. September 11 announces the new trend toward exclusionism. "Everything is dividing."

January 1995

For a variety of reasons, there is a high probability that the U.S. will be involved in a major war during the next ten years. The extent to which EWT's forecast for war within a few years is contrary to expectations is revealed in this quote from Time magazine regarding the signing of the Strategic Arms Reduction Treaty: "The fact that the ceremony went almost unnoticed testifies to how effectively Washington and Moscow have worked to dispel the once rampant dread of nuclear holocaust." That "rampant dread" occurred throughout all but the final years of a 46-year bull market. Can you imagine such an agreement having gone "almost unnoticed" in the 1950s, '60s, '70s or '80s? The disappearance of the long-standing fear to the point of complete complacency is marking a social mood peak.

February 1995

North Korea, for nearly five decades a fierce Communist regime, and now (therefore) bankrupt and starving, has lifted restrictions on trade with the United States and has agreed to allow U.S. merchant ships into its ports for the first time since 1949. The first shipload of oil arrived on January 18, 1995.

May 1995

175 governments are meeting to sign a treaty to stop the spread of nuclear weapons beyond the five countries that admit to having them (U.S., China, Russia, France, U.K.). The U.S. Secretary of State called it "one of the most important treaties of all time," an expression of how much the U.S. wants to keep such weapons away from Iraq and Iran.

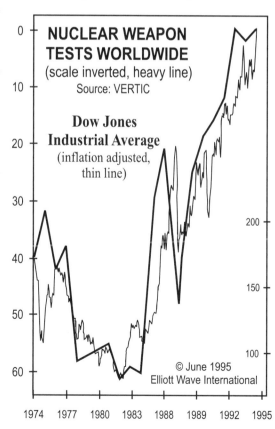

July 1995

Is the thick line in the chart on the previous page some kind of annual average of stock prices, which it resembles so closely? No, it is a chart of the number of nuclear weapons tests annually, inverted. Tests had been rising during the bear market and reached a high in 1982 that coincided with the stock market bottom in inflation-adjusted terms. From there, testing declined persistently as the bull market progressed. It jumped sharply in 1986-87, peaking as the stock market crashed. Then it resumed its decline as stocks resumed their advance. Bomb testing actually reached zero in 1993, and has stayed near there since. This line is ready to reverse direction, though, as France has just announced that it will resume nuclear testing in the Pacific. Social mood doesn't really trend with the stock market, does it?

Japan has conceded that it faces a banking crisis. Its banks now have nearly $500 billion worth of "problem" loans outstanding. This figure will increase as Japan's deflation continues. Watch financial and social developments in Japan carefully, as that country's experiences are an advance warning of what the U.S. will face over the next ten years.

August 1995

In bear markets, anger, fear and the urge to destroy overcome the social conscience. Remorse, on the other hand, is a bull market trait born of the larger trend toward inclusionist impulses. Historic expressions of it would be expected to appear at bull market tops, when the inclusionist mood trend is at its extreme. Today, the climate is that of a Grand Supercycle top, and regret has reached an extreme in a worldwide drive for forgiveness. The peaking social mood has brought apologies for a host of transgressions that are decades, generations, and even centuries old. After years of bickering, the Japanese government reached a "compromise" apology for its part in World War II. At a recent press conference, President Clinton resisted considerable public pressure to ask forgiveness for bombs dropped on Japan eight administrations ago. A group of ethicists and historians has decided that financial compensation and a formal government apology is due victims of secret human radiation experiments conducted in the U.S. during the Cold War. Though not exactly apologizing, the U.S. has just normalized relations with Vietnam, its bitterest enemy, and one of its longest standing, since World War II.

The United Church of Canada has apologized to a host of native tribes for sins of the past. Southern Baptists, the nation's largest Protestant denomination, have asked forgiveness for defending slavery in the 1800s. (The sect was founded in 1845 in a show of support for slavery.) The Catholic Church apologized to "every woman" in the world for centuries of relegation to "the margins of society"; then it apologized to the Czech Republic for the Catholic church's role in the 16th Century wars that followed the Protestant Reformation; then it agreed to join Protestants in ceremonies repenting the Crusades against Muslims and Jews 900 years ago! According to a Vatican spokesman, the Pope is "pushing hard toward unity."

September 1995

In the atonement department, two more figures have come forward to apologize to millions of people. Norma McCorvey, a.k.a. Jane Roe of Roe vs. Wade fame, has joined the right-to-life movement to make amends for her 1969 decision to fight for women's right to an abortion, and a one-time Ronald McDonald apologized to "kids everywhere for selling out to concerns who make millions by murdering animals."

October 1995

The craze is in force worldwide. International markets are being flooded with new offerings, as the governments of Spain, France, Indonesia and Holland sell off state-owned companies. In some countries, retail investors are offered incentives that pay them back for declines of less than 10%, while others are enticed by discounts on their telephone, gas or utility bills. Another common lure is shares on the installment plan. International corporate offerings are also high,

The Group: Presidents, premiers and heads of delegations pose for a commemorative photo Sunday.
— USA Today, October 25, 1995

as companies in holdout countries like Germany are, according to one international newspaper, "finally embracing the equity culture." If you have any doubts about whether equities have conquered the world and are now at a higher level of adoration than gold was in 1980, consider this paragraph from the Financial Times: "A partial devaluation of the maira at the start of the year, inflation of over 80 percent, negative interest rates, and fears of bank failure have persuaded many Nigerians that the stock market is the best place for their savings."

Israel and the PLO have reached their third agreement in three years. The latest one calls for Palestinian self rule and the withdrawal of Israel from parts of the West Bank.

In what may turn out to be the grandest among historic signs of a long term peak in social mood, New York City has just hosted "history's greatest gathering of world leaders." It was the political equivalent of the "Harmonic Convergence" gathering in August 1987. The above photo is the latest and most comprehensive in a series of "peak mood" photos of world leaders embracing or signing peace accords that EWT has reproduced since September 1993. This photograph is a candidate for being the snapshot that represents the ultimate top in a Grand Supercycle bull market. In past years, the leaders of the world have not gathered for a photo like this one because tensions between nations would not allow their leaders to stand together in the same room. In the fall of 1995, however, the U.N.'s media director said the photo of 185 leaders was a relatively simple matter because "everybody loves each other." EWT once characterized major mood peaks as involving "amorphous feelings of love," where "everybody's a good guy." That description certainly fits the mood in most of the world today, this picture being a concrete expression of it.

In 1941 and 1942, when the Dow was at a bottom that has yet to be revisited, the Pentagon, the world's largest office building, was constructed. Since it was during a bear market of Supercycle degree, it is only natural that the purpose of the building was to wage war. At the top of a Grand Supercycle degree bull market, it is equally fitting that the world's largest non-military office building, the International Trade and Commercial Center, is being constructed in Washington. "No one has figured out how to fill the building," says an article, but one idea is to fill the space with employees of the International Monetary Fund and the World Bank, which organizations will presumably "assume a much higher profile (in) an increasingly interconnected world market." Given the history of divisive politics in large degree bear markets, this monument to harmony and centralization is undoubtedly marking the peak.

517

Australians hold 'Sorry Day'

The Atlanta Journal-Constitution, May 27, 1998

The Pope's in Confessional and Jews Are Listening

The New York Times, January 8, 1997

VATICAN REPENTS FAILURE TO SAVE JEWS FROM NAZIS

The New York Times, March 17, 1998

Great Britian will Apologize for High Tea Tax

The British are to apologize today for the high taxes that incited the Boston Tea Party.

Richmond Times-Dispatch, December 16, 1998

IRS to Send Apology To 20,000 Taxpayers

THE WALL STREET JOURNAL, June 8, 1998

Govt. To Pay, Apologize For Experiments

UPI Focus, October 30, 1997

Argentina to Apologize for Its Role in Holocaust

REUTERS, June 12, 2000

CEOs Now Love to Say 'Sorry'

Apologies, if sincere, soothe angry public

The New York Times, November 30, 1997

"We beg God's pardon, and we ask the Jewish people to hear our words of repentance."

Archbishop Olivier de Berranger, in an apology from the Roman Catholic Church in France for remaining silent while more than 75,000 Jews were deported by French authorities during World War II.

NEWSWEEK, October 13, 1997

November 1995

On October 16, the Million Man March of black men on Washington was unquestionably a peak mood event. One headline described the event as "Harmony and Unity from Start to Finish." Black men came together to apologize for the race's past treatment of women (another in a string of worldwide mass apologies) make business contacts and "declare that they will be responsible for themselves and their families, not to demand that government bail them out," a highly laudable goal. This mass expression of positive mood among American blacks is similar to that of 1963, when Martin Luther King marched peacefully on Washington in a display of pride and the desire for equality.

December 1995

In another development that is highly reminiscent of 1966, the USA is No. 1 again. The World Competitiveness Report rates the U.S. as the world's most productive nation, three listings ahead of Japan, which had topped the rankings for seven consecutive years until 1993. A Business Week cover raves that the "American Economy Is the Most Productive in the World," which means "Higher Living Standards Seem Inevitable." Newsweek says "America is Back." It supports the contention by noting that peace agreements in the Mideast and Bosnia occurred because the United States "is the only power with the military and moral force to get what it wants. And that's not likely to change for years." This occurrence is a brief echo of the old days, and the reaction to it a reflection of euphoric social mood.

January 1996

In Japan, much of the news focuses on the financial sector, where stocks have lost half their value, the economy remains stagnant, and once-mighty banks have been forced to pay premium interest rates on their borrowings. That's right; the economy is in the tank and interest rates are now rising. Meanwhile, the country's financial experts are continually "playing down fears" about "the nature of the difficulties" on the one hand, while on the other allowing many lending institutions to hide the full extent of their bad debts for fear that it will spook the markets. In one failed credit cooperative, a full audit of the damages revealed that just 10% of the institutions' assets were providing a return. The losses, which were 50% higher than originally reported, exceeded the country's entire deposit insurance fund.

"Fortunately, it means almost nothing for the financial markets," responds one optimistic American analyst (a champion of diversification, no doubt). Eventually, bickering bureaucrats and bankers may find a way to unload the bad debts on the Japanese public, but polls show that the public will not tolerate "getting shafted again." So far, just $6.8 billion of the problem has been liquidated at taxpayers' expense. The bailout of even this tiny portion prompted a public outcry that cost Japan's top financial bureaucrat his job. Many observers say that the news is not all bad in Japan, as consumer prices have seen their biggest fall in 39 years. In actual fact, that is very bad news, as it screams deflation. Japan, the country that has suffered the longest in a bear market, is becoming an emotional pressure-cooker looking for release.

May 1996

The craze is not only domestic, of course, but worldwide. Doors to the global bull market are swinging open to investors as far away as Macedonia, where the Skopje Stock Market is set to bring stock trading to one of most isolated regions of the former Yugoslavia. India's National Stock Exchange plans to introduce stock index futures trading for the first time since 1969, the year after the last Cycle degree top. At present, seventeen second- and third-world countries are initiating futures exchanges. Emerging market equity indices now attract $5 billion, up from $200 million in 1993. In Europe, governments expect to raise a record $55 billion with the sale

MOLDOVA PLANS FIRST DIP INTO CAPITAL MARKETS

FINANCIAL TIMES, October 21, 1996

Germans Dive Into The Equity Culture

Germany yesterday took a big step toward becoming a nation of shareholders as the shares of Deutsche Telekom got off to a racing start on the Frankfurt and New York stock markets.

Mr. Theo Waigel, the country's finance minister, said the Telekom issue showed Germans were no longer "anti-share." He praised the DM20bn flotation as the "high point of German privatization history."

FINANCIAL TIMES, November 9, 1996

Russia Prepares Biggest Sell-Off

FINANCIAL TIMES
November 15, 1996

Uzbekistan Plans Big State Sell-Off

Uzbekistan is to sell off state shares in at least 300 medium-sized enterprises to newly created investment funds. Mr. Abdullah Abdukadirov, deputy chairman of the state property committee, said that 30 percent stakes in 300 enterprises would be put up for sale next month.

"Our goal is to attract the average guy, not the big guys with big bucks," Mr. Abdukadirov said.

FINANCIAL TIMES
September 25, 1996

Jakarta To Revive Sell-Off Impetus

FINANCIAL TIMES, August 12, 1996

Czechs Privatize At A Breakneck Pace

Chicago Tribune, July 7, 1996

Small Investors Pushed Aside in Peru Telecom Privatization

The Peruvian government appears to have mishandled its first big exercise in popular capitalism. After attracting thousands of ordinary Peruvians to apply for shares in Telefonica del Peru, it has drastically scaled down the numbers of shares available to them in order to accommodate stronger-than-expected demand from international investors.

Almost a quarter of a million Peruvians have responded to an intense advertising campaign to buy shares in the company. Throughout June, they flocked to banks and stockbroking agencies to make small deposits against orders for shares. The local Telefonica offering had been designed to start building a broad-based shareholder community.

FINANCIAL TIMES, July 4, 1996

of state-owned enterprises, including Deutsche Telekom, a $10 billion offering. Telekom will "market the shares" with a multi-million dollar advertising campaign. Italy has just elected a center-left government that is intent on selling government businesses. The sale of major government-owned firms in Peru and Brazil will quintuple the volume of Latin American offerings from $2 billion in 1995 to $10 billion this year. Japan will sell two crown jewels, its tobacco and telephone holdings (it needs the money to cover tax shortfalls). If all goes well, Japanese offerings will reach 2.4% of the total Japanese market capitalization. At the peak in 1989, offerings were 1.3% of Japanese market cap.

September 1996

Neither the TWA bombing nor the Centennial Park bombings have been solved. This is due to a new trend in terror. The terrorists take no credit. Their first goal is to get away. By succeeding, they achieve their second goal: "to shake their enemies with horror." The director of the FBI says we're in "for a very difficult time with respect to continuation of these types of things."

October 1996

"The longest sought, hardest fought prize in arms control history," a treaty banning all nuclear explosions, has been signed by the world's nuclear powers. This is the latest and probably the greatest of all the international milestones of cooperation that EWT has cited since 1992. The treaty itself is great news, but its implication is that today's social mood is the polar opposite of that during World War II in Supercycle wave (IV), which means that Supercycle wave (V) is peaking out.

Michael Jackson's Star May be Fading in the USA but It Burns Brightly Here

TEHRAN, Iran — Many young Iranians can't seem to get enough of the eccentric American singer, whose videos, copied off MTV, are coveted possessions. In fact, about anything of U.S. origin — from Palmolive soap to Levis jeans — seems downright irresistible.

Ever since the 1979 Islamic revolution, when Iran held 52 Americans hostage for 444 days, the two countries have had no official relations. Now, enticed by the USA's image as forbidden fruit and frustrated with the way their revolution has turned out, ordinary Iranians in this sprawling, gritty capital of 10 million view the USA as a fantasy land of material and technological magnificence.

"Of course you know Americans are loved," said a middle-age Tehrani who, like many people, asked not to be identified. "Unfortunately, Iranians can't help themselves."

Iranians, eager for a resumption of ties, seize on every sign of a thaw.

Iranians want Americans to come back, or they want to visit the USA. Visa applications are up nearly 50% this year even though Iranians must spend thousands of dollars to travel to neighboring countries with U.S. embassies just to apply.

Even government officials who are obliged to spout the anti-American line find some things about the USA to admire.

"There are many things about America that make you worry, like the homeless," said the mayor of Tehran, Gholam Hossein Karbaschi. But Karbaschi, who visited the United Nations twice, added, "I like your Broadway Street."

—USA Today, December 2, 1996

December 1996

In the wake of election day, a whole host of signature signs of a peak in social mood have appeared. The U.S. political season has ended in a spirit of "cooperation." The battle for the White House was hardly a battle at all, as it began with both parties sounding inclusionist themes at their respective conventions. Observers wonder whatever happened to the political rifts that were supposedly ripping the country apart in 1994. Party positions have drifted together, as Clinton promises to balance the budget and end welfare while the Republicans win Congress by stifling Newt Gingrich and the rhetoric of revolution. Now the talk in Washington is of "cooperation over confrontation and reconciliation over revolution."

Another traditionally intense rivalry that reached a low point with the stock market in 1980 is the U.S.' relationship with Iran. According to recent press accounts, Iranians 16 years later are infatuated with the U.S. and its culture. They can't get enough of Michael Jackson or Western movies. Or as one headline put it, Iranians have taken "A Shine to USA."

There were two more pictures of historic rendezvous by world leaders in November. When Castro met the Pope and re-established ties between Cuba and the Vatican, he called it "a miracle." Bill Clinton was shown doing the wave with an assortment of Asian leaders in a successful summit that reportedly cleared the way for series of future summits with China.

Finally, there is this item from a subscriber who works in the administration building at the Los Alamos Nuclear Laboratory in New Mexico. Access to the building has been closely monitored by uniformed, machine-gun toting guards for the 50-year history of the nuclear weapons lab, which contains some of the planet's most highly classified secrets. New monitors wear jackets, ties and no guns. "For the first time, we have greeters rather than guards," he says.

The events in Russia will surely stand as one of the bull market's most impressive feats. Even though GDP continues to fall at a rate of 4% a year (after a 50% decline in industrial production since 1991), the investment scene in Moscow is as vibrant as in New York. The outlook is even better according to all of the panelists on a recent Bloomberg analysts forum. Boris Yeltsin even changed his country's November 7 holiday from Revolution Day, which commemorated the victory of communism, to a celebration more in keeping with a Grand Supercycle peak. It's now the "Day of Accord and Reconciliation."

With Yeltsin calling the shots again, one analyst insisted that the Russian stock market was primed for a big rally: "a gain of 100 or 200% is not out of the question." Russian citizens are being readied with the initiation of the first Western style mutual fund, which "could lure $20 billion in savings that Russians now stash under the mattress." Vimpel Communications, a Russian cellular telephone company, is said to be a new breed of Russian company, which means it is freely traded on the American stock market. On November 15, on the first day of American trading for Vimpel ADRs, which raised almost twice as much as the company expected and did it two weeks earlier, soared 48% from their offering price. The three-year-old firm now has a market capitalization of $700 million, seven times annual sales.

The same thing happened to the cash-strapped Russian government when it turned to the international bond market for funds. In its first international debt offering since the 1917 Bolshevik revolution, it was hoping to get $300 million. Despite continued contraction in the economy, routine Mafia hits on prominent businessmen, revelations that most Russian firms do not pay tax bills, entrenched communist politicians, a "backlash against foreign investment" and a long history of turning on capitalists, international investors so love Russia that they more than tripled the size of the offering to $1 billion. Bids for the 5-year notes that pay 9.36% per year exceeded $2 billion even as the Financial Times reported that the government's inability to collect taxes or control spending created "a danger that the state might simply wither away."

This unprecedented willingness to throw money at a sinking ship of state says volumes about the pathological optimism of investors. Investors are so blinded by bullishness that no one has stopped to consider investment in Russia as a serious breach of fiduciary responsibility and perhaps even morality. As Alan Abelson put it, buying Russian bonds is "kind of like lending money to the Gambino family." In the July issue, *The Elliott Wave Theorist* noted that this detachment of morality and money is common in the late stages of an investment mania. "Investing" becomes an end in itself, regardless of all other considerations. The thing that will restore the underlying link between moral and investment values is a bear market.

January 1997

Bull market tops bring social reconciliation, the larger the degree of the top, the more significant the reconciliation. Britain's Prince Andrew has just returned the Stone of Scone, the coronation seat of Scottish kings, to Scotland (see next page). It was stolen by the English 700 years ago. In December, Portugal atoned for the expulsion of Jews 500 years ago. To set the stage to receive urgently needed food, North Korea has apologized to South Korea for its September military incursion. The apology is the first in 50 years of open hostility. Guatemala has ended a 36-year civil war, Central America's longest.

Stone Of Scone Back In Scotland

With prayers, pipers and some political nuance, the legendary Stone of Scone was placed in its new home in Scotland on Saturday, seven centuries after it was stolen by an English king. The rough-hewn block of gray sandstone, weighing 458 pounds, was the coronation seat of Scottish kings until it was carried away as war booty by King Edward I in 1296.

The New York Times
December 1, 1996

In a heretofore unimaginable triumph for inclusionism, a California school district has recognized "Ebonics," or black English, as the primary language of many black students. Based on this new standard, sentences such as "I be eatin" and "I ain't got no coffee" will be considered correct and used as "a starting point" to teach standard English.

February 1997

Israeli and Palestinian leaders reached agreement on the withdrawal of Israel from Hebron and parts of the West Bank. Egypt's Hosni Mubarak celebrated by noting, "War has gone out of style."

March 1997

A host of new stock market standards were set over the past month. They include the initiation of trading on the Palestinian stock exchange and the launch of Egypt's first mutual fund.

April 1997

[After technology] the second most common defense of higher prices has been the expansion of international markets. On March 13, The Wall Street Journal touched the heart of motley fools everywhere with this front page story:

Global Growth Attains A New Higher Level That Could Be Lasting

The wave of stories about the end of the U.S. business cycle, which began last fall, has been expanded to the point that they now insist the entire world will defy the rhythm of the ages. "We've entered a golden age that will last for decades," says an Argentine economist. Even the UN Secretary General, who "often deals with troubled countries that have had no growth for years, sees the world entering 'a new golden age.'" World growth estimates are put at 4% for the next 20 years. Never mind that we've just gone an unprecedented two decades without a bear market or that in that time, 4% annual growth was never achieved. This will be the year, says the International Monetary Fund, and then the world will have 20 more just like it!

June 1997

Mania Watch

It is now common knowledge that diversification into foreign stocks is a badge of safety. Some analysts conclude that "everything is in place for a bonanza in the international primary equity market this autumn." This belief is held in many countries, which is why half of Norway's oil revenues will soon be shifted from low-risk government bonds to foreign equities. USA Today pinpointed the location of 14 African stock exchanges in a recent issue and noted the relative value of African company earnings. "Fund managers see this, and they salivate," said a mutual fund observer. It's not a craze; it's prudence, you see.

More Evidence of a Grand Supercycle Peak

In May 1997, "five years after the Cold War ended," President Clinton has traveled to the Hague "to formally declare victory for the West." NATO's former sworn enemy, Russia, has now joined the organization, an event that would have been considered outrageous fantasy any time between 8 and 80 years ago. This is a tangible result of the euphoric social mood brought on by a worldwide Grand Supercycle top. Several celebrants, including President Clinton, described the agreement as a "great day" for peace. It is indeed, but it is occurring at a time in the social cycle that is akin to 1929. A brief three years later, warmonger Adolf Hitler reached the peak of his public popularity in Germany. Great days for peace come at major social-mood turning points, just as do the blackest days of war.

July 1997

In 1992, *The Elliott Wave Theorist* introduced the idea of waxing inclusionism as an aspect of bull markets. This concept holds that bull markets are accompanied by an expansion in the size of social units. Boundaries weaken, and the relaxation of once-strained relationships allows former antagonists to bury the hatchet and form all manner of alliances and covenants. Over the last five years, we have chronicled this phenomenon in the extension of the world community through treaties, trade pacts, apologies for past transgressions, "peace keeping" efforts and a succession of photographs in which world leaders have expressed their mutual goodwill.

June 1997 brought so many inclusionary developments that we hardly have room for them. On the issue of race, a poll showing whites' increasing acceptance of blacks (61% approve of black-white marriages vs. 45% in 1994 and 4% in 1958) was followed quickly by the introduction to Congress of a bill apologizing for slavery, a Clinton initiative to "bridge the nation's racial divide," and word that reconciliation with blacks has "become a priority for the religious right."

The debate over smoking is one of the few areas where this bull market has promoted exclusion rather than inclusion. Bull markets have their Puritanical streak (Prohibition in the 1920s is the classic example), and the anti-smoking campaign that established smoking sections in restaurants in the mid-1980s, bumped smoking from commercial flights in the late 1980s and evicted smokers from the workplace in the early 1990s has continually gained steam. Nonetheless, cigarette makers and anti-smoking advocates have managed to reach a historic settlement. The same thing happened near the highs for Cycle wave III. Back then, the deal called for warning labels and no TV advertising. This time, it's bigger warning labels, more stringent advertising restrictions, the gradual removal of nicotine, billions in health care contributions and a host of other concessions that befit the larger degree of the current peak. The settlement is a classic example of how a bull market in mood overcomes all obstacles to unite even the most divergent social forces.

In other cultural convergences, the U.S. has agreed to the addition of three nations to NATO, England has apologized for its role in the potato famine of 1845-1851, Germany and France have compromised to keep the European currency on track for adoption in 1999, the Group of Seven has turned into the Summit of the Eight with Russia's inclusion, the first regular-season inter-league baseball games between the National and American leagues have been played, and the National Basketball Association has expanded to include a women's basketball league. In coming days, we'll also witness another Earth Summit, the introduction of a new $50 bill designed to make it easier for the visually-impaired to discern the value of the currency, and a new wheelchair-bound Barbie doll. As we noted in 1992, in periods of rising social mood, "even mythical aliens are included in the brotherhood of the universe." July will see the world's largest gathering of UFO enthusiasts ever, in Roswell, New Mexico.

A moderate Iranian cleric has won a landslide election in Iran. The surprise winner was not the choice of the ruling conservative mullahs. "In the closing days of the campaign, [Mohammed Khatami] barnstormed

> ## *Roswell's Desert Swarm*
> Washington Post, July 5, 1997

> ## *Thousands Gather in Roswell*
> San Francisco Chronicle, July 2, 1997

> ### *Now landing in Roswell:*
> ## Crush of tourists invading NM town for UFO festivities
> Dallas Morning News, July 1, 1997

across the country in a campaign bus and attracted crowds so jubilant that the police could barely contain them." Inclusionism has even reached Iran.

August 1997

The bull continues to add to its list of historic achievements. Twenty-eight eastern European countries and former Soviet republics entered into a partnership with NATO. In one manner or another, virtually all of Europe is in the same fold. On the religious front, the "winds of ecumenism" are "breaking denominational barriers." The Pope said he hopes to reach a formal reconciliation with the Eastern Orthodox Church by the year 2000. Their separation dates to the Great Schism of 1054. Catholics have also settled a "searing theological debate" with Lutherans over the means of eternal salvation. Division on the question contributed to the Protestant Reformation in the 16th Century. Britain has unveiled sweeping plans to give Scotland a parliament for the first time since 1707. As President Clinton said July 13, this may be "the greatest time in all human history."

September 1997

This is the greatest stock mania in Western history. Do your bullish friends think they can safely wait until after the market turns down to act? Tell them to ask the Asians. Last Thursday, the stock indexes of Hong Kong, Singapore, Malaysia and Indonesia fell 4%, while the Philippine market was down 9%, in one day. (It's down another 6% tonight!) The Far Eastern economies seem peachy, yet stock markets in the region have collapsed 30% to 75%! We are determined to be on the right side of the U.S. trend when it changes. Long-time readers will recall EWT's bullish fervor as the market bottomed in the early 1980s. The start of the Great Bear Market promises to even more exciting.

Queen Atones for Wrongs Done by British Rulers in India

Queen Elizabeth II laid a wreath of marigolds Tuesday at a park in Amritsar, India, where British colonial troops massacred 300 Indians. The gesture, along with a speech the night before, were apology enough for the descendants of some victims.

The 10-minute wreath-laying ceremony also convinced some others in the northern border city of the British monarch's goodwill, and they welcomed her with pomp and joyful shouts.

—The Associated Press, October 14, 1997

Pope says Church should seek forgiveness for past

Pope John Paul said on Thursday that the entire Roman Catholic Church should use the forthcoming start of the third millennium as a chance to seek forgiveness for its past errors and sins.

—Reuters, October 23, 1997

The planet gets ready to party
Pessimism is passé, fin de siècle foreboding is out

For the moment, there are no large or even middling-scale wars on Earth. No superpower confrontations. No significant famines or programmes of genocide. No immediate likelihood of global economic cataclysm or the vaporisation of world financial markets. To a mature planet-watcher, this week's corrective declines in world stock markets have been no more frightening than a single snowflake falling from a lapis lazuli sky.

—Financial Times, November 2, 1997

November 1997

In the day-of-atonement department, there are now more high-level multi-decade or -century apologies being issued than we can safely count. Lutherans have withdrawn their condemnation of Catholics as a "new era of friendship" dawns on the "once warring denominations." French Catholics have repented for "silence on the Holocaust." Queen Elizabeth traveled to India and apologized personally for a 1919 massacre by British soldiers. Pope John Paul said on October 22 that the "entire Roman Catholic Church should use the start of the third millennium as a chance to seek forgiveness for its past errors and sins."

And finally, in early October, several hundred thousand "contrite white men" assembled at the Washington Mall to confess their sins and promise to do better. This Promise Keepers march, along with last

The march becomes the thing

Mass gatherings are becoming the way to get message across

By Scott Bowles
USA TODAY

PHILADELPHIA — By the hundreds of thousands, black women came here Saturday, standing shoulder to shoulder in the latest national rally to promote the power of family, community and God.

In the end, the power of such marches may not be the message so much as the number of messengers.

"I haven't heard a word of what's been said up there, and I don't care," said Emma Wilkes, 53, who caught a bus from Trenton, N.J., to attend the Million Woman March in Philadelphia's historic downtown. "The point isn't what one person has to say. The point is all of us coming together."

The Million Woman March was inspired by the Million Man March in Washington in 1995, and came on the heels of the Promise Keepers' rally at the nation's capital earlier this month. Each event called for participants to take a more active role in their families and neighborhoods, and each drew between 300,000 and close to 1 million people.

"Anyone can say that they believe in family values, or in doing more at their churches," says Ann Hardy, 41, who recruited a busload of women in suburban Detroit for the trek. "But it

means more when you see how many thousands of people are willing to give up their time to come here and say it together. That's what makes the message powerful."

The events also may inspire similar gatherings in the future. Several group leaders at the Million Woman rally said that they are considering a joint march of black men and women sometime before the year 2000 as a pro-family demonstration.

Marches also can add a sense of community for those people who feel isolated by their personal difficulties, sociologist Tom Rosenfeld says.

"It can have a profound effect to be with thousands of other people who are going through some of the same problems that you are," says Rosenfeld, author of *The Race Effect: Cultural Diversity in America.* "It can serve as massive group therapy, and send people back home energized with new ideas."

Myriad ideas wafted over the loudspeakers as an eclectic group of women took the lectern in front of Philadelphia's Museum of Art. Speakers included singer Faith Evans, Rep. Maxine Waters, D-Calif., and actress Jada Pinkett.

Winnie Madikizela-Mandela, the former wife of South African presi-

dent Nelson Mandela, gave a 20-minute speech on issues ranging from threats to the global environment to the bond between American and African women.

It brought Alisha Reynolds to tears. Reynolds, 38, of Los Angeles, who came to the march after discovering her sister was diagnosed with breast cancer, says she was stunned by the speeches and the turnout.

"I really feel like I gained three or four new sisters," Reynolds said. "One of them made it through

(breast) cancer, which gave me a lot of hope. I didn't know what to expect when I was heading out here."

Neither did many of the participants and organizers, who had purposely excluded large mainstream civil rights groups in organizing the event.

"This was an example of what we can do without money or big-name people to coordinate things," participant Ellen Worley said. "This was simply about us working with each other. That's what makes it special."

By Jay Gorodetzer, Reuters

Making a point: Carolyn Mungin of Washington, D.C., joins other Million Woman March participants as they sing the black national anthem. The gathering was the largest dedicated to issues vital to women.

By Chris Lane, AP

Traffic jam: Hundreds of thousands of women march in show of solidarity Saturday on Philadelphia's Benjamin Franklin Parkway.

week's Million Women March and last year's Million Man March, represents a display of mass expression that has not been seen since the demonstrations of the late 1960s. The difference is that these participants aren't marching against anything. At a Grand Supercycle top, there is not really anything to protest. Yet the urge to join together is so strong, "The March Becomes the Thing." "Mass Gatherings Are Becoming the Way to Get Message Across." What message? Strength. Unity. Atonement. Harmony. Said one of the hundreds of thousands of black women gathering for the latest Philadelphia be-in: "I haven't heard a word of what's been said, and I don't care. The point isn't what one person has to say. The point is all of us coming together." Exactly. Bull markets bring homogeneity; bear markets bring polarity. This is a historic extreme in the former.

December 1997

Countless headlines insist that the "Asian Skid Poses Little U.S. Threat." Now each new day brings word of the great Asian fire sale. Even U.S. banks have rushed in because "the domino collapse of once proud Asian economies may not be all red ink after all. On the contrary, it could be a bonanza." For even the most remedial students of mass psychology, however, Asia is a crystal-clear window to "the approaching chaos" alluded to in the final chapter of *At the Crest of the Tidal Wave*. In financial historian J.K. Galbraith's vernacular, it is experiencing the "final common feature" of a financial euphoria, "anger and recrimination." The classic symptoms of this post-bubble backlash have emerged in all the countries affected by plunging markets. The December 2 Wall Street Journal tells of a sweeping wave of "resentment": "From Thailand to South Korea, casualties of the region's market meltdowns are casting blame far and wide."

In each country, the severity of these symptoms is directly proportional to the extent and duration of the fall. In Japan, where the decline began five years ago and has erased more than 60% of the Nikkei's value, five different prime ministers have been booted, and the social system faces nothing less than "revolution." In Thailand, where the market has fallen 78% since its peak in 1994, protestors have taken to the streets, the prime minister has been sacked in a populist uprising, and "even cosmopolitan Thais" say the U.S. is trying to plunder Thailand. "It's a war without bullets," one American-educated Thai told the WSJ. Malaysia is down more than 40% since February. There, the prime minister has declared speculation "immoral" and suggested his country is the victim of a Jewish plot. Analysts issuing negative forecasts have been branded "traitors."

January 1998

Deflation

Much of the back-room plotting and many of the headlines that surround events in Asia are about efforts to "restore confidence" no matter what. This top-of-page-one headline expresses the prevailing sentiment: "Japan Calls For Calm in Face of Fall in Confidence." *At the Crest*'s central expectation of a debt/credit contraction hinged upon this change in attitude: "The only thing holding today's debt pyramid together is confidence. [A deflationary crisis] will actually occur when the confidence that supports it erodes and then dissolves."

That erosion appears to have begun; the Tokyo markets face a "Death Spiral," notes a headline. Falling stock prices force banks to sell more shares and tighten lending, which causes bankruptcies that "create further selling pressure." "It's difficult to know what the authorities can do." Actually, it's impossible. Deflation is a state of social mind, and politicians and bankers can do nothing to change it.

February 1998

All one need do now is observe the Indonesian situation. Its economy was booming until last July, when its stock market peaked. David Knox Barker's K-Wave Report notes that now, less than 10% of the companies listed on the Jakarta Stock Exchange are considered financially viable, which gives Indonesia virtually no chance of repaying its $130 billion-worth of corporate and government debt. A January 9 article noted that Indonesia risked "defaulting on foreign debt. Spooked investors fear a moratorium on payments to overseas creditors." Two weeks later, the moratorium appeared a virtual certainty: "Talk of Moratorium Grows," said a headline. "Everybody's avoiding the word 'standstill;' everybody's avoiding the words 'major rescheduling summit,' but everyone knows that it's just days away." On January 28, a three-month halt on debt payments was declared. According to the IMF, the freeze is not a moratorium, however. It is a "pause." Good thing. "Once one country declares a debt moratorium," says Barker, "others will have no choice but to follow. As the crisis deepens in Asia and spreads to Eastern Europe and South America, countries will balk at seeing capital exported to pay off astronomical debts. The natural progression of moratorium forcing moratorium is inevitable in coming months." Moratorium means no interest payments. It means that the promises to pay are temporarily (and usually that means permanently) void.

Evidence of a Grand Supercycle Peak

In 1998, the civil rights movement reached Wall Street, and the denizens of finance happily stepped forward to greet it. In January, the heads of all the big Wall Street firms, Alan Greenspan, Robert Rubin and the President, got together to kick off Jesse Jackson's three-day conference on the hiring of minorities in the securities industry, investing in black-owned firms and raising "the level of sophistication of black investors."

Jackson, Clinton combine forces in Wall Street blitz

Political, corporate allies press for racial diversity

Speaking in the Windows on the World restaurant near the top of the 110-story World Trade Center on the famed financial street, Mr. Clinton urged business leaders to help him build "one America," the catch-all label he often uses for his ongoing race initiatives.

Mr. Clinton came to New York on the 69th anniversary of the birth of the Rev. Martin Luther King Jr. at the invitation of the Rev. Jesse Jackson, a King disciple who has launched his own civil rights and economic crusade within corporate America.

It was a glittering gathering of Mr. Jackson's political and corporate allies, government officials and Wall Street bankers, brokers and investors.

—The Dallas Morning News, January 16, 1998

As the President addressed the gathering, a sign over his head perfectly expressed the social force behind the event. It said: "Expanding the Marketplace; Inclusion, the Key to Economic Growth and Opportunity." Inclusion is the very word we have used to describe the waxing perceived brotherhood of men and nations that brings people together in bull markets. To steal a few words from the President's speech commemorating the event, bull markets "promote community instead of chaos." Undoubtedly, Clinton was more right than he realized when he added, "We are all lost in an inescapable web of mutuality. We see it every day on Wall Street."

May 1998

During 1997, an "unbelievable torrent" of $66 billion came into the U.S. market from abroad. That was more than the total for the previous nine years combined. Foreign buying is a classic sell signal.

Cultural Trends

The peak of Intermediate (3) last August was accompanied by the Earth Summit, NATO expansion and Russia's addition to the Group of Seven. Near the April highs, the drought of major international peace agreements was broken by (another) peace agreement for Northern Ireland. When the Irish government approved the agreement April 23, "30 years of conflict" (once again) ended. Ireland's prime minister called it the first concurrent act of self-determination by the people of Ireland since 1918. He added that the deal ended Britain's 828-year claim to sovereignty.

That deal was part of a quickening drumbeat of developments reflecting the Grand Supercycle scale of the social-mood turn that is underway. The next most significant event in this regard was probably the German Bundestag's "signing of a death warrant for the D-Mark." By a vote of 575 to 35, German legislators gave Helmut Kohl authorization to approve the replacement of the D-Mark with the Euro (despite opposition by 60% of the population). The vote was considered the most important hurdle in next January's enactment of a true European union. By May 3, most of the countries in Western Europe were expected formally to join Germany in actions that would "irrevocably bind their currencies together." Since joiners will not be allowed to leave, this is a rather strong expression of inclusionism, as well as a setup for future conflict.

In another first of major-degree proportion, the Dalai Lama revealed April 24 that he could be the last spiritual Tibetan leader. "If an institution that came into being 600 years ago loses relevance, it is logical to scrap it," he said. The line of Tibetan "god-kings" stretches back to the 15th century. (If the Pope makes a similar announcement, we will conclude that this turn is bigger than Grand Supercycle.) The Dalai added that the Tibetan people should keep pace with the times by becoming totally democratic.

June 1998

As we go to press, Russia is experiencing a financial "meltdown" that has led to a "profound political crisis." South Korea is under pressure from workers who rioted on May 1 and conducted nationwide strikes on May 28. Back in the U.S.A., however, the economy is humming, unsavory words are being removed from Webster's dictionary and the Chicago Bulls are rolling toward another NBA final.

The long rolling top in the world stock market has, however, exposed many of the fault lines for the next downward swing in global social mood. In many cases, like Indonesia, the pressure points are showing up exactly where anyone with a history book and a long-term chart of the Dow would expect. The tension between Pakistan and India is another example in which the fracturing mood has chosen the exact same social setting to announce its presence. A series of wars between the two countries began in 1965, a year before the peak of Cycle III. The triple top that preceded the last major bear market was marked by India's declaration of its nuclear capability in 1966, its refusal to sign a non-proliferation agreement on the high of 1968, and Pakistan's initiation of its own nuclear program in 1972, a few months from the final high of January 1973. This time around, the Dow high has been accompanied, once again, by India's refusal to sign a nuclear non-proliferation agreement and a showcasing of its nuclear capabilities. India conducted five nuclear tests May 11-13. Pakistan responded with its own tests on May 28. As *The Elliott Wave Theorist* showed in July 1995, total global nuclear tests have been inversely correlated to the stock markets since at least 1974. The chart is updated. Note that the dip at the end is accounted for entirely by the 10 tests since the Dow's high. India's bomb tests met with immediate popular adulation while Pakistan's response was propelled by the demands from angry mobs. Non-proliferation groups worry that the tests could mark a new wave of nuclear muscle-flexing. This chart, combined with our expectations for the Dow, confirms their fears.

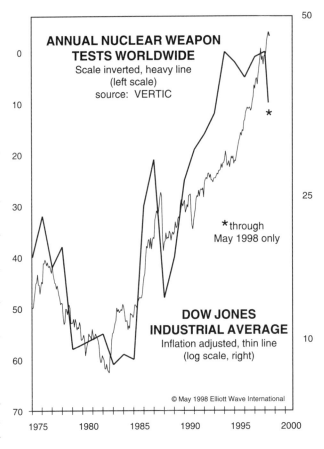

That move in the Dow can't be too far in the future. President Clinton has just announced a $7 billion-per-year federal "War on Terror," complete with an anti-terror "czar." This is scary news. The government's War on Intemperance in the 1920s and 1930s led to a massive increase in the size of the alcoholic beverage industry and spawned criminal gangs to run it. The government's War on Drugs (czar and all) has transformed a marginal activity into one of the largest industries in world history, and a violent, criminal one to boot. All government programs produce the opposite of what is intended. What will be the results of a government War on Terror? If you think they will be anything other than a massive increase in terrorism, you should explain why this time will be an exception.

September 1998

The Moscow exchange is down 85% from its high last August, and the futures market for the ruble has been shut down. It was hard for us to imagine that any money managers wanted to own Russian stocks, or Latin American stocks, or stocks on any tertiary exchange. Of course, our attitude then seems self-evident now, but a year ago, it attracted a puzzled look as if we had muttered something in Martian.

October 1998

As we have pointed out many times, the stock craze was a worldwide phenomenon. It is now officially deceased in the east, but the west careens onward oblivious. In the once-remote financial backwater of Spain, "market-crazed Spaniards" have "a greater demand for economic knowledge." Demand for this "knowledge" is evident in a surge in the ratings of a round-the-clock financial news station at the daily close. Closing levels constitute knowledge because "informed" investors know how far the market is from its high and thus can always calculate the exact minimum distance of the next rally.

Given the drama that it foresees, is *At the Crest* too dangerous to advertise? It already is in one country. Here is an e-mail we got from Russia:

Dear New Classics Library: Thank you for the possibility to get the copyrights of the book, *At the Crest of the Tidal Wave*, by R. Prechter. But unfortunately, due to the last economic crisis in Russia, it has become too dangerous for us to publish that book right now. We hope that very soon we will have the chance to publish that book.

Read it while you can.

December 1998

A Peek at the Future

The emotional drain of the latest high in the Dow has caused a handful of our domestic subscribers to pack it in. It is interesting to compare their frustration to the near total affirmation we receive from many foreign subscribers. As D.C. in Mildura, Australia puts it: "From the financial press here in Australia over the past few months, one could be excused for thinking they were publishing excerpts from your book rather than reporting actual economic events from around the world." In Hong Kong, where the decline is deeper, the feedback we receive reflects an even stronger sense of conviction that *At the Crest's* vision is correct. Here is a letter we received from the heart of the bear market:

> If I read *At the Crest* last year, I would be much better off and my parents wouldn't have lost so much money. I returned to Hong Kong from [California in June 1997], to witness the historical handover of Hong Kong back to China and to start a new university job. The first thing my mother told me to do was to buy an apartment because in her own words, "If prices keep on increasing, you will never be able to afford one." Being a physician, if I cannot afford one, how many other citizens [would] be able to? Prices more or less quadrupled as everyone went into a speculative frenzy. Even taxi drivers and little old ladies in the market were talking about the stock market and the real estate market. I concluded that it was crazy to buy at that point. The stock market was something else; anything to do with Mainland China would appreciate no matter what. A penny stock called CNPC, which explores oil on the mainland, went from an IPO of 10 cents to $5 within a matter of months. Then, there were the "Red Chips," companies that do business in China. You could pretty much put China onto anything and it [would] turn into gold. My friends installed terminals in their clinics and stopped seeing patients. Many of them were boasting how much money they were making, certainly much more than most doctors. A friend of mine put all his savings into the stock market and borrowed up to the limit of margin requirements. Even my wife bought a couple of Chinese "H-shares" based on tips from my mother-in-law! (Investment for my wife usually means T-bills). Then, on October 28 [1997], everything came apart. First, the index fell from 16,600 to 12,000. It maintained that level long enough to lure back in the optimists. Then, it went down to 8000. Everybody started blaming the hedge funds and George Soros. To those skeptics who sneer at the predictions in *At The Crest*, I only have this to say; you have to live through it to believe it, but it really can happen, even if it seems impossible at the moment, just as it was in Hong Kong [in] June [1997].
>
> —Dr. Wu, Hong Kong
> November 17, 1998

In June 1997, EWT profiled the craze in Red Chips, mainland Chinese stocks traded on the Hong Kong exchange, and noted, "In 1898, the British leased Hong Kong for 99 years, until July 1, 1997. The mania in Red Chips is likely to end on approximately the same day that Hong Kong's century of progress does." The actual high was August 7, 1997. At that time, Chinese speculators were convinced that the mathematics of investing had been adjusted to account for the "hidden value" in companies that had the inside track on harnessing the great growth economy of the 21st century. "The euphoria surrounding these stocks," EWT noted in June 1997, "makes the U.S. stock market seem tame." Comparisons of that experience to today's U.S. market would be just about right. Only 18 months ago, China was going to carry the economic torch into the next millennium. That flame has passed back to the United States, where it burns just as intensely in the public's imagination.

We think people were right in 1997 when they said, "Asia is the future." The gory details now include a 7% quarterly GDP decline in Hong Kong, the island's biggest quarterly decline ever. The figure dwarfs the previous record of 4.7% set in the third quarter of 1974.

Over the past year, property values have declined 40%. In China, competition is so fierce as deflation takes hold that Beijing is now setting minimum prices for 21 different industries. Despite the measures, prices fell almost 3% in October alone. Angry investors have staged the "boldest protest in the Chinese capital since the 1989 Tiananmen Square demonstrations." Gitic corporation, the shining financial star behind the office towers, five-star hotels and six-lane highways of Gangzhou and one of the highest fliers of 1997, has been shut down.

A broader look at Asia offers an even more gruesome portrait. Car sales are off 70% in Thailand. Jakarta office rental rates fell by half from April to June 1998. Japan's bad public-sector debt amounts to 20-25% of GDP. Bad private-sector debt pushes the total figure to as much as 60%. The only industry that is growing is the "alibi" business, in which agencies create fake lives for the unemployed. "We often take on the role of pretend employer," explains a man who runs an agency in Tokyo's nightlife district. We could go on and on, but you get the idea. The news is going to get still worse. As it rolls in, Americans have a huge advantage over their Asian counterparts. They can see the headlines months and months ahead of time. Most, however, will have to "live through it to believe it."

January 1999
Perspective

In half the world, from Tokyo to Moscow, the financial "tidal wave" has already crashed, devastating stocks, bonds and many currencies and placing citizens, financial institutions and governments under extreme stress. In most of the rest of the world, from Europe to South America, it has curled over. In the U.S., it is still cresting. Your assessment of our outlook for deflation spelled out in *At the Crest* probably depends upon where you live. Final judgment awaits more time. The global monetary wheel is grinding more slowly than expected but also inexorably. U.S. stock market indicators continue to reflect the atmosphere of a Grand Supercycle top. There is every reason to stay the course.

"Sky-high price-earning ratios" attained by stocks like Yahoo! and Amazon.com are cited as the key piece of evidence that "reveal how optimistic American investors are." The incredible exploding valuations of the Internet frenzy, now recognized as the "biggest speculative mania in history," are another direct throwback to Japan in the late 1980s.

The front page of The Wall Street Journal reported on America's "Culture of Optimism" on December 22. Here, under the banner "Joy To the World," the WSJ records that the S&P and NASDAQ attained all-time highs despite political chaos, dropping bombs and fraying economic fundamentals because of "the ebullient national personality of the U.S., an immeasurable quirk that without question adds to the gross domestic product and to social harmony." America, the "most optimistic nation on earth," has an irrepressible natural resource, or "good feelings premium," which it places on the economy, political figures who project optimism and Internet stocks. From our perspective, it is an amazing article because it accurately identifies the driving force behind the bull market. The economy is a reflection of "a generic, almost metabolic, human optimism," says the author of *Optimism: The Biology of Hope*. The dean of one of the nation's top business schools adds, "When I'm optimistic, I'm more likely to make commitments of capital, to spend and to take risks.'" As *The Elliott Wave Theorist* has always stressed, this positive group emotion is in fact the root of all bull markets.

What the article does not say, however, is that there is a natural countervailing pessimism (also known as a bear market) that enters the picture from time to time. In that light, we note that the article characterizes Americans with the same unwaveringly positive traits that Japanese writers attributed to their country's people in 1989. In November 1989, a month before the Nikkei's peak, for instance, the author of *The Japan That Can Say No* appeared in Time suggesting that Japan's bull market was a racial trait. Japan's leadership in technology would help it "build a new world history." At Japan's great peak, countless other articles and books on both sides of the Pacific extolled the virtues of Japanese management techniques and declared its business habits and educational system far superior to its slothful American counterparts. Now that the S&P is at an all-time high and the Nikkei is down more than 65%, the situation is reversed. We believe the outcome here will be the same as it was there.

March 1999

A Bubble Remembered

Few know that they are living through a mania when it is raging. Manias are obvious to the majority only in retrospect. Paul Montgomery recently published the graphs below and on the next page using data from Bryan Taylor (Global Financial Data, Alhambra, CA). As you can see, in just a single decade, Japan's Nikkei index has returned to its 1950s-1960s value in terms of both the DJIA and Japan's own bonds. The two-decade bubble has been fully deflated relative to these measures.

Despite the surface implication of these graphs, Japan's share market deflation is not over, for two reasons. First, every manic advance in the price of an investment has been ultimately more than fully retraced. The Nikkei has a long way down to go before that happens. Second, the U.S. market is itself complet-

---

Joy to the World:
Despite Everything, America Still Embraces A Culture of Optimism
Impeachment? Iraq Tensions? Humbug! Markets Soar, Polls Rise, Masses Spend — The Good-Feelings Premium

What will it take to shake America's confidence?

Certainly not the impeachment of the President, the chaos in the House leadership, an air raid on Iraq that was of questionable effectiveness, or a fraying global economy.

In the capital in recent days, pundits and politicians have been wondering whether it's indifference or ignorance that's keeping Americans from sharing in their gloom. But across the economic and cultural terrain of the most optimistic nation on Earth, the answer heard again and again is "perspective." Life goes on.

Yesterday, investors demonstrated their bullish faith, pushing the Dow Jones Industrial Average up 85.22 to 8988.85. Meantime, both the NASDAQ Composite Index and the Standard & Poor's 500-stock index hit new record highs. Consumers continued to shop, not wildly but not cautiously. And people were mindful of, but not riveted to, the serious yet manageable events playing out in Washington.

All of this is a reminder of the ebullient national personality of the U.S., an immeasurable quirk that without question adds to the gross domestic product and to social harmony.

In the U.S., nobody likes a sourpuss, as the public opinion polls continually remind the dour Republican leadership in Congress, and as Jimmy Carter learned during his one-term presidency. Regardless of political point of view, leaders who project optimism – Bill Clinton, the man from Hope, Ronald Reagan, the man from Hollywood – confound their critics with high approval ratings. Even after impeachment, Clinton's ratings remain high.

Larry J. Kimbell, director of the Business Forecasting Project at UCLA's Anderson School, is accustomed to making precise, fact-based projections using a computer model. But he doesn't hesitate to hazard a guess at the value of optimism and America's appetite for risk-taking: It adds half a percentage point to growth in gross domestic product.

—The Wall Street Journal, December 22, 1998

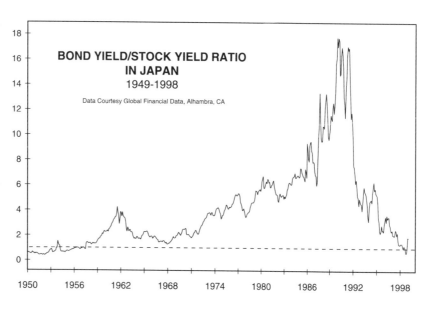

BOND YIELD/STOCK YIELD RATIO
IN JAPAN
1949-1998

Data Courtesy Global Financial Data, Alhambra, CA

ing a historic mania, which means that when U.S. stock prices turn down, the Nikkei will have to fall just to keep these two graphs in equilibrium. The two stock markets need not rise and fall simultaneously, as they have already proved during the 1990s. Their multi-month trends may diverge. However, before the long global deflation is over, they will have achieved the same goal: a complete retracement of their manias.

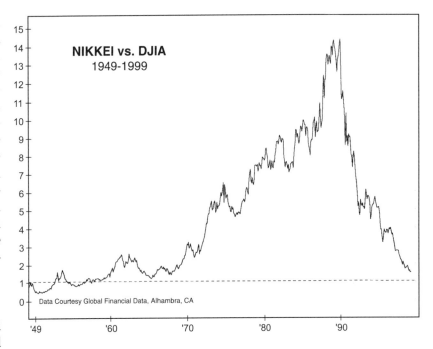

June 1999

According to an e-mail we received, former Fed chairman Paul Volcker made this observation on May 14: "The fate of the world economy is now totally dependent on the growth of the U.S. economy, which is dependent on the stock market, whose growth is dependent on about 50 stocks, half of which have never reported earnings."

July 1999

To catch one of the last great Grand Supercycle photo opportunities (for the first six, see Chapter 18 of *The Wave Principle of Human Social Behavior*), set your VCR to record the world news of July 15. That's the day the "Reconciliation March" will complete a four-year journey to atone for the raping, looting and murdering of Jewish and Muslim "infidels" by Christian Crusaders in July 1099. "Thousands of Western Christians from all walks of life are retracing" the steps of their ancestors "to express repentance and seek forgiveness for the atrocities of the Crusades." The walk began in France in 1995 and has moved through Europe, the Balkans, Asia Minor and now into the Middle East.

Apology for Crusades Given 900 Years Later

To most, the Crusades are ancient history.

Not to Prince Albrecht zu Castell-Castell, a descendant of one of the Christian knights who nearly a millennium ago conquered Jerusalem and massacred Muslims and Jews in the name of God.

Yesterday, the German aristocrat with white hair and ruddy cheeks finally got a chance to apologize to descendants of the Muslim warrior Saladin for his ancestor's crimes, which he said have burdened his conscience for years.

Castell-Castell was one of dozens of Western Christians who delivered apologies to Israel's chief rabbi, the top Muslim cleric and anyone in the streets of Jerusalem who would listen.

Yesterday marked the 900th anniversary of the Crusaders' conquest of Jerusalem in 1099.

—Richmond Times-Dispatch, July 16, 1999

This event binds together two of history's most monumental moments of collective human expression. In linking these two manias from the first and last centuries of the millennium, we can see the constancy, connectedness and contradictions of social mood. According to the inclusionistic mindset of the reconcilers now marching on Jerusalem, there is an obvious conflict between the savagery and intense faith of the Crusaders. "Exactly 900 years ago Christians visited this land with a sword and a spirit of vengeance in a manner contrary to teachings and character of Jesus," says one of the group's leaders. Of course, the social mood then was one of extreme exclusionism. At this end of the rising Millennium wave, it is the opposite.

Someday, observers will look back at the last days of the great bull market and be just as perplexed by the behavior of its participants. Perhaps the most glaring contradiction will be how great things were right before the bottom fell out. Things today are so great that people are literally marching all over the world saying "Forgive me" for misdeeds that took place nearly a millennium before they were even born. Things today are so great that the President of the United States has announced a $1 trillion dollar "addition" (projected, of course) to the budget surplus and proposed the elimination of all federal debts by 2015.

The bullish urge to expand all social circles is so strong that anti-social individuals are classified as diseased. A cottage industry has sprouted to combat this "very pervasive" "under-diagnosed and undertreated" disorder. An array of books, tapes and a $6860 intensive four-week course are commonly prescribed. For the seriously shy, a whole host of new anti-depressants have come on the market. The pharmaceuticals industry sees it as "a huge new market in social anxiety." Anti-social behavior is also under attack at the corporate level. A study of "mood linkage in work" groups by a team of researchers finds that "depression" and "negativity" do not belong in "fast-paced, highly interactive, group-dependent" working environments. Crime rates have fallen (this time by a whopping 11%), IRS agents are turning nice (seizures of property are down 98%), and there is a shortage of rats. Everyone says, "It doesn't get any better than this." In coming times, Christians will probably be charging back to Palestine, once again to do battle. At the thought of the events at the preceding millennial cusp, they will simply shake their heads and say, "What were they thinking?"

September 1999

In 1992, *The Elliott Wave Theorist* introduced the concept of inclusionism by noting that it was a function of the "size of people's unit of allegiance, the group that they consider to be like themselves" and added, "At the peak, there is a perceived brotherhood of men." It turns out, however, all of humankind is not inclusive enough to contain sentiment at this Grand Supercycle peak.

"Influenced by developing scientific and ethical scholarship showing animals to have far higher levels of cognition and social development than previously believed," lawyers have created a "whole new field of animal law" that intends to remove "a fundamental principle of American law that animals have no rights." A federal appeals court gave a human zoo visitor "the right to sue to get companionship for chimpanzees." The 66th annual pigeon shoot was cancelled in Hegins, Pa. after the Pennsylvania Supreme Court sided with lawyers seeking an injunction on the grounds of animal cruelty. Animal Law, the first scholarly journal dedicated to legal protections for animals, is now being published by the same law school that published the first environmental law journal in the late 1960s, when social mood was also putting in a long-term peak. The Great Apes Project has been formed to win human rights for all great apes. It expects to bring a measure before the New Zealand legislature that would grant great apes the right to life, the right not to suffer cruel or degrading treatments and the right not to take part in all but the most benign experiments.

The president of a San Francisco-based animal defense group offered this description of the Grand Supercycle progression toward ever greater inclusionism: "Society first moved away from women and wives as property, then it moved away from African Americans as property. Now a large segment of people are beginning to move away from the concept of animals as property."

> ### All in the Family:
> # *Human Rights for Apes?*
> In recent years, evidence of cognitive and genetic similarities between humans and apes have resulted in the Great Apes Project – an international campaign to win specific human rights for all great apes. The project has now culminated in a drive to make sure that New Zealand's new Animal Welfare Bill contains a clause allowing great apes the right to life, the right not to suffer cruel or degrading treatment and the right not to take part in all but the most benign experiments.
>
> Philosopher Peter Singer of Monash University in Melbourne predicts that, although legal rights for rats are unlikely, we will see a gradual broadening of the "sphere of moral concern" to include species beyond the great apes.
>
> "The case is clear for [great apes]. Like humans, they are entitled to certain rights," he says. And, if we deny rights to chimps, we will logically have to deny those same rights to intellectually disabled children, too, he adds.
>
> —New Scientist, July 20, 1999

The eclipse of August 11 was an even bigger communal gathering event than the Harmonic Convergence at the top in August 1987. As trading came "to a near halt at stock exchanges" across Europe, millions of Europeans gathered in the "band of totality" to celebrate. The German autobahn was clogged all day for more than 200 miles "yet there were few signs of bitterness or frustration." "It was euphoric," said a hotel receptionist. "You had the feeling that people had put everything behind them." According to Newsweek, "More people watched the total solar eclipse of 1999 than have seen any other such phenomena since the dawn of time." And they were euphoric.

In February 1933, the same month the Dow tested this century's low of 41 in 1932, the Reichstag was burned down by the Nazis, and the Weimar Republic effectively came to an end. In a sign of a completed advance from the Supercycle low, the historic "symbol of German unity," will be re-occupied by the German government on September 1.

May 2000

In a direct parallel to 1968, the year of the market's speculative peak in Cycle wave III, a genuine protest movement hit Washington D.C. on April 7 of this year. The three-day demonstration at the International Monetary Fund had all the divisive intensity of its late 1960s' cousin, but it lacked one important element: a unified opposition. As columnist James Toranto points out, this was different from the anti-war movement of 32 years ago. "It must be frustrating to be a young left-wing demonstrator in 2000, longing for the glory days of the Vietnam era. Back then, protestors had a clear and simple message: End the war. By contrast, nothing of consequence unites today's demonstrators. Today, you name it, and someone is against it." There were blocs within the blocs. Among the various groups with economic complaints, there were anti-traders, anti-globalizationists and anti-trusters. There was even an anti-debt faction. "Cancel the WHOLE Debt," said one of the signs that will probably come in handy in the not too distant future. All of this diversity shows is that social protest need not be about anything in particular. It comes is an expression of impulsive emotion, not reason.

The other important aspect of the uprising is that the target all of these disparate antagonists could agree on was the IMF. When the global decline started in Asia in 1997, *The Elliott Wave Theorist* called the battle against the IMF "a crystal-clear window to 'the approaching chaos'" alluded to in the final chapter of *At the Crest of the Tidal Wave*.

If a moderate sell-off yields this kind of negative emotional release after just a few weeks, imagine what a grinding decline over the course of a few years will yield. By the end of the bear market, protests will turn to violent confrontation.

June 2000

The late post-peak burst of positive social sentiment has carried into the political realm, as a major trade deal with Communist China was reached May 23. A vote by the U.S. House seals the granting of normal trade ties to China. The passage of this historic measure places another arrow on our chart of Grand Supercycle milestones from *The Wave Principle of Human Social Behavior*. Will it be the last? We cannot say, but, if it is, it is interesting that these historic reconciliations followed the same geographic course, from Europe to China, as the progression of hostility shown for the bear market of the 1930s and 1940s.

The trade ties that are now being restored originally ceased after the Communists took over China in 1949, where the final arrow in the last Supercycle degree bear market appears. Hopes today are as bright as they were faint in 1949. The vote is considered a huge victory for the "salivating" U.S. business community and its drive to gain access to "the expanding Chinese marketplace of 1.3 billion." According to USA Today, the measure marks the culmination of an "irresistible" 150-year-old "fantasy." In the past, these dreams have always been dashed. Our Elliott wave count for the Dow suggests that it will happen again. The goodwill represented by the "permanent" embrace of these two trade partners should fade as hostility develops with surprising speed.

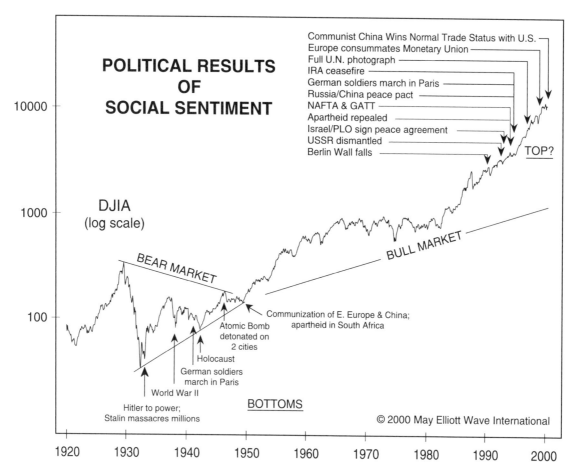

POLITICAL RESULTS OF SOCIAL SENTIMENT

Communist China Wins Normal Trade Status with U.S.
Europe consummates Monetary Union
Full U.N. photograph
IRA ceasefire
German soldiers march in Paris
Russia/China peace pact
NAFTA & GATT
Apartheid repealed
Israel/PLO sign peace agreement
USSR dismantled
Berlin Wall falls

TOP?

DJIA (log scale)

10000

1000

100

BEAR MARKET

BULL MARKET

Communization of E. Europe & China; apartheid in South Africa

Atomic Bomb detonated on 2 cities

Holocaust

German soldiers march in Paris

World War II

Hitler to power; Stalin massacres millions

BOTTOMS

© 2000 May Elliott Wave International

1920   1930   1940   1950   1960   1970   1980   1990   2000

September 2000

Foreigners make their biggest commitments when major trends are about to reverse. As Bob Prechter explained in *Prechter's Perspective*, "No crowd buys stocks of other countries intelligently. For decades, heavy foreign buying in the U.S. stock market has served as an excellent indicator of major tops." Over the years, this observation has served *The Elliott Wave Theorist* well. In the late 1980s, for instance, after years of disinterest, foreigners became net buyers of Japanese stocks, and EWT used the inflow of foreign money to identify the termination phase of one of the biggest bull markets in history.

The chart of the Dow and foreigners' net purchases of U.S. equities illustrates how beautifully the pattern has held through the U.S. bull market of the 1990s. The solid lines show the flood of foreign buyers within a month of each high, and the dotted lines show them rushing back out again on the months of the big lows. Early in the decade, when stocks were a bargain, foreigners were net sellers. They did not sustain net purchases until the Dow crossed 8000 in 1997. In fact, since the topping process began as the advance/decline line peaked in April 1998, foreigners have purchased a net total of $200 billion worth of U.S. stocks, 50% more than in all the rest of the 1990s. The record of $29 billion came in February, one month after the all-time peak in the Dow and a month before the NASDAQ's record high. The latest figure, for May, shows monthly net buying of $6 billion in U.S. stock. This is well above the net sales of more than $10 billion near the bottom in 1998. Given the degree of trend change, the next important low should be accompanied by a reading that is at least equivalent to that of 1998.

Figures since June are not yet available, but the probability is that no net outflows have occurred. The upward trend in the market and anecdotal evidence of ongoing foreign interest in U.S. financial markets suggest that foreigners are piling back in. A prime example of unprecedented interest on the part of foreigners comes from Germany, a country whose risk-averse inhabitants

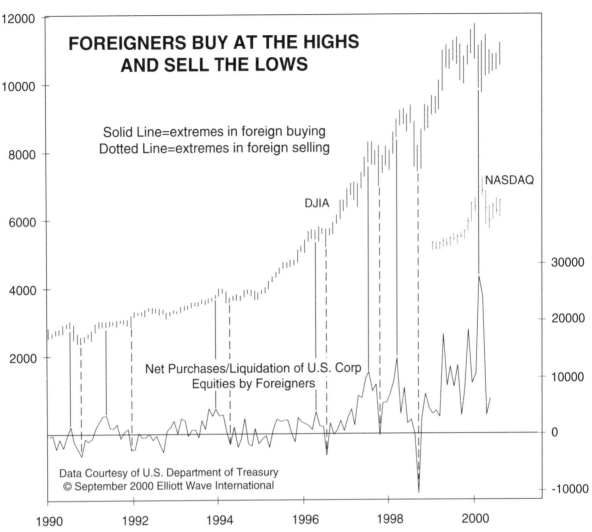

**FOREIGNERS BUY AT THE HIGHS
AND SELL THE LOWS**

Solid Line=extremes in foreign buying
Dotted Line=extremes in foreign selling

NASDAQ

DJIA

Net Purchases/Liquidation of U.S. Corp
Equities by Foreigners

Data Courtesy of U.S. Department of Treasury
© September 2000 Elliott Wave International

did not even buy German stocks until the later half of the 1990s. These days, the Germans are buying obscure U.S. stocks and listing them on a board they call the "High Risk Market." Says one source, "The Hamburg Stock Exchange now offers a new specialty: microcap U.S. stocks. A new trading board currently features about 40 companies, all of them based in North America, few with any deep connection to Europe. Yet some of these stocks generate more trading volume in Hamburg than they do in the U.S."

October 2000

Remember "red chip fever?" That was the speculative craze that focused on shares of companies through which China's communist party was expected to take over Hong Kong beginning July 1, 1997. In June 1997, *The Elliott Wave Theorist* identified the red chip frenzy as an extension of the worldwide mania for financial assets that was likely to end around July 1, 1997, the day of the island's reunion with mainland China. The Hang Seng topped a month later and fell 46% in three months. This past March, the Hang Seng rallied back to an all-time high (about 8% above the July 1997 peak) amidst another speculative frenzy, this time for Internet stocks. When Hong Kong tycoon Li KaShing offered a piece of his Internet empire, Tom.com, almost half a million prospective investors "thronged local banks, a response unmatched since the red chip boom." Predictably, that euphoria has also been followed by a swoon.

So far, the Hang Seng is off 20%, and investors are clearly clinging to their hopes for higher prices. Despite layoffs and a decline of 75% in its value since March, Tom.com completed a secondary offering in early September. On September 25, hundreds "shrugged off the gloom" and lined up at banks to buy another offering, this time in the city's subway system. The potential for a long-lasting break in the Hang Seng is suggested by the fact that the bullish sentiment is less than the white-hot tones of 1997 and March 2000. The Hong Kong subway offering is a bit less speculative because the subway actually makes money. Also, "unlike Tom.com, police weren't needed to control the crowds." On the mainland, the stock indexes have formed a double top with the highs of 1997.

As in 1997, a historic political moment is marking the turn. By an overwhelming margin, the U.S. Senate voted on September 19 to "permanently normalize" trade ties with China. The vote "puts the world's largest communist country on a clear path to full economic integration with the West." Do you agree with the pundits, who say that this event is "bullish?" This vote is the bull market counterpoint to the communist takeover of the China at the bottom in 1949, which marked the end of the last Supercycle degree bear market in inflation-adjusted terms. As we summarized the prevailing view last July, "Hopes today are as bright as they were faint in 1949." It pays to invest contrarily to widely held views. Since EWFF made that statement, the Hang Seng has declined 20%. The impulsive pattern of this retreat, along with the doggedly bullish sentiment that persists in spite of it, indicate that it has much further to go.

November 2000

The flood of articles about popular uprisings (see collage) is just a small sample of the conflicts that have spilled into the streets in recent weeks as a result of the waxing bear market mood. In October alone, there were more protests and demonstrations than we have room to mention. Several, like the Arab-Israeli riots/demonstrations, the protests before the IMF and the European gas price revolt were actually an ongoing succession of mass uprisings that have energized millions all over the world.

This upheaval is a deeply significant consequence of the long-term turn in social mood. The potential for such a vivid exhibition of mass human emotion falling back upon itself was first identified by EWT in 1985. EWT called for a two-step sequence in which a "positive minded

Industry fears more GM protests
Chemical Week

Unrest puzzles campuses; some blame recent riots on boredom, not beliefs

The Acquittal Last Month of 28 Greenpeace protesters, accused of causing criminal damage to a field of genetically modified (GM) crops in the U.K. has raised fears among biotechnology suppliers. The protesters were acquitted on the grounds that they were protecting surrounding fields from GM pollen contamination

PROTESTERS OPPOSE CLOSING OF I-644 OVERPASSES
St. Louis Post-Dispatch

Protest of Coca Crop Eradication

McDonalds under fire: Protesters try to halt rise of fast-food giant in Italy

Earlier this month Fausto Bertinotti, leader of the Refounded Communist party, led 100,000 protesters to a McDonald's branch in Piazzo della Repubblica in Rome. The Turin-based Slow Food movement, which champions traditional cooking and eating, joined yesterday's protests.

The huge scale and rapid sweep of the European fuel-tax revolt caught much of the continent's political leadership off guard. Like [Tony Blair], most tended to dismiss the early signs of a gathering storm as yet another symptom of something widely derided in Europe as the "French disease." It was in France that the protests began.

THOUSANDS DEMONSTRATE ON CAMPUS

Tensions escalated between some of the several thousand protesters and State Police facing each other outside last night's presidential debate. For several minutes, nothing happened. Then suddenly, the police rushed the protesters, swinging batons and spraying pepper spray into the crowd, forcing protesters behind barricades.

Actor Rob Schneider from the film *Deuce Bigalow: Male Gigolo* led a sit-in protest at P&G's headquarters in Cincinnati.

PROTESTS SPREAD AS RISING ANGER REUNITES ARABS

Beijing Protest by Falun Sect Brings Arrest of Hundreds

At Rally, Suffolk Residents Protest Illegal Immigration

Waving American flags and red, white and blue balloons, 200 Suffolk County residents opposed to illegal immigrants and day laborers in their communities held a boisterous town hall meeting in Centereach, N.Y., yesterday and called for tougher enforcement of immigration laws.

Protesters Contend It's Unsafe Walking to Santa Ana School
Los Angeles Times

Organizers planned the rally on Orange County Pedestrian Safety Day because "it's a perfect time to show our concern."

PROTEST MARCHERS TARGET VIOLENCE AGAINST WOMEN AND WORLDWIDE POVERTY

People power ousts Slobodan Milosevic

save-the-world social concern" at the final highs gives way to "rebellious, angry social concern" as stock prices start to fall. This progression is consistent with what has happened in the realm of mass social expression. Remember the Million Man March in 1995 and the Million Woman March in 1997? These and several other marches during the same period of roaring stock gains were "calls for unity" in which up to 1 million gathered and vowed to "take a more active role in their families and neighborhoods."

In April 1998, the month the average NYSE stock peaked but before the Dow and most major averages started down, a slow escalation in the size and number of protests started with student demonstrations in Indonesia. A month later, the upheaval led to the ousting of Indonesia's long-time dictator and the establishment of a democratically elected government. Similar Indonesian uprisings foreshadowed the peak of Supercycle (III) in 1929 and Cycle III in 1966. Since 1998, anti-IMF/World Bank protests have also gathered steam and become steadily more contentious. At the most recent meeting in Prague, bear market forces were stunningly successful. In addition to shortening the conference by a day, the beliefs of the "anti-capitalist" mob penetrated to the heart of the proceedings, as this report from the Economist reveals: "Instead of pondering how to sell the merits of unfettered free markets to the street protesters outside, the ministers inside were considering the advantages of interfering in two of them: the markets for currencies and for oil."

The U.S. has already beaten them to the punch with the release of oil from its Strategic Petroleum Reserve. In June 1998, EWT also anticipated this backlash against market forces as an inevitable by-product of the coming bear market: "History shows government intervention tends to wane in bull markets and grow in bear markets." Its rapid rate of growth and marriage to the spreading protest movement is a powerful symbol of the strength of this downturn.

GE 1974-2000 = phi x 100

General Electric was one of the last stocks to complete its bull market with a final high on August 28. As late as October 5, GE, the only original member of the Dow Jones Industrial Average, was within a fraction of its all-time peak. Subscriber Alvery Bartlett points out that GE expanded from a September 1974 low of 0.625 to 60.5. As the chart shows, GE advanced nearly to 100 times the Fibonacci ratio in a fine-looking Elliott wave pattern that began a few months before the overall bull market and finished a few months after its completion. While we are not about to say that GE can't try to make it up to 62.5 just to make it perfect, the long term picture is what counts. While the Dow achieved a 20x multiple from the 1974 low, GE achieved a 100x multiple, five times as much. In the process, the company switched a good part of its focus from manufacturing to finance (its holdings and thus its bubble-era valuation include CNBC). When the markets collapse, so will the finance business. GE's consumer products aren't nearly as good as they were during wave III (1942-1966). We want to be the first to say it out loud: GE is going to go way down over the next four years.

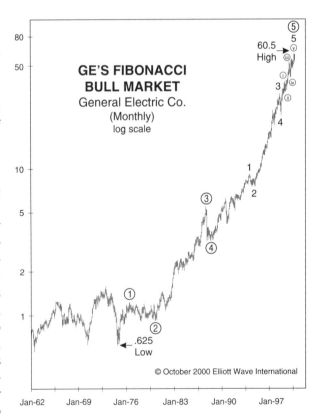

GE'S FIBONACCI BULL MARKET
General Electric Co.
(Monthly)
log scale

© October 2000 Elliott Wave International

December 2000
Talking About Revolution

A month ago, EWFF observed a worldwide flood in popular unrest and called it a "deeply significant consequence of the long-term turn in social mood." In November, the number and size of these mass eruptions accelerated to an even faster rate. Once again there were many more uprisings than we have room to cover, but here's one addition to last month's collage.

Dot-Com Boom Spurs Angry Protests

Protest groups such as the Yuppie Eradication Project and AARGG! (All Against Ruthless Greedy Gentrification), promise an unruly campaign against the technology industry's "colonization" of the Mission District and the "Starbuckization" of San Francisco.
—November 27, 2000

The sweeping emotion of today's protest events is so powerful that even the participants seem shocked. As one middle-aged Republican holding a "Bush or Revolution" sign put it, "I never in a million years thought I'd be out here holding up a sign like this." The response to the election stalemate is entirely consistent with *The Elliott Wave Theorist*'s original call for a transition from "save-the-world social concern" to "rebellious, angry social concern." This quote from the same middle-aged Republican demonstrates that the transition from the great show-of-unity marches in 1995 through 1997 is definitely in place: "Anger? That's an understatement. The thought of revolution is terrible, but I speak to many people from all walks of life all across the country and it is not far from their minds."

May 2001

A subscriber asks about Japan:

Japan's bear market is a mature one with household share ownership now 10% versus the U.S. at over 50%. While in the U.S. it is likely to take time (a lot of time) to kill the equity culture, this has been dead and buried in Japan for years. Can things get any worse?!
—Paul K., Tokyo

The cultural effects of the bear market are obviously much more fully developed in Japan than in the United States. So, Japan presents a view to the U.S.' future, as *The Elliott Wave Theorist* has suggested for several years. In addition to the washout we have witnessed in Japan's equity culture, recent months have brought a wave of nationalism and punk rock. Genuine political upheaval has also arrived with the election of a reform-minded prime minister. Can things get any worse? Indeed they will. Before the bear market is over, the Japanese will probably elect someone who is not even a member of the Liberal Democratic Party. Remember, manias tend to be more than fully retraced, and Japan's mania goes back to at least 1982 when the Nikkei was at 6850, less than half of current levels, and probably to 1974 when it was near 3000. In other words, the bear market is still in mid-trend.

IT'S "1973" IN JAPAN

1973 in the U.S.

INFLATION ADJUSTED DJIA (Monthly) 1966-1982

NIKKEI (Monthly) 1990-present

2000 in Japan

© May 2001 Elliott Wave International

One cultural clue to that fact is the emergence of "super platform" shoes. Last year, platform soles of up to nine inches became popular among "girl fashion gangs" and women who want to emulate the gangs' look. A similar excess for men hit the U.S. footwear market in 1973 when the bear market in inflation-adjusted terms was only about half over. For the Japanese market, then, this appears to be cultural confirmation that the bear market has a ways to go. In the U.S., where soles have just started to rise, the message for people who remember 1970s relics like the one shown here is, don't buy stocks on the Nikkei too soon.

June 2001

Global conflict is a by-product of a downturn in social mood. This inescapable tension between nations and distinct social groups is best illustrated by our long-term chart of the "Political Results of Social Sentiment" (see June 2000 entry) which shows Hitler's rise to power, World War II, the Holocaust and the dropping of two atomic bombs on Japan between the bear market lows of 1932, 1942 and 1949.

Social clashes take myriad forms, but one bellwether rift that has an almost perfect record of erupting into open hostility right at the onset of major downturns is in the Mideast. The chart shows that relations between Jews and Arabs in Israel (or Palestine before 1948) have been particularly responsive to the start of important bear markets since 1929 when *The Year of the Great Crash* says, "All hell had broken loose in Palestine. At the end of August, a series of relatively inconsequential disputes concerning the privileges of worship for Jews and Moslems erupted into an orgy of bloodletting." The violence came a few days before the Dow's final high.

If major hostilities are defined as wars or mob violence that result in mass killings, each of the headlines on the chart marks a significant outbreak. All were preceded by periods of easing tension (or at least an absence of bloodshed) and followed by further clashes. The greatest stretch of peaceful cooperation between the two sides is shown by the Era of Good Feelings table at the

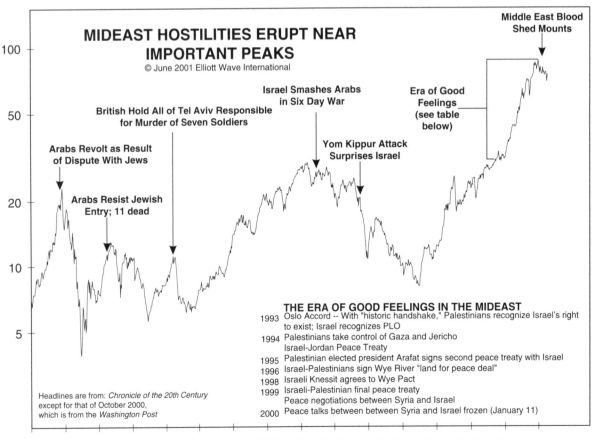

MIDEAST HOSTILITIES ERUPT NEAR IMPORTANT PEAKS
© June 2001 Elliott Wave International

Middle East Blood Shed Mounts

Israel Smashes Arabs in Six Day War

British Hold All of Tel Aviv Responsible for Murder of Seven Soldiers

Era of Good Feelings (see table below)

Arabs Revolt as Result of Dispute With Jews

Yom Kippur Attack Surprises Israel

Arabs Resist Jewish Entry; 11 dead

THE ERA OF GOOD FEELINGS IN THE MIDEAST

1993 Oslo Accord -- With "historic handshake," Palestinians recognize Israel's right to exist; Israel recognizes PLO
1994 Palestinians take control of Gaza and Jericho
Israel-Jordan Peace Treaty
1995 Palestinian elected president Arafat signs second peace treaty with Israel
1996 Israel-Palestinians sign Wye River "land for peace deal"
1998 Israeli Knessit agrees to Wye Pact
1999 Israeli-Palestinian final peace treaty
Peace negotiations between Syria and Israel
2000 Peace talks between between Syria and Israel frozen (January 11)

Headlines are from: *Chronicle of the 20th Century* except for that of October 2000, which is from the *Washington Post*

1925 1930 1935 1940 1945 1950 1955 1960 1965 1970 1975 1980 1985 1990 1995 2000

bottom of the chart. It started on September 13, 1993 with the famous handshake between the prime minister of Israel and the chairman of the Palestine Liberation Organization. Historians said the historic handshake was a symbol of "a major breakthrough after a century of conflict." *The Elliott Wave Theorist* identified it as a product of the century-long advance in stock prices that would mark a long-term top rather than a great new era for Palestinian and Israeli relations. The next seven years of bull market yielded productive talks but no lasting peace. As late as January 30 2000, the Houston Chronicle reported that the "tide of history" was moving the "Mideast toward peace."

In reality, however, the tide had already reversed. In July 2000, the same paper would mark the moment by reporting that "Syrian-Israeli peace negotiations have been frozen since mid-January." The exact date was January 11, three days before the Dow's all-time high. By last summer, the anxiety level was clearly rising fast as the Palestinians threatened to declare statehood and another peace conference failed to produce a breakthrough for the first time since 1993.

As stocks entered their September-October swoon, Palestinian sections of Israel exploded in a continuous wave of rioting. By December the depth of anger was evidenced by this headline: "As Arafat Embraces Revolt, His Sagging Popularity Rises." Israel responded with the election of hardliner Ariel Sharon. In the first half of May, the situation bordered on open warfare. "Is It War Yet?" asked one headline on May 20. On May 21, the Bush administration criticized Israel for using U.S.-supplied warplanes against Palestinians for the first time since the 1967 war, which was a year after the peak of Cycle III. Finally, on May 22, the day of the Dow's high, there was a "glimmer of hope" as Sharon talked of compromise and ordered Israeli forces "only to return fire if shot at."

Past signals have usually come at and after long-term turns; 1967 was an exception, being between the highs of 1966 and 1968. The conflict may ease briefly, but a historic sell signal has clearly been issued by the open warfare. The Mideast's record as an early register of negative social mood suggests that a major bear market and thus the trend toward global hostility has only just begun.

August 2001

One of *At the Crest of the Tidal Wave*'s key points was the global reach of the bear market, to wit, "The conclusions in this book pertain almost equally to every other stock exchange around the world." Another sign of the large degree of the trend change is that no matter how forcefully the bear tears into one financial community after another, it still manages to catch participants by surprise. The "latest financial crisis" in Argentina and Turkey shows that the bear market's capacity for astonishing its still-unwitting participants may actually

Barak Halts Peace Talks With Syria

Prime minister demands that Damascus rein in Hezbollah guerrillas after three Israeli soldiers are killed in the wake of a top Lebanese ally's slaying.

—Los Angeles Times, February 1, 2000

Israeli-Palestinian Peace Talks Run Aground

Summit ends in discord over West Bank land transfers. Barak downplays difficulties, but negotiator for other side cites 'crisis.'

—Los Angeles Times, February 4, 2000

Setbacks to Mideast Peace

—The New York Times, February 9, 2000

EXPLOSIONS
IN THE MIDEAST

The violent Palestinian riots have gone well beyond their proximate cause, an ill-chosen visit to a Muslim and Jewish holy site by a right-wing Israeli politician. They now raise the serious question of whether Palestinian leader Yasser Arafat is able, or willing to stop the violence.

The government of Israeli Prime Minister Ehud Barak, having gone further in concessions to the Palestinians than anyone would have imagined a year ago, can now legitimately question whether any agreement reached with Arafat would stand up.

Arafat's intentions are opaque, especially his refusal to try to halt the violence. He has appeared to abdicate to extremists in the streets.

—The Commercial Appeal
October 13, 2000

be rising. Unlike the "Asian crisis" of 1997 and Russia's default in 1998, flight from Argentine and Turkish bonds has not produced a wholesale liquidation of emerging market debt. As the media continually notes, the side effects of Argentina and Turkey have been "substantially less severe." One report refers to the latest turbulence as a "second crisis of globalization."

But if the scenario laid out in *At the Crest* is accurate, the events of 1997 and 1998 are not separate events. They are just the opening paragraphs in an exposé that will reveal the term "emerging markets" to be "a euphemism that means low-priced stocks of undercapitalized companies in politically shaky countries with little or no history of capitalism." In 1995, *At the Crest* predicted that these emerging markets, the "cats and dogs" of the global bull market, would "soon be submerging markets." This is exactly what happened. Actually the first domino, Thailand, topped in July 1995, before *At the Crest* was off the presses. Since then, despite the best efforts of the IMF, one after another has toppled. Some, like South Korea, Brazil and Chile, have managed double tops with slight new highs, but many that were at the center of the initial phase of the crisis, like Malaysia, Indonesia and Russia, are well below their 1997 peaks in dollar terms.

In fact, even Argentina's "troubles" can be directly traced to the decline of 1997, as its main stock market index peaked in July of that year. In 1998, its economy followed the market down. Now, after a decade of stability, the deterioration has reached the political realm. Argentina's extremely unpopular president stands almost no chance of surviving a tumultuous election season. In neighboring Chile, Peru and Brazil, a sudden uncertainty has also shattered a long period of political tranquility. In racially divided Peru, for instance, a native Peruvian has been elected and will rule the country for the first time in 500 years. His predecessor, Alberto Fujimoro, fled the country amidst social and economic crisis late last year. The sudden disappearance of stability is the result of the bear market, which has been pressing down in these fringe regions for years now. It is also a direct throwback to 1930, when political dynasties were thrown out of all four countries.

"Should we worry?" asks a USA Today article. "Not too much, most economists say." Why? Because:

Experts Say U.S. Economy Can Stand on Its Own

The long-term pattern in the Dow and the World Index illustrates very clearly, however, that the U.S. cannot support the weight of the world.

September 2001

The latest from Japan is that it now realizes it has a deflation problem and is readying to combat it with inflationary fiscal policies.

In a related revelation, the parallel between the 2000-2001 NASDAQ and the 1989-1991 Nikkei collapse (see January 2000 entry in Chapter 1 and January 2001 entry in Chapter 6), has hit the mainstream papers. The story rose to the top of USA Today's front page on August 20. "NASDAQ Mirrors Nikkei Slump," re-

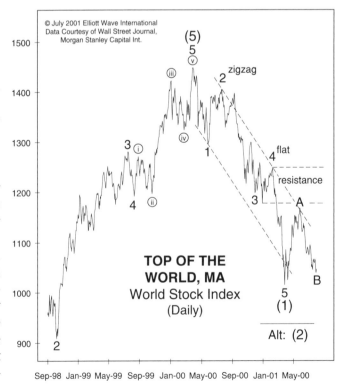

© July 2001 Elliott Wave International
Data Courtesy of Wall Street Journal,
Morgan Stanley Capital Int.

TOP OF THE WORLD, MA
World Stock Index
(Daily)

ported the nation's largest daily paper in an article that could have been lifted directly from the January 2000 and 2001 issues of EWFF. Of course, there is an important difference. In its coverage of the "remarkable similarity" between the Nikkei and the NASDAQ, EWFF was speaking prospectively about the potential for sharp declines in the OTC indexes. Yes, the parallel appears to be very much on track, but, at the moment, it is bullish, not bearish as the papers presume. Based on our analysis, the NASDAQ is approximately where the Nikkei was in February 1991, when, after several months of sideways action, it rose more than 20% in a little less than a month.

Even in the particulars, the reaction to the bursting of the NASDAQ resembles that of the Nikkei in 1990/1991. Does this sound familiar? "The securities industry has an inherently bullish bias. '[Brokers] are always bulls. Even if they think a stock is too expensive, they will recommend to buy.' [Nomura] 'called the bottom eighteen times.'" It is from an article about the backlash against Japanese securities firms in the February 1991 issue of Institutional Investor. The U.S. is conforming to the Japanese model as *The Elliott Wave Theorist* long contended that it would. In the second quarter, U.S. GDP came in at 0.2%, setting the stage for all-consuming public debate about whether the U.S. is or is not in a recession. Look for this fact to go unnoticed: the Japanese economy rebounded to a growth rate of 10% in the second quarter of 1991. Still, the Nikkei never even approached the March 1991 high. In fact, a decade later, it's down 70% from its all-time high and at its lowest point since 1984.

September 11, 2001

Sometimes it takes an appalling drama to stir people from lethargy and make them pay attention to matters of grave importance. If your friends and family have yet to wake up to the Wave Principle's crucial message, please do your part to help them realize where we are in the social cycle and why it matters. Comfort and safety come from understanding. If you can see the big picture clearly, both past and future, you will be able to make fruitful decisions calmly.

Understanding the Engine of Social Trends

The radical thesis of *The Wave Principle of Human Social Behavior and the New Science of Socionomics* was unmistakably manifest in the raucous social comedy of the 1990s, and now it is playing out in the first act of a developing worldwide social tragedy that will last years. The primary thesis of this book is that changes in social mood cause and therefore precede changes in the character of social events. In contrast to this idea, most people erroneously try to divine the implications of events in attempts to forecast financial markets and people's collective feelings. Their approach cannot work because markets are driven by natural trends in mass psychology, and events resulting from those psychological trends come afterward. It is the changes in such trends, as indicated by turns in the stock market, that signal a coming change in the tenor of social events.

Socionomics explained why global atrocities followed the 1929-1932 crash and continued during most of the rest of the bear market pattern, which ended in 1949. It also explained why the worldwide peace initiatives and unprecedented acts of reconciliation of the 1990s followed nearly half a century of social mood uptrend. The dramatic, historic pictures shown in HSB to convey the power of these moods were not placed there simply for academic purposes. This is real life we're talking about. You have to live near those events to sense that fact.

Forecasting the Tenor of Social Events

At the Crest of the Tidal Wave forecast in no uncertain terms that severe social unrest would follow the onset of what was then the approaching — and is now the developing — Grand Supercycle bear market:

SOCIAL IMPLICATIONS

A long term trend toward a positive social mood always leads to times of peace and political cooperation, such as we enjoy today. An extreme trend change in social mood toward the negative always leads to calamities. The average level of conflict during the bear market will be far greater than it was during the bull market and will lead to periods of turmoil, not just in financial markets, but in society. Indeed, the trends now implied by long term market patterns have always produced dramatic social upheaval. The last time a bear market of the currently projected magnitude took place was 1720 to 1784, a period that began with a market crash, ended with the Revolutionary War, and led to a deep and global five-year depression.

The coming trend of negative social psychology will be characterized primarily by polarization between and among various perceived groups, whether political, ideological, religious, geographical, racial or economic. The result will be a net trend toward anger, fear, intolerance, disagreement and exclusion, as opposed to the bull market years, whose net trend has been toward benevolence, confidence, tolerance, agreement and inclusion. Such a sentiment change typically brings conflict in many forms, and evidence of it will be visible in all types of social organizations. Political manifestations will include protectionism in trade matters, a polarized and vocal electorate, separatist movements, xenophobia, citizen-government clashes, the dissolution of old alliances and parties, and the emergence of radical new ones. Tariffs will become popular, regardless of the fact that virtually everyone knows they are dangerous and wrong, because they are a consequence of an increasingly negative psychology involving fear, envy and a misguided attempt at self-defense. Xenophobia will be practiced regardless of people's generally good intentions, because fear and hatred become pervasive in major bear markets regardless of whether or not they are justified. There will also be a danger that governments will impose police-state type controls as a consequence of the bear market. Such periods often end with emotional political oustings, whether by vote, resignation, impeachment, coup or revolution.

The worst economic and social programs are years away, but advance planning is incalculably better than trying to react when it is too late.

October 2001

Global Markets

In August, we discussed the bearish wave pattern in the World Stock Index and asserted, "On a global scale: it's a bear market." A continued sell-off in August and September places a large exclamation point on our bearish forecast. Like the NASDAQ, the World Stock Index should get a reprieve in the coming months, but the longer-term message of this five-wave decline is that the bear market that began in March 2000 is still in the early stages of a large-degree correction.

January 2002

The debt bomb is going off. So far, it's progressing very much in line with the debacle depicted in *At the Crest of the Tidal Wave*. Argentina, with its rapid descent from wage cuts and austerity measures to pension fund seizures, frozen bank accounts and "total anarchy," offers the latest and most intense glimpse of the liquidation process. We could fill a whole newsletter with the repercussions. For now, it will have to suffice to echo what *The Elliott Wave Theorist* has been saying about Japan for much of the last decade. It is a window into the future. The situation in

Argentina should be studied closely as a key to how the unwinding depression will play out in many parts of the world. In time, the food riots, unprecedented political instability (Argentina has had five presidents in two weeks!) and attacks on the banks and international monetary authorities that "created the problem" will be seen as the norm in many countries. The lack of "contagion effect" to neighboring countries so far has led many to conclude that the impact on the global economy "will be limited for investors because they had a lot of time to prepare for this." We see this contained fear as one of the scariest aspects of the whole situation. It shows yet another area in which investors and creditors have taken on a complacency that is completely out of bounds with historic precedent.

April 2002

As the negative social psychology of the bear market grabs hold, one of the key social forecasts featured in *At the Crest of the Tidal Wave* was a call for a global trade war:

> Political manifestations will include protectionism in trade matters. Tariffs will become popular, regardless of the fact that virtually everyone knows they are dangerous and wrong, because they are a consequence of an increasingly negative psychology involving fear, envy and a misguided attempt at self defense.

On March 5, George Bush "set the wheels in motion for a global trade war" by imposing stiff tariffs on imported steel. The move "triggered retaliation the world over." The new tariff is another direct parallel to the "recovery" of 1930 when the Smoot-Hawley trade tariff bill worked its way through Congress against a backdrop of recovering stock prices. Bush "contradicted his own free trade advocacy" for the same reason Hoover signed Smoot-Hawley into law in June 1930. Not doing so would have been political suicide. Obviously, George Bush knows these tariffs are dangerous and wrong. Just six weeks before he imposed them, he was attacking protectionists for holding out a "false comfort." Like September 11, it is a harbinger of the global tension, exclusionism and xenophobia that will mark the real "new era." It is also another great reminder of how fast reason can fly out the window, when the emotional reality of a bear market slaps the unprepared across the face.

May 2002

In many areas, bear market psychology is picking up speed. A typical example are the harbingers of exclusionism and xenophobia discussed last month. On April 13, we got word of a wave of anti-Semitic attacks in Europe. According to a new study, 2001 and 2002 "stand in contrast to a steady decline in anti-Semitic activity that continued from 1995 to 1999." On April 23, Jean-Marie Le Pen shocked the world by taking second place in France's preliminary presidential vote. "Le Pen is a symptom of a wider political malaise: fear of globalization, gloomy declinism, ugly xenophobia," reports the Washington Post. The Post added, "When it comes to France, this resentment is most loudly expressed as hatred of America." In an attack on U.S. Marines in Puerto Rico, perpetrators blame U.S. culture rather than the Catholic church for the church's sex scandal. Along with Latin American condemnation of the U.S. over a failed Venezuelan coup, the spread of anti-U.S. sentiment can be seen fanning out across the globe. Obviously, it is gaining a foothold in contingents that are thought to be far less radical than those that attacked the World Trade Center on September 11. This is the opposite of the global embrace that the U.S. and its democratic, free-market ideals enjoyed during the bull market.

December 2002
The Curl of the Tidal Wave

One of the bolder assertions contained in [Bob Prechter's 2002 book] *Conquer the Crash* is the scope of the bear market, which is described on page 95: "Make no mistake: It's a global story." In 2001, when the global depression arrived in Argentina, EWFF identified it as a sure sign that the turn was every bit the Grand Supercycle event called for in *At the Crest of the Tidal Wave*. But five months later, when political chaos, bank runs and protests disturbed daily life in Argentina, analysts breathed a collective sigh of relief because the social unrest failed to jump the tracks to the rest of South America. They spoke too soon. EWFF said that the "contained fear" was one of the scariest aspects of Argentina's fall: "It shows yet another area in which investors and creditors have taken on a complacency that is completely out of bounds with historic precedent." Eight months later, the International Monetary Fund bailed out Brazil, the region's biggest economy, with the biggest loan in IMF history. Despite the effort to stem the tide, the turmoil has infected the rest of the continent. In addition to Brazil, Paraguay, Uruguay, Bolivia and Peru have experienced economic setbacks and political instability. In recent days, Venezuela has been literally shut down by strikes aimed at ousting President Hugo Chavez. As we noted in anticipating this growing epidemic last January, South America's social unrest is a direct parallel to that of 1930, the last bear market of similar degree.

In recent weeks, the trouble infected Europe, which "is going from bad to worse." After rapidly ratcheting down growth estimates in late October and November, the European Commission just admitted that growth will probably go negative in the first quarter of 2003. "It is difficult to paint the situation with roses when in reality the situation is much darker," said the president of Italy's largest retailer. The telltale signs — "collapsing confidence," sick currencies and shattered myths about collective regional advance — are in place. Back in 1996, these symptoms were a disease that was called the Asian contagion. Now, as it prepares to spread to the U.S., it is clear that we are witnessing the global deflationary depression forecast in *At the Crest of the Tidal Wave* and *Conquer the Crash*. This is another parallel to 1929-1932, when America's troubles were widely seen as a European import.

The rising incidence of social conflict predicted by socionomics is escalating rapidly. In late November, Muslims in Nigeria went berserk over a newspaper article's assertion that the prophet Muhammad would have been happy to marry a candidate from the upcoming Miss World pageant. The pageant was moved to London after a three-day riot left 100 Christians and Muslims dead. It ended on Friday, November 23. Socionomics provides the background to understand why there was also a riot in South Korea, in fact, on the same day. This one was over the acquittal of two U.S. army soldiers, so the riots are completely unconnected by any external signs. The internal connection — the emerging global depression, in the psychological sense of the word — governs their synchronicity, at least generally if not specifically. Like so much of the violence of the past two years, these two events do have one external thing in common: Anger toward America. This is not a good sign for the social future of the U.S. It indicates that the global anti-Americanism discussed in May is accelerating at a rapid rate. This is confirmed by intensifying anti-American protests and hunger strikes in South Korea. A Pew Research survey of 38,000 people in 44 countries found that U.S. favorability ratings have slipped significantly in virtually every country. The Grand Supercycle bear market has social implications, and we have only glimpsed their breadth and extent.

January 2003

Spanning the Globe

In 2002, not one major stock market posted a gain. Of 375 stock indexes tracked by Bloomberg, 318, or 85% were down for the year. Most of the winners were gold and silver stock averages or relatively small, out-of-the way markets like Pakistan, Kuwait and Zimbabwe. This year, EWFF has chronicled the spread of the economic consequences of the bear market from Argentina to the rest of South America and, most recently, to Europe. The following table shows some of the damage that was done in 2002 and since the start of the bear market for each respective index.

2002 REVIEW

The December 2001 issue of The Elliott Wave Financial Forecast called for lower stock prices in 2002. The first column shows the results for the major averages. The second shows the decline for the bear market to date (BMTD) in each respective index.

MARKET	2002	BMTD
DJIA	-16.80%	-29.00%
S&P 500	-23.40%	-43.30%
NASDAQ	-31.50%	-74.00%
Dow Utilities	-26.80%	-48.50%
Dow Transports	-12.50%	-39.10%
Russell 2000	-21.60%	-37.60%
Wilshire 5000	-22.10%	-44.30%
S&S/TSX (Canada)	-13.90%	-45.70%
FTSE 100 (England)	-24.50%	-43.20%
CAC (France)	-33.80%	-49.20%
Dax (Germany)	-43.90%	-61.00%
Nikkei (Japan)	-18.60%	-78.00%
Hang Seng (Hong Kong)	-18.20%	-49.30%
DJ World Stock Index	-20.10%	-45.00%

February 2003

In 1999, *The Wave Principle of Human Social Behavior* theorized that a long-term shift in the direction of social mood would have an observable effect on people's style of thinking. It surmised that a waxing negative mood correlates to a collective rise in "credulity, dullness of focus and magical thinking, fuzziness of thinking." HSB went on to describe the opposing influences of bull and bear thought this way:

> Practical thinking manifests itself in philosophic defenses of reason, self-providence, individualism, peacemaking and a reverence for science. Magical thinking manifests itself in philosophic attacks on reason, self-abnegation, collectivism, witch hunts, war-making and reverence for religion.

Abundant evidence now suggests that the clear, unifying cognition that produces positive outcomes in a bull market has, in fact, given way to the slippery and counterproductive decision making of a bear. A big surge in fuzzy thinking is very clear in a host of different developments including: Witches being hunted down and killed in Mexico, India, Uganda, Mozambique and the Central African Republic; a newly "receptive" scientific inquiry into the legend of Bigfoot; a "news" account of "credible" encounters with Elvis; a new Elvis-oriented church; and a hit TV show that mediates discussions between pets and their owners.

Another big story that has been layered with appeals to bearish mental impulses is the one about the Raelians, a group that was formed when its founder says he had contact with aliens that are responsible for the creation of all life on earth. The Raelians hit the publicity jackpot simply by claiming to have followed in the footsteps of their alien creators and produced the first human clone. A month later, the story continues to make headlines even though the Raelians have never offered any evidence of a successful cloning. The reason is that, in making their claim, the Raelians touched several hot-buttons in the public's bearish psyche, like the possibility of collective non-conformity, the danger posed by "alien" threats and rising fears about science, all with a smattering of gratuitous sex thrown in on the side (Raelians believe physical pleasure is the way to enlightenment). Combine these bear market preoccupations with a motherlode of credulity and you have the makings of a whole self-contained fantasy world.

A more pervasive and serious illustration of the danger posed by bear market thinking is the big surge in the impetus to make war. Within the U.S., the bull market in this mindset dates back to September 2001. In the immediate aftermath of September 11, *The Elliott Wave Theorist* noted that the attack on the U.S. was unlikely to provoke an immediate global war. EWT added, however, that it could be the "sparking event" that would eventually lead to world war, "even if the U.S. and its allies appear to win an initial victory."

This is exactly what seems to be happening. The quick rout in Afghanistan has led to the current conflict with Iraq. The reason behind the forecast is the same reason that an invasion of Iraq will not end the long term march toward a more serious global conflict: This is a bear market of Grand Supercycle degree, which has much longer to run. Major wars generally don't take place until the end of, or even after, the downtrends in social mood that create them. In the larger scheme, Iraq (if it goes well, which it may not) is likely to be remembered as another preliminary skirmish. Comparing the dynamics surrounding the pending war to those of the first Gulf War, which was the result of a much smaller Primary degree bear market from 1987 to 1990, this encounter's Grand Supercycle scale is apparent in the much greater potential for divisiveness and destruction. In 1990, the war had a unifying effect because the U.S. entered it during a resurrection of the bull market. The current mobilization has caused a split between the West and the Arab world, between the U.S. and Europe, and within the U.S. The rising stakes are also visible in the lethal capability of the weapons being drawn by the combatants. According to a media monitoring service, the most commonly used phrase of 2002 was "weapons of mass destruction." Does Iraq have them? Will the U.S. use nuclear weapons to try and disable them? Will enemies of the United States counterattack with bioterror? Earlier this week, the U.S. Secretary of Health said such attacks are "inevitable." The spread of these threats is also apparent in North Korea's resumption of uranium processing and willingness to arm potential U.S. adversaries.

The uncertainty surrounding this endeavor is correspondingly higher than in 1990, when Iraq's attack of Kuwait was a clear act of aggression. This time, the motivation is shrouded in Kafkaesque confusion. The enemy of the West is al-Qaeda, a widely dispersed religious group based primarily in Saudi Arabia, yet the U.S. wants to attack Iraq, where no al-Qaeda representatives are now known to operate. Because the war has already breached U.S. borders, fuzzy thinking extends deep within the U.S. where the Office of Homeland Security has been established along with new laws that give government unprecedented secret access to massive amounts of private information. All al-Qaeda members are of Middle Eastern origin, yet U.S. airport "screeners" stop and search teenage Caucasian girls and African-American grandmothers in wheelchairs. Vigilantes are offering to police U.S. borders. The chaos has only begun.

Another sign of the bearish influences at work here is the religious conviction that underlies much of the polarization. Already, the Pope has referred to the violence across the world as a "clash of civilizations that at times seems inevitable." This conflict is most pronounced in the Holy Land, where Israel is fighting a "wide and extensive" battle against a suicidal enemy. The more their adversaries bomb, the more power flows to "right-wing nationalist religious parties." The hardline Likuds just won re-election. Even left wing Israelis are losing the "hopes of reconciliation — seemingly so reasonable just a few year ago." "Liberals have come to countenance the wisdom of walls." A "dovish" Israeli historian now says the conflict can be managed but not solved. He calls the idea of separation "a kind of magic medicine" that "reflects desperation." Only the transition to the entirely new thought patterns of a bear market can explain the shift from a desire for reconciliation to the vision of separation as "magic."

March 2003

On a global basis, an expansion of downside leadership has actually been going on for years. In 1995, when *At The Crest of The Tidal Wave* published its call for a "slow motion economic earthquake that will register 11 on the financial Richter scale," Thailand was the first domino to fall. Since then, *The Elliott Wave Theorist* and *The Elliott Wave Financial Forecast* have anticipated virtually every step of the contagion's westward advance, into the rest of Asia in 1996-98, up through South America in 2002 and over to Europe at the end of last year. The Europe index (see chart next page) confirmed our extremely bearish count by being one of the first major averages to break the lows of 2002. As Europe raced back to new lows, the European Central Bank revealed that the European economy was unlikely to recover at all in 2003. The pattern portends even greater selling pressure ahead. Europe's economic fall puts the still-unfolding depression on the same path it took in 1929-1930, when the problems were seen as a European import.

EUROPE LEADS THE WAY LOWER
S&P Europe Index
Daily

© February 2003 Elliott Wave International

April 2003

The primary factor hinting that the Iraqi conflict will turn into a much bigger problem than the last Persian Gulf War is that this war has started in the midst of a bear market. In 1991, the bull market was off and running again when the U.S. got involved. Besides the wave count, the biggest reason to suspect that the bear market is in place is the air of confidence surrounding this most destructive and uncertain human endeavor. As U.S. engagement approached in January 1991, investors were far less confident. In fact, leading up to that time, the Investors Intelligence survey of advisory sentiment registered more bears than bulls for 26 straight weeks (www.chartcraft.com). This week, bulls outnumber bears for a 23rd straight week!

July 2003

A rash of international agreements, trade pacts and summits echo the global harmony of the Grand Supercycle-degree peak. One that clearly reflected the recent upswing in world stock markets was a reconciliation between the United States, Germany, France and Russia at the latest economic summit. At the stock market lows in March, relations were strained to the breaking point. Near the recent highs, the differences spawned by the war with Iraq were set aside and a series of trade pacts were reached. The underlying shakiness of international relations is evident, however, in the limited scope of the deals. Instead of the sweeping, continent-wide agreements that were signed in the 1990s, most were two-country pacts. The U.S. signed deals with Chile and Singapore; China hooked up with Hong Kong and India, and India made a deal with Egypt. In another subtle twist, some of the deals were more exclusionary than inclusionary. India's agreement with Egypt, for instance, was a "preferential trade pact." Other treaties were downright hostile to open markets. The Trade Pact of Gene-Altered Goods allows countries to bar imports of genetically modified products even if there is not enough information to prove that the products are dangerous.

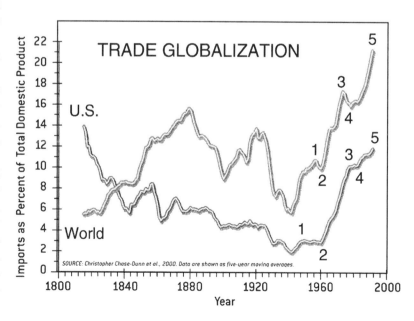

TRADE GLOBALIZATION

Imports as Percent of Total Domestic Product

SOURCE: Christopher Chase-Dunn et al., 2000. Data are shown as five-year moving averages.

Year

Since the 1940s, there has been a five-wave rise in imports as a percent of total domestic product. According to the latest figures from Global Insight, imports accounted for 18.8% of the world's economic activity this year, a decline from 20% in 2000. The Scientific American article that included the chart states, "It is very likely that international trade will continue to expand." This optimistic extrapolation confirms that sentiment is about right for a much greater decline. Our analysis confirms this contrarian view from a former trade negotiator: "All the trade negotiations are in trouble." Back in mid-1998, near the opposite side of the Grand Supercycle degree peak in stocks, *The Elliott Wave Theorist* reported on a "new consensus" in which markets had gained the upper hand. "Almost everywhere, even the liberals are much like traditional moderate conservative parties." EWT applauded the triumph but added, "As social scientists, we know what the implications of the celebration are: that trend is ending. This trend and that of the stock market are likely on parallel paths."

The New York Times reports that our reversal forecast is now appearing in subtle but profound ways. For one thing, it's the wealthy nations that are digging in their heels. "At times, they have even erected new barriers." Exporters to the U.S. are seething over new American farm subsidies. Cambodia's commerce secretary says, "Everything is dividing." Added the former head of Argentina's central bank, "Everyone is questioning globalization." Globalization, universally regarded as good and proper in 1998, is today the focus of intense public opposition. The anger against it is so strong that trade meetings have to be held in obscure hamlets that can be sealed off from the outside world. This is an apt metaphor for the prospects of these negotiations and a clear signal that the bear market is far from over. If it had ended last October, the anger would at least be subsiding.

In related turmoil, a sign of a renewed decline has flashed with the outbreak of a "new cycle of violence" in the Mideast. For the first time since the all-time highs, a lull in the fighting occurred in May as the Dow [rose] toward 9000. Suicide bombings and retaliatory Israeli strikes were halted as a U.S. "road map" for peace was discussed. In another fleeting throwback to the promise of the 1990s, the plan was accepted by Palestinian and Israeli prime ministers on June 4, the day of the peak in the Dow Transports. On June 6, the day of a key reversal from a multi-month peak in the NASDAQ 100, however, Hamas, the armed Palestinian Islamic group, broke off talks. Two days later, attacks were underway once again.

December 2003

The mini-euphoria surrounding the secondary peak in stocks has inspired the Bush administration to repeal the March 2002 steel tariffs, but the writing is on the wall for the rest of the bear market. Now that the U.S. has shut out foreign competition in the steel industry, other nations have been given the go-ahead to respond with similar barriers. As the next leg down picks up speed, the skirmishes reflected in these headlines (see next page) will give way to more serious confrontations. Widespread economic deterioration will be pinned on this escalating tension. Don't believe it for a second. The emerging trade war didn't cause the decline. It is a result of a bear market in social mood; one that fits perfectly with the experience of 1930 and was fully anticipated in EWI's long-term forecast. Since the unfolding bear market is the biggest in more than 200 years, the anti-trade actions taken over the next few years will be the most sweeping in the history of the U.S. As protectionism grows, some will actually cheer its onset as more rational voices wonder, "How can this be happening?" The answer is that bear markets are breeding grounds for fear and stupidity, and nothing brings these traits to the fore like a good tit-for-tat trade war.

Dimming Hopes for Free Trade
—The Washington Post, Nov. 23, 2003

Alan Greenspan warned yesterday that "creeping protectionism" threatens the world economy
— *Knight Ridder* Nov. 21, 2003

U.S. to Impose Duties on China TV Sets

The U.S. Commerce Department has accused Chinese manufacturers of selling color television sets at below market value in the United States and will levy duties of as much as 46 percent on color TV imports. — *CBS MarketWatch* Nov. 24, 2003

China Adds Threat to U.S. Trade Tensions
— L.A. TIMES, Nov. 21, 2003

Tax Break Row With EU
—*Dow Jones*, Nov. 24, 2003

On the Verge of a Trade War?
— Business Week, Nov. 24, 2003

EU Promises Retaliation
—The Wall Street Journal, Nov. 11, 2003

SPARKS FLY OVER STEEL; TRADE WARS
THE ECONOMIST NOV. 15, 2003

Bush Urges American Firms to Pull Out of Britain

George Bush's administration has called on US companies in Britain to relocate jobs to America in an astonishing move that could trigger a major trade war. —*Knight Ridder*, Nov. 17, 2003

March 2004

A USA Today survey found that enthusiasm for free trade among high-income Americans has dropped dramatically since the last year of the bull market. According to the poll, the percentage of households with income of $100,000 or more in favor of actively pursuing free trade has fallen in half, from 57% in 1999 to 28% in 2004. Suddenly, "there's a lot of emotion in the debate over the off-shoring of U.S. jobs." The fear has produced a rush of protectionism in the form of legislative bills that prohibit state and federal governments from subcontracting jobs to foreign countries. But what about the countermeasures trading partners will take and the inefficient business practices these new laws will undoubtedly engender? *At the Crest of the Tidal Wave* revealed that, in a bear market, protectionist measures become popular "regardless of the fact that virtually everyone knows they are dangerous and wrong because they are a consequence of an increasingly negative psychology."

August 2004

By late June, the potential for a cascading financial calamity was readily apparent in an emerging Russian credit squeeze. Even more revealing were the assurances that there "was no cause for panic." When the lines started to form outside Russian banks, the headlines put out an urgent call for "Calm." "The current crisis has an artificial ring to it," said a Russian newspaper on June 28. "Banks have money, but they have stopped sharing it." In a sudden flash of recognition, the chairman of Russia's central bank insisted, "The current problems are only psychological."

551

But he went on to say, "There is no crisis." We agree with his first sentence but not the second; psychology is the *reason* for crises.

Russia is experiencing serious financial spasms. Its problems are compounded by its long history of anti-capitalist activity, which puts it on the leading edge of the backlash against the beneficiaries of the old bull market. Jailed Yukos Oil founder Mikhail Khodorkovsky is the Russian equivalent of Martha Stewart, except that he probably is innocent. Still, his own lawyer says he has no hope of a successful trial. This is clearly another symptom of the global "eat the rich" syndrome discussed in past issues. As the bear market in social mood intensifies, it will spread a lot further.

December 2004

In Europe, the seriousness of divisive social forces that are now emerging broke into the open when the murder of film maker Theo van Gogh by Muslim radicals sparked a wave of "tit for tat violence" in the Netherlands. The traditionally tolerant society is experiencing a "growing trend towards fanaticism." Opinion polls show that most Dutch people "feel threatened by the presence of foreigners, especially fundamental Muslims, who oppose the openness of Western society." "The Muslim community has lived side-by-side with the Dutch for years." Some say the problem can be contained within Holland, but the racist taunts at soccer games in Spain and England suggest that the European Justice Commissioner is right when he contends that it can happen anywhere in the EU. In fact, it probably will. By the time the bear market is over, the EU country that doesn't experience violence against immigrants and minorities will probably be the exception.

March 2005
A Grand Supercycle at Twilight

As the Dow Industrials, the single-best meter of social mood, pushes to a new high for its bear market rally, the social scene is experiencing a quick burst of the global goodwill and harmony that ruled back in the 1990s. Once again, the aura of a positive mood peak is in the air as formerly combative country leaders have exchanged handshakes (Bush and various European leaders), enacted a major global treaty (Kyoto) and engineered a democratic election in a former totalitarian stronghold (Iraq). Remember the remarkable cessation of hostilities that took place between Israel and the PLO in the 1990s? The peace ended, on que, with the bull market in 2000 and intensified throughout the bear market decline. But the four-year high in social mood, as measured by the Dow Industrials, has now produced a "formal end to more than four years of fighting." Back in 2003, English writer Christopher Wilson said the royal family was waiting for the "right moment" to announce a wedding between Prince Charles and his former mistress. "They're waiting to spring it on the public," he said in a BBC documentary. "When the wind is in the right direction, everybody's feeling good. That's the moment [it] will come out." Word of the marriage came February 10.

It's clearly only a countertrend peak, as all of these events floated above a witches brew of global disparagement and hostility. In Britain, for instance, the locals just aren't taking to the royal wedding the way they did to Prince Charles' first wedding at the start of the bull market in 1981. As one reviewer noted, "Camilla is no Diana-alike and Charles is a dork. The magic is gone." Even the queen, Charles' mother, will not attend the ceremony. Despite the truce in Israel and Iraq's elections, bombings in both places continue. Unlike the unified global trade pacts and summits of the 1990s, the Kyoto global warming treaty actually creates tension instead of alleviating it: "This is Australia and the United States against the rest of the world." Bush and European leaders were all smiles as the president completed a fence-mending trip through Europe, but once he departed, big-time friction surfaced. For the first time, signs of a potential split in the 50-year alliance between the U.S. and all of Europe appeared when George Bush refused to negotiate with Iran regarding its nuclear capabilities and the U.S. house voted 411-2 to warn the EU that it must not lift its arms embargo with China. As one political observer noted, "Imagine a world where Russia and the European Union, and Russia and China, and the EU and China, all find more in common with each other than with the United States. The seeds of such an anti-U.S. entente were planted in Europe last week." In the downtrend in social mood, these seeds will surely sprout into serious conflict.

May 2005
Global Wrap

After a half century of reconciliation and cooperation, for instance, Europe is suddenly battling xenophobic and racist demons. As it now stands, polls suggest that France will reject the European Union's constitution in the upcoming May vote. When the EU was formed in 1999, *The Wave Principle of Human Social Behavior* stated that its consummation "following 1500 years of repeated conflict" was "consistent with the Elliott wave case that an uptrend of Grand Supercycle degree is ending." Some contend that the no vote will mean the "fall of Europe." Others say Europe will be left "divided, confused and unable to proceed for a time." Socionomics says it doesn't matter how the French vote, the atmosphere of peace and harmony is over for quite a while. During the bear market, the independent nations of Europe will rediscover their borders and rekindle the animosities that kept them apart for centuries. This burgeoning instability is precisely why EWI did not include the euro in the Stable Currency Benchmark. As we say on our web page (stablecurrencybenchmark.com), "The euro is a currency managed by a group of trading partners who have been historically distinct if not involved in warring with each other."

Another Grand Supercycle turning point cited by EWFF in 2000 is the signing of a U.S. trade deal with Communist China. When the U.S. Senate voted to "permanently normalize" trade ties with China in September 2000, EWFF weighed in with this bearish assessment: "This vote is the bull market counterpoint to the communist takeover of China at the bottom in 1949, which marked the end of the last Supercycle degree bear market in inflation-adjusted terms." The chart shows the performance of China's main stock index since. After two stabs to slightly higher highs in 2001, Chinese shares joined the global bear market and are now down 49%. In recent weeks, Chinese stocks plunged to a new bear market low. Even as they did, the media continues to drone on about China's global leadership. Yes, China is leading the way, but so far, there is virtually no mention of the direction that it is taking the rest of the world, which is down. Here's a headline that sets the new tone: "In China, Sinking Stocks Stir Middle-Class Protest." The Wall Street Journal article says Chinese investors are now lighting themselves on fire and blowing themselves up to protest large stock market losses.

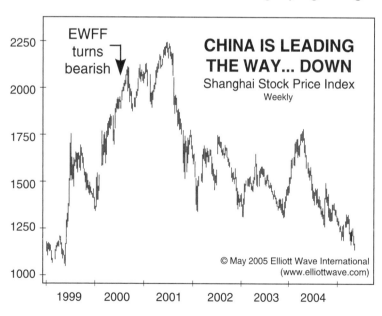

April spawned a spontaneous and continuous stream of anti-Japan protests "all over China." At the root of the outburst is Japan's invasion of China 3/4 of a century ago. It took place in 1937. After five decades of peace between the two nations, many are baffled about the timing of China's rage. "I have little clue as to why now," said Japan's trade minister. But socionomics explains why: bear markets bring anger and nationalism. They also tend to awaken the mass emotions and trends that were in place at similar-degree declines. China's anti-Japan movement is a reaction against its outside oppressors at the last Supercycle-degree low. In Russia, deep-seated authoritarian impulses are resurfacing; the National Bolsheviks are once again a functioning party. Half the population says Stalin played a "positive role in the country's history." These longings, at the outset of the decline, are just a glimpse of a much more bearish tone that will emerge as Grand Supercycle wave Ⓘⓥ progresses.

July 2005
A Bearish Tradewind Blows In

Read this excerpt from *Conquer the Crash*:

Bear markets engender trade protectionism. When fear makes people defensive, they often act on impulse, without full regard to reason. Protectionism is correctly recognized among economists of all stripes as destructive, yet there is always a call for it when people's mental state changes to a defensive psychology. Voting blocs, whether corporate, union or regional, demand import tariffs and bans, and politicians provide them in order to get re-elected. If one country does not adopt protectionism, its trading partners will. Either way, the inevitable dampening effect on trade is inescapable.

The U.S.-Sino trade relationship is suddenly crumbling. In addition to the clear parallel to Smoot-Hawley in July 1930, when the end of another important second wave rally ushered in the Great Depression, the emerging trade tension is accompanied by a misplaced sense of confidence that a trade war can't happen just because it is "rash," "unreasonable" and downright "insane." In addressing the textile trade dispute between China and the U.S., for instance, one expert noted, "If the trade dispute on textiles deteriorates further, the global trade system could be hurt." He therefore predicted that concerned parties would "compromise by taking a step back." But the irrationality at the center of the unfolding conflict is precisely the bear market result that *Conquer the Crash* anticipated.

The bipartisan Schumer-Graham China Free Trade bill would slap a 27.5% tariff on Chinese goods. Early this week, when 67 of 100 U.S. senators supported the measure, pundits quickly discounted its chances. "It'll never pass the House," said one. On Thursday, Senators Schumer and Graham decided to temporarily shelve their bill when China revealed that it is likely to make its exchange rate more flexible, perhaps within two months. The agreement, if it comes to fruition, will probably be the focus of much celebrating, but the resulting euphoria will be an echo of September 2000 when the U.S. senate voted to permanently recognize trade ties with China.

There's a big difference between this latest "trade deal" and those of the all-time highs. A new tone governs the debate, and it's clearly away from the laissez-faire trend of the last half century. It's the will of the people, and the politicians will find a way to express it. "Lawmakers from both parties had stockpiled bills to punish China," notes one article. China is actually forcing the issue with bids to buy Unocal and Maytag. Both bids are from companies that are owned by the Chinese government. The former head of the CIA, James Woolsey, calls the effort a "conscious long-term effort to take over . . . as much of the American economy as possible." (What else, we would like to know, is China suppose to do with its billions of dollars worth of paper "assets" in its banking system?) The media are already framing these events as a primary cause of the recent brief stock market swoon, saying stocks fell because Wall Street smelled the "prelude to a trade war, and it doesn't like what it sees." But remember, the above quote and others like it in EWFF, EWT, *At the Crest of the Tidal Wave* and scores of media interviews that we have done in the late 1990s when protectionism was a 1930s relic.

September 2005
Foreign Markets Join In

Many foreign stock markets pushed on after the recent tops in the major U.S. averages. "We're seeing a healthy diversification toward overseas markets," a portfolio manager explained in USA Today. "Americans have ignored (foreign markets) for too long." The same issue proclaims,

"Emerging Markets On Rise." As *The Elliott Wave Financial Forecast* pointed out in September 2000, foreigners always commit funds when major trends are about to reverse.

February 2006
Putting the Il Back in Illegal Aliens

Another manifestation of a bear market is the attitude toward immigration. First, recall what *The Elliott Wave Theorist* said on the subject in October 2003: "The U.S. will increase restrictions on immigration." Last month, over two years after our forecast, the U.S. House of Representatives passed the "toughest immigration legislation in more than a decade." The bill includes "provisions that once seemed unthinkable to many lawmakers, like the construction of five fences across 698 miles of the United States border with Mexico." As EWT has noted, in bear markets, "people build walls and fences to shut out those perceived to be different." Tom Tancredo, the Colorado congressman behind the fence idea (he also wants to add one along the border with Canada), marvels at his sudden move into the mainstream. "I would have said to you a month ago or so, 'Yeah, it's definitely the case that I am a pariah.' But it has changed. I'm respected. It leaves me speechless." It was only last summer that Business Week's cover story on "Embracing Illegals" stated that companies "are getting hooked on the buying power of 11 million undocumented immigrants." "Let's be real: the U.S. is not about to arrest and herd millions of men, women and children into boxcars for transport back across the Rio Grande," said an editorial in the same issue. "That's a nativist's fantasy that will never come to pass." But we caution such editorialists that in a major bear market, nativist and other fantasies of exclusion typically become stark reality. And the brunt of this bear market is still to come.

March 2006

As in 2000, stock investment today is by no means an even flow across various sectors of the market; the majority of the money is funneling into one relatively risky area. In 2000 that area was technology; this time it's foreign stock markets. According to ICI, 75% of the mutual fund flows went into international funds. A good example of the focal point is AIM Investments Developing Markets fund. The gross weekly sales of this fund, which invests in countries such as Russia, Brazil and Egypt, was up 500% from a year earlier. The recent surge in interest only strengthens EWFF's call for a surprising plunge in foreign shares. The faster investors plunge into foreign markets, the more sure we are that they will soon want out. So we'll stick by our call for a selling contagion.

Cultural Trends

Back in the 1990s, news channels and network news shows suffered through a slow news phase that got so pronounced some feared that the well of hard news was drying up. Late in the 1990s when columnists actually started to complain, EWT said just wait a while, "The bear market, when it arrives, will (unfortunately) reinvigorate the news game." With a deluge of racial hostilities, exploding shrines, cartoon riots and geopolitical rifts, we can declare that the reinvigoration is underway. It's definitely the news boom EWT was looking for, because it bears a striking resemblance to the bear market blueprint presented in *At the Crest of the Tidal Wave*. Here's what the book said to look for once the negative social mood wore away the peace and political cooperation that was left over from the old bull market:

> Conflict during the bear market will be far greater than it was during the bull market and will lead to periods of turmoil in society. The coming trend of negative social psychology will be characterized primarily by polarization between and among various perceived groups, whether political, ideological, religious, geographical, racial or economic. The result will be a net trend toward anger, fear, intolerance, disagreement and exclusion. Such a sentiment change typically brings conflict in many forms, and evidence of it will be visible in all types of social organizations. Political manifestations will include a polarized and vocal electorate, separatist movements, xenophobia, the

dissolution of old alliances and parties, and the emergence of radical new ones. Xenophobia will be practiced regardless of people's generally good intentions, because fear and hatred become pervasive in major bear markets regardless of whether or not they are justified.

The book concluded that the "worst economic and social problems are years away," but their time is approaching. The cracks in the global community are widening so fast that the same author who wrote on the strictly positive impact of "globalization" in 1999 now writes on the "Spread of Global Fissures," saying, "The world is drifting dangerously toward a widespread, religious and sectarian cleavage, the likes of which we have not seen for a long, long time." Where there was once the promise of an ever-growing interconnectedness, some now perceive a threat that the world will "go Dark Ages" and be ruled by "pitchfork wielding xenophobes." A survey of headlines from around the world over just the last few days turns up one bear market manifestation after another. A summary of some of the items and their socionomic significance follows:

- **In Africa:** Maiduguri, Nigeria is a city that "had never witnessed any major religious crisis" until February 18-19. According to a Nigerian newspaper called The Vanguard, it was then that Muslim fanatics incensed by the publishing of images of Mohammed in a Danish editorial cartoon "wreaked havoc on churches and other business premises owned by Christians." More than 70 people were killed. Vanguard's portrayal of the carnage certainly fits ATC's "turmoil" forecast. The newspaper describes a "mindless orgy of violence" in which "traders' shops and goods went up in flames before their eyes. Their business life has once again reverted to the toddler stage." One survivor insisted that the dead got the better end of the deal because those "who are living yet do not have a source of livelihood. 'All I have ever owned went up in flames before my eyes and rather than salvage them, I had to run for my life. I am back to square one for no fault of mine.'"

- **In Iraq:** *The Wave Principle of Human Social Behavior* describes a bull market as a period of relatively practical thinking in which reason is relatively more highly valued, while bear markets bring attacks on reason and greater reverence for religion. Another recent sign of faith's victory over logic was the bombing of the Golden Mosque in Samarra. The resulting violence between Shiite and Sunni Muslims "has convulsed the nation and raised fears of civil war." Ismael Zayer, editor in chief of Al Sabah al Jadid, a daily newspaper, said, "People are marching by order of clerics and stopping by order of clerics."

- **In Iran:** President Mahmoud Ahmadinejad believes Israel should be wiped off the map, denies that the Holocaust took place and rules his country with an eye toward Armageddon in the not-too-distant future. In recent weeks, he kicked out U.N. inspectors and said Iran will go ahead with its nuclear development plans. A newly-adopted policy shift by the United States will try "not just to contain Tehran's nuclear ambitions but also to topple the Iranian government." But the L.A. Times points out, "Iran's current regime enjoys considerable popularity," not in spite of Ahmadinejad's deeply bearish diatribes toward Israel and the United States but because of them.

- **In Israel:** With the Hamas landslide victory in the Palestinian parliamentary election, Israel's situation in the Gaza strip went from unstable to virtually unmanageable. It's primary response is to cut off funding to what is essentially a welfare state, but this may not be a feasible course of action. If they try to starve Hamas, Iran has promised to step in with support that will increase its influence in the region. The Israelis may be forced to deal with a government that is responsible for many suicide bombings and does not believe in their right to exist. The tension will rise just as it has at the outset of every major stock market decline of the last 100 years (see "Mideast Hostilities Erupt Near Important Peaks" chart, June 2001 entry).

- **In Turkey:** Even former friends are turning hostile. The Washington Post says a "pop culture war is raging between the United States and Turkey." In a new movie, Valley of the Wolves, U.S. soldiers shoot small children at point blank range, blow up Muslim clerics and "to top it all off, display utter contempt for Turkish foreign policy." The villain is a U.S. Army commander who declares, "I am the son of God." The movie, says a prominent Turkish commentator, plays on the "inner feelings, unsatisfied feelings of Turkish public opinion." The film is a smash hit. After opening February 3, it set a box office record.

- **In France:** The rising influence of religion is evident even on the catwalks of Paris. The hood shown here is representative of a "change of mood" that some designers are privately referring to as the "Muslimization of fashion." The fall lines display a marked acceleration in the body "cover-up" that EWFF talked about as "inevitable" in the July 2005 and December 2004 issues. "The mood is now for a chaste sobriety, with sturdy fabrics, thick leggings and even ankle-length hemlines." EWT's first major pop culture report in 1985 stated, "Hemlines and stock prices appear to be in lock step." The balance of the evidence suggests that stocks will fall in line with hemlines.

- **In the United States:** Last month EWFF covered the anti-immigration wave that is suddenly embedding itself into the American political landscape. In an era of intensifying political polarization, the move to enforce immigration laws and seal off U.S. borders is the one area where the far right and left are actually coming together. A similarly radical bearish alliance is evident in hawkish responses to Iran by liberals and conservatives alike. In USA Today's "Common Ground" column, a liberal Democratic strategist and a conservative columnist agreed: "If in the next nine months or so, Iran continues to develop nuclear weapons, we must attack." And that's the liberal talking. Asked if that will inflame anti-American hatred in the Muslim world, he answers, "Of course, but frankly, so what?"

Just as the will to attack Iraq unified U.S. politicians in 2003, a unifying force today among U.S. politicians is a shared fear of foreigners. This reality is also clear from the bipartisan uproar that erupted when the U.S. administration approved a Middle Eastern company's purchase of port management rights. As one political contributor noted, the episode "demonstrates how steeped American politicians are in Arabophobia. The default attitude of this country toward the Muslim world is suspicious and hostile." The drive to reverse the port decision is a perfect example of the "misguided attempts at self-defense" that *At The Crest* cites as a typical bear market response. It has to be "a consequence of an increasingly negative psychology" because during the preceding 25 years when social mood was rising, foreign firms acquired the same rights at 80% of U.S. ports and nobody said a thing about it.

- **At the U.N.:** With the corruption surrounding its oil-for-food program in Iraq and its apparent powerlessness against disease and ethnic fighting in parts of Africa, the U.N.'s lack of effectiveness is becoming an issue. These failures are minor to what's coming.

- **At the Olympics:** Even as the Dow clings to the 11,000 mark the fading of the Olympic spirit is visible. A Wall Street Journal commentary on "Why [the Olympics] Should Come to an End" offered the following as a "proposal to increase harmony and goodwill among nations. Cancel the Olympics forever." As the major averages catch up to this sentiment, it will get very serious consideration.

August 2006

The July 2005 issue of *The Elliott Wave Financial Forecast* argued that "A new tone governs the [free trade] debate, and it's clearly away from the laissez-faire trend of the last half century. It's the will of the people, and the politicians will find a way to express it." On July 25, the five-year push to complete a new global trade pact collapsed. This is an economic expression of "the sudden wave of violence" covered in the latest issue of *The Elliott Wave Theorist*. Realize that it was intransigence on the part of the supposedly "developed" world, namely the U.S. and Europe, that stalled the process. Reason cannot stand against the reactionary force of a bear market. The primitive brain stem is in control.

September 2006

To The Ends of the Earth

Another remnant of the old mania fever is visible in a burst to new highs by a cluster of small African stocks and bonds. The Nigeria Stock Exchange Index, for example, surged over 50% to a new all-time high from April to early August. "Sudden interest in emerging markets such as Zambia is indicative of the constant search for high yield and a willingness to go far to get it," reports the Financial Times. This willingness persists despite steep losses of up to 50% and 60% in markets on distant shores in recent months. Business Week, which has a stellar track record of capping rallies with positive features, recently put out this "Emerging Giants" cover story discussing why Brazil, Russia, India, China "and even Egypt" may soon rule the business world. No matter how troubled the world seems to get, a raft of other headlines suggest that investors cannot be swayed from their affection for foreign shares. In the Middle East, for example, where markets in Lebanon, Jordan, Qatar, UAE and Saudi Arabia are down from 30%-60% (with oil still hovering around $70, we might add), Bloomberg reports: "Mideast Stocks and Currencies 'Shrug off' Violence." In China, "Bank Fraud Fails to Damp Investor Frenzy for Share Sales." "Traders Unfazed by Gathering Terror," says the New York Post. Explains one investment strategist, "Western investors want to be at the party."

October 2006

An analyst with Fitch Ratings warns, "Credit growth has been zooming across the whole of Eastern Europe, and that has tended to be a precursor to banking troubles." Fifteen different economies are above the 15% annual "speed limit" that generally precipitates credit woes. In Lithuania, Estonia, Ukraine and Kazakhstan, year-over-year credit growth ranges from 41% to 50%. Still, Reuters reports, "Global investors are better able to cope with sudden surprises. This time they reckon things are different and lessons have been learned. The risk of contagion is seen as small."

November 2006

> Sobering military developments in Vietnam and continued tension in North Korea last week failed to affect the stock market in the slightest degree.
> —The Trader column, Barron's, February 26, 1968

The higher stocks extend, the more intense the social divergence becomes. The quote above shows just how precisely the Dow Jones Industrial Average's bullet-proof veneer to war in Iraq and tension with North Korea resembles the social disorder that ruled as the index carried to another B-wave peak in 1968. As *The Elliott Wave Theorist*'s November Special Report notes, the war in Iraq fits with a high degree B-wave like that of 1968, when a countertrend rally within a major bear market accompanied the war in Vietnam. President Bush recently verified the tightness of the correlation when he compared a worsening tone in Iraq to the 1968 Tet Offensive, which is "often seen as a turning point in the Vietnam War." Like 1968, The Washington Post says October 2006 has the look of a "tipping point" when civilian and U.S. casualties shook "both the military command in Iraq and the political establishment in Washington."

Recent tension with North Korea also follows the pattern of a geopolitical standoff in 1968. In that year, the Dow stormed higher even as North Korea "shocked the world" by seizing the USS Pueblo, a U.S. spy ship, off its shores. The impasse ended in December 1968, the month that the Dow Industrial Average hit its B-wave peak. With its first-ever nuclear test, North Korea shocked the world again on October 9. After a period of heightened tension—one North Korean general even stated that war was inevitable—the most recent highs brought some thawing. On October 31, North Korea agreed to rejoin nuclear disarmament talks. As troop deployments along both sides of Korea "demilitarized zone" attest, tension is basically a fixture of North Korea's foreign relations, but it does tend to wane right at important peaks. Notice that the peaks of 1994, 1998 and especially the larger peak of 2000 were accompanied by agreements or "near breakthroughs."

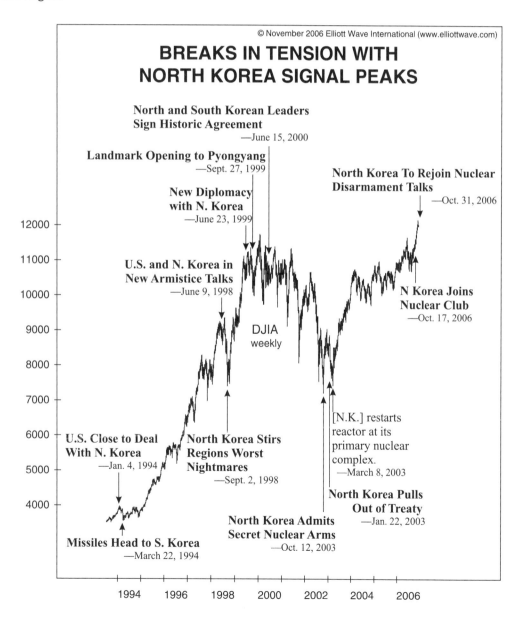

The bear market corollary is that the conflict is greatest near major lows. Following the Korean War in the early 1950s, which came near the end of a Supercycle bear market pattern in the inflation-adjusted Dow, one of the most contentious periods was 2002. After Bush identified North Korea as a member of the "Axis of Evil," North Korea marked the lows of October 2002 and March 2003 by admitting to processing highly enriched uranium for use in atomic bombs, expelled nuclear inspectors, pulled out of the nuclear non-proliferation agreement and fired missiles within 200 miles of Japan. As long as the Dow continues to rally, the conciliations of recent days will persist, but the resumption of the bear market will ultimately bring a return to more serious conflict. The larger degree of the current peak is confirmed by the nuclear stakes. North Korea may not push the button, but its acquisition of nuclear weapons has certainly gotten the attention of its non-nuclear neighbors and aspiring despots everywhere. The October bomb test is the first since 1998, the front end of the great peaking process. It may go down as the spark that ignited a new nuclear arms race.

December 2006

The Japanese Model Points Lower

Back in January 2000, EWFF pointed out the "remarkable similarity" between the NASDAQ 100 of 1999 and the Japanese Nikkei of 1989. Noting that the Nikkei subsequently fell 65%, EWFF stated, "Such analogies rarely work to perfection, but given the striking replication of a year-long trading pattern, this one bears watching." The NASDAQ eventually fell 78%. In recent months, *The Elliott Wave Financial Forecast* has shown some of the ways in which U.S. stocks continue to take their cue from the Japanese experience. In addition to facing the same deflationary pressures, the U.S. is now borrowing from Japan everything from a proposed reduction in margin requirements to the popularity of platform shoes (see October 2006 in Chapter 3 and May 2001 entry in this chapter). Once again, the Nikkei appears to be blazing the trail to much lower levels. After peaking ahead of most other major global stock markets on April 7, the Nikkei registered a countertrend rally high on June 14. The index is poised for the start of a powerful decline.

April 2007

Through February, the unprecedented liquidity-fueled flight to the riskiest possible financial assets pushed emerging markets to all-time highs, but the potential for a much more sustained collapse is embodied by record amounts of mutual fund cash pouring into the sector and the widely-held belief that emerging markets are a vital part of the average investor's portfolio. "Don't be scared to make emerging markets a permanent part of your diversified portfolio," says a February issue of a national news magazine. The depth of investors' faith in these traditionally volatile shares is captured by the premium on emerging market bonds. According to JPMorgan's EMBI+ Index, spreads between U.S. Treasuries and emerging market issues hit a record low of 164 basis points in February. "Emerging markets are in a much healthier financial position than they have ever been," says the manager of an emerging market fund.

As we explained with respect to runs on Vietnamese and Chinese shares in last month's issue (Chapter 1), a mania always progresses down through less sophisticated investment classes, and few of the current long-running mania tactics are as unrefined and captivating as B-R-I-C, an acronym/rallying cry for investment in Brazil, Russia, India and China. Talk about simplistic; the expression itself is said to be responsible for profits. Says the Asia Times, "The coining of BRIC was a boon for the emerging markets. The snappy acronym summed up the macroeconomic forces that were reshaping the planet. The acronym sparked myriad new investment funds and trading strategies, boosting capital flows into the emerging markets and trading commissions for investment banks."

Australia has the right look too, but ABRIC is not so catchy. It may be appropriate, however, as the prefix "a" means "not" and these markets should head in the opposite direction of their 2002-2007 rally. In fact, the full retracement principle for manias suggests that these gains will ultimately be erased. BRIC, in other words, will very likely become bric-a-brac.

August 2007

A [key] indicator is foreigners buying U.S. stocks. This chart of the Dow and foreigners' net purchases of U.S. equities shows how the correlation held for U.S. shares through the bull market of the 1990s. After briefly fleeing the U.S. market in a record net selling month last December, foreigners jumped into the U.S. market like never before in May. The new record was a full third higher than the old one, which was set in February 2000, one month after the Dow Industrials' 2000 peak and one month before the NASDAQ's all-time high. The first

five months of the year produced what was easily the biggest gusher of net foreign buying in history. The record suggests that falling prices lie directly ahead for the U.S. market. The same goes for most foreign markets as global mutual fund sales reveal that the portfolios of U.S. investors are stuffed to the gills with stocks from far off places. Notes Prechter, "No crowd buys stocks of other countries intelligently."

November 2007

Social Portents of Extreme Behavior in the Resurging Russian Bear
(by Alan Hall)

Investors' infatuation with Russia during the two rising waves in the RTSI (1995-1997 and 1999-2007, shown on chart) accompanied financial manias in the U.S. and Europe. This was Russia's first taste of a roaring stock market, and the excitement is still palpable today.

As EWI has noted, in the late stages of a bull run, extrapolation of the recent uptrend becomes so intuitive and popular that non-professionals—including Playboy playmates, media commentators and politicians—become experts on the stock market. Putin recently offered his first short-term analysis at a government meeting on August 22: "For us, it wasn't such a critical fall, but more like a correction with regard to the previous unprecedented growth...." When the call for more bull market is easy and natural, the market is usually near a top.

Below is a chart of the Russian Trading System Index from its inception. Our Elliott wave count in the RTSI shows that a clear five-wave advance beginning in 1999 is near completion. During this time, the RTSI increased by sixty-fold. This index should soon begin its biggest bear market since the five-wave pattern began. The minimum probable drop—a move into the area of the fourth wave of 2004—would more than halve the value of the index.

Such a decline should produce financial and social events of a character comparable to those seen during comparable declines in the past. Viewed in the context of Russian history, this outlook has serious geostrategic implications.

February 2008

One more sign of a top in place is a Newsweek cover story, which ostensibly warns of burgeoning recession in the U.S. But the article quickly redirects readers to an ongoing bull market in places like India and China. The story announces a "new economic order" in which emerging markets "de-couple" from a U.S. downturn and continue rising on their own. "What decoupling means is this: even as the globe's economic engine, the United States, has stalled, optimists believe that the train cars it has been pulling for the last several decades may finally be able to chug along under their own power." The April 2007 issue of EWFF made a case for the opposite result, noting that JP Morgan's EMBI Plus Sovereign Index of spreads between U.S. Treasuries and emerging market issues had just hit a record low. After trading slightly lower through May of last year, this index is anything but bullish for emerging markets. In fact, the chart shows the spread rising fast. As the bear market intensifies, it should easily surpass the "crisis" levels of September 2001, when a 10 percentage point difference separated the yield between U.S. Treasuries and emerging market debt. Many emerging-market indexes will likely plunge even more dramatically than the U.S. stock market.

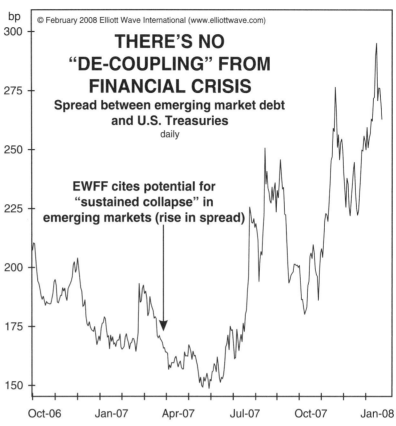

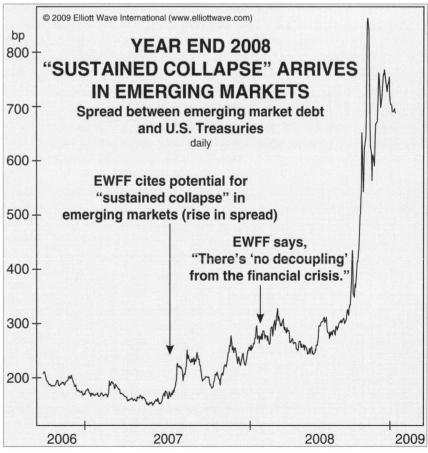

May 2008

The General Casts Its Lot

Back in 2000, the first leg of the bear market didn't really sink its teeth in until the fall months. One sure sign of a more serious bear market was a peak in the most venerable Dow stock, General Electric. In November 2000, EWFF showed this long-term picture of an exquisite Fibonacci rise in "the only original member of the Dow Jones Industrial Average," and stated, "GE is going to go way down." The chart at right shows the 65% decline that followed over the next 28 months. It also shows a corrective rally that had retraced 50% of the decline before an October 2, 2007 peak, which should be the end of GE's b-wave advance. A c-wave decline should take GE well below its February 2003 low of $21.30, so another even more serious plunge has probably begun.

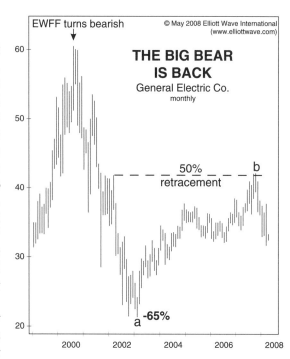

Once again, the weakness in GE probably heralds stormy weather ahead for the market as a whole; or should we say, "hole"? GE gapped over 11% lower on April 11 after it fell short of its own earnings estimates. The fall was attributed to its exposure to the financial sector, which is certainly substantial. But GE is also broadly diversified globally, and we suspect that the sell-off resulted at least as much from the first hint of shrinkage in GE's global growth rates. As *Conquer the Crash* says, "Make no mistake about it: It's a global story." And no firm is a better global bellwether than GE. And if the dollar has bottomed, revenues from overseas sales should decline as well.

The worldwide scope of this bear market is confirmed by another sector that EWI pegged as the front edge of the decline back in 2005: housing. Here's the latest update on global home prices from The New York Times: "The collapse of the housing bubble in the United States is mutating into a global phenomenon, with real estate prices down from the Irish countryside and the Spanish coast to Baltic seaports and even in parts of India." In England, confidence in the U.K. housing market slipped to its lowest point in at least 30 years, which a closely watched survey of English appraisers described as "the gloomiest reading since the survey began in 1978." Every bursting bubble announces itself with a flash of public recognition, and here it takes the form of a rash of expert predictions that "some countries, like Ireland, will face an even more wrenching adjustment than the United States, with the possibility that the downturn could turn into wholesale collapse."

There's still evidence of fundamental economic strength outside the U.S. An April 18 story about corporate earnings notes that big U.S. businesses that sell to customers abroad are proving resilient, but Kelvin Davidson, an economist at Capital Economics in London, notes that the boom in house prices was actually much bigger outside the U.S. and, "If anything, people should be more worried than in the U.S." This chart from the International Monetary Fund shows how much more

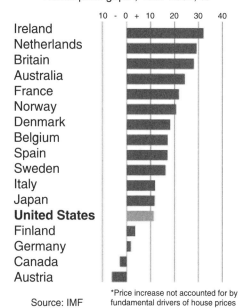

Through the roof

House price gaps*, 1997-2007, %

Ireland
Netherlands
Britain
Australia
France
Norway
Denmark
Belgium
Spain
Sweden
Italy
Japan
United States
Finland
Germany
Canada
Austria

Source: IMF

*Price increase not accounted for by fundamental drivers of house prices

out-of-whack with the fundamentals home prices are in most countries than they are in the U.S. Global business may be holding up, but don't forget that it took more than a year for the Dow Jones Industrial Average to acknowledge the U.S. housing bust with a peak of its own. Global home prices are reversing amidst a slowing global economy and well-developed credit crunch, so the transition to EWFF's "across-the-board decline in financial assets" should happen much faster.

August 2008

Last year, with investors crowding into international mutual funds at a record rate, EWFF said that "falling prices lie directly ahead for most foreign markets as global mutual fund sales reveal that the portfolios of U.S. investors are stuffed to the gills with stocks from far-off places."

That forecast echoed *Conquer the Crash*'s call for a bear market that is global in scope. As of now, the Dow Jones Euro Stoxx Index of 50 EU blue chips is down 23.5%; India's Sensex is off 29%; and China's Shanghai Composite is down a whopping 47%, all compared with a 14.2% decline in the Dow Jones Industrials. But, hey: Wasn't overseas diversification supposedly the antidote to the bear market? Despite greater declines in many foreign markets, the financial media continued to say so, even as recently as a month ago. On June 30, for instance, a financial daily insisted, "The U.S. economy is most at risk." In mid-July, however, the media finally noticed the bear market's global scope. In a typical piece, Der Spiegel, Germany's most popular magazine, spotted an "Economic Tempest" overtaking Europe:

> Spain, Ireland and Denmark are either in a recession or on the brink. Italy is stagnating. France is weakening fast. And Germany, the sturdy locomotive of European growth, is suddenly faltering—dashing most residual hopes that Europe could escape the upheaval in the United States.

Other stories now reveal, "the eurozone is tipping into a deeper downturn than America." The international sales of U.S. multinationals, which were supposed to "fuel growth" a few short months ago, are slumping. The MSCI World Index opened the year with a 15% decline, its worst start since 1970. The global bear market carries the same foundation as the American bear. According to Moody's, "creditworthiness is deteriorating around the world." We even see the same post-mania backlash against former bull market paragons. EWFF has been discussing similar U.S. recriminations in recent issues. In Pakistan, investors stoned the Karachi Stock Exchange when the Pakistani Securities and Exchange commission removed a 1% daily limit on price declines. The head of the Small Investors Association is demanding "that all stock prices be frozen." In Brazil, the 1.5 million strong Landless Workers Movement is seizing offices, railroads and factories. One plant occupation included a gunfight in which two people were killed. Wall Street is responding by "chasing returns" in even more obscure "places like Nigeria and Oman." But the launch of an exchange-traded fund that will invest exclusively in "frontier markets" signals that the worldwide mania for stocks is making a late break for the ends of the earth, where it will undoubtedly perish, probably very rapidly. The Pakistani experience suggests that it will not be a quiet death.

September 2008

On the occasion of Russia's invasion of Georgia, the U.S. Secretary of State said, "This is not 1968 and the invasion of Czechoslovakia, where Russia can invade its neighbor, occupy a capital, overthrow a government and get away with it." She's right, it is 2008. But otherwise the statement is dead wrong. In fact, it is a more serious juncture in a cycle of one higher degree. So it should come as no surprise that the Russian bear is awake and ready to renounce the pacifism that ended the Cold War in the 1990s. In fact, this is precisely what our own Alan Hall said Russia would do in "Social Portents of Extreme Behavior in the Resurging Russian Bear," a socionomic study of Russia that came out in November. Noting that Russia appeared to be making an important top, Hall stated:

This situation bears watching, because it has serious implications for Russia and the rest of the world. ...The ex-Soviet republic [of Georgia] is of strategic interest to both Moscow and Washington because it has energy pipelines that skirt Russia. The U.S. supports Georgia's desire to bring its pro-Russian separatist regions under control, but Russia has military plans to stop any move to secure these regions. ...Russia has the potential to become once again one of the world's great dangers, bringing increased potential for conflict.

The MICEX index of Russian blue chip stocks is down more than 30% from a December 12 peak. Bear markets unleash powerful desires for restriction and control. With Russia's invasion of Georgia, we might even say the trend is moving toward flat-out authoritarianism. Actually we don't have to, the Financial Times just recognized "The New Age of Authoritarianism" on August 12, and the New York Times concurred on August 17 by saying, "It is at least a season. Springtime for autocrats, and not just the minor-league monsters of Zimbabwe and the like, but the giant regimes that seemed so surely bound for the ash heap in 1989."

And it's not just Russia. In Italy, where fascists held power through the last Supercycle degree bear market in the 1930s, "Party Pooper Laws Pile Up." A range of new laws are now in place banning everything from lawn mower use on the weekends to popcorn in movie theaters (its consumption can interfere with the watching of a film). In the U.S., the bans and restrictions are not quite as intrusive yet, despite bans on smoking and trans fats. But just wait. More serious civil rights are coming into play. Congress has allowed the FBI to conduct warrantless investigations beginning this fall. The new guidelines allow the agency to open an investigation of an American, conduct surveillance, pry into private records (online and off) and take other investigative steps "without any basis for suspicion." So it's happening here too. This should not be a surprise since the just completed Grand Supercycle bull market emerged from a bear market that ended with another fight for freedom, the American Revolution.

October 2008

Japan is another window into the future of the U.S. market and economy. Under the headline, "The Japanese Model Points Lower," the December 2006 issue of *The Elliott Wave Financial Forecast* noted that the Nikkei "is poised for the start of a powerful decline." The chart shows how the Nikkei has, in fact, led the way down with a 38% slide from February 2007 through September 18.

More broadly, EWFF noted that U.S. stocks appeared to be ready to "take their cue from the Japanese experience." "With each passing month," one economist notes, "America is looking more and more Japanese." Another says that the latest $700 billion mortgage fund means "the risk of ending up like Japan, with 10 years of stagnation, is now much lessened." We disagree with this latter statement, and Japan illustrates why. Remember when U.S. officials wagged their fingers at Japan and said our central bank was too smart to allow deflation? Ironically,

"Once again, blazing the trail to much lower levels."
—*The Elliott Wave Financial Forecast*

A MODEL DECLINE
Nikkei weekly

Down 38% so far

© October 2008 Elliott Wave International (www.elliottwave.com)

today's frantic U.S. government efforts to "fix" the downtrend is in fact just one more addition to our list of parallels. In August 1992, the Japanese initiated "price keeping operations" under a comprehensive economic package in which it tried to support stock prices by buying from trust banks during market declines. According to Lead Capital, these operations continue to this day in the form of an "estimated 100 trillion yen ($770 billion) national pension fund. The Japanese government has also put new curbs on short selling and allocated new government funds towards the purchase of stocks." Along the way, Japan also goosed the economy with at least 11 different stimulus efforts. Similar to what the U.S. Treasury is attempting to do now, Japan "flooded the economy with cash only to see banks hoard the money." See what we mean about psychology? "The result has been a series of recessions and persistent deflation." After nearly 20 years, the Nikkei is still down nearly 70% from its late 1989 peak of 38,957. U.S. efforts to stop an even more virulent form of the same economic pressure should be no more effective.

Another similarity is the U.S.'s ever-more striking resemblance to Japan's economy. The only reason Japan experienced a series of recessions rather than a depression is that the larger global economy cushioned its contractions. Deflation's tenacity in the face of every official effort to eliminate it is very clear in these headlines since 2003.

At Last an End to Deflation
—Japan Echo, December 2003

Japanese Deflation Seen Coming to End Soon
—The Wall Street Journal, June 2004

Deflation Defeated
—The Financial Times, November 2004

Bank of Japan Sees End to Deflation
—The New York Times, December 2005

Japan Takes Step Toward Declaring End to Deflation
—The Wall Street Journal, July 2006

Japan CPI Suggests End of Deflation Near
—The Financial Times, April 2008

The next series of headlines will announce deflation's return—not just to Japan but to the whole world. When it was solely in Japan, a robust export economy softened deflation's impact. With global economies locked in decline, the Japanese struggle will seem milder by comparison.

The World View

One of the extraordinary properties that made the Great Asset Mania the greatest of all time was its lack of any apparent ideological or geographic limits. This feat and a dramatic re-imposition of limits is shown below by the boom and bust in Vietnamese and Chinese stocks. In March 2007, EWFF forecast the reversal saying, "An investment frenzy within the same Hanoi

EVEN THE
COMMUNISTS
ARE SELLING
weekly

Shanghai Corp. **-70%**

Ho Chi Minh
Stock Index

-69%

© October 2008 Elliott Wave International (www.elliottwave.com)

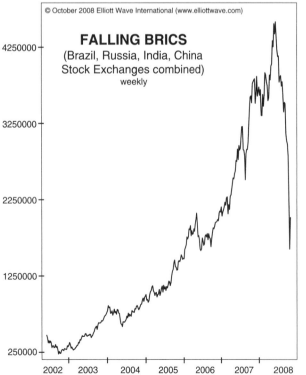

© October 2008 Elliott Wave International (www.elliottwave.com)

FALLING BRICS
(Brazil, Russia, India, China
Stock Exchanges combined)
weekly

populace that was consumed by communism at the lows in the 1970s is signaling the end of the last phase in the Great Asset Mania." Even though both averages have been down as much as 70%, their respective declines are not yet complete.

Another window into the mania's global dominance is the action in BRIC shares. As EWFF explained in April 2007, BRIC is an "acronym/rallying cry" for investment in Brazil, Russia, India and China. Here's EWFF assessment of the approach from that time:

> These markets should head in the opposite direction of their 2002-2007 rally. In fact, the full retracement principle for manias suggests that these gains will ultimately be erased. BRIC, in other words, will very likely become bric-a-brac.

The chart below left shows an index of all four BRIC countries, which topped in May; it's now down 60% in five months. After the BRIC nations topped, a June 16 Wall Street Journal article reported that the passion for fat returns was moving on to "places like Nigeria and Oman. As stocks in the U.S. and other developed markets flounder, financial services firms are creating investment vehicles designed to tap into some of the tiniest—albeit fastest growing—economies in the world." Some of the other "opportunities" covered were in Bangladesh, Bulgaria, Lebanon and Jordan. When July brought the creation of an exchange-traded fund in "frontier markets," EWFF stated that the launch "signals that the worldwide mania for stocks is making a late break for the ends of the earth, where it will undoubtedly perish, probably very rapidly." The Credit Suisse Global Frontier Index is down 50%.

"Make no mistake about it: It's a global story," warned *Conquer the Crash*. The scope of the crisis was largely hidden until very recently. Only a few weeks ago, "America-

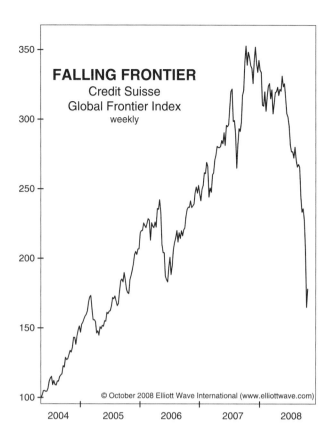

FALLING FRONTIER
Credit Suisse
Global Frontier Index
weekly

© October 2008 Elliott Wave International (www.elliottwave.com)

bashing in some countries" hit levels "not seen since 2003" as turmoil on Wall Street was initially "greeted with a smug chorus of ridicule from nearly every European country." The speed and scope of the downtrend is shown by the latest news from across the Atlantic...

Shockwaves Took Europe by Surprise

When the US authorities allowed Lehman Brothers to fail last month, nobody expected that the decision would trigger a wave of nationalisations, rescues and government interventions across Europe.

A "shockwave" toppled "financial institutions in Iceland, Belgium, Britain and Germany; causing investors and customers to question the stability of even the soundest lender.

—Financial Times,
October 3, 2008

And the Pacific...

US Financial Quake Rocks Asia

For the most part, Asian banks have remained unscathed and economies relatively robust compared with other parts of the world. But tumbling Asian stock markets, marked on Monday by near-panic selling, is signaling just how little confidence there is among bankers and investors that the $700 billion bailout of U.S. banks will end the financial crisis.

—Time, October 7, 2008

Ironically, some bears on U.S. equities had been recommending foreign stock shares. As we have said all along, though, investments per se were at risk, and cash was the place to be. This is the opposite of the "go global" mantra that prevailed less than six months ago. Already it buys a lot more stock than it did then.

Chapter 8

The Dark Side of Financial Euphoria Creeps to the Fore

Sky-high valuations, permissive accounting standards and the ever-more benevolent aura of the bull market spawn a deluge of recrimination befitting a Grand Supercycle reversal. When a 200-year accumulation of arrogance and complacency is displaced by rage and despair, Enron and Martha Stewart's insider trading case signal the wave of the future. Cash reigns supreme. After a respite, the backlash returns. The ultimate bear market consequences, depression and deflation, arrive.

March 1995

Historically euphoric sentiment toward the long term trend remains in place. Take a look at the latest annual figure for Canadian analyst Charles Cummings' "Dow Risk." This indicator is an amalgam of four measures of fundamental value based on yield, earnings, book value and monetary factors. As you can see on the chart at right, 1994 set another all-time record, which is, incredibly, *double* the figure at the 1966 high of wave III!

A record high valuation has been in place for several years now, so investors have gotten used to it. Bulls today fall into two camps, rationalizing the long standing warning as false because either 1) it is a new era, so the indicators don't matter, or 2) the indicators are flawed.

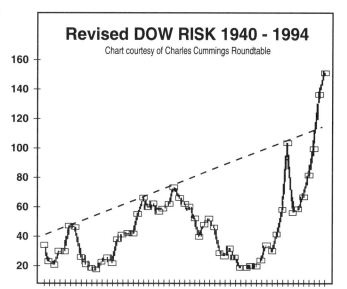

Under the February 7 WSJ headline, "Flaws in Market Gauges Make Stocks *Seem* Expensive," an article reports on explanations by analysts and money managers as to why not just one indicator of value, *but all of them*, are misleading.

The longer a valuation indicator stays in extreme territory, the bigger the ensuing move. People are receiving very little in the way of solid assets when they buy a share of the DJIA today. Why is the Dow's value so high? The subhead on the Barron's cover of February 6 certainly reveals one reason: "According to our Big Money Poll, America's portfolio managers see *rising stock prices, tame inflation and a steady economy*." In other words, their outlook reflects what has now become a mantra in the investment community: "It's the *best of all possible worlds* for stocks and the economy."

July 1995

Investors who buy markets when they are cheap and sell them when they rise in value follow a safe road to investment wealth. By contrast, today's investors have gained paper profits in the past two to four years by buying stocks dear with the hope of selling them dearer or with no intention of selling them at all. Right now, they look smart. History provides a few examples of times when the public looked right for awhile: 1720, 1830-1835, 1926-1929, 1968, and now. I use the term paper profits deliberately. Anyone who has been comfortable buying at these levels of valuation will not sell in time to avoid the bear market, as he has no historical parameters for doing so.

Evidence of unconstrained optimism abounded in June and reached new heights. June 19-23 were particularly jam-packed days. "How To Love the Market and Stop Worrying" is a headline in the June 19 Forbes. The movie title, "How I Learned To Stop Worrying and Love the Bomb" was satirical; this headline is in earnest. Using the ever-popular linear extrapolation of past trends, it assures readers that even if the market is to lose 1/3 of its value (apparently the worst imaginable scenario), the only sensible thing to do with your money is put it all in stocks now. The June issue of Smart Money offers an article entitled "Nowhere To Go But Up," which counsels, "Get invested right now. America's mutual fund managers...will be forced to drive prices forever higher." Says one broker, "There are some stocks that should be bought and never sold."

September 1995

At the end of June, U.S. stocks were worth 76.5% of the Gross Domestic Product. The only months on record in which market capitalization was a higher percentage of GDP were August 1929, November-December 1968, and December 1972. At the July high in the Dow, this ratio undoubtedly surpassed the 1929 extreme of 77.4%, putting the stock market at a Grand Supercycle degree of overvaluation by this measure. Meanwhile, Ned Davis has noted that the underlying financial situation today is far weaker than in those previous times. GDP growth was 60% higher than the long term rate of interest at the 1929 high and 90% higher at the 1966 high. Today the economy is growing at a rate 30% below the long term interest rate. The euphoria and denial required to maintain the current stock market valuation is unprecedented in U.S. history.

November 1995

I.Q. Trends (La Jolla, CA) shows a market that is more overpriced than ever. The service's Blue Chip Trend Verifier, a ranking of the over- or undervaluation of 350 stocks based on dividend yields, now lists only 14 as undervalued. That is 4% of the total, which is the lowest percentage in the 29-year history of the service. For the record, on the close of October 19, the yield on the DJIA was 2.37%, its lowest ever.

January 1996

Since many young NASDAQ stocks have no earnings, a new standard has emerged: revenue multiples. At Objective Systems and Macromedia, where stock options have elevated lowly mailroom employees to paper millionaires, analysts now consider price to revenue ratios of more than 40x to be reasonable.

Hints of Coming Social Unrest

In mid-November, near the end of a five-month stock market decline of 21%, an investor in Thailand attempted to dramatize the plight of small investors by shooting himself on the floor of the Bangkok stock exchange on live television. Others picketed the exchange because of requirements that investors sell stock when they can't meet their margin calls. Instead of forcing investors to stick to the rules, the government will provide access to two funds with $1.2 billion that will help margined investors "avoid losses for up to three years," which means that taxpayers will take the losses.

March 1996

At the Crest explained that relative stock valuation rests on three measures against price: (1) book or liquidation value of the companies and (2) their dividend yield (3) *relative* to the safest interest rate available elsewhere. We have created a chart that includes the third variable, expressed as the bond/ stock yield ratio, from figures provided by Paul Montgomery.

As you can see, if you thought stocks were expensive in 1928 and 1929, those years have nothing on 1987, 1991, 1992, 1993, 1994, 1995 and 1996 to date. Note that even if stock values fall all the way back into the rectangle that defines the normal range for this century, *they will still be at exorbitant levels* within that range, which includes 1937, 1966 and 1968, years in which all but one of the biggest bear markets of the past 80 years began. A wise man once said, "Don't confuse brains with a bull market." In the past five years, bullish analysts have benefited from the fact that the

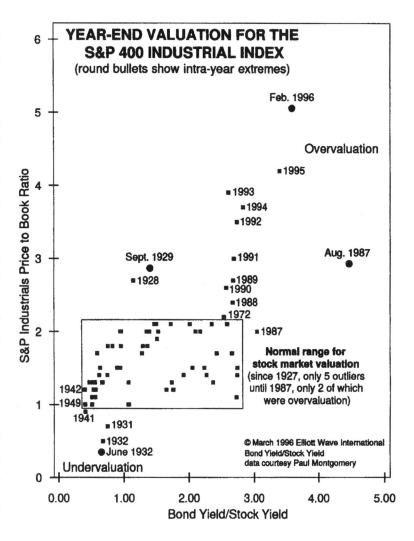

stock market has done something it has not done in 276 years, and it has done it for five years in a row. Because the bulls ignore value and disdain market timing, they will not get out before being financially destroyed.

July 1996

One brokerage firm reasons that too many observers are calling this a mania for it to be one. The "real craze," says a report, is the way the "superb performance of the stock market" is being compared to past manias. "All past manias had one thing in common: the prices to which the object of speculation rose bore no relationship to any measurement of underlying value. That could not be further from the truth of the U.S. stock market today." That a major brokerage firm could make this statement when almost every objective measure of stock market valuation is at or near all-time highs is astounding. The Q ratio, which is the stock market's total value divided by the replacement value of corporate assets, is 20% higher than in 1929. With the Dow dividend yield at 2.17%, the lowest ever, its price/dividend ratio is 30% higher than at the 1929 high. The total value of U.S. equities was 90.4% of GDP at the end of the first quarter, another record high.

One subscriber notes that a single day's trading on the NYSE and NASDAQ exchanges now surpasses the volume for all of 1929, yet the population of the U.S. has only doubled since then. This data suggests a far greater level of public participation today than in 1929. The reality is that values are so far from the norm that some commentators are bound to recognize the mania for what it is. Their doing so does not constitute a mass recognition of the folly, which is properly denoted by the word panic. When the public reaches the point of recognition, you will know it.

More Evidence of a Grand Supercycle Peak

The popularity of lotteries and other government-approved gambling projects has been building rapidly since 1989. The gambling industry now covers most of the country, with casinos in 26 states and lotteries in 34. Americans took 154 million trips to casinos in 1995, a 23% increase over 1994. Spending on the activity doubled to $20.3 billion. Corporate giants like ITT Corp. and Hilton Hotels have moved in on turf that was the exclusive domain of mobsters like Bugsy Siegel during Supercycle wave (IV). British Airways has introduced in-flight gaming, and U.S. carriers want to offer the same service. Bear Stearns estimates that interactive home wagering could go from $0 to $10 billion in four years. The government of Liechtenstein recently launched a lottery on the Internet. In Thailand, police broke up a syndicate that ran a daily lottery based on the last two numbers of a Thai stock index. One bookie continued to field bets on his mobile phone as he was paraded before television crews.

In his book, *Manias, Panics and Crashes*, Charles Kindleberger explains the relationship between manias and fraud this way: "Fortunes are made, individuals wax greedy, and swindlers come forward to exploit that greed. ...Swindling grows with prosperity." In an article on the proliferation of investment scams, the nation's largest newspaper noted that "all kinds of people are looking for easy ways to strike it rich." Lately, the risk tolerance and gullibility of many victims has spiked to an all-time high and left regulators "shaking their heads." Comparator Systems (see chart in Chapter 1), which has been accused of operating as a borderline fraud for more than a decade, was pushed up in four trading days the same percentage as the Dow Jones Industrial Average rose over Supercycle wave (III)'s 87 years from 1842 to 1929! (Both rises were followed by a crash.) Wireless cable schemes promising 400% returns have relieved 20,000 "investors" of $250 million. Another scam artist took 1192 investors for $50 million. How? One simple thought (the re-sale of frequent flyer miles) and an appeal to "people's lust for high yields."

The spate of gambling and swindles indicates that many are engaging in a furious dash to "get theirs" before the good faith of the bull market is extinguished. (They're getting theirs, all

---

Once a Long Shot for Success, **Internet Casinos Are Packing Them In**
Seattle Times, November 23, 1997

Atlantic City Growing a New $4 Billion Casino

Biggest Boom Since Gambling's Debut **In-Flight Gambling**
Dallas Morning News, July 7, 1996

Betting Booms On Campus **Is Ready To Take Off**

Colleges become a haven for gambling **For Shreveport,** THE WALL STREET JOURNAL
Milwaukee Journal Sentinel **the Gamble Has Paid Off** May 24, 1996

Gamble: November 10, 1996 The Times-Picayune, July 24, 1996

Huge Casino Project Does the Unthinkable: It Rattles Las Vegas

Venetian Will Add 6,000 Rooms To Already-Glutted City

Betting on a State Gaming Boom THE WALL STREET JOURNAL, December 4, 1997

Casino operators ready to roll into cash-hungry cities **Gambling In Iowa Saw 1995 Surge**
San Francisco Chronicle, May 15, 1996 Omaha World-Herald, July 11, 1996

Bill Boosts Boom

In Florida Betting **Indiana County Hopes Riverboat Casino Launches Economic Boom**
Sun Sentinel, May 19, 1996 THE PLAIN DEALER, August 11, 1996

---

right.) When the trend of increasing prosperity stops, Kindleberger says, fraudulent exploitation only "increases further." A study of history's great manias shows that once the top is in, tight credit and falling prices will intensify the urge, and simultaneously the need by many people in financial trouble, to strike it rich. Headlines like "Fraud Charge Ends the Good Life," from The New York Times, will probably leave the impression to historians that scandal snuffed out the bull. But this is not the case. Social mood has simply changed and is now demanding payment in full for ethical breaches, past and present. The costs will stagger many established players because they are likely to be commensurate with the degree of the trend change. The Swiss banking community, for instance, has been forced to admit that it holds at least $34 million in deposits from victims of the holocaust. The banks, which benefited from this policy for half a century, are now paying a heavy public relations toll for its use. The coming bear market will ultimately kill investment speculation flat. While gambling will persist, the industry will probably get seedier and eventually be driven underground.

August 1996

A good example of how today's attitude toward stocks and bonds will ultimately accentuate rather than soften the coming economic contraction is a Business Week cover story on stock options. The story, headlined "Options for Everyone," noted that "millions of U.S. workers are learning for the first time what the options game is all about" because "stock options are filtering down to an ever-increasing number of rank-and-file corporate employees." Newly established accounting standards will insure that corporations can issue options without taking a charge against earnings. Already, the total number of shares reserved for management and employees is more than 10% of outstanding shares. By "tying everyone to the stock price," companies say they have created a powerful performance incentive. In the bear market, however, the effect will be inverted. As prices fall and those options become worthless, the reward for striving will evaporate, and therefore to some degree, so will the striving.

October 1996

"If your strategy is to buy a high quality company, you want to buy that company regardless of price." *Regardless of price?* Can you imagine reading such a statement at a bottom, when it would actually be timely? At the next bottom, as at all previous ones, the consensus will be "Sell that company regardless of price!"

December 1996

This bull market passed an overvaluation equivalent to 1929's long ago, in 1987 by many measures and in 1992 by all others. For example, at the 1929 high, the DJIA yielded 2.89% per year in dividends (a 34.6x multiple). It now yields 2.00% (a 50x multiple), making Dow stocks 45% more overpriced than at that famous high. Wall Street writers are using barrels of ink to explain why this measure of value is meaningless, which is just another symptom of the historic optimism that has produced the multiple.

New Rules for Wall Street

As the Dow Jones Industrial Average flirts with the stunning level of 7,000, several leading analysts on Wall Street are counseling that the old rules no longer apply when judging whether the stock market has soared beyond reason.

These market watchers, whom some call the New Era group, divine a new period for stocks that is defined by low inflation and the public's keen attraction to stock mutual funds. When the old standbys for valuing stocks are adjusted for these factors, they assert, stock prices look either perfectly reasonable or, at worst, modestly high.

New Era analysts argue that measures that worked well in the past must be updated now that the investment climate has changed. Among that group is Abby Joseph Cohen, co-chairwoman of the investment policy committee at Goldman Sachs & Co.

"I have been a New Era person since 1991," she says, explaining that changes in the behavior of the baby boom generation were a catalyst for her fresh market perspective.

The issue of whether stocks have reached unsustainable heights has become more pressing as investors appear to be holding firm in their belief that stocks will continue lurching upward, with only brief dips and pauses. A poll of 1,014 mutual fund investors taken at the end of last year by Louis Harris and Associates found that 86 percent thought that the annual returns from the stock market in the next 10 years will be 14 percent or better.

—Seattle Post-Intelligencer, February 11, 1997

March 1997

According to a New York Times article headlined "Analysts redefine Valuation of Stocks," a rising school of stock market experts, known as the "New Era group," has readjusted values to account for low inflation and the "public's keen attraction to stock mutual funds." A more direct admission of turning bullish because prices have risen a long way we could not imagine.

November 1997

On August 6, 1997, the Dow Jones Industrial Average yielded 1.61% in annual dividends, making it 1.8 times as overvalued as it was on the top day in 1929. In other words, if the Dow drops approximately 45% to 4600 (and dividends remain unchanged), it will reach a yield valuation equal to that of September 3, 1929, from which the Dow fell 89%! This is the downside potential we mean to imply with terms such as "Grand Supercycle degree top."

Although the price/dividend ratio has a 100-year record of signaling major bear markets with every drop below 3%, bulls cavalierly dismiss the indicator as having lost touch with these "new era" times. The old rule is broken, they say, because companies now buy back loads of their own shares, "paying" shareholders in the form of higher stock prices. After the decline of October 27, the president of the NYSE even suggested that it was a great opportunity for firms to buy back their own shares. This corporate behavior simply reflects wild-eyed optimism about the future; boards of directors would rather commit capital to the stock market than their own business plans! Corporations made a similar choice in the late 1920s, lending cash to the call money markets where it was used by mutual funds to buy up the shares of the lenders. When the market retreats, these programs will be acknowledged as a total waste of a most precious corporate asset.

Our (lack of) valuation chart, updated from March 1996, is shown at right. The October high is marked with a bullet (which appears to be aimed at a certain aging, infirm bull).

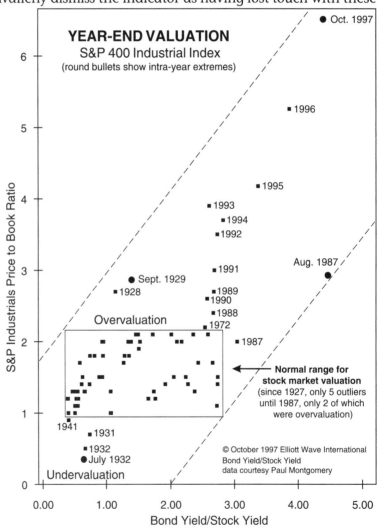

December 1997

With respect to dividend yield and replacement value of corporate assets, the U.S. stock market is more overvalued than any stock market in recorded Western financial history, going back 300 years. (Among major markets worldwide, only the Nikkei reached a higher valuation, and it has accordingly collapsed.)

Countless headlines insist that the "Asian Skid Poses Little U.S. Threat." Now each new day brings word of the great Asian fire sale. Even U.S. banks have rushed in because "the domino collapse of once proud Asian economies may not be all red ink after all. On the contrary, it could be a bonanza." For even the most remedial students of mass psychology, however, Asia is a crystal-clear window to "the approaching chaos" alluded to in the final chapter of *At the Crest of the Tidal Wave.*

In financial historian J.K. Galbraith's vernacular, it is experiencing the "final common feature" of a financial euphoria, "anger and recrimination." The classic symptoms of this post-bubble backlash have emerged in all the countries affected by plunging markets. The December 2 Wall Street Journal tells of a sweeping wave of "resentment": "From Thailand to South Korea, casualties of the region's market meltdowns are casting blame far and wide." In each country, the severity of these symptoms is directly proportional to the extent and duration of the fall. In Japan, where the decline began seven years ago and has erased more than 60% of the Nikkei's value, five different prime ministers have been booted, and the social system faces nothing less than "revolution." In Thailand, where the market has fallen 78% since its peak in 1994, protestors have taken to the streets, the prime minister has been sacked in a populist uprising, and "even cosmopolitan Thais" say the U.S. is trying to plunder Thailand. "It's a war without bullets," one American-educated Thai told the WSJ.

AHN YOUNG-JOON / Associated Press

Riot police in Seoul confront shareholders who called for a stock market shutdown to prevent further declines.

Atlanta Journal-Constitution, December 4, 1997

Malaysia is down more than 40% since February. There, the prime minister has declared speculation "immoral" and suggested his country is the victim of a Jewish plot. Analysts issuing negative forecasts have been branded "traitors."

Another important leavening agent that is largely unique to the final leg of the Grand Supercycle bull has been the financial bailout. Since the U.S. government rescued Lockheed in 1971, financial bailouts have become so commonplace that the potential for systemic risk is not even debated, even though the size of the bailouts and the warranties that they imply are suddenly expanding at exponential rates. Thanks to the "successful" bailout of Mexico in 1995, for instance, an attempted rescue of Asia's struggling tigers was all but foreordained. Five months ago, the Asian bailout amounted to a single $1.1 billion loan. Now it is increasing at an almost parabolic rate; from $68 billion at the November summit of Pacific nations to $78 billion a week later to $55 billion for just one country, Korea, as of December 2.

January 1998

The ever-increasing IMF bailout, which we covered last month (it has since been "speeded up") is another sign that investors have stepped off the "magic stairway," as Anne Crittenden put it in EWT's Special Report from December. When you hear that the Secretary of the Treasury and the chairmen of the Federal Reserve, the New York Stock Exchange and the Commodity Futures Trading Commission are meeting again to iron things out, remember this line from the report: "Our efforts to escape invariably make our sufferings worse."

It makes us shudder to think that many of these meetings are now taking place in the White House "situation room." The potential for damage is contained in the hubris of a senior American official who says, "Someone is going to have to teach the [South Korean] president-elect how to talk to the markets. He doesn't quite have the language down yet." This is from a man who thinks it is a good idea to take billions of hard-earned U.S. tax dollars and use them to prop up shaky investment schemes perpetrated by good-ole-boy political-commercial deal-makers in a land halfway across the globe. When such schemes dissolve, the money disappears. It does not "flow into other investments." It's just *gone*.

June 1998

"Sky-high price-earning ratios" attained by stocks like Yahoo! and Amazon.com are cited as the key piece of evidence that "reveal how optimistic American investors are." The incredible exploding valuations of the Internet frenzy, now recognized as the "biggest speculative mania in history," are another direct throwback to Japan in the late 1980s.

July 1998

Despite years of underperformance, many low-priced stocks are more expensive today than Japanese stocks were in 1989. Ray DeVoe (DeVoe Report, Legg Mason Wood Walker, New York City) notes that when the three biggest stocks are taken out of the NASDAQ, the rest have a P/E multiple of 91 compared with 68 for both the NASDAQ as a whole and the Nikkei at its all-time high in 1989.

September 1998

This time last year, Wall Street analysts were calling for a 10% growth in first quarter S&P profits. The final numbers showed a 1.3% increase. Second quarter hopes were for a 13% rise. The quarter came in at 2.3%. In an environment where record high P/E multiples have been justified by the expectation of big profit leaps down the road, this slowing represents a huge shortfall. The bull market's ability literally to rise above these disappointments may have been its last great achievement. Companies had become "experts at managing expectations," The New York Times explained in early July. In the final days of the bull market, analysts were reduced to an almost hypnotic state in which companies could "jawbone down earnings forecasts" then announce "positive surprises" a few days later. Weyerhauser is one of countless examples. In early July, the firm "beat expectations" even though earnings were below the consensus estimate of 36 cents in mid-June. It did this by lowering the "consensus estimate" two weeks before the second quarter ended.

In recent weeks, estimates for overall S&P earnings continue to anticipate an imminent return to the profit growth that companies need to justify their stock prices. Forecasts still call for a rapid reversal to 11.9% growth in the fourth quarter and a whopping 19.1% next year. The sole basis for this newfound effort to forecast a leap in growth is the enduring psychological coercion of the bull market, which has deeply subverted the objectivity of Wall Street research houses.

What Analysts Want To Believe

In 1983, EWT nailed another aspect of the latter stages of the forecasted bull market, predicting an "unbelievable institutional mania for stocks," i.e., euphoria among financial sophisticates, not just the public. Indeed, the experts have been explaining away, ignoring and denying the existence of the crumbling fundamentals. At a July conference of analysts, Microsoft's CFO spent an hour "making a fairly persuasive case that Microsoft's tremendous stock price fails to recognize the fact that its growth rate continues to slow, and that, for a whole host of reasons, it faces tough times ahead." When he had finished, the audience was not fazed in the least. In fact, attendees wanted to know what the point was. So, the CFO put it another way: "The stock is overvalued." Barron's reports that "200 or so analysts found this absolutely hilarious."

When the chief executive of an electronics firm cited a recession in his firm's sector of the economy for his decision to slash his work force and cut capital spending, analysts accused the executive of blaming the economy for his firm's mistakes. "They were in a state of denial," the manufacturing executive said. "Everyone wanted to believe that everything was going to be good."

Bull Market Accounting Standards

On April 10, accountants began peeling back layers of financial inconsistencies at Cendant Corp. On July 21, Cendant auditors announced that they had been "deceived" by outright fraud in Cendant's discount shopping club unit. "The best planned and performed audit may not detect material misstatements if there is intentional, collusive fraud by a company's financial management," said Ernst & Young. On August 28, USA Today pronounced the fraud "astonishing" and reported that "Accountants Were Told To Doctor Numbers."

The discovery of "fictitious revenue" at Cendant Corp. is part of a slow awakening to the realization that the fundamentals of many companies, weak as they have become, are not even what they purport to be. Financial improprieties at Sunbeam, Oxford Health, Green Tree Financial, Boston Chicken and Mercury Financial have also been reported. Jim Grant (Grant's Interest Rate Observer, New York City) and a few other skeptics had been covering the more polished forms of financial legerdemain for years. For instance, Grant's pointed out that reported earnings of GE were within 2.37% of the analytical consensus for 20 quarters in a row. "The odds of such a display of clairvoy-

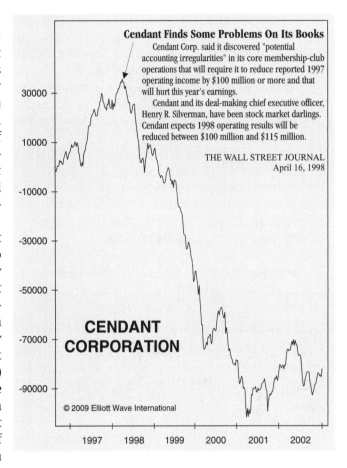

Cendant Finds Some Problems On Its Books

Cendant Corp. said it discovered "potential accounting irregularities" in its core membership-club operations that will require it to reduce reported 1997 operating income by $100 million or more and that will hurt this year's earnings.

Cendant and its deal-making chief executive officer, Henry R. Silverman, have been stock market darlings. Cendant expects 1998 operating results will be reduced between $100 million and $115 million.

THE WALL STREET JOURNAL
April 16, 1998

CENDANT CORPORATION

© 2009 Elliott Wave International

ance on Wall Street are 1 in 50 billion." In 1993, Grant's first discussed the dubious nature of Coca Cola Co.'s financial performance, noting that when Coke spun off its bottling division, it established the equivalent of two sets of books. The pristine set allowed the corporate parent to nail its ambitious growth targets while Coca Cola Enterprises housed the debt and capital expenditures that were integral to the business.

The financial press ignored several follow-up stories by Grant's until a new scrutiny emerged August 5 with a story in The New York Times. It said Coca-Cola was "under fire" for "skirting the spirit of accounting rules" when it spun off its bottling division in 1986. "This is an old worn-out point of view," the company retorted. This headline from an August 11 article in USA Today shows an unmistakable popular recognition of long-running deterioration in the quality of corporate earnings:

Cooking the Books Proves Common Trick of the Trade
—USA TODAY, August 11, 1998

The story reveals that "publicly traded firms routinely massage their earnings" with "smoke-and-mirrors accounting methods" and "controversial efforts to manage earnings." The real news, of course, is that this has been true for years, but the emerging shift in social mood is beginning to shatter the collective financial delusion. These stories can "now be told" because people are disposed to listen to them. As the bear market unfolds, many more "scandalous" cases will be revealed.

On July 20, opposition from the technology industry and other sectors forced the Federal Accounting Standards Board to abandon the last and most modest in a series of proposals that would have forced companies to make some allowance for the cost of stock options in their earnings statements. Options have become the "Currency of an Opulent Age," notes a recent Wall Street Journal headline. Combined with another miracle of modern accounting, the corporate stock re-purchase plan, options have helped financial engineers mask wavering corporate fundamentals as they literally hold their stocks up. Like options, buy-backs do not show on corporate income statements, but they do reduce the number of shares outstanding, thus increasing per-share earnings. Since 1995, IBM has earned $18.2 billion and repurchased $21.3 billion in its own stock. In the second quarter, Intel had net income of $1.12 billion as it bought up $1.74 billion of its own shares.

A bear market will lay waste to this "virtual cash machine." Columnist Roger Lowenstein compares the dispersal of options to Morgan bank's distribution of hot stock issues to favored clients at bargain prices in the 1920s. This time, however, the difference is that there is nothing secret about the practice. "No one will be able to say, as in the '30s, 'How could we know?'" Lowenstein noted. "This time, the tune will be, 'We didn't want to know.'" Such are the demands at the peak of an equity culture.

October 1998

By bailing out financial gamblers, the IMF and the Fed are continuing to import deflation. When the IMF sends $100 billion into Russia's black hole or $30 billion to Brazil, when the Fed

---

Long-Term Capital Bailout Prompts Calls for Action on Regulating Derivatives
The New York Times
December 15, 1998

Clinton Seeks Global 'New Deal' To End 'Boom and Bust' Cycles

President Clinton warned yesterday that the global march toward democracy and free markets in recent years is imperiled by the international economic slump, and called for what would amount to a worldwide version of the New Deal, measures designed to curb the excesses of unfettered capitalism.

Washington Post, October 17, 1998

Tsuang urges global war on speculators

Bloomberg, September 24, 1998

Blair to urge full overhaul of IMF and World Bank

UK prime minister says financial turmoil highlights failings of 1940's institutions

Tony Blair will today call for a comprehensive overhaul of the International Monetary Fund and World Bank, saying they have failed to provide economic stability in a world of massive cross-border capital flow.

FINANCIAL TIMES
September 21, 1998

Malaysia Invokes Extreme Powers, Jails Critics

KUALA LUMPUR, Malaysia—The government here has jailed a popular former deputy prime minister and several of his allies, invoking an internal security law that permits indefinite detention without charges.

THE WALL STREET JOURNAL
September 22, 1998

World Bank warns Big Five over global audit standards

The World Bank has told the Big Five global audit firms to stop putting their names to accounts published in the Asian economies unless they are drawn up using high-quality international financial reporting standards.

FINANCIAL TIMES
October 19, 1998

KOREA: RAGE AND DESPAIR

Will the economic pain spark a ruinous upheaval?

BusinessWeek
August 17, 1998

Germany's Schroeder Backs Controls

PARIS—German Chancellor-Elect Gerhard Schroeder gave his strongest endorsement yet of placing greater controls on international capital flows and restructuring the global financial system.

THE WALL STREET JOURNAL, October 1, 1998

Japan, at last, acts to stem world economic crisis.

USA Today, October 13, 1998

---

pledges to back up bank loans of $3.75 billion to bail out a wealthy gamblers' hedge fund that goes bankrupt, when the "plunge protection team" ("an emergency council of America's top financial officials that operates with its own special staff in the shadows of the U.S. Treasury," according to dejanews.com) hints that it will buy S&P futures if the stock market looks dicey, you know that these officials are hell-bent on importing deflation to the U.S. by destroying U.S. taxpayers' and depositors' money as fast as they can. Of course, they do not realize they are doing this, which reflects the essence of the history of monetary policy.

One country has already tried intervention. In August, the government of Hong Kong spent 13% of the world's third-largest currency reserves to buy the equivalent of $12.5 billion worth of stock, 6% of the entire HK stock market. Its stock market is exactly unchanged since the last day of that program. Said some traders quite correctly, "The government might end up owning the stock it buys for years." Yes, and when it finally decides to sell the shares, it will be a bottom. Columnist Holman W. Jenkins, Jr. once said in The Wall Street Journal, "A woefully common misapprehension is that adults in positions of authority know what they are doing."

January 1999

Here is a headline from 1988: "Analysts' Adjustments Make Japanese Stocks Look Cheap." In that story, the P/E ratio valuation of Japanese stocks was recalculated allowing for cultural and accounting differences (translation: it was a rationalization of absurd prices). That last-minute analytical adjustment was child's play compared to the methods now being used to justify the astronomical prices of U.S. Internet companies. Since most pure Internet plays have no earnings to work with (many of them, we suspect, are trading on differences in their price-to-loss ratios), research houses have concocted a host of different measures that compare an Internet company's market capitalization to everything from marketing dollars spent to electricity consumed.

A conservative method, according to one firm's valuation study called "Teaching an Old Dog New Tricks," is "Theoretical Earnings Multiple Analysis." TEMA "captures the long-term wealth generation potential" by measuring "long-term target operating margins" and "forward revenue forecasts" to provide "a relative sense" for the earnings power of a business. By these means, analysts are able to develop "realistic theoretical earnings power" which "imply forward P/E multiples." However, when forward P/E multiples are discounted for "upside premium assumptions" in the highest quality Internet stock covered, they still carry multiples twice as high as Japanese P/Es in December 1989.

Not mentioned amidst all the relative sensing and long-term targeting is that the Internet is a rapidly changing medium with virtually no barriers to competition, aggressive pricing and an ever-growing number of well-financed, profit-starved computer geniuses. TEMA, then, is not an analytical tool but simply a rationalization designed to feed the gold-rush mentality of the day. As "Internet-driven valuations" spread to conventional stocks (so long as they have a web site), experienced analysts are finding it almost impossible to deal with "the conviction that certain exceptional companies shouldn't have any valuation ceilings." The following paragraph is from the January 4 WSJ:

> "It's frustrating," says an analyst [with a major mutual fund company]. As a stock picker at a firm with many billions in assets, he can schedule face-to-face meetings with Internet company executives, or confer with industry experts anytime he wants their thinking. But with Internet stocks governed mostly by the chatter of online investor groups, [the firm's] elite privileges seem meaningless. "Perhaps I should have spent more time in the chat groups," [the professional analyst] ruefully says.

"Earnings per share insurance" is another good example of the ways in which the mounting decline is actually pushing economic agents further out on a limb. To compensate for "the most gruelingly competitive commercial-insurance markets in years," insurers are "getting closer to insuring all the vital components of corporate earnings."

April 1999

A new book, *Dow 36,000*, is based on the assumption that the risk premium, or extra return investors receive for betting on the uncertainty of stocks over bonds' guaranteed return, is "heading for its proper level: zero." This is opposite the conclusion suggested by Paul Montgomery of Universal Economics. Montgomery has long used the bond yield/stock yield ratio to track investors' valuation of stocks vs. bonds. Needless to say, at this point, historic demand for stocks has pushed their yields to negligible levels. Bonds now yield nearly five times as much as stocks, an unprecedented amount.

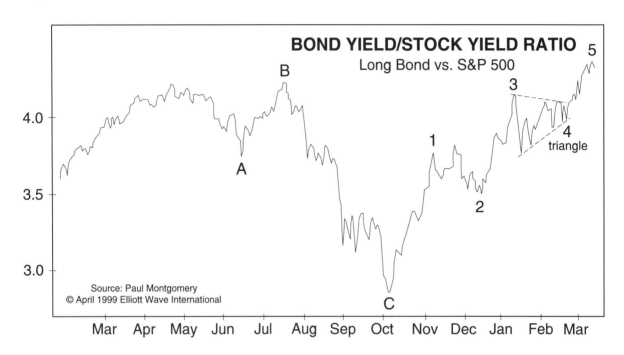

P/E Multiples Compound

William R. Emmons of the Federal Reserve Bank of St. Louis performed a service in his June 1998 article, "The Current P/E Ratio: Higher Than You Think." First, recall the observation in Chapter 10 of *At the Crest* that P/E is a mostly irrelevant ratio when it comes to valuing stocks. This is due partly to the fact that earnings lag stock prices, thus pitting their trends against each other, making P/E a rubber benchmark. Indeed, the ratio is often high near the end of a recession after the first advance in a bull market, thus giving a false bearish message. Emmons makes this point and then explains the implications of today's very high P/E ratio, which is in place during an economic expansion. Here is his conclusion:

> P/E ratios reached in January 1997 and 1998 [we can now add 1999] are without historical precedent for a mature expansion. At the current level of stock prices, a decline in corporate earnings of 30%, as occurred in the recessionary period of 1989-91, would cause the market P/E ratio to soar to 40 — a level never before seen in the U.S. stock market. Thus, from a cyclically-adjusted historical perspective, stock prices are unprecedentedly high.

After adjustment, then, we find the same message from P/E that we get from the valid ratios of valuation: price/dividend, bond yield/stock yield and price/book value. They all say that stock prices are so high today that top tick in 1929 looks cheap by comparison. The following chart updates Emmons's study. And that was using figures as of a year ago!

Grant's Interest Rate Observer (30 Wall St., New York, NY) put extreme P/Es in a similar perspective with a table comparing the leaders of the last three technology-related stock bubbles

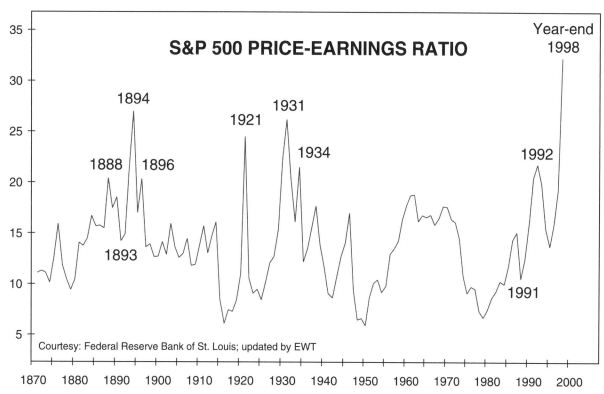

to the current one. The tally shows RCA had its highest multiple of 72.5 in 1929, Xerox hit 122 in 1962 (it was 63.4 at the 1968 peak) and Apple's high was 150 in 1980 (48.9 at the peak for the sector). All three of these extremes were in the same ballpark. Today, AOL has a P/E of 578, Yahoo's is at 569 and eBay's is 3,324. Amazon.com's P/E is listed as n/a because it has no E. In terms of these leaders, the current stock market top is infinitely more euphoric than past ones. This is the difference between prior Cycle and Supercycle tops and today's Grand Supercycle top, which *Elliott Wave Principle* said in 1978 was the degree that would be coming to an end.

May 1999

Disasters in the making are moving through society with unprecedented speed. This fact is apparent from "Minute Trading." The standard price pattern in "minute" shares, quick bursts of profitability followed by extended periods of bloodletting, causes this activity to be dismissed as only an isolated fringe of scam artists capitalizing on ignorant neophytes. Granted, it is also the leading edge of this bull market.

Now that the mania has exposed the irrelevance of earnings, investors have dropped the pretense of searching for value or even a decent "story." Minute trading marks the clear advance of the financial bubble into that gray area in which promoters tread the line between orchestrated stock jobbing and outright embezzlement. The mania books, like Kindleberger's *Manias, Panics and Crashes*, explain that, in time, it will not really matter if the minute traders were swindled or simply swept off their feet by financial euphoria. They will pay for their incaution either way. For as long as the market basks in the twilight of the bull market, however, there is no general concern because everyone is, or least ought to be, getting rich.

June 1999

Further proof of an unprecedented dumbing down of the investment climate is the article, "Rethinking a Quaint Idea: Profits," from The Wall Street Journal. It says, "One of the sacred tenets of business — you have to make money — suddenly looks almost like a quaint artifact of an outdated era." The executive vice president of a start-up industrial company says that his financial advisors talked his firm out of becoming profitable by 2000. "The attitude is almost antiprofit. In this marketplace, the more money you lose, the more valuable you are." We cannot wait to see if this sentiment is uttered during the next economic contraction. In another revolutionary redefinition, some "equity-income [mutual fund] managers aren't convinced the 'income' component of 'equity income' makes sense any more." The average yield on equity income funds, which have historically been regarded as more conservative funds that perform better in a decline, has fallen to 1.5%. In other words, when it comes to investment, there are virtually no conservatives to be found even where one would normally find them.

July 1999

The financial bailouts of the last few years are also instruments of the coming debt implosion. By using them, officials have basically booby-trapped much of the global financial landscape. In March, we saw the first taste of how quickly these traps will shut. U.S. Treasury Secretary Robert Rubin told a congressional panel that much of the $4.9 billion in loans sent to Russia last summer by the International Monetary Fund "may have been siphoned off improperly." Can you imagine a private institution so easily losing $4.9 billion to crooks? Even if you could, can you imagine it handing over an equal amount immediately thereafter? Well, just two weeks after losing the $4.9 billion, the IMF agreed to extend $4.8 billion in fresh loans! You have to hand it to these government agencies. No one else can destroy money faster. In countries where the rescues have appeared to work, the damage will be even greater, as phony confidence has attracted more funds for the bonfire.

Beware the approach of financial fascism. Russia has decided that in order to satisfy the IMF enough to get another $22b. of mostly American tax money, it will impose price controls on goods and currency controls on citizens and disallow retail pricing in dollars. This is a recipe for chaos, which will induce a cry for yet more controls. Likewise, Brazil's plan to entice an international bailout package involves raising taxes. Government screws up, and the citizens pay. Even the U.S. will not be immune to such impulses when financial pressures increase.

October 1999

Where to now? Well, our bullet chart of stock-market valuation offers a host of newly relevant targets. EWT first published this chart in March 1996. This issue updates the chart once again, and this time, the dot marking the current valuation looks like Pluto does in a depiction of our solar system: way out there. Most important, the message of this chart is now popularly "refuted" by "new theories" about "the right price for stocks."

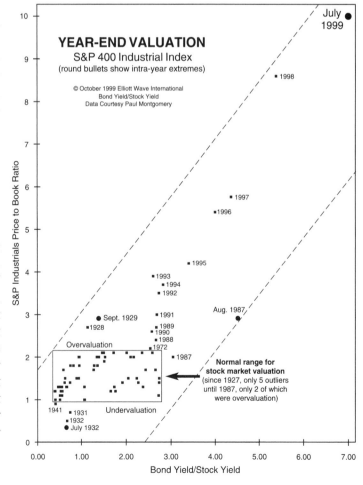

584

With its "Dow 36,000" headline, the Atlantic Monthly, which is not a financial magazine, opines that a proper valuation for the Dow is 3.6 times its current level. This would place the valuation dot somewhere out in the Milky Way, dismissing three centuries of the stock market's valuation of industrial development as absurdly underpriced. This exercise in modern valuation theory is the ultimate example of a point made in EWT's May 1997 Special Report, "Bulls, Bears and Manias": In a stock mania, valuation levels are meaningless. They only become meaningful in a bear market when the gravity of falling prices returns them to their historic orbit.

The trip back toward Earth has always meant a return at least to the historical average. So, how far does the Dow Jones Industrial Average have to fall to produce reasonable values? Based on a 1.56% dividend yield at the August 25 closing high in the Dow, the index was 1.85 times as overvalued as it was on the top day in 1929. In other words, at 6100, the Dow would have a yield valuation equal to that of September 1929, from which it fell 89%. At 4500, it will approach the 40-year average valuation based on dividends. At 2600, it will approach typical Cycle degree bear market dividend payout levels. These levels assume no decline in dividends, which would be an absurd assumption. Every mania holds the seeds of an economic depression because it ties the average person's finances to the bull market. When the market falls after a mania, it is not just a few fat cat investors who are affected, but everyone. Dividends will fall substantially a few years from now, and the market will see that development coming and price stocks accordingly.

The Economy

The "new era" has been officially endorsed by the U.S. government, as the Bureau of Economic Analysis has reclassified software purchases as investments rather than spending!

The gains created by this bookkeeping breakthrough are more than offset by unrecognized expenses and other questionable practices like the padding of profits with gains from stocks in corporate pension funds. In 1998, earnings from pension surpluses inflated the earnings of the S&P 500 by 3%. Stock options are another huge expense that has not been deducted from earnings. According to one study, for instance, Microsoft's net income of $7.8 billion for its most recently completed fiscal year would have been a loss of $12 billion if its options were fully expensed. As *The Elliott Wave Theorist* pointed out in our September 1998 special report on the weakness of Cycle V fundamentals versus those of Cycle III, accounting standards have eroded as the bull market has aged. The flip side of these papered-over cracks in the fundamentals is that in a bear market they will be an enormous weight on growth.

Combined with the unprecedented global economic dependence on a rising U.S. stock market, the likelihood is that they will exert their drag with stunning speed. And what good is an option to buy a stock above its current value? At many firms, option programs are already becoming a huge source of employee discontent rather than an incentive, as employee's presumed "earnings" are melting away. Despite all these shenanigans and all this risk, the only danger that economists see is that the economy might overheat! The only clear parallel to the dependence of today's prosperity upon the stock market is 1929, when the stock market downturn was exactly coincident with the downturn in the economy.

November 1999

In another late-breaking milestone, Martha Stewart "struck stock market gold" October 19 with the sale of 14% of her firm to the public. Stewart's first book, *Entertaining*, came out in 1982 as the bull market was taking off. Since then, she has become "the queen of gracious living," a self-made billionaire "credited with creating a lifestyle industry." She is not the first bull-market hero to equitize her persona, but she may be the most fully valued. The Martha Stewart company has a capitalization of $1.7 billion and earnings of $14 million, which makes her an excellent "role model" according to one consultant, who added, "we need them because it gives women hope and desire to strive." Overvaluation is now a social virtue.

MARTHA, INC.

Inside the growing empire of America's lifestyle queen

It's a taping day at Martha Stewart's Westport (Conn.) studio, and the spotless halls are humming with activity. Helen Murphy, the new chief financial officer at Martha Stewart Living Omnimedia Inc. (MSO), nervously gets ready to tape a presentation to investors. Permeating every part of the building is Stewart herself, chairman, CEO, and founder. Her husky voice rises from the speakers as dozens of screens show her juggling beanbags for her daily TV show.

It's a fitting image. Anyone who spends more than a few minutes with America's most famous homemaker learns that she is one heck of a juggler. On a recent day, Stewart, 58, rose at her usual 5:30 a.m. to work out in Westport before zipping into Manhattan to prepare Greek food with a guest chef, meet with her magazine staff, share dessert with restaurateur Warner LeRoy for the TV show, make a cookie tree on Letterman, and attend a party for her publisher.

The dizzying routine seems to be working. Stewart's Web site racked up record Christmas sales, while her holiday TV special reached 7.8 million households. Recently, the former caterer pulled off her best party yet: a hot initial public offering on Oct. 19. Shares of Martha Stewart Living Omnimedia opened at $18 and quickly doubled, to about $36—as Stewart herself served brioches and freshly squeezed orange juice from a striped tent near the New York Stock Exchange

What really has investors salivating, though, is Stewart's fledgling Web business. Organized around the core content areas, the site, with more than 1 million registered users, offers traditional how-to advice, chat rooms, and related merchandise. Internet and direct sales accounted for roughly 13% of revenues in 1999. This year, online sales should surpass catalog sales. Still, the Net remains a money-loser because of heavy investment in staff and site development.

Even those who scoff at Stewart's perfect-housewife image admit that she's a stunningly savvy entrepreneur. Her company, which raised $149 million in its IPO, posted record sales of $49.8 million in the third quarter, although the investment in e-commerce shrank profits to $1.9 million, down from $4.7 million a year earlier. Stewart controls 60% of the shares and 96% of the votes.

FLOOD OF MAGIC. What gave Stewart the capital to buy her independence was a new arrangement with Kmart, which guaranteed millions in royalties. Kmart wanted to flood key corners of its store with Martha Stewart magic, and it was willing to give her control over her product to do it. Instead of consulting on a few floral sheet patterns, Stewart's people could produce thousands of different products and get astounding play with Kmart shoppers.

With stock that's now worth almost $1 billion, she can also afford a place in Manhattan that's big enough to house her cherished cats and dogs. She'll still have five other houses: two in Westport, two in East Hampton, N.Y., and her favorite retreat—in Seal Harbor, ME.

—Business Week, January 17, 2000

The Redistribution of Wealth?

The chart (next page) of the wealth held by the richest 1% of U.S. households offers another perspective on just how top heavy the bull market has become. Notice how much lower and thus relatively stable the last peak was at the end of Cycle III in the mid-1960s. The most recent figure of 40.1% is a projection for 1997 based on changes in asset prices. The figure for 1999 is not yet known, but, with most of the growth in wealth now coming directly from the stock market and the market's thinning since the spring of 1998, 1999 will challenge 1929's all-time record of 44.2%. Since 1997, it is known that the net worth of the world's richest person, Bill Gates, nearly tripled to about $100 billion in July. According to Forbes' 1999 list of the world's richest people, near the summer highs, Gates was worth about 1% of GDP, which is roughly equal to the 50 richest Americans on its 1982 list. As a percentage of GDP, the wealth of the 50 richest Americans is 4.5 times the level of the top 50 in 1982. In the 1930s, the wealth distribution problem was "solved" by a falling market and tax rates of better than 90% for the wealthiest

Americans. In the second half of 1999, the same social forces can be seen stirring, as the "growing gulf between the haves and the have-nots" has suddenly become an issue. Within days of the S&P high, the seeds of a new social movement were visible in a rash of headlines like this one: "Income Inequalities Reach 'Grotesque' Gap, U.N. Says." The Republican Presidential front runner has even attacked his party for trying to "balance the budget on the backs of the poor." As the chart shows, a bear market is nature's way of redistributing wealth, but apparently, at a trend change as big as this one, people just cannot wait to get in there and lend a hand.

January 2000

The dividend yield on the Dow fell to an all-time low of 1.32% on December 31. At this point, a 100% increase in yield will still leave it below its low at the peak of Supercycle (III) on the top day in 1929! As noted in *At the Crest of the Tidal Wave*, dividend yield is the ultimate test of faith for investors, as it shows how willing they are to forgo the certainty of a cash payout for the possibility of a capital gain down the road. The chart of the percentage of NYSE, NASDAQ and AMEX firms offering a dividend shows that as of 1998, nearly four out of five firms were being bought solely for their potential to produce capital gains.

Another valuable thing about dividends is that they can sometimes provide insight into the extent of the next long-term move in stock prices. The chart on the following page from *At The Crest* (also shown in *The Wave Principle of Human Social Behavior*) shows that the reversals from extremes in the dividend yield have always been commensurate with the degree of the trend that created them. So, in coming this far, the dividend yield has confirmed that the current trend change will mark a Grand Supercycle degree reversal of the 200-year uptrend in stock prices. It has also offered the first glimpse of a very different world to come, one in which surviving firms will have to pay back skittish investors a huge percentage of their initial investment via dividends just to get them to hold their shares.

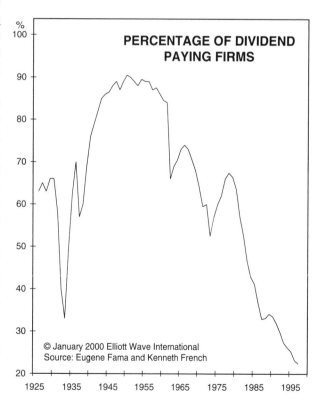

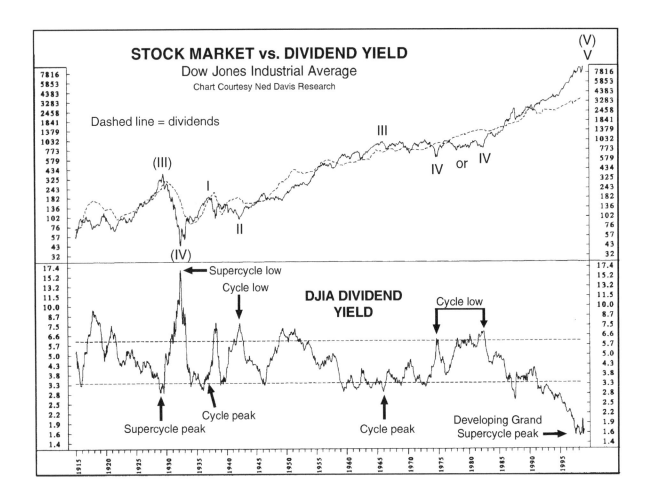

STOCK MARKET vs. DIVIDEND YIELD
Dow Jones Industrial Average
Chart Courtesy Ned Davis Research

Dashed line = dividends

DJIA DIVIDEND YIELD

February 2000

A Long Build-Up has Led to this Peak

The transition to deflation is now moving at a rapid pace. However, the process has actually been unfolding in subtle but profound ways for two decades. Much of the early contraction was concealed in the form of corporate restructurings, buy-backs and mergers that pumped up stock prices at the expense of revenues and companies' prospects for long-term growth. In a great article called "The Profit Illusion Game" from the Fall 1999 issue of American Outlook, author Charles Parlato shows how the emasculation of book value, serial mergers, the stock repurchase game and earnings enhancements techniques have already contributed mightily to the prospects for deflation. The bull market's attendant accounting gimmicks will also get a lot more ink as the blinding light of the new era gives way to sober reflection and recrimination.

March 2000

The high potential for nightmare trading scenarios in which sales go unrecognized and successful short positions go uncovered underscores our "cash is king" advice in the February issue of *The Elliott Wave Theorist*. The following chart of mutual fund cash levels further accentuates the case, as it currently displays an utter contempt for cash. The latest available reading of 4.2% cash is the lowest ratio since the stock-market peak of January 1973, right before the biggest stock-market decline since the 1930s.

In a growing list of industries, professionals are being paid in equity rather than dollars. "Stock options, once an employee-only perk, are becoming the scrip of choice for many. Lawyers may have been the first to demand equity, but now corporate recruiters, publicists, landlords,

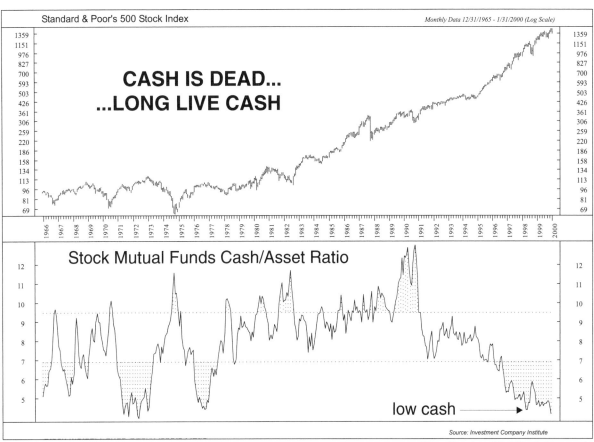

Chart Courtesy Ned Davis Research

contractors, writers, Web site developers and even massage therapists are seeking options, too." Some advertising executives are "so keen to get a piece of a juicy Internet stock" that they are moving the best talent and ad spots away from bigger established clients and supplying them to Internet start-ups that can pay in the currency of the day. When these options expire worthless and the cash-paying customers are long gone, the luster of cash will burn brighter than ever.

April 2000

Another indication that a historic extreme in brand awareness has reached its zenith is that in recent months, even individuals have become brands. A number of them, including Dick Clark, Donna Karan, Tommy Hilfiger, Ralph Lauren, Martha Stewart and C. Everett Koop, have become publicly traded companies. All are down substantially from their close on their first day of trading, but the effort literally to buy heroes continues to spread. The latest development is at the venture capital level, where numerous promoters are busily launching Internet investment funds with superstar athletes because "athletes have tremendous brand presence." Many venture capitalists and investors expect to get in on the ground floor of the "new paradigm," but the elevator is actually on the penthouse floor. If the bull market is topping as we assert, then these are the final death throes of brand name imaging per se.

May 2000

Anger and RecrimiNation

When the global decline started in Asia in 1997, *The Elliott Wave Theorist* called the battle against the IMF "a crystal-clear window to 'the approaching chaos' alluded to in the final chapter of *At the Crest of the Tidal Wave*. In financial historian J.K. Galbraith's vernacular, society is now experiencing the 'final common feature' of a financial euphoria, 'anger and recrimination.'

The classic symptoms of this post-bubble backlash have emerged in all the countries affected by plunging markets." At that time, it did not include the United States. Its arrival on U.S. shores has been signaled by more than just an [April] IMF protest. According to the SEC, investor complaints are pouring in. Just four days after the April 14 smash in the NASDAQ, the following headline appeared in USA Today: "Losing Investors play blame game." "The pain of stock market losses is making some people lash out in anger," says the story. Some warned of a conspiracy between market strategists and the media while others blamed day traders, politicians, the judge who ruled against Microsoft and bearish TV commentators. The Wave Principle is great at times like this because it is the one tool that identifies the true source of all the agitation and conflict. From this vantage point above the fray, we can stand ready to pick up valuable assets when everyone else is casting them aside.

The Timing of Bailouts

In the past three decades, the U.S. government has taken to bailing out losing enterprises. These actions derive from the same egalitarian impulse behind its attacks on successful companies at major social mood tops. Rather than acting to prevent *success*, though, the government acts to prevent *failure*. The overall economic result is still destructive, as saving one enterprise endangers its competitors and wastes both productive resources and tax money at the same time, but this fact is irrelevant to the socionomic observation that impulsive social mood is the engine of these actions.

When do bailouts occur? Bailouts occur near stock market lows, when the mood is the opposite of that near peaks. As you can see in the following chart, Lockheed Aircraft and Penn Central Railroad applied for aid in March and May 1970, as the stock market was crashing into its biggest low in 28 years. (Aid was approved in December 1970 and August 1971.) In another bailout of Penn Central and several other northeastern railroads, Congress created Conrail in 1974, the final year of the biggest bear market since 1937-1942. (It took two separate "federal investments" of $2.1 billion in 1976 and $1.2 billion in 1980, as real stock prices continued falling, to keep Conrail on track.) The government's initial rescue of Continental Illinois came in May 1984, at the bottom of a fear-laden "wave

TIMING OF APPLICATIONS FOR U.S. GOVERNMENT BAILOUTS VS. AGGREGATE STOCK PRICES

Resolution Trust Corp. created

Continental Illinois

Chrysler

Lockheed

Penn Central

Conrail created

© May 2000 Elliott Wave International

two" stock market correction. (It was completed with a $4.5 billion FDIC package in late July.) Following the 1987 crash and the sluggish, mostly sideways year of 1988, Congress established the Resolution Trust Corp. on February 6, 1989. Its creation marked the beginning of the biggest financial bailout in U.S. history. The crisis lasted through the 1990 bear market (which brought the Value Line index down to its 1987 low) and abated by mid-1993, when the RTC had liquidated or paid off the debts of 90% of the failed institutions it had taken over.

Although a bailout involves the use of force — taking tax money and using it to shore up an enterprise that no one will support voluntarily — it is psychologically the opposite of an attack. While free competition in fact requires allowing failure, the force wielded by the government is intended, however erroneously, to benefit competition by keeping the number of competitors in the marketplace higher than it would be otherwise.

June 2000

Valuation

Stock market valuation in March 2000 will probably stand as the outer limit for centuries (see chart next page). Notice the bullets marking the S&P 400's valuation in September 1929 and July 1932. These show what happens when the gravitational pull of normalcy reasserts itself after a historic overvaluation. The trip back always takes investor psychology past average valuations to at least the low end of the normal range shown by the box in this chart, now dwarfed in size by the utterly outrageous extremes attending the stock mania of the 1990s. Now that tech stocks are in retreat, one of the popular things to say is that the "rationale for the boom" got out of hand, and the decline marks a return to common sense. This sudden onset of sanity has reputedly produced the rebirth of the "old economy" and thus, relative strength for the Dow. The mantra is, "valuation matters again." If history is any guide, the bulls had better hope this is false.

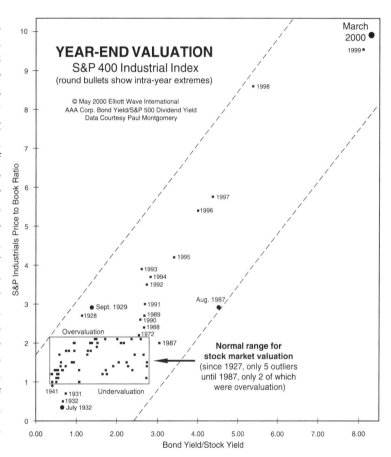

Financial Shenanigans Coming to Light

Some of the lame excuses for optimism are being outed. As *The Elliott Wave Theorist* noted in our 1998 Special Report on the relative weakness of the fundamentals in Cycle V vs. Cycle III, "the enduring psychological coercion of the bull market" has compensated for Cycle V's obvious fundamental shortcomings with the general acceptance of accounting standards that overstate the quality of companies' financial performance. The exposure of fallacious bull-market bookkeeping has been a subject of ongoing discussion in EWFF. For our purposes, the importance is not the transgressions themselves, but the timing of their discovery and repudiation. This process actually started within a few days of the peak of the advance/decline line in April 1998, when a long advance in Cendant Corp. was revealed to be influenced by "fictitious revenue."

This process has accelerated in the wake of the NASDAQ's retreat. There is now "growing concern among accounting professionals that many companies are relying on financial alchemy to burnish their results." Instead of peripheral corporate players and outright fraud, the charges of "financial engineering" are now being leveled against stalwarts like Microsoft, Dell and Cisco Systems for accounting practices that have been known to be in place for years. Less than a month after Cisco was tabbed as the new stock-market bellwether, its aggressive acquisition strategy was profiled as a "modern house of cards" in Barron's.

Days later, Cisco's reported earnings surpassed analysts' expectations by one cent for the 12th straight quarter, yet failed to produce the usual upside pop. In fact, the stock plunged. It is now down 33% from its high. In another sudden reversal, First Call, the keeper of Wall Street's main yardstick for measuring quarterly results, which had "become more indulgent in recent years about letting companies and analysts slice earnings any way they see fit," has challenged a company's effort to omit the losses of its Internet subsidiary in its first quarter numbers. "Excluding Internet losses is beyond the pale," said the firm's research director.

The return to sobriety is uncovering all kinds of techniques that have allowed firms to pyramid stock-market gains and pad profits. Some of the most widespread offenses center around stock option plans. As EWFF noted in October, stock options carry an additional psychological weight because instead of acting as an incentive, they become a "huge source of employee discontent" in a bear market. The full-fledged arrival of this burden announced itself to our ears in the form of a radio report in which the reporter stated that workers everywhere "are experiencing the dark side of stock options." "It's all about bringing the stock up," said one of several employees who were "too nervous to give their names." Nobody came right out and said it, but from the mixture of shock, desperation and hope in the voices, it was clear that what these people really wanted to know was this: how come nobody told them that stocks go down?

July 2000
The "New Reality" Bites

There is a common theme in the press now. Writers are calling the stock market setback a "new reality," or "rational exuberance" or "the culling of the weak." As we said last month, and as the history surrounding the declining side of the South Sea and Nikkei charts (see Chapter 1) illustrates, "a sudden onset of sanity" is not a bullish thing because it is a sure sign that the increasingly delusional psychology that created the mania has stopped waxing and has begun to wane.

Last month, we reported that the exposure of slack bull market accounting standards and outright frauds was worth watching as an indication that the "return to sobriety" was gaining ground. Even as stocks rallied modestly in June, there were further revelations about boomtime financial practices. The New York Times revealed on June 13, for instance, that in a declining market, stock options can be as hard on investment performance as they were a lift on the way up. In various academic papers and commentaries, "economists and investors warn [that] companies and their shareholders will find themselves paying a heavy price for something they thought was a free lunch."

Another big story focused on Cendant Corp., the same firm that our September 1998 issue placed at the leading edge of revelations about slack bull market accounting standards. It turns out that Cendant's accounting shenanigans date all the way back to its initial public offering in 1983. As columnist Floyd Norris notes, "For investors, the most interesting question is not whether" the firm's founder "will go to jail. It is how this fraud managed to go on so long." The answer, according to a professor of accounting who has studied a report on Cendant's bookkeeping practices, is that "auditors were fooled because, in some measure at least, they wanted to be

---

Financial Scam Artists Thrive on Investors' Naiveté and Greed

The Mob Goes Downtown

A stock scam shakes Wall Street, while investigators say there's more to come

The most far-reaching federal indictment of mob-led stock fraud, bribery and extortion took place last week in New York City. Mobsters have found the fringes of the stock market particularly ripe for the picking.

U.S. News & World Report, June 26, 2000

MILWAUKEE JOURNAL SENTINEL, July 9, 2000

Financial Frankensteins Terrorize All Americans

According to the Securities and Exchange Commission and the North American Securities Administrators Association, scammers pitching phony securities cost U.S. investors at least $10 billion a year.

USA Today, July 6, 2000

Investors Beware! Internet Scams Are Seductive, Costly

The Commercial Appeal, July 2, 2000

---

fooled." This, at bottom, is the thesis of socionomics. The social mood dictates how people treat real data. From 1983 through 1999, public mood was in a bull market. This year, it all changed, and so has the socially perceived reality.

A steady stream of big-time financial scams gave the world its first hard look at the scale of financial fraud that bull market psychology has refused to expose. On June 15, reports revealed the "largest securities fraud sting in history," as the FBI arrested 120 people and broke up "a ring of organized crime on Wall Street" that has been operating for five years. Five days later, the damage done by "the mob" was eclipsed by a money laundering scheme that was many times as large. According to accounts, there is no hope of ever getting to the bottom of it. A federal probe into whether $7 billion was illegally diverted out of Russia has been "stymied" by Russian officials. The SIPC, the government's insurance fund for the securities industry, announced on June 20 that it had paid out $31 million in connection with a Texas scam. The payment is its largest ever.

When the Royal Bank of Canada was charged with stock manipulation, a Toronto paper said, the "practice of manipulating stock prices and pension fund performance has been suspected for so long, the only real surprise is that Canada's largest bank got caught first." This acceleration in the size and scope of fraud exposure is exactly what *The Elliott Wave Theorist* has said we should expect in a post-mania environment. EWT first made this prediction in August 1991 with reference to Japan and the collapse in the Nikkei. Scams and scandals grow with prosperity and then become even more severe as financial distress pushes many schemes over the edge.

August 2000

The following graph of the bond/stock yield ratio shows that stock market overvaluation is still making history. On July 20, the AAA-rated bond yield pushed to 8.57 times the stock yield. This is the highest stock valuation relative to bond market valuation in history, and by a huge margin. The all-time high in the ratio was achieved against a lower second wave high in the Dow, S&P and NASDAQ. This fact is not simply of academic importance, as there is a crucial precedent for this condition that speaks directly to the situation now. The last time this happened was on October 2, 1987, one trading day before the start of the 1987 crash.

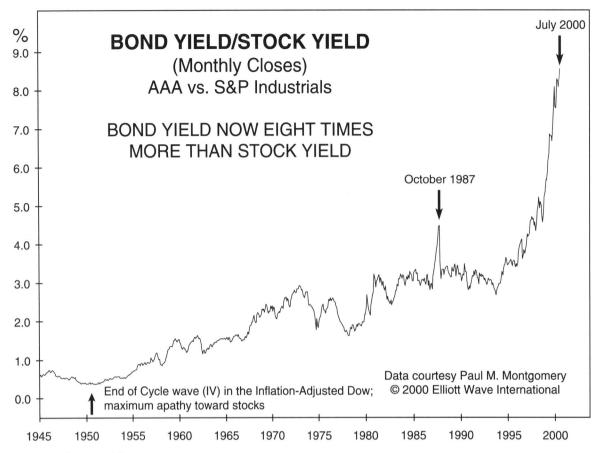

September 2000

Many of the bull-market accounting gimmicks that we have covered in the recent issues of EWFF are alternate forms of financial leverage. In many cases, this is quite literally the case because firms have financed options and buy-back schemes with corporate debt. In other cases, companies are drawing cash reserves down so low that their creditworthiness is compromised. The trend poses "systemic, long-term risk" to companies' debt ratings, says one specialist. All it took was a two-month decline of 16% in the Dow to expose this weakness. The same practices that goosed the numbers on the way up will drag them down in a bear market.

The latest revelations concern the "magic" of pension fund accounting. A quarter of the firms in the S&P applied gains from pension fund increases to their 1999 earnings. "If the stock market were to go down dramatically and the surpluses were to disappear, the impact on reported earnings would be very dramatic and very adverse." As the July issue noted and accountants are starting to realize, stock options will be as much of a burden on investment performance on the way down as they were a lift on the way up. This headline [is] from the August 25 USA Today: "People Crave Stock Options But Don't Understand Them." The unprecedented naivete that surrounds these instruments will prove to be directly proportional to the outrage the public will express at the next major bottom.

December 2000

The persistent conflict between the social effects of the bear market and investors' relentlessly bullish outlook for stocks also suggests that the downtrend will soon reassert itself. EWFF has been commenting on the schism between the rising tide of financial scandal and investors' willingness to buy and hold stocks for several months, but the latest wave of mutual fund investigations has raised the dissonance to epic levels. According to one survey, 84% of investors refuse to sell, or plan to buy more, even though 67% of the same group doesn't trust corporate management, 65%

doesn't trust auditors and 79% questions the reliability of corporate financial statements. In an article headlined, "Rich See More Risk Everywhere, But Stocks Offer Some Solace," The Wall Street Journal reported that "a real dynamic tension" exists between investors' position in the market and their rising concern about financial security. A story on a similar survey was headlined, "Wealthy Investors Losing Faith in Wall Street." But respondents said that they still "believe there will be positive returns." By strategists' conservative estimates that means a "normal" up year of "10 to 12 percent gains." The survey was called a "powerful wake-up call for Wall Street." Any further advance will only heighten the tension, which means the real wake-up call will be the torrential stock market decline that comes when investors finally move to align their portfolios with their increasingly "negative attitudes" toward the financial world. The form and extent of the post-mania countertrend suggest that this bearish resolution is imminent.

One common form of financial leverage that has been exposed in recent weeks is high-tech companies' "portfolio investments" in (what else?) other high-tech firms. Recent accounts reveal that many companies like GE, Intel, Microsoft and Cisco "made many such investments at rock-bottom prices and were able to sell at handsome mark-ups during the mania."

Another revelation focuses on loans to customers. The public is now learning that many of their favorite tech companies pumped up performance by lending start-ups the money to buy their products. So, mounting bankruptcies mean sales don't just slow, they disappear from prior quarters. "It is only going to get worse," reported The Wall Street Journal on November 24. "High-tech equipment makers world-wide are exposed to the problems like never before."

March 2001

In the middle of last year, when the financial community was reassuring itself that the decline in stocks was a good thing because it meant that "valuation matters again," *The Elliott Wave Financial Forecast* said, "the bulls had better hope this is false." Our reason is that periods of historic overvaluation are always followed by return trips past average valuation to the low end of the normal range or beyond. What's more, as Bob Prechter has pointed out, major stock market declines bring economic contractions. Normally, fast-falling stock prices produce lower P/Es, but if the accompanying economic contraction is swift and powerful enough, the decline in earnings will push the P/E ratio up. As the following item from Floyd Norris' March column in the N.Y. Times points out, this is what is happening now:

NASDAQ Stocks Pricey Despite Drop

As the red ink flows, the NASDAQ 100 is setting new standards for a price-earnings ratio by a major index. The index is now trading at 811 times the combined earnings of the companies in the index. The surge in the price-earnings ratio means stocks in the NASDAQ 100 are now exceptionally expensive on the basis of the companies' ability to actually make money.

In other words, the P/E ratio for NASDAQ stocks is going up even though stocks are collapsing (in fact, partly because stocks are collapsing). With the NASDAQ off a hefty 60%, one can only imagine how far down it will have to go to achieve a "normal" P/E. The deteriorating fundamentals have the potential to push a whole range of valuation measures even further out into deep space before they start their trip back to undervaluation.

"Value" shoppers should keep this in mind as the temptation to nibble on stocks that look cheap intensifies. Consider, for instance, the undervaluation index of "select blue chip stocks" published by Geraldine Weiss at Investment Quality Trends (LaJolla Calif.). After reaching an all-time low of 2% in April 1998, falling prices for most stocks helped lift the percent of undervalued stocks to 14% in December 2000. Since then, however, as the market has continued to fall, the index has declined by half to 7%. Even once-sacrosanct utility payouts have been threatened in recent months. And we haven't even seen an official recession! Rest assured that further economic contraction is coming.

July 2001

In the March 28 issue, *The Elliott Wave Financial Forecast* posited that even as the market began to rally, the rising wave of resentment toward analysts and other bull market luminaries would ironically intensify. [The Dow Jones Industrial Average rallied about 25% from March 22, 2001 through May 22, 2001.–Ed.] We made that prediction because social actions lag social mood. The specific forecast has certainly come to pass, as the volume of lawsuits, investigations and shareholder rebellions has gone to new highs in recent weeks. In the first stage of a decline, investors are too focused on hope to muster any appetite for vengeance. As soon as the bottom is in, however, psychology has completed its reversal, and an anger commensurate with the decline emerges. Here is a small sample of the places investors are looking to pin the blame:

U.S. Banks Face Huge Claims Over Dot-Coms
—USA TODAY, June 22, 2001

Fuzzy Accounting Raises Flags

Wall Street banks are facing an avalanche of expensive litigation, with as many as 100 class-action lawsuits, demanding tens of billions of dollars in damages. The banks are being accused by investors of allegedly rigging the flotations of Internet companies during the dot-com boom.
—The Times (of London), May 29, 2001

EWFF also identified many of the particulars on the approach to the final highs. Less than three weeks before the NASDAQ's all-time peak, for instance, we anticipated the accounting crisis depicted in the headline above. As far as we know, this is a forecast that did not appear anywhere else.

It is a forecast that intrigues us because in addition to demonstrating the depth of insight that a socionomic grasp makes possible, it confirms our best guess about why socionomics works in the first place. To understand, we must review our discussion of the triune brain and its evolution in Chapter 8 of *The Wave Principle of Human Social Behavior*. The most recently developed portion of the human is the neocortex, which houses the human capacity for processing ideas using reason. Researchers have shown that the neocortex is subservient to a far more impulsive and primitive portion of the brain known as the limbic system. As one scientist says: "The limbic system is where we live, and the neocortex is basically slave to that."

According to the theory sketched out in HSB, in matters of survival, particularly those that are defined by highly subjective human interactions, the rational faculties of the neocortex are no match for the emotion-based survival instincts that inhabit the limbic system:

> How can seemingly rational professionals be so utterly seduced by the opinion of their peers to the effect that they will not only hold, but change opinions collectively? Recall that the neocortex is functionally disassociated from the limbic system. This means not only that feelings of conviction may attach to utterly contradictory ideas in different people but that they can do so in the same person at different times. In other words, the same brain can support opposite views with equally intense emotion, depending upon the demands of survival perceived by the limbic system. This fact relates directly to the behavior of financial market participants, who can be flush with confidence one day and in a state of utter panic the next.

The expanding controversy over accounting standards is a perfect example of the same brains taking the opposite view based on the demands of survival. As of the late 1990s, many thousands of analysts altered the tenets of the profession to a point at which book value, dividends, profits and total earnings did not matter. Contending otherwise was grounds for dismissal; in fact, analysts lost their jobs because they refused to adopt the new standard. Now, however, succeeding in the same job requires a single-minded devotion to judging earnings.

The change revolves around a very specific event at a very specific time. On March 10, 2000, the direction of the NASDAQ switched from up to down and the influence of social mood on millions of limbic systems reversed. On the approach to that high, the accountants themselves were consumed with hope and denial. Afterward, the essence of the job became to doubt the numbers. USA Today's June 22 story notes, "accounting experts, analysts and academics" all agree "companies are twisting the numbers to show better results."

September 2001
Can the Market Bail Out One More Bailout?

Once again, the International Monetary Fund appeared to rescue a teetering financial system with an August 23 bailout of Argentina. The timing is about right as the May 2000 issue of *The Elliott Wave Theorist* explained, "Bailouts occur near stock market lows." An updated version of the chart from that issue is shown here. In recent years, the bailouts of Mexico in early 1995, South Korea, Thailand and Indonesia in December 1997, and Brazil, Pakistan and Long Term Capital Management in 1998 were all completed after the lows were in place.

Over the course of the bull market, the lows

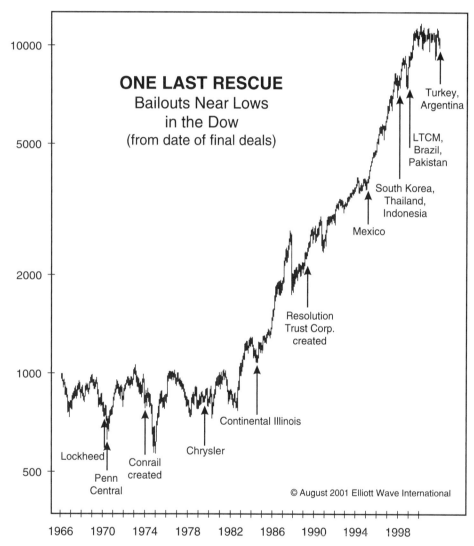

ONE LAST RESCUE
Bailouts Near Lows
in the Dow
(from date of final deals)

Turkey, Argentina

LTCM, Brazil, Pakistan

South Korea, Thailand, Indonesia

Mexico

Resolution Trust Corp. created

Continental Illinois

Chrysler

Conrail created

Lockheed

Penn Central

© August 2001 Elliott Wave International

associated with the bailouts on this chart have never been broken. Notice that the same cannot be said for the bailouts of the 1970s. During the Cycle degree bear market of 1966-1982, bailouts were always ultimately followed by new lows. If the Dow's bull market is intact, the bull market bailout pattern should hold. The deal with Argentina should mark the end of the latest crisis and be followed by a new high in the Dow. If the March 22 low of 9106 is broken, it will be the first breach of a bailout low in more than 20 years, a clear signal that the Dow is back in bear-market mode. It will also mark the beginning of the end for the IMF's rescue efforts. Without the true source of its success, the bull market, the IMF will wither fast. By the first important stock market low, its purse will be empty and its policies the object of bitter discord and derision.

October 2001

Into the Bottomless Bailout Pit

Last month, EWFF stated, "If the March 22 low at 9106 is broken, it will be the first breach of a bailout low in more than 20 years, a clear signal that the Dow is back in bear market mode." Six days after the September 17 break of 9106, the international financial crisis discussed in last month's issue reached the U.S. mainland as Congress passed a bill that will attempt to rescue the U.S. airline industry. And "the line of U.S. bailout supplicants" is growing fast in Washington. "Bailout fever is in the air," reported one columnist. The speed and scope of the need is another big hint that the era of the successful financial rescue has ended.

November 2001

Remember back in 1999 and early 2000 when the mania was in full bloom and academics offered "proof" of a new era in valuations in all the leading investment journals? Even though valuation levels as measured by virtually every method are still higher than at almost any time in history, the same Ivy League economists are getting access to the same opinion pages to concoct variations on the same theme. "There is no reason to believe" price/earnings multiples are "historically high" although, at 22, P/Es are still historically high. In a Wall Street Journal op-ed piece headlined, "Don't Sell Out," a Princeton economics professor asserts, "The market today appears to be fairly valued." Another Wall Street

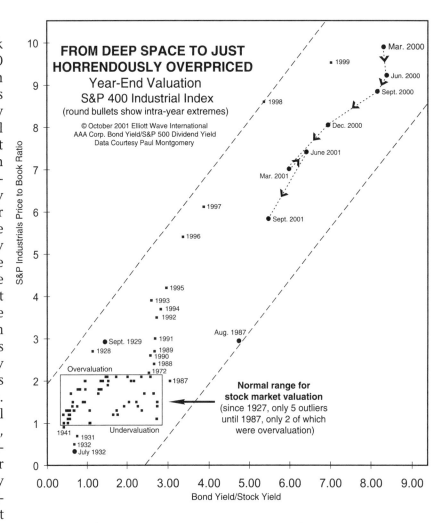

Journal article says, "Veteran Value-Fund Managers See Bargains Everywhere." No one seems to recall that the entire basis for sky-high valuations was a technology-induced earnings boom that failed to materialize. In fact, earnings are in a free fall, and the innovation that was used to justify the new set of valuation rules is feeding the deflationary spiral.

When the S&P 500 finally broke down in March 2000, a belief in slightly more rational valuation levels suddenly set in. "The mantra is 'valuation matters again,'" EWFF noted in June 2000. "If history is any guide, the bulls had better hope this is false." EWFF identified the March 2000 bullet on the preceding chart as the "outer limit" of valuation extreme and asserted that the trip back to at least the low end of the normal range shown by the box at the bottom of the chart had begun. The updated version of our chart shows a quarterly progression that is racing back toward the "normal range" box. As in 1930-1932, the downward pull on valuations has been relentless.

The long-term chart of year-end Dow dividend yields offers another perspective on what happens when valuation matters again. Viewed from year-to-year, the long-term movement from over- to undervaluation is usually a fast trip with very little intervening volatility. In fact, since the early 1900s, every time the Dow has fallen through 3.47% and then reversed by more than 20%, it has continued past the 102-year average dividend yield of 4.34%. With the rise to above 2%, the Dow has now completed such a reversal. At current dividend levels, it would take a further Dow decline to 4126 to return the dividend yield to this long-term average. As noted, however, rising yields never stop at the average level. A replay of the minimum reversal would take the Dow's yield to 5.36%, which equates to a Dow of 3340. A return to 7.2%, the average extreme for the eight advances since 1907, would be attained with a Dow of 2487.

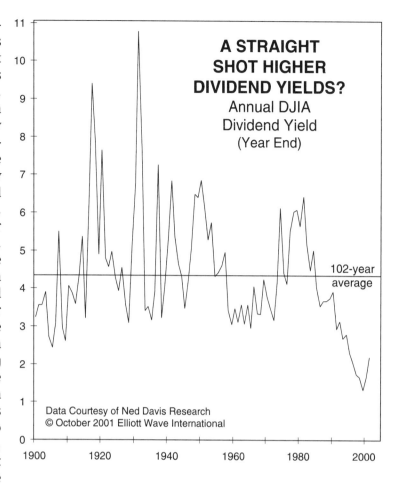

A STRAIGHT SHOT HIGHER DIVIDEND YIELDS?
Annual DJIA
Dividend Yield
(Year End)

102-year average

Data Courtesy of Ned Davis Research
© October 2001 Elliott Wave International

These figures are actually conservative estimates because the current cash payout to shareholders is anything but assured. The October 10 USA Today reveals that even "blue-chip firms are struggling with cash." Ford Motor Co. has already blown through so much of its cash horde that it has slashed its dividend by 50%. Others firms like TRW and Dana Corp. have followed suit. Considering the high degree of the trend change, a potential for a 50% cut in the average dividend strikes us as very likely. With such a reduction, a yield rise past 9% would put the Dow back below 1000. *At the Crest of the Tidal Wave*'s triple-digit forecast for the Dow still strikes many as impossible, but if the craving for cash continues on its historic path, it won't stop there. At 9%, the dividend yield would be only slightly better than halfway to the high of 16% in 1932, the last Supercycle-degree decline. This time we're talking about an unprecedented Grand Supercycle decline, so there is no telling how high yields could go.

December 2001

Enron Corp.'s imminent [bankruptcy] will easily be the largest bankruptcy ever, topping the old record (Texaco in 1987) by almost 70%. With respect to deflation and the lending standards of the future, the nature of the energy trading firm's business is even more important than its size. As one headline notes, "Enron Soared on [financial] Innovation, Fell as Debt Scared Away Investors." One story says Enron's "bewildering series" of financial makes it "a black hole...a witches brew of bankruptcy." The "forensic accountants" have been called in to sort out a mess that will lead on to a seemingly endless series of financial catastrophes.

January 2002

A Fool on the Hill

Some still insist the stock market cannot experience a 1929-1932-type collapse because margin buying is not the problem that it was in 1929. A recent editorial in Upside magazine says, for example, "The number of people leveraging their stock savvy to buy shares in great companies with money they don't have is not nearly the number in the 1920s, nor do banks lend money to buy stocks on the margin as they did in the 1920s." But *The Elliott Wave Theorist* and *The Elliott Wave Financial Forecast* have continually warned that financial leverage is actually far more abundant than it was in the 1920s. Over the years, we have observed its presence and potential for destruction in everything from financial such as stock options to bull market accounting standards. We have also continually noted that the real difference between 1930 and the current "margin call" is that back in 1930 the buyers actually got called. This time around, the "sophistication" of many forms of modern financial leverage means that the full extent of the exposure cannot be known until the confidence that underlies them has washed away. This is what happened at Enron. When the marketplace suddenly "lost confidence" in its impossibly complex "off balance sheet" financing structures, Enron went straight to bankruptcy court. Within days, Enron retirees were lining up in front of the Subcommittee on Consumer Affairs to tell how they lost everything in Enron stock. This is what we meant when we said that the extent of the margin problem could only be known in retrospect. The best way to keep a tally on the size of the margin call will be to keep an eye on Congress and other venues of recrimination. Be careful, however; it is not likely to be a pretty sight. Here's how the Enron fiasco opened at hearings on December 18:

Mr. Chairman, Members of the committee:

Good Morning. I am William H. Mann, senior analyst for The Motley Fool. As it is not often that a Fool gets the chance to address the United States Senate, I am honored by the invitation to speak before you today about Enron...

This is only the fact finding stage. Late in the downtrend and into the early part of the next uptrend, they'll start in with the "reforms." This fool is a harbinger of the hare-brained and eventually quite harmful "solutions" the watchdogs are likely to come up with.

February 2002

The advance shown on this chart is a representation of the bull market in cash. It is formed by inverting NASDAQ prices to show the purchasing power of cash relative to shares of the NASDAQ. As the NASDAQ declines, the amount of stock a holder of cash can buy rises. This is good news for those that have to buy stocks because it shows that by employing strate-

HEARD ABOUT THE BIG BULL MARKET?

© February 2002 Elliott Wave International

2000   2001

gies that optimize the timing of purchases they can actually stockpile purchasing power while everyone else is getting hammered. In March 2000, for instance, *The Elliott Wave Financial Forecast* showed the chart of mutual fund holdings (updated below) and declared, "Cash is Dead... Long Live Cash." At the time, many new economy believers were taking stock options in lieu of currency, and EWFF said this was a huge mistake. Anyone who cashed out at that time knows exactly what we meant. The purchasing power of that cash in terms of NASDAQ shares grew more than 350% by September 21.

The mutual fund cash levels in the chart reveal that cash is still in a new bull market. Mutual fund cash levels are not even halfway to 12%, their usual bear market extreme, while record high bankruptcies, soaring corporate losses and dividend reductions indicate that the demand for cash within the economy is expanding at the fastest rate in years. S&P 500 firms reduced their dividend payouts by 3.3% last year; that's the biggest decline in 50 years and the first back-to-back decline in the dividend rate since 1970-1971.

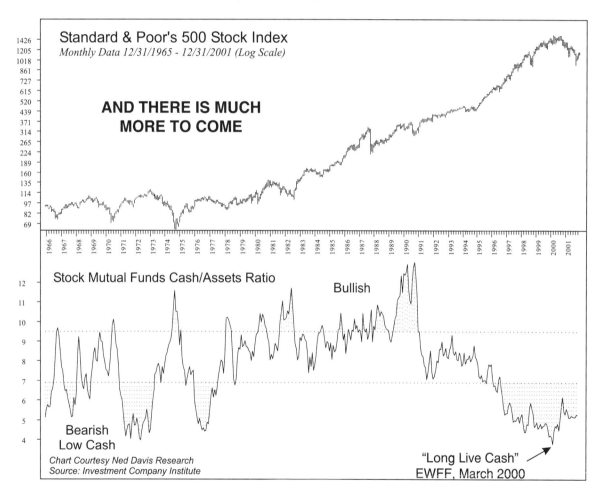

Sentiment remains bullish as investor disdain for the safest haven on the planet is still running high. One inside observer reports that money managers are "doubling down" on stocks because their clients will not tolerate big cash positions. "Managers believe it is the best hope for their survival." Actually, cash itself is the single best ticket to being around for the ride to the next big top. When a true bottom is finally at hand, the masters of cash management will have mountains of buying power to put to work on true values.

All Enron, All the Time

"Twenty minutes ago, the only topics on the nation's radar screen were Afghanistan and terrorism. Now there's Enron," says a USA Today column on "How Enron Stole Center Stage." One of the big mysteries is why the public suddenly cannot get enough dirt on Enron. "A few years ago, it would hardly have seemed possible," Business Week notes. "The nation's attention, from the halls of Congress to Main Street, has been riveted on an accounting scandal, a subject so abstruse it rarely makes the front page."

But there it is on page 1, day after day after day. Here's what the front page of yesterday's Wall Street Journal had to say:

> Tuesday was the day that the smoldering corporate accounting scandal, which started with Enron Corp. and quickly spread to Arthur Andersen LLP, reached a wide group of U.S. companies and seriously singed their stock prices. Accounting problems surfaced at companies ranging from banking to oil, prompting fears of new mini-Enrons and spurring a sell-off of shares at the slightest whiff of such trouble.

The steamroller is moving so fast we can hardly keep up. The number of Congressional investigations has risen to double digits and the lawsuits are likely to climb into the thousands. Today's news is that the Government Accounting Office will bring suit against the White House. The Washington Post says it is the first such suit in the GAO's 80-year history and "the highest profile court fight between Congress and an administration since Watergate." The gathering mass and momentum of the scandal verify that a 200-year, Grand Supercycle-degree uptrend ended in the first quarter of 2000.

The public's "growing sense of anger" over Enron and now, corporate America in general, is no surprise to our subscribers. It is the latest and, to date at least, the greatest manifestation of the financial scandals that *The Elliott Wave Theorist* predicted would be an inevitable byproduct of the long-term reversal in social mood. Since the advance-decline line turned down in April 1998, EWT and *The Elliott Wave Financial Forecast* have continued to give readers sneak peeks at the drama that is now unfolding. Many of you are clearly catching on, because you have been sending us keen insights into its eventual extent. One alert subscriber noted, for instance, that Enron is a twin to the Insull Utility Trust scandal that broke in the wake of the crash in 1929. Then as now, financial pioneers used the most "innovative" instruments of the day to gain maximum leverage on a fast-rising social mood and amassed a towering utilities empire. Of the now fallen modern-day version, The New York Times says, "Proving Fraud May Be Elusive." It was much the same in the 1930s when founder Samuel Insull was "acquitted of embezzlement, fraud and violation of the bankruptcy laws." Nevertheless, "he became an example of the corruption and fraud which contributed to the Great Depression. The revelation of corporate duplicity brought to light during the investigation led to a public outcry for reform." The same steamrolling public opinion is clearly on the loose, again.

The almost rabid mass attraction to once mundane audit matters is another sign of a big-time trend change. In February 2000, one month after the peak in the Dow, EWFF added "that the bull market's attendant accounting gimmicks will also get a lot more ink." At the time, EWFF said, "For our purposes, the importance is not the transgressions themselves, but the timing of their discovery and repudiation." As the news rippled through the financial community, the market was actually rallying in wave ②. It is most important to realize that the latest, much larger series of accounting scandals has emerged in a similar countertrend wave of one larger degree. The first news story about Enron's shaky finances actually broke last March, when the market hit a short-term bottom. But the media firestorm didn't start until the wave b rally was clearly underway. As one headline put it, Enron is a story that "Waited To be Told." What was it waiting for? It was waiting to provide the perfect psychological set-up for the next leg down. Remember, third waves are the "point-of-recognition" waves, which means they offer the consensus a rare moment of clarity. During the set up for wave ③ in June 2000, we said the "return to sobriety" was bearish, not bullish, for stocks because it meant that the "delusional psychology that created the mania has begun to wane." Here are a couple more headlines suggesting that the latest dose of reality will be even more damaging to stock prices:

New Realism May Set the Corporate Mood
The New York Times, January 20, 2002

In Recession, Face Brutal Facts, Thrive
USA Today, November 27, 2001

The second one illustrates that the grand illusion has not dissipated. According to a column by a famous CNBC anchor, "more realistic" means "savvier than ever." The truth is that most investors still do not have a clue. The USA article on thriving in a recession hints that the moment when they finally start to "get it" may not be that far off. The article offers a quote from Vietnam veteran Jim Stockdale, who lived through most of the last major bear market in a Hanoi prison camp with the help of this philosophy: "You must never confuse faith that you will prevail in the end with the need for discipline to confront the most brutal facts of your current reality, whatever they might be." The Enron scandal and its recent "spread to other large, complex companies" shows that investors are waking up to what they did not want to know during the bull market. A new bear market reality is taking form in the newly stringent accounting mindset. After a 250-point drop on January 29, the biggest one-day decline since the panic low of September, The Wall Street Journal noted, "Signs of toughening stances by auditors and regulators emerged, raising questions as to how many more corporate managements will be forced to restate their earnings and abandon cozy accounting treatments that easily passed muster a few months ago." The fate of "goodwill" is a great example of how the atmosphere surrounding the public's beloved fundamentals has shifted from up to down. (One column comes right out and tells managers they should "Dare To Keep Your Stock Price Low"). Goodwill accounting principles have been altered in a way that will crush the earnings of many firms for years to come. Because of the changes, firms that were buying up everything in sight, are now searching for ways to break apart. Tyco International, which was formerly known as the "grand acquirer," has dumped its dealmaking apparatus and put out this message: "Everything is for sale." Since the beginning of the year when rumors of accounting irregularities again hit the street, Tyco has fallen by 50%.

The collapse fits right in with our forecast for the bear market. In late 1999, EWFF said, "The flip side of papered-over cracks in the fundamentals is that in a bear market they will be an enormous weight on growth. The likelihood is that they will exert their drag with stunning speed." Enron's near-total destruction took 14 months. Then, Time magazine reported, "It's the scariest type of scandal: a total system failure." If the system is a total failure and the media can only inform investors of the next failure after it is over, and the numbers that investors are supposed to use to do their own homework cannot be relied upon, the only answer is to sell. But virtually all the experts say the moral of the Enron story is to do the opposite:

Diversify, Diversify, Diversify
The Wall Street Journal, January 18, 2002

This is "the most important rule, by far, for successful investors," they say. But *At the Crest of the Tidal Wave* challenged the diversification gospel with this statement: "Extracting oneself from investments in Singapore, Taiwan, France and Brazil, or from junk bonds and exotic real estate packages upon which no one is bidding, will be a nightmare in a bear market." The longer the bear market wears on, the truer this statement becomes, yet the more insistently the experts fall back on diversification. A Wall Street Journal headline says, "Many Investors Pick Stocks For Lack of Other Options." It highlights a preference for junk bonds, real estate and foreign markets, all of which are ongoing or pending disasters. Another article says that most investors are being told to get used to single-digit returns, but they can still score big if they emphasize "extremely compelling opportunities," like small-cap stocks, REITs and high yield bonds. In other words, the "magic answer" of diversification is being used to herd investors into the very things that *At the Crest* said were the most important to avoid.

An extension of the Enron lesson is what it has reputedly taught investors about their all-important retirement accounts. Recall that the whole 401(k) boom that contributed mightily to the mania is founded in a deep-seated desperation for higher yields. *At the Crest* traced the roots of this great yield hunger to the early 1990s when investors decided there was "nowhere else to go." By August 1999, EWFF reported that many were actually using the "compulsory" buying in 401(k) accounts to suggest that the bubble could not break, since too many people needed the money. But break it did, and some pensioners were wiped out. Instead of safely removing clients' most vital retirement funds to the sidelines, "brokers and human resource professionals across the country" are "reworking their portfolios and shifting money from fallen stars to safer investments." Safer means sectors that have fallen less or typically rebound in the early stages of an economic recovery or have simply not fallen yet. Pension funds remain perfectly positioned for maximum damage.

March 2002
What's Beyond Enron

Last month, we showed how perfectly the Enron scandal fits the blueprint for a Grand Supercycle-degree bear market. This month the river of recriminations broke its banks. The potential for a flood of Enron-style revelations into virtually any sector of the economy is signaled by word that the Federal Reserve is "stepping up" its scrutiny of securitized credit-card debt and mortgages as well as a Fortune exposé that offers investors "More Reasons to Get Riled Up." Fortune points out that Enron's $63 billion in market losses is nothing compared to the $155 to $423 billion in market cap that disappeared from 10 other firms. "Let's get mad at them, too," says the magazine. "Let's put our anger and righteous outrage in all the places they belong."

Meanwhile, Enron has evolved into what one Washington attorney called "an eerie financial witch hunt" that is comparable to the Salem witch trials. The still-expanding demand for dirt on Enron is apparent by its arrival on the cover of the National Enquirer. The tabloid claims to have the "untold story" in its latest issue. When it comes to Enron, however, the only story the media has left untold is what's driving the fascination. EWFF covered the socionomic dynamics eight months ago in a section which stated, "The rational faculties of the neocortex are no match for the emotion-based survival instincts that inhabit the limbic system. The expanding controversy over accounting standards is a perfect example of the same brains taking the opposite view based on the demands of survival."

When stocks were rising, investors had all the basis they needed to bend accounting standards into the most lenient system imaginable. As the optimism of the bull market is displaced by more bearish dispositions, a new scrutiny has fallen into place. This produces scandals like

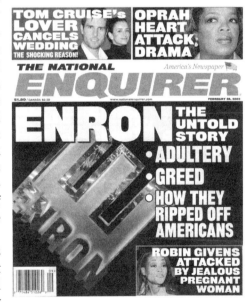

Enron, which are natural consequences of a declining social mood. As we said last month, Enron is a twin to the Insull Utility Trust that marked the scandal phase of the last Supercycle-degree reversal. The February 15 issue of Jim Grant's Interest Rate Observer (30 Wall Street, New York City, www.grantspub.com) followed with a great description of the earlier utility-turned-financial empire and its dismemberment by Congress, the media and the public. Grant recognizes the scandal for what it is: the work of a bear market. He adds that its scale is even larger than that of Insull and agrees with a reader who says, "The 1930s are starting to look pretty good." His assessment corroborates a very important point from last month's issue: The "gathering mass and momentum of the scandal" verifies that a 200-year, Grand Supercycle-degree uptrend ended in the first quarter of 2000.

May 2002

Financial magazine covers continue to flash bold headlines encouraging investors to "Seize the Moment" by buying stocks. "All is Forgiven," says Kiplinger's latest cover, adding, "Top Managers Welcome You Back To the Road To Riches." Most investors bought into the financial media's preeminent "buy and hold" mantra and simply stayed with stocks. While they did not sell in September, many withdrew psychologically. The magazine covers signal that the memory of the pounding of 2000-2001 has receded and that investors are ready to get their heads back in the game.

This may be more dangerous than ever because of the rising wall of post-boom recriminations. The spreading financial scandals and investigations are a predictable result of the reversal in stock prices. EWFF readers know this because EWFF anticipated their arrival in the late 1990s and has been following their rising stature over the last two years. At this point, what interests us is their expanding scope. They are now gaining impetus at an unprecedented rate. As armies of investigators dig deeper into Enron's financial black hole, the New York state attorney general is "using his savvy political instincts" to prosecute Wall Street. On April 29, the SEC got on board with its own probe into whether "big brokerage firms misled small investors with overly optimistic research."

As Bob Prechter has explained, investors relish a good witchhunt in the wake of a great peak because it frees them from accountability. The public's appetite for scandal is rooted in the same delusional psychology that created the bubble in the first place. Since the mood has shifted from up to down, however, it takes a destructive form. In this case, it also creates a tremendous psychological tension because the optimism they are rebelling against still exists. In fact, investors are still acting on the very advice of the advisors they are trying to string up. Like all psychological dissonance, this growing imbalance must be resolved. It won't take many clear-eyed investors to tip the scale to the downside. As a wisened few finally smell the coffee and sell, the exact location of the put-call ratio won't matter. The psychology is in place for a hard break from current levels.

July 2002

From Bad to Worse

This week's Time magazine cover focuses on the end of the world while Newsweek digs into the Martha Stewart insider trading debacle with a front-page story on "Martha's Mess." According to yesterday's Washington Post, "The exploding scope and volume of these still-unfolding corporate and accounting scandals have begun to weigh heavily on the stock market." Subscribers know the truth, a declining social mood, as reflected by the stock market, has produced attacks on the leaders, companies and social units that were the focus of the advance. These are the results of the trend change that were forecast in past issues. Their scope is indicative of the degree of the decline.

July 2, 2002

ISRAEL'S EMERGENCY ROOMS • THE FIRESTARTER MYSTERY

Newsweek

July 1, 2002: $3.95

An Insider Trading Scandal Tarnishes the Queen of Perfection

MARTHA'S MESS

July 1, 2002

Can the scandals and end-of-the-world rhetoric get any worse? Since these are the lagging effects of falling stock prices and stocks have just fallen close to their bear market lows, they surely will. The important point now is that the recriminations have expanded through the decline of 2002. Despite this negative news environment, EWFF turned bearish because the "market is in full reversal of a mania in which the public enjoyed a rare, extended fulfillment of its wildest expectations." Just as the market rose through the "best of all possible worlds" in the mid-1990s, EWFF said it should descend through a cloud of gloom. By falling through an intensifying cycle of negative news, the market has confirmed that this is no ordinary bear market. As the Dow fell more than 16% in three months, every new low was accompanied by a trembling headline, from war in the Mideast, to nuclear confrontation to "The End of the World." Just as it peaked temporarily at positive extremes on the way up, countertrend rallies will start near outbreaks of severe pessimism like this week's cover on apocalyptic concern, but a Grand Supercycle bear market cannot get where it is going without passing through these kinds of events and fears.

Since financial scandals are a natural consequence of a reversing mania, the focus on Wall Street and "America's Corporate Meltdown" is another reason to take the bad news at face value this time around. As today's USA Today notes, "The litany of corporate and executive malfeasance appears to grow broader and deeper each day." Yesterday, it was Worldcom's announcement that its earnings were inflated by more than $7.5 billion. The day before, it was a media feeding frenzy over Martha Stewart's trading misadventures. "White-collar crime is spinning through the roof," says a column. "Phony earnings, inflated revenues, conflicted Wall Street analysts, directors asleep at the switch — this isn't just a few bad apples," says a Fortune cover story. "This is our Watergate," says a CNBC commentator. "How about jail time for Wall Street crooks," suggests another pundit.

"Focus on My Salad"

Newsweek says Martha Stewart is not going to jail, and it offers no evidence of impropriety. Still, there she is on the front page as the tarnished "queen of perfection" because Martha Stewart embodies the descending mood. She reflects the public's vulnerability and anger with such perfection that television stations across America had to show the image of her chopping salad, laughing nervously and declaring that she "will be exonerated of any ridiculousness." In March, EWFF anticipated the intensifying glare of the bear market mood with this comment: "The next, more personal phase of this process will focus on the individuals that benefited the most from the rising mood." As the stock market approached its final highs, no one was a more direct beneficiary than Martha Stewart. Her persona was so entwined in the rising mood that she took it public. In October 1999, when her market capitalization rose to $1.7 billion on sales of just $14 million, EWFF said overvaluation had risen to the "level of a social virtue." Over the next five months, Martha Stewart shares fell almost 74% and hinted at a whole new social order. But no one noticed until recent weeks because that is when the new more destructive order was in place. Now CNBC and the scandal sheets track her decline tick for tick.

October 2002

Back in the fall of 1999 when the bull market was just a few months from its final highs, Martha Stewart's public image became such a bankable commodity that Wall Street sold shares in it. *The Elliott Wave Financial Forecast* offered the following socionomic explanation for her incarnation as a high-flying IPO:

> Martha Stewart "struck stock market gold" October 19 with the sale of 14% of her firm to the public. Stewart's first book, *Entertaining*, came out in 1982 as the bull market was taking off. Since then, she has become "the queen of gracious living," a self-made billionaire "credited with creating a lifestyle industry." She is not the first bull-market hero to equitize her persona (the World Wrestling Federation went public on the same day), but she may be the most fully valued. The Martha Stewart company has a capitalization of $1.7 billion and earnings of $14 million, which makes her an excellent "role model" according to one consultant, who added, "we need them because it gives women hope and desire to strive." Overvaluation is now a social virtue.

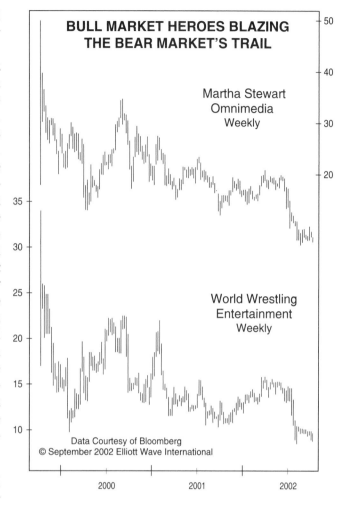

BULL MARKET HEROES BLAZING THE BEAR MARKET'S TRAIL

Martha Stewart Omnimedia Weekly

World Wrestling Entertainment Weekly

Data Courtesy of Bloomberg
© September 2002 Elliott Wave International

2000   2001   2002

Stewart's stock, along with that of World Wrestling Entertainment (the former WWF), did not wait for the peak in the rest of the market to turn down. This chart shows that both were such delicate manifestations of the long-term uptrend that they ran to all-time peaks the moment they went public and have been working their way lower ever since. Their initial breaks foreshadowed the peak of the major averages in the first quarter of 2000, as EWFF indicated that they would in November 1999. The forecast was based on an understanding of the hero-making dynamics of a bull market. "The operative principle of social mood is that every bull market has its champions," explained *The Elliott Wave Theorist* in 1998. "These heroes are of their times, and their images become vulnerable when the wind changes."

The bear market has guided Stewart's image with the same precision as the bull. In September, the now "tarnished queen of perfection" beat the NASDAQ to a new low when she refused to testify before Congress about insider trading charges and had her case forwarded to the Justice Department. "Everything negative that could happen has happened," said the author of a Stewart biography. "A curtain has been drawn back in a way that is causing her excruciating and irreparable damage."

But the curtain to "everything negative" has nothing to do with Martha Stewart. This is clear from the alleged offense, which would not even have been prosecuted in the bull market, and the fact that corporate executives everywhere face similar attacks. The more fully that they leveraged the benevolent effects of a rising social mood, the more likely it is that they now face the slings and arrows of angry shareholders, politicians and community activists.

January 2003

[A] critical parallel to the Grand Supercycle bear market that began in 1720 is that we continue to unwind a mania, one that was even bigger than the South Sea Bubble. As the bull market came to a close and the bear market took its first steps, knowledge of this simple fact has served as an extraordinary forecasting device. In addition to the direction and tenor of the new trend, it has allowed us to predict many specifics like this one:

2002 Indelibly Stamped as the Year of the Scandal

The Associated Press, December 26, 2002

In 2002, "executives were led away in handcuffs, business leaders took the Fifth Amendment" and the "fabric of corporate America was tearing apart." Business Week featured 15 separate covers featuring the fall of financiers and recrimination against corporate governance, accounting malfeasance and other bull market business practices such as mergers. Time magazine's "persons of the year" are three "whistle blowers" against "the swashbuckling economy of the '90s." In "Anger and RecrimiNation" right after the start of the decline in May 2000, EWFF identified the rising sense of outrage in the United States as the "final common feature" of a financial euphoria. "If a moderate sell-off yields this kind of negative emotional release after just a few weeks, imagine what a grinding decline over the course of a few years will yield." We are starting to find out.

Here again, the size of the scandals and the public's pervasive interest in them confirm the high degree of the turn. Scandals are what happen as people slowly snap out of a mania's trance. Some are even starting to recognize the fury of blame and recrimination for what it is, a patterned, post-mania response to a collective euphoria. This story from The New York Times actually unlocks the dynamic:

After a Boom, There Will Be Scandal. Count on It.

It was, it seemed, the year when corporate America went crooked as it never had before, when chicanery took the place of integrity, when wrongdoing exploded in ways that could not have been anticipated. Then again, maybe it wasn't. Despite all the surprise and anguish set off by corporate scandals, for many Wall Street historians and fraud aficionados, the year almost fits into a pattern, as the re-emergence of a moment that has become something of a tradition in the financial world. Most everyone knows of the business cycle of boom and bust, but what is less well known is capitalism's cycle of scandal. Indeed, experts said, the emergence of frauds after the end of a market bubble is a predictable result of human nature.

—December 16, 2002

If it was so predictable, why were we so alone in predicting it? How come no matter how bad things get and how long they stay that way, virtually everyone is sure that they cannot get any worse? The word on all the fraud, for instance, is that it is now out in the open. "2003 is not expected to witness the number of scandals that made 2002 a year of tarnished reputations in the executive suite," says one report. "I can't help but think, on the corporate fraud issues, the pressure is going to be lessened in 2003," says an investment strategist. The reason that he "can't help but think" a certain way is due to the residual force of a 200-year rise that ended three years ago. We see the effect of the very same feelings with respect to countless other crises that are actually predictable consequences of the reversal from a manic high. All of these headlines from the last few days were anticipated in 1998 and 1999 and early 2000 issues of *The Elliott Wave Financial Forecast* and *The Elliott Wave Theorist*:

Options Frenzy: What Went Wrong

Executives' Ownership Stake Put Extreme Focus on Stock; Creating a 'House of Cards'

—Wall Street Journal, December 17, 2002

Financial TV Shows Suffer Hard Times

—USA Today, December 17, 2002

Earnings 'Time Bomb' Looms as Pension Fund Losses Mount

—Bloomberg, December 20, 2002

More Investment Banker Layoffs Ahead

—American Banker, December 30, 2002

North Korea Raises The Nuclear Stakes

—The Atlanta Journal-Constitution, January 1, 2002

No matter how fully bad tidings dominate the investment scene, Wall Street's seers refuse to believe that they will keep stocks from rising in the coming year. The collage of 2003 forecasts shows that the tenacious grip of the old bull's psychology is holding fast.

2003 Forecasts

Economic Indicators Point to Promising 2003
--After a year of mostly distressing economic news, things appear to be looking up a bit for 2003.
—The Florida Times-Union, 12/20/02

BusinessWeek

The Bull in the Crystal Ball
Strategists and portfolio managers see a Dow rally in '03. But then, they saw one in '02, too.
—December 30, 2002

Recovery at hand
—The Atlanta Journal Constitution, 12/22/02

money
YOUR **BEST** MOVES FOR **2003**

Confidence Is Growing That Economic Pickup Is Real Deal This Time
—Investors Business Daily, December 2, 2002

EDITORIAL
Stock Markets Will Be Volatile But Better in 2003
—Knight Ridder, November 3, 2002

Why Stocks Still Rock
December 2002

FORTUNE
Investor's Guide 2003
GET BACK IN THE MARKET
January 1, 2003

Wave Goodbye to the Bears
History suggests the next bull market has already started
Financial Times, November 30, 2002
For the agile and discerning, 2003 will provide a reason to smile again.
—BusinessWeek, December 30, 2002

"Investors want to be in stocks for next year. Returns will be double digit."
—Money Manager, 12/15/02, Denver Post

S&P, others suggest moving money into equities, reducing cash holdings
"We believe the S&P 500 and Nasdaq may advance approximately 15 percent by year-end," said S&P's chief investment strategist.
—Milwaukee Journal Sentinel, Dec 15, 2002

March 2003

Valuation

On January 7, 2000, when the Dow Jones Industrial Average was one week from its all-time high, *The Elliott Wave Financial Forecast* pointed to the all-time low in the Dow dividend yield as a key indicator of the scope of the upcoming decline. Noting that a 100% increase in dividends would still leave the Dow's yield below that of 1929, EWFF said that the record low payout offered "the first glimpse of a very different world to come, one in which surviving firms will have to pay back skittish investors a huge percentage of their initial investment via dividends just to get them to hold their shares." In recent weeks, the beginning of the effort actually to provide investors with a cash return on their investments was signaled by Microsoft's announcement of its first-ever dividend. In January, Fortune reported, "Battered, Angry Investors Are Clamoring for Dividends." As much as companies would like to comply, however, "companies are desperate for cash." Even many utilities, "the classic widow-and-orphan, sleep-at-night stocks," have cut or eliminated "once-sacred dividends." At 2.42%, the Dow's dividend yield still hasn't even returned to where it was at the market's peak in 1929. By the end of the bear market, however, history says investors will get the cash they crave. The Dow's payout surpassed 7% at the start of the Cycle degree bull market in 1982; this time it should go much higher. At the last Supercycle degree low in 1932, the Dow was yielding about 17%. The Grand Supercycle degree of the bear market indicates that this time investors will hold out for even higher yields. Over the course of Supercycle wave (V), the percentage of dividend-paying firms dropped from more than 90% near the lows of the 1940s to 20% in 2000. As the bear market wears on, this figure should trend back toward the 90% level.

April 2003

One of the psychological aspects of a bear market is investors' costly tendency to reject falling equity prices as evidence of a trend change, no matter how dramatically or insistently the market places them before their eyes. A watchful subscriber submitted the following example from a column in his local paper:

> Oddly, as an investor, I find myself unexpectedly calm. Call it fatalism if you like, but I feel I don't have to agonize over any big decisions, as there doesn't seem to be anything I can do. Whatever will happen will happen.

A bear market is a series of hard choices brought on by an initial belief that there is no choice. In fact, all this person has to do to avoid financial devastation is to make a simple phone call. Like many investors, this columnist is obviously still caught in this first phase. Eventually, it gives way to an equally irrational secondary reaction, "I've been robbed." At this point, much of the initial serenity is lost. There is evidence that this moment is approaching for many investors. In a series of e-mails to our office and in news articles, we are hearing more and more about, "'surprising' swings that suggest the markets may be rigged." The (London) Evening Standard recently delivered word of a "secret" committee whose mission it is to stabilize stock prices. In a strange contradiction, however, the article went on to state that the existence of the U.S. government's "plunge protection team" was revealed by the Washington Post more than 5 years ago. If it is unknown to most people, it is only because nobody believed in or cared about market manipulation when stocks were going up. In a bull market, investors want all the credit for their gains. In a bear market, they want losses to be the object of forces that are beyond their control.

Of course, just because people are paranoid about government manipulation doesn't mean that the government won't try it. As EWT has explained before, however, the market and social mood are too big to be pushed around for any significant duration. The extent to which the government tries manipulation is the extent to which it will accelerate deflation's destruction of U.S. taxpayers' and depositors' money. How successfully has the Fed stopped the 75% NASDAQ decline and the 50% S&P decline? Just the belief in the existence of plunge protectors plays right into the psychology of the decline. As EWT explained in 1998, "Hope-filled bulls will hold on for the slaughter and irresolute bears will give up their positions." It was the other way around in 1985: the evil institutions were driving the little guy out. This is more evidence that there really is an all-powerful force conspiring against the average investor. It's his own participation in the collective mood.

August 2003
And Cash Is Still Trash

On a 1-, 2-, 3- and 5-year basis, cash outperformed the S&P through June 30. And for all but the latest one-year span, stocks weren't even close. Still, investment advisors are as fearless as ever when it comes to thrusting their clients' money into stocks. Here's a good example of the urgency of the herding instinct at the current juncture:

Can This Portfolio Be Saved?

Our Panel Advises Couple Who Once Sought Safety in Cash and Needs to Return to Stocks

Two years ago, Mike Ford suffered a $100,000 loss in his retirement account and moved much of his money out of stocks, avoiding the worst of the bear market.

Now, the 60-year-old retiree in Pasadena, Calif., has a different problem: He and his wife, Susan, 57, still have more than half their $722,000 portfolio in cash or cash-like investments and they're wondering how to reach some ambitious financial goals, including buying a vacation home.

—The Wall Street Journal, July 9, 2003

Wall Street sirens are calling individuals back like never before. Advice ranges from "invest all retirement accounts in stocks, including a 40% allocation to international stocks" to a "more conservative" 55% allocation to stocks and a 45% stake in corporate and high-yield junk bonds. A third advisor threw in "a small stake in real-estate investment trusts." Zero consideration was given to cash. In fact, it's become a "problem." In our opinion, these recommendations are all financial death traps.

The secret motivation for these unrelentingly aggressive stances is the same as it was when stocks were rising: desperation. In August 1999, *The Elliott Wave Financial Forecast* exposed this chink in the armor of the mania with the following comment: "One investment consultant argues that the 'current stock market does not fit the definition of a classic speculative bubble' because too many investors need the money. 'They are buying not because it is discretionary investing but rather because it is compulsory investment for the 401(k) retirement plans.'" By March 2000, the compulsion had produced an "utter contempt for cash" so powerful that EWFF recognized it as the start of a new bull market — in cash. The key to the imminence of its next wave higher in value is the mention of the vacation home in the second paragraph. It shows that the commitment of the investment community is still based on hopes and wishes rather than sound investment principles and hard data. If the bear market were over, there would be no such talk. Advisors would be clinging to the fact that a 30-day certificate of deposit has returned a solid 3% over the last three years while the S&P has lost an average of 11.4% in each year. Instead, low yields on certificates of deposit and money markets are cited as the No.1 reason for investing in stocks and risky bonds. Investors needed the money at the top, but that reality didn't save them; it hurt them. Now that they really need the money, the selloff is likely to be much more painful.

January 2004

Another "Year of the Scandal"?

The Elliott Wave Theorist explained back in August 1991 that scandals are what happen when the psychology of investors is "in transition from an earlier state of happy acceptance and trust" to "a full fledged bear market psychology of mistrust and avoidance." The emphasis on the word "transition" supports our take on the current scene, which is that the explosion of scandals is a sign of movement toward a much deeper bear market. In year-end reviews, most financial pages have tabbed the phenomenon a defining trait of 2003. "Reports of corporate chicanery have come all too regularly since the discovery of arcane and esoteric accounting schemes at Enron more than two years ago. But this year, the misdeeds went distressingly mainstream," said The New York Times. "Another Scandalous Year," summarized The Economist. No matter how bad the scandals have gotten, however, there has been no concern about a residual effect on stock prices. Under its scandal headline, for instance, the Economist notes, "Despite the headlines, things are looking up in the boardroom." The other "story of the year" is the return of stock market euphoria. The incongruous optimism that surrounds the scandals confirms that the market is nowhere close to a bear market bottom.

Investors' almost unfathomable detachment from history is illustrated by a fiasco that the Financial Times has dubbed Tulip Bulbs II. More than 100 Dutch investors contributed about

$100 million to fund the development new varieties of tulips. In a page drawn straight from the Tulip Bulb mania of 1637, even after NovaCap Florales Future went bankrupt, officials denied it was a "speculative investment vehicle." They maintained that by investing "only in later stage tulip bulb development" they had "reduced the risk to investors."

The aftermath of a mania is a breeding ground for illicit financial behavior because swindlers work extra hard to raise new funds to keep their schemes afloat, and formerly law abiding losers go astray in a desperate bid to get lost money back. Another factor at work in the current environment is that gullibility levels, as measured by the sentiment data, have continued to ascend. The eventual scope of the current plague is anyone's guess, but a potential treasure trove of booty has been exposed by Parmalat, an Italian dairy firm that managed to issue billions of dollars worth of "collateralized debt obligations." As the bankrupt firm's "tangled investment web" unraveled in late December, The Wall Street Journal revealed that CDOs are a type of security in which corporate loans are repackaged to offer "varying amounts of risk." An accompanying chart revealed two types, "funded" CDOs, which are backed by assets and "synthetic" CDOs, "which are only hypothetically backed by assets." Since the Dow peaked in 2000, the issuance of funded deals has declined while synthetic deals have skyrocketed from $50 to $500 billion. The potential for rampant CDO abuse was demonstrated by Parmalat's founder. As he was being hauled off to jail, he reportedly claimed he was innocent of wrongdoing because many of the assets he was reputed to have manipulated didn't actually exist.

The still-germinating stage of the new age of financial scandal is also evident in investigators' Inspector Clouseau-like advance on the heart of the financial world. "The Parmalat affair was astonishing in its simplicity and amateurishness," reports Wednesday's Wall Street Journal. And yet, it went on for more than a decade. In their attacks on the mutual fund industry and the New York Stock Exchange, regulators are continually finding misdeeds that have been right in front of their faces for years. Eliot Spitzer is becoming deeply despised for his attacks, but the reality is that Wall Street has mostly itself to blame for his successes. Just one tip from a former insider at Canary Capital led to a chain reaction of mutual fund firings, indictments and millions in fines. As the bear market wears on, Wall Street will turn more violently against itself. Eventually, the "sophistication" that went into the creation of things like CDOs will shift to the enforcement side of the table. In time, regulators will acquire the knowledge and access they need to tear the lid off of hedge funds, Freddie Mac, Fannie Mae and other "creative" users of . Here's a headline that captures the self-destructive emotion behind these inquests and hints at its eventual effect:

Franklin Punishes 3 For Frequent Trading
—USA Today, December 23, 2003

When the bear market is over and silence has descended upon the trading floors, we will hear wistful stories of those who were destroyed in the bear market for doing what they were richly rewarded for doing in the bull market.

July 2004
Phase II of the Recrimination Wave

For the first time since the Depression, traders will be able to sell stocks short without waiting for an uptick. In a sure sign that the peak sentiment of the Supercycle-degree bull market rise from 1932 is still very much intact, the Securities and Exchange Commission has dropped the rule that "was adopted during the Depression when short sellers were blamed for the 1929 crash." With the decision, the U.S. government demonstrates, once again, its impeccable knack for acknowledging trends after they have run their course. The re-leveling of the playing field for short sellers confirms that the market is probably on the precipice of a decline that should be as historically significant as that of 1929. It is similar to the repeal of Glass-Steagall (passage of the Financial Modernization Act) in November 1999, which came two months before the Dow's all-time peak.

Near the spring highs, even the most scurrilous corporate victims of the bear market meat grinder were catching a few breaks: Enron's bankruptcy plan was approved by the SEC; World-com emerged from bankruptcy (it's now MCI); Tyco's former chief executive, whom Business Week classified as "destined for a swift conviction" in October 2002, got a reprieve thanks to a hung jury; and the most serious charge against Martha Stewart was dropped. At the same time, there are subtle signs that the post-bubble backlash that accompanied the decline from 2000 has resumed. Several of the old scandals have regained momentum. In coming weeks, the media will surely pounce on the indictment of Enron's former leader Kenneth Lay, the trial of former Worldcom CEO Bernie Ebbers and Martha Stewart's arrival at the Big House.

The Sarbanes-Oxley law is a perfect illustration of how the Wave Principle takes concrete form. In a response to the loss and disappointment of the bear market, this law tightens financial controls and makes key executives personally responsible for the accuracy of corporate accounts. It was signed into law in July 2002 as wave ① down was approaching its conclusion. It takes effect and will start to bite into corporate capital budgets in mid-November. "I feel like a bad storm's coming," said the chief information officer of a major firm. The author of a white paper on Sarbanes-Oxley implementation added that a "sense of panic" over Sarbanes-Oxley "is not unique." With competitive pressures mounting like never before, Congress' many moves to slap restrictions on firms will be onerous. In fact, the timing is so bad, with the U.S. losing its stature as the world's top producer, that historians will probably wonder why the government piled on the way it did. Socionomists, on the other hand, will know.

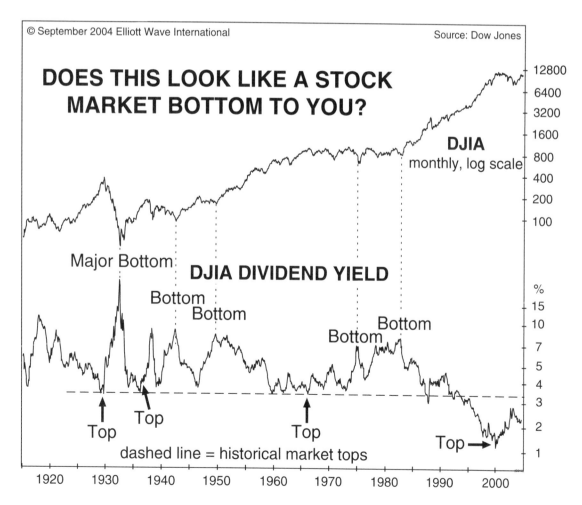

October 2004

According to the great Dow theorist George Schaefer, Charles H. Dow, for whom Dow Theory is named, "always gave first consideration to values. When the low point of a bear market is being approached, values will give us the first indication of a change in trend." At such times, Schaefer said good dividend paying issues should be purchased and held until yields for the Dow Industrials fall back into the 3% to 3½% area. But the chart on the previous page shows that no such buying opportunity is at hand because the bear market has not yet even managed to push the Dow dividend yield up through the 3-to-3½% range that is the normal Dow selling area (horizontal dashed line on chart). At 2.11%, the dividend yield still has to rise by 50% to get to a traditional topping point, so there is no way Dow or Schaefer would be buying stocks now. Despite 45 months of a bear market, nearly every time-tested valuation standard, from yield to P/E to the price-to-book value ratio, remains historically overvalued.

November 2004

The Bear Sets Its Sights on The Bottom Line

As EWFF has continually pointed out over the course of the past few months, Primary ③ is a reality-recognition wave that will expose and break down many of the delusional beliefs and behaviors of the old bull market. The deconstruction of the old uptrend is now so strong that it is being mentioned in the media. In a recent column headlined, "A New Morality Makes Old Deceptions Expensive for Wall Street," for instance, Floyd Norris of The New York Times observed, "Lying may be a sin, but on Wall Street there has always been a spirit of understanding for those who merely help others to deceive. But that is changing, and this is a case of today's new morality being applied to yesterday's conduct."

"In an effort to lift the cloud depressing shares" of her stock, Martha Stewart went straight to jail on October 8. Martha's crime is lying to protect herself from insider trading allegations, but, from a socionomic perspective, her big problem is that she is wrestling with forces that are beyond her control. There is nothing she can do to get back the "Teflon" she enjoyed as a revered icon of the bull market. The harder she tries, the deeper her public persona is likely to sink because her image is now a magnet for negative publicity and social attacks. The building pressure of negative judgment is evident in the action of Citicorp shares, which dropped to a new low for the year amid the shutdown of its scandal-plagued Japanese bank and a record fine for hedge-fund sales abuses. As Gretchen Morgensen notes in The New York Times, the scope of the shenanigans is growing larger every day: "Like the universe itself, corporate chicanery just seems to keep on expanding. Unlike earlier versions, however, the latest scandals tend to implicate not just individual companies but entire industries."

February 2005

According to the literary scholar Daniel Mendelsohn, in classic Greek literature, tragedy is almost always "punishment for hubris." As EWFF and *The Elliott Wave Theorist* have explained, no one is a stronger candidate for a calamitous fall from grace than the sitting U.S. president. George W. Bush boasts of the "political capital" gained by his November re-election, but, at 2.9%, his margin of victory was actually the narrowest re-election since 1828. As Bill Clinton's last four years attest, second terms are notoriously difficult to navigate. A few days before his inauguration, the Christian Science Monitor noted, "His challenge is to avoid the trap of second-term hubris, and beyond that, to recognize that he's still in the White House by the skin of his teeth, with only a bare majority of public support." Instead, Bush put forward one of the most ambitious global visions ever articulated by a U.S. President. As he pushed to "end tyranny" in "every nation" (of which there are close to 200). Bush laid the groundwork for dashed hopes by stating, "The United States will not ignore your oppression or excuse your oppressors. When you stand for your liberty, we will stand with you."

He made no mention of Iraq, where the costs and casualties from the U.S. "stabilizing" effort are spiraling higher. Reporter Seymour Hersh writes, "Despite the deteriorating security situation in Iraq, the Bush administration has not reconsidered its basic long-range policy goal in the Middle East, the establishment of democracy throughout the region." Overconfidence is the perfect set-up for a tragedy. The lesson of all tragedies, Mendelsohn reveals, is that the arrogant are ultimately leveled by a "failure to bend," which "inevitably results in terrible fracture." Bush's "astonishingly ambitious" agenda is being advanced at a time when fractures are already extremely well developed along political, generational and religious lines.

Bush's high-handed inaugural puts him on the fast track toward the "bigger slide" than Nixon's that EWFF and EWT have forecast in recent issues. At least Nixon enjoyed a big jump in popularity at the start of his second term; Bush's approval ratings have barely bounced. Another reason to expect Bush's second term to rival Nixon's is that his presidency has shown the same marked tendency to avoid blame when the market rallies and suffer it when stocks slump. After the market peaked in early 2002, Bush's approval ratings leveled off from stratospheric heights, and articles appeared saying the public wanted to know "What Went Wrong?" and "Who Dropped The Ball?" The hostile Newsweek cover is from May 2002, when the final leg of wave ① down was getting underway. At such times, the bear market impulse manifests itself in a sudden willingness to examine the "inside story of missed signals" and "intelligence failures" that were overlooked when stocks were heading higher. Remember, the basis for Nixon's collapse was the Watergate break-in, which took place in June 1972 when the market was still rising. But scandal did not come until

later, after the market began falling. Nixon was finally driven out of office in August 1974, two months before the S&P 500 reached a major low.

When the Bush administration launched an unprecedentedly aggressive attack on Iraq, the market began rising and there was almost no public opposition. Presidential assertions of evidence of weapons of mass destruction in Iraq went largely unchallenged by the media even after presidential claims about Iraqi purchases of Nigerian uranium were revealed to be false in March 2003. Bush's popularity stayed high through the end of 2003. But, as we noted last month, Bush's approval rating started to sink when the averages turned lower in the first quarter of 2004. This headline from one day after the Dow Jones Industrial Average peaked on February 19, 2004 marks a clearly coincident reversal in Bush's popularity:

Poll Sees Big Rise In Bush Negatives

After the S&P peaked in March, another damaging inquiry into 9/11 was underway. This Newsweek cover is from April 5, 2004. The abuse of Iraqi prisoners at Abu Ghraib also took

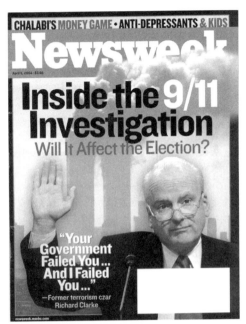

place in late 2003 when the market was rising. In mid-January, 2004, the Dow and S&P continued higher, so there was no uproar in the U.S. media even though the U.S. military revealed at that time that a criminal inquiry into allegations of abuse of Iraqi prisoners at Abu Ghraib was underway. CNN and The Miami Herald reported on the abuse. Reuters and NBC reporters were even among the abused, but the "story stayed largely under the radar" — until May 2004 when the market completed a corrective decline. That same month the film *Fahrenheit 9/11*, a documentary comprising information that was fully available throughout the course of rally from October 2003 to March 2004, won the top prize at the Cannes Film Festival. With its "scathing portrayal of White House actions," *Fahrenheit* also became the highest grossing documentary film in history. Thanks to the rally off the August lows, however, Bush's popularity bounced back enough for him to win re-election in November. This month, with the averages within a few weeks of their countertrend peaks, *Fahrenheit 9/11* failed to garner a single nomination for an Academy Award.

As the market falls in a genuine renewal of the bear market, Bush's fortunes will fall with it. Something else will get the blame for bringing down Bush, just as Watergate got the blame for bringing down Richard Nixon. But the real impetus will be the same force that finally pushed Nixon out: a large-degree bear market in social mood.

March 2005

Some formerly beleaguered leaders, like Martha Stewart, are back on the high ground of 1999. Even though she's been in jail, Stewart's star is soaring, with the landing of roles in two TV shows and a company stock that has soared back to heavenly heights. After collapsing to about $5 near the lows of October 2002, Martha Stewart Living Omnimedia shares rose to $37, right where they were one day after MSO came to market in October 1999. MSO's price/earnings ratio cannot be calculated because the firm lost $7.5 million in the fourth quarter of 2004.

It expects to lose more than twice that amount in the first quarter of 2005. "Jail can give beaten CEOs and burned-out celebrities the martyr's halo," explains Thursday's Washington Post. As long as the trend is rising, MSO can bask in its optimistic potential of the future. But Stewart's smiling visage on the cover of the March 7 Newsweek suggests that another peak is near. A similarly beaming Martha appeared on a January 2000 cover of Business Week, just as the Dow was topping. Newsweek says Stewart will emerge from prison "thinner, wealthier and ready for prime time." As the bear market reasserts itself, Stewart will find her return to the business world a lot less accommodating than her jail cell. According to a February 11 story about the "Evolving Saga of America's CEO," CEOs took their lumps in January when 92 got the boot or retired, the highest figure since February 2001 when 119 CEO changes took place. "The CEO is on

the hot seat," says John Challenger, who heads a Chicago outplacement firm. "Mistakes aren't forgiven." That goes double for Martha Stewart because bull market favorites tend to get singled out for special attention on the downside.

April 2005

A Change of Heart for Stocks

The de-equitization of American social life is reaccelerating. Recall what the March 4 EWFF said would happen to Martha Stewart's stock, as supporters hailed her triumphant release from prison. Within hours, Martha Stewart Living Omnimedia was cascading lower in a decline that reduced its value by 45% in 13 days. The market's harsh response to "the new Martha" is just a small hint of the rejection that stock market totems and icons will experience in the newly emerging phase of decline.

May 2005

A common argument against deflation is that it is impossible because the Federal Reserve can simply create inflation by expanding the money supply. *Conquer the Crash* carefully explains why this premise is false. History shows that major deflations happen every century, and minor deflations happen often. The chart below is based on an earlier version by Comstock Partners (www.comstockfunds.com). In the 1980s, Comstock observed a series of "rolling depressions" in which certain sectors deflated dramatically after gorging on easy credit. From the farm belt and lesser-developed country loans in the mid-to-late 1970s to the oil industry in the early 1980s, real estate and junk bonds in the mid-to-late 1980s and Wall Street in the late 1990s, different sectors and financial instruments succumbed to a binge-purge cycle in which they pumped up performance by overindulging in easy money. Once economic growth slowed or interest rates rose high enough to make servicing the accumulated debt impossible, restructuring or default resulted. Although financially ruinous for the companies and industries that were caught in the

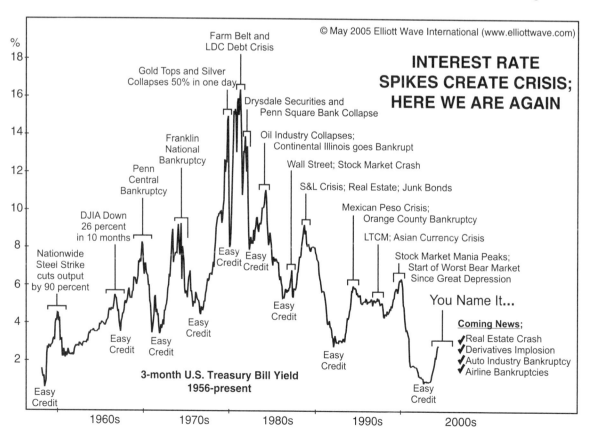

617

vortex of falling prices, diminishing collateral values and margin calls, crises since the 1940s have generally been contained to the sectors with excessive exposure to bad debts.

Once again interest rates are headed for the purge phase of a minor cycle, but this time it is in the context of the very late stages of a *major* cycle. This time, therefore, the implosion and its deflationary effect is not likely to confine itself to any one economic group. As CTC explained, the current level of system-wide debt is unprecedented and is becoming unmanageable. Total credit market debt is now $36.9 trillion, more than triple the U.S. GDP of $12 trillion (see figure 11-5 in CTC). The figure does not even include some whole new risk exposures such as credit default swaps, which by some estimates now total more than $8 trillion, or 2/3 of GDP. Since the secular trend of interest rates peaked in 1981, each successive deflationary episode has co-incided with a smaller rise in rates. The reason is that ever-increasing debt burdens have meant that companies' balance sheets have been more sensitive to interest rate movements and even modest rate increases have created stress and default.

With its progression of higher peaks into 1980 and lower peaks since then, this chart is a graphic representation of the Kondratieff wave that was discussed in Chapter 12 of CTC. In 1980, inflation gave way to disinflation, which now should give way to outright deflation. The down portion of this wave is scheduled to bottom in 2010-2014.

June 2005
The Jury Finds In Favor of the Bear

Back in mid-1998 — immediately after the Value Line Geometric average made its all-time high — the story of cooked books at Sunbeam was one of the first accounting scandals to break. When it did, EWT identified it as a part of "a slow awakening" to an emerging social mood downturn that was "beginning to shatter the collective financial delusion. These stories can 'now be told' because people are disposed to listen to them. As the bear market unfolds, many more 'scandalous' cases will be revealed."

On the far side of the peak, Sunbeam has returned to the spotlight as its acquirer sued Morgan Stanley for not disclosing accounting fraud when it purchased the firm in 1998. As the trial closed, The New York Post reports that Morgan's attorney "warned jurors that if they didn't let Morgan Stanley off the hook, it would hurt the American economy. 'What would be the purpose of severely hurting one of our two top investment banks? We're talking about hurt-ing a pillar of our economy. . . that's not justice, that's self-destruction . . . Are you so angry at Morgan Stanley?'"

The jury's answer? Absolutely. After a five-weeks of complex financial testimony, the jury returned a verdict worth $604.3 million to the plaintiff in less than two days. An additional $850 million in punitive damages was awarded with less than four hours of deliberation. The winning side said the $1.4 billion judgment "should send a clear message." Yes, it does, and that message is: "It's a bear market." The first hint of scandals in 1998 signaled the start of the bear market's discovery phase. It should ultimately become the most punitive in the history of Wall Street.

September 2005

A few days before the NASDAQ's all-time high in March 2000, in a section in which we urged subscribers to "Take Cash, Not Options," *The Elliott Wave Financial Forecast* showed the steady drop in equity mutual fund cash levels and proclaimed the start of a new reign for King Cash.

This turned out to be sage advice, as the subsequent decline in the S&P overtook that of 1973-1974 to become the largest since the Great Depression. Don't look now, but the ratio of mutual fund cash to assets has just slipped to 3.9%, below it's level in March 2000. So despite a 22% net loss in the S&P over the last five years, mutual funds are even more fully invested than they were at the pinnacle of the greatest stock market mania in history. During the first leg of the bear market, the ratio never climbed above 6%, compared with an average high of 11.3% at prior bottoms in 1974, 1982, 1987 and 1990. The ratio's inability even to approach double digits is one of the guarantees that 2002 did not see the final bear-market low. Considering the high degree of the bear market and the cash-friendly deflationary forces that are accompanying it, this ratio should easily exceed the 12.9% high on this chart before the bear market ends.

This table shows how the return on cash has crushed the return on stock indexes over the last five years. Instead of marveling over the fact that cash's return was accomplished with virtually no risk to its holders, sentiment toward this most liquid of assets is not far from the "utter contempt" level of March 2000. A Slate.com columnist excoriates corporate leaders for hoarding "Useless Mountains of Cash." "CEOs need to stop saving and start spending," says the article. S&P 500 firms now hold more than $634 billion in cash, an increase of 54% in just over two years and 92% from five years ago. Obviously, corporate chieftains see something that most investors and fund managers do not. The faster growth rate of corporate cash over the last two years is significant because the rise came during a period of economic recovery. The table illustrates what it is they see: in a world threatening deflation, excess supply and slack demand mean that returns in short term bills are better than the best efforts corporations have to offer. Thus, cash at S&P firms now equals 7.7% of their market value, up from 3.6% in 2000. The man on the street may not agree just yet, but CEOs recognize that an asset's ability to hold value is the first order of business. The so-called "global savings glut" shows that this principle is being firmly embraced in many other parts of the world.

FIVE YEARS INTO ITS BEAR MARKET KING CASH GETS NO RESPECT

S&P 500
monthly, log scale

% Cash in U.S. Equity Mutual Funds

Source: Investment Company Institute
© September 2005 Elliott Wave International (www.elliottwave.com)

CASH AIN'T TRASH
Five Year Return
12/31/99 to present

INDEX	Simple Price Change	Annual Price Change	Annual Price Change (Div. Reinvested)
Dow Jones Wilshire 5000	-12.82%	-2.40%	
Dow Jones Industrial Average	-9.57%	-1.76%	0.22%
S&P 1500 Supercomposite	-11.92%	-2.22%	-0.74%
S&P 500	-17.98%	-3.44%	-1.93%
NASDAQ Composite	-47.89%	-10.88%	-10.50%
CASH 6-month T-bills	13+%	2.62%	3½%

Source: Bloomberg

November 2005
Blame It On Martha

In March, when Martha Stewart's stock was soaring to a countertrend high with the Dow Industrials, *The Elliott Wave Financial Forecast* offered this forecast:

Stewart's star is soaring, with the landing of roles in two TV shows and a company stock that has soared back to heavenly heights. Stewart's smiling visage on the cover of the March 7 Newsweek suggests that another peak is near. As the bear market reasserts itself, Stewart will find her return to the business world a lot less accommodating than her jail cell.

Eight months later, the Industrials are down 7%, her stock is off more than 50%, while ratings for her prime time version of *The Apprentice: Martha Stewart* started lower than expected and fell from there. "The doyenne of domesticity's carefully constructed TV comeback has met with a chilly reception from viewers." One problem is that reality/survival shows are popular in the transition to a declining phase, and Martha's public image has always thrived on the more purely positive vibe of a rising trend.

December 2005

Who Needs Savings?

One of the most impressive pictures of the epic public faith in the rising trend is the chart of personal savings rates over the last 40 years, which depicts a rising sense of fearlessness. The source of this emotion is clearly the bull market. The savings rate peaked in August 1982, the exact month of the low in stocks, and plunged with every major advance of the bull market. In 1999, when the monthly savings rate (as it was then devised) fell below zero for the first time, here's what EWFF had to say about it:

> The draining of bank accounts right before final highs is a time-honored tradition. Dramatic peaks in consumers' willingness to bet on the future instead of conserve for it have been forerunners to almost every important stock market high since 1970. We have no doubt that the ratio will re-enter the more normal realm and create a colossal version of the more earthbound peaks of 1972, 1976, 1983, 1987 and 1990.

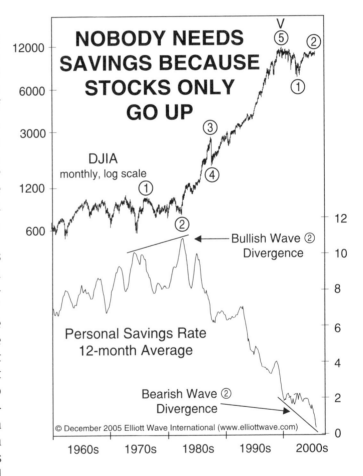

EWFF's forecast of a rise back toward positive territory for the savings rate happened immediately. U.S. statisticians simultaneously re-configured the definition of savings so the rate would not go negative. Adding money market instruments to the savings total, the government "adjusted" the rate back to a positive level. As Elliott Wave International has pointed out with respect to several of these recalibrations, such as Dow Jones' decision to reconfigure the DJIA to include high-flying technology companies in late 1999, these changes are themselves signs of trend extremity. The initial move below zero and its recalculation did, in fact, correspond to a market peak and a rise in the savings rate from 1.85% in March 2000, the month of the all-time high in the S&P, to

2.23% in November 2002, one month after a market low. The current plunge to historically low levels is evidence of wave ②'s extraordinary capacity for regenerating, in this case superseding, the psychology of the prior peak. Notice that the wave ② decline that ended in August 1982 created a similar divergence in the opposite direction. At this point, savings are so widely shunned that even the U.S. government's reconstituted monthly number is below zero.

Savings rates, then, have joined mutual fund cash levels, New York Stock Exchange seat prices and various measures of long-term bullish sentiment (such as the duration for Investors Intelligence's record long bullish consensus) in achieving record levels. These extremes in the absence of any corresponding all-time highs in the three major stock indexes—the Dow, NASDAQ or S&P 500—are powerful evidence that the last three years of rising stock prices is a countertrend bear market rally that will be completely retraced.

According to one account, this "startling trend" means people are spending more than 100% of their after-tax income. Because of the average household's stock and real estate holdings, many economists insist that the lack of savings is not a problem. Consumers are "figuring that the unprecedented increase in property values will bail them out of the financial shortfall. 'It's human nature,'" says a Federal Reserve Board economist. That's certainly true, but it is completely unprecedented, and, it comes precisely at the point in the wave pattern when humans can be counted on to try to re-experience the glory of a prior peak. In normal times, people keep savings on hand because they realize that stocks and real estate are uncertain stores of value.

Several stories contend that this is the first savings rate deficit since the Great Depression, but this is probably untrue. Discretionary income for the 1920s and 1930s is unavailable, but savings and income data from the U.S. Census Bureau show that the savings rate surely rose from 1929 to 1932. According to the data, savings fell 15% but the savings rate had to rise because income fell much harder, at 55%. Financial assets are now considered synonymous with "money in the bank." This rare belief is rock-solid evidence that the unfolding peak is a 200-year event that almost no one is prepared for. When people are scared, they find ways to scrimp and save. At this point, they are anything but scared; in fact, the savings rate says they are as bold as they have ever been.

May 2006

An aspect of the reversal that no one ever counts on in the midst of a mania is the high level of fraud that invariably attaches itself to the hottest sectors. This was the basis for the following statement in the July issue: "This time there is no mistaking who the Enrons of the bust phase will be. They will be the firms now pedaling adjustable-rate, no-interest/nothing-down and assorted other types of 'sub-prime' mortgages." The next wave of scandals is probably still growing, because in-too-deep participants generally do whatever it takes to stay solvent as the reversal takes place, but its outline is clearly visible in articles like this one from MarketWatch on April 9:

Home Is Where the Fraud Is

Mortgage scams cost billions

Once a nuisance to a handful of lenders, mortgage fraud has blossomed into one of the fastest-growing white collar crimes in the country.

The fulfillment of these 2005 forecasts about the housing market confirms that a Grand Super-cycle version of the Supercycle real estate busts of the 1830s and 1930s is underway. These are just the warm-up acts. If there is a banker out there who took this advice from *Conquer the Crash*, "Sell off your largest-percentage mortgages and get into safer investments," it's time to sit back and enjoy the show.

July 2006

This is a key chart showing the unprecedented resolve of bullish fund managers since the month after stocks bottomed in 2002. *The Elliott Wave Financial Forecast* showed a similar version of this graph under the headline, "Cash Is Dead...Long Live Cash," on March 3, 2000, right before the start of the first leg of the bear market in the S&P. Historically, a penetration of the 5% level, denoted by the gray areas on the chart, has signaled a rally in cash holdings and a corresponding decline in stocks. Notice that besides recording the lowest cash-to-assets level on record, 3.8% in September, this measure has been locked below 5% for three-and-a-half years! As we have noted before with respect to the incredible string of net bullish readings in Investors Intelligence's weekly survey of investment advisory sentiment (InvestorsIntelligence.com), this unyielding bullish resolve is a long-term negative for stocks, with Grand-Supercycle-level bearish implications. It will take a commensurate run of net bearish readings to balance this extreme.

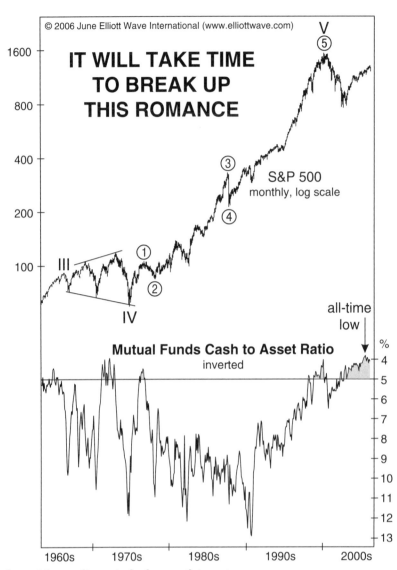

August 2006

Re-Recrimination Bears Down

After a brief reprieve in early 2004, a July 2004 EWFF piece considered the potential for "Phase II of the Recrimination Wave," citing "subtle signs that the post-bubble backlash that accompanied the decline from 2000 has resumed." Clear evidence of an even nastier renewal of the offensive against the most aggressive practitioners of bull market accounting practices, for instance, came in the middle of last year when WorldCom and Tyco's executives were finally sentenced to up to 25 years in prison. Another stride came early this year as the NASDAQ 100 reached its peak, and Tyco, a conglomerate that was assembled through the bull market of the 1990s, announced a plan to split into three separate companies. The stock dropped like a brick on the news.

In the wake of the May highs, the rumbling turned into a torrent. Evidence of a new onslaught of recrimination includes the return of Martha Stewart bashing ("Everyone Hates Martha," NY Post, July19); the criminalization of the "once celebrated practice" of creating millionaires out of Silicon Valley secretaries through backdating stock options ("Stigma Emerges, Glitter Fades for Stock Options," San Jose Mercury News, July 23); and the Enron saga's re-arrival on the front page ("Guilty Verdicts For Enron Brass," May 25 Business Week). When Ken Lay died of a heart attack in July, The Houston Chronicle quoted the former Enron leader's preacher saying that his "heart simply gave out." But the extremely negative force of the unfolding decline will not let Lay lie in peace (pun intended). His memory continues to be sullied by an endless series of Internet speculation about his Elvis-like survival and a ruthless roasting by late-night comedians. We count numerous jokes about Lay's eternal damnation, such as, "Don't know if this is a coincidence or not, but Ken Lay died last week and today, Hell filed for bankruptcy," from Jay Leno. Another sign of reputation trashing is the resumption of government attacks on Microsoft. The European Union just socked the software company with a $356 million penalty because it refuses to surrender the code to its Windows operating system to rivals. Microsoft faces additional fines of $3.82 million a day, beginning on July 31, unless it provides "complete and accurate technical specifications." The socionomic motivation behind these "anti-trust" attacks was discussed fully in the May 2000 issue of *The Elliott Wave Theorist* and was applied to a recent wave of attacks on Google in these pages in February.

Of course, *The Elliott Wave Financial Forecast* called for the opening of whole new fronts of scandalous revelations in the next phase of the bear market, and it appears to be happening as advertised. We cited real estate and hedge funds in particular as likely focal points, and lengthening rap sheets in both fields suggests that they will in fact be hotbeds of scandal in the months ahead. Here's the latest from Forbes, for instance:

Attack of the Real Estate Rip-Offs

Urge to cash in on the housing bubble has spawned an industry of schemers
—July 21, 2006

In the hedge fund industry, the scandal meter is rising fast. The SEC brought 29 civil cases against hedge funds in 2005 (compared with 10 in 2002), and several fund companies have collapsed or shut down in recent months. The Fed's entrance into a whole new world of financial fraud is signaled by the establishment of a presidential task force that is now "looking into hedge-fund fraud." "Amid Rising Fraud," the chairman of the Securities and Exchange Commission said Tuesday that he will "push for new emergency regulations of the high-risk investment pools." Fraud in the $1.2 trillion hedge-fund industry poses an "emerging threat" to investors, says U.S. Deputy Attorney General Paul McNulty. In what promises to be one of the understatements of the next several years, Bloomberg reports, "The potential for wrongdoing in the lightly regulated investment pools makes them ripe for scrutiny." Just as the SEC was formed in the 1930s and mutual fund regulations went on the books, government oversight and controls over the hedge fund industry will be greatly expanded in the years ahead. Many of the changes will be inspired by trading, compensation and reporting standards that are now commonly accepted. However, in the light of the coming bear market and the attendant transformation to a pessimistic social mood, these same practices will shock and appall the public.

Another throwback to the early 1930s that EWFF touched on in July 2004 is "a post-crash backlash against collusive pricing strategies." At that time, EWFF observed the June 2004 passage of the "Antitrust Criminal Penalty Enhancement and Reform Act," a law that will now be applied fully to a deluge of price fixing cases that are suddenly appearing. "Price Fixing Scandal Plagues BP," says a typical headline from July 17. Just within the last few weeks, major collusion cases have been brought in the pricing of kitchen and bathroom fixtures, credit cards, air freight, airlines and semiconductors. Of the semiconductor case, in which 34 states are bringing price-fixing allegations against seven global semiconductor companies, one state's Assistant Attorney General says, "I have never seen a price-fixing case where there is so widespread, so continuous an exchange of confidential price information among competitors or over so long a time period." Here again, everyone wants to know, "How did it go on for so long?" The answer is precisely the same one that we offered in the July 2000 EWFF when the markets were in a similar post-peak position and a wave of discoveries about boomtime financial practices were making their appearance. It is based on socionomic causality: After a major bull market peak, acceptance and trust engendered by the optimism of rising share prices gives way to suspicion and control. At really big turns, it's not hard to see—unless you are blinded by the anger and recriminatory impulses of the bear market.

September 2006

A Bull Market in Scapegoats

When bubbles burst, they invariably unleash a negative social response against the most aggressive and successful exploiters of the preceding advance. Credit default swaps (CDS) are one relatively new financially engineered product that is rapidly climbing to the top of our growing list of likely targets. To give you an idea of how confusing and untrackable the market is, we've seen estimates of total market cap ranging from $7 billion to $17 trillion. At their current rate of growth, Lehman Brothers projects that the volume of CDSs, which allow hedge funds and others to speculate on the ability of companies to pay their bank debt, will quadruple in 12 months. Due to the "insatiable demand for high-yield debt," Bloomberg reports, "competition from investors for the highest yields is so great that borrowers are turning lenders away." Sudden prices swings of 30% and 80% earlier this month in the credit default swaps of Verizon and Rentokil, respectively, signals the potential for a violent reversal. The volatility was due to changes in their corporate structure rather than any business breakdown. The damage done by an actual economic contraction, which is fast approaching, will undoubtedly be catastrophic.

As likely scapegoats, *At The Crest of the Tidal Wave* listed "speculators, short sellers, pool operators, you name it," and hedge funds certainly fit the bill on all three counts. A small taste of the fury that is starting to percolate is a concerted series of attacks against "naked short sellers," traders who purportedly profit from selling shares they have not bothered to borrow. The extent of this practice is an open question, but what is clear is that the prevailing Stock Borrow program originated one year before the start of the bull market in 1982, and after 25 years is only now being vehemently assailed. "I've been pouring kerosene on myself and setting myself on fire because I think there are global, systemic issues with naked short selling," says a vocal critic. Another says that regulators and stock exchanges should call for "multimillion-dollar fines." "They need to make a few examples out of people," says the chairman of a software firm whose stock was reputedly the target of naked short selling. The urge to "get even" will run very strong, in both senses. The more that investors' portfolios suffer from a market decline, the more furious they will become. By now, subscribers are well aware of the dynamic and the danger inherent in clinging to old bull market forms and ideas. In the next phase of decline, however, it will pay to be mindful of the speed and scope of the retribution. In another typical post-peak revelation, a recent study showed that 41% of buyout candidates experienced "abnormal and suspicious" trading activity ahead of the public announcement of offers. So, Martha Stewart's wave ① scandal was probably just the tip of an insider trading iceberg, one of many that will grow larger as the discord and anger of wave ③ down sinks in.

October 2006

People recently have been quoting the "Fed model" to claim that today's stock prices are low. But there is no valid basis upon which to say stocks are cheap. You might remember our graph of stock valuations on the basis of two tried-and-true measures: book value and the yield on stocks vs. corporate bonds. The chart updates the picture. The box in the lower left-hand corner shows the area of fluctuation for all decades up to the last two, the only previous outlying years on the upside being 1928 and 1972. Stock prices will eventually come back to the box and almost assuredly below it, since extremes in the downward direction tend to follow extremes in the upward direction (observe 1929 and 1932). In the past, the market has never stayed outside the box for more than a year. It has now been above it from 1987 through 2006, an unbelievable 20 years! Way back in 1983 (the stone age), EWT predicted a "mania" for stocks to occur for the first time since the 1920s. But that word hardly suffices to describe what happened. "Obsession" is perhaps

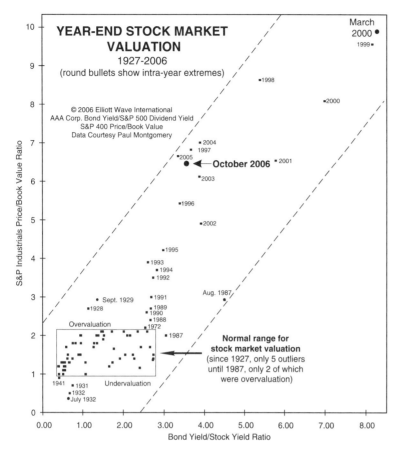

YEAR-END STOCK MARKET VALUATION
1927-2006
(round bullets show intra-year extremes)

© 2006 Elliott Wave International
AAA Corp. Bond Yield/S&P 500 Dividend Yield
S&P 400 Price/Book Value
Data Courtesy Paul Montgomery

S&P Industrials Price/Book Value Ratio

Bond Yield/Stock Yield Ratio

← October 2006

Overvaluation

Undervaluation

Normal range for stock market valuation
(since 1927, only 5 outliers until 1987, only 2 of which were overvaluation)

a better word for the psychological condition of 1999 and 2000. At this point rising stock prices are treated almost as a birthright. In a 10/16 review of the now defunct real estate mania, Lisa Prevost of The Boston Globe comments, "Practicality was almost illogical." We will hear these words about the stock obsession one day, too. Until then, we have to play the cards we are dealt.

November 2006
The New Scandal Era Picks Up Steam

One of the great tip-offs that the first leg of the bear market was indeed underway was a big surge in "the exposure of slack bull market accounting standards and outright frauds," which EWFF discussed in the June and July 2000 issues. Similar harbingers of the next decline are definitely in the air. With pressure from Congress and "a wide-ranging Government Accountability Office investigation" mounting, the SEC says that it plans to bring more enforcement actions in 2007, which until now have receded every year since the bottom in 2002. SEC chairman Christopher Cox is expected to pay "very close attention to the basics of securities regulation, which is to root out the bad guys." The number of companies under investigation "in the ever-widening stock-options scandal" recently surged past 150. It's a "red alert," with the SEC's Cox issuing "a chilling warning" about more charges to come. Everyone wants to know who's next to get nailed, but the key question is, "Why now?" The FBI's criminal division is calling it the "newest trend in investor fleecing," but option backdating itself backdates to at least the mid-1990s. Reports indicate that 13.6% of options granted to top executives since 1996 were backdated or otherwise manipulated. On the way up, options were the greatest thing since sliced bread because they fed people's appetite for building wealth. But, in a bear market, as EWFF suggested in October 1999, "the flip" side of this bull market windfall "is that they will be an enormous weight on growth."

Another result of the market's four-year advance is rising pressure to repeal the stringent Sarbanes-Oxley accounting standards, which were originally adopted at the bottom of wave **a** in 2002. The following article marks the re-birth of the bear market "flip" back to more severe restrictions:

Options Scandal Seen Vindicating Reforms

Perhaps the Sarbanes-Oxley corporate governance reforms were not too harsh after all. A quick flip through the latest bombshell report on a corporate scandal — this one on the likely backdating of stock options — suggests many of the requirements of the law were justified. Some corporate governance experts now say the scandal shows that Sarbanes-Oxley does not go far enough.

—Reuters, October 20, 2006

February 2007

According to the Financial Times, John Lipsky, the deputy managing director of the International Monetary Fund, "a long-standing optimist," is "radically reshaping the fund's thinking on financial market issues, something that has come as quite a culture shock for the more cautious IMF staff. With everything looking much more positive, Mr. Lipsky is charging ahead with a radical plan for the IMF." "The mindset has shifted somewhat," he says. "The challenge is not to stave off imminent risks but to take advantage of the benign environment." His statement suggests that actually the risks are more imminent and powerful than he can envision. EWFF's real-time observations of the reversal in 2000 records very clearly that the same mindset shift proved to be a last straw. Somehow it makes perfect sense that the IMF is lowering its guard against the financial meltdown just in time to face its first real emergency since the organization was founded in 1944 to address the liquidity constraints of a depression that was already over.

March 2007

Let the Backlash Begin

After months of study, financial regulators rejected calls for more oversight of hedge funds on Saturday, February 24. In announcing its first policy directive on the subject since the failure of LTCM, the President's Working Group on Financial Markets, a.k.a. the Plunge Protection Team, said no regulations are needed because "the current system for preventing market collapse and widespread investor losses is 'working well.'"

The group, which comprises the heads of the SEC, Treasury Department, Federal Reserve and the Commodity Futures Trading Commission, declined to "tamper with an innovative industry that has created billions of dollars in wealth and liquidity." Despite a string of hedge fund failures in recent years and calls for tighter regulation in Germany and Canada, the PPT refused to create any new rules or impose limits on lending to hedge funds or trading strategies. While we always advocate free markets, government officials vacillate on this subject. This "unanimous policy directive" is a sure-fire sign of an extremely entrenched bull market psychology; we are quite sure that when the decline that is now forming approaches its lows, the U.S. Treasury Secretary will not be saying he prefers "to let the market operate without undue meddling from overseers," as he did on Saturday. Keel Capital is evidence of the industry's belief in the PPT's placid view. This U.S. hedge fund decided to close down because they could find nothing to short! The closure came one day before the Dow experienced its largest decline since the end of the last bear phase in March 2003. The fund's owners cited hedge funds themselves as the cause of the "dampened volatility" and said it may well "lead to long periods of lower volatility in the future." We'll see how that one goes.

The first initial public offering of a U.S. hedge fund, Fortress Investment Group, which came out at $18.50 a share on February 8 and immediately traded up to $35, signals hedge funds' critical role in the unfolding drama. Another story reveals that the world's largest financial institutions are also jumping on the bandwagon with the equivalent of a retail hedge fund offering a "copycat hedge fund to people with as little as $1,000 to invest." It is no coincidence that these instruments, known as long-short funds and sold through mutual funds, are being peddled to individuals at a time when "returns of these exclusive investments to millionaires are drying up." It takes us back to the great opening of the IPO market to little guy investors in 1999. In the second half of that year, a three-year "campaign to get the public in IPOs" was successfully completed and a Datek Services commercial showed a "modern-day investment mob crashing through the doors and windows of the NYSE" as an announcer proclaimed that "the tools of serious trading" are "now available to everyone." Based on the precedent of the original Tulip Mania 350 years ago, the November 1999 issue of EWFF stated, "These offerings are significant because they are generating a whole new wave of enthusiastic and totally unsophisticated investors. Joe Granville called this class of investors the 'bagholders' because it always appears at or after a market peak with an aggressive attitude that demands, 'Gimme that bag!'" At the current juncture, the public's lunge for the hedge fund bag combined with the PPT's clean bill of health creates a powerful set-up for a long assault on financial assets.

The Special Section in the January issue (see Chapter 1) tabbed 2007 the "year of financial flameout," and that's certainly being borne out by recent developments. The front edge of that collapse is visible in key finance stocks such as Citigroup and Merrill Lynch, which started down ahead of the blue chip averages. Various other bank stocks and Goldman Sachs held up with the Dow, but they are now hurrying to catch up. Here's how one trader described the initial plunge at dealbreaker.com: "Goldman fell six bucks. People were going nuts. There were no bids for five or six points. We haven't seen that kind of thing for years. This was no high-flying tech stock. It was Goldman-f*ing-Sachs. For a minute I wondered if they had blown up Broad Street. Maybe Goldman Sachs no longer existed." In time, many may wish it hadn't existed.

April 2007

Some contend that the bearish significance of high margin levels is mitigated by high cash levels, but they refer to absolute amounts, not percentages. Mutual funds, for example, hold close to their lowest cash percentages ever, and as far as we can tell, the capital in hedge funds and elsewhere is beyond fully committed; it's leveraged. So "cash" is not likely to save the day.

Coming Soon To a Jail Cell Near You

Resident CNBC bull Jim Cramer captured the general feeling in the wake of the first leg down this way: "Our short national nightmare is over." The quote and a lot of others like it remind us of historian John Brooks' comment on the crash in 1929-1932: "It was possible to believe one had experienced and survived it when in fact it had no more than just begun." The strength of the street's happy-go-lucky attitude is evidenced by captains of disasters staging comebacks. Brian Hunter, the energy trader behind hedge fund Amaranth Advisors' September collapse, is raising money and intends to open a "multibillion dollar commodity investment vehicle." Nick Leeson, the trader who single-handedly brought down the 233-year old Barings Bank back in 1995, is also back in the game. These last two items may be important as they connect the front and back ends of the Great Asset Mania, revealing its amazing durability and tolerance for even the most egregious failures. This magnanimity will undoubtedly change fast in the bear market's next phase. At the lows, there will likely be formal restrictions on who trades and how they do it.

Bear markets bring recrimination. Practices that were routine during the bull market suddenly become vilified. The 2000-2002 downturn gave us Enron, Tyco, Martha Stewart and Adelphia. We cannot say exactly who the culprits will be this time, but they will probably be some of the most successful and aggressive exploiters of the old uptrend. Their transgressions will be common bull market practices, and the accused will defend themselves by saying "Everyone else was doing it." In the interest of justice, however, (and the enforcement of a whole new social mood), many will be punished. The forces of the new trend can be seen in the stir that surrounds a video interview in which Cramer boasted about orchestrating price movements in a various stocks several years ago. The webcast was made in December, but didn't spread rapidly over the Internet until recent weeks. Cramer discussed one illegal strategy and said it was quite safe because the Securities and Exchange Commission "never understands this." It's not the transgression, but the delayed fury that now surrounds the tape that is telling. It shows that investors are itching for a fight. Soon, charges of manipulation and the need for reform will be flooding out. Along these lines, a flurry of stories on indictments and investigations involving insider trading, buyouts and various Ponzi schemes hit the headlines in recent weeks. This is just the first puff of smoke of what promises to be a huge mushroom cloud.

The bursting of the credit bubble will be the key fundamental effect of Cycle wave **c**. It will make a grand appearance in coming months, but, as this updated chart of 3-month Treasuries and credit crises over the last 40 years shows, it is rooted in a succession of easy money episodes. The most relevant is 2003's half-century low in rates that gave us nothing-

627

down, low-rate balloon mortgages, pay-me-later car loans, record high junk bond issuance and a dizzying array of credit that are probably not fully understood by any living person. EWFF first published this chart in May 2005 and noted then that the only difference this time is the much larger size of the completing credit cycle: "Therefore the implosion and its deflationary effect is not likely to confine itself to any one economic group." With this observation in mind, we forecasted "Real Estate Crash," "Auto Industry Bankruptcy," "Airline Bankruptcies" and " Implosion." The first three are all well underway. A meltdown is not yet apparent, but the following headline about credit default obligations hints at its unraveling:

CDOs Face Severe Ratings Cuts – Moody's
—Bloomberg, March 27, 2007

Last month's discussion of the subprime mortgage implosion included an updated chart of EWI's SubPrime Lenders Index (Chapter 2). Of the stocks that comprise this index, we said, "one or more of these companies will probably declare bankruptcy." It didn't take long for the first candidate to appear. New Century Financial, one of the index's components, is de facto bankrupt. The official announcement should be forthcoming. This stock is down 98% from its high at 66.95 on December 20, 2004. Its recent delisting from the NYSE brought a symbol change from NEW to NEWC. Given the potential for more debt "nukes," it's an appropriate designation. We keep seeing headlines along these lines, "Bernanke Doesn't See Subprime Woes Spreading," but evidence of a wider fallout is mounting fast. Fund manager and fellow bear Bill Fleckenstein quotes an industry source saying, "Subprime loan bulks are fetching a max of 70 cents on the dollar. Two middle-market mortgage banking firms we work with went to bid with $100 mil of Alt-A product they typically get 108-110 for, and the bids came back at 68 and 50, respectively. These are Alt-A loans. Not even subprime!" This is the real world of deflation that we discuss in these pages.

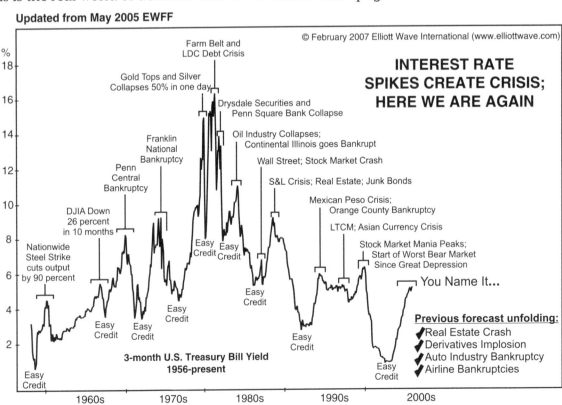

Updated from May 2005 EWFF

628

The scope of the situation is evident in the fact that a bailout, the modern answer to every big-time credit bust, is already being discussed in the mortgage arena. With "homeowners by the millions" falling behind, "cries for a government bailout are starting to echo through Washington." On March 28, activist Jesse Jackson called on consumers struggling with subprime mortgages to take to the streets and urged the federal government to step in and help them secure their homes. "What we must do now is begin to ask for some bailout of victims of this crisis," Jackson said. The current bailout fever aligns the subprime meltdown with a previous major mortgage bailout movement that emerged in the early 1930s, during the last significant U.S. deflation.

According to Jim Grant (Grant's Interest Rate Observer), over an 18-month period in 1933-34, 27 states enacted stays on mortgage foreclosures. A critical difference this time, however, is the timing of the bailout exhortations. Bailouts generally come near lows; the push for this one hit within days of the stock market's peak, which means it will only expand to unrivaled proportions as the bear market and economic contraction roll in. But it won't work. Chrysler and Continental Illinois were "too big to fail;" the unfolding crisis will be "too big to bail."

May 2007

Based on our knowledge of the Wave Principle and a study of the great bull markets of the last century, it is a virtual certainty that a giant wave of investigation, scandal and humiliation will be the end result of the next market reversal. Of course, heads are not yet rolling because stock prices, unlike home prices, are still near their highs. At this point, hedge funds are a conspicuously tight knit group. In fact, New York magazine notes that they cling together within a few blocks of one another on the Upper East Side of Manhattan or Greenwich, Connecticut. "Hedge-fund managers tend to move in the same small, concentric circles. 'They're generally image-conscious, they like to congregate, and credibility is generated by affiliation and by proximity,' says a [real estate] executive with hedge-fund clients in Greenwich and New York." Based on his reading of the 1930s backlash, our insider says the "incestuous" relationships between hedge funds operators and their bankers will sour quickly. "I spent countless hours reading the Pecora Commission hearings [held by Congress in the 1930s]," he said. "Soon, these men will turn on each other out of a need to survive and the subsequent market historians will have a field day."

It's not possible to say exactly who will get hanged, but the hindsight of the last Supercycle-degree bear market provides some perspective. In February 1933, Bernard Baruch offered his take to the U.S. Congress by first quoting Mackay's Tulip Mania description from *Extraordinary Popular Delusions*. "Everyone imagined that the passion for tulips would last forever. People of all grades converted their property into cash and invested it in flowers. Foreigners became smitten with the same frenzy and poured into Holland from all directions." Baruch then added:

> You will recognize some of these expressions. It seems incredible that so solid a nation as the Dutch should nearly ruin itself on such a thought, but is it any more credible than that we would go into debt to pay thirty times earnings power, and even more, for common stocks of the "New Economic Era" on the theory that we also were going to "banish" poverty by selling billions in manufacturers to an almost bankrupt world by the expedient of continually lending our customers more money? We built a tinsel tower of paper prosperity out of debts and speculative hopes and such other things as dreams are made of.

Twenty years ago, in 1987, the Dow's valuation based on dividend yield exceeded 1929's valuation. After a brief respite from there to 1991, the Dow's dividend yield has ever since remained more expensive than it was in 1929. On this and many other bases, it has been the wildest period of financial optimism in history, by many multiples, in both duration and extent. Generally, we "know" how it's going to end, but in many real ways, we don't. This bubble is so huge and has permeated so deeply and broadly into society that the concrete social consequences will have to be experienced as they unfold in order to believe they could happen. If we were to forecast in detail now the social disruptions that in fact will happen over the next 15-20 years, it would be labeled fantastical. *Conquer the Crash* tried to come close, but we are beginning to think that even the strong descriptions there are too conservative.

July 2007

The unwinding process will be sped along by a flood of revelations about illicit hedge fund and investment banking activities. Just as Enron, Tyco and a host of other primary beneficiaries of the late 1990s bull market run became the focus of scandals, hedge funds and the banks that enabled them are starting to become a focal point for scrutiny. This is the leading edge of the "giant wave of investigation, scandal and humiliation" that we alluded to in the May issue. In a story about the Bear Stearns blow-up, The Economist even uses the word that EWI has long identified with this downside of the cycle: "The recriminations are likely to grow." In a glimpse of the vicious infighting to come, hedge funds urged regulators to investigate investment banks for allegedly manipulating the mortgage bond market. "The funds accuse the banks of protecting their own positions in by propping up the prices of dodgy mortgages bought under the pretext of helping struggling borrowers."

In another sign, Congress launched investigations into the compensation schemes and taxation of hedge funds and many of the they trade. Several U.S. representatives also tried to put off Blackstone Group's initial public offering. Last month, EWFF classified Blackstone's IPO as a bearish signal. The signal was strengthened considerably on June 22 when the firm had to advance the deal by a week to beat the tsunami of recriminations that is now on a collision course with the hedge fund industry. On Tuesday, the Securities and Exchange Commission added a "broad-based investigation into the troubled subprime mortgage market" and "issues surrounding the secondary market for these instruments." As one pundit put it, hedge funds' antagonists are in "a no-lose situation politically." "Industry leaders have made themselves ready targets thanks in part to annual payouts that sometimes reach more than $1 billion and extravagant displays of wealth such as [Blackstone chairman Stephen] Schwarzman's 60th birthday party in New York on Feb. 13, which featured a performance by Rod Stewart and a video greeting from President George W. Bush."

Another important measure of sentiment that is showing a historically unprecedented level of optimism is the percentage of mutual fund cash levels relative to assets. A revised figure from the Investment Company Institute shows that mutual fund cash dropped to just 3.6% in March, an all-time record low. The reading breaks the lows of 3.9%, which came six months before a major stock peak in 1973, and 4.0%, which accompanied the March 2000 top in the S&P and NASDAQ.

© July 2007 Elliott Wave International (www.elliottwave.com)
Source: Investment Company Institute

KING CASH IS READY TO RULE
Cash as % of Assets in Equity Mutual Funds
monthly

S&P 500

Mutual Fund Cash to Assets Ratio

new all-time low→

October 2007

Wait 'Til Congress Hears About the Missing Money

Back in July, EWFF directed readers' attention to a "tsunami of recriminations that is now on a collision course with the hedge fund industry." Hedge funds are suddenly under assault from so many directions that we can't keep up. The SEC, Congress and foreign securities regulators have been taking on hedge funds at every turn. Investigations into insider trades ("SEC Scrutinizes Hedge Funds in Insider-Trading," Bloomberg September 18), market manipulation ("US Senator Aims to Stop Energy Market Manipulation," September 17) and a long-standing privacy ("Turbulent Markets May Change UK and US's Hedge Fund Stance," Forbes September 4) are underway. The potential for a huge haul of charges and penalties (and probably indictments too) is clear in a drive to increase hedge fund taxes. In England, the head of the Labour Party set the tone by drawing an unfavorable comparison to the mafia. "Private equity makes the Cosa Nostra look like a model of openness and transparency," said Jack Dromney. "They fleece all of us by not paying their fair share of tax." Parliament is considering raising the tax rates on private equity firms from the capital gains rate of 10% to an income tax of 22%. In the U.S., the stakes are even higher as Congress is considering raising hedge fund taxes from the capital gains rate of 15% to an ordinary income tax rate of as much as 35%. Hedge fund managers' dim comprehension of the forces that are massing against them is obvious by their main argument against increased taxation—it reduces the returns they deliver to pension fund clients. We predict that they will soon escape paying taxes altogether due to portfolio losses.

The Big Bailout Bluff

Last week, a consortium of the USA's three largest banks—Citigroup, Bank of America and JP Morgan Chase—agreed to create a super fund (called M-LEC) of $80 billion "to buy distressed securities from SIVs [Structured Investment Vehicles]." Of course, like the Fed's loans for only the very best paper, the super fund will buy only high-quality mortgages, not the sub-prime or Alt-A stuff.

Do you think this plan will work? First let's examine what the SIVs did to get themselves in trouble. As AP (10/16) reports,

> The SIVs used short-term commercial paper, sold at low interest rates, to buy longer-term mortgage-backed securities and other instruments with higher rates of return. With the seizure of the credit markets, many SIVs had trouble selling new commercial paper to replace upcoming obligations on older paper.

Their plan, in other words, was the equivalent of a perpetual motion machine: "Money for Nothing," as the song title goes. But the world does not work like that. Oversized interest rates often mean that the investment is in fact sucking money out of principal. Sometimes investors can get away with the gambit for awhile, but eventually somebody pays the bill. The collapse in sub-prime mortgages and in the commercial paper that supported them has simply adjusted the value of the principal to make up for the outsized returns that these investors got over the past five years. But guess what: The money that banks owe on their commercial paper didn't change. Sounds like trouble. And here is what they are doing about it:

> This time around, the banks hope to not only prevent credit problems from spreading, but also are bailing themselves out. (AP, 10/16)

This idea is the equivalent to trying to levitate yourself by pulling on your legs. These banks are going to offer more commercial paper to buy mortgage assets; in other words, they are going to borrow more short-term money in order to buy long-term assets from themselves! That is, if they can borrow the money in the first place. One of the casualties in the rout was the commercial paper market; investors are realizing that it backs a lot of lousy mortgage debt, so they are backing away from investing in the commercial paper that backs the mortgages.

The last time banks colluded to hold up an entire market was October 1929. It didn't work.

If you have any exposure to illiquid mortgage investments, look upon this superfund as a gift. As soon as these banks pledge to buy one of your long-term, mortgage-backed securities, *sell it to them.*

What collateral will these banks use to back the $80 billion in commercial paper they hope to sell to finance this scheme? They can't use mortgages, because the market doesn't want them. As one article says, "Analysts say that investors have all but stopped buying SIV-affiliated commercial paper." Will the new commercial paper become obligations of the banks? There appears to be no other alternative. In other words, depositors' money may end up backing this paper. One thing seems certain: the banks are digging themselves deeper into a hole. If you still have deposits in debt-laden banks despite our entreaties, you might want to take this late opportunity to move them.

November 2007

From M-Lec to Blech!

Most big bull runs ultimately lead to government or financial industry rescues that bring a high level of scrutiny and recrimination to the perpetrators of mania-era schemes. In recent days, we've already seen the initiation of the first major bailout. This month's issue of *The Elliott Wave Theorist* covers the consortium of U.S. banks—Citigroup, Bank of America and JPMorgan Chase—and their effort to create a super fund (called M-LEC) that proposes to buy $80-$100 billion of Structured Investment Vehicles or SIVs. So far their attempts have failed because few want to buy their paper. According to the book *Collateralized Debt Obligations and Structured Finance*, SIVs are "offshore entities" (based primarily in the Cayman Islands) set up to purchase AA-rated investments with up to eight-times leverage. The advantage of SIVs is the "fact that credit default swap spreads are often wider for the same credit than those in the capital markets." As it turns out, there's a reason for the discrepancy. The lack of liquidity and price transparency makes the off-market instruments big losers in periods of widening spreads, which is exactly what happens when a credit bubble bursts.

The October EWT revealed the flaws in the latest bailout scheme. Another problem was timing, which is displayed in the following chart of past bailouts. In the course of the healthy bull market of the 1980s and 1990s, bailouts happened at or immediately after big lows. This is the secret of their success; they typically come at the most dire financial moments, which is fueled by an extreme in pessimism that creates major stock market lows. A rebound always appears to rescue even the most heinous financial concoction. The September 2001 issue of EWFF suggested an alternate fate in big bear markets. With a proposed bailout of Argentina on the table, EWFF asserted that the stock market would fall straight through the efforts to shore up the country's debt. This turned out to be an accurate assessment, as the Dow declined 30% thereafter despite heavy lending by the International Monetary Fund to Argentina. A bailout of Brazil in 2002, however, did coincide with a low. But the fascinating aspect of the SIV bailout attempt is that it was needed before the stock market even headed down. The market experienced a smaller version of this failure back in June when brokerage firms tried to assemble a bailout for two Bear Stearns hedge funds. The effort was abandoned at the peak in mid-July when Bear Stearns told clients that the hedge fund assets were "almost worthless." As we said here in April: "Chrysler and Continental Illinois were 'too big to fail;' the unfolding crisis will be 'too big to bail.'"

Another difference between the current deal and most of the others on the chart is its proximity to Wall Street. This time the players left holding the bag are not investors in foreign bonds and securities or the U.S. government but the "money-center" firms themselves. This is another sign that the fault lines associated with this bailout run very, very deep.

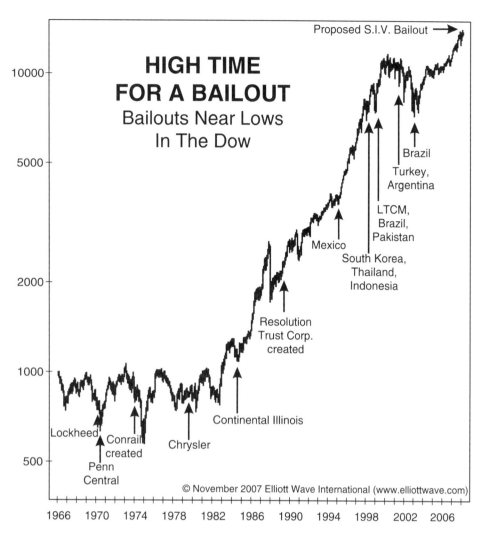

HIGH TIME
FOR A BAILOUT
Bailouts Near Lows
In The Dow

Proposed S.I.V. Bailout →

Brazil
Turkey,
Argentina
LTCM,
Brazil,
Pakistan
Mexico
South Korea,
Thailand,
Indonesia
Resolution
Trust Corp.
created
Continental Illinois
Lockheed
Conrail
created
Chrysler
Penn
Central

© November 2007 Elliott Wave International (www.elliottwave.com)

December 2007

Increasing fear manifests in certain behaviors. For one thing, bankers become fearful of lending. Depositors' fear is also a factor. Just a few weeks ago the Local Government Investment Pool run by the Florida State Board of Administration, which held the assets of many state government organizations, had such a run that it suspended withdrawals. Does anyone think that its current and former depositors will blithely add more money to this fund just because the Fed says it can make more credit available? Well, it could happen. But if the trend is now toward greater fear in society, it won't. One of the most entertaining articles in recent memory is one from Bloomberg on December 4, about the fund in Florida. The portion italicized will be suitable for framing:

> On Nov. 30, an advisory panel of local governments in the Florida pool held a conference call with members of the State Board of Administration. The SBA put out a "Preferences Survey" for discussion, and Question No. 1 was "What percent of your current holding would you withdraw in December 2007, if it meant you would receive 99 cents on the dollar?" The next three questions were exactly the same, except with 98 cents on the dollar, 95 cents on the dollar and 90 cents on the dollar. *The municipal officials on the call would have none of it. They want 100 cents on the dollar. Anything less, they said, would be unacceptable.*

News flash for these investors: *You can't tell the market what you will or won't accept. It tells **you**.*

Another line in the article expresses the problem correctly, failing only in expressing the futility of a solution:

> They were a pretty conciliatory and reasonable bunch. They kept saying that what was needed was to restore confidence and trust in the fund.

Good luck changing the mood of the crowd.

The Economy and Deflation

Over two years ago, when the real estate mania was in full swing, we showed a graph of REITs juxtaposed with Time magazine's July 2005 "Home $weet Home" cover (see Chapter 2). We thought it was a good way to illustrate a peak in real-estate fever. We published an update recently in the August 2006 issue against the S&P Supercomposite Homebuilding index. Well, our graphic instincts must be pretty good, because almost the same illustration has just appeared in USA Today, making the same point in retrospect. We are flattered, of course, and look forward to seeing newspapers and magazines publishing some of our current illustrations two years from now.

The key question now is whether the media alarm on housing is a sign of a bottom or an important new phase in which the delusionary psychology of the old bull market is erased by a new bear market reality. At such times, the entrenched optimism of the old bull market is reversed and a negative social mood begins to manifest itself in the economy. The charts that follow suggest strongly that the latter scenario is the correct one. While most economists continue to dispel notions of a recession, stories about a harsh new economic reality are starting to appear. It is focused most dramatically on housing because housing is at the front edge of the great fall.

The chaos in housing is crucial because it remains the leading edge of the great transformation. Don't forget that it was only four months ago that headlines in Fortune and The Wall Street Journal declared that the economy was in the midst of its greatest-ever boom. Here are the headlines we showed in the August issue:

The Greatest Economic Boom Ever
—Fortune, July 12, 2007

The Best Economy Ever
—The Wall Street Journal, July 31, 2007

EWFF strongly disagreed, citing a "clearly weakening" picture based on the connection between housing's "ravaging tidal wave" and the economy. According to the latest data, the median price of new homes just dropped 13% from a year earlier. Several key indicators show that the economy is on the threshold of a similar fall.

Housing Stops

One key indicator with a long history of success in pre-dating economic downturns is housing starts, which are approaching the 1-million-a-month level that has preceded all recessions of the last 40 years. At 48%, the chart shows that the decline in starts is at a point that has never failed to accompany a recession. In percentage terms, the only comparable reversal was the one that preceded the last housing debacle in 1990. In that case, however, the decline in starts lasted over six years. This time an equivalent decline took just 20 months. The faster speed should translate into a more serious economic contraction.

Help-Wanted Advertising

Some say the Internet is turning the Index of Help Wanted Advertising into an obsolete economic indicator, but it worked pretty well back in 2001, when the Internet was nearly as ubiquitous as it is today. In February 2001, EWFF anticipated that year's recession with the help of a collapse that took the Help Wanted index to its lowest level since 1993. The index is plunging once again; this time to its lowest level ever. The index's unblemished track record is shown by the shaded areas indicating recessions on the chart. There is a complementary decline in the share price of Monster.com, the most popular Internet classified website. Together, these forward-looking measures of employment clearly signal a contraction. Meanwhile, the three-month rate of change in non-farm U.S. payroll employment is rolling over. One strong down month will probably take it to the zero level, which would be another strong signal that a recession is at hand.

Big Ticket Items

Sellers of major amenity items like recreational vehicles are feeling the pinch, too. For the first time in six years, sales of motor homes and travel trailers are falling just as they did before every recession over the last 30 years. At Winnebago, sales are in their third straight year of decline, and they came off the hitch with a 20% drop in September. "This has actually been a little bit longer downturn than anything that

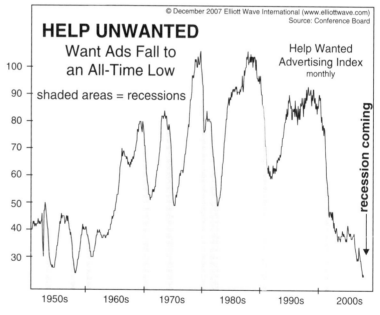

we've seen over the last 30 years," said Winnebago's chief executive. Shares in the five largest RV companies are down anywhere from 20% to 47%. "No one needs a new RV," explains a fund manager with RV holdings. "When people are boisterous, [RV makers] have good years, and when they're cautious, sales are down. I wish I had started selling sooner." Somehow, the longer the big break lower takes to arrive, the more surprised people seem to be when it digs in.

Waning Momentum

One of the most important long-term economic signals was identified by Bob Prechter in *At the Crest of the Tidal Wave*: the "ability to render real" the bullish psychology of a rising wave. Bob observed that translating "ebullience into actual capital production" fades in fifth waves relative to the preceding third wave. Chapter 1 of *Conquer the Crash* captures a host of different economic measures showing the weaker output of Cycle wave V in the 1980s and 1990s versus Cycle wave III in the 1950s and 1960s. The chart of year-over-year GDP growth shows the slackening

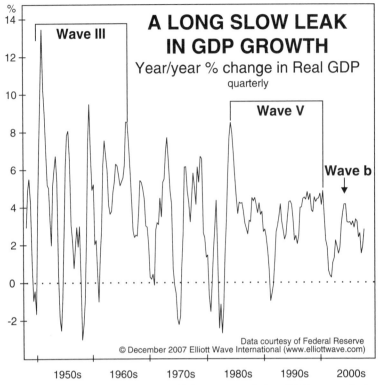

strength of the economy in Cycle wave V and wave **b**. The still-lower peak in GDP growth in wave **b** occurred despite and because of a record high issuance of debt that continued to mount even as growth trailed off.

Considering the current expansion's relatively low increase in real wages, record high exposure to credit card and mortgage debt and the first year-to-year decline in home values in the lives of most homeowners, consumers remain remarkably sanguine. The rarity of the recession bars in recent decades on these long-term charts probably explain why. Most consumers today are not familiar with economic contraction. After 1933, contractions become shorter and less frequent, most likely due to the exponential rise in credit inflation. The GDP chart shows that year-to-year growth slipped below the zero line for just one brief period in the last 25 years. This probably contributes to consumers' willingness to spend freely despite the relentless approach of the next recession. The importance of defensive measures like paying down debt and saving more are not familiar to many people today. While reckless spending has kept a modicum of growth in place, a dire consequence is that more people will be far more exposed when the job losses hit. These charts say that contraction is on its way, and if *Conquer the Crash* is correct, it will be the harshest downturn in memory for everyone under the age of 80.

February 2008

Cracking a Financial Crime Wave

If there is one attribute that assures a bright future for socionomics, it is its uncanny knack for solving crimes before they are even committed. In the case of the great housing bust, for instance, the list of culprits keeps getting longer and longer. Back in July 2005, when housing stocks were topping and the industry was still perceived as a bastion of respectability, EWFF issued the following statement:

> This time there is no mistaking who the Enrons of the bust phase will be. They will be the firms now peddling adjustable-rate, no-interest/nothing-down and assorted other types of 'subprime' mortgages.

The recent wave of lawsuits, indictments and convictions shows just how massive the search for the bad guys behind the housing bust has become. Recent front page headlines include "Fraud Seen As Driver in Wave Of Foreclosures," (December 21, Wall Street Journal), "Housing Scams Rising, FBI Says," (January 14, USA Today) and "Broke Homeowners Linked to Arsons," (MSN Money, January 28). According to the NY Times, a "wave of lawsuits is beginning to wash over the troubled mortgage market and the rest of the financial world. Homeowners are suing mortgage lenders. Mortgage lenders are suing Wall Street banks. Wall Street banks are suing loan specialists. And investors are suing everyone." The FBI announced earlier this week that it is investigating 14 companies, including lenders, developers and Wall Street banks, for accounting fraud "and other crimes related to the subprime lending crisis."

Or, how about this one from the January 21 Chicago Tribune:

New Alarm: Option-ARM 'Liars Loans'

Housing is a veritable mushroom cloud of litigation and prosecution. Socionomically, we're more interested in its size, speed and spread than the crimes themselves because these factors tell us the most about the direction and force of social mood. Scams and scandals appear in the wake of every mania. The bigger the crime wave, or more precisely the greater the effort to pursue criminals, the bigger the underlying change in social mood. In this case, the size of the collapse is also indicated by how long the fraud persisted after the bubble burst. Most of the "Liar Loans" mentioned above, for instance, were issued after the 2005 peak, and the most recent loans are faring the worst. According to the Mortgage Asset Research Institute, nine out of ten applicants overstated income and almost 60% did so by more than 50%!

Subprime fraud is pervasive, but what about the rest of the financial world? If the bust is spreading, as we contend, the backlash against the bull market's institutions, instruments and heroes should be making its way into other areas of the markets. Here's how EWFF expressed this principle in November:

> Up until now, the sufficiency of mark-to-model accounting attested to the level of trust prevailing at the end of a Grand Supercycle bull market. But as more markets top out, the revelations of fraud should spike as drowning traders flail—and eventually fail—to stay above water.

The largest loss ever attributed to a single trader, a $7.2 billion snafu by Société Générale's Jerome Kerviel, certainly fits the bill. It is a classic case of the calamity that results when a mania ends and over-leveraged traders, who built their reputations on the back of higher and higher price surges, try to trade, then scam their way out of a fast-falling market. "He'd taken winning positions for a long time and thought he had the benefit of the doubt," says one prosecutor. But in 2008, he leveraged his bet. "Ahead of worldwide markets experiencing a steep sell-off, the junior-level trader bet the market would recover." The specifics are difficult to see ahead of time, but the inevitability of it is not, given the position of social mood. We can now make additional inferences based on the scope of the fraud. The "biggest ever" tag says that it must be a big decline. Then there is the speed of the reversal. It was only a few days ago that Société Générale earned the following distinction:

Awards: January 2008 | Volume21/No1

Risk Awards 2008

Equity Derivatives House Of the Year—Société Générale

Things will happen even faster now. And the changes will be profound. In bestowing Société Générale "equity house of the year" honors, Risk noted that its "losses were minor and relatively manageable." The word "were" refers back to a gentler time. As *Conquer the Crash* explained, are far more toxic now because of the losses inherent in a trend change from up to down.

It is traditional to discount the representative value of because traders will presumably get out of losing positions well before they wreak destruction. Well, maybe. It is at least as common a human reaction for speculators to double their bets when the market goes against a big position. At least, that's what bankers might do with your money.

Banks are also discovering that many of the exotic financial instruments that helped them leverage the uptrend will now keep them lashed to the downtrend. The havoc-wreaking potential of one instrument, credit-default swaps, was covered in the September 2006 issue of EWFF:

> When bubbles burst, they invariably unleash a negative social response against the most aggressive and successful exploiters of the preceding advance. Credit-default swaps (CDS) are one relatively new financially engineered product that is rapidly climbing to the top of our growing list of likely targets. Sudden prices swings of 30% and 80% earlier this month in credit-default swaps signals the potential for a violent reversal. The damage done by an actual economic contraction will undoubtedly be catastrophic.

CDSs allow investors to buy securities that are essentially a bet on whether a company or securitized package of loans will default. They can place these bets whether they own the underlying security or not. So on the way up, credit-default swaps helped perpetuate the rise because many bondholders who became bearish never sold; they just bought the CDSs that they expected to rise as the prospects of repayment diminished. In down times, however, as academics Henry Hu and Bernard Black recently discovered, the risk of default rises sharply because the CDS' return in the event of default is worth much more than a struggling business or dwindling stream of mortgage payments. "Thanks to explosive growth in credit , debt-holders such as banks and hedge funds have often more to gain if companies fail than if they survive," say Hu and Black. Of course, the larger question is whether the holders of $43 trillion in bets on the soundness of corporations can survive. As Washington Post columnist Steven Pearlstein notes, "The credit-default swap has become central to modern global finance. If the losing side is unable to make good on even a fraction of a percent of those contracts, it could set in motion a financial chain reaction that could easily rival the subprime debacle." The numbers suggest that the subprime problem could be small by comparison.

March 2008
The Long, Un-winding Road

At an investment conference in Florida earlier this month, we had the opportunity to feel the pulse of advisors and investors. The consensus opinion—that investors should ignore the stock market's 20%-24% decline since October and instead focus on holding for the long term—was not too surprising. Obviously, we've heard "buy and hold" espoused at these gatherings before, but the forceful, endless repetition of this bull-market mantra was somewhat unexpected.

Considering the early bear market juncture of social mood, however, it fits right in. As this chart of the average holding period for a NYSE stock illustrates (next page), investors actually turn up the hope and cling most tenaciously to their shares in bear markets. In bull markets they may espouse the buy and hold approach, but the chart shows that they don't actually practice what they preach. The average holding period plunged through the last 60+ years of advancing stock prices and fell to a low of just 9 months in 2007. The decline brought the average below the previous record lows of just under one year in 1929, the end of the last bull market of Supercycle degree. Upward spikes on the chart end near bear markets in the early 1940s, 1974 and 1990. Also notice that the most bruising period for stocks, the 13 years that followed the 1929 peak, produced the longest holding periods. So, the harder stocks fall, the tighter the grip of investors gets. This is a graphic depiction of Bob Prechter's phrase "slope of hope" that keeps investors nervously eyeing, and then wistfully recalling their break-even levels as stocks continually break to new lows.

Ironically, while at bottoms investors are most attached to the stocks they already own, their willingness to buy new stocks at such junctures is virtually non-existent. At the major lows of 1932, 1974, or 1980-1982, the public dared not consider stock market investing, let alone for the long term. At each of these optimum buy points, stocks were railed against, ignored, or at best, treated as vehicles for garnering quick profits. Recall the now-infamous August 1979 Business Week cover that proclaimed the "Death of Equities," near the end of a 14-year long bear market. By contrast, wide-spread lip service to buy and hold reflects a powerfully entrenched optimistic social mood, which, contrarily, is a very bearish market signal. The forcefulness of the opinion is being ratcheted up now because prices are not keeping pace with the previous trend. Advisors advocate holding for the long term, mainly as a method to placate worried investors. But as *At the Crest* noted, buy and hold is a stance, not a philosophy:

> Properly applied, the phrase "focus on the long term" is in no way synonymous with "close your eyes and buy." Sometimes it means "get out and wait."

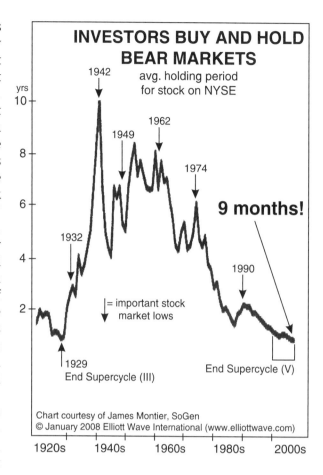

INVESTORS BUY AND HOLD BEAR MARKETS
avg. holding period for stock on NYSE

↓ = important stock market lows

9 months!

1929 End Supercycle (III)

End Supercycle (V)

Chart courtesy of James Montier, SoGen
© January 2008 Elliott Wave International (www.elliottwave.com)

One sign of buy and hold's fading efficacy is visible in the table that compares the return on cash to the return on stocks since the beginning of this decade. While the buy-and-hold sentiment is as strong as ever, that stance has been bested by a completely risk-free return for eight years. Cash will continue to outperform until stocks are no longer fashionable, at which time the market will be near a bottom.

There is a host of other problems with "buying and holding for the long term." One big one is that the notion of "long term" is variable. Is it 5 years, 8 years, 11.3 years? Each investor's situation is somewhat unique, but there is no investor who was better off holding through the 20- and 14-year periods of non-rising stock prices shown on the chart of the Dow (next page). The chart also reveals that real values—stocks denominated in real money, which is gold—are crashing. EWT and EWFF have discussed

EIGHT-YEAR TOTAL RETURN
12/31/99 to 2/21/08
Transaction costs excluded

INDEX	Total Return
CASH 3-month T-bill	+29.24%
S&P 500	+5.39%
NASDAQ Composite	−40.53%
Dow Jones Wilshire 5000	+13.95%
Dow Jones Industrial Average	+26.97%

this important behavior before, but note that the previous two times that real stock values crashed marked long-term bear market periods. Since the early 1920s, there has never been a period when real stock values crashed and the market wasn't in a long-term bear market. So far, it has been eight years since the early 2000 top, which is about half the time of the average of

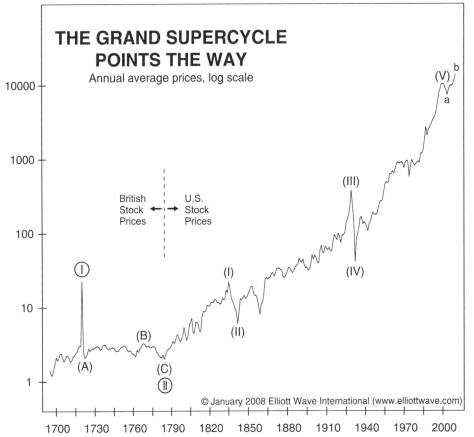

the two previous long-term periods of non-rising stock values. And real stock values dropped an average of 90% in the two previous declining phases on the chart. This history suggests that in both time and intensity, this bear market is a long way from over, in which case a buy and hold stance will ultimately prove devastating to one's portfolio.

Observe that the market experiences long periods of rising and falling prices. A successful long-term investor needs to identify when the market is in each of these phases because they last from one to two *decades*. "To do it properly," *At the Crest* notes, "you must have a method of anticipating long term trends." This is where Elliott becomes so valuable. As the chart at the bottom of the previous page shows, January 2000 marked the completion of a full five-wave advance from at least 1974, likely from 1932, and possibly from the end of the Revolutionary War. The decline to 2002 and subsequent rally to 2007 were waves **a** and **b** of an ongoing bear market. Wave **c** down is now underway. So the investment-conference crowd is absolutely correct: It is time to focus on the long term. But the Wave Principle, a crash in real values, and investors' determination to stay the course all say that this is no time to hold out hope for stock-market gains. The long-term trend is toward cash and this remains our forecast.

The Best Investment During Recessions

The most important question is not whether the Dow beat gold or vice versa but whether making either investment would have been better than taking no risk at all. The tables on the next page show that ten-year Treasury notes beat both gold and the Dow during recessions since 1945, *and they did so far more reliably*. T-notes provided a capital gain in ten of the 11 recessions, and of course they provided interest income during all of them. And the transaction costs are low. The average total return in T-notes per recession is a full 10%, beating both stocks and gold. The average total return after transaction costs is 9.82%, beating the Dow's 6.87% and gold's 4.80%. If you compound these figures over 11 recessions, the difference is substantial. It is far greater when we include the major declines in stock prices during the economic contractions of the 1930s and figure in the transaction costs of buying and selling gold.

So if you want to make money *reliably and safely* during recessions and depressions, you should own bonds whose issuers will remain fully reliable debtors throughout the contraction. Of course, as *Conquer the Crash* makes abundantly clear, finding such bonds in *this* depression, which will be the deepest in 300 years, will not be easy. CTC forecast that in this depression most bonds will go down and many will go to zero. This process has already begun. This time around, you have to follow the suggestions in that book to make your debt investment work.

O.K., Then, So What Is the Economy Usually Doing When Gold Goes Up?

If gold isn't going up when the economy is contracting, when is it going up? The table on the next page answers the question: *All the huge gains in gold have come while the economy was expanding*. This is true of the three most dramatic gold gains of the past century:

1. Congress changed the official price of gold from $20.67 to $35 per ounce in 1934, during an economic expansion. The gain against the dollar was 69%.

2. The entire bull market from 1970 to 1980 occurred during an economic expansion, aside from $2.60 worth of gain in the 1970 recession and $87 worth of gain during the recession of 11/73 to 3/75. In other words, of the $815 per ounce that gold rose from 1970 to 1980, $725 worth of it came while the economy was expanding.

3. The entire bull market from 2001 to the present occurred during an economic expansion, aside from the first eight months, when gold edged up $22. In other words, of the $748 per ounce that gold has risen since February 2001, $726 worth of it has come while the economy was expanding.

Even lesser rises in gold, such as the two big rallies during the 1980s, came during economic expansions. So the biggest gains in gold, by far, have occurred while the economy was in *expansion, not contraction*.

BEHAVIOR OF THREE KEY
MARKETS DURING RECESSIONS

GOLD Recession Start	Recession End	Length in Months	Start Value	End Value	Capital Gain/Loss	Income	Total Return	Total Return w/ 2008 Transaction Costs
(15th of month)	(15th of month)							
Feb 1945	Oct 1945	8	35	35	0.00%	0.00%	0.00%	-4.00%
Nov 1948	Oct 1949	11	35	35	0.00%	0.00%	0.00%	-4.00%
Jul 1953	May 1954	10	35	35	0.00%	0.00%	0.00%	-4.00%
Aug 1957	Apr 1958	8	35	35	0.00%	0.00%	0.00%	-4.00%
Apr 1960	Feb 1961	10	35	35	0.00%	0.00%	0.00%	-4.00%
Dec 1969	Nov 1970	11	35.35	37.95	7.36%	0.00%	7.36%	3.36%
Nov 1973	Mar 1975	16	91.5	178.25	94.81%	0.00%	94.81%	90.81%
Jan 1980	Jul 1980	6	684	619.5	-9.43%	0.00%	-9.43%	-13.43%
Jul 1981	Nov 1982	16	412.25	403.25	-2.18%	0.00%	-2.18%	-6.18%
Jul 1990	Mar 1991	8	363.6	366	0.66%	0.00%	0.66%	-3.34%
Mar 2001	Nov 2001	8	260.9	275.6	5.63%	0.00%	5.63%	1.63%
	Average:	10.18182				Average:	8.80%	4.80%
© March 2008 Elliottwave International						Median:	0.00%	-4.00%

DJIA		Length in Months	Start Value	End Value	Capital Gain/Loss	Income	Total Return	Total Return w/ 2008 Transaction Costs
(15th of month)	(15th of month)							
Feb 1945	Oct 1945	8	158.2	185.5	17.26%	2.55%	19.80%	19.78%
Nov 1948	Oct 1949	11	176	186.4	5.91%	5.86%	11.77%	11.75%
Jul 1953	May 1954	10	268.7	322.5	20.02%	4.22%	24.24%	24.22%
Aug 1957	Apr 1958	8	487.3	447.5	-8.17%	3.03%	-5.13%	-5.15%
Apr 1960	Feb 1961	10	630.1	648.8	2.97%	2.93%	5.90%	5.88%
Dec 1969	Nov 1970	11	784	759.7	-3.10%	3.85%	0.75%	0.73%
Nov 1973	Mar 1975	16	874.5	773.4	-11.56%	7.03%	-4.53%	-4.55%
Jan 1980	Jul 1980	6	868.6	901.5	3.79%	2.96%	6.75%	6.73%
Jul 1981	Nov 1982	16	954.1	1021.4	7.05%	8.20%	15.25%	15.23%
Jul 1990	Mar 1991	8	2980.2	2948.5	-1.06%	2.47%	1.40%	1.38%
Mar 2001	Nov 2001	8	10031.3	9872.4	-1.58%	1.21%	-0.37%	-0.39%
	Average:	10.18182				Average:	6.89%	6.87%
© March 2008 Elliottwave International						Median:	5.90%	5.88%

T-NOTES		Length in Months	Start Value	End Value	Capital Gain/Loss	Income	Total Return	Total Return w/ 2008 Transaction Costs
(15th of month)	(15th of month)							
Feb 1945	Oct 1945	8	100	102.7167	2.72%	1.29%	4.01%	3.87%
Nov 1948	Oct 1949	11	100	103.8969	3.90%	1.98%	5.88%	5.74%
Jul 1953	May 1954	10	100	104.4658	4.47%	2.43%	6.90%	6.76%
Aug 1957	Apr 1958	8	100	110.036	10.04%	2.57%	12.61%	12.47%
Apr 1960	Feb 1961	10	100	103.8428	3.84%	3.54%	7.38%	7.24%
Dec 1969	Nov 1970	11	100	104.1723	4.17%	7.00%	11.17%	11.03%
Nov 1973	Mar 1975	16	100	95.45263	-4.55%	9.02%	4.47%	4.33%
Jan 1980	Jul 1980	6	100	102.879	2.88%	5.33%	8.21%	8.07%
Jul 1981	Nov 1982	16	100	119.0004	19.00%	18.76%	37.76%	37.62%
Jul 1990	Mar 1991	8	100	102.1924	2.19%	5.62%	7.82%	7.68%
Mar 2001	Nov 2001	8	100	100.1729	0.17%	3.19%	3.36%	3.22%
	Average:	10.18182				Average:	9.96%	9.82%
© March 2008 Elliottwave International						Median:	7.38%	7.24%

Why is such the case? Simple: During expansions, liquidity is available, and it has to go somewhere. Sometimes it goes into stocks, sometimes it goes into gold, and sometimes it goes into both. During times of extreme credit inflation, such as we have experienced over the past three decades, the moves in these markets during economic expansions are likewise extreme. When recession hits, liquidity dries up, and investors stop buying. During *depressions*, they sell assets with a vengeance.

Let's apply the Wave Principle to the silver market. The April 18, 2006 issue of EWT predicted an imminent top in silver, with a price projection of $21.70 and a backup projection of $16.61:

> In 1980, silver peaked just beyond the line that connects the tops of waves ① and ③. Silver's rise in 1967-1980 created a neat Fibonacci price tapestry. Wave ③ peaked very close to a 233% gain from the top of wave ①, and wave ⑤ peaked very close to a 610% gain from the top of wave ③, a 2.618 relationship, achieving approximately a 34x multiple for the rise from the low of wave ②. In the current bull market, wave ③ peaked almost exactly at a 61.8% gain from the top of wave ①. If wave ⑤ soars to the same 2.618 relative percentage gain as the former wave ⑤, it will peak near **$21.70**, achieving approximately a 5x multiple for the rise from the low of wave ②, which is a Fibonacci .146 relationship to the same part of the former bull market. Observe that the first two peaks (in 2002 and 2004) occurred slightly beyond Fibonacci numbers: **$5** and **$8**. Likewise this projection would bring wave ⑤ slightly beyond **$21**. A repeat of these aspects of the wildest silver market ever, though, seems a lot to expect. A 100 percent gain (1.618 x .618) to near **$16.61** would bring the price just beyond the 1→3 resistance line (see chart below), which is what happened at the peak in 1980.

Silver topped 2½ weeks later and fell 37 percent. But the peak price just above $15 did not match either of the price projections. Though silver corrected for over a year, 2006 proved not to be the final top. I had labeled wave ④ as a triangle, clearly the best labeling even in retrospect. But wave ④ was a zigzag, and the peak in 2006 was only the top of wave (3) of ⑤. The price projection of $21.70, however, is looking very good. The high so far is $21.32, and once again the wave structure appears nearly terminal while market sentiment is extreme. As shown in the chart, silver has met its resistance line on arithmetic scale, and bulls outnumber bears so lopsidedly that the 21-day average of daily readings has reached 91 percent and the 10-day average 95 percent, while the peak daily reading hit an amazing 98 percent. The wave count is nearly satisfied, although ideally it should end after one more new high to complete wave 5 of (5) of ⑤. A slight new high would give this top the same profile as that of 2006.

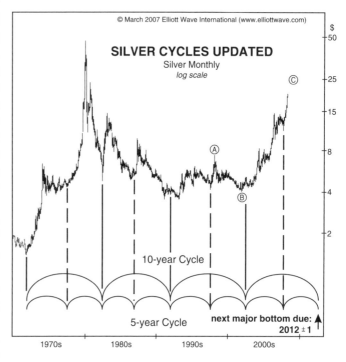

If this analysis of silver is accurate and silver does peak this year and begin a bear market, gold is likely to go down with it. As we have already seen, gold tends to perform less well during economic contractions, so the economy is likely to peak along with gold. This conclusion fits our long-standing observation that silver is an excellent predictor of recessions: When it goes down substantially, recession follows. Despite the recent torrent of bad news, the economy has yet to go into recession. So all this analysis fits our view: The economy is on its last legs, and the precious metals are nearing a top right along with it.

The chart at right shows how this five-wave bull market in silver fits into the larger picture: It is wave ⓒ of an Ⓐ-Ⓑ-ⓒ counter-trend rally. This chart also updates our silver cycles from two years ago. They have continued to work, as the 5-year cycle coincided with the low in August 2007, and the 10-year cycle still points to a low in 2012 (± a year). This is also a projected year for a major low in the stock market. So everything still points to a deflationary collapse bottoming about four years from now.

April 2008

We have said it before, but given the popularity of gold and silver it bears repeating: When almost all investors hold a bullish opinion about a given market, there are scant few left to carry an asset much higher. The 10-day Daily Sentiment Index percentage of bulls maxed out at a record high of 93.8% for gold and 95.1% for silver. Metals fever is so strong now that an early 1980s' tradition of bringing a geiger counter to the beach is back in vogue. Last month, EWFF cited the historic optimism and contended that the uptrend in both markets was near exhaustion. Gold's breakneck $129.00 collapse in just 3½ days (13%) indicates that the forecasted multi-month decline is underway.

The St. Patrick's day reversal in silver and gold got our attention because it was on the same day in 1837 that the deflationary depression that accompanied Supercycle wave (II) kicked off. In that case, the big bust began with a downside implosion in the cotton markets. Here's how Charles Albert Collman describes that fateful day in *Our Mysterious Panics 1830-1930*:

> The panic struck Wall Street with brutal suddenness. A swift packet had flown from the South on the wings of the wind. The packet brought news of commercial disaster. In

A COMPLETE RALLY

spot gold
weekly, log scale

area of the
previous
fourth wave

© April 2008 Elliott Wave International (www.elliottwave.com)

1999 2000 2001 2002 2003 2004 2005 2006 2007 2008

the rich city of New Orleans, the greatest cotton houses in the country had gone under with staggering losses. Nearly one-fifth of the bank directors were insolvent. The great land boom had crashed. The cotton corner was broken. How would all this react upon Wall Street? The answer soon came. The firm of J.L. & S. Josephs & Company stopped payment in consequence of the New Orleans failures.

Bear Stearns' meltdown to just $2.84 also hit on March 17. Thanks to the Federal Reserve and its guarantee of nearly $30 billion in Bear Stearns paper, Bear Stearns didn't collapse (in the legal sense) the way J.L. Josephs did in 1837. But as the March 14 analysis in *The Elliott Wave Theorist* points out, the potential for a brutally sudden economic reversal is likely signaled by gold's turn lower. EWT also notes that "silver is an excellent predictor of recessions." Economic statistics are lagging indicators, but they still can impart useful information in helping to confirm the message of forward-looking market-based indicators. The following chart shows the excellent track record of just such an economic indicator, the three-month rate of change in U.S. non-farm employee payrolls (NFEP). Declines below zero in three-month payrolls preceded or accompanied each of the last eight recessions. In February 2001, EWFF showed another notch below the zero line and said that it signals "recession ahead." The recession of 2001 started the next month.

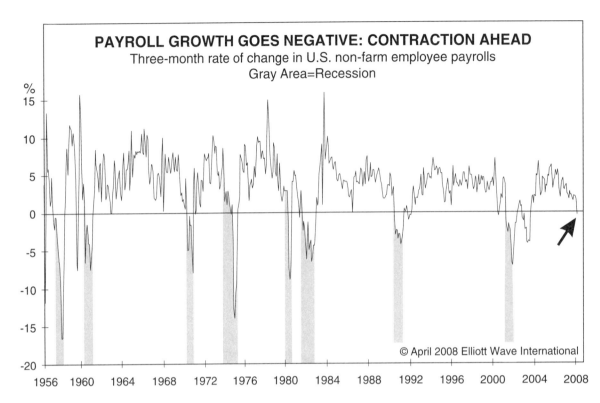

PAYROLL GROWTH GOES NEGATIVE: CONTRACTION AHEAD
Three-month rate of change in U.S. non-farm employee payrolls
Gray Area=Recession

© April 2008 Elliott Wave International

The NFEP rate of change just crossed the zero line again. This time we modified the headline on the chart to "contraction" ahead because recession is too nice a word for what's coming. Other economic measures suggest a slide of radical proportions. According to the durable goods orders for February, demand for machinery fell 13% *in one month*. The decline is the largest since comparable records were initiated in 1992. March brought a similar month-to-month plunge in the Conference Board's consumer confidence index. The 12-point decline to 64.5 puts consumers about where they were in March 2003 when war with Iraq was imminent. Consumers' expectations for the economy over the next six months are even more dire. The index just fell to 47.9, its lowest level since December 1973, which was the beginning of the worst economic contraction since the Great Depression.

In February, we talked about the "survival mentality" in which consumers "rein in spending, cut coupons and reduce consumption." This point in the cycle is where it comes into full play. Consumers are developing a craving for falling prices. In fact, some are returning to a price-reducing strategy that went out with the vestiges of the deflationary depression that started with the panic of 1837.

At Megastores, Hagglers
Find No Price Set in Stone

Shoppers are discovering an upside to the down economy. They are getting price breaks by reviving an age-old retail strategy: haggling. A bargaining culture once confined largely to car showrooms and jewelry stores is taking root in major stores like Best Buy, Circuit City and Home Depot, as well as mom-and-pop operations. Haggling was once common before department stores began setting fixed prices in the 1850s.

—The New York Times, March 23, 2008

As subscriber S. Osborne notes, the trend shows that the "socionomic shift to a deflationary environment is fully underway. People once flocked to stores like the now bankrupt Sharper Image, Fortunoff and Harvey Electronics and bragged about how much they spent (or wasted). Now people go to formerly 'fixed price' big box stores and haggle over the price of an iPod and big screen television and then boast about saving money." Sometimes it takes longer than expected, but the wheel of social psychology never fails to come around again.

May 2008

The Rich Get Ravaged

Wealth tends to skew toward a few well-positioned financiers in high-degree fifth waves. At the very end of such moves, income distribution becomes extremely lopsided and emerging bear market sentiments against the rich start to become more pronounced. One of the ways to identify the completion of a fifth wave is that skewed wealth becomes a hot topic. EWFF spotted one such moment in November 1999.

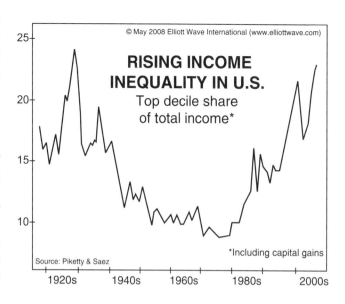

In recent weeks, the media, once again, noticed that the very richest are getting richer and ever more exclusive. The chart from the April 16 issue of the Financial Times shows that 1% of the population accounted for almost 25% of total income in 2006. Given the additional market gains in 2007, 1929's record high was probably surpassed last year. "There is anger about a system that permits bankers to earn huge bonuses when finance booms while taxpayers pick up the bill when banks fail," says the Financial Times. Even wealthy financiers seem to agree that the rich are just too rich these days. "Now is the time to admit that for the rich, for the mega-rich of this country, that enough is never enough, and it is therefore incumbent upon government to rectify today's imbalances," says the manager of the world's biggest bond fund. Warren Buffett, the world's richest man, advocates tax hikes and steep inheritance taxes for the super rich. Efforts to correct the imbalance through taxes are completely unnecessary. As EWFF noted in November 1999, "A bear market is nature's way of redistributing wealth." This effect is clearly evident by the sharp plunge on the chart, from 2000 to 2003. The picture now shows an apparently completed five-wave rise from the 1970s, which is one more reason to believe that income distribution will be equalized by a bear market. Of course, that won't stop the politicians from piling on as mood positions the crowd against those that prospered most during the bull market. "Progressive" tax policies will prove regressive in the years ahead.

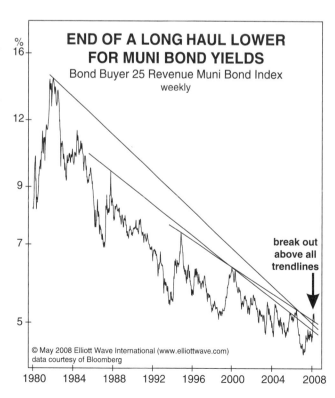

A Bear Hug For States and Cities

Last month we covered the unfolding bear market in muni bonds. The long-term chart shows muni bond yields smashing through three key long-term trendlines.

One of the reasons that munis are such a bad investment now is that they, by their very nature, are dependent on government, and government's specialty is compounding the effects of a bear market by taking actions that rely on the prior uptrend. A new law passed by the state of Wisconsin is a good example. It will allow its largest county to borrow $270 million to cover unfunded pension liabilities. The debt will carry an interest rate of 6%, but issuers figure they can "wind up making money on the deal" if they can match their long-term investment return of 8%. These kinds of assumptions will backfire badly in a bear market. There's plenty more where that came from; The Wall Street Journal says that unfunded liabilities now exceed $1 *trillion* nationally.

The crisis should arrive in a hurry. One reason is that taxpayers are already operating under the influence of an emerging bear market. They are in no mood for a bigger tax bite; the battle lines for a fight are already forming. In Virginia, commuters are choosing long commutes over higher taxes to pay for more roads. When New Jersey tried to fund a "gold-plated" pension scheme with years and years of rising highway tolls, the plan was shot down by a series of protest rallies and a plunge in the governor's approval rating from 47% to 34%. As the contracting economy squeezes budgets tighter, local governments will threaten to cut back on parks, libraries, fire, police and trash hauling to excite the people and the press. Then they'll try to raise money any way they can. Golf course and parking fees and taxes of all kinds will increase. Costs for services like fire, ambulance, police and trash hauling will be converted to a pay-as-you-go basis. Other services will be outsourced, and prisons, stadiums and toll roads sold to raise funds. As things get really tight, some cities will borrow for current expenses, which is the last step before bankruptcy. Before the bear market is over, even the most entrenched politicians will lose their jobs, and outsiders will get into office by promising to cut out the dead wood.

June 2008
The Devil Wears Pinstripes

Here's another EWFF comment from April 2007 that provides powerful confirmation that the bear market is out of hibernation: "Practices that were routine during the bull market suddenly become vilified." No pursuit is more representative of the late stages of the bull market than speculation, and nothing is being more vilified as wave (3) down arrives. Suddenly, buying and selling things strictly for profit is an evil act. In China, Vietnam and India, where some of the last white-hot vestiges of the Great Mania resided until the end of last year, speculators are being castigated and curtailed. India shut down futures trading in certain markets while Vietnam and China limited exports of rice. Presidential candidate Clinton vows to "punish speculators for driving up oil prices," and some within the U.S. Congress have taken aim at "large institutional investors." A new bill "aimed at speculators" will attempt "to limit the opportunity people have to maximize their profits because a lot of the rest of us are paying through the nose," said Sen. Joseph Lieberman, who is considered a moderate.

Here is one more area in which wave **c** down is picking up where wave **a** down left off in 2002-2003. Just as Enron broke under the weight of collapsing off-balance sheet investments, banks are now contending with undisclosed billions in rotting variable interest entities. Bloomberg reveals that VIEs are "a post-Enron version of special-purpose vehicles," the very same investments that sank the energy trading firm in 2001. "They never got the real problem fixed after Enron," says the man who was the SEC's chief accountant when the Enron scandal broke. "When people find out how little the Financial Accounting Standards Board did, they are going to be shocked." These are the revelations that EWFF alluded to in 2006 when we stated, "Move over Enron, the really big scandals are ready to start popping." That forecast was premature, but you can bet that the financial geniuses of the world didn't use the extra time to clean up their books. They dug themselves in deeper and insured that the problems will ultimately be whoppers. Look for the size and scope of the scandals, as well as the supposed fixes, to be far more onerous than those of the early 2000s.

August 2008
Cash's Invisible Reign Made Visible

With respect to cash and its status as the preeminent financial asset, we are starting to wonder if investors will ever come around to our point of view, which, as we explained in March, is that there are times when "the phrase 'focus on the long term' means "get out and wait.'" As we also pointed out, the last eight years are clearly one of these times, as cash has outperformed all three major stock averages over this period. A July 3 *USA Today* article shows how this outlook is actually becoming more farsighted as the bear market intensifies:

3-month Treasuries Beat S&P 500 for Past 10 Years

The article says, "Investors who bought stocks for the long run are finding out just how long the long run can be." But the farther back in time cash's dominance stretches and the rockier the stock market gets, the farther investors seem to move from ever taking anything off the table. After stating that "there can be times, long times, when stocks won't beat T-bills," a professor and popular buy-and-hold advocate is cited as "optimistic that the next 10 years will be better than the past decade." In March EWFF stated, "Cash will continue to outperform until stocks are no longer fashionable." There is no sign that such a condition is even close to happening.

It's somewhat amazing that cash is not capturing anyone's fancy because a tremendous society-wide thirst for cash is spreading fast. "In a deflation," EWFF has stated, "Rule No. 1 is to unload everything that isn't nailed down. Rule No. 2 is to sell whatever everything remaining is nailed to." The banking system is surely deflating, because, echoing EWFF's wording again, "Desperate American Banks Are Selling Everything That Isn't Nailed Down." SunTrust is selling its stock in Coca-Cola, an asset the bank held for *90 years*. Merrill Lynch sold its founding stake in Bloomberg as well as various other subsidiaries. Meanwhile, "Americans are selling prized possessions online and at flea markets at alarming rates." Pawnshops and auction sites are booming. At Craigslist.org, the number of for-sale listings soared 70% in eight months. This fits with our review of Craigslist's prospects when it was getting started in 2005: "This is just the set-up phase. Once the global garage sale really gets rolling, truly astounding volumes of dirt-cheap goods will be available on-line and elsewhere." The global garage sale is on. The chart of the U.S. savings rate shows that the bull market in cash has come to life.

A 30-year downtrend in savings rates ended at minus 2.3% in August 2005. In May 2008, the savings rate skyrocketed to 5% (see chart). This jolt may be somewhat overstated due

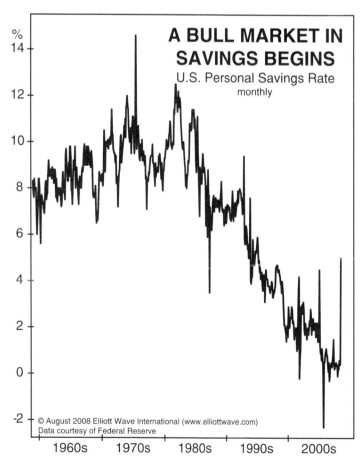

A BULL MARKET IN SAVINGS BEGINS
U.S. Personal Savings Rate
monthly

© August 2008 Elliott Wave International (www.elliottwave.com)
Data courtesy of Federal Reserve

to the arrival of the government's stimulus checks, but the burst should be the start of a critical new mindset among consumers. When the government showered the economy with $600 checks, many did something they never would have thought of through most of the bull market: They put the money in the bank, which is exactly what the administration did not want. In fact, federal, state and local governments are desperate for the tax revenue that a little ripple-effect spending would have generated. According to the National Conference of State Legislatures, states must close a $40 billion shortfall in the current fiscal year. "The problem today is that tax revenue is vanishing," says a story about the sudden appearance of the worst fiscal crisis in New York since 1975. Even cities like East Hampton, New York, where someone paid $103 million for an oceanfront house last year, are out of money. "Nobody understands how it happened," says one resident. The pages of this newsletter show otherwise. If we are right, a deflationary decline is depleting and destroying cash flows in novel new ways that no one alive has experienced before.

September 2008
The Rise and Fall of Moral Hazard

Everyone knows there's no such thing as easy money. Still, it never fails—easy-credit environments invariably lead to an orgy of lending followed inevitably by crisis and default in what seemed to be robust sectors of the economy. Our long-term chart of interest rates back through the late 1950s shows this never-ending, binge-purge, credit cycle, which was first published by *The Elliott Wave Financial Forecast* in May 2005 (with the help of some original research by Comstock Partners). The chart at the top of the next page shows our original depiction along with a series of forecasts on the right hand side, while the updated version below shows how it is playing out. The basic concept is simple: When money goes on sale (i.e., rates are low), certain borrowers will almost always find a way to gorge on readily available credit. When the accumulated debt becomes unserviceable due to rising rates or falling collateral values, default and failures result. As the charts show, up until now the damage was mostly contained to certain regional economies and market sectors. These pictures reveal something else now pertinent to realize about falling rates. They aren't always a panacea for debt-carrying firms and individuals. At the interest rate peak in 1980, for instance, the problem only *started* for farmers and less-developed countries (LDCs). As they struggled to re-pay their high-cost loans in a period of falling commodity prices *and* falling rates, it took nearly a whole decade to work through the resulting defaults and bail-out refinancings. Keep in mind that the 1980s were a period of disinflation or falling rates of inflation. The difficulty now is a turn toward outright deflation, one that will do far greater damage because systemic debt levels are much higher. As EWFF said in May 2005:

> This time the implosion and its deflationary effect is not likely to confine itself to any one economic group. The current level of system-wide debt is unprecedented and is becoming unmanageable.

Since we made that statement, total U.S. credit-market debt has increased 35% to almost $50 *trillion*. EWFF also noted at the time that it takes smaller and smaller rate increases to induce "stress and default." This cycle, all it took was a rise to just over 5%. By the time yields on 3-month U.S. T-bills hit that level in February of last year, the purge phase was well underway, even if the media had yet to pick up on it. The text on the previous page shows that events are adhering closely to EWFF's forecast. Now that the storm is raging, it's easy to forget how serene the environment was back in 2005. At the time, real estate was soaring. The auto industry was barreling along selling SUVs like they were going out of style (which, it turns out, they were), airlines were coasting on the coattails of low rates and low fuel costs, and the volume of was expanding higher by the trillions. The updates accompanying the charts tell quite the opposite story. But just as the disinflation of the 1980s took two full decades to play out, the unfolding deflationary purge will play out in defaults and foreclosures that will also last years. The housing industry's reversal is still just the first hint of the trouble ahead for those that are still heavily indebted.

THE "NEWS" ARRIVES

Real Estate

Status: According to Zil-low.com, one-third of U.S. homes are worth less than their owners owe, and 20% of transactions happening across the country are foreclosures.

Prognosis: On track toward *Conquer the Crash's* forecast for an average price decline of 90%.

Implosion

Status: The mortgage industry experience in which untallied billions in collateralized debt obligations have vaporized is just the tip of the iceberg. Let's take just one as-yet-unexploded derivative class as an example: the market for credit default swaps. It is worth an estimated $43 to $62 trillion. Any further economic weakness will make widespread losses in the credit default swap market unavoidable—even for many of those who took the default side of the swap. For an idea of how extensive and surprising the derivative losses are going to be, consider that Warren Buffett's Berkshire Hathaway is among the firms already booking losses on these instruments. The world's richest man is the one who said " are financial weapons of mass destruction."

Prognosis: The sky is the limit for this mushroom cloud.

Autos

Status: Speculation is "rife over whether the three car makers can survive in their present form." According to UniCredit, the credit default swaps market places the likelihood of a GM bankruptcy at 84%, while Ford has a 75% chance of default. Chrysler is already failing in its efforts to secure funding.

Prognosis: At least one and as many as all three U.S. car makers will go under. Foreign entities might pick up some of the pieces. Surviving entities and their work forces will be substantially smaller and more fragmented.

Airlines

Status: Delta and Northwest filed for bankruptcy in September 2005. Frontier and three other small carrier bankruptcies in April 2008 signals a new round of failures.

Prognosis: Creditors will lose, and airlines will re-form.

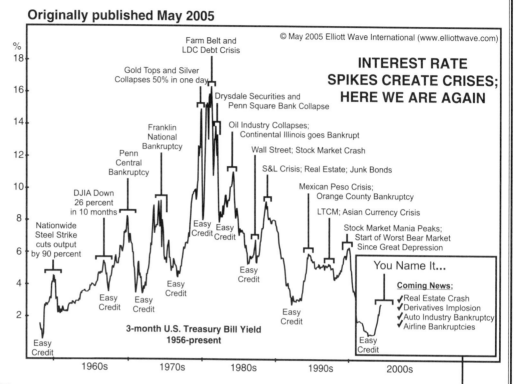

Originally published May 2005

© May 2005 Elliott Wave International (www.elliottwave.com)

INTEREST RATE SPIKES CREATE CRISES; HERE WE ARE AGAIN

3-month U.S. Treasury Bill Yield 1956-present

You Name It...

Coming News;
✔ Real Estate Crash
✔ Derivatives Implosion
✔ Auto Industry Bankruptcy
✔ Airline Bankrupticies

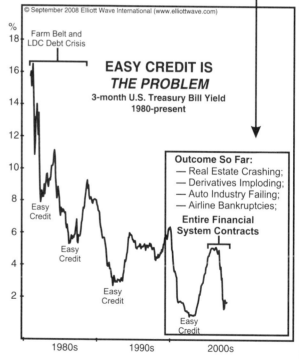

© September 2008 Elliott Wave International (www.elliottwave.com)

EASY CREDIT IS *THE PROBLEM*
3-month U.S. Treasury Bill Yield 1980-present

Outcome So Far:
— Real Estate Crashing;
— Derivatives Imploding;
— Auto Industry Failing;
— Airline Bankruptcies;

Entire Financial System Contracts

The Role of the Bull Market

How did things come to this? Simply put, a bull market in social mood held sway over the credit markets just as it did the stock market. To track the interaction between the two, we turn to one of the great breakthroughs in the age of financial engineering—the financial bailout. Bailouts first garnered national attention in the 1970s when the U.S. government stepped in to guarantee $250 million in loans to Lockheed Aircraft (1971). Their periodic appearances since then have come so regularly that EWFF speculated in 2001 that they can be used to identify bull and bear markets based on their timing in relation to the trend. As EWFF explained in 2001, typically "bailouts occur near stock market lows" in a bull market. During

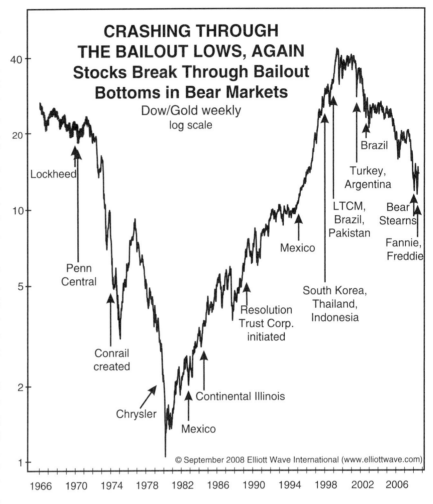

CRASHING THROUGH THE BAILOUT LOWS, AGAIN
Stocks Break Through Bailout Bottoms in Bear Markets
Dow/Gold weekly
log scale

Lockheed
Penn Central
Conrail created
Chrysler
Mexico
Continental Illinois
Resolution Trust Corp. initiated
Mexico
South Korea, Thailand, Indonesia
LTCM, Brazil, Pakistan
Turkey, Argentina
Brazil
Bear Stearns
Fannie, Freddie

© September 2008 Elliott Wave International (www.elliottwave.com)

these phases, the stock market lows that occurred near major bailouts invariably remained intact. The same cannot be said for the bailouts of the 1970s. During the Cycle degree bear market of 1966-1982 the Dow/gold chart shows that bailouts that coincided with apparent stock market lows were always ultimately followed by *lower* lows. The February-August 2001 World Bank bailout of Turkey and Argentina was significant because it encompassed what many were calling a solid stock market low in March 2001. The breach of this low in September 2001 helped confirm the presence of a new long-term bear market. It was the first breach of a bailout low in more than 20 years, "a clear signal that the Dow is back in bear-market mode." A bailout of Brazil in late August 2002 confirmed the bear market in the Real Dow (Dow/Gold), as the market continued lower. There is a simple socionomic explanation for this pattern. As we have noted many times, government is the ultimate consensus organization and as such commits to trends near their exhaustion point and subsequent reversal. Bailouts come at lows because that is when the outlook is most dire. In bull markets, these lows go unbroken. In a long-term bear market, prices keep declining beneath the bailout lows.

The latest U.S. government rescue efforts clearly confirm the ongoing bear market. In mid-March, the Fed helped to finance JP Morgan's takeover of Bear Stearns. In mid-July, after the S&P breached its March 17 lows, "Treasury officials moved quickly to bring forward government rescue plans" when prospects of a regularly scheduled Fannie Mae bond sale soured. So, the bailouts keep coming at lower lows, signaling further declines ahead. This is different from what happened in 1982, when the first Mexican bailout came at a higher low, marking an upside divergence with the trend in stock prices and indicating the start of a bull market.

If there is such a thing as a hard sell signal, this may be it. The chart of the Dow offers a deeper look at just how entrenched, and unsuccessful, bailout attempts have been over the last 18 months. In addition to Bear Stearns and the Fannie/Freddie rescue efforts, the Fed created two new loan programs, the Term Auction Facility (TAF) and the Term Securities Lending Facility (TSLF), in an effort to lend to troubled banks and eventually to brokerage houses. In essence, the Fed is "temporarily" swapping the pristine U.S. Treasury bonds in its own portfolio for dicey mortgages held by these lending institutions. This has contributed to a 43% degradation in the Fed's own balance sheet: the percentage of U.S. Treasuries they hold as collateral for Federal Reserve Notes is down from near 95% to under 55% (see chart below). Short of holding a sign that says, "Will Inflate For Food," the Fed is throwing everything it has at the still nascent force of deflation. The net gain for all this effort is a Dow that is still down nearly 19% from its October peak. The Dow chart shows just the highlights. Many other financial "victims," from money market investors who saw their shares "break the buck" to holders of auction-rate bonds that were frozen by market failures, have been bailed out. Don't forget the seven Federal Reserve rate cuts from August 2007 to April 2008, three of which were "surprise cuts" that accompanied the August (2007), January and March 2008 market lows, all of which were subsequently broken. In March, the U.S. Treasury also allowed broker-dealers to use the Discount Window for the first time since the Great Depression. This is a far cry from the end of Supercycle Wave I when the Second Bank of the United States, the equivalent of the today's Fed, was disbanded (in 1836) and the markets and troubled firms were basically left to their own devices.

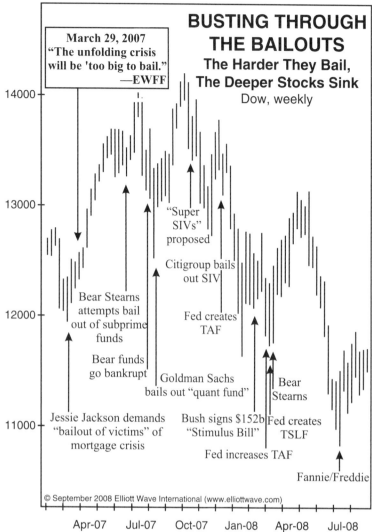

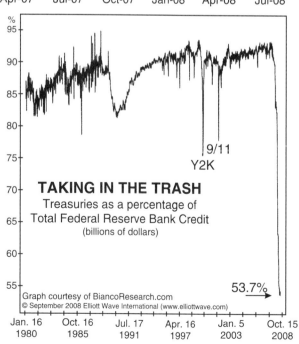

The argument against bailing out failing sectors and firms is that it can create a "moral hazard." Moral hazard is said to happen when borrowers and lenders take risks that they otherwise would not because they do not bear the full consequences of a failure to repay, leaving a third party (usually taxpayers) to cover their obligations. By our reckoning, an unprecedented moral hazard was in place prior to the 2007 stock market peak because, as far as we know, this is the first time in history that government pursued and attempted bailouts *before* nominal stock prices had even started to decline! At the tail end of the great rise in social mood, the dislocations engendered by 200 years of rising prices were so pronounced that consequences began to play out even before the mood trend changed. Moreover, complacency had become so extreme that Treasury officials, Wall Street and even the knowledgeable members of the money classes could see no larger threat to the system. This complete loss of fear means that a long rise in moral hazard has almost surely run its course. As risk aversion, tightening credit standards and a bear market in stocks intensify, a new prudence should emerge.

The abject failure of many bailout efforts will contain another important lesson. As EWFF said when the first bailout call went out in early 2007, "It won't work. The unfolding crisis will be 'too big to bail.'" The big question at this point is whether "the powers that be" recognize the limitations of their power. It is possible that the Federal government will attempt to make good on all past promises to lend and re-pay loans, but *Conquer the Crash* asserts that the more likely outcome is that the U.S. will at some point be forced to let nature take its course. This moment is fast approaching as home prices continue to decline sharply, and "top economists" are starting openly to question whether a cash injection into Fannie and Freddie "will be enough to bolster the economy." According to one headline, Fed Chairman Ben Bernanke is now trying to "Define What Institutions Fed Could Let Fail." Says another, "Paulson Might Weigh Whom to Hurt in Any Fannie, Freddie Rescue." As Cycle wave **c** ratchets lower, this calculus will get way too complex. The economy is only just starting to roll over, and defaults are spreading fast to the commercial real estate sector. Beyond commercial real estate lies the corporate bond market and private-equity debt, much of which, it turns out, was issued on the basis of "overly optimistic assumptions." Payments on these debts are starting to be marked "past due." When everything falls at once, the Fed is likely to say that the only recourse is for everyone to buckle down and take bitter medicine. This happened on a smaller scale in 1980 when Paul Volcker clamped down with a series of rigorous rate increases. The result was a quick burst of deflation in the first quarter of 1980 when commodities and financial assets, as well as gold and silver, all went down simultaneously. The same thing should happen now but on a much larger scale.

Coming Events for EWI's Subscribers

We spend much of our time describing coming financial, economic and social events due in this bear market. But we should also talk about what will happen for those individuals positioned in the safest cash equivalents in the world, held in the safest banks in the world. Here is a short list:

Our *cash* will continue to gain value.
Our *shorts* will continue to gain value.
We will be able to buy lots of stuff at the bottom.
And we will not have to ━━━━━━━━➤

October 2008

The bull market is over, but the bailout craze is running at "fever pitch." In less than a month, the Federal government moved to issue a *trillion* dollars in U.S. Treasuries to back bailout loans; took over Fannie Mae and Freddie Mac, as well as the world's largest insurance company, American International Group (AIG); and banned short selling on financial and other stocks. As these pages discussed last month, it won't work.

Obviously, we still await the all-important "uncle point" in the government's bid to stave off decline, but as the September issue of *The Elliott Wave Theorist* noted, the markets "are not so dumb as to wait for it. They can already see the end of the road, and are moving ahead of it." Outside of the market, the first concrete sign of an end to the era of moral hazard is the decision to let Lehman Brothers go bankrupt. With more than $600 billion in pre-bankruptcy assets, Lehman was easily the largest Chapter 11 filing in history. WorldCom, the prior record holder, had "merely" $100 billion in assets. Lehman was also bigger and more diversified than Bear Stearns, which was deemed too big to fail just last March. Another signal of the bailout plan's eventual fate is what happened to the stock market after AIG became the property of U.S. taxpayers. In contrast to the temporary lows that coincided with Bear Stearns' shotgun marriage to JPMorgan Chase last March and the federal "protection" extended to Fannie/Freddie in mid-July, the stock market greeted AIG's surprise takeover by falling, and not to just any level. It fell below the Dow's Minor wave 1 low of 10,827.70 on July 15. It did so again early

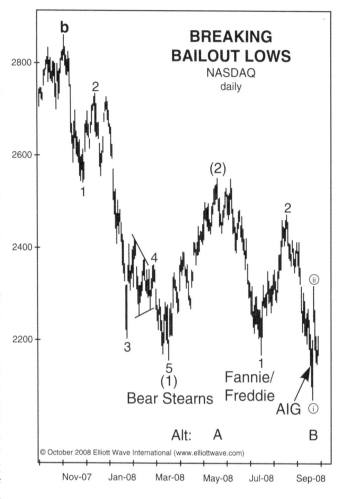

this week after the Feds hatched a plan to create a whole new government agency that will purchase distressed financial assets of up to $700 billion at a time. The biggest financial bailout in history was followed by the biggest point decline in the history of the Dow. This action confirms that the bear market is alive and kicking. As EWFF noted here last month, "In a long-term bear market, prices keep declining beneath the bailout lows." The chart shows the key break of the bailout low in the NASDAQ.

Another multifaceted indicator of the bear market's presence and extraordinary downside potential is all the different ways in which the bailouts are backfiring. The effort isn't opening up the credit markets as so many had hoped, for example; it's closing them. Bank of America refused to extend any further loans to McDonald's for espresso machines, citing its financial commitment to take over Merrill Lynch. "Even well-known brands such as McDonald's face difficulties financing expansions," says Bloomberg. Then there's the "reverse auction" pricing mechanism that will use actual market prices to establish a value for distressed assets in the Treasury's $700 billion bailout plan. As EWFF has previously discussed, the complete inability to establish prices in this environment of obfuscation and manipulation is one of the keys to keeping the fantasy of solvency alive. This step toward more accurately assessing asset values is bad news for regional banks, as it will suddenly give them "a more concrete way of benchmarking just how far their own assets have declined." The takeover of Fannie and Freddie also cratered the value of their preferred stock, which accounts for 11% of the core capital of the average bank. Apparently the bailout cowboys never saw that one coming. Moreover, one of the more punitive edicts from the Securities and Exchange Commission, the ban on short selling, won't help liquidity; it will hurt it. This unintended bearish consequence was covered on page 200 in *Conquer the Crash*:

Sometimes authorities outlaw short selling. In doing so, they remove the one class of investors that must buy. Every short sale must be covered, i.e., the stock must be purchased to close the trade. A ban on short selling creates a market with no latent buying power at all, making it even less liquid than it was. Then it can dribble down day after day, unhindered by the buying of nervous shorts.

Once the government-sponsored short squeeze of September 19 was over, this is exactly what happened. Stocks dribbled lower through Wednesday. As of the September 18 low, the Dow was down 26% from its October 2007 peak despite one bailout after another, each one weakening the federal balance sheet in ways that will undoubtedly contribute to the severity of the decline.

Finally, there is the whole point of the government's extraordinary actions, the restoration of confidence. "The government needs to step in and inspire confidence," goes the oft-repeated refrain. Of course, the harder anyone tries to prop up confidence, the less confident people get. "The only way it will work," says columnist Jonathan Weil of Bloomberg, "is if people like you, think other people like you, think other people like you, will think it will work." Here's how President Bush sees it: "At first, I thought we could deal with the problem one issue at a time. The house of cards was much bigger and started to stretch beyond Wall Street. When one card started to go, we worried about the whole deck going down." We did a double-take on this statement. Did the President of the United States describe the U.S. financial system as a "house of cards?" Indeed he did, and, in doing so, he took the words right out of *Conquer the Crash*: "Confidence is the only thing holding up this giant house of cards." The presidential avowal of a position that was once considered by some to be among the most radical statements offered in CTC goes straight to the book's main point—at its core, it's a psychological process. The deflationary depression therein described must surely be unfolding.

As the scope of the problem expands, the full absurdity of the Treasury/Fed bailout gambit will be plain to see. Notice, for instance, that all of the bailouts to date, from the $700 billion federal slush fund for collapsing financial assets to the ban on short selling, are aimed at the financial sector which *is already wiped out*. This is so because government, by socionomic definition, moves only by consensus and therefore is always the last to act. It follows trends and attempts to respond *after* social mood has produced its effects. It is well known that Fed chairman Ben Bernanke is a student of the Great Depression, and he is famous for his belief that that financial catastrophe could have been avoided if the Fed had only nipped it in the bud. But these charts [showing declines of up to 99% in key financial stocks like Fannie Mae] (in Chapter 2, October 2008) show how laughable this stemming-of-the-tide idea really is. Bernanke is trying to calm the waves by raising up sunken ships. If he wants at least to look as if he were holding things up, he should do something to shore up a sector that is still standing. Of course, this won't work either, because any instrument at his disposal still rests upon the sand we call social mood, which is simply too powerful to be nudged in the direction desired by any central banker. Witness the backlash from the public about the latest bailout scheme. The sideshow is that government can always be counted on to move too late and in a direction that will do more harm than good.

Will Heavy Hitters Turn the Market Around?

We are aware that institutions with immense buying power—for example the Federal Reserve and the Treasury of the United States—are lined up on the bullish side. The legendary billionaire Warren Buffett also agrees that it's time to buy, and Friday's New York Times gave him space to say so. He also has harsh words for our investment stance:

Buy American. I am.

Today people who hold cash equivalents feel comfortable. They shouldn't. They have opted for a terrible long-term asset, one that pays virtually nothing and is certain to depreciate in value. Indeed, the policies that government will follow in its efforts to alleviate the current crisis will probably prove inflationary and therefore accelerate declines in the real value of cash accounts.

—Warren Buffett, in The New York Times,
October 17, 2008

As you can see, Buffett agrees with others that the government's policies virtually guarantee inflation and moreover that stocks will provide a safe haven from it. But consider: The Fed and the government, by jamming down interest rates, by borrowing and spending at a record rate and more recently by offering unlimited liquidity to the banking system, created the greatest inflation ever over the past eight years, causing the dollar to plunge against other currencies. Yet during this time the dollar value

EIGHT-YEAR TOTAL RETURN
12/31/99 to 10/17/08
Transaction costs excluded

Index	Total Return
CASH 3-month T-bill	+31.04%
S&P 500 including dividends	-26.16%

of cash held in T-bills has *risen* 31 percent while the dollar value of the S&P, *including* dividends, is *down* 26 percent. So, stock investors have been losing doubly, on a falling dollar *and* falling stock prices. Another way to look at it is to incorporate the fact that the dollar is down vs. other major currencies by one-third, in which case we may say that T-bill investors have held onto 100 percent of their buying power, while stock investors since 2000 have lost more than half of theirs. The S&P will have to double in order to bridge that gap. And it surely seems to require a fresh point of view about inflation to explain why that gap is even there. Could it be that aggressive credit inflation saps companies' strength and *ruins* them?

The market usually deceives people who argue for outcomes based on seemingly logical mechanistic causes. If someone told you in 1998 that oil would rise 14 times in price, would you have guessed that the Dow Jones Transportation Average, which is filled with companies that prefer oil prices to be low, would go up almost the whole time and make a new all-time high within two months of the high in oil? It sounds illogical, but as you know, *our* logic said it was "All the Same Market" in an environment where credit liquidity supported both speculation *and* commerce. Old-timers will also recall the period from 1979 to 1984, when interest rates were so high as to be in double digits. At that time, few could see any good reason to give up that return to buy stocks, but that's when you should have bought, and we said so. Today cash yields almost nothing, and few can see any good reason to give up their stocks to hold cash, but that is where you should be. Isn't it wonderful how counter-intuitive the market is?

It may be pertinent that in his career, Buffett has weathered three declines of 40 to 50 percent, which occurred in 1973-1974, 1987 and 2000-2002. So this amount may be his benchmark for a buying opportunity. There are other benchmarks, however, and we will become interested in looking for a bottom only when the long term indicators—including the dividend yield, the price/book value ratio, the price/earnings ratio and the percentage of cash in mutual funds—show a sold-out market. To date, they all continue to reveal that the stock market is still historically, if not absurdly, overpriced.

Bailouts Point Down, Not Up

What about the bailouts? Can government bring back the bubble? The answer, as *Conquer the Crash* said well before the bailouts began, is no. The reason we can be so definitive is that we know from history that the bailouts come after the mania is over. So, the more that the effort escalates (and it is already the largest in history), the more assurance we have that the mania is past. In fact, the latest news is not the bailouts themselves but the markets' response to them. The October issue cited a critical character shift in which bailout measures suddenly failed to produce the rallies that they had through the course of the bull market and the early days of the bear. We cited the decline following AIG's bailout as a trigger point. It happened again on September 29, when the announcement of the biggest financial bailout in history was followed by the biggest point decline in the history of the Dow Jones Industrial Average. The need for a still bigger fix was expressed this way by President Bush, "If money isn't loosened up, this sucker could go down." When a $700 billion "financial stability" measure was finally passed and rushed into law on October 3, the market closed down again. After an unheard-of coordinated global interest rate cut on October 8, the Dow plunged again. As we've said since March 2007, the problem is "too big to bail," and the government's failure to stem the bearish tide, (the Dow is still down 17% since the introduction of the $700 billion bailout plan on September 28) is a definitive signal that the mania's upside energy is all but spent.

November 2008

It's hard to believe, but since last month's issue of *The Elliott Wave Financial Forecast* observed the "fever pitch" of the government bailout effort, authorities took these stunning measures: The Senate passed the most aggressive bailout bill in history, world central banks orchestrated a globally coordinated rate cut, the U.S. government announced a plan to own direct stakes in U.S. banks and Congress placed another stimulus package on a fast track for approval. Last month EWFF flatly stated, "It won't work." The 27% decline from the end of September to the October 10 interim low illustrates what we meant by "won't work." The series of charts on the next page shows why. Powerful bearish forces are tugging on the stock market, and the charts illustrate what they are: downside waves of Grand Supercycle, Supercycle, Cycle, Primary and Intermediate degrees. These charts reveal the potential size of the remaining stock market decline in the bear market. The five-wave rally that ended in 2000 marks the top of a Grand Supercycle impulse wave, which means that the decline that began last October is now correcting the entire Grand Supercycle and Supercycle degree advances from 1784 and 1932, respectively. As the idealized Elliott wave chart shows, ABC corrections most often find a low near the bottom of the area of the previous fourth wave. The charts at the bottom of each row show two other important dynamics that EWFF discussed earlier this year: the once-colliding and now coincident Cycle degree forces and the unmistakable bear market in the Dow denominated in gold (Real Dow), which is real money. Because of the latent strength of the Great Asset Mania, which provided the psychological basis for the massive credit inflation, wave **b** managed to carry the Dow Jones Industrials denominated in dollars to a new all-time high against the headwind of a collapsing Real Dow. In March, we said that the nominal Dow would play catch-up to the Real Dow, and it surely is. As the late 2008 charts in all prior chapters demonstrate, the former speculative fevers that allowed the diverging behavior have passed into history with the bursting of the commodity

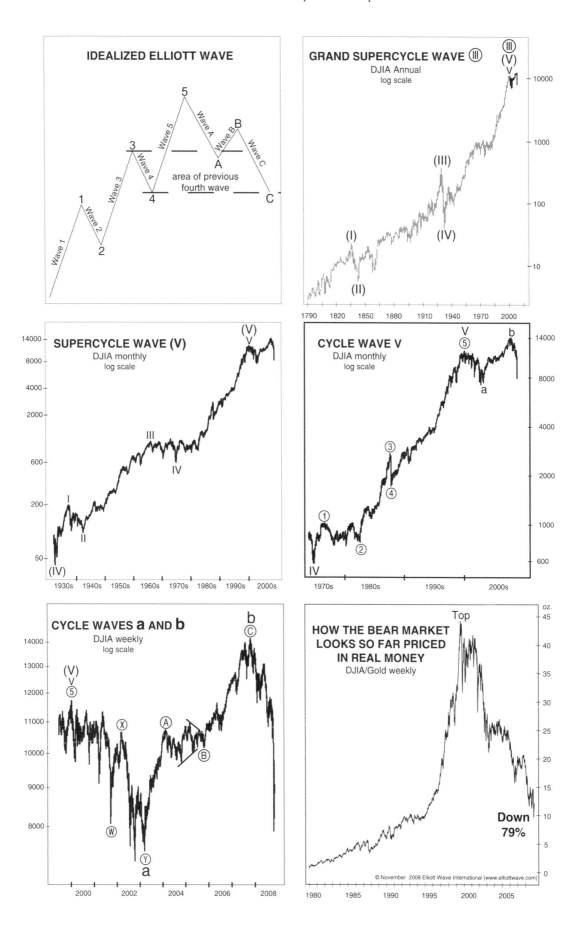

IDEALIZED ELLIOTT WAVE

GRAND SUPERCYCLE WAVE ⓘⓘⓘ
DJIA Annual
log scale

SUPERCYCLE WAVE (V)
DJIA monthly
log scale

CYCLE WAVE V
DJIA monthly
log scale

CYCLE WAVES a AND b
DJIA weekly
log scale

HOW THE BEAR MARKET LOOKS SO FAR PRICED IN REAL MONEY
DJIA/Gold weekly

Down 79%

© November 2008 Elliott Wave International (www.elliottwave.com)

bubble in July, and they should stay away on a long term basis. This clears the way for investors to feel the full force of the 79% decline in the Real Dow. The markets will get as carried away on the downside as they did to the upside over the previous 13 years.

Valuations

October 28 brought the second biggest Dow point gain on record, as "the cheapest valuations in more than two decades lured investors back into equities." Is this latter statement true? A close look at history and corporate America's cash-generating outlook reveals that stocks are anything but cheap at current levels. Let's look first at dividends. In a CNBC appearance on October 22, Joe Kernan asked Steve Hochberg if an uptick in the Dow's dividend yield, from 1.5% to 3.5%, was reason to be bullish. In the context of history, the answer is that 3.5% is closer to a *top* than a bottom. The chart shows the Dow Industrials plotted against the Dow's dividend yield from 1915 to the present. Observe the dashed horizontal line running through the dividend yield. For 80 years, the only time that the Dow's dividend yield touched or slightly broke this line was when the market was near a top. The dashed circles on the right side of the chart depict the beginning and end of an unprecedented 15-year period of historic overvaluation, when the dividend yield broke decisively beneath the horizontal line and stayed there. As our CNBC encounter demonstrates, due to this unprecedented anomaly, low dividend yields have come to be viewed as normal. They are anything but. The dividend yield's long stay below its bottom ticks of 1929, 1968 and 1987 actually represents the greatest overvaluation in history and is one of the most dramatic illustrations of the Great Asset Mania's mesmerizing influence.

The move back above the horizontal line is proof that the mania is dead and that the bull market in cash is breaking out to the upside. Now that the dividend yield is above the key horizontal line, it should not only stay there for many years, but history also dictates that it should continue to rise a long way. In fact, the average level of dividend yield at prior bear market bottoms is approximately 6.5%, which means that today's 3.7% dividend yield remains shockingly overvalued. The Dow would have to fall beneath 5000 to equal the average dividend yield at prior bear market lows. And that would be if dividends remain as they are. But this is no average

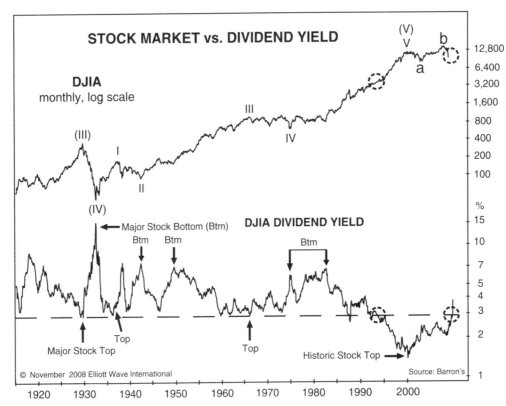

660

bear market. This is a Grand Supercycle bear that should exceed the extreme of 16% in 1933. This will take considerable price compression, as the dividend cuts of recent months by cash-strapped companies are only just beginning. Companies will slash more furiously in the future to save money, and stocks prices will chase dividends lower to produce the high yields that come at every major bear market bottom.

Dividends are one of the best valuation measures, because they are a crucial component of the total return equation, and there is no way to manipulate reports of the cash that companies give back to shareholders. Either they pay or they don't. By contrast, the miracle of financial engineering reveals that earnings can be spun in various ways. For instance, back in 2002, Standard and Poor's lowered the stock market's price/earnings ratio across the board to make the market appear more reasonably valued by changing from reported earnings to operating earnings, thus excluding "non-recurring" expenses. Another problem with current P/Es is that E is subject to the performance of another e, the economy, which is contracting in a way that few economists yet fathom (see Economy & Deflation section below). Finally, the E in the P/E lags the market, so while some may claim that the current P/E level appears reasonable, as the stock market continues to decline corporate earnings will continue to shrink. When earnings go negative, the papers print "--" or "NA" for not applicable. To remain applicable through the next market phase, they need to offer the Earnings/Price ratio, which would allow for comparisons as losses mount.

The Economy & Deflation

In January, when a Wall Street Journal survey showed that economists believed there was only a 42% chance of recession, *The Elliott Wave Financial Forecast* contended that a contraction was inescapable. "As deflation catches investors, consumers and businesses by surprise," EWFF concluded, "various measures of economic output will drop through the floors established by the recessions of 1973-1975 and 1980-1982."

The latest surveys show that economists are finally starting to face the music. According to the October WSJ Economic Forecasting Survey, the probability of a recession over the next 12 months is up to 89.3%, but what economists are still missing is the depth of the coming decline.

The average call is for Gross Domestic Product to *gain* 0.6% in 2008 and 1.3% in 2009. The most dire forecast for next year is for a 0.5% GDP decline.

These forecasts are wildly optimistic. The economy always lags the markets, and the markets are not anticipating a mild contraction. Last month, EWFF cited declines ranging from 67% to 99% in eight different financial stocks, as representative of the unfolding economic wreck and said, "The financial stocks have simply 'set the tone.' Look for the bricks and mortar of the economy to feel the force of this move at any moment." To represent the bear market's imminent move into the mainstream, we added a ninth chart of Wal-Mart (see October 2008 entry in Chapter 2), which was still hovering near a six-year high. It has since fallen 23%, as retail sales hit a pothole. The third consecutive

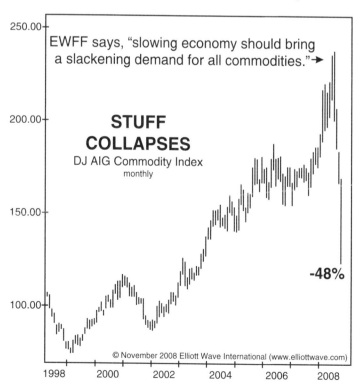

EWFF says, "slowing economy should bring a slackening demand for all commodities."➤

STUFF COLLAPSES
DJ AIG Commodity Index
monthly

-48%

© November 2008 Elliott Wave International (www.elliottwave.com)

monthly drop of 1.2% in September retail sales marks the first three straight months of decline since at least 1992. The late break in the commodity markets paints a vivid picture of deflation snapping into place.

The 48% cratering in the Dow Jones AIG Commodity Index (previous page) confirms that *Conquer the Crash's* deflationary depression is on. According to the latest reports, U.S. GDP fell 0.3% in the third quarter. From 1929 to 1933, GDP fell by 45.6%, so much larger declines will follow. More sensitive economic measures are already hinting at them. In September, we showed a picture of consumer confidence and said a previously "forecasted plunge is clearly underway." And plunge it did. This month's Conference Board figure fell to 31, the lowest reading in the 41-year history of the index. Considering the relatively benign economic environment through the 1950s and 1960s, it is probably the lowest ebb in consumer confidence since at least 1949, the end of the last Supercycle-degree bear (in inflation-adjusted terms). Consumer spending dipped at an annual rate of 3.1% between July and September, the largest three-month drop since the second quarter

of 1980. That was before the October Consumer Confidence reading fell 38% from September to October; so future spending will surely contract further. On the manufacturing side, Industrial Production plunged 2.8% in September, the biggest one-month decline since December 1974, the final month of the last bear market of at least Cycle degree. What about the global economic engine that was supposed to compensate for U.S. short-comings just a few short months ago? The Baltic Dry Index is another index that expresses the global scope of the downturn. It measures the demand for shipping capacity through dry bulk shipping rates. It is down more than 90%—since May 23, only five months ago! In the third quarter of 2007, Bloomberg reports that Volvo received 41,970 European orders for new trucks. In the third quarter of 2008, it got just 155. That's no misprint. Orders fell 99.63%. "We're heading toward the sharpest downturn I've ever seen in Europe," said Volvo's Chief Executive Officer.

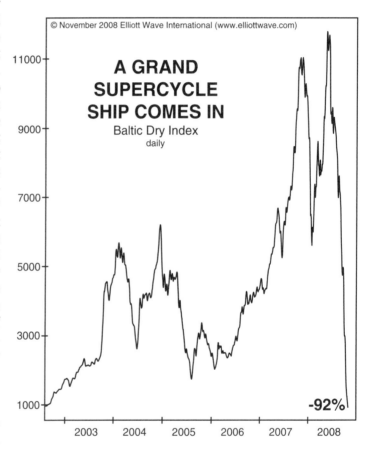

Employment doesn't yet reflect the scope of the downturn, but joblessness is already starting to emerge as public enemy No.1. "Unemployment claims, already well into recession territory, are rising even faster than expected," says the Associated Press. Unemployment hit 24.9% in the wake of the last Supercycle degree bear market in 1933. Given the degree of this decline and the powerful signs of contraction in the most responsive economic indicators, this record may fall by the wayside. Even if it survives, the work life of most people will be changed in ways almost no one has yet imagined.

CONCLUSION

By three methods we may learn wisdom: first, by reflection, which is noblest; second, by imitation, which is easiest; and third by experience, which is the bitterest. — Confucius

In 1983, *The Elliott Wave Theorist* issued the forecast that begins this book, calling for a mania that would "combine elements of 1929, 1968 and 1973 all operating together, and to an even greater extreme." It also stated that "major trend signals" would be given "two and three years before the final top, and the market will just keep on going." Ironically, this was so true that even we were unprepared for the extent of it. The chart below shows the NASDAQ's great March 2000 peak sandwiched between the 1998 and 2007 peaks in two separate compositions of the Value Line (arithmetic and geometric). The bubble's incredible staying power surprised us. Most of Elliott Wave International's forecasting errors can be traced to the rising trend's ability "to just keep on going."

In the interest of full disclosure, many of the resulting miscalculations are included in this book. In a number of areas, such as the unprecedented escalation in bids for coffee shops and real estate, Elliott Wave International first identified a connection between the rising trend in stocks based on parallel moves in past bull markets of high degree. When the stock market reversed for good, we asserted that these coincident trends would turn down with it. In 1996, for instance, *The Elliott Wave Theorist* tied the coffee-shop craze to similar society-wide caffeine binges during the manias of the 1920s and the South Sea Bubble in 1720 (see entry from September 1996 in Chapter 3). Citing the correlation and an apparent completion of a rise in Starbucks' stock price, *The Elliott Wave Financial Forecast* called for a reversal in Starbucks' shares in December 2001 (see

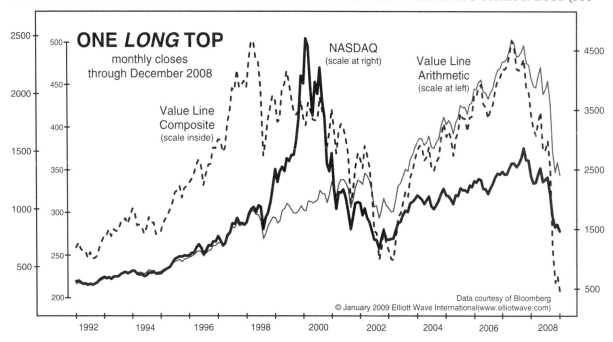

December 2001 entry in Chapter 3). Instead, Starbucks continued on to new highs, eventually reaching $40 a share in November 2006, which we (once again) identified as a long-term peak. Knowledge of coincident real estate crashes in the late 1830s and 1930s led us to inform readers of a likely repeat. Here again, we were ahead of the peak (see entry of January 2002 in Chapter 3). We were also too quick to call for a reversal in the luxury sector (see December 2002 entry in Chapter 1), small-cap shares (September 2003 in Chapter 4) and emerging markets (March 2003 in Chapter 7).

We thought the financials (see April 2004 entry in Chapter 2), hedge funds and commodities were all finished before their time. In February 2003, when the hedge-fund phenomenon and its twin, the commodity bull market, were still in the early stages of their mid-2000s boom, *The Elliott Wave Financial Forecast* argued that "as the economic downturn reasserts itself, [hedge funds and commodities] should get hit hard." Of course, the economy continued on, so we were early on all three counts. It is important to observe that our model of causality held true: while the trend was up, it was up for everything; when it finally reversed, everything reversed.

By 2007, as the Dow and S&P managed to slip to new all-time highs (unaccompanied by the NASDAQ), the mania characteristics in each area became more exotic and ripe for a reversal. In each case, EWI was on the scene pounding the table as their respective peaks were achieved. The Hedge Fund Index (shown in Chapter 5, October 2008) topped in July 2007, and in December 2007 the economy began a contraction that by the end of 2008 had already become the biggest since the 1930s.

It's 1837 All Over Again, As Food Riots Break the Mania's Back

Commodities turned out to be the final holdout. When global food riots hit in mid-2008, we were convinced that the last domino was about to fall and that an "across-the-board" plunge was near:

The Elliott Wave Financial Forecast, May 2008

The Reuters/Jefferies CRB Index eked out a new high on Tuesday, but with the outcry over food and energy costs rising to fever pitch, we are more convinced than ever that the trend is ending and the start of deflation is near. One reason is that it reveals another link to the deflationary collapse of 1837-1842. Last month, we discussed the similarities with respect to the financial arena, but the parallel to early 1837 may be even more compelling with regard to commodities. In the wake of Supercycle wave (V), fears of surging commodity prices took much longer to arrive (eight years vs. two years in 1837), but this month it boiled over in a manner that is strikingly similar to 1837. According to *Gotham: A History of New York City*, the price of flour jumped from $4.87 in December 1834 to $12.00 a bushel, or a gain of 144%. Wheat futures are at $8.24 a bushel, up a comparable 171% over the last three years. A spasm of semi-organized opposition to price rises is also common to both periods. In 1837, spiral food prices led demonstrators to fill New York City streets and carry signs demanding, "Bread, Meat, Rent, Fuel! Their Prices Must Come Down!" A series of "flour riots" followed. Word of a current global version of this turmoil appeared in the recent April 14 issue of The Wall Street Journal:

> Rioting in response to soaring food prices recently has broken out in Egypt, Cameroon, Ivory Coast, Senegal and Ethiopia. In Pakistan and Thailand, army troops have been deployed to deter food theft from fields and warehouses. World Bank President Robert Zoellick warned in a recent speech that 33 countries are at risk of social upheaval because of rising food prices.

According to a flood of news accounts, a jump in rice is fueling anger and "fears of unrest" in Asia, while in New Jersey, truckers pulled their rigs off the road and others slowed to a crawl on major highways to protest high fuel prices. "In wealthy Japan, soaring food prices have forced a pampered population to contemplate the shocking possibility of a long-term—perhaps permanent—reduction in the quality and quantity of its food."

English Prime Minister Gordon Brown calls the growing "food crisis" a threat to world stability. "World food markets have been seized with panic," said one news account. If there is a difference, it is that this time around, the affected population spans the globe. Here are two more headlines from April 17:

Runaway Prices Fuel Chinese Unrest
—Globe and Mail

Meat Price Begin To Soar Out of Control
—Warsaw Business Journal

If the parallel holds, relief will come in the form of a market-induced reversal in commodity prices.

A month later we zeroed in on soaring oil prices:

The Elliott Wave Financial Forecast, June 2008

If there is a fly in our forecast for an imminent break in the economy, it is crude oil prices. A slowing economy should bring a slackening in demand for all commodities, especially oil, which continued to bubble higher with a run through $130 a barrel in May. A key feature of the forecast is investor psychology, which continues to ripen. On a 60-day basis, the Daily Sentiment Index just hit 90% bulls, displaying the most persistent optimism toward oil on record. Readings such as this are almost non-existent. In fact, the only other market to achieve this record is soybeans (and the accompanying bean meal), which hit a 60-day DSI of 90% bulls on March 3, the exact day of the soybean top so far.

The case for an end in oil's rise is growing even stronger, as the current social environment is saturated with discussions, books and cartoons that focus on high (and ever higher) energy prices. "All Memorial Day weekend, gas prices were the topic of conversation," said one newspaper. In another rare signal, crude has attained that rare state, even for a mania, in which more bullish forecasts themselves are believed to drive prices higher. Here's the headline from one of the most popular general interest sites on the web:

$200 Oil Prediction Rocks Market
—Drudge Report

According to Bloomberg, oil initially climbed above $130 after three Wall Street firms "raised their price forecasts" and then, after falling back, moved back over $130 when Morgan Stanley said prices "May Reach $150." If forecasts drove prices, they might have something there. But when extreme forecasts are cited as driving prices, it is almost invariably very late in the game.

The oil chart offers something more substantive, a complete, or nearly complete, bull market pattern. Observe the five-wave form of the rally from December 21, 1998 ($10.35). The parallel trendchannel formed by this advance is not an Elliott wave channel, but it does encompass all price action of the past 9½ years. The fifth wave has carried to the upper line, which signals that the rally is nearing an end. Oftentimes, prices will "throw over" the upper channel for a brief period. Coming back within the channel then confirms the top, after which a strong and sustained decline ensues. Either way, be ready for an oil reversal.

From July to December 2008, the commodity markets fell 56% while crude oil fell more than 70%. Here's the updated chart that appeared partway down, in the November 2008 issue of EWFF:

Mania Expiration Opens the Door to Its Antithesis
The commodities' plunge, which was swifter than the one from 1929 to 1933, combined with a 43.5% decline in the Dow Jones Industrial Average from October 2007 to October 2008, the bursting credit bubble and the October 2008 confirmation of a new low in the Dow Jones Transportation Average, all spoke decisively to the mania's termination. On October 15, 2008, *The Elliott Wave Financial Forecast* issued a Special Report that examined the speculative evidence and declared that the bubble was, in fact, over:

END OF THE MANIA ERA
Like Dracula rising from his coffin after being consumed by fire, this Great Asset Mania has come back from the dead again and again. Does it have what it takes to rise once more? Or has it finally received a fatal stake to the heart?

The answer may seem obvious. The Dow Jones Industrial Average is down 30% this year. Governments around the world have taken historic measures and appear impotent in the face of the fall. Bank runs have started, and a majority of Americans say that not a recession but a depression is underway. How can stocks come back from that?

Students of the mania and its many mutations remember, however, that the society-wide drive for higher prices has had a monstrous penchant for springing back to life. Time and again, the Great Asset Mania has released from one sector, producing a violent fall from record heights, only to grab another whole new class of assets. Subscribers are well aware of the mania's rotation from technology in 2000 to housing in 2005, to the financial sector in early 2007 and then to commodities in 2008. Fundamental justifications, ranging from an infinite demand for semiconductors to peak oil to Chinese demand, proved bogus in every case. Why can't the financial crowd drive some new asset class to freakish new heights now? It is an important question because so long as the mania lives, the potential for a leavening of equity and bond prices lives with it.

History tells us there's never been anything like this extended mania, but it also shows us that a mania, and presumably a succession of them, cannot live forever. The basic engine behind a mania is that paying too much for a piece of paper is rational because someone (a greater fool) will always be there to pay an even higher price. There comes the breaking point, however, when people take the opposite view, determining that they will never be that fool again. As *The Elliott Wave Theorist*'s 1997 study, "Bulls, Bears and Manias," put it:

> A mania is not simply a "big bull market." It is something else, and it not only behaves differently, but it resolves differently as well, which is why the difference is worth knowing. [This is] the most important observation about the market's action following a mania: every mania is followed by a decline that ends below the starting point of the advance. ...Manic markets are akin to people abusing "speed." In foregoing sleep, amphetamine abusers disrupt the healthy ebb and flow of consciousness that is required for healthy long-term functioning, just as manias disrupt the ebb and flow of prices that is required for healthy long term advance. Like manias, amphetamine abusers perform abnormally well for awhile...until they crash. When they crash, they reach a state worse than the one they were in when they began the abuse, just as a market does after a mania.

The Great Mania took longer than any other, but by measuring its vital signs against those registered over the course of the prior 13 years, EWFF determined that the resolution described in "Bulls, Bears and Manias" was, in fact, at hand. The evidence is presented in the October 2008 entries that finish all eight chapters of this chronicle. EWFF completed its assessment by stating:

> We cannot say with certainty that some nook of the financial world won't bound higher during the next selling respite. In fact, there is precedent for a residual bubble in some obscure investment vehicle. It happened after Supercycle wave (I) ended with the crash of 1837. Investors went crazy buying and selling—are you ready for this?—mulberry bushes. But the psychological reversal presented here and in *The Elliott Wave Theorist* over the last 13 years covers the full breadth of the mania's topping process. To conclude, the weight of the evidence overwhelmingly favors the mania's termination. The October 2007 DJIA peak represents the start of a major bear market in nominal terms that ultimately should last for years. With a 44% decline (DJIA) in one year's time span, the first phase of the bear is well along.

667

The most exotic of modern-day tulips will expire; that's certain. But, on the positive side, individuals with cash will prosper, and companies with well-established roots will weather the storm. Those that can adjust to the changing business environment will survive and eventually thrive as many competitors will be out of business or dramatically reduced in size. If this is the first you've heard of the mania and its unfolding collapse, there is good news. Even at 9000, the Dow is at a historically high valuation level with respect to dividends and earnings. For investors still exposed to stock market risk, there is an opportunity to pursue the defensive strategies profiled in *Conquer the Crash*. But don't delay. The mania endpoint implies an equal and opposite downside response, so the developing negative social force will quickly find its way to the doorstep of those who are oblivious to its presence. Don't be one of them.

An Important Clue: The Smaller They Are the Harder They Fall

The mania's incredible staying power is evident in the "One Long Top" chart that begins this Conclusion. The chart shows that the initial peak came in April 1998, when the Value Line Composite hit its all-time high. The NASDAQ's all-time peak, the most forceful upward surge, came two years later, and the Value Line Arithmetic average topped more than nine years later, in July 2007. The Value Line Arithmetic's continued rise, as the NASDAQ managed to retrace just 50% of its value from 2002-2007, reveals a continuing public thirst for new price highs.

But it also shows the mania's diminishing strength. The geometric version, which is commonly referred to as the Value Line Composite, failed to accompany the Value Line Arithmetic to a new peak in 2007. This was a subtle but critically important statement about the unfolding bear market. The averages comprise the same 1650 stocks. In the arithmetic version, there is a dollar-for-dollar effect on the index value, which means share contributions to the index become minimal as they approach zero. In the geometric version, stocks contribute according to their percentage change. So, lower priced shares do not lose their influence on the overall index value.

The Value Line Composite has been dismissed for years now, because any index that is not acting bullishly becomes ignored. But there is a very important reason to pay close attention to the geometric version and the greater influence of heavily devalued shares. Its underperformance is due to the influence of the downside leaders that best reflect the force of the unfolding bear market. In October 2007, *The Elliott Wave Financial Forecast* noted that financial services, banks, homebuilders and retail stocks were out in front and stated that "the bear market already appears underway" in these key sectors. The Dow Industrials fell more than 40% over the next year. Similarly, the potential for much further weakness over the course of the bear market is signaled by the Value Line Composite's break of the Cycle wave **a** low in 2002. The weakest stocks are getting weaker faster. Most of the bust lies ahead, and the Value Line geometric is a window into that future.

Fannie Mae and The Infinite Possibilities in a Journey Toward Zero

The performance of the Value Line is instructional for another reason. One of the reputed advantages of betting on a bull market as opposed to a bear is that a rising stock can theoretically go to infinity (and in the throes of the upward flight that finished in October 2007, many fully expected this outcome) while a bear market can fall only to zero. But back in September 2001, *The Elliott Wave Financial Forecast* pointed out that one critical trait of the unfolding bear market is that theoretically the same formerly high flying stocks can plunge, sometimes by "80%, 90% and 98%," an infinite number of times. This tendency was well illustrated by various technology stocks. As the stock market turned down in late 2007, this major bear market trait, which EWI dubbed the "infinity or bust principle," was very much in play once again, this time across the breadth of the economy. One prime example is the collapse of the Federal National Mortgage Association, a.k.a. Fannie Mae. To many, Fannie's collapse was an overnight sensation, but it actually began years earlier. In fact, it was in March 2002 that *The Elliott Wave Financial Forecast* recognized that the wheels had actually started to come off.

[In] the coming downturn, Fannie Mae and Freddie Mac, the "government sponsored enterprises" that have pushed home ownership into the depths of the population, will be extremely vulnerable.... Fannie Mae and Freddie Mac will be getting the worst of the downturn from every angle.

Here's a chart that shows the rise behind Fannie Mae when EWFF made this statement.

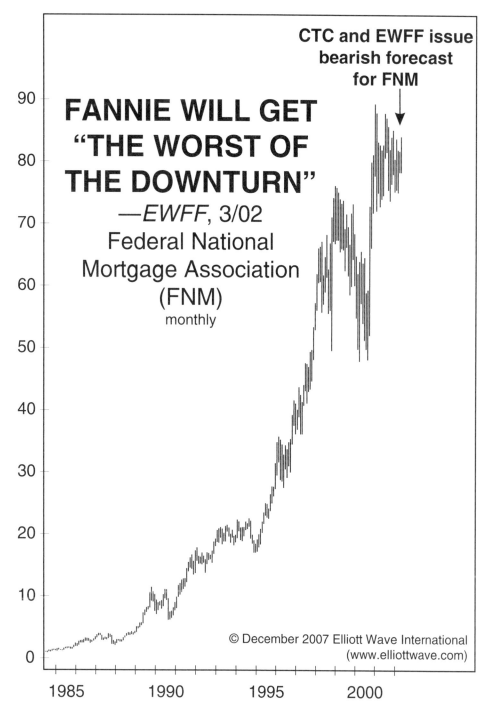

Like the market as a whole, Fannie didn't go to pieces in 2000. It lingered near its highs for months on end. As it did, EWFF fleshed out the bearish case. Here's a sampling of the commentary EWI offered as Fannie Mae approached its peak and hovered there for several years.

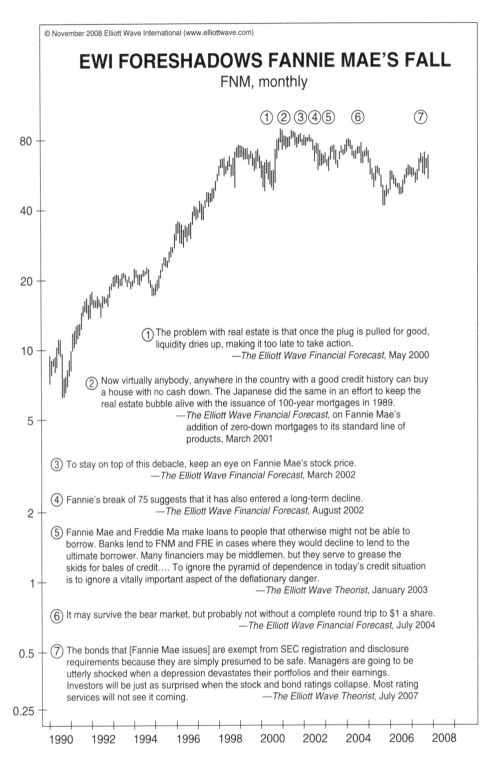

EWI FORESHADOWS FANNIE MAE'S FALL
FNM, monthly

① The problem with real estate is that once the plug is pulled for good, liquidity dries up, making it too late to take action.
—*The Elliott Wave Financial Forecast*, May 2000

② Now virtually anybody, anywhere in the country with a good credit history can buy a house with no cash down. The Japanese did the same in an effort to keep the real estate bubble alive with the issuance of 100-year mortgages in 1989.
—*The Elliott Wave Financial Forecast*, on Fannie Mae's addition of zero-down mortgages to its standard line of products, March 2001

③ To stay on top of this debacle, keep an eye on Fannie Mae's stock price.
—*The Elliott Wave Financial Forecast*, March 2002

④ Fannie's break of 75 suggests that it has also entered a long-term decline.
—*The Elliott Wave Financial Forecast*, August 2002

⑤ Fannie Mae and Freddie Ma make loans to people that otherwise might not be able to borrow. Banks lend to FNM and FRE in cases where they would decline to lend to the ultimate borrower. Many financiers may be middlemen, but they serve to grease the skids for bales of credit.... To ignore the pyramid of dependence in today's credit situation is to ignore a vitally important aspect of the deflationary danger.
—*The Elliott Wave Theorist*, January 2003

⑥ It may survive the bear market, but probably not without a complete round trip to $1 a share.
—*The Elliott Wave Financial Forecast*, July 2004

⑦ The bonds that [Fannie Mae issues] are exempt from SEC registration and disclosure requirements because they are simply presumed to be safe. Managers are going to be utterly shocked when a depression devastates their portfolios and their earnings. Investors will be just as surprised when the stock and bond ratings collapse. Most rating services will not see it coming. —*The Elliott Wave Theorist*, July 2007

The bearish bounty finally arrived in the second half of 2007 as the great housing bust set in and quickly took back almost everything Fannie Mae gained in the 1990s. In November 2007, when many economists suggested that Fannie Mae and Freddie Mac be used to maintain the "flow of reasonably priced loans to creditworthy home purchasers," EWFF said that "Such measures are a pipe dream" and added that the 70% plunge in Fannie was still just the down payment on a "new bear market reality." Here's the chart:

As published in the EWFF, November 29, 2007

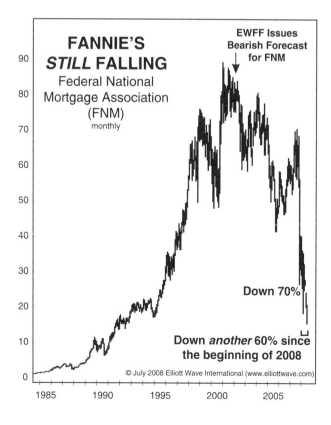

Seven months later, on July 10, EWI posted this "Fannie's *Still* Falling" chart:

The principle was further illustrated a month later when Bob Prechter appeared on Bloomberg TV. Noting that Fannie was now so deeply depressed that it was best viewed on log scale, which presents its price in percentage terms, Bob showed the following chart on August 20, 2008:

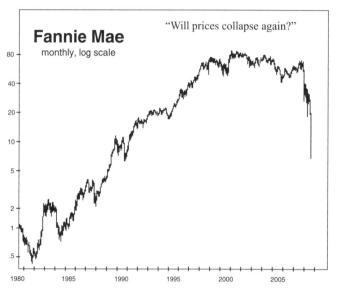

Here's how Bob described the downside opportunity that remained for Bloomberg's TV audience:

> People wonder why people are shorting [Fannie Mae] at $18. "It's already down from $89, isn't that enough?" And then it goes to $9, and they are still shorting it. Well, now it's $4.50. And this chart shows why. If you look at the low way back in 1981, it was 40 cents. Somebody might look at this today and say it's got 90% more to go even though it's down 95%. That's hard to conceive of, but that's what happens in severe, severe bear markets.

Even after a decline of better than 95%, Fannie Mae packed plenty of downside punch. In fact, by the second week of September, it was down another 85%. The following chart is the September 12, 2008, version as shown to visitors to Elliott Wave International's website, elliottwave.com.

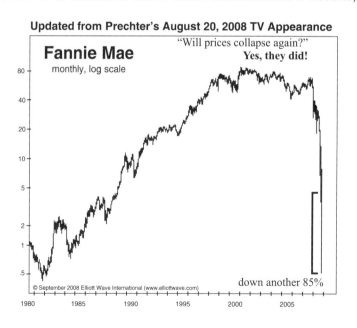

"It's not too late to take advantage of everything that these charts have to say about the overall stock market and economy," EWI's website stated. Over the next month, the Dow Jones Industrial Average fell 30% and the economy entered a free fall. And Fannie Mae continued to present downside opportunities. Even after it went bankrupt and became a ward of the state in September, the December 2008 issue of EWFF pointed out, Fannie registered another 87% decline.

Taking the Bear by Its Horns

The share price of Fannie Mae offers a prime example of our "infinity or bust" principle. That little squiggle at the bottom of the chart, which is blown up to produce the inset, illustrates the infinite space between Fannie's stock value and the zero figure that it will likely one day achieve. The latest upward blip illustrates how the Slope of Hope generates new, highly profitable entry points for the alert bear. It came when Fannie announced its plans for a reverse stock split, which will give sellers the advantage of even higher price points. No matter how crushing, this decline finds ways to create massive downside opportunities.

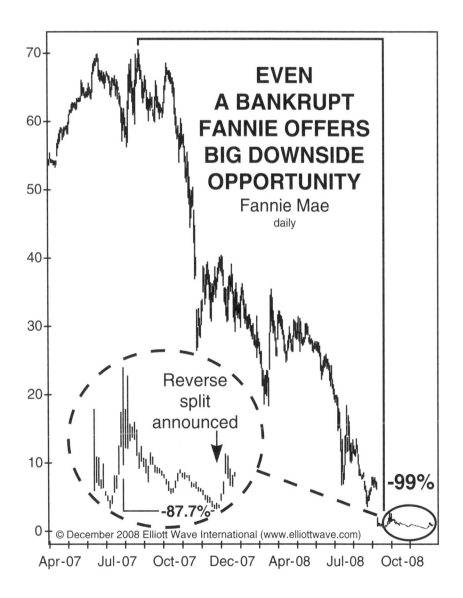

Fannie Mae's decline highlights the persistence of the downside as well as a big-time bear market's remarkable capacity for summoning the optimism of the preceding bull market. *Everyone knows* that speculative bubbles always burst, leading to a rapid depreciation of share prices. During the bubble era, this most elementary law of finance was suspended for so long that a whole generation of investors lost all fear of falling prices. By the time the Dow Jones Industrial Average reached its all-time highs in October 2007, the only fear most investors struggled to overcome was the fear of being left behind by stock-rich friends and neighbors. This is not to suggest a causal relationship but that, after 200 years of advance, social mood is so elevated investors are impervious to the potential for further damage, even in the face of massive declines. It will take the selling and continual disappointments of a complete Elliott wave to reawaken the public's visceral fear of falling prices.

How the Crash of 1987 "Pushed Things Along"

After 200 years of rising stock prices, the October 1987 crash reversed the usual effect of scaring off investors. Investors didn't cringe at the prospects for stocks, they binged on them. Here's how New York Times financial writer Joe Nocera explained the impetus in 1997:

> The famous crash of 1987, when the stock market fell more than 500 points in one day, pushed things along. Rather than causing people to flee back to banks with their money, the crash, in the end, caused people to embrace the market with renewed fervor. Within months the market had earned back every penny — and it kept going up. Ultimately, the people who felt foolish were those who had panicked and gotten out of the market. Thus was a new lesson learned. Just as Americans now "know" that when the market went down — even when it went down 500 points in a day — they should simply invest more heavily. The lesson of the 1987 crash was that the market will always bounce back.

Sentiment data from the American Association of Individual Investors survey confirms that investors were almost immediately emboldened by the crash of 1987 (47% bulls to 22% bears in the week of November 6); this was a Fibonacci 13 years from the 1974 low. This book begins in 1995 because that was the first year of the most intense phase of the mania. If the mania has expired as we suspect, the most intense speculative frenzy finally came to a halt after another 13 years, when the decline of 2008 hit investors harder than the decline of 1929-1930.

The crash of 2008, which occurred a Fibonacci 34 years from the 1974 low, has been followed by countless reminders of the quick recovery after 1987. "The story of the 1987 crash and the subsequent long bull market that followed [is] a comforting story for investors," says Forbes. Under the headline, "Certain Financial Truths Remain," the Baltimore Sun reports, "When everything seems upside down, when century-old banks fall like bowling pins, when even 'safe' investments seem risky, there are still eternal truths investors can embrace. This, too, shall pass. Financial panics always end. It took less than two years for stocks to recover from the 1987 crash." Mainstream advisors will not let the public forget it. "Investors who resisted the urge to sell in 1987 suffered, but their portfolios eventually bounced back," says a Braintree, Mass.-based investment strategist, "When you cash out, you never recover," concludes a typical October 2008 advisory.

Having to wait two years to get back to even is the most bearish imaginable scenario for many. Older investors might have been able to recall a grimmer fate, but the bull market carried on so long that it substantially thinned their ranks. At this point, those who can reflect on anything remotely similar to the events of recent years are few and far between. "Legendary financier" Leon Levy, who started on Wall Street in 1948, offered a fuller perspective. In his 2002 memoir, *The Mind of Wall Street*, Levy referred to the late 1990s as "my bubble" and noted "eerily similar" parallels "to just before the crash of 1929." He also cited a "pattern of generational forgetting" as one of the factors behind the bubble. "Basically, we all live three lives: our life, the lives of our parents, and those of our children. Events within our experience, particularly our youth, remain the most visceral in memory but events that lie beyond the horizon of these generations tend to be more abstract, if only because they don't have an immediate connection to our lives." In a demonstration of how those ties and the psychological impact of the greatest investment debacles are lost over the course of a 200-year bull market, however, Levy did not live to see the final highs in nominal terms. He died in 2003.

For every seasoned pro with some grasp of the reality of the mania, there were many thousands of investors with no mania knowledge, experiential or otherwise, to fall back on. Many of the biggest were newer to the markets than the bull market itself. A typical example was "supertrader" and hedge fund operator Kenneth Griffin, whose newspaper profiles never failed to mention that he "started trading out of his dorm room at Harvard in 1987." By the mid-2000s, Griffin's Citadel Investment Group was one of the largest hedge funds in the world, reputedly accounting for 1% of all trading activity in New York, London, and Tokyo. In September 2008, however, Citadel was on the ropes with billions in losses. In October, the firm lost billions more, and The New York Times reported that Griffin held an "emergency conference call that transfixed Wall Street." "I've never seen a market as full of panic as I've seen in the last seven to eight weeks," Griffin said. "To call it a dislocation doesn't go anywhere near what we've seen." (History, however, has seen it all before.) In December, Citadel announced that it would close offices, lay off workers and halt redemptions as its two main funds were down close to 50%. According to The New York Times, the magnitude of the crisis and its effect on their business came as a "real shock" to hedge fund managers like Griffin. All at once, banks cut back on hedge fund lending — "essentially turning off a financial spigot that the funds relied upon to goose their returns" — as the economy tanked, investors became risk averse and new regulations and taxes loomed. "Add it all up, and managing a hedge fund looks much less attractive than it used to." The predicament suggests powerfully that we have reached the critical point envisioned in the last few sentences of *Elliott Wave Principle*. This is that moment that comes right after "the fifth wave of the fifth wave" has topped out; "the laws of nature will have to be patiently relearned."

Beneath the Rubble of the Big Turn, A Secret Message

For most, the lessons will come through involuntary attendance in the school of hard knocks. But the quote at the top of this chapter highlights the cleverness of another method, the study of history, upon which this book is founded. By applying the Wave Principle and history of similar episodes, EWI managed to shield subscribers from the negative consequences of an all-time bust. In addition to providing critical instructions in the importance of an independent and contrary approach, the Great Asset Mania is worthy of further study because it unlocks the investment world's deepest secret: that the true engine of market trends is the endogenous ebb and flow of social mood, which extends into all aspects of human life. At the social mood peak of 2000, this reality was as tangible as ever. Chapter 3 covers many of the ways in which the optimism that was so brilliantly reflected in the stock averages swept through virtually every layer of social interaction, from convents to grade schools to prime time TV to the bright lights of Times Square.

It was wonderful to be around for it. Another promising aspect of the mania is how it opens our eyes to the true cause of social change. In a normally trending market, events can be mistaken for causes, because a well-established trend creates news that reflects its direction. It lags, but the lag is not obvious. At the great social mood peak of 2000, the news environment was uniformly positive. Years and years of rising stock prices had produced a cloudless sky, lit by the bright sun of "the New Economy." But the sky darkened nonetheless. Initially, the only outward manifestation of the downturn was the reversal in stock prices. It took a full six months for the second significant manifestation, a sense of confusion over the perfect prospects for the future and the tumbling stock averages, to appear and confirm the bear market. Puzzlement over the incongruity was recorded by the Associated Press with the following comment from an economist on August 20, 2000: "The news is terrific — inflation, earnings growth, interest rates, dollar, Fed — but the market is flat. What's up with that?" The serene social setting at the beginning of the great bear market is the ultimate proof that waves of optimism and pessimism are guiding human social behavior.

Another clue is how the bear market completely refashioned the social scene. *The Wave Principle of Human Social Behavior* describes the characteristics of a negative mood change as a polar shift from an increase in concord, inclusion, happiness, forbearance, confidence and daring in a bull market to waxing discord, exclusion, depression, intolerance, defensiveness and fear in a bear. Many of the post-2000 passages in this book record these changes. From the September 11, 2001, attacks on the World Trade Center to the nascent global trade tension and the reverberating recriminations covered in Chapter 8, a high-degree shift in the direction of social mood is apparent. In 2001 and 2002, personalities that the crowd rallied around on the way up were the same ones the social mood lined up to tar and feather on the way down. The initial leg down delivered a wave of indictments, bankruptcies, lawsuits and prison terms that reflected the bearish tide just as HSB and other EWI forecasts said they would. From Enron to Worldcom, Martha Stewart Omnimedia, Computer Associates and Tyco, we captured the epic swing.

Elliott Wave International's fuller, society-wide approach to financial analysis held up. No, we didn't get it all right, but the preceding chapters show that there was nothing murky about our vision for the great peak. The stark contrast to popular expectations is illustrated by the following retrospective comparing the euphoria that accompanied the "New Millennium" to the troubled world that actually ensued. The article appeared across the top of The Detroit News and Free Press front page on February 23, 2003:

Millennium Sparkle Fades Into Darkness
Looming war, corporate scandals, economic downturn take toll on American psyche

The first shells exploded in Sydney and Tokyo, then over Moscow, Egypt's pyramids, the Parthenon, the Eiffel Tower, Big Ben, and finally, the Millennium celebration reached America with fireworks over Manhattan and Washington D.C.

"It was all about hope: You felt it was a turning point for the world," recalled 48-year old Neal Harkness, who watched the made-for-TV spectacle with a few friends from his living room. The lights stayed on at midnight – Y2K was a false alarm. The Dow hovered comfortably around 11,500.

"Never before have we had such an opportunity to move toward what generations have prayed for: peace on earth and a better life for all," said President Clinton, who would lament the legacy of governing during such an era of good fortune.

Only 1,100 days later, Neal Harkness stood on the frozen lawn of Detroit's Grand Circus Park to shout out against looming war, corporate sleaze, a tattered economy, a splintered United Nations, a new millennium malaise spreading through the American psyche like some kind of time-release depressant.

"Things are worse now than I ever imagined they could get," Harkness said. "We don't time these things."

We never do. We can only see from a distance how history plays these tricks, humbling us with unimaginable crisis in times of plenty, or making folly of fear with breakthroughs when all seems bleak.

"The notion of hubris will inevitably be punished," said Jonathan Marwil, a University of Michigan history lecturer. "History doesn't answer us the way we think it will."

This last comment is completely consistent with the Wave Principle, which structures history to confound intuitive expectations at every turn. The other bearish events demonstrate the incalculable value offered by an understanding of the Wave Principle. Virtually every facet of the "time release depressant" cited in the article above — war in the Mideast, corporate recriminations, a tattered economy, splintered United Nations and a millennium malaise — was anticipated in the pages of *The Elliott Wave Financial Forecast*, *Conquer the Crash* and *The Elliott Wave Theorist*. EWI's long-term forecast included the irony in a night of fireworks, which *The Elliott Wave Financial Forecast* predicted with this comment from the January 2000 issue: "It was fitting that as the Dow reached its all-time closing high on New Year's Eve, fireworks were going off around the world. The global festivities will probably be long remembered as an end rather than a beginning of a golden era."

From there, it was not a straight line down in the Dow/gold ratio, but after the article appeared in 2003, stocks rallied in nominal terms for more than four years as the dollar collapsed in value. During that time, Martha Stewart emerged from her prison cell and returned to her corporate post. Other corporate kingpins-turned-scoundrels were acquitted (such as Richard Scrushy of HealthSouth in June 2005). Burdensome Sarbanes-Oxley accounting rules, which were imposed near the lows in 2002, were relaxed in 2007, right on time for the top.

In late 2008, the effects of a bear market returned full force as the ebullience surrounding all-time highs once again began to be displaced by a seething public anger. In companies and governments everywhere, there is an increasingly frantic effort to get to the bottom of what went wrong. Suddenly, in case after case, juries, Congressional committees, attorneys general and the police are digging hard to discover "who knew" what about inappropriate activities that took place in happier times. The size of the scams reflects the size of the turn. The bigger the bear market, the bigger the bad boys and their exposed deeds. From that principle derives EWFF's 2007 assertion that in the approaching decline the scams and scandals would be massive:

> Bear markets bring recrimination. A flurry of stories on indictments and investigations involving insider trading, buyouts and various Ponzi schemes hit the headlines in recent weeks. This is just the first puff of smoke of what promises to be a huge mushroom cloud.

At a reputed $50 billion, the Madoff Ponzi scheme is the largest ever by a wide margin. The best explanation for its ability to maintain upward momentum despite continual reports and investigations of fraud is the collective delusion and literally mind-numbing euphoria of Grand Supercycle proportions. As one investor told The New York Times, "something about" the fund's chairman Bernard Madoff "inspired trust." That something was the bull market; it took its conclusion and the start of a powerful downturn to break that trust. As the bear market builds, a NY Times article on lavish Wall Street bonuses reveals, "questions are being asked. Scrutiny is intensifying." So it goes across the universe of investments. In many cases, these crackdowns and prosecutions are far from healthy, as they direct energy into largely destructive channels. Over time, they will become mechanisms through which scorned investors, consumers and voters shift blame and vent the rage of a bear market. The widespread belief that the market has already bottomed will ultimately provide more fuel for disappointment and fury. There is more to come.

As the collapse of 2008 set in, the papers became convinced that cash was in some type of blow-off that would end badly.

Cash Could Be Next Bubble to Burst—Hooray
Cash is a rising bubble that's bound to burst.
—Motley Fool, December 22, 2008

"Is Cash a Bubble?" echoes the December 20 issue of Barron's. The answer is *no*. There are some important distinctions that explain why. For one thing, a bubble requires an over-extension of credit to purchase investments for profit, and there's no way to borrow your way to a big position in cash. If there were, it wouldn't be cash. So, by definition, cash is not exposed to the margin calls and forced selling that create the stunning bust of every bubble. Another reason that cash cannot be the focus of a bubble is that people don't buy it hoping to resell it to someone else at a higher price. They buy it because they think it is worth exactly what it is. Cash is about keeping what you have; a bubble is about getting rich.

When all is said and done, the gains and losses from the bubble and its aftermath will be the greatest ever, but they will not be the most important legacy of the bubble years. The mania's great gift is what it teaches us about our nature. These lessons are just as accessible to the bulls who suffered heavy losses as they are to the handful of bears who sensed the new direction and profited by it. The intellectual spoils will fall to the few who treat the experience as a once-in-many-lifetimes happening they were privileged to witness. The passage from the great bull market to the great bear is the biggest display of socionomic fireworks in at least 300 years, maybe 1,000. Those who can apply this knowledge to their lives and understanding of the world will be rich indeed.

—Peter Kendall

Appendix A

A Capsule Summary of the Wave Principle

The Wave Principle is a detailed description of stock market behavior. In the 1930s, R.N. Elliott, a retired corporate accountant, studied the fluctuations of market prices in yearly, monthly, weekly, daily, hourly and half-hourly increments. He isolated specific patterns of movement, or "waves," that recur in market price data. He named, defined and illustrated those patterns and described their variations. He then described how these structures link together to form larger versions of those same patterns, how those in turn link to form identical patterns of the next larger size, and so on. A complete pattern can last anywhere from a few minutes to centuries. The basis of the Wave Principle is quite simple: Waves in the same direction as the wave of one larger degree develop in five waves, and waves in the opposite direction develop in three waves (or a variation thereof). Figure 1 shows the Wave Principle in idealized form. Each set of numbers, (1), ① or I, denotes a different size, or degree, of trend change.

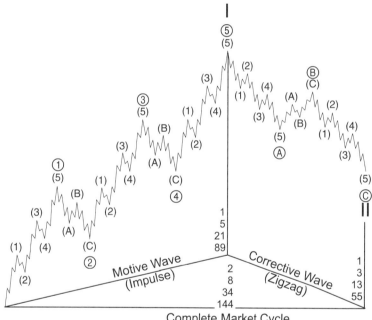

Pattern Analysis

Until a few years ago, the idea that market movements are patterned was highly controversial, but recent scientific discoveries have established that pattern formation is a fundamental characteristic of complex systems, which include financial markets. Some such systems undergo "punctuated growth," that is, periods of growth alternating with phases of non-growth or decline, building fractally into similar

Number of Waves at Each Degree

	Motive (Impulse)	Corrective (Zigzag)	Cycle
Largest waves	1	1	2
Largest subdivisions	5	3	8
Next subdivisions	21	13	34
Next subdivisions	89	55	144

Figure 1

patterns of increasing size. This is precisely the type of pattern identified in market movements by R.N. Elliott some seventy years ago.

The basic pattern Elliott described consists of motive waves (denoted by numbers) and corrective waves (denoted by letters). A motive wave comprises five subwaves and moves in the same direction as the trend of the next larger size. A corrective wave comprises three subwaves (or a variation thereof) and moves against the trend of the next larger size. As Figure 1 shows, these basic patterns link to form five- and three-wave structures of increasingly larger degree.

In Figure 1, the first small sequence is a motive wave (called an "impulse") ending at the peak labeled (1). This pattern signals that the movement of one larger degree is upward. It also signals the start of a three-wave corrective sequence, labeled wave (2).

Waves (3), (4) and (5) complete a larger motive sequence, labeled wave ①. Exactly as with wave (1), the five-wave structure of wave ① signals that the movement at the next larger degree is upward and signals the start of a three-wave corrective downtrend of the same degree as wave 1. This correction, wave ②, is followed by waves ③, ④ and ⑤ to complete a motive sequence of the next larger degree, labeled wave I. Once again, a three-wave correction of the same degree occurs, labeled wave II. Note that at each "wave one" peak, the implications are the same regardless of the size of the wave. The accepted notations for labeling Elliott waves at every degree of trend are shown here.

Within a corrective wave, waves A and C may

Wave Degree	5s With the Trend					3s Against the Trend		
Grand Supercycle	Ⓘ	Ⓘ	Ⓘ	Ⓘ	Ⓥ	ⓐ	ⓑ	ⓒ
Supercycle	(I)	(II)	(III)	(IV)	(V)	(a)	(b)	(c)
Cycle	I	II	III	IV	V	a	b	c
Primary	①	②	③	④	⑤	Ⓐ	Ⓑ	Ⓒ
Intermediate	(1)	(2)	(3)	(4)	(5)	(A)	(B)	(C)
Minor	1	2	3	4	5	A	B	C
Minute	ⓘ	ⓘ	ⓘ	ⓘ	ⓥ	ⓐ	ⓑ	ⓒ
Minuette	(i)	(ii)	(iii)	(iv)	(v)	(a)	(b)	(c)
Subminuette	i	ii	iii	iv	v	a	b	c

be motive waves, consisting of five subwaves. This is because they move in the same direction as the next larger trend, as within waves 2 and 4 in Figure 1. B waves, however, are always corrective waves, consisting of three subwaves, because they move against the larger downtrend. These forms have numerous tendencies regarding the relative length of waves, channel or wedge-shaped boundaries, complexity, pattern alternation and so on. For a complete list, see *Elliott Wave Principle*.

Each type of market pattern has a name and a geometry that is specific and exclusive under certain rules and guidelines, yet variable enough in other aspects to allow for a limited diversity within patterns of the same type. If indeed markets are patterned, and if those patterns have a recognizable geometry, then regardless of the variations allowed, certain relationships in extent and duration are likely to recur. In fact, real world experience shows that they do. The most common and therefore reliable wave relationships are discussed in *Elliott Wave Principle*.

Applying the Wave Principle

The practical goal of any analytical method is to identify market lows suitable for buying (or covering shorts) and market highs suitable for selling (or selling short). The Wave Principle is especially well suited to these functions. Nevertheless, the Wave Principle does not provide *certainty* about any one market outcome; rather, it provides an objective means of assessing the relative *probabilities* of possible future paths for the market. At any time, two or more valid wave interpretations are usually acceptable by the *rules* of the Wave Principle. The rules are highly specific and keep the number of valid alternatives to a minimum. Among the valid alternatives, an analyst will generally regard as preferred the interpretation that satisfies the largest number of *guidelines* and will accord top alternate status to the interpretation satisfying the next largest number of guidelines, and so on. Alternate interpretations are an essential aspect of investing with the Wave Principle, because in the event that the market fails to follow the preferred scenario, the top alternate count becomes the investor's backup plan.

Fibonacci

Within the progression of five- and three-wave structures lies a mathematical wonder known as the Fibonacci sequence. The sequence results from adding adjacent numbers to obtain the next value, i.e. 0+1=1, 1+1=2, 2+1=3. The result is 1, 1, 2, 3, 5, 8, 13, 21, 34, 55, 89, 144, 233, 377 and so on into infinity. In the 13th Century, Leonardo Fibonacci introduced this sequence in a popular book on mathematics.

Elliott had no knowledge of Fibonacci when he catalogued the patterns of the Wave Principle. He found out about the Fibonacci sequence when Charles Collins, an investment writer and manager who helped establish Elliott on Wall Street in the 1930s, revealed its presence within the Wave Principle to him. The number of waves at each degree produces the sequence, as you can see at the bottom of Figure 1.

Success for the Model

Robert Prechter investigated the Wave Principle in the early 1970s when he was on a quest to find the most reliable guide to the future course of stock prices. Through his mastery of its tenets, Prechter produced the insightful passage that begins this book, which itself extended a 70-year record of accurate stock market forecasts from four other pioneering Elliotticians.

That record begins with R.N. Elliott. In 1941, when the nations of the world were on a collision course toward the most destructive war in the history of the world, Elliott postulated the emergence of a great bull market that would last decades. (See *R.N. Elliott's Masterworks*.) In the ensuing years, Hamilton Bolton, Charles Collins, A.J. Frost and Prechter forecasted the ups and downs within the larger wave that Elliott had forecast.

Elliott's forecasted wave was the fifth — and therefore final — wave of an even larger sequence from the late 1700s, as depicted in Figure 2 in the Introduction of this book. Since fifth waves sport the most exuberant sentiment in an Elliott wave progression and because the forecasted advance was to be a fifth wave of even higher degree than that of the 1920s, Prechter correctly anticipated that it would end with a swell of enthusiasm for stocks and speculation that would surpass any stock mania on record.

Some critics contested Elliott Wave International's outlook strictly on the basis of this 200-year time frame. How could the horse and buggy economy of two centuries ago have any bearing on modern-day financial markets? If bull and bear markets were mechanical systems driven by external causes, they might have a point. Prechter's radical contention is that waves do not respond to various social actions but rather derive from endogenous, self-regulating changes in social mood, which in fact induce people to take social actions. We address this topic in Appendix B.

Another way to gauge the effectiveness of a theory is the breakthroughs that follow in its wake. In Figure 1, notice the similarity between waves (1) - (2), ① - ② and I - II. This is the idea of market cycles as fractals, or compositions of smaller units of the same design that link together to create a self-similar whole. Three decades after Elliott's pioneering work, a mathematician named Benoit Mandelbrot examined cotton prices and discovered a fractal. Mandelbrot's work spawned the science of fractal geometry, a style of organization that permeates natural forms, both animate and inanimate. Elliott called his last book *Nature's Law, The Secret of the Universe*, a bold claim to be sure. But nothing has shaken it. In fact, the scientific evidence is steadily rolling his way.

Appendix B

A Primer on Socionomics

R.N. Elliott knew almost immediately that he had opened the door to something that was much more than a technical approach to stock market analysis. The first chapter of his first treatise on the Wave Principle was titled "Rhythm In Nature." In it, Elliott wrote, "Man is no less a natural object than the sun or the moon. [The Wave Principle] is a phenomenon that has always functioned in every human activity." Over the last 20 years, Robert Prechter has demonstrated and expanded upon this insight. He formalized the effort in 1999 with *The Wave Principle of Human Social Behavior and the New Science of Socionomics*. The book substantiates Elliott's claim to having discovered a law of nature by finding support for the Wave Principle in everything from the structure and function of the human brain and the biology of unconscious herding to world history and popular culture. Socionomics has launched a whole new approach to social science. The link between trends in stock prices and everything from music, movies and fashion to politics and war is continually examined in Elliott Wave International's monthly publications and by the Socionomics Institute.

Understanding socionomics requires comprehending the contrast between two postulations:

(1) **The standard presumption**: Social mood is buffeted by economic, political and cultural trends and events. News of such events affects the social mood, which in turn affects people's penchant for investing.

(2) **The socionomic hypothesis**: Social mood is a natural product of human interaction and is patterned according to the Wave Principle. Its trends and extent determine the character of social action, including economic, political and cultural trends and events.

The contrast between these two positions comes down to this: The standard presumption is that in the social setting, events govern mood; the socionomic hypothesis recognizes that mood governs events. In both cases, the stock market is seen as an efficient mechanism. In the first instance, it presumably revalues stocks continually and rationally in reaction to events; in the second, it revalues stocks continually and impulsively as the independent social mood changes. We will now investigate some presumed "outside forces" to see which of these views and their relationship to the stock market can be supported by the standard presumption and which ones are supported by the socionomic hypothesis.

The Economy

The standard presumption is that the state of the economy is a key determinant of the stock market's trends. All day long on financial television and year after year in financial print media, investors debate the state of the economy for clues to the future course of the stock market. If this presumed causal relationship actually existed, then there would be some evidence that the economy leads the stock market. On the contrary, for decades, the Commerce Department of the federal government has identified the stock market as a leading indicator of the economy, which is indeed the case.

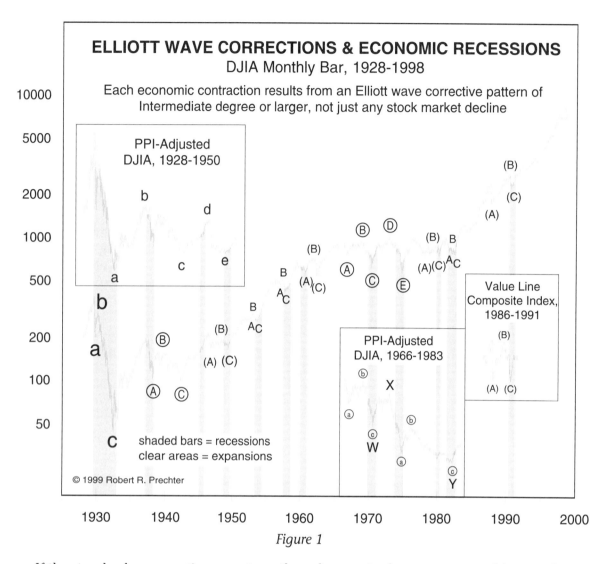

Figure 1

If the standard presumption were true, then changes in the economy would coincide with or precede trend changes in aggregate stock prices. However, a study of Figure 1 will show that changes in the economy coincide with or follow trend changes in aggregate stock prices. Except for the timing of the recession of 1946 (which supports neither case), all economic contractions came upon or after a downturn in aggregate stock prices, and all economic recoveries came upon or after an upturn in aggregate stock prices.[1] In not one case did a contraction or recovery precede a change in aggregate stock prices, which would repeatedly be the case if investors in fact reacted to economic trends and events. This chronology persists back into the nineteenth century as far as the data goes.

The socionomic hypothesis explains the data. Changes in the stock market immediately reflect the changes in endogenous social mood. As social mood becomes increasingly positive, productive activity increases; as social mood becomes increasingly negative, productive activity decreases. These results show up in lagging economic statistics as expansions and recessions. The standard presumption has no explanation for the relative timing of these two phenomena.

Elections

The standard presumption is that election results are a key determinant of the stock market's trends. As an election approaches, commentators debate the effect that its outcome will have on stock prices. Investors argue over which candidate would likely influence the market to

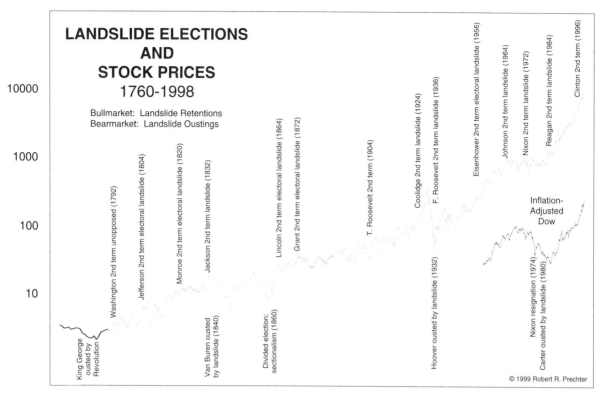

Figure 2

go up or down. "If so-and-so gets elected, it will be good/bad for the market," we often hear. If this causal relationship were valid, then there would be evidence that a change in power from one party's leader to another affects the stock market. On the contrary, there is no study that shows such a connection.

A socionomist, on the other hand, can show the opposite causality at work. Examine Figure 2 and observe that strong and persistent trends in the stock market determine whether an incumbent president will be re-elected in a landslide or defeated in one. In all cases where an incumbent remained in office in a landslide, the stock market's trend was up. In all cases where an incumbent was rejected by a landslide, the stock market's trend was down.[2] In not one case did an incumbent win re-election despite a deeply falling stock market or lose in a landslide despite a strongly rising stock market.[3]

The socionomic conclusion is this: When social mood waxes positive, as reflected by persistently rising stock prices, voters desire to retain the leader who symbolizes their upbeat feelings and who they presume helped cause the conditions attending them.

When the social mood becomes more negative, as reflected by persistently falling stock prices, voters decide to throw out the incumbent who symbolizes their downbeat feelings and who they presume helped cause the conditions attending them.

The political policies of the incumbent and his challenger are irrelevant to this dynamic. The key is a desire for change per se, not any particular type of change. The standard presumption has no explanation for reconciling the relationship between these phenomena.

Peace & War

"Surely," says the supporter of the conventional view, "if war broke out, that would affect social mood and the stock market." Such a comment would be, and is, an assumption. It is unsupported by argument or history. As to argument, many people assume that war is a dangerous

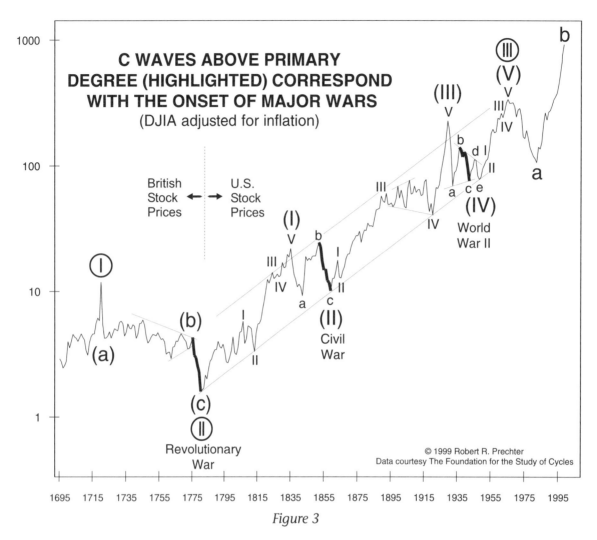

Figure 3

enterprise that would cause concerned investors to sell. Many historians, on the other hand, argue that war is good for the economy, which by conventional logic would make it good for the stock market. As this reasoning is contradictory, so is the historical record. The Revolutionary War took place entirely during a falling stock market in England. The Civil War took place entirely during a rising stock market in the U.S. World War I saw the stock market rise in the first half and fall in the second half. World War II saw the opposite, as the stock market fell in the first half and rose in the second. During the Vietnam War, it went up, down, up, down and up, finishing about unchanged. In sum, there is no data to support the conventional view, and all the data taken together contradict it.

Socionomics, in contrast, points out a consistent correlation with a consistent rationale. Because social mood governs the character of social activity, a persistently rising stock market, reflecting feelings of increasing goodwill and social harmony, should consistently produce peace, and a persistently falling stock market, reflecting feelings of increasing ill will and social conflict, should consistently produce war. Figure 3 bears out this expectation. Long rises in the stock market unerringly result in climates of peace, while sharp declines result in major wars.

The Revolutionary War took place during a major bear market from 1720 to 1784. The Civil War broke out shortly after the end of the bear market from 1835 to 1959. World War II started during the bear market from 1929 to 1949 (inflation-adjusted terms). In every case, a rising social mood eventually brings an end to the war and a period of peace and cooperation.[4]

Other Political Results

The standard presumption is that political developments have a significant impact on stock market trends. The following excerpts from *The Wave Principle of Human Social Behavior and the New Science of Socionomics*, published in 1999, addresses this presumption:

> Shall we apply this concept to today's environment as we enter 1999? The character of today's social events is as bright as any time in history. Look around and witness how the upswing in common temper has produced events during this decade that are so positive as to have been previously unimaginable. Officials have pronounced the forty-year-long Cold War officially over; the U.S.S.R. has freed Eastern Europe, creating what The Wall Street Journal called "a period of euphoria unequaled in the postwar era"; China appears to be on the long-term road to adopting capitalism and freedom; U.S. political leaders have promised a perpetually balanced Federal budget by constitutional amendment; the U.S. won its first war in 46 years; South Africa ended apartheid three and a half centuries after the Dutch arrival in South Africa and 45 years after its adoption as official government policy; and countless political and religious leaders have reached conciliation after decades, centuries and in some cases millennia of animosity.

> The response of today's conventional analysts to these conditions is as optimistic as it was in the late 1920s. For example, State Department Policy Planner Francis Fukuyama, in his widely praised New York Times bestselling book, declares 'the end of history as such' because political risks have been obliterated by the global triumph of Western liberal democracy. World officials agree, expressing joy that a new golden age of world peace and prosperity has begun. The public agrees; as a result of all this truly wonderful news, the Consumer Confidence statistic in 1998 approached its highest levels of the past 25 years. The vast majority of citizens, public and private, including all conventional futurists, economists and political analysts, are bullish on the stock market, the economy and the future as far as the imagination can project. However, you, as a reader of this paper, have the basis for a more reliable perspective.

Summary

As social mood becomes more positive, people buy more stocks, behave more productively, vote for more incumbents, have more children, blow off fewer bombs and act peacefully toward their neighbors. Conversely, as social mood becomes more negative, people sell more stocks, behave less productively, vote for more challengers, have fewer children, blow off more bombs and act belligerently toward their neighbors. All this correlation is consistent with the idea that all these activities have a common engine, which is social mood. Of course, social mood dynamics produce countless other manifestations, such as trends in art, music, entertainment, mores and fashion, to name but a few.

Because social mood change, as revealed by stock market's form, is patterned according to the Wave Principle, we can propose a larger socionomic hypothesis, that the Wave Principle ultimately shapes the dynamics underlying the character of all human social activity.

NOTES

¹ The converse is true as well, as long as we define "downturn in aggregate stock prices" as the onset of an Elliott wave correction (see letter labels in Figure 1). Thereafter, the resulting recession may occur in wave A, C or both.

² To this summary we may add Richard Nixon, who, after being re-elected in a landslide as the DJIA rose to an all-time high, was forced to resign during the 1973-1974 bear market.

³ Narrowly contested elections sometimes hinge on near-term market trends and/or the lagging performance of the economy, as in the cases of Truman in 1948 and George Bush in 1992.

⁴ This is where historians get the bizarre notion that war is good for the economy. Actually, each war is triggered by an extreme low in mood, typically in the climate of economic depression. The social mood then reverses naturally and brings about both increased productivity and peace.

Index

NEW CLASSICS LIBRARY

Elliott Wave Principle
A.J. Frost and
Robert R. Prechter, Jr.
$29

Conquer the Crash
Robert R. Prechter, Jr.
$27.95

2-BOOK BOXED SET

Pioneering Studies in Socionomics
&
The Wave Principle of Human Social Behavior
Robert R. Prechter, Jr.
$59

View from the Top of the Grand Supercycle
Robert R. Prechter, Jr.
$29

Market Analysis for the New Millennium
edited by
Robert R. Prechter, Jr.
$39

At the Crest of the Tidal Wave
Robert R. Prechter, Jr.
$49

Prechter's Perspective
edited by
Peter Kendall
$27

R.N. Elliott's Market Letters (1938-1946)
edited by
Robert R. Prechter, Jr.
$89

The Complete Elliott Wave Writings of A. Hamilton Bolton
edited by
Robert R. Prechter, Jr.
$89

The Elliott Wave Writings of A.J. Frost and Richard Russell
edited by
Robert R. Prechter, Jr.
$89

R.N. Elliott's Masterworks
edited by
Robert R. Prechter, Jr.
$34

Beautiful Pictures
Robert R. Prechter, Jr.
$39

How to Forecast Gold and Silver
Robert R. Prechter, Jr.
$179

The Theory of Elementary Waves
Lewis E. Little
$27.71